Eighth Ed

The Psychology of Women and Gender

Margaret W. Matlin

SUNY Geneseo

With Rebecca D. Foushée

LINDENWOOD University

CENGAGE

Australia • Brazil • Canada • Mexico • Singapore • United Kingdom • United States

The Psychology of Women and Gender,
Eighth Edition
Margaret W. Matlin
with Rebecca D. Foushée

SVP, Higher Education Product Management:
Erin Joyner

VP, Product Management, Learning
Experiences: Thais Alencar

Product Director: Laura Ross

Product Manager: Cazzie Reyes

Product Assistant: Jessica Witczak

Vendor Content Manager: Manoj Kumar,
Lumina Datamatics Limited

Digital Delivery Quality Partner: Allison
Marion

Manufacturing Planner: Ron Montgomery

Inventory Analyst: Seth Cohn

IP Analyst: Deanna Ettinger

IP Project Manager: Chandrakumar
Kumaresan, Integra Software Services

Production Service: Lumina Datamatics Ltd

Designer: Nadine Ballard

Cover and Interior Images Sources: Trevor
Williams/DigitalVision/Getty Images;
Petri Oeschger/Moment/Getty Images;
mediaphotos/E+/Getty Images; pixelfit/E+/Getty
Images; visualspace/E+/Getty Images;
LordHenriVoton/E+/Getty Images

For product information and technology assistance,
contact us at **Cengage Customer & Sales Support,
1-800-354-9706 or support.cengage.com.**

For permission to use material from this text or product,
submit all requests online at **www.copyright.com.**

Library of Congress Control Number: 2022900029

ISBN: 978-0-357-65817-8
LLF ISBN: 978-0-357-65821-5

Cengage
200 Pier 4 Boulevard
Boston, MA 02210
USA

Cengage is a leading provider of customized learning
solutions with employees residing in nearly 40 different
countries and sales in more than 125 countries around the
world. Find your local representative at **www.cengage.com.**

To learn more about Cengage platforms and services, reg-
ister or access your online learning solution, or purchase
materials for your course, visit **www.cengage.com.**

Printed at CLDPC, USA, 02-22

To the students in our Psychology of Women and Gender classes

About the Authors

Margaret W. Matlin earned her bachelor's degree from Stanford University and her PhD from the University of Michigan. She currently holds the title of Distinguished Teaching Professor of Psychology, Emerita at SUNY Geneseo, where she taught courses in the Psychology of Women for 39 years.

Dr. Matlin received the State University of New York Chancellor's Award for Excellence in Teaching in 1977. She has also won three national teaching awards: the American Psychological Association Teaching Award for 4-year institution in 1985, the American Psychological Foundation's Distinguished Teaching Award in 1995, and the Society for the Psychology of Women's Heritage Award in 2001, for lifetime contributions to the teaching of the psychology of women.

Rebecca D. Foushée earned her PhD from Virginia Tech. For the past 24 years, she has taught courses in Developmental Psychology and the Psychology of Women and Gender at The University of Alabama in Huntsville, Fontbonne University, Washington University in St. Louis, and Lindenwood University, where she currently holds the title of Professor of Psychology.

Dr. Foushée has received several research and teaching awards throughout her career, including the APA Division 6 Frank A. Beach Award in 1997 and an APA Dissertation Award in 1998, the Joan Goostree Stevens Award for Excellence in Teaching in 2006, the Emerson Award for Excellence in Teaching in 2006, the Lindenwood University Professor of the Year Award in 2018, and the NCAA Roars Excellence in Teaching Award in 2020.

Four General Themes About the Psychology of Women and Gender

Theme 1   Psychological gender differences are typically small and inconsistent.

Theme 2   People react differently to men and women.

Theme 3   Women are less visible than men in many important areas.

Theme 4   Women vary widely from one another.

Pages 28 through 30 discuss the four themes in greater detail.

Brief Contents

Contents

5 Gender Comparisons in Cognitive Abilities and Attitudes About Achievements   143

6 Gender Comparisons in Social and Personality Characteristics   173

Preface

Dr. Margaret W. Matlin began writing the first edition of *Psychology of Women and Gender* in 1983. By this point, she had taught courses on the psychology of women for 9 years. Every year, she tried a different textbook. One book was too brief. Another was too psychodynamic. The third book was a collection of research articles that didn't capture women's voices.

One of her goals in writing the first edition of *Psychology of Women and Gender* was to demonstrate how the empirical research about women and gender often contradicts popular opinion. A second goal was to include women's descriptions of their experiences and thoughts, because her own students were especially responsive when they heard women's own words. Her third goal was to create pedagogical features that would help students learn and remember the material more effectively.

These three goals are even more important now than they were in the 1980s. The amount of research about women and gender has increased dramatically. For instance, *PsycINFO* shows that about 11,300 journal articles were published—listing "women" or "gender" as a keyword—during the period from 1980 through 1985. In contrast, *PsycINFO* shows 122,577 journal articles from 2015 through 2020 that list these same two keywords. Students therefore need a textbook that captures the research in a clear, well-organized fashion.

In addition to those three goals, this text emphasizes a fourth goal—social justice. During the 1970s and 1980s, Dr. Matlin's personal emphasis on social justice became clarified. The Vietnam War forced her to become an activist: Why should people in the United States, devalue the lives of people in Southeast Asia and assume the *obligation* to decide what is best for them? With the rise of feminism during the 1970s, it was easy to translate those same concerns to the issue of gender. Why should people—throughout the world—devalue the lives of women and gender minorities and also assume that these people have the *obligation* to make decisions about women's lives? She felt compelled to write about this problem and to encourage students to think about this inequality. Social justice is therefore an overarching feature of this textbook.

For the eighth edition, Dr. Rebecca Foushée joined as a coauthor. She is a developmental psychologist, a member of APA Divisions 2 and 35, and an award-winning professor who has taught psychology of women and gender courses for more than two decades. She shares a passion for intersectional and interdisciplinary perspectives, as well as a dedication to critically analyzing how social and economic inequalities in societies around the world affect the lives of women and gender minorities. Together, they share a goal of advocating for social justice through the transformative processes of education and research.

Organization of This Book

Another important feature of this textbook is its organization. The various topics in the women and gender course does not align themselves in a linear fashion. It was impossible to place the chapters in either a clearly topical order or a clearly lifespan-developmental order. Therefore, there are two approaches when writing the eight editions of *Psychology of Women and Gender.*

For example, the introductory chapter of this eighth edition presents general concepts and several important cautions about research methods and biases. Chapter 2 explores how stereotypes help to shape gender-related expectations and behavior. Chapters 3 and 4 examines sex and gender development throughout infancy, childhood, and adolescence.

The following nine chapters (Chapters 5–13) considers important components of women's lives prior to late adulthood. These include cognitive and social gender comparisons (Chapters 5 and 6), work experiences (Chapter 7), love relationships (Chapter 8), sexuality (Chapter 9), childbirth (Chapter 10), physical health and psychological health (Chapters 11 and 12), and gender and victimization (Chapter 13).

Some of the material in Chapters 5 through 13 also foreshadows the descriptions of older women, whose lives are examined in Chapter 14. Chapter 8 considers the long-term romantic relationships of older women, Chapter 9 sexuality and aging, and Chapter 11 relevant health issues. Following those nine topical chapters, Chapter 14 returns to the lifespan-developmental framework to focus specifically on gender during middle age and late adulthood. Chapter 15, the concluding chapter of this textbook, assesses the current status of the psychology of women and gender, women of color, the men's movement, and recent trends in feminism.

The combination of lifespan and topical approaches provides a cohesive framework that students appreciate. In addition, each chapter is self-contained, because each section within a chapter has its own section summary. Therefore, instructors who prefer a different organizational framework can easily rearrange the sequence of topics within the course. For example, an instructor could move the section on menopause from Chapter 14 to the earlier section on menstruation in Chapter 4.

A second organizational feature is the four general themes about the psychology of women and gender (refer to pages 28–30). These themes can be traced through many aspects of women's lives. In addition, the four themes help to provide continuity for a course that might otherwise seem overwhelming to both instructors and students.

Pedagogical Features of This Book

Professors and students have provided positive feedback about the variety of special features that facilitate learning about the psychology of women and gender. This book is intended for students from a variety of backgrounds. It includes extensive learning aids to make it readable for students who have taken only an introductory course in psychology. However, *Psychology of Women and Gender* should also be appropriate for advanced-level students, because the coverage of topics is complete and the references are extensive. To help all students, *Psychology of Women and Gender* (8th ed.) continues to include the following pedagogical features:

- **Topical outlines** provide students with an overall structure at the beginning of each chapter.
- The **writing style** is clear and interesting and includes many examples and quotations in which girls and women describe their own experiences.

- All of the **key terms** appear in boldface type, and they are defined within the same sentence and in the glossary section. Some professors choose to assign chapters in a nonlinear order. To accommodate this preference, a key term is defined in each chapter where it appears. For example, the term *social constructionism* is defined in Chapter 1, as well as in several subsequent chapters. Students can also consult the pronunciation guide for terms that have potentially ambiguous pronunciations.
- Informal **demonstrations** encourage active involvement and clarify the procedures used in important research studies.
- **Section summaries** help students review the major concepts in one section of a chapter before they begin the next section. This feature increases an instructor's flexibility, as noted on page XVIII. Section summaries are also helpful to those students who do not read an entire chapter in one sitting. They can read one or two sections and then take a break. When they return to read the remaining sections, they can refresh their memory by reviewing the previous section summaries.
- The **end-of-chapter review questions** encourage students to clarify and synthesize concepts. Some instructors also use these questions as writing assignments or as topics for class discussion.
- A **list of key terms** at the end of each chapter invites students to test themselves on important concepts. The page number on which the term is defined is listed, if students want to check their accuracy.
- The **recommended readings** suggest extra resources for students who want to explore the topics in each chapter in greater detail. Each reference is annotated to clarify its scope. Most of these readings are books, but a few chapters in books and comprehensive journal articles are included.
- Finally, the **subject index** is very comprehensive. The detailed index in this textbook will be especially helpful to students who want background information when writing a paper, who are curious about a particular topic, or who want to share some information with a friend.

New Material in This Book

Instructors and students who have read previous editions of this textbook continue to be enthusiastic about a variety of features, including the pedagogical features, the writing style, the scholarly information, and the sequence of topics. Accordingly, this eighth edition retains the same topic sequence as in the seven earlier editions. However, this new edition includes more extensive coverage about women of color who live in the United States and Canada, consistent with the increasing information available in books and journal articles. Similarly, this edition includes more cross-cultural and intersectional perspectives, as well as updated examples and terminology throughout the text to emphasize gender diversity, inclusion, and equity among people of all genders and sexualities. Also included are more recent quotations for the eighth edition; the older quotes were retained only if there was no appropriate replacement.

This eighth edition of *The Psychology of Women and Gender* is thoroughly revised. It now features a total of 3,270 references, and about 538 of these references are new to this edition. A few references to classic studies remain, but a majority of citations throughout the text were published in 2005 or later. This new edition therefore reflects changes in women's lives, changes in their perspectives about themselves, and changes in society's attitudes toward women and gender and sexual minorities.

In addition to updated references, *Psychology of Women and Gender* (8th ed.) includes the following new pedagogical features:

- New chapter learning objectives that define learning outcomes for instructors and help students organize their learning.
- New "Did You Know?" sections at the beginning of each chapter, to pique students' interest in the material and foreshadow many of the key issues examined in each chapter.
- A new glossary section that outlines the definitions of key terms used throughout the text.

For professors familiar with *Psychology of Women* (7th ed.), the following brief guide outlines some of the major changes in this new edition:

- **Chapter 1** features updated information about intersectionality, White privilege, biracial individuals, Asian American women, and Native American women.
- **Chapter 2** includes updated discussion of women in the media, recent research about the changes in stereotypes, additional research on benevolent sexism, an expanded discussion of heterosexism, and a new demonstration.
- **Chapter 3** includes additional information about the biological bases of sex and gender, places greater emphasis on the role of parents' encouragement of gender stereotypes in their children, and discusses new information regarding girls' education in nonindustrialized countries.
- **Chapter 4** has less emphasis on menstruation, so that more research can be included about cultural identity among Latina and Muslim American adolescents, as well as current research about lesbian relationships among Asian American and Latina adolescents.
- **Chapter 5** includes new research on neurological bases of cognitive abilities, examines several new studies about gender similarities and differences in a variety of cognitive areas, including mathematics performance, as well as gender comparisons in students' definitions of success.
- **Chapter 6** includes recent research on gender comparisons in the content of language samples, attitudes about social justice, and leadership, as well as an expanded of the role of congruity theory.
- **Chapter 7** includes an expanded discussion of immigrant women's employment experiences, emphasizes the impact of systemic racism and socioeconomic inequalities on women's financial stability, and includes recent studies on employment in traditionally female occupations as well as information about nonmaternal child care.
- **Chapter 8** includes updated research about ideal partners, arranged marriages, same-sex marriages, and Diamond's (2009) dynamical systems approach to sexual orientation.
- **Chapter 9** has been updated to include research on bisexuality and transgender women's sexuality, as well as media influences on sexuality.
- **Chapter 10** includes updated information about ethnicity and smoking during pregnancy, the cesarean-section problem, and research about lesbian mothers.
- **Chapter 11** provides updated information about social status and women's health in the United States, women's health in developing countries, and LGBTQ+ experiences with health-care systems.

- **Chapter 12** features a discussion of therapists' diagnostic biases, additional information about gendered racism, an expanded section on eating disorders, information about cultural attitudes of psychological disorders, as well as updated guidance about psychotherapy with people of color.
- **Chapter 13** examines sexual harassment and sexual assault of women in the military, updated research about police responses to rape reports, and new information about the abuse of women in Asia, Latin America, and Africa.
- **Chapter 14** features new information on gender differences in post-retirement income, reorganized sections on family relationships and older women of color, and current research about successful aging.
- **Chapter 15** provides updated information about women of color and the feminist movement, new examples about the men's movement, and new options for becoming an activist.

Instructor Resources

Additional instructor resources for this product are available online. Instructor assets include an Instructor's Manual, PowerPoint® slides, and a test bank powered by Cognero®. Sign up or sign in at www.cengage.com to search for and access this product and its online resources.

Acknowledgments

We would like to thank the people who have provided ideas, references, perspectives, and encouragement for the current and previous editions of this text.

Our continuing thanks go to: Mary Roth Walsh, Lucinda DeWitt, Helen Severance White, Donald E. White, Arnie Matlin, Jerry Mize, Amy Hillard, Alice Alexander, Cheryl Anagnopoulos, Harriet Amster, Linda Anderson, Julianne Arbuckle, Illeana Arias, Carole Beal, Cheryl Bereziuk, Nancy Betts, Beverly Birns, Janine Buckner, Krisanne Bursik, Joyce Carbonel, Wendy C. Chambers, Joan Chrisler, Gloria Cowan, Mary Crawford, Kay Deaux, Darlene DeFour, Lucinda DeWitt, Sheri Chapman De Bro, Nancy DeCourville, Mary Ellen Dello Stritto, Amanda Diekman, Claire Etaugh, Joan Fimbel DiGiovanni, Elaine Donelson, Gilla Family, Sandy R. Fiske, Susan K. Fuhr, Grace Galliano, Margaret Gittis, Sharon Golub, Beverly Goodwin, Gloria Hamilton, Michele Hoffnung, Chris Jazwinski, Patricia Kaminski, Linda Lavine, Liz Leonard, Beth Lux, Kim MacLean, Laura Madson, Melanie Maggard, Wendy Martyna, Peggy Moody, Nina Nabors, Agnes O'Connell, Maureen O'Neill, Michele A. Paludi, Letitia Anne Peplau, Jean Poppei, Wendy M. Pullin, Rebecca Reviere, Carla Reyes, Zoa Rockstein, Janis Sanchez-Hucles, Barbara Sholley, Linda Skinner, Myra Okazaki Smith, Natalie Smoak, Susan Snelling, Hannah Steinward, Noreen Stuckless, Beverly Tatum, Jennifer Taylor, Lori Van Wallendael, Wendy Wallin, Barbara S. Wallston, Dolores Weiss, Yvonne V. Wells, Barbara J. Yanico, and Cecilia K. Yoder.

1   Introduction

Learning Objectives

After studying this chapter, you will be able to …

1-1 Describe the central concepts in the psychology of women and gender.

1-2 Summarize the history of the psychology of women as a discipline.

1-3 Explain intersectionality, gender, and ethnicity.

1-4 Outline potential problems and biases in research on the psychology of women and gender.

1-5 Summarize the primary themes of the textbook.

Did You Know?

- If a corporation refuses to consider hiring a man for a receptionist position, then this corporation is practicing sexism (p. 4).
- If you believe that women should be highly regarded as human beings, then you are a feminist (p. 6).
- In the 2020s, Asian American women are much more likely than White women to graduate from college (p. 17).
- An important problem in research on gender is that researchers' expectations can influence the results of the study (p. 21).
- In general, popular media sources emphasize gender differences rather than gender similarities (p. 28).
- Gender differences are larger when researchers observe people in real-life situations rather than in a laboratory setting (p. 29).

In the modern world, although we can find many examples of women's success in the news, other reports are often grim. Sometimes we read about good news and bad news in the same week. For example, as we were updating this chapter, various news organizations were celebrating the inauguration of Kamala Harris as the first woman, and the first woman of color, to serve as vice president of the United States. Although this historic achievement reflected significant progress, this news was juxtaposed with economic reports that women, and especially women of color, lost significantly more jobs than men throughout the COVID-19 pandemic, jeopardizing their families' financial stability and economic well-being (Boesch & Phadke, 2021).

Another article was featured in the *Chronicle of Higher Education*, a newspaper that focuses on colleges and universities. Researchers from the Eos Foundation found that women earn more degrees than men, and 60% of women working in colleges and universities occupy professional jobs. However, only 24% of the highest paid core employees are women. On medical campuses the disparity is even worse, with only 12% of women occupying the highest paid positions of power. Women of color have even less representation and comprise only 2.5% of these high-status positions (Silbert & Dubé, 2021).

In many ways, women's lives are improving. However, even in the twenty-first century, women are frequently treated in a biased fashion. This biased treatment is often relatively subtle, but it can also be life threatening.

Furthermore, the popular media and the academic community frequently neglect women and issues important to them. For example, we searched for topics related to women in the index of a current introductory psychology textbook. Pregnancy isn't mentioned, even though pregnancy is an important part of most women's lives. The topic of rape is also missing from the index. However, the listings under the letter *R* do include receptor sensitivity curves, as well as multiple references to reflexes and to rapid eye movements.

This book explores a variety of psychological issues that specifically concern women. For example, women are more likely than men to experience life events such as menstruation, pregnancy, childbirth, and menopause. Other experiences such as rape, domestic violence, and sexual harassment are also more likely for women than for men. In addition, when we study the psychology of women, we can focus on women's experiences in areas that usually emphasize the male point of view. These areas include achievement, work, sexuality, and retirement.

Still other important topics compare females and males. Are boys and girls *treated* differently? Do women and men differ substantially in their intellectual abilities or their social interactions? These topics, which are neglected in most psychology courses, will be an important focus throughout this book.

In this chapter, our exploration of the psychology of women and gender begins with some key concepts in the discipline. Next, we'll briefly consider the history of the psychology of women. The third section of this chapter provides background about women of color to give context for the discussion of ethnicity, gender, and intersectionality in later chapters. Then we'll explore some of the problems and biases that researchers often face when they study the psychology of women and gender. In the final section, we'll describe the themes of this book, as well as several features that can help you learn more effectively.

1-1 Central Concepts in the Psychology of Women and Gender

Learning Objectives

To describe the central concepts in the psychology of women and gender, you can ...

1-1-1   Differentiate between the concepts of sex and gender.

1-1-2   Explain how the concepts of sexism, racism, classism, ableism, and heterosexism impact people's lives.

1-1-3   Differentiate among liberal feminism, cultural feminism, radical feminism, and women-of-color feminisms.

1-1-4   Explain how the similarities perspective and social constructionism account for gender differences.

1-1-5   Explain how the differences perspective and essentialism arguments account for gender differences.

Let's first consider two related terms, *sex* and *gender,* that are crucial to the psychology of women. Other central concepts that we'll examine include several forms of bias, various approaches to feminism, and two psychological viewpoints on gender similarities and differences.

Sex and Gender

The terms *sex* and *gender* have provoked considerable controversy (e.g., Caplan & Caplan, 2009; Kimball, 2003; LaFrance et al., 2004). **Sex** is a relatively narrow term that typically refers to physical and biological characteristics relating to reproductive anatomy, such as *sex chromosomes* or *sex organs* (Kimball, 2003). Sex is typically assigned at birth based on the appearance of external genitalia and refers to the condition of being male, female, or intersex (APA, 2015). In cases of ambiguous genitalia, the goal is to assign a sex that will likely be congruent with the child's gender identity (MacLaughlin & Donahoe, 2004). In contrast, *gender* is a broader term. **Gender** refers to the psychological characteristics and social categories that human culture creates (APA, 2015; Golden, 2008) and implies the psychological, behavioral, social, and cultural traits associated with being male, female, or nonbinary. For example, a friend showed a photo of her 7-month-old son, who the photographer had posed with a football. This photographer was providing gender messages for the infant, his mother, and everyone who sees the photo. These gender messages tell us that this small infant needs to learn know how to run fast, knock down other people, and become a hero. In contrast, imagine an infant girl you know. It's probably challenging to create a mental image of her accompanied by a football.

Cisgender refers to individuals who have a match between the sex they were assigned at birth, their reproductive anatomy or biological sex, and their gender identity (APA, 2015; Schilt & Westbrook, 2009). **Transgender** is an umbrella term for people whose gender identity, expression, or behavior does not conform to the sex they were assigned at birth. This textbook focuses on psychology rather than on biology. As a result, you'll read the word *gender* more often than the word *sex*. For example, you'll read about gender comparisons, gender roles, and gender stereotypes.

Unfortunately, psychology articles and books often fail to maintain the distinction between sex and gender (Kimball, 2003). In fact, a highly regarded scholarly journal is called *Sex Roles,* although a more appropriate title might be *Gender Roles.*

A useful related phrase is *doing gender* (Golden, 2008; Lorber, 2005b; Schilt & Westbrook, 2009; C. West & Zimmerman, 1998a). According to the concept of **doing gender**, you express your gender when you interact with other people; you also perceive gender in these other people, such as an infant posed with a football. For example, you provide gender messages to other people by your appearance, your tone of voice, and your conversational style. At the same time, you perceive the gender of your conversational partner, and you probably respond differently to a male than to a female.

The phrase *doing gender* emphasizes that gender is an active, dynamic process rather than something that is stable and rigid. In addition, it's virtually impossible to stop doing gender because it's part of our actual identity (Lorber, 2005b). In fact, the next time you are speaking with another person, think about whether you can stop expressing your own gender and perceiving the gender of this other person.

The Extent of Social Biases

An important term throughout this book is *sexism* (which probably could be reconceptualized as *genderism*). **Sexism** is bias against people on the basis of their gender. A person who believes that women cannot be competent lawyers is sexist. A person who believes that men cannot be competent preschool teachers is also sexist. Sexism can reveal itself in many forms, such as social behavior, media representations of women and men, and job discrimination.

Sexism can be blatant. For example, a student in one of our psychology of women courses was attending a recruitment session for prospective high school teachers. She was dressed in a suit that was similar to the suit of a male student standing behind her in line. The interviewer greeted her by saying, "Hi, kid, how are you doin'?" The same interviewer greeted the young man by saying, "Hi, good to meet you," and then he extended his arm for a handshake. However, sexism can also be more subtle: Some people use the word *girl* when talking about a 40-year-old woman. Would they use the word *boy* when talking about a 40-year-old man?

In this book, we will emphasize sexism. However, numerous other biases permeate our social relationships. In each case, one social category is considered normative or standard, whereas the other categories are considered deficient (Canetto et al., 2003). For example, **racism** is bias against people on the basis of racial or ethnic groups. Research suggests that White preschoolers tend to choose other White children as their friends, even when the classroom includes many Black children (Katz, 2003).

As we'll learn throughout this book, sexism and racism combine in complex ways. For instance, the experiences of women of color may be quite different from the experiences of White men (Brabeck & Ting, 2000; Kirk & Okazawa-Rey, 2001; Zigerell, 2018).

Let's consider another social bias in which a person's category membership can influence their social position. **Classism** is bias that is based on social class. Social class is defined by such factors as income, occupation, and education. As with sexism and racism, classism provides special privileges to some people based on their social category. In contrast, U.S. residents who live below the poverty level do not have enough money to pay for their basic needs, such as food, housing, transportation, and medical care.

Surprisingly, psychologists have paid little attention to social class, even though this factor has a major impact on people's psychological experiences (Fine & Burns, 2003; Lott & Bullock, 2010; Ocampo et al., 2003). In the United States, for instance, the chief executive officers of corporations earn approximately 431 times as much as their lowest-paid employees (Belle, 2008), and since 1978, the average compensation for CEOs has grown 940%, while the average worker's compensation has grown only 12% (Mishel & Wolfe, 2019). Executives and entry-level employees certainly have different experiences, as we will learn in Chapter 7. Unfortunately, psychologists typically assume that they can leave social class to sociologists (Ostrove & Cole, 2003). However, Chapter 11 shows that social class clearly affects people's physical health, and Chapter 12 shows that social class clearly affects people's psychological well-being (Belle, 2008).

An additional problem is called **ableism,** or bias against people with disabilities (Olkin, 2008; Weinstock, 2003). Just as psychologists ignore social class, they also ignore disability issues—even though disabilities have a major impact on people's lives (Asch & McCarthy, 2003). In Chapter 11, we'll learn how ableism can create inequalities for people with disabilities, both in the workplace and in personal relationships (Olkin, 2008).

Another important problem is **heterosexism** (also called **sexual prejudice**), which refers to bias against anyone who does not identify as exclusively heterosexual. Heterosexism therefore harms people who identify as lesbian, gay, bisexual, or another sexual minority. Heterosexism appears in the behaviors of individuals and in the policies of institutions, such as the legal system (Garnets, 2008; Herek, 2009).

Heterosexism encourages many people to believe that male–female romantic relationships should be considered normative, and therefore people in same-gender relationships do not have the same rights and privileges (Lorber, 2005b; Garnets, 2008). In Chapters 2 and 8, we will explore heterosexism in detail, and in Chapters 4, 8, 9, 10, and 12, we will also discuss the life experiences of lesbians, bisexual women, and women who identify as sexual minorities.

In Chapter 14, we will emphasize **ageism**, or bias based on chronological age. Ageism is typically directed toward older people (Schneider, 2004; Whitbourne, 2005). Individuals can reveal ageism in terms of biased beliefs, attitudes, and behaviors. For example, a teenager may avoid sitting next to an older person. Institutions can also exhibit ageism, for instance, when an older adult applies for a job.

Feminist Approaches

A central term throughout this book is **feminism**, the principle that values women's experiences and ideas; feminism also emphasizes that women and men should be socially, economically, and legally equal (Anderson, 2010; Pollitt, 2004). As Rozee and her colleagues (2008) point out, "Feminism is a life philosophy, a worldview, a blueprint for justice" (p. ix).

We need to emphasize several additional points about feminists. First, reread the definition of feminism, and notice that it does *not* exclude men. In fact, men as well as women can be feminists. Many books and articles discuss men who are feminists (e.g., Jensen, 2017; Kilmartin, 2007; Lorber, 2005b; A. J. Lott, 2003). Think about this: You probably know some men who advocate feminist principles more than some of the women you know. We'll discuss male feminists and the growing discipline of men's studies in the final chapter of this book.

Second, many of your friends would qualify as feminists, even though they may be reluctant to call themselves feminists (Cohen, 2008; Dube, 2004; Pollitt, 2004). You have probably noticed someone say, "I'm not a feminist, but I think men and women should be treated the same." This person may mistakenly assume that a feminist must be a person who hates men. However, remember that the defining feature of feminism is a high regard for women, not antagonism toward men.

Third, feminism encompasses a variety of ideas and perspectives, not just one feminist viewpoint (Dube, 2004; Rozee et al., 2008). Let's consider four different theoretical approaches to feminism: liberal feminism, cultural feminism, radical feminism, and women-of-color feminisms.

1. **Liberal feminism** emphasizes the goal of gender equality, giving women and men the same rights and opportunities. Liberal feminists argue that people can achieve this goal by passing laws that guarantee equal rights for women and men (Chrisler & Smith, 2004; Enns & Sinacore, 2001).

   Liberal feminists emphasize that biological factors have relatively little effect on gender differences. In addition, these gender differences are relatively small, and they would be even smaller if women had the same opportunities as men (Enns, 2004a; Lorber, 2005b). Women and men who are liberal feminists believe that everyone benefits if culture's rigid gender roles can be transformed (Goldrick-Jones, 2002).

2. **Cultural feminism** emphasizes the positive qualities that are presumed to be stronger in women than in men—qualities such as nurturing and care-taking. Cultural feminism therefore focuses on gender differences that value women rather than on the gender similarities of liberal feminism (Chrisler & Smith, 2004; Enns, 2004a; Lorber, 2005b). In addition, cultural feminists often argue that society should be restructured to emphasize cooperation rather than aggression (Enns & Sinacore, 2001; Kimball, 1995).

3. **Radical feminism** argues that the basic cause of women's oppression lies deep in the entire sex and gender system rather than in some superficial laws and policies. Radical feminists emphasize that sexism permeates societies, from the personal level in male-female relationships to the national and international levels (Chrisler & Smith, 2004). Radical feminists often argue that societies need to dramatically change their policies on sexuality and on violence against women (Enns, 2004a; Goldrick-Jones, 2002).

4. **Women-of-color feminisms** point out that the other three types of feminism overemphasize gender. Women-of-color feminists emphasize that feminism must pay attention to other human dimensions such as historical forms of oppression, ethnicity, and social class (Baca Zinn et al., 2001; Chrisler & Smith, 2004; Lorber, 2005b; Smith, 2011). For example, Gearon (2021) explains that Indigenous feminism is intersectional, with a focus on decolonization, sovereignty of Indigenous peoples, and human rights for Indigenous women and their families. Transnational feminism similarly focuses on systematic forms of oppression rooted in the historical forces of colonization and globalism (Grabe & Else-Quest, 2012). Womanism, or Black feminism (Boisnier, 2003; Walker, 1983), and the Mujerista feminism movements highlight the intersectionality of ethnicity, race, and gender in shaping the lives of women of color (Bryant-Davis & Comas-Díaz, 2016).

   According to these perspectives, we cannot achieve a genuinely feminist approach by making a few minor adjustments to liberal feminism, cultural feminism, or radical feminism (Enns, 2004a). For example, the life of a Black lesbian woman is substantially different from the life of a White lesbian woman (Lorde, 2001). If we want to understand the experiences of a Black lesbian woman, we must begin with her perspective, rather than initially focusing on White lesbian women and then "adding difference and stirring" (Baca Zinn et al., 2001).

In Chapter 15, we'll further explore perspectives on feminism and women's studies. A central point, however, is that feminism isn't simply one unified point of view. Instead, feminists have created a variety of perspectives on gender relationships and on the ideal pathways for achieving better lives for women. To clarify the four feminist approaches discussed in this section, try Demonstration 1.1.

Demonstration **1.1**

Differentiating Among the Four Approaches to Feminism

Imagine that, in a discussion group, each of these eight individuals makes a statement about feminism. Read each statement and note whether the approach represents liberal feminism, cultural feminism, radical feminism, or women-of-color feminisms. The answers are on page 34.

1. Cora: "The way marriage is currently designed, women are basically servants who spend most of their energy improving the lives of other people."____
2. Marta: "Too many feminists think that White women are at the center of feminism, and the rest of us are out at the edges of the feminist circle."____

(continues)

Demonstration 1.1 *(continued)*

3. Nereyda: "Laws must be made to guarantee women the right to be educated the same as men; women need to reach their full potential, just like men do."___
4. Sylvia: "My goal as a feminist is to value the kind of strengths that have traditionally been assigned to women, so that women can help society learn to be more cooperative."___
5. Maria: "Society needs to change in a major way so that we can get rid of the oppression of women."___
6. Michelle: "I consider myself a feminist. However, I think that many feminists just don't pay enough attention to factors such as social class and ethnicity."___
7. Stuart: "I think women should be given exactly the same opportunities as men with respect to promotion in the workplace."____
8. Terry: "Because women are naturally more peaceful than men, I think women need to organize and work together to build a peaceful society."___

Source: Based on Enns (2004a).

Psychological Approaches to Gender Similarity and Difference

When psychologists examine gender issues, they usually favor either a similarities perspective or a differences perspective. Let's explore these two approaches. Before you read further, however, be sure to try Demonstration 1.2.

Demonstration 1.2

Reading a Paragraph

Chris was really angry today! Enough was enough. Chris put on the gray suit, marched into work, and went into the main boss's office and yelled, "I've brought in more money for this company than anybody else and everybody gets promoted but me!" The boss saw Chris's fist slam down on the desk. There was an angry look on Chris's face. They tried to talk, but it was useless. Chris just stormed out of the office in anger.

Source: Based on Beall 1993, p. 127.

The Similarities Perspective

Psychologists who emphasize the **similarities perspective** believe that men and women are generally similar in their intellectual and social skills (Hyde, 2005a). These psychologists argue that social forces may create some temporary differences. For example, women may act more submissive than men in the workplace because women typically hold less power in that setting (Kimball, 1995; B. Lott, 1996). Supporters of the similarities perspective also tend to favor liberal feminism. By deemphasizing gender roles and strengthening equal rights laws, they say, gender similarities will increase still further.

If the similarities perspective is correct, then why do women and men often *seem* so different? Take a moment to consider how you interpreted Demonstration 1.2. Most people conclude that Chris is a man, although this paragraph does not mention Chris's gender. Instead, readers construct someone's gender based on their cultural knowledge about gender. Read that paragraph again. What phrases influenced your conclusions?

Social constructionism provides a useful perspective for understanding gender. According to **social constructionism**, individuals and cultures construct or invent their own versions of reality based on prior experiences, social interactions, and beliefs (Gergen & Gergen, 2004; Lorber, 2005b; Marecek et al., 2004). A young woman develops a female identity, for example, by learning about gender through her social interactions in her culture. As we discussed on page 4, she is continually "doing gender."

Social constructionists argue that we can never objectively discover reality because our belief system always influences our observations (Marecek et al., 2004; Yoder & Kahn, 2003). In the United States, cultural norms and perspectives still consider women to be different from men. As a result, people in the United States tend to perceive, remember, and think about gender in a way that exaggerates the differences between women and men. The views in this textbook (and most other psychology of women textbooks) support both the similarities perspective and the social constructionist view.

The Differences Perspective

In contrast to the similarities perspective, other psychologists interested in women's studies emphasize the differences perspective. The **differences perspective** argues that men and women are generally different in their intellectual and social abilities. Feminist psychologists who support the differences perspective usually emphasize women's positive characteristics that have been undervalued, primarily because they are associated with women (Lorber, 2005b). These psychologists might emphasize that women are more likely than men to be concerned with human relationships and caregiving. As you might guess, those who favor the differences perspective also tend to be cultural feminists. Critics of this perspective point out a potential problem: If we emphasize gender differences, we will simply strengthen people's stereotypes about gender (Clinchy & Norem, 1998).

People who endorse the differences perspective typically believe that essentialism can explain gender differences. **Essentialism** argues that gender is a basic, unchangeable characteristic that resides *within* an individual. The essentialists emphasize that women are more concerned than men with caregiving because of their own inborn nature, not because society currently assigns women the task of taking care of children (Hare-Mustin & Marecek, 1994; Kimball, 1995).

According to the essentialist perspective, all women share the same psychological characteristics, which are very different from the psychological characteristics that all men share. Essentialism also emphasizes that women's psychological characteristics are universal and occur in every culture. This proposal is not consistent with women-of-color feminisms. This proposal is also not consistent with the findings from cross-cultural research (Chrisler & Smith, 2004; Lonner, 2003; Wade & Tavris, 1999). We'll explore the similarities and differences perspectives in more detail in Chapter 6.

Section Summary

Central Concepts in the Psychology of Women

1. *Sex* refers only to biological characteristics related to reproduction (e.g., sex chromosomes, anatomy); in contrast, *gender* refers to psychological characteristics (e.g., gender roles). The term *doing gender* means that we display gender in our social interactions and we perceive gender in other people during those interactions.
2. This book explores several kinds of social biases, such as sexism, racism, classism, ableism, heterosexism, and ageism.
3. Feminism emphasizes that women and men should be socially, economically, and legally equal. Women and men who hold these beliefs are feminists; however, many people believe in feminist principles, even if they do not identify themselves as feminists.
4. Four feminist perspectives discussed in this section are liberal feminism, cultural feminism, radical feminism, and women-of-color feminisms.
5. Psychologists typically favor either a gender similarities perspective (often combined with social constructionism) or a gender differences perspective (often combined with essentialism).

1-2 A Brief History of the Psychology of Women

Learning Objectives

To summarize the history of the psychology of women as a discipline, you can …

1-2-1   Describe how early theories of gender in the history of psychology discriminated against women.

1-2-2   Explain how Helen Thompson Wooley and Leta Stetter Hollingworth helped counteract gender bias in psychology.

1-2-3   Summarize the factors leading to the emergence of psychology of women as a discipline.

1-2-4   Describe the current status of the field of the psychology of women and gender.

Psychology's early views about women were generally negative (Kimball, 2003). Consider the perspective of G. Stanley Hall, who founded the American Psychological Association and pioneered the field of adolescent psychology. Unfortunately, however, he opposed college education for young women because he believed that academic work would "be developed at the expense of reproductive power" (G. S. Hall, 1906, p. 592; Minton, 2000). As you might imagine, views like Hall's helped to encourage biased research about sex and gender. Let's briefly examine some of this early work, then trace the emergence of the psychology of women, and finally outline the discipline's current status.

Early Studies of Gender Comparisons

During the late 1800s and the early 1900s, most of the early researchers in psychology were men. The early research on gender typically focused on gender comparisons, and it was often influenced by sexist biases (Bem, 2008; Caplan & Caplan, 2009; Milar, 2000). It's important to remember that women could not vote in the United States until 1920. The justification for this position was that women had inferior intelligence and reasoning skills (Benjamin, 2007).

During that early era, a few women made valiant attempts to contribute to the discipline of psychology (Furumoto, 2003; Pyke, 1998; Scarborough & Furumoto, 1987). For instance, psychologist Helen Thompson Woolley (1910) claimed that this early research on gender was permeated with "flagrant personal bias, ... unfounded assertions, and even sentimental rot and drivel" (p. 340). Her own research demonstrated that men and women had similar intellectual abilities. Furthermore, women actually earned higher scores on some memory and thinking tasks (Benjamin, 2007; H. B. Thompson, 1903).

Leta Stetter Hollingworth (1914) also studied gender bias. For example, she demonstrated that women's menstrual cycles had little effect on their intellectual abilities, a conclusion that contradicted a popular belief (Benjamin, 2007; Klein, 2002). This first generation of female psychologists used their research findings to argue that women and men should have equal access to college education (LaFrance et al., 2004; Milar, 2000).

The Emergence of the Psychology of Women as a Discipline

Research on the psychology of women did not advance significantly until the 1970s (Rutherford & Granek, 2010; Walsh, 1987). By that point, the number of women in psychology had increased. Feminism and the women's movement gained recognition on college campuses, and colleges added numerous courses in women's studies (Howe, 2001a; Marecek et al., 2003; Rosen, 2000). This rapidly growing interest in women had an impact on the field of psychology. For example, the Association for Women in Psychology was founded in 1969. In 1973, a group of American psychologists established an organization that is now called the Society for the Psychology of Women; it is one of the largest divisions within the American Psychological Association (Chrisler & Smith, 2004; Denmark et al., 2008).

In 1972, a group of Canadian psychologists submitted a proposal for a symposium—called "On Women, By Women"—to the Canadian Psychological Association. When this organization rejected their proposal, they cleverly decided to hold this symposium at a nearby hotel. Shortly afterward, these feminist leaders formed the Canadian Psychological Association Task Force on the Status of Women in Canadian Psychology (Pyke, 2001). In both the United States and Canada, the psychology of women or the psychology of gender has become a standard course on many college campuses (Marecek et al., 2003).

Beginning in the 1970s, the research on the psychology of women also expanded dramatically. Researchers began to explore topics such as women's achievement motivation, domestic violence, sexual harassment, and other topics that had previously been ignored (Kimball, 2003; LaFrance et al., 2004).

However, the work done in the 1970s typically had two problems. First, feminist scholars did not realize that the issue of gender was extremely complicated. For example, most scholars optimistically thought that just a handful of factors could explain why so few women held top management positions. As you'll learn in Chapter 7, the explanation encompasses numerous factors.

A second problem with the 1970s framework was that people sometimes blamed women for their own low status. For instance, in trying to determine why women were scarce in management positions, researchers from this era typically constructed two answers: (1) Women were not assertive enough, and (2) they were afraid of success. Researchers ignored an alternative idea: The *situation* might be faulty because of biased institutional policies and stereotypes (LaFrance et al., 2004; Marecek et al., 2003). Gradually, however, many researchers became less interested in gender differences. Instead, they began to examine gender discrimination and sexism (Unger, 1997).

The Current Status of the Psychology of Women and Gender

In the modern psychology era, we emphasize that questions about the psychology of women are likely to require complex answers. Furthermore, research in this area continues to increase rapidly. For example, we conducted an Internet search of the online psychology database in ProQuest for January 2015 to March 2021. This search revealed that 178,573 scholarly articles mention the topics of women, gender, or feminism. Four journals that are especially likely to publish relevant articles are *Psychology of Women Quarterly, Sex Roles, Feminism & Psychology,* and *Canadian Woman Studies/Les cahiers de la femme.*

A related development is that psychologists are increasingly aware of how factors such as ethnicity, social class, age, and sexual orientation interact in complex ways with gender. As you'll read throughout this book, we typically cannot make statements that apply to *all* women. Contrary to the essentialist approach, women are definitely not a homogeneous group!

The current field of the psychology of women is also interdisciplinary. In preparing all eight editions of this book, we have consulted resources in areas as varied as biology, medicine, sociology, anthropology, history, philosophy, religion, media studies, political science, economics, business, education, and linguistics. In the 2020s, research in the psychology of women is especially lively because women now earn the majority of psychology Ph.D. degrees—for example, 79% in 2019 in the United States and 67% in Canada in 2016 (Statistics Canada, 2016; American Psychological Association, 2020).

Still, research on the psychology of women is relatively young, and many important issues are not yet clear. At several points throughout this textbook, you will read a sentence such as, "We don't have enough information to draw conclusions." Our students tell us that these disclaimers irritate them: "Why can't you just tell us what the answer is?" In reality, however, the conflicting research findings often cannot be summarized in a clear-cut statement.

Another issue is that our knowledge base continues to change rapidly. New research often requires us to revise a previous generalization. As a result, this current edition of the textbook is substantially different from the seven earlier editions. For example, the coverage of gender comparisons in cognitive abilities bears little resemblance to the material on that topic in the first edition. Other topics that have changed dramatically include women and work, women's physical health, and older women.

The field of psychology of women and gender is especially challenging because women, men, and nonbinary individuals continue to change as we move further into the twenty-first century. You'll learn, for example, that the number of women working outside the home has changed dramatically. On many different dimensions, women in the 2020s are psychologically different from women in earlier decades. It is fascinating to contemplate the future of the psychology of women toward the end of the twenty-first century.

Section Summary

A Brief History of the Psychology of Women

1. Most early research on gender examined gender differences and emphasized female inferiority; however, Helen Thompson Woolley and Leta Stetter Hollingsworth conducted research that was not biased against women.
2. Gender research was largely ignored until the 1970s, when the psychology of women became an emerging field in both the United States and Canada. However, researchers in that era underestimated the complexity of the issues; in addition, women were often blamed for their own low status.
3. Modern research on gender is widespread and interdisciplinary; the knowledge base continues to change as a result of this research.

1-3 Women and Ethnicity

Learning Objectives

To explain intersectionality, gender, and ethnicity, you can ...

1-3-1 Describe the concepts of White privilege and White-as-normative in relation to gender and ethnicity.

1-3-2 Identify key experiences that have shaped the lives of Latina women in the United States.

1-3-3 Identify how historical factors have shaped Black women's experiences in the United States.

1-3-4 Describe how Asian American women's experiences have been shaped by historical events and discrimination.

1-3-5 Analyze which historical factors have impacted the lives of Native American women.

1-3-6 Explain the concept of intersectionality.

1-3-7 Analyze how U.S.-centered nationalism contributes to unequal treatment of women and minorities.

Earlier in this chapter, we introduced the term *racism,* or bias against certain ethnic groups. In this section, we'll specifically focus on ethnicity to provide a framework for future discussions. When we consider the psychology of women, it is important to examine ethnic diversity so that we can establish an accurate picture of all women's lives rather than simply the lives of White women.[1] It is also important to appreciate how women construct or make sense of their own ethnic identity (Madden & Hyde, 1998).

---

[1]At present, our terminology for this dominant ethnic group is in flux. We will use the terms White or European American to refer to people who do not consider themselves to be Black or African American, Latina/Latino, Asian American, or Native American.

Let's begin by exploring a concept called "White privilege" and then consider some information about ethnic groups. Our final topic is U.S.-centered nationalism, a kind of bias in which U.S. residents believe that the United States holds a special status that is superior to other countries.

The White-Privilege Concept

According to Peggy McIntosh (2001), cultures and cultural norms in the United States and Canada are based on a hidden assumption that White individuals have a special status. According to the **White-privilege concept**, White people are given certain privileges based on their skin color (Chisholm & Greene, 2008; Kendall, 2012). Furthermore, White people often take these privileges for granted. In contrast, people from other ethnic groups often lack this special status. For example, if a White woman is late for a meeting, people do not conclude, "She is late because she's White." In contrast, if a Latina woman is late, White people often assume that her behavior is typical of Latina individuals. Similarly, a White woman can use a credit card and not arouse suspicions. In contrast, when a Black woman uses a credit card, some White people may wonder if she stole the card (McIntosh, 2001; Wise, 2008).

However, psychologists point out that White people seldom realize the advantages of having white skin (Corcoran & Thompson, 2004; Ostenson, 2008; Rose, 2008). They may protest that they have never been treated better than people of color. Some White people may insist that they are "color blind." However, White people who ignore someone's ethnicity are neglecting an important part of that person's identity (Blais, 2006; Rose, 2008).

A concept related to White privilege can be called the **White-as-normative concept**, which points out that being White is the normal standard in U.S. culture (Lorber, 2005b). In observing a sociology class in which students from different ethnic groups were discussing their ethnic identity, a White woman said, "I don't have an ethnic identity; I'm just normal."

White individuals often think that Black people, Latinas/os, Asian Americans, and Native Americans belong to ethnic groups—but that White people do not (Peplau, Veniegas et al., 1999; Weedon, 1999). In fact, each of us has an ethnic heritage.

Let's return to the central concept of White privilege. McIntosh (2001) reports that, as a White woman, she knows that her children will be taught material that focuses on their ethnic group. In contrast, a child from any other ethnic background has no such guarantee. For instance, Aurora Orozco (1999) was born in Mexico and came to California as a child. She recalls a song the students sang in her new U.S. school:

> The Pilgrims came from overseas
> To make a home for you and me.
> Thanksgiving Day, Thanksgiving Day
> We clap our hands, we are so glad. (Orozco 1999, p. 110)

Orozco felt as though her own ethnic heritage was invisible in a classroom where children were supposed to clap their hands in celebration of their Pilgrim ancestors. Keep in mind the White-privilege concept and the White-as-normative concept as we consider women who are Latina, Black, Asian American, and Native American.

Women of Color

Figure 1.1 displays the estimated number of U.S. residents in the major ethnic groups as of 2019. Figure 1.2 indicates the ethnic origins of people who live in Canada. Let's briefly consider each of the groups so that you have a context for future discussions about ethnicity.

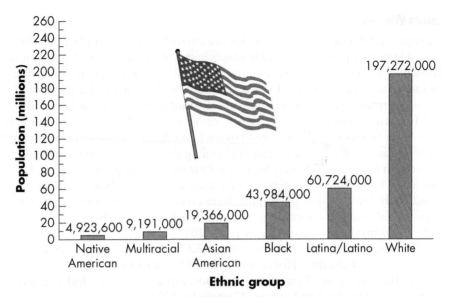

FIGURE **1.1** Estimated U.S. population in 2019, by ethnic group.

Note: Some individuals listed two or more races, and so they are tallied for each applicable category.

Source: https://www.census.gov/quickfacts/fact/table/US

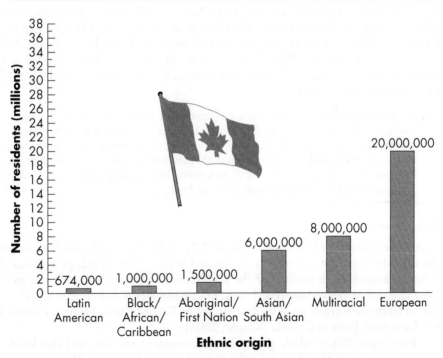

FIGURE **1.2** Estimated self-reported ethnic origins of Canadian residents, based on 2016 data.

Source: https://www12.statcan.gc.ca/census-recensement/2016/as-sa/98-200-x/2016016/98-200 -x2016016-eng.cfm

Latina Women

As Figure 1.1 reveals, Latinas/Latinos are currently the second-largest ethnic group in the United States. At present, most individuals in this ethnic group prefer these terms rather than *Hispanic,* the term often used by governmental agencies (Castañeda, 2008; Fears, 2003), and more than half of individuals who would be classified as *Hispanic* by the U.S. Census actually prefer labels that reference their country of origin, such as Cuban, Colombian, or Mexican (Taylor, Lopez, Martinez, & Velasco, 2012) One problem is that *Hispanic* focuses on Spanish origins rather than on Latin American identity. Unfortunately, though, the term *Latinos* has an *-os* (masculine) ending that renders women invisible when speaking about both males and females. We will follow the current policy of using *Latinas* to refer to women of Latin American origin and *Latinas/os* to refer to both genders (Castañeda, 2008). Incidentally, Latin American feminists have created a nonsexist alternative that incorporates both the *-as* and the *-os* endings; it is written *Latin@s*. Others have proposed *Latinx* or *Latine* as neutral alternatives (Carbajal, 2020).

Mexican Americans constitute about 62% of the Latina/o population in the United States (Noe-Bustamante, Flores, & Shah, 2017). Incidentally, Mexican Americans often refer to themselves as *Chicanas* or *Chicanos,* especially if they feel a strong political commitment to their Mexican heritage (Castañeda, 2008).

Any exploration of ethnicity must emphasize the wide diversity of characteristics and experiences within every ethnic group (Castañeda, 2008; Sy & Romero, 2008). For example, Latinas/os share a language and many similar values and customs. However, a Chicana girl growing up in a farming community in central California has different experiences from a Puerto Rican girl growing up in New York City. Furthermore, a Latina woman whose family has lived in Iowa for three generations has different experiences from a Latina woman who recently left her Central American birthplace (Martin, 2004).

Donna Castañeda (2008) described how she and other Latinas need to navigate two cultures, frequently crossing borders between their Latina heritage and the cultures in which they now live. As she writes:

> The notion of border crossing has a deep resonance for me each time I go home to visit my family. In a family of seven children, I have been the only person to go to college, and on top of that I went on to get a Ph.D. Each homecoming is like moving from one world into another, from one self to another. The transitions are now much smoother for me than in earlier years, but only after a process of coming to understand that at any point in time I am more than one person, one dimension. (Castaneda 2008, p. 264)

Black Women

If you re-examine the U.S. data in Figure 1.1, you'll notice that Black Americans constitute the third-largest ethnic group in the United States. Some Black people may have arrived recently from African nations or the Caribbean, whereas the families of others may have lived in North America since the 1700s. In Canada, Black individuals are likely to have emigrated from the Caribbean, African nations, or Great Britain. However, about half of Black residents were born in Canada (Knight, 2004).

Every non-White ethnic group has encountered racism, and this book will provide many examples of racial bias. In the United States, however, Black people's experiences with racism have been especially well documented (Rose, 2008; Schneider, 2004). Breonna Taylor and Sandra Bland are two examples of Black women who died in police custody (Klein, 2020) and are among countless other Black women, Indigenous women, and people of color who have been targeted due to racial bias (Ritchie, 2017). For example, Amanda Gorman (2021a) is a Harvard University graduate, the first ever National Youth Poet Laureate, and at 22, made history as the youngest inaugural poet in U.S. history when she read her poem *The Hill We Climb* at the inauguration of President Joseph Biden and Vice President Kamala Harris in January 2021. A few weeks later, however, she was racially profiled by a local security guard as she attempted to enter her apartment because she looked "suspicious." As she posted on Twitter, "This is the reality of black girls: One day you're called an icon, the next day, a threat" (Gorman, 2021b).

People often use the terms *Black* and *African American* interchangeably. In general, we'll use the term *Black* because it is more inclusive (Boot, 1999). *African American* seems to ignore many U.S. residents who feel a strong connection to their Caribbean roots (e.g., Jamaica, Trinidad, or Haiti), as well as Black people who live in Canada. As the Black poet Gwendolyn Brooks, former U.S. poet laureate, said in an interview, she likes to think of Black people as family who happen to live in countries throughout the world. She feels that *Black* is a welcoming term, like an open umbrella (B. D. Hawkins, 1994).

Asian American Women

As with Latinas/os, Asian Americans come from many different countries. Asian Americans include Chinese, Filipinos, Japanese, Vietnamese, Koreans, South Asians (e.g., people from India, Pakistan, and Bangladesh), and more than 30 other ethnic-cultural groups (Chan, 2008). Consider a Laotian woman who is one of the 10,000 Hmong refugees who now live in Minnesota (Vang, 2008). She may have little in common with a Taiwanese woman living in Toronto's Chinatown or a South Asian woman who is a physician in New Jersey. Many Asian American women have professional careers. However, women who are Filipino, Korean, and Chinese garment workers often experience some of the most stressful labor conditions in the United States and Canada (Vō & Scichitano, 2004).

Asian Americans are often stereotyped as the ideal or model minority group, and in fact they are often academically successful (Nance, 2007; Schneider, 2004). For example, 71% of college-age Asian American women in the United States have earned at least a bachelor's degree, in contrast to 45% of White women EducationData.org, 2019). However, some colleges report that a significant number of their Asian American students have low grade-point averages (Nance, 2007). Others have argued that the model minority myth can lead to misperceptions of Asian Americans and neglect of their mental health and social support needs (Cheng, Chang, O'Brien, Budgazad, & Tsai, 2017).

Throughout this book, we'll learn that women from an Asian background sometimes face discrimination (Chan, 2008; Lorber, 2005b). For instance, Dr. Madhulika Khandelwal describes her experiences as a professor at the University of Massachusetts, Boston: "Stereotypically [Asians] are presumed to have had limited access to English before arriving in America. They are considered followers rather than leaders. And the women are portrayed as either downtrodden or sexual 'exotics'" (Khandelwal, Collision, 2000, p. 21). Dr. Khandelwal also reported that people often praise her for her excellent mastery of English, even though English is her first language.

Native American and First Nations Women

Native Americans and First Nations people[2] may share a common geographic origin and a common history of being invaded, dispossessed, and regulated by White colonizers. However, their languages, values, and current lifestyles may have little in common (Hall & Barongan, 2002; James, 2006; McLeod, 2003). In the United States, for example, Native American people have more than 250 different tribal languages and about 560 separate native backgrounds (Smithsonian Institute, 2007; Trimble, 2003).

Many Native American women struggle as they try to integrate their personal aspirations with the values of their culture. For example, a Native American teenager explained this conflict: "As a young woman, I should have been starting a family. When Grandma told them I was going to college, they'd look away. But in my eyes, going to college wasn't going to make me less Indian or forget where I came from" (Garrod et al., 1992, p. 86).

Further Perspectives on Ethnicity

We have learned that each ethnic group consists of many different subgroups. Even if we focus on one specific subgroup—perhaps Chinese Americans—the variability *within* that one subgroup is always large (American Psychological Association, 2003; Chan, 2008). Whenever we examine whether ethnic groups differ from one another, keep in mind the substantial diversity within each group.

The within-group diversity is increased still further because millions of people in the United States and Canada are biracial or multiracial. Unfortunately, however, psychologists have not conducted much systematic research about biracial or multiracial individuals (Gillem, 2008). Furthermore, some of the research shows that multiracial individuals may experience challenges such as experiencing conflict from having to "choose" between multiple ethnic or racial identities (Gaither, 2015). However, research also shows that multiracial individuals often experience benefits, because they have access to a greater number of cultural communities (Gaither, 2015; Shih & Sanchez, 2005).

Let's return to a very important point about racism: It is important to continually examine the perspective that routinely considers White people to be normative. In the United States and Canada, most White students have learned a perspective in which the "normal human" is male, White, middle class, able-bodied, heterosexual, and young (Cushner, 2003). When students enroll in a course about the psychology of women and gender, they often report that they needed to rethink their assumptions about social categories.

We also need consider another issue related to ethnicity, called *intersectionality*. The concept of **intersectionality** emphasizes that each person belongs to multiple social groups based on categories such as ethnicity, gender, sexual orientation, and social class (Cole, 2009; Crenshaw, 1989). For instance, a White lesbian woman may experience a disadvantage because she differs from the heterosexual "standard." However, compared to lesbian women who are not White, she experiences a racial privilege (Shields, 2008).

Intersectionality points out that we cannot simply add a person's social categories together and come up with a clear-cut social identity. For instance, a Black woman may

---

[2]In referring to people whose ancestors lived in Canada before the arrival of European Americans, most Canadians use either of two terms, *First Nations* or *Aboriginal* (James, 2006; Smithsonian Institute, 2007). The two terms are used somewhat interchangeably, although some people limit the term *First Nations* to descendents of the original inhabitants of Saskatchewan and Manitoba (McLeod, 2003).

sometimes emphasize her ethnicity, and she may sometimes emphasize her gender (Bowleg, 2008). Furthermore, a person who experiences discrimination in one dimension may experience privilege in another dimension, as in the case of a White woman (Cole, 2009). Page 3 of this chapter emphasizes that the psychology of women is an extremely complex topic. The concept of intersectionality certainly increases the complexity of the important issues. You'll read more about intersectionality throughout this book.

U.S.-Centered Nationalism

So far, we have applied the "normative" concept to gender and several other social categories. Now let's focus on a related bias, in which residents of the United States consider their country to be normative.

According to the principle of **U.S.-centered nationalism**, the United States is dominant over all other countries in the world, which are believed to have lower status. U.S.-centered nationalism reveals itself in many ways that may be invisible to U.S. residents (Hase, 2001). For example, my colleagues in Canada have e-mail addresses that end in "ca." The e-mail address for Japanese residents ends in "jp," and those in Greece end in "gr." This pattern is standard in most countries. However, residents of the United States do not need to add any extra letters to their e-mail addresses, because the United States occupies a position of privilege.

In other words, U.S. residents are considered "normal," whereas the other countries have "second-class status." If you are a U.S. resident, and this point doesn't seem accurate, how would you feel if Japan were the normative country, and every U.S. e-mail address required the "us" ending?

To illustrate U.S.-centered nationalism, suppose that you read an article tomorrow and discovered that soldiers in another country (say, Italy or France) had been torturing political prisoners who are citizens of the United States. Some of these prisoners have been held for more than a year in solitary confinement without any trial. Others have been stripped naked and forced to sodomize one another. Still others have been beaten and had their heads forced down a toilet. All of these tortures have been forbidden by the international laws specified by the Geneva Conventions. How would you respond? Would you be outraged that anyone would treat U.S. citizens so cruelly?

Now, switch countries, so that U.S. soldiers are the torturers, and the people from the other nation are being tortured. Does the torture seem more justified, because of U.S.-centered nationalism? During the summer of 2004, the world learned that U.S. soldiers had in fact been using these specific kinds of torture on citizens from Iraq and from several European countries who were being held in prisons in Iraq and Cuba.

U.S.-centered nationalism is a challenging topic to discuss in the United States (Hase, 2001). It's difficult for students to hear their own country criticized. This attitude is often strengthened by students' educational experiences. If you grew up in the United States, for example, students at your high school were probably encouraged to respect and value people from ethnic groups other than their own. However, were you taught to value other countries equally—or did everyone simply assume that the United States had a special, privileged status compared with the rest of the world? Try searching for examples of U.S.-centered nationalism in the news, in academic settings, and in people's conversations.

Throughout this book, we will explore biases such as sexism, racism, and ageism—situations in which one group has a more powerful position than other groups. We need to keep in mind that U.S.-centered nationalism creates similar problems of inequality on an international level rather than on the interpersonal or intergroup level.

Section Summary

Women and Ethnicity

1. Social and cultural norms in the United States and Canada suggest that being White is normative; as a result, White individuals may mistakenly believe that they do not belong to any ethnic group.
2. Latinas/os share a language with one another as well as many values and customs. However, their other characteristics vary tremendously. Latinas often comment that they must frequently cross boundaries between Latina culture and other cultures.
3. Black Americans constitute the third-largest ethnic group in the United States. Black people in the United States and Canada differ from one another with respect to their family's history.
4. Asian Americans also come from diverse backgrounds. Although they are considered the ideal minority, they often experience discrimination and stressful work conditions.
5. Native Americans and Canadian Aboriginal peoples share a common geographic origin and history. However, they represent numerous different native backgrounds.
6. The variability within any ethnic group—or subgroup—is always large.
7. The limited research about multiracial individuals does not show consistent disadvantages or advantages.
8. An important concept called *intersectionality* emphasizes that each person belongs to many social groups, based on categories such as ethnicity, gender, sexual orientation, and social class. This complexity makes it difficult to study individual differences in psychology.
9. Another form of bias that is related to ethnic bias is U.S.-centered nationalism, in which U.S. residents believe that their nation has higher status than other countries.

1-4 Potential Problems and Biases in Current Research

Learning Objectives

To outline potential problems and biases in research on the psychology of women and gender, you can ...

1-4-1   Describe the five main stages in which bias can negatively impact the research process.

1-4-2   Identify the three main problems that can occur with hypothesis development in scientific research.

1-4-3   Describe the four main sources of bias in designing research studies in psychology.

1-4-4   Explain how research expectancies can influence the outcomes of psychological research.

1-4-5   Differentiate between practical and statistical significance in research results.

1-4-6 Describe how mistakes in data interpretation can skew research results.

1-4-7 Explain how bias in communicating research results contributes to bias in our understanding of gender differences.

1-4-8 Identify the main characteristics of critical thinking.

Earlier in this chapter, we noted the biased research that characterized the early history of the psychology of women. Let's now explore the kinds of problems that sometimes arise when contemporary researchers conduct studies on the psychology of women and gender.

Researchers in all areas of psychology face the problem of potential biases. However, take a moment to consider why biases could raise even more problems in research on the psychology of women. After all, researchers are likely to have strong pre-existing emotions, values, and opinions about the topics being investigated (Caplan & Caplan, 2009; LaFrance et al., 2004). In contrast, consider people who conduct research in visual shape perception. As they were growing up, they probably did not acquire strong emotional reactions to topics such as the retina and the visual cortex. Gender is certainly more controversial! Pre-existing emotions about gender issues seem to be especially strong in connection with research on women who do not conform to the traditional feminine stereotypes, such as unmarried women or lesbian mothers.

Figure 1.3 shows how biases and inappropriate procedures can influence each step of research. Psychologists are trained to carefully consider each phase of research to eliminate these problems. Fortunately, most current studies avoid obvious flaws, but students must still learn how to evaluate psychological research. However, this psychology course can raise your awareness about biases in research. Let's examine each phase of this research in more detail, and then we'll consider the more general issue of critical thinking in psychology.

Formulating the Hypothesis

Researchers are often strongly committed to a certain psychological theory. If this theory is biased against women, then the researchers may expect to find biased results before they even begin to conduct their study (Caplan & Caplan, 2009; McHugh & Cosgrove, 1998). For example, Sigmund Freud argued that women actually enjoy suffering. Notice that psychologists who endorse that perspective would be biased if they conduct research about women who have been emotionally or physically abused.

A second problem is that psychologists may formulate a hypothesis based on previous research that is unrelated to the topic they want to study. Several decades ago, for example, researchers wanted to determine whether children were psychologically harmed when their mothers worked outside the home. Psychologists' own biases against employed mothers led them to locate studies showing that children raised in low-quality orphanages often developed psychological problems. A child whose mother works outside the home for 40 hours a week has a different life compared to a child raised in an institution without a mother or father. Still, those early researchers argued that the children of employed mothers would develop similar psychological disorders.

The final way that biases can influence hypothesis formulation concerns the nature of researchers' questions. For example, researchers studying Native American women typically examine issues such as alcoholism or suicide (Hall & Barongan, 2002). If researchers have a biased attitude that these women are somehow deficient, they will not ask questions that

I. Formulating the hypothesis

    A. Using a biased theory
    B. Formulating a hypothesis on the basis of unrelated research
    C. Asking questions only from certain content areas

II. Designing the study

    A. Selecting the operational definitions
    B. Choosing the participants
    C. Choosing the researcher
    D. Including confounding variables

III. Performing the study

    A. Influencing the outcome through researcher expectancy
    B. Influencing the outcome through participants' expectancies

IV. Interpreting the data

    A. Emphasizing statistical significance rather than practical significance
    B. Ignoring alternate explanations
    C. Misinterpreting correlational data
    D. Making inappropriate generalizations

V. Communicating the findings

    A. Leaving out analyses that show gender similarities
    B. Choosing a title that focuses on gender differences
    C. Journal editors rejecting studies that show gender similarities
    D. Secondary sources emphasizing gender differences instead of gender similarities

FIGURE **1.3** How bias can influence research during five different stages.

can reveal the strengths of these women. For example, do women with extensive tribal experience have more positive attitudes about growing old?

So far, we have reviewed several ways in which biases can operate in the early stages of hypothesis formulation. Specifically, biases can influence the psychologists' theoretical orientation, the previous research they consider relevant, and the topics they investigate.

Designing the Study

An important early step in designing a research study is selecting the operational definitions. An **operational definition** describes exactly how researchers will measure a **variable** (or characteristic) in a study. Consider a study investigating gender comparisons in empathy. **Empathy** is your ability to experience the same emotion that someone else is feeling. For our operational definition, we might decide to use people's answers to a question such as "When your best friend is feeling sad, do you also feel sad?" In other words, we will measure empathy in terms of self-report.

This operational definition of empathy may look perfectly innocent until we realize that it contains a potential bias. Women and men may really be similar in their personal thoughts about empathy. However, men may be more hesitant to *report* that they feel empathic. After all, gender stereotypes emphasize that men should not be overly sensitive.

Imagine, instead, that we measure empathy by observing people's facial expression while they watch a sad movie. Then we might have reached a different conclusion about gender comparisons in empathy. Ideally, researchers should test a hypothesis with several different operational definitions to provide a richer perspective on the research question.

The second source of bias in research design is the choice of participants. Psychologists typically conduct research with participants who are college students, who are primarily rom middle-class homes and historically of White ethnicity. As a result, we know relatively little about people of color and people who are economically disadvantaged (B. Lott, 2002; Saris & Johnston-Robledo, 2000). The selection of research topics can also influence the choice of participants. Studies about mothers with low incomes and about female criminal behavior have disproportionately focused on Black and Latina women. In contrast, studies on body image or salary equity have usually been limited to White women.

A third source of bias in designing a study is the choice of the person who will actually conduct the study. For example, think how the gender of the researcher may make a difference (e.g., F. Levine & Le De Simone, 1991; Sechzer & Rabinowitz, 2008). Let's imagine that a researcher wants to compare women's and men's interest in babies by interviewing the participants. If the researcher is a man, some male participants may be embarrassed to demonstrate a strong interest in babies; gender differences may be large. The same study conducted by a female researcher could produce minimal gender differences.

In research design, a final source of bias is the problem of confounding variables. A **confounding variable** is any characteristic, other than the central variable being studied, that is not equivalent under all conditions; this confounding variable has the potential to influence the study's results. In studies that compare women and men, a confounding variable is some variable—other than gender—that is different for the two groups of participants.

Suppose, for example, that we want to compare the spatial ability of college men and women. A potential confounding variable might be the amount of time they have spent on video games and other activities that emphasize spatial ability. College men are more likely than women to have experience with these activities. Therefore, any gender difference in spatial ability might be traceable to the discrepancy in the amount of spatial *experience* rather than to a true difference in the actual spatial *ability* of college women and men.

The reason we must be concerned about confounding variables is that we need to compare two groups that are as similar as possible in all relevant characteristics except the central variable we are studying. Careless researchers may fail to take appropriate precautions to rule out confounds.

For example, suppose that a group of researchers want to study whether sexual orientation influences psychological adjustment, and they decide to compare married heterosexual women with women who are lesbians. The two groups would not be a fair comparison. For example, some of the lesbian women may not currently be in a committed relationship. Depending on the goals of the researchers, a more appropriate study might compare heterosexual women in a committed relationship and lesbian women in a committed relationship.

Each of these problems in designing a study may lead us to draw the wrong conclusions. The choice of participants in some research—for example, college students are a common choice for researchers—means that we know much more about them than about other groups of people. Furthermore, the operational definitions, the gender of the researcher, and confounding variables may all influence the nature of the conclusions (Caplan & Caplan, 2009).

Performing the Study

Psychologists may run into further problems when they actually perform the study. One potential bias at this point is called researcher expectancy (Caplan & Caplan, 2009; Rosenthal, 1993). According to the concept of **researcher expectancy**, the biases that researchers bring to the study can influence the outcome. If researchers expect males to perform better than females on a test of mathematics ability, they may somehow treat the two groups differently. As a result, males and females may respond differently (Halpern, 2000). Any researcher—male or female—who has different expectations for males and females can produce these expectancy effects.

Researchers in other areas of psychology also have expectations about the outcome of their research, but those expectations may be subtle. In gender research, however, the investigators may be aware of which participants are female and which are male. Suppose that researchers are rating female and male adolescents on their degree of independence in working on a difficult task. The researchers' ratings may reflect their expectations and stereotypes about female and male behavior. These researchers may rate male adolescents higher than female adolescents on a scale of independence, even though they might not find gender differences if they objectively tallied the adolescents' actual behavior. As we noted on page 27, it is important for researchers to choose their operational definitions carefully to minimize the impact of potential biases.

Furthermore, the participants—as well as the researchers—have typically absorbed expectations and stereotypes about their own behavior (Jaffee et al., 1999). For example, popular culture says that women are expected to be moody and irritable just before their menstrual periods. Suppose that a woman is told that she is participating in a study on how the menstrual cycle affects mood. Wouldn't you predict that she would supply more negative ratings during the premenstrual phase of the cycle? In contrast, if she had been unaware of the purpose of the study, she might have responded differently. When you read about a study that uses self-report, keep this potential problem in mind.

In summary, the expectations of both the researchers and the participants may bias the results and distort the conclusions. As a result, the conclusions will not be accurate.

Interpreting the Data

When researchers study the psychology of women and gender, they can misinterpret the data in many ways. For example, some researchers confuse statistical significance and practical significance. As we'll discuss in Chapter 5, a difference between male and female performance on a math test may be *statistically* significant. **Statistical significance** means that the results are not likely to occur by chance alone. In the mathematical formulas used in calculating statistical significance, the sample size has a major influence on statistical significance.

Imagine that a standardized geometry test was given to 10,000 males and 10,000 females. A statistical analysis of the data reveals that the males scored significantly higher than the females. However, suppose that a close inspection reveals that the males received an average score of 40.5, in contrast to the females' average score of 40.0. Even though the difference might be statistically significant, this difference has little *practical* significance. **Practical significance**, as the name implies, means that the results have some meaningful and useful implications for the real world (Halpern, 2000). A half-point difference in these hypothetical geometry scores would have no imaginable implications for how males and females should be treated with respect to teaching geometry. Unfortunately, researchers often discuss only statistical significance, when they should also discuss whether a gender difference has practical significance.

When researchers interpret the data they have gathered, a second potential problem is that they may ignore alternative explanations. Suppose that females score higher than males on a test that measures anxiety. This difference might really be caused by males' reluctance to *report* any anxiety that they might feel rather than by any gender differences in true anxiety. In interpreting this study, researchers must consider alternative explanations.

A third problem when researchers try to interpret the findings is that they may misinterpret correlational data. Consider this hypothetical study: Suppose that some researchers find that there is a positive correlation between the number of years of education that a woman has completed and her score on a test of feminist attitudes. That is, a woman with many years of education is likely to have a high score on on this test of feminist attitudes.

Let's explore this third problem in more detail. Suppose that the researchers conclude that the years of education *cause* women to become more feminist. As you may know, the problem with this conclusion is that correlation is not necessarily causation. Yes, an advanced education may provide information that encourages women to adopt feminist beliefs. However, it may also be likely that women who are feminists are more eager to pursue additional years of education. Yet another explanation could be that it is some third variable (such as the feminist beliefs of a woman's parents) that encourages her to pursue an advanced education and also to hold feminist beliefs. In summary, the third problem with misinterpreting the research results is that researchers may reach an incorrect interpretation of correlational data.

A fourth and final problem in data interpretation occurs when researchers make inappropriate generalizations (Caplan & Caplan, 2009). For example, researchers may sample unusual populations and draw conclusions from them about the psychological characteristics of more typical populations. Suppose that you are investigating infants who had been exposed to abnormally high levels of male hormones before they were born. Unfortunately, researchers may overgeneralize and draw conclusions about the way that male hormones influence *normal* infants (Halpern, 2000). Other researchers might examine a sample of White female and male college students and then assume that their findings apply to all people, including people of color and people who have not attended college.

In summary, the interpretation phase of research contains several additional possibilities for distorting reality. Researchers have been known to ignore practical significance, bypass alternative explanations, misinterpret correlations, and overgeneralize their findings.

Communicating the Findings

After researchers conduct their studies and perform the related analyses, they usually want to report their findings in writing. Other sources of bias may now enter. Psychologists continue to be preoccupied with gender differences, and a gender similarity is seldom considered startling psychological news (Bohan, 2002; Caplan & Caplan, 2009; LaFrance et al., 2004). Therefore, when researchers summarize the results of a study, they may leave out a particular analysis showing that females and males had similar scores. However, they are likely to report any gender *difference* that was discovered. As you can imagine, this kind of selective reporting will underrepresent the gender similarities found in research, and it will overrepresent the gender differences.

Biases are even likely to influence the choice of a title for a research report. For instance, a study examining aggression might be titled "Gender Differences in Aggression," even if it reported one statistically significant gender difference and five comparisons that showed gender similarities! The term *gender differences* focuses on dissimilarities, and it suggests that we need to search for differences. A more neutral term is *gender comparisons*.

After researchers have written a report of their findings, they send their report to journal editors, who must decide whether it deserves publication. Journal editors, along with the researchers themselves, may be more excited about gender differences than about gender similarities (Halpern, 2000). This selective-publication bias can therefore overrepresent gender differences still further so that gender similarities receive relatively little attention.

Even further distortion occurs when the published journal articles are discussed by secondary sources, such as textbooks, newspapers, and magazines. For example, an introductory psychology textbook might discuss one study in which men are found to be more aggressive than women and ignore several other studies that report gender similarities in aggression.

The popular press is especially likely to distort the research. For instance, a local newspaper featured an article titled, "He thinks, she thinks." The article included a sketch of the brain, with one hemisphere in pink and the other in blue.

In an attempt to entice their audience, the media may even misrepresent the species population. For example, a magazine article on stress during pregnancy emphasized the research conducted with rats (Dingfelder, 2004). However, the article included a large photo of a distressed-looking pregnant woman. Many readers might conclude from the misleading article that a mother's prenatal stress clearly causes disorders in human babies. When you have the opportunity, try Demonstration 1.3 to discover whether you find similar media biases.

Demonstration **1.3**

Analyzing Media Reports About Gender Comparisons

Locate a magazine, website, or news source that you normally read. Identify any reports on gender comparisons or the psychology of women. Check Figure 1.3 as you read each article. Can you discover any potential biases?

In addition, can you find any areas in which the summary does not include enough information to make a judgment (e.g., the operational definition for the relevant variables)?

Critical Thinking and the Psychology of Women and Gender

As we have discussed, it helps to be cautious when you encounter information about gender and to carefully inspect published material for a variety of potential biases. This vigilance is part of a more general approach called critical thinking. **Critical thinking** consists of the following four components:

1. Ask thoughtful questions about what you read.
2. Look for potential biases at each step of the research process, as outlined in Figure 1.3 (page 22).
3. Determine whether the conclusions are supported by the evidence that has been presented.
4. Suggest alternative interpretations of the evidence.

One of the most important skills you can acquire in a course on the psychology of women and gender is the ability to think critically about the issues. As Elizabeth Loftus (2004) emphasizes, "Science is not just a giant bowl of facts to remember, but rather a way of thinking. … An idea may *seem* to be true, but this has nothing to do with whether it actually is true" (p. 8).

Unfortunately, popular culture does not encourage critical thinking (Halpern, 2004b). We are often asked to believe the messages that are presented without asking thoughtful questions, determining whether the evidence supports the conclusions, or suggesting other interpretations. As a result, people may consider emotional-sounding evidence to be more important than research-based statements (Scarr, 1997).

Because accuracy is an important aim of research, it is important to identify and eliminate the sources of bias that can distort accuracy and misrepresent women. It is also helpful to use critical-thinking skills to examine the research evidence (Halpern, 2004b). Only then can we have a clear understanding about women and gender.

Section Summary

Potential Problems and Biases in Current Research

1. When researchers formulate their hypotheses, biases can influence their theoretical orientation, the research they consider relevant, and the topics they choose to investigate.
2. When researchers design their studies, biases can influence how they choose their operational definitions, participants, and the people who conduct the research; another bias is the inclusion of confounding variables.
3. When researchers perform their studies, biases may include researcher expectancy as well as the participants' expectations.
4. When researchers interpret their results, biases may include ignoring practical significance, overlooking alternative explanations, misinterpreting correlational data, and overgeneralizing the findings.
5. When researchers communicate their findings, gender differences may be overreported; the title of the paper may emphasize gender differences; journal editors may prefer articles that demonstrate gender differences; and the popular media may distort the research.
6. An important part of critical thinking is being alert for potential biases; critical thinking requires you to ask thoughtful questions, determine whether the evidence supports the conclusions, and propose alternative interpretations for the evidence.

1-5 About This Textbook

Learning Objectives

To summarize the primary themes of the textbook, you can …

1-5-1   Identify four main themes in the text that provide a framework for the study of the psychology of women and gender.

1-5-2   Differentiate between gender as a *subject variable* and as a *stimulus variable*.

1-5-3   Analyze which experiences of women have traditionally been invisible to researchers.

1-5-4   Explain the differences between within-subject and between-subject differences.

The psychology of women and gender is an extremely important topic. Our scientific understanding of the ways in which gender shapes almost every aspect of our lives from cradle to grave is constantly evolving. Therefore, we've made every effort to create a textbook that can help you understand and remember concepts about the psychology of women and gender. Let's first consider the four themes of the book, and then we'll examine some features that can help you learn more effectively.

Themes of the Book

The subject of the psychology of women is impressively complex. Furthermore, the discipline is relatively young, and we cannot yet identify a large number of general principles that summarize this diverse field. Nevertheless, you'll find several important themes woven throughout this textbook. The themes are also listed inside the front cover so that you can easily learn them. Let's discuss the themes now to provide a framework for a variety of topics you will encounter in your textbook.

Theme 1: Psychological Gender Differences Are Typically Small and Inconsistent.

The earlier section on research biases noted that published studies may exaggerate the gender differences as being relatively large. However, even the *published* literature in psychology shows that gender similarities are usually more impressive than gender differences. In terms of permanent, internal psychological characteristics, women and men simply are not that different (Basow, 2001; Bem, 2008; Hyde, 2005a). In gender research, one study may demonstrate a gender difference, but a second study—apparently similar to the first—may demonstrate a gender similarity (Unger, 1998; Yoder & Kahn, 2003). Many traditional studies of gender differences have relied on the notion that gender is a binary construct. This perspective assumes that people can be divided into two separate categories—women and men. It also assumes that people who fit into those two categories are either similar to or different from each other in reliable and measurable ways. In reality, people's scores on a wide variety of psychological variables do not neatly fall into one gender category or the other. Gender is not a binary construct and instead exists on a continuum that includes female, male, nonbinary, and transgender individuals.

You'll recognize that Theme 1 is consistent with the similarities perspective that we discussed on page 8. Theme 1 also specifically rejects the notion of essentialism. As we noted earlier, essentialism argues that gender is a basic, stable characteristic that resides within an individual.

Let's clarify two points, however. First, we are emphasizing that men and women are *psychologically* similar; obviously, their sex organs make them anatomically different. Second, men and women acquire some different skills and characteristics in various cultures because they occupy different social roles in those cultures (Eagly, 2001; Yoder & Kahn, 2003). Men are more likely than women to be chief executives, and women are more likely than men to be receptionists. However, if men and women could have similar social roles in a culture, then those gender differences might be almost nonexistent.

Throughout this book, we will learn that gender differences may appear in some social contexts but not in others. Gender differences are most likely to occur in the following three contexts (Basow, 2001; Unger, 1998; Yoder & Kahn, 2003):

1. When people evaluate themselves rather than when a researcher records behavior objectively.
2. When people are observed in real-life situations (where men typically have more power) rather than in a laboratory setting (where men and women are fairly similar in power).
3. When people are aware that other people are evaluating them.

In these three kinds of situations, people drift toward stereotypical behavior. Women tend to respond the way they think women are supposed to respond; men tend to respond the way they think men are supposed to respond.

Theme 1 focuses on **gender as a subject variable**, or a characteristic within a person that influences the way they act. This book will present evidence that the gender of the participant or the subject (i.e., the person who is being studied) typically has little impact on behavior.

Theme 2: People React Differently to Men and Women.

We just pointed out that gender as a subject variable is usually not important. In contrast, gender as a *stimulus variable* is important (Bem, 2004). When we refer to **gender as a stimulus variable**, we mean a characteristic of a person to which other people react. When psychologists study gender as a stimulus variable, they might ask, "Do people react differently to individuals who are nonbinary or female than to individuals who are male?" Gender is an extremely important social category. To illustrate this point, try ignoring the gender of the next person you meet!

Throughout the book, we will emphasize that gender is an important stimulus variable. In general, we will learn that males are often more valued than females (Lorber, 2005a). For example, many parents prefer a boy rather than a girl for their firstborn child. In Chapter 2, we will also discuss how males are represented more positively in religion and mythology, as well as in current language and the media. In addition, men are typically more valued in the workplace.

When people react differently to men and women, they are demonstrating that they believe in gender differences. We could call this phenomenon "the illusion of gender differences." As you will discover, both men and women tend to exaggerate these gender differences.

Theme 3: Women Are Less Visible Than Men in Many Important Areas.

Men are typically featured more prominently than women in areas that our culture considers important. A quick skim through the daily headlines will convince you that males and "masculine" topics receive more emphasis (Berkman, 2004).

In Chapter 2, we will discuss the research on all forms of media, confirming that men are represented more than women are. Another example is that girls and women are relatively invisible in the classroom, because teachers tend to pay more attention to males than to females (Sadker & Sadker, 1994). Women may also be relatively invisible in the English language. In many respects, this language has traditionally demonstrated **androcentrism:** The male experience is treated as the norm (Basow, 2001; Bem, 2008, Rozee et al., 2008). Instead of *humans* and *humankind,* many people still use words such as *man* and *mankind* to refer to women and men.

Psychologists have helped to keep some important topics invisible. For example, psychology researchers seldom study major biological events in women's lives, such as menstruation, pregnancy, childbirth, and breast feeding. Women *are* visible in areas such as women's magazines, the costume committee for the school play, and low-paying jobs. However, these are all areas that many cultures do not consider important or prestigious.

As we noted in a previous section, women of color are even less visible than White women. Until recently, women of color were also relatively invisible in psychology research (Guthrie, 1998; Holliday & Holmes, 2003; Winston, 2003). In Chapter 2, we will emphasize how women of color are often absent in the media. Although some Black women have now achieved visibility in the media, women of color are still largely absent in primary roles. This lack of representation extends to economically disadvantaged women as well.

Theme 4: Women Differ Widely from One Another.

In this textbook, we will explore how women differ from one another in their psychological characteristics, their life choices, and their responses to biological events. In fact, individual women show so much variability that we often cannot draw any conclusions about women in general (Kimball, 2003). Notice that Theme 4 contradicts the essentialism perspective, which argues that all women share the same psychological characteristics and that these are very different from men's psychological characteristics.

Think about the variability among women you know. They probably differ dramatically in their aggressiveness or in their sensitivity to other people's emotions. Women also vary widely in their choices in terms of careers, marital status, sexual orientation, desire to have children, and so forth. Furthermore, women differ in their responses to biological events. Some women have problems with menstruation, pregnancy, childbirth, and menopause; others find these experiences neutral, somewhat positive, or even wonderful!

In the previous section, we discussed ethnicity, and we noted that the diversity within each ethnic group is remarkable. Throughout this book, when we examine the lives of women in countries outside the United States, we will gather further evidence that women vary widely from one another.

We have emphasized that women show wide variation. As you might imagine, men show a similarly wide variation among themselves. These within-gender variabilities bring us full circle to Theme 1 of this book. Whenever variability *within* each of two groups is large, we probably will not find a statistically significant difference *between* those two groups. In the case of gender, we seldom find a large difference between the average score for females and the average score for males. In Chapter 5, we will discuss this statistical issue in more detail. The important point to remember now is that women show wide within-group variability, and men also show wide within-group variability.

How to Use This Book Effectively

We have designed several features of this textbook to help you learn the material more effectively. Read this section carefully to make the best use of these features.

Each chapter in this book begins with an outline. When you start a new chapter, be sure to read through the outline to acquaint yourself with the scope of the chapter. Learning objectives at the beginning of each chapter and major reading sections focus your attention on the key concepts and let you know what you can do to show mastery of the chapter content.

The third feature in each chapter is a Did You Know? feature. You will find references to the page number where each item is discussed. These items will encourage you to think about some of the controversial and surprising findings you'll encounter in the chapter.

The chapters contain a number of demonstrations, such as Demonstrations 1.1 (page 7) and 1.2 (page 8). Try them yourself, or invite your friends to try them.[3] Each demonstration is simple and requires little or no equipment. The purpose of the demonstrations is to make the material more concrete and personal. According to research about human memory, material is easier to remember if it is concrete and is related to personal experience (Matlin, 2009; T. B. Rogers et al., 1977).

In the text, key terms appear in boldface type (e.g., **gender**) and they are defined in the same sentence. We have also included some phonetic pronunciations, with the accented syllable in italics. (Our students say they feel more comfortable about using a word in discussion if they know that their pronunciation is correct.) Concentrate on these definitions, because an important part of any discipline is its terminology.

Many textbooks include summaries at the end of each chapter, but this book contains summaries at the end of each major section. For example, Chapter 1 contains five section summaries. This feature can help you review the material more frequently, so that you can feel confident about mastering small, manageable portions of the textbook before you move on to new material. At the end of each section, you can test yourself to determine whether you can recall the important points. Then check the section summary to determine whether you were accurate. Incidentally, some students have mentioned that they learn the material more effectively if they read one section at a time, then take a break, and review that section summary before reading the next portion.

A set of 10 chapter review questions appears at the end of each chapter. Some questions test your specific recall, some ask you to draw on information from several parts of the chapter, and some ask you to apply your knowledge to everyday situations.

At the end of each chapter is a list of the key (boldface) terms, in the order in which they appear in the chapter. Try testing yourself to check whether you can define each term. This list of terms also includes page numbers so that you can check on the terms you find difficult. Furthermore, each term appears in the subject index at the end of the book.

A final feature, also at the end of each chapter, is a list of several recommended readings. These are important articles, books, or special issues of journals that are particularly relevant to that chapter. These readings should be useful if you are writing a paper on one of the relevant topics or if you find an area that is personally interesting to you. We hope you'll want to go beyond the information in the textbook and learn on your own about the psychology of women and gender.

---

[3]Some colleges and universities have a policy that students—as well as faculty members—cannot ask other people to complete a survey unless their Institutional Review Board has approved the project. Your course instructor can tell you whether your institution requires this procedure.

Section Summary

About This Textbook

1. Theme 1 states that psychological gender differences are typically small and inconsistent; gender differences are more likely (a) when people evaluate themselves, (b) in real-life situations, and (c) when people are aware that others are evaluating them.
2. Theme 2 states that people react differently to men and women; for example, males are typically considered more valuable than females.
3. Theme 3 states that women are less visible than men in many important areas; for instance, many languages are androcentric.
4. Theme 4 states that women vary widely from one another; for example, they vary in their psychological characteristics, life choices, and responses to biological processes.
5. Features of this book that can help you learn more effectively include chapter outlines, learning objectives, Did You Know? statements, demonstrations, boldfaced key terms, section summaries, chapter review questions, lists of key terms, and recommended readings.

Chapter Review Questions

1. Define the terms *sex* and *gender*. Then decide which of the two terms you should use in discussing each of the following topics: (a) how boys learn "masculine" body postures and girls learn "feminine" body postures; (b) how hormones influence female and male fetuses prior to birth; (c) a comparison of self-confidence in older men and women; (d) the development during puberty of body characteristics such as pubic hair and breasts in women.
2. Apply the two terms *feminism* and *sexism* to your own experience. Do you consider yourself a feminist? Can you identify examples of sexism you have observed during the past week? How do the terms *feminism* and *sexism*—as used in this chapter—differ from their popular use in the media?
3. Define each of the following terms, and then give an example: *racism, classism,*

heterosexism, ableism, ageism, White privilege, the *White-as-normative concept,* and *U.S.-centered nationalism.*
4. Describe the four kinds of feminism discussed in this chapter. How are the similarities perspective and the differences perspective (with respect to gender comparisons) related to those four kinds of feminism? How are social constructionism and essentialism related to these two perspectives?
5. Describe the early research related to gender and the psychology of women. In the section on problems in research, we discuss biases that arise in formulating hypotheses. How might these problems be relevant in explaining some of this early research?
6. Turn back to Figures 1.1 and 1.2. Does the information about the diversity of racial and ethnic groups match the diversity at your own college or university? If not,

what are the differences? How does the information on ethnicity relate to two of the themes of this book?

7. Imagine that you would like to examine gender comparisons in leadership ability. Describe at least four biases that might influence your research.

8. Suppose that you read an article in a news magazine that concludes, "Women are more emotional than men." From a critical-thinking perspective, what questions would you ask to uncover potential biases and problems with the study? (Check Figure 1.3 to determine whether your answers to Questions 7 and 8 are complete.)

9. Describe each of the four themes of this book, and provide an example for each theme, based on your own experiences. Do any of the themes contradict your previous ideas about women and gender? If so, how?

10. What is the difference between gender as a subject variable and gender as a stimulus variable? Suppose that you read a study comparing the aggressiveness of men and women. Is gender a subject variable or a stimulus variable? Suppose that another study examines how people judge aggressive men versus aggressive women. Is gender a subject variable or a stimulus variable?

Key Terms

sex (p. 4)
gender (p. 4)
cisgender (p. 4)
transgender (p. 4)
doing gender (p. 4)
sexism (p. 4)
racism (p. 5)
classism (p. 5)
ableism (p. 5)
heterosexism (p. 5)
sexual prejudice (p. 5)
ageism (p. 6)
feminism (p. 6)

liberal feminism (p. 6)
cultural feminism (p. 6)
radical feminism (p. 7)
women-of-color feminisms (p. 7)
similarities perspective (p. 8)
social constructionism (p. 9)
differences perspective (p. 9)
essentialism (p. 9)

White-privilege concept (p. 14)
White-as-normative concept (p. 14)
intersectionality (p. 18)
U.S.-centered nationalism (p. 19)
operational definition (p. 23)
variable (p. 23)
empathy (p. 23)
confounding variable (p. 23)

researcher expectancy (p. 24)
statistical significance (p. 24)
practical significance (p. 25)
critical thinking (p. 27)
gender as a subject variable (p. 29)
gender as a stimulus variable (p. 29)
androcentrism (p. 30)

Recommended Readings

Caplan, P. J., & Caplan, J. B. (2009). *Thinking critically about research on sex and gender* (3rd ed.). Boston: Pearson. Paula Caplan is a well-known psychologist whose work on the psychology of women is discussed throughout this textbook. She and her son Jeremy—a memory-cognitive neuroscientist at the University of Alberta—wrote this excellent book on applying critical-thinking principles to the research on gender.

Chrisler, J. C., & Golden, C. (Eds.). (2018). *Lectures on the psychology of women* (5th ed.). Long Grove, IL: Waveland Press. This excellent book features 22 chapters written by prominent researchers in the psychology of women; the topics include poverty, body weight, and sexual harassment.

Enns, C. Z. (2004a). *Feminist theories and feminist psychotherapies* (2nd ed.). New York: Haworth. We strongly recommend this book, especially because of its clear descriptions of different approaches to feminism and its excellent overview of feminist therapy, a topic we'll discuss in Chapter 12.

Scarborough, E., & Furumoto, L. (1987). *Untold lives: The first generation of American women psychologists*. New York: Columbia University Press. If you are searching for interesting women in the early history of psychology, this book is ideal. It focuses not only on these important women but also on the forces that shaped their lives.

Answers to Demonstrations

Demonstration 1.1:   1. radical feminism; 2. women-of-color feminisms;   3. liberal feminism;   4. cultural feminism;   5. radical feminism;   6. women-of-color feminisms;   7. liberal feminism;   8. cultural feminism

Courtesy of Robert Sullivan

2 Gender Stereotypes and Other Gender Biases

Learning Objectives

After studying this chapter, you will be able to ...

2-1 Describe instances of biased representations of women and men.

2-2 Summarize beliefs about women and men.

2-3 Summarize the personal consequences of gender stereotypes.

Did You Know?

- Historians and archaeologists have typically paid great attention to men's lives, whereas they often ignore contributions made by women. (p. 38)
- When people read a sentence such as "Each student took his pencil," they typically think of a male student, rather than a student of another gender. (pp. 43–44)
- Black women and men are fairly well represented on prime-time television, but Latina/o, Asian, and Native American actors are rarely featured. (p. 46)
- Men typically have more traditional stereotypes about gender than women do. (p. 54)
- People are most likely to be biased against a woman's competence when she is acting in a stereotypically masculine fashion. (p. 57)
- Research shows that approximately half of lesbian women and gay men report that they have been verbally harassed about their sexual orientation. (p. 63)
- When parents are asked to explain why their daughter gets high grades in mathematics, they tend to attribute her success to hard work. In contrast, parents tend to attribute their son's high grades to his mathematical ability. (p. 68)
- When college students make judgments about the personality characteristics that they consider most important for themselves, women and men tend to prefer similar items. (p. 51)

We each live in a sea of stereotypes. Some stereotypes are obvious, such as ethnicity, country of origin, family income, age, and—of course—gender. Other stereotypes are less prominent, but many people are persuaded that they are completely valid. These include stereotypes about a person's birth order, amount of education, and political beliefs. Some stereotypes are unique to a particular population. For instance, at my college in upstate New York, many students from New York City and Long Island are convinced that the upstate students are not very sophisticated. Furthermore, many students from upstate New York believe that the students from "the city" are not especially friendly.

Stereotypes are the beliefs and assumptions that we associate with particular groups of people. For example, a series of studies showed that students at Yale University tended to associate the word "America" with the word "White" (Devos & Banaji, 2005). Throughout this book, we will consider a variety of stereotypes, for instance, about ethnicity, disabilities, and age. However, we will primarily focus on gender stereotypes.

Gender stereotypes are the beliefs that we associate with women, men, and nonbinary, transgender, or genderqueer people (Fiske, 2004; Kite et al., 2008; D. J. Schneider, 2004; James et al., 2016). In other words, stereotypes refer to our thoughts about a social group; these thoughts may not correspond to reality (Whitley & Kite, 2010).

Some gender stereotypes may be partly accurate (Kite et al., 2008). For example, men may be, on average, less likely than women to ask for directions to a destination (Rosette, Mueller, & Lebel, 2015). However, this stereotype may not apply to every individual man or woman on Earth. Theme 4 emphasizes that people differ widely from one another, no matter which psychological characteristic you are considering. No stereotype can accurately describe everyone (Eagly & Koenig, 2008; Kite et al., 2008). However, we all hold gender stereotypes—even psychologists who study stereotypes!

Several additional terms are related to stereotypes. For example, **prejudice** is an emotional reaction or attitude toward a particular group of people (Eagly & Koenig, 2008; Ostenson, 2008; Whitley & Kite, 2010). The term "prejudice" usually refers to a negative attitude, but it can also refer to a positive attitude. For instance, in many situations, people have a positive attitude toward women because they consider women to be warm and friendly (Eagly & Koenig, 2008).

The term **discrimination** refers to biased treatment of a particular group of people (Crosby, 2008; Glaser, 2005; Whitley & Kite, 2010). For example, the chief executive of a corporation may have prejudiced attitudes about women's leadership ability. This executive can discriminate against women by refusing to promote them to the executive level.

Table 2.1 contrasts the three major terms. The most general term, **gender bias**, includes all three issues: gender stereotypes, gender prejudice, and gender discrimination.

Let's begin our examination of gender stereotypes by noting how women have been represented in history, philosophy, and religion and how they are currently represented in language and the media. In the second section of this chapter, we focus on the content of contemporary stereotypes: What are the current stereotypes? The third section explores how these stereotypes can influence our thinking, our behavior, and even our own identity.

TABLE **2.1**

Comparing Three Kinds of Gender Bias About Women

Term	Brief Definition	Example
Stereotype	A relatively fixed, overly simplified concept or belief of the attitudes and behaviors considered normal and appropriate for women in a particular culture	Chris believes that women aren't very smart.
Prejudice	Emotional reactions or negative attitudes toward women	Chris doesn't like female lawyers.
Discrimination	Differential treatment of the members of different gender groups that often involves negative, hostile, and injurious treatment of people in the rejected groups	Chris won't hire women for a particular job.

2-1 Biased Representations of Women and Men

Learning Objectives

To describe instances of biased representations of women and men, you can …

2-1-1   Identify how gender bias emerges from stereotypes, prejudice, and discrimination toward others.

2-1-2   Summarize how women's contributions to society and culture have historically been invisible.

2-1-3   Describe how traditional philosophical views have emphasized negative views of women's roles in society.

2-1-4   Summarize how various religious perspectives describe the nature and roles of women.

2-1-5   Explain how gender-specific terms and the masculine generic in language perpetuate gender bias.

2-1-6   Describe how women are portrayed in stereotyped ways in the media.

2-1-7   Describe how women of color and women with low incomes are represented and misrepresented in media.

2-1-8   Summarize how stereotyped representations of women in media influence perceptions of reality.

A systematic pattern emerges when we examine how women and men are portrayed. As we'll learn in this section, women have been described as the "second sex" (de Beauvoir, 1961). Consistent with Theme 2, women are often represented as being inferior to men. In addition, consistent with Theme 3, women are frequently invisible. As you read about gender biases in history, religion, language, and the media, think about how they may have shaped your own beliefs about women and men.

Gender Biases Throughout History

A few pages of background discussion cannot do justice to a topic as broad as humans' legacy of gender bias. However, we need to consider several topics to appreciate the origin of current views about women.

The Invisibility of Women in Historical Accounts

Prior to the 1960s, the field of "women's history" did not exist (Kessler-Harris, 2007). In recent decades, scholars have pointed out that we know little about how half of humanity has fared throughout history (Brubaker & Smith, 2004; Erler & Kowaleski, 2003; Roberts, 2008). Archaeologists interested in prehistoric humans typically focused on tools associated with hunting, which was most often men's activity. They ignored the fact that women provided most of the diet by gathering vegetables and grains, raising crops, caring for farm animals, and bringing products to market (Stephenson, 2000; Wiesner, 2000).

Occasionally, however, researchers have made surprising discoveries. For example, in the early Middle Ages (300–900 C.E.), women apparently fought in some battles, because women's bodies have been found on battlefields. In some areas, women have been buried with their weapons (Pohl, 2004). In addition to warfare, medieval nuns also produced illuminated manuscripts and texts, contributing to knowledge creation and scholarly activities that have traditionally been attributed only to men (Radini et al., 2019).

However, women are often missing from the history books because their work was typically confined to home and family. Women artists often expressed themselves in music, dance, embroidered tapestries, and quilting. These relatively anonymous art forms were less likely to be preserved than men's artistic efforts in painting, sculpture, and architecture (Wiesner, 2000).

In recent years, however, feminist historians have examined women's contributions beyond the home and family (Erler & Kowaleski, 2003; Kessler-Harris, 2007). During the sixteenth century, for instance, Lavinia Fontana painted portraits in Bologna, Italy (C. P. Murphy, 2003; Pomeroy, 2007). Furthermore, Artemesia Gentileschi was an active artist who lived in Rome and Florence during the seventeenth century (Pomeroy, 2007). To learn about women artists, search online for the National Museum of Women in the Arts.

In addition, many women's accomplishments have been forgotten. Did you know that women often presided over monasteries before the ninth century (Hafter, 1979)? Did your history books tell you that the Continental Congress chose Mary Katherine Goddard to print the official copy of the Declaration of Independence in 1776? Traditional historians—whether consciously or unconsciously—have ensured women's invisibility in most history courses (Bolden, 2002; Frenette, 2008).

Fortunately, scholars interested in women's history continue to uncover information about women's numerous accomplishments. Many college history and art courses now focus on women's experiences, making women central rather than peripheral (Djen, 2007). You can locate more information about women's history by searching online for the National Women's History Alliance and the Women's Rights National Historical Park.

Philosophers' Representation of Women

Philosophers throughout the centuries have typically depicted women as inferior to men. For example, the Greek philosopher Aristotle (384–322 B.C.E.) believed that women could not develop fully as rational beings and that women are more likely than men to be envious and to tell lies (Stephenson, 2000).

Later philosophers often adopted the same framework. For instance, Jean-Jacques Rousseau (1712–1778) argued that the function of women was to please men and to be useful to them (Hunter College Women's Studies Collective, 1995). In other words, this prominent Enlightenment philosopher was definitely not enlightened about the roles of women! Rousseau's views were echoed by political figures. For example, the French emperor Napoléon Bonaparte (1769–1821) wrote: "Women are nothing but machines for producing children" (cited in Mackie, 1991, p. 26).

Before the twentieth century, perhaps the only well-known philosopher whose views would be acceptable to current feminists was John Stuart Mill (1806–1873). Mill was a British philosopher whose viewpoint was strongly influenced by his wife, Harriet Taylor Mill (1807–1858). John Stuart Mill argued that women should have equal rights and opportunities to own property, to vote, to be educated, and to choose a profession. John Stuart Mill is prominently featured in philosophy textbooks, but these textbooks have often omitted his views on women (Hunter College Women's Studies Collective, 1995).

Gender Biases in Religion and Mythology

We've learned that history and philosophy have not been kind to women. In addition, women are often treated differently from men in traditional religion and in mythology. Women are typically less prominent than men. Furthermore, women are frequently portrayed with negative characteristics, although every religion includes some positive characteristics. Table 2.2 presents a summary of how various religions portray women.

TABLE **2.2**

Gender Differences in Traditional Religion and Mythology

Religion	Examples of Gendered Bias in Traditional Beliefs and Practice	Twenty-First Century Practice
Judaism	**Negatives** • Women are portrayed negatively in some traditional prayers for men such as "Blessed art Thou, O Lord our God, King of the Universe, that I was not born a woman." • Women were created from Adam's rib and caused original sin. • Marriage and family law largely favored men over women. **Positives** • "Jewishness" is passed down matrilineally, through the mother. • Women were viewed as more faithful.	Expectations for women's participation and religious behavior differ widely depending on type of Judaism practiced. For example, women in Orthodox and Conservative movements are more restricted, while women in Reform and Reconstructionist movements have equal opportunities to serve as rabbis and participate in religious ceremonies.
Christianity	**Negatives** • Women should avoid leadership positions, "keep silent in the churches," and be subordinate to men. • Women were created from Adam's rib and caused original sin. **Positives** • Women are seen as virtuous and saintly, especially when they nurture men and small children and engage in self-sacrifice.	Women are pastors, bishops, and lay leaders in several Protestant Christian denominations but are restricted from the highest leadership positions in others, such as in Catholic and some Protestant orders.

(continues)

Religion	Examples of Gendered Bias in Traditional Beliefs and Practice	Twenty-First Century Practice
Traditional Chinese Religious Philosophy	*Negatives* • The feminine *yin* represents darkness, ignorance, and evil, and the *yang*, the masculine side, represents light, intellect, and goodness. • Chief virtue of women is obedience to father, then husband, then grown son, and practices such as foot-binding and chastity were valued. *Positives* • "Feminine" virtues such as softness, fertility, and nonaggression were viewed as healthier than traditionally masculine traits.	More traditional Confucianist views of *yin* and *yang* have become more balanced in modern times. Additionally, Daoist and Buddhist belief systems have historically provided more vocational and social opportunities for women in religious spaces.
Islam	*Negatives* • Beginning in the Middle Ages, views of women in Islam became more restricted and became influenced by social customs and traditions. *Positives* • Women historically had rights and opportunities that were broad and not limited to domestic spaces. • Muhammad and the Quran emphasize the equal treatment of women and men, with their roles in society as complementary instead of competing (Ahmed, 1992; Saleh, 1972).	In the current era, Islamic cultures vary widely in their treatment and views of women.
Hinduism	*Negatives* • A woman is typically defined in terms of her husband. • Unmarried women and widows have no personal identity. *Positives* • Kali is an especially powerful Hindu goddess. It is believed that she emerges from the bodies of admirable deities, destroys her enemies, and drinks their blood. • Numerous Hindu communities are matriarchal.	Schools now allow young women to learn the Vedas and sacred scriptures that were previously limited to only men of a certain class or caste (Pechilis, 2004).

Consider the difference between Adam and Eve in the story shared by Jews and Christians. Because men are created in "God's image" and women are created from men, they are therefore secondary in the great scheme of things (Bem, 2008). Historically in Judaism, women are relatively invisible in the Torah (Ruth, 2001; R. J. Seigel et al., 1995), and in some forms of Christianity, women are expected to be silent and subordinate to men (Sawyer, 1996).

In the twenty-first century, Jewish women have become rabbis and scholars, and many ceremonies designed for men and boys have been adapted for women and girls (P. D. Young, 2005). Women have also assumed leadership responsibilities in Protestant religions, although women still cannot hold higher positions within the Catholic church (P. D. Young, 2005).

Additional religions have also promoted negative views of women. In traditional Chinese Confucianism, the masculine yang was viewed as being preferable to the feminine yin (Levering, 1994; Pauwels, 1998). Alternatively, Buddhist and Daoist traditions have viewed women's roles in Chinese society and religion more positively (Adler, 2006).

The Islamic religion as written in the Quran (or Koran) emphasizes the equal treatment of women and men (Ali, 2007; Sechzer, 2004; Ussem, 2005). Islamic cultures vary widely in their treatment of women (Ali, 2007; El Safty, 2004). In some modern practices of Islam, women experience restrictions and unequal treatment, although these restrictions are more often due to patriarchal interpretations of Islam and cultural traditions rather than Islam itself (Ahmed, 1992; Saleh, 1972).

In Hinduism, a woman is typically defined in terms of her husband, and unmarried women and widows often have no personal identity (Siegel et al., 1995). However, some Hindu goddesses, such as Kali, are viewed as quite powerful (Wangu, 2003).

When we combine views of women from various religions and from classical Greco-Roman mythology, we can derive two conflicting views of women:

1. *Women are evil.* Women can bring harm to men, and like the goddess Kali, may even be bloodthirsty.
2. *Women are virtuous.* Women can also be virtuous and saintly, especially when they nurture men and small children. For example, the Virgin Mary represents the essence of caring and self-sacrifice.

Notice that these portrayals are sometimes negative and sometimes positive. However, each representation emphasizes how women are *different* from men. These traditions illustrate **androcentrism** or the **normative-male problem**: Men are the standard of comparison, whereas women are "the second sex."

Gender Biases in Language

Language—as well as religion—frequently encourages a second-class status for women. Specifically, people often use either subordinate or negative terms to refer to women. We'll also learn that women are often invisible in language, for example, when the term *he* is used in reference to both men and women (Weatherall, 2002). Incidentally, in Chapter 6, we'll consider a related topic, comparing how women and men use language.

Terms Used for Women

In many situations, people use different terms to refer to men and women, and the two terms are not parallel (Adams & Ware, 2000; Gibbon, 1999). For example, people call DeShawn Washington, M.D., a doctor, whereas they may call Elena Garcia, M.D., a *female* doctor. This usage implies that being a male doctor is "normal" and that a female doctor is an exception.

Sometimes, the female member of a pair of words has a much more negative, sexualized, or trivial connotation than the male member does. Think about the positive connotations of the word *bachelor*—a happy-go-lucky person, perhaps with many romantic partners. How about *spinster?* Here the connotation is much more negative. Similarly, compare *master* with *mistress, major* with *majorette, sculptor* with *sculptress,* and *wizard* with *witch* (Adams & Ware, 2000; Gibbon, 1999; Weatherall, 2002).

Language may also infantilize women. For example, people often refer to adult women as *girls* or *gals* in situations where adult men would not be called *boys.* Words really do matter! According to the research, when a news article uses these biased terms to describe a woman, people judge her to be less competent than when she is described in gender-neutral terms (Dayhoff, 1983).

The Masculine Generic

Suppose that you are reading an anthropology book, and it says, "Man has often shown a tendency to paint animals in his artistic representations." Be honest: Did you imagine a woman painting an animal?

The example of *man* illustrates a problem called the *masculine generic.* The **masculine generic** (sometimes called the **androcentric generic**) is the use of masculine nouns and pronouns to refer to all human beings—of all genders—instead of referring only to men (Wodak, 2005).

Table 2.3 shows some of these masculine generic terms. A teacher may have told you that *his* actually includes *her*, as in the sentence, "Each student took his pencil." Essentially, you were supposed to consider *his* in this sentence as gender neutral, even though any female content is invisible (Adams & Ware, 2000; Romaine, 1999; Wayne, 2005; Weatherall, 2002).

We have clear research evidence that these masculine generic terms are not actually gender neutral. Approximately 50 studies have demonstrated that terms such as *man* and *he* produce more thoughts about men and boys, instead of thoughts about other genders (e.g., M. Crawford, 2001; Lambdin et al., 2003; Madson & Shoda, 2006; Rozee et al., 2008; Weatherall, 2002). The issue is no longer simply a grammatical one; it is also both political and practical.

Demonstration 2.1 illustrates part of a classic study, conducted by John Gastil (1990). Gastil presented a number of sentences that used a masculine generic pronoun (e.g., "The average American believes he watches too much TV"). Other sentences used a gender-neutral pronoun (e.g., "Pedestrians must be careful when they cross the street"). Gastil asked participants to describe the mental image that each sentence evoked.

TABLE **2.3**

Examples of Masculine Generic Terms

businessman	patronize
manpower	he/his/him (to refer to both genders)
chairman	salesman
master of ceremonies	mankind
forefather	workmanship
Neanderthal	man man-made
fraternal twins	

Source: American Psychological Association (2010) and Doyle (1995).

Demonstration 2.1

Thoughts for Masculine Generic and Gender-Neutral Pronouns

Ask a friend to read sentence 1. Then ask the friend to describe any thought that comes to mind. Repeat the process with the remaining sentences. For each of the target (T) sentences, note whether your friend's description of their thought represents a male, a female, or some other answer.

	1. Fire hydrants should be opened on hot days.
(T)	2. The average American believes he watches too much TV.
	3. The tropical rain forests of Brazil are a natural wonder.
(T)	4. Pedestrians must be careful when they cross the street.
	5. The apartment building was always a mess.
(T)	6. After a patient eats, he needs to rest.
	7. In the corner sat a box of worn-out shoes.
(T)	8. Teenagers often daydream while they do chores.

Did your friend supply more male descriptions for sentences 2 and 6 than for sentences 4 and 8? To obtain a broader sample of replies, have several friends respond to this demonstration, or combine data with other classmates.

As Figure 2.1 shows, women participants reported four times as many male images as female images when they responded to sentences containing *he*. In contrast, women reported an equal number of male and female images (i.e., a 1:1 ratio) when they responded to sentences containing *they*. Figure 2.1 also shows that men, in responding to the *he* sentences, reported an astonishing 13:1 ratio of male images to female images, but only a 4:1 ratio in response to the *they* sentences. In short, masculine generic terms produce more thoughts about males than do gender-neutral terms.

The masculine generic issue also has important implications for people's career choices. For example, Briere and Lanktree (1983) presented students with different versions of a paragraph describing careers in psychology. Students who had been presented with the gender-neutral version rated psychology as a more appealing career for women than did those who had been presented with the masculine generic version. Furthermore, college students rate psychology counselors more positively if the counselors use gender-neutral language rather than masculine-generic language (M. E. Johnson & Dowling-Guyer, 1996).

People have clearly increased their use of gender-neutral language. For example, most writers now use the term *people* rather than the masculine generic term *man*. In addition, most college students prefer to read gender-neutral language (Parks & Roberton, 1998a, 1998b, 2000). People who have low scores on a test of gender bias are especially likely to

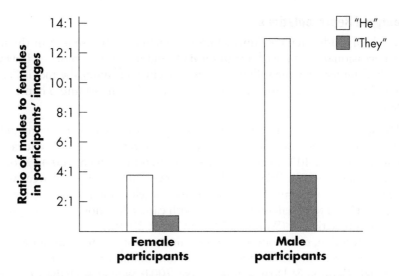

FIGURE **2.1** Ratio of male images to female images, as a function of the pronoun condition and the gender of the participant.
Source: Based on Gastil (1990).

prefer this gender-neutral language (Swim et al., 2004). Furthermore, Parks and Roberton (1998a) discovered that some male students make positive comments about gender-neutral terms. For example, a male college student reported:

> Being a male myself, it's easy to think that people are making mountains out of molehills. ... But I think that if the roles were reversed, I would want change. ... It wouldn't be fair if I was part of womankind, so it shouldn't be fair for women to be part of mankind. We should all be part of humankind. (Parks and Roberton 1998a, p. 451)

Organizations such as the American Psychological Association (2020) strongly caution against gender-biased language. Table 2.4 offers some appropriate suggestions for gender-neutral language.

Gender Biases in the Media

An advertisement for shoes in an upscale U.S. magazine shows a woman sprawled in an awkward position on a living-room floor, as if she were a murder victim. Another ad shows a woman about age 20 applying antiwrinkle cream; the text says to use this cream *before* your first wrinkle. Can you imagine switching the genders—using a corpselike male model to advertise men's shoes or running an ad to encourage 20-year-old men to purchase an antiwrinkle cream? If you want to decide whether an advertisement is sexist, here's a test that is usually helpful: Switch the genders and note whether the revision seems bizarre.

In Chapter 3, we'll consider media directed toward children. Here, let's first examine gender stereotypes found in media directed toward adults, and then we'll discuss the effects of these stereotyped representations.

Stereotyped Representations

Hundreds of studies have examined how women are represented in the media. You may find an occasional example of nurturant dads and intellectual moms. However, the research generally demonstrates the following eight conclusions about the media. These conclusions support both Theme 2 (differential treatment of women) and Theme 3 (invisibility of women).

- *Women are relatively invisible.* The research shows that women are underrepresented in the media. For example, only 37% of prime-time TV news broadcasts feature female anchors, 40% of online news is written by women, and 41% of print news is written by women (Women's Media Center, 2019). The only areas where women account for more than 50% of the bylines in television and online news outlets include topics related to female-dominated health care, education, and lifestyle, entertainment, and leisure activities (Women's Media Center, 2019).

  In addition, men dominate entertainment. For example, about 60 to 70% of the speaking actors in prime-time television and online streaming entertainment shows are male (Lauzen & Dozier, 2002; Perse, 2001; Women's Media Center, 2019; Ziegler, 2008). Furthermore, we rarely observe women athletes on TV. Even though they comprise 40% of all athletes, media coverage of women's sports is only 4 to 6% of the total sports coverage, and female sportscasters are equally rare (R. L. Hall, 2008; The Tucker Center & tptMN, 2014). Compared to women, men are also more likely to appear in films and advertisements (Ganahl et al., 2003; A. G. Johnson, 2001; Women's Media Center, 2019).

  Other forms of technology also emphasize male perspectives. For instance, only 35% of computer clip-art images are female (Milburn et al., 2001). In addition, even though they represent 39% of all gamers, women are seldom featured in video games. Only 5% of video games feature exclusively female protagonists, partly because fewer than 10% of video-game designers are female (Burgess et al., 2007; "Online," 2004; Sarkeesian & Petit, 2019).
- *Women are relatively inaudible.* Women are not presented much, and they are *heard* even less (Perse, 2001). Try to recall a typical advertisement. Whose voice of authority is praising the product's virtues? Usually, it is a man's voice. The percentage of men in these voice-overs has remained fairly constant in recent years. Studies in the United States report that 70–90% of voice-overs are male. Similar data are reported

TABLE **2.4**

Suggestions for Nonsexist Language

1. Use the plural form. "Students can monitor their progress" can replace "A student can monitor his progress."

2. Use "you." The sentence "Suppose that you have difficulty recalling your Social Security number" is less sexist—and also more engaging—than "Suppose that a person has difficulty recalling his Social Security number."

3. Eliminate the pronoun. "The student is typically the best judge of the program" can replace "The student is usually the best judge of his program."

Source: Based on American Psychological Association (2020).

in Australia, Denmark, France, Great Britain, Japan, Saudi Arabia, Spain, and Turkey (Arima, 2003; Bartsch et al., 2000; Furnham & Mak, 1999; Hurtz & Durkin, 1997, 2004; Nassif & Gunter, 2008; Uray & Burnaz, 2003; Valls-Fernandez & Martinez-Vicente, 2007).

- *Women are seldom shown working outside the home.* For example, advertisements, popular magazines, and comic strips are much more likely to show men—rather than women—in an employment setting (Arima, 2003; Glascock & Preston-Schreck, 2004; Morrison & Shaffer, 2003; D. J. Schneider, 2004). Researchers have confirmed this same pattern in both Korea and Spain (Kim & Lowry, 2005; Valls-Fernandez & Martinez-Vicente, 2007).

  Seventeen and other magazines aimed at female adolescents also tend to minimize the importance of pursuing a career (Schlenker et al., 1998; Willemsen, 1998). The articles on physical appearance and finding a boyfriend consistently outweigh the articles about career planning and independence.

- *Women are shown doing housework.* Here, unfortunately, the percentages probably capture reality accurately. Commercials seldom show men taking care of children or performing household chores, whether the sample is gathered in North America, Europe, the Middle East, Asia, or Africa (Arima, 2003; Bartsch et al., 2000; Furnham & Mak, 1999; Furnham et al., 2000; Ibroscheva, 2007; G. Kaufman, 1999; Kim & Lowry, 2005; Mwangi, 1996; Nassif & Gunter, 2008; Perse, 2001; Royo-Vela et al., 2006; Royo-Vela et al., 2007; Vigorito & Curry, 1998). When men actually do household chores, they tend to be humorously incompetent. The problem is so pervasive that the British Advertising Standards Authority recently banned sexist gender stereotypes from commercial advertising because of their harmful effects (Tiffany, 2019).

- *Women and men are represented differently.* The media are likely to treat men more seriously than women. For example, when a woman runs for elected office, it's difficult to find a news article that does not mention her hairstyle, her "figure flaws," or her clothing choices (Pozner, 2001; Van der Pas & Aaldering, 2020). Interestingly, the only categories of ads in which women appear more often than men are for beauty products and clothing (Ganahl et al., 2003). In addition, sports commentators refer to male athletes as "men," whereas the female athletes are called "girls," consistent with the biased language we discussed earlier in this section (R. L. Hall, 2008).

- *Women's bodies are used differently from men's bodies.* Magazines, online media, and television rarely show images of women with larger bodies, except in weight-loss ads (Bennett, 2007; Greenwood & Pietromonaco, 2004). In action comic books, video games, and animated cartoons, the women have exaggerated bodies, with enormous breasts and tiny waists (Burgess et al., 2007; Ziegler, 2008).

  Furthermore, if you analyze advertisements, you'll notice that the women are more likely than the men to serve a decorative function. Women recline in seductive clothes, caressing a car, or they drape themselves coyly on the nearest man. In contrast, the men are strong and muscular, and they typically adopt a rigid, dignified body posture (Stankiewicz & Rosselli, 2008). Advertisements in countries as different as Bulgaria and Korea also feature these stereotyped representations (Ibroscheva, 2007; Nelson & Paek, 2005).

  Physical attractiveness is definitely more important for women than for men. On prime-time television, for instance, 65% of the compliments about appearance are directed toward women, even though they represent only 40% of the actors (Lauzen & Dozier, 2002; Women's Media Center, 2019).

- *Women of color are underrepresented, and they are often shown in a particularly biased way.* In the United States, Black individuals are now represented in a reasonable number of TV programs and fashion magazines (Millard & Grant, 2006). However, they are seldom shown in romantic relationships (Perse, 2001).

  Other women of color such as Latina, Asian American, and Native American women—are virtually invisible in the media (Boston et al., 2001; Millard & Grant, 2006; Molinary, 2007; Perse, 2001; Women's Media Center, 2019). Hovland and her colleagues (2005) conducted an interesting media analysis on Korean and U.S. women's magazines. They discovered that 30% of the women depicted in Korean women's magazines were White. In contrast, only 2% of women in comparable U.S. women's magazines appeared to be Korean or members of any other Asian ethnic group.

  In the earlier discussion of women and religion, we noted that religions represent women as either saints or sinners. The same polarized representation is often true for women of color in the media. Most women of color are either "good girls" or "bad girls"—either asexual or hypersexualized. The characters are seldom well enough developed to reveal the interesting combination of traits depicted in the media for White individuals (Coltrane & Messineo, 2000; Vargas, 1999). In summary, women of color are both underrepresented and misrepresented by the media (Women's Media Center, 2019).

- *Women who are economically disadvantaged are underrepresented, and they are often shown in a particularly biased way.* In Chapter 1, we noted that psychologists have paid remarkably little attention to socioeconomic status. Media researchers also ignore socioeconomic status. However, some research shows that prime-time television and other media primarily feature middle-class or wealthy individuals (Mantsios, 2001). If you are looking for women from lower-income backgrounds on television, you'll need to watch reality television shows, such as *Teen Mom* or *Here Comes Honey Boo-Boo,* or talk shows, such as *Dr. Phil.* Though problematic, it's been standard practice and considered acceptable to include women who are economically disadvantaged if they are promiscuous or if they come from dysfunctional families (Lott & Bullock, 2010; Mantsios, 2001).

  In news sources or magazines, you'll rarely find any article about women who are economically disadvantaged unless it describes health issues or public assistance. These articles seldom capture the difficulty of raising a family under these conditions (Bullock et al., 2001). Furthermore, about half of the women from economically disadvantaged backgrounds who are featured in magazine articles are Black—a much higher percentage than in the real world (D. J. Schneider, 2004).

  Now that you are familiar with some of the representations of women in the media, try Demonstration 2.2. You can also analyze magazine advertisements to assess stereotyped representations. Pay particular attention to any nontraditional advertisements. Does the female physician in the advertisement look both confident and competent? How about the father changing the baby's diaper?

Demonstration 2.2

The Representation of Women and Men on Television

Keep a pad of paper next to you during the next five television shows you watch so that you can monitor how women and men are represented. Use one column for women and one for men, and record the activity of each individual who appears on screen for more than a few seconds. Use simple codes to indicate what each person is doing, such as working at a job (W), doing housework (H), or performing some activity for other family members (F). In addition, record the number of female and male voice-overs in the advertisements. Can you detect any other patterns in the representations of women and men, aside from those mentioned in the text?

How are social class and ethnicity represented on these shows? Can you identify any nonstereotypical examples?

A common practice now is to share your views with the advertisers via e-mail or reaching out directly to companies on social media. Sponsors are often sensitive to public opinion. For example, Unilever vowed to drop sexist stereotypes from its ads in response to public pressure and research showing that only 2% of ads showed intelligent women (Sweney, 2016). Similarly, PepsiCo dropped plans to develop a less messy version of Doritos, dubbed "Lady Doritos," in response to public criticism (Sullivan, 2018).

The Effects of Stereotyped Representations

Does the biased representation of women in the media simply *reflect* reality, or does it actually *influence* reality? Although the topic has not been extensively studied, we have evidence for both options (Kite et al., 2008; D. J. Schneider, 2004):

- *Yes, the media do reflect reality.* For instance, the media often reflect the realities that women are often invisible and silenced and that they are more likely than men to do housework. The media also reflect the reality that people often believe that women should be decorative. However, the ads certainly do *not* reflect reality in other respects. For example, do you have any female friends who obsess about a nearly invisible age spot or who invite neighbors in to smell their toilet bowl?
- *Yes, the media can actually influence reality by changing some people's attitudes and cognitive performance.* For example, research has shown that after viewing stereotyped ads, both men and women held less feminist attitudes (MacKay & Covell, 1997). Furthermore, after watching stereotyped ads, women were less interested in leadership roles (Davies et al., 2005).

However, a carefully conducted study by Janice Yoder and her colleagues (2008) compared college women who had viewed traditional, stereotyped television advertisements versus college women who had viewed nontraditional, nonstereotyped TV ads. Surprisingly, these two groups reported similar career goals and focus on achieving success. It's possible that stereotyped and nonstereotyped advertisements might have different effects for women who have not attended college.

The media can also influence our attitudes toward other people (M. J. Levesque & Lowe, 1999). For example, J. L. Knight and Giuliano (2001) asked students to read an article about a female athlete and rate her on a number of dimensions. If the article emphasized her athletic skills rather than her attractiveness, the students rated her higher in talent, aggressiveness, and heroism.

The media can influence people's cognitive performance. For instance, Wilhelm Hurtz and Devin Durkin (2004) asked a group of community residents to listen to popular songs interspersed with radio advertisements that were either gender neutral or gender stereotyped. Next, they saw a list of gender-stereotyped personality characteristics. Finally, they were asked to recall those personality characteristics. The people who had heard the gender-stereotyped ads—rather than gender-neutral ads—actually remembered a greater number of those stereotyped personality characteristics.

Section Summary

Biased Representations of Women and Men

1. "Gender stereotype" is a term that refers to the beliefs and assumptions that we associate with women, men, and nonbinary individuals. Prejudice applies to emotional reactions, and discrimination indicates biased behavior.
2. We have little information about women's activities throughout history, although feminist researchers have discovered some nontraditional accomplishments. In general, philosophers have emphasized women's inferiority.
3. Judaism and Christianity both depict women's inferiority; traditional Chinese beliefs, the Islamic religion, and Hinduism also tend to portray negative images of women. Various religions and ancient myths have often represented women as either evil people or as virtuous mothers.
4. The linguistic terms used for women often emphasize their secondary status; many of these terms are negative or infantilizing.
5. Numerous studies have demonstrated that the masculine generic encourages people to think about men more often than women; gender-neutral terms can be easily substituted.
6. The media frequently represent women in a stereotyped fashion. Women are represented less than men are. They are seldom shown working outside the home; more often, they are shown doing housework. The media treat men more seriously; women's bodies are also represented differently.
7. Women of color and women who are economically disadvantaged are particularly likely to be underrepresented or to be represented in a stereotypical fashion.
8. The media's stereotyped representations of women reflect cultural values. Furthermore, the media can sometimes influence people's gender roles, their attitudes toward others, and their cognitive performance.

2-2 People's Beliefs About Women and Men

Learning Objectives

To summarize beliefs about men and women, you can ...

2-2-1   Analyze how communal and agentic stereotypes relate to perceptions of women and men.

2-2-2   Explain how gender stereotypes intersect with other factors such as ethnicity, economic status, and sexual orientation.

2-2-3   Identify subject variables that influence gender stereotypes.

2-2-4   Explain how researchers measure implicit gender stereotypes.

2-2-5   Evaluate how gender stereotypes affect attitudes about women's competence.

2-2-6   Describe how gender stereotypes influence attitudes toward women's pleasantness.

2-2-7   Differentiate between hostile and benevolent forms of sexism.

2-2-8   Compare how gender discrimination varies in countries around the world.

2-2-9   Describe how heterosexism affects the lives of LGBTQ+ people.

2-2-10   List the factors that correlate with heterosexism.

In the first section of this chapter, we looked at how women and men are represented in history, philosophy, religion, mythology, language, and the media. These representations certainly help to shape people's beliefs about gender. Let's now turn to the man and woman on the street—or, more likely, on the college campus. What is the nature of their gender stereotypes? How can we assess these stereotypes? Why is sexism such a complex topic? What kinds of thinking produce these stereotypes and keep them powerful? How can gender stereotypes influence people's social interactions? Finally, how do strong gender stereotypes contribute to heterosexism?

The Content of Stereotypes

Gender stereotypes are so pervasive that they extend to a wide range of human behaviors (Barnett & Rivers, 2004; Kite et al., 2008). For example, most people believe that males earn higher grades than females in math classes, although we'll learn in Chapter 5 that females' grades are usually better. Most people also assume that male leaders are more effective than female leaders, although we'll refute that stereotype in Chapter 6. In addition, most people believe that men are more likely than women to have a heart attack, yet we'll learn in Chapter 11 that this stereotype is inaccurate.

In this section, however, we'll focus primarily on people's stereotypes about women's and men's personality characteristics. Before you read any further, try out Demonstration 2.3. Rather than assess your own stereotypes or beliefs about men and women, try to guess what *most people* think. You will probably find that most of your answers are accurate.

Demonstration 2.3

Stereotypes About Women and Men

For this demonstration, you will guess what most people think about women and men. Put a W in front of those characteristics that you believe most people associate with women more than with men. Put an M in front of those characteristics associated with men more than with women.

_____	self-confident	_____	emotional
_____	dependent	_____	talkative
_____	gentle	_____	loud
_____	greedy	_____	physically strong
_____	kind	_____	compassionate
_____	caring	_____	patient
_____	competitive	_____	modest
_____	nervous	_____	courageous
_____	active	_____	inventive
_____	capable	_____	powerful

The answers at the end of the chapter are based on responses obtained by several researchers (Cota et al., 1991; Ghavami & Peplau, 2013; Street, Kimmel, & Kromrey, 1995; J. E. Williams & Best, 1990; J. E. Williams et al., 1999).

If you check the list of personality characteristics associated with women and with men, you'll realize that those two lists are somewhat different. According to theorists, the term **communion** emphasizes a concern for your relationship with other people. Terms associated with communion (such as *gentle* and *warm*) are usually stereotypically feminine. In contrast, the term **agency** describes a concern with your own self-interests. Terms associated with agency (such as *self-confident* and *competitive*) are usually stereotypically masculine (Rudman & Glick, 2008).

Interestingly, however, women's agency scores have been increasing during the past 20 years (Kite et al., 2008). Furthermore, when college students in the United States, Germany, Chile, and Brazil were asked to consider gender roles in the year 2050, they estimated that women would demonstrate more agency than they do now. However, men were not expected to demonstrate more communion (Diekman & Goodfriend, 2006; Diekman et al., 2005; Wilde & Diekman, 2005).

Let's now examine the stereotypes about men and women from various ethnic groups. Then we'll consider whether several subject variables influence our stereotypes.

Stereotypes About Women and Men from Different Ethnic Groups

In addition to simple stereotypes about women's and men's personality, people also create stereotypes about women and men from different ethnic groups (Deaux, 1995;

D. J. Schneider, 2004; Ghavami & Peplau, 2013). To study the intersectionality of gender and ethnicity stereotypes, Ghavami and Peplau (2013) asked college students to generate adjectives that they believed would be stereotypically associated with people from five different ethnic groups. These intersectional groupings were based on gender (i.e., men and women) and ethnicity (i.e., Asian Americans, Black Americans, Latina/o Americans, Middle Eastern Americans, or White Americans).

Table 2.5 combines the data from all participants and shows some commonly listed terms for each target group. As you can observe, people do not have one unified gender stereotype when they judge women and men in all five ethnic groups. Instead, people combine information about the gender and ethnicity of the target, so that they create a variety of gender stereotypes. Consistent with the intersectionality hypothesis, women and men across some ethnic groups share some stereotypes. This intersection of gender and ethnicity makes it difficult to talk simply about gender stereotypes *or* ethnicity stereotypes, because these

TABLE **2.5**

Intersectionality: Common Stereotypes for Men and Women from Different Ethnic Groups in the United States

White Women	White Men
Intelligent, Attractive	Intelligent, Assertive
Rich, Materialistic	High Status, Successful
Arrogant, Racist	Arrogant, Racist
Black Women	**Black Men**
Athletic, Loud	Athletic, Loud
Dark skin, Hair weaves	Dark skin, Tall
Assertive, Confident	Dangerous, Violent
Asian American Women	**Asian American Men**
Intelligent, Quiet	Intelligent, Quiet
Shy, Family-oriented	Shy, Nerdy
Good at math, Short	Good at math, Short
Latina Women	**Latino Men**
Feisty, Loud	Macho, Jealous
Hard workers, Good cooks	Hard workers, Day laborers
Dark skin, Attractive	Dark skin, Short
Middle Eastern Women	**Middle Eastern Men**
Religious, Covered	Religious, Wear turban
Attractive, Submissive	Rich, Sexist
Dark skin, Oppressed	Dark skin, Terrorists

Source: Based on Ghavami & Peplau (2013).

stereotypes are not uniformly shared by men and women across each ethnic group. For example, the "attractive" stereotype is something shared among White men, White women, Latina women, and Middle Eastern women. The "loud" stereotype is shared among Black women, Black men, and Latina women. "Assertiveness" is a shared stereotype between Black women and White men.

Furthermore, we apparently create subtypes within each of these gender–ethnicity categories. For example, the stereotypes often distinguish between the "good women" and the "bad women" in each ethnic group.

Scholars who study ethnicity note that Black women are stereotyped as either warm but sexless "Mammies"—a stereotype preserved since the slavery era—or sexually promiscuous women (C. M. West, 2008). Latina women are portrayed, with similar polarization, as either chaste, self-sacrificing virgins or sexually promiscuous women (Baldwin & DeSouza, 2001; Peña, 1998). Asian American women are presented as either shy, submissive young women or as threatening and manipulative "dragon ladies" (LeEspiritu, 2001; Matsumoto & Juang, 2004). Unfortunately, however, researchers haven't systematically studied people's stereotypes about Native American or First Nation women (Russell-Brown, 2004).

The research on ethnic subtypes within gender stereotypes illustrates the complexity of these stereotypes. No simple, unified stereotype represents all women. Instead, stereotypes often reflect ethnicity, economic status, and other characteristics of the group being judged (Lott & Saxon, 2002). Notice that this perspective is consistent with the concept of intersectionality that we considered in Chapter 1. Specifically, the concept of **intersectionality** emphasizes that each person belongs to many social groups based on characteristics such as gender, ethnicity, sexual orientation, and social class (Cole, 2009; Crenshaw, 2017). As a result, we cannot consider just one dimension of a person's identity, such as gender. Although women across ethnic groups may share some common experiences, women from different ethnic groups also have experiences that are unique to their ethnicity.

Subject Variables That Could Influence Stereotypes

We've just learned that various characteristics of the target—the person we are judging—can influence our stereotypes. For example, ethnicity as a *stimulus* variable can affect these stereotypes. Now let's switch topics and examine characteristics of the *subjects*—the people who hold these stereotypes. Subject variables are sometimes important in research about gender. (You may want to review the distinction between stimulus variables and subject variables on page 29.)

Are stereotypes influenced by subject variables such as gender, ethnicity, and the culture in which we are raised? Alternatively, do we all share the same gender stereotypes, no matter what our own background may be? The answer seems to be somewhere between these two possibilities.

Consider the influence of the respondents' gender. Typically, men and women hold similar gender stereotypes, but men's stereotypes are somewhat more traditional (e.g., Baber & Tucker, 2006; Bryant, 2003; Frieze et al., 2003; D. J. Schneider, 2004). Within each gender, however, there are substantial individual differences in the strength of these stereotypes (Monteith & Voils, 2001). Consistent with Theme 4, some women hold strong gender stereotypes; other women believe that men and women are quite similar. Men also show this pattern of individual differences.

In contrast, the respondents' ethnicity does not have a consistent influence on gender stereotypes (R. J. Harris & Firestone, 1998; Levant et al., 1998). Furthermore, there is no consistent relationship between a person's country of residence and the overall strength of their stereotypes (Best & Thomas, 2004; Désert & Leyens, 2006; Frieze et al., 2003; J. E. Williams & Best, 1990; J. E. Williams et al., 1999). Instead, the research shows that people in many different cultures share similar gender stereotypes (Rudman & Glick, 2008). For instance, people typically believe that men are more outgoing and ambitious. In contrast, people typically believe that women are more dependent and agreeable (Best & Thomas, 2004; Matsumoto & Juang, 2004).

In summary, then, people do have different stereotypes about women than about men. Furthermore, gender as a subject variable is somewhat important; men have somewhat stronger stereotypes than women do. However, it is difficult to recognize any consistent effect for the other two subject variables, ethnicity and culture. Finally, there are large individual differences within any group of individuals. Now try Demonstration 2.4 before you read further.

Demonstration **2.4**

Using the Implicit Association Test to Assess Implicit Attitudes Toward Social Groups

Log onto the Internet and visit a site called "Project Implicit": https://implicit.harvard.edu/implicit/demo. You can examine your own attitudes about gender, ethnicity, sexual orientation, people with disability, and older adults. Be certain to follow the caution to make your responses as quickly as possible. More leisurely responses might assess explicit attitudes rather than implicit attitudes.

Implicit Gender Stereotypes

So far, we have focused on **explicit gender stereotypes**, the kind you supply when you are aware that you are being tested. For instance, suppose that a researcher asks some students, "Do you believe that math is more strongly associated with men than with women?" Most socially aware students would answer "No." An explicit question like this implies that it's not appropriate to hold rigid stereotypes. As a result, students typically supply a socially desirable response rather than an honest "Yes" (Fazio & Olson, 2003; Kite et al., 2008; Klonis et al., 2005). Notice, then, that these traditional explicit measures may underestimate the strength of people's gender stereotypes.

Since the late 1990s, psychologists have conducted numerous studies using different techniques. **Implicit gender stereotypes** are the automatic stereotypes you reveal when you are not aware that your gender stereotypes are being assessed (Rudman & Glick, 2008). This research typically uses the Implicit Association Test (IAT), which you tried in Demonstration 2.4. The IAT is based on the principle that people can mentally pair words together very rapidly if they are related. However, they take significantly more time to pair unrelated words (Greenwald &

Nosek, 2001; Greenwald et al., 1998; Whitley & Kite, 2010). For example, White Americans respond quickly when White people are paired with positive words, but they respond relatively slowly when Black people are paired with positive words (Lane et al., 2007).

Consider the research that Nosek and his colleagues (2002) conducted using the IAT. The participant sits in front of a computer screen that presents a series of words. On a typical trial—in which the pairings were *consistent* with gender stereotypes—the participant would be told to press the key on the left if the word was related to math (e.g., *calculus* or *numbers*) and also if the word was related to males (e.g., *uncle* or *son*). This same participant would press the key on the right if the word was related to the arts (e.g., *poetry* or *dance*) and also if the word was related to females (e.g., *aunt* or *daughter*). Notice that these pairings should be easy if people hold a gender stereotype that the math terms are related to males and the art terms are related to females.

Then the instructions shifted so that the pairings are *inconsistent* with gender stereotypes. Now, on a typical trial, the participant should press the left key for a word related to math and also for a word related to females. This same participant should press the right key for a word related to the arts and also for a word related to males. In all cases, the researchers instruct the participants to respond as quickly as possible; the researchers do not want the participants to consciously consider their responses.

The results of this research typically show that the participants respond significantly faster to the stereotype-consistent pairings than to the stereotype-inconsistent pairings (Nosek et al., 2002; Nosek et al., 2007; Whitley & Kite, 2010). In other words, math and males seem to go together, whereas the arts and females seem to go together. The research therefore suggests that people reveal strong gender stereotypes using an implicit measure, although they might deny these stereotypes if they were concerned about providing socially desirable responses on an explicit measure (Glick & Fiske, 2007; Hewstone et al., 2002).

Several researchers have used different methods for assessing implicit gender stereotypes. These studies confirm that we do have different stereotypes about women as compared to men (Cacciari & Padovani, 2007; Duffy & Keir, 2004; Osterhout et al., 1997).

The Complexity of Contemporary Sexism

At the beginning of this chapter, we introduced three intertwined concepts: stereotypes, prejudice, and discrimination. In the previous discussion, we focused on stereotypes. Now we'll consider prejudice (biased attitudes), and we'll also explore the complexity of current sexism.

In 1989, a Texas state senator remarked, "Do you know why God created women? Because sheep can't type" (Kenneth Armbrister, cited in Starr, 1991, p. 41). That quotation is clearly sexist—no doubt about it! In contrast, present-day sexism is typically less obvious and more subtle, elusive, and complex. Let's examine three components of prejudice: (1) attitudes toward women's competence, (2) attitudes toward women's "pleasantness," and (3) a related topic, a scale designed to test the complicated ambivalent sexism that is now fairly common. Finally, we'll consider several studies that focus on discrimination against women in interpersonal interactions.

Attitudes Toward Women's Competence

Many studies in the past few decades have focused on people's attitudes about women's competence (e.g., Beyer, 1999b; Goldberg, 1968; Haley, 2001; Swim et al., 1989). In some studies, students are asked to make judgments—under well-controlled circumstances—about either a man or a woman.

Consider, for example, a study by Abel and Meltzer (2007), who asked undergraduate students to evaluate a written essay about work opportunities. Everyone received the same essay, but they were randomly assigned to one of two groups. Half of the students were told that the author who wrote the essay was Dr. Michael Smith, and half were told that the author was Dr. Mary Smith. After reading the essay, the students rated it on a variety of dimensions. For example, they provided a rating of the overall quality of the essay, using a scale in which 1 equaled poor and 7 equaled excellent. Those who thought that the professor was a male gave the lecture an average rating of 5.3, whereas those who thought that the professor was a female gave the lecture an average rating of 4.8. This difference was statistically significant.

Other research by Susan Fiske and her coauthors (2002) and Peter Glick and his coauthors (2004) asked students and nonstudents from 16 different countries to rate categories of people, such as men and women. The participants rated men as being significantly more likely than women to be associated with status and power.

We should note that some of the research has failed to find negative attitudes about women's competence. In contrast, here are the circumstances in which women's competence is most likely to be devalued:

- Males are more likely than females to downgrade women, especially if the participants have traditional attitudes (Abel & Meltzer, 2007; Eagly & Mladinic, 1994; Frieze et al., 2003; Haley, 2001).
- People are more likely to rate women less favorably than men when they don't have much information about the person's qualifications (Swim et al., 1989).
- Bias against women may be strongest when a woman is acting in a stereotypically masculine fashion (Eagly et al., 1992; Eagly & Mladinic, 1994; Fiske & Stevens, 1993; Fiske et al., 1993).

Notice that this bias against strong, competent women presents a double bind for women. On the one hand, if these women act stereotypically feminine, then they are not likely to be persuasive. On the other hand, if women act masculine and assertive, then people often give them negative evaluations.

Attitudes Toward Women's Pleasantness

People don't think that women are especially competent, but they *do* think that women are generally pleasant and nice. As we noted on page 37, prejudice is an attitude that can be positive as well as negative (Eagly & Koenig, 2008). A series of studies was conducted by Alice Eagly, whose work on gender comparisons forms the core of Chapter 6. In this research, college students were asked to rate the category "men" and the category "women" on scales with labels such as "pleasant–unpleasant," "good–bad," and "nice–awful" (Eagly, 2001, 2004; Eagly & Mladinic, 1994).

Compared to men, women typically receive more positive ratings on these "pleasantness" scales. For example, the subtype "macho men" receives the lowest rating; these men are rated as much less pleasant than the somewhat comparable female subtype "sexy women." Additional studies confirm that people give women more positive ratings than they give men, and they also consider women to be warmer than men (Fiske et al., 2002; Glick et al., 2004; Whitley & Kite, 2006).

We also know that people are not equally positive about all kinds of women. For example, W. D. Pierce and his colleagues (2003) asked Canadian university students to rate their attitude toward three types of people: "man," "woman," and "feminist." Figure 2.2 shows their responses on a scale where −2 was the most negative rating, 0 was neutral, and +2 was the most positive rating. As you can tell from the results presented in the chart, people gave much higher ratings to "woman" than to "man." However, they gave the lowest ratings to "feminist," consistent with other research (Anderson, 2010). Before you read any further, try out Demonstration 2.5 on page 58.

Demonstration **2.5**

The Ambivalent Sexism Inventory

The following items are selected from Glick and Fiske's (1996) Ambivalent Sexism Inventory. For each item, indicate the degree to which you agree or disagree with each statement, using the following scale:

0	1	2	3	4	5
disagree strongly	disagree somewhat	disagree slightly	agree slightly	agree somewhat	agree strongly

_____ 1. Many women are actually seeking special favors, such as hiring policies that favor them over men, under the guise of asking for equality.

_____ 2. Women should be cherished and protected by men.*

_____ 3. Most women fail to appreciate fully all that men do for them.

_____ 4. Many women have a quality of purity that few men possess.

_____ 5. A good woman should be set on a pedestal by her man.*

_____ 6. Most women interpret innocent remarks or acts as being sexist.

_____ 7. Once a woman gets a man to commit to her, she usually tries to put him on a tight leash.**

_____ 8. In a disaster, women should be rescued before men.

_____ 9. Women seek to gain power by getting control over men.

_____ 10. No matter how accomplished he is, a man is not truly complete as a person unless he has the love of a woman.

When you have finished this test, check the scoring instructions at the end of the chapter on page 75. You may also want to ask friends to take the test to determine whether these friends show the same gender differences that Glick and Fiske found.

*Set on a pedestal = uplifted and viewed with high regard
**Put him on a tight leash = restrict his extracurricular activities with friends and acquaintances

Note: The complete test includes 22 items, some of which are worded so that a highly sexist person would disagree with them. This textbook's shortened version of the Ambivalent Sexism Inventory.

Source: From Glick and Fiske, Ambivalent Sexism Inventory. Copyright © 1995 by Peter Glick and Susan T. Fiske. Reprinted with Permission.

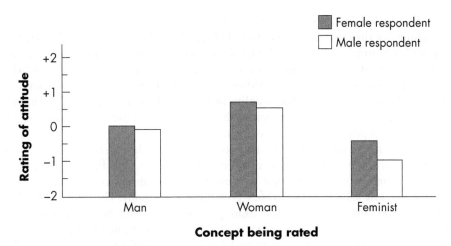

FIGURE **2.2** Attitudes toward the concepts "man," "woman," and "feminist," as a function of respondents' gender. (Note: +2 = extremely favorable; –2 = extremely unfavorable.)

Source: Based on Pierce et al. (2003).

Ambivalent Sexism

We have learned that contemporary sexism is complicated. People may think that women are not very competent, but they *are* fairly nice—unless they happen to be feminists.

Peter Glick and Susan Fiske (1996, 2001a, 2001b) have examined the complexity of sexism with a scale they call the Ambivalent Sexism Inventory. They argue that sexism is a prejudice based on a deep ambivalence toward women rather than on a uniform dislike of women. This scale contains items that tap two kinds of sexism: hostile sexism and benevolent sexism.

Hostile sexism, the more blatant kind of sexism, is based on the idea that women should be subservient to men and should "know their place." Hostile sexism is primarily directed toward nontraditional women, such as female professionals and feminists.

Benevolent sexism is a more subtle kind of sexism that argues for women's special niceness and purity. Benevolent sexism is primarily directed toward traditional women, such as stay-at-home-mothers (Fiske, 2004; Fiske et al., 2002). In general, people believe that hostile sexism is worse than benevolent sexism (Swim et al., 2005). Furthermore, deeply religious students tend to be higher than other students in benevolent sexism, but these religious students are not higher in hostile sexism (Burn & Busso, 2005). You may initially think that benevolent sexism cannot be harmful. However, it still emphasizes that women are *different* from men and that they are also weaker.

Notice that these two different kinds of sexism are consistent with the two different representations of women in religion and mythology (pages 40–42) as well as with the mixture of negative and positive attitudes toward women that we have just discussed (pages 56–58). All of these general tendencies reflect an ambivalence toward women. **Ambivalent sexism** therefore combines both hostile sexism and benevolent sexism.

Demonstration 2.5 on page 58 is a short version of Glick and Fiske's (1996) Ambivalent Sexism Inventory. In the United States, many studies with this inventory have shown that male participants typically score somewhat higher than female participants on the benevolent sexism subscale. However, men score much higher than women on the hostile sexism subscale (Glick & Fiske, 1996, 2001b).

The Ambivalent Sexism Inventory has also been tested with 15,000 men and women in 19 countries throughout the world (Glick et al., 2000; Glick et al., 2004). The researchers found both hostile sexism and benevolent sexism in all of these countries. The studies also confirmed that gender differences are larger on the hostile sexism subscale than on the benevolent sexism subscale. In addition, Glick and his colleagues obtained data from the United Nations about gender equality in each of these 19 countries. Gender equality was based on measures such as women's share of the earned income and the percentage of high governmental positions held by women.

Let's consider the results for countries with low gender equality. These respondents tended to be high in both hostile sexism and benevolent sexism. This finding makes sense for hostile sexism: When people believe that women should be subservient to men, women will probably receive low salaries and hold few government positions. The relationship between gender equality and benevolent sexism is more puzzling. However, benevolent sexism also helps to justify gender inequality. It assumes women are pleasant, helpless people whom men must protect from having too much responsibility in the workplace (Glick & Fiske, 2001a, 2001b).

Studies investigating women's perceptions of and experiences with benevolent sexism suggest that women experience benevolent sexism more often than hostile sexism (Kuchynka et al., 2018; Oswald, Baalbaki, & Kirkman, 2019). Experiencing the protective paternalism inherent in benevolent sexism affects women's self-efficacy, self-esteem, engagement, and psychological well-being across a variety of contexts. For example, experiencing benevolent sexism, rather than hostile sexism, may discourage women for pursuing careers in STEM disciplines, especially when they are still unsure about that career direction (Kuchyna et al., 2018). Women exposed to benevolent sexism while completing a challenging task display impaired cardiovascular recovery following the task (Salomon, Burgess, & Bosson, 2015). However, experiencing benevolent sexism within the context of intimate relationships is associated with higher self-esteem and decreased self-doubt (Oswald, Baalbaki, & Kirkman, 2019). In short, the research on the Ambivalent Sexism Inventory highlights both the subtlety and the complexity of contemporary sexism. It also illustrates that the two different kinds of sexism are widespread throughout the world.

After decades of effort from feminist advocates, in September 2017, Saudi Arabia became the last country in the world to allow women to drive cars.

Gender Discrimination in Interpersonal Interactions

So far in this section, we've examined the nature of stereotypes and prejudice. We'll now explore gender discrimination. As you'll learn, people in the United States behave differently toward men and women, both in laboratory research and in real life.

Discrimination in the United States

Bernice Lott conducted the classic laboratory research in the United States. Specifically, she observed pairs of unacquainted students from behind a one-way mirror while they worked together to build a structure (Lott, 1987; Lott & Maluso, 1995). This research showed that the women seldom responded negatively to their partners (either male or female). However, the men made many more negative comments to their female partners than to their male partners.

The conclusions from these laboratory studies are echoed in research on real-life gender discrimination (e.g., Anthis, 2002; Landrine & Klonoff, 1997; Nielsen, 2002; Wessler & De Andrade, 2006). For example, Janet Swim and her colleagues (2001) found that undergraduate women reported an average of one or two nontrivial sexist remarks and behaviors every week. One category of sexist remarks emphasized traditional gender-stereotyped remarks (e.g., "You're a woman, so fold my laundry"). Another category involved demeaning comments and behaviors (e.g., a woman who was talking with friends was told by a man, "Yo, bitch, get me some beer!"). A third category included sexual comments and behaviors, such as a remark about a woman's breasts.

Other researchers have confirmed that sexist comments and behaviors occur fairly often for Black female students and for female students from several different ethnic backgrounds (Matteson & Moradi, 2005; DeBlaere & Moradi, 2008). This section on gender discrimination in the United States provides abundant evidence for Theme 2: Women are often treated differently from the way men are treated.

In Chapter 7, we will explore other forms of interpersonal discrimination when we examine sexism in the workplace. In Chapter 12, we'll learn that interpersonal discrimination may contribute to the relatively high rate of depression in women (Matteson & Moradi, 2005; Schmitt et al., 2002; Swim et al., 2001). The interpersonal discrimination that women experience does not evaporate quickly. Instead, these gender-biased experiences often reduce the overall quality of women's lives.

Discrimination in Other Cultures

Most of the research discussed in this textbook focuses on the United States, Canada, and other English-speaking countries. In many countries, however, the kind of discrimination we've just discussed would be considered relatively minor.

On the other end of the spectrum, women in Scandinavian countries experience less discrimination than women in the United States. For example, the percentage of women in Parliament (the highest government assembly in these countries) ranges from 38% in Iceland to 47% in Finland and Norway (Statista Online Database, 2019). The current percentage of women in the U.S. Senate is only 17%. The U.S.-normative perspective encourages U.S. citizens to assume that women are especially well treated in our society. In many cases, this perspective is true. Sadly, however, this textbook will identify many exceptions to this assumption.

Heterosexism

Our earlier discussion of contemporary sexism emphasized that people make a major distinction between men and women. People may be hostile toward women or may be benevolent toward women, but an important conclusion is that they think women are psychologically *different* from men. As we also emphasized in our discussion of Theme 2, people react differently to men and women. We'll learn throughout this chapter that people tend to divide the world into two categories, male and female.

Traditional notions of gender categorization and gender identity are based on the gender binary, which is a system of conceptualizing gender as having two opposing and opposite groups (i.e., "male and female" or "men and women"). For example, people with a **cisgender** identity have a gender identity that corresponds with the sex they were assigned at birth.

However, in reality, gender identities are not binary and span many categories. People who identify as **genderqueer** express a gender identity that is beyond the traditional binary and is not exclusively male or female. Individuals who are **gender nonconforming** may not identify as transgender but do not conform to traditional gender norms. People who are **transgender** have a gender identity or gender expression that differs from the sex they were assigned at birth. **Trans** is an umbrella term for anyone on the transgender spectrum, which may include people who identify as transgender, gender nonconforming, genderqueer, cross-dressing, gender fluid, pangender, polygender, two-spirit, androgynous, or any other nonbinary identity. People with **intersex** conditions are born with reproductive anatomy or genitals that do not necessarily match their genes, sex chromosomes, or hormones, or they have bodies that are atypical of cisgender women and men.

When cultures emphasize strict gender categorization based on binary categories, love relationships are impacted (Garnets, 2008). Specifically, gender categories encourage people to believe that a person from the category "male" must fall in love with a person from the other category, "female." Some people are troubled by same-gender love relationships (Anderson, 2010).Romantic relationships and sexual orientation do not fit into simple binary stereotypes that have traditionally been characterized by "heterosexuality" and "homosexuality." **Heterosexuality** is a sexual orientation in which a cisgender man or woman experiences sexual attraction for someone of the opposite sex or gender. **Asexuality** is a sexual orientation in which people have low sexual attraction to others. **Bisexuality** is a sexual orientation characterized by psychological, emotional, and sexual attraction to both women and men. **Demisexuality** is a sexual orientation in which someone is only sexually attracted to a person with whom they have formed a strong emotional connection. **Pansexuality** is a sexual orientation in which someone experiences sexual, romantic, or emotional attraction toward someone's personality, regardless of their sexual orientation or gender identity. **Sapiosexuality** refers to an orientation in which someone finds intelligence sexually attractive or arousing, independent of other factors such as appearance.

Chapter 4 examines how adolescent young women begin to explore their sexual orientation. In Chapter 8, we will discuss potential explanations for sexual orientation as well as the love relationships of women who have nonheterosexual orientations. Additionally, Chapter 9 focuses on sexuality issues, Chapter 10 discusses motherhood, and Chapter 14 examines the love relationships of older women with nonheterosexual orientations.

In this section, however, let's focus on heterosexism. As Chapter 1 notes, **heterosexism** is a belief system that devalues lesbian, gay, and bisexual individuals—or any group that is not exclusively heterosexual (Garnets, 2008; Herek, 2007; Whitley & Kite, 2010). A related term, **sexual prejudice**, is a negative attitude that individuals hold against someone because of their sexual orientation (Garnets, 2008; Herek, 2004).

Researchers have measured attitudes toward both heterosexual and LGBTQ+ individuals, using the IAT, as discussed on pages 55–56. The IAT results typically show more positive attitudes toward heterosexual people (Dasgupta & Rivera, 2006a). However, people who know many lesbian women and gay men are less likely to demonstrate heterosexism (Dasgupta & Rivera, 2006b).

We have emphasized that sexism places men in the center and women on the periphery. Similarly, heterosexism places heterosexual individuals in the center and everybody else on the periphery. Let's examine some examples of heterosexism.

Examples of Heterosexism

Many different types of heterosexism reveal that cultural norms in the United States value people who love someone from a different gender category rather than someone from the same gender category. For instance, many lesbian women and gay men report that their partners are not welcome at family celebrations. Furthermore, more than half of high school lesbian women and gay men have been verbally harassed about their sexual orientation (D'Augelli et al., 2002; Wessler & De Andrade, 2006).

Gregory Herek (2007) conducted a survey throughout the United States of adults who had identified themselves as lesbian, gay (male), or bisexual. About half of the respondents reported that they had experienced verbal abuse. Furthermore, about 20% said that they had been physically attacked or their property had been damaged.

Consider an example provided by a woman who described how she and some women friends were walking in a public park when three men threatened them. Even though the women said they did not want to fight, the men attacked them. One woman had her nose broken, another was knocked unconscious, another had a gash on her cheek, and another was severely bruised (Herek et al., 2002).

We've learned that gay men and lesbian women frequently experience interpersonal discrimination—heterosexist biases, verbal harassment, and physical assault— because of their sexual orientation. They also face institutional discrimination; that is, the government, corporations, and other institutions discriminate against people with nonheterosexual orientation. For example, same-sex parents experiencing divorce or separation still experience discrimination with regards to child custody and parental rights, due to bias in the legal system that privileges biological parents over nonbiological parents (Haney-Caron & Heilbrun, 2014).

Factors Correlated with Heterosexism

Attitudes toward people with nonheterosexual orientation are complex. In general, men are more negative than women in their attitudes toward gay men and lesbian women (Dasgupta & Rivera, 2006a; Herek, 2002a; Whitley & Kite, 2010). Men are also much more likely than women to commit antigay hate crimes (Herek et al., 2002). Furthermore, people generally have more negative attitudes toward gay men than toward lesbian women (Dasgupta & Rivera, 2006b; Herek, 2002a). To assess your own attitudes toward lesbian women and gay men, try Demonstration 2.6.

Demonstration 2.6

Attitudes Toward People Who Identify as LGBTQ+

Answer each of the following items either yes or no. (Please note that the original questionnaire was designed for heterosexual people, so some items may seem inappropriate for respondents with nonheterosexual orientation.)

1. I would not mind having LGBTQ+ friends.
2. I would look for a new place to live if I found out that my roommate was LGBTQ+.
3. I would vote for an LGBTQ+ person in an election for a public office.
4. Two adults of the same gender holding hands in public is disgusting.
5. Identifying as LGBTQ+, as far as I'm concerned, is not sinful.
6. I would mind being employed by an LGBTQ+ person.
7. I would decline membership in an organization if it had LGBTQ+ members.
8. I would not be afraid for my child to have an LGBTQ+ teacher.
9. LBGTQ+ people are more likely than heterosexual people to commit deviant sexual acts, such as child molestation.
10. I perceive the LGBTQ+ movement as a positive thing.

To obtain a rough idea about your attitudes, add the number of "yes" answers you provided for items 1, 3, 5, 8, and 10. Next, add together the number of "no" answers you gave for items 2, 4, 6, 7, and 9. Then, combine these two subtotals; scores close to 10 indicate positive attitudes toward LGBTQ+ people.

Source: Adapted from Kite and Deaux (1986).

In addition, people with traditional gender roles are more likely than nontraditional people to express sexual prejudice (Basow & Johnson, 2000; Whitley & Ægisdóttir, 2000; Whitley & Kite, 2010). Also, people with heterosexist attitudes tend to be politically conservative, religiously conservative, and racist (Horvath & Ryan, 2003; Kite & Whitley, 2002). However, students often become more tolerant and less heterosexist as they go through college (Hewitt & Moore, 2002).

Sometimes a group of committed activists can transform their community's social biases. For example, Antigonish is a town of 5,000 people in a rural region of Nova Scotia, Canada. A group at St. Francis Xavier University worked together with the Antigonish Women's Resource Center on a variety of programs related to gender and sexual diversity (Marple & Latchmore, 2005). This coalition held a fundraiser that was attended by 200 community members. In addition, high school students gained permission for their school to support a Gay–Straight Alliance at their school.

Section Summary

People's Beliefs About Women and Men

1. People believe that men and women differ substantially on a number of personality characteristics. They consider women to be higher in communion and men to be higher in agency.
2. During the past 20 years, people have supplied increasingly higher scores when they rate women's agency.
3. People have different stereotypes about women and men from different ethnic groups. For each ethnic group, however, there are stereotypes about women that emphasize both "good women" and "bad women."
4. Men tend to have more traditional stereotypes than women do, but ethnicity and country of residence do not have a consistent effect on stereotype strength.
5. Psychologists have developed the Implicit Association Test (IAT), which assesses the strength of stereotypes in terms of response speed. The IAT typically reveals stronger gender stereotypes than rating-scale measures of stereotypes.
6. Women's competence is likely to be downgraded when (1) evaluators are male rather than female, (2) little other information is available, and (3) women act in a stereotypically masculine fashion.
7. People typically rate women higher than men on scales assessing pleasantness; however, feminists receive relatively low ratings.
8. Men typically earn higher scores than women on both the benevolent sexism and the hostile sexism subscales of the Ambivalent Sexism Inventory.
9. Research in the United States shows evidence of gender discrimination in interpersonal interactions (e.g., negative statements about women and sexist comments). Sexism in cultures that have more rigid and traditional gender role expectations has more serious consequences than in cultures that do not.
10. Heterosexism is encouraged by strict gender categorization. Lesbian women and gay men frequently experience harassment, and many are physically assaulted. Men are more likely than women to show sexual prejudice. People with traditional gender roles are also more likely to show sexual prejudice.
11. Students often become less heterosexist as they go through college. Activists can also encourage their communities to become more supportive of sexual diversity.

2-3 The Personal Consequences of Gender Stereotypes

Learning Objectives

To summarize the personal consequences of gender stereotypes, you can ...

2-3-1   Describe how the social cognitive approach helps explain stereotypical thinking and other cognitive errors.

2-3-2   Explain how gender polarization perpetuates gender differences between women and men.

2-3-3   Explain how androcentric bias influences conceptualizations of what is normative.

2-3-4   Identify stereotypes that lead to biased judgments and attributions about the knowledge and competencies of others.

2-3-5   Analyze how stereotypes can affect people's memories about past events.

2-3-6   Explain how processes such as self-fulfilling prophecy and gender stereotype threat influence behavior.

2-3-7   Explain why the concept of androgyny is problematic in understanding gender bias.

2-3-8   Explain how people internalize gender stereotypes into their own self-concepts.

So far, we have examined many stereotypes related to gender, and we have discussed gender prejudice and gender discrimination. However, gender stereotypes can also have an important effect on our own cognitive processes, behavior, and gender identity (Eagly & Koenig, 2008; Schaller & Conway, 2001; Whitley & Kite, 2010). Let's now explore these three areas.

Gender Stereotypes and Cognitive Errors

One personal consequence of gender stereotypes is that they encourage us to make cognitive errors—that is, errors in our thought processes. The social cognitive approach explains how these errors arise. This approach also provides a useful theoretical explanation for gender stereotypes and stereotypes based on categories such as ethnicity, sexual orientation, economic status, disability status, and age. According to the **social cognitive approach**, stereotypes are belief systems that guide and simplify the way we process information, including information about gender (Schaller & Conway, 2001; Sherman, 2001; Whitley & Kite, 2010).

One cognitive process that seems nearly inevitable is our tendency to divide the people we meet into social groups (Brehm et al., 2005; Macrae & Bodenhausen, 2000; D. J. Schneider, 2004). We categorize people as female or male, White people or people of color, people with high occupational status or people with low occupational status, and so forth.

The social cognitive approach argues that stereotypes help us simplify and organize the world by creating categories. The major way we categorize people is on the basis of their gender (Harper & Schoeman, 2003; Kunda, 1999; D. J. Schneider, 2004). This process of categorizing others on the basis of gender is habitual and automatic (Rudman & Glick, 2008).

The problem, however, is that this process of categorizing and stereotyping often encourages us to make errors in our thinking. These errors, in turn, produce further errors. Specifically, because we have a stereotype, we tend to perceive women and men differently, and this perception adds further "evidence" to our stereotype. A strengthened stereotype leads to an even greater tendency to perceive the various genders differently. As a result, stereotypes are especially resistant to change (Macrae & Bodenhausen, 2000; Rudman & Glick, 2008).

As you read this section on cognitive errors, keep in mind that we don't always think in terms of stereotypes. For example, the social setting can modify our thinking (Glick &

Fiske, 2007). However, let's examine several ways that gender stereotypes may encourage cognitive errors:

- People tend to exaggerate the contrast between women and men.
- People tend to perceive the male as normative and the female as nonstandard.
- People tend to make biased judgments on the basis of stereotypes.
- People tend to selectively remember information that is consistent with gender stereotypes.

Exaggerating the Contrast Between Women and Men

We tend to exaggerate the similarities within a group and exaggerate the contrast between groups (T. L. Stewart et al., 2000; Van Rooy et al., 2003). When we divide the world into two groups—male and female—we tend to perceive all males as being similar, all females as being similar, and the two gender categories as being different from each other; this tendency is called **gender polarization** (Bem, 1993, 2008). Gender polarization encourages people to downgrade individuals who deviate from this rigid role definition. For example, we learned on page 37 that many people have a positive attitude toward women in general, but they have a negative attitude toward feminists.

As we will emphasize throughout this textbook, the characteristics of women and men tend to overlap. Unfortunately, however, gender polarization often creates an artificial gap between women and men. People tend to believe that gender differences in psychological characteristics are larger than they really are (J. A. Hall & Carter, 1999; Hyde, 2005a). Human cognitive processes seem to favor clear-cut distinctions, not the blurry differences that are more common in everyday life (Van Rooy et al., 2003).

The Normative Male

As we discussed earlier in this chapter, the normative male concept (or androcentrism) means that the male experience is considered the norm—that is, the neutral standard for the species as a whole. In contrast, the female experience is a deviation from that supposedly universal standard (Basow, 2001; Bem, 1993, 2008).

One example of the normative-male principle is that, when we are presented with the word *person,* we tend to believe that this individual is a male rather than a female (M. C. Hamilton, 1991; Merritt & Kok, 1995; Miller et al., 1991). For example, Merritt and Harrison (2006) tested 192 college students by describing a person named "Chris" in a completely gender-neutral situation. The students thought that Chris was male 69% of the time and female only 31% of the time. Furthermore, all 192 students reported that they did indeed assign a gender to Chris. Here's another example of the normative-male principle: Both adults and children usually refer to a stuffed animal as "he," unless this toy has clearly feminine clothing (Lambdin et al., 2003).

We have already reviewed evidence of androcentrism in Chapter 1; the early history of the psychology of gender assumed that the male is normative. Our discussions of masculine generic language and the representation of gender in the media also reflect androcentrism. In addition, androcentrism is apparent in the workplace, family life, and medical care (Basow, 2001; Bem, 2008), as we will read in later chapters of this book.

Making Biased Judgments About Females and Males

Many stereotypes are based on grains of truth, so these stereotypes may be at least partly accurate (Schaller & Conway, 2001). However, our stereotypes may also lead us to interpret certain behaviors in a biased manner (Blair, 2001). For example, people often provide stereotyped interpretations when they judge men's and women's emotional reactions (M. D. Robinson & Johnson, 1997).

Chingching Chang and Jacqueline Hitchon (2004) conducted a representative study about biased judgments. They gave U.S. undergraduate students an advertisement for either a male political candidate or a female political candidate. Let's focus on the condition in which the ads did not mention the candidate's knowledge about certain gender-stereotyped areas of expertise. After reading the advertisement, the students were instructed to rate the candidate's competence in these areas. Even though the students had no relevant information, they judged that female candidates would be more competent than the male candidates in "women's issues," such as children and health care. Furthermore, they judged that the male candidates would be more competent than the female candidates in "men's issues," such as the economy and national security. When we make judgments—and we lack relevant information—we fall back on gender stereotypes.

Naturally, several variables influence our tendency to make stereotyped judgments. For example, we are especially likely to use a stereotype if we are busy working on another task at the same time (Macrae & Bodenhausen, 2000; D. J. Schneider, 2004). In contrast, specific information about individuals can sometimes be so persuasive that it overrides a stereotype (Kunda & Sherman-Williams, 1993). For example, a woman may be so well qualified for a job that her strengths outweigh the "problem" that she is female.

Many studies have been conducted on a particular kind of judgment called attributions. **Attributions** are explanations about the causes of a person's behavior. Chapter 5 discusses how people make attributions about *their own* behavior. In this current chapter, we'll discuss how people make stereotypical attributions about the behavior of *other individuals*.

The research on attributions shows that people often think a woman's success on a particular task can be explained by effort—she tried hard (D. J. Schneider, 2004; Swim & Sanna, 1996; Yarkin et al., 1982). For example, researchers have examined parents' attributions for their children's success in mathematics. When a daughter does well in math, parents often attribute her success to hard work. In contrast, they often attribute their son's math success to his high ability (Eccles, 1987). Notice the implications of this research: People think that females need to try harder to achieve the same level of success as males.

Let's review what we know so far about the social cognitive approach to gender stereotypes. Stereotypes often simplify and bias the way we think about people who belong to the social categories of "female" and "male." Because of gender stereotypes, we often exaggerate the contrast between women and men. In addition, we may consider the male experience to be standard, whereas the female experience is a deviation from that standard. In addition, we sometimes make biased judgments about females and males, for instance, when we assess their expertise about stereotypically masculine or feminine topics. Research in social cognition also emphasizes one final component of stereotypes: people's memory for gender-stereotyped characteristics.

Memory for Personal Characteristics

In many cases, people recall gender-consistent information more accurately than gender-inconsistent information (e.g., Cann, 1993; D. F. Halpern, 1985; T. L. Stewart & Vassar, 2000). For instance, Dunning and Sherman (1997) asked participants to read a sentence such as "The women at the office liked to talk around the water cooler." During a later memory test, the researchers presented a series of sentences and asked the participants to decide whether each sentence was old (i.e., exactly the same as a sentence presented earlier) or new.

The most interesting results in this study concerned people's judgments about new sentences that were consistent with the gender stereotype implied by a sentence presented earlier (e.g., "The women at the office liked to gossip around the water cooler"). People erroneously judged that 29% of these sentences were old. In contrast, other new sentences were *inconsistent* with a gender stereotype (e.g., "The women at the office liked to talk sports around the water cooler"). In this inconsistent condition, people erroneously judged that only 18% of these sentences were old.

Apparently, when the participants in this study read the original sentence about women talking around the water cooler, they sometimes made gender-consistent inferences (e.g., that the women must be gossiping). As a result, when they later read a sentence that explicitly mentioned gossiping, that sentence seemed familiar. In contrast, the sentences about sports were less likely to seem familiar.

The research in social cognition shows that we are especially likely to recall stereotype-consistent material when we have other tasks to do at the same time, such as remembering other information, and when we have a strong, well-developed stereotype (Hilton & von Hippel, 1996; Ottati et al., 2005; Sherman, 2001). When we are undistracted and when the stereotype is weak, we may sometimes remember material inconsistent with our stereotypes.

Gender Stereotypes and Behavior

We began the previous section by discussing the content of gender stereotypes and the complex nature of contemporary sexism. We've just examined the social cognitive approach, which helps us to understand how errors in our thinking can arise. However, if we focus entirely on our thought processes, we may forget an extremely important point: Stereotypes can influence people's behavior. That is, stereotypes can affect actions and choices, in other people and in ourselves.

Stereotypes can influence behavior through a **self-fulfilling prophecy**: Your expectations about someone may lead them to act in ways that confirm your original expectation (Rosenthal, 1993; Skrypnek & Snyder, 1982; Smith, 2004). For example, if parents expect that their daughter will not do well in mathematics, she may become pessimistic about her ability in that area. As a result, her math performance may drop (Eccles et al., 1990; Jussim et al., 2000).

A related problem is called stereotype threat (Steele, 1997). Imagine you belong to a group that is hindered by a negative stereotype, and someone reminds you that this group performs poorly on a particular task. When you work on this specific task, you may experience **stereotype threat**; your performance may suffer (K. L. Dion, 2003; Marx & Stapel, 2006a, 2006b; Smith, 2004; C. M. Steele et al., 2002).

Consider a classic study by Shih and her colleagues (1999), in which all the participants were Asian American college women. In the United States, one stereotype is that Asian Americans are "good at math" (compared to other ethnic groups). In contrast, another stereotype is that women are "bad at math" (compared to men).

One group of Asian American women in this study were asked to indicate their ethnicity and then answer several questions about their ethnic identity; afterward, they took a challenging math test. These women answered 54% of the questions correctly. A second group of Asian American women did not answer any questions beforehand; they simply took the same math test. The women in this control group answered 49% of the questions correctly. A third group began by indicating their gender and then answering several questions about their gender identity; afterward, they took the same math test. These women answered only 43% of the questions correctly.

Apparently, when Asian American women are reminded of their ethnicity, they perform relatively well. However, when Asian American women are reminded of their gender, they experience stereotype threat and perform relatively poorly (Shih et al., 1999). This effect of stereotype threat appears most often when people are *aware* of their own group's stereotypes, but not necessarily when they are *unaware* of the stereotypes (Gibson, Losee, & Vitiello, 2014).

Additional research shows that Latina college women are more vulnerable to stereotype threat than White college women are (Gonzales et al., 2002). Other research focuses on knowledge about politics. In general, women score lower than men on surveys of political knowledge. However, women performed as well as men when they were tested by a female researcher who said that no gender differences had been detected on this particular test of political knowledge (McGlone et al., 2006).

However, people are not always at the mercy of gender stereotypes (Fiske, 1993; Jussim et al., 2000). We are not marionettes, with other people pulling our strings. Our own self-concepts and abilities are usually stronger determinants of behavior than are the expectations of other people. Still, we should be concerned about the potentially powerful effects of gender stereotypes because these stereotypes help to maintain important gender inequities (Jussim et al., 2000; Smith et al., 2007).

Applying Gender Stereotypes to Ourselves

In this chapter we have explored these topics: (1) the representation of gender stereotypes in religion, language, and the media; (2) the nature of people's current gender stereotypes; and (3) the influence of gender stereotypes on our thinking and our behavior. However, stereotypes not only describe our perceptions about the typical characteristics of women and men. They also describe how women and men *ought* to behave (Eagly, 2001). According to the traditional view, women should try to be "feminine" and men should try to be "masculine." Do people actually internalize these stereotypes, so that women and men have extremely different standards about the person they should be? As you'll soon learn, the answer to this question is complicated (Guimond et al., 2006; Wood & Eagly, 2010).

Assessing Self-Concepts About Gender

Researchers have developed several different scales to assess people's ideas about their own gender-related characteristics. By far the most popular scale has been the Bem Sex-Role Inventory (BSRI). Sandra Bem designed this test to assess how people rate themselves on a variety of psychological characteristics (Bem, 1974, 1977).

The BSRI provides one score on a femininity scale and one score on a masculinity scale. A person who scores high on both scales would be classified as **androgynous** (pronounced an-DRAH-jih-nuss). In the 1970s, psychologists often urged both women and men to develop more androgynous characteristics.

Hundreds of studies have been conducted to try to discover whether androgynous individuals might possess any unusual advantages (Oswald & Lindstedt, 2006). However, most contemporary psychologists have become disenchanted with androgyny. They argue that the concept of androgyny has several problems. For example, the research shows that androgynous people are *not* more psychologically healthy than other people.

Also—according to critics—androgyny tempts us to believe that the solution to gender bias lies in changing the individual. The critics emphasize that we should try instead to reduce institutional sexism and discrimination against women. Interestingly, Sandra Bem herself argued against the concept of androgyny (Bem, 1983). She urged psychologists to turn their attention to a different question explored throughout this textbook: Why do cultures place such a strong emphasis on gender?

Internalizing Gender Stereotypes

Contemporary researchers continue to explore how people internalize gender stereotypes into their own self-concepts. For example, your own gender concept actually consists of a wide variety of different gender-related characteristics (Oswald & Lindstedt, 2006). Some of these characteristics are based on personality traits, but others are based on characteristics such as your interests and your perception of yourself in close relationships (Wood & Eagly, 2010).

In addition, a person's identity typically depends on several social categories. For example, Settles (2006) studied Black women who were undergraduate and graduate students at a variety of U.S. universities. These women considered their identity as a Black woman to be more important than either their identity as a woman or their identity as a Black person. Notice how these results support the concept of intersectionality. In fact, these women locate their identity in the intersection between their ethnicity and their gender.

Furthermore, the research demonstrates that social context clearly matters. For instance, many women say that they would act stereotypically feminine if they were in a social situation where most people were strangers (C. J. Smith et al., 1999).

Another example of social context is the comparison group that people use when rating themselves (Guimond et al., 2007). For example, Guimond and his colleagues (2006) asked French high school and college students to rate their personal characteristics in comparison to people of a *different* gender. In this context, the gender differences in self-rating were large. In another condition, the researchers asked students to rate their personal characteristics in comparison to people of the *same* gender. In this context, the gender differences in self-rating were small.

In summary, people do not have a simple, consistent gender identity. Instead, this identity is complex, and it depends on factors such as ethnicity and social context.

Are Gender Stereotypes Personally Important?

So far, we've learned that people tend to incorporate gender stereotypes into their own self-concepts, at least in some situations. But do they believe that these gender stereotypes are crucial aspects of their own personality? Auster and Ohm (2000) asked U.S. undergraduates to rate each characteristic on the BSRI according to how important they felt it would be to have this characteristic. Table 2.6 lists the 10 characteristics that each gender judged to be most important. As you might expect, the lists are remarkably similar. In fact, seven items appear on both the women's and men's lists.

Conclusions About Applying Gender Stereotypes

In this discussion, we've learned that people tend to adopt flexible self-concepts about gender. We should not oversimplify the conclusions in our current discussion about applying gender stereotypes to ourselves. In fact, women and men often have similar perspectives about their gender-related characteristics. Consistent with Theme 1, gender differences in psychological characteristics are usually small. As we'll emphasize throughout this textbook, women and men do not live on different psychological planets with respect to their beliefs, abilities, and personal characteristics.

As one final exercise for this chapter, try Demonstration 2.7, to discover some potential stereotypes that you may have about gender, ethnicity, and a wide variety of other social categories.

TABLE **2.6**

Top 10 Traits That Female and Male Students in the United States Consider Most Important for Themselves

Female Students	Male Students
1. Loyal	1. Loyal
2. Independent	2. Defends own beliefs
3. Individualistic	3. Willing to take a stand
4. Defends own beliefs	4. Understanding
5. Self-sufficient	5. Independent
6. Understanding	6. Ambitious
7. Ambitious	7. Willing to take risks
8. Self-reliant	8. Self-reliant
9. Sensitive to the needs of others	9. Self-sufficient
10. Compassionate	10. Has leadership abilities

Source: With kind permission from Springer Science Business Media: *Sex Roles,* "Masculinity and Femininity in Contemporary American Society: A Reevaluation Using the Bem Sex-Role Inventory" Vol. 43, 2000, pp. 499–528, Carol J. Auster.

Demonstration 2.7

Confronting Your "-Isms"

For at least the next two weeks, keep a list of the immediate response that you have to a person who is different from yourself. This person may seem different from you in terms of gender, ethnicity, appearance, accent, age, sexual orientation, social class, disability, religion, or nationality. Don't try to censor your immediate reaction. Instead, listen to your "inner DJ," and record your response immediately. (Be sure to keep a piece of paper or some other recording device handy so that you can quickly capture your reactions!)

Then try to analyze what evidence you focused on to reach your conclusion. For example, if you heard someone speaking with an accent that seemed characteristic of another region of the country, did you draw a conclusion about their personal characteristics? Also, do you think you learned this perspective from your family, friends, culture, or the media? Finally, think what you can do to overcome these stereotypes.

Sources: Gibson (2008); Gibson & Lindberg (2006).

Section Summary

The Personal Consequences of Gender Stereotypes

1. One consequence of gender stereotyping is that we make errors in our cognitive processes; these errors are relevant for the social cognitive approach to stereotypes.
2. According to the social cognitive approach to stereotypes, people tend to (1) exaggerate the contrast between women and men, (2) consider the male experience to be normative, (3) make biased judgments about females and males, and (4) remember gender-consistent information more accurately than gender-inconsistent information.
3. Stereotypes can influence behavior through self-fulfilling prophecies, according to research on topics such as parents' expectations for their children's mathematical abilities. Also, the research on stereotype threat shows that people's own gender stereotypes can undermine their performance on tests when the instructions emphasize their gender.
4. In specific settings, many people adopt flexible self-concepts about gender rather than internalizing rigid gender stereotypes. In addition, ethnic group and social context influence a person's self-concept.
5. Women and men in U.S. colleges tend to rate themselves similarly on gender-related traits that they consider to be important.

Chapter Review Questions

1. How would you define the term *gender stereotype?* Based on the information in this chapter, why might a stereotype of a female not accurately represent a specific woman whom you know? Why or why not?
2. What topics related to women have historians previously ignored? Mention several reasons why women have not received much attention in history books.
3. We discussed in this chapter how women often seem invisible; for example, men are normative, whereas women are secondary. Summarize the information about women's relative invisibility, mentioning history, religion, mythology, language, and the media. How is this issue relevant to the social cognitive research on androcentrism?
4. In this chapter, we highlighted that people often hold more positive views about men than about women. Discuss this statement, citing support from philosophers, religion, mythology, language, and the media. Then discuss why the issue is more complicated when we consider the current research on ambivalent sexism.
5. What does the research show about people's stereotypes regarding women from various ethnic groups (i.e., when ethnicity is a stimulus variable)? Similarly, what does the research show about how a person's ethnicity influences their gender stereotypes (i.e., when ethnicity is a subject variable)?

6. What is heterosexism, and how are gender stereotypes related to heterosexism? The social cognitive approach proposes that our normal cognitive processes could encourage people to develop stereotypes about many social categories, such as lesbian women and gay men. Describe how the four cognitive biases (listed on pages 67–69) could encourage these stereotypes.

7. The social cognitive approach proposes that our gender stereotypes arise from normal cognitive processes, beginning with the two categories "men" and "women." Describe some of the cognitive biases that would encourage people to believe that women are more talkative than men (a stereotype that actually is not correct).

8. What is a self-fulfilling prophecy? Why is it relevant when we examine how stereotypes can influence behavior?

Identify one of your own behaviors that is more gender stereotyped than you might wish, and point out how a self-fulfilling prophecy might be relevant.

9. Women and men are represented differently in the media and in cultural gender stereotypes, yet people may not incorporate these stereotypes into their own self-concepts. Discuss this statement, using material from throughout the entire chapter.

10. Throughout this chapter, we discussed cross-cultural research. How do gender biases and stereotypes operate in cultures outside the United States? Propose three additional topics related to gender that would be especially interesting to explore.

Key Terms

stereotypes (p. 36)
gender stereotypes (p. 37)
prejudice (p. 37)
discrimination (p. 37)
gender bias (p. 37)
androcentrism (p. 42)
normative-male problem (p. 42)
masculine generic (p. 43)
androcentric generic (p. 43)

communion (p. 52)
agency (p. 52)
intersectionality (p. 54)
explicit gender stereotypes (p. 55)
implicit gender stereotypes (p. 55)
hostile sexism (p. 59)
benevolent sexism (p. 59)
ambivalent sexism (p. 59)

cisgender (p. 62)
genderqueer (p. 62)
gender nonconforming (p. 62)
transgender (p. 62)
trans (p. 62)
intersex (p. 62)
heterosexuality (p. 62)
asexuality (p. 62)
bisexuality (p. 62)
demisexuality (p. 62)

pansexuality (p. 62)
sapiosexuality (p. 62)
heterosexism (p. 62)
sexual prejudice (p. 63)
social cognitive approach (p. 66)
gender polarization (p. 67)
attributions (p. 68)
self-fulfilling prophecy (p. 69)
stereotype threat (p. 69)
androgynous (p. 70)

Recommended Readings

Anderson, K. J. (2010). Benign bigotry. *The psychology of subtle prejudice*. New York: Cambridge. Kristin Anderson's book is an excellent choice if you want more information about prejudice. Three chapters that are especially relevant for this chapter focus on prejudice against feminists, LGBTQ+ individuals, and people of color.

Rudman, L. A., & Glick, P. (2008). *The social psychology of gender: How power and intimacy shape gender relations*. New York: Guilford. Throughout your textbook, you'll read about Laurie Rudman's and Peter Glick's research. We strongly recommend this book to anyone interested in the social components of gender!

Schneider, D. J. (2004). *The psychology of stereotyping*. New York: Guilford Press. In this clear and well-organized book, the author explores the content of certain stereotypes, and he also examines how children develop stereotypes about race and gender.

Whitley, B. E., Jr., & Kite, M. E. (2010). *The psychology of prejudice and discrimination* (2nd ed.). Belmont, CA: Wadsworth. Bernard Whitley and Mary Kite are well known for their studies about sexism, ageism, and heterosexism. This excellent textbook includes interesting quotations and media reports about biases, as well as a clear discussion of the relevant research.

Answers to Demonstrations

Demonstration 2.3: Most people believe that the following items are characteristics of women (W): dependent, gentle, kind, caring, nervous, emotional, talkative, compassionate, patient, modest. They also believe these items are characteristic of men (M): self-confident, greedy, competitive, active, capable, loud, physically strong, courageous, inventive, powerful.

Demonstration 2.5: Add together the total number of points from the following items: 1, 3, 6, 7, 9. These items represent the hostile sexism subscale. Then add together the total number of points from items 2, 4, 5, 8, and 10. These items represent the benevolent sexism subscale. Adding these two subscale scores together provides an index of overall sexism.

Monkey Business Images/Shutterstock.com

3 Infancy and Childhood

Learning Objectives

After studying this chapter, you will be able to …

3-1 Explain how early experiences during infancy and childhood shape gender typing, gender development, and gender stereotypes.

3-2 Summarize factors that shape gender typing.

3-3 Explain how children conceptualize gender during infancy and childhood.

Did You Know?

- During the first few weeks of prenatal development, most mammalian females and males have similar sex glands and external genitals (p. 80).
- When adults think that they are interacting with a baby girl, they typically judge that the baby is more delicate and feminine than if they think they are interacting with a baby boy; this finding is consistent with social constructionism (p. 84).
- Mothers talk more about anger to their sons than to their daughters; they talk more about sadness to their daughters than to their sons (p. 91).
- A boy who acts feminine is more likely to be rejected by other children, compared to a girl who acts masculine (p. 91).
- Teachers typically give more educational feedback to boys than to girls (p. 98).
- Children who consume more media tend to have stronger gender stereotypes (p. 99)
- By the age of 6 months, infants can perceive that a male face belongs in a different category from a series of female faces (p. 105).

One hot summer day in South Carolina, a little girl was attending the birthday party of another preschooler. The children managed to stay cool by taking off their clothes and wading in the backyard pool. The little girl's mother picked her up from the party, and the two began discussing the afternoon's events. The mother asked how many boys and how many girls had attended the party. "I don't know," the child replied. "They weren't wearing any clothes" (C. L. Brewer, personal communication, 1998).

As we'll learn in this chapter, children's and adults' conceptions of gender are often surprisingly different. After all, adults would point out that it's typically easier to determine a child's gender *without* any clothing. However, we'll also learn that children can be quite knowledgeable. For example, even preschoolers are well informed about cultural gender stereotypes.

In this chapter, we will discuss a process called gender typing. **Gender typing** includes how children acquire their knowledge about gender and how they develop their gender-related personality characteristics, preferences, skills, behaviors, and self-concepts (Liben & Bigler, 2002; Ruble et al., 2006). We'll start by considering the early phases of development, during the prenatal period and infancy, and then we'll discuss some theoretical explanations of gender typing. In the second section of this chapter, we'll examine factors that contribute to children's gender typing. These factors—such as the school system and the media—virtually guarantee that children growing up in the United States will be well informed about the importance of cultural norms regarding gender. In the final section, we'll focus on children's knowledge and stereotypes about gender; as we'll learn, even infants can tell the difference between female and male faces.

3-1 Background on Gender Development

Learning Objectives

To describe biological influences on and theories of gender development, you can...

3-1-1   Explain how genes, chromosomes, and hormones contribute to the development of sex and gender.

3-1-2   Identify factors that may contribute to atypical development and/or intersex conditions.

3-1-3   Compare and contrast various cultural preferences for male and female children.

3-1-4   Describe the *social constructionism* perspective, and identify common stereotypes for girls and boys across cultures.

3-1-5   Describe the social learning approach to gender development.

3-1-6   Explain how gender schemas contribute to gender identity.

Some important biological components of gender—such as the sex organs—develop during the **prenatal period**, the time before birth. Culture then conveys many messages about gender during **infancy**, the period between birth and 18 months of life. An adequate theory about gender development must be sufficiently complex to explain the societal forces that encourage children's gender typing. The theory must also emphasize that children contribute to their own gender typing by actively working to mentally process their lessons about gender.

Prenatal Sex Development

At conception, an egg with 23 chromosomes combines with a sperm, which also has 23 chromosomes. Together, they form a single cell that contains 23 chromosome pairs. The 23rd pair is called the **sex chromosomes**; these are the chromosomes that determine whether the embryo will be genetically female or male. In typical prenatal sex development, the other 22 chromosome pairs determine all the additional physiological and psychological characteristics.

The egg from the mother always supplies an X sex chromosome. The father's sperm, which fertilizes the egg, contains either an X chromosome or a Y chromosome. If an X chromosome from the father fertilizes the egg, then XX represents the chromosome pair, and the child will be a genetic female. If a Y chromosome from the father fertilizes the egg, then XY represents the chromosome pair, and the child will be a genetic male.

Consider the irony of this situation. Culture emphasizes the importance of gender—whether someone is an XX person or an XY person (Beall et al., 2004). However, this outcome is determined simply by whether a sperm bearing an X chromosome or a sperm bearing a Y chromosome is the first to penetrate the egg cell!

Typical Prenatal Development

Female and male embryos differ in their chromosomes. However, until about 6 weeks after conception, female and male embryos are virtually identical in all other characteristics (M. Hines, 2004). For instance, each human fetus has two sets of primitive internal reproductive systems. The internal female system, called Müllerian ducts, will eventually develop—in females—into a uterus, egg ducts, and part of the vagina. The internal male system, called Wolffian ducts, will eventually develop into the male internal reproductive system, which includes structures such as the prostate gland and the vesicles for semen (Federman, 2004).

The sex glands (or **gonads**) of males and females also appear identical during the first weeks after conception. If the embryo has an XY chromosome pair, a tiny segment of the Y chromosome called the SRY gene is responsible for sending a "message" that activates Sox9 gene expression and guides the gonads to develop into male testes, beginning about 6 weeks after conception (Hanley et al., 2000; Kashimada & Koopman, 2010). In contrast, if the embryo has an XX chromosome pair, the gonads begin to develop into female ovaries, beginning about 8 to 10 weeks after conception (Blakemore et al., 2009; Fausto-Sterling, 2000; M. Hines, 2004).

In about the third month after conception, the fetus's hormones encourage further sex differentiation, including the development of the external genitals. In males, the testes secrete two substances. One of these, the Müllerian inhibiting hormone, shrinks the (female) Müllerian ducts. The testes also secrete **androgen,** one of the male sex hormones. High levels of androgen encourage the growth and development of the Wolffian ducts (Blakemore et al., 2009). Androgen also encourages the growth of the external genitals. (Refer to Figure 3.1.) The genital tubercle becomes the penis in males.

Later in females' prenatal development, the ovaries begin to make **estrogen,** one of the female sex hormones. However, researchers currently believe that estrogen does not play an important role in the development of female organs (Blakemore et al., 2009). Consistent with the "invisible female" theme, we know much less about prenatal development in females than in males (Crooks & Baur, 2005; Fitch et al., 1998). For instance, an article in the prestigious *New England Journal of Medicine* shows an elaborate figure labeled "Factors Involved in the Determination of Male Sex"—but no comparable figure for the female sex (Federman, 2004). Researchers know, for example, that the genital tubercle develops into the clitoris in females. (Refer to Figure 3.1.) However, it isn't clear whether this developmental process requires a specific hormone or whether a clitoris simply develops when androgen is absent.

For decades, scientists assumed that female prenatal development was a passive, "default" process. However, a few investigations have explored the actual mechanisms that guide female developmental pathways. Those studies have revealed that female differentiation is not, in fact passive, but actively regulated by genetic and epigenetic factors (Leung & Adashi, 2019; Smith, Wilhelm, & Rodgers, 2014; Zhao et al., 2017).

In summary, typical sexual development follows a complex sequence before birth. The first event is conception, when genetic sex is determined. Female and male embryos are anatomically identical for the first weeks after conception. As we have learned, four additional processes then lead to the differentiation of females and males: (1) the development of the

Undifferentiated before sixth week

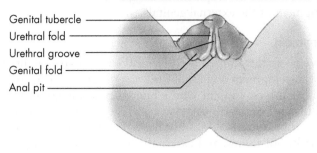

Genital tubercle
Urethral fold
Urethral groove
Genital fold
Anal pit

Seventh to eighth week

Male **Female**

Glans
Area where foreskin (prepuce) forms
Urethral fold
Urogenital groove
Genital fold (becomes
shaft of penis or labia minora)
Labioscrotal swelling
(becomes scrotum or labia majora)
Anus

Fully developed by twelfth week

Male **Female**

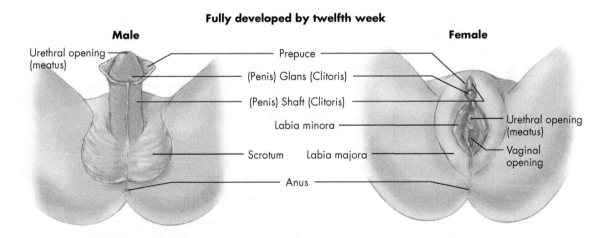

Urethral opening
(meatus)
Prepuce
(Penis) Glans (Clitoris)
(Penis) Shaft (Clitoris)
Labia minora
Urethral opening
(meatus)
Scrotum Labia majora
Vaginal
opening
Anus

FIGURE **3.1** Prenatal development of the external genitals.
Source: Based on Crooks & Baur (2008).

internal reproductive system, (2) the development of the gonads, (3) the production of hormones, and (4) the development of the external genitals.

Atypical Prenatal Development

The elaborate scenario we've just examined is the typical one. As you might expect from such a scenario, prenatal development sometimes takes a different pathway (Blakemore et al., 2009). The result is an intersex infant whose biological sex is not clearly female or male. An **intersex individual** is born with sex characteristics that are not clearly female or clearly male. An intersex person also does not have the chromosomes or an internal reproductive system, gonads, hormones, and external genitals that are either consistently female or consistently male. In other words, the world does not have just two binary sex categories, female and male (Golden, 2008; S. J. Kessler, 1998; Marecek et al., 2004). In fact, experts estimate that intersex individuals represent about 0.05 to 1.7% of the general population, depending on how intersex conditions are classified, making them about as common as having red hair (United Nations, 2015). Let's consider two examples of atypical prenatal development.

One atypical pattern is called **congenital adrenal hyperplasia**; in one form of this condition, genetic females (XX) receive as much androgen as males do during prenatal development. The excess androgen causes their genitals to appear somewhat masculine at birth (Pasterski, 2008). The traditional medical treatment has been surgery—even though surgery is not medically necessary—so that the genitals can appear more feminine (M. Hines, 2004; MacLaughlin & Donahoe, 2004; Ruble et al., 2006).

A second atypical pattern is called **androgen insensitivity syndrome**, a condition in which genetic males (XY) produce normal amounts of androgen, but a genetic condition makes their bodies not respond to androgen (Fausto-Sterling, 2000; M. Hines, 2004; Pasterski, 2008). As a result, the genital tubercle does not grow into a penis; the external genitals appear female. These children are usually labeled girls because they lack a penis. However, they have a shallow cavity instead of a complete vagina, and they have no uterus. This syndrome is usually discovered when they do not begin to menstruate at the normal time of puberty (M. Hines, 2004).

To us, the most interesting aspect of atypical prenatal development focuses on some important questions: Why do many cultures force all infants into either the female category or the male category (Basow, 2006; Golden, 2008; S. J. Kessler, 1998)? Why can't we accept that some people are intersex—neither female nor male? Why do physicians typically recommend surgery for intersex individuals, so that the external genitals can appear to be either clearly feminine or clearly masculine?

Many intersex adults now argue that intersex children should not be forced to adopt one sex or gender just because it is socially acceptable (Colapinto, 2000; Fausto-Sterling, 2000; Golden, 2008; Navarro, 2004; United Nations, 2015). As one intersex adult writes:

> I was born whole and beautiful, but different. The error was not in my body, nor in my sex organs, but in the determination of the culture.... Our path to healing lies in embracing our intersexual selves, not in labeling our bodies as having committed some "error." (M. Diamond, 1996, p. 144)

In Chapters 1 and 2, we pointed out that gender polarization forces us to perceive the two genders as being very different from one another. Carla Golden (2008) writes that feminist psychology is about conceptualizing the world differently. From this new viewpoint, can we overcome gender polarization and acknowledge that we humans are not limited to just two options?

People's Responses to Infant Girls and Boys

We consider a person's sex—the label "female" or "male"—to be extremely important, as noted in previous chapters and in the discussion of intersex individuals. You probably know many women who choose, during their pregnancy, to learn the sex of their baby several months before childbirth. Interestingly, when a woman chooses *not* to know the baby's sex, she is likely to find that her friends and relatives may become insistent: "Couldn't you just do me a favor and ask the doctor? I want to crochet some booties for your baby, and I need to know what color to make them!"

Parental Preferences About Sex of Children

Several decades ago, researchers in the United States and Canada found that most men and women preferred a boy for their firstborn child. More recent research shows no clear-cut pattern of parents' stated preferences about the sex of their offspring (Blakemore et al., 2009; Marleau & Saucier, 2002; McDougall et al., 1999; Pollard & Morgan, 2002), although if parents are asked if they could only have one child, they continue to voice a slight preference for having a boy instead of a girl (Newport, 2018).

However, more subtle measures seem to reveal the preferences of parents in the United States and Canada. For example, Gonzalez and Koestner (2005) examined 386 birth announcements in Canadian newspapers. Two researchers rated each birth announcement—without knowing the sex of the newborn—for the amount of happiness and the amount of pride it revealed. The results showed that parents were more likely to express pride following the birth of a boy. They were also more likely to express happiness following the birth of a girl. Now try Demonstration 3.1, which examines people's ideas about the preferred sex of a baby.

Demonstration **3.1**

Preferences for Males Versus Females as the Firstborn Child

You've just read that most U.S. parents no longer express clear-cut preferences for the gender of their offspring. However, some individuals you know may have strong opinions on the topic. To try this demonstration, locate 10 women and 10 men who do not have children, and ask them whether they would prefer a boy or a girl as their firstborn child. Be sure to select people with whom you are comfortable asking this question, and interview them one at a time.

After noting each person's response, ask for a brief rationale for the answer. Do your male and female respondents differ in their preferences? Do you think their responses would have been different if they had filled out an anonymous survey?

In some other cultures, however, parents do have strong preferences for boys. Favoritism toward boys is so strong in India and Korea that many women seek prenatal sex determinations. If the fetus is female, the mother often requests an abortion (Bellamy, 2000; Blakemore et al., 2009; Carmichael, 2004).

Selective abortion and female infanticide are also common in China, where the excess male population has important social consequences. In some regions of China, for instance, the preference is so strong that about 110 infant boys are born for every 100 infant girls, down from a peak of 121 infant boys for every 100 girls in the late 2010s (Tang, 2021). This pattern of selective abortion means that many heterosexual Chinese men of marrying age have difficulty finding a spouse (Glenn, 2004; Hudson & den Boer, 2004; Pomfret, 2001; Zeng & Hesketh, 2016). However, one ironic outcome of this development is that the reduced number of women in society has led to a push for greater equality for Chinese women in the twenty-first century (Zeng & Hesketh, 2016).

The bias against female babies also appears in other cultures, even those that do not practice selective abortion (Croll, 2000; Gonzalez & Koestner, 2005). For example, C. Delaney (2000) reported that residents of Turkish villages often say, "A boy is the flame of the hearth, a girl its ashes" (p. 124).

This antifemale bias is an important example of Theme 2 of this book: People often respond differently to females and males. This information about prenatal preferences demonstrates that, unfortunately, the bias begins even before the child is born (Croll, 2000; Rajvanshi, 2005).

The bias against female infants may also have important health consequences. For example, the Asian Center for Human Rights (2016) estimates that antifemale bias, sex-selective abortion, infanticide, and childhood neglect lead to 1.5 million girls "going missing" per year worldwide.

People's Stereotypes About Infant Girls and Boys

Do people think baby girls are different from baby boys? Let's first examine parents' stereotypes. In a classic study, Katherine Karraker and her colleagues (1995) investigated 40 mother-father pairs, two days after their infant daughter or son had been born. The researchers made certain that the daughters were objectively similar to the sons in terms of size and health. All the parents were asked to rate their newborn infant on a number of scales.

As presented in Figure 3.2, parents of girls rated their daughters as being relatively weak, whereas parents of boys rated their sons as being relatively strong. Notice that the parents also thought that the girls were more fine-featured, delicate, and feminine, in comparison to the sons. More recent studies show similar findings (Blakemore et al., 2009). Other research demonstrates that parents treat daughters and sons differently by choosing "gender appropriate" room decorations and toys (Basow, 2006; A. Pomerleau et al., 1990).

We have learned that parents respond somewhat differently to their infant daughters than to their infant sons. Strangers also show this same tendency to make distinctions based on gender. For instance, have you ever assumed an infant was a boy, and then learned this infant was a girl? Most of us find this experience puzzling. We try to maintain a nonsexist perspective, yet we find ourselves immediately justifying this gender transformation: "Oh, of course, I didn't notice her long eyelashes," or "Yes, her hands are so delicate."

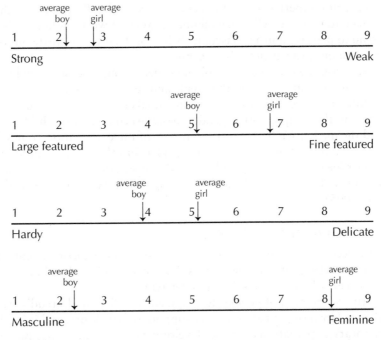

FIGURE **3.2** Average ratings for newborn girls and boys on four dimensions.

Source: Based on Karraker et al. (1995).

In general, the research evidence confirms that strangers judge infants differently when they are perceived to be female rather than male (e.g., Archer & Lloyd, 2002; Condry & Condry, 1976; Delk et al., 1986; Demarest & Glinos, 1992; C. Lewis et al., 1992). However, many adults who live in a relatively liberal community may not judge infants in terms of gender stereotypes (Plant et al., 2000).

Marilyn Stern and Katherine Karraker (1989) reviewed the research in which infants had been given male or female labels. More than two-thirds of the studies showed at least one gender-label effect; that is, the gender label "boy" or "girl" had a significant influence on people's ratings of the infant. In general, the differences were largest when people judged infants' activities and physical characteristics. The differences were generally smallest when people judged developmental achievements and personality characteristics (Golombok & Fivush, 1994).

In addition, relatives and friends may convey gender stereotypes through their choice of greeting cards that they send to parents of a newborn. In general, cards for boys show physical activity and action toys, whereas the cards for girls emphasize the baby's sweetness (Bridges, 1993). Parents therefore receive strong gender messages as soon as they open the envelopes.

Notice that these studies on adults' treatment of infants tend to support a social constructionist approach (Reid et al., 2008). As we discussed in Chapter 1, **social constructionism** argues that we tend to construct or invent our own versions of reality based on our prior experiences and beliefs. For example, if we are told that an infant is female, we tend to perceive delicate, feminine behavior. If we are told that the same infant is male, we tend to perceive sturdy, masculine behavior. That is, we create our own versions of reality, based on our prior beliefs about gender.

This discussion suggests we can explain gender typing at least partly by the way people respond to infant girls and boys: Both parents and strangers make some gender distinctions. However, differential treatment by these individuals is certainly not the complete answer. As we'll learn in this chapter, other gender messages come from a child's peers, the school system, and the media. We'll also learn that part of the explanation comes from girls' and boys' own ideas about the importance of gender. In other words, children may initially acquire gender ideas from other people and other institutions. However, children can exaggerate or modify these ideas still further through their own patterns of thought (Basow, 2008; Zack, 2005).

Theories of Gender Development

How can we account for the development of gender? What theories explain how children acquire their knowledge about gender, as well as their gender-related personality characteristics, preferences, self-concepts, skills, and behaviors?

One early explanation of gender development was Sigmund Freud's elaborate psychoanalytic theory. However, research has not supported that theory, and it is seldom discussed in contemporary explanations for the development of gender (e.g., Bussey & Bandura, 2004; Denmark & Paludi, 2008; Rudman & Glick, 2008; Ruble et al., 2006).

In our discussion of gender development, we will focus on two contemporary perspectives. These perspectives emphasize two different processes that operate during child development: the social learning approach and the cognitive developmental approach.

In previous decades, these two approaches were considered rival theories. We now must conclude that gender development is such a complex process that neither explanation is sufficient by itself. Instead, children apparently acquire their information about gender by *both* of these important methods (Bem, 1981, 1993; Bussey & Bandura, 2004; Powlishta et al., 2001; Ruble et al., 2006). To be specific:

1. In the social learning approach, children learn gender-related *behaviors* from other people.
2. In the cognitive developmental approach, children actively synthesize and create their own *thoughts* about gender.

The Social Learning Approach

The social learning approach argues that the traditional principles of learning explain an important part of gender development (Bandura & Bussey, 2004; Blakemore et al., 2009; Bussey & Bandura, 2004; B. Lott & Maluso, 2001).
More specifically, the **social learning approach** proposes two major mechanisms for explaining how girls learn to act "feminine" and how boys learn to act "masculine":

1. Children are rewarded for "gender-appropriate" behavior, and they are punished for "gender-inappropriate" behavior.
2. Children observe and imitate the behavior of people from their own gender category.

Let's first discuss how rewards and punishments might operate. Jimmy, age 2, races his toy truck, producing an impressive rumbling-motor sound. His parents smile, thereby rewarding Jimmy's "masculine" behavior. If Jimmy had donned his sister's pink tutu and waltzed around the dining room, his parents might actively try to discourage him. Now imagine how Sarah, also age 2, could win smiles for the pink tutu act. However, in some families, she might earn frowns for the rumbling-truck performance.

The research shows that parents respond more positively when children play "gender consistent" play patterns (Ruble et al., 2006). According to this first component of the social learning approach, children directly learn many gender-related behaviors, based on positive and negative responses from other people. As we'll soon realize, adults and other children often praise a girl for a behavior that they would condemn in a boy ... and vice versa (Fabes & Martin, 2000).

According to the second of the two social learning components, children also learn by observing others and imitating them, a process called **modeling** or **observational learning**. Children are especially likely to imitate a person of their own gender or a person who has been praised for a behavior (Blakemore et al., 2009; Bussey & Bandura, 2004; Carli & Bukatko, 2000; B. Lott & Maluso, 2001). For example, a little girl would be particularly likely to imitate her mother if someone had praised her mother for her actions. Also, children frequently imitate characters from books, films, and television, as well as real people (Bussey & Bandura, 2004).

Direct learning, by means of rewards and punishments, is an important way that very young children learn "gender-appropriate" behavior. As children grow older, the second component (modeling) becomes active. Children can now observe the behavior of others, internalize that information, and imitate that behavior later (Bussey & Bandura, 1999, 2004; B. Lott & Maluso, 2001; Trautner & Eckes, 2000). Now let's discuss how our gender schemas and other cognitive processes contribute to a lifetime of learning about gender.

The Cognitive Developmental Approach

Whereas the social learning approach emphasizes *behaviors,* the cognitive developmental approach emphasizes *thoughts.* More specifically, the **cognitive developmental approach** argues that children are active thinkers who seek information from their environment; children also try to make sense of this information and organize it in a coherent fashion (Gelman et al., 2004; Olson & Dweck, 2008; Reid et al., 2008).

One important concept in the cognitive developmental approach is called a *schema*. A **schema** (pronounced *skee*-mah) is a general concept that we use to organize our thoughts and attitudes about a topic (Blakemore et al., 2009). As we noted in Chapter 2 (page 66), we humans seem to automatically sort people into groups.

At a relatively early age, children develop powerful **gender schemas**; they organize information into two conceptual categories, female and male (Zack, 2005). These gender schemas encourage children to think and act in gender-stereotyped ways that are consistent with their gender schemas (Blakemore et al., 2009; C. L. Martin & Ruble, 2004; C. L. Martin et al., 2002, 2004).

A child's gender schema may include relatively important information, such as the fact that the kindergarten teacher consistently instructs children to form a boys' line and a girls' line (Bem, 1981, 1993). The schemas may also include trivial information, such as the observation that children's drawings of females show more prominent eyelashes than their drawings of males. As children grow older, their gender schemas become more complex and also more flexible (C. L. Martin & Ruble, 2004).

According to the cognitive developmental approach to gender development, children actively work to make sense of their own gender (Blakemore et al., 2009; Gelman et al., 2004; Kohlberg, 1966). One of the first major steps in gender development is **gender identity**, or girls labeling themselves as girls and boys labeling themselves as boys. Most children provide the "correct" label by the time they are 1 1/2 to 2 1/2 years old (C. L. Martin et al., 2004). Notice, incidentally, that this "two-category system" is rigid; it does not provide any flexibility for an intersex child, a transgender child, a gender-fluid child, a nonbinary child, or a child whose family tries to avoid gender labels.

Soon after children label themselves, they learn how to classify other males and females. At this point, most children begin to prefer people, activities, and things that are consistent with their own gender identity (Kohlberg, 1966; C. L. Martin et al., 2002; Powlishta et al., 2001; Rudman & Glick, 2008). A child who identifies as a girl, for example, is more prone to like feminine objects and activities. A woman in one of my classes provided a useful example of these preference patterns. Her 4-year-old daughter asked about the sex of every dog she met. If it was a "girl dog," she would run up and pat it lovingly. If it was a "boy dog," she would cast a scornful glance and walk in the opposite direction. According to the cognitive developmental approach, girls prefer stereotypically feminine activities because these activities are consistent with their female gender identity.

General Comments About Theories of Gender Development

We have explored two major theoretical approaches to development; both of these theories are necessary to account for children's gender typing. Together, they suggest the following:

1. Children's behaviors are important, as proposed by the social learning approach.
   a. Children are rewarded and punished for gender-related behavior.
   b. Children model their behavior after same-gender individuals.
2. Children's thoughts are important, as proposed by the cognitive developmental theory.
   a. Children develop powerful gender schemas.
   b. Children use gender schemas to evaluate themselves, other people, and other things.

Both the social learning and the cognitive developmental approaches work together to account for children's development of gender typing (e.g., Bussey & Bandura, 1999, 2004; C. L. Martin et al., 2002, 2004). To some extent, children *behave* before they *think*. In other words, the two components of social learning theory may begin to operate before children have clear gender schemas or other thoughts about gender (Warin, 2000). As children's cognitive development grows more sophisticated, however, their ideas about gender schemas enhance their ability to learn gender-typed behavior, through direct learning and modeling (Reid et al., 2008).

For the remainder of this chapter, we turn our attention to the research about children's gender development. We'll first consider the external forces that encourage gender typing. These forces include the parents, peers, and teachers who reward and punish children's gender-related behavior, as well as the media that provide models of gender-stereotyped behavior. Then we'll consider how children's thoughts about gender develop from infancy to late childhood.

Section Summary

Background on Gender Development

1. During typical prenatal development, male and female embryos initially appear identical; male testes begin to develop at 6 weeks, and female ovaries begin to develop at about 8 to 10 weeks.

2. An embryo's neutral external genitals usually grow into either female or male genitals during prenatal development.

3. In atypical prenatal development, an intersex infant is born; this child is neither clearly male nor clearly female. For example, genetic females with congenital adrenal hyperplasia (excess androgen) have external genitals that appear masculine. Also, genetic males with androgen insensitivity syndrome may have external genitals that appear female.

4. Parents in the United States are typically uncomfortable with intersex infants because they do not fit into one of the two "acceptable" gender categories.

5. Most parents no longer have a strong preference for male offspring in the United States and Canada. In contrast, gender preferences are so strong in some countries (e.g., India, Korea, and China) that female fetuses may be aborted.

6. Parents and strangers tend to judge infant girls and infant boys differently.

7. We can best explain gender typing by combining two approaches: (a) the social learning approach (children are rewarded for "gender-appropriate" behavior and punished for "gender-inappropriate" behavior, and children imitate the behavior of same-gender individuals) and (b) the cognitive developmental approach (children's active thinking encourages gender typing, and children use gender schemas for evaluation).

3-2 Factors That Shape Gender Typing

Learning Objectives

To summarize factors that shape gender typing, you can...

3-2-1 Explain how parents contribute to gender typing in infants and children through activities, conversations, and attitudes.

3-2-2 Describe how peer interactions among infants and children contribute to gender typing.

3-2-3 Explain how nontraditional behavior and gender segregation in children contributes to gender typing.

3-2-4 Analyze how gender prejudice, standards, and attractiveness contribute to gender typing in infants and children.

3-2-5 Provide examples of how teachers contribute to gender typing in the classroom.

3-2-6   Analyze why there is a gender gap between industrialized and nonindustrialized countries in terms of girls' education.

3-2-7   Explain how media exposure contributes to gender typing.

3-2-8   Describe how biased representations in children's books contributes to gender typing.

In the previous section, we discussed two general explanations for gender typing. The social learning approach emphasizes that parents often reward gender-typed behavior more than "gender-inappropriate" behavior; also, parents and the media typically provide models of gender-typed behavior. The cognitive developmental approach emphasizes that children actively construct their gender schemas based on messages they learn from parents and other sources. Let's explore several important factors that shape gender typing, beginning with parents and then moving on to peers, schools, and the media. As you'll learn, each factor contributes to children's development of gender roles.

Parents

We learned earlier that parents react somewhat differently to male and female infants. Those reactions tend to be stereotyped because parents do not yet know their child's unique characteristics (Jacklin & Maccoby, 1983). When children are older, however, the parents know much more about each child's individual personality (B. Lott & Maluso, 1993). Therefore, parents often react to older children on the basis of each child's personality characteristics in addition to their gender (Blakemore et al., 2009; Reid et al., 2008).

In this section, we'll discover that parents sometimes encourage gender-typed activities and conversational patterns. They also treat sons and daughters somewhat differently with respect to two social characteristics: aggression and independence. However, parents often do not make as strong a distinction between boys and girls as you might expect (R. C. Barnett & Rivers, 2004; Blakemore et al., 2009; Leaper, 2002; Ruble et al., 2006). We'll also consider the factors related to parents' gender-typing tendencies.

Gender-Typed Activities

Parents encourage gender-typed activities when they assign chores to their children. As you might expect, parents are likely to assign girls to domestic chores, such as washing the dishes or taking care of younger children, whereas they assign boys to outdoor work, such as mowing the lawn or taking out the garbage (Blakemore et al., 2009; Ruble et al., 2006; Sy & Romero, 2008).

Research in Asia shows that girls typically perform more time-consuming chores than boys do, whereas boys are allowed more time for schoolwork (Croll, 2000). Furthermore, in nonindustrialized cultures, boys have roughly twice as much free time as girls do (McHale et al., 2002).

Studies suggest that parents often encourage their children to develop gender-typed interests by providing different kinds of toys for daughters than for sons (Leaper, 2002; Reid et al., 2008). However, parents frequently have gender-neutral responses to children's play patterns (Idle et al., 1993; Ruble et al., 2006). In other words, if parents notice that 3-year-old Tanya likes playing with the Fisher-Price gas station, they won't interfere by handing her a doll.

In general, however, girls are allowed greater flexibility than boys, as far as the toys they play with (Basow, 2008; Reid et al., 2008; E. Wood et al., 2002). That is, parents are much more worried about boys being "sissies" than about girls being "tomboys." One likely explanation is that adults tend to interpret feminine behavior in a boy as a sign of gay tendencies, but they are less likely to view masculine behavior in a girl as a sign of lesbian tendencies (Kite et al., 2008; Sandnabba & Ahlberg, 1999).

We have learned that male children are more likely than female children to *receive* strong messages about "gender-appropriate" behavior. Similarly, the research shows that male adults are more likely than female adults to *give* these messages (Blakemore & Hill, 2008; Leaper, 2002; Ruble et al., 2006). For example, fathers are more likely than mothers to encourage their daughters to play with stereotypically feminine items, such as tea sets and baby dolls, and to encourage their sons to play with stereotypically masculine items, such as footballs and boxing gloves.

In summary, parents do seem to promote some gender-typed activities in their children. As we'll soon discover, however, many parents conscientiously try to treat their sons and daughters similarly.

Conversations About Emotions

Another kind of gender-typed activity focuses on conversations. For example, mothers talk more to infant daughters than to infant sons (Clearfield & Nelson, 2006). With older children, parents are especially likely to talk to daughters about other people and about emotions (Blakemore et al., 2009; Bronstein, 2006; Clearfield & Nelson, 2006; Reid et al., 2006).

One of the most interesting aspects of parent–child conversations is that parents typically discuss different emotions with their daughters than with their sons (Chance & Fiese, 1999; Fivush & Buckner, 2000; Leaper, 2002). For example, Fivush (1989) examined mothers' conversations with children between the ages of 2 1/2 and 3 years. During a session that lasted about half an hour, 21% of mothers discussed anger with their sons, whereas none of mothers discussed anger with their daughters. Instead, they talked with their daughters about fear and sadness.

Mothers are especially likely to discuss sadness in detail with their daughters, in order to discover exactly why their daughters had been sad on a particular occasion (Fivush & Buckner, 2000). Also, mothers speak in a more emotional fashion when interacting with their daughters than with their sons (Fivush & Nelson, 2004). Fathers, as well as mothers, are much more likely to discuss sadness with their daughters than with their sons (S. Adams et al., 1995; Fivush & Buckner, 2000; Fivush et al., 2000).

Parents also tend to pressure boys to avoid expressing sadness or fear (Blakemore et al., 2009). Not surprisingly, then, studies of 3- and 4-year-olds show that girls are more likely than boys to spontaneously talk about sad experiences (Denham, 1998; Fivush & Buckner, 2000).

In Chapter 12, we'll learn that when women are sad they often spend time trying to figure out the precise nature of their sadness, an activity that may lead to higher rates of depression in women than in men (Nolen-Hoeksema, 1990, 2003). Early family interactions may set the stage for these gender differences during adulthood.

Attitudes About Aggression

Do parents respond differently to aggressiveness in their daughters, as opposed to their sons? The findings are somewhat inconsistent. Some studies show that parents are more likely to discourage aggression in their daughters, but other studies show few differences

(Basow, 2008; Powlishta et al., 2001; Ruble & Martin, 1998). One possibility is that parents treat preschool girls and boys similarly. However, once the children begin elementary school, parents may discourage aggression somewhat more in their daughters than in their sons (Blakemore et al., 2009).

Try Demonstration 3.2 when you have a chance. What do your own observations suggest about parents' responses to aggressive daughters and aggressive sons?

Parents can also provide information about aggression and power in other ways. As the second component of social learning theory emphasizes, some boys learn to be aggressive by imitating their aggressive fathers. Furthermore, children notice in their own families that fathers make more decisions. Fathers may also use physical intimidation to assert power. By observing their parents, children often learn that physical aggression and power are "boy things," not "girl things."

Attitudes About Independence

Do parents respond differently to independence in their daughters, as opposed to their sons? Similar to the situation with aggression, the findings are somewhat inconsistent. For example, parents tend to give the same kind of verbal directions to their daughters and their sons (e.g., Leaper et al., 1998). However, in research on toddlers, parents are more likely to leave boys alone in a room, whereas they are more likely to supervise girls (Bronstein, 2006; Grusec & Lytton, 1988).

When children reach school age, parents are also more likely to provide cautions to their daughters than to their sons (Leaper, 2002; Morrongiello & Hogg, 2004; Ruble et al., 2006). Parents specifically allow their sons to be more independent about playing away from home (Blakemore et al., 2009).

However, as Blakemore and her colleagues write, "In many ways, contemporary parents treat boys and girls very similarly overall, and they are likely to treat particular children differently than others, depending on factors such as their age, birth order, or temperament" (p. 287).

Demonstration **3.2**

Tolerance for Aggression in Sons and Daughters

For this demonstration, you will need to find a location where parents are likely to bring their children. Some possibilities include grocery stores, toy stores, public parks, and fast-food restaurants. Be sure to choose places where you can observe others unobtrusively and where you will not "stick out" or be considered a suspicious individual if you're not there with your own children (i.e., playgrounds, schools). Observe several families with more than one child. Be alert for both verbal and physical aggression from the children, directed toward either a parent or a sibling. What is the parent's response to this aggression? Does the parent respond differently to aggression, depending on a child's gender?

Individual Differences in Parents' Gender Typing

We have learned that parents may encourage gender-typed activities. Furthermore, they often spend more time talking about sadness with their daughters than with their sons. However, parents do not consistently encourage aggression or independence in their sons more than in their daughters (Leaper, 2002; Powlishta et al., 2001; Ruble & Martin, 1998).

Consistent with Theme 4 (individual differences), parents vary widely in the kinds of gender messages they provide to their children. Some parents treat their sons and daughters very differently, whereas others actively try to avoid gender bias (Blakemore et al., 2009; Ruble et al., 2006).

Relatively few studies have focused specifically on the relationship between ethnicity and parents' treatment of sons and daughters. Factors such as an ethnic group's social class can have an important influence on the results (Hill, 2002; Reid et al., 2008; Raffaelli & Ontai, 2004). However, there is some evidence that Black mothers tend to be less gender-biased than mothers of other ethnicities (Flannagan & Perese, 1998; Hill, 2002; Reid et al., 2008).

As you might expect, parents' personal ideas about gender can have an important effect on the kind of messages they give their sons and daughters (Bem, 1998; Ruble et al., 2006). For example, parents with traditional attitudes about gender tend to disapprove of their children adopting the characteristics of other genders (Blakemore & Hill, 2008).

A study by Tenenbaum and Leaper (1997) observed Mexican American fathers interacting with their preschool children in a feminine setting: playing with toy foods. Fathers who had traditional attitudes toward gender did not talk much with their children in this setting. In contrast, nontraditional fathers asked their children questions such as "What is on this sandwich?" and "Should we cook this egg?" By asking these questions, the fathers are sending a message to their children that men can feel comfortable with traditionally feminine tasks.

In other research, Fiese and Skillman (2000) asked a parent to tell a story to their 4-year-old child, focusing on the parent's own childhood experience. Mothers and fathers who had traditional attitudes about gender were likely to talk with their children in a gender-stereotypical fashion. For instance, they told about three times as many stories about achievement to their sons as they did to their daughters. In contrast, nonstereotyped parents told about the same number of achievement-related stories to their sons and daughters.

Before we move on, let's review the general conclusions about parents. Parents often encourage gender typing by their reactions to their children's "masculine" and "feminine" activities. They also discuss emotions, especially sadness, more with their daughters than with their sons. Parents are somewhat more likely to *discourage* aggression in their daughters, rather than their sons. In addition, they are somewhat more likely to *encourage* independence in their sons, rather than their daughters. Parents' gender-related messages about aggression and independence may be somewhat stronger when children reach school age. However, nontraditional parents typically provide fewer gender messages.

When we take everything into account, parents don't seem to be as consistent about encouraging gender typing as the articles in the popular media would suggest. We need to consider additional forces that are responsible for gender typing, including three factors that reveal greater gender bias: peers, schools, and the media.

Peers

Once children in the United States and Canada begin school, a major source of information and attitudes about gender is their **peer group**—that is, other children of approximately their own age. A child may have been raised by relatively nonsexist parents. However, on the first day of class, if Naomi wears her hiking boots and Jamal brings in a new baby doll, their peers may respond negatively. According to the research, peers seem to be more influential than parents in emphasizing gender typing (Maccoby, 2002).

Peers encourage gender typing in four major ways: (1) Children reject their peers who act in a nonstereotypical fashion; (2) they encourage gender segregation; (3) they are prejudiced against children of other genders; and (4) they have different standards for treating boys and girls. As you read this discussion, consider how social learning theory and gender schema theory would explain each topic's contribution to children's gender typing.

Rejection of Nontraditional Behavior

In general, children tend to reject peers who act in a fashion that is more characteristic of other genders (Basow, 2006; Blakemore et al., 2009; Rudman & Glick, 2008). For example, children tend to think that girls should not play aggressive electronic games about fighting (Funk & Buchman, 1996). Women who had been tomboys as children often report that their peers were influential in convincing them to act more feminine (B. L. Morgan, 1998). As we learned in the discussion of social learning theory, children are rewarded for "gender-appropriate" behavior, and they are punished for "gender-inappropriate" behavior (Bussey & Bandura, 2004).

Nontraditional boys usually experience even stronger peer rejection than girls do (Bussey & Bandura, 2004; Ruble et al., 2006; Rudman & Glick, 2008). For example, Judith Blakemore (2003) asked children between the ages of 3 and 11 to judge whether they would like to be friends with a child who violated traditional stereotypes. The children were especially likely to say that they would dislike a boy who wore a girl's hairstyle or a girl's clothing, who played with a Barbie doll, or who wanted to be a nurse. In contrast, they judged girls significantly less harshly for comparable role violations. Interestingly, when a boy often participates in pretend play with girls, he tends to be unpopular with other boys (Colwell & Lindsey, 2005).

Peers contribute to an unwritten **boys' code**, a set of rigid rules about how boys should speak and behave (Cox, 2018; Pollack, 1998). This code explicitly specifies that boys should not talk about their anxieties, fears, and other "sensitive" emotions. As we read in the discussion of the cognitive developmental approach, children's gender schemas are often extremely rigid. Furthermore, boys' schemas become even more rigid when their peers are present (Basow, 2008; Cox, 2018).

Gender Segregation

The tendency to associate with other children of the same gender is called **gender segregation**. Children in the United States and Canada begin to prefer playing with same-gender children by age 2 or 3 years, even on tasks where gender is completely irrelevant (Blakemore et al., 2009; Kite et al., 2008). Gender segregation then increases until early adolescence (C. P. Edwards et al., 2001; Maccoby, 1998, 2002; Rudman & Glick, 2008). In one study, for instance, more than 80% of 3- to 6-year-old children clearly preferred to play with another child of the same gender (C. L. Martin & Fabes, 2001).

One problem with gender segregation is that these single-gender groups encourage children to acquire—and practice—gender-stereotyped behavior (Fabes et al., 2003; Maccoby, 1998, 2002; Rudman & Glick, 2008). In these "separate cultures," boys learn that they are supposed to be physically aggressive, and they should not admit that they are sometimes afraid. Girls learn to express their emotions and to be sensitive to their friends' problems (Rose & Rudolph, 2006; Underwood, 2004).

A major problem with gender segregation is that children who grow up playing with only same-gender peers will not learn the broad range of skills they need to work well with both females and males (Fagot et al., 2000; Rudman & Glick, 2008; Shields, 2002). Furthermore, these different activities, in turn, strengthen children's gender schemas, so that the "boy" category seems distinctly different from the "girl" category (Fabes et al., 2003; Ruble et al., 2006).

Girls and boys also learn that the boys' group has greater power (Blakemore et al., 2009; Rudman & Glick, 2008). This inequality encourages a sense of **entitlement** among the boys; the boys will feel that they *deserve* greater power simply because they are male rather than female (McGann & Steil, 2006; L. M. Ward, 1999).

This preference for playing with children of the same gender continues to increase until about the age of 11 (Blakemore et al., 2009; Maccoby, 1998). As romantic relationships develop in early adolescence, boys and girls then increase the amount of time they spend together (Rudman & Glick, 2008).

Gender Prejudice

A third way in which peers encourage gender typing is with prejudice against members of other genders (Carver et al., 2003; Narter, 2006; Rudman & Glick, 2008). As we discussed in connection with gender schema theory, children develop a preference for their own gender.

For example, Powlishta (1995) showed 9- and 10-year-old children a series of brief videotaped interactions between children and adults. After viewing each video, the children rated the child in the video, using a 10-point scale of liking that ranged from "not at all" to "very, very much." As demonstrated in Figure 3.3, girls liked the girl targets in the videos better than the boy targets, and boys preferred the boy targets to the girl targets.

Similarly, in a study with Brazilian 3- to 10-year-olds, children gave positive ratings to same-gender children and negative ratings to children of the other gender (de Guzman et al., 2004). This kind of gender prejudice arises from children's clear-cut gender schemas, and it reinforces children's beliefs that females and males are very different kinds of people.

Gender prejudice is far from innocent. For example, Kuhn (2008) describes how boys have verbally harassed her third-grade daughter, and they also repeatedly tell her that girls can't play sports. In addition, the boys frequently physically assault her by slapping her bottom as they pass by. Unfortunately, surveys indicate that young girls frequently experience this kind of hostility (Leaper & Brown, 2008; Rudman & Glick, 2008; Wessler & De Andrade, 2006).

Different Standards

A fourth way in which peers promote gender typing is that they use different standards when they interact with boys than they use with girls. One of the most interesting examples of differential treatment is that children respond to girls on the basis of their physical attractiveness, but attractiveness is largely irrelevant for boys.

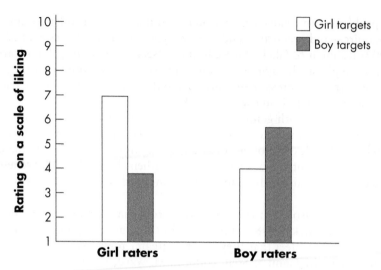

FIGURE **3.3** Ratings supplied by female and male children for the girls and boys in videos. The data show prejudice against other genders.

Source: From Powlishta, K. (1995). Intergroup processes in childhood. *Developmental Psychology, 31*, 781–788. ©1995 by the American Psychological Association. Reprinted with permission.

In a classic study, Gregory Smith (1985) observed middle-class White preschoolers for 5-minute sessions in a classroom setting on five separate days. He recorded how other children treated each child. Were the other children prosocial—helping, patting, and praising the child? Or were the other children physically aggressive—hitting, pushing, or kicking the target child? Smith then calculated how each child's attractiveness was related to both the prosocial and aggressive behavior that the child received.

The results showed that attractiveness (as previously rated by college students) was correlated with the way the girls were treated. Specifically, attractive girls were much more likely to receive prosocial treatment. Figure 3.4 shows a strong positive correlation.

In other words, the "cutest" girls were most likely to be helped, patted, and praised. In contrast, the less attractive girls received few of these positive responses. However, Smith found no correlation between attractiveness and prosocial treatment of boys; attractive and less attractive boys received a similar number of prosocial actions.

Gregory Smith (1985) also found a comparable pattern for physical aggression scores. That is, the less attractive girls were more likely to be hit, pushed, and kicked, whereas the "cutest" girls rarely received this treatment. However, attractiveness was not related to the aggression directed toward boys. Young girls learn a lesson from their peers that will be repeated throughout their lives: Physical attractiveness is important for females, and pretty girls and women will receive better treatment. Boys learn that physical attractiveness is not especially relevant to their lives.

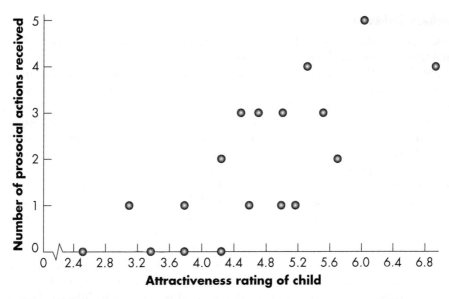

FIGURE **3.4** Positive correlation between attractiveness and prosocial treatment of girls (r = + .73).

Source: G. J. Smith (1985).

Researchers have not examined the influence of peers on gender typing as thoroughly as the influence of parents (Maccoby, 2002). However, we have learned that children have several different ways of influencing their peers. Specifically, they frequently reject children who don't conform to gender norms. They also encourage gender segregation, so that boys and girls have minimal contact with one another. In addition, they frequently express prejudice against children of other genders. Finally, they may have different standards for treating their peers, for example, by emphasizing attractiveness for girls but not for boys.

School

The typical child in elementary school in the United States spends more waking hours in school with teachers than at home with family members. As a result, teachers and schools have numerous opportunities to influence gender typing (Blakemore et al., 2009; Maher & Ward, 2002; Ruble et al., 2006). For example, children's textbooks and even the displays on classroom bulletin boards may underrepresent females (Sadker & Zittleman, 2007a).

The structure of a school also provides evidence that boys are treated differently and valued more than girls (Theme 2). Specifically, most principals and other high-prestige officials are men, whereas about 80% of those who teach "the little kids" are women (Meece & Scantlebury, 2006; Sadker & Zittleman, 2007b).

Let's investigate how teachers' behavior can favor boys. Then we'll consider how gender-fair programs can encourage children to become less gender stereotyped. Finally, we'll consider a serious problem in some developing countries, where girls are much less likely than boys to receive a good education.

Teachers' Behavior

In the early 1990s, the media began to publicize an important problem: Girls do not receive equal treatment in the classroom (Grayson, 2001; Rensenbrink, 2001; Sadker & Zittleman, 2007b). The publicized reports highlighted the invisibility of girls in the educational system, a point that is clearly consistent with Theme 3 of this textbook. According to the reports, classroom teachers often select activities that appeal to boys and they typically pay more attention to boys in the classroom (Maher & Ward, 2002; Meece & Scantlebury, 2006).

More specifically, research suggests that boys generally receive more positive feedback in the classroom than girls do (Sadker, Sadker, & Zittleman, 2009). Boys are also more likely to be recognized for their creativity, called on in class, and included in class discussions (Basow, 2008; Ruble et al., 2006; Sadker & Sadker, 1994). Teachers also tend to offer more specific suggestions to boys than to girls (Blakemore et al., 2009; Sadker & Zittleman, 2007a, 2007b). Incidentally, both female and male teachers typically pay more attention to boys than to girls (Blakemore et al., 2009; Basow, 2004).

Furthermore, teachers emphasize gender roles through a variety of messages. For example, a friend showed me an invitation to a Mother's Day tea party, which her 5-year-old son had brought home from school. The invitation urged mothers to wear "tea-party dresses" and fancy hats. The event was described as a good way to teach children about proper etiquette. The following month, the fathers received invitations to a Father's Day celebration. The invitation did not mention clothing or etiquette. Instead, fathers were encouraged to discuss their professions. Think about the messages provided to the children in the class, and also to their parents!

Students' Characteristics and Teachers' Treatment

Female students of color are especially likely to be ignored in the classroom. In early school years, Black girls speak up in the classroom. However, teachers may discourage their assertiveness. By fourth grade, they may become more passive and quiet (Basow, 2004). In addition, teachers do not typically encourage Black girls to take on academic responsibilities, such as tutoring or showing a new student how to prepare an assignment (Grant, 1994). These outcomes are particularly stark in situations in which a "demographic divide" occurs, where students of color are taught by White teachers. Over time, these interactions impact students' perceptions of teachers as well as their motivation levels and academic achievement. Students of all ethnicities generally report more positive ratings of Latino/a and Black teachers than White teachers (Cherng & Halpin, 2016).

Social class is another factor that influences teachers' behavior (Maher & Ward, 2002). Teachers may encourage a child from a middle-income family to learn independently. In contrast, they often emphasize simple memorization for a girl from a lower-income family (B. Lott, 2003; Rist, 2000).

Some people claim that U.S. schools have a "war on boys," so that boys earn low grades. The data actually show that boys and girls earn similar grades if they come from middle-income and high-income families. However, in low-income families, boys are more likely than girls to earn low grades, and they are more likely to be held back in school (Basow, 2008; Corbett et al., 2008; Entwisle et al., 2007).

In short, several factors in the school system may operate so that girls are short-changed. Luckily, most of us have known several inspirational teachers who value girls and boys equally. However, in many cases, teachers may ignore girls, they may not give girls appropriate feedback, and they may not encourage girls to be academically competent. In addition, the school system may convey important messages about the roles of women and men.

Encouraging Change in Schools

So far, our exploration of gender and education has emphasized that school structure and teachers' behavior often favor boys over girls. Many colleges and universities in the United States that train teachers now require courses about gender and ethnic diversity. However, teacher education textbooks devote only 3% of their content to gender-related issues (Sadker & Zittleman, 2007b). Still, the media coverage of the "silenced female" problem has alerted teachers about the need for more equal attention to girls and boys (Maher & Ward, 2002). As a result, many teachers are concerned about gender-fair education.

Educators have designed several classroom programs that explore children's stereotypes (Bigler, 1999a; Maher & Ward, 2002; Wickett, 2001). For instance, Bigler (1995) found that children in some classroom conditions were more likely to make gender-stereotyped judgments if the teachers had emphasized gender, for example, by instructing girls and boys to sit on opposite sides of the classroom.

However, there is little recent research on how schools can reduce children's gender stereotypes, partly because government funding of these pilot projects decreased, beginning in the 1980s (Sadker & Zittleman, 2007b). Another reason for the lack of research is that well-learned stereotypes are difficult to erase with just one brief intervention. Children actively construct their gender schemas, so a more comprehensive approach toward minimizing gender bias across grade levels may help schools reduce inappropriate stereotypes about gender.

Gender and Education in Nonindustrialized Countries

At the international level, we often encounter a more extreme problem about education for young girls. In every region of the world, women are still less likely to have formal schooling than men (Evans, Akmal, & Jakiela, 2019). In many countries, boys are much more likely than girls to be enrolled in school. For instance, only 39% of countries worldwide have equal numbers of girls and boys enrolled in school (United Nations Children's Fund, 2013).

There are numerous reasons for the gender gap in school enrollments. For example, in East Africa, many parents withdraw their daughters from school because of the custom of early marriages for young girls. Other parents withdraw their daughters when they discover that the school has toilets for boys, but not for girls (Mulama, 2008).

United Nations data also show that there are about 774 million illiterate adults in the world, and about two-thirds of them are women (Stromquist, 2007; UNESCO Institute for Statistics, 2010; United Nations Children's Fund, 2013). Where food and other essentials are limited, the education of girls is considered a luxury. Literacy rates for women in nonindustrialized countries vary greatly. For example, 97% of women in Cuba can read, in contrast to 50% in nearby Haiti (UNESCO, 2007).

Unfortunately, girls who have not been educated will experience lifelong disadvantages. As adults, they will not be able to read newspapers, write checks, sign contracts, or perform numerous other activities that can help them to become independent and economically self-sufficient (M. Nussbaum, 2000; UNESCO Institute for Statistics, 2010).

In addition, educated women are more likely to obtain employment. Educated women typically postpone marriage, and they have much lower birth rates than uneducated women. Infant mortality is also lower. Their children are usually healthier, and these children are more likely to go to school (W. Chambers, 2005; UNESCO Institute for Statistics, 2010). In other words, women's education has widespread effects on the health and well-being of people in nonindustrialized countries.

There is a wide gap between nonindustrialized countries and wealthy countries, with respect to factors such as education and family income. In addition, the governments of wealthy countries—such as the United States - rarely subsidize literacy programs or other socially responsible projects that could make a real difference in the lives of women in the less wealthy countries (Lipson, 2003; Mortenson & Relin, 2006).

One woman living in the Canary Islands, off the coast of North Africa, described why she regrets that she never learned to read:

> The greatest treasure that exists in life is to read and understand what one is reading. This is the most beautiful gift there is. All my life I have wished to learn to read and write, because, to me, knowing how to do so meant freedom. (Sweetman, 1998, p. 2)

The Media

So far, we have considered how parents, peers, and schools often treat girls and boys differently. Children also receive gender messages from many other sources. For example, the educational software designed for preschoolers has twice as many male main characters as female main characters (Sheldon, 2004). Fortunately, organizations such as the National Academy of Sciences have developed educational resources that feature women's achievements ("Wonder Girls," 2007).

Children's toys provide additional gender messages. As you might expect, girls typically choose to play with dolls and stuffed animals, whereas boys prefer mechanical toys, vehicles, and action figures (Blakemore & Centers, 2005; Cherney & London, 2006; Reid et al., 2008).

Even children's clothing conveys messages about gender. For example, parents of infant girls can now buy tiny shoes that are shaped like high heels. If you are shopping for a preschool girl, you can purchase bikini underwear and T-shirts featuring "Born to Shop" slogans (Cummings & O'Donohue, 2008; Lamb & Brown, 2006).

Most of the research on gender and the media examines how male- and female characters are represented in television and video games or in books. Let's explore these two areas in more detail.

Television and Video Games

Preschoolers age 0 to 2 average more than 20 hours of screen time per week, and most of that time consists of watching television (Chen & Adler, 2019; Paik, 2001). By the time teenagers graduate from high school, they have spent about 18,000 hours in front of the TV set, in contrast to about 12,000 hours in classroom instruction (D. G. Singer & Singer, 2001). In addition, about 85% of children aged 6 to 11 reported that they played a video game within the last month (Dill & Thill, 2007).

In Chapter 2, we examined stereotyping in programs intended for adult audiences. Now let's consider the television and video games aimed at children. As we'll learn, 18,000 hours of television can provide a strong "education" in gender stereotypes. In addition, with hundreds of cable channels—as well as DVDs and Internet programs—children have many opportunities to learn about stereotypical behavior!

Males appear much more frequently than females in children's television programs and advertisements (Blakemore et al., 2009; Huntemann & Morgan, 2001; Ruble et al., 2006). For instance, a sample of television advertisements aimed at children included 183 boys and only 118 girls (M. S. Larson, 2003).

Males and females also perform different activities in children's television programs. For example, males are more likely to be represented in the workplace, whereas females are typically presented as caregivers (Ruble et al., 2006; Van Evra, 2004). Males also display more leadership and ingenuity. Furthermore, the males in television programs are frequently violent, using guns, lasers, and karate kicks to destroy other people. Clearly these programs contribute to children's gender schemas that males are often aggressive (Gunter et al., 2003; Johnson et al., 2008; Kundanis, 2003; Ruble et al., 2006).

Is there a correlation between time spent watching television and gender stereotyping? In a classic study, Signorielli and Lears (1992) selected 530 fourth- and fifth-graders so that the sample resembled the distribution of ethnic groups in the United States. Then they statistically controlled for other important variables such as gender, ethnic group, reading level, and parents' education. The correlation between TV viewing and gender stereotyping was statistically significant. In general, the research tends to show modest correlations between television viewing and gender stereotypes (e.g., Huntemann & Morgan, 2001; Perse, 2001; Ruble et al., 2006; Ward & Freedman, 2006).

Most of the media research focuses on television programs. In general, however, the large number of masculine video games encourages boys to use these games more often than girls do. The games also help boys develop more extensive computer skills (Dill & Thill, 2007; Rubel et al., 2006; Subrahmanyam et al., 2002).

Cautious parents who want to raise nonstereotyped children might consider limits on screen time. Parents could also encourage their children to watch programs in which women are competent and men are nurturant. In addition, parents can select educational and entertaining videos that avoid stereotypes. Television and videos have the potential to present admirable models of female and male behavior, and they could even make children less stereotyped. Unfortunately, the media have not yet lived up to that potential.

Books

Are books more successful than electronic media in presenting gender-fair material? Unfortunately, most of the main characters in children's picture books are males, usually by a ratio of about 2 to 1 (Blakemore et al., 2009; R. Clark et al., 2003; M. C. Hamilton et al., 2006). Males also appear more often in the books' illustrations (Blakemore et al., 2009; Gooden & Gooden, 2001).

What are the males and females doing in these books designed for young children? Men are portrayed in a wider variety of occupations compared to women (Gooden & Gooden, 2001; Ruble et al., 2006). Also, boys help others, they solve problems independently, and they play actively. In contrast, girls need help in solving their problems, and they play quietly indoors (D. A. Anderson & Hamilton, 2005; M. C. Hamilton et al., 2006; Ruble et al., 2006).

Most authors still portray males in stereotypically masculine roles (Diekman & Murnen, 2004). Furthermore, a study of 200 best-selling children's books showed many more mothers than fathers. Mothers also interacted much more frequently with their

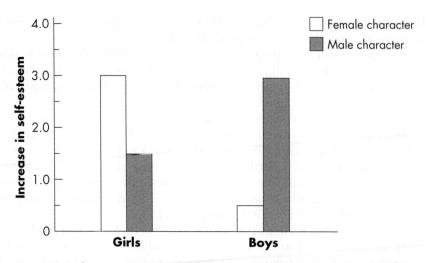

FIGURE **3.5** Improvement in girls' and boys' self-esteem (compared to baseline) after hearing stories about a female character or a male character.

Source: Based on Ochman (1996).

children, compared to fathers. Sadly, not one book showed a father kissing or feeding a baby (D. A. Anderson & Hamilton, 2005). Children's books therefore convey the message that child care is the responsibility of mothers (Basow, 2008).

Unfortunately, the biases in children's books can have important consequences for children. For example, in a classic study by Jan Ochman (1996), children watched videos of an actor reading a series of stories. Each story required the main character to solve a problem, which then enhanced this character's self-esteem. The same stories were presented to classrooms of 7- to 10-year-olds. However, a boy was the main character for half of the classes, and a girl was the main character for the remaining classes.

Ochman administered a standard measure of self-esteem at the beginning of the study. Then the children saw the video stories over a period of about 6 weeks. Finally, Ochman measured the change in the children's self-esteem. Girls had a greater increase in self-esteem if they heard the stories about an achieving girl, rather than an achieving boy. The boys showed a comparable pattern; their self-esteem increased after they heard stories about an achieving boy, rather than an achieving girl.

Think about the implications of Ochman's research. Suppose that children read stories about strong, competent boys, but not girls. The boys are likely to experience a boost in self-esteem. Meanwhile, the girls' self-esteem will not be improved.

One consideration for conscientious parents and teachers is to review the books that children read, to make sure that competent females and nurturant males are well represented. They can also be alert for alternative resources. For example, the website A Mighty Girl has a large collection of books, toys, and movies that encourage confidence and courage in girls and break them out of stereotypes. In addition, a feminist magazine called *New Moon* is edited by girls and young women. (Refer to Figure 3.6.)

FIGURE **3.6** *New Moon,* a magazine for girls and young women, discusses issues such as gender, racism, and ecology.

Section Summary

Factors That Shape Gender Typing

1. Parents tend to encourage gender-typed activities, for instance in choosing toys and assigning chores. These tendencies are especially strong for fathers (rather than mothers) and for sons (rather than daughters).
2. Parents discuss different emotions with daughters than with sons. Parents also treat sons and daughters somewhat differently with respect to children's aggression and independence, but the differential treatment is not consistent.
3. Parents' ethnicity is not consistently related to their gender typing. However, nontraditional parents are likely to treat their daughters and sons similarly.
4. Peers react negatively to another child's nontraditional behavior, especially in boys; peers also encourage gender segregation.
5. Children are typically prejudiced against peers of other genders, and they use different standards (e.g., attractiveness) when interacting with girls rather than boys.
6. Many schools encourage gender typing through the distribution of men's and women's occupations in the school system. Teachers also give boys more attention and useful feedback in the classroom, compared to girls.
7. Educators have developed some programs to help children reduce stereotypes, but these programs are frequently not comprehensive enough to have an important impact. In many nonindustrialized countries, boys are more likely than girls to attend school and to learn to read.
8. Children's television, media, video games, and books continue to underrepresent females and to present males and females in stereotyped activities.
9. According to research, reading books and watching television can influence children's ideas about gender.

3-3 Children's Knowledge About Gender

Learning Objectives

To explain how children conceptualize gender during infancy and childhood, you can...

3-3-1   Explain how infants differentiate among genders.

3-3-2   Provide examples of how children understand gendered stereotypes of activities, occupations, and personality.

3-3-3   Identify which factors are related to children's gender stereotypes.

We've just outlined several important ways in which children receive gender messages from the surrounding culture. Now let's discuss how well children learn their gender lessons: What do they know about gender, and what kind of stereotypes do they hold? In Chapter 2, we explored adults' stereotypes. As you'll learn, many of these ideas about gender are well established before children begin kindergarten.

Keep in mind a point we emphasized in connection with the cognitive developmental explanation of gender typing: Children actively work to create gender schemas, and these schemas encourage them to act in a manner that is consistent with their gender. In the previous section, we learned that parents, peers, schools, and the media all provide lessons about gender stereotypes. Here, we'll discuss how children's own thought processes also encourage gender stereotypes (Blakemore et al., 2009; Gelman et al., 2004).

Let's begin by discussing infants' early information about gender. Then we'll examine children's use of gender labels, their knowledge about gender-stereotyped activities and occupations, and their knowledge about gender-stereotyped personality characteristics. We'll also examine some factors that could influence the strength of children's stereotypes.

Infants' Basic Information About Gender

Interestingly, infants can make distinctions related to gender even before they learn to talk. For instance, they can categorize photos of males and females into two different groups (Blakemore et al., 2009; Golombok & Hines, 2002; Ruble et al., 2006). In a representative study, Katz and Kofkin (1997) showed 6-month-old infants a series of images of the heads and shoulders of different women. When the infant lost interest in these female stimuli, the researchers presented a new picture, showing either a male or a female.

Katz and Kofkin found that the 6-month-olds in this study looked significantly longer at the picture of a male than at the picture of a female. In other words, these young infants are "telling" us that the new (male) image belongs to a different category than the old (female) images they had seen previously. Infants also looked longer at a picture of a female after seeing a series of picture showing males. Infants' knowledge about gender is certainly not very sophisticated, but it does set the stage for children's gender concepts.

Children's Usage of Gender Labels

As you can imagine, gender knowledge is much easier to test in children who are old enough to talk. For instance, almost all 3-year-olds already state that they are a girl or a boy when talking with others (Gelman et al., 2004; Narter, 2006; Ruble et al., 2006).

However, as illustrated in the birthday-party anecdote at the beginning of this chapter, children's ideas about gender often differ from adults' perspectives. Young children frequently believe that clothing is the most accurate way to determine a person's gender. Most children can provide gender labels such as "lady" and "man" before the age of 2 (Blakemore et al., 2009; Ruble et al., 2006). However, children typically cannot explain the differences between females and males until they are 6 or 7 years old (Ruble et al., 2004). Let's now examine children's stereotypes about females and males.

Children's Stereotypes About Activities and Occupations

At an early age, children have clear ideas about activities that are "gender consistent." As the cognitive developmental approach argues, children actively construct gender schemas. For instance, 2-year-old children look significantly longer at a picture of a man performing a "feminine" activity, compared to their looking time for each of the other combinations of the person's gender and the nature of the activity (Serbin et al., 2002). In other words, this man's nonstereotyped behavior was very puzzling.

Older children often protest when they encounter nonstereotypical behavior. For example, Lori Baker-Sperry (2007) discussed a classic fairy tale, Cinderella, with a group of first-grade girls. One girl asked whether Cinderella has babies after she is married. Baker-Sperry answered that the book does not say, and she solicited their thoughts. The same girl replied,

"She should have babies, and she will change diapers, right?" Baker-Sperry then asked, "If they have babies, do you think the prince will change diapers?" The entire group responded in a loud chorus, "No!" (p. 722).

Children also make gender-stereotyped choices about their own activities. For example, when 4- and 5-year-olds chose a picture to color, 75% of boys selected a picture of a car, a baseball player, or some other "masculine" scene, whereas 67% of girls selected a picture of a cat, a ballet dancer, or some other "feminine" scene (Boyatzis & Eades, 1999).

By the age of 5, most children also show strong preferences for "gender-appropriate" toys, and the magnitude of these preferences is large (Cherney & London, 2006; C. F. Miller et al., 2006; Davis & Hines, 2020). Furthermore, adults often have difficulty persuading children to play with toys considered appropriate for another gender (Fisher-Thompson & Burke, 1998). Also, children remember a greater number of gender-stereotypical toys and activities, compared to neutral or nonstereotypical activities (Cherney, 2005; F. M. Hughes & Seta, 2003; Susskind, 2003).

Children's gender schemas also extend to occupations (Blakemore et al., 2009; Gelman et al., 2004; Liben et al., 2002). For instance, Gary Levy and his colleagues (2000) interviewed younger children (ages 3 to 4) and older children (ages 5 to 7), using questions such as those in Demonstration 3.3. As in this demonstration, the study required a choice; researchers told children to respond either "a woman" or "a man." As represented in Table 3.1, even the younger children have well-developed gender stereotypes about occupations.

Demonstration 3.3

Children's Beliefs About Men's and Women's Occupations

With a parent's permission, enlist the help of a child who is between the ages of 4 and 7 years. Then ask the child each of the following four questions. After obtaining each answer, ask the child, "Why do you suppose that a (man or woman, depending on the child's answer) would be best for that job?"

1. An airplane pilot is a person who flies an airplane for other people. Who do you think would do the best job as an airplane pilot, a woman or a man?
2. A clothes designer is a person who draws pictures of and makes clothes for other people. Who do you think would do the best job as a clothes designer, a woman or a man?
3. A car mechanic is a person who fixes cars for other people. Who do you think would do the best job as a car mechanic, a woman or a man?
4. An office assistant is a person who types up letters and mails things for other people. Who do you think would do the best job as a secretary, a woman or a man?

After asking all four questions, ask the child which job they would like best and which one would be worst. (For younger children, you may need to remind them what each employee does.)

Source: Based on G. D. Levy et al. (2000).

TABLE **3.1**

Children's Judgments About the Relative Competence of Women and Men in Four Gender-Stereotyped Occupations

	Child's Age Group	
	Younger	Older
	(3- to 4-year-olds)	(5- to 7-year-olds)
"Feminine" occupations		
Percentage who judged women more competent	75%	78%
Percentage who judged men more competent	25%	22%
"Masculine" occupations		
Percentage who judged women more competent	32%	7%
Percentage who judged men more competent	68%	93%

Source: G. D. Levy et al. (2000).

Sadly, children also show strong gender stereotypes when thinking about their own future occupations. For example, in another part of the study, Levy and his colleagues (2000) asked children to choose which emotion they would feel if they grew up to have each of the four occupations described in Demonstration 3.3.

According to the results, girls typically said that they would be happy with a stereotypically feminine occupation, but they would be angry or disgusted with a stereotypically masculine occupation. Boys typically said that they would be happy with a stereotypically masculine occupations, but they would be extremely angry and disgusted with a stereotypically feminine profession. We have learned throughout this chapter that gender roles often restrict boys more than they restrict girls.

Other research confirms that children's ideas about future occupations are gender stereotyped (Etaugh & Liss, 1992; Helwig, 1998). For instance, Etaugh and Liss (1992) found that not even one boy in their study of kindergartners through eighth-graders named a career choice for themselves that would be considered "feminine."

Children's Stereotypes About Personality

Young children also have gender stereotypes about personality. For example, children between the ages of 2 1/2 and 4 tend to believe that strength and aggression are associated with males. In contrast, softness and gentleness are associated with females (Heyman, 2001; Powlishta, 2000; J. E. Williams & Best, 1990). By the age of 5, children have also developed stereotypes about girls' and boys' responses to emotional events (Rudman & Glick, 2008; Widen & Russell, 2002).

In a representative study focusing on children's stereotypes, 8- to 10-year-old children looked at a series of photographs of women, men, girls, and boys (Powlishta, 2000). The children rated each photo on several gender-related personality characteristics, such as "gentle" and "strong." Consistent with previous research, the children rated female photos significantly higher than male photos on the stereotypically feminine characteristics, and they rated male photos significantly higher than the female photos on the stereotypically masculine characteristics.

Factors Related to Children's Gender Stereotypes

Several factors influence the strength of children's stereotypes. We mentioned earlier that boys have stronger stereotypes about career choices than girls do. Ethnicity and social class probably have a complex relationship with children's gender stereotypes. Unfortunately, we do not have large-scale studies that explore these issues.

Are children's gender ideas influenced by their family's views? Parents who have strong gender stereotypes about child rearing are likely to have children with stronger gender stereotypes (O'Brien et al., 2000; Powlishta et al., 2001; Ruble et al., 2006).

As you might expect, children's age influences their stereotypes (Lobel et al., 2000; Powlishta et al., 2001; Ruble et al., 2006). Some studies assess children's knowledge about culturally accepted gender stereotypes. The older children clearly know more than the younger children. After all, the older children have had more opportunities to learn their culture's traditional notions about gender.

However, other studies assess the flexibility of children's stereotypes. A typical question might be: "Who can bake a cake? Can a woman do it, can a man do it, or can they both do it?" Older children are generally more likely than young children to reply, "Both can do it." In other words, older children are typically more flexible than younger children. We can conclude that older children know more about gender stereotypes, but they also believe that people do not need to be restricted by these stereotypes (Blakemore, 2003; Ruble et al., 2006; Trautner et al., 2005).

Finally, children vary widely in their beliefs about gender, consistent with Theme 4. Their own unique interests often lead them to specific experiences with stereotypical and nonstereotypical activities (Basow, 2006; Liben & Bigler, 2002; Ruble et al., 2006). These experiences, in turn, shape their beliefs and their knowledge about gender.

Section Summary

Children's Knowledge About Gender

1. Even 6-month-old infants show some ability to distinguish between males and females, and 2-year-olds can label men and women.
2. Children have well-developed stereotypes about women's and men's activities, occupations, and personality characteristics; they are also gender stereotyped about their own future occupations.
3. Parents who have traditional ideas about gender usually have children with stronger gender stereotypes. Furthermore, older children are more knowledgeable about stereotypes, but they have more flexible beliefs.

Chapter Review Questions

1. Infant boys and girls are similar until the 6th week after conception. By the time they are born, they differ in their gonads, internal reproductive systems, and external genitals. How do these three kinds of differences emerge during normal prenatal development? Also, explain why some infants may not be clearly female or clearly male.

2. According to a well-known proverb, "Beauty is in the eye of the beholder." Apparently, the masculinity or femininity of an infant is also in the eye of the beholder. In what ways do both parents and strangers perceive differences between male and female infants?

3. Five-year-old Darlene is playing with a doll. How do social learning theory and the cognitive developmental approach explain her behavior?

4. Imagine that a family has twins, a girl named Yasmine and a boy named Halil. Based on the information on families and gender typing, how would you predict that their parents would treat Yasmine and Halil? Discuss four areas in which parents might respond differently to boys and girls: (a) gender-typed activity, (b) discussion of emotion, (c) aggression, and (d) independence.

5. Discuss four ways in which peers encourage gender typing. How might skillful teachers minimize gender typing? What other precautions should these teachers take to increase the likelihood that girls and boys will receive fair treatment in the classroom?

6. In what way do television, electronic media, video games, and books convey gender stereotypes? How could these media influence children's toy preferences and other gender-typed activities?

7. Suppose that you are working at a day-care center where you interact with children between the ages of 6 months and 5 years. What evidence do we have that the 6-month-olds already know some information about gender? Also describe what the older children of different ages will probably know about gender and gender stereotypes.

8. As children grow older, they know more about gender stereotypes; however, these stereotypes are also more flexible. Describe the research that supports this statement. What implications does this statement have for the influence of peers on gender typing?

9. Are gender stereotypes more restrictive for boys than for girls? Are fathers more likely than mothers to encourage these stereotypes? Discuss this question, being sure to mention parents' reactions to their children's gender-related activities, children's ideas about occupations, and any other topics you consider relevant.

10. Children actively work to construct their ideas about gender. Discuss several ways in which they create gender schemas. With respect to the four topics examined in the discussion about peers, how could these gender schemas encourage children to treat their male and female peers differently?

Key Terms

gender typing (p. 78)

prenatal period (p. 79)

infancy (p. 79)

sex chromosomes (p. 79)

gonads (p. 80)

androgen (p. 80)

estrogen (p. 80)

intersex individual (p. 82)

congenital adrenal hyperplasia (p. 82)

androgen insensitivity syndrome (p. 82)

social constructionism (p. 85)

social learning approach (p. 86)

modeling (p. 87)

observational learning (p. 87)

cognitive developmental approach (p. 87)

schema (p. 87)

gender schemas (p. 87)

gender identity (p. 88)

peer group (p. 94)

gender segregation (p. 94)

entitlement (p. 95)

Recommended Readings

Blakemore, J. E. O., Berenbaum, S. A., & Liben, L. S. (2009). *Gender development*. New York: Psychology Press. This book addresses gender comparisons and theories of gender development, as well as the social forces that shape children's development.

Klein, S. S. (Ed.). (2007). *Handbook for achieving gender equity through education* (2nd ed.). Mahwah, NJ: Erlbaum. This superb handbook features 31 chapters on topics such as patterns of education in other countries, gender equity in teacher education, and gender equity in a variety of content areas.

Ruble, D. N., Martin, C. L., & Bebenbaum, S. A. (2006). Gender development. In W. Damon & R. M. Lerner (Series Eds.) & N. Eisenberg (Vol. Ed.). *Handbook of child psychology*, Vol. 3. *Social, emotional, and personality development*

(6th ed., pp. 858–952). Hoboken, NJ: Wiley. This excellent chapter provides a clear, comprehensive overview of children's gender development, including an interesting summary of children's knowledge about gender.

National Center on Parent, Family, and Community Engagement. (2020). *Healthy gender development and young children: A guide for early childhood programs and professionals*. This document provides many resources for promoting healthy gender development in children, as well as an overview of the stages of gender development in childhood and many references for further reading. Available from the Office of Head Start through the U.S. Department of Health and Human Services website: https://eclkc.ohs.acf.hhs.gov/publication /healthy-gender-development-young-children.

Rolf Bruderer/Tetra Images, LLC / Alamy Stock Photo

4   Adolescence

Learning Objectives

After studying this chapter, you will be able to ...

4-1 Explain how puberty and menstruation affect girls and young women during adolescence.

4-2 Describe factors that influence self-concept and identity development during adolescence.

4-3 Analyze how gender influences education and career planning.

4-4 Summarize how gender impacts interpersonal relationships in adolescence.

Did You Know?

- In the United States, adolescents are relatively likely to say that they support feminist principles such as gender equality; they are less likely to say that they are feminists (p. 126).
- For all major ethnic groups in the United States, women are more likely than men to attend college (p. 132).
- Adolescent girls and boys are equally interested in pursuing careers that are prestigious (p. 133).
- According to the research, most adolescents get along fairly well with their parents (p. 135).
- Young lesbian women are more likely to "come out" to their mothers than to their fathers (p. 139).

A young Black woman described why she decided to leave her inner-city home to pursue a college education:

> I just decided that I wanted to go to college.... I didn't want to be poor. I didn't want to live in the projects. I wanted to have a home and drive a nice car. But now I'm a big girl, and I understand that education is more than getting a paycheck.... It's a continual exploration. It's a continual wealth of knowledge, even after you get your degree, there's still so much that you don't know. Education is a process. You live the experience and graduate. You get your credentials, then, the next week, you turn on the television and learn that something brand new happened in the field that you graduated from. It's like an ongoing evolution of knowledge. It's pretty neat. (Ross, 2003, p. 70)

This young woman's narrative explains how girls and young women today can construct a thoughtful life for themselves—one that is not constrained by stereotypical ideas of gender. In this chapter, we'll explore physical and psychological changes during adolescence, focusing on the changes where gender plays a particularly important role.

During **puberty,** a young girl experiences the *physical* changes that lead to sexual maturity. In contrast, **adolescence** refers to the *psychological* changes that occur during puberty; adolescence is the transition phase between childhood and adulthood (Blakemore et al., 2009). For girls, the major biological milestone of puberty is **menarche** (pronounced *men*-ar-key), or the beginning of menstruation.

In contrast, no specific event marks the end of adolescence and the beginning of adult-hood, a transition that historically received little attention from researchers (Collins & Steinberg, 2006; Smetana et al., 2006). We usually associate the beginning of adulthood with milestones such as living separately from our parents, completing college, holding a job, and finding a romantic partner. However, none of these characteristics is essential for adulthood.

Adolescents often find themselves caught between childhood and adulthood. Adults may sometimes treat adolescents as children—a mixed blessing that eases their responsibil-ity but limits their independence and their sense of competence (Zebrowitz & Montepare, 2000). Adolescents also receive mixed messages about issues of sexuality and the transition into adulthood (Collins & Steinberg, 2006; Posner, 2006). Parents tell them not to grow up too quickly. On the other hand, their role models tend to be adolescents who have grown up too quickly: sexy teenage television and movie stars, teens in ads, social medial influ-encers, and maybe even the girl next door (Cope-Farrar & Kunkel, 2002; Gleeson & Frith, 2004; Voelker, Reel, & Greenleaf, 2015).

In this chapter, we will examine four important topics for adolescents who identify as cisgender and transgender young women: (1) puberty and menstruation, (2) self-concepts, (3) education and career planning, and (4) interpersonal relationships. We'll mention other relevant topics (such as cognitive abilities, sexuality, and eating disorders), but later chap-ters will discuss them more completely.

4-1 Puberty and Menstruation

Learning Objectives

To explain how puberty and menstruation affect girls and young women during adolescence, you can...

4-1-1   Summarize the physical changes that happen to girls and young women during puberty.

4-1-2   Describe the stages of the menstrual cycle.

4-1-3   Explain why some people experience menstrual pain.

4-1-4   Summarize reasons why the concept of premenstrual syndrome is controversial.

4-1-5   Explain why research on mood swings during menstruation is problematic.

4-1-6   Identify various treatments for premenstrual syndrome.

4-1-7   Analyze why some cisgender women experience positive reactions to the menstrual cycle.

4-1-8   Compare cross-cultural attitudes toward menstruation.

Let's begin by discussing the physical changes that girls experience as they enter adoles-cence. We'll briefly consider puberty before we examine menstruation in greater detail.

Puberty

Most girls enter puberty between the ages of 9 and 13; the average age at menarche is 12 (Chumlea et al., 2003; Ellis, 2004; La Greca et al., 2006). In general, Black and Latina girls in the United States reach menarche somewhat earlier than White girls. Furthermore, White girls tend to reach menarche somewhat earlier than Asian American girls (S. E. Anderson et al., 2003; Chumlea et al., 2003; Ellis, 2004). Unfortunately, data is not currently available for Native American girls. Researchers do not have a satisfactory explanation for ethnic differences. However, body weight, stress, socioeconomic status, and nutrition seem to be important factors (Adair & Gordon-Larsen, 2001; K. K. Davison et al., 2003; Joos, Wodzinski, Wadswirth, & Dorn, 2018; Kelly, Zilanawala, Sacker, Hiatt, & Viner, 2017; Posner, 2006).

Menarche is seldom depicted in television programs or films. When the popular media do focus on menarche, most of the messages are negative (Kissling, 2002, 2006). In real life, young women's emotional reactions to menarche vary widely (Chrisler, 2017). However, some of them enjoy sharing the excitement and talking about their mixed emotions with their female peers (Fingerson, 2006; Stubbs, 2008). Efforts within the framework of the global menstrual hygiene movement have increased research support for understanding the multiple ways in which menarche affects the lives of girls, young women, and transgender youth (Critchley et al., 2020; Nahata et al., 2019; Sommer et al., 2015).

Young women who can communicate with a trusted adult often feel more comfortable about menstruation (Piran & Ross, 2006). However, other young women report largely negative reactions from family members (Costos et al., 2002). As Johnston-Robledo and Chrisler (2017) suggest, social stigma still surrounds the onset of menarche and menstruation. In short, the variety of emotional messages about menarche provide evidence for the individual differences theme of this textbook.

During puberty, young girls experience the most dramatic physical changes they have undergone since infancy. Specifically, at around 10 to 11 years of age, they experience a transformation in their **secondary sex characteristics**, which are features of the body related to reproduction but not directly involved in it. These characteristics include breast development and pubic hair (Ellis, 2004; Fechner, 2003; Summers-Effler, 2004).

During puberty, girls also accumulate body fat through the hips and thighs. Girls in the United States often resent this body fat, because cultural norms in the United States emphasize slender bodies (La Greca et al., 2006; Piran & Ross, 2006; Posner, 2006).

Biological Aspects of the Menstrual Cycle

The average cisgender woman menstruates about 450 times during her life. Naturally, then, this discussion of the menstrual cycle is relevant for most girls and women for 30 to 40 years after menarche. We will discuss menstruation in the current chapter, and we will return to this topic in Chapter 14, when we discuss menopause.

The hypothalamus, a structure in the brain, is crucial in menstruation because it monitors the body's level of estrogen during the monthly cycle. When estrogen levels are low, the hypothalamus signals the pituitary gland, another brain structure. The pituitary gland produces two important hormones: follicle-stimulating hormone and luteinizing hormone.

In all, four hormones contribute to the menstrual cycle (Chrisler, 2017; Federman, 2006):

1. Follicle-stimulating hormone acts on the follicles (or egg holders) within the ovaries, making them produce estrogen and progesterone.
2. Luteinizing hormone is necessary for the development of an ovum (or egg).
3. Estrogen, primarily produced by the ovaries, stimulates the development of the endometrium, which is the lining of the uterus.
4. Progesterone, also primarily produced by the ovaries, regulates the system. When the level of luteinizing hormone is high enough, progesterone stops the release of that hormone.

Figure 4.1 illustrates several major structures in menstruation, together with other important organs in the female reproductive system. The two **ovaries**, which are about the size of walnuts, contain the follicles that hold the **ova**, or eggs, and produce estrogen and progesterone.

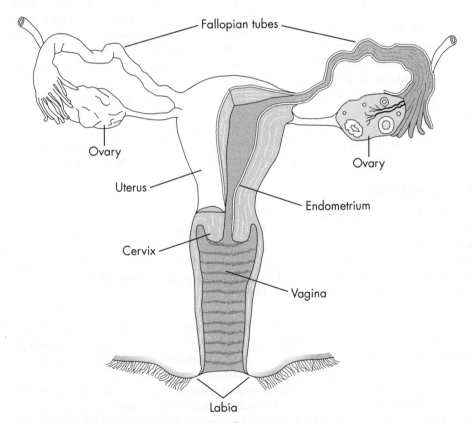

FIGURE **4.1** Female internal reproductive organs.

Note: On the right-hand side of the diagram, the interior of a cisgender women's ovaries, the fallopian tube, and the uterus are portrayed.

On about the 14th day of the menstrual cycle, one of the eggs breaks out of its follicle; this process is called **ovulation** (pronounced ov-you-*lay*-shun). The egg moves from an ovary into a fallopian tube and then into the **uterus**, the organ in which a fetus develops. Suppose that the egg is fertilized and implanted in the endometrium lining of the uterus. The endometrium can then serve as a nourishing location for this egg to mature during pregnancy. However, if the egg is *not* fertilized and implanted, the egg disintegrates on its way out of the uterus, and the endometrium is shed as menstrual flow.

The most important concept to remember is that brain structures, hormones, and internal reproductive organs are carefully coordinated to regulate the menstrual cycle (Chrisler, 2017). They operate according to a **feedback loop**: When the level of a particular hormone is too low, a structure in the brain is signaled, and the chain of events repeats itself, producing more of that hormone. Later on, when the level of a hormone is too high, a signal to a structure in the brain begins a chain of events that decreases that hormone.

In more detail, after ovulation the empty follicle matures into a round structure that secretes progesterone and estrogen. Therefore, the levels of both of these hormones rise. Then the feedback loop operates, leading to a rapid decrease in the production of both progesterone and estrogen. With such low levels of these hormones, the endometrium can no longer be maintained. The endometrium is then sloughed off, and it passes out of the vagina as menstrual flow. The low level of estrogen signals the hypothalamus, causing a new cycle to begin.

Note the checks and balances that are required to orchestrate the menstrual cycle (L. L. Alexander et al., 2021). This complex set of interactions first encourages the production of an egg, next leads to menstrual flow if no fertilized egg is implanted, and then begins another cycle.

Incidentally, you may have learned that women who live together—for instance as roommates—will tend to have synchronized menstrual cycles. However, research suggests no empirical evidence for this phenomenon (Schank, 2006; Yang & Schank, 2006).

Menstrual Pain

Menstrual pain, or **dysmenorrhea** (pronounced diss-men-or-*ree*-ah), typically refers to painful cramps in the abdomen. It may also include headache, nausea, dizziness, fatigue, and pain in the lower back (Chrisler, 2017; Crooks & Baur, 2008; Taylor, 2005). Dysmenorrhea is not the same as premenstrual syndrome, or PMS, which we will discuss in the next section. How common is menstrual pain? Estimates range from 50 to 75% for high school girls and college-age women (Golub, 1992; A. E. Walker, 1998).

In some cultures, women expect that menstruation will be painful. It's important to know that menstrual pain is clearly not imaginary. The contractions of the uterus that cause menstrual pain are encouraged by prostaglandins (pronounced pross-tuh-*glan*-dins). **Prostaglandins** are substances that the body produces in high concentrations just before menstruation, and they can cause severe cramps (Chrisler, 2017).

Researchers have discovered that women who experience high anxiety report having more menstrual pain than women who experience less anxiety. Some researchers have suggested that women who experience high anxiety focus more attention on their cramps, which could increase their intensity (Sigmon, Rohan et al., 2000). However, we must think critically about correlational results such as these. Another possibility may be that women who experience relatively strong menstrual pain (and perhaps other forms of pain) experience more anxiety as a consequence of these unpleasant experiences. Given the evidence, menstrual pain is probably caused by a combination of physiological and psychological factors.

Many different treatments have been used to reduce menstrual pain. Some drugs are helpful, including those that inhibit the synthesis of prostaglandins (e.g., ibuprofen). Exercise, a heating pad, muscle relaxation, adequate sleep, and dietary changes often produce additional relief (Chrisler, 2017; Golub, 1992).

The Controversial Premenstrual Syndrome

Menstrual pain is well accepted as being part of the menstrual cycle. In contrast, premenstrual syndrome is controversial among both professionals and laypeople (Chrisler, 2017, 2018). **Premenstrual syndrome (PMS)** is the name given to the cyclical set of symptoms that may occur a few days before menstruating. The list of symptoms often includes headaches, breast soreness, swelling, nausea, increased sensitivity to pain, allergies, and acne—as well as various psychological reactions. These psychological reactions typically include depression, irritability, anxiety, dizziness, and low energy (Caplan & Caplan, 2009; Chrisler, 2018; Chrisler et al., 2006).

One reason that PMS is controversial is that researchers do not agree on its definition (Chrisler, 2018; Figert, 1996). Read the previous list of symptoms once more, and add other symptoms that you've learned about in popular accounts of PMS. Some critics have discovered as many as 200 different symptoms presumably connected with PMS or its more serious form, called premenstrual dysphoric disorder or PMDD (Chrisler, 2018; Gottheil et al., 1999; Kaiser, Janda, Kleinstäuber, & Weise, 2018). When you have the opportunity, try Demonstration 4.1.

Think of the problem created by this confusing variety of symptoms. One researcher may be studying women whose primary symptom is anxiety; another may be studying women with headaches. How can researchers study PMS systematically when we don't even have a clear-cut operational definition for the problem? Furthermore, no blood test or other biochemical test can assess whether a woman is experiencing PMS (Chrisler, 2018; Gottheil et al., 1999).

Demonstration **4.1**

People's Opinions About Premenstrual Syndrome (PMS)

Make a list of 8 to 10 adolescent and adult women whom you know quite well—well enough to ask them about premenstrual syndrome! You can question them in person or by e-mail, but emphasize that you want them to answer the questions seriously. If they *don't* answer seriously, what does this tell you about people's discomfort with the topic of menstruation?

Here are three questions you might ask, but be sure to create some of your own questions:

1. How would you define the premenstrual syndrome (PMS)?
2. What would you list as three especially important examples of PMS?
3. Do you think that researchers have clearly established that women behave differently during the days just before their periods, as opposed to, say, two weeks after they menstruate?

Another reason that PMS is so controversial is that some experts claim that virtually all menstruating women experience it. This claim is unfair because it suggests that all women are at the mercy of biological factors such as their "raging hormones" (Chrisler, 2018). Note that this belief encourages the stereotype that women are irrational and overly emotional (Chrisler, 2017; Rudman & Glick, 2008).

An alternative view argues that PMS is a myth that some cultures create. The "culture explanation" is consistent with research demonstrating that women in India and China report different symptoms from women in the United States, for example (Chrisler, 2018). This perspective, if taken too far, would be equally unfair because some women do experience certain symptoms more often premenstrually than at other times in their cycle.

Our discussion of PMS takes an intermediate position between the two extremes of the biologically driven explanation and the psychological-cultural explanation. Apparently, a small percentage of women (maybe 5 to 10%) have significant symptoms that are related to their menstrual cycle (Chrisler et al., 2006; D. Taylor, 2005). Some of those symptoms are severe enough that a diagnosis of PMDD may be assigned (Hantsoo & Epperson, 2015). Other women do not have any symptoms at all. This situation is an example of your textbook's theme of large individual differences among women. We cannot make a statement that holds true for all women.

Let's examine the aspect of PMS that has received the most attention from the popular media, the negative mood swings that are presumed to occur during the menstrual cycle. We'll also consider methods of coping with PMS, as well as evidence that women sometimes report positive reactions to menstruation.

Mood Swings

Much of the research that supposedly supports the concept of PMS is actually plagued by biases (Caplan & Caplan, 2009; Ussher, 2006). For example, many researchers ask women to recall what their moods have been during various times throughout the previous weeks of their menstrual cycle.

You can anticipate some problems with this kind of retrospective study. For example, the popular media often discuss PMS and negative moods. As a result, women may recall their moods as being more negative premenstrually than they actually were (Chrisler, 2017). Most of the carefully controlled research has produced results that should make us skeptical about the mood-swings component of PMS (e.g., Chrisler, 2018; Caplan & Caplan, 2009; Offman & Kleinplatz, 2004).

Let's consider a classic study that is critical of the PMS concept. Hardie (1997) asked 83 menstruating women who were university employees to keep records in a booklet titled *Daily Stress & Health Diary*. Each day, for 10 weeks, they recorded their emotional state, stress level, general health, exercise, laughter, crying, menstrual bleeding, and so forth. At the end of the 10 weeks, the women completed a questionnaire about women's health issues. Included in this questionnaire was a crucial item: "I think I have PMS."

To assess PMS, Hardie used an operational definition that several others have used: A woman's mood during the premenstrual phase needs to be more depressed and emotional than during other parts of her menstrual cycle. Not one of the 83 women met this criterion for two menstrual cycles during the 70-day study. In addition, the women who believed they had PMS did *not* have more negative emotions premenstrually than did the women who reported no PMS. In other words, both groups actually reported similar cyclic changes.

The psychological-cultural explanation for PMS argues that some cultures clearly accept PMS as an established fact, even though it cannot be systematically documented (Caplan & Caplan, 2009; Chrisler, 2017). With this kind of cultural endorsement, women believe that PMS is normal. If a woman is feeling tense and she is premenstrual, she often blames her emotions on PMS (Cosgrove & Riddle, 2001a; Hardie, 1997; Ussher, 2006). For example, one woman explained how she often interprets her emotions: "I feel irritable for some reason and then I'll think about why I am irritable and then I'll think, oh, well, it's the week before my period and sometimes I'll say, well, maybe that's what it is" (Cosgrove & Riddle, 2001a, p. 19).

Why is the concept of PMS so widespread, if relatively few women seem to have severe symptoms? Joan Chrisler and her colleagues (2006) surveyed female college students and found that they tended to think that most other women had more severe symptoms than they themselves experienced. This perception therefore allows women to believe that PMS is a genuine problem for other women.

Unfortunately, this concept of PMS encourages people to think that many women are out of control for several days each month. People who endorse the PMS concept may hesitate before they support a female candidate for a job (Chrisler, 2018). (Incidentally, try Demonstration 4.2 before you read further.)

Demonstration **4.2**

Positive Aspects of Menstruation

If you are a woman who has menstrual cycles, complete the following questionnaire, which is based on the Menstrual Joy Questionnaire (Chrisler et al., 1994; J. Delaney et al., 1988). If you do not have menstrual cycles, ask a friend who does if they would be willing to fill out the questionnaire.

Instructions: Rate each of the following items on a 6-point scale. Rate an item 1 if you do not experience the feeling at all when you are menstruating; rate it 6 if you experience the feeling intensely.

_____ high spirits
_____ affection
_____ sexual desire
_____ self-confidence
_____ vibrant activity
_____ creativity
_____ revolutionary zeal
_____ power
_____ intense concentration

Did you or your friend provide a positive rating for one or more of these characteristics?

Hormonal factors may indeed cause premenstrual problems in a small percentage of women (Hantsoo & Epperson, 2015; Kaiser, Janda, Kleinstäuber, & Weise, 2018) However, two other factors are probably more important:

1. Psychological factors, such as anxiety and strong endorsement of traditionally feminine gender roles (Chrisler, 2017; Sigmon, Dorhofer et al., 2000; Sigmon, Rohan et al., 2000).
2. Cultural factors, such as some cultures' belief that PMS is a well-established fact and some cultures' emphasis on biological explanations (Chrisler, 2017, 2018; Cosgrove & Riddle, 2001b).

Coping with the Premenstrual Syndrome

It's difficult to talk about coping with or treating PMS when we have no clear-cut definition of the problem and no comprehensive theory about its origins.

The research we just discussed would suggest that women could monitor their emotional reactions throughout the menstrual cycle to determine whether tension or anxiety is just as likely to occur during phases that are *not* premenstrual. In this case, psychotherapy may be helpful (D. Taylor, 2005).

When health professionals believe that PMS is a genuine, biologically driven problem, they often recommend physical exercise as therapy. They also suggest avoiding salt, sugar, and caffeine (Chrisler, 2017; Kissling, 2006; D. Taylor, 2005). None of these remedies can hurt, although their value has not been established. Some physicians recommend antidepressants that drug companies market for women who believe that they experience PMS or, in more severe cases, PMDD (Hantsoo & Epperson, 2015). These drugs can cause side effects, and they are not necessary for most women (Kissling, 2006; D. Taylor, 2005; Ussher, 2006). As Chrisler and Caplan (2002) conclude:

> Taking medication may provide apparent serenity to individual women, but it does nothing to alleviate the oppressive conditions that contributed to the stress and tension that caused them to report severe PMS. PMS is a form of social control and victim blame that masquerades as value-free. (p. 301)

Positive Reactions to the Menstrual Cycle

Joan Chrisler and her colleagues realized that the menstruation questionnaires focused only on negative aspects of menstruation. Furthermore, the popular press had generated hundreds of articles on the negative—and often exaggerated— aspects of changes associated with the menstrual cycle (Chrisler, 2018; Chrisler & Levy, 1990; Chrisler et al., 1994). Surely some cisgender women must have occasional positive reactions to menstruation! Therefore, Chrisler and her colleagues (1994) decided to administer the Menstrual Joy Questionnaire (J. Delaney et al., 1988). Try Demonstration 4.2 on page 119, which is similar to that questionnaire.

Interestingly, some cisgender women in this study first completed the Menstrual Joy Questionnaire. They typically rated their level of arousal relatively positively when they later completed a different questionnaire about menstrual symptoms. Compared to women who had not been initially encouraged to think about the positive side of menstruation, these women were more likely to report feelings of well-being and excitement, as well as bursts of energy (Chrisler et al., 1994).

Research in the United States and Canada confirms that many cisgender women have some positive responses to menstruation, such as increased energy, creativity, and psychological strength (Aubeeluck & Maguire, 2002; Chrisler & Caplan, 2002; S. Lee, 2002).

We need to emphasize that menstrual cramps and other problems will not disappear if you simply adopt a more positive attitude. However, the issues may be easier to deal with if you know their cause and remind yourself that other cisgender women share similar experiences. Isn't it interesting that so little research has been conducted on the potentially positive side of menstruation?

Cultural Attitudes Toward Menstruation

Throughout this book, you'll often perceive a contrast between people's beliefs about women and women's actual experiences. For example, people's stereotypes about women (Chapter 2) often differ from women's actual cognitive skills (Chapter 5) and women's social characteristics (Chapter 6). Similarly, we will learn in this discussion that cultural attitudes about menstruation often differ from women's actual experiences.

Some cultures around the world have a taboo against contact with menstruating women (Gottlieb, 2020; Usher, 2006). For example, in many parts of India, women of the Hindu faith are prohibited from participating in normal daily activities while menstruating (Garg & Anand, 2015). Many similar menstrual practices reflect a belief in female pollution and the devaluation of women (J. L. Goldenberg & Roberts, 2004; Kissling, 2006; T. Roberts & Waters, 2004). These attitudes toward menstruation are consistent with Theme 2 of this book: The cultural community may have negative attitudes about something associated with women—in this instance, their menstrual periods (Chrisler, 2018; Usher, 2006).

Most White people also have negative attitudes toward menstruating women. In a classic study, participants were told that they would be working on a problem-solving task with a female student (T. Roberts et al., 2002). At one point, the participants watched this woman open her handbag. By "mistake" either a hair clip or a wrapped tampon fell out of her bag. Later in the session, the real participants were instructed to evaluate this woman. Both male and female participants rated the woman as being less competent and less likeable if her handbag had contained a tampon, rather than a hair clip.

Throughout most of the United States, the topic of menstruation is not only negative but also relatively absent, consistent with Theme 3 of this book. We usually do not openly discuss menstruation (Kissling, 2003, 2006). Instead, people enlist euphemisms, or more pleasant ways of saying the same thing. For example, the word *menstruation* is rarely mentioned on television. An ad referring to "that time of the month" probably does not mean the date the car payment is due.

Furthermore, in Aída Hurtado's (2003) study of Latina adolescents, 55% of the young women had never talked with either parent about menstruation. Many of the adolescents in her study emphasized the secrecy of disposing of sanitary napkins, which one woman noted was "more complicated than making tamales" (p. 52).

In the United States, young women's attitudes may be shaped by advertisements that specifically make them believe that menstruation is a problem (Chrisler, 2018; Erchull et al., 2002; Merskin, 1999). For example, Jessica Oksman (2002) examined a total of 36 issues of *Seventeen* and *Mademoiselle* magazines. She found that 46 advertisements emphasized that menstruation is something secretive, and it must be concealed. For instance, a typical ad pointed out that "nobody needs to know." In contrast, she found only 1 positive message about menstruation: "It is a symbol of strength, beauty, spirit. It is woman. It is you." Imagine how much more positive young women would feel about menstruation if they encountered 46 messages like this and only 1 that encouraged secrecy.

Section Summary

Puberty and Menstruation

1. Adolescence begins at puberty; for girls, menarche is the crucial milestone of puberty.
2. The menstrual cycle features a feedback loop, and it requires a complex coordination of brain structures, hormones, and internal reproductive organs.
3. Dysmenorrhea, or menstrual pain, is common in women. Dysmenorrhea is partly caused by prostaglandins, but psychological factors also play an important role.
4. Premenstrual syndrome (PMS) is a controversial set of symptoms that presumably includes headaches, breast soreness, depression, and irritability. PMS is challenging to study because it cannot be clearly defined. Consistent PMS-related mood swings seem to be relatively rare.
5. The psychological-cultural explanation of PMS suggests that psychological factors play a role and that cultural expectations encourage women to use PMS as an explanation for negative moods that occur on the days before their menstrual period.
6. Because of the controversy about the origins and nature of PMS and premenstrual dysphoric disorder (PMDD), it is difficult to make recommendations about treating these conditions.
7. Some women report increased energy and other positive reactions to menstruation.
8. Menstrual myths and other negative attitudes are found in many cultures, including the United States. White Americans judge menstruating women to be less competent and less likeable, compared to other women. In addition, U.S. media directed at adolescent girls suggest that menstruation should be kept secret.

4-2 Self-Concept and Identity During Adolescence

Learning Objectives

To describe factors that influence self-concept and identity development during adolescence, you can ...

4-2-1   Analyze how gender affects self-esteem during adolescence.

4-2-2   Describe various factors that impact body image and perceived physical attractiveness.

4-2-3   Summarize factors that are associated with developing a feminist identity.

4-2-4   Explain how gender intersects with cultural identity development during adolescence.

4-2-5   Describe how puberty may affect individuals who identify as transgender.

As we've learned, adolescent young women experience a major transition when they reach menarche. Adolescents are developing the cognitive capacity to think abstractly, so they often ask complex questions about their identity. A person's **identity** is their self-rating of personal characteristics in the physical, psychological, and social dimensions (Reid et al., 2008; Rhodes et al., 2007; Whitbourne, 2008). We'll consider five components of identity in this section: self-esteem, body image, feminist identity, cultural identity, and transgender identity.

Self-Esteem

According to researchers, cultural norms in the United States emphasize the importance of self-esteem (Crocker & Park, 2004a, 2004b). **Self-esteem** is a measure of how much you like and value yourself (Malanchuk & Eccles, 2006). Do adolescents of different genders differ in self-esteem? Several researchers have reported a modest gender difference in adolescents' self-esteem (e.g., Bleidorn et al., 2016; J. Frost & McKelvie, 2004; Quatman & Watson, 2001). However, other researchers have reported that adolescent girls and boys have similar self-esteem, at least in some conditions (e.g., Bialecka-Pikul et al., 2019; Kling & Hyde, 2001; Meece & Scantlebury, 2006; D. Wise & Stake, 2002).

With mixed results like these, how can we draw any conclusions? Fortunately, researchers who study gender comparisons can use a technique called meta-analysis. **Meta-analysis** provides a statistical method for integrating numerous studies on a single topic. Researchers first locate all appropriate studies on the topic. Then they perform a statistical analysis that combines the results from all these studies. The meta-analysis yields a single number that tells us whether a particular variable has an overall effect. For example, a meta-analysis of the gender-comparison research in self-esteem can statistically combine numerous previous studies into one enormous "super-study." This meta-analysis can provide a general picture of whether people differ in self-esteem depending on their gender.

Two important meta-analytic studies have been conducted on gender comparisons of self-esteem. Each study examined more than 200 different gender comparisons (Kling et al., 1999; Major et al., 1999). Both studies concluded that the average male scores are slightly—but significantly—higher in self-esteem than the average female scores. However, when these two groups of researchers examined the data in greater detail, they found that the gender differences are minimal in childhood, early adolescence, and later adulthood. In contrast, the gender differences are somewhat larger during late adolescence.

Furthermore, the gender differences in self-esteem are relatively large for White Americans, but they are relatively small for Black Americans. These findings are consistent with other research (Buckley & Carter, 2005; Denner & Griffin, 2003; Malanchuk & Eccles, 2006).

In addition, Major and her colleagues (1999) found that gender differences are relatively large among lower-class and middle-class participants. In contrast, when these researchers examined students from upper-class, well-educated families, the gender differences were very small. It's possible that these families have the resources to encourage their daughters to overcome traditional gender roles (Major et al., 1999).

Let's review this topic. Gender comparisons in self-esteem are inconsistent. The results of the gender comparison depend on several personal characteristics such as age, ethnicity, and social class.

Body Image and Physical Attractiveness

In Chapter 3, we learned that physical attractiveness is more important for preschool girls than for preschool boys. Compared to less attractive little girls, cute little girls are more likely to be patted and praised—and less likely to be hit and pushed. However, physical attractiveness is generally irrelevant for little boys (G. J. Smith, 1985). It's not surprising, then, that 11-year-old girls are more likely than 11-year-old boys to spend time thinking about their physical appearance (Lindberg et al., 2006).

This emphasis on female attractiveness is exaggerated during adolescence. A young woman learns to conceptualize herself as an object that can be viewed and judged by other people (Lindberg et al., 2006; Tiggemann & Boundy, 2008). Furthermore, young women constantly receive the message that attractive features and physical beauty are the most important dimensions for girls and women (Buckley & Carter, 2005; Galambos, 2004; Tolman et al., 2006). Their skin must be clear, their teeth straight and gleaming, and their hair perfect.

Young women are especially likely to receive the message that they must also be slender. Young women who have bodies that are above average size are the target of numerous negative comments from other people (Hunt, 2007). Some young women are so concerned about being slender that they develop life-threatening eating disorders. (We will discuss these disorders and how cultural norms in the United States emphasize thinness in more detail in Chapter 12.) This intense focus on body weight extends beyond those with eating disorders as well. In some studies, young Black women are less likely to emphasize thinness, but the results are not consistent (Kornblau et al., 2007; Poran, 2006).

The media encourage this emphasis on beauty and slenderness, and young women are well aware of this message (Botta, 2003; C. A. Smith, 2008). Furthermore, a variety of research approaches suggest that women are less satisfied with their bodies if they have been reading mainstream fashion magazines, rather than magazines portraying normal-sized women (Pollitt, 2004; Sengupta, 2006). Research examining the relationships between social media exposure, self-esteem, and body image suggests similar outcomes. When adolescent and young adult women spend many hours per week consuming social media, they experience reduced body satisfaction and lower self-esteem over time (de Vries, Peter, de Graaf, & Nikken, 2016; Makwana, Lee, Parkin, & Farmer, 2018). Try Demonstration 4.3 (below) to appreciate the narrow perspective that teen magazines provide to adolescent girls.

Demonstration **4.3**

Representation of Females in Teen Magazines

Locate several magazines intended for adolescent girls. *Seventeen, Teen Vogue,* and *Teen People* are popular choices (Tyre, 2004). Glance through the magazine for photos of women in either advertisements or feature articles. What percentage of these women would be considered above average size? How many are portrayed as slender, thin, or below average size? Then inspect the magazines for ethnic representation. If you find any women of color, are they pale-skinned, with features typical of White women, or do they seem typical of other ethnic groups?

Notice the body posture of the women pictured. Would a young man seem ridiculous in these positions? What percentage of the photos seems aimed at encouraging sexual relationships? How many of the women appear competent? What other messages do these images provide for high school women?

Women of color are especially likely to comment that women who represent themselves are missing from the fashion magazines. However, Black women often appear—in degrading roles—in hip hop and rap music videos (Sharpley-Whiting, 2007). Try Demonstration 4.3 when you have the opportunity to browse through teen magazines.

Unfortunately, young women's general self-concepts are often shaped by whether they believe they are attractive. Researchers have found that physical appearance is the strongest predictor of self-worth in adolescent girls. For adolescent boys, however, athletic competence is a stronger predictor of self-worth (Denner & Griffin, 2003; Kwa, 1994). Notice, then, that young women feel valued for their bodies' *appearance*. In contrast, young men feel valued for their bodies' *performance* in athletics.

Researchers have discovered that young women who participate in athletics can often escape from the dominant appearance-based messages presented to adolescent girls. Not surprisingly, young female athletes often have higher self-esteem than young women who are not athletes (Hall, 2008; Tracy & Erkut, 2002; J. Young & Bursik, 2000). Exercise often increases women's sense of control over their lives (Vasquez, 2002). However, when young women athletes internalize cultural messages that being slender is ideal, they sometimes display symptoms of the female athlete triad. This condition is characterized by disordered eating, menstrual dysfunction, and low bone mineral density, all of which can lead to long-term health complications (Brown, Dewookler, Baker, & Dodich, 2017).

Young women's participation in sports has increased dramatically since 1972, when Title IX was enacted, guaranteeing equal access to educational and sport opportunities for all genders. In fact, about 3 million high school girl athletes play competitive sports each year (Hall, 2008; Zittleman, 2007). The media are now somewhat more likely to feature female athletes, and these images of strong women might make a difference. Adolescent girls watching the victorious women athletes in sports such as basketball, tennis, and soccer may realize that women's bodies exist in a variety of forms, all of which can be competent, athletic and attractive (Dowling, 2000; Strouse, 1999).

Feminist Identity

In Chapter 1, we emphasized that **feminism** is the principle that values women's experiences and ideas; in addition, feminism emphasizes that people of all genders should be socially, economically, and legally equal (Pollitt, 2004; Rozee et al., 2008). Earlier in the present chapter, we noted that adolescents have the capacity to think abstractly and to contemplate their personal identity. As a consequence, they may consider abstract questions such as "What do I believe about women's roles?" and "Am I a feminist?"

Demonstration **4.4**

Assessing Feminist Identity

If you are a woman, rate each of the following items using a 5-point scale. Rate an item 1 if you strongly disagree; rate the item 5 if you strongly agree. If you are a man or are nonbinary, think of a woman you know well who shares your ideas about women's issues, and try to answer the questionnaire from her perspective. Then check page 142 for further instructions.

(continues)

```
_____  1. I want to work to make the world a fairer place for
            all people.
_____  2. I have become increasingly aware that society is sexist.
_____  3. I am very interested in women writers and other aspects
            of women's studies.
_____  4. I think that most women feel happiest being a wife and
            mother.
_____  5. I do not want to have the same status that a man has.
_____  6. I am proud to be a strong and competent woman.
_____  7. I am angry about the way that men and boys often
            treat me.
_____  8. I am glad that women do not have to do construction work
            or other dangerous jobs.
_____  9. I owe it to both women and men to work for greater
            gender equality.
_____  10. I am happy being a traditional female.
```

Note: These items are similar to the 39-item Feminist Identity Development Scale, developed by Bargad and Hyde (1991). The reliability and validity of the items in this shortened version have not been established.

Most of the research about feminist values and identity has surveyed college students in late adolescence and emerging adulthood. It would be useful to conduct research on the development of a feminist identity from early adolescence through late adulthood, using a more diverse sample of people (Saunders & Kashubeck-West, 2006).

In both the United States and Canada, many people are likely to say that they support feminist ideas such as gender equality. However, they are less likely to claim a **feminist social identity** by saying, "Yes, I am a feminist" (Cohen, 2008; Dube, 2004; Pollitt, 2004).

Researchers have identified several factors that are associated with feminist beliefs. For example, people who support feminist beliefs are more likely than other people to have a complex mental schema of themselves (Bursik, 2000). People who have a feminist social identity are also more likely to be very knowledgeable about feminism, through friends, college classes, social media, or feminist magazines and books. They are also more likely to have a positive evaluation of feminists (Nelson et al., 2008; A. Reid & Purcell, 2004).

In addition, women are more likely than men to consider themselves feminists (Burn et al., 2000; Henderson-King & Zhermer, 2003; Toller et al., 2004). Furthermore, people who are not gender stereotyped are more likely to consider themselves feminists (Saunders & Kashubeck-West, 2006; Toller et al., 2004). In related research, Bronstein and her coauthors (2007) found that high school girls with supportive, nurturant parents were especially likely to have "moral courage," speaking up when they witnessed injustice.

Now assess your answers to Demonstration 4.4 by reviewing the answers at the end of the chapter (page 142). Also, answer one additional question: Do you consider yourself a feminist?

Cultural Identity

We can define **cultural identity** as the ideas and customs associated with a social grouping such as country of origin, ethnic group, or religion (Markus, 2008). Some evidence suggests that young girls of color are more likely than young boys of color to be interested in maintaining their cultural traditions, but the results are not consistent (K. K. Dion & Dion, 2004; Meece & Scantlebury, 2006).

Other studies focus on the nature of adolescents' ethnic identity rather than on gender comparisons. In general, young White Americans are not concerned about their ethnic identity (Peplau et al., 1999; Poran, 2002). We noted this issue in Chapter 1. When being White is considered standard or normative, White individuals don't notice their privileged status. In fact, White people often believe that they don't "have" a race (Markus, 2008; McIntosh, 2001).

Some young girls of color may initially try to reject their ethnicity. For example, Zulay Regalado (2007) emphasized that she had avoided family gatherings with her boisterous Cuban American relatives. At the age of 18, however, she decided to join them and, as she wrote, "For the first time in eighteen years, instead of wishing myself to be anywhere but the dinner table … I was comfortable with who I am" (Regalado, 2007, p. 65).

Also, here is a Black woman's description of herself:

> For a long time it seemed as if I didn't remember my background, and I guess in some ways I didn't. I was never taught to be proud of my African heritage. Like we talked about in class, I went through a very long stage of identifying with my oppressors. Wanting to be like, live like, and be accepted by them. Even to the point of hating my own race and myself for being a part of it. Now I am ashamed that I ever was ashamed. I lost so much of myself in my denial of and refusal to accept my people. (Tatum, 1992, p. 10)

Sadly, the White-as-normative attitudes are strikingly evident in beauty contests. For instance, Vietnamese immigrant communities in the United States often organize beauty contests in which the winners are young Vietnamese women who most resemble White women. In fact, many contestants even undergo plastic surgery so that their eyes, chin, and nose can appear more "American" (Lieu, 2004). Furthermore, women who enter the "Miss India" pageant in India are expected to attend a 6-week training session that includes a near-starvation diet and skin bleaching so that they can appear more "White" (Runkle, 2004).

In the years following the September 11, 2001, bombing of the World Trade Center, the Muslim American cultural group has frequently experienced discrimination (Sirin & Fine, 2008). Even 16-year-old Muslim American girls—described as "typical teenagers"—were arrested and subjected to weeks of interrogation (Zaal et al., 2007).

Mayida Zaal and her coauthors (2007) use the phrase, "the weight of living at the hyphen" (p. 165) to describe the challenge of being both Muslim and American. Muslim Americans who live in the United States come from more than 80 countries. However, many other Americans view Muslims as potential traitors in this era of increased surveillance (Ibish, 2008; Nguyen, 2005; Sirin & Fine, 2008). In fact, 44% of respondents in a U.S. poll said that Muslim Americans should be denied the civil liberties that other U.S. citizens experience (Friedlander, 2004).

Given this complex situation, how do Muslim American teenagers make sense of their own identity? Sirin and Fine (2007) asked participants in their study to draw sketches to represent their Muslim American identity. Selina, a 15-year-old young woman, drew two connecting rivers, as shown in Figure 4.2. As portrayed in this image, the two streams mingle to represent a fluid sense of identity. The media often emphasize the superficiality of teenagers, a perspective that clearly misrepresents the complex identities they can create for themselves (Sirin & Fine, 2007, 2008).

FIGURE **4.2** A drawing that illustrates how a 15-year-old represents her identity as a Muslim American.

Source: From "Muslim American Youth," S. Sirin & M. Fine. Copyright 2007. Reprinted with permission of New York University Press.

Transgender Identity

The prefix "trans" means "across" or "beyond." A **transgender person** moves across or beyond the gender boundaries as they are traditionally defined in U.S. culture (Golden, 2008). Some women and men do not identify with the gender they were assigned at birth and instead identify as transgender. In addition, some individuals transcend these binary categories of "woman" and "man" and instead identify as nonbinary (APA, 2015; Wilchins, 2004). A college student named Katherine Roubos, who chooses this third-category alternative, says that being a transgender person isn't scary, but "it's about this person living a life" ("A Safe Crossing," 2008, p. 30).

Some transgender people decide to have gender confirmation surgery, so that their bodies align with their gender identity (Lawrence, 2008). In other words, they want to express their own identity, rather than adopting society's expectations. This may sound atypical until you think that many women decide to have surgery to make their breasts larger (Golden, 2008) and men increasingly have pectoral or calf implants to enhance their muscular physiques (Singh, Keaney, & Rossi, 2018). Furthermore, as we read on page 79 in Chapter 3, physicians still regularly perform surgery for intersex infants, so that the external genitals can appear to be either clearly feminine or clearly masculine. Why does genital surgery seem "normal" for infants, but "abnormal" for adults who want to have surgery so that they can live in a body that is consistent with their gender identity?

Many major corporations now provide health benefits that include gender-affirming surgery. These surgeries are also covered under federally funded health care programs, such as Medicare and Medicaid, although some individual states still provide limited care and discriminate against transgender individuals (Baker, McGovern, Gruberg, & Cray, 2016). Furthermore, Title IX prevents colleges and universities from discriminating against transgender individuals

Section Summary

Self-Concept and Identity During Adolescence

1. The average male may score slightly higher in self-esteem than the average female. Meta-analyses show that this gender difference is relatively large during late adolescence, in White Americans, and in people with relatively little education.
2. Physical attractiveness is emphasized for adolescent young women. The current emphasis on thinness and beauty can lead to eating disorders and excessive concern about personal appearance.
3. People who say they are feminists are typically familiar with feminism, and they evaluate feminists positively. People in general are relatively likely to support feminist perspectives, but they are less likely to say that they are feminists.
4. Young girls of color may initially ignore their ethnic identity but strengthen it during adolescence. Some young women of color undergo plastic surgery so that they can appear more like White women. Muslim American young women often work to create an identity that integrates multiple cultures.
5. Transgender individuals move across or beyond the traditional gender boundaries.

4-3 Education and Career Planning

Learning Objectives

To analyze how gender influences education and career planning, you can ...

4-3-1 Describe negative experiences that adolescent girls commonly experience in middle and high school.

4-3-2 Identify which factors contribute to gender differences in pursuing math and science careers.

4-3-3 Describe how gender discrimination in colleges and universities impacts women's educational experiences.

4-3-4 Summarize gender differences in career aspirations among adolescents.

4-3-5 Identify factors that influence young women's interest in pursuing nontraditional careers.

In Chapter 3, we read that young girls are often relatively marginalized in the elementary-school classroom, whereas boys receive more attention. Now we'll examine young women's educational experiences and early career planning. In Chapter 5, we'll consider a related topic: gender comparisons in cognitive skills and achievement motivation. Then Chapter 6 will focus on gender comparisons in social and personality characteristics. A background in all these topics will prepare us to discuss women and employment in Chapter 7. Let's now explore young girls' experiences in middle school and high school, early encounters with math and science, experiences in higher education, and career choices.

Young Girls' Experiences in Middle School and High School

Some of the adolescent characteristics we've discussed in this chapter make it especially challenging for girls to achieve academic success. Their bodies are changing, they may be preoccupied with their physical appearance, and they may be tempted to starve themselves. They may also have low self-esteem. Many girls in middle school (junior high) and high school feel marginalized in the classroom (Levstik, 2001; Sadker & Zittleman, 2007b).

Young girls may also be the target of sexual comments, sexual bullying, and other forms of sexual harassment (Leaper & Brown, 2008; Ormerod et al., 2008; Paludi, 2007; Shute et al., 2008). When the academic environment is not friendly to girls, they will study less, choose less rigorous courses, and select less challenging careers (Eccles, 2004).

In addition, many schools do not emphasize either ethnic equality or social-class equality (J. L. Hochschild, 2003; Ostrove & Cole, 2003; Wigfield et al., 2006). For example, Sarahi Salamanca was once told by her high school guidance counselor "Well, unfortunately, people like you don't go to college and there's no money for people like you to go to college" (Immigrants Are Us, n.d.). In spite of this discrimination, she attended college and became founder and CEO of DREAMer's Roadmap, an organization that helps undocumented students in the United States navigate the challenges of attending college. She was named to Forbes 30 under 30 in 2016 and has won numerous national awards since her high school experience (Salamanca, 2019).

The research shows that young girls are most likely to maintain their academic aspirations if their middle schools or high schools make gender equality a priority, institute a mentoring system, and have high expectations for women. The research also shows that parents' encouragement has a strong impact (Betz, 2008; Li & Kerpelman, 2007). For instance, research about Latina adolescents in Los Angeles showed that mothers frequently discuss academic achievement with their daughters (Hyams, 2006; Romo et al., 2006). Teachers can be especially helpful if the family members do not support their daughters' achievements (Erkut et al., 2001; Fort, 2005b; Wigfield et al., 2006).

Early Experiences in Math and Science

Zelda Ziegler remembers sitting in a high school classroom, preparing to take an engineering exam. She was the only young woman among those taking the test. The proctor stood in front of the room and announced that the exam would be reasonable. "Nobody would have trouble with it except for one person—and she knows who she is" (J. Kaplan & Aronson, 1994, p. 27). Fortunately, Ziegler was not discouraged by these words. She went on to earn a Ph.D. degree in chemistry and now acts as a mentor for young women interested in science.

Most current adolescent girls don't face such overt sexism. One reason is that high school girls and boys are now equally likely to enroll in upper-level math courses. Still, some girls experience more subtle biases (Lacampagne et al., 2007; Leaper & Brown, 2008). For example, math and science teachers may convey higher expectations to male students than to female students (Duffy et al., 2001; Piran & Ross, 2006). Teachers may also give male students more helpful feedback and greater encouragement to pursue careers in math and science (Wigfield et al., 2006).

Several additional factors contribute to the gender differences in pursuing careers in math and science:

1. Male peers may react negatively toward female peers who are interested in these areas (Brownlow et al., 2002; Stake, 2003). These peers may also make young girls feel like outsiders (Dingel, 2006).
2. Female students often feel less competent and effective in these "stereotypically male" courses, even though they may actually perform very well (Dingel, 2006; Tenenbaum & Leaper, 2003; Wigfield et al., 2006). In contrast, they may actively seek "stereotypically female" courses, which are more consistent with their long-term goals, and where they are more confident about their skills (Evans & Diekman, 2009; Oswald, 2008).
3. Parents often believe that boys are more skilled in science than girls are (Tenenbaum & Leaper, 2003; Wigfield et al., 2006).

Some national organizations and some local school systems have developed innovative programs to encourage young girls to pursue careers in math and the sciences (Lacampagne et al., 2007; Stake, 2003; Weisgram & Bigler, 2007). For example, Carolyn Turk (2004) describes her experiences in a program designed for high school girls who were interested in engineering. As she writes, "If I hadn't stumbled into that summer program, I wouldn't be an engineer" (p. 12). In these academic settings, young women can learn to take risks, make mistakes, develop a peer group, and enjoy being successful in a nontraditional area (Stake & Nickens, 2005).

In addition, parents can support their daughter's interest in nontraditional fields by seeking nonsexist career guidance. They can also encourage her college plans and value her academic interests (Betz, 2006; Song, 2001). Furthermore, teachers can identify young girls who are gifted in science and math and then encourage parents to support their daughter's interest in these nontraditional areas (Eccles et al., 2000; Reis, 1998).

Gender Issues in Higher Education

In the United States and Canada, women are currently more likely than men to pursue higher education. For example, 56% of all full-time university students in Canada are female (Statistics Canada, 2017). Women also constitute 56% of all full-time students enrolled in U.S. colleges and universities (Macfarland et al., 2017). As Table 4.1 portrays, this gender difference holds for all five major ethnic groups in the United States, although the gap is largest for Black women and men. Furthermore, you'll probably be surprised to learn that U.S. women now earn 53% of all the Ph.D. degrees awarded in U.S. universities (Okahana & Zhou, 2018).

In contrast to the gender ratio for students, relatively few college professors are women. At present, only 47% of all full-time faculty members at U.S. colleges and universities are women (AAUP 2020). If a young woman wants to pursue a science degree, she will find that female faculty members are even less present. For instance, women constitute only 20% of the approximately 1,500 chemistry faculty in the United States (Wang & Widener, 2019).

The Academic Environment in Higher Education

In some cases, female college students may receive a message that they have entered a male-dominated environment where they are not welcome. In the 1980s, some observers referred to this situation as the "chilly classroom climate." When this **chilly classroom climate** operates, faculty members treat men and women differently in the classroom, and women may feel ignored and devalued. As a result, some women may participate less in discussions and may be less likely to feel academically competent (Basow, 2004; Betz, 2006).

Research on the chilly classroom climate has been mixed (K. L. Brady & Eisler, 1995, 1999; M. Crawford & MacLeod, 1990; Fencl & Scheel, 2006). However, gender discrimination is more likely in male-dominated disciplines such as math, science, and engineering (J. Steele et al., 2002). Furthermore, students of color are more likely than others to experience a chilly climate (Janz & Pyke, 2000).

Women of Color and Higher Education

As we learned in Table 4.1, Black women are much more likely than Black men to attend college. The reasons for this discrepancy are not clear. However, theorists suggest that part of the problem is a cultural climate that values athletic ability, and it emphasizes athletes' high salaries more than academic achievement in young Black men (Etson, 2003).

Students of color often receive the message that they do not fit well in a college setting (Molinary, 2007; Mooney & Rivas-Drake, 2008; Pinel et al., 2005). As one young Puerto Rican woman said, "People sort of see me differently because I'm Hispanic and I'm smart. I feel sometimes that they want to put me down. I have had several incidents where people will look at my skin color and think I'm dumb, and they immediately think 'She's not bright, she's not smart'" (Reis, 1998, pp. 157–158). Students of color often comment that some faculty members seem to have low expectations for their performance (Fouad & Arredondo, 2007).

TABLE **4.1**

Male and Female Enrollment in U.S. Colleges and Universities in 2015–2016, as a Function of Ethnic Group

Ethnic Group	Percentage of Students	
	Women	Men
White	55%	45%
Black	62.2%	37.8%
Latina/o	57.9%	42.1%
Asian	52%	48%
Native American	53%	47%

Source: Based on Lorelle L. Espinosa, Jonathan M. Turk, Morgan Taylor, and Hollie M. Chessman. (2020). *Race and Ethnicity in Higher Education: A Status Report.* American Council on Education.

Financing a college education is often an issue for women of color, especially in immigrant families. Latina/o and Asian American parents typically want their daughters to attend college (Marlino & Wilson, 2006). However, many are reluctant to let their daughters attend a college far from home (Sy, 2006; Sy & Brittian, 2008). Rosa Hernandez is a Latina university graduate who addressed this problem creatively. She had her parents come to her university and follow her through a complete day of classes, work, and studying in the library. After this first-hand experience, Rosa's parents realized why she wanted to study at this university (Silvera, 2008).

In general, Native Americans are the ethnic group about which researchers often have the most limited data. However, an important program for Native Americans in the United States is called **tribal colleges**, which are 2- and 4-year institutions that provide a transition between native culture and the predominately White "mainstream" culture. At present, there are 32 fully accredited tribal colleges, most of which are located on reservations west of the Mississippi River (Pember, 2008). These colleges train Native American students—primarily women older than 20—in fields such as health care. After completing their education, most return to work in their own community ("New England Tribal College," 2004; Williams, 2007). In Canada, several dozen colleges and universities are actively recruiting Aboriginal students, and the government has also committed funds to Aboriginal higher education (Birchard, 2006).

Our discussion so far has focused on the difficulty of blending school with peer relationships, early experiences in math and science, and the challenges of higher education. Now let's turn to young women's career plans.

Career Aspirations

A variety of studies have asked adolescents about their career aspirations. In general, adolescent girls and boys have similar career goals. Here are some of the findings:

1. In general, adolescent boys and girls have similar aspirations about entering prestigious careers (e.g., Astin & Lindholm, 2001; Betz, 2008; C. M. Watson et al., 2002). However, a nationwide survey asked first-year college students about their top reasons for going to college. The results showed that 63% of women—in contrast to only 51% of men—responded, "To prepare myself for graduate or professional school" ("This Year's Freshmen," 2007, p. A41).
2. Adolescent girls are more likely than adolescent boys to choose careers that are considered nontraditional for their gender (Bobo et al., 1998; C. M. Watson et al., 2002). For example, relatively many women aspire to become doctors, compared to the number of men who aspire to be nurses.
3. Adolescent girls are more likely than adolescent boys to report that they have been effective in gathering information about their future careers (Gianakos, 2001).
4. When considering their future careers, adolescent girls are more likely than adolescent boys to emphasize the importance of marriage and children (Betz, 2008; Mahaffy & Ward, 2002; Zhou, 2006). The majority of adolescent women and men also believe that mothers should not work full-time until their children are at least in grade school (Weinshenker, 2006).

What personal characteristics are typical for women who aspire to high-prestige, nontraditional careers? Not surprisingly, they receive high grades in school (C. M. Watson et al., 2002).

They also tend to be independent, self-confident, assertive, emotionally stable, and satisfied with their lives (Astin & Lindholm, 2001; Betz, 1994; Eccles, 1994). Notice that the young women who plan to pursue nontraditional careers typically have the academic characteristics and personality traits that are important for these careers. They also tend to express feminist attitudes, and they are not constrained by traditional gender roles (Flores & O'Brien, 2002; Song, 2001).

Women who plan on prestigious nontraditional careers typically have a supportive and encouraging family, and this factor is important for both White women and women of color (Betz, 2008). Other important factors are female role models and work experience as an adolescent (Flores & O'Brien, 2002; Lips, 2004).

Most of the research in this area examines the career paths of women from relatively affluent families who can afford to send their daughters to college. However, the family situations of many young women are very different. For example, Patton (2008) describes Antonique, a 20-year-old woman from Detroit who is experiencing homelessness. She also dropped out of high school several months before graduation. At the time Antonique was interviewed, she had a 1-year-old child, with a second child to be born several months later. She wants to complete her high school degree and then go to college and become a social worker, a goal that seems very difficult to reach. Yes, we occasionally hear about a young woman like Liz Murray (2008) who once experienced homelessness and then went on to graduate from Harvard University. However, Liz is one of very few exceptions.

Section Summary

Education and Career Planning

1. High-school teachers and school systems may treat young women in a biased fashion; they may also discriminate on the basis of ethnicity and social class. Parental encouragement has an important impact.
2. Adolescent girls may be discouraged from pursuing careers in math and science. However, innovative programs and supportive parents can encourage these young women to pursue nontraditional careers.
3. In the United States and Canada, women are now more likely than men to go to college. Current research has not documented widespread discrimination against female students.
4. Women of color sometimes report that they do not feel comfortable in academic environments, and finances are frequently a barrier. Tribal colleges provide an option for Native American and Aboriginal students.
5. Adolescent girls are similar to adolescent boys with respect to their aspirations to, about prestigious careers, but young women are more likely than young men to choose nontraditional careers.
6. Young women are more likely than young men to gather career information, and they are also more likely to emphasize marriage and children.
7. Factors associated with women's choice of a prestigious nontraditional career include high grades, self-confidence, emotional stability, and feminist beliefs. Also, their parents and families are typically supportive.

4-4 Interpersonal Relationships During Adolescence

Learning Objectives

To summarize how gender impacts interpersonal relationships in adolescence, you can ...

4-4-1 Describe gender differences in family relationships during adolescence.

4-4-2 Describe why close friendships are important for adolescent girls' development.

4-4-3 Explain how gender stereotypes and cultural norms impact heterosexual romantic relationships during adolescence.

4-4-4 Identify factors that impact the development of romantic relationships among LGBTQ+ youth.

So far in this chapter, we have explored three clusters of issues that are important to young women: (1) puberty and menstruation; (2) self-concept and identity; and (3) education and career planning. However, adolescent girls are perhaps most concerned about their social interactions.

Consider Ruby, a 14-year-old Black girl, who has six younger siblings. Her narrative illustrates the centrality of interpersonal relationships for adolescent girls. For example, she describes how the women in her family provide a circle of support when she wants to discuss her future plans: "[My mother] says if I want something, I can always accomplish it. I believe that, too. And my aunt and my grandmother. There's lots of people" (J. M. Taylor et al., 1995, p. 42). Ruby also emphasizes the support offered by her classmates, for example, when they elected her to a special team in her history class: "The kids are all—I guess they accepted me for that, so maybe they like me. ... You know you're wanted" (p. 42).

In this final section of the chapter on adolescence, we will begin by exploring relationships with family members. Then we'll examine connections with peers, specifically in friendships and in love relationships.

Family Relationships

If you believe the popular media, you might conclude that adolescents and their parents inhabit different cultures, interacting only long enough to snarl at each other. The data suggest otherwise (Collins & Steinberg, 2006; Smetana et al., 2006). Most adolescents, both girls and boys, actually get along reasonably well with their parents. They may disagree on relatively minor issues such as music, personal style, or messy rooms. However, they typically agree on more substantive matters such as religion, politics, education, and social values (W. A. Collins & Laursen, 2006; Smetana et al., 2003; Smetana et al., 2006).

Furthermore, current theories of adolescent development emphasize the strong emotional bond between many adolescents and their parents (W. A. Collins & Laursen, 2004, 2006). For example, Judith Smetana comments,

> Yes, there are increases in disagreement, but it's usually in the context of warm, supportive relationships ...We now know that teens don't break away from parents. Healthy development is establishing individuality but remaining connected. (cited in Appelman, 2008)

The family is likely to be a strong basis of identification for young women of color, especially if the family can serve as a source of resiliency when these young women experience ethnic or gender discrimination (Vasquez & De las Fuentes, 1999). The research also suggests that both in the United States and in other cultures, adolescent girls typically feel closer to their mothers than to their fathers (W. A. Collins & Laursen, 2004; Gibbons et al., 1991; Smetana et al., 2006).

In most areas, adolescent girls and boys report similar family experiences. However, you may remember that parents are more likely to discuss fear and sadness with their daughters, compared to their sons (Chapter 3). Interestingly, adolescent girls are much more likely than adolescent boys to endorse statements such as "In our family, it's okay to be sad, happy, angry, loving, excited, scared, or whatever we feel" (Bronstein et al., 1996). These family discussions may encourage young women to emphasize their emotional experiences. We'll explore some of the consequences of this emphasis on emotions in Chapter 12, when we discuss depression.

As some young women mature, they may become aware of gender issues in their families. For example, young Latina and Portuguese American women report that their parents give young men many more privileges and much more freedom (Ayala, 2006; Raffaelli, 2005). These young women also report that their parents strictly prohibit all forms of sexual activity. Young Asian American women also learn that they must not express any evidence of sexual desires and sexual activity (Chan, 2008). The parents' concerns have important implications for young women's romantic relationships, a topic we'll discuss at the end of this chapter.

Friendships

In Chapter 6, we'll examine gender comparisons in friendship patterns during adulthood. We have less information about adolescent friendships. In general, adolescent girls' friendships seem to be somewhat closer and more intimate than adolescent boys' friendships (Erdley & Day, 2017). However, the gender differences are small, and some studies report no significant gender differences (Collins & Steinberg, 2006; Smetana et al., 2006; Monsour, 2002).

A more interesting question focuses on the importance of close friendships in the lives of adolescent girls. Young women consider loyalty and trust to be essential in these friendships (B. B. Brown et al., 1997; L. M. Brown et al., 1999). For example, Lyn Mikel Brown (1998) studied a group of White adolescents from lower income socioeconomic groups. These young women reported that their relationships with girlfriends provided a support system in an environment that often seemed hostile.

Another important part of young women's friendships is intimate conversations. A Latina teenager discusses her best friend: "I go to her because I wouldn't feel comfortable telling other people, you know, like, real deep personal things" (Way, 1998, p. 133).

The research on friendships illustrates a central choice that weaves through women's lives. At many turning points, from youth through older adulthood, women face conflicts between doing something that is best for themselves or doing something for another person, such as a parent, a female friend, a male friend, or a spouse (Eccles, 2001).

In two later chapters of this book, we will examine topics related to women's focusing on themselves: cognitive ability and achievement (Chapter 5) and work (Chapter 7). Several other chapters emphasize women in relationships: social characteristics (Chapter 6), love relationships (Chapter 8), sexuality (Chapter 9), and pregnancy, childbirth, and motherhood (Chapter 10). As you'll learn, women frequently have to balance their own needs and priorities against the wishes of other people who are important in their lives.

Romantic Relationships

For most individuals, adolescence marks the beginning of romantic relationships. We'll explore these experiences in more detail in Chapter 8, but let's consider some of the issues that young women face in heterosexual and lesbian relationships during adolescence. Before you read further, try Demonstration 4.5 on page 137, which focuses on early heterosexual romances.

Demonstration **4.5**

Gender and Love Relationships

For each of the following quotations, try to guess whether the person describing the love relationship is male or female. Then check the answers, which are listed at the end of the chapter.

_____ Person 1: "Um, we're both very easygoing. Um, we like a lot of affection. Um, not like public affection, but um, just knowing that we, we care for each other. Um, uh, it doesn't even have to be physical affection, just any type. We like cuddling with each other. Um, we enjoy going out and doing things with each other and each other's friends. We enjoy high action things together. Um, pretty much, we have a very open relationship, and we can talk about anything."

_____ Person 2: "I think after a while, like, (person) following me around, and wanting to be with me all the time, and maybe the fact that I had a lot to say and had the power … I'd just, like, I don't know, I still think like that. I don't know why but (person) … was getting too serious by following me around all the time and, you know, wanting to spend every minute of the day. … You know I'm, like, 'I do have friends I need to talk to.' … I was just, like 'Aaah! Go away!'"

_____ Person 3: "It's like … you know … we love each other so much … it's great. We have so much fun. We get mad at each other sometimes, and, you know, we make up, and, you know, we hug. It's great. I mean (person) is wonderful! … We, like, we just have a lot of fun, and we have a lot of heartache, but it's perfect because of that, you know. If it was all fun all the time, what's wrong? And if it's bad all the time, something's wrong. It's right in the middle. It's right where it should be."

_____ Person 4: "I'm not really a relationship person. If I meet someone, I want to be able to, you know, to uh, you know … not have any restraints or anything. Basically, I run into someone who I think is cool and all that about twice a month…. The friends before are friends after. Most of them are probably physical. Um, I don't have any regrets."

Source: Based on Feiring (1998).

Heterosexual Relationships

As you recall from Chapter 3, young girls and boys practice gender segregation; they tend to inhabit different worlds for many years. As a result, they reach early adolescence with only limited experience regarding other genders (Compian & Hayward, 2003; Rudman & Glick, 2008). Furthermore, young women often have very idealized visions about romance (Lamb & Brown, 2006; Rudman & Glick, 2008; Smetana et al., 2006).

How do young women figure out how they should interact with unfamiliar others in a romantic relationship? An important source of information is the media, including movies, television, music, magazines, online sources, and computer games (J. D. Brown et al., 2006; Galician, 2004; J. R. Steele, 2002). Not surprisingly, the media usually portray gender-stereotyped and heteronormative romances. The media also suggest that a boyfriend is an absolutely necessity for a high school-aged girl.

Consider the title of a typical article in a magazine aimed at female adolescents: "Why Don't I Have a Boyfriend? (And How Do I Get One?)" (2001). This article suggests, for example, that if a young woman is too busy studying to meet a boyfriend, she should go to the library to find a likely candidate. Basically, the magazines emphasize that young women need to be creative and persistent in pursuing potential boyfriends (Rudman & Glick, 2008).

If you believe the media reports that are directed toward adults, you would think that adolescent romance is rare, but adolescent sexuality is widespread. However, Hearn and her colleagues (2003) surveyed Black and Latina females between the ages of 12 and 14. According to their results, 94% of these teenagers reported having had a crush on someone, but only 8% reported having had penile-vaginal intercourse.

Some researchers focus on understanding adolescent romantic relationships, but unfortunately, a majority of the research focuses on White teenagers (Raffaelli, 2005; Smetana et al., 2006). The researchers report tremendous individual differences in the gender typing of adolescents' romantic relationships, consistent with Theme 4 of this book (Hartup, 1999; Tolman, 2002). For example, check the answers to Demonstration 4.5. As you'll learn, some adolescents behave in a gender-stereotypical fashion but some clearly transcend these stereotypes.

Research on early heterosexual romances suggests that these relationships typically last an average of about 4 months, but relationships last longer in late adolescence (B. B. Brown, 2004). Both girls and boys are likely to describe their romantic partners in terms of positive personality traits, such as "nice" or " funny." However, young boys are somewhat more likely to mention physical attractiveness, whereas young girls are somewhat more likely to emphasize personal characteristics, such as support and intimacy (Feiring, 1996, 1999b). In Chapter 8, we'll discover that men's greater emphasis on attractiveness in a dating partner continues through adulthood. However, as adolescent boys grow older, they place more emphasis on care and commitment in a relationship (Blakemore et al., 2009).

In Chapter 9, we'll examine an important component of heterosexual romantic relationships during adolescence: decision making about sexual behavior. As we'll learn, these decisions can have a major impact on a young woman's life, especially because they may lead to pregnancy and life-threatening sexually transmitted infections.

However, when a young woman has a boyfriend who respects her and values her ideas, these romantic relationships can encourage her to explore important questions about her identity and self-worth (Barber & Eccles, 2003; Furman & Shaffer, 2003;

R. W. Larson et al., 1999). She may notice how her interactions with this boyfriend affect her own personality (Feiring, 1999a). She can also think about the qualities that she truly wants in an ideal long-term relationship (W. A. Collins & Sroufe, 1999). Clearly, this self-exploration will have an important impact on her personal values during adulthood, as well as her romantic relationships.

Lesbian Relationships

In Chapter 8, we will examine many aspects of lesbian relationships during adulthood. Adolescent girls who are just beginning to discover their lesbian identity rarely observe positive lesbian images in the movies or on television (O'Sullivan et al., 2001). Psychology researchers also pay more attention to adolescent gay men than to adolescent lesbian women. As Theme 3 points out, women are less obvious than men. In addition, psychology researchers typically focus on observable problems (Welsh et al., 2000). Young lesbian women have fewer problems, because they are not at high risk for health problems as other adolescent populations, such as pregnancy.

However, young lesbian women are likely to hear negative messages about lesbian women and gay men from their peers. In one study, 99% of lesbian and gay youth reported that they had heard antigay remarks in their schools ("Lesbian, gay, bisexual," 2001). Adolescent lesbian women are also more likely than their heterosexual female peers to be threatened or attacked (Prezbindowski & Prezbindowski, 2001). They may also receive negative messages from their parents, who sometimes believe that being a gay man or lesbian woman is a sin. Adolescent LGBTQ+ youth also experience a three times higher risk for suicide than heterosexual youth (Whitaker, Shapiro, & Shields, 2015).

Fortunately, adolescents may find a school or community support group for LGBTQ+ young people (D'Augelli et al., 2002; Garnets, 2008; Marple & Latchmore, 2005). Furthermore, the American Academy of Pediatrics published a six-page article about how pediatricians can support and help LGBTQ+ adolescents (Frankowski, 2004). These kinds of social-support systems can help to reduce adolescents' sense of isolation.

Lesbian women report that they were about 11 years old when they were first aware of their attraction to other girls. This early attraction frequently takes the form of an intense friendship (Blakemore et al., 2009; D'Augelli et al., 2002; Garnets, 2008). Lesbian women are likely to have their first same-gender relationship at the median age of 18 (Savin-Williams, 2007). They frequently have a period of questioning their sexual orientation, often explaining to themselves that they are simply feeling an intense emotional connection with another female, rather than a sexual connection (Garnets, 2008).

Young lesbian women are most likely to first "come out" to a friend (D'Augelli, 2003). If they come out to their parents at some point, they are more likely to disclose to their mother rather than to their father, according to surveys conducted in the United States and Canada (D'Augelli, 2002, 2003; Savin-Williams, 1998, 2001). In Asian and Latina/o cultures, however, many young lesbian women know that they must not discuss their sexual orientation with their parents (Chan, 2008; Garnets, 2008; Molinary, 2007).

Consistent with Theme 4, young women have widely varying experiences if they do come out to their parents. At first, parents may react with shock or denial (Savin-Williams, 2001). However, some young women reported a more positive reaction. As one teenager explained, "We've always been very close, very close, and talk about everything. No secrets from her! … This gave me hope in coming out to her. Shortly thereafter I told her I was dating Naomi. ... But you know, she seemed to know it before I did!" (Savin-Williams, 2001, p. 67). Fortunately, most parents eventually become tolerant or even supportive of their daughters' lesbian relationships (Savin-Williams & Dubé, 1998).

As we'll learn in Chapter 8, lesbian women typically overcome most negative messages from their community and family, and they construct positive self-images. For example, D'Augelli and his coauthors (2002) surveyed 552 lesbian and bisexual high school girls in the United States and Canada. They found that 94% of these young girls reported that they were glad to identify as either lesbian or bisexual.

In Chapter 3 and in this chapter, we have considered how children and adolescents develop gender typing. We discussed in Chapter 3 that children develop elaborate ideas about gender throughout their childhood, especially because their family, their peers, their schools, and the media often provide clear gender messages.

In the current chapter, we have examined how puberty and menstruation help define young women's views of themselves. We have also noted that gender may influence an adolescent's self-esteem, body image, feminist identity, cultural identity, and transgender-identity. Gender also has important implications for an adolescent's career planning and interpersonal relationships.

In the following chapters, we will change our focus to examine adult women. We'll first explore gender comparisons in cognitive and achievement areas (Chapter 5) and gender comparisons in personality and social areas (Chapter 6). Next we'll consider women in work settings (Chapter 7) as well as in social relationships (Chapters 8, 9, and 10). In Chapters 11, 12, and 13, we will focus on issues women face with respect to health, psychological disorders, and violence. Then we will return to a developmental framework in Chapter 14, when we consider women's journeys during middle age and old age. Our final chapter examines some trends in gender issues that we are facing in the twenty-first century.

Section Summary

Interpersonal Relationships During Adolescence

1. Despite some disagreements, adolescent girls generally get along well with their families. They typically feel closer to their mothers than to their fathers. Young girls are more likely than young boys to discuss emotional experiences with family members.
2. Compared to adolescent men, adolescent girls may have friendships that are somewhat more intimate, and they value this intimacy.
3. Adolescents' heterosexual relationships show wide individual differences in the extent to which they are gender stereotyped. These relationships can encourage them to explore important questions about their identity.
4. Adolescent lesbian girls often hear negative messages from both peers and parents, but some lesbian girls find support in their community. Their experiences differ widely when they come out to their parents. Most adolescent lesbian and bisexual young women are positive about their sexual orientation.

Chapter Review Questions

1. In the section on menstruation, we examined two topics that the popular media sometimes mention: menstrual pain and premenstrual syndrome (PMS). What did you learn in this section that was different from the impressions the media convey?

2. Throughout this book, we have discussed the social constructionist perspective, in which people construct or create their own versions of reality, based on prior beliefs, experiences, and social interactions. How does this perspective help explain the following issues: (a) premenstrual syndrome, (b) young women's emphasis on slenderness, (c) transgender identity, and (d) heterosexual romantic relationships?

3. This textbook emphasizes that research findings about gender comparisons often vary, depending on the researchers' operational definitions (e.g., how you measure the relevant variables). How is this statement relevant when we consider the research on feminist identity and cultural identity?

4. Think about a woman you know who has a career in mathematics, science, or something similar. Consider the factors we examined in this chapter that encourage women to pursue this kind of occupation. Which factors seem to have helped this woman to achieve her goal? Did she have to overcome barriers that often limit women from these careers?

5. Portions of this chapter examined ethnic comparisons. Describe information about relevant comparisons, including age of menarche, self-esteem, and experiences with higher education.

6. Compare adolescent boys' and girls' career aspirations. What factors influence these aspirations for young women? Although we did not consider similar research about young men, what factors might influence the aspirations of adolescent boys?

7. Relate the material in the section on self-concept to the material on career aspirations and to the material on social interactions. Focus on the struggle between commitment to one's own pursuits and commitment to social relationships.

8. We mentioned parents in connection with nontraditional careers, family relationships, and romantic relationships. Discuss this information, and speculate how parents can also be important in a young woman's attitudes toward menstruation, body image, feminist identity, and cultural identity.

9. Imagine that you are teaching high school. A group of teachers has obtained a large grant for a program on improving the lives of adolescent girls. Review the topics in this chapter, and suggest 8 to 10 important topics that this program should address.

10. Chapter 5 focuses on gender comparisons in cognitive abilities and interests in achievement. Chapter 6 explores gender comparisons in social and personality characteristics. To prepare for these two chapters, make a list of gender comparisons on these dimensions, based on your knowledge from the chapter you have just completed. Be sure to include the experiences in academic settings in middle school, high school, and college, as well as early experiences in math and science, career aspirations, and friendships.

Key Terms

puberty (p. 112)	secondary sex characteristics (p. 114)	ovaries (p. 115)	uterus (p. 116)
adolescence (p. 112)		ova (p. 115)	feedback loop (p. 116)
menarche (p. 112)		ovulation (p. 116)	

dysmenorrhea (p. 116)

prostaglandins (p. 116)

premenstrual
syndrome (PMS)
(p. 117)

identity (p. 122)

self-esteem (p. 123)

meta-analysis (p. 123)

feminism (p. 125)

feminist social
identity (p. 126)

cultural identity
(p. 127)

transgender person
(p. 128)

chilly classroom
climate (p. 132)

tribal colleges (p. 133)

Recommended Readings

Chrisler, J. C., & Golden, C. (Eds.). (2018). *Lectures on the psychology of women* (5th ed.). Long Grove, IL: Waveland Press. Several chapters in this excellent book are relevant to the topic of adolescence. Some especially relevant chapters discuss women's body image, women and sport, menstruation, and lesbian relationships.

Denmark, F. L., & Paludi, M. A. (Eds.). (2017). *Psychology of women: A handbook of issues and theories* (3rd ed.). Santa Barbara, CA: ABC-CLIO. If you are searching for helpful overviews about female adolescents, I would recommend several chapters in this handbook, including topics such as developmental theory, the menstrual cycle, and career development.

Denner, J., & Guzmán, B. L. (Eds.). (2006). *Latina girls: Voices of adolescent strength in the United States.* New York: New York University Press. I especially appreciate this book because it often includes the Latina adolescents' own words, as well as quantitative data, and it includes Latinas from different regions of

the United States. I also admired the editors' emphasis on the young women's positive, healthy behaviors.

Goldwasser, A. (Ed.). (2007). *Red: The next generation of American writers—teenage girls—on what fires up their lives today.* New York: Hudson Street Press. In 2006, writer Amy Goldwasser invited young women—between the ages of 13 and 19—to send nonfiction essays about their thoughts and their lives. This book features 58 well-chosen short essays about topics such as family members, body issues, friendships, romance, and popular culture.

Sirin, S. R., & Fine, M. (2008). *Muslim American youth: Understanding hyphenated identities through multiple methods.* New York: New York University Press. This thought-provoking book illustrates how Muslim American teenagers often experience negative reactions from other Americans; still, they can creatively construct a complex identity for themselves.

Answers to Demonstrations

Demonstration 4.4: You can informally assess your feminist identity by adding together the ratings that you supplied for Items 1, 2, 3, 6, 7, and 9 and then subtracting the ratings that you supplied for Items 4, 5, 8, and 10. Higher scores indicate a stronger feminist identity.

Demonstration 4.5: Person 1 is a male; Person 2 is a female; Person 3 is a female; Person 4 is a male.

Pressmaster/Shutterstock.com

5 Gender Comparisons in Cognitive Abilities and Attitudes About Achievements

Learning Objectives

After studying this chapter, you will be able to…

5-1 Summarize major issues surrounding research on gender comparisons.

5-2 Describe gender comparisons in cognitive abilities.

5-3 Explain how gender is related to attitudes about achievement.

Did You Know?

- In general, people across multiple age ranges earn similar scores on a wide variety of tests that assess cognitive ability (p. 148).
- The largest gender difference for any measure of cognitive ability is that men are typically faster than women in mentally rotating a geometric shape (pp. 157–158).
- According to several studies, men are often more confident than women when they judge their own academic abilities (pp. 164–165).
- Women are more likely than men to find that their self-confidence is influenced by the evaluations provided by other people (pp. 166–167).

Once, a friend sent me an article titled "He Thinks, She Thinks," by Linda Marsa (2007), which appeared in *Discover* magazine. The article emphasizes that societal factors cannot explain gender differences. Instead, Marsa claims, "Our brains are hardwired differently, and these anatomical variations in architecture and function illuminate some of the reasons why men and women seem to come from different planets" (Marsa, 2007, p. 12). Without citing any relevant research, Marsa then claims that these brain differences account for the different ways that she and her husband organize the task of fixing breakfast, as well as the difference in their ability to focus their attention on other topics during times of crisis, such as when their pet cat had been injured.

The article does quote psychiatrist Nancy Andreasen, who emphasizes that men and women "are more alike than they're different, and even when there are variations, there is a significant overlap between the sexes" (Marsa, 2007, p. 12). However, Marsa did not elaborate on this point, because the remainder of her article emphasized brain differences.

As you can probably guess from Theme 1 of this textbook, the information in Chapter 5 generally supports Dr. Andreasen. Unfortunately, however, when people who are not experts discuss gender comparisons in thinking, they almost always emphasize gender *differences* (Hyde & Grabe, 2008). Meanwhile, they ignore the substantial evidence for gender *similarities* (Hyde, 2005a; Zell, Krizan, & Teeter, 2015).

Furthermore, people who are not experts typically highlight biological explanations for the small number of comparisons that reveal significant gender differences (Sechzer & Rabinowitz, 2008). You need to know, however, that social and cultural explanations play a very important role in accounting for gender differences.

In the present chapter, we will focus on two broad questions regarding gender comparisons:

1. Do people of different genders differ in their cognitive abilities?
2. Do people of different genders differ in their attitudes related to motivation and success?

By addressing these two questions, we will also gain some background information needed to answer another important question. In Chapter 7, we'll learn that men and women tend to pursue different careers. For example, men are much more likely than women to become engineers. Can we trace these gender differences in career choice to major gender differences in cognitive skills (such as ability in math) or to major gender differences in motivation (such as attitudes about success)? We will focus here—in Chapter 5—on the school-related comparisons that assess intellectual abilities and achievement motivation.

In contrast, in Chapter 6 we will emphasize interpersonal gender comparisons, specifically, social and personality characteristics. Can we trace these gender differences in career choice to gender differences in social and personality qualities, such as communication patterns, helpfulness, or aggressiveness?

5-1 Background on Gender Comparisons

Learning Objectives

To summarize major issues surrounding research on gender comparisons, you can ...

5-1-1   Describe five areas of caution in conducting research on gender comparisons.

5-1-2   Explain how meta-analysis improves our understanding of actual gender differences.

Before we address any specific gender comparisons, let's consider some research issues that are relevant both here and in Chapter 6. We'll first examine several cautions about the way psychologists conduct their research and interpret it. Then we'll briefly describe a statistical technique, called meta-analysis, which can summarize a large number of studies that focus on the same topic.

Cautions About Research on Gender Comparisons

As we learned in Chapter 1, a variety of biases can have a powerful effect when psychologists conduct research about either women or gender comparisons. In addition, we need to be cautious about interpreting the results of the research. Let's consider five specific cautions that are relevant to the current chapter:

1. Biased samples can influence results.
2. People's expectations can influence results.
3. If we measure some ability, and then we create one graph for the scores of men and another graph for the scores of women, the two distributions of scores will overlap substantially.
4. Researchers seldom find gender differences in all situations.
5. The cognitive gender differences are not large enough to have a major influence on a person's career choice.

Let's examine each caution in more detail:

1. *Biased samples can influence results.* Almost all the research on cognitive abilities focuses on college students, so this research is not representative of the general population (D. F. Halpern, 2000). We know almost nothing about adults who have not attended college. In addition, most of the research on gender comparisons examines White men and women in the United States and Canada (Eccles et al., 2003; McGuinness, 1998; Sechzer & Rabinowitz, 2008). Our conclusions about gender comparisons might be different if these studies had included other genders or people of color.

2. *People's expectations can influence results.* As we noted in Chapter 1 (pages 20 to 27), biases can interfere at every stage of the research process. For example, researchers who expect to find gender differences will tend to find them (Caplan & Caplan, 2009; Sechzer & Rabinowitz, 2008). The participants also have expectations about cognitive gender differences (Caplan & Caplan, 2009; Nosek et al., 2002). We considered this issue in Chapter 2, in connection with stereotype threat.

3. *If we measure some ability, and then we create one graph for the scores of men and we add another graph for the scores of women, the two distributions of scores will overlap substantially.* To discuss the concept of overlap, we need to consider frequency distributions. A **frequency distribution** tells us how many people in a sample receive each score.

Imagine that we give a vocabulary test to a group of women and men. Then we use their scores to construct a hypothetical frequency distribution for each gender, as demonstrated in Figure 5.1. Notice the tiny section in which the frequency distribution for the men overlaps with the frequency distribution for the women. In Figure 5.1, men and women received the same scores only in that one small region, roughly between 54 and 66.

When the two distributions display such a small overlap, this pattern tells us that the two distributions are very different. As portrayed in the hypothetical distributions in Figure 5.1, the average man received a score of 40, whereas the average woman received a score of 80.

In real life, however, distributions of female and male characteristics rarely show the large separation and the small overlap illustrated in Figure 5.1. They are much more likely to demonstrate *a small separation* and *a large overlap,* such as the one represented in the hypothetical distributions in Figure 5.2 (Blakemore et al., 2009; Gallagher & Kaufman, 2004b; A. J. Stewart & McDermott, 2004). Notice that most men and most women earn scores in the large region that extends roughly between 35 and 85. As we have often emphasized in our discussion of Theme 1, men and women are reasonably similar. As a result, their scores will overlap considerably. Notice in Figure 5.2 that the average man received a score of 57 and that the average woman received a score of 63.

This 6-point difference between the average scores appears trivial when we compare it to the variability *within* each distribution, a range of about 50 points. As Theme 4 emphasizes, women differ widely from one another in cognitive abilities; men also show wide variation (A. J. Stewart & McDermott, 2004).

4. *Researchers seldom find gender differences in all situations.* You are certainly familiar with this issue from our earlier discussion of Theme 1. Throughout this chapter, as well, you will notice that we cannot make general statements about gender differences.

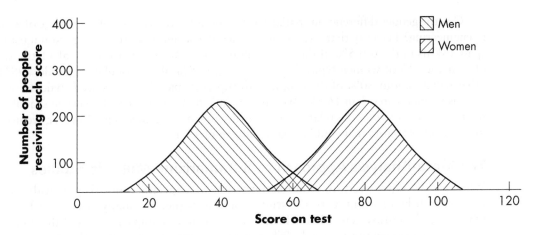

FIGURE **5.1** Scores achieved by women and men on a hypothetical test.

Note: The small overlap indicates a large gender difference.

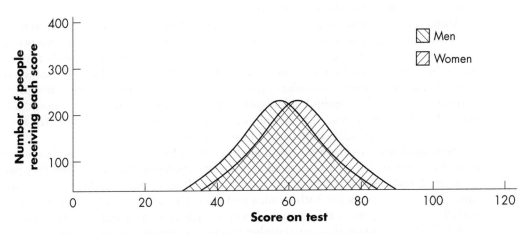

FIGURE **5.2** Scores achieved by women and men on a hypothetical test.

Note: The large overlap indicates a small gender difference.

Instead, the gender differences often disappear when we test certain kinds of people or when we examine particular situations (Caplan & Caplan, 2009; D. F. Halpern, 2006b; Hyde & Grabe, 2008). This observation suggests that gender differences can be modified; they are not inevitable (D. F. Halpern, 2004a). In short, many people of all genders have remarkably similar psychological characteristics in many situations.

5. *The cognitive gender differences are not large enough to be relevant for a person's career choice.* Let's consider engineering as a career choice. At present, only about 16.5% of U.S. engineers are women (Bureau of Labor Statistics, 2020). Engineering clearly requires spatial skills, and the research suggests that men are somewhat more likely than women to earn higher scores on tests of spatial ability.

Can the gender difference in spatial skills account for the very small percentage of women in engineering? Let's say that a career in engineering would require that a person must have spatial skills in the top 5% of the general population. According to some calculations, 7% of men and 3% of women typically place in the top 5% of the population (Hyde, 1981). In other words, about 30% of the people with superior spatial abilities are female. However, 30% is much greater than 16.5%. We can conclude that the gender difference in spatial skills might partially explain the relative absence of women in engineering. However, we need to look for other factors that could explain that gap of 13.5%.

The Meta-Analysis Approach to Summarizing Multiple Studies

When psychologists want to obtain an overview of a specific topic, they typically review the research by examining all the studies on that topic. For many years, psychologists who wanted to draw general conclusions about gender comparisons used the **box-score approach** to reviewing research. When using the **box-score approach** (also called the **counting approach**), researchers read through all the appropriate studies on a given topic and draw conclusions based on a tally of their outcomes (Hyde & Grabe, 2008). Specifically, how many studies show no gender differences, how many show higher scores for women, and how many show higher scores for men?

Unfortunately, however, the box-score approach often produces ambiguous tallies. Suppose that researchers locate 16 relevant studies; 8 of these studies find no gender differences, 2 show higher scores for women, and 6 show higher scores for men. One researcher might conclude that no gender differences exist, whereas another might conclude that men score somewhat higher. The box-score approach does not provide a systematic method for combining individual studies. Let's consider a more useful alternative, called "meta-analysis," a technique we mentioned earlier in this book, for example, in connection with gender comparisons in self-esteem.

Meta-analysis provides a statistical method for combining numerous studies on a single topic. Researchers first try to locate all appropriate studies on the topic. Then they perform a statistical analysis that combines the results from all these studies, taking into account the variability of the scores for both women and men. This analysis calculates the size of the overall difference between two groups of people, such as women and men. For example, for verbal ability, a meta-analysis can combine numerous previous studies into one enormous superstudy that can provide a general picture of whether gender has an overall effect on verbal ability.

A meta-analysis yields a number known as effect size, or d. For instance, if the meta-analysis of numerous studies shows that men and women received exactly the same overall score, the d would be zero. Now consider the d for the gender difference in height; here, the d is 2.0. This is a huge difference! In fact, the overlap between the male and female distributions for height is only 11% (Kimball, 1995).

Compared to a d of 2.0 for gender comparisons of height, the d values for psychological gender comparisons are relatively small. In an important study, Janet Hyde (2005a) examined 128 different meta-analysis measures that focused on gender comparisons in cognitive skills. She found that 30% of these gender comparisons were in the "close-to-zero" range (d less than 0.11), 48% had a small effect size (d = 0.11 to 0.35), 15% had a moderate effect size (d = 0.36 to 0.65), and only 8% had a large effect size (d greater than 0.65).

In other words, the clear majority of these comparisons of cognitive abilities showed either no gender difference or a small gender difference. Importantly, these studies provide stronger evidence for moving beyond the gender binary in psychological research (Hyde et al., 2019). With all these important methodological issues in mind, let's now consider the actual research on cognitive gender comparisons.

Section Summary

Background on Gender Comparisons

1. In considering research on gender comparisons, we need to emphasize that biased samples and expectations can influence results.
2. Frequency distributions for the scores of men and women typically show a large overlap; in other words, most people receive similar scores, regardless of their gender.
3. Gender differences that are present in some situations are typically absent in others; also, the cognitive gender differences are not large enough to be relevant when people make career choices.
4. The meta-analysis technique provides a systematic statistical method for integrating studies on a single topic and for drawing conclusions about that topic. These meta-analyses demonstrate that fewer than 10% of the gender comparisons show a large difference in cognitive abilities.

5-2 Cognitive Abilities

Learning Objectives

To describe gender comparisons in cognitive abilities, you can ...

5-2-1 Summarize which cognitive abilities appear to be similar among people of different genders.

5-2-2 Describe how memory functions differently among people of different genders.

5-2-3 Explain which general verbal abilities are similar, and which differ, among people of different genders.

5-2-4 Analyze the reasons why boys appear to have higher rates of reading disabilities than girls.

5-2-5 Explain why actual gender differences in math ability do not match most people's stereotypes regarding math ability.

5-2-6 Identify which spatial abilities appear to differ across the genders.

5-2-7 Explain why mental rotation tasks provide mixed evidence for gender differences in spatial ability.

5-2-8 Describe how biological explanations account for gender differences in cognitive abilities.

5-2-9 Provide examples of how experience affects performance on cognitive tasks.

5-2-10 Describe gender differences in attitudes about mathematics.

We've covered some of the background information about gender comparisons. In this second section, we'll examine the research on gender comparisons in cognitive abilities. The third section of this chapter will explore topics related to achievement motivation.

In this current section, we'll first examine some areas that show gender similarities, and then we'll focus on four kinds of cognitive abilities for which we have some evidence of gender differences: (1) memory, (2) verbal ability, (3) mathematics ability, and (4) spatial ability. Then we'll consider some potential explanations for these gender differences.

Cognitive Abilities That Show No Consistent Gender Differences

Before we examine the four areas that show occasional gender differences, let's first consider some general categories where gender similarities are typical.

General Intelligence

One major area in which women and men are similar is general intelligence, as measured by total scores on an IQ test (D. F. Halpern, 2001; Herlitz & Yonker, 2002; Hines, 2007; Johnson et al., 2008; Nisbett et al., 2012). People who construct intelligence tests often eliminate test items that show a gender difference. As a result, the final versions of the intelligence tests usually reveal gender similarities (D. F. Halpern, 2006a). However, IQ scores for men show greater *variability* than IQ scores for women (Johnson et al., 2008).

Other research also shows gender similarities in general knowledge about history, geography, and other basic information (Meinz & Salthouse, 1998). Furthermore, let's dispel a popular belief. The media often claims that women are better than men at "multitasking," or performing two tasks at the same time, and research suggests people believe this common stereotype (Szameitat et al., 2015). However, researchers in cognitive psychology have not reported systematic gender differences in this area (Hirsch, Koch, & Karbach, 2019).

Complex Cognitive Tasks

Several other challenging intellectual tasks show no overall gender differences. For example, men and women are equally competent when they form concepts and when they solve a variety of complex problems (Ellis et al., 2008; Kiefer & Shih, 2006; Kimura, 1992; Meinz & Salthouse, 1998). Men and women are also similar in their performance on a variety of creativity tasks (Baer & Kaufman, 2008; Ellis et al., 2008; Ruscio et al., 1998).

Furthermore, you may have learned about gender differences in "learning style," with girls learning best in a cooperative environment and boys learning best in a competitive environment. However, researchers have not discovered gender differences in learning style (Hyde & Lindberg, 2007). In fact, learning styles themselves are one of the most pervasive myths in psychology and reflect a form of *psychological essentialism* (Nancekivell, Shah, & Gelman, 2020). This incorrect way of thinking about cognitive abilities is similar to the notion of gender essentialism that we discussed in Chapter 1.

We have learned that women and men are typically similar in their general intelligence and complex cognitive abilities. Keep these important similarities in mind as we explore the four areas in which modest gender differences have sometimes been identified.

Memory Ability

The research on gender differences in memory ability is mixed, primarily because humans have and use various kinds of memory skills. Although men perform better on some types of memory tasks, women outperform men on other types of memory tasks.

In one kind of memory task, people read a list of words. After a delay, they are asked to remember the words. In general, women are somewhat more accurate on this kind of memory skill (Herlitz & Rehnman, 2008; Herlitz & Yonker, 2002; Larsson et al., 2003; Maitland et al., 2004; Thilers et al., 2007).

However, the nature of the items on the list may influence the results (Herrmann et al., 1992; Rubin et al., 1999). For instance, Colley and her colleagues (2002) gave women and men a list of items to remember. The list was labeled either "Grocery store" or "Hardware store." The items on the list were equally likely for both kinds of stores (e.g., *nuts, salt,* and *disinfectant*). Let's consider some representative results. As demonstrated in Figure 5.3, women recalled many more items than men from the "grocery" list, but women and men recalled a similar number of items from the "hardware" list.

The research also suggests that women tend to be more accurate than men in remembering events from their own lives (Colley et al., 2002; Ellis et al., 2008; Fivush & Nelson, 2004). As you may recall from Chapter 3, mothers are more likely to discuss emotional topics with their daughters, rather than their sons. As a result, girls have more opportunities to practice remembering these personal events (Fivush & Nelson, 2004). The gender differences in memory for life events is therefore consistent with the research in cognitive psychology, which demonstrates that people with practice and expertise in a specific area remember this material more accurately than nonexperts (Matlin, 2009; Schmid Mast & Hall, 2006).

Let's now shift to memory tasks for nonverbal material. Women tend to be more accurate than men in recognizing faces (Ellis et al., 2008; Herlitz & Yonker, 2002; Lewin & Herlitz, 2002). Women's greater accuracy even holds true for recognizing faces from a different ethnic group. For instance, Swedish women performed better than Swedish men in recognizing the faces of people from the South Asian country of Bangladesh (Rehnman & Herlitz, 2007). Women are also more accurate than men in recalling details about a person's hair and clothing (Schmid Mast & Hall, 2006).

FIGURE **5.3** Performance on a memory task, as a function of participants' gender and the kind of memory task.
Source: Colley et al. (2002).

In general, women are also better than men in remembering objects that they have observed at an earlier time and also in remembering *where* they have observed these objects, according to a meta-analysis by Voyer and his colleagues (2007) on these two specific skills. However, men and women are similar in remembering abstract shapes (Ferguson et al., 2008; Herlitz & Yonker, 2002). According to a meta-analysis of visual-spatial working memory, men have a slight advantage in this type of memory, which involves the ability to remember images, patterns, and sequences of events. But the overall gender difference is small ($d = 0.155$) and is dependent on both age and specific type of task (Voyer, Voyer, & Saint-Aubin, 2017).Other studies suggest that some neurological differences exist in how men and women activate their working memory networks during working memory tasks. For example, it appears that women's memories tend to show higher activation in the limbic and prefrontal areas of the brain, but men's memory systems tend to be distributed throughout the parietal regions of the brain related to spatial processing (Hill, Laird, & Robinson, 2014).

In summary, some studies suggest that men perform somewhat better than women on certain types of memory tasks, such as those related to working memory. However, women generally earn somewhat higher scores on memory tests for words, life events, faces, and objects. Even when studies demonstrate gender differences in memory, it is important to remember that the differences are small and dependent on the performance of specific memory tasks.

Verbal Ability

Women score somewhat higher than men on a small number of verbal tasks, although the overall gender similarities are more striking (Caplan & Caplan, 2009). Let's explore three areas of research: general studies, standardized language tests, and data about reading disabilities.

General Verbal Ability

Research on gender comparisons in preschoolers' verbal ability suggests that girls have larger vocabularies than boys have before the age of 2, but these gender differences disappear by 3 years of age (N. Eisenberg et al., 1996; Huttenlocher et al., 1991; Jacklin & Maccoby, 1983). Furthermore, the similarities are more striking than the differences when we consider vocabulary in young school-age children (Hyde & Grabe, 2008; Hyde & Lindberg, 2007; Kidd & Lum, 2008). Therefore, if you plan to teach elementary school, the girls and boys in your class should be comparable in their language skills.

Throughout elementary and middle school, it appears that girls do have a slight advantage in other verbal abilities. A meta-analysis of assessment data collected from more than 10 million children in the United States indicated that girls outperform boys on reading ($d = 0.19$) and language arts ($d = 0.29$) and demonstrate moderate performance advantages in writing ($d = 0.45$; Peterson, 2018).

When we consider adolescents and adults, the research shows gender similarities in language skills such as spelling, vocabulary, word associations, reading comprehension, and learning a second language (Madu & Kasanga, 2005; Maitland et al., 2004; Ritter, 2004). However, women seem to be somewhat better at **verbal fluency**, or naming objects that meet certain criteria, such as beginning with the letter S (Barel & Tzischinsky, 2018; D. F. Halpern, 2000, 2001; D. F. Halpern & Tan, 2001; Maitland et al., 2004; Ullman et al., 2008).

In general, women score higher than men on tests of writing ability (Ellis et al., 2008; D. F. Halpern, 2004a, 2006a; D. F. Halpern, Benbow et al., 2007; Reilly, Neumann, & Andrews, 2019). However, it isn't clear whether this gender difference has practical implications for women's success in the classroom and on the job.

We emphasized earlier that meta-analysis is the ideal statistical tool for combining the results of a number of studies on a specific topic. Janet Hyde and Marcia Linn (1988) conducted a meta-analysis on overall gender comparisons in verbal ability. The average effect size (d) was only 0.11, just slightly favoring women. This value is very close to zero, and so Hyde and Linn concluded that overall gender differences do not exist.

Other researchers have reached the same conclusions about verbal abilities, based on standardized test scores for U.S. students (Feingold, 1988; Hedges & Nowell, 1995; Willingham & Cole, 1997). Ironically, researchers seldom study the two general areas in which women occasionally have the advantage, memory and verbal abilities. In contrast, there is much more research about mathematical and spatial abilities, areas in which men may have an advantage (D. F. Halpern, 2000).

We've examined gender comparisons in general verbal ability, from preschool up to adulthood. Let's now explore the related topic of reading disabilities.

Reading Disabilities

The research suggests that boys are more likely than girls to have language problems. For instance, school systems report reading disabilities about four or five times as often for boys as for girls (D. F. Halpern, 2000; Quinn & Wagner, 2015; Shaywitz et al., 1990).

However, Sally Shaywitz and her colleagues (1990) suggested that teachers might target more active, less attentive boys as having reading disabilities. What happens when researchers use objective statistical measures to classify the children?

According to Shaywitz and her coauthors (1990), an objective measure of the term **reading disability** should refer to poor reading skills that are not accounted for by the level of general intelligence. These researchers used this operational definition to study children in Connecticut. Their data showed that roughly the same number of boys and girls met the criterion of having reading disabilities. Specifically, boys were about 1.2 times more likely than girls to have reading disabilities.

Michael Rutter and his coauthors (2004) performed a similar analysis of children's reading disabilities in New Zealand. They used a definition of reading disability that was similar to the one used by Shaywitz and her colleagues (1990). When they included general intelligence in their analysis, they found that boys were about twice as likely as girls to have reading disabilities. In other words, the New Zealand study produced a more extreme ratio of boys to girls, in comparison to the American study.

Suppose that boys really are two times as likely as girls to have reading disabilities, which some studies support (Quinn & Wagner, 2015). This gender difference is significant. However, we still need to ask why schools identify reading problems four to five times more often in boys than in girls, often referred to as *ascertainment bias* (Quinn & Wagner, 2015). Other research shows that boys have more trouble focusing their attention, whereas girls are more skilled at controlling their behavior (Else-Quest et al., 2006). It's likely that teachers target the more active, less attentive boys as having reading disabilities. These boys may be referred to a reading clinic on the basis of their behavior, rather than their poor reading skills (Shaywitz et al., 1990).

An equally disturbing problem is that many girls may have genuine reading disabilities, but sit quietly in their seats and hide their disabilities (J. T. E. Richardson, 1997). These well-behaved, neglected girls will miss out on the additional tutoring in reading that could help them thrive in school. As Chapter 3 emphasized, girls are often overlooked in our schools, and because of this they lose out on educational opportunities.

Throughout this section on verbal skills, we have learned about a general pattern of minimal gender differences, based on a variety of measures. However, we also have to conclude that boys are more likely than girls to have reading disabilities.

Mathematics Ability

Performance in mathematics is the cognitive ability that receives the most attention from both researchers and the popular press (Halpern, Benbow et al., 2007). Media reports would lead you to expect large gender differences in math ability, favoring boys. However, adolescent boys and girls in both the United States and Canada now complete the same number of math courses during high school (Lacampagne et al., 2007; Shapka et al., 2008; Spelke & Grace, 2007). In addition, you'll discover that most of the research shows gender similarities in math ability (Halpern, Aronson et al., 2007). Furthermore, girls actually receive higher grades in math courses, especially during middle and early high school years. The only measure on which boys consistently perform better than girls is the mathematics section of the SAT. Let's examine the details.

General Mathematics Ability

Most comparisons of boys' and girls' ability on mathematics achievement tests show gender similarities. Consider, for example, a meta-analysis of 100 studies, based on standardized-test scores of more than 3 million students. (This analysis did not include math SAT scores, which we'll consider shortly.) By examining across all samples and all tests, Janet Hyde and her colleagues (1990) found a d of only 0.15. (Refer to Figure 5.4.) As represented in this figure, the two distributions are almost identical.

Janet Hyde and her colleagues (2008) provide additional evidence of gender similarities on standardized math exams. These researchers analyzed test scores for 7.2 million students in 10 U.S. states. They found consistent gender similarities for students of all ages, from 2nd grade through 11th grade, even when the tests included complex math problems. An additional meta-analysis of 242 studies published between 1990 and 2007 and representing data from 1,286,350 people demonstrates a d of only 0.05 in terms of mathematics ability. Together, these studies indicate that there are no gender differences in mathematics ability among people of all genders (Lindberg, Hyde, Peterson, & Linn, 2010). The results of the research on general math abilities make a clear statement about gender similarities in mathematics.

Other research has examined gender differences in math performance; science, technology, engineering, and mathematics (STEM) interest; and advanced placement credits among twelfth-grade students in the United States. Using National Center for Education Statistics data, Cunningham, Ralph, Mulvaney Hoyer, and Sparks (2015) report that more high school boys than girls express interest in math-related courses. However, the differences are small, and girls actually earn more advanced placement credits than boys in those courses (Cunningham et al., 2015). Similarly, Ceci, Ginther, Kahn, and Williams

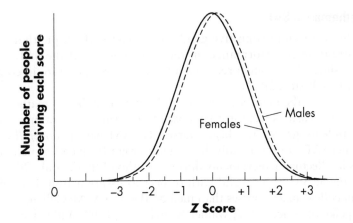

FIGURE **5.4** Performance of females and males on all mathematics tests except the SAT, showing an effect size (*d*) of 0.15.

Source: Copyright © 1990 by the American Psychological Association. Adapted with permission. Figure 1 (adapted), p. 149, from Hyde, J. S., Fennema, E., & Lamon, S. J. (1990). Gender differences in mathematics performance: A meta-analysis. *Psychological Bulletin, 107(2),* 139–155. doi:10.1037/0033-2909.107.2.139.

(2014) suggest that although slight gender differences in spatial and mathematical reasoning still exist, the differences are not based in biology. Across the world, the gap in STEM performance has been narrowing since the early 2000s (Ceci et al., 2014). Despite the slight gender differences in mathematics ability that exist throughout the school years, the perception that math is a "masculine" domain unfortunately persists (Makarova, Aeschlimann, & Herzog, 2019).

Grades in Mathematics Courses

I often ask students in my classes to raise their hands if they have been told that boys receive higher average scores on the math section of the SAT, a common entrance exam for college and university admission. The hands fly up. Then I ask how many have been told that girls receive higher average grades in mathematics courses throughout middle and early high school grades. The hands all drop. In fact, representative studies show that girls earn higher grades in fifth-, sixth-, eighth-, and tenth-grade mathematics as well as in college math courses (Caplan & Caplan, 2009; Crombie et al., 2005; Ellis et al., 2008; D. F. Halpern, 2004a, 2006b; Kimball, 1989, 1995; Willingham & Cole, 1997). Women also earn higher grades in related areas, such as high-school science courses and college-level statistics (Brownlow et al., 2000; D. F. Halpern, 2004a; M. Stewart, 1998).

Meredith Kimball (1989, 1995) proposed that female students perform better when dealing with familiar situations, such as exams on material covered in a mathematics course. In contrast, male students perform better when dealing with unfamiliar situations, especially the kinds of math problems included on the SAT. In any event, Kimball points out that girls' high grades in math courses deserve wider publicity. This publicity would encourage female students, their parents, and their teachers to be more confident about girls' and women's competence in mathematics.

The Mathematics SAT

Of all the research in cognitive gender differences, the topic that has received the most media attention is performance on the math portion of the SAT. For instance, the data for 2017 show that women received an average score of 516, in contrast to 531 for men (The College Board, 2020).

However, is the math SAT test a valid index of ability in mathematics? A test has high **validity** if it measures what it is supposed to measure. For example, the SAT is supposed to predict students' grades in college courses. The SAT has high *overall* validity because people with higher SAT scores generally do earn higher grades in college math courses. The SAT also predicts intellectual achievements during adulthood (Park et al., 2007). However, the math portion of the SAT is not valid with respect to its prediction that women will earn lower grades in college math courses than men do (De Lisi & McGillicuddy-De Lisi, 2002; Spelke, 2005; Spelke & Grace, 2007; Wainer & Steinberg, 1992; Willingham & Cole, 1997).

In other words, the math SAT underestimates women's actual math performance. This problem means that colleges and universities are sending many rejection letters to female students who would be likely to earn *higher* math grades than the male students who receive acceptance letters. Based on validity studies such as these, some colleges and universities have stopped using the SAT or have modified the math SAT requirements (Ceci & Williams, 2007a; Hoover, 2004; Tugend, 2019).

Spatial Ability

Most people are familiar with the first two cognitive abilities discussed in this chapter: verbal ability and mathematics ability. In contrast, spatial abilities are less well known. **Spatial abilities** include understanding, perceiving, and manipulating shapes and figures (Lawton & Hatcher, 2005). Spatial ability plays a role in many everyday activities, such as playing electronic games, reading road maps, and arranging furniture in an apartment.

Researchers agree that spatial ability is not unitary (Caplan & Caplan, 2009; Chipman, 2004). Many researchers propose three components: spatial visualization, spatial perception, and mental rotation. The research indicates that mental rotation tests are the only spatial tasks that reveal large gender differences. Let's consider each of the three components separately.

Spatial Visualization

Tasks that use **spatial visualization** require complex processing of spatially presented information. For example, an embedded-figure test requires you to locate a particular pattern or object that is hidden in a larger design. Demonstration 5.1a illustrates three examples of an embedded-figure test. As a child, you may have tried similar games, perhaps searching for faces in a picture of a woodland scene.

Many individual studies and meta-analyses have shown that men and women perform fairly similarly on tasks requiring spatial visualization (e.g., Ellis et al., 2008; Sanz de Acedo Lizarraga & García Ganuza, 2003; Scali & Brownlow, 2001; Scali et al., 2000). For example, one meta-analysis of 116 studies produced a d of 0.19, a small gender difference suggesting that men are slightly better on this task (Voyer et al., 1995). Refer again to Figure 5.4 for a graph of a similar effect size ($d = 0.15$). As portrayed in this chart, the overlap for the two distributions is substantial.

Let's consider one component of spatial visualization, the ability to learn map information. Some studies find that men perform better, but other similar studies report no gender differences (Bosco et al., 2004; C. Davies, 2002; Ellis et al., 2008; Henrie et al.,

Demonstration **5.1**

Examples of Tests of Spatial Ability

Try these three kinds of tests of spatial ability.

a.   *Embedded-Figure Test.* In each of the three units, study the figure on
     the left. Then cover it up and try to find where it is hidden in the figure
     on the right. You may need to shift the left-hand figure to locate it in
     the right-hand figure.

b.   *Water-Level Test.* Imagine that this woman is drinking from a glass
     that is half-filled with water. Draw a line across the glass to indicate
     where the water line belongs.

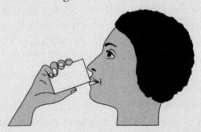

c.   *Mental Rotation Test.* If you mentally rotate the figure on the left-hand
     side, which of the five figures on the right-hand side would you obtain?

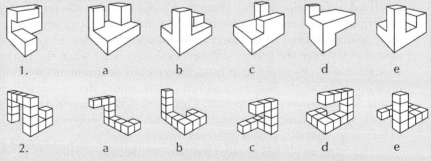

The answers to these three tests appear at the end of the chapter.

1997; Lawton & Kallai, 2002). Related research indicates that men are better than
women at finding their way back to the starting point from a distant location. However,
other similar studies reveal no gender differences (Halpern & Collaer, 2005; Lawton &
Morrin, 1999; Saucier et al., 2002; Schmitz, 1999). As we have learned, the picture is
mixed; gender differences in spatial visualization are not consistent.

Spatial Perception

In **spatial perception** tests, participants are asked to identify a horizontal or vertical location without being distracted by irrelevant information. One example of this skill, a water-level test, appears in Demonstration 5.1b.

Meta-analyses of gender comparisons for spatial perception show that men receive somewhat higher scores; effect sizes are in the range of 0.40 (Nordvik & Amponsah, 1998; Voyer, Nolan, & Voyer, 2000; Voyer, Voyer, & Bryden, 1995). However, some studies report no gender differences on the water-level test (Ellis et al., 2008; Herlitz et al., 1999). Still another study found that gender differences were erased following a brief training session (Vasta et al., 1996).

Mental Rotation

A test of **mental rotation** measures the ability to rotate a two- or three-dimensional figure rapidly and accurately. The two problems of Demonstration 5.1c illustrate this skill. The mental rotation task produces the largest gender differences of all skills, when measured in terms of performance speed. Men tend to respond faster than women. The effect sizes for mental rotation are generally in the range of 0.50 to 0.90 (Ellis et al., 2008; D. F. Halpern, 2001, 2004a; Nordvik & Amponsah, 1998; Ritter, 2004).

Even though the gender differences for mental rotation tasks are relatively large, we still need to keep the data in perspective. An effect size as large as 0.90 is certainly larger than any other cognitive effect size. However, 0.90 is trivial compared to the effect size of 2.00 for height, discussed earlier (Kimball, 1995). Also, some researchers in Canada, the United States, and Spain report no consistent gender differences (Brownlow & Miderski, 2002; Brownlow et al., 2003; D. F. Halpern & Tan, 2001; Robert & Chevrier, 2003; Sanz de Acedo Lizarraga & García Ganuza, 2003). Other studies show that the appearance of gender differences depends on whether participants are presented with either 2D or 3D stimuli (Roberts & Bell, 2003). Data on developmental factors that may influence mental rotation abilities and gender differences is mixed (Johnson & Moore, 2020). Additional studies suggest that gender differences on mental rotation tasks depend on how the task is described to participants. For example, Sharps and his colleagues (1994) found that men performed much better than women when the instructions emphasized the usefulness of these spatial abilities in stereotypically masculine professions, such as piloting military aircraft. However, the gender differences disappeared when the instructions emphasized how these abilities could help in stereotypically feminine occupations, such as interior decoration. Similarly, Roberts and Bell (2000) found that familiarity with a mental rotation task also impacts performance. Their data demonstrate that when college women and men are given a chance to become familiar with a computerized mental rotation task prior to testing, gender differences in mental rotation disappear.

Olga Favreau (1993) pointed out that statistically significant gender differences often arise from studies in which most men and women actually receive similar scores. Refer to Figure 5.5, which Favreau derived from earlier research by Kail and his colleagues (1979). As represented in this figure, most men and women received scores between 2 and 8. The statistically significant gender difference can be traced almost entirely to 20% of the women who had very slow mental rotation speeds (Favreau & Everett, 1996).

Fortunately, both women and men can improve their mental-rotation ability by practicing mental-rotation strategies. For example, they become more skilled if they

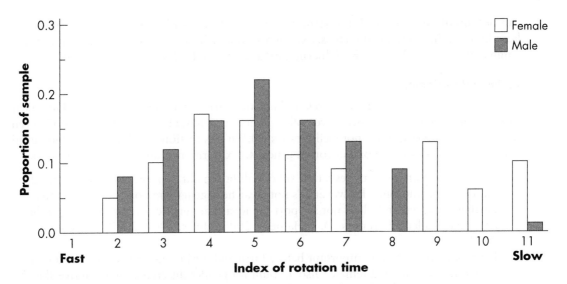

FIGURE **5.5** Amount of time required to mentally rotate a geometric figure, showing a large overlap between males' scores and females' scores.

Note: Faster scores represent better performance.

Sources: Based on Favreau (1993) and Kail et al. (1979).

practice the kind of video games where players need to rotate geometric shapes (Feng et al., 2007; Halpern, Aronson et al., 2007; Terlicki & Newcombe, 2005; Terlicki et al., 2008; Wright et al., 2008).

What can we conclude about spatial abilities? Even the most well-established gender difference—mental rotation—turns out to be elusive. The gender differences seem to decrease when the instructions emphasize that a spatial skill is related to a traditionally feminine area of interest. Furthermore, only a small sample of women seem to have difficulty with mental rotation. Also, scores on spatial tests improve with modest training.

In short, this erratic gender difference should not have major implications for women's lives. Furthermore, the gender differences in spatial skills cannot explain why only 12% of U.S. engineers are women, which was the question we considered at the beginning of this chapter.

Explaining the Gender Comparisons

We began this chapter by considering a large number of cognitive skills on which men and women are similar. Then we learned that the gender differences for most cognitive skills are minimal. However, the gender differences on a few tasks are somewhat larger, so we'll investigate some potential reasons for the difference.

Let's first consider the biological explanations, and then we'll examine the factors that focus on people's experiences, as well as their attitudes. However, it is important to note that the various explanations can be intertwined. For instance, suppose that you spend many weeks playing computer games that emphasize spatial knowledge. This experience can potentially modify both the structure of your brain and your attitudes. Therefore, keep in mind that biological factors, experience, and attitudes cannot be divided into three completely separate lists (D. F. Halpern, 2004a, 2007; D. F. Halpern & Ikier, 2002).

Biological Explanations

It's ironic that the media and some researchers are extremely eager to embrace a biological explanation of gender differences (Brescoll & LaFrance, 2004; Hyde & Lindberg, 2007), even though those differences are not well established.[1] In this section, we'll divide the biological explanations into three major categories: genetics, sex hormones, and brain organization.

1. A genetic explanation suggests that spatial ability might be a recessive trait carried on the X chromosome. However, it's not clear how genetic factors would operate. Furthermore, research does not support the idea that genetic factors directly produce cognitive gender differences (D. F. Halpern, 2000; Hines, 2004, 2007; Newcombe, 2007b).

2. Hormones are critically important before birth and during puberty. Could the level of hormones in males and females also account for gender differences in cognitive skills? However, it's not clear how hormonal factors would operate. In addition, the results are often complex or contradictory (Hampson & Moffat, 2004; Newcombe, 2007b). Furthermore, in some of the studies, the research methods were not carefully controlled (M. Hines, 2004, 2007).

3. The last category of biological explanations focuses on brain organization, specifically, the potential gender differences in brain lateralization. **Lateralization** means that the two halves (or hemispheres) of the brain function somewhat differently. In humans, the left hemisphere tends to be faster and more accurate on language tasks, and the right hemisphere tends to be faster and more accurate on spatial tasks.

A typical lateralization theory might argue that men use only the right hemisphere to perform spatial tasks. In contrast, women may use both hemispheres to perform all cognitive tasks (D. F. Halpern, 2000; M. Hines, 2004). This approach argues that women work slowly on a spatial task because only a small portion of the right hemisphere is available to process this spatial information.

However, there's little evidence that men actually *do* have more complete lateralization, and the results of studies are often contradictory (Clements et al., 2006; Hyde & Lindberg, 2007; Sommer et al., 2004; Sommer et al., 2008). For example, one study was widely cited in the media as "proof" that men's brains show more lateralization (B. A. Shaywitz et al., 1995). However, the media failed to mention that only 11 of the 19 female participants showed the balanced-hemisphere pattern proposed by lateralization theory (Favreau, 1997).

Still other studies report gender similarities in lateralization, or else only weak gender differences (D. F. Halpern & Collaer, 2005; Hyde & Lindberg, 2007; Medland et al., 2002; Ullman et al., 2008). For instance, Frost and her colleagues (1999) studied language processing in a large sample of men and women. The brain-imaging data revealed gender similarities: Both women and men showed strong lateralization, with most activity in the left hemisphere (Gernsbacher & Kaschak, 2003). In addition, no one has yet shown that

---

[1]Biological factors—such as genetics and brain structure—are clearly important in accounting for individual differences in various cognitive abilities. For example, these biological factors help explain why some people earn high scores on a math test, whereas other people earn low scores. As emphasized in this discussion, however, biological factors cannot adequately account for gender differences on cognitive tasks.

these brain differences actually *cause* the gender differences on cognitive tests (Caplan & Caplan, 2009; D. F. Halpern, 2000; Hyde & Lindberg, 2007).

Conceivably, at some time in the future, researchers might identify a biological factor that helps to explain gender differences. However, keep in mind that the differences requiring explanation are typically small and inconsistent. Additionally, simply identifying a biological difference doesn't tell us anything about how that biological difference came to be, or whether it has anything to do with the behavioral, cognitive, or psychological gender differences we are trying to measure. In summary, it helps to be cautious about assuming that cognitive gender differences can be explained by genetics, hormones, or brain structure.

Experience as an Explanation

Many theorists have suggested additional approaches to explaining cognitive gender comparisons. For example, let's consider how men and women differ in the amount of experience they have had with mathematics and spatial tasks.

1. As we noted on page 154, male and female students now take a similar number of math courses during high school (Chipman, 2004; De Lisi & McGillicuddy-De Lisi, 2002). However, boys are more likely to belong to a chess club, be members of a math team, learn about numbers in sports, and have more experience with computers (J. Cooper & Weaver, 2003; J. E. Jacobs et al., 2004; Newcombe et al., 2002).

   Compared to girls, boys also have more experience with maps, video games, and other spatial tasks. As we noted earlier, this additional practice helps boys perform a mental-rotation task relatively quickly and accurately (D. F. Halpern & Ikier, 2002; Roberts & Bell, 2000; Sanz de Acedo Lizarraga & García Ganuza, 2003).
2. Parents and teachers may provide different experiences for boys and girls (Wigfield et al., 2002). For example, parents spend more time explaining science concepts to their sons than to their daughters (Crowley et al., 2001; Tenenbaum et al., 2005).
3. The media seldom feature women in nontraditional situations. When elementary textbooks show how people use mathematics, they often include more pictures of boys than girls. The girls also appear primarily in helping roles (Kimball, 1995). Similarly, computer magazines include more pictures of boys than girls. When a picture does show a woman using a computer, the text frequently includes a stereotypical comment, such as the attractive colors produced by the printer (Burlingame-Lee & Canetto, 2005). These ads imply that women focus on superficial "feminine" aspects of computers, rather than their usefulness in math and science.

Attitudes as an Explanation

We have reviewed several *biological* explanations for gender differences, as well as explanations that focus on mathematics and spatial *experience*. Let's now examine gender differences in *attitudes* about mathematics.

1. Parents' and teachers' attitudes can influence their children's self-confidence indirectly. For instance, if parents and teachers hold strong stereotypes about girls' poor performance in math and science, they may convey these stereotypes to their daughters (Bhanot & Jovanovic, 2005; Hyde, 2007; J. E. Jacobs et al., 2004). Teachers may have especially low expectations for Black and Latina girls (S. Jones, 2003; Ruffins, 2007).
2. By the age of 11—or even earlier—boys often perceive themselves as more competent in math than girls do, even though boys may actually receive lower grades (Byrnes, 2004; Crombie et al., 2005; Rudman & Glick, 2008; Skaalvik & Skaalvik, 2004).

In addition, boys typically have more positive attitudes toward mathematics than girls do (Cunningham, Ralph, Mulvaney Hoyer, and Sparks, 2015; E. M. Evans et al., 2002).

3. By about the age of 10, many students believe that math, computers, and science are primarily associated with men (J. Cooper & Weaver, 2003; Räty et al., 2004; J. L. Smith et al., 2005). As noted in Chapter 3, people tend to prefer activities that are consistent with their gender roles. Accordingly, many girls may avoid math because it seems "too masculine" (Makarova, Aeschlimann, & Herzog, 2019).

4. Stereotype threat may decrease girls' performance on mathematics and spatial tests. In Chapter 2, we introduced the concept of **stereotype threat**; if you belong to a group that is hampered by a negative stereotype, and you are reminded about your membership in that group, your performance may suffer (Chipman, 2004; Davies & Spencer, 2004; Gibson, Losee, & Vitiello, 2014; C. M. Steele et al., 2002). Take a moment to review the important study by Shih and her colleagues (1999) about stereotype threat, which we discussed on pages 69–70.

Now, imagine that a young woman is beginning to take a challenging math test. Suppose that she thinks to herself, "This is a test where women just can't do well." She is likely to have many more negative thoughts than a young man with similar math ability (Cadinu et al., 2005). As a result, she might make more errors on this important test.

Researchers have conducted numerous studies about stereotype threat in connection with mathematics (e.g., Good et al., 2003; Gresky et al., 2005; J. L. Smith, 2004; Smith et al., 2005). Most of them report that women earn lower scores when stereotype threat is present than when it is absent. Furthermore, when Dustin Thoman and his colleagues (2008) told college women that men score higher on math tests because they try harder, these women actually *improved* their math scores.

We have discussed three categories of factors that can contribute to the gender differences in spatial and mathematics tasks. These three categories focus on gender differences in biology, experience, and attitudes. However, as Janet Hyde and Amy Mezulis (2001) concluded, "If the extensive examination of gender differences over the past several decades has taught us anything, it may be that gender differences are (1) often small in magnitude and (2) low in frequency compared with the vast similarities between the sexes" (p. 555). Furthermore, not one of these cognitive gender differences is so substantial that it has major implications for the career performance of women and men, a topic we will explore in Chapter 7.

Section Summary

Cognitive Abilities

1. No consistent gender differences are found in areas such as general intelligence, general knowledge, concept formation, problem solving, or creativity..

2. On memory tasks, women are more skilled than men in remembering life events, recognizing faces, and remembering objects they had been exposed to previously. However, women and men are equally skilled in remembering abstract shapes.

3. At present, gender differences in verbal skills are minimal, but boys are somewhat more likely than girls to have reading disabilities.

(continues)

> **Section Summary** *(continued)*
>
> 4. Gender differences in mathematics ability are negligible on most tests. Girls generally receive higher grades than boys in their math courses. However, men generally receive higher scores on the SAT mathematics test, a test that underpredicts women's college math grades.
> 5. Gender differences are minimal on spatial visualization tasks, moderate on spatial perception tasks, and more substantial on mental rotation tasks. Still, most men and women receive similar scores on mental rotation tests. Also, gender differences on mental rotation tests disappear when the task is described as a feminine one or when people receive training on the task.
> 6. Biological explanations for gender differences in cognitive skills include genetics, hormones, and brain organization (e.g., brain lateralization); however, research does not strongly support any of these explanations.
> 7. Social explanations for gender differences in cognitive skills include several that emphasize gender differences in experience (extracurricular activities, illustrations in books and magazines, and treatment by adults). Several other social explanations focus on math attitudes (parents' and teachers' attitudes, perceptions of math competence, beliefs about math being masculine, and stereotype threat).

5-3 Attitudes About Achievement

Learning Objectives

To explain how gender is related to attitudes about achievement, you can ...

5-3-1   Summarize similarities and differences in achievement motivation among the genders.

5-3-2   Describe which factors affect people's levels of self-confidence on challenging tasks.

5-3-3   Describe gender differences in people's reactions to evaluations from others.

5-3-4   Identify factors that influence how people make attributions for their success.

So far, we've learned that women and men are generally similar in their cognitive abilities. The cognitive differences are never large enough to explain the tremendous imbalances in the gender ratios found in many professions. Some observers argue that these imbalances can be traced, instead, to women's lack of motivation: Perhaps women simply don't want to achieve? In this section, we'll explore aspects of **achievement motivation**, which is the desire to accomplish something on your own and to do it well (Hyde & Kling, 2001).

In a classic article, Arnold Kahn and Janice Yoder (1989) noted that many theorists have claimed that women are missing from certain prestigious fields because they have personal "deficiencies" that inhibit their achievement. However, the research actually shows that women are *more* likely than men to (a) have positive attitudes toward school, (b) spend time studying, and (c) earn higher grades (Ellis et al., 2008; Halpern, 2006a; Van de gaer et al., 2007). Women are also less likely than men to drop out of school and more likely to enroll in college (Eccles et al., 2003; Wigfield et al., 2006).

Demonstration 5.2

Reactions to Comments from Other People

Imagine that you have given a presentation on a project to an important group of people. Afterward, someone approaches you and says that you did a very good job: You used wonderful examples, and your ideas were interesting. Someone else rejects everything you had to say and disagrees with all your proposals. Then a third person comments, not on the content of your presentation but on your excellent speaking style.

How much would the feedback from these other people influence your self-confidence? Would your confidence rise or fall, depending on the nature of the comments, or would your self-evaluations tend to remain fairly stable?

Source: Based on T. Roberts (1991, p. 297).

As we'll discover in this section, the research reveals gender similarities in almost every area related to attitudes about achievement. Personal deficiencies cannot explain the gender differences in career patterns. In Chapter 7, we will explore several more valid explanations. Now, try Demonstration 5.2.

Let's begin our exploration of motivation by discussing gender similarities in people's desire for achievement. We'll learn that women and men sometimes differ in self-confidence, although gender similarities are often reported. Our next topic addresses gender comparisons in people's personal definitions of success. We'll also learn that women and men usually provide similar explanations for their achievements.

Achievement Motivation

To measure achievement motivation, researchers often ask the study participants to examine drawings of people in various situations and then to create stories based on these drawings. A person receives a high achievement motivation score if these stories emphasize working hard and excelling. The research, conducted with both Black and White participants, shows that men and women are similar in achievement motivation (Eccles et al., 2003; Hyde & Kling, 2001; Krishman & Sweeney, 1998; Mednick & Thomas, 1993).

Men and women are also similar in their **intrinsic motivation**, which is your tendency to work on a task for your own satisfaction, rather than for rewards such as money or praise (Grolnick et al., 2002). Furthermore, men and women are equally likely to emphasize motivation when they describe important events in their lives (Travis et al., 1991).

Now try Demonstration 5.3 (below) before reading further.

Confidence in Your Own Achievement and Ability

Self-confidence is another concept that is intertwined with achievement motivation. As we'll learn, gender differences do sometimes emerge in two areas: (1) Men often report more self-confidence than women do, and (2) men's self-confidence may be less influenced by the evaluations provided by other people.

Demonstration **5.3**

Defining Personal Success

A study by Laura Dyke and Steven Murphy (2006) asked successful women and men to define describe how they defined success for themselves. Below are several randomly selected definitions. For each quotation, guess whether the person is a woman or a man. Then check page 172 to find out whether you guessed correctly.

_____ 1. Success for me on a personal level is being happy, being at ease with myself, being able to sleep at night knowing that the decisions I am making are reasonable decisions, to be content in the direction that my life is going.

_____ 2. Well there are two things. I do like the outside recognition and certainly had a lot of that [in a previous job] ... I do enjoy that but the rest of the success is being good at a challenging job, being recognized as being good at it and knowing myself that I have done a good job.

_____ 3. I think it's just if you have peace of mind, and it has to do with family, your job, your friends, and if you can really just go home and only really worry about the files on your desk, and not have any other concerns about how your marriage or children are doing, where the next bump is coming from, or that you don't have debtors banging on your door. I think peace of mind and good health.

_____ 4. My success would be measured by acceptance by clients, being able to communicate with those people, establish myself as a key player. I really want to be considered one of the key players in the industry ... Someone asked me when I took this job what my goal was in this company, and I said by the time I am finished in 3 years I want my face on the cover of a business magazine.

_____ 5. So success would be defined as applying energy to relationships that are symbiotic and that way you can grow as a person, you can grow as a mentor to people. One of my biggest successes is helping people grow in their own jobs, to actually help them develop their careers and things. From my perspective the money comes naturally anyway so it's not a problem.

_____ 6. Probably the biggest thing for me is the freedom to pursue what I feel I would like to achieve as a person or to explore as a person in the time that I have. So my idea of success is to free myself as much as possible from feeling what I'm doing seems just to maintain the lifestyle or just to maintain money, just to get enough money, as much as possible.

Source: With kind permission from Springer Science+Business Media: Sex Roles, "How We Define Success: A Qualitative Study of What Matters Most to Women and Men," Vol. 55, 2006, pp. 357–71, L. S. Dyke and S. Murphy.

Level of Self-Confidence

Boys and girls may not differ significantly in their academic self-confidence (Stevens et al., 2007). However, several studies suggest that men are more self-confident about their ability than women are (Eccles et al., 2003; Ellis et al., 2008; Furnham, 2000).[2] In a representative study, Pallier (2003) administered a test of general knowledge to college students. Men gave much higher estimates of their scores on this test, compared to women. However, their actual scores were similar. Let's consider several factors that can influence gender differences in self-confidence.

1. *The Type of Setting.* Researchers have found that gender differences in self-confidence are larger when people make public rather than private estimates (J. Clark & Zehr, 1993; Daubman et al., 1992; Lundeberg et al., 2000). Women are especially likely to give low estimates for their grade-point average when another student has already announced that they have low grades (Heatherington et al., 1993, 1998). One possible explanation is that women are more likely than men to be modest when they are with other people (Daubman et al., 1992; Wosinska et al., 1996).

2. *The Type of Task.* Gender differences in self-confidence tend to be larger on a task that is considered traditionally masculine, rather than one that is considered neutral or traditionally feminine (S. Beyer, 1998; Eccles et al., 2003). For instance, Brownlow and her colleagues (1998) compared the strategies of contestants on the TV game show *Jeopardy.* On stereotypically masculine topics, men bet a higher percentage of their earnings than the women did. On neutral and stereotypically feminine topics, men and women used similar betting strategies.

3. *Personal Characteristics of the Individual.* Chatard and his colleagues (2007) asked French high school students to recall their score on an important mathematics examination that they had completed two years earlier. For students with strong stereotypes about gender differences in math ability, the boys overestimated their scores and girls underestimated their scores. For students who believed in gender similarities in math ability, girls and boys provided similar estimates.

Furthermore, Buchanan and Selmon (2008) studied **self-efficacy**, which is a person's belief that they have the ability to achieve a goal. They found that Black women, Black men, and White women had higher self-efficacy if they had nontraditional beliefs about gender roles. In contrast, for White men, there was no relationship between self-efficacy and gender roles.

Be sure to try Demonstration 5.2, on page 164, above before reading further.

Self-Confidence and Evaluation Provided by Others

Now let's consider a second issue, focusing on the *stability* of a person's self-confidence. Specifically, Tomi-Ann Roberts and Susan Nolen-Hoeksema (1989, 1994) demonstrated that comments from other people can influence women's self-confidence. In contrast, men's self-confidence is more stable. Compared to these findings, how did you respond to Demonstration 5.2?

In an important study on responses to other people's comments, Roberts and Nolen-Hoeksema (1989) asked students to work on a series of challenging cognitive tasks.

---

[2]People sometimes assume that women are underconfident. An alternative viewpoint is that men are overconfident and that women have the appropriate level of self-confidence (Hyde & Mezulis, 2001; Tavris, 1992).

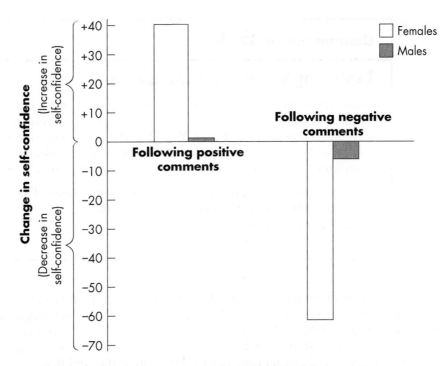

FIGURE **5.6** Change in self-confidence, following either positive or negative comments.

Note: Negative numbers indicate a decrease in self-confidence; positive numbers indicate an increase.

Sources: Based on T. Roberts and Nolen-Hoeksema (1989).

After several minutes, the participants rated their self-confidence in terms of the likelihood that they could do well on the task. A few minutes later, half of the participants—chosen at random—received positive comments from the researcher (e.g., "You are doing very well" or "You are above average at this point in the task"). The other half of the participants received negative comments (e.g., "You are not doing very well" or "You are below average at this point in the task"). Several minutes later, they all rated their self-confidence a second time.

Figure 5.6 presents the change in self-confidence between the first and the second rating period. Notice that the men's self-confidence ratings were not significantly changed by the nature of the comments other people made. In contrast, the women's self-confidence rose dramatically after receiving positive comments, and it fell even more dramatically after receiving negative comments.

This research has been replicated in the workplace, after bank employees had been evaluated by their supervisor (M. Johnson & Helgeson, 2002). Once again, women were more responsive to the feedback from other people. But why should men and women react differently to people's comments? One reason is that women may be more likely than men to believe that other people's evaluations are accurate assessments of their performance (Johnson & Helgeson, 2002; Roberts & Nolen-Hoeksema, 1994). Furthermore, women may be more likely to use the information from these evaluations in assessing their own performance, even when the evaluations are not accurate (Van Blyderveen & Wood, 2001).

Demonstration 5.4

Explaining Successful Performance

Think about the last time you received a good grade on a test. A number of different factors could have been responsible for your success. Four possible factors are listed below. You have 100 points to divide among these four factors. Assign points to reflect the extent to which each factor contributed to your success; the points must add up to 100.

_____ I have high ability for the subject that was covered on that test.
_____ I put a lot of effort into studying for that test.
_____ The test was easy.
_____ It was just luck.

When we first read about these gender differences in response to others' comments, we'll confess that we were dismayed. Men apparently trust their own judgments, whereas women seem to adjust their self-confidence in response to whatever comments they happen to hear. But then we recalled the male-as-normative issue, which we discussed on page 67 in Chapter 2. Maybe we shouldn't conclude that men are stable and that women are fickle. Instead, men may be overly rigid, not questioning their initial judgment. In contrast, women may be appropriately flexible, willing to listen and respond to new information. Ideally, people *should* respond to an evaluation when it comes from well-informed experts. These are examples of how to avoid female deficit interpretations of research findings.

Personal Definitions of Success

Before reading further, be sure to try Demonstration 5.3, and then refer to page 172 to check whether your guesses were accurate. Lorraine Dyke and Steven Murphy (2006) selected highly successful professional women and men in the Ottawa region of Canada. A trained interviewer then asked each person to define success for themselves. Demonstration 5.3 includes representative quotations from each of six individuals.

Dyke and Murphy found that women were somewhat more likely than men to emphasize a balance between professional achievement and personal relationships, rather than focusing primarily on their profession. Furthermore, men were more likely than women to emphasize material success. Still, your results from Demonstration 5.3 might suggest that the gender differences are not clear-cut.

Attributions for Your Own Success

Try Demonstration 5.4 before reading further. This demonstration asks you to make attributions about your own performance on an achievement task. **Attributions** are explanations about the causes of your behavior.

Check your answers to Demonstration 5.4. When people have been successful on an achievement task, they often attribute that success to some combination of four factors: (1) ability, (2) effort, (3) task easiness, and (4) luck. Keep your own answers to this demonstration in mind as we examine the research on gender comparisons in the relative importance of ability.

Incidentally, this topic of attributions may seem familiar, because we examined a similar topic in connection with gender stereotypes in Chapter 2. In that chapter, we learned that the *gender of the stimulus* often influences attributions. Specifically, when people make judgments about men, they tend to attribute the success of men to their high ability. In contrast, when they make judgments about women, they tend to attribute the success of women to other factors, such as an easy task or luck.

In this chapter, though, we are examining the *gender of the person making the judgments*. Several classic studies suggested that men are more likely than women to give credit to their own ability (e.g., Deaux, 1979). However, two meta-analyses concluded that gender differences in attributional patterns are minimal (D. Sohn, 1982; Whitley et al., 1986). Other studies also conclude that women and men are generally similar in the reasons that they provide for their success or failure (Mednick & Thomas, 1993; Mezulis et al., 2004; Wigfield et al., 2002).

Let's consider several factors that influence whether women and men have different patterns of attribution for their own success on a task.

1. **The Type of Setting.** When other people are around, men are more likely than women to credit their own ability. When men and women provide attributions in private, their responses are typically similar (J. H. Berg et al., 1981).
2. **The Type of Task.** Men are more likely than women to use the "ability explanation" on stereotypically masculine tasks such as earning high grades in mathematics (C. R. Campbell & Henry, 1999; A. K. F. Li & Adamson, 1995). Similarly, women are more likely than men to use the "ability explanation" on stereotypically feminine tasks such as earning high grades in an English course (S. Beyer, 1998/1999; R. A. Clark, 1993). However, when women are told that they earned a *low* score on a math test, they tend to attribute this poor performance to a lack of math ability (Kiefer & Shih, 2006).
3. **The Age of the Individual.** Between the ages of about 13 and 25, females and males tend to have similar attribution patterns. However, among people older than 25, men are more likely than women to say, "I did well because I have high ability" (Mezulis et al., 2004).

At the beginning of this section on achievement motivation, we noted that theorists have often favored a "women are deficient" rationale to explain why women are less likely than men to hold prestigious positions in society. However, the discussion of achievement motivation, self-confidence, and attributions reveals the same pattern we have discussed throughout most of this chapter. Consistent with Theme 1, people are typically similar on most tasks. When gender differences do emerge, they can usually be traced to characteristics of the social setting or the specifics of the task. With attribution patterns, the gender differences are so small and readily modifiable that a blame-the-person explanation does not seem useful.

We have emphasized in this chapter that women resemble men in both cognitive ability and motivational factors. In Chapter 6, we will continue our search for explanations about the lack of women in prestigious occupations. Specifically, we will consider gender comparisons in social and personality characteristics. Then, in Chapter 7, we will turn our attention to women's work experiences to try to identify external factors that account for gender differences in employment patterns.

Section Summary

Achievement Motivation and Attitudes About Success

1. Women and men are similar in their achievement motivation and intrinsic motivation.
2. Men are sometimes more self-confident than women on achievement tasks, especially (a) on tasks involving public estimates of self-confidence, (b) on traditionally masculine tasks, and (c) when a person has strong beliefs about gender differences.
3. Comments from other people are more likely to influence women's self-confidence than men's.
4. Women are somewhat more likely than men to define personal success in terms of a balance between professional achievement and personal relationships.
5. Women and men tend to use similar attributions when explaining their successes. However, gender differences may emerge (a) when making statements in public, (b) when performing gender-stereotyped tasks, and (c) for adults older than 25.

Chapter Review Questions

1. Suppose that your local newspaper carries the headline: "Test Shows Men Are More Creative." The article reports that men had an average score of 78 on a creativity test compared to an average score of 75 for women. Based on the cautions discussed at the beginning of this chapter, why would you be hesitant to conclude that the gender differences in creativity are substantial?

2. Recall the cognitive abilities for which researchers have reported no consistent gender differences. Think of several people whom you know well. Do the conclusions about those abilities match your observations about these individuals?

3. When we examined gender comparisons in memory, we noted that the research in this area is mixed. Describe the specific gender comparisons that researchers have conducted, and note whether these results apply to the women and men whom you know well.

4. Imagine that a third-grade teacher tells you that the girls in her class are much better readers than the boys. What would you answer, based on the information in this chapter?

5. The sections on mathematics and spatial abilities revealed inconsistent gender differences. Which areas showed the smallest gender differences, and which showed the largest? Which potential biological and/or social explanations might account for these differences?

6. Imagine that your local newspaper features an article that claims there are large gender differences in math ability. You decide to write a letter to the editor; describe four points that you would emphasize in your letter.

7. The research on topics related to achievement motivation illustrates how gender differences rarely apply to all people in all situations. Describe some variables that determine whether gender differences will occur in self-confidence and in attributions for one's own success.

8. We discussed two factors that influence whether women and men differ with respect

to self-confidence in achievement settings. Keeping these factors in mind, think of a concrete situation in which gender differences are relatively large. Then think of an example of a situation in which gender differences are probably minimal.

9. In Chapter 6, we'll learn that—in comparison to men—women are somewhat more attuned to the emotions of other people. How is this sensitivity to emotions related to an observation in the current chapter that women are somewhat more attuned to social factors and other people's emotions when they make judgments about self-confidence and attributions for success? Also, how is sensitivity to others related to the discussion of self-confidence on pages 164 to 168?

10. To solidify your knowledge in preparation for the chapter on women and work (Chapter 7), think of a prestigious profession that employs relatively few women. Review each of the cognitive abilities and motivational factors discussed in this chapter. Do any of these factors sufficiently explain the relative absence of women in that profession?

Key Terms

frequency distribution (p. 146)

box-score approach (p. 148)

counting approach (p. 148)

meta-analysis (p. 148)

verbal fluency (p. 152)

reading disability (p. 153)

validity (p. 156)

spatial abilities (p. 156)

spatial visualization (p. 156)

spatial perception (p. 158)

mental rotation (p. 158)

lateralization (p. 160)

stereotype threat (p. 162)

achievement motivation (p. 163)

intrinsic motivation (p. 164)

self-efficacy (p. 166)

attributions (p. 168)

Recommended Readings

Ceci, S. J., & Williams, W. M. (Eds.). (2007b). *Why aren't more women in science? Top researchers debate the evidence.* Washington, DC: American Psychological Association. Here is an excellent book that examines an extremely important question about women and science. The editors chose superb researchers to provide a variety of perspectives on this topic.

Gallagher, A. M., & Kaufman, J. C. (Eds.). (2004). *Gender differences in mathematics: An integrative psychological approach.* New York: Cambridge University Press. It's not clear why the editors chose the term "gender differences," rather than "gender comparisons." However, I strongly recommend this book, which includes 15 chapters that address the research on gender and math.

Halpern, D. F., Aronson, J., et al. (2007). *Encouraging girls in math and science.* Washington, DC: National Center for Education Research. This book is an excellent resource for both psychologists and educators, providing clear summaries of the relevant research, as well as important recommendations about policy and practice.

Wigfield, A., et al. (2015). Development of achievement motivation and engagement. In R. M. Lerner (Series Eds.) & M. Lamb (Vol. Ed.), *Handbook of child psychology and developmental science:* Vol. 3. *Socioemotional processes* (7th ed., pp. 657–700). Hoboken, NJ: Wiley. Surprisingly few resources focus on topics related to achievement. This chapter is especially useful for a general orientation about achievement, as well as information about gender comparisons.

Answers to Demonstrations

Demonstration 5.1: a.1: Rotate the pattern so that it looks like two mountain peaks, and place the leftmost segment along the top-left portion of the little white triangle. a.2: This pattern fits along the right side of the two black triangles on the left. a.3: Rotate this figure about 100 degrees to the right, so that it forms a slightly slanted z, with the top line coinciding with the top line of the top white triangle. b. The line should be horizontal, not tilted. c. 1c, 2d.

Demonstration 5.3: Numbers 1, 2, and 4 are women; Numbers 3, 5, and 6 are men.

6   Gender Comparisons in Social and Personality Characteristics

Learning Objectives

After studying this chapter, you will be able to …

6-1 Describe gender differences in communication patterns.

6-2 Identify gender similarities and differences in characteristics related to helping and caring.

6-3 Describe gender differences in characteristics related to aggression and power.

Did You Know?

- Women tend to make eye contact with their conversational partners more than men do, especially when talking with someone of the same gender (p. 181).
- During the Nazi holocaust, non-Jewish women were more likely than non-Jewish men to save the lives of Jewish people (p. 188).
- According to self-reports, men and women are equally satisfied with their friendships (p. 193).
- Men are more likely to be persuaded by a woman who uses tentative language than by a woman who uses assertive language (p. 202).

A popular magazine featured an article titled "Uncommon Valor." Think of the word *valor*. Many people envision a heroic man rescuing a helpless woman. However, the stories were refreshingly gender balanced. Yes, 24-year-old Ryan Lane had rescued five people from a flood in Kansas. However, the feature story described how Roxanna Vega, 16 years old, rescued her young cousins after their mother had deliberately driven over a cliff. When the car crashed, Roxanna had broken her back, ankle, and arm, yet she struggled up the 160-foot cliff to get help from passing motorists (Jerome & Meadows, 2003).

In Chapter 5, we learned that gender similarities are common when we consider cognitive abilities and achievement. In this chapter about social and personality characteristics, we'll once again learn about many gender similarities, although we'll discuss several small to moderate gender differences (Eagly, 2001; M. C. Hamilton, 2001; J. D. Yoder & Kahn, 2003). For example, we'll learn that men are typically more likely than women to be heroic rescuers, although the overall differences in helping behavior are not large (S. W. Becker & Eagly, 2004).

In Chapter 6, we will explore gender comparisons in three areas: (1) communication patterns, (2) characteristics related to helping and caring, and (3) aggression and power. The social constructionist approach is especially useful when we consider these socially oriented topics. According to the **social constructionist approach**, we construct or invent our own versions of reality, based on prior experiences, social interactions, and beliefs. The social constructionist approach often focuses on language as a mechanism for categorizing our experiences—for example, our experiences about gender (K. J. Gergen & M. M. Gergen, 2004; Lorber, 2005b; Marecek et al., 2004).

Here's an example of the way we construct personality characteristics. Quickly answer the following question: Who are more emotional, men or women? Most people immediately respond, "Women, of course" (Brody, Hall, & Stokes, 2016; J. R. Kelly & Hutson-Comeaux, 2000). But what kinds of emotions did you consider? Only sadness and crying? Why don't we include anger, one of the primary human emotions? When a man pounds his fist into a wall in anger, we don't comment, "Oh, he's so emotional." Cultural norms in the United States construct the word *emotional* to emphasize the emotions that are typically associated with women.

Notice, too, that we interpret a behavior differently, depending upon who is displaying the behavior. Suppose that you are entering a classroom, and you meet someone sitting alone and crying. If the person is a man, you are likely to think that he is upset about a genuinely important problem (L. Warner & Shields, 2007). Now imagine that the person is a woman. Would you judge her problem to be equally important?

The final section of this chapter explores how social constructionism also shapes the way we perceive aggression. Specifically, we define the word *aggression* primarily in terms of the kinds of aggression associated with men. The social constructionist approach forces us to consider alternative interpretations of our communication patterns and our social interactions (K. J. Gergen & M. M. Gergen, 2004). When social constructionists examine gender, they focus on a central question: How do cultural norms create gender and maintain it in our communication patterns and in our interpersonal relationships?

You and I do not construct gender independently. Instead, cultural norms provide us with schemas and other information. All this information operates like a set of lenses through which we can interpret the events in our lives (Bem, 1993). In Chapters 2 and 3, we examined how the media provide cultural lenses for both adults and children. Women are typically represented as gentle, nurturant, and submissive, whereas men are represented as independent, self-confident, and aggressive. Cultural norms establish different social roles for women and men, so we should find that people usually want to uphold these ideals (Popp et al., 2003; Shields, 2005).

Before you read further in this chapter, refer to pages 145–147 and re-read the five cautions about research on gender comparisons in cognitive skills. These cautions are also relevant when we consider gender comparisons in social and personality characteristics. For example, we read in Chapter 5 that the social setting influences people's academic self-confidence and their attribution patterns. However, the social setting has a relatively modest impact on cognitive and achievement tasks because people typically perform these tasks in relative isolation.

The social setting is more important when we consider social and personality characteristics. Humans talk, smile, help, and act aggressively in the presence of other people. The social setting provides a rich source of information that people examine to make sense of the world (J. D. Yoder & Kahn, 2003). If the social setting has such an important influence on whether people act in a gender-stereotyped fashion, then a characteristic such as "nurturant" is not an inevitable, essential component of all women. Furthermore, a characteristic such as "aggressive" is not an inevitable, essential component of all men.

Several factors related to the social setting have an important influence on the size of the gender differences in social and personality characteristics (Wester et al., 2002; J. D. Yoder & Kahn, 2003; Zakriski et al., 2005). Here are some examples:

1. *Gender differences are usually largest when other people are present.* For instance, women are especially likely to react positively to infants when other people are nearby.
2. *Gender differences are generally largest when gender is prominent and other shared roles are minimized.* For example, at a singles' bar, a person's gender is very relevant, so gender differences are likely to be large. In contrast, at a professional conference—where men and women have the same occupations—the work role will be emphasized, and gender differences will be relatively small.
3. *Gender differences are usually largest when the behavior requires specific gender-related skills.* For example, men might be especially likely to volunteer to change a tire or perform a similar skill traditionally associated with cultural norms related to masculinity.

Notice, then, that gender differences are especially prominent when a social setting encourages us to think about gender and to wear an especially powerful set of gender lenses. In other social settings, however, women and men usually behave with remarkable similarity. Now let's explore our first topic, which focuses on verbal and nonverbal communication patterns. Later, we'll consider characteristics related to helping and caring, as well as characteristics related to aggression and power.

6-1 Communication Patterns

Learning Objectives

To describe gender differences in communication patterns, you can ...

6-1-1 Provide examples of how women and men differ in talkativeness, interruptions, and language styles with others.

6-1-2 Describe how women's and men's language is often similar in terms of content.

6-1-3 Summarize gender differences in nonverbal communication between women and men.

6-1-4 Explain how people differ in decoding the nonverbal communication of others.

6-1-5 Differentiate between power and social status versus social learning explanations of nonverbal communication.

The term *communication* typically suggests verbal communication, or communication with words. However, communication can also be nonverbal. **Nonverbal communication** refers to all forms of human communication that do not focus on the actual words—including tone of voice, facial expression, body language, and even how far you stand from another person.

Both verbal and nonverbal communication are essential in our daily interactions. Unless you are reading this sentence before breakfast, you've probably already spoken to many people, smiled at them, and perhaps avoided eye contact with others. Let's now examine gender comparisons in both verbal and nonverbal communication.

Verbal Communication

John Gray's classic best-selling book, *Men Are from Mars, Women Are from Venus,* claims that men and women "almost seem to be from different planets, speaking different languages" (Gray, 1992, p. 5). However, Gray's book is based on speculation and informal observations rather than actual research. In reality, people of all genders are fairly similar in their patterns of verbal communication. The research also shows great individual differences—*within* each gender—in verbal communication patterns. Furthermore, social factors frequently influence whether the studies show gender similarities or gender differences (Athenstaedt et al., 2004; R. C. Barnett & Rivers, 2004; R. Edwards & Hamilton, 2004; Shields, 2002). Let's consider the research.

Talkativeness

According to the long-standing stereotype, women talk for hours. In reality, however, several studies show no substantial gender differences in the length of college students' conversations with their friends, their oral descriptions, and their written descriptions of vivid memories (Athenstaedt et al., 2004; Mehl et al., 2007; Niedźwieńska, 2003). Men and women are also equally talkative when they are being interviewed on talk shows (Brownlow et al., 2003).

In other research, men are *more* talkative than women, based on data gathered in elementary classrooms, college classrooms, and college students' conversations (Aries, 1998; M. Crawford, 1995; Eckert & McConnell-Ginet, 2003; Romaine, 1999; Thomson et al., 2001). In short, the research shows mixed results, but it does not support the "talkative woman" stereotype.

Interruptions

Researchers have discovered that interruptions can take multiple forms. Sometimes, people interrupt others to "take over" the conversation through intrusive interruptions. Suppose that you are telling a story about meeting a famous person. A listener interrupts after your first two sentences to say, "Oh, that sounds like the time I...." When researchers examine this kind of intrusive interruption, they find that men tend to interrupt more frequently than women do (Athenstaedt et al., 2004; Ellis et al., 2008). Other times, people interrupt others to request clarification, express support, or agree with the person talking. These types of affiliative, or supportive, interruptions are more common among women than men (Anderson & Leaper, 1998).

Some of the research on interruptions compares conversations between men in positions of power and women in positions of lower interpersonal power. These studies typically find that men in powerful positions interrupt others more than women do (Hancock & Rubin, 2015). However, in these cases, the interruptions can be at least partially explained by their relative level of interpersonal power, rather than gender (R. C. Barnett & Rivers, 2004; Romaine, 1999). Other research suggests that men interrupt significantly more often than women do in conversations with strangers and in competitive task settings. Still, gender differences may be minimal in other settings (Aries, 1996, 1998; Athenstaedt et al., 2004; C. West & Zimmerman, 1998b).

Language Style

Some theorists suggest that women's language style is very different from men's (e.g., Lakoff, 1990; Tannen, 1994). In reality, the gender differences are more subtle (Mulac et al., 2001;

Thomson et al., 2001; Weatherall, 2002). Boys and men are likely to curse more often and to use a larger vocabulary of obscene words, in comparison to girls and women (Blakemore et al., 2009; Jay, 2000; Newman et al., 2008; Pennebaker et al., 2003). However, other research shows only minimal gender differences in politeness during conversations or in writing style (S. Mills, 2003; Timmerman, 2002).

How about hesitant phrases such as "I'm not sure" or "It seems that"? This type of speech is called *tentative speech,* and it includes disclaimers like "I might be interpreting this incorrectly, but ..." as well as tag questions such as "It's a nice day, isn't it?" (Lakoff, 1990). A review of the literature suggests that women are more likely than men to use this speech pattern, often because it serves as a signal of greater interpersonal sensitivity to others rather than reflecting a lack of assertiveness (Leaper & Robnett, 2011; Mulac et al., 2001). Once again, however, the social setting can be important. For example, Carli (1990) found that people rarely used these hesitant phrases when they were talking with another person of the same gender. In contrast, when a woman was talking with a man, the woman was much more likely than the man to use this hesitant speech pattern.

The Content of Language

We have discussed how women and men talk, but what do they talk about? R. A. Clark (1998) asked students at the University of Illinois to report on all topics mentioned in their most recent conversation with a student of the same gender. Women and men were equally likely to talk about four categories of topics: (1) a person of another gender; (2) a person of the same gender; (3) academic issues; and (4) jobs. The only statistically significant gender difference was that men were more likely than women to talk about sports.

In general, women and men also use similar kinds of words in their conversations. Matthew Newman and his colleagues (2008) gathered data on the spoken and written language of 14,000 people. Next, they calculated the percentage of the time that each speaker talked about positive emotions, negative emotions, social processes, and so forth. As you would expect with such a large sample, some of the gender differences showed statistical significance. However, represented in Table 6.1 the gender differences did not show practical significance.

Let's consider one other important point about conversations. In our list of three generalizations about gender comparisons (page 174), we noted that gender differences are small when shared roles are emphasized. S. A. Wheelan and Verdi (1992) observed professionals in business, government, and service-oriented occupations who were attending a four-day group relations conference. This is clearly a setting in which work-related roles would be prominent. The researchers found that the men and the women were similar in the number of statements that challenged the leadership and also in the number of statements that supported other people's remarks.

The groups in Wheelan and Verdi's study met for many hours; most other studies have recorded relatively brief conversations. In Chapter 2, we learned that stereotypes are especially likely to operate when people do not have enough information about a person's qualifications. When people initially meet each other, these stereotypes may inhibit a competent woman's comments. As time passes, however, other group members begin to appreciate the woman's remarks, and their expectations become less gender based. As a consequence, gender differences typically grow smaller as conversations become longer (Aries, 1998).

TABLE **6.1**

Gender comparisons in the Relative Number of Sentences About a Variety of Topics, During Conversations with Same-Gender Friend (Newman et al., 2008).

Category	Examples	Relative Number of Words for Women	Relative Number of Words for Men
1. Positive emotions	happy, good	2.49	2.41
2. Negative emotions	nervous, hate	2.05	1.89
3. Social words	share, brother	9.54	8.51
4. Cognitive processes	think, know	7.35	7.17
5. Occupation	work, class	2.34	2.50
6. Sex	lust, pregnant	0.30	0.27

Source: Copyright 2008 From Discourse Processes 45 (3), "Gender Differences in Language Use: An Analysis of 14,000 Text Samples" by Matthew L. Newman, Carla J. Groom, Lori D. Handelman, and James W. Pennebaker. Reproduced by permission of Taylor & Francis Group, LLC., http://www.taylorandfrancis.com.

Demonstration **6.1**

Gender Differences in Body Posture

Which of these figures is a girl, and which is a boy? What cues are you using when you make your decision?

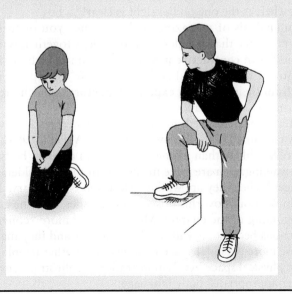

Nonverbal Communication

Try turning off the sound on a television game show and observing the nonverbal behavior. A transcript of the conversation between Mr. Game Show Host and Ms. Contestant would fail to capture much of the subtle communication between these two people. The nonverbal aspects of conversation are extremely important in conveying social messages. As we'll learn, gender differences are often substantial in certain kinds of nonverbal behavior, such as personal space, body position, and smiling.

Let's examine several components of nonverbal communication, beginning with the nonverbal messages that people send by means of their personal space, body posture, visual gaze, and facial expression. A fifth topic, decoding ability, examines gender comparisons in *interpreting* these nonverbal messages. As we'll read throughout this section, gender differences in nonverbal communication are typically larger than other kinds of gender differences (J. A. Hall, 1998). We'll also consider explanations and implications of these gender comparisons. Now try Demonstration 6.1 before you read any further.

Personal Space

The term **personal space** refers to the invisible boundary around each person—a boundary that other people should not invade during ordinary social interactions. You are probably most aware of personal space when a stranger comes too close and makes you feel uncomfortable. In general, women have smaller personal-space zones than men, regardless of whether they are interacting with others in real-life situations or in virtual environments as avatars (LaFrance & Henley, 1997; Nishihara & Okubo, 2015; Payne, 2001). As a result, when two women are talking to each other, they typically sit closer together than two men do.

Body Posture

Gender differences in body posture develop early in life. The drawings in Demonstration 6.1 were traced from yearbook pictures of two fifth-graders, and then other cues about gender—such as clothing—were equated. You can easily identify that the figure on the left is girl, whereas the one on the right is clearly a boy.

An analysis of magazines will convince you of further gender differences in body posture. Notice that females keep their legs together, with their arms and hands close to their bodies in **contractive postures** that convey submissiveness (LaFrance & Vial, 2016). In contrast, males sit and stand with their legs apart, and their hands and arms move away from their bodies in **expansive postures**, which are linked to feelings of power and dominance (Carney, Cuddy, & Yap, 2015).

Men appear relaxed; however, even when resting, women keep their postures more tensely contained (Bate & Bowker, 1997; J. A. Hall, 1984). When talking to another person, men are less likely than women to maintain an erect body posture (J. A. Hall et al., 2001). When walking, men are more likely to shift their shoulders from side to side; women seldom "swagger" when they are walking (Johnson & Tassinary, 2005).

Think about how this observation meshes with the gender differences we discussed at the beginning of the chapter. Men often use more "conversational space" in their verbal interactions because they may talk for longer and they may interrupt more often. Similarly, men use more personal space (distance from other people), and their own postures require greater physical space. As Demonstration 6.1 illustrates, even young children have mastered "gender-appropriate" body language.

Visual Gaze

When we consider gaze, gender as a subject variable is important. Research shows that women typically gaze more at their conversational partners than men do (Briton & Hall, 1995; LaFrance & Henley, 1997). This gender difference emerges during childhood; young girls spend more time making eye contact with their conversational partners.

Gender as a stimulus variable is even more powerful than gender as a subject variable. Specifically, people gaze at women more than they gaze at men (J. A. Hall, 1984, 1987). As a result, two women speaking to each other are likely to maintain frequent eye contact. In contrast, two men in conversation are likely to avoid making eye contact with each other for long periods of time. Prolonged eye contact is relatively uncommon between two men.

Facial Expression

Gender differences in facial expression are substantial. The most noticeable difference is that women smile more than men do (Ellis et al., 2008; Else-Quest et al., 2006; Kalat & Shiota, 2007). In a meta-analysis of 418 gender comparisons of smiling frequency, the d was 0.41 (LaFrance et al., 2003).

The magazines you examine in Demonstration 6.2 are likely to reveal smiling women and somber men. An inspection of yearbooks will probably confirm this gender difference. For example, in a classic study, Ragan (1982) examined nearly 1,300 portrait photographs and found that women were nearly twice as likely as men to smile broadly. In contrast, men were about eight times as likely as women to show no smile.

Gender differences in smiling are especially large when people interact with strangers (LaFrance et al., 2003). Furthermore, the gender differences are relatively large when people pose, for instance, for a yearbook photo, or when they know that someone is filming them. In contrast, women and men have more similar facial expressions in candid photos (J. A. Hall et al., 2001; LaFrance et al., 2003).

Demonstration **6.2**

Gender Differences in Smiling

For this demonstration, you will first need to assemble some online news articles that contain photos of people. Inspect the photos to identify smiling faces. (Let's define a smile as an expression in which the corners of the mouth are at least slightly upturned.) Record the number of women who smile, and divide it by the total number of women to calculate the percentage of women who smile. Repeat the process to calculate the percentage of men who smile. How do those two percentages compare? Does the gender comparison seem to depend on the kind of magazine you are examining (e.g., fashion and lifestyle sites versus news sites)?

Next, locate a high-school or college yearbook. Examine the portraits, and calculate the percentages of women and of men who are smiling. How do these two percentages compare?

The gender difference in smiling has important social implications. For example, positive responses, such as smiling, can affect the person who receives these pleasant messages. For example, you are likely to move closer to someone who is smiling (Miles, 2009). Furthermore, you often act in a more competent fashion when someone is smiling (P. A. Katz et al., 1993; Word et al., 1974). Therefore, when a typical man and woman interact, the woman's smiles and other positive reactions may encourage a man to feel competent and self-confident (Athenstaedt et al., 2004). However, the typical man does not smile much to encourage a woman.

The gender difference in smiling also has a more negative interpretation. You may have noticed that some women smile bravely when someone makes fun of them, tells an embarrassing joke in their presence, or sexually harasses them. In fact, social tension is a strong predictor of smiling in women. In other words, women often smile because they feel uncomfortable or embarrassed in the current social setting, not because they are enjoying the social interaction (J. A. Hall & Halberstadt, 1986; LaFrance et al., 2003). Related research shows that women are more likely than men to be aware that they are using false smiles, rather than genuine smiles (Woodzicka, 2008).

A related issue is that men and women may "send" different messages through their facial expressions. For instance, when people judge adults' facial expressions, they are more likely to detect anger in a man's facial expression (Becker et al., 2007; Shields et al., 2006).

Let's consider a study by Algoe and her colleagues (2000) in more detail. These researchers asked college students to make judgments about the facial expressions of adult men and women in photographs. These photos were carefully chosen so that the men and women showed similarly intense emotions.

As part of this study, Algoe and her colleagues (2000) asked people to judge a photo of either an angry man or an angry woman. In both cases, the person was described as an employee involved in a workplace incident. Figure 6.1 reflects that the man was judged to be

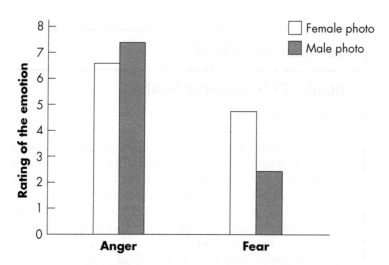

FIGURE **6.1** Ratings of anger and fear when judging the photo of an angry female or male employee.
Note: Minimum rating = 0; Maximum rating = 8
Source: Based on Algoe et al. (2000).

somewhat angrier than the woman. Furthermore, the angry woman was judged to be showing a moderate amount of fear, much more than the angry man showed. Apparently, when people interact with an angry woman, they perceive that she is actually somewhat afraid.

Other research demonstrates that people also perceive more sadness than anger in a woman's ambiguous facial expression. In contrast, they perceive more anger than sadness in a man's ambiguous facial expression (Plant et al., 2004).

Decoding Ability

So far, we have examined evidence of gender differences in several kinds of nonverbal behavior: personal space, body posture, visual gaze, and the facial expressions that people send to others. Decoding ability is different because it requires *receiving* messages, rather than sending them. Specifically, **decoding ability** refers to your skill in interpreting another person's nonverbal behavior and figuring out what emotion that person is feeling. A person who is a skilled decoder can examine a friend's facial expression, posture, and tone of voice and determine whether that person is in a good mood or a bad mood.

The research shows that women are more likely than men to decode nonverbal expressions accurately (L. R. Brody & Hall, 2000; Lim et al., 2008; Shields, 2002). For example, one meta-analysis of the research yielded a moderate effect size ($d = 0.41$); women were better decoders in 106 of 133 gender comparisons (J. A. Hall, 1984; J. A. Hall et al., 2000). Girls are also more accurate decoders than boys are (Bosacki & Moore, 2004; Einav & Hood, 2008; McClure, 2000). For adults, the gender difference in decoding also holds true cross-culturally, as demonstrated in studies conducted in Greece, New Guinea, Japan, and Poland (Biehl et al., 1997; J. A. Hall, 1984).

So far, we have reviewed gender differences in decoding emotion from facial expressions. Bonebright and her colleagues (1996) examined people's ability to decode emotion from voice cues. They instructed trained actors to record paragraph-long stories, each time using their voice to portray a specified emotion—fear, anger, happiness, or sadness—or neutrality. Then, undergraduate students listened to each recorded paragraph and tried to determine which emotion the speaker was trying to portray.

As represented in Figure 6.2, women were significantly more accurate than men in decoding voices that expressed fear, happiness, and sadness. These gender differences were small but consistent. No gender differences were found for neutral expressions or for anger—the one emotion where we might have expected men to be more accurate.

Potential Explanations for Gender Differences in Communication

Consistent with Theme 4 of this textbook, we must consider the large individual differences within each gender (R. Edwards & Hamilton, 2004). Still, we need to explain the gender differences in some kinds of verbal and nonverbal communication. Specifically, men often talk more, interrupt more, have larger personal-space zones, use more relaxed postures, gaze less, and smile less. Men also tend to be less skilled at decoding other people's facial expressions. Let's consider two explanations, which primarily address the gender differences in decoding ability and in smiling.

Power and Social Status Explanations

Researchers such as Marianne LaFrance and her coauthors argue that the most effective explanation for gender differences in communication is that men have more power and social status in many cultures (Helwig-Larsen et al., 2004; LaFrance et al., 2003;

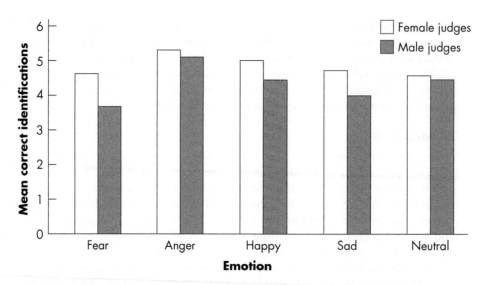

FIGURE **6.2** Men's and women's accuracy in decoding emotions from vocal cues.

Note: Maximum score = 6.

Source: With kind permission from Springer Science+Business Media: *Sex Roles,* "Gender Stereotypes in the Expression and Perception of Vocal Affect" Vol. 34, 1996, pp. 429–445, Terri L. Bonebright.

A. J. Stewart & McDermott, 2004). Powerful people are allowed to talk for a long time; less powerful people must listen. Powerful people don't need to smile, whereas low-power people are supposed to smile, even if they do not feel happy (Athenstaedt et al., 2004; LaFrance et al., 2003; Pennebaker et al., 2003).

Marianne LaFrance and Nancy Henley (1997) are especially interested in explaining the gender differences in decoding ability. They argued that low-power individuals must be especially attentive to powerful individuals so that they can respond appropriately. A low-ranking assistant must be vigilant for signs that the boss is angry, because those signs suggest that the boss shouldn't be interrupted or brought any bad news. In contrast, the boss doesn't need to be equally sensitive. According to the power-based explanation, the boss has little to gain from decoding the assistant's facial expression.

LaFrance and Henley (1997) argue that modern cultures usually assign dominant status to men and subordinate status to women. Therefore, even when a man and a woman are equivalent in other characteristics—such as age and occupation—the man will generally have more power. With that status, the man will use the verbal and nonverbal communication patterns that are characteristic of a boss, leaving the woman in the position of a relatively submissive assistant.

Social Learning Explanations

Judith Hall and her colleagues believe that social status and power cannot account for the gender differences in nonverbal decoding ability (J. A. Hall, 2006; J. A. Hall et al., 2005). For example, Hall and her colleagues (2001) studied interactions between high-status university employees and low-status university employees. They found that high-status employees smiled just as much as low-status employees.

Instead, researchers such as Hall and her colleagues argue that cultures provide roles, expectations, and socialization experiences that teach men and women how to communicate (Athenstaedt et al., 2004; J. A. Hall et al., 2000; Pennebaker et al., 2003; Weatherall, 2002). In other words, these researchers emphasize a social learning approach, which we discussed in Chapter 3.

According to the social learning approach, children are reinforced for behavior that is consistent with their gender. They are also punished for behavior that is more typical of other genders. Thus, a young girl may be scolded and told, "Let's put a smile on that face!" when she has been frowning. If she values the approval of other people, she will tend to smile more often. The girl also notices that women often smile and gaze intently at their conversational partners. In contrast, a boy will be criticized if he uses "feminine" hand gestures. A boy can certainly notice stereotypically masculine body movements by observing the men in his family, his community, and the media. A child who identifies as nonbinary may display behavior that is consistent with all genders and be either punished or reinforced for their behavior.

Girls also learn that they are supposed to pay attention to people's emotions, so they are likely to develop sensitivity to facial expressions. In addition, girls learn that they are supposed to care about people's emotional well-being, and a smile makes people feel welcome and accepted. Boys are less likely to learn these skills.

Conclusions

As with so many debates in psychology, both perspectives are probably at least partially correct. Our own sense is that the power hypothesis and the social learning approach combine fairly well to explain the gender differences in the communications that people send to others. However, the social learning approach seems more relevant than the power hypothesis in explaining people's ability to decode the emotions of other people. Consistent with J. A. Hall and Halberstadt's (1997) argument, We've known some executives and other individuals in powerful social positions who are skilled at reading other people's emotions from relatively subtle cues. Social sensitivity makes some people popular, and so they rise to positions of power.

Even if we aren't certain about the explanations, some gender differences remain. What should we do about them? With respect to verbal communication, women should feel comfortable about claiming their fair share of the conversation. Women do not have to smile when they are unhappy, and they do not need to occupy the smallest possible space on a couch. Men can interrupt less, they can smile more, and they can sit so that they occupy less space.

In discussing how communication patterns can be changed, let's remember that women do not have to necessarily strive to be more masculine in their behavior. This reaction would assume that male behavior must be normative. I recall an article in a magazine—intended for women executives—that urged woman to master high-powered, masculine verbal and nonverbal behavior. However, as we'll read later in the chapter, this strategy may backfire.

Furthermore, we cannot assume that women are the only ones who need to change their behavior. Instead, we should note that men may have learned inappropriate communication strategies. They have much to gain from adopting some of the strategies typically associated with women.

Section Summary

Communication Patterns

1. The social constructionist perspective helps us understand how cultures create different standards for the ideal social behavior of women and men.
2. Gender differences are largest when other people are present, when gender roles are emphasized, and when a task requires gender-related skills.
3. Research often reveals no gender differences in talkativeness, or else men talk more than women; in some settings, men also interrupt more.
4. With respect to language style, women may be less likely than men to use profanity; also, women use tentative language and hesitant phrases (e.g., "I'm not sure...") more often when talking with men than when talking with other women.
5. Gender differences in the content of conversations are usually minimal.
6. Women generally maintain smaller personal-space zones than men do, and their posture is more contractive and less relaxed.
7. Compared to men, women often gaze more at their conversational partners, especially when speaking with someone of the same gender.
8. Women usually smile more than men do, but their smiles may indicate social tension rather than pleasure. Also, people may misread women's angry facial expressions as being partly fearful.
9. Women are generally more accurate than men at decoding nonverbal messages that other people send, both in the United States and in other countries.
10. Some gender differences in communication can be traced to gender differences in power; however, social learning explanations (e.g., roles, expectations, and socialization) are equally important.
11. To change communication patterns, we must not emphasize how women should become more "masculine." Instead, men could benefit from adopting some of the strategies that are usually associated with women.

6-2 Characteristics Related to Helping and Caring

Learning Objectives

To identify gender similarities and differences in characteristics related to helping and caring, you can ...

6-2-1   Explain how altruistic behavior differs, depending on the gender of the helper.

6-2-2   Summarize gender differences in patterns of nurturance and empathy.

6-2-3   Differentiate between the justice vs. care approach to moral judgment and behavior.

6-2-4   Describe gender differences in attitudes about social justice.

6-2-5   Explain how women and men differ in their friendship styles and behaviors.

Demonstration 6.3

A Personal Dilemma

Suppose you have been anticipating settling in with a special television program: an old movie you have always wanted to experience, a sports championship game, or a binge-watch session with your favorite program. Just as you are all settled in and the show is about to begin, your best friend calls and asks you to help with something you had promised several days ago you would do—for example, painting a room or hanging pictures. You had assumed that your friend would need you sometime during the week but had not expected it to be right now. You want nothing else but to stay in your comfortable chair and watch this show, but you know your friend will be disappointed if you do not come over to help (R. S. L. Mills et al., 1989). For purposes of this demonstration, assume that you cannot record the program for future viewing. What would you choose to do in this dilemma?

Take a moment to think about a person helping someone else. Try to imagine the scene as vividly as possible. Now think about your imaginary scenario. Is this helpful person a man or a woman?

In the United States, we have two different stereotypes about gender differences in helpfulness. Men are considered more helpful in activities requiring heroism; they are supposed to take risks, even to help strangers. In contrast, women are considered more helpful and generous in offering assistance and emotional support to family members and close friends (Eisenberg et al., 2006; Frieze & Li, 2010). In later chapters, we'll explore how women provide this less obvious kind of helpfulness when we discuss child care (Chapter 7), love relationships (Chapter 8), and care of elderly relatives (Chapter 14).

Furthermore, women's paid employment often emphasizes this nonobvious kind of helpfulness. Women are more likely than men to choose occupations in the "helping professions," such as nursing and social work (Eagly & Diekman, 2006; Frieze & Li, 2010).

In summary, helpfulness actually includes both the high-profile activities that are stereotypically masculine and also the less obvious activities that are stereotypically feminine. Let's consider several topics related to helping and caring: altruism, nurturance, empathy, moral judgments involving social relationships, attitudes about social justice, and friendship. Try Demonstration 6.3 before you read further.

Altruism

Altruism means providing unselfish help to others who are in need, without anticipating any reward. Research with children and with adults shows gender similarities (N. Eisenberg et al., 1996). For example, one meta-analysis of 182 gender comparisons yielded an overall effect size (d) of only 0.13 (Eagly & Crowley, 1986). Gender similarities are common, although men are more helpful on tasks that are physically dangerous or require expertise in a traditionally "masculine" area (Eisenberg et al., 2006; Ellis et al., 2008; Rankin & Eagly, 2008).

Let's consider a classic study that demonstrated gender similarities. Researchers distributed questionnaires to adult visitors at a Canadian science museum (R. S. L. Mills et al., 1989). Each person read three stories, such as the one in Demonstration 6.3, and was instructed to choose between two specified options. The results showed that both women and men selected the altruistic choice 75% of the time. In other words, the researchers found no gender differences in responses to this hypothetical scenario not involving danger.

An important article by Selwyn Becker and Alice Eagly (2004) examined helpfulness in more dangerous situations. Specifically, they studied **heroism**, which they defined as risking one's life for the welfare of other people. One category of heroes that Becker and Eagly considered was the list of Carnegie Hero Medal recipients. This award is given to individuals in the United States and Canada who risk their own life to save the lives of other people (e.g., from drowning or electrocution). Becker and Eagly discovered that 9% of these individuals were women.

The next category of heroes that Becker and Eagly considered was individuals whose helpfulness was less dangerous, although still very risky. Here, the majority of these individuals were women. For instance, 57% of "living kidney donors" were women. In other words, women are somewhat more likely than men to undergo pain and potential medical problems, in order to help another person.

The last category in Becker and Eagly's study was the individuals who earned the title "Righteous Among the Nations." These were non-Jewish people who risked their lives during the Nazi holocaust to save Jews. For this category, 61% were women.

Alice Eagly and her colleagues believe that the pattern of gender differences in helpfulness can be explained by social roles (S. W. Becker & Eagly, 2004; Eagly, 2001; Rankin & Eagly, 2008). A **social role** refers to a culture's shared expectations about the behavior of a group that occupies a particular social category, for example, the social category "men." Men typically have greater size and strength than women, which means that they are more likely to perform activities requiring these physical characteristics, such as saving someone from drowning. Their heroism is also more public.

What about women's heroism? The social-role explanation points out that women's social role is partly based on their giving birth to children. They are therefore more likely to take care of children, most often in a home setting. Their kind of heroism is less likely to require physical strength and more likely to occur in private. For example, most people who rescued Jews during the Nazi holocaust were very careful to conceal their heroism. In summary, then, both men and women can be heroic, but the nature of their heroism is somewhat different (Rankin & Eagly, 2008).

Nurturance

Nurturance is a kind of helping in which someone gives care to another person, usually someone who is younger or less competent. The stereotype suggests that women are more nurturant than men (Cole et al., 2007). Furthermore, women rate themselves higher on this characteristic than men do (Feingold, 1994; Frieze & Li, 2010; P. J. Watson et al., 1994).

Here's a related question: Do women find babies more interesting and engaging than men do? As we've learned before, the answer to this question depends on the operational definitions that researchers use. For example, women and men are equally responsive to babies when the operational definition requires a physiological measure (e.g., heart rate). However, when the operational definition is based on self-report, women rate themselves as being more attracted to babies (Berman, 1980; M. C. Hamilton, 2001).

Judith Blakemore (1998) examined whether preschool girls and boys differ in their interest in babies. She asked parents to observe their children interacting with an unfamiliar baby on three separate occasions—for example, when a family with a baby came to visit in the home. The analysis of the ratings showed that preschool girls scored higher than boys in their amount of nurturance toward the baby, degree of interest in the baby, and kissing and holding the baby. Studies suggest that girls tend to be more nurturant than boys when interacting with babies (Blakemore et al., 2009).

However, Blakemore (1998) noted that some parents had rated themselves as being tolerant of "girl-like behavior" in their sons. Interestingly, these parents tended to have sons who were highly interested in babies and very nurturant toward these babies. It appears, then, that preschool girls are often higher than boys on behavioral measures of both nurturance and interactions with a baby, although some preschool boys can overcome the stereotypes.

Empathy

You demonstrate **empathy** when you (1) understand the emotion that another person is feeling, (2) you experience that same emotion, and (3) you are concerned about that person's well-being (Frieze & Li, 2010; Hatfield et al., 2008). When empathic people learn that someone has lost a contest, they can experience the same feelings of anger, frustration, embarrassment, and disappointment that the person who lost feels. According to the stereotype, women are more empathic than men. However, the actual research shows substantial gender differences only when the results are based on self-reports (Blakemore et al., 2009; Cowan & Khatchadourian, 2003; N. Eisenberg et al., 2006). The research findings will remind you of our discussion about responsiveness to babies:

1. *Women and men are equally empathic when the operational definition requires physiological measures.* Specifically, measures such as heart rate, pulse, skin conductance, and blood pressure typically show no gender differences in empathy.
2. *Women and men are equally empathic when the operational definition requires nonverbal measures.* For example, some studies have measured empathy in terms of the observer's facial, vocal, and gestural measures. A typical study examines whether children's facial expressions change in response to hearing an infant cry. Using this nonverbal measure, boys and girls usually do not differ in their empathy.
3. *Women are more empathic than men when the operational definition is based on self-report.* To assess empathy, a typical questionnaire includes items such as "I tend to get emotionally involved with a friend's problems." Studies with adolescents and adults usually find that women report more empathy than do men (Frieze & Li, 2010). Furthermore, men who rate themselves relatively high in "feminine characteristics" also report that they are high in empathy (Karniol et al., 1998).

In related research, K. J. K. Klein and Hodges (2001) examined empathic accuracy. A person is high in empathic accuracy if they can correctly guess which emotions another person is experiencing. In the control condition, women earned higher scores in empathic accuracy. However, people were equally accurate if (a) they received feedback on their accuracy or (b) if they were paid when their empathic accuracy was high.

In summary, the research demonstrates that gender differences in self-reported empathy are far from universal. As we have emphasized, we cannot answer the question of whether men or women are more empathic unless we know how empathy is measured and whom we are studying. Once again, this is an example of Theme 1: Gender differences certainly are not found in every condition.

Moral Judgments About Social Relationships

Do men and women differ in the way that they make moral judgments about other people? As you can imagine, this question has important consequences for the way we interact with other people. Lawrence Kohlberg (1981, 1984) had proposed a theory of moral development, and he argued that men are more likely than women to achieve sophisticated levels of moral development. Carol Gilligan disagreed with this perspective, and she developed a feminist perspective on moral development (Clinchy & Norem, 1998). Specifically, Gilligan and several other theorists have argued that women are *not* morally inferior to men, but they do "speak in a different voice" (Gilligan, 1982; Gilligan & Attanucci, 1988; Jordan, 1997).

Gilligan (1982) contrasted two approaches to moral decision making. She argued that men tend to support a justice approach. According to the **justice approach**, each individual is part of a hierarchy in which some people have more power and influence than others. Gilligan argued that women tend to support a care approach. According to the **care approach**, individuals are interrelated with other people in a web of connections. Notice, then, that Gilligan's approach favors the **differences perspective**, which tends to emphasize that men and women are different from each other.

In contrast, the **similarities perspective** tends to minimize gender differences, arguing that men and women are generally similar. As you know from Theme 1, this textbook typically favors the similarities perspective. With respect to helping and caring about other people, women and men do not live on separate planets.

Most of the research on moral judgments has supported the similarities perspective. When men and women make these judgments, they typically respond similarly (e.g., Brabeck & Brabeck, 2006; Brabeck & Shore, 2002; W. L. Gardner & Gabriel, 2004).

An occasional study shows that men are somewhat more likely than women to endorse the "caring" perspective. Consider a study by Skoe and her coauthors (2002). In one part of this study, college students rated the importance of moral dilemmas that focused on the justice approach, as well as moral dilemmas that focused on the care approach. Women thought that the "care dilemmas" were slightly more important than the "justice dilemmas." However, men were even more likely to endorse the "care dilemmas," rather than the "justice dilemmas." These results contradict Gilligan's proposal that women are more likely than men to focus on caring and interpersonal relationships.

Furthermore, a meta-analysis by Jaffee and Hyde (2000) found gender similarities in 73% of the 160 studies they examined. The *d* was 0.28, indicating only a small gender difference. Men and women seem to live in the same moral world, sharing similar basic values that include both justice and care (Brabeck & Shore, 2002; Kunkel & Burleson, 1998).

It's likely that Gilligan's theory was initially appealing because it matched people's stereotypes that men are hierarchical and women are interconnected (Brabeck & Shore, 2002; Schmid Mast, 2004). However, psychologists have pointed out an important problem. If we were to glorify women's special nurturance and caring, then would be less likely to recognize and develop their own competence in that area (H. Lerner, 1989; Tavris, 1992).

Attitudes About Social Justice

For several years, I have collected quotations that focus on social justice and compassion for groups that experience disadvantages. One of my favorite quotes comes from an unusual source, the Greek philosopher Thucydides, who lived from about 460 to 400 B.C. Thucydides was once asked when there would be justice in Athens. He replied, "There will be justice in Athens when those who are not injured are as outraged as those who are."

In general, the research suggests that women are somewhat more likely than men to endorse social justice issues, indicating that they are concerned about people who are frequently "injured" in our society. If you emphasize **social justice**, you are concerned about the well-being of a large group of people who experience discrimination and danger, such as people of color, people who identify as LGBTQ+, people who have been displaced from their home countries, and people who are living in a war zone.

Fortunately, we have an excellent resource for information about gender comparisons in social-justice attitudes. Every year in the United States, approximately 240,000 first-year college students complete a survey that asks them about their personal characteristics, their attitudes about education, and their opinions about political issues and social justice (Stolzenberg et al., 2020). Table 6.2 displays how women and men compare on a variety of social-justice issues. As represented in this table, women are somewhat more likely than men to express concern for the well-being of other people, including those from social categories that often experience injustice.

These data on college students are echoed in the general U.S. population. For example, Eagly and Diekman (2006) examined data from the General Social Survey during the years from 1973 to 1998. They compared women and men on "social compassion attitudes" for the years 1973 to 1998. Their analysis showed, for example, that women are somewhat more likely than men to *support* (1) gun control and (2) the reduction of income differences between the rich and poor. They are also more likely to *oppose* (1) police brutality and (2) racial discrimination in housing.

Neither of these surveys provide evidence that men and women live on different planets, with respect to their attitudes about social justice. You probably have some male friends who are much more socially compassionate than some of your female friends. Still, the modest "gender gap" is intriguing.

Friendship

For many decades, psychologists ignored the topic of friendship; aggression was a much more popular topic! However, many books and articles have discussed issues relevant to gender comparisons in friendship (e.g., Blakemore et al., 2009; Fehr, 2004; Foels & Tomcho, 2005; Rose & Rudolph, 2006). Let's consider three components of gender comparisons in friendship: (1) Do the friendships of girls and boys differ? (2) Are there gender differences in the nature of women's and men's friendships? (3) Do women and men use different strategies to help their friends?

The Nature of Girls' and Boys' Same-Gender Friendships

As we learned in Chapter 3, children show gender segregation; that is, they tend to play with children of the same gender. In general, girls tend to have a smaller number of friends than boys

TABLE **6.2**

Gender Comparisons in College Students' Attitudes About Social-Justice Issues

	Percentage of Students Who Responded	
Questionnaire Item	Men	Women
1. The federal government should do more to control the sale of handguns.	64%	80%
2. A national health-care plan is needed to control everybody's medical costs.	65%	74%
3. Same-sex couples should have the right to legal marital status.	59%	72%
4. Wealthy people should pay a larger share of the taxes than they do now.	60%	61%
5. Affirmative action in college admissions should be abolished.	53%	43%
6. Federal military spending should be increased.	32%	24%
7. Racial discrimination is no longer a major problem in America.	25%	16%

Note: On items 1, 2, 3, and 4, *higher* scores reflect greater concern for social justice. On items 5, 6, and 7, *lower* scores reflect greater concern for social justice.

Source: Copyright 2011 The Regents of the University of California Press. All Rights Reserved.

do. Furthermore, girls are more likely than boys to have friends who do not know each other. In contrast, boys are more likely than girls to have friends who all belong to the same group (Blakemore et al., 2009).

When people engage in **self-disclosure**, they reveal information about themselves to another person. Girls are more likely than boys to engage in self-disclosure with their friends. In contrast, boys are more likely than girls to engage in sports or games with rules with their friends (Blakemore et al., 2009; Rose & Rudolph, 2006).

The Nature of Women's and Men's Same-Gender Friendships

Try to imagine two women who are good friends with each other, and think about the nature of their friendship. Now do the same for two men who are good friends. Are female-female friendships basically different from male-male friendships? You can probably anticipate the conclusion we will reach in this section: Athough gender differences are observed in some components of friendship, gender similarities are more striking (Marshall, 2010).

We find gender similarities when we assess what friends do when they get together. Specifically, both female friends and male friends are most likely to just talk. They are generally less likely to work on a specific task or project together. And they rarely meet for the purpose of working on some problem that has arisen in their friendship (Duck & Wright, 1993; Fehr, 2004; P. H. Wright, 1998). Another gender similarity is that women and men report the same degree of satisfaction with their same-gender friendships (Brabeck & Brabeck, 2006; Crick & Rose, 2000; Foels & Tomcho, 2005). However, women also value physical contact with the friend, whereas men mention this less often (Brabeck & Brabeck, 2006).

According to research in both Canada and the United States, women are slightly more likely than men to value self-disclosure and to engage in self-disclosure with their friends (Dindia & Allen, 1992; Fehr, 2004; Marshall, 2010). However, both women and men typically believe that self-disclosure increases the intimacy of a friendship (Fehr, 2004; Monsour, 1992).

Why do women tend to be more self-disclosing? One reason is that women value talking about feelings more than men do. As we've already discussed, women receive greater training in emotions. In addition, cultural norms in the United States create powerful pressure for men with regard to self-disclosure. Men may *want* to self-disclose but often choose not to share their private feelings with other men (Fehr, 2004; Winstead & Griffin, 2001).

Research by Beverley Fehr (2004) compares women's and men's perspectives on qualities that are important for a close, intimate friendship. Try Demonstration 6.4 now to test whether you can predict which characteristics women rate higher than men do.

Demonstration **6.4**

Characteristics of Intimate Friendships

Beverley Fehr (2004) conducted a study at the University of Winnipeg in which she asked female and male students to indicate how important certain characteristics would be for an intimate friendship. For five of the items below, women gave higher ratings to the characteristics than men did; for the remaining five, women and men supplied similar ratings of importance. Select the five characteristics that you think revealed gender differences. The answers appear at the end of this chapter, on page 205.

1. If I need to talk, my friend will listen.
2. If I have a problem, my friend will listen.
3. If someone were insulting me or saying negative things behind my back, my friend would stick up for me.
4. No matter who I am or what I do, my friend will accept me.
5. Even if it feels as though no one cares, I know my friend does.
6. If I need to cry, my friend will be there for me.
7. If something is important to me, my friend will respect it.
8. If I do something wrong, my friend will forgive me.
9. If I need cheering up, my friend will try to make me laugh.
10. If something is bothering me, my friend will understand how I feel.

Source: Based on Fehr (2004).

How Women and Men Help Their Friends

Several researchers have focused on how people help their friends in real-life settings. These studies often show that women are more helpful (D. George et al., 1998; S. E. Taylor, 2002). For example, George and his colleagues (1998) asked 1,004 community residents to describe a recent situation in which they helped a friend of the same gender. Compared to men, women reported spending more time helping their friend.

Women and men may also differ in the kind of help they provide to their friends. When a friend has a problem, women tend to report that they would encourage the friend to talk about it. Men report that they would tend to split their vote evenly between the "let's talk about it" strategy and a strategy such as encouraging the friend to make a list of pros and cons about possible solutions to the problem (Belansky & Boggiano, 1994).

Several recent studies have explored whether women and men differ in the kind of emotional support they offer their friends. As you might expect, the research shows that the gender differences are subtle rather than widespread. For example, both women and men are much more likely to offer sympathy or advice to a worried friend, rather than changing the subject or telling the friend not to worry (MacGeorge et al., 2004). However, men are somewhat more likely than women to blame their same-gender friends for a problem they have (MacGeorge, 2003). Taking everything into account, MacGeorge and her coauthors (2004) comment on the idea of two different cultures—a Mars culture and a Venus culture—that cannot communicate with each other. As these researchers conclude, "The different cultures thesis is a myth that should be discarded" (p. 143).

Section Summary

Characteristics Related to Helping and Caring

1. Overall gender differences in helpfulness are not strong; men are more likely to help on dangerous tasks and on tasks requiring expertise in masculine areas. When helping family members and friends, women may help more.
2. The research on heroism is consistent with Eagly's social role theory; men are likely to be more heroic when the tasks require physical strength, and women are more likely to be heroic when the tasks require secrecy.
3. Research shows gender similarities when nurturance is measured in terms of physiological measures, but women are more nurturant in terms of self-report measures. Preschool girls may show more interest in infants than most preschool boys do; however, boys who have been reared in nontraditional households are very nurturant toward babies.
4. In general, women and men do not differ in empathy; gender similarities are common for physiological and nonverbal measures, but women are typically more empathic on self-report measures.
5. Carol Gilligan (1982), who supports the gender-differences perspective, proposed that men favor a justice approach, whereas women emphasize a care approach. However, most of the research supports a similarities perspective.
6. Women are somewhat more likely than men to express concern about social-justice issues such as racism and government spending on the military.

(continues)

Section Summary *(continued)*

7. Girls tend to have a smaller number of same-gender friends, whereas boys tend to have friends who belong to the same group; girls are more likely to self-disclose to their friends.

8. Men and women have similar friendship patterns in terms of the activities that same-gender friends engage in when they get together and in terms of satisfaction with their friendships; women are typically somewhat more self-disclosing than men are.

9. Women tend to report spending more time helping their friends and using somewhat different helping strategies; however, the gender differences are relatively small.

6-3 Characteristics Related to Aggression and Power

Learning Objectives

To describe gender differences in characteristics related to aggression and power, you can …

6-3-1   Explain the social constructionist perspective to gender and aggression.

6-3-2   Differentiate between physical and relational aggression.

6-3-3   dentify factors that are related to gender and aggression.

6-3-4   Explain how women and men differ in their interest in leadership opportunities.

6-3-5   Differentiate between transformational and transactional styles of leadership.

6-3-6   Explain why women are less likely to be rated by others as effective leaders.

6-3-7   Describe situations where women are more persuasive, and situations where men are more persuasive.

We have learned that the research on helping and caring does not permit simple conclusions about gender differences. The situation is similar for the research associated with aggression and power.

In the previous section, we focused on characteristics that are stereotypically associated with women. In this section, we will focus on characteristics that are stereotypically associated with men (Schmid Mast, 2005). An important central topic in this cluster is **aggression,** which we'll define as behavior that is directed toward another person, with the intention of doing harm (Blakemore et al., 2009; J. W. White, 2001).

Let's begin by considering some issues raised by social constructionists about the nature of aggression, and next we'll examine the research on aggression. Then we'll shift our focus from aggression to power, as we examine the topics of leadership and persuasion. In other words, we will begin by discussing the negative components of aggression, and we will end by examining the more positive components of power.

Gender and Aggression: The Social Constructionist Perspective

As we read in the introduction to this chapter, social constructionists argue that we actively construct our schemas of the world. This point also holds true for theorists and researchers trying to make sense out of human behavior. As a result, researchers who are studying aggression are often guided by the way scholars have constructed the categories. The customary language has limited the way that researchers tend to view aggression (Marecek, 2001a; Underwood, 2003; J. W. White, 2009). Consequently, the cultural lenses that researchers wear will often restrict their perspectives (Ostrov et al., 2005).

In particular, researchers have frequently constructed aggression so that it is considered a male characteristic. To appreciate this point, reread the definition of aggression in the second paragraph of this section. What kinds of aggression do you visualize—hitting, shoving, and other kinds of physical violence? True, but aggression can be verbal as well as physical. When someone makes an extremely negative, hurtful comment about you, it can have a profound effect on your self-esteem. Still, traditional cultural perspectives usually prevent us from recognizing the kinds of aggression that might be more common in women (White, 2009).

Social constructionists point out that each culture devises its own set of lenses (K. J. Gergen & Gergen, 2004; M. M. Gergen, 2010; Matsumoto & Juang, 2004). As a result, cultural communities may differ in their construction of social behaviors such as aggression. For example, M. G. Harris (1994) reported on female members of Mexican American gangs in the Los Angeles area. The young women she interviewed stated that they had joined the gang for group support, but also because of a need for revenge. One young woman emphasized, "Most of us in our gangs always carry weapons. Guns, knives, bats, crow-bars, any kind.... Whatever we can get hold of that we know can hurt, then we'll have it" (p. 297). In a cultural community that admires physical aggression, gender differences may disappear as both women and men adopt violent tactics (Miller-Johnson et al., 2005).

Throughout our discussion of aggression, keep in mind the cultural lenses that we wear. Also, remember that the way we frame our questions has an important influence on the answers we obtain.

Comparing Physical Aggression with Relational Aggression

We have noted that our cultural lenses typically encourage us to perceive aggression from a male perspective. That perspective emphasizes **physical aggression**, which is intentional aggression that could physically harm another person. In general, men are more likely than women to demonstrate physical aggression.

Let's consider the research on gender comparisons in crime rates, an important index of physical aggression. The data on crime show that men are more likely than women to be the offenders in almost every category of criminal behavior (C. A. Anderson & Bushman, 2002). For example, in the United States, men account for 78.9% of the arrests for violent crime, including murder, robbery, and assault (U.S. Department of Justice, Federal Bureau of Investigation, 2020). In Canada, men account for 75% of those who are charged with a violent crime (Savage, 2019). We'll return to this topic in Chapter 13 when we consider sexual assault and the abuse of women.

What can we conclude from these data on criminal behavior? Women are clearly capable of committing horrifying acts of aggression, both in their home community and in the military services. For instance, when the newspapers reported that American soldiers had been terrorizing Iraqi citizens at Abu Ghraib Prison, one of the most chilling photos showed a petite and perky American soldier, Lynndie England. She had a wide grin on her face, as she dragged a naked Iraqi man around on a leash (Cocco, 2004). Yes, women may be somewhat more likely to commit crimes now than in earlier eras, leading to a narrowing gender gap in crime statistics (Estrada, Bäckman, & Nilsson, 2016). Still, the gender differences in physical aggression remain relatively large.

Now let us consider a different kind of aggression, one that threatens interpersonal relationships (e.g., Crick, Casas, & Nelson, 2002; Remillard & Lamb, 2005; A. J. Rose et al., 2004). **Relational aggression** is aggression that could harm another person through intentionally manipulating interpersonal relationships, such as friendships (Crick et al., 2004; Frieze & Li, 2010). For example, someone may spread a lie about a person or intentionally exclude a person from a group. This kind of aggression requires substantial cognitive sophistication, compared to hitting or other physical forms of aggression (Blakemore et al., 2009). Interestingly, adults have more difficulty recognizing relational aggression, compared to both physical aggression and prosocial (positive) behavior (Ostrov et al., 2005).

Relational aggression is often more common in women than in men, although some studies report no gender differences (Archer & Coyne, 2005; Basow et al., 2007; Ellis et al., 2008; Geiger et al., 2004). Furthermore, girls are more likely than boys to report that relational aggression is very upsetting (Crick & Nelson, 2002).

In a representative study, Jamie Ostrov and his colleagues (2004) studied 3- to 5-year-old children who attended a preschool program. These researchers observed groups of three same-gender children, who had been instructed to use a crayon to color in a picture—such as a cartoon of Winnie the Pooh—on a white sheet of paper. Each observation period began by placing three crayons in the center of the table. One crayon was an appropriate color, such as an orange crayon for coloring Winnie the Pooh. However, the other two crayons were white—clearly useless for coloring on white paper. As you might expect, the children in this condition wanted to have the orange crayon, rather than a white one, and they tried different tactics to take this crayon away from the child who was currently using it. Trained observers recorded measures of physical aggression, such as hitting or pushing another child. They also recorded measures of relational aggression, such as spreading rumors about a child or ignoring a child.

As represented in Figure 6.3, the boys were more likely than the girls to use physical aggression. However, the girls were more likely than the boys to use relational aggression. For example, in one group of three girls, Girl 3 was holding the only useful crayon. Girl 1 said to Girl 2, "I gotta tell you something" (p. 367). She then got out of her seat to whisper something in Girl 2's ear, clearly excluding Girl 3 from the private interchange. Studies like these help us to reinterpret the myth that women are nonaggressive. However, in emphasizing girls' use of relational violence, we must not ignore the harmful consequences of men's physical violence.

Other Factors Related to Gender and Aggression

So far, we have learned that girls and women may be relatively high in physical aggression but that boys and men are relatively high in relational aggression. What other factors play a role in gender comparisons?

For many years, psychologists seemed convinced that men are consistently more aggressive than women. However, a breakthrough in our understanding of gender and aggression came from a classic review of previous studies, conducted by Ann Frodi and her colleagues (1977). According to the studies they examined, men were often found to be more aggressive. However, only 39% of these studies showed men being more aggressive than women for all the research conditions.

The analysis by Frodi and her colleagues has now been joined by additional research and meta-analyses (e.g., Archer, 2004; L. R. Brody, 1999; Graham-Kevan & Archer, 2005).

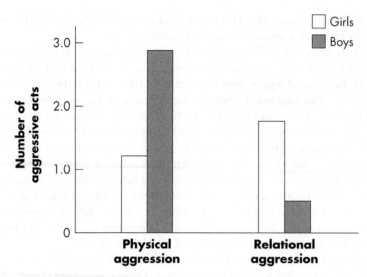

FIGURE **6.3** The number of acts of physical and relational aggression delivered by boys and girls.
Source: Based on Ostrov et al. (2004).

These reports inform us that gender differences in aggression depend on factors such as operational definitions and the nature of people's relationships.

For example, the gender differences are relatively large when researchers measure spontaneous aggression. Men are more likely than women to show spontaneous, unprovoked aggression—the kind of aggression that cannot be traced to a specific cause. In contrast, suppose that a person has been insulted, which provides a specific excuse for an aggressive response. In the case of provoked aggression, both men and women are likely to respond aggressively (C. A. Anderson & Bushman, 2002; Archer, 2004; L. R. Brody, 1999).

A second factor is the nature of the relationship between the two individuals. This factor has a more complex influence on gender comparisons in aggression: Specifically, when two research participants have never met before, women can be as aggressive as men. However, when the participants have met briefly—in a research setting—men are more aggressive (Carlo et al., 1999; Lightdale & Prentice 1994). What happens when people are in an intimate relationship, for example, if they are dating or married? In some cases, men and women are equally likely to be violent, but men typically inflict more physical injury (Archer, 2004; McHugh et al., 2008; Richardson, 2005).

When you think about gender and aggression, keep in mind the general principle that the psychological characteristics of people of all genders always show a substantial overlap (Archer, 2004). For example, some studies have compared boys and girls on measures of observed physical aggression (e.g., Archer, 2004; Favreau, 1993; Frey & Hoppe-Graff, 1994). In these studies, most of the boys and girls were similarly nonaggressive, and the gender differences could be traced to a small number of aggressive boys.

Also, researchers and theorists are less likely to study the kind of aggression in which women may be as aggressive or more aggressive. As a result, people tend to believe that women are rarely aggressive. This myth of the nonaggressive woman has several disadvantages for society:

1. If women perceive themselves as weak and nonaggressive, some of them may believe that they cannot defend themselves against men's aggression.
2. Some people associate competitiveness with aggression, so women may sometimes be denied access to professions that value competition.
3. Aggressiveness may be perceived as normal for men, so some men may choose not to inhibit their aggressive tendencies.

In short, both women and men suffer when we hold stereotyped ideas of the gender differences in aggression.

Leadership

So far, we have considered only the negative characteristics associated with power, such as physical and relational aggression. In contrast, leadership can play an important positive role associated with power. Let's explore gender comparisons in three areas related to leadership: (1) interest in leadership, (2) style of leadership, and (3) leadership effectiveness. However, try Demonstration 6.5 before you read further.

Demonstration **6.5**

Leadership Styles

Imagine that you have completed college, and you are applying for a job. Try to imagine what characteristics your new boss will have. Place a check mark in front of every item you would *most* like to have in an ideal boss.

_____ 1. My boss will be optimistic and enthusiastic about the organization's goals.

_____ 2. My boss will give rewards when employees do satisfactory work.

_____ 3. My boss will have personal characteristics that encourage me to respect them.

_____ 4. My boss will focus on mentoring employees and will try to figure out what each person needs.

_____ 5. My boss will wait until a problem becomes serious before trying to fix the problem.

_____ 6. My boss will communicate with employees about the values of the organization's mission.

_____ 7. My boss will pay special attention to employees' mistakes.

  Now read the section on leadership to determine which leadership style you prefer.

Sources: Based on Eagly et al. (2003) and Powell & Graves (2003).

Interest in Leadership

Compared to men, women may be less interested in being a leader. For example, women often judge themselves to be less suitable for a leadership position (Bosak & Sczesny, 2008). They are also less likely to believe that it would be possible for them to become leaders (Killeen et al., 2006). Furthermore, women are less likely to feel comfortable in a leadership position. In fact, it may take a special incentive for a woman to decide that she will be a leader (Lips & Keener, 2007). Women in leadership positions sometimes also experience stereotype threat, a concept we discussed in Chapter 2 (Hoyt & Murphy, 2016).

Several organizations are developing courses that encourage women to recognize that they could become effective leaders. For example, the University of Michigan invited female faculty members in medicine, science, and engineering to join a program that provided leadership training and networking opportunities. The program helped to increase the number of women who serve as the chairs of academic departments and important committees (Stewart & LaVaque-Manty, 2008).

Similarly, Jessica Daniel designed a workshop for junior-level women of color in psychology. At this workshop, senior women discussed how they had become leaders, and they encouraged the junior women to think how they could use their ethnic identities as a source of strength in becoming leaders (Porter & Daniel, 2007).

Leadership Style

Researchers who study leadership often refer to two effective kinds of leadership styles (Eagly, 2007; Eagly & Carli, 2007; Eagly et al., 2003). Leaders who have a **transformational style of leadership** will inspire employees, gain their trust, and encourage them to develop their potential skills (Porter & Daniel, 2007). The term "transformational" makes sense because these leaders encourage employees to *transform* themselves. In Demonstration 6.5, items 1, 3, 4, and 6 represent a transformational boss.

In contrast, leaders who have a **transactional style of leadership** will clarify the tasks that employees must accomplish, rewarding them when they meet the appropriate objectives and correcting them when they do not meet these objectives. The name "transactional" makes sense because the leader focuses on straightforward exchanges: "If you do X, I will give you Y." In Demonstration 6.5, items 2, 5, and 7 represent a transactional style.

Alice Eagly and her colleagues (2003) conducted a meta-analysis of 45 studies that focused on the kind of leadership style adopted by men and women. As you might predict, the results were complex. However, women leaders were slightly higher on the transformational dimension. Women leaders were also slightly higher on the "reward" aspect of transactional leadership (item 2), but slightly lower on the other aspects of transactional leadership (items 5 and 6). However, it's important to note that some studies fail to find gender differences in leadership style (e.g., Barbuto et al., 2007).

Leadership Effectiveness

Which gender is actually more effective in the leadership role? Eagly and her coauthors (2003) performed a meta-analysis of the research conducted with an assessment technique called the Multifactor Leadership Questionnaire (MLQ). Women scored somewhat higher than men on the MLQ ($d = 0.22$). Furthermore, research in the United States shows that companies with the largest percentage of women in top-management positions are also those that have the best financial performance (Eagly, 2007).

But how do people rate female leaders, compared to male leaders? As you might expect, the answer depends on the nature of the task (Van Vugt & Spisak, 2008). However, the research shows that female leaders receive negative ratings when they use a highly power-oriented leadership style or when they claim to be an expert about a stereotypically masculine topic (Chin, 2004; Lips, 2001; J. Yoder et al., 1998). Traditionally masculine males are especially likely to give negative ratings to female leaders (Rivero et al., 2004). Alice Eagly proposed a **role congruity theory** of prejudice to explain why people rate women leaders more harshly (Eagly & Karau, 2002). According to this theory, people tend to perceive women in leadership positions as not behaving in a manner consistent with the "female" role in society, which leads to prejudice against women leaders.

All this research on leadership ability has important implications for women and work, the topic of our next chapter. Specifically, the research tells us that women are, if anything, somewhat more effective as leaders. However, the research also tells us that people react differently to male and female leaders, consistent with Theme 2.

Unfortunately, few of the studies on leadership examine intersectionality factors in women's lived experiences. We don't know, for example, whether Black men and women differ in their leadership style. We also don't know whether ethnicity influences people's ratings of male and female leaders. For instance, would people be more or less likely to rate a woman of color negatively if she held a leadership position in a traditionally masculine field? People might also assume that a woman of color was appointed to a leadership position primarily because of affirmative action (Chin, 2007).

Persuasion

How do people respond to the persuasive efforts of men and women? In general, the research shows that men are more persuasive than women (Carli, 2001; Carli & Eagly, 2002). This gender difference can be partly traced to stereotypes about women. As we read in Chapter 2 (pp. 57–58), people think women are friendly and nice, but not especially competent. Suppose that a woman tries to influence other people, and she therefore violates this stereotype. She is likely to encounter a variety of problems (Carli & Bukatko, 2000).

Consider, for example, a study by Bowles and her coauthors (2007). These researchers asked participants to imagine that they were senior managers in a corporation, trying to decide whether to hire a job candidate for a position that required working well with other employees. The participants then examined a description of the job candidate, who was either male or female and who either did not ask for a higher salary or did ask for a higher salary.

Bowles and her colleagues (2007) found that the evaluations of the male job candidate were similar, whether or not he asked for a higher salary. In contrast, the evaluations of the female job candidate were significantly less positive when she asked for a higher salary. In other words, women who request higher salaries may be less likely to be hired. Furthermore, both male and female participants downgraded the female job candidate if she had requested a higher salary. This study contradicts the pattern you will read in other studies in this section, where women are often more sympathetic than men in evaluating a strong woman.

Our discussion of leadership pointed out that female leaders are downgraded if they use a high-power style. Similarly, women may be less persuasive if they appear too masculine.

For example, men are not persuaded by a woman who uses assertive language. Instead, they are persuaded when a woman uses the kind of tentative language we discussed earlier, such as "I'm not sure" (Buttner & McEnally, 1996; Carli, 1990, 2001; Eagly & Carli, 2007).

Interestingly, though, *women* are often more persuaded by a woman who uses assertive language than by a woman who uses tentative language (Carli, 1990). A female politician who plans to give a persuasive speech to voters therefore faces a double bind: If she is too assertive, she'll lose the men, but if she is too tentative, she'll lose the women!

Other research shows this same pattern of gender differences in response to a competent, assertive woman (Carli & Eagly, 2002). For example, Dodd and her colleagues (2001) asked students to read a vignette focusing on a conversation among three friends: one woman and two men. In the story, one of the men makes a sexist comment, and the woman either ignores it or confronts it. The results of the study showed that the male students liked the woman more if she ignored the comment rather than confronted it. In contrast, the female students liked the woman more if she confronted the comment rather than ignored it.

Women also face a problem if they use nonverbal behavior that appears too masculine. An interesting analysis by Linda Carli and her colleagues (1995) compared women who used a competent nonverbal style and men who used the same style. A competent nonverbal style includes a relatively rapid rate of speech, upright posture, calm hand gestures, and moderately high eye contact when speaking. A male audience was significantly more influenced by a man who used this competent style than by a woman who used this same style.

According to other research, women are more successful if they act modest. In contrast, men are more successful if they are boastful and self-promoting (Carli & Eagly, 2002; Rudman, 1998). Again, behavior associated with high social status is not acceptable when used by a person with relatively low social status (Carli, 1999; Carli & Bukatko, 2000; Rudman, 1998).

As you can tell, subtle sexism persists in social interactions. A competent woman finds herself in a no-win situation. If she speaks confidently and uses competent nonverbal behavior, she may not persuade the men with whom she interacts. But if she speaks tentatively and uses less competent nonverbal behavior, she will not live up to her own personal standards—and she might not persuade other women. Keep this issue in mind when you read about women's work experiences in Chapter 7.

Throughout this chapter, we have compared women and men on a variety of social and personality characteristics. For example, we noted occasional gender differences in communication patterns, helpfulness, aggression, and leadership. However, gender similarities are typically more common. Furthermore, every characteristic we discussed demonstrates a substantial overlap in the distribution of female scores and the distribution of male scores.

In summary, we can reject the claim that men and women are from different planets and have little in common. The title of John Gray's (1992) book, *Men Are from Mars, Women Are from Venus,* was certainly enticing enough to produce a best-seller. However, its message does not match the gender similarities found in psychology research. Furthermore, in Chapter 7, we'll continue to search for factors that could explain why women are seldom employed in certain high-prestige occupations and why women are treated differently from men in the workplace. In the chapter you've just read, we have learned that major gender differences in social and personality characteristics are not powerful enough to explain why there are so few women in some occupations.

Section Summary

Characteristics Related to Aggression and Power

1. According to the social constructionist perspective, scholars in the United States have emphasized the stereotypically masculine components of aggression. They have usually ignored the kinds of aggression that might be more common in females; they have also paid little attention to gender similarities in other cultures and subcultures.
2. Researchers currently differentiate between two kinds of aggression. Men are typically higher in physical aggression, whereas women are typically higher in relational aggression.
3. Gender differences in physical aggression are inconsistent. These gender differences are relatively large when spontaneous aggression is measured, and when individuals either do not know each other at all or when they have an intimate relationship.
4. Men are usually more interested than women in becoming a leader.
5. Women are slightly more likely than men to adopt a transformational leadership style and to reward employees who meet objectives (part of the transactional style). However, women are somewhat less likely to adopt other parts of the transactional style.
6. Women score somewhat higher than men on an assessment of leadership effectiveness. However, women who are leaders are likely to be downgraded when they act in a traditionally masculine fashion and when they are rated by traditionally masculine males.
7. According to the research, women tend to be downgraded if they ask for a higher salary. In addition, women face a double bind when they want to be persuasive. If they act stereotypically masculine, they won't persuade men; if they act less assertive and more stereotypically feminine, they won't persuade women.

Chapter Review Questions

1. In the discussion of communication styles, we learned that men seem to take up more space than women, whether we use the word *space* to refer to physical space or, more figuratively, to conversational space. Discuss this point, making as many gender comparisons as possible.
2. Imagine that two college students—a man and a woman—are sitting next to each other on a bench somewhere on your college campus. They have never met before, but they begin a conversation. Compare how they would act, with respect to verbal communication (talkativeness, interruptions, language style, language content) and nonverbal communication (personal space, posture, visual gaze, facial expression, decoding ability).
3. Revisit Chapter 3, and review the social learning and cognitive developmental approaches to gender development (pp. 86–88). Describe how these two approaches could explain each of the gender differences in verbal and nonverbal communication. How could the power explanation and the social status explanation in this chapter (pp. 183–186) account for gender differences in communication?

4. The social constructionist perspective emphasizes that cultural lenses shape the way we ask questions. In particular, these lenses influence the choices that psychologists make when they select topics for research. Summarize the topics of helpfulness, aggression, leadership, and persuasion, emphasizing how the nature of the results could be influenced by the kinds of issues studied in each area (e.g., aggression in stereotypically masculine areas).

5. According to stereotypes, women care about interpersonal relationships, whereas men care about dominating other people. As with many stereotypes, this contrast contains a grain of truth. Discuss the grain of truth with respect to helping, friendship, aggression, leadership, and persuasion. Then list the number of *similarities* shared by men and women.

6. What kinds of factors influence gender differences in aggression? Combining as many factors as possible, describe a situation in which gender differences are likely to be exaggerated. Then describe a situation in which gender differences are likely to be small.

7. Some researchers argue that gender differences are likely to emerge in areas in which men and women have had different amounts of practice or training. Using the chapter outline on page 173, discuss how differential practice might account for many of the gender differences.

8. Page 176 lists three circumstances in which we tend to find large gender differences in social and personality characteristics. Describe what these factors would predict about gender comparisons in the following situations: (a) a male professor and a female professor who have similar status are discussing a professional article they have both read; (b) a group of male and female students are asked to talk about the nurturing support that they have given to a younger sibling; (c) a lecture hall is filled with people, and the presentation system is not working. The speaker asks for volunteers to figure out the problem. Who will help?

9. In most of this chapter, we focused on the gender of the *subject*. However, we also discussed the gender of the *stimulus*. How do people react to male and female leaders and to women who are trying to influence other people? Why is the phrase "double bind" often relevant to this question?

10. To solidify your knowledge in preparation for studying women and work (Chapter 7), think of a profession in which relatively few women are employed. Review each of the social and personality characteristics that this chapter discusses. Note whether any of these factors provides a sufficient explanation for the relative absence of women in that profession.

Key Terms

social constructionist approach (p. 174)

nonverbal communication (p. 176)

personal space (p. 180)

contractive posture (p. 180)

expansive posture (p. 180)

decoding ability (p. 183)

altruism (p. 187)

heroism (p. 188)

social role (p. 188)

nurturance (p. 188)

empathy (p. 189)

justice approach (p. 190)

care approach (p. 190)

differences perspective (p. 190)

similarities perspective (p. 190)

social justice (p. 191)

self-disclosure (p. 192)

aggression (p. 195)

physical aggression (p. 196)

relational aggression (p. 197)

transformational style of leadership (p. 200)

transactional style of leadership (p. 200)

role congruity theory (p. 201)

Recommended Readings

Barnett, R., & Rivers, C. (2004). *Same difference: How gender myths are hurting our relationships, our children, and our jobs.* New York: Basic Books. This is the book to buy for friends who believe that men and women come from different planets. In contrast to the standard pop psychology, Barnett and Rivers' book critically evaluates the gender-difference myths in areas such as emotions, power, and helping behavior.

Chrisler, J. C., & McCreary, D. R. (Eds.). (2010). *Handbook of gender research in psychology* (Vols. 1–2). New York: Springer. This comprehensive handbook about gender and the psychology of women includes sections on relevant topics such as gender comparisons in communication, aggression, and altruism. New York: Springer.

Eckert, P., & McConnell-Ginet, S. (2003). *Language and gender.* New York: Cambridge University Press. Here is an excellent book that approaches language and gender from the perspective of linguistics, rather than psychology; it also conveys the subtlety of gender comparisons in language use.

Underwood, M. K. (2003). *Social aggression among girls.* New York: Guilford. In recent years, many books have been published about aggression in girls and women. Most are intended for either a general audience or for researchers. This book is both readable and scholarly.

Answers to Demonstrations

Demonstration 6.4: The statements that women were more likely than men to endorse are numbers 1, 2, 5, 6, and 10. No gender differences were found for numbers 3, 4, 7, 8, and 9.

7   Gender and Work

ESB Professional/Shutterstock.com

Learning Objectives

After studying this chapter, you will be able to ...

7-1 Describe background factors that are related to women's employment.

7-2 Identify factors that increase gender discrimination in the workplace.

7-3 Summarize women's experiences in selected occupations.

7-4 Describe factors that impact how women coordinate employment with personal life.

Did You Know?

- More than half of U.S. women are employed outside the home (p. 209).
- On average, women earn about 82% of what men earn in the workplace (p. 216).
- Men who are employed in traditionally female occupations—such as nursing—are often quickly promoted to management positions (p. 220).
- Women and men in the same profession, such as medicine, are typically similar in their personality characteristics and academic experiences (p. 228).

During the week when we were editing this chapter on women and work, we were happy to learn that the Paycheck Fairness Act was passed by the U.S. House of Representatives and sent to the U.S. Senate for review (Smith, 2021). This proposed labor law would amend the Fair Labor Standards Act of 1938, extend the Equal Pay Act of 1963, and make it illegal for employers to pay unequal wages to women and men who perform substantially similar jobs. The Paycheck Fairness Act has been introduced to every session of the U.S. House of Representatives since 1997, and if passed, it would help close the wage gap between women's and men's income. However, the bill has yet to be passed by the U.S. Senate and has died in committee during every session since 1997.

We immediately checked with the National Committee on Pay Equity (2021) to determine the size of the wage gap. If we consider all full-time U.S. workers—who work during an entire year—women earn 82% of the wages that men earn. Specifically, the median wage for men is $57,456 and the median wage for women is $47,299. In other words, half of the men earn more than $57,456 and half of the women earn more than $47,299; the difference in these salaries is $10,157. This is the gender wage gap, and we'll consider more information about it on pages 216 to 219.

Women experience a "promotion gap" as well as a "wage gap." A few years ago, a student described her mother's experience with gender discrimination. Her mother—whom we will call Ms. W.—had worked at the same small business for 14 years. She knew every aspect of the business, from supervising the factory to managing the office. Several years ago, Ms. W. learned that her boss had decided to hire a man to help with some of her work. This man had the same educational credentials and much less job experience, yet he would earn twice the salary that Ms. W. was earning. Furthermore, Ms. W. would be responsible for training this new employee. At this point, Ms. W. decided to leave that job and pursue a new career.

As we will learn throughout this chapter, the gender differences in work-related skills and characteristics are often small, consistent with Theme 1 of this book. Even so, consistent with Theme 2, women and men are often treated differently. For example, women frequently face barriers with respect to hiring, salary, treatment, and advancement in the workplace.

Let's begin this chapter by exploring some general information about women and work, and next we'll consider several kinds of discrimination in the workplace. We'll then examine a variety of traditional and nontraditional occupations. In the final section of the chapter, we'll discuss how women coordinate their employment with family responsibilities.

7-1 Background Factors Related to Women's Employment

Learning Objectives

To describe background factors that are related to women's employment, you can …

7-1-1   Describe which factors predict whether women will be employed outside the home.

7-1-2   Identify some specific barriers that immigrant women face in the workplace.

7-1-3   Explain why TANF regulations are counterproductive for some women.

7-1-4   Describe which factors make access discrimination more likely for women who are applying for jobs.

7-1-5   Explain how employer stereotypes are related to access discrimination.

7-1-6   Define affirmative action and explain how it is intended to reduce discrimination in the workplace.

To eliminate confusion, we first need to introduce some terms related to work. The general term **working women** refers to two categories:

1. **Employed women**, or women who work for pay. Employed women may receive a salary or be self-employed.
2. **Nonemployed women**, or women who are not paid for their work. They may do work for their families in their own homes, or for volunteer organizations, but they receive no money for these services.

As this chapter demonstrates, employment has become an increasingly important part of women's lives in the United States. For example, in 1970, 43% of women over the age of 16 were employed. That percentage has now increased to 57% (Bureau of Labor Statistics, 2019). The comparable percentage in Canada is 61%. Some employment rates for women in other countries are 54% for Japan, 51% for France, and 61% for Sweden (The World Bank, 2021).

Here is another change: The number of women has increased dramatically in some fields that were once reserved for men (M. R. Walsh, 1990). For the first time ever in 2019, 50.5%, or more than half, of U.S. medical school students were women (Heiser, 2019).

In previous eras, law schools also enrolled very few women. Ruth Bader Ginsburg, a former Supreme Court Justice, was one of nine women in 1956 when she enrolled at Harvard Law School. The Law School also enrolled 500 men that year. The Dean of the Law School gathered the nine women together at the beginning of the year, and he demanded to know why they had decided to come to law school (Strebeigh, 2009). In 1960, women comprised 3.5% of students enrolled in law school, but by 2020, 54% of U.S. law school students were women (Enjuris, 2020). It's encouraging to know that the percentage of women in the professional pipelines has steadily increased over time.

In this chapter, we will examine areas in which women have made progress in recent decades, as well as areas in which women still face disadvantages. Let's begin this first section by considering some basic information about women's employment. Then we'll briefly explore two issues that are critical for women in the workplace: child care and financial assistance, and discrimination in hiring.

General Information About Employed Women

What situations or characteristics predict whether a woman works outside the home? One of the best predictors of women's employment is her educational background. As portrayed in Figure 7.1, U.S. women with at least a master's degree are much more likely than women with less than four years of high school to be employed outside the home (Bureau of Labor Statistics, 2019). Education and employment are also highly correlated in Canada; 84% of women with a graduate degree and 70% of women with a university degree are currently employed, compared to 40% of women who had attended high school but had not graduated (OECD, 2019).

Several decades ago, one of the best predictors of a woman's employment was whether she had young children. However, data in the United States suggest that women with preschool children do not differ from other women in their rate of employment (Bureau of Labor Statistics, 2019; Halpern, 2006).

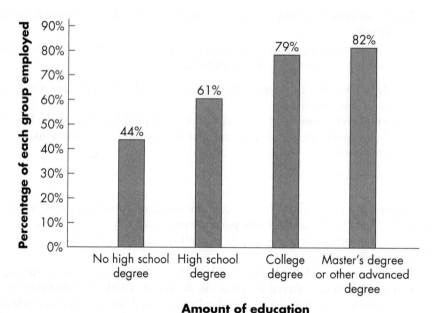

FIGURE **7.1** Percentage of women in the U.S. labor force, as a function of education.

Source: Based on Bureau of Labor Statistics (2019).

The current data also reveal that ethnicity is not strongly related to participation in the labor force. For example, U.S. data show employment for 54.5% of White women, 63.2% of Latina women, 58.3% of Black women, and 63.2% of Asian American women (Bureau of Labor Statistics, 2019). However, women of color are underrepresented in most high-salary occupations (DeFour, 2008).

Immigrant women make up a little over 7% of the workforce in the United States, and face different barriers to employment than native-born women (American Immigration Council, 2017). Although 57% of immigrant women have at least a college degree, and 13.5% have a graduate level degree, their educational degrees, professional licenses, and work experience in another country may not be given full credit when they apply for job in the United States (American Immigration Council, 2017; Berger, 2004; Naidoo, 2000). Furthermore, many immigrants experience discrimination, because U.S. residents are concerned about competition for jobs, although these fears are not supported by economic data (Costa, Cooper, & Shierholz, 2014; Deaux, 2006).

The situation for immigrant women in Canada is similar to that of the United States. For instance, of the Asian women immigrants in Canada, 47% have had at least some university education, in contrast to only 30% of women who list their ethnicity as "Canadians" (Finnie et al., 2005). In general, however, immigrants' salaries are significantly lower than those of nonimmigrants with comparable training (Berger, 2004; Hesse-Biber & Carter, 2000).

Partly due to these barriers, immigrant women in the United States and Canada tend to work in occupations that either do not reflect their educational training or are concentrated in lower paying occupations in the service, health care, education, hospitality, and agricultural industries (American Immigration Council, 2017; Bureau of Labor Statistics, 2019; Chang, 2016). Social support and educational initiatives show promise for helping immigrant women overcome additional employment barriers such as language, expectation adjustments, and acculturative stress (Greenwood, Adshead, & Jay, 2017; Msengi, Arthur-Okor, Killion, & Schoer, 2015).

In summary, education and immigrant status are related to women's employment situation. However, two factors that are *not* related to employment are parental status and ethnicity. In contrast with earlier eras, women of all ethnicities, with or without children, are employed in the labor force.

Women, Employment, and Financial Assistance

In the United States, an important long-standing debate has focused on mothers who are not currently employed in jobs outside the home. Often, women do not seek external employment because the cost of paying for child care would exceed their wages, which is particularly true for women who work occupations that have low levels of compensation (Morrissey, 2017). In addition, 56% of women with young children report that, if possible, they would prefer to stay home and take care of their children rather than work outside the home, because of the lack of available or high-quality child-care options in their regions (Saad, 2015). Women with young children who do not have additional sources of income from a spouse or partner, extended family members, or external employment, as well as those who do not have sufficient child-care options available, may sometimes need financial assistance from governmental sources.

Since 1996 in the United States, a program called Temporary Assistance for Needy Families (TANF) has existed—in theory—to assist women who are economically disadvantaged. Unfortunately, this program has historically operated in a discriminatory, unfair, and racist manner. It disproportionately targets women of color and indigenous women and creates limitations and regulations that have tragic consequences for many women (CBPP, 2021; Lein & Schexnayder, 2007).

The long-term goal of the original TANF policy was for a mother to earn enough money for the family to eventually be self-sufficient (Kahne, 2004; Stevens, 2008). Unfortunately, very few families manage to meet this goal (Lein & Schexnayder, 2007; Belle, 2008). In addition, each of the 50 states is allowed to decide which individuals are "desperate" enough to need financial assistance, and many states choose to allocate TANF funds to programs that do not directly support women and their families (CBPP, 2021).

Furthermore, women in the TANF program in most states are specifically discouraged from pursuing education beyond the level of high school (Belle, 2008; Ratner, 2004). Imagine, for example, that a college student who is a mother wants to escape from an abusive marriage. If she leaves the marriage and applies for TANF funding to support her children, she will be forced to leave college and earn a minimum wage in a low-level job (Evelyn, 2000).

A few states include the option of higher education for TANF recipients. For example, the state of Maine created the "Parents as Scholars" program. This program allows TANF recipients to attend college, with the long-term goal of empowering them and helping them move out of poverty. Here is a comment from a 39-year-old woman, now a college senior with a 3.7 grade point average:

> My self-esteem has greatly improved. For most of my life I believed I was not intelligent enough to go to college. When I began school I was very nervous and stressed about whether I could succeed; I have! I now feel confident in my ability to think, process, and produce answers both academically and personally. (Deprez et al., 2004, p. 225)

You already know from Figure 7.1 that a woman's education is one of the best predictors of her employment. Compared to college graduates, women without college degrees are significantly more likely to live in poverty (Deprez et al., 2004; Mathur et al., 2004). The current TANF policy has not solved the employment problem, and it also has important consequences for the children of these women. The current TANF program is obviously shortsighted for both women and their children.

Discrimination in Hiring Patterns

Consider the following classic study. Rhea Steinpreis and her colleagues (1999) wrote to psychology professors, asking them to evaluate the qualifications of a potential job candidate. All the professors received the same, identical resume; however, half the resumes used the name "Karen Miller" and half used the name "Brian Miller." Of those who thought that the candidate was a woman, 45% said that they would hire her. Of those who thought that the candidate was a man, 75% said that they would hire him. Incidentally, female professors were just as likely as male professors to demonstrate this biased hiring pattern. This evidence of discrimination is especially worrisome because this study surveyed psychology professors, who are well aware of the research on gender stereotypes (Powell & Graves, 2003).

The term **access discrimination** refers to discrimination used in hiring—for example, rejecting well-qualified women applicants or offering them less attractive positions. Once women have been hired, they may face another kind of discrimination, called treatment discrimination, which we'll discuss later in this chapter. In later chapters, we will encounter additional examples of access discrimination during hiring when we consider women with disabilities (Chapter 11) and women who are above average size (Chapter 12).

When Does Access Discrimination Operate?

As you might guess, the research on access discrimination is complex. Several factors determine whether women face access discrimination when they apply for work.

1. *Employers who have strong gender stereotypes are more likely to demonstrate access discrimination.* In general, supervisors who endorse traditional gender roles tend to avoid hiring women (Masser & Abrams, 2004; Powell & Graves, 2003). In addition, people who consider themselves strongly religious are likely to have negative attitudes toward employed women (Harville & Rienzi, 2000).
2. *Access discrimination is particularly likely to operate when the applicant's qualifications are ambiguous.* For instance, employers will hire a man rather than a woman when both candidates are not especially qualified for a job. In contrast, employers are less likely to discriminate against a woman if they have abundant information that she is well qualified and if her experience is directly relevant to the proposed job (Powell & Graves, 2003).
3. *Employers often discriminate against women candidates who are assertive.* We discussed this tendency at the end of Chapter 6. According to related research, people believe that strong, assertive women are not socially skilled (Hopkins, 2007; Phelan et al., 2008; Rhode & Williams, 2007). As a result, these women may not be hired.
4. *Access discrimination is particularly likely to operate when women apply for a prestigious position.* For example, the Canadian government designed a program of awarding research grants to attract outstanding professors to Canadian universities. Unfortunately, only 17% of the approximately 1,000 awards went to women, although 26% of all the full-time Canadian faculty members were women (Birchard, 2004).
5. *Access discrimination often operates for both women and men when they apply for "gender-inappropriate" jobs.* In general, employers and career-placement consultants select men for jobs when most of the current employees are men, and they select women when most of the employees are women (Lawless & Fox, 2005; Powell & Graves, 2003).

In summary, a woman is less likely to be considered for a job when the evaluators hold strong stereotypes, when a woman's qualifications are ambiguous, or when she is considered too assertive. She is also less likely to be considered when the position is prestigious, and when the job is considered appropriate for men.

How Does Access Discrimination Operate?

We examined gender stereotypes in some detail in Chapter 2. Unfortunately, people's stereotypes about women may operate in several ways to produce access discrimination (Lawless & Fox, 2005; Powell & Graves, 2003; Rudman & Glick, 2008; Schmader et al., 2007; Steinberg et al., 2008).

1. *Employers may have negative stereotypes about women's abilities.* An employer who believes that women are typically unmotivated and incompetent will probably react negatively to a specific woman candidate.
2. *Employers may assume that the candidate must have certain stereotypically masculine characteristics to succeed on the job.* Female candidates may be perceived as having stereotypically feminine characteristics, even if they are actually assertive and independent. As you know from Chapter 2, people's stereotypes can bias their memory and their judgment.

3. *Employers may pay attention to inappropriate characteristics when female candidates are being interviewed.* The interviewer may judge a woman in terms of her physical appearance, parental status, and personality. They might ignore characteristics relevant to the executive position that she is seeking. In this situation, called **gender-role spillover**, beliefs about gender roles and characteristics spread to the work setting (Rudman & Glick, 2008). Employers are likely to emphasize the kinds of stereotypically female traits we discussed in Chapter 2.

In each case, note that stereotypes can encourage employers to conclude that a man ought to receive a particular position. In fact, employers may hire a moderately qualified man, instead of a more qualified woman (Powell & Graves, 2003).

What Is Affirmative Action?

Affirmative action is designed to reduce access discrimination and other biases in the workplace and other institutions. According to federal law in the United States, every company that has more than 50 employees must establish an affirmative action plan. **Affirmative action** means that an employer must make special efforts to consider qualified members of underrepresented groups during hiring, as well as decisions about salary and promotion (Crosby et al., 2003). Affirmative action also means that the employer has actively worked to remove any barriers that prevent genuine equality of opportunity. Most often, the underrepresented groups are women and people of color.

The average U.S. citizen is not well informed about affirmative action (Crosby, 2004, 2008; Crosby et al., 2006). You may observe news-show hosts or politicians claiming that the government is forcing companies to hire unqualified women instead of qualified men. They may also claim that the government sets quotas, for instance, about the specific number of Black individuals that a company must hire. Neither of these claims is correct (Crosby et al., 2006). Instead, affirmative action specifies that (1) companies must encourage applications from the underrepresented groups, based on ethnicity and gender, and (2) companies must make a good-faith effort to meet the affirmative action goals they have set (Bisom-Rapp et al., 2007).

The goal of affirmative action is to make sure that fully qualified women and people of color are given a fair consideration in the workplace, to compensate for past or present discrimination (Cleveland et al., 2000). For example, a company's administrators may discover that the company employs a smaller percentage of women than the data indicate to be available for a specific job title. The administrators must then analyze their procedures to determine whether the hiring procedures are somehow biased (Sincharoen & Crosby, 2001).

Research demonstrates that those U.S. companies with affirmative action programs do indeed have greater workplace equality for women and people of color (Crosby et al., 2003). A comparable program in Canada, called Employment Equity, has shown similar success (Konrad & Linnehan, 1999).

Some people think that affirmative action will produce **reverse discrimination**, in which a woman would be hired instead of a more highly qualified man. However, reverse discrimination is relatively rare. According to a study of 3,000 U.S. affirmative action court cases, only 3 cases represented had to do with reverse discrimination (Blau et al., 2006; Crosby et al., 2003).

The research also shows that affirmative action can provide an advantage for White employees. Specifically, White individuals actually learn more cognitive skills and conflict-resolution skills if they interact frequently with people from other ethnic groups (Hurtado, 2005). In addition, data suggest that the people who benefit most from affirmative action are White women (Crenshaw, 2006).

Section Summary

Background Factors Related to Women's Employment

1. Women's employment status is influenced by factors such as education and immigrant status; parental status and ethnicity are not strongly related to being employed.
2. The current TANF policy on financial assistance for economically disadvantaged women has long-term consequences for U.S. women; for example, women may be forced to leave a career-oriented college program to earn money in a low-level job.
3. Women are especially likely to experience access discrimination when (a) the employer has strong gender stereotypes, (b) the applicant's qualifications are ambiguous, (c) the applicant is assertive, (d) the position is prestigious, and (e) they apply for "gender-inappropriate" jobs.
4. Gender stereotypes encourage access discrimination because employers may (a) have negative stereotypes about women, (b) believe women lack "appropriate" stereotypically masculine characteristics, and (c) pay attention to characteristics that are irrelevant for the positions women are seeking.
5. Affirmative action policy specifies that companies must make appropriate efforts to consider qualified members of underrepresented groups in work-related decisions.

7-2 Discrimination in the Workplace

Learning Objectives

To identify factors that increase gender discrimination in the workplace, you can...

7-2-1 Define treatment discrimination and identify some factors that lead to the gender wage gap.

7-2-2 Differentiate between the glass ceiling, labyrinth, sticky floor, and glass escalator concepts.

7-2-3 Identify how gender is related to promotions and sexual harassment at work.

7-2-4 Explain how heterosexism creates disparity in the workplace for lesbian women.

7-2-5 Summarize possible solutions for reducing discrimination in the workplace.

So far, we've discussed one kind of discrimination against women: the *access discrimination* that women face when applying for a job. A second problem, **treatment discrimination**, refers to the discrimination that women encounter after they have obtained a job. Let's examine salary discrimination, promotion discrimination, other workplace biases, and the discrimination that lesbian women experience in the workplace. We'll also consider what people can do to combat workplace discrimination.

Discrimination in Salaries

The most obvious kind of treatment discrimination is that women earn less money than men do. As of 2020, as we noted earlier, U.S. women who worked full time earned only 82% of the median[1] annual salary of men (National Committee on Pay Equity, 2021). Let's make this discrepancy more vivid: The average female college graduate will earn $1.2 million less during her lifetime than the average male college graduate, if both of them work full time (E. F. Murphy, 2005).

As Figure 7.2 portrays, the gender gap in salaries holds true for White, Black, Latina, and Asian American women (Bureau of Labor Statistics, 2019; Steinberg et al., 2008). However, comparable data for Native American workers are not available. Canadian workers also experience a gender gap. The research demonstrates that Canadian women who

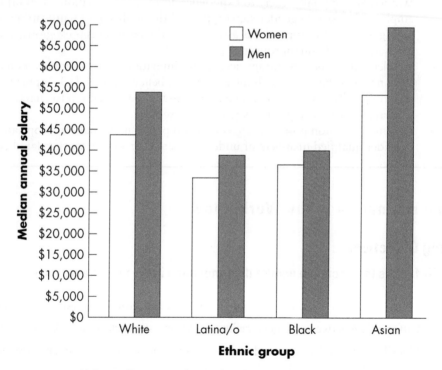

FIGURE **7.2** U.S. median annual salaries for full-time employment (aged 15 and older), as a function of gender and ethnic group.

Source: Institute for Women's Policy Research (2019).

---

[1]The median is the exact midpoint of a distribution; in this case, it is a dollar amount above which half the men were receiving higher salaries and below which half were receiving lower salaries.

worked full time earned only 87% of the average[2] annual salary of men (Pelletier, Patterson, & Moyser, 2019). Regardless of ethnicity, women earn less than men across most occupations. This is what scientists call a *main effect* for gender in terms of the wage gap.

Salary discrimination cannot be explained by gender differences in education (Dey & Hill, 2007; Institute for Women's Policy Research, 2009; Statistics Canada, 2006). Women earn substantially lower salaries at every educational level. For instance, studies have demonstrated that men with associate degrees actually earn more money each year than women with bachelor's degrees (Dey & Hill, 2007). In other words, these women attend college for approximately 2 more years than these men do, and the women then earn lower salaries.

One important reason for the discrepancy in salaries is that men enter jobs that pay more money (Bergmann, 2006; Lovell et al., 2007; Rudman & Glick, 2008). Lawyers, who are usually men, earn more than twice as much as social workers, who are usually women. However, men earn more than women, even in the same job (E. F. Murphy, 2005; Rudman & Glick, 2008). For instance, male lawyers have a median annual income of $120,848 versus $86,560 for female lawyers. Male social workers have a median annual income of $60,480 versus $50,544 for women (Bureau of Labor Statistics, 2020).

Other variables that can explain part of the wage discrepancy include gender differences in the number of years of work experience and family responsibilities. However, studies conducted in the United States and Canada demonstrate that women are simply paid less than men, even when other factors are taken into account (Blau & Kahn, 2006; Dey & Hill, 2007).

Researchers have reported similar wage gaps in countries other than the United States and Canada. For instance, in Great Britain, Switzerland, and Germany, women earn between about 65% and 75% of men's pay. The gap is even larger in Japan, where women earn about 50% of men's pay. However, in countries such as Norway, Denmark, and Australia, women earn close to 90% of men's pay (Powell & Graves, 2003). The salary gap is smaller in countries in which the government has instituted a policy of pay equity.

Let's examine two more specific aspects of the salary gap: (1) a concept called "comparable worth" and (2) women's reactions to receiving lower pay.

Comparable Worth

Most people are willing to agree that a man and a woman with equivalent performance at the same job should receive the same salaries. That is, women and men should receive equal pay for equal work.

Comparable worth is more complicated. The concept of **comparable worth** argues that women and men should receive equal pay for different jobs when those different jobs are comparable—that is, when the jobs require equal training and equal ability (Lips, 2003; Lovell et al., 2007).

People who favor comparable-worth legislation argue that we can attribute much of the gender gap in wages to **occupational segregation**; as we noted, men and women tend to choose different occupations. Specifically, "women's jobs" (such as librarians and child-care workers) pay less than "men's jobs" (such as engineers and tree-trimmers). Consistent with Theme 3 of this book, the work that women do is devalued in terms of the actual

---

[2]In contrast to the median, the average is calculated by adding together every person's salary and dividing by the number of people. Because the U.S. data and the Canadian data used different measures to represent the typical salary, they cannot be directly compared.

Demonstration 7.1

Gender Comparisons in Salary Requests

Ask a number of friends to participate in a brief study. Ideally, you should recruit at least five men and five women. (Make sure that the two groups are roughly similar in average age and work experience.) Ask them the following question:

"I want you to imagine that you are an undergraduate who has been employed as a research assistant to Dr. Lee, who is a professor of psychology. You will be working with him all summer, entering data that are being collected for a summer research project. What hourly salary do you believe would be appropriate for this summer job?"

When you have gathered all the data, calculate the average wage the men suggested and the average wage the women suggested.

The text lists the salary requests that students provided in a study several years ago. Do you find a similar wage gap in the requests you gathered?

Source: Based on Bylsma and Major (1992).

---

dollar value placed on their accomplishments in the workplace. In other words, these female-stereotypical jobs pay less, simply because it is women—rather than men—who do this work (Lips, 2003; Lovell et al., 2007; E. F. Murphy, 2005).

In general, the strategy behind comparable worth is to pay the same salaries for "men's jobs" and "women's jobs" that have been matched on characteristics such as education, previous experience, skills, level of danger, and supervisory responsibilities (Lips, 2003; Lovell et al., 2007). By this reasoning, a woman with a bachelor's degree who works with children in a day-care center should earn a larger salary than a mechanic with a high-school degree who works with air conditioners. So far, however, comparable worth legislation has had only limited success.

Reactions to Lower Salaries

How do women feel about their lower salaries? One answer to this question comes from research in which women and men decide how much they ought to receive for doing a particular job. According to research in both the United States and Canada, women specify lower salaries, suggesting that they are satisfied with less money (Bylsma & Major, 1992; Heckert et al., 2002; Hogue & Yoder, 2003; McGann & Steil, 2006; Steinberg et al., 2008).

Now try Demonstration 7.1, which illustrates a classic study by Bylsma and Major (1992). These researchers found that undergraduate men and women who received no additional information provided very different salary requests. Specifically, men asked for an average of $6.30, whereas women asked for an average of $5.30. In a study that was similar, Hogue and Yoder (2003) found that men asked for an average of $10.27, whereas women asked for $7.48. With respect to salary, men seem to have a greater sense of **entitlement**;

based on their membership in the male social group, they believe that they have a right to high rewards (McGann & Steil, 2006).

How do women react to the overall gender gap in wages? Both women and men know that women actually earn lower wages (McGann & Steil, 2006). However, women are typically more concerned about women's lower wages than men are (Desmarais & Curtis, 2001). For instance, Reiser (2001) asked 1,000 men and women a variety of questions that focused on anger. She found that 62% of the women and only 38% of the men agreed with the statement, "It makes me angry when men have greater job opportunities and rewards than women" (p. 35). Still, isn't it surprising that 38% of the women and 62% of the men were *not* concerned about this inequity?

Now let's consider a more personal question. In general, women are not especially angry about *their own* salaries: Why aren't women outraged? One reason may be that they often fail to acknowledge that they have the right skills for the job (Hogue & Yoder, 2003; Steinberg et al., 2008).

Faye Crosby identified another important reason. According to her research on the **denial of personal disadvantage**, many women are reluctant to acknowledge that they—personally—are the victims of discrimination (Crosby, 2008; Crosby et al., 2006; Steinberg et al., 2008). Yes, they know that *women in general* experience discrimination. However, if a woman acknowledges that she herself is underpaid, then she must explain this inequity. She may be reluctant to conclude that her boss and the organization that employs her are villains. Unfortunately, if she continues to deny her personal disadvantage, she is not likely to fight for pay equity and other social justice issues.

Discrimination in Promotions

We've learned that women earn lower salaries than men, even in comparable occupations. A related problem is that women are less likely than men to be promoted into the top leadership positions in universities, corporations, and other organizations (Duehr & Bono, 2006; Goldman et al., 2006; Hogue & Lord, 2007; Hoyt & Blascovich, 2007; Rudman & Glick, 2008).

A relevant term that has been especially popular is "the glass ceiling." The **glass ceiling** is an invisible but rigid barrier that seems to prevent women and people of color from reaching the top levels in many professional organizations (Atwater et al., 2004; Betz, 2006).

However, Alice Eagly and Linda Carli (2007) suggest that the glass-ceiling metaphor is no longer appropriate. They reject that term for a variety of reasons. For example, a "a glass ceiling" implies that women and men have had equal opportunities—throughout their early employment—until they suddenly encounter this glass ceiling. Furthermore, in recent years, women and people of color do occasionally make it to the most prestigious leadership positions, such as the president of a corporation and the president or vice president of the United States.

Eagly and Carli (2007) propose a different metaphor, called the "labyrinth." According to their concept of the **labyrinth metaphor**, women in search of a promotion will encounter many difficulties along the route, including dead ends, detours, and puzzling pathways. To successfully reach the goal at the end of the labyrinth, women must be extremely competent, and they also need to develop flexible strategies that blend warmth and compassion with strength and decisiveness.

Labor theorists have created a different metaphor to describe a problem that women are statistically more likely to encounter. The metaphor of the **sticky floor** describes the situation of women who are employed in low-level jobs with no chance of promotion (Gutek, 2001; Whitley & Kite, 2010). Many women are office workers, cashiers, and servers. They are likely to remain in these jobs throughout their work life, never being considered for positions with greater responsibility (Padavic & Reskin, 2002). In fact, these women have no opportunity to even find the entrance to a labyrinth, let alone reach the glass ceiling.

A fourth metaphor describes another component of gender bias. The **glass escalator** phenomenon applies to men who enter fields that are often associated with women, such as nursing, teaching, library science, and social work; in these occupations, men are often quickly promoted to management positions (Furr, 2002; Whitley & Kite, 2010; J. D. Yoder, 2002). The glass escalator whisks them up to a more prestigious position. For example, a male teacher in elementary special education was asked about his career choice. He replied, "I am extremely marketable in special education. That's not why I got into the field. But I am extremely marketable because I am a man" (C. L. Williams, 1998, p. 288).

In short, women generally face discrimination with respect to promotion (Eagly & Karau, 2002; Whitley & Kite, 2010). The three stereotypes that we mentioned on pages 213–214 in connection with hiring patterns also operate when women are eligible for a promotion (Sczesny, 2003). After reviewing the research on treatment discrimination, Mark Agars (2004) concluded, "It is clear that substantial discrepancies in gender distributions at high levels of organizations are attributable, at least in part, to gender stereotypes" (p. 109).

Other Kinds of Treatment Discrimination

In addition to discrimination in salary and promotions, women experience treatment discrimination in other areas. For example, several studies suggest that women in the workplace are more likely than men to receive negative evaluations (e.g., Chrisler & Clapp, 2008; Settles et al., 2006). As we read in Chapter 2 and Chapter 6, women are often downgraded for their performance, especially if they are assertive (Chin, 2004; Rivero et al., 2004).

For women teaching at colleges and universities, students provide other forms of treatment discrimination. For instance, students rate young male professors as more conscientious and interested in their material, compared to young female professors (Arbuckle & Williams, 2003). Students also think that their male professors should be entertaining, but their female professors should be caring and nurturing (Sprague & Massoni, 2005). Women professors in a variety of academic fields systematically receive lower teaching evaluations than their male counterparts (Mengel, Sauermann, & Zölitz, 2019; Mitchell & Martin, 2018).

Sometimes the treatment discrimination depends on the gender of the students. For example, undergraduate men are more likely than undergraduate women to give their female college professors poor ratings on their teaching performance and classroom interactions (Basow, 2004; Basow et al., 2006).

In addition, students often assume that their male professors have had more education than their female professors (J. Miller & Chamberlin, 2000). When students address their female professors who have Ph.D. degrees, they are likely to call them "Miss —" or "Ms. —," instead of "Dr. —" (Laube et al., 2007; Wilbers et al., 2003).

Another form of treatment discrimination is sexual harassment, a topic we'll explore in Chapter 13. **Sexual harassment** refers to unwanted gender-related behavior, such as sexual coercion, offensive sexual attention, sexual touching, and hostile verbal and physical behaviors that focus on gender (Fitzgerald et al., 2001; Gutek, 2007). Women frequently experience this kind of treatment discrimination, when other workers convey the message that women are sexual objects or incompetent employees. For example, a Black female firefighter recalled her first encounter with her White male supervisor:

> The first day I came on, the first day I was in the field, the guy told me he didn't like me. And then he said: "I'm gonna tell you why I don't like you. Number one, I don't like you cuz you're Black. And number two, cuz you're a woman." And that was all he said. He walked away. (J. D. Yoder & Aniakudo, 1997, p. 329)

You won't be surprised to learn, then, that women in blue-collar jobs are typically more likely than men to report negative interactions in the workplace (Betz, 2006; Settles et al., 2006). In addition, women may be excluded from informal social interactions where employees may exchange important information and form useful friendships. Women of color are especially likely to be left out of the social interactions and mentoring (Fassinger, 2002). In addition to facing other forms of discrimination, women certainly do not have equal opportunities in informal social interactions.

Discrimination Against Lesbian Women in the Workplace

In Chapter 2, we noted that **heterosexism** is a belief system that devalues lesbian women, gay men, and bisexual women—any group that is not heterosexual. Lesbian women frequently face heterosexism in the workplace. As you might guess, many employers refuse to hire individuals who are known to be openly gay. For example, public schools often discriminate against hiring people who identify as lesbian, gay, and bisexual as teachers. The unjustified argument is that these individuals may try to persuade young people to adopt a nonheterosexual orientation. Furthermore, in some parts of the United States, employers can fire employees for any reason they choose, including being a lesbian woman or a gay man (Horvath & Ryan, 2003; Peplau & Fingerhut, 2004).

The research suggests that people who are open and accepting of their LGBTQ+ identity are higher in self-esteem (Badgett, 2008). Sadly, many jobs seem to require that LGBTQ+ individuals refrain from being open about their gender or sexual orientation. Many lesbian women say they spend so much energy trying to hide their sexual orientation that their work is less productive (Badgett, 2008; Hambright & Decker, 2002). Lesbian women may also internalize some of the prejudiced beliefs they encounter in their coworkers (Herek, 2009).

Should lesbian women, gay men, and bisexual individuals disclose their sexual orientation to potential employers? Openness makes sense for people who plan to be "out" in their work setting, if they wouldn't want to work in a heterosexist environment (Wenniger & Conroy, 2001). However, some lesbian women prefer to receive the job offer first and then come out gradually to coworkers. As you know from this chapter, bias is less likely when people are already familiar with an employee's high-quality work. Incidentally, lesbian women and gay men workers sometimes find that their labor unions can support them when they encounter workplace discrimination (Hunt & Boris, 2007).

In a related study, undergraduates judged the qualifications of a potential job applicant, using a scale from 0 to 100. The description of the job applicant's characteristics were identical, except for gender and sexual orientation. The students gave a rating of 85 to the heterosexual man, 81 to the gay man, 80 to the lesbian woman, and 76 to the heterosexual woman (Horvath & Ryan, 2003). These results are not especially hopeful for anybody other than heterosexual men, except for the fact that there was only a 9-point range among all four ratings.

The research also provides interesting perspectives on lesbian women and their work experiences. For instance, several studies show that lesbian workers earn higher salaries than heterosexual female workers. One explanation is that lesbian women are almost twice as likely as heterosexual women to have at least a bachelor's degree, and education is correlated with a person's income. Another explanation is that lesbian women are more likely than other women to pursue nontraditional careers, which also pay better than traditionally feminine careers (Peplau & Fingerhut, 2004).

What to Do About Treatment Discrimination

The title of this section is daunting: How can we possibly try to correct all the forces that encourage gender discrimination in the workplace? A few guidelines may be helpful with respect to the actions of both individuals and institutions.

Individuals can have an impact on their own work experiences as well as on the experiences of other women:

1. It is helpful for women to be aware of the conditions in which stereotypes are least likely to operate, for example, when the job applicant's qualifications are clear-cut rather than ambiguous. Find work you enjoy. Then develop skills and experiences that are especially relevant to your occupation, so that you are clearly well qualified (O'Connell, 2001). It is also beneficial to know your legal rights (Rhode & Williams, 2007).
2. Join relevant organizations, use online sources, and make connections with other supportive people (Kimmel, 2007; Padavic & Reskin, 2002; Wenniger & Conroy, 2001). Feminist organizations may be especially helpful. For example, a survey of female psychologists showed that many regarded feminism as "a life raft in the choppy, frigid waters of gender discrimination" (Klonis et al., 1997, p. 343).
3. Locate someone who has achieved success in your profession; ask whether she can serve as a mentor (Hart, 2008; O'Connell, 2001; Rhode & Williams, 2007). Employees who have mentors are likely to be especially successful and satisfied with their occupation (Padavic & Reskin, 2002).

In reality, however, individual employees cannot overcome the major problem of gender discrimination. It is often in their best interests for institutions to become more diversified and change. For example, a company's sales may increase if their workplace diversity resembles the diversity in the real world outside that company (Cleveland et al., 2000; Powell & Graves, 2003). In addition, corporations and firms that are led by women are more profitable (Sandberg, 2019). Finally, gender discrimination is legally prohibited. Organizations that are genuinely committed to change can take the following precautions:

1. Understand affirmative action policies and take them seriously; make sure that women are well represented in the pool of candidates for hiring and promotion. Develop guidelines within the organization (Karsten, 2006; Wetchler, 2007).
2. Appoint a task force to examine gender issues within the organization. The chief executive must make it clear that the group's recommendations will be valued and carried out. Diversity training sessions are useful if their objective is genuine change (Powell & Graves, 2003).
3. Train managers so that they can evaluate candidates fairly, reducing gender stereotypes (Gerber, 2001; Rhode & Williams, 2007). For example, managers who rate employees might ask themselves questions such as, "How would I evaluate this performance if the person were a man rather than a woman?" (Valian, 1998, p. 309).

Realistically, creating gender-fair work experiences requires a massive transformation of cultures, beginning with nonsexist child rearing, acceptance of feminist concerns, and appreciation for the contributions of women and other underrepresented groups. Implementing policies that ensure equal pay for comparable work would also help reduce the gender pay gap (Karsten, 2006; J. D. Yoder, 2000). A truly gender-fair work world would also provide a comprehensive national child-care plan, and it would ensure that men would perform an equal share of child-care and housework responsibilities—a topic we'll examine at the end of this chapter.

Section Summary

Discrimination in the Workplace

1. For all ethnic groups, the average woman earns less than the average man; the wage gap remains, even when factors such as occupation, education, and work experience are taken into account.
2. "Comparable worth" means that women and men would receive the same pay for occupations that require similar education, previous experience, skill, and other relevant factors.
3. A man typically feels entitled to a higher salary, compared to a woman. Also, a woman often demonstrates "denial of personal disadvantage"; she does not express concern that she herself is underpaid.
4. Women experience discrimination in terms of promotion; Eagly and Carli's metaphor of a labyrinth is more descriptive than the glass ceiling metaphor. Other related kinds of gender discrimination are called the sticky floor and the glass escalator.
5. Women may also experience other kinds of treatment discrimination, such as lower evaluations from supervisors and—in the case of professors—from students; women may also face sexual harassment and exclusion from social interactions.
6. Lesbian women are especially likely to experience workplace discrimination; they may be fired because of their sexual orientation, and they may feel that they need to hide their sexual orientation. Lesbian women often earn higher salaries than other women, partly because they are more likely to have at least a bachelor's degree.
7. The actions of individuals and institutions can address some aspects of treatment discrimination. However, a genuine solution depends on more widespread societal change.

7-3 Women's Experiences in Selected Occupations

Learning Objectives

To summarize women's experiences in selected occupations, you can ...

7-3-1   Discuss the pros and cons for women who work in traditional female-dominated occupations.

7-3-2   Describe how working in the domestic and garment factory industries affect the lives of women.

7-3-3   Describe characteristics of women who work in traditionally male-dominated, high-prestige professions.

7-3-4   Identify factors that impact the workplace climate for women in high-prestige professions.

7-3-5   Describe the experiences of women who work in traditionally male-dominated, blue-collar occupations.

7-3-6   Differentiate between person-centered and situation-centered explanations for women's scarcity in certain occupations.

We have learned that women face access discrimination when they apply for work. They also encounter several types of treatment discriminations once they are employed. In this section, we will examine women's work experiences in several specific occupations.

News reports in the United States often feature women who are physicians, heads of corporations, and astronauts. Women who are nurses, cashiers, and cafeteria workers do not make headlines. Even though the majority of employed women hold jobs in clerical and service occupations, the work of millions of these women is relatively unappreciated.

Let's begin by discussing some traditionally female occupations. Then we'll examine two areas in which fewer women are employed: the traditionally male professions and traditionally male blue-collar work. We will then examine why women are so scarce in nontraditional occupations.

Employment in Traditionally Female Occupations

Table 7.1 lists some representative occupations that are traditional for women. Notice the percentage of employees who are women. Furthermore, roughly half of all female professional or technical workers are in traditional areas such as nursing and pre-college teaching.

This observation does not imply that something is wrong with traditionally female occupations. In fact, our children would probably be better off if we genuinely valued the people who work in day-care centers and in elementary schools. However, women in traditionally female jobs frequently struggle with problems such as low income, underutilization of abilities, and lack of independence in decision making.

Similar employment patterns operate in Canada, where the gender pay gap can be explained by differences in occupational choice, part-time versus full-time employment, and educational attainment (Pelletier, Patterson, & Moyser, 2019). For example, 70% of all employed women work in teaching, health-care occupations such as nursing, clerical positions, or occupations such as sales or service. In contrast, only 31% of employed men work in one of these three areas (Statistics Canada, 2004).

Surprisingly, however, women in traditionally female occupations report the same level of job satisfaction as people in other occupations (Buchanan, 2005). As we discussed on page 219, women tend to report that they are not disadvantaged, as far as factors such as salary.

It's also important to know that the work considered traditional for women may be quite different in developing countries. About 80% of women in Western Europe work in service occupations, but in sub-Saharan Africa, 65% of the women in the labor force work in agriculture (United Nations, 2000). We even observe different work patterns within the same continent. For example, consider two countries in West Africa. In Sierra Leone, the men are responsible for the rice fields; in Senegal, women manage the rice fields (Burn, 1996).

TABLE **7.1**

Percentage of Workers in Selected Traditionally
Female Occupations Who Are Women

Occupation	Percentage of Workers Who Are Women
Preschool teacher	99%
Dental hygienist	94
Administrative assistant	93
Registered nurse	87
Bank teller	80

Source: Based on Bureau of Labor Statistics (2019).

Perhaps the only characteristic that all these traditionally female occupations have in common is relatively low pay (Ehrenreich, 2001). As we discussed in connection with welfare, many of these workers earn wages that are below the poverty level, even if they have worked for more than 25 years (Lovell et al., 2007). For example, some teacher's aides in upstate New York make as little as $16,000 a year, although they have worked for 25 years on the job. They often need to take a second job, just to pay for basic living expenses (Saunders & Mulligan, 2008).

You probably know many women who work as secretaries, librarians, and other occupations listed in Table 7.1. Let's consider two traditionally female jobs that may be less familiar: domestic work and work in the garment industry. Consistent with Theme 3, this kind of women's work is generally underappreciated; women do the work, but few people notice (Zandy, 2001). Furthermore, women are especially likely to be exploited in these jobs.

Domestic Work

Many women emigrate from the Caribbean, Latin America, and other developing countries. They come to the United States to live and work in private homes, doing child care and other domestic work until they can earn a green card, which will allow them to find better jobs. They may be expected to work every day—with no time off and no health insurance—for a fraction of the minimum-wage salary. Many of the women report that their employers insult them, do not let them leave the house, and treat them much like modern-day slaves (B. Anderson, 2003; Boris, 2003; Hafiz & Paarlberg, 2017; Zarembka, 2003). For example, one woman reported:

> I work hard. I don't mind working hard. But I want to be treated with some human affection, like a human being.... I don't get any respect.... Since I came here this woman has never shown me one iota of ... human affection as a human being. (Colen, 1997, p. 205)

Many immigrant domestic workers do not know their legal rights (Onti-veros, 2007). In New York City, women who worked as nannies decided to organize a group called the "Domestic Workers' Union." These organizers went to parks and playgrounds, because dozens of nannies frequently go there with their employees' children. The organizers passed out fliers, inviting the women to meetings where they could learn more about their rights, as well as information about child development (J. Fine, 2007). Still, the problem of poorly treated domestic workers remains underappreciated.

Garment Work

A **sweatshop** is a factory that violates labor laws regarding wages and working conditions. Several years ago, I showed my psychology of women class a video about sweatshops. Afterwards, a young Chinese American woman—whom I will call "Ling"—said to us, "I worked in a sweatshop in New York City." Ling then described the inhumane working conditions in this clothing sweatshop.

Later, I asked Ling to write down some of the details. Ling wrote that at the age of 17, she was urged to quit high school so that she could work longer hours. She then worked every day at this sweatshop, from about 8:00 in the morning until as late as 1:00 the next morning, with just a 15-minute break for lunch. Several months later, Ling's mother began to work on a garment, without asking for the supervisor's permission. The supervisor then punched Ling's mother in the chest, and the family called the police to report the assault. The manager then fired the entire family.

Ling was one of the fortunate ones. She took this opportunity to complete high school and then enroll at SUNY Geneseo. As Ling wrote:

> Unfortunately, many young people still work there in order to live in the United States, and they are still suffering long working hours, low wages, and terrible working conditions. They are losing their sense of being interesting human beings day by day, and becoming boring and dehumanized machine-like humans.... After all these experiences, my American dream is that all workers deserve to have humane working conditions, living wages so that they can survive, and reasonable working hours, and that we will make better changes until these basic needs are met for all workers of all occupations.

Fortunately, Ling's story has a positive outcome. She graduated from my college with a strong academic record, and she is now employed as a union organizer. However, sweatshops still operate in many North American cities, from Los Angeles to Toronto (Bao, 2003; I. Ness, 2003; Seidman, 2007). These sweatshops typically employ recent immigrants from Asia and Latin America.

Furthermore, about half of all the clothing you can purchase in the United States was made in another country, typically under extremely poor working conditions. In Latin America, these sweatshops are called *maquiladoras* (pronounced mah-kee-lah-door-ahs) or *maquilas,* and they are typically run by U.S. corporations. In Latin America, a young woman may earn only 16 cents an hour, which cannot cover the cost of her food and housing (Bilbao, 2003). The work hours are also inhumane. In a typical shoe factory in China, for example, the women work from 8:00 A.M. to 9:30 P.M., six days a week (Pak, 2019). As one woman commented, "When my children called me, I cried" (Pak, 2019).

These sweatshop workers cannot earn an education, save money, or train for a better job. In addition to the long hours, low pay, and unsafe working conditions, the women who work in these sweatshops often experience sexual harassment and physical abuse. If they try to organize a union, they may be fired; many have even received death threats (Bender & Greenwald, 2003a; Bilbao, 2003).

Tai Hongling inspects a pair of Kenneth Cole shoes before they are shipped to the United States

The sweatshop issue cannot be addressed without looking at economic systems to discover who is making the greatest profits from our clothing industry (Seidman, 2007). It certainly isn't the sweatshop workers! You can obtain more information from the websites of organizations that promote sweatshop reform, such as the Chinese Staff and Workers' Association, the National Mobilization Against Sweatshops, the National Labor Committee, the Workers' Action Center (Canada), and the United States Students Against Sweatshops. To bring the sweatshop issue closer to home, try Demonstration 7.2.

Demonstration **7.2**

Where Were Your Clothes Made?

Go to your closet or your dresser and search each item of clothing for a label indicating where it was made. Record each location. What percentage was made in the United States or Canada, and what percentage was made in other countries? Later, when you have the opportunity, look in your college bookstore or other location that sells caps and sweatshirts featuring your college's logo. Where were these items made?

Employment in Traditionally Male, High-Prestige Professions

Ironically, we have far more information about the relatively small number of women employed in the prestigious "male professions" than we have about the much larger number of women employed in traditionally female jobs. Unfortunately, this emphasis on nontraditional professions creates an impression that employed women are more likely to be executives and highly trained professionals, rather than clerical workers. A more accurate picture of reality appears in Table 7.2, which lists the percentage of workers who are women in several of these high-prestige occupations. Use Table 7.1 to compare the two groups.

Let's consider some of the characteristics of women in traditionally male professions. Then we'll examine the climate in which these women work.

Characteristics of Women in High-Prestige Professions

In general, the women who work in stereotypically masculine occupations are similar to the men in those areas. For example, Lubinski and his colleagues (2001) sent questionnaires to men and women enrolled in the most prestigious U.S. graduate programs in math and science. The men and women reported highly similar academic experiences and attitudes toward their future careers. According to other research, men and women also tend to be similar in their attitude toward working in groups, rather than working alone (Hartman & Hartman, 2007).

To some extent, these similarities may occur because only those women with personal characteristics appropriate for that occupation would choose it for a career and persist in it (Cross & Vick, 2001; Eccles, 2007; Frome et al., 2008). For example, women who pursue nontraditional careers tend to be high achievers in their specific area of expertise (L. L. Sax & Bryant, 2003).

As we would expect, women and men in the same profession also tend to be similar in cognitive skills. For example, Cross (2001) found that men and women in science and engineering had earned similar scores on standardized tests, as well as similar grades in graduate school.

Other research suggests that men and women have corresponding professional expectations, motivation, fascination with the discipline, and work involvement (R. C. Barnett

TABLE **7.2**

Percentage of Workers in Selected Traditionally Male Professions Who Are Women

Occupation	Percentage of Workers Who Are Women
Aerospace engineer	12%
Computer programmer	21
Architect	28
Dentist	29
Lawyer	37

Source: Bureau of Labor Statistics (2019).

& Rivers, 2004; T. D. Fletcher & Major, 2004; Preston, 2004). However, one area in which gender differences often appear is general self-confidence (Cross, 2001). This finding is not surprising. As we observed in Chapter 5, men are more self-confident than women in some achievement settings.

The Workplace Climate for Women in High-Prestige Professions

In Chapter 4, we noted that some young female students may face a chilly classroom climate in their academic classrooms. The chilly climate may continue for some women in their graduate training and in their professions (Betz, 2006; Fort, 2005; MacLachlan, 2006; Preston, 2004; Stewart & LaVaque-Manty, 2008; Valian, 2006). For example, women typically receive less mentoring than men do (Anyaso, 2008; Nolan et al., 2008; Stewart & LaVaque-Manty, 2008; "Welcoming women," 2004).

Unfortunately, when women apply for jobs, they may find that they are evaluated in terms of their physical appearance, rather than their job-related competence (Bhattacharjee, 2007a; Dowdall, 2003). Women scientists are also much less likely than men to be hired by prestigious universities (Kuck et al., 2007). After women are hired, they may feel that their male colleagues have negative attitudes toward women and ignore women's contributions (Bergman, 2003; Preston, 2004; Settles et al., 2006). Furthermore, women are seldom nominated for prestigious national awards (Bhattacharjee, 2007b; Mervis, 2007).

Earlier in this chapter, we noted several forms of treatment discrimination. Unfortunately, treatment discrimination has an important effect on the professional environment. For instance, Dr. Frances Conley (1998), a prominent neurosurgeon, described how the male neurosurgeons would call her "honey" in front of patients.

We learned on page 57 that women are downgraded if they are too self-confident and assertive; this principle also applies in the high-prestige professions. For example, Heilman and her colleagues (2004) asked students to rate successful male and female employees who were described in vignettes. The students liked the men much more than the women. In other words, a woman who is competent, confident, and assertive may encounter negative reactions from her coworkers.

Another problem for women in these high-prestige, traditionally male professions is that men may treat them in a patronizing fashion (Preston, 2004). For instance, one female astronomer remarked, "You will go through three or four days of professional meetings and never once hear the word 'her' used. Every scientist is 'he'" (Fort, 2005b, p. 187). In summary, women in high-prestige careers receive many messages that they are not really equal to their male colleagues.

Employment in Traditionally Male Blue-Collar Jobs

At one time, Barbara Quintela worked as an administrative assistant for $10 an hour. When her husband left her—and their five children—she managed to persuade a school administrator to let her enroll in a high-school training program for electricians. After a grueling interview with eight hostile administrators, she was accepted into an apprenticeship program that later paid $22 an hour. As she said, "I like getting dirty, running wires, digging ditches, getting into crawl spaces. I would never want to go back to being a secretary. I can't afford to be a secretary" (J. C. Lambert, 2000, p. 6). Most women in blue-collar jobs report that the pay is attractive, especially compared to the salaries for jobs that are traditionally female dominated.

TABLE **7.3**

Percentage of Workers in Selected Traditionally Male
Blue-Collar Occupations Who Are Women

Occupation	Percentage of Workers Who Are Women
Firefighter	4%
Carpenter	3
Pest control employee	3
Electrician	3
Plumber	2

Most of the information on working women describes women in such traditionally male professions as medicine, law, and college teaching. In contrast, women in blue-collar jobs are discussed less often. Women are slowly entering these fields, but the percentages are still small (England, 2006; Bureau of Labor Statistics, 2019). Table 7.3 lists some representative employment rates for women in these jobs.

Women in blue-collar jobs often report that they are held to stricter standards than their male coworkers. For example, a Black woman firefighter was forced by her White male supervisor to recertify after her vehicle skidded into a pole during an ice storm. In contrast, a male colleague received no penalty when his vehicle accidentally killed an elderly pedestrian who was crossing a street (J. D. Yoder & Aniakudo, 1997). Women firefighters frequently comment that they would probably have to keep proving—for the rest of their lives—that they are competent workers (J. D. Yoder & Berendsen, 2001).

Men often claim that women are physically unable to handle the work (Milkman, 2007). Furthermore, sexual harassment is common in these jobs (S. Eisenberg, 1998; Frye, 2017; Parker, 2018). In a survey of female firefighters, 41 out of 44 women reported that they had experienced at least some sexist reactions on the job (J. D. Yoder & McDonald, 1998).

Fortunately, some women report that they develop good working relationships with their male colleagues (Padavic & Reskin, 2002; J. D. Yoder, 2002). For instance, a White female firefighter described the friendship she shared with her Black male coworkers:

> It's neat. Because I think a lot of them . . . we kind of have a bond, too. And they understand more what I go through than a White guy would. So, yeah. They're pretty together guys. They've come through the fire too, I think, in a lot of ways. (J. D. Yoder & Berendsen, 2001, p. 33)

Other women mention additional advantages to blue-collar work, such as a sense of pride in their own strength and satisfaction in doing a job well (Cull, 1997; S. Eisenberg, 1998). Some women also enjoy serving as a role model and encouraging young women to pursue work in these nontraditional areas (Coffin, 1997).

Why Are Women Scarce in Certain Occupations?

Why do relatively few women work in the traditionally male professions or in the traditionally male blue-collar jobs? Researchers have identified two major classes of explanations.

According to **person-centered explanations** (also called the **individual approach**), female socialization encourages women to develop personality traits and skills that are inappropriate for these "male occupations" (Hesse-Biber & Carter, 2000). One example of a person-centered explanation would be to claim that women are somehow less motivated than men. However, as we learned in Chapter 5, women and men are similar in areas related to motivation and achievement.

Most current research and theory in the psychology of women supports a second explanation for the scarcity of women. According to **situation-centered explanations** (or the **structural approach**), the characteristics of the organizational situation explain why women are rarely employed in these traditionally masculine occupations; personal skills or traits cannot be blamed (Hesse-Biber & Carter, 2000). For example, access discrimination may block women's opportunities. If women do manage to be hired, they face several kinds of treatment discrimination when they try to navigate the labyrinth that leads to promotion (Eagly & Carli, 2007; Powell & Graves, 2003). Also, people in prestigious positions may be unwilling to help new women employees.

Note that the person-centered explanations and the situation-centered explanations suggest different strategies for improving women's employment conditions. For example, if a woman aspires to a management position in a corporation, the person-centered explanations propose that women could take courses in handling finances, conducting meetings, and assertiveness training.

In contrast, the situation-centered explanations propose strategies that are designed to change the situation, not the person. For instance, companies could train managers to use objective rating scales (Gerber, 2001). They could also enforce affirmative action policies, and promote women to high-ranking positions (Crosby, 2008; Etzkowitz et al., 2000).

Although these suggestions sound excellent, they will not occur spontaneously. It might be helpful to remind executives that corporations will benefit if they hire competent women and treat them fairly (Krieger, 2007; Powell & Graves, 2003; Strober, 2003). When executives publicly state that a woman employee is competent, other employees will also value her contributions (Yoder, 2002).

Furthermore, the gender gap in many professions will continue as long as women continue to do the majority of housework and child care (England, 2006; Myersson Milgrom & Petersen, 2006). We will examine this issue in the next section of this chapter.

Section Summary

Women's Experiences in Selected Occupations

1. Women are especially likely to be exploited in two low-income, traditionally female jobs: domestic work and work in the garment industry (including sweatshops).
2. Women who are employed in traditionally male, high-prestige professions are generally similar to the men in these professions in terms of cognitive skills, personal characteristics, and work involvement. However, the women are often lower in self-confidence.
3. Many women in traditionally male, high-prestige professions may face treatment discrimination, sexist attitudes, and patronizing behavior.

(continues)

Section Summary *(continued)*

4. Women in blue-collar jobs may face biased treatment from the men on the job, but they value the salary and the sense of pride they gain from their work.
5. Person-centered explanations argue that women are underrepresented in traditionally male occupations because they lack the relevant personality characteristics and skills.
6. Situation-centered explanations provide a more appropriate explanation for the findings; they emphasize that access discrimination and treatment discrimination may limit women's success.

7-4 Coordinating Employment with Personal Life

Learning Objectives

To describe factors that impact how women coordinate employment with personal life, you can …

7-4-1   Identify factors that increase gender disparities in the division of household responsibilities for married women.

7-4-2   Explain how gender disparities in household chores impact women's satisfaction in marriage.

7-4-3   Summarize how taking care of children affects marital satisfaction and marital success.

7-4-4   Explain how children are impacted by maternal employment.

7-4-5   Describe how role strain affects employed women's physical and mental health.

Most college women plan to combine a career with family life (Gutek & Gilliland, 2007; Hoffnung, 2004). However, the popular media often claim that an employed woman with a family must be overwhelmed (R. C. Barnett & Rivers, 2004; Bennetts, 2007). Every day, she must juggle multiple commitments, to her work, her spouse, her children, and the mental load of managing household responsibilities (Daminger, 2019). According to television comedies, fathers are incompetent in taking care of their children, even though we all know loving, competent fathers.

Online articles and popular magazines imply that numerous well-educated women are quitting their jobs to escape the time crunch and enjoy life at home. However, those articles are typically based on small samples of White, upper-class women (Prince, 2004). These magazines seldom include articles about how women can successfully blend employment and family life (Bennetts, 2007; Wildgrube, 2008).

As we have noted throughout this textbook, reality often differs from the myth presented by the media. In this section, we'll discover that employed women may find it challenging to combine their many roles. However, Moen (2008) points out that the majority are not dropping out of their careers, as some articles imply. Let's discover how employment influences three components of a woman's personal life: (1) her marriage, (2) her children, and (3) her own well-being.

Marriage

In 50% of all married couples in the United States, both the wife and the husband are employed (Bureau of Labor Statistics, 2019). The comparable figure for Canada is 78% (Moyser, 2017). Try Demonstration 7.3 before you read further, and then we'll consider two questions:

1. How do families divide their household responsibilities?
2. Does a woman's employment influence marital satisfaction?

Dividing Household Responsibilities

While writing this chapter, we read an article posted on a popular website aimed at working women trying to balance work from home with family responsibilities during the COVID-19 epidemic (DealsInsight, 2020). The authors of this article provided seven suggestions for creating work–life balance that included hiring someone to help with daily chores, finding a nanny for the children, creating a strict schedule for everyone throughout the day, and defining daily "kitchen hours." But *none* of the suggestions mentioned that women should expect their household partners to do some of the work! This article also assumed that women would be the managers of the household, which reflects the often unrecognized cognitive load that women carry in dividing household responsibilities.

Throughout this chapter, we've often noted that women are treated unfairly in the world of work. When we consider how married couples divide household tasks, we find

---

Demonstration **7.3**

Division of Responsibility for Household Tasks

Think about a married heterosexual couple with whom you are familiar; it might be your parents, the parents of a close friend, or your own current relationship with someone of the other gender. For each task in the following list, place a check mark to indicate which member of the pair is primarily responsible. Is this pattern similar to the division of housework we are discussing in this chapter?

Task	Wife	Husband
Shopping for food	_____	_____
Cooking	_____	_____
Washing the dishes	_____	_____
Laundry	_____	_____
Vacuuming	_____	_____
Washing the car	_____	_____
Gardening	_____	_____
Taking out the trash	_____	_____
Paying the bills	_____	_____
Household repairs	_____	_____

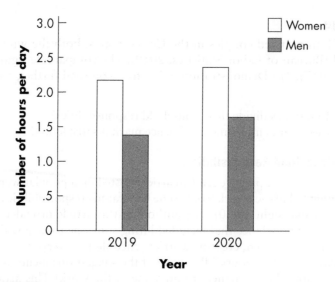

FIGURE **7.3** U.S. amount of time spent on housework, as a function of gender and ethnic group.
Source: Based on Bureau of Labor Statistics (2019).

additional evidence of unfairness, particularly in heterosexual relationships. Figure 7.3 presents data from the Bureau of Labor Statistics (2019) regarding gender differences in household duties. As demonstrated in the chart, on average, women in the United States spend more time than men on housework.

Several studies in the United States suggest that men do somewhat more housework if they are married to employed women. However, men still perform between only 30% and 40% of the household tasks in two-job families (Coltrane & Adams, 2001a; Crosby & Sabattini, 2006; Perry-Jenkins et al., 2004). A Canadian study showed that men performed a median of about 7 hours of housework each week, in contrast to a median of about 13 hours for women (Statistics Canada, 2005c).

Women are much more likely than men to do the cooking, cleaning, laundry, dishwashing, and shopping. The only indoor chores that men are more likely to do are household repair and paying bills (Eagly & Carli, 2007). Another issue is that men seldom take responsibility for noticing when a household task needs to be done; instead, the typical husband waits for his wife to remind him (Coltrane & Adams, 2008). Daminger (2019) has argued that the cognitive labor involved with managing households is a gendered phenomenon that creates inequality in heterosexual relationships. Women are more likely than men to perform this labor, which includes stressful tasks such as anticipating needs, making decisions, and monitoring household organization and progress. Because this cognitive labor involves non-obvious mental tasks, rather than obvious physical tasks, it is less recognizable to others and often goes unacknowledged by women's partners (Daminger, 2019).

Unfortunately, many men do not acknowledge how little housework they do; only 52% of men in one study agreed with the statement "Men typically don't do their share of work around the house" (Reiser, 2001, p. 35). Earlier in the chapter, we noted a wage gap between the salaries of employed men and employed women. Because women spend so much time on housework, there is also a leisure gap for employed men and women (Coltrane & Adams, 2008; Such, 2006; Weinshenker, 2005).

What factors influence the division of household tasks? As Figure 7.3 demonstrates, U.S. women do more housework than men do. Another factor is the couple's belief system. Research in the United States and in 13 European countries shows that men tend to share the housework more equally if they are nontraditional and politically liberal (Apparala et al., 2003; Sabattini & Leaper, 2004).

How do the men explain their lack of responsibility for household tasks? Although many men may be more sensitive, one man explained, "People shouldn't do what they don't want to do.... And I don't want to do it" (Rhode, 1997, p. 150). Earlier in this chapter, we noted that men often feel entitled to higher salaries than women receive. Apparently, many men also feel entitled to leave the housework to their wives (Crosby & Sabattini, 2006; Steil, 2000). Furthermore, even college students tend to believe that men are entitled to perform less than half of the housework (Swearingen-Hilker & Yoder, 2002). Surprisingly, many women do not express anger toward their greater work in the home (Dryden, 1999; Perry-Jenkins et al., 2004), just as they fail to acknowledge that they are underpaid (refer to page 219). At some point in the near future, try Demonstration 7.4.

Satisfaction with Marriage

According to the research, a woman's employment status typically does not influence either her marital satisfaction or the stability of her marriage (Bennetts, 2007; Rogers, 1996;

Demonstration **7.4**

College Students' Plans About Careers and Parenthood

Conduct an informal survey of your friends, ideally at least five women and five men. (Choose people who would feel comfortable discussing this topic with you.) Ask them each individually the following questions:

1. After you have finished your education, do you plan to seek employment? How many hours would you expect to work each week?
2. After you have finished your education, do you perceive yourself becoming a parent? (If the answer is no, you do not need to ask additional questions.)
3. Suppose that you and your partner have a 1-year-old child. How many hours a week would you expect to work outside the home? How many hours a week would you expect your partner to work outside the home?
4. How many hours a week do you expect to spend taking care of the baby? How many hours a week would you expect your partner to spend in child care?

Note the percentage of respondents who plan to be employed when they are the parents of a 1-year-old child. If you surveyed both women and men, did you notice any differences in their patterns of responses?

Viers & Prouty, 2001; L. White & Rogers, 2000). Furthermore, there is no correlation between an increase in a woman's salary and a couple's likelihood of divorce (Rogers & DeBoer, 2001).

Some studies even show that marriages are more stable if the woman is employed (R. C. Barnett & Hyde, 2001). However, some women in high-powered occupations decide to quit when the workload is too overwhelming. Unfortunately, these women often then find that their egalitarian marriages suddenly become traditional; their husbands expect them to do all the housework and child care (Stone, 2007).

Marital satisfaction is related to other workload-related factors. For example, it's no surprise that an employed woman is usually happier with her marriage if her husband performs a relatively large percentage of the housework (Coltrane & Adams, 2001b; Padavic & Reskin, 2002; Steil, 2000). In contrast, a woman whose husband performs relatively little housework is at risk for depression (C. E. Bird, 1999), as we'll learn in Chapter 12.

In summary, women who work outside the home may be busier than nonemployed women. However, the two groups of women seem to be equally satisfied with their marriages.

Children

In the United States and Canada, most young women expect to combine a career with motherhood (Hoffnung, 2000, 2004). Still, a substantial number plan to give up their career once they have children (Riggs, 2001). Demonstration 7.4 explores this question with your own friends.

The reality is that most mothers in the United States do work outside the home. In the United States, 71% of mothers with children under the age of 18 are currently employed (Bureau of Labor Statistics, 2021). The data are comparable for Canada, where 75% of mothers with children under the age of 16 are currently employed (Canadian Press, 2016). These observations suggest two important questions concerning the children of employed women:

1. How are the child-care tasks divided in two-parent families?
2. Does a mother's employment influence children's psychological adjustment?

Taking Care of Children

In the previous section, we learned that women perform more housework than men do. Who's taking care of the children? The research suggests that fathers in the United States have substantially increased their child-care responsibilities since similar studies were conducted 30 years ago (R. C. Barnett, 2004; Gottfried & Gottfried, 2008; Halpern, 2005; Pleck & Masciadrelli, 2004).

Still, researchers conclude that mothers perform most of the child care. For example, a large-scale study of U.S. residents included data on adults who had children younger than 18 years of age. In this study, the men spent about 50 minutes a day in child care, in contrast to 1 hour and 45 minutes for the women (Bureau of Labor Statistics, 2004a). In general, fathers tend to spend their child-care time playing with their children, whereas mothers are in charge of tasks such as diapering and discipline (Stone, 2007).

Other studies provide similar data; mothers perform between 60% and 90% of child-care tasks (Laflamme et al., 2002; Pleck & Masciadrelli, 2004; Statistics Canada, 2005c). If we combine the hours spent on housework and the hours spent on child care, we realize that mothers devote many more hours working in the home, in comparison to fathers (Bureau of Labor Statistics, 2019; M. Fine & Carney, 2001).

When fathers perform a high proportion of the child care, children show greater cognitive and social skills than when fathers seldom provide child care. The children are also higher in self-esteem, and they have fewer behavioral problems (Coltrane & Adams, 2001b; Deutsch et al., 2001). Apparently, children benefit from having two caring adults actively involved in their lives. Furthermore, fathers who spend more time in child care are healthier and more caring toward other people than are uninvolved fathers.

These fathers also have better relationships with their children (bell hooks, 2000a; Pleck & Masciadrelli, 2004). In other words, both fathers and children may benefit from the time they spend together.

Francine Deutsch and her colleagues have studied married couples who share their child-care activities reasonably equally (Deutsch, 1999, 2001; Deutsch & Saxon, 1998a, 1998b). Many fathers report the unexpected benefits of sharing child care. For example, a fire inspector who is married to an administrative assistant commented:

> [I've gained] time with my wife. I mean it's not much time, but whatever time there is in the evening. If one of us had to do everything, then we wouldn't have the time together. I enjoy spending time with my wife too (as well as the kids). It's crazy sometimes, crazy most days, but I love my life. I love the way it is and I can't see living any other way. (Deutsch, 1999, p. 134)

Many women have no partner who can—even theoretically—share in the care of the children. Mothers who are single, separated, divorced, or widowed are likely to work outside the home for economic reasons. These families are especially likely to need the income to pay for basic needs. For these women, however, the logistical problems of arranging for child care and transporting children become even more complicated. In addition, these mothers usually have sole responsibility for nurturing their children, helping them with homework, and disciplining them (Halpern, 2005).

Maternal Employment and Children

Many people respond negatively to "nontraditional" families, with mothers employed full time (Brescoll & Uhlmann, 2005; Riggs, 2005). They also tend to believe that a mother's employment has a negative impact on her children (Newcombe, 2007a; Tan, 2008). Mothers who do not work outside the home also believe that children are harmed by their mother's employment (Johnston & Swanson, 2006, 2007).

The research contradicts these beliefs about maternal employment. We need to emphasize that the topic of maternal employment and children's adjustment is complex. Researchers have conducted a variety of studies. However, the most extensive research comes from a series of reports based on 1,261 children from many communities throughout the United States. These reports have been published by the National Institute of Child Health and Human Development (NICHD) Early Child Care Research Network (2002, 2004, 2005, 2006).

The nature of the conclusions about maternal employment depends on a wide variety of variables, such as the quality of the child care, the age of the child, the economic background of the family, and the mother's sensitivity to her child's needs (Brooks-Gunn et al., 2002; Marshall, 2004; NICHD Early Child Care Research Network, 2004, 2005, 2006).

In general, the cognitive development of children who have been in a day-care setting is similar to that of children cared for by their mother at home (NICHD Early Child Care Research Network, 2005, 2006; Gottfried & Gottfried, 2008). When families with low incomes have high-quality day care, the children score higher on cognitive tasks, compared to children cared for at home (Loeb et al., 2004; NICHD Early Child Care Research Network, 2005, 2006).

Children who spend more time in day care interact slightly more negatively with their playmates (NICHD Early Child Care Research Network, 2006). However, children in *high-quality* day care are generally more cooperative, and they have fewer behavior problems, compared to home-care children (Marshall, 2004; NICHD Early Child Care Research Network, 2004, 2005, 2006).

In addition, most infants who spend time in a day-care center have the same kind of emotional closeness to their mothers as do children whose mothers do not work outside the home. The only exception is children who have poor-quality day care and whose mothers are not sensitive to their needs (NICHD Early Child Care Research Network, 2001, 2005).

Other research shows that employed mothers tend to encourage their children to be independent (Johnston & Swanson, 2002). Furthermore, children whose mothers work outside the home have an important advantage: Their mothers provide models of competent women who can achieve in the workplace (Casad, 2008).

In summary, the overall picture suggests that children's development is not substantially affected by nonmaternal care (NICHD Early Child Care Research Network, 2005, 2006; Tan, 2008). However, U.S. families face an important problem. Children clearly benefit from good day care, but high-quality child care at a reasonable price is not widely available (Brooks-Gunn et al., 2002; NICHD Early Child Care Research Network, 2006).

In the United States, we claim that our children are a top priority. However, child care is expensive—a particular problem for families with low incomes. For example, in the United States, migrant workers harvest 85% of hand-picked fruit and vegetables (Kossek et al., 2005). Suppose that you were a migrant worker, and affordable child care was not available. You would probably bring your children work with you, where they would be exposed to rain, excessive heat, pesticides, and dangerous farm equipment.

In many European countries, parents can enroll their children in a variety of programs at no cost or at a minimal charge (Poelmans, 2005). However, the United States is one of a few industrialized countries that does not have comprehensive child-care policies (Bub & McCartney, 2004; Marshall, 2004). We clearly need to develop family-friendly work policies (Halpern, 2005, 2008; Patterson, 2008).

Personal Adjustment

We have examined the marriages of employed women, as well as their children. But how are the women themselves doing? Do they experience role strain? How is their physical and mental health?

Role Strain

Michelle Wildgrube is a partner in a law firm, a wife, and the mother of two girls. When she told her 11-year-old daughter that she was writing an article about finding balance between work and family, her daughter responded, "You can't do that, you don't have time" (Wildgrube, 2008, p. 31).

Wildgrube—and her daughter—are describing **role strain**, which occurs when people have difficulty fulfilling all their different role obligations. For example, in research with both Canadian nurses and Canadian physicians, women reported excessive workloads and high levels of role strain (Bergman et al., 2003; K. Thorpe et al., 1998).

According to similar research in the United States, employed mothers in every ethnic group experience some kind of role strain between their jobs and their family responsibilities (Crosby & Sabattini, 2006; Powell & Graves, 2003). It's important to emphasize that women in low-paying, exhausting work are especially likely to experience role strain (Lundberg-Love & Faulkner, 2008).

However, many employed women say that they would miss their work identity if they stopped working outside the home. For example, at the age of 23, Leslie Bennetts (2007) discovered a career that matched her skills and interests. As she wrote, "Coming upon journalism was like finding the key that fit the lock…. *So this is what I'm supposed to do with my life!*" (p. 288).

Physical Health

We might imagine that role strain could lead to poor physical health for employed women. However, the data suggest that employed women are, if anything, healthier than non-employed women (Crosby & Sabattini, 2006). Only one group of employed women has substantial health problems: women who have low-paying or unrewarding jobs, several children, and/or an unsupportive husband (Cleveland et al., 2000; Lundberg-Love & Faulkner, 2008).

Mental Health

What can we conclude about the mental health of employed women? As you might expect, the answer depends on their job satisfaction. Employed women are often happier and better adjusted—compared to nonemployed women—if their work role is an important part of their positive self-concept and if their work allows them some degree of independence (Ahrens & Ryff, 2006; Betz, 2006, 2008). Many women enjoy the challenge of a difficult task and the enormous pleasure of successfully achieving a long-term occupational goal.

Furthermore, many women find that their multiple roles provide a buffer effect (Ahrens & Byff, 2006; R. C. Barnett & Hyde, 2001; Betz, 2006). Specifically, employment can act as a buffer against family problems, and family life can act as a buffer against problems at work. When these roles are generally positive, the benefits of multiple roles seem to outweigh the disadvantages.

Research also demonstrates that woman's self-esteem is often enhanced by employment. In general, employed women report a greater sense of competence, accomplishment, and life satisfaction, compared to nonemployed women. Employed women are also less likely to be depressed or anxious (Betz, 2006; Cleveland et al., 2000; S. J. Rogers & DeBoer, 2001). Research in Japan and South Korea shows similar results (Kikuzawa, 2006; Park & Liao, 2000).

Throughout this book, we have noted that psychologists often neglect the important issue of social class (Lott & Bullock, 2010). Unfortunately, most of the research on employment has focused on well-educated women who have relatively high levels of freedom and autonomy in their jobs. We need additional research that focuses on women who are raising several children without a partner, and who have a low-paying, unsatisfying job. These women probably do not benefit from having multiple roles.

Furthermore, we cannot ignore the fact that employed women experience a leisure gap; their housework and child-care responsibilities are much greater than those of employed men (D. L. Nelson & Burke, 2002). Women cannot solve this problem by simply learning how to manage their time more effectively. Instead, couples need to navigate through work–family conflicts so that they can share the workload more equally (Casad, 2008; Crosby & Sabattini, 2006; MacDermid et al., 2001).

Most important, society would benefit from acknowledging the reality of employed women and dual-earner families. Companies that design genuinely family-friendly policies for their employees might discover that these policies are actually good for families and businesses (Casad, 2008; Tan, 2008).

Section Summary

Coordinating Employment with Personal Life

1. Among married families in the United States—when both members are employed—men do only about 30 to 40% of the household tasks.
2. In general, a woman's employment status is not related to her marital satisfaction.
3. In the United States, women perform the clear majority of child-care tasks; however, both children and their fathers benefit from fathers' involvement with child care.
4. In general, children in day care do not experience disadvantages with respect to cognitive abilities, social relationships, or maternal attachment.
5. The quality of day care has an important influence on children's psychological development; unfortunately, many families cannot afford high-quality day care.
6. Employed women may experience role strain from conflicting responsibilities, but many report that their work enhances their feeling of competence.
7. Employed women are as healthy and as well adjusted psychologically as nonemployed women; women with satisfying jobs seem to be even healthier and better adjusted.

Chapter Review Questions

1. In many ways, women's work experiences have changed dramatically during the past few decades. Turn to the chapter outline on page 207 and describe which factors have changed and which ones have stayed reasonably constant.
2. The beginning of Chapter 7 discusses "Women, Employment, and Financial Assistance." Where have you previously learned information about this topic: from other classes, from the media, or from people you know? Which aspects of this chapter's discussion match your previous information, and which aspects are new?
3. Based on this chapter's examination of access discrimination, describe a situation in which a woman would be especially likely to face access discrimination when she applies for a job. What five factors would make a woman least likely to face access discrimination? How should affirmative-action regulations operate in hiring situations?
4. What kinds of treatment discrimination do women usually face in the workplace?

Discuss the research on this topic, and supplement it with some of the issues mentioned in the section on women's experiences in selected occupations.

5. Some people claim that the wage gap can be entirely explained by the fact that women are more likely than men to stop working once they have children and that women have less education than men. How would you respond to this claim? How does the concept of comparable worth apply to women's and men's salaries?

6. Compare the experiences of employed women and employed men with respect to the labyrinth metaphor, the sticky floor, and the glass escalator. Also compare the personal characteristics of men and women who have the same high-prestige occupation.

7. Outline the two general kinds of explanations that have been offered for women's under-representation in certain jobs (pp. 231–232). Review the section summaries in Chapters 5 and 6, and note which of these two explanations is most

supported by the evidence from cognitive and social gender comparisons.

8. Suppose that you know several women who earn lower salaries than comparable men in the same company, yet they don't seem very upset by the discrepancy. How would you explain why they are not angry? What similar process operates when a woman considers the gap in the amount of housework and child care that she and her partner perform?

9. Imagine that you are a 25-year-old woman and that you have decided to return to your former job after the birth of your first baby. Suppose that a neighbor tells you that your child will probably develop psychological problems if you work outside the home. Cite evidence to defend your decision.

10. Imagine that you are part of a new task force in your state or province. This task force has been instructed to make recommendations to improve the situation of women in the workplace. Based on the information in this chapter, make a list of 8 to 10 recommendations.

Key Terms

working women (p. 209)

employed women (p. 209)

nonemployed women (p. 209)

access discrimination (p. 212)

gender-role spillover (p. 214)

affirmative action (p. 214)

reverse discrimination (p. 214)

treatment discrimination (p. 215)

comparable worth (p. 217)

occupational segregation (p. 217)

entitlement (p. 218)

denial of personal disadvantage (p. 219)

glass ceiling (p. 219)

labyrinth metaphor (p. 219)

sticky floor (p. 219)

glass escalator (p. 220)

sexual harassment (p. 220)

heterosexism (p. 221)

sweatshop (p. 226)

maquiladoras (maquilas) (p. 226)

person-centered explanations (p. 231)

individual approach (p. 231)

situation-centered explanations (p. 231)

structural approach (p. 231)

role strain (p. 238)

Recommended Readings

Eagly, A. H., & Carli, L. L. (2007). *Through the labyrinth: The truth about how women become leaders.* Cambridge, MA: Harvard Business School Press. Alice Eagly and Linda Carli are well known for their research about gender roles, gender comparisons, and evaluations based on gender. This interesting book would be especially relevant for women aspiring to become leaders and executives.

Marcus-Newhall, A., Halpern, D. F., & Tan, S. J. (Eds.). (2008). *The changing realities of work and family.* Malden, MA: Wiley-Blackwell. I strongly recommend this book as a resource on combining work and family, as well as a guide for changes that need to be addressed in the United States.

Murphy, E. F. (2005). *Getting even: Why women don't get paid like men—and what to do about it.* New York: Simon & Schuster. Evelyn Murphy served as the Lieutenant Governor of Massachusetts from 1987 to 1991, and she has also held executive positions in corporations. This well-written book provides information about the gender gap—and steps that individuals can take to bridge the gap.

Paludi, M. A. (Ed.). (2008). *The psychology of women at work* (Vols. 1–3). Westport, CT: Praeger. Michele Paludi is the editor of this useful resource, which examines issues related to employment, including perspectives on obstacles, self-image, and family. All three volumes include "In My Own Voice" features, in which women describe their personal experiences related to the research-based chapters.

8 Love Relationships

iStockPhoto/Serts

Learning Objectives

After studying this chapter, you will be able to …

8-1 Identify characteristics that define dating and heterosexual relationships.

8-2 Explain how gender impacts marriage and divorce.

8-3 Describe factors that characterize romantic relationships among lesbian and bisexual women.

8-4 Describe factors that characterize the lives of single women.

Did You Know?

- When looking for an ideal marriage partner, people value honesty, good personality, and intelligence (p. 247).
- According to recent research, heterosexual women tend to have more stable relationships if their romantic partner is a feminist (p. 252).
- People's satisfaction with their marriage often drops during the first 20 years of marriage, but it typically increases later in life (p. 256).
- In at least half of current first marriages in the United States, the couples had lived together before they were married (pp. 261–262).
- In general, lesbian women have higher self-esteem if they have accepted their identity (p. 265).
- In the United States, Black women and Latina women are more likely than White women to have never married (p. 279).

During the week when I was editing this chapter on love relationships, I checked the People.com website to catch up on celebrity relationships in the news. Shailene Woodley and Aaron Rodgers are celebrating their engagement, but Jennifer Lopez and Alex Rodriquez have called off theirs. Michael B. Jordan and Lori Harvey have made their relationship Instagram official, and Great Britain's Prince William and Kate Middleton are celebrating 10 years of marriage! No matter how many times we read about love and marriage, most people are eager for more. Movies, Internet series, and television shows sometimes focus on power or danger or money. However, these topics are clearly outnumbered by themes about romantic love (Fletcher, 2002; Hedley, 2002a, 2002b). Social psychologists Laurie Rudman and Peter Glick (2008) provide the following definition of romantic love:

> Romantic love refers to the intense attachments formed between people who are in love, including feelings of wanting to merge with another person, sexual attraction, and the desire to protect the other's welfare. (Laurie Rudman and Peter Glick (2008), p. 205)

Does this definition seem accurate to you? Would you delete any of these components or include any additional items? How might this definition change for people who identify as asexual or sapiosexual in their sexual orientation?

The previous chapter focused on women and work, a central issue in the lives of contemporary women. In Chapters 8, 9, and 10, we'll examine women's close personal relationships as we consider love, sexuality, and motherhood. Our four major topics in the current chapter about love relationships are (1) dating and heterosexual relationships, (2) marriage and divorce, (3) lesbian and bisexual women, and (4) single women. As you'll learn, these four categories are much more fluid than they may initially seem.

8-1 Dating and Heterosexual Relationships

Learning Objectives

To identify characteristics that define dating and heterosexual relationships, you can …

8-1-1   Describe which factors people in the United States identify as ideal characteristics in romantic partners.

8-1-2   Compare and contrast how Westernized and non-Westernized cultures describe ideal romantic partners.

8-1-3   Describe how the evolutionary-psychology and social-roles approaches explain gender differences in romantic preferences.

8-1-4   Identify aspects of romantic relationships that women and men emphasize in heterosexual love relationships.

8-1-5   Summarize the factors that lead to relationship satisfaction in heterosexual relationships.

8-1-6   Describe gender differences in how women and men cope with the end of a romantic relationship.

We'll begin by talking about heterosexual relationships, which is the category represented most frequently in the media. Notice that the title of this section uses the word *dating*. Dating is common among adolescents and adults, when "dating" means that two people are romantically involved and spend substantial amounts of time together creating intimacy and getting to know each other (e.g., Morr Serewicz & Gale, 2008; Rudman & Glick, 2008; Wekerle & Avgoustis, 2003). We will refer to "dating" because popular culture has not yet invented a term that is appropriately broad.

Let's first consider the characteristics that heterosexual people perceive as desirable in an ideal romantic partner; we'll then discuss two explanations for gender differences in this area. Next, we'll compare people with respect to several characteristics of love relationships. Our final topic will focus on couples who break up.

The Ideal Romantic Partner

Before you read this section on ideal partners, try Demonstration 8.1. You may be convinced that you can tell whether a man or a woman wrote these dating profiles, but be sure to check the answers. Let's first consider U.S. studies on this topic and then explore research from additional cultures.

> # Demonstration **8.1**
>
> ## The Ideal Partner
>
> This demonstration contains portions of online dating profiles from Bumble and OkCupid. We have left out any mention of the gender of the potential partner; otherwise, this portion of the online dating profile is complete. In front of each description, put a W if you think the writer of the profile is a woman or an M if you think the writer is a man.
>
> _____ 1. I love any movie where they spontaneously break out into song, can only eat three pieces of pizza, and probably work too much.
>
> _____ 2. I like when I randomly decide to call an old friend and they say, "I was just thinking about you!"
>
> _____ 3. I'm energetic and restless at times. If I don't get out of the house at least once a day, I go a little stir-crazy. I'm always climbing or going for a run outside.
>
> _____ 4. I have to admit, I like life's simple pleasures. I'm looking for someone who's as easy-going as I am and wants to relax and enjoy life.
>
> _____ 5. I may be young, but I'm wise beyond my years. I've learned to be genuine, responsible, and yes, a little feisty.
>
> _____ 6. I host my own podcast and would love to know if you've ever listened to it. Tell me what you're currently listening to. Maybe it's me!
>
> _____ 7. I haven't dated much in recent years because I've been so focused on my career. Now I'm ready to meet the person who will pull my head out of the books and bring me a bit of happiness.
>
> _____ 8. My favorite books all evoke some emotion in me. I'd love to talk about which works of literature have inspired tears in your eyes.
>
> _____ 9. I know my way around an Excel spreadsheet. I'm not afraid to put that out there. I also am a huge college football fan, an amateur chef, and owner of a lucky dog named Bolero.
>
> _____ 10. I drink massive amounts of coffee, love anything ridiculous or bizarre, and will shamelessly use my dog to flirt with you.
>
> Check the accuracy of your answers at the end of this chapter (page 281).

Research in the United States

What do women and men want in their romantic partners? Young adolescents tend to emphasize physical attributes; older adolescents emphasize their compatibility with their partner (Collins & Steinberg, 2006).

The ideal characteristics also depend on whether people are discussing a sexual partner or a marriage partner (Impett & Peplau, 2006; Li & Kenrick, 2006). For example, Regan and Berscheid (1997) asked undergraduates at a Midwestern university to rank a variety of personal characteristics in terms of their desirability for (a) a partner for sexual activity and (b) a partner for a long-term relationship such as marriage. Table 8.1 shows the five most important characteristics for each type of relationship, for women judging men and for men judging women.

As demonstrated in the table, both women and men emphasized physical attractiveness when judging an ideal sexual partner. However, a statistical analysis showed that men were more likely than women to rank physical attractiveness as the most important characteristic.

Note, however, that the preferred characteristics shift when people judge an ideal marriage partner. The gender differences are small for a marriage partner, because both women and men value honesty, good personality, and intelligence. However, physical attractiveness is somewhat more important for men.

Other research confirms that physical appearance is extremely important when people first meet a potential romantic partner. Also, attractiveness and slimness are especially important when men are judging women (Fletcher, 2002; J. H. Harvey & Weber, 2002; Travis & Meginnis-Payne, 2001). We will return to this topic later in this book, when we discuss people's reactions to women with disabilities (Chapter 11) and women who are above average size (Chapter 12).

How accurate were you in guessing the gender of the people who wrote online dating profiles in Demonstration 8.1? You may have hesitated because several of these profiles

TABLE **8.1**

Characteristics That Men and Women Consider Most Important for a Sexual Partner and a Marriage Partner, Listed in Order of Importance

	Women Judging Men	Men Judging Women
Sexual partner	Physically attractive	Physically attractive
	Healthy	Healthy
	Attentive to my needs	Overall personality
	Sense of humor	Attentive to my needs
	Overall personality	Self-confident
Marriage partner	Honest or trustworthy	Overall personality
	Sensitive	Honest or trustworthy
	Overall personality	Physically attractive
	Intelligent	Intelligent
	Attentive to my needs	Healthy

Source: Copyright 1997 From Journal of Psychology & Human Sexuality 9 (1), "Gender Differences in Characteristics Desired in a Potential Sexual and Marriage Partner" by Pamela C. Regan and Ellen Berscheid. Reproduced by permission of Taylor & Francis Group, LLC., http://www.taylorandfrancis.com.

could have been written by either a man or a woman. Several systematic studies of dating profiles in both the United States and Canada confirm that men are more likely than women to emphasize physical attractiveness in describing an ideal partner. In contrast, women are more likely than men to emphasize the financial status of an ideal partner (Fales et al., 2016). Memory studies demonstrate a similar pattern of results. Specifically, people recalled more cues about a man's financial prospects, but they recalled more cues about a woman's attractiveness (De Backer et al., 2007).

However, the research also shows that both men and women tend to specify that an ideal partner should be warm, romantic, kind, and sensitive, and also have a good sense of humor (Lance, 1998; E. J. Miller et al., 2000). Furthermore, Theme 4 operates in the choice of a romantic partner; there is more variation *within* each gender than *between* the genders.

You may wonder whether women are looking for strong, dominant men or for nice guys. Urbaniak and Kilmann (2003) found that female undergraduates were much more likely to prefer a man who said he was "kind and attentive and doesn't go for all that macho stuff," rather than a man who said he knew how to get what he wants and "doesn't go in for all that touchy-feely stuff" (p. 416). Furthermore, Burn and Ward (2005) found that college women were more satisfied with their romantic relationships if their male partner was low in traditionally masculine characteristics. Any reader of this textbook who happens to be a kind, considerate man, in search of a female partner, will be pleased to know that nice guys usually finish first, not last!

Cross-Cultural Research

Most of the participants in research on ideal romantic partners have been White men and women living in the United States and Canada. In general, people in Westernized cultures provide similar responses. However, when we move beyond Westernized cultures, we may find different patterns for romantic relationships (Hamon & Ingoldsby, 2003; Hatfield & Rapson, 2006; Reis & Aron, 2008).

In many developing countries, couples are not expected to marry for love. For example, some marriages in India are arranged by the couple's parents (Hatfield et al., 2007), and this tradition often continues even when young men and women immigrate to the United States. For example, here is a representative ad from matrimonial section of the website *India Abroad* (2018): "U.S. born citizen, doctor doing residency in radiology. Handsome looking, 29 yrs, 5'6". Preferred doctor and U.S. citizen."

Different cultures value somewhat different characteristics in a romantic partner. In general, however, women are more likely than men to believe that a partner should be well educated and have good financial prospects (Greitemeyer, 2007; Walter et al., 2020). In contrast, men are more likely than women to believe that a partner should be physically attractive (Eastwick & Finkel, 2008; Higgins et al., 2002; Winstead et al., 1997).

In a classic cross-cultural study, Hatfield and Sprecher (1995) asked college students in the United States, Russia, and Japan to rate a number of characteristics that might be important in selecting a marriage partner. Gender similarities were found for many characteristics. However, Figure 8.1 demonstrates that women in all three cultures are more likely than men to emphasize financial prospects in a spouse. Figure 8.2 demonstrates that men in all three cultures are more likely than women to emphasize physical attractiveness. Other cross-cultural research confirms that women value a man's financial status, and men value a woman's physical attractiveness (Eastwick et al., 2006; Ellis et al., 2008; Walter et al., 2020).

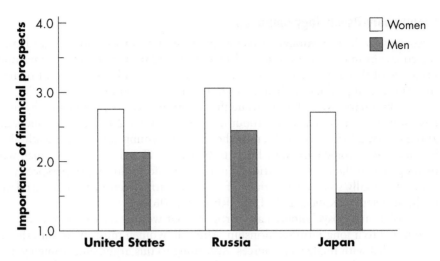

FIGURE **8.1** Importance of financial prospects in a spouse, for women and men in three cultures.
Source: Hatfield and Sprecher (1995).

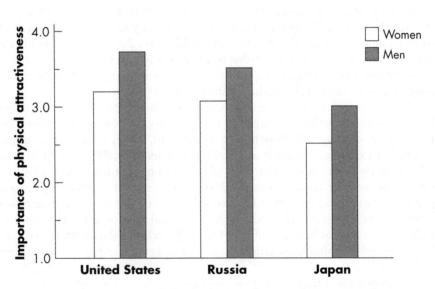

FIGURE **8.2** Importance of physical attractiveness in a spouse, for women and men in three cultures.
Source: Hatfield and Sprecher (1995).

Explanations for Gender Differences in Patterns of Preference

One of the most controversial topics in the research on love relationships is whether evolutionary explanations or social roles can best account for gender differences in romantic preferences. Let's compare these two approaches.

Evolutionary-Psychology Approach

According to the **evolutionary-psychology approach**, various species gradually change over the course of many generations so that they can adapt better to their environment. A basic principle of this approach is that both men and women have an evolutionary advantage if they succeed in passing on their genes to the next generation.

Evolutionary psychologists argue that their approach can explain why men and women have somewhat different views about ideal mates (Buss, 2000; A. Campbell, 2002; Fletcher, 2002; Geary, 2005). Specifically, men should prefer young, attractive, healthy-looking women because those women are most likely to be fertile. Therefore, these women will pass on the men's genes to the next generation. Contrary to the evolutionary perspective, however, the research actually shows that ratings of women's attractiveness are not correlated with either health or fertility (Kalick et al., 1998; Rhodes, 2006).

Evolutionary psychologists also propose that women try to select a partner who will be committed to a long-term relationship. After all, women must make sure that their children are provided with financial resources. According to this argument, women search for reliable men who also have good incomes. Evolutionary psychologists emphasize that culture has little influence on gender differences in mate selection (Buss, 1998; Buss & Schmitt, 2019).

The Social-Roles Approach

Many feminist psychologists object to the evolutionary approach. They argue, for example, that the theory is highly speculative about evolutionary forces that operated many thousands of years ago (Eagly & Wood, 1999; Hatfield et al., 2007). Feminists also point out that the evolutionary approach has failed to identify any genetic mechanism for these proposed gender differences (Hyde, 2002). In addition, evolutionary psychology cannot account for same-gender romantic relationships (Surra et al., 2004).

Furthermore, the research shows that people are equally interested in maintaining long-term relationships, regardless of sexuality or gender (Diamond & Blair, 2018; L. C. Miller et al., 2002; Popenoe & Whitehead, 2002; Umberson, Thomeer, & Lodge, 2015). For example, in a study at a California university, 99% of female students and also 99% of male students said that they planned to be in a long-term relationship with just one sexual partner (Pedersen et al., 2002). Research on relationships among sexual and gender minorities suggest that relationship quality and long-term success outcomes are similar to those found in cisgender or heterosexual relationships (Diamond & Blair, 2018). In fact, some studies have found that LBGTQ+ relationships experience somewhat higher long-term relationship satisfaction than their cisgender and heterosexual peers (Chonody, Killian, Gabb, & Dunk-West, 2020).

An explanation that seems much more credible to us—and to most other feminists—emphasizes that social factors can effectively explain gender differences in preference patterns. According to the **social-roles approach**, men and women often occupy different social roles; they are also socialized differently, and they experience different social opportunities and social disadvantages (Eagly & Wood, 1999; S. S. Hendrick, 2006; Johannesen-Schmidt & Eagly, 2002; Schmitt, 2008). For example, women have more limited financial resources in many cultures, as we learned in Chapter 7. As a result, women often focus on a partner's ability to earn money.

In support of the social roles approach, research demonstrates that women are especially likely to prefer high-income men if they live in countries where women have limited educational and financial opportunities (Eagly & Wood, 1999; Eastwick et al., 2006;

Demonstration **8.2**

Friendship-Based Love

If you are currently in a love relationship, rate the following statements based on that relationship. Alternatively, rate a previous love relationship that you experienced or a love relationship of a couple whom you know fairly well. For each statement, use a scale in which 1 = strongly disagree and 5 = strongly agree. Then add up the total number of points. In general, high scores reflect a love relationship that is strongly based on friendship.

_____ 1. My love for my partner is based on a deep, long-lasting friendship.

_____ 2. I express my love for my partner through the activities and interests we enjoy together.

_____ 3. My love for my partner involves solid, deep affection.

_____ 4. An important factor in my love for my partner is that we often laugh together.

_____ 5. My partner is one of the most likable people I know.

_____ 6. The companionship I share with my partner is an important part of our love.

_____ 7. I feel I can really trust my partner.

_____ 8. I can count on my partner in times of need.

_____ 9. I feel relaxed and comfortable with my partner.

Source: Based on Grote and Frieze (1994).

Kasser & Sharma, 1999). In contrast, in more egalitarian countries, women can earn their own incomes, so they don't need to find wealthy husbands. Contrary to the predictions of evolutionary psychology, culture *does* affect mate preferences (Eastwick et al., 2006; Travis & Meginnis-Payne, 2001).

Characteristics of Heterosexual Love Relationships

We have examined women's and men's ideal romantic partners. However, do women and men differ in their thoughts about an established love relationship? Furthermore, what factors predict satisfaction with a love relationship?

Gender Comparisons

To some extent, women and men emphasize different aspects of love in their current romantic relationships. For example, women are significantly more likely than men to report that they have a relationship based on friendship (K. L. Dion & Dion, 1993; Schmitt, 2008; Sprecher & Sedikides, 1993). When describing their romantic relationship, women are more likely than men to report commitment, liking, and satisfaction—all positive emotions. However, women also report more sadness, depression, hurt, and loneliness. In other words, compared to men, women appear to experience a wider range of both positive and negative emotions (Impett & Peplau, 2006; Sprecher & Sedikides, 1993).

However, in many other respects, the gender similarities are more striking. For example, both women and men typically say that the essential features of their love relationships are trust, caring, honesty, and respect (C. Hendrick & Hendrick, 1996; Rousar & Aron, 1990). Both women and men also report similar strategies for maintaining a romantic relationship, such as acting cheerful toward the partner and expressing love for this person. Still, the research suggests that women actually perform more of this "relationship-maintenance work" (Impett & Peplau, 2006; Steil, 2001a).

Factors Related to Satisfaction with the Relationship

Before you read further, try Demonstration 8.2, which is based on a classic study by Grote and Frieze (1994). This questionnaire assesses the friendship dimension of a love relationship. We just noted some gender differences in emphasizing friendship. Other research suggests that both men and women are more satisfied with a love relationship if it is based on friendship (Grote & Frieze, 1994; J. H. Harvey & Weber, 2002). People who have friendship-based relationships also report a greater degree of reciprocal understanding. In addition, relationships that are based on friendship lasted longer. Couples who strive to maintain equity and balance in various aspects of their relationships also rate their relationships as more satisfying (Frieze, Ciccocioppo, & Khosla, 2018). Furthermore, people who are emotionally and sexually faithful to their romantic partners also tend to be more satisfied with their relationships (Schmookler & Bursik, 2007).

In Chapter 6, we learned that women are sometimes more likely than men to disclose personal information about themselves. In their romantic relationships, however, women and men have similar self-disclosure patterns (Hatfield & Rapson, 1993). In addition, both men and women are more satisfied with their love relationship if both partners are skilled at expressing their emotions (Lamke et al., 1994; Sternberg, 1998). The strong, silent man or the mysteriously uncommunicative woman may seem appealing in the movies. However, in real life, people prefer a person with sensitivity and other interpersonal skills.

As we noted earlier in this textbook, people sometimes have negative opinions about feminists. Some research on feminism and relationship satisfaction would probably surprise them. Laurie Rudman and Julie Phelan (2007) studied a group of college students and a group of older adults, all of whom were in heterosexual relationships. All the participants provided information about their own attitudes toward feminism, as well as the feminist attitudes of their partner. In both groups, the women who had feminist romantic partners tended to report more stable relationships—as well as greater sexual satisfaction—in comparison to women with nonfeminist romantic partners. Furthermore, in the older group of adults, men who had feminist partners tended to report more stable relationships—as well as greater sexual satisfaction—in comparison to men with nonfeminist partners. Before you read further, try Demonstration 8.3.

Breaking Up

Suppose that a couple have been dating for about a year, and then they break up. Who suffers more? Choo and her coauthors (1996) asked heterosexual college students to think back on a romantic relationship that had broken up and to assess their emotional reactions immediately after the breakup. Men and women reported similar negative emotions (anxiety, sadness, and anger), as well as similar guilt. As Choo and her colleagues (1996) suggest,

---

Demonstration **8.3**

Coping with a Breakup of a Love Relationship

Think about a person you once dated and felt passionate about, but then the two of you broke up. Read each of the items below, and place an X in front of each strategy you frequently used to cope with the breakup. (If you have not personally experienced a breakup, think of a close friend who has recently broken up with a romantic partner, and answer the questionnaire from that person's perspective.)

_____ 1. I tried to figure out what I might have done wrong.
_____ 2. I took alcohol or drugs.
_____ 3. I talked to my friends, trying to figure out if there was anything we could do to save the relationship.
_____ 4. I thought about how badly my partner had treated me.
_____ 5. I kept busy with my schoolwork or my job.
_____ 6. I told myself: "I'm lucky to have gotten out of that relationship."
_____ 7. I engaged in sports and other physical activities more than usual.

Source: Based on Choo et al. (1996).

"Men and women are more similar than different. In most things, it is not gender, but our shared humanity that seems to be important" (p. 144).

However, women felt more joy and relief following the breakup. How can we explain these results? The research by Choo and her coauthors suggests that women are usually more sensitive to potential problems in a relationship. In other words, women may anticipate a breakup, and they worry about potential danger signs (Chethik, 2006).

Let's explore this issue further. As we discussed in Chapter 6, women are relatively skilled in decoding the emotions in a person's facial expressions. In contrast, a man may not recognize signs of sadness or anger in a person's facial expression. In other words, women tend to be better "mind-readers" than men (Fletcher & Boyes, 2008). Some additional research also suggests that it's easier to detect romantic interest in a man's facial expression, compared to a woman's facial expression (Place et al., 2009). Combining these two factors, a woman may be better at picking up signs of discontent. As a result, a woman may be less shocked when the breakup does occur.

How do women and men cope with a breakup? Choo and her colleagues (1996) asked their respondents to recall how they had responded to the end of their love relationship. Demonstration 8.3 presents some of the items. The researchers found that women and men were equally likely to blame themselves for the breakup (Questions 1 and 3 of Demonstration 8.3). They were also equally likely to take alcohol and drugs following the breakup (Question 2). Men were more likely than women to try to distract themselves from thinking about the breakup (Questions 5 and 7). However, women were somewhat more likely than men to blame their partner for the breakup (Questions 4 and 6).

Why were women more likely than men to blame their partner for the breakup? One possibility is that women typically work harder than men do to maintain a relationship. When a breakup occurs, women may realistically blame their partner for not investing more effort in the relationship.

Section Summary

Dating and Heterosexual Relationships

1. In research in the United States, both women and men value physical attractiveness as an important characteristic for an ideal sexual partner, but men emphasize it more. Both women and men value characteristics such as honesty and intelligence in an ideal marriage partner, but men still emphasize attractiveness more than women do.

2. Cross-cultural research about ideal romantic partners suggests that men are more likely to emphasize physical attractiveness, whereas women are more likely to emphasize financial status.

3. To explain why men emphasize physical attractiveness in a romantic partner—and why women emphasize good financial prospects—evolutionary psychologists theorize that people emphasize characteristics that are likely to ensure passing their genes on to their offspring.

4. According to the social-roles explanation, men and women typically occupy different social roles. For instance, women tend to have low incomes, so they emphasize a partner's financial status. They are socialized differently, and they also have different opportunities and disadvantages.

5. Women are significantly more likely than men to say that their love relationships are based on friendship; women also report a wider range of emotions in their relationships. Most other gender differences in evaluations of love relationships are minimal.

6. Romantic relationships are typically more satisfying if they are based on friendship and equitable effort, if both partners can express their emotions, and if both partners are feminists.

7. When couples break up, women and men experience similar negative emotions. However, women are also more likely than men to experience joy and relief; they are also more likely to blame their partner for the breakup.

8-2 Marriage and Divorce

Learning Objectives

To explain how gender impacts marriage and divorce, you can …

8-2-1   Differentiate between factors that impact women and men's satisfaction with marriage.

8-2-2   Summarize the characteristics of happy, stable marriages.

8-2-3   Differentiate between traditional and egalitarian marriages.

8-2-4   Describe how ethnicity impacts marriage patterns among Latina, Black, and Asian American women.

8-2-5   Identify factors that increase the likelihood of divorce.

8-2-6   Explain how divorce affects women psychologically and financially.

What do college students think about marriage? The research suggests that women are significantly more likely than men to anticipate getting married (Blakemore et al., 2005). However, college women who are nontraditional tend to say that they will keep their own last name, rather than adopting their husband's last name (Blakemore et al., 2005; Hoffnung, 2006).

Our theme of individual differences in women's lives is especially important when we discuss women's experiences with marriage. Here is a report from Lili, who at the time was 53 years old:

> "I married right out of school, and I don't want to be married anymore. But what's out there for me?" … Her children were adults. The marriage was "dead." She felt stuck in a relationship and a household that gave her little pleasure. "To tell you the truth," she said, "if I could start over, maybe I'd skip getting married entirely. My women friends are the best. I'm thinking now, the thing is to stay single, have the occasional affair with a man, maybe adopt a kid, spend your free time enjoying your girlfriends." (Cantor et al., 2004, p. 81)

Contrast that description with the observations of feminist author Letty Cottin Pogrebin (1997), who emphasizes that marriage can be a source of strength and joy:

> All I know is what I've had—34 years with a devoted partner who is my lover and closest friend. I know how it feels to live with someone whose touch excites, whose counsel calms, whose well-being matters as much as my own. I know that simple contentment is a kind of euphoria, that the familiar can be as intoxicating as the exotic, and that comfort and equality are, over the long haul, greater aphrodisiacs than romanticized power plays. I know how soul-satisfying it is to love someone well and deeply and to be loved for all the right reasons. I know how much more layered life is when everything is shared—sorrow and success, new enthusiasms, old stories, children, grandchildren, friends, memory…. We're what's called a good fit. (Pogrebin 1997, p. 37)

In Canada, the average ages for a first marriage are 29.6 years for women and 31 years for men (Cardus, 2020). In the United States, the average ages for a first marriage are slightly younger—28.1 years for women and 30.5 years for men (U.S. Census Bureau, 2020. In 2020, about 50% of U.S. women were married, a decrease from earlier eras (U.S. Census Bureau, 2020). Figure 8.3 shows the percentages of married women in four major ethnic groups of U.S. residents; unfortunately, the current data do not include information about Native Americans (U.S. Census Bureau, 2020). Also note the percentages of divorced women in this figure.

It's also important to keep in mind that the traditions of other countries may be very different. For example, in Afghanistan, more than half of adolescent girls are married before they are 16, and about three-quarters of adolescent girls and young women have arranged marriages (Raj, Gomez, & Silverman, 2008).

Let's begin our examination of marriage and divorce by first discussing marital satisfaction. Then we'll explore the distribution of power in marriage and marriage patterns among women of color. Our final topic in this section is the realities of divorce.

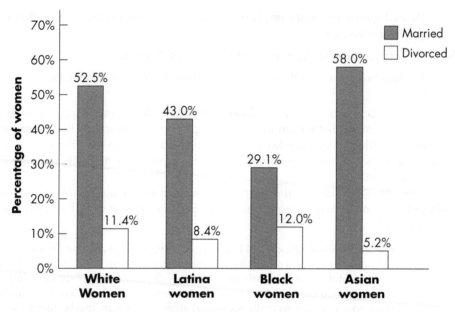

FIGURE **8.3** Percentages of women (age 15 or older) who label their status as married and divorced, in four major ethnic groups of U.S. residents.
Source: Based on data from U.S. Census Bureau (Current Population Reports 2020).

Marital Satisfaction

How happy are women with their marriages? Let's explore how marital satisfaction changes over time, how men and women compare in terms of marital satisfaction, and how certain characteristics are associated with happy marriages.

Satisfaction During Various Periods of Marriage

Surveys reveal that young married couples are probably the happiest people in any age group (Karney & Bradbury, 2004). A few years after the wedding, however, many married people report feeling less romantic and more dissatisfied (Burpee & Langer, 2005; Neff & Karney, 2005; Noller, 2006). They may realize that they had different expectations for marriage (Noller & Feeney, 2002).

People who have been married 20 to 24 years tend to be the group that is least satisfied with their marriage. However, for couples who have children, marital satisfaction generally improves during the next decade, once the children have left home (Chethik, 2006; J. Jones et al., 2001). Couples who have been married at least 35 years also report relatively little conflict in their relationship (Bachand & Caron, 2001). The reasons for this increased satisfaction are not clear, but they may include factors such as reduced conflict over parenting issues after the children leave home, as well as an increase in economic resources.

In general, same-sex couples, couples who are child-free, couples with higher incomes, and older adults tend to be the happiest in terms of marital satisfaction across the lifespan (Crouch et al., 2014; Gabb, Klett-Davies, Fink, & Thomae, 2013).

Gender Comparisons in Marital Satisfaction

Women are more likely than men to wish that they could change some aspects of their marriage (Vangelisti, 2006). Also, women are more sensitive than men to problems in their marital relationships (Amato et al., 2007; K. K. Dion & Dion, 2001b). Women's sensitivity is consistent with our earlier observation that women are somewhat better than men at anticipating potential problems in a dating relationship. In general, however, current research tends to emphasize gender similarities in marital satisfaction (Amato et al., 2007; Kurdek, 2005; Verhofstadt et al., 2007).

Characteristics of Happy, Stable Marriages

In a happy, long-lasting marriage, both partners feel that their emotional needs are fulfilled, and each partner enriches the life of the other. Both people understand and respect each other, as noted in Pogrebin's (1997) comment at the beginning of this section.

Researchers have found that a variety of psychological characteristics are correlated with happy, stable marriages (Amato et al., 2007; Bradbury et al., 2001; Cutrona et al., 2005; Dindia & Emmers-Sommer, 2006; Fincham, 2004; Fitness, 2006; Frieze, Ciccocioppo, & Khosla, 2018; Hazen et al., 2006; Noller, 2006; Perry-Jenkins et al., 2004; Prager & Roberts, 2004; Rauer & Volling, 2005; Wickrama et al., 2004):

1. Emotional stability.
2. Good communication skills and understanding.
3. A greater number of positive comments and expressions of affection, rather than negative comments and responses.
4. Strong conflict-resolution skills.
5. Trust in the other person.
6. Mutual support.
7. The belief that each spouse is genuinely concerned about the other person's well-being.
8. Flexibility.
9. Equal sharing of child care and household tasks.
10. Equal sharing in decision making.

Happily married couples even interpret their spouse's actions differently than unhappy couples do. For example, suppose that Issac gives a gift to his wife, Rachel. If Rachel is happily married, she is likely to think to herself, "How wonderful! Issac wanted to do something nice for me! However, if Rachel is unhappily married, she might think, "He's probably giving me these flowers because he's feeling guilty about something." Unpleasant interactions can also be explained in either a positive or a negative light. These explanatory patterns could make a happy marriage even happier, but they could encourage more conflict in an unhappy marriage (Fincham, 2004; Fitness, 2006; Karney & Bradbury, 2004).

Distribution of Power in Marriages

We have emphasized individual differences throughout this book, and the variation in marital roles is also substantial. In a heterosexual **traditional marriage**, the husband is more dominant than the wife, and both partners maintain traditional gender roles. The wife can make most of the decisions about housework and child care, but the husband has the ultimate authority in family decisions. The husband protects the wife, and he also controls the money (Rudman & Glick, 2008). Traditional marriages are especially common among people from a conservative religious background (Impett & Peplau, 2006; S. E. Smith & Huston, 2004).

However, most U.S. and Canadian marriages are somewhat less traditional, moving closer to an egalitarian marriage (Amato et al., 2003; Ogletree, 2015). In an **egalitarian marriage**, both partners share power equally, without traditional gender roles. The wife and the husband have equal responsibility for housework, child care, finances, and decision making. Egalitarian marriages also emphasize companionship and sharing. These marriages are based on a true friendship in which both partners really understand and respect one another (Impett & Peplau, 2006; Pessin, 2018). Same-sex couples are significantly more likely to experience egalitarian marriage than heterosexual couples, sharing equitably in child care duties and household chores (Crouch et al., 2014; Garcia-Navarro & Green, 2014; Peplau & Fingerhut, 2007).

In an egalitarian marriage, both partners also share many of the same interests. For example, a husband who had been married 16 years remarked:

> I started out pretty traditional. But over the years it made sense to change. We both work, and so we had to help each other with the kids. … And we worked together at church, and we both went whole hog into the peace program. So that got shared. I don't know; you can't design these things. You play fair, and you do what needs doing, and pretty soon you find the old ways don't work and the new ways do. (P. Schwartz, 1994, p. 31)

Marriage and Women of Color

We do not have a large number of systematic studies about marriage patterns in ethnic groups that are not White (Caughlin & Huston, 2006). However, some resources provide partial information. Throughout this section, keep in mind the diversity within each group (Bryant & Wickrama, 2005; Chan, 2008; Jankowiak & Paladino, 2008). For instance, Latin American families in the United States differ from one another because of the wide range of family income, education, country of origin, location of current residence, and level of acculturation.

Latina/o Relationships

In general, Latinas/os emphasize that they have an important obligation to their family (de las Fuentes et al., 2003; Parke, 2004; Torres, 2003). One of the key concepts connected with Latinas/os in heterosexual relationships is *machismo* (pronounced mah-*cheez*-mo). Social scientists have traditionally defined **machismo** as the belief that men must show their manhood by being strong, sexual, and dominant over women in relationships (de las Fuentes et al., 2003; Molinary, 2007). The machismo perspective also emphasizes that men should not do housework (Hurtado, 2003).

The parallel concept for women is *marianismo* (pronounced mah-ree-ah-*neez*-mo) Social scientists have traditionally defined **marianismo** as the belief that women must be chaste until marriage; they must also be passive and long suffering, giving up their own needs to help their husbands and children (de las Fuentes et al., 2003; Hurtado, 2003; Molinary, 2007). *Marianismo* is based on the Catholic representation of the Virgin Mary, who serves as an important role model for Latina women. *Machismo* and *marianismo* complement each other in a traditional Latina/o marriage:

> Love and honor your man—cook his meals, clean his house, be available and ready when he wants to have sex, have and care for his children, and look the other way at marital

infidelities. ... In return, he will agree to protect you and your children, work, pay the bills. (M. Fine et al., 2000, p. 96)

How well do *machismo* and *marianismo* capture the relationship between heterosexual Latinos and Latinas in everyday life? Many Latina women emphasize that their Catholic faith inspires them to help other people (Molinary, 2007). However, most Latinas/os do report more traditional attitudes than White or Black people. Recent immigrants to the United States and Canada are especially likely to emphasize these attitudes (Steil, 2001b; Torres, 2003).

Still, the stereotype of the dominant husband and the completely submissive wife does not apply to most contemporary Latin American families (Matsumoto & Juang, 2008; Molinary, 2007). Fewer than half of Latinos and Latinas believe that marriages should adopt this pattern of inequity. Furthermore, both Latina women and Latino men believe that they can effectively influence their partners by being honest and by talking with each other (Beckman et al., 1999).

The *marianismo* model also fails to describe women's roles for the millions of Latina women who work outside the home, most often in the service, agricultural, or hospitality industries (Bureau of Labor Statistics, 2015). These Latinas cannot remain in the home, passive or totally focused on their husbands and children. In short, many Latinas and Latinos have created marriage patterns that differ from the models of *marianismo* and *machismo*.

Latina women in same-sex marriages are less likely to receive support from community and family sources, largely due to the larger prevalence of Catholic religious norms within their community and stigma toward LGBTQ+ individuals (Bell et al., 2014). However, Latina married lesbian couples are more likely to have college degrees, to both be employed, and to have higher incomes than their Latina peers in heterosexual relationships (Gates & Kastanis, 2013).

Black Women

Most of the early research about Black women and family dynamics disproportionately focused on the most economically disadvantaged families. Much of this early research failed to acknowledge how structural racism and persistent economic inequality in the United States created poverty among Black families and negatively impacted their family relationships (Hanks, Solomon, & Weller, 2018). Furthermore, those researchers have often criticized Black women for working outside the home and for being strong figures in their own homes (Bryant & Wickrama, 2005; Gadsden, 1999; McLoyd et al., 2005).

The research does support the idea that Black heterosexual couples may be more egalitarian than couples from some other ethnic backgrounds (Dodson, 1997; McLoyd et al., 2005; Tucker & James, 2005). For example, some researchers have examined decision-making power in Black families (J. L. McAdoo, 1993; Parke, 2004). Most of these families are close to the egalitarian model. The husband and the wife contribute equally to decisions about what car to buy, what house to buy, child rearing, and other similar issues.

Black women who identify as lesbian or bisexual are more likely than their heterosexual peers of other ethnic groups to become mothers, sometimes due to the norms of compulsory motherhood and heterosexuality prevalent in the Black community (Reed, Miller, & Timm, 2011). However, their experience of "triple jeopardy" in their communities, due to intersecting gender, sexuality, and ethnic minority statuses, can lead to higher levels of minority stress and interpersonal relationship dysfunction in some couples

(Calabrese et al., 2015; Hill, Woodson, Ferguson, & Parks, 2012). Unfortunately, many Black sexual minority couples are less likely to receive support from their families or communities than women of other ethnicities (Glass & Few-Demo, 2013).

Asian American Women

Asian American parents expect their children to marry someone from their own ethnic group, and the children typically do so (Chan, 2003). When people have recently emigrated from Asian countries, they may encounter conflict between the traditional customs from their country of origin and contemporary gender roles in the United States (Chan, 2003; K. K. Dion & Dion, 2001a; Vang, 2008). Consider a Korean couple who immigrated to the United States and now work together in a family business. The husband comments:

> After she started working her voice got louder than in the past. Now, she says whatever she wants to say to me. She shows a lot of self-assertion. She didn't do that in Korea. Right after I came to the U.S., I heard that Korean wives change a lot in America. Now, I clearly understand what it means. (Lim, 1997, p. 38)

In contrast, consider his wife's comments:

> In Korea, wives tend to obey their husbands because husbands have financial power and provide for their families. However, in the U.S., wives also work to make money as their husbands do, so women are apt to speak out at least one time on what they previously restrained from saying. (Lim, 1997, p. 38)

We've noted the relative power of the wife and the husband in heterosexual Latina/o, Black, and Korean couples. When Hindu couples immigrate to the United States from India, the traditional wife is supposed to quietly obey her husband and in-laws. She should consider the goddess Sītā to be her role model, and she must therefore be self-sacrificing, faithful, and uncomplaining (Gupta, 1999; Pauwels, 2008; Tran & Des Jardins, 2000).

Traditional Hindu couples also divide decision-making power along gender-stereotypical lines. Specifically, wives are primarily responsible for decisions concerning food and home decoration. In contrast, husbands are primarily responsible for decisions requiring large sums of money, such as buying a car and deciding where to live (Dhruvarajan, 1992; Parke, 2004).

Asian American and Pacific Islander (AAPI) women in same-sex marriages are less likely to have graduated from college than their heterosexual peers. However, they are both more likely to be employed outside the home than their heterosexual peers and tend to earn higher incomes than their peers in different-sex relationships (Kastanis & Gates, 2013). Additionally, approximately 80% of AAPI women in same-sex marriages are married to someone of a different ethnicity (Kastanis & Gates, 2013), a rate much higher than other ethnic groups.

In summary, families of color are guided by cultural traditions that vary widely, consistent with Theme 4 of this book. However, couples from all cultures frequently create their own marriage styles that differ greatly from the norms of their culture, whether they are in heterosexual or same-sex or gender relationships.

Divorce

So far, most of our discussion has focused on relatively upbeat topics such as dating and marriage. As you know, however, divorce has become more common in many cultures around the world. For example, the divorce rate in Canada is now about four times as high as it was in 1968, with a 32.5% rate (Stevenson, 2021). According to current predictions, between 40% and 65% of first marriages recently taking place in the United States and Canada will eventually end in divorce (Amato et al., 2007; Coleman et al., 2006).

In the United States, as Figure 8.3 on page 256 demonstrates, the different ethnic groups have somewhat different divorce rates. The highest rate is for Black couples, the lowest for Asian American couples (Kitzmann & Gaylord, 2001; U.S. Census Bureau, 2020). Furthermore, divorce rates are lowest for people who have completed college (Deveny, 2008).

Even though attitudes toward divorce are not as negative as they were several decades ago, the divorce experience is still extremely stressful for most people (McCarthy & McCarthy, 2006). Let's consider four aspects of divorce: (1) cohabitation and divorce, (2) the decision to divorce, (3) psychological effects, and (4) financial effects.

Cohabitation and Divorce

In more than half of first marriages in the United States, couples had lived together before marriage (Horowitz, Graf, & Livingston, 2019; Smock & Gupta, 2002). According to research in the United States and Canada, couples who live together before marriage are more likely to get divorced than those who have not lived together (Amato et al., 2007; Smock & Gupta, 2002; Surra et al., 2004). Does this mean that a couple should avoid cohabiting because it is likely to cause divorce? An equally likely explanation is that people who live together before marriage are relatively nontraditional. Nontraditional people may also feel fewer constraints about seeking a divorce (Smock & Gupta, 2002; Surra et al., 2004).

The Decision to Divorce

Who is more likely to initiate divorce, men or women? Folk wisdom might suggest that the men are most eager to leave a marriage. However, you'll recall that women are more likely to anticipate problems in a dating relationship. In fact, the data suggest that wives initiate divorce more often than husbands do (Coleman et al., 2006; McCarthy & McCarthy, 2006; Rudman & Glick, 2008). For instance, one survey focused on men and women who had experienced a divorce when they were between 40 and 69 years old. The results revealed that 66% of women said that they had asked for the divorce, in contrast to 41% of men. Furthermore, 14% of women said that their spouse's request for a divorce had surprised them, in contrast to 26% of men (Enright, 2004).

The three major reasons that women listed for a divorce were physical or emotional abuse, infidelity, and drug or alcohol use (Enright, 2004). In Chapter 13, we will discuss detailed information about the abuse of women. However, it's important to note that many religious leaders in the United States believe that divorce should be the last resort for a woman, even for one who has been abused (Levitt & Ware, 2006).

Many women report that they contemplated a divorce for years. Consider the following example:

> Jane Burroughs knew 10 years into her marriage that it wasn't working. She and her husband argued constantly. He made all the decisions; she felt she had no say. But instead of divorcing, she stayed for 21 more years, when her children were grown. … Burroughs, now 58, concedes it was the most difficult experience of her life and one that triggered conflicting emotions. (Enright, 2004, p. 62)

Psychological Effects of Divorce

Divorce is especially painful because it creates so many different kinds of transitions and separations, in addition to the separation from a former spouse (Baca Zinn & Eitzen, 2002; Ganong & Coleman, 1999). When a woman is divorced, she may be separated from friends and relatives previously shared by the couple.

Divorce is one of the most stressful changes a person can experience (Enright, 2004; M. A. Fine, 2000; Kitzmann & Gaylord, 2001). Depression and anger are often common responses, especially for women. In addition, mothers typically need to help children cope with the reality of divorce (Cantor et al., 2004; J. M. Lewis et al., 2004).

However, divorce can lead to some positive feelings. Women who felt constrained by an unhappy marriage may also feel relief (Baca Zinn & Eitzen, 2002). As one woman said, "For me, the divorce was not difficult. I had been living in loneliness for years by the time my marriage ended, so that being alone felt uplifting, free" (Hood, 1995, p. 132). Many women also report that their divorce lets them know they are stronger than they had thought. In fact, some say that the divorce actually had some long-range positive effects (Coleman et al., 2006; Enright, 2004; McKenry & McKelvey, 2003).

Financial Effects of Divorce

Despite the occasional positive effects of divorce, one consequence is painful: A woman's financial situation is almost always worse following a divorce, especially if she has children (Rice, 2001a). In Canada, two-thirds of divorced single mothers and their children live in poverty (Gorlick, 1995). In the United States, less than half of divorced fathers actually pay the mandated child support (Baca Zinn & Eitzen, 2002; Stacey, 2000). Black mothers are even more likely than White mothers to face financial problems (McKenry & McKelvey, 2003) due to both structural racism and the gender wage gap, as we discussed in Chapter 7. These financial problems often increase a woman's depression and anger.

Section Summary

Marriage and Divorce

1. Marital satisfaction is high during the newlywed period, but it often drops during subsequent years. For couples who have children, satisfaction is lowest during the first 20 to 24 years of marriage, and then it may increase after the children have left the home.
2. Women are more likely than men to report positive emotions about their marriage, but they are also more sensitive than men to marital problems.
3. Happy marriages are more common among people who have strong communication skills and conflict-resolution skills, who trust and support each other, and who share equally.
4. Marriages can be categorized along a continuum between traditional and egalitarian.
5. Some Latinas and Latinos emphasize *machismo* and *marianismo* in their marriages, but many advocate more egalitarian marital patterns. Black families may be more egalitarian than families from other ethnic backgrounds. Asian American families are likely to experience conflicts between traditional Asian values and contemporary gender roles in the United States and Canada.

(continues)

Section Summary *(continued)*

6. A couple who lives together before marriage is more likely to get divorced, but the explanation for this tendency is not clear.
7. Women are more likely than men to initiate divorce, most often because of physical or emotional abuse, infidelity, and substance abuse.
8. Divorce is almost always stressful, especially because it creates depression and anger. Women may experience some positive effects, such as relief and a sense of strength. However, most divorced women experience financial problems that can have serious implications for their well-being.

8-3 Lesbian and Bisexual Women

Learning Objectives

To describe factors that characterize romantic relationships among lesbian and bisexual women, you can …

8-3-1 Describe how heterosexism and bias affect the psychological adjustment of people who identify as a sexual minority.

8-3-2 Describe characteristics of lesbian relationships.

8-3-3 Explain why experiencing multiple forms of prejudice impacts the lives of lesbian women of color.

8-3-4 Discuss how *Obergefell v. Hodges* (2015) affected the legal status of lesbian relationships.

8-3-5 Describe characteristics of bisexual women and their relationships.

8-3-6 Discuss why Diamond's research provides evidence for fluidity in women's sexual orientation.

8-3-7 Describe how biological, social constructionist, and dynamical systems approaches explain sexual orientation.

Rita and Sandy are a lesbian couple who have been together for 16 years. Reflecting on their first 10 years, Rita describes how she had thought that their relationship could not get any better:

> And now, between ten and sixteen years, I'm thinking, this is just excellent! Our relationship is just getting deeper and deeper and more loving and more loving, and of course, like any relationship, we've had our roller coaster. We've had our ups and downs and we'll continue to have our problems and work them out. It's hard to describe the deepness of the love. It keeps growing and growing and growing. So I can't imagine what it's going to be like in another sixteen years.

Then Sandy adds:

> And we're grateful for each other and we're both very verbal about thanking each other and being grateful to each other, respecting each other. I think that's really important. (Haley-Banez & Garrett, 2002, pp. 116–117)

A **lesbian woman** is psychologically, emotionally, and sexually attracted to other women. This definition includes both cisgender and transgender women who are attracted to other women. Our discussion of sexual orientation emphasizes love, intimacy, and affection, as well as sexual feelings.

Some psychologists use the term **sexual minority** to refer to anyone who has a same-gender attraction (L. M. Diamond, 2002). This term therefore includes lesbian women, gay men, bisexual women, bisexual men. The term *sexual minority* may also refer to other sexual orientations, such as pansexual, sapiosexual, and asexual (Brotto & Yule, 2017; Morandini, Blaszczynski, & Dar-Nimrod, 2017). Sexual minority couples are more common than many people believe. For instance, data from the U.S. Census demonstrates that same-gender couples live in 99.3% of all the counties within the United States (Pawelski et al., 2006), and there are approximately 646,000 same-gender couples in the United States (Williams Institute, 2019).

In Chapter 1, we introduced the term **heterosexism**, or bias against lesbian women, gay men, and people who identify as bisexual, asexual, pansexual, or any other nonheterosexual orientation (Herek, 2009). In the United States, an important consequence of heterosexism is that many people judge heterosexual relationships to be different from lesbian, gay, bisexual, and other nonheterosexual relationships (S. D. Smith, 2004). Try Demonstration 8.4 to appreciate how heterosexist thinking pervades our culture.

Demonstration **8.4**

Heterosexist Thinking

Answer each of the following questions, and then explain why each one encourages us to reassess the heterosexist framework.

1. Suppose that you are walking to class at your college and you witness a man and a woman kissing. Do you think, "Why are they flaunting their heterosexuality?"
2. Close your eyes and picture two women kissing each other. Does that kiss seem sexual or affectionate? Now close your eyes and imagine a woman and a man kissing each other. Does your evaluation of that kiss change?
3. Suppose that you have an appointment with a female professor. When you arrive in her office, you notice that she is wearing a wedding ring and has a photo of herself and a man smiling at each other. Do you say to yourself, "Why is she shoving her heterosexuality in my face?"
4. If you are heterosexual, has anyone asked you, "Don't you think that heterosexuality is just a phase you'll outgrow once you are older?"
5. In all the public debates you've experienced about sexual orientation, has anyone asked any of the following questions?

   a. The divorce rate among heterosexuals is now about 50%. Why don't heterosexuals have more stable love relationships?

(continues)

Demonstration 8.4 *(continued)*

    b. Why are heterosexual men so likely to sexually harass or rape women?

    c. Why do heterosexual people place so much emphasis on sex?

Sources: Based partly on L. Garnets (2008) and Herek (1996).

An important point is that lesbian women are no longer routinely excluded from research in psychology. In fact, while preparing this chapter, we conducted a search on an electronic resource called PsycINFO. Impressively, 1,961 professional articles had been published with the term *lesbian* in the title, for research conducted between January 2010 and May 2021.

In Chapter 2, we examined heterosexism and bias based on sexual orientation, and in Chapter 4 we discussed the coming-out experience of adolescent lesbian girls. In Chapter 7, we emphasized antilesbian prejudice in the workplace. In upcoming chapters, we will discuss sexuality issues among lesbian women (Chapter 9), the research on lesbian mothers (Chapter 10), and the experiences of lesbian women whose life partners have died (Chapter 14).

In this section of Chapter 8, we'll first discuss the psychological adjustment of lesbian women. Next we'll explore several characteristics of lesbian relationships, the experiences of lesbian women of color, and the fluid nature of sexual orientation. We'll then address the legal status of lesbian relationships, as well as information about bisexual women. Our final topic will be potential explanations for sexual orientation.

The Psychological Adjustment of Lesbian Women

A large number of studies have shown that the average lesbian woman is similar to the average heterosexual woman in terms of mental health and life satisfaction (e.g., Herek & Garnets, 2007; J. F. Morris & Hart, 2003). However, many of these articles have major problems with research design (Cochran & Mays, 2006). In contrast, consider a carefully designed study by Rothblum and Factor (2001). This study compared the mental health of 184 pairs of lesbian women and their biological sisters who were heterosexual. Notice what makes the research well controlled: Each lesbian woman in this study resembles a well-matched heterosexual woman. The results showed that the two groups were equivalently well adjusted, except that the lesbian women were higher in self-esteem.

In other carefully designed research, lesbian and heterosexual women are similar on almost all psychological dimensions, except that lesbian women often score higher on positive characteristics such as "being self-sufficient," "being self-confident," and "making decisions easily" (Garnets, 2008).

In Chapter 2, our discussion of heterosexism and sexual prejudice emphasized that many sexual minority individuals are victims of hate crimes (e.g., Herek, 2009). Not surprisingly, lesbian, gay, and bisexual individuals who have experienced hate crimes or abuse are likely to report problems such as depression, anxiety, and substance abuse (Bontempo & D'Augelli, 2002; Herek & Garnets, 2007; I. L. Meyer, 2003). In other words, hatred has real-life consequences for the well-being of millions of people in North America.

Largely due to a history of experiencing discrimination and bias, women who identify as LGBTQ+ who have had a history of adverse experiences are unfortunately at higher risk for suicidal ideation and suicide than heterosexual women (Blosnich, Nasuti, Mays, & Cochran, 2016; Lyons et al., 2019).

Students in our classes sometimes ask whether people who accept their lesbian or gay identity are better adjusted. The research shows that people who accept their lesbian identity have higher self-esteem than those who have not accepted their lesbian identity (Garnets, 2008; Herek & Garnets, 2007; J. F. Morris et al., 2001).

In spite of exposure to societal stigma and discrimination, many lesbian women create their own communities, and warm, supportive networks develop from the "families" they choose. These communities are especially helpful when lesbian women are rejected by their birth families (Szymanski & Owens, 2009; Haley-Banez & Garrett, 2002). However, these women are more satisfied with their lives and less depressed if their family and friends support their lesbian identity (Beals & Peplau, 2005).

Characteristics of Lesbian Relationships

For most people in the United States—whether they identify as lesbian, gay, bisexual, non-heterosexual, or heterosexual—being in a love relationship is an important determinant of their overall happiness (Peplau et al., 1997). Surveys suggest that between 40% and 65% of lesbian women are currently in a steady romantic relationship (Badgett, 2008; Peplau & Beals, 2004). In other words, many lesbian women consider that being part of a couple is an important aspect of their life.

Let's now look more closely at several aspects of lesbian relationships. Specifically, how do most lesbian relationships begin? How is equality emphasized in these relationships? How happy are lesbian couples? How do they respond when the relationship breaks up?

The Beginning of a Relationship

Lesbian women want many of the same qualities in a romantic partner that heterosexual women emphasize. These include characteristics such as dependability and good personality (Peplau & Beals, 2004). The research suggests that most lesbian couples begin their relationship as friends and then fall in love (Diamond, 2006; Peplau & Fingerhut, 2007; S. Rose, 2000). For many adolescent girls and young women, a romantic relationship is a major milestone in coming out and identifying as a lesbian (M. S. Schneider, 2001).

An important hallmark of a strong relationship is emotional intimacy. As we'll learn, lesbian couples are likely to emphasize emotional closeness. In contrast, physical attractiveness is relatively unimportant as a basis for a lesbian love relationship. Lesbian women who create dating profiles rarely emphasize physical characteristics (Peplau & Spalding, 2000; C. A. Smith & Stillman, 2002).

Equality in Lesbian Relationships

The balance of power is extremely important in lesbian relationships. Furthermore, couples are happier if both members of the pair contribute equally to the decision making (Garnets, 2008).

In Chapter 7, we learned that women do most of the housework in heterosexual marriages, even when both the husband and the wife work full time. As you might expect, lesbian couples are especially likely to emphasize that housework should be divided fairly (Peplau & Fingerhut, 2007).

Satisfaction

Some of the research on lesbian couples shows that their satisfaction with their relationship is much the same as for heterosexual couples and gay couples (Diamond, 2006; Herek, 2006; Peplau & Fingerhut, 2007). Other research shows that lesbian couples have stronger relationship quality and fewer conflicts than heterosexual married couples (Balsam et al., 2008). Try Demonstration 8.5 before you read further.

Demonstration **8.5**

Assessing Commitment to a Relationship

Answer the following questions about a current or a previous love relationship. Or, if you prefer, think of a couple you know well, and answer the questionnaire from the perspective of one member of that couple. Use a rating scale where 1 = strongly disagree and 5 = strongly agree. These questions are based on a survey by Kurdek (1995). This is a shorter version. Refer to page 281 to discover which relationship dimensions these items assess.

Rating   Question

_____ 1. One advantage to my relationship is having someone to count on.

_____ 2. I have to sacrifice a lot to be in my relationship.

_____ 3. My current relationship comes close to matching what I would consider my ideal relationship.

_____ 4. As an alternative to my current relationship, I would like to date someone else.

_____ 5. I've put a lot of energy and effort into my relationship.

_____ 6. It would be difficult to leave my partner because of the emotional pain involved.

_____ 7. Overall, I derive a lot of rewards and advantages from being in my relationship.

_____ 8. Overall, a lot of personal costs are involved in being in my relationship.

_____ 9. My current relationship provides me with an ideal amount of equality.

_____ 10. Overall, alternatives to being in my relationship are appealing.

_____ 11. I have invested a part of myself in my relationship.

_____ 12. It would be difficult to leave my partner because I would still feel attached to them.

Source: Kurdek, L. A. (1995). *Family Relations, 44,* 261–266. (Table 1). Copyright © 1995 by the National Council on Family Relations. Reprinted with permission.

Demonstration 8.5 contains some of the questions from a classic survey, designed by Lawrence Kurdek (1995), that measures relationship commitment. In this survey, Kurdek's sample of lesbian couples had commitment scores that were similar to the scores of married couples. The results also showed that the lesbian couples were more committed to the relationship than were heterosexual couples who were dating, but not living together.

Psychological intimacy is likely to be strong in lesbian couples (Garnets, 2008). One woman described this sense of caring and intimacy:

> What has been good is the ongoing caring and respect and the sense that there is somebody there who really cares, who has your best interest, who loves you, who knows you better than anybody, and still likes you … and just that knowing, that familiarity, the depth of that knowing, the depth of that connection [make it] so incredibly meaningful. There is something spiritual after awhile. It has a life of its own. This is what is really so comfortable. (Mackey et al., 2000, p. 220)

Breaking Up

We do not have extensive information about how lesbian partners break up their love relationships. However, the general pattern seems to be similar to the heterosexual breakup pattern (Balsam, Rothblum, & Wickham, 2017; Diamond, 2006; Peplau & Beals, 2001).

When relationships end, both lesbian and heterosexual women report some negative emotions and some positive emotions (Diamond, 2006). Similar to heterosexual unions, predictors of lesbian couple dissolution include young age at marriage, relatively short dating periods prior to marriage, and sexual infidelity (Balsam et al., 2017). However, there is evidence that lesbian relationships are less stable than other relationships, such as those between gay men or heterosexual couples (Balsam et al., 2017; Rosenfeld, 2014). Lesbian couples are less likely to have support for their relationship from other family members—a factor that often keeps heterosexual couples together. However, lesbian couples are more likely to have support from their extensive friend networks during and after a break-up, and this factor actually *increases* the likelihood that they will break up (Balsam et al., 2017).

Lesbian Women of Color

Lesbian women of color often comment that they face a triple barrier in U.S. society: their ethnicity, their gender, and their sexual orientation (R. L. Hall & Greene, 2002; Herek & Garnets, 2007). In earlier chapters, we discussed a concept called *intersectionality*. **Intersectionality** argues that it's important to consider several social categories together, rather than independently (Cole, 2009; Crenshaw, 2017).

For example, we cannot consider just gender, or just sexual orientation, or just ethnicity. After all, a woman who is lesbian and Latina typically encounters a different kind of discrimination than a woman who is lesbian and White. This perspective is consistent with Theme 4, which argues that there are large individual differences in women's experiences. The social category called "sexual orientation" is similarly diverse. Let's therefore consider some of the ways in which heterosexism is experienced by women who are Latina, Black, and Asian American.

Many lesbian women of color face an extra barrier because some ethnic cultural norms have even more traditional views of women than those associated with mainstream cultural norms in the United States. For example, Black churches often show sexual prejudice toward lesbian and gay individuals (Cole & Guy-Sheftall, 2003; B. Greene, 2000a).

A Latina who is lesbian may have a different experience than a Black woman who is lesbian. Her family may believe that she cannot fulfill the roles that her family and community may expect of her—such as marrying, being obedient to her husband, and rearing her children in a traditional fashion (Torres, 2003). Because of these restrictions, a Latina lesbian may decide to marry and try to ignore her attraction to other women (Castañeda, 2008).

Another issue is that some cultures may be more traditional than those typically found in the United States with respect to discussing sexuality. For example, some Asian cultures believe that sexuality shouldn't be discussed (C. S. Chan, 2008; Takagi, 2001). Asian or Asian American parents may also feel that a lesbian daughter has rejected their cultural values (C. S. Chan, 2008; Hom, 2003).

In addition, many conservative heterosexual people of color believe that only White people face the "problem" of having gay men and lesbian women in society (Fingerhut et al., 2005; J. F. Morris, 2000). Furthermore, non-White sexual minority individuals may be more worried than White sexual minority individuals that their parents will reject them because of their sexual orientation (Dubé et al., 2001). As a result of these two factors, lesbian women of color may not adopt a strong lesbian identity, and they may be even less open than in White communities (Fingerhut et al., 2005).

Many lesbian women of color can find organizations and community groups that provide support, especially in urban regions of the United States (J. F. Morris, 2000). For example, lesbian Latinas in the New York City area can attend winter holiday parties, read brochures on health care written in Spanish by lesbian Latinas, and march in the Puerto Rican Day parade with a contingent of lesbian Latinas and gay Latinos. Racism and heterosexism may still be present, but these groups can provide a shared sense of community.

Some regions of the United States and Canada have Asian American lesbian and gay social organizations, support groups for parents of Asian American lesbian and gay children, and conferences that focus on relevant issues. However, critics emphasize that much work still needs to be done to include lesbian and gay perspectives within the framework of contemporary Asian American issues (Duong, 2004; Fingerhut et al., 2005; Takagi, 2001).

Lesbian women of color often create positive environments for themselves, even though they might appear to be living on the margins of mainstream society. They refuse to let themselves be confined by labels, they develop powerful friendships, and their activism strengthens their own lives, as well as the lives of lesbian communities (R. L. Hall & Fine, 2005).

Legal Status of Lesbian Relationships

In 2015, the United States Supreme Court ruling on the *Obergefell v. Hodges* case made same-gender marriages legal in all 50 states. This ruling finally brought marriage equality to lesbian and gay couples after decades of discrimination and inconsistency in marriage laws at the state level. Prior to 2015, lesbian women could only legally marry each other in a few states in the United States, and therefore struggled with structural inequality as well as a lack of societal acknowledgement for their relationships. For example, Linda Garnets is a professor at UCLA, and she conducts research about lesbian relationships. She describes her personal perspective during the pre-*Obergefell v. Hodges* era:

> I am in a 22-year relationship that I know is a life partnership, but it has no legal status because same-gender marriages are illegal. My partner and I cannot be jointly covered by insurance, inheritance laws, or hospital visitation rules.... A good friend of ours was dying, and the hospital would only let her partner of 12 years see her if she pretended to be her sister. She was not considered "immediate family" by the hospital rules. (Garnets, 2008, p. 235)

Why was gaining marriage equality so important for lesbian couples? One obvious reason is personal: Two women want to recognize their commitment to each other. Studies of marital satisfaction among lesbian couples who were legally married in Massachusetts prior to *Obergefell v. Hodges*, and among lesbian couples in Canada following legalized same-sex marriage in 2005, suggested similar rates of physical, psychological, and financial well-being as heterosexual couples (Ducharme & Kollar, 2012; MacIntosh, Reissing, & Andruff, 2010). Studies such as these provided evidence that marriage equality is psychologically beneficial for nonheterosexual couples.

A second reason is political: Many want to overcome the heterosexist bias that makes lesbian couples less obvious within society (Garnets, 2008). However, similar to heterosexual couples, lesbian couples also sometimes experience ambivalence toward saying "I do" now that legal marriage is available for all adults in the United States (Bosley-Smith & Reczak, 2018).

A third reason is practical. In the United States, the General Accounting Office has calculated that two people who are married can receive more than 1,000 federal and state benefits and protections, in comparison to two people who are an unmarried couple (General Accounting Office, 2004; Peplau & Fingerhut, 2007).

As of 2020, same-gender marriages are permitted in 29 countries around the world, including Canada, the Netherlands, Belgium, Iceland, Sweden, Norway, Portugal, Spain, Argentina, Australia, the United States, and South Africa, among others (Human Rights Campaign, 2021).

Bisexual Women

Heather Macalister, a psychology professor, describes her personal perspectives on sexual attraction:

> Growing up I assumed I was straight, as most of us do, and when I was about seventeen I discovered that some of the people I was attracted to were women. I was pretty excited about this. I thought it was neat to be open-minded, a freethinker, to place other criteria for attraction above gender or sex. I frankly never considered referring to myself as "bisexual." It wasn't until later when the cumbersome "I'm open-minded, a free-thinker. I place other criteria for attraction above gender or sex!" left people confused that I began using the label "bisexual" for their cognitive convenience. But I still feel like it's missing something. I'm not hung up on gender or sex or sexual orientation, and I'm just attracted to whomever I'm attracted to. (Macalister, 2003, pp. 29–30)

A **bisexual woman** is a woman who is psychologically, emotionally, and sexually attracted to both women and men; a bisexual woman therefore refuses to exclude a possible romantic partner on the basis of that person's gender (Berenson, 2002; Macalister, 2003). In general, women are more likely to have experienced attraction to both women and men than attraction only to women (L. M. Diamond, 2002, 2005; Rust, 2000). We'll discover that bisexuality presents a dilemma for a culture that likes to construct clear-cut categories (Macalister, 2003).

Characteristics of Bisexual Women

Bisexual women often comment that the nature of their attraction to women and men may differ. For example, one woman explained: "I feel a greater physical attraction to men, but a greater spiritual/emotional attraction to women" (Rust, 2000, p. 212). In short, bisexuality creates a flexible identity rather than a clear-cut life pathway (Rust, 2000).

Social scientists have not conducted much research on the adjustment of bisexual women. However, they seem to be similar to other women (Balsam et al., 2005; Ketz & Israel, 2002). Also, bisexual women and lesbian women are equally satisfied with their lives and with their current sexual identity (Balsam et al., 2005; Rust, 1996).

Bisexual women who come from a background of mixed ethnicity often find that their mixed heritage is consistent with their bisexuality. After all, their experience with ethnicity has taught them from an early age that many cultures construct clear-cut ethnic categories. As a result, they are not surprised to encounter clear-cut cultural categories of sexual orientation (Duong, 2004; Rust, 2000).

Attitudes Toward Bisexual Women

Bisexual women often report that they have been rejected by both the heterosexual and the lesbian communities, and there is some evidence that people who identify as bisexual experience more discrimination than other sexual minority groups (Mereish, Katz-Wise, & Woulfe, 2017). Because of sexual prejudice, heterosexual people may condemn bisexual women's same-gender relationships. In fact, heterosexual individuals rate bisexual women more negatively than they rate lesbian women (Herek, 2002b; Whitley & Kite, 2010). Many heterosexual people also believe that bisexual people are frequently unfaithful to their partners (Ketz & Israel, 2002; Peplau & Spalding, 2000). In contrast, lesbian women often argue that bisexual women are "buying into" heterosexism and therefore deny that they are lesbian women (Ketz & Israel, 2002; Whitley & Kite, 2010). As a result, both heterosexual and bisexual people often fail to understand women who identify as bisexual (Robin & Hamner, 2000).

In Chapter 2, we emphasized that people like to have precise categories for men and women, so that everyone fits neatly into one category or the other. Prejudice against lesbian women can be partly traced to the fact that they violate the accepted rules about categories: You shouldn't have a romantic relationship with someone who belongs to your own gender category. Bisexual individuals provide an additional frustration for people who like precise categories, because they cannot be placed into either the "clear-cut lesbian" or the "clear-cut heterosexual" category. People who have a low tolerance for ambiguity definitely feel uncomfortable about people who identify as bisexual.

The Fluidity of Female Sexual Orientation

During the 1990s, researchers who were interested in the topic of lesbian and gay sexual orientation favored a straightforward model. Specifically, a young person would feel unhappy about their heterosexual relationships. Then they would enter a period of sexual questioning, which would end with the adoption of a lesbian, gay, or bisexual identity.

Current researchers realize that this model is too simplistic, because it does not acknowledge the diverse pathways by which sexual orientation develops, especially for women (Baumeister, 2000; L. M. Diamond, 2002, 2003b, 2005, 2007, 2008; Vohs & Baumeister, 2004). One problem with the older research is that most of the sexual minority individuals who had shared their stories were openly gay men who were exclusively attracted to other men. Consistent with Theme 3 of this textbook, earlier research focused on sexual minority *men* rather than on sexual minority *women*.

We now know that sexual orientation can be a fluid, changing process rather than a rigid category. Consider, for example, the research of Lisa M. Diamond (2002, 2003b, 2005). She began by interviewing 80 women between the ages of 18 and 25 who had identified themselves as "nonheterosexual women," a term that could include lesbian and bisexual women. Diamond located these women in college courses on sexuality, in college campus groups, and in community events sponsored by lesbian, gay, and bisexual organizations.

Diamond has continued to interview these women over a period of 8 years. Of the women who had identified themselves as lesbians in the first interview, some described a "classic" development of their lesbian identity. These **stable lesbians** had focused on girls and women during childhood, and this interest had continued during adolescence. However, a larger number of women in Diamond's study could be classified as **fluid lesbians** because they had questioned or changed their lesbian sexual identity at some point. Consider the following description, provided by one woman who qualifies as a fluid lesbian:

> After I graduated from college … I found myself, not necessarily only attracted to both sexes, but also slightly more open-minded to the notion that maybe … maybe I can find something in just a person, that I don't necessarily have to be attracted to one sex versus the other. (L. M. Diamond, 2005, p. 126)

Interestingly, many of the women in Diamond's research also emphasized that they disliked having to fit themselves into someone else's labels or categories. In fact, by the time that Diamond had interviewed her sample of women in 2005, two-thirds of these women had considered themselves to be "unlabeled" at some period of time in their lives (Diamond, 2007).

In this chapter, we have emphasized the variation in women's romantic relationships, consistent with Theme 4. As we've just learned, research also suggests that a woman's sexual orientation can vary throughout her lifetime. In the last part of this section on lesbian and bisexual women, we will discover the implications of this fluidity for theories of sexual orientation.

Theoretical Explanations About Sexual Orientation

When we try to explain how lesbian women develop their psychological, emotional, and sexual preference for women, we might also consider another question: How do *heterosexual* women develop their psychological, emotional, and sexual preference for men? Unfortunately, theorists rarely mention this question.[1] Because of heterosexist bias, it is considered both "natural" and "normal" for women to be attracted exclusively to men. This assumption implies that lesbianism is unnatural and abnormal, and abnormalities require an explanation (Baber, 2000; Nencel, 2005).

However, heterosexuality is actually more puzzling. After all, research in social psychology shows that we prefer people who resemble ourselves, not people who are different. On this basis, we should actually prefer those of our own gender.

Articles in the popular press proclaim that biological factors are the most important determinate of sexual orientation. In reality, we do not have strong evidence for a biological explanation for the sexual orientation of lesbian or bisexual women. Meanwhile, psychologists who favor social constructionist explanations theorize that both social forces and our thought processes tend to shape a woman's sexual orientation. We'll also consider a perspective developed by Lisa M. Diamond (2007, 2008; Diamond & Rosky, 2016), which is based on the dynamical systems approach.

---

[1]One exception is an excellent article by Hyde and Jaffee (2000), which suggests that adolescent girls are encouraged toward heterosexuality by means of traditional gender roles and numerous antigay messages.

Biological Explanations

Researchers who favor biological explanations are much more likely to study gay men than lesbian women. For example, an article in the *Wall Street Journal* was titled "Brain Responses Vary by Sexual Orientation, New Research Shows" (2005). However, lesbian women were marginalized in this particular study because it discussed only gay men. Other research examines members of nonhuman species exposed to abnormal levels of prenatal hormones. These research areas are too far removed to offer compelling explanations for women's sexual orientation.

Other research examines humans to determine whether genetic factors, hormonal factors, or brain structures determine sexual orientation (e.g., Hershberger, 2001; LeVay, 1996; Savic et al., 2005). Some of the research suggests, for example, that a particular region on the X chromosome may contain genes for same-gender sexual attraction. However, this research focuses almost exclusively on gay men, not lesbian women or bisexual people (Peplau, 2001; Savic et al., 2005). Many of these studies also have serious methodological flaws that other researchers have pointed out (e.g., Diamond & Rosky, 2016; J. M. Bailey et al., 2000; J. Horgan, 2004; Hyde & DeLamater, 2006; L. Rogers, 2001).

Let's consider one of the few studies on genetic factors that examined lesbian women. Bailey and his colleagues focused on lesbian women who happened to have an identical twin sister (J. M. Bailey et al., 2000). Of these women, 24% had twin sisters who also identified as lesbian. This is a fairly high percentage, but these lesbian twins shared the same home environment, as well as the same genetic makeup. Furthermore, if genetic factors guarantee sexual orientation—and each twin pair has identical genes—why isn't that figure closer to 100% (L. Rogers, 2001)? Other conceptually similar research shows weak support for the purely biological approach to women's sexual orientation (J. M. Bailey et al., 1993; Hyde, 2005b; Pattatucci & Hamer, 1995).

In short, biological factors may be responsible for a small part of women's sexual orientation; however, relatively few studies examine either lesbian or bisexual women. We should note, incidentally, that research suggests somewhat stronger support for the role of biological factors in male sexual orientation (Baumeister, 2000; Fletcher, 2002; Hershberger, 2001; Vohs & Baumeister, 2004). Clearly, however, the popular press has overemphasized the importance of biological factors in explaining sexual orientation in women (J. Horgan, 2004).

The Social Constructionist Approach

Other research and theories suggest that women's sexual orientation is more influenced by our culture, the social norms, and situational factors, rather than by biological factors (Baumeister, 2000; L. M. Diamond, 2003b; Vohs & Baumeister, 2004). Furthermore, note that these sociocultural explanations emphasize the individual differences among women in their erotic orientations (Vohs & Baumeister, 2004).

The **social constructionist approach** argues that cultures create sexual categories, which we use to organize our thoughts about our sexuality (Baber, 2000; Bohan, 1996; C. Kitzinger & Wilkinson, 1997). Social constructionists reject an essentialist approach to sexual orientation. In other words, sexual orientation is not a fundamental aspect of an individual that must be acquired either before birth or in early childhood.

The social constructionists propose that, based on their life experiences and cultural messages, most women in the United States initially construct heterosexual identities for themselves (Baber, 2000; Carpenter, 1998). However, some women review their sexual and romantic experiences and decide that they identify as either lesbian or bisexual (Bociurkiw, 2005; L. M. Diamond, 2007).

The social constructionist approach argues that sexuality is both fluid and flexible, consistent with our earlier discussions. For example, women can make a transition from being heterosexual to being lesbian by re-evaluating their lives or by reconsidering their political values (C. Kitzinger & Wilkinson, 1997).

To examine the social constructionist approach, Celia Kitzinger and Sue Wilkinson (1997) interviewed 80 women who had previously identified as heterosexual for at least 10 years and who, at the time of the study, strongly identified themselves as lesbian women. These women reported how they re-evaluated their lives in making the transition. For example, one woman said:

> I was looking at myself in the mirror, and I thought, "That woman is a lesbian," and then I allowed myself to notice that it was me I was talking about. And when that happened, I felt whole for the first time, and also absolutely terrified. (p. 197)

However, we need to emphasize an important point: Some lesbian women recognize that their sexual orientation is truly beyond their conscious control (Golden, 1996). These women had considered themselves different from other women at an early age, usually when they were between 6 and 12 years old.

In short, the social constructionist approach acknowledges that the "categories" *heterosexual, bisexual,* and *lesbian* are fluid and flexible, and exist more as a continuum of sexual attraction rather than dichotomous categories. This approach also explains why some women consciously choose their sexual orientation, while others know from an early age that they identify as a sexual minority.

The Dynamical Systems Approach

According to Lisa M. Diamond (2007, 2008; Diamond & Rosky, 2016), an appropriate model of female sexual orientation needs to focus on how women's sexual orientation may change over time. As we read on pages 271–272, Diamond's own research has examined the developmental changes that nonheterosexual women experienced during an interval of more than 10 years. Diamond (2007, 2008) searched for a model that could explain how complex changes can occur over a period of many years, and she discovered a perspective called the *dynamical systems* approach.

Originally, physicists and mathematicians developed the dynamical systems approach to explain complicated changes in the physical world. Then developmental psychologists applied this perspective to topics such as infants' motor development.

When applied to woman's sexual orientation, the **dynamical systems approach** proposes that a woman may experience new sexual feelings that occur in specific situations, and then she thinks about these experiences. If these cycles of sexual feelings and interpretations keep occurring, this woman eventually creates a new perspective about her sexuality.

Diamond (2007, 2008; Diamond & Rosky, 2016) therefore emphasizes that changes in a woman's sexuality may not occur in a systematic, linear fashion. Consistent with Diamond's own research findings and the perspective of other researchers, she argues that the experiences of nonheterosexual women are much more fluid and complex (Peplau, 2001; Peplau & Garnets, 2000).

The most comprehensive theory of sexual orientation may actually include a biological predisposition that encourages some women to develop a lesbian or bisexual orientation (L. M. Diamond, 2003c, 2008). Social constructionism also plays an important role. However, a woman's continuing reinterpretations of her sexual experiences can influence whether she will develop a heterosexual, lesbian, or bisexual identity. In other words, sexual orientation is not a clear-cut category but a continuing process of self-discovery that operates within a continuum of sexual desire, rather than a category.

Section Summary

Lesbian and Bisexual Women

1. Lesbian women are psychologically, emotionally, and sexually attracted to other women; however, heterosexist cultural norms portray heterosexual relationships as very different from sexual-minority relationships.
2. Research demonstrates that lesbian and heterosexual women are equally well adjusted; lesbian women who accept their lesbian identity are typically higher in self-esteem than other lesbian women who do not accept their identity.
3. The research shows that most lesbian relationships begin with friendship and that lesbian couples tend to emphasize emotional closeness.
4. Lesbian couples are happier when decision making is evenly divided; in general, lesbian couples and heterosexual couples are equally satisfied with their relationships.
5. Lesbian couples and heterosexual couples have somewhat similar emotional reactions to breaking up; however, lesbian relationships are somewhat less stable than other relationships.
6. According to the intersectionality perspective, it is important to consider several social categories at the same time; for instance, a woman who is a Latina lesbian may have different perspectives from a woman who is a Black lesbian.
7. Lesbian women of color are often reluctant to disclose their sexual orientation if their ethnic community has conservative values; however, many lesbian women of color belong to supportive organizations in their community.
8. The legalization of same-gender marriages in the United States has been beneficial for many reasons. These reasons include increased personal fulfillment, increased recognition in society, and legal equality.
9. A diverse assortment of countries throughout the world permit either same-gender marriages or partnerships.
10. Bisexual women illustrate that women can be attracted to both women and men; unfortunately, these women may face rejection by both the lesbian and the heterosexual communities.
11. The majority of lesbian women report that they have had a fluid pattern of sexual identity, with some heterosexual interest, rather than a consistent lesbian identity.
12. Biological research seldom focuses on lesbian women or bisexual people; we do not currently have conclusive evidence that biological factors are responsible for a major part of women's sexual orientation.

(continues)

Section Summary *(continued)*

13. The social constructionist approach emphasizes that female sexual orientation is typically flexible, and women can reconstruct their identity to make transitions between heterosexual and lesbian orientations.
14. Diamond's dynamical systems approach argues that a woman's sexual orientation is often complex, because it involves nonlinear cycles of sexual feelings and interpretations of those feelings.

8-4 Single Women

Learning Objectives

To describe factors that characterize the lives of single women, you can ...

8-4-1   Describe characteristics that are associated with single women.

8-4-2   Define singlism and explain why it negatively impacts women.

8-4-3   Summarize the advantages and disadvantages of being single.

8-4-4   Discuss factors that characterize single women of color.

As of 2020, 35% of adult women have never married (Wang, 2020). In Canada, 73% of 18- to 34-year-old people have never been married, and 17% of individuals in this group say they have no intention of getting married (Angus Reid Institute, 2018).

The category "single women" includes those who have never married. However, it also overlaps with many groups we have already considered. For example, this category includes women who are either in a dating relationship or living with a romantic partner. Women who are separated or divorced are also included. So are lesbian and bisexual women who are not currently married. Finally, some of these single women are widows, a group that we will consider in Chapter 14.

This section on single women focuses on women who have never married, because they are not considered elsewhere in the section. However, all the other groups of single women share some of the same advantages and disadvantages that these never-married women experience. Before you read further, try Demonstration 8.6.

Characteristics of Single Women

Psychologists and sociologists seldom conduct systematic research about single women, even though they constitute a substantial percentage of adult women (Byrne, 2009; M. S. Clark & Graham, 2005; B. M. DePaulo, 2006).

The data suggest that single women are slightly more likely than married women to work outside the home (Bureau of Labor Statistics, 2004b). Many single women are highly educated, career-oriented individuals. These women often report that being single allows them flexible work hours and geographic mobility (Byrne, 2009; DeFrain & Olson, 1999).

Demonstration **8.6**

Attitudes Toward Single Women

Imagine that a friend has invited you to a family picnic with their extended family. They are giving you a brief description of each relative who will be there. For one relative, Melinda Taylor, they say,

"I really don't know much about her, but she is in her late 30s and she isn't married."

Try to imagine Melinda Taylor, given this brief description.

Compare her with the average woman in her late 30s, using the following list of characteristics. In each case, decide whether Melinda Taylor has more of the characteristic (write M), the same amount of the characteristic (write S), or less of the characteristic (write L).

_____ friendly
_____ bossy
_____ intelligent
_____ lonely
_____ disorganized
_____ attractive
_____ warm
_____ good sense of humor
_____ good conversationalist
_____ unhappy
_____ feminist
_____ politically liberal

Do you recognize any pattern to your responses?

Many single women have chosen not to marry because they never found an ideal partner. For example, *Time* magazine conducted a survey of 205 never-married women. One question asked, "If you couldn't find the perfect mate, would you marry someone else?" (T. M. Edwards, 2000, p. 48). Only 34% of these women replied that they would choose to marry a less-than-perfect spouse. Other women remain single because they believe that happy marriages are difficult to achieve (Huston & Melz, 2004).

Single, never-married women typically receive the same scores as married women on tests that measure psychological distress (N. F. Marks, 1996). Furthermore, single women score higher than married women on measures of independence, and some research shows that they have lower rates of psychological disorders (Byrne, 2009). Other research shows that single women and married women are similar in their life span, and both groups tend to live longer than divorced women (Fincham & Beach, 1999; Friedman et al., 1995). In summary, single women are generally well adjusted, and they are frequently satisfied with their single status.

Attitudes Toward Single Women

What kinds of answers did you provide in Demonstration 8.6? Also, think about the comments aimed at never-married women when you were growing up. The word **singlism** refers to bias against people who are not married (B. M. DePaulo & Morris, 2005, 2006). For example, single women report that they have received less respect and poorer service at restaurants, compared to married women (Byrne & Carr, 2005). They also experience more housing discrimination (B. M. DePaulo & Morris, 2006; Morris et al., 2007). However, most people—including some single women—are not aware of this singlism bias (Morris et al., 2008).

Furthermore, research shows that college students tend to describe single people as egocentric, lonely, shy, unhappy, insecure, and inflexible (Byrne, 2009; B. M. DePaulo & Morris, 2005, 2006). However, these college students also describe single people as being sociable and friendly, so the students do acknowledge some positive characteristics of single people.

Remaining single is more respectable than it was in earlier eras (Baca Zinn & Eitzen, 2002; Cantor et al., 2004). One reason is that the number of well-educated, economically self-sufficient women has increased over time (Whitehead, 2003). In 1970, only 10% of 25- to 29-year-old women were unmarried, compared to 40% by 2003 (U.S. Census Bureau, 2005). Many media sources also represent single women in a positive fashion.

Advantages and Disadvantages of Being Single

When single women are asked to identify the advantages of being single, they frequently mention freedom and independence (B. M. DePaulo & Morris, 2005; K. G. Lewis & Moon, 1997). Single people are free to do what they want, according to their own preferences. In fact, single women are more likely than married women to spend their time in leisure activities, travel, and social get-togethers (Lee & Bhargava, 2004). Single women also have more freedom to choose the people with whom they want to spend time (B. M. DePaulo & Morris, 2005).

In addition, single women mention that privacy is an advantage for them. They can be by themselves when they want, without the risk of offending someone. By learning to be alone with themselves, many women also say that they have developed a greater level of self-knowledge (Brehm, Miller et al., 2002).

When single women are asked about the disadvantages of being single, they frequently mention loneliness (T. M. Edwards, 2000; Rouse, 2002; Whitehead, 2003). One woman reported, "I am not a widow, but I'm the same as a widow. I'm a woman living alone, going home to an empty house" (K. R. Allen, 1994, p. 104).

However, most single women create their own social networks of friends and relatives (Rouse, 2002). Many have housemates with whom they can share their joys, sorrows, and frustrations. Others create a group of friends who can enjoy social activities togeer. In summary, single women frequently develop flexible support systems for caring and social connection.

Single Women of Color

We noted that little research has been conducted on the general topic of single women. This is especially true for single women of color in the United States, although researchers in other countries are more open to studying the topic of single women's lives (Ang, Lee, & Lie, 2020; Apostolou, O, & Esposito, 2020; Lesch & van der Watt, 2018).

In some communities, unmarried women serve a valuable function. For example, in Chicana (Mexican American) culture, an unmarried daughter is expected to take care of her elderly parents or to help out with nieces and nephews (Flores-Ortiz, 1998).

Compared to other women, there is more research on Black women who are single, especially because they spend a longer proportion of their lives as singles (Tucker & James, 2005). The research demonstrates, for example, that many Black women prefer to remain single, rather than to marry a man who currently has limited employment possibilities (Baca Zinn & Eitzen, 2002; Jayakody & Cabrera, 2002). Supportive friendships often provide invaluable social interactions for single Black women (Denton, 1990).

Surveys show that Asian American single women are frequently expected to fulfill the unmarried-daughter role (Ferguson, 2000; Newtson & Keith, 1997). Many Asian American women also report that they choose to remain single because they want to pursue an advanced education or because they have not found an appropriate marriage partner (Ferguson, 2000).

Researchers have historically failed to provide a balanced description of the attitudes, social conditions, and behaviors of single women. Future research may provide a more complete understanding of the diversity of single women from all ethnic backgrounds. Furthermore, as Bella DePaulo and Wendy Morris (2005) emphasize:

> Enlightened citizens come to realize that you don't need to be a man to be a leader, you don't need to be straight to be normal, you don't need to be White to be smart, and you don't need to be coupled to be happy. (p. 78)

Section Summary

Single Women

1. Researchers typically do not study single women; however, these women are reasonably similar to married women on various measures of adjustment and health.
2. "Singlism" refers to bias against people who are not married. Single women report some housing discrimination. Surveys indicate some negative attitudes about single people, but remaining single is now more acceptable than in earlier decades.
3. Single women tend to value their freedom to pursue their own leisure activities, but many mention that loneliness is a disadvantage; most single women create alternative social networks.
4. Unmarried Latina women are often expected to take care of elderly family members. Many Black single women emphasize the importance of supportive friends. Some Asian American women stay single to take care of elderly family members; others stay single to pursue advanced educational degrees.

Chapter Review Questions

1. At several points in this chapter, we discussed cross-cultural studies as well as research focusing on women of color in the United States. Summarize this research with respect to the following topics: (a) the ideal romantic partner, (b) marriage, (c) lesbian women, and (d) single women of color.

2. What is evolutionary psychology, and how does it explain women's and men's choices for an ideal romantic partner? Why is it inadequate in explaining cross-cultural research? How can the social-roles theory account for that research? Finally, why would evolutionary psychology have difficulty accounting for lesbian relationships?

3. The issue of power is an important topic in this chapter. Describe the division of power in traditional and egalitarian marriages, as well as in lesbian relationships. Also discuss how power operates for married women of color.

4. Discuss how this chapter contains many examples of the theme that women differ widely from one another. Be sure to include topics such as patterns of living together, reactions to divorce, sexual orientation, and the social relationships of single women.

5. Discuss gender comparisons that were described throughout this chapter. Be sure to include topics such as the ideal sexual partner, the ideal marriage partner, reactions to breaking up, satisfaction with marriage, and the decision to seek a divorce.

6. We noted that people who like clear-cut categories often experience frustration when they try to understand lesbian and bisexual women. Discuss Lisa Diamond's research about the fluid nature of sexual orientation, the experiences of bisexual women, and theories about sexual orientation.

7. Lesbian, bisexual, and single women all have lifestyles that differ from the traditional norm. What are people's attitudes toward women in these three groups?

8. Imagine that you are having a conversation with a friend from your high school, whom you know well. This friend tells you that she thinks that lesbian women are more likely than heterosexual women to have psychological problems and relationship difficulties. She also opposes same-gender marriages. How could you address her concerns by using information from this chapter?

9. Suppose that you continue to talk with the high-school friend mentioned in Question 8, and the conversation turns to people who have never married. She tells you that she is worried about a woman you both know who doesn't seem to be interested in dating or finding a life partner. How would you respond to your friend's concerns?

10. During the past few decades, people's behaviors and attitudes about love relationships have changed a great deal. Using the chapter outline on page 243 as a guideline, describe between five and ten substantial changes.

Key Terms

evolutionary-
    psychology
    approach (p. 250)
social-roles approach
    (p. 250)
traditional marriage
    (p. 257)
egalitarian marriage
    (p. 258)

machismo (p. 258)
marianismo (p. 258)
lesbian woman
    (p. 264)
sexual minority
    (p. 264)
heterosexism (p. 264)

intersectionality
    (p. 268)
bisexual woman
    (p. 270)
stable lesbians
    (p. 272)
fluid lesbians (p. 272)

social constructionist
    approach (p. 273)
dynamical systems
    approach (p. 274)
singlism (p. 278)

Recommended Readings

Amato, P. R., Booth, A., Johnson, D. R., & Rogers, S. J. (2007). *Alone together: How marriage in America is changing.* Cambridge, MA: Harvard University Press. Here is an excellent resource about research on heterosexual marriages. Although the analyses are complex, the writing style is clear and interesting.

DePaulo, B. M. (2006). *Singled out: How singles are stereotyped, stigmatized, and ignored, and still live happily ever after.* New York: St. Martin's Press. Bella DePaulo is a social psychologist, and her excellent book combines scholarly research with well-chosen narratives.

Diamond, L. M. (2008). *Sexual fluidity: Understanding women's love and desire.* Cambridge, MA: Harvard University Press. Lisa Diamond's book provides in-depth information about the lives of the women whom she interviewed in her research on nonheterosexual women. Diamond includes many quotations from these women, as well as potential theories that could account for sexual orientation.

Vangelisti, A. L., & Perlman, D. (Eds.). (2006). *The Cambridge handbook of personal relationships.* Mahwah, NJ: Erlbaum. I strongly recommend this superb handbook; about half of the chapters provide information relevant to this chapter on love relationships.

Answers to Demonstrations

Demonstration 8.1: 1. F; 2. F; 3. M; 4. M; 5. F; 6. F; 7. M; 8. F; 9. M; 10. M.

Demonstration 8.5: Kurdek's (1995) questionnaire, the Multiple Determinants of Relationship Commitment Inventory, assesses six different components of love relationships. On the shortened version in this demonstration, each of six categories is represented with two questions: Rewards (Questions 1 and 7), Costs (Questions 2 and 8), Match to Ideal Comparison (Questions 3 and 9), Alternatives (Questions 4 and 10), Investments (Questions 5 and 11), and Barriers to Leaving the Relationship (Questions 6 and 12). High relationship commitment was operationally defined in terms of high scores on Rewards, Match to Ideal Comparison, Investments, and Barriers to Leaving and low scores on Costs and Alternatives.

Carina König/EyeEm/Alamy Stock Photo

9 Sexuality

Learning Objectives

After studying this chapter, you will be able to ...

9-1 Describe background research on women's sexuality.

9-2 Explain which factors impact peoples' attitudes and knowledge about sexuality.

9-3 Identify characteristics of sexual behavior and sexual disorders.

9-4 Describe birth control, abortion, and alternatives for managing pregnancy.

Did You Know?

- In the textbooks designed for middle-school and high-school students, the discussions of sexuality typically emphasize biological factors (p. 286).
- The gender differences in sexual desire are larger than most other psychological gender differences (p. 290).
- Most U.S. parents say that they want high-school sex-education courses to include the topic of birth control (p. 295).
- Suppose that some college students are reading a story about a dating couple named Maria and José, but it's not clear whether they are sexually involved; men are more likely than women to believe that Maria wants to have a sexual relationship with José (p. 300).
- During sexual activity, women are often concerned about their physical attractiveness (p. 303).
- During adolescence, a girl in the United States is about three times as likely as a girl in Canada to become pregnant (p. 307).
- When women with an unwanted pregnancy have an abortion, they typically do not experience serious psychological consequences (p. 313).
- The current research suggests that teen mothers who remain single are much more likely than married teen mothers to return to school after the birth of their baby (p. 313).

When editing this chapter about sexuality, we decided to check a variety of entries on Google. The most general search—for the topic "sexuality"—yielded about 1,280,000,000 entries "Human male sexuality" had about 99,500,000 entries, but "human female sexuality" had only about 88,600,000. Many of the top entries on the list for "human female sexuality" included links to medical websites with information related to topics of women's sexual dysfunction, or stories and links about "what women want" in sexual interactions or trying to understand the "enduring enigma of female sexual desire." Although these topics are important, they represent a limited perspective of women's sexual experiences and include only a fraction of the topics that would be considered especially important by feminist psychologists who specialize in women's sexuality.

With more than 1.28 billion Google entries about sexuality, we might expect people to be well informed about the topic. However, the studies suggest otherwise. Mariamne Whatley and Elissa Henken (2000) asked people in Georgia to share some of the "information" they had heard about a variety of sexual topics. Some people believed, for instance, that a woman can become pregnant from kissing, from dancing too close to a man, or when having sexual intercourse during her menstrual period (rather than midcycle).

People in this survey also reported that gynecologists have found snakes, spiders, and roaches living in women's vaginas. Still others told how they had heard that a tampon, inserted into the vagina, can travel into a woman's stomach. Apparently, people can be seriously misinformed about both pregnancy and women's sexual anatomy!

Our chapter begins with some background information about women's sexuality. In the second section, we'll discuss people's attitudes and knowledge about sexuality. We'll then consider sexual behavior and sexual disorders. The final section examines the topics of birth control and abortion. Later on, in Chapter 11, we will discuss the related issue of sexually transmitted infections.

9-1 Background on Women's Sexuality

Learning Objectives

To describe background research on women's sexuality, you can …

9-1-1   Compare and contrast the essentialism and social constructionist perspectives on sexuality.

9-1-2   Identify major components of women's sexual anatomy.

9-1-3   Summarize the general phases of the human sexual response.

9-1-4   Describe gender comparisons in people's sexual responses.

9-1-5   Describe how sexual desire varies among humans.

In most of this chapter, we focus on people's attitudes toward sexuality and on women's sexual behavior; sexuality is much more than just a biological phenomenon (Easton et al., 2002; Fine & McClelland, 2006; Marecek et al., 2004). To provide a helpful context for these topics, however, we'll first address some background questions. What theoretical approaches to sexuality are currently most prominent? What parts of a woman's body are especially important in her sexual activities? What sexual responses do women typically experience? Furthermore, are there gender differences in sexual desire?

Theoretical Perspectives

Feminist psychologists have suggested that discussions about sexuality often represent a limited perspective on the topic (L. M. Diamond, 2004; Fine & McClelland, 2006, 2007; Marecek et al., 2004; Tiefer, 2004). For instance, consistent with Theme 3, researchers frequently consider men's sexual experiences to be the normative standard; they tend to ignore women's sexuality (Fassinger & Arseneau, 2008).

This androcentric emphasis is reflected in descriptions of sexuality in several textbooks designed for middle-school and high-school students. In one textbook, for example, the word *penis* is defined as "the male sexual organ," whereas *vagina* is defined as "receives penis during sexual intercourse" (cited in C. E. Beyer et al., 1996). Critical analyses of multiple elementary and middle school textbooks find similar examples of heterosexist bias and stereotypical representations of female sexuality (Deckman, Fulmer, Kirby, Hoover, & Mackall, 2018; Puchner & Klein, 2012). Consistent with much of the sexuality research, the woman's partner is assumed to be a man.

Here's another bias in the pre-college textbooks about sexuality: Sexual experiences are often presented from a purely biological framework, so that hormones, brain structures, and genitals occupy center stage (Tolman & Diamond, 2001a; J. W. White et al., 2000). Furthermore, these discussions often assume that the biological processes apply universally to all women (Peplau, 2003; Tiefer, 2004).

This overemphasis on biology is consistent with the essentialist perspective. As we discussed earlier in this book, **essentialism** argues that gender is a basic, stable characteristic that resides within an individual. According to the essentialist perspective, all women share the same psychological characteristics (Marecek et al., 2004).

Theme 4 of this textbook emphasizes widespread individual differences, including differences in women's sexual responses. In contrast, essentialism ignores these individual differences (Baber, 2000). When researchers adopt this essentialist perspective, they often neglect the social and cultural framework. That framework is especially important because sexuality is so prominent in our popular culture.

In contrast to the essentialist perspective, social constructionism emphasizes that social forces have an important impact on our sexuality. As we discussed in earlier chapters, the **social constructionist approach** argues that individuals and cultures construct or invent their own versions of reality based on prior experiences, social interactions, and beliefs. For example, cultural norms in the United States suggest that men are supposed to have sexual desires, but women's sexual desires are rarely mentioned (Fine & McClelland, 2006; Tolman, 2002). However, in another culture, women may be considered highly sexual (Easton et al., 2002; Fontes, 2001; Tiefer, 2004).

According to social constructionists, cultures even construct the basic sexual vocabulary (Fassinger & Arseneau, 2008; Marecek et al., 2004). For instance, consider the phrase "to have sex." How people define this phrase depends on their gender, sexual orientation, developmental cohort, and cultural background (Rothblum, 2000; Sewell, McGarrity, & Strassberg, 2017; Sewell & Strassberg, 2015; Twenge, Sherman, & Wells, 2017).

Let's briefly discuss women's sexual anatomy and sexual responses, because we need to establish some background information. As you'll soon learn, however, women's sexuality is far more subtle and complex than anatomy and biological responses (Fassinger & Arseneau, 2008).

Female Sexual Anatomy

Figure 9.1 shows the external sexual organs of an adult cisgender woman. The specific shapes, sizes, and colors of these organs vary greatly from one woman to the next (Foley et al., 2002). Ordinarily, the labia fold inward, so that they cover the vaginal opening. However, this diagram shows the labia folded outward, so that the urethral and vaginal openings can be more clearly observed.

Notice the labia majora are the "large lips," or folds of skin, located just inside a woman's thighs. Located between these two labia majora are the labia minora, or "small lips." The upper part of the labia region forms the clitoral hood, which partially covers the clitoris. As we will learn later in this section, the **clitoris** (pronounced *klih*-tuh-riss) is a small sensitive organ that plays a central role in women's orgasms. The clitoris has a

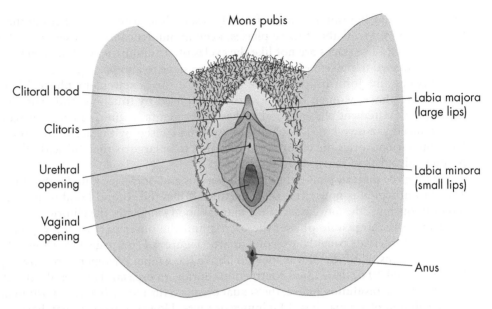

FIGURE **9.1** Female external sexual organs.

high density of nerve endings, and its only purpose is to provide sexual excitement (Foley et al., 2002).

Urine passes through the urethral opening. As Figure 9.1 displays, the vaginal opening is located between the urethral opening and the anus. The **vagina** is a flexible canal through which menstrual fluid passes. During heterosexual intercourse, the penis enters the vagina. During vaginal birth, the infant passes out through the canal.

At this point, you may want to return to Figure 4.1, on page 115, to review several important internal organs that are relevant for women's sexuality. In addition, many women report that their breasts are sexually sensitive, especially in the nipple region (Stayton et al., 2008). In other words, breast sensations are often an important part of women's sexuality.

Sexual Responses

Women typically report a variety of reactions during sexual activity, and they emphasize that emotions and thoughts are extremely important. Furthermore, certain visual stimuli, sounds, and smells can influence arousal (L. L. Alexander et al., 2021; Stayton et al., 2008). Let's consider the general phases that many women experience during sexual activity, and then we'll discuss some gender comparisons.

General Phases

William H. Masters and Virginia Johnson (1966) wrote a book, called *Human Sexual Response,* which summarized their research on individuals who readily experienced orgasms during sexual activity. As you can imagine, these findings should not be overgeneralized; women's sexuality shows much more variety than the neatly ordered sequence of events that Masters and Johnson described (L. L. Alexander et al., 2021; Basson, 2006; Crooks & Baur, 2008; Levin, 2008).

Masters and Johnson described four phases, each focusing on changes in the genitals. However, as you read about these phases, keep in mind a caution raised by C. Wade and Cirese (1991): "The stages are not like the cycles of an automatic washing machine; we are not programmed to move mechanically from one stage to another" (p. 140).

Masters and Johnson called the first phase the "excitement phase." During the **excitement phase**, women become sexually aroused by touching and erotic thoughts. During the excitement phase, blood rushes to the genital region, causing **vasocongestion** (pronounced vaz-owe-kun-*jess*-chun), or swelling caused by the accumulation of blood. Vasocongestion causes the clitoris and the labia to enlarge as they fill with blood; it also produces droplets of moisture in the vagina.

During the **plateau phase**, the clitoris shortens and draws back under the clitoral hood. The clitoral region is now extremely sensitive. When the clitoral hood is moved through physical touching, the movement of the clitoral hood stimulates the clitoris.

During the **orgasmic phase**, the uterus and the outer part of the vagina contract strongly, at intervals roughly a second apart. (Figure 4.1, on page 115, shows the female internal organs, with the uterus located above the vagina.) Women typically experience between 3 and 10 of these rapid contractions during an orgasm (Foley et al., 2002).

During the **resolution phase**, the sexual organs return to their earlier unstimulated size. The resolution phase may last 30 minutes or more. However, women may have additional orgasms without going directly into the resolution phase.

As we noted earlier, the clitoris is extremely important when women experience an orgasm (L. L. Alexander et al., 2021; Crooks & Baur, 2008, p. 344). Orgasms result from stimulation of the clitoris, either from direct touching in the clitoral area or from indirect pressure. Physiologically, the orgasm is the same, no matter what kind of stimulation is used (Hyde & DeLamater, 2006). However, current feminist researchers and theorists emphasize that women's experiences of sexuality do not focus simply on genitals and orgasms during sexual activity. Emotional closeness and communication are vitally important (Conrad & Milburn, 2001; O'Sullivan, 2006; J. W. White et al., 2000). These relationship factors are especially important for people who identify as asexual or demisexual, who may still sometimes engage in sexual activity with a partner (Antonsen, Zdaniuk, Yule, & Brotto, 2020; Brotto et al., 2010; Zheng & Su, 2018).

Gender Comparisons in Sexual Responses

The studies by Masters and Johnson and by other researchers allow us to conclude that people are reasonably similar in the nature of their sexual responses. For example, people experience similar phases in their sexual responses. Sexually aroused people experience vasocongestion, and their orgasms are physiologically similar.

In addition, people have similar psychological reactions to orgasm, and they use similar adjectives to describe orgasms (Mah & Binik, 2002). Read Demonstration 9.1 and try to guess whether a man or a woman wrote each passage. Vance and Wagner (1977) asked people to guess which descriptions of orgasms were written by women and which were written by men. Most respondents were unable to guess at better than a chance level. In general, men reach orgasms more quickly than women (Crooks & Baur, 2008), although "faster" does not always mean "better."

In general, then, people are reasonably similar in these internal, physiological components of sexuality. However, we'll discover that gender differences are larger in some other aspects of sexuality, such as sexual desire and its consequences.

Demonstration 9.1

Psychological Reactions to Orgasm

Try to guess whether a woman or a man wrote each of the following descriptions of an orgasm. Place an W (woman) or an M (man) in front of each passage. The answers appear at the end of the chapter, on page 315.

_____ 1. A sudden feeling of lightheadedness followed by an intense feeling of relief and elation. A rush. Intense muscular spasms of the whole body. Sense of euphoria followed by deep peace and relaxation.

_____ 2. To me, an orgasmic experience is the most satisfying pleasure that I have experienced in relation to any other types of satisfaction or pleasure that I've had, which were nonsexually oriented.

_____ 3. It is like turning a water faucet on. You notice the oncoming flow but it can be turned on or off when desired. You feel the valves open and close and the fluid flow. An orgasm makes your head and body tingle.

_____ 4. A buildup of tension which starts to pulsate very fast, and there is a sudden release from the tension and a desire to sleep.

_____ 5. It is a pleasant, tension-relieving muscular contraction. It relieves physical tension and mental anticipation.

_____ 6. A release of a very high level of tension, but ordinarily tension is unpleasant, whereas the tension before orgasm is far from unpleasant.

_____ 7. An orgasm is a great release of tension with spasmodic reaction at the peak. This is exactly how it feels to me.

_____ 8. A building of tension, sometimes, and frustration until the climax. A tightening inside, palpitating rhythm, explosion, and warmth and peace.

Source: Based on Vance and Wagner (1977, pp. 207, 210).

Sexual Desire

Our students tell us that their high-school sex-education programs offered some basic information about the anatomy of sex organs, but the rest of the messages focused on "just say no," including the dangers of pregnancy and sexually transmitted infections. Were your high-school experiences similar? Very few students can recall learning about "sexual desire," especially in connection with women (Fine & McClelland, 2006, 2007; Tolman, 2002).

Sexual desire is defined as a need to engage in sexual activities, for either emotional or physical pleasure (L. M. Diamond, 2004; Impett et al., 2008). Sexual desire is associated with a variety of sex hormones, such as estrogen and testosterone. However, social and cultural factors are just as important. In many communities in the United States, for instance, people believe that teenage girls are not supposed to feel sexual desire (Cantor et al., 2004; Tolman & Diamond, 2001a).

Feminist researchers have concluded that the gender differences in sexual desire are larger than most other psychological gender differences (e.g., Antonsen, Zdaniuk, Yule, & Brotto, 2020; Diamond, 2008; Hyde & DeLamater, 2006; Peterson & Hyde, 2010a, 2010b; Zheng & Su, 2018). Compared to women, men (a) think about sex more frequently; (b) masturbate more often; (c) want sexual activities more frequently; (d) initiate sexual activities more frequently; (e) are more interested in sexual activities without a romantic commitment; and (f) prefer a greater number of sexual partners (Impett & Peplau, 2003; Miller et al., 2004; Mosher & Danoff-Burg, 2005; Ueda, Mercer, Ghaznavi, & Herbenick, 2020; Vohs & Baumeister, 2004).

How can we explain these gender differences in sexuality? One factor may relate to biological differences. A cisgender woman's clitoris is not as large as a cisgender man's penis, so men may be simply more familiar with sexual sensations due to their more obvious externalized genitalia (Hyde & DeLamater, 2006). Women may also have more general concerns about pregnancy than men, and in some rare cases experience anxiety or fear related to becoming pregnant and giving birth (Poggi, Goutaudier, Séjourné, & Chabrol, 2018). As we'll soon learn, the sexual double standard may inhibit women's sexual activities. However, gender differences in hormones are probably not relevant (Hyde & DeLamater, 2006). Furthermore, some portion of these gender differences might be traceable to using male-normative standards—for instance, focusing on traditional definitions of sexual intercourse rather than other measures of sexual desire or activity (Peplau, 2003). However, it is important that researchers pay more attention to gender comparisons in the subjective *quality* of sexual desire, rather than simply the *strength* of sexual desire (Tolman & Diamond, 2001a).

It is also important to study people's motives for sexual activity. Suppose that a woman has sexual interactions for her personal pleasure or to increase the intimacy of a relationship. She typically feels relatively positive about herself in these situations. In contrast, she usually feels more negative if she has sexual interactions for avoidance reasons, for example, to avoid a breakup in her relationship (Impett et al., 2005; Impett & Tolman, 2006).

Many different factors influence people's sexual interactions. However, the gender differences in sexual desire help us understand several topics throughout this chapter, such as masturbation, sexual scripts, and variations in sexual desire.

Section Summary

Background on Women's Sexuality

1. Feminist psychologists argue that discussions of sexuality have paid relatively little attention to women's perspectives and that the discussions overemphasize biological factors (consistent with essentialism), rather than social and cultural factors (consistent with social constructionism).
2. In terms of women's sexual organs, the clitoris plays a central role in women's orgasms.

(continues)

Section Summary *(continued)*

3. Emotions and thoughts are central to women's sexual responses. Individual differences are large, and sexual responses do not follow a rigid sequence; Masters and Johnson (1966) described four phases of sexual response: excitement, plateau, orgasm, and resolution.
4. Women's orgasms produced by direct stimulation of the clitoris are similar to those produced by indirect stimulus; modern researchers and theorists emphasize aspects of sexuality other than genitals and orgasms.
5. Women and men are similar in their psychological reactions to orgasm, but men are often higher in some components of sexual desire.

9-2 Attitudes and Knowledge About Sexuality

Learning Objectives

To explain which factors impact peoples' attitudes and knowledge about sexuality, you can ...

9-2-1 Define the sexual double standard and explain how it negatively impacts attitudes about women's sexuality.

9-2-2 Explain how sexual scripts guide norms for sexual behavior.

9-2-3 Discuss how parents, schools, and media sources contribute to people's sexual education.

The previous section emphasized the biological side of sexuality—the swelling genitals and the contracting uterus. Let's now turn to the humans who possess these sex organs as we address several questions such as these: What are people's attitudes about sexuality? What are the basic social norms in the United States? What kind of knowledge about sexuality do young people acquire from their parents, schools, and the media? Before you read further, however, try Demonstration 9.2.

Attitudes About Sexuality

The majority of people in the United States believe that nonmarital intercourse is acceptable, for example, in a committed relationship (Twenge, Sherman, & Wells, 2015). In one study, only 12% of Canadian participants and 29% of U.S. participants said that sex before marriage is always wrong (Widmer et al., 1998). However, attitudes varied widely across the other 22 countries in this study. Less than 5% of respondents in Austria, Germany, and Sweden said that premarital sex was always wrong, in contrast to 35% in Ireland and 60% in the Philippines. Another cross-cultural analysis of 40 countries found that attitudes about nonmarital and premarital sex vary, depending on a culture's economic development, women's participation in the labor force, religiosity, and levels of marriage success (Barber, 2017).

In the United States, men typically have more permissive attitudes toward sexual behavior than women do (Brehm et al., 2002; Fenigstein & Preston, 2007). For example,

---

Demonstration **9.2**

Judgments About Sexual Behavior

Suppose that you discover some information about the sexual behavior of a 25-year-old unmarried person whom you know slightly. Items 1 through 4 provide information about four possible people. Rate the person in terms of this person's *moral values*. Try to rate each person separately, without considering the other three persons.

| 1 | 2 | 3 | 4 | 5 |

Poor moral values   Good moral values

_____ 1. A man who has had no sexual partners
_____ 2. A man who has had 19 sexual partners
_____ 3. A woman who has had no sexual partners
_____ 4. A woman who has had 19 sexual partners

Source: Based on M. J. Marks and Fraley (2005).

---

a meta-analysis demonstrated that men are significantly more permissive about casual sex; the *d* for this gender difference was 0.45, a medium-sized effect (Peterson & Hyde, 2010b). Gender as a *subject variable* seems to be moderately important.

How about gender as a *stimulus* variable? Do people judge a man's sexual behavior differently from a woman's sexual behavior? Before the 1960s, most people in the United States held a **sexual double standard**: They believed that premarital sex was more appropriate for men than for women (Hatfield & Rapson, 2005; Sprecher, 2006). In general, primetime television dramas demonstrate the double standard (Aubrey, 2004; Kim et al., 2007). Also, the research shows that nonfeminists are more likely than feminists to support the sexual double standard (Bay-Cheng & Zucker, 2007).

However, let's consider the research conducted by Michael Marks and R. Chris Fraley (2005). Demonstration 9.2 is a greatly simplified version of their study; also, each of the participants in their study rated only one person. These researchers tested both undergraduate students and people who responded to their online questionnaire. The participants in both samples gave a lower rating to a person who had 19 sexual partners, compared to a person who had zero sexual partners. Surprisingly, however, the participants supplied about the same ratings for the male target as for the female target. In other words, these researchers did *not* find evidence of a sexual double standard.

What happens when researchers use more subtle techniques to assess the sexual double standard? In a second study, Michael Marks and R. Chris Fraley (2006) asked students to read a story about the sexual history of either a woman or a man. The story also included positive and negative comments that others had made, with respect to the main character's sexual experiences. The stories were identical, except for the gender of the main character.

The research participants were then asked to estimate how many positive and negative comments that they had read about the main character. The results showed that people recalled more positive comments about the man (compared to the woman) and more negative comments about the woman (compared to the man).

Notice an interesting situation. When people provide direct ratings, there's not much evidence for the sexual double standard. When the measurement is more subtle—as in the second study—people have relatively positive memories of a sexually active man, compared to a sexually active woman.

If you check back to page 55 in Chapter 2, you'll remember that direct ratings often show little evidence of gender stereotypes, whereas subtle measurement techniques reveal substantial gender stereotypes.

In many cultures outside North America, the double standard frequently has life-threatening consequences for women. For example, in some Asian, Middle Eastern, and Latin American cultures, people expect a man to uphold the family honor by killing a daughter, a sister, or even a mother who is suspected of engaging in "inappropriate" sexual activities (Pauwels, 2008; Whelehan, 2001; Zeigler, 2008). Between 5,000 and 20,000 of these honor killings occur each year around the world (D'Lima, Solotaroff, & Pande, 2020; Kiener, 2011). People typically ignore the same sexual activity in a male family member.

Sexual Scripts

A script for a play describes what people say and do. A **sexual script** describes the social norms for sexual behavior, which we learn by growing up in a culture (Bowleg et al., 2004; DeLamater & Hyde, 2004; Rudman & Glick, 2008). Cultural norms in the United States provide a sexual script for most heterosexual couples: Men initiate sexual relationships. In contrast, women are expected either to resist or to comply passively with their partner's advances (Impett & Peplau, 2002, 2003; Greene & Faulkner, 2005; Morokoff, 2000).

According to the traditional script, for example, the woman is supposed to wait for her date to kiss her; she does not initiate kissing (Morr Serewicz & Gale, 2008). Only one person is in charge in this script-based kind of relationship. In most long-term relationships and marriages, the man's erotic schedule may regulate sex. However, women in egalitarian relationships typically feel free about expressing their erotic interests, and they also feel free to decide not to have sex (Peplau, 2003).

In far too many cases, men reject the standard sexual script, and they commit sexual assault (Bartoli & Clark, 2006). **Sexual assault** refers to unwanted sexual contact, which includes sexual touching as well as rape. **Rape** can be defined as sexual penetration without the individual's consent, obtained by force or by threat of physical harm. As we discuss in Chapter 13, people can be raped, not just by a stranger—but also by an acquaintance, a current or past romantic partner, or even a spouse.

Sex Education

Take a moment to think about your early ideas, experiences, and attitudes about sexuality. Was sex a topic that produced half-suppressed giggles in the school cafeteria? Did you worry about whether you were too experienced or not experienced enough? Sexuality is an important topic for adolescents and many preadolescents. In this section, we will examine how children and adolescents learn about sexuality—at home, at school, and from the media.

Parents and Sex Education

Young women are much more likely to learn about sexuality from their mothers than from their fathers (Crooks & Baur, 2008; Raffaelli & Green, 2003). Furthermore, parents are not likely to talk about pleasurable aspects of sexuality (Conrad & Milburn, 2001; Tolman & Diamond, 2001a, 2001b). As a consequence, certain topics are never discussed. For example, fewer than 1% of students in a college human sexuality course reported that a parent had mentioned the word *clitoris* (Allgeier & Allgeier, 2000). Other women recall receiving mixed messages from their parents, such as "Sex is dirty," and "Save it for someone you love" (O'Sullivan et al., 2001; K. Wright, 1997).

Some studies have examined parent–child communications among women of color. Latina and Asian American adolescents often report that sex is a forbidden topic with their parents, who may have conservative ideas about dating (Chan, 2008; Hurtado, 2003; Raffaelli & Green, 2003). Black mothers seem to feel more comfortable than Latina or White mothers in speaking to their daughters about sexuality. For example, one Black mother reported, "I can't remember a specific age when I first talked. ... I'm real open with my daughter as far as sex and things like that" (O'Sullivan et al., 2001, p. 279).

Although parents have difficulty discussing sexuality with their children, many young people say that they appreciated these conversations. For example, one young woman commented,

> First my mother, and later my father, talked to me at separate times about sex. I was enlightened by these conversations, and they created a closer bond and increased confidentiality and trust among all of us. I was very thankful that both of my parents talked with me about sex. I realized that they really cared about my well-being, and I appreciated their efforts to say to me what their parents did not say to them. (Crooks & Baur, 2008, p. 344)

Schools and Sex Education

What do schools in the United States teach about sexuality? Many sex-education programs focus on the reproductive system, in other words, an "organ recital." Students don't learn about the connections between sexuality and emotions. They seldom learn about LGBTQ+ perspectives, and many programs specifically avoid the discussion of contraceptives. As a result, sex education in school often has little impact on students' sexual behavior (Feldt, 2002; Fine & McClelland, 2006, 2007; T. Rose, 2003).

Following policy recommendations first made by the U.S. government in 1981, and later expanded in 1996, many school programs emphasized an oversimplified approach called, "Abstinence Only Until Marriage" (AOUM). These AOUM programs typically included scientific misinformation and scare techniques (Bartell, 2005; Fine & McClelland, 2006, 2007). For example, many of these programs showed a video called "No Second Chance." At one point in the video, a student asks a school nurse, "What if I want to have sex before I get married?" The nurse replies, "Well, I guess you'll just have to be prepared to die" (Fine & McClelland, 2007, p. 1006).

Furthermore, these AOUM programs do *not* decrease teenagers' sexual activity or their rate of sexually transmitted diseases (Hauser, 2009; Fine & McClelland, 2006, 2007; Santelli et al., 2017). Still, from 1996 to 2017, the U.S. government spent more than $2 billion dollars on these ineffective programs (Quindlen, 2009; Santelli et al., 2017).

However, some communities in the United States have developed a more comprehensive approach to sexual education. In addition to providing accurate information, these programs address values, attitudes, and emotions. They also provide strategies for making informed choices about sexuality (B. L. Barber & Eccles, 2003; Florsheim, 2003). A comprehensive educational program helps students to develop skills and behaviors, such as how to discuss contraceptives with a partner and how to actually use them.

Teenagers who participate in these comprehensive programs—as opposed to the abstinence-only programs—typically postpone sexual relationships until they are older. They also have a lower pregnancy rate (Kohler, Manhart, & Lafferty, 2008; S. L. Nichols & Good, 2004).

We often are presented with reports about parents protesting sex education in the schools. However, most parents would prefer that high-school sex-education classes take a comprehensive approach. For example, one large-scale U.S. survey reported that only 36% of adult responders favored abstinence-only programs. In contrast, 82% wanted sex-education classes to include information about birth control (Bleakley et al., 2006; Escobar-Chaves et al., 2005).

The Media and Sexual Information

So far, we've learned that parents frequently avoid discussing sexuality with their children. Furthermore, many schools provide inadequate and incorrect information. Where else could adolescents learn about sex? Well, they might discuss the topic with other adolescents. However, most of us wouldn't want children to rely on the accuracy of their friends' information. Another source of information—or misinformation—is the media.

According to one survey, many adolescents report that they have learned information about sexual issues from the media: 40% pointed to television and movies, and 35% mentioned magazines (Hoff & Greene, 2000).

Let's first consider the analyses of magazines (e.g., Kim & Ward, 2004). For example, many adolescent girls and young women read *Seventeen* or *Cosmopolitan,* which emphasize heterosexuality and provide narrowly defined sexual scripts about how they can make themselves alluring to adolescent boys and young men (Nelson & Paek, 2005).

Furthermore, adolescent girls and young women often report feeling that they cannot attain the perfect image of female sexuality portrayed in magazines. These images often suggest that girls and young women are a combination of innocence and seductiveness (Kilbourne, 2003; J. L. Kim & Ward, 2004). For instance, one magazine ad portrays a woman dressed in an old-fashioned white dress, but the dress is unbuttoned and pulled down over one shoulder. How can real-life adolescent girls and young women make sense of this mixed message that they should be both sexually innocent and sexually active?

Meanwhile, what do adolescent boys and young men learn from the male-oriented magazines that they read? These magazines typically portray women as sex objects, and suggest that men can improve their sex lives by taking specific steps (C. N. Baker, 2005; L. D. Taylor, 2005).

Television has been a target of much research about sexuality in the media. Surprisingly, only 5% of the television ads on U.S. network stations show any sexual content (Hetsroni, 2007a). What about the content of the TV shows themselves? A meta-analysis showed an actual decrease between 1975 and 2004 in kissing, petting, and implied intercourse on network television. The only increase during these years was for programming about gay and lesbian relationships (Hetsroni, 2007b).

In general, adolescents who watch many hours of TV shows with sexual content are *less* likely to believe that sexual intercourse can have negative consequences such as pregnancy or sexually transmitted diseases. As a result, adolescents may be more likely to initiate sexual intercourse before they graduate from high school (Martino et al., 2005).

Online and digital media sources are also an important source of information—and misinformation—about sexuality (Escobar-Chaves et al., 2005; Guttmacher Institute, 2017). For example, 19% of heterosexual youth and 40 to 78% of LGBTQ+ youth report learning information about sexual behavior and sexual health issues through digital media sources (Guttmacher Institute, 2017). Unfortunately, some of this information is learned through referencing online pornography, as 42% of 10- to 17-year-olds report having seen pornography online; 27% report that they intentionally viewed those sources (Collins et al., 2017). Additionally, adolescent girls and boys who consume large amounts of sexualized online and digital media, including video games, are more likely to objectify themselves and others (Karsay, Knoll, & Matthes, 2018).

Section Summary

Attitudes and Knowledge About Sexuality

1. Most people in the United States believe that sex before marriage is acceptable in some circumstances. The double standard about sexuality is no longer widespread, but it does operate in some situations.
2. In some Asian, Middle Eastern, and Latin American cultures, a woman may be killed for suspected sexual activity, whereas a man is allowed sexual freedom.
3. Sexual scripts specify what women and men in a certain culture are supposed to do in sexual interactions; for example, in many cultures men are usually supposed to take the initiative in sexual activity.
4. Children and adolescents typically report that their parents do not discuss pleasurable aspects of sexuality when discussing issues related to sex.
5. Many schools have historically adopted "abstinence-only" sex-education programs; these programs contain misinformation and have been shown to have no long-term effect on reducing pregnancy rates.
6. The more comprehensive school programs discuss emotions and decision-making strategies; these programs decrease pregnancy rates. The media frequently portray sexuality, but they seldom convey the negative consequences of sexual activity.
7. Media sources are a source of information—and misinformation—for sexual knowledge. Adolescents who consume many hours of media content tend to have more stereotypical views of sexuality and higher rates of objectification toward themselves and others.

9-3 Sexual Behavior and Sexual Disorders

Learning Objectives

To identify characteristics of sexual behavior and sexual disorders, you can ...

9-3-1 Describe factors that characterize adolescent sexual behavior.

9-3-2 Identify key gender differences in the sexual behavior of heterosexual adults.

9-3-3 Explain why people sometimes experience communication issues in sexual interactions.

9-3-4 Describe characteristics of lesbian women's sexuality.

9-3-5 Describe how women's sexuality changes in older adulthood.

9-3-6 Summarize common sexual problems that women experience and therapies for those problems.

9-3-7 Describe how traditional gender roles contribute to sexual disorders in women.

We began this chapter by noting that the discussion of sexuality is often centered on men, biology, and messages such as "just say no." The second section examined cultural attitudes about sexuality and scripts for sexual behavior, as well as how children learn about sexuality from their parents, their schools, and the popular media.

With this information in mind, let's consider the sexual behavior of heterosexual adolescents and adults, how couples communicate about sexuality, and sexual behavior among lesbian, transgender, and older women. Our last topic in this section is a brief description of sexual disorders.

Sexual Behavior in Heterosexual Adolescents

Adolescent girls are more likely to have early heterosexual experiences if they reached puberty before most of their peers (Bergevin et al., 2003; Weichold et al., 2003). Other important predictors of girls' early experiences include low self-esteem, poor academic performance, poor parent–child relationships, low family income, extended exposure to sexually explicit media, and the early use of alcohol and drugs (Centers for Disease Control and Prevention, 2008; Crockett et al., 2002; Escobar-Chaves et al., 2005; Farber, 2003; Furman & Shaffer, 2003; Halpern, 2003; Sieverding et al., 2005; Spencer et al., 2002).

Ethnicity is another factor that is related to adolescent sexual experience. In the United States, for example, Black female adolescents are likely to have their first sexual intercourse one or two years before White or Latina female adolescents (Joyner & Laumann, 2002; O'Sullivan & Meyer-Bahlburg, 2003; Stayton et al., 2008). Asian American female adolescents are typically the least likely to have early sexual experiences (Chan, 2008). In Canada, adolescents born in other countries and immigrating to Canada are much less likely than Canada-born adolescents to have early sexual experiences (Maticka-Tyndale et al., 2001).

As you might imagine, peer pressure encourages some teenagers to become sexually active (Hatfield & Rapson, 2005; O'Sullivan & Meyer-Bahlburg, 2003). These teenagers may risk unwanted pregnancies and sexually transmitted infections; we will examine these topics later in this chapter and in Chapter 11. In other words, biological, psychological, cultural, and social variables all have an impact on adolescent girls' sexual experiences.

On college campuses, students often report *hooking up* with others. Although there is no precise definition for this term, **hooking up** usually refers to a sexual encounter in which two people—who are not in an established relationship or are uncommitted—have sexual interactions that may range from behaviors such as nongenital touching to oral sex or intercourse (Bogle, 2008; Garcia, Reiber, Massey, & Merriwether, 2012). According to Michael Kimmel (2008), hookups are similar to the standard formula, in which men dominate and women comply. Hookups actually follow the traditional script of male initiative and female submission (Rudman & Glick, 2008).

For many adolescents, personal values are critically important when they make decisions about sexual behavior (Carpenter, 2005; Tolman, 2002). For instance, one adolescent girl was neither judgmental nor prudish, but she had decided not to be sexually active as a teenager. As she explained:

> I have certain talents and certain gifts, and I owe it to myself to take care of those gifts. I'm not going to just throw it around, throw my body around. And I see that sexuality is part of that. The sexual revolution—I guess we grew up in that—I think a lot of it has cheapened something that isn't cheap. (Kamen, 2000, pp. 87–88)

Romance novels portray idealized images of young women being blissfully transformed by their first sexual experience. However, many women do not have positive memories of their first heterosexual intercourse (Conrad & Milburn, 2001; Straus, 2007). The experience may also be physically painful (Tolman, 2002). In addition, adolescent girls are twice as likely as adolescent boys to report feeling bad about themselves after an early experience with heterosexual intercourse (Brady & Halpern-Felsher, 2007). Furthermore, about 10% of high-school girls say that they were forced to have sexual intercourse (Centers for Disease Control and Prevention, 2008; S. L. Nichols & Good, 2004).

In contrast, some adolescent girls recall a highly positive experience:

> We were totally in love. We wanted this to be the best experience of our lives. We were at his apartment and we had done everything right. We had talked about it, planned for it, saw this as the highest expression of our joint future. He was very caring, very slow with me. I felt empowered, beautiful. It was a great night. (P. Schwartz & Rutter, 1998, p. 97)

In summary, adolescent girls often learn about sexuality in a less-than-ideal way. As we read earlier in this section, parents, schools, and the media seldom help young people make informed decisions about sexuality. In addition, many adolescent girls' early sexual experiences may not be as romantic or joyous as they had hoped.

Sexual Behavior in Heterosexual Adults

Any survey about sexual behavior inevitably runs into roadblocks. How can researchers manage to obtain a random sample of respondents—who represent all geographic regions, ethnic groups, and income levels—on a sensitive topic such as sexuality? Sociologist Edward Laumann and his colleagues (1994) conducted a classic U.S. survey of sexual behavior. They interviewed 3,432 adults about a wide range of topics. The results revealed, for example, that 17% of men claimed to have had more than 20 sexual partners during their lifetime, in contrast to 3% of women. A meta-analysis of 12 earlier studies confirmed a general trend for men to report a somewhat greater number of sexual partners, with a *d* of 0.25 (Oliver & Hyde, 1993).

Do you wonder how men can report more sexual partners than women do? It's possible, for example, that men are more likely than women to count oral sex as a sexual encounter. However, the major reason may be that men are more likely than women to exaggerate the number of partners they have had (Miller et al., 2004; Willetts et al., 2004).

Surveys also show that masturbation is much more common for men than for women (Hill, 2008; Hyde & Oliver, 2000; Peterson & Hyde, 2010a). Peterson and Hyde (2010b) reported a *d* of 0.53, a medium-sized gender difference.

Some of the gender differences in masturbation can be traced to the more obvious prominence of the male genitals (Oliver & Hyde, 1993) and to gender differences in sexual desire, discussed on pages 289–290. As researchers note, it's interesting that this basically risk-free sexual activity is missing from many women's sexual scripts (Baber, 2000; Shulman & Horne, 2003).

Communication About Sexuality

We mentioned earlier in this section that parents often feel uncomfortable talking about sex with their children. Actually, most couples also feel uncomfortable talking with *each other* about sexual activity (Hickman & Muehlenhard, 1999).

One problem, however, is that it's difficult to convey some messages about sexuality. Suppose that you are a woman, and you want to convey to a man, "I'm not certain whether I'm interested in sexual activity." Most women report that they have trouble verbally communicating this message (Brehm et al., 2002; O'Sullivan & Gaines, 1998). Now try imagining how you would convey this ambivalent message *nonverbally* to a romantic partner, and you can anticipate some communication difficulties. Women may try to convey their uncertainty, but men may not understand the message (Tolman, 2002).

A related study at a university in Ontario, Canada, showed that 65% of women and 53% of men preferred that a partner ask for consent before engaging in sexual activity. In contrast, 35% of women and 47% of men preferred to assume consent unless the partner indicated otherwise (Humphreys & Herold, 2007).

In another study, Humphreys (2007) presented an ambiguous sexual scenario, and she asked students to make judgments. Men were significantly more likely than women to perceive that this scenario described a situation that was acceptable, consensual, and clear. Women and men do not live on separate planets, but men are somewhat more likely to assume that there's a "green light" for sexual activities!

It's possible that a woman may hesitate to say no to a man's sexual advances because she doesn't want to hurt his feelings. Patricia Morokoff and her colleagues (1997) developed a Sexual Assertiveness Scale for women. Try Demonstration 9.3, which includes some of the questions from the Sexual Assertiveness Scale. Then check the answers at the end of the chapter. Were you fairly accurate in predicting the women's answers? If relevant, did this exercise provide any new insights into your own communication patterns with respect to sexual activity?

In general, people are reluctant to talk with their partner about the sexual activities that they like or dislike. However, those who provide more self-disclosure are likely to be more satisfied with the sexual aspects of their relationship (Byers & Demmons, 1999). This correlation is consistent with some information from Chapter 8: Married couples are more satisfied with their relationship if they have good communication skills.

Demonstration **9.3**

The Sexual Assertiveness Scale for Women

The items listed in this demonstration were shown to women students at a large state university in northeast United States. The women were asked to rate each item, using a scale where 1 = disagree strongly and 5 = agree strongly. Your task is to inspect each item and estimate the average rating that the women supplied for that item (e.g., 2.8). When you have finished, check page 315 to learn how the women actually responded. (Note: This demonstration is based on Morokoff et al., 1997, but it contains only 6 of the 18 items; the validity of this short version has not been established.)

_____ 1. I let my partner know if I want my partner to touch my genitals.

_____ 2. I wait for my partner to touch my breasts instead of letting my partner know that's what I want.

_____ 3. I give in and kiss if my partner pressures me, even if I already said no.

_____ 4. I refuse to have sex if I don't want to, even if my partner insists.

_____ 5. I have sex without a condom or latex barrier if my partner doesn't like them, even if I want to use one.

_____ 6. I insist on using a condom or latex barrier if I want to, even if my partner doesn't.

Source: Copyright © 1997 by the American Psychological Association. Adapted with permission. Appendix (adapted), p. 804, from Morokoff, P. J., Quina, K., Harlow, L. L. Whitmire, L., Grimley, D. M., Gibson, P. R., and Burkholder, G. J. (1997). Sexual Assertiveness Scale (SAS) for women: Development and validation. *Journal of Personality and Social Psychology*, 73(4), 790–804. Doi: 10.1037/0022–3514.73.4.790. No further reproduction or distribution is permitted without written permission from the American Psychological Association.

Sexuality in Lesbian, Bisexual, and Transgender Women

Most of this chapter focuses on heterosexual relationships. How does sexuality compare in lesbian, bisexual, and transgender relationships? Unfortunately, there is much less research on sexuality in these relationships.

However, the available research suggests that lesbian couples value emotional intimacy and nongenital physical contact, such as hugging and cuddling (Klinger, 1996; McCormick, 1994; Peplau & Garnets, 2000). In contrast, heteronormative cultural norms in the United States tend to define sexual activity in terms of genital stimulation and orgasm. Researchers who use that operational definition of sexual activity might conclude that lesbian couples are less sexually active than heterosexual couples or gay men couples (Fassinger & Arseneau, 2008; Matthews et al., 2006; Peplau & Fingerhut, 2007).

When lesbian women do engage in genital sexual activity, they are more likely than heterosexual women to experience an orgasm (Fassinger & Arseneau, 2008). One likely explanation for this difference is that a woman may know what her female partner will probably find enjoyable, and men do not have this personal experience. Also, lesbian couples may communicate more effectively and be more sensitive to each other's preferences. Lesbian couples may also engage in more kissing and caressing than heterosexual couples do (Hatfield & Rapson, 1996; Herbert, 1996). They are also more likely than heterosexual women to respond positively to sexualized images of women (Chivers, 2017).

Laura S. Brown (2000) wrote that lesbian women are like the early mapmakers who must construct their own maps about the unknown territories of lesbian sexuality. After all, the well-established maps—or scripts—represent heterosexual territory.

Research with women who identify as bisexual suggests that women outnumber men among this sexual orientation category, with 5.5% of women reporting a bisexual identity, but only 2% of men identifying as bisexual (Copen, Chandra, & Febo-Vazquez, 2016). Similar to lesbian women, bisexual women respond positively to images of other women (Chivers, 2017). They are also more likely to display sexual fluidity than men, and longitudinal studies suggest that bisexual women's sexual fluidity tends to be rather stable over time (Diamond, 2008; Katz-Wise & Hyde, 2015).

What research is available on transgender women's sexuality suggests that gender affirming care can positively impact relationship satisfaction over time (Defreyne et al., 2021). Additionally, specific sexual orientation varies among transgender women, much as it does among cisgender women, and remains highly stable over time prior to, during, and after transitioning (Defreyne et al., 2021; Gaither et al., 2017).

Older Women and Sexuality

Cisgender women's reproductive systems change somewhat as women grow older. As we'll discuss in Chapter 14, estrogen production drops rapidly at menopause. As a result, the vagina loses some of its elasticity and may also produce less moisture (Foley et al., 2002). However, these problems can be at least partly corrected by using supplemental lubricants. Also, women who have been sexually active throughout their lives may not experience vaginal changes (Hyde & DeLamater, 2006; McHugh, 2006). Furthermore, it's worth questioning the popular belief that a decrease in hormone levels actually causes a decrease in sexual interest; no solid research supports that proposal (McHugh, 2006; Rostosky & Travis, 2000).

Researchers often report that the *frequency* of genital sexual activity declines as women grow older (Burgess, 2004; Dennerstein et al., 2003; McHugh, 2006). However, a woman's age doesn't have a strong influence on either sexual interest or her enjoyment of sex (Burgess, 2004; Laumann et al., 2002). The best predictors of a woman's sexual satisfaction are her feeling of well-being and her emotional closeness with her partner, rather than more "biological" measures such as vaginal moisture (Bancroft et al., 2003).

In a study by Mansfield and her colleagues (1998), many older women emphasized the importance of "sweet warmth and constant tenderness" and "physical closeness and intimacy." As one woman wrote, "Touching, hugging, holding, become as or more important than the actual sex act" (p. 297). Notice, then, that these studies emphasize a broad definition of sexuality, rather than a focus on the genitals.

In general, older women maintain the physiological capability to experience an orgasm as well as an enthusiastic interest in sexual relationships. However, they may no longer have a partner. In addition, some heterosexual older women may have male sexual partners who are no longer able to maintain an erection. These men may stop all caressing and sexual activities once intercourse is not possible (Ellison, 2001; Kingsberg, 2002; McHugh, 2006).

Another problem is that people in the United States seem to think that older women should be asexual (Gergen, 2008; McHugh, 2006; Schwartz, 2007). Sexuality seems to be condemned more in older women than in older men (C. Banks & Arnold, 2001). Cultural norms in the United States construct portrayals of grandmothers baking cookies in the kitchen, not cavorting in the bedroom. Some cultures are generally negative about sexuality. For example, cultural norms in Uttar Pradesh in Northern India suggest that people do not expect older women to be sexually active. In contrast, in sex-positive cultures, such as the San of Africa or Chinese Taoists, sexuality is considered healthy for older people (Whelehan, 2001).

Sexual Disorders

A **sexual disorder**, or sexual dysfunction, is a disturbance in sexual arousal or in sexual responding that causes mental distress (L. L. Alexander et al., 2021; Hyde & DeLamater, 2006). According to some estimates, 43% of women have had sexual experiences that were less than ideal (Laumann et al., 2002; Tiefer, 2006). Sexual dissatisfaction is relatively high among women who have limited education, economic problems, or general depression (Basson, 2007; Heiman, 2007; Shifren & Ferrari, 2004).

Let's examine two relatively common sexual problems in women, and then we'll discuss how traditional gender roles are partly responsible for sexual problems. In addition, we'll briefly discuss therapy for sexual problems, including some thought-provoking questions raised by feminist theorists and researchers (e.g., Kaschak & Tiefer, 2001; Tiefer, 2004, 2006).

Low Sexual Desire

As the name suggests, a woman with **low sexual desire** has little interest in sexual activity, and she is distressed by this lack of desire (Basson, 2006; Hyde & DeLamater, 2006; LoPiccolo, 2002). As we noted earlier in this chapter, women tend to be somewhat lower in sexual desire than men.

A disorder of low sexual desire may be caused by a variety of psychological factors. These may include a general problem such as depression, anxiety, or dissatisfaction with her romantic partner (Hyde & DeLamater, 2006; O'Sullivan et al., 2006; Wincze & Carey, 2001).

Some lesbian women also experience low sexual desire. In many cases, a lesbian couple may be compatible and loving. However, they no longer have sexual interactions because the more sexually interested member of a lesbian couple is reluctant to pressure her less enthusiastic partner (M. Nichols & Shernoff, 2007).

Female Orgasmic Disorder

A woman with **female orgasmic disorder**, also called anorgasmia or orgasmic dysfunction, experiences sexual excitement, but she does not reach orgasm. The diagnosis of female orgasmic disorder should be applied only if a woman is currently unhappy about her sexual experiences (Heiman, 2007).

One frequent cause of female orgasmic disorder is that women who are accustomed to inhibiting their sexual impulses have difficulty overcoming their inhibitions, even in a relationship where sex is approved. Many women may not have orgasms because their partners do not provide appropriate sexual stimulation. Unfortunately, female orgasmic disorder is a relatively common sexual problem (Baber, 2000; Heiman, 2007).

How Gender Roles Contribute to Sexual Disorders

Sexual problems are often complex. Some are caused by a painful medical problem, psychological trauma, or problems in a couple's interactions (Crooks & Baur, 2008; Offman & Matheson, 2004; Wincze & Carey, 2001).

Gender roles, stereotypes, and biases frequently contribute to sexual problems. As feminist researchers have pointed out, a heterosexual relationship is typically an unequal playing field, with the man having more power (Tiefer, 1996; Tolman & Diamond, 2001b). Here are some reasons that gender roles can create or intensify sexual problems:

1. Many people believe that a man should be sexual and aggressive, whereas a woman doesn't need to enjoy sexual activity (Sanchez et al., 2005, 2006).
2. Many cultures emphasize the length, strength, and endurance of a man's penis. When a man focuses on these issues, he probably won't think about how to make the romantic and sexual interactions pleasurable for his partner (McHugh, 2006).
3. Physical attractiveness is emphasized more for women than for men, and so a woman may focus on her physical appearance, rather than on her own sexual pleasure (Impett et al., 2006).

Let's consider additional information about women and physical attractiveness. We discussed how cultural norms emphasize female attractiveness in the chapters on adolescence and love relationships. We will also consider this issue in Chapter 12 in connection with eating disorders and in Chapter 14, on older women.

Many cultures frequently judge women on the basis of their attractiveness. As a result, a woman may experience **self-objectification**; she adopts an observer's view of her body—as if her body were an object (Lamb, 2008; McHugh, 2006; T. Roberts & Waters, 2004). In a cleverly designed study, Tomi-Ann Roberts and Jennifer Gettman (2004) encouraged one group of young women to think about words related to their body's competence, such as *healthy, energetic,* and *strong.* Young women in a second group were encouraged to think about "objectifying" words such as *attractive, shapely,* and *slender.* Compared to the women in the "physical competence" condition, those in the "objectifying" condition felt more ashamed, disgusted, and anxious about themselves.

In summary, culture emphasizes men's sexuality, and it focuses on male genitals. In contrast, women's sexual enjoyment receives little attention. In addition, self-objectification encourages women's sexual problems.

Therapy for Sexual Disorders

Sex therapists have developed several techniques to address women's sexual disorders. For example, in **cognitive restructuring**, the therapist tries (1) to change people's inappropriately negative thoughts about some aspect of sexuality and also (2) to reduce thoughts that interfere with sexual activity and pleasure (Basson, 2006; Wincze & Carey, 2001).

Leonore Tiefer (1996, 2001, 2004, 2006) is one of the leading feminist sex therapists. She argues that the traditional biologically based approaches to sex therapy are too limited. As she notes,

> The amount of time devoted to getting the penis hard and the vagina wet vastly outweighs the attention devoted to assessment or education about sexual motives, scripts, pleasure, power, emotionality, sensuality, communication, or connectedness. (Tiefer, 2001, p. 90)

So far, unfortunately, sex therapists have not devised a comprehensive program that addresses gender inequalities and education in a relationship, while also correcting specific problems in sexual responding. The answer is not simply a pill for women that is the equivalent of Viagra for men (McHugh, 2006). Instead, an ideal comprehensive program would award equal value to women's and men's pleasurable experiences. Tenderness, emotional closeness, and communication are also essential (Basson, 2006; Crooks & Baur, 2008; O'Sullivan et al., 2006).

Section Summary

Sexual Behavior and Sexual Disorders

1. Important predictors of women's early sexual experiences include a variety of psychological and family-related factors. Most women report that their first experience with heterosexual intercourse was not positive; about 10% of high-school girls report that their first experience was forced intercourse.
2. The research shows that men report more sexual partners than women; men are also much more likely to report masturbating.
3. Couples often experience difficulty in communicating about sexual issues; in an ambiguous situation, men often assume that their female partner is interested in sexual activity.
4. An important component of communication is sexual assertiveness; couples who discuss their preferences about sexual activities are more likely to be satisfied with the sexual aspects of their relationships.
5. Lesbian couples typically value nongenital physical contact; compared to heterosexual women, they are more likely to experience an orgasm, partly because of better communication.
6. Many older women experience subtle changes in their sexual responses, but not necessarily decreased enjoyment; however, lack of a partner is often an important obstacle to older women's sexual activities.
7. A woman who has a disorder called low sexual desire has little interest in sexual activity, and she is unhappy about this situation. Depression, other psychological problems, and relational issues may contribute to this disorder.
8. A woman who has female orgasmic disorder feels sexual excitement but does not experience orgasm, and she is unhappy about this situation. Gender roles and other psychological factors are often responsible.
9. Gender roles contribute to sexual disorders in several ways: (a) People often believe that men should be sexual and aggressive, but women should not be interested in sex; (b) sexuality research emphasizes the male perspective; and (c) physical attractiveness is emphasized for women more than for men, so that women may experience self-objectification.
10. Therapy for sexual disorders may use techniques such as cognitive restructuring, as well as a broader perspective that includes gender equality and communication, rather than developing the female equivalent of Viagra.

9-4 Birth Control, Abortion, and Other Alternatives

Learning Objectives

To describe birth control, abortion, and alternatives for managing pregnancy, you can …

9-4-1 Describe the various types of birth control methods that are designed to prevent pregnancy.

9-4-2 Summarize relevant factors related to birth control use.

9-4-3 Identify factors that create obstacles to using birth control.

9-4-4 Explain how people in developing countries manage pregnancy.

9-4-5 Describe people's psychological reactions to abortion.

9-4-6 Summarize the long-term effects on children who are born from unwanted pregnancies.

9-4-7 Describe the pros and cons of choosing alternatives to abortion.

Birth control and abortion continue to be highly controversial topics in the twenty-first century. The most publicized data about birth control and abortion in the United States typically focus on teenagers. Unfortunately, U.S. adolescents are more likely to give birth than adolescents in any other industrialized country in the world (Sedgh et al., 2015; Singh & Darroch, 2000; World Bank, 2019).

Table 9.1 on page 306, presents estimated birth rates for adolescents in Canada, the United States, and many countries in Western Europe. Keep these birth rates and abortion rates in mind, because we need to examine why the birth rate for U.S. adolescents is so much higher than in other comparable countries (Klein et al., 2005).

In this section, we will first discuss methods of contraception, as well as women's decisions about contraception. Later we'll examine some information about abortion and other alternatives. Because this is a psychology of women textbook, we will primarily focus on women's experiences. Still, we need to keep in mind that issues such as teen pregnancy have widespread political and economic consequences. Consider, for instance, that the United States spends billions of dollars each year in costs related to teen pregnancy. However, in New York State, every dollar spent on family planning saves at least three dollars later, just on the cost of prenatal and newborn care (Family Planning Advocates of New York State, 2005).

Birth Control Methods

If a sexually active heterosexual woman uses no form of birth control whatsoever, she has an estimated 85% chance of becoming pregnant within 1 year (Hatcher et al., 2004). Table 9.2 describes the major forms of birth control, together with some information about their effectiveness.

You'll note that abstinence is the only method of birth control that is 100% effective in preventing pregnancy. In earlier decades, people who recommended abstinence might have been considered prudish. However, sexual intercourse presents not only a substantial risk of pregnancy for women and transgender men but also a significant risk of contracting

TABLE **9.1**

Annual Rate of Adolescent Births and Abortions (per 1,000 women, ages 15–19) for Canada, the United States, and 9 Countries in Western Europe

Country	Birth Rate	Abortion Rate
Netherlands	4	7
Denmark	4	14
Belgium	4	8
France	5	15
Norway	5	13
Finland	6	13
Spain	7	13
Portugal	8	8
Canada	8	14
United Kingdom	12	20
United States	17	15

Note: Several countries in Western Europe are missing because data on abortion were not available.
Source for birth data: World Bank (2019).
Source for abortion data: Guttmacher Institute. (2015). *Adolescent pregnancy and its outcomes across countries.* https://www.guttmacher.org/fact-sheet/adolescent-pregnancy-and-its-outcomes-across-countries.

a deadly disease. As we will discuss in Chapter 11, very few birth control methods can reduce the risk of contracting HIV/AIDS. Even condoms cannot completely prevent the transmission of this disease. Yes, they make sex safer, but not completely safe.

Incidentally, Table 9.2 does not list two behavioral birth control methods: (1) withdrawal (removal of the penis before ejaculation) and (2) the rhythm method, also known as natural family planning (intercourse only when a woman is least fertile). These methods are not listed because their effectiveness is unacceptably low (Guttmacher Institute, 2008; Hatcher et al., 2004).

Emergency Contraception: A New Option

Suppose that Jessica and DeShawn have been lovers for about a year. They have been very conscientious about using condoms, except that one night the condom breaks. Or suppose that a female college student is raped by an acquaintance, and she is deeply concerned about becoming pregnant. In cases like these, women have an option called **emergency contraception**, or hormone pills that prevent pregnancy by inhibiting ovulation and by producing other changes in the cervix and the uterus (Landau et al., 2006).

You may have learned about "Plan B," one of the more effective forms of emergency contraception. It is important to know that emergency contraception is a form of birth control —rather than a form of abortion—because it *prevents* pregnancy (Planned Parenthood, 2010).

An important caution about emergency-contraception pills is that they must be taken as soon as possible after intercourse. These pills are available in many drugstores—without

TABLE **9.2**

Major Contraceptive Methods

Method	Effectiveness When Used Consistently	Possible Side Effects and Disadvantages
Abstinence	100% effective	No physical disadvantages (assuming no sperm contact whatsoever).
Tubal sterilization (severing of woman's fallopian tubes)	99% effective	Minor surgical risk; typically not reversible; possible negative emotional reactions.
Vasectomy (surgery to prevent passage of sperm in a man)	99% effective	Minor surgical risk; typically not reversible; possible negative emotional reactions.
Oral contraceptives (synthetic hormones taken by woman)	99% effective	Slight risk of blood-clotting disorders, particularly for women over 35 and those who use nicotine products; other medical side effects possible; must be taken regularly.
Condom (sheath placed on penis)	98% effective	Must be applied before intercourse; may decrease pleasure for man.
Diaphragm and spermicidal cream	94% effective	Must be applied before intercourse; may irritate genital area.

a doctor's prescription—for women 17 years of age or older (Gardner, 2009; Harper et al., 2008; Landau et al., 2006).

Let's now examine the traditional forms of birth control, in more detail. We also need to consider the personal characteristics related to using birth control, the obstacles that prevent its use, and family planning in developing countries.

Who Uses Birth Control?

Many heterosexual women who are sexually active use either an unreliable birth control method (such as withdrawal or rhythm) or no contraception at all. Because these women do not always use effective birth control methods, they often have unplanned pregnancies. Figure 9.2 shows, for example, that approximately 750,000 U.S. teenagers become pregnant each year (Klein et al., 2005; Martin, Hamilton, Osterman, & Driscoll, 2019). If we consider women of all ages in the United States, about half of all pregnancies were unintended at the time of conception (Guttmacher Institute, 2005).

Here are some relevant factors related to women's birth control use:

1. *Social class.* Women from the middle and upper socioeconomic classes are more likely to use birth control (Farber, 2003; Klein et al., 2005).
2. *Ethnicity.* In the United States, birth control use is higher for White women and Asian American women than for Latina women and Black women (Kaiser Family Foundation, 2003). We do not have comparable data about other ethnic groups.

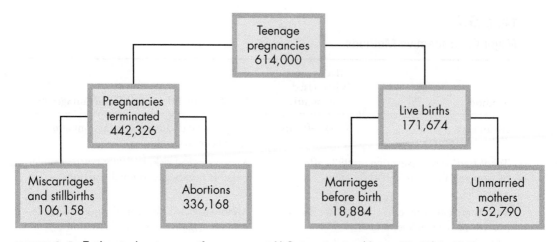

FIGURE **9.2** Estimated outcomes for pregnant U.S. teenagers (Ages 15–19) in 2019.
Source: Calculations based on data from Livingston & Thomas (2019), Martin et al. (2021), and Sedgh et al. (2015).

3. *Level of education.* Women who have had at least some college education are somewhat more likely than other women to use birth control (E. Becker et al., 1998). However, according to one study, 48% of women who had at least a master's degree reported that they did not consistently use contraception (Laumann et al., 1994). In other words, about half of these well-educated women could face an unplanned pregnancy.

4. *Feminist beliefs.* Female students who consider themselves to be feminists are more likely than nonfeminist female students to engage in safer sex behavior (Yoder et al., 2007).

5. *Personality characteristics.* Research on adolescents shows that girls are more likely to use contraceptives if they have high self-esteem and if they dislike taking risks (E. Becker et al., 1998; N. J. Bell et al., 1999; Pearson, 2006). Consider a representative study on risk taking by Odgers and her coauthors (2008). They found that girls who had used alcohol and other risky drugs during early adolescence were much more likely than nonrisk takers to become pregnant before the age of 21.

Obstacles to Using Birth Control

Why are approximately half of all U.S. pregnancies unplanned? The problem is that many obstacles stand in the way of using effective birth control. A woman who avoids pregnancy must have adequate knowledge about contraception. She must also have access to it, and she must be willing to use it on a consistent basis. In Canadian and U.S. surveys of sexually active young adults, only about 25 to 40% reported using a contraceptive when they last had intercourse (Fields, 2002; Statistics Canada, 2000).

In more detail, here are some of the obstacles to using birth control:

1. Parents and educators often avoid discussing birth control with young people because they "don't want to give them any ideas." As a result, many young people

are misinformed or have gaps in their knowledge (Fine & McClelland, 2006; Kaiser Family Foundation, 2003; Klein et al., 2005).

2. Some young women cannot obtain contraceptive services or products, so they use less reliable forms of birth control (Feldt, 2002; Hyde & DeLamater, 2006). Other women in the United States have no health insurance, or their health insurance does not cover birth control (American College of Obstetricians and Gynecologists, 2015; Guttmacher Institute, 2001).

3. Many young women have sexual intercourse without much planning. In a survey of Canadian female college students going to Florida over spring break, 13% reported that they had sex with someone they had just met (Maticka-Tyndale et al., 1998). In a sample of U.S. college students, 26% reported having had intercourse with someone they had met earlier the same night. Casual sex does not encourage conversations and careful planning about contraception strategies (M. Allen et al., 2002; Hyde & DeLamater, 2006; S. L. Nichols & Good, 2004).

4. People may not think rationally about the consequences of sexual activity. For example, sexually inexperienced women often believe that they themselves are not likely to become pregnant during intercourse (Brehm et al., 2002; Hyde & DeLamater, 2006). A survey of adolescents in the United States revealed another example of irrational thinking. Specifically, 67% of adolescent girls in this sample reported that they use condoms "all the time." However, only 50% of these same young women said that they had used condoms during the last time they had sexual intercourse (Kaiser Family Foundation, 2003). A Canadian survey reported a similar discrepancy (H. R. L. Richardson et al., 1997).

5. Traditional women believe that if they were to obtain contraception, they would be admitting to themselves that they planned to have intercourse and are therefore not "nice girls." In fact, college students downgrade a woman who is described as providing a condom before sexual intercourse (D. M. Castañeda & Collins, 1998; Hynie et al., 1997; Tolman, 2002).

6. People often believe that birth control devices will interrupt the lovemaking mood, because they are not considered erotic or romantic (Fine & McClelland, 2006; Perloff, 2001). Condoms and other contraceptives are seldom mentioned in movies, television, romantic novels, and magazines, as Demonstration 9.4 illustrates. We can observe a woman and a man undressing, groping, groaning, and copulating. The one taboo topic seems to be contraception! Interestingly, women who read romance novels are especially likely to have negative attitudes toward contraception (Diekman et al., 2000).

7. Many young women are forced to have sexual intercourse, often with a much older man (Centers for Disease Control and Prevention, 2004a; Fine & McClelland, 2006; Klein et al., 2005). When a 14-year-old girl has a partner who is a 21-year-old man, she may have less power to persuade him to wear a condom.

Earlier in the chapter, we noted that ideally, schools would develop more comprehensive sex-education programs. This would ensure that adolescents within the community receive appropriate information before they become sexually active, especially because many adolescents are not well informed about contraception (Fine & McClelland, 2006).

Unfortunately, it's difficult to change people's sexual behavior. Even a carefully designed program—with relevant information and training in communications skills—may not increase college students to use condoms more frequently (Tulloch et al., 2004).

Demonstration 9.4

Contraception as a Taboo Topic

For the next two weeks, keep a record of the number of times couples in sexual relationships appear in the media. Monitor television programs, movies, stories in magazines, books, and online, as well as any other source that seems relevant. In each case, note whether contraceptives are mentioned, shown, or even hinted at.

Another issue is the need to increase the representation of contraceptives in the media. People might use contraceptives more often if the women in movies or shows were shown discussing birth control methods with their gynecologists and if the men carefully adjusted their condoms before the steamy love scenes.

Contraception and Family Planning in Developing Countries

A country's fertility rate is measured in terms of the average number of children a woman will have in her lifetime. The fertility rate is 2.0 in the United States and 1.5 in Canada. In general, the highest fertility rates are in Africa, for example, 7.2 in Niger, 7.1 in Guinea Bissau, and 6.5 in Mali ("List of countries," 2009).

In general, the developing countries and regions that have the highest female literacy rate tend to have the lowest fertility rates (Winter, 1996). For example, if we consider the entire country of India, 31% of high-school-age girls are in school, and the average adult woman has 3.7 children. Kerala, one of the states in India, has the highest level of family planning in that country (Department of Health and Family Planning, 2010). In Kerala, 93% of high-school-age girls are in school, and the average adult woman has only 2.0 children (B. Lott, 2000). Notice that this number is identical to the average number for U.S. women.

When women are well educated, they are likely to take control of their lives and make plans for the future. By limiting their family size, they can increase their economic and personal freedom (P. D. Harvey, 2000). They can also provide better care for the children they already have.

The use of contraceptives throughout the world has been rising steadily, with between 50% and 60% of couples practicing contraception (David & Russo, 2003; Townsend, 2003). Still, millions of unmarried couples do not have access to family planning. In fact, during the next 5 minutes, about 950 women throughout the world will have conceived a pregnancy that is not wanted (David & Russo, 2003). Each woman will need to make choices about continuing with a pregnancy, giving the child up for adoption, or having an abortion. Let's now explore the controversial topic of abortion and the alternatives.

Abortion and Other Alternatives

Many women face a difficult decision when they find that they are pregnant: Should they terminate the pregnancy, or should they continue the pregnancy? Women of all ages choose to have an abortion. However, in this section, we will focus specifically on adolescent girls. There are about 750,000 teen pregnancies in the United States each year (Klein et al., 2005; Martin, Hamilton, Osterman, & Driscoll, 2019).[1] Figure 9.2 shows estimates of the outcomes for these young women. Suppose that a young woman is pregnant, and she does not experience a miscarriage. She will need to make an extremely important decision: Should she carry the pregnancy to term, or should she seek an abortion? Should she choose marriage, or should she become a single mother? Should she give up her baby for adoption?

Before 1973 in the United States, many abortions were performed illegally, often by untrained individuals in unsanitary conditions. Each year, an estimated 200,000 to 1,200,000 illegal abortions were performed and about 10,000 women died from these illegal abortions (Gorney, 1998). Before 1973, countless other women attempted to end an unwanted pregnancy themselves. They swallowed poisons such as turpentine, and they tried to stab coat hangers and other sharp objects through the cervix and into the uterus (Baird-Windle & Bader, 2001; Gorney, 1998).

According to the U.S. Supreme Court's *Roe v. Wade* decision in 1973, women have the legal right to choose abortion. However, throughout the United States, health-care professionals who perform abortions have been harassed or even murdered by pro-life groups. Abortion clinics have also been bombed (Baird-Windle & Bader, 2001; Feldt, 2002; Planned Parenthood, 2009).

Incidentally, Figure 9.2 also shows the number of miscarriages for U.S. teenagers. Here's some interesting information about one of the major causes of miscarriages. Cigarette smoking nearly doubles a woman's chances of having a spontaneous miscarriage and losing her baby (Mendola et al., 1998; Mills, 1999; Ness et al., 1999). Researchers have known for many decades that smoking causes fetal death. However, pro-life groups have not yet harassed the tobacco companies.

Let's also emphasize an important point about abortions: *No one recommends abortion as a routine form of birth control.* Providing more comprehensive education about sexuality is more effective in preventing pregnancy in the first place, which means that adolescent girls and women do not then need to consider the abortion alternative (Adler et al., 2003; Kohler, Manhart, & Lafferty, 2008). As portrayed in Table 9.1 on page 306, the adolescent abortion rate is higher in the United States than in most other countries on this list.

Worldwide, about 50 million abortions are performed each year for women of all ages. About 40% of these abortions are illegal (Caldwell & Caldwell, 2003; E. M. Murphy, 2003; United Nations, 2000). Worldwide, about 120 women die every 5 minutes from an unsafe abortion (David & Russo, 2003). Most of these deaths could have been avoided by using effective birth control methods and legal abortion procedures.

About one-quarter of all pregnancies in the United States and Canada are terminated by means of a legal abortion (Singh et al., 2003; Statistics Canada, 2000). Abortion may be a controversial issue, but the safety aspect of abortion is not controversial. A woman in the United States is about 30 times more likely to die as a result of childbirth than as a result of a legal abortion (Adler et al., 2003). Let's now consider the psychological aspects of abortion.

---

[1] Unfortunately, no comparable analysis is available for the options faced by pregnant teenagers in Canada. However, as Table 9.1 portrays, a teenager in Canada is only about one half as likely as a U.S. teenager to give birth. Also, the abortion rate is somewhat lower in Canada.

Women's Psychological Reactions to an Abortion

Most women report that their primary reaction following an abortion is relief (David & Lee, 2001; Russo, 2008a). Some women experience sadness, a sense of loss, or other negative feelings. Consistent with Theme 4 of this textbook, individual differences in emotional reactions are large (Needle & Walker, 2008; Russo, 2008b). However, according to the best-controlled studies, the typical woman who has an abortion experiences no long-term negative psychological effects, such as problems with depression, anxiety, or self-esteem (Lee, 2003; Munk-Olsen et al., 2011; C. P. Murphy, 2003; Russo, 2008).

What factors are related to psychological adjustment following an abortion? In general, women who cope most easily are those who have the abortion early in their pregnancy (Allgeier & Allgeier, 2000). Another important psychological factor related to adjustment is **self-efficacy,** or a woman's feeling that she is competent and effective (Major et al., 1998). Not surprisingly, adjustment is also better if the woman's friends and relatives can support her decision (N. E. Adler & Smith, 1998; David & Lee, 2001).

Children Born to Women Who Were Denied Abortions

So far, we have considered the well-being of the mothers. Let's now turn to the well-being of the unwanted children. Abortion has been legal in the United States since 1973, so researchers cannot accurately examine that question in this country. However, several studies in other countries provide some answers. Consider a long-term study conducted with 220 children whose mothers had been denied abortions in the former Czechoslovakia (David et al., 1988; David et al., 2003). Each of these children was carefully matched—on the basis of eight different variables such as social class—with a child from a wanted pregnancy. As a result, the two groups were initially comparable.

The results have shown that, by 9 years of age, the children from unwanted pregnancies had fewer friends and responded poorly to stress, compared to children from wanted pregnancies. By age 23, the children from unwanted pregnancies were more likely to report that they had marital difficulties, drug problems, conflicts at work, and trouble with the legal system (David et al., 1988). Ongoing research about these two groups continued to show psychological problems when these unwanted children are adults, whereas the wanted children had relatively few problems (David & Lee, 2001; David et al., 2003; Russo, 2008b).

Other similar studies show that many mothers of unwanted children continue to report negative emotions and a lack of concern about those children many years later (J. S. Barber et al., 1999; Needle & Walker, 2008; Sigal et al., 2003). Taking these implications for children's lives into account may help governments make informed decisions about abortion policies.

Alternatives to Abortion

Unplanned pregnancies can be resolved by methods other than abortion. For example, people who oppose abortion often suggest the alternative of giving the baby up for adoption, and this might be an appropriate choice for some women. However, adoption often creates its own kind of trauma and pain when the birth mother continues to feel guilty (David & Lee, 2001; Feldt, 2002; Fessler, 2006). One woman who gave up her daughter for adoption described how her anguish continued for many years afterwards:

> I am shocked at how much it has impacted my life. I really tried to move on and forget. I tried to do what they said, but it didn't work ... it was supposed to work; everybody said so. But it didn't. No matter how many degrees I got, how many credits I had, how many years I worked, I was still empty. (Fessler, 2006, p. 12)

Another alternative is to deliver the baby and choose the motherhood option. In many cases, an unwanted pregnancy can become a wanted baby by the time of delivery. However, hundreds of thousands of babies in the United States are born each year to mothers who do not want them. Unfortunately, most teenage mothers encounter difficulties in completing school, finding employment, fighting poverty, and obtaining health care. In addition, teenage mothers often confront cultural biases (Hellenga et al., 2002; S. L. Nichols & Good, 2004; Russo, 2008a).

Some people believe that marriage is the ideal solution to an unwanted pregnancy. However, research suggests that teen mothers who remain single are actually more than three times as likely as married teen mothers to return to school after the baby is born (Fine & McClelland, 2007).

We have learned that none of these alternatives—abortion, adoption, or motherhood—is free of problems. Instead, preventing the pregnancy seems to create fewer psychological issues than the other alternatives.

Section Summary

Birth Control and Abortion

1. In the United States, about 750,000 adolescent girls become pregnant each year; pregnancy rates are much lower in Canada and Western Europe.
2. No birth control device offers problem-free protection from both pregnancy and sexually transmitted infections; abstinence is the only genuinely safe option. Emergency contraception is an option, but not every woman can easily access this option.
3. Many heterosexual, sexually active women do not use reliable birth control methods. Contraceptive use by women is related to social class, ethnicity, education, feminist beliefs, self-esteem, and risk taking.
4. Couples avoid using birth control because of inadequate information, unavailable contraceptive services, inadequate planning, irrational thinking, reluctance to admit they are sexually active, and the belief that birth control devices are not romantic. If a teenage girl has a much older sexual partner, she often has difficulty convincing him to wear a condom.
5. Some developing countries have instituted family planning programs, whereas others lack these programs. Literacy is strongly correlated with women's contraceptive use.
6. Before *Roe v. Wade*, thousands of U.S. women died each year from illegal abortions; legal abortions are much safer than childbirth.
7. Following an abortion, most women experience a feeling of relief; adjustment is best when the abortion occurs early in pregnancy, when the woman feels competent, and when friends and family are supportive.
8. Children born to women who have been denied an abortion are significantly more likely to experience psychological and social difficulties, compared to children from a wanted pregnancy.
9. In general, a woman who gives up her child for adoption often feels guilty, even many years later; women who choose the motherhood option typically face many difficulties. Pregnancy prevention is therefore the preferable solution.

Chapter Review Questions

1. At several points throughout this chapter, we have learned that sexuality has traditionally been male centered. Address this issue, focusing on topics such as (a) theoretical perspectives on sexuality, (b) sexual scripts, and (c) sexual disorders. Also, compare how the essentialist perspective and the social constructionist perspective approach the topic of sexuality.
2. In the first section of this chapter, we noted that men and women differ more in the intensity of sexual desires than in most other psychological gender comparisons. What are some of the potential consequences of this difference, with respect to sexual behavior and sexual disorders?
3. In many sections of this chapter, we discussed adolescent girls. Describe the experiences an adolescent girl might face as she discusses sexuality with her parents, listens to a sex-education session in her high school, has her first experience with sexual intercourse or sexual contact, makes decisions about contraception, and tries to make a decision about an unwanted pregnancy.
4. How are gender roles relevant in (a) the initiation of sexual relationships, (b) sexual activity, (c) sexual disorders, and (d) decisions about contraception and abortion?
5. Describe the information in this chapter that would be helpful for a sexually active woman to know regarding communication about sexuality, self-objectification, and methods of birth control.
6. Describe attitudes about sexuality in the twenty-first century. Does the sexual double standard still hold true in the United States?
7. What information do we have about sexuality in lesbian couples, bisexual women, and transgender women, including sexual activity and sexual problems? Why would a male-centered approach to sexuality make it difficult to decide what "counts" as sexual activity in a lesbian, bisexual, or transgender relationship? Why is this same problem relevant when we consider older women and sexual activities?
8. Describe the two sexual disorders discussed in this chapter. Why might older women be especially likely to experience these disorders? Briefly describe the general approach to therapy for sexual disorders, including the feminist perspective on sex therapy.
9. Imagine that you have received a large grant to reduce the number of unwanted pregnancies at the high school you attended. What kinds of programs would you plan in order to achieve both immediate and long-term effects?
10. Discuss the information that we have about unwanted pregnancies. Include such topics as (a) the safety of abortion; (b) a woman's psychological reactions to an abortion; (c) the consequences for a child whose mother had been denied an abortion; and (d) the consequences for a mother who has given up her baby for adoption.

Key Terms

essentialism (p. 286)
social constructionist approach (p. 286)
clitoris (p. 286)
vagina (p. 287)
excitement phase (p. 288)
vasocongestion (p. 288)
plateau phase (p. 288)
orgasmic phase (p. 288)
resolution phase (p. 288)
sexual desire (p. 289)
sexual double standard (p. 292)
sexual script (p. 293)
sexual assault (p. 293)
rape (p. 293)

hooking up (p. 298)

sexual disorder
(p. 302)

low sexual desire
(p. 302)

female orgasmic
disorder (p. 302)

self-objectification
(p. 303)

cognitive restructuring
(p. 303)

emergency
contraception
(p. 306)

self-efficacy (p. 312)

Recommended Readings

Crooks, R., & Baur, K. (2017). *Our sexuality* (13th ed.). Cengage Learning. Several excellent textbooks on human sexuality have been published over the years. One feature that is especially interesting and informative in this textbook is the quotations from real people about aspects of their own sexuality.

Fine, M., & McClelland, S. I. (2006). Sexuality education and desire: Still missing after all these years. *Harvard Educational Review, 76,* 297–338. We strongly recommend this interesting and informative review article, which emphasizes the weaknesses of abstinence-only education, as well as the power of young women's desires.

Klein, J. D., et al. (2005). Adolescent pregnancy: Current trends and issues. *Pediatrics, 116,* 281–286. Here is a comprehensive article about factors related to adolescent pregnancy. You can also access this article on the website of the American Academy of Pediatrics.

Tiefer, L. (2004). *Sex is not a natural act and other essays.* Boulder, CO: Westview Press. We strongly recommend this book, which provides a feminist perspective on sexuality, rather than a biological approach. The book includes some theoretical essays, but also some intended for the general public.

Answers to Demonstrations

Demonstration 9.1: 1. F; 2. M; 3. F; 4. F; 5. M; 6. M; 7. M; 8. F.

Demonstration 9.3: 1. 2.7; 2. 2.7; 3. 4.2; 4. 4.1; 5. 4.6; 6. 4.4. Note that a woman who is high in sexual assertiveness would provide high ratings for Items 1, 4, and 6; she would provide low ratings for Items 2, 3, and 5. Also note that respondents answered numbers 5 and 6 inconsistently—as both having sex without a condom and insisting on a condom.

Miramiska/Shutterstock.com

10 Pregnancy, Childbirth, and Motherhood

Learning Objectives

After studying this chapter, you will be able to ...

10-1 Understand how pregnancy affects people physically, emotionally, and financially.

10-2 Explain how the childbirth process impacts people physically, socially, and psychologically.

10-3 Summarize how motherhood impacts women's lives.

Did You Know?

- Psychologists have conducted little research on the psychological aspects of pregnancy and childbirth (p. 319).
- About one-third of pregnant women in developed countries do not receive any prenatal care prior to childbirth (p. 320).
- Women who are pregnant during very stressful events are at risk for premature delivery (p. 323).
- People tend to show either hostile sexism or benevolent sexism toward a pregnant woman, depending on the circumstances (p. 324).
- Medical complications are often reduced during childbirth if a helpful, experienced person is present (p. 359).
- Children raised by lesbian mothers resemble children raised by heterosexual mothers in characteristics such as intelligence, psychological adjustment, and popularity (pp. 336–337).
- Approximately half of mothers in the United States experience postpartum blues within a few days after the birth of their first child; common symptoms include crying, sadness, and irritability (p. 339).

A student in one of my classes gave me a book that her mother wrote about the topic of motherhood, when my student had been a toddler. One of my favorite parts describes the range of emotions that mothers experience:

> Sometimes single and/or childless friends want to know something about what it is like to be a parent. The best I can come up with is: after a child enters your home, your physical and mental feelings are heightened to degrees you never imagined possible. One has never before experienced such exhaustion, impatience, frustration, or fright. However, one has also never experienced such happiness, pride, or love. (Santoro, 1992, p. 9)

In this chapter, you'll discover many examples of Theme 4, that women vary widely from one another. However, consistent with Karla Santoro's description, this chapter also emphasizes how each woman experiences a wide variation within her own emotions.

The world currently has more than 7 billion inhabitants, each of whom was produced by a pregnancy. Shouldn't the sheer frequency of this personally important event make it a popular topic for psychological research? Still, the topic of pregnancy rarely appears in psychology journals published in the United States (Greene, 2004; Johnston-Robledo &

Barnack, 2004; Hoffnung, 2011; Rice & Else-Quest, 2006). Furthermore, these articles almost always focus on topics such as teen pregnancy, unwanted pregnancy, and drug abuse during pregnancy. In contrast, psychologists tend to ignore the experiences of women who are happy to be pregnant and are looking forward to being mothers (Matlin, 2003).

Most studies of pregnancy also focus primarily on the experiences of cisgender women or people who are born with uteruses. Studies of pregnancy among transgender people who give birth after having socially or medically transitioned or both are rare, but they suggest that transgender people frequently experience discrimination from health-care systems regarding their pregnancies (Leung et al., 2019; Light, Obedin-Maliver, Sevelius, & Kerns, 2014). Research suggests that 23 to 30% of transgender people delay or avoid seeking medical care due to discrimination and cisnormative bias from health-care providers (Jaffee, Shires, & Stroumsa, 2016; Kcomt, Gorey, Barrett, & McCabe, 2020). Another barrier to pregnancy for transgender people is the risk of being misgendered. As one transgender male participant in a research study stated:

> I just didn't like leaving the house at all because I knew that I was going to be read as pregnant female, and it just ugh. After I'd worked so hard the past couple of years to get [people to see me as male]. (Hoffkling, Obedin-Maliver, & Sevelius, 2017, p. 4)

The media provide another context in which the motherhood sequence is limited. In Chapter 8, we learned that the theme of love dominates music, television, and entertainment. Sexuality—the focus of Chapter 9—is equally prominent. However, pregnancy and childbirth are relatively rare topics, consistent with Theme 3. One exception is reality shows such as *Maternity Ward* or *Teen Mom*, which exaggerate the amount of medical intervention required during childbirth or focus on teen pregnancy (Luce et al., 2016; Morris & McInerney, 2010).

Let's examine pregnancy, childbirth, and motherhood in more detail. As you'll learn, each of these three phases has important psychological components.

10-1 Pregnancy

Learning Objectives

To understand how pregnancy affects people physically, emotionally, and financially, you can ...

10-1-1 Describe the major biological components of pregnancy.

10-1-2 Summarize how pregnancy affects people's bodies and physical health status.

10-1-3 Analyze the range of both positive and negative emotions that individuals experience during pregnancy.

10-1-4 Explain how hostile and benevolent sexism negatively affect people who are pregnant.

10-1-5 Describe how pregnancy affects people's employment experiences.

What are the major biological components of pregnancy? How do people react to pregnancy, both emotionally and physically? Also, how do other people react to those who are pregnant? Finally, how do people combine pregnancy with their employment?

The Biology of Pregnancy

In a typical pregnancy, the egg and the sperm unite while the egg is traveling down a fallopian tube. The fertilized egg continues along the fallopian tube and then floats around in the uterus. When it is about six days old, it may implant itself in the thick tissue that lines the uterus (Pobojewski, 2008). If a fertilized egg does not implant itself, then this tissue is sloughed off as menstrual flow. This is the same menstrual flow that occurs when an egg has not been fertilized. However, if implantation does occur, this tissue provides an ideal environment in which a fertilized egg can develop into a baby.

Shortly after the fertilized egg has implanted itself, the placenta begins to develop. The **placenta**, which is connected to the growing embryo, is an organ that allows oxygen and nutrients to pass from the mother to the embryo (Crooks & Baur, 2008). The placenta also helps transport the embryo's waste products back to the mother's system. This amazing organ even manufactures hormones. By the end of a cisgender woman's pregnancy, her estrogen and progesterone levels are much higher than they were before her pregnancy (L. L. Alexander et al., 2021).

Prenatal care is essential for identifying and treating any complications related to pregnancy, and health-care professionals can also provide relevant information (Crooks & Baur, 2008). However, only 75% of women in the United States receive adequate prenatal care, a rate that is much lower than in other developed countries (Osterman & Martin, 2018). In developing countries, that percentage is much lower. In Somalia, for instance, only 31% of women have one or more prenatal visit during their pregnancy (World Bank, 2019). Globally each year, approximately 300,000 women die from pregnancy related causes; 99% of those deaths occur in the developing world (Sprimont, 2020; World Health Organization, 2016). For example, 1 out of every 260 women in Yemen dies during pregnancy or childbirth (English & Swangin, 2019).

Physical Reactions During Pregnancy

Pregnancy affects virtually every organ system in a woman's body, although most of the consequences are relatively minor. The most obvious changes are weight gain and a protruding abdomen. During pregnancy, many women also report breast tenderness, frequent urination, and fatigue (L. L. Alexander et al., 2021; Boston Women's Health Book Collective, 2008; Crooks & Baur, 2008).

Nausea is another especially common symptom during the first trimester. It is often called "morning sickness," even though it may occur at any time of the day (Feeney et al., 2001; Murkoff et al., 2002). Surveys in the United States suggest that 50 to 90% of pregnant women will experience nausea and vomiting during the first three months of pregnancy (Lacasse et al., 2009).

Our general theme about the wide range of individual differences holds true with pregnancy, as with other phases in women's lives. For instance, the majority of women are less interested in sexual activity during pregnancy, but some actually report more interest in sex (Crooks & Baur, 2008; Haugen et al., 2004). Furthermore, pregnant couples often enjoy other forms of sexual expression.

Emotional Reactions During Pregnancy

All I seem to think about is the baby.... I'm so excited. I'd love to have the baby right now. Somehow this week I feel on top of the world. I love watching my whole tummy move. (Lederman, 1996, p. 35)

I think I, in a sense, have a prepartum depression—already! ... Over Easter, when I was home from teaching, it just really hit me how I would be home like that all the time.... I was very depressed one day just kind of anticipating it and realizing how much of a change it was going to be, because I had been really active with my teaching, and it had been a pretty major part of my life now for four years. (Lederman, 1996, p. 39)

These quotations from two pregnant women illustrate how individual women respond differently to the same life event, consistent with Theme 4. In pregnancy, the situation is especially unpredictable because each woman may experience a wide variety of emotions during the 9 months of her pregnancy. For example, those two quotations, although very different in emotional tone, could have come from the same woman.

Positive Emotions

At some point in their lives, the majority of women in the United States, about 86%, choose to become pregnant and to remain pregnant (Livingston, 2018; Lobel et al., 2008). If a woman has hoped to be a mother, and she learns that she is pregnant, she typically experiences a rush of positive emotions, excitement, and anticipation.

The clear majority of pregnant women also remain within the normal range of emotions throughout their pregnancy. In fact, pregnant women tend to have a relatively low incidence of psychiatric disorders (Russo & Tartaro, 2008). Most women adapt well, and the stress levels do not harm the developing fetus (DiPietro, 2004; Johnston-Robledo & Barnack, 2004; Lobel et al., 2008). Women who are characteristically optimistic or high in agreeableness are especially likely to adapt successfully to being pregnant (Hamilton & Lobel, 2008; Lobel et al., 2008; Peñacoba Puente, Carmona Monge, Carretero Abellán, & Marín Morales, 2011).

Many women also report feeling wonder and awe at the thought of having a new, growing person inside their own bodies. In a study of married heterosexual couples, many husbands also shared this sense of wonder in creating a new life (Feeney et al., 2001).

Most married women also sense that other people approve of their pregnancy. After all, in many cultures around the world, women who are married are expected to have children due to pressure from social and cultural norms, so friends and family members typically offer social support (Morling et al., 2003). Social support is correlated with better psychological well-being and with better physical health (Lobel et al., 2008).

For many women, pregnancy represents a transition into adulthood. They may describe a sense of purpose and accomplishment about being pregnant, especially in societies such as the United States where pronatalism is a cultural norm for women (Leifer, 1980; Mollen, 2014). Another positive emotion is the growing sense of attachment that pregnant women feel toward the developing baby (Bergum, 1997; Condon & Corkindale, 1997). One woman reported:

When I had my first scan, the man explained everything, like this is his leg, this is his foot, little hands, little head. I couldn't see his other leg and asked "Where's his other leg then?" Then they pushed him round and showed me his other leg. It was quite nice. That's when you realize you are having a baby, when you actually see it on the scan. (Woollett & Marshall, 1997, p. 189)

In addition, many pregnant women find pleasure in anticipating the tasks of motherhood and child rearing, which they believe will provide a tremendous source of satisfaction. As we'll learn in the section on motherhood, their expectations may be different from reality.

Negative Emotions

Pregnant women typically express some negative feelings, fears, and anxieties, such as concern about the pain of childbirth (Feeney et al., 2001; Melender, 2002; Walker, 2007). Some women report that their emotions are fragile and continually changing.

Some women report that their self-image declines as their body grows bigger (Philipp & Carr, 2001). Women in the United States often say that they feel fat and ugly during pregnancy, especially because cultural norms in the United States value more slender bodies.

Interestingly, however, these women's romantic partners may feel otherwise. For example, C. P. Cowan and Cowan (1992) questioned heterosexual married couples who were expecting a baby. They noted that most husbands responded positively. For instance, one man named Eduardo was looking at his wife, and he remarked, "The great painters tried to show the beauty of a pregnant woman, but when I look at Sonia, I feel they didn't do it justice" (p. 59). Fortunately, many women are able to overcome cultural concerns about weight. They are excited to see their abdomen swell, to feel the baby move, and to anticipate a healthy pregnancy.

Women may worry about their health and bodily functions, especially in cases of medically high-risk pregnancy (Johnston-Robledo & Barnack, 2004; McCoyd, Curran, & Munch, 2020). These anxieties are heightened by the increasing evidence that smoking, alcohol, a variety of drugs, and environmental contaminants can harm the developing fetus (Bailey et al., 2008; Newland & Rasmussen, 2003; Streissguth et al., 1999). Incidentally, studies in both the United States and Canada show that many pregnant women try to stop smoking cigarettes during their pregnancy, but it's difficult to break this addiction (Bailey et al., 2008; N. Edwards & Sims-Jones, 1998). About 7% of women in the United States smoke cigarettes during pregnancy, and the smoking rate during pregnancy is highest for White and Native American women, intermediate for Black women, and lowest for Latina and Asian-American women (Arias et al., 2003; Drake, Driscoll, & Mathews, 2018; Hamilton et al., 2007; Hoyert et al., 2000).

An important part of women's negative reactions to pregnancy is caused by other people beginning to respond differently to them, as we will learn in the next section. They are categorized as "pregnant women"—that is, women who have no identity aside from the responsibility of a growing baby (Philipp & Carr, 2001). Women may also begin to perceive themselves in these terms.

A woman's overall response to pregnancy depends on a variety of factors. These factors include her physical reactions to pregnancy, whether the pregnancy was planned, her relationship with the baby's co-parent if one is present, and her economic status (Molinary, 2007; Tolman, 2002; Walker, 2007). Additionally, individual personality factors such as neuroticism and agreeableness, as measured by the NEO Five-Factor Inventory, may also mediate women's reactions to pregnancy (Peñacoba Puente et al., 2011).

We can understand how an unmarried, pregnant 16-year-old may have predominantly negative emotions if her romantic partner and family have rejected her, and she must work in a lower-income job to earn an income. Her problems will be intensified if she is one of the hundreds of thousands of pregnant people in the United States who cannot afford prenatal care (S. E. Taylor, 2002; P. H. Wise, 2002). We can also understand predominantly positive emotions from a happily married 30-year-old who has hoped for this pregnancy for 2 years, and whose family income allows her to buy stylish maternity clothes that she can wear to her interesting, fulfilling job (Feeney et al., 2001).

During pregnancy, some women will experience a **miscarriage**, or an unintended termination of pregnancy—prior to the 24th week of pregnancy—before the fetus is viable and developed enough to survive after birth (Crooks & Baur, 2008). For instance, in Figure 9.2 (p. 308), we learned that—each year—an estimated 15% of pregnant teenagers in the United States experience a miscarriage. We cannot provide an accurate estimate of miscarriage rates for teenagers or for pregnant women of any age because a large percentage of miscarriages occur during early pregnancy, outside a medical setting. As you can imagine, some women will experience intense sorrow about this loss (Bueno, 2019; McCreight, 2005). Others feel a sense of relief or else mixed emotions.

Some women are pregnant during extremely stressful events. For example, some women lived through a major earthquake or a hurricane. Others have friends or relatives who died during catastrophes such as mass shooting events or the COVID-19 epidemic. In situations like these, the research shows that a woman has an increased risk of premature delivery and a low-birthweight infant (Harville et al., 2009; Lilliecreutz, Larén, Sydsjö, & Josefsson, 2016; Lobel et al., 2008). In some cases, a woman's partner may begin to abuse her when she is pregnant, or a partner may increase the severity of habitual abuse. These women are also at risk for premature delivery and a low-birthweight infant (Frieze, 2005).

In summary, a person's emotional reaction to pregnancy can range from excitement and anticipation to worry, a loss of identity, and grief. Consistent with Theme 4 of this book, the individual differences can be enormous. For most people, pregnancy is a complex blend of both pleasant and unpleasant reactions.

Attitudes Toward Pregnant Women

Most women experience three major gynecological events during their lifetime: menarche, pregnancy, and menopause. Menarche and menopause are highly private events, which women discuss only with intimate acquaintances. In contrast, pregnancy is public, especially in the last trimester. In fact, complete strangers often feel free to pat the stomach of a pregnant woman and offer unsolicited comments to her (Quindlen, 2008). Can you imagine these same people taking such liberties with a woman who was *not* pregnant?

According to research by Michelle Hebl and her colleagues (2007), people's attitudes toward pregnant women depend on the context. These researchers arranged for young women to go to a retail store, in two different contexts. In half of the situations, the woman was instructed to ask a store employee if she could apply for a job. In the other half, the woman was instructed to ask for help in choosing a gift for her sister.

The second variable in this study was whether or not the woman looked pregnant. Half the time in each situation, the woman wore a "pregnancy prosthesis," which had been professionally constructed to resemble the stomach of a woman who was 6 to 7 months pregnant. The other half of the time, the woman did not wear a prosthesis. Meanwhile, observers unobtrusively watched and coded the way that the store employee interacted with the woman.

In Chapter 2, we discussed two kinds of sexism that people are likely to display toward women. **Hostile sexism**, the more blatant kind of sexism, is based on the idea that women should be subservient to men and should "know their place." When the woman in this study asked to apply for a job, the store employees displayed significantly more hostile sexism to the woman who appeared pregnant than to the woman who did not appear pregnant. After all, the employees may have thought that this woman is pregnant, so she certainly should not be out looking for a job! Other studies have confirmed this bias against hiring a pregnant woman for a job (Bragger et al., 2002; Hackney et al., 2021).

Benevolent sexism, the more subtle kind of sexism, argues for women's special niceness and purity. When the woman in the study by Hebl and her colleagues (2007) asked for help in buying a gift, the employees showed significantly more benevolent sexism to the pregnant-looking woman than to the nonpregnant-looking woman. After all, the employees likely thought that this woman is pregnant, so she may need extra help. Naturally, a pregnant woman may appreciate help on some tasks. However, the store employees in this study were overly helpful and even patronizing. Other research confirms that people are especially likely to help a pregnant woman, for example, if she has dropped her keys (Walton et al., 1988).

Employment During Pregnancy

In past decades, White women in the United States and Canada typically stopped working outside the home once they became pregnant. However, Black women have historically had different expectations. Being a good mother never meant that a woman should stay at home full time (P. H. Collins, 1991; 2000). Similarly, across the world, pregnant women are often expected to work in the fields or to perform other physically exhausting tasks, sometimes until labor begins (S. Kitzinger, 1995).

In modern times in the United States, many women plan to have both a career and children, especially if the women are college graduates (Hoffnung, 2003, 2004, 2010). However, as you might expect from the research on hostile sexism, potential employers tend to avoid hiring a pregnant job applicant (Masser et al., 2007). Both female and male employers show this same tendency (Cunningham & Macan, 2007).

The research shows that employed pregnant women often continue at their jobs until shortly before their due date (Boston Women's Health Book Collective, 2008; Hung et al., 2002; Mozurkewich et al., 2000). Unfortunately, most U.S. women cannot take time off during late pregnancy or after the baby is born, without a loss of income (Blades & Rowe-Finkbeiner, 2006; Halpern et al., 2008).

According to the research, a woman's pregnancy is typically not affected if her job involves normal physical exertion (Hung et al., 2002; Klebanoff et al., 1990). However, she is slightly more likely to have a premature delivery if her job is physically demanding, if she works on the night shift, or if her job involves prolonged standing without the opportunity to sit down (Mozurkewich et al., 2000). Try Demonstration 10.1 to explore how job expectations for women vary depending on pregnancy status.

Demonstration **10.1**

Pregnancy Status and Ideal Job Descriptions

Do a quick Internet search of jobs advertised for women. For the first set of terms in your search, enter the phrase "jobs for pregnant women" and note the web pages that show up. What types of jobs are listed as ideal for pregnant women? How much do these jobs typically pay, according to the Bureau of Labor Statistics? How intellectually or physically challenging are these jobs?

(continues)

Demonstration 10.1 *(continued)*

For your second internet search, enter the phrase "jobs for women" and note the web pages that show up. What types of jobs are listed as ideal for women in general? How much do these jobs typically pay, according to the Bureau of Labor Statistics? How intellectually or physically challenging are these jobs?

Consider all the reasons why the jobs for "pregnant women" versus "women" might differ. How might the difference in pay for the jobs listed affect women's economic situation? What might be the factors that impact why these types of jobs differ?

Section Summary

Pregnancy

1. Pregnancy and childbirth receive surprisingly little attention in psychological research and in the media.
2. At the beginning of pregnancy, the fertilized egg implants itself in the tissue that lines the uterus.
3. Even in developed countries, many women do not receive prenatal care.
4. Although individual differences are great, several common physical reactions to pregnancy include weight gain, fatigue, and nausea.
5. Women vary greatly in their emotional reactions to pregnancy. Positive emotions include feelings of excitement and wonder, growing attachment, and the anticipated pleasure of motherhood.
6. Negative emotions include changeable emotions, concerns about physical appearance, health worries, and concern about other people's reactions.
7. An unknown percentage of pregnant women also experience a miscarriage. If life events are extremely stressful, there is an increased risk of premature delivery and a low-birthweight infant.
8. When people interact with a woman who looks pregnant, they tend to show hostile sexism if she is doing something considered nontraditional, such as applying for a job. They show benevolent sexism if she is doing something traditional, such as shopping for a gift.
9. Potential employers are relatively unlikely to hire a pregnant job applicant.
10. Most women can work outside the home without affecting their pregnancy; however, a physically demanding job and nonstandard work hours are associated with a slightly higher risk of premature delivery.

10-2 Childbirth

Learning Objectives

To explain how the childbirth process impacts people physically, socially, and psychologically, you can …

10-2-1   Explain what happens to people's bodies during the process of childbirth.

10-2-2   Discuss the positive and negative impacts of cesarean delivery on the physical health of mothers.

10-2-3   Describe how cultural and social factors affect women's experiences during childbirth.

10-2-4   Identify factors that can improve the psychological experience of childbirth for people.

Women in the United States currently have an average of 2.1 children, and Canadian women have an average of 1.5 children (Livingston, 2018; Worldometer, 2020). Even though childbirth is so common, psychologists virtually ignore this important topic. Interesting questions, such as women's emotions during childbirth, are rarely asked. In fact, most of our information comes from nursing journals, such as *Birth*. Let's consider the biology of childbirth, cesarean births, social factors affecting the childbirth experience, and emotional reactions to childbirth. Then we'll discuss some modern practices that are likely to improve women's childbirth experiences.

The Biology of Childbirth

Labor for childbirth begins when the uterus starts to contract strongly. The labor period is divided into three stages. During the first stage, the uterus contracts about every 5 minutes. Also, the dilation of the cervix increases to about 10 centimeters (4 inches), a process that may last anywhere from a few hours to at least a day (L. L. Alexander et al., 2021; Feeney et al., 2001).

The second stage of labor lasts from a few minutes to several hours. The contractions move the baby farther down the vagina. When a woman is encouraged to push during this second stage, she usually says that this is the most positive part of labor (Boston Women's Health Book Collective, 2008; Kitzinger, 2003). Women report feelings of strong pressure and stretching during this stage. The contractions often become extremely painful and stressful (Soet et al., 2003). This stage ends when the baby is born. The photograph below illustrates the end of the second stage of labor.

The third stage of labor, which usually lasts less than 20 minutes, is clearly an anticlimax. The uterus continues to contract, which separates the placenta from the uterine wall. The placenta is then expelled along with some other tissue that had surrounded the fetus (Kitzinger, 2003). The levels of estrogen and progesterone drop during this third stage, so that both of them are drastically lower than they were several hours earlier.

Birth normally happens after 40 weeks' gestation. A **preterm birth** (also called a **premature birth**) is defined as less than 37 weeks' gestation; a preterm birth places a child at risk for medical complications. The research in the United States shows that women with little education, women experiencing high levels of stress, and women who are very thin are at risk for a preterm birth. Also, Black women are almost twice as likely as White, Latina, and Asian American mothers to have a preterm birth. After adjusting for factors such as the age of the mother and her level of education, Black women are still more likely than other women to have a preterm birth. Researchers have found that these disparities likely result from differences in health prior to pregnancy, as well as differences in stress level during pregnancy and exposure to systemic racial discrimination (Alhusen, Bower, Epstein, & Sharps, 2016; Giscombé & Lobel, 2005; R. L. Goldenberg & Culhane, 2005; Haas et al., 2005).

Cesarean Births

Currently, cesarean births constitute about 32% of all deliveries in the United States and about 28% in Canada (OECD, 2021). In a **cesarean birth** (pronounced sih-*zare*-ee-un; often called a **cesarean section** or a **C-section**), the physician makes an incision through the woman's abdomen and into the uterus to deliver the baby.

Some cesarean sections are necessary if a vaginal delivery would be risky— for example, because the baby's head is larger than the mother's pelvis (L. L. Alexander et al., 2021). However, a C-section carries health risks for both a mother and the baby (R. Walker et al., 2002). A C-section can also be a traumatic experience (Johnston-Robledo & Barnack, 2004). Women who have had cesarean births tend to have more negative perceptions of both their birth experiences and their newborn infants (Lobel & DeLuca, 2007).

Critics argue that the rate of C-sections is high because they are more convenient for the medical staff and other similar reasons (M. C. Klein, 2004; Young, 2003). The research shows that the C-section rate can be reduced when hospitals adopt appropriate precautions (Chaillet & Dumont, 2007).

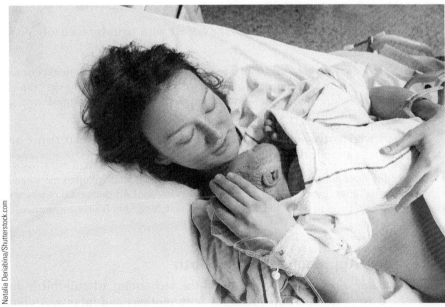

Natalia Deriabina/Shutterstock.com

A childbirth scene, showing the end of the second stage of labor.

Social Factors Affecting the Childbirth Experience

A variety of factors can influence the health of both the mother and her newborn ("Challenging Cases," 2004; Hoyert et al., 2000). For example, a Canadian study by Gagnon and her colleagues (2007) showed that medical complications were less likely when a woman had just one nurse attending her throughout labor, rather than a sequence of different nurses. (Fortunately, this study controlled for the length of time that the woman was in labor.) Another study in a hospital in the African nation of Botswana reported that women required significantly less pain medication if they had been accompanied by a female relative during labor and delivery (Madi et al., 1999).

For women in many cultures—as diverse as Scandinavian countries and Mayan communities in Latin America—childbirth is considered a normal process rather than a medical achievement. In these cultures, women expect to have attendants with them during childbirth (DeLoache & Gottlieb, 2000; Klaus et al., 2002; Whelehan, 2001). Many hospitals in the United States now offer a doula *(doo-lah)* option. A **doula** is a woman experienced in childbirth who provides continuous support to a family throughout labor and delivery (Zeldes & Norsigian, 2008).

Emotional Reactions to Childbirth

Women's emotional reactions to the birth of their child can vary as widely as their reactions to pregnancy (Hoffnung, 1992; Johnston-Robledo & Barnack, 2004). For some women, childbirth can be a peak experience of feeling in tune with the birth. For instance, one woman described her intense joy when her firstborn arrived:

> When I saw him and heard him cry, I was overwhelmed with emotion, and when the nurse placed him in my arms I felt that I had *knowledge* of something very powerful that made life completely comprehensible. I remember feeling very light, as if every burden was lifted from me. (de Marneffe, 2004, pp. 93–94)

Another woman describes how she coped with pain by focusing on the child who would be born:

> I don't think one should focus on the pain, that women should have to experience pain. But in the pain there is an experience of being inward and involved in feeling the pain—not enjoying it but taking hold, enduring, or whatever you do to handle it—and knowing that it is going to produce a child. (Bergum, 1997, p. 41)

Fathers who participate in the birth of their child may also experience intense joy, as in this description provided by a new:

> I couldn't have imagined the incredibly powerful feelings that engulfed me when I saw Kevin slip out of Tanya. I was right there, and this was my son! All the next day whenever he began to cry or nurse, I was in tears. I'm still transfixed watching him. It's the most amazing experience I ever had. (C. P. Cowan & Cowan, 1992, p. 71)

Alternative Approaches to Childbirth

Impressive advances have been made in the technology of childbirth during the past 70 years. Death rates are now lower for both mothers and infants. An unfortunate side effect of this high-tech approach, however, is that births in hospitals may focus on expensive equipment, fetal monitoring, and sanitizing every part of the mother (Chalmers, 2002; Kitzinger, 2003; Wolf, 2001).

Many health-care advocates suggest that the childbirth experience should be made more comfortable and emotionally satisfying for women. Specifically, **natural childbirth** includes the following components (L. L. Alexander et al., 2021; Boston Women's Health Book Collective, 2008; Kitzinger, 2003; Simkin et al., 2008; Young, 2009):

1. Empathic health-care providers who can encourage a woman's sense of empowerment during pregnancy and childbirth.
2. Education about pregnancy and childbirth, to reduce fear and dispel myths.
3. Relaxation techniques and exercises designed to strengthen muscles.
4. Controlled breathing and other focusing techniques that can distract attention away from the pain of the contractions.
5. Social support throughout childbirth from the baby's father, the mother's partner, or a person trained as a caregiver.

The natural-childbirth approach also emphasizes that the vast majority of births are normal. During labor and delivery, the pregnant woman deserves respectful care that encourages her to make informed choices about her labor and delivery. Here are some relevant components (Boston Women's Health Book Collective, 2008; M. C. Klein, 2004; Simkin et al., 2008; Young, 2009):

1. If she chooses, she can move around during labor, and she can sit upright during childbirth.
2. Anesthetics should not be used unless desired or necessary.
3. The physician should not artificially induce labor or perform a cesarean section simply because it may be more convenient.

Professionals who emphasize natural childbirth point out that this method does not eliminate pain. Childbirth is still a stressful experience. However, natural childbirth seems to provide a number of substantial benefits. The mothers report more positive attitudes, less anxiety, and reduced pain. They also require less medication (Chalmers, 2002; Young, 1982, 2009).

This approach to childbirth emphasizes that the mother's wishes should be taken seriously. This approach helps redistribute power, so that women in childbirth have more control over their own bodies. Women can make choices about how they want to give birth, rather than being passive and infantilized.

Basically, it is important for professionals to recognize that childbirth is an important psychological event in which a family structure is modified and new relationships are formed. Mothers, not technology, should be at the center of the childbirth experience (Chalmers, 2002; Dahlberg et al., 1999; Pincus, 2000).

Try Demonstration 10.2 to learn about the childbirth experiences of several people you know. Also, can you detect any changes in childbirth procedures for people with the most recent birth experiences?

Demonstration 10.2

Comparison of Childbirth Experiences

Locate people who had babies very recently, about 10 years ago, about 20 years ago, and in some year long before you were born. If possible, include your own mother or close relatives in your interview. Ask each of these people to describe their childbirth experience in as much detail as possible. After each person has finished, you may wish to ask some of the following questions, if they were not already answered:

1. Were you given any medication? If so, do you remember what kind?
2. How long did you stay in the hospital?
3. Did the baby stay with you in the room, or were they returned to the nursery after feedings?
4. Was a relative or friend allowed in the room while you were giving birth?
5. When you were in labor, were you encouraged to lie down?
6. Did you have "prepared childbirth"?
7. Do you recall any negative treatment from any of the hospital staff?
8. Were you treated like a competent adult?
9. Do you recall any positive treatment from any of the hospital staff?
10. If you could have changed any one thing about your childbirth experience, what would that have been?

Section Summary

Childbirth

1. The three stages in labor are dilation of the cervix, childbirth, and expulsion of the placenta. Social factors can influence the duration of labor and the amount of pain medication required.
2. Two potential problems during childbirth are preterm births and cesarean sections.
3. Social factors, such as the continuity of care and exposure to racism, can affect birth outcome.
4. Emotional reactions to childbirth vary widely. Some women report an intensely positive experience; others focus on coping with the pain. The baby's co-parent may also have intense emotional reactions.
5. Natural childbirth emphasizes factors such as empathic health-care providers, education, relaxation, focusing techniques, and social support; this approach generally produces a more satisfying childbirth experience.
6. The natural-childbirth approach also focuses on allowing women in labor to make relevant choices; it discourages the unnecessary use of high-technology procedures.

10-3 Motherhood

Learning Objectives

To summarize how motherhood impacts women's lives, you can …

10-3-1 Describe some common stereotypes about motherhood.

10-3-2 Summarize the negative experiences that some people have during the few weeks following childbirth.

10-3-3 Describe the positive factors associated with motherhood.

10-3-4 Compare and contrast motherhood experiences among Black, Latina/o, and Asian American parents.

10-3-5 Analyze how parents who identify as LGBTQ+ navigate the challenges and successes of parenthood.

10-3-6 Describe the benefits and challenges of breastfeeding for new parents.

10-3-7 Explain how post-partum depression differs from major depression and describe when it is most likely to occur.

10-3-8 Summarize the challenges of employment for people who are working outside the home following childbirth.

10-3-9 Identify the advantages and disadvantages for people who choose childfree lifestyles.

10-3-10 Describe the psychological experiences of people who experience infertility.

The word *motherhood* suggests some stereotypes that are well established, although contradictory; we'll consider these stereotypes in the first part of this section. Next we'll analyze how those stereotypes contrast with reality. We'll also examine the motherhood experience of two groups of women that differ from White heterosexual mothers: women of color and lesbian women. We'll then focus on two issues of concern to many women who have just given birth: postpartum depression and breastfeeding. The final topics in this chapter focus on the decision about returning to the workplace, the option of deciding not to have children, and the issue of infertility.

Stereotypes About Motherhood

For many people, the word *motherhood* inspires a rich variety of pleasant emotions such as warmth, strength, protectiveness, nurturance, devotion, and self-sacrifice (Ganong & Coleman, 1995; Johnston & Swanson, 2003b, 2008; Swanson & Johnston, 2003). According to the stereotype, motherhood is completely happy and satisfying, a notion that is perpetuated by media portrayals of the "Perfect Mother" (Johnston & Swanson, 2008; Simkin et al., 2008; J. Warner, 2005). Furthermore, the motherhood stereotype emphasizes that a woman's ultimate fulfillment is achieved by becoming a mother (P. J. Caplan, 2000, 2001; P. J. Caplan & Caplan, 2009; Johnston & Swanson, 2003b).

The motherhood stereotype also specifies that a mother will feel perfectly competent as soon as she sees her newborn, and her "natural" mothering skills will take over (Johnston

& Swanson, 2003b; Johnston-Robledo, 2000). She is also completely devoted to her family, and she shows no concern for her own personal needs (S. J. Douglas & Michaels, 2004; Ex & Janssens, 2000; Johnston & Swanson, 2003b). As you might imagine, many mothers feel guilty when they cannot live up to this impossible standard of perfect mothering (P. J. Caplan, 2001; S. J. Douglas & Michaels, 2004; J. Warner, 2005).

Cultural norms in the United States are actually ambivalent about motherhood, although the negative aspects are generally less prominent. The media exaggerate the faults of some mothers, while simultaneously ignoring their positive attributes. Chapter 2 suggested that women in classical mythology and religion are sometimes saints and sometimes villains. Stereotypes about mothers provide similar ideas of these two extremes (P. J. Caplan, 2001).

The Reality of Motherhood

Many lofty phrases pay tribute to motherhood, but the role is actually accorded low prestige (P. J. Caplan, 2000; Hoffnung, 1995, 2011). In reality, U.S. society considers money, power, and achievement to be much more prestigious than motherhood (J. Warner, 2005). It's clear that mothers do not receive the appreciation they deserve.

Furthermore, none of the stereotypes captures the rich variety of emotions that mothers actually experience. Columnist Anna Quindlen (2001) describes this perspective:

> My children have been the making of me as a human being, which does not mean that they have not sometimes been an overwhelming and mind-boggling responsibility … I love my children more than life itself. But just because you love people doesn't mean that taking care of them day in and day out isn't often hard, and sometimes even horrible. (Quindlen 2001a, p. 64)

Before you read further, try Demonstration 10.3, which we'll discuss later in this chapter. Let's now explore the reality of motherhood in more detail. We'll first consider a long list of negative factors and then examine the more abstract but intensely positive factors.

Demonstration 10.3

Infant Mortality Rate

Look at the list of 15 countries on page 333, and think about which ones are likely to have a low infant mortality rate (i.e., a low rate of an infant dying within the first year of life). All 15 countries have at least a reasonably good health-care system, and their infant mortality rates range between 3 and 7 infant deaths per 1,000 infants. Rate these countries, placing a 3 in front of the countries that you think would have the lowest rates, so they are the *safest* for infants. Place a 7 in front of the countries that you think would have the highest rates, so they are the *least safe* for infants. Continue rating the 15 countries, using a scale that ranges from 3 to 6. The answers appear at the end of the chapter.

(continues)

Demonstration 10.3 *(continued)*

	Australia		Japan		Belgium
_____	Australia	_____	Japan	_____	Belgium
_____	Greece	_____	France	_____	Czech Republic
_____	Cuba	_____	Sweden	_____	Ireland
_____	Israel	_____	Germany	_____	Italy
_____	Denmark	_____	United States	_____	Canada

Note: These data represent infant mortality rates for 2019, the most recent international data available.

Source: World Bank (2019).

Negative Factors

A newborn infant certainly creates pressures and stress for the mother. Many of these problems will seem relatively trivial when the infant is older (Hayden et al., 2006). However, here are some of the negative factors that women often mention during the first weeks after childbirth:

1. Child care is physically exhausting, and sleep deprivation is also common (Huston & Holmes, 2004; Simkin et al., 2008; J. F. Thompson et al., 2002). Because infant care takes so much time, new mothers often feel that they can accomplish very little other than taking care of the infant.

2. Roughly 40% of all infants in the United States are born to women who are not married (Martin, Hamilton, Osterman, & Driscoll, 2021). The father or co-parent (if any) may not live in the same house, and the mother may not have adequate income to raise children.

3. Co-parents who do live in the same home usually help much less with child rearing than mothers had expected. As we noted in Chapter 7, mothers usually take the major responsibility for child care, including unpleasant tasks such as changing diapers (Genesoni & Tallandini, 2009; Gjerdingen & Center, 2005; Rice & Else-Quest, 2006).

4. For several weeks after childbirth, women report that they feel leaky and dirty, coping with after-birth discharges. They are also likely to feel pain in the vaginal area, the uterus, and the breasts (Simkin et al., 2008).

5. New mothers seldom have training for the tasks of motherhood; they often report feeling incompetent. As a result, they may wonder why no one warned them about the difficulty of child care or how their life would change after the baby was born (Boston Women's Health Book Collective, 2008; Gager et al., 2002; J. Warner, 2005).

6. Pregnant women often create an idea of the glowing baby they expect to cuddle in their arms. In reality, babies cry much more than parents expect, and they do not smile until they are about 2 months old (Kail, 2010; Simkin et al., 2008).

7. Because parenting is done at home, mothers of newborns may have little contact with other adults (Johnston & Swanson, 2008). A single mother may have limited social interactions with other adults. This kind of isolation further encourages the marginalization of women, already an important issue throughout this book.

8. Because the biological parent's attention has shifted to the newborn, the baby's co-parent may feel neglected. Many mothers in heterosexual relationships comment that their male partners make them feel inadequate. However, parents and nonparents are equally positive about the quality of their marriage (Huston & Holmes, 2004).

9. Women feel disappointed in themselves because they do not match the standards of the ideal mother, the completely unselfish and perfect woman. Cultural norms portray that stereotype of motherhood—but no one really lives up to that stereotype (P. J. Caplan & Caplan, 2009; Quindlen, 2005).

10. People frequently blame mothers—more than co-parents—for most of the problems that infants and children may develop, such as aggressive behavior or school phobia (P. J. Caplan & Caplan, 2009).

However, the most horrifying of all these negative factors is that a large number of infants throughout the world die at an early age. The most common measure is called the **infant mortality rate**, which is the annual number of deaths prior to the first birthday, per 1,000 live births. For instance, in Benin, Burkina Faso, Chad, Nigeria, Sierra Leone, and other sub-Saharan African countries, more than 50 out of every 1,000 infants die before their first birthday (World Bank, 2021). Globally, the infant mortality rate is 29 deaths per 1,000 live births (World Health Organization, 2018). Some so-called developed countries also have a much higher child death rate than most people expect. Check your responses to Demonstration 10.3 against the answers on page 348. Did you guess that the United States has the worst record among the 15 countries on this list?

Furthermore, the maternal mortality risk in the world's least developed countries due to complications of pregnancy and childbirth, is 40 times higher than the maternal mortality risk in Europe and almost 60 times higher than the rate in Australia and New Zealand (World Health Organization, 2019).

Positive Factors

Motherhood also has its positive side, although these qualities may not predominate early in motherhood. Some women discover that an important positive consequence of motherhood is a sense of their own strength. As one woman told me, "I discovered that I felt very empowered and confident, like, 'Don't mess with me! I've given birth!'" (T. Napper, personal communication, 1998). Sadly, we often focus so much on childbirth's negative consequences for women that we fail to explore the life-enhancing consequences. One mother described her new perspective:

> I had a child at 46. Before that, although I loved being with other people's children, anytime something went wrong and the child irritated me, I would think to myself, How could I ever stand the full-time responsibility of being a mother? Somehow, becoming a mother changed that. There is an intangible, indescribable bond intrinsic to the relationship, which in the long run transcends the petty everyday irritating occurrences. (Boston Women's Health Book Collective, 2005, p. 311)

Parents often point out that a child can be fun and interesting, especially when they can perceive the world from a new viewpoint, through the perspective of a child. In addition, one mother explained how her children developed an important part of her personality: "My kids have opened up emotions in me that I never knew were possible; they have slowed down my life happily" (Villani, 1997, p. 135). Many women suggest that having children helped them to identify and develop their ability to nurture (Bergum, 1997).

In heterosexual relationships, many fathers are very competent in caring for their children (R. C. Barnett & Rivers, 2004; Deutsch, 1999). Fathers also express their admiration and affection for their partner. In these families, marital satisfaction increases after children are born (Shapiro et al., 2000). These couples typically say that they enjoy the sense of unity and feeling like a family (Feeney et al., 2001).

Summarizing the comments of many mothers, Hoffnung (1995) wrote:

> The role of mother brings with it benefits as well as limitations. Children affect parents in ways that lead to personal growth, enable reworking of childhood conflicts, build flexibility and empathy, and provide intimate, loving human connections.... They expand their caretakers' worlds by their activity levels, their imaginations, and their inherently appealing natures. Although motherhood is not enough to fill an entire life, for most mothers, it is one of the most meaningful experiences in their lives. (Hoffnung 1995, p. 174)

If you were to ask a mother of an infant to list the positive and negative qualities of motherhood, the negative list would probably contain more items and more specific details. Most mothers find that the positive side of motherhood is more abstract, more difficult to describe, and yet more intense (Feeney et al., 2001). The drudgery of dirty diapers is much easier to talk about than the realization that this complete human being was once part of your own body, and now this baby breathes and gurgles and hiccups independently.

Also, shortly after birth, babies develop ways of communicating with other humans. The delights of a baby's first tentative smile are undeniable. An older baby can interact even more engagingly with adults by making appropriate eye contact and conversational noises. Most parents also enjoy watching their babies develop new skills. They also value the intimate, caring relationships they develop with their children (Feeney et al., 2001). Motherhood has numerous joyous aspects. Unfortunately, societies have not yet devised creative ways to diminish the negative aspects so that we can appreciate the joys more completely.

Motherhood and Women of Color

The U.S. Census Bureau (Hamilton, 2021) provides information for each major ethnic group about the average number of children that a woman would be expected to have in her lifetime. (Keep in mind that many women in each group do not have any children.) These ethnic-group differences are smaller than many people expect: 2.3 for White women, 2.5 for Black women, 2.2 for Asian American women, 2.5 for Native American women, and 2.6 for Latina women (Livingston, 2015).

The data on family size may be fairly similar, but the motherhood experiences for women of color often differ from White mothers' experiences.

For example, Hoffnung (2010) conducted a study of women who had graduated from several East Coast colleges. Part of her study compared White women with women of color, who were Black, Latina, or Asian American. Fourteen years later, the women of color who were mothers were significantly more likely than White mothers to be employed full time.

In general, however, mothers who are not White are surprisingly underrepresented in the social science research. Women of color are also missing from the articles in popular magazines that idealize mothers (Johnston & Swanson, 2008). Additionally, intersectional perspectives on motherhood suggest that women of color are disproportionately impacted by structural racism in U.S. society that promotes antinatalist ideas that they should *not* become mothers (Fikslin, 2021). Women of color in the United States also have two to three times higher rates of infant and maternal mortality than White mothers (Petersen et al., 2019; Urban Indian Health Institute, 2016).

Fortunately, we do have some information about the role of extended families. In Black families, for example, the networks of grandmothers, aunts, siblings, and close family friends are especially important among mothers (Kirk & Okazawa-Rey, 2001; H. P. McAdoo, 2002; Parke, 2004). However, the cultural expectations of caregiving and being a "strong" family member can sometimes cause Black women stress in family relationships (Nelson, Cardemil, & Adeoye, 2016).

The extended family is also important for Latina/o families (Cisneros, 2001; Harwood et al., 2002; Matsumoto & Juang, 2004). For instance, many immigrants from Latin America move in with relatives who are already established in the United States. As a result, young Latina/o children are likely to be cared for by members of their extended family (Parke, 2004).

Some ethnic groups emphasize values in motherhood that would not be central for White mothers. For example, many Native American mothers emphasize the continuity of generations, with grandmothers being central to childbirth and caregiving (A. Adams, 1995).

Asian American perspectives on motherhood depend on the family's country of origin and the number of generations that the family has lived in North America (Parke, 2004). However, cultural beliefs may conflict with the U.S. medical model when women from Asia emigrate to the United States. For instance, Hmong women who have come to the United States from Southeast Asia are uncomfortable with the prospect of being examined by a male obstetrician when they are pregnant (Symonds, 1996).

Lesbian Mothers

Lesbian women become mothers by a variety of pathways. The largest number are women who had a child in a heterosexual relationship and later identified as lesbian women. Other lesbian women adopt their children. Still others decide to conceive by donor insemination, for example through a sperm bank (Pawelski et al., 2006; Peplau & Fingerhut, 2007). As you might imagine, it's difficult to estimate how many lesbian women are raising children. According to data from the U.S. Census Bureau, about 15% of same-sex parents in the United States are raising children under the age of 18 (Bajko, 2020). An estimated 12% of lesbian mothers living in Canada are raising children under the age of 16 (Statistics Canada, 2016).

Several studies have compared the parenting styles of lesbian mothers and heterosexual mothers. The two groups are similar in characteristics such as their parenting quality, enthusiasm about child rearing, warmth toward children, and self-esteem (Golombok et al., 2003; S. M. Johnson & O'Connor, 2002; C. J. Patterson, 2003; Pawelski et al., 2006). However, compared to heterosexual mothers, lesbian mothers in one study were more likely to engage in imaginative play with their children and less likely to spank them (Golombok et al., 2003). Additionally, children raised by lesbian mothers tend to perform better in school (Mazrekaj, De Witte, & Cabus, 2020).

Other research—including a meta-analysis by M. Allen and Burrell (2002)—has compared the adjustment of children raised in lesbian households and children raised in heterosexual households. According to studies in the United States, Canada, and England, the children in the two groups are similar in characteristics such as intelligence, development of gender roles, self-esteem, psychological well-being, social adjustment, popularity with peers, and positive feelings about their family (Foster, 2005; Fulcher et al., 2008; Golombok et al., 2003; Herek, 2006; S. M. Johnson & O'Connor, 2002; C. J. Patterson, 2003; Pawelski et al., 2006; Savin-Williams & Esterberg, 2000; Stacey & Biblarz, 2001; M. Sullivan, 2004).

Our students sometimes ask whether children raised by lesbian women have trouble being accepted by the wider community, especially because of the problem of sexual prejudice. Although some children feel uncomfortable talking about their mothers' sexual orientation, most are positive about their mothers' nontraditional relationships (S. M. Johnson & O'Connor, 2001; Pawelski et al., 2006). Many children also report that they are more accepting of all kinds of diversity, compared to the children of heterosexual parents (D. Johnson & Piore, 2004; C. J. Patterson, 2003; Peplau & Beals, 2004).

As we have learned, the research confirms that children raised by lesbian women are well adjusted and that they do not differ substantially from children raised by heterosexual parents. In light of these findings, professional organizations have emphasized that the courts should not discriminate against lesbian mothers in custody cases and that lesbian women should be allowed to adopt children (e.g., American Academy of Pediatrics, 2002a, 2002b; American Psychological Association, 2004).

However, in many parts of the United States, lesbian parents also face discrimination in numerous ways that heterosexual parents would never anticipate. For example, a hospital security guard refused to let two lesbian parents visit their child in the pediatric ward of a California hospital. As the guard said, the regulations allowed "only parents" on the ward (M. Sullivan, 2004, p. 177).

Breastfeeding

Currently, about 84% of mothers in the United States breastfeed their newborn infants, and approximately 58% continue to nurse their babies for at least 6 months (CDC,

iStockPhoto/JLco - Julia Amaral

Numerous studies demonstrate that children raised by lesbian mothers are similar in psychological adjustment to children raised by heterosexual mothers.

2017). Mothers who breastfeed are likely to be better educated than mothers who bottle feed (Heck et al., 2003; J. A. Scott et al., 2004; Slusser & Lange, 2002). Mothers who are in their 30s or older are also more likely than younger mothers to breastfeed (Chalmers et al., 2009; Johnston-Robledo & Fred, 2008; J. A. Scott et al., 2004; Slusser & Lange, 2002). According to surveys, White and Asian American mothers are most likely to breastfeed, Latina mothers are less likely, and Black mothers are least likely to breastfeed their infants (Kruse et al., 2005; R. Li & Grummer-Strawn, 2002; Slusser & Lange, 2002).

As you might expect, women are more likely to nurse successfully if their friends and the hospital staff members are knowledgeable, supportive, and encouraging (Avery et al., 2009; Kruse et al., 2005; Zeldes & Norsigian, 2008). Early encouragement in breastfeeding is also more likely in hospitals that favor vaginal births, rather than cesarean sections (Rowe-Murray & Fisher, 2002). However, many mothers with cesarean sections nurse their babies, as described by one mother:

> I'd sit on the couch, scoop him up ... and place him on a fat cushion by my side. I'd tuck his feet behind me and lie his head to my breast, and he would latch right on. These first moments of sucking brought such a physical and emotional release. I'd sigh and stare into his eyes or close my eyes and drift. Eventually he'd pop off my nipple, give a contented "ah," and fall asleep. (Boston Women's Health Book Collective, 2008, p. 250)

Health-care professionals have devised programs to encourage mothers to breastfeed. For example, mothers in lower-income groups are more likely to breastfeed if they have received guidance from women who had successfully breastfed their own infants (e.g., Ineichen et al., 1997; Schafer et al., 1998).

Mothers who breastfeed typically report that nursing is a pleasant experience of warmth, sharing, and openness (Houseman, 2003; Lawrence, 1998). In contrast, mothers who bottle feed their babies are more likely to emphasize that bottle feeding is convenient and trouble free.

The research demonstrates that human milk is better for human infants than is a formula based on cow's milk. After all, evolution has encouraged the development of a liquid that is ideally designed for efficient digestion.

Breast milk also protects against allergies, diarrhea, infections, and other diseases (American Academy of Pediatrics, 2001, 2005; Kitzinger, 2003; Simkin et al., 2008). In addition, breastfeeding offers some health benefits for mothers, such as reducing the incidence of breast cancer and ovarian cancer (Simkin et al., 2008; Lawrence, 1998; Slusser & Lange, 2002).

Because of the health benefits, health professionals typically encourage breastfeeding. This precaution is especially important in developing countries where sanitary conditions make bottle feeding hazardous. However, health professionals should not make mothers feel inadequate or guilty if they need to bottle feed their babies (Else-Quest et al., 2003; Johnston-Robledo & Fred, 2008; Zeldes & Norsigian, 2008). Some mothers are unable to breastfeed their infants, which unfortunately can lead to stigma regarding bottle feeding (Moss-Racusin, Schofield, Brown, & O'Brien, 2020).

Postpartum Disturbances

U.S. cultural norms expect mothers to be delighted with their young infants, anticipating a blissful motherhood. However, a significant number of women develop psychological disturbances during the **postpartum period**, which extends from 0 to 6 weeks after birth. Take a moment to review the list of ten negative factors on pages 333–334. Imagine that you are a new mother who is exhausted from childbirth, and you are also experiencing most of these negative factors. In addition, suppose that your infant is not yet old enough to smile delightfully. Under these stressful circumstances, you can easily imagine how a mother might experience these emotional problems (Mauthner, 2002).

Two different kinds of postpartum problems occur relatively often. The most common kind of problem is called **postpartum blues** or **baby blues**, a short-lasting change in mood that usually occurs during the first 10 days after childbirth, and it occurs in many different cultures. According to some estimates, at least half of new mothers in the United States experience postpartum blues (Boston Women's Health Book Collective, 2008; G. E. Robinson & Stewart, 2001). Common symptoms include crying, sadness, insomnia, irritability, anxiety, and a lack of confidence, as well as feeling overwhelmed (O'Hara & Stuart, 1999). Postpartum blues are probably a result of the emotional letdown following the excitement of childbirth, combined with the sleeplessness and other life changes that a new baby brings. Most women report that the symptoms are gone within a few days. However, it is important for women to be well informed about this problem. Talking with other mothers is often helpful (Boston Women's Health Book Collective, 2008; Mauthner, 2002; G. E. Robinson & Stewart, 2001).

Postpartum depression is a more intense and serious condition, typically involving feelings of extreme sadness, exhaustion, sleep disturbances, despair, lack of interest in enjoyable activities, loss of interest in the baby, and feelings of guilt (Boston Women's Health Book Collective, 2008; Kendall-Tackett, 2005; Simkin et al., 2008). Postpartum depression usually begins to develop within 6 months after childbirth, and it may last for many months (G. E. Robinson & Stewart, 2001).

Postpartum depression is also associated with physical issues, such as fatigue, nausea, and backaches (Webb et al., 2008). An additional consideration is that depressed mothers tend to interact less effectively with their infants, placing them at risk for health and psychological issues (Bartlett et al., 2004; P. S. Kaplan et al., 2002; Kendall-Tackett, 2005).

Postpartum depression affects about 10 to 15% of women who have given birth (P. S. Kaplan et al., 2002; Kendall-Tackett, 2005; L. J. Miller, 2002). It is also reported in many different cultures (e.g., des Rivieres-Pigeon et al., 2004; E. Lee, 2003; Wang et al., 2005; Webster et al., 2003). One U.S. mother described her struggle with postpartum depression:

> To not have any hope. ... It's like you're suffocating or you're in a little prison. ... And to wake up and to dread the day, I think, was the most hardest for me. To get up and go, "Oh, my God, I've got to go through another day." I mean, I never thought about killing myself. I never had those thoughts. I just thought I wanted to dig a big hole and have no one ever find me. (Mauthner, 2002, p. 189)

Postpartum depression is similar to other kinds of depression that are not associated with children. In fact, it may be the same as other forms of depression (G. E. Robinson & Stewart, 2001; Stanton et al., 2002). We will explore depression in more detail in Chapter 12. Fortunately, most cases of depression can be successfully treated, so it is important for women to discuss this issue with a professional (Boston Women's Health Book Collective, 2008).

Social factors are also important, according to research in the United States, Canada, and Europe. For instance, women who experience major life stress during pregnancy are more likely to develop postpartum depression. As a result, women who are socioeconomically disadvantaged are at risk (L. J. Miller, 2002; Simkin et al., 2008).

Women who lack social support from a partner, relatives, or friends are also likely to develop postpartum depression (Feeney et al., 2001; G. E. Robinson & Stewart, 2001; Thorp et al., 2004). In contrast, researchers found a low rate of postpartum depression among Hmong women who had emigrated from Southeast Asia to a community in Wisconsin (S. Stewart & Jambunathan, 1996). The researchers also noted that these women received high levels of support from their spouses and family members in this community.

The origins of both postpartum blues and postpartum depression are controversial. We noted that the levels of progesterone and estrogen drop sharply during the last stages of childbirth. Women's popular magazines are likely to emphasize these hormonal factors as a cause of psychological conditions (R. Martínez et al., 2000). However, the relationship between hormonal levels and postpartum disorders is weak and inconsistent (Mauthner, 2002; G. E. Robinson & Stewart, 2001). In contrast, as we just discussed, social factors do play an important role in postpartum disturbances.

Keep in mind that many women do not experience either the blues or depression following the birth of their baby. Earlier in this chapter, we noted that some women experience little discomfort and few psychological problems during pregnancy. In Chapter 4, we suggested that many women do not have major premenstrual or menstrual symptoms, and we'll learn in Chapter 14 that most women pass through menopause without any trauma. In short, women differ widely from one another. The various phases in a woman's reproductive life do not inevitably bring emotional or physical problems.

Employment Following Childbirth

Should women work outside the home after the birth of a child? The popular media and public opinion basically suggest a "no win" dilemma. If you have a young child, you should *definitely* stay home and be a full-time mother. However—especially if you are well educated—you should *definitely* work outside the home, rather than wasting all that education by not living up to your potential (Boston Women's Health Book Collective, 2008; Johnston & Swanson, 2003a, 2004; Rice & Else-Quest, 2006).

There's a further complication: Suppose that a woman does decide to work outside the home after she has given birth. People often judge employed mothers to be less competent than employed women who have no children (Correll et al., 2007; Heilman & Okimoto, 2008; Cuddy & Fiske, 2004).

Earlier in the chapter, we examined the bias against a pregnant woman in the workplace. The bias persists when a woman seeks employment after the baby is born. Additionally, the stigma associated with childbirth can often lead to women leaving the workforce following the birth of children, if they are already employed (Fox & Quinn, 2015).

We have seen abundant evidence for Theme 4 throughout this chapter: During pregnancy, childbirth, and motherhood, women differ widely from one another. Marjorie H. Klein and her colleagues (1998) discovered another aspect of individual variation: Women differ widely in their reactions to combining motherhood and employment. These researchers surveyed 570 women in two Midwestern cities; each woman had recently given birth. Overall, they found that the length of the women's maternity leave—before returning to work—was not correlated with mental health measures such as depression, anxiety, anger, and self-esteem.

However, Klein and her colleagues (1998) then conducted a separate analysis for women who considered their employment an important part of their identity. In general, these women tended to be more depressed if they had a relatively long maternity leave. In other words, staying home with a baby on an extended maternity leave may actually be harmful for those women who really value their work role.

In another part of the same study, Klein and her colleagues (1998) compared the mental health of three groups of women: homemakers, women employed part time, and women employed full time. One year after childbirth, these three groups of women did not differ on measures of depression, anxiety, anger, or self-esteem.

We learned in Chapter 7 that children do not experience increased problems if someone other than their mother takes care of them. Similarly, mothers who choose to work outside the home are no more likely than other mothers to experience mental health issues. In fact, women who are engaged in more than one role (e.g., mother and employee) often have better physical and psychological health than women who have only one role (R. C. Barnett & Hyde, 2001). In short, mothers ideally would assess their own personal situations and preferences so that they can make informed decisions about this crucial question.

Unfortunately, there's another important factor related to the issue of employment following childbirth. Employees in the United States are entitled to take up to 12 weeks of maternity leave if they meet specified criteria. However, they receive *unpaid* leave. Among 41 rich industrialized countries, the United States is the only country that does not offer or require paid maternity leave (Livingston & Thomas, 2019). The informed decisions that mothers make—following childbirth—are clearly limited by the reality of family income.

Deciding Whether to Have Children

During the 1970s, most married women did not need to make a conscious decision about whether to have a child. Almost all married women anticipated becoming mothers, with little awareness that they actually had a choice. However, attitudes have changed. In the United States, for example, about 14% of women will never have children (Miller, 2018; Simon, 2008; Warren & Tyagi, 2003). Some of these women may choose not to have children because they are unmarried or they do not want to be mothers. Still other women may not have children because they, or their partners, are infertile.

Let's consider how other people view these "childfree" women. We'll also explore some advantages and disadvantages of deciding not to have children.

Demonstration **10.4**

Attitudes Toward Childfree Women

For this demonstration, you will need some volunteers—ideally, at least five people for each of the two scenarios described. Read the following paragraph to half of the volunteers, either individually or in a group.

> Kendra and Isaiah are an attractive couple in their mid-forties. They will be celebrating their twentieth wedding anniversary next year. They met in college

---

(continues)

Demonstration 10.4 *(continued)*

and were married the summer after they received their undergraduate degrees. Isaiah is now a very successful attorney. Kendra, who earned her Ph.D. degree in social psychology, is a full-time professor at the university. Kendra and Isaiah have no children. They are completely satisfied with their present family size because they planned to have no children even before they were married. Because both have nearby relatives, they often have family get-togethers. Kendra and Isaiah also enjoy many activities and hobbies. Some of their favorites are biking, gardening, and taking small excursions to explore nearby towns and cities.

After reading this paragraph, pass out copies of the rating sheet on page 343 and ask volunteers to rate their impression of Kendra.

Follow the same procedure for the other half of the volunteers. However, for the sentence "Kendra and Isaiah have no children" and the following sentence, substitute this passage: " Kendra and Isaiah have two children. They are completely satisfied with their present family size because they planned to have two children even before they were married."

Compare the average responses of the two groups. Do they rate Kendra as more fulfilled if she is described as having two children? Does she have a happier and more rewarding life?

1	2	3	4	5
Less fulfilled				More fulfilled

1	2	3	4	5
Very unhappy				Very happy

1	2	3	4	5
Unrewarding life				Rewarding life

Source: With kind permission from Springer Science+Business Media: *Sex Roles*, "Gendered Norms for Family Size, Employment, and Occupation: Are There Personal Costs for Violating Them?" Vol. 36, 1997, p. 211, Karla Ann Mueller.

Attitudes Toward Women Choosing Not to Have Children

Many people believe that all women should have children, a viewpoint called **compulsory motherhood** or **pronatalism** (Boston Women's Health Book Collective, 2008; Coltrane, 1998; Mollen, 2014). A few decades ago, a young woman who did not plan to have children would have been viewed very negatively. Unfortunately, attitudes toward childfree women are still somewhat negative (Bays, 2017; P. J. Caplan, 2001; Morison et al., 2016; Mueller & Yoder, 1999; Simon, 2008).

For example, Demonstration 10.4 is a modified version of two scenarios tested by Karla Mueller and Janice Yoder (1997). These researchers found statistically significant differences in the way that college students in Wisconsin rated the women in the two scenarios. Table 10.1 displays the results on the three dimensions included in this demonstration. The ratings for the childfree woman would probably be somewhat more negative in a general population that includes nonstudents (Simon, 2008).

Married couples also report that they receive advice about the ideal family size from many different people, including their parents, friends, and acquaintances (Boston Women's Health Book Collective, 2008; Casey, 1998; Mueller & Yoder, 1999). Childfree couples are informed that they are self-centered and too career-oriented. Couples with one child are told—incorrectly—that an only child will face emotional problems. Couples with four or more children are told that they are mentally unstable, because they won't be able to pay enough attention to each child (Blayo & Blayo, 2003; Kantrowitz, 2004).

Note that cultural norms seem to admire only a narrow range of options. A couple may have two or three children, but many people will criticize them for fewer than two or more than three. Interestingly, however, Mueller and Yoder (1999) also studied married couples and found that family size was not correlated with the couples' actual satisfaction. In other words, those with no children were just as happy as those with one, two, three, or more children.

Advantages and Disadvantages of Being Childfree

Married couples provide many reasons for not wanting to have a child (Boston Women's Health Book Collective, 2008; P. J. Caplan & Caplan, 2009; Ceballo et al., 2004; Jokela et al., 2009; Megan, 2000; Townsend, 2003; Warren & Tyagi, 2003):

1. Parenthood is an irrevocable decision; you can't take children back to the store for a refund.
2. Some couples are afraid that they will not be good parents. This fear is encouraged by the myth of the Perfect Mother.

TABLE **10.1**

Ratings of a Childfree Woman and a Woman with Two Children, on Three Different Characteristics

	Rating of Woman in Scenario	
Characteristic	Childfree Woman	Woman with Two Children
Fulfillment	4.0	4.4
Happiness	3.5	4.3
Rewarding life	3.5	4.2

Note: 5 is the highest level of the attribute.
Source: With kind permission from Springer Science+Business Media: *Sex Roles*, "Gendered Norms for Family Size, Employment, and Occupation: Are There Personal Costs for Violating Them?" Vol. 36, 1997, p. 216, Karla Ann Mueller.

3. Parenthood is extremely stressful. It's a well-kept secret, but parents actually report more symptoms of depression than nonparents who are the same age (Simon, 2008).
4. Some couples realize that they don't have the energy required to raise children.
5. Some couples realize that they genuinely do not enjoy children.
6. Some couples are reluctant to give up a satisfying and flexible lifestyle for a more child-centered orientation.
7. Children can interfere with educational and vocational plans.
8. Raising children can be extremely expensive, especially if they will attend college.
9. People can spend time with other people's children, even if they don't have children of their own.
10. Some couples do not want to bring children into a world threatened by overpopulation, nuclear war, terrorism, climate change, structural inequality and racism, and other serious global problems.

Still, people who are enthusiastic about parenthood provide many reasons for having children (Boston Women's Health Book Collective, 2008; Ceballo et al., 2004; de Marneffe, 2004; Jokela et al., 2009; McMahon, 1995; Simon, 2008):

1. Parenthood offers a lifelong relationship of love, connection, nurturance, and social interactions with other human beings; children can enrich people's lives.
2. Parents have a unique chance to be responsible for someone's education and training; in raising a child, they can clarify their own values and instill them in their child.
3. Parents can watch their children grow into socially responsible adults who can help the world become a better place.
4. Parenthood is challenging; it offers people the opportunity to be creative and learn about their own potential.
5. Through parenting, people can fulfill their relationship with their spouse, and they can become a "family."
6. Children can be a source of fun, pleasure, and pride.

Infertility

You probably know a woman who has wanted to have children, but pregnancy does not seem to be a possibility. For example, one woman wrote:

> How had having a baby, getting pregnant, become such an obsession with me? All I could think was that there must be a mechanism that clicks in once you try to get pregnant that, instead of allowing you to accept that you cannot, compels you to keep trying, no matter what the odds or cost. ... I never would have suspected, until I tapped into it, just how powerful the desire could be. (Alden, 2000, p. 107)

By the current definition, **infertility** is the failure to conceive after 1 year of heterosexual intercourse without using contraception (Carroll, 2005; Pasch, 2001). An estimated 10 to 15% of couples in the United States are infertile (Beckman, 2006; A. L. Nelson & Marshall, 2004). In the United States, women are especially likely to have infertility problems if they have had infections that can damage the reproductive system, as well as poor medical care (Mundy, 2007). Women who are between 30 and 40 years of age are less likely than younger women to become pregnant. However, women older than 35 are now more likely than in previous decades to become pregnant, often with reproductive technology (Gregory, 2007; Lobo, 2005).

Some women manage to reconcile their initial sadness. Consider the conclusion reached by the woman in the previous quote: "It came to me that it really was a choice between two good things—having a child and not having a child. Our life without a child seemed good to me. I caught a glimpse that it was what was right for us, for the best" (Alden, 2000, p. 111).

Some women have looked forward to children as a central part of their lives. They experience stress and a real sense of loss, and they report that people give them unsolicited advice about fertility options (Perry, 2005). However, comparisons of fertile and infertile women show that the two groups do not differ in their relationship satisfaction or self-esteem (Beckman, 2006; Stanton et al., 2002).

Still, the research does suggest that women who are infertile—and want to have children—have higher levels of distress and anxiety than women who are fertile (Ceballo, Graham, & Hart, 2015; L. L. Alexander et al., 2021; Stanton et al., 2002). We need to emphasize an important point: According to researchers, the infertility causes the distress and anxiety. Distress and anxiety do not cause couples to become infertile. Also, individual differences in psychological reactions to infertility are substantial, consistent with Theme 4 of this book (Parry, 2005; Raque-Bogdan & Hoffman, 2015; Stanton et al., 2002).

One source of psychological strain for people facing infertility is that they may live with the constant hope, "Maybe next month. ..." They may see themselves as "not yet pregnant," rather than as permanently childless. As a result, they may feel unsettled, caught between hopefulness and mourning the child they will not have.

Women of color face an additional source of strain when they experience infertility. In one study, Ceballo (1999) interviewed married Black women who had tried to become pregnant for many years. These women often struggled with racist health-care providers who seemed astonished that a Black woman would be infertile. As these women explained, White women seem to believe that infertility is "a White thing" because they believe that Black women are highly sexualized, promiscuous, and fertile. One woman pointed out how she began to internalize these racist messages; she almost believed that she was "the only Black woman walking the face of the earth that cannot have a baby." Unfortunately, psychologists have often neglected to study the impact of infertility on the lives of women of color (Ceballo et al., 2015; Pasch, 2001; Stanton et al., 2002).

Many couples who are concerned about infertility decide to consult health-care professionals for an "infertility workup," which includes a medical examination of both partners. About half of couples who seek medical treatment will eventually become parents (A. L. Nelson & Marshall, 2004). They will use one of a wide variety of reproductive technologies, which are often stressful and extremely expensive. Health insurance plans rarely cover these costs (Beckman & Harvey, 2005; Gregory, 2007, Mundy, 2007).

However, many women will not become pregnant, even after medical treatment, or they may experience miscarriages. Eventually, some will choose to adopt (Ceballo et al., 2004; Gibbons et al., 2006). Others will decide to pursue other interests. A woman who might have focused on the regret of infertility in earlier eras can now shift her emphasis away from what is not in her life, so that she can fully appreciate the many positive options available in her future (Alden, 2000).

Section Summary

Motherhood

1. The stereotypes about motherhood reveal our ambivalence about mothers: Mothers are supposed to feel happy and contented, but they are also blamed for children's problems.
2. Motherhood has a strong negative side because mothers may feel exhausted, over-worked, physically uncomfortable, incompetent, unrewarded, isolated, guilty, disappointed by failing to be the "ideal mother," and responsible for children's problems.
3. In addition, some children die before they are 1 year of age; the neonatal mortality rate is extremely high in low-income regions such as sub-Saharan Africa.
4. Motherhood also has a strong positive side; the benefits include a sense of women's own strength, pleasurable interactions with children, and increased nurturing skills, as well as abstract, intense joys.
5. College-educated mothers of color are more likely to be employed, compared to their White counterparts. Extended familes tend to be especially important for Black, Latina, and Native American mothers. Asian American women who have immigrated to the United States may encounter conflicts between their cultural beliefs and U.S. medical practice.
6. Extensive research on lesbian mothers reveals that they do not differ from hetero-sexual mothers in their parenting skills or the adjustment of their children. However, lesbian families currently face numerous legal obstacles.
7. Breastfeeding provides benefits for a mother's interactions with her infant, as well as for the health of both the infant and the mother.
8. About half of new mothers experience the short-term depression called postpartum blues; between 10 and 15% experience the more severe postpartum depression.
9. Despite popular beliefs, the psychological well-being of mothers of infants is similar for homemakers, women employed part time, and women employed full time; those with multiple roles may even experience benefits to their physical and psychological health.
10. At present, attitudes toward childfree women are somewhat negative; attitudes toward women with large families are also somewhat negative.
11. Childfree couples say that the disadvantages of parenthood include the irrevocability of the decision to have a child, the interference with lifestyle and work, and the expenses.
12. Couples who want to have children cite advantages such as the pleasurable aspects of children, the opportunity to educate children, and the challenge of parenthood.
13. Women who are infertile are similar to women with children in terms of their marital satisfaction and self-esteem, but they may be more anxious; many women manage to refocus their lives when childbirth seems unlikely.

Chapter Review Questions

1. Pregnancy and childbirth both involve biological processes. However, social factors are also very influential. Describe how social factors can operate during pregnancy and childbirth.

2. This chapter emphasizes ambivalent feelings and thoughts more than any other chapter in the book. Address the issue of ambivalence with respect to six topics: (a) emotional reactions to pregnancy, (b) emotional reactions to childbirth, (c) the reality of motherhood, (d) the decision to have children, (e) returning to the workplace after childbirth, and (f) reactions to infertility.

3. Describe how people react to pregnant women. How might these reactions contribute to women's emotional responses to pregnancy? Be sure to discuss both hostile and benevolent sexism.

4. Contrast the high-tech approach to childbirth with the natural-childbirth approach. List the reasons that the natural-childbirth approach would make women feel more in control of their experience during childbirth.

5. Throughout this chapter, we have seen that stereotypes often do not match reality. Address this issue with respect to some of the problems of motherhood.

6. In the chapter on women and work (Chapter 7), we discussed Francine Deutsch's (1999) research on families in which the mother and father take almost equal responsibility for child care. Based on the information in this chapter, describe how an ideal father would offer the best possible support during pregnancy, childbirth, and the initial months following birth.

7. What are the stereotypes about women of color who are mothers, and how is reality different from these stereotypes? What are the stereotypes and the reality for lesbian mothers?

8. Childbirth educators have made impressive changes in the way childbirth is now approached. However, motherhood is still extremely stressful. Imagine that our society valued motherhood enough to fund programs aimed at decreasing the difficulties that women experience during the postpartum phase. First, review those sources of stress. Then describe an ideal program that would include education, assistance, and social support.

9. Psychologists have conducted less research on pregnancy, childbirth, and motherhood than on any other topic in this book. Review this chapter, and suggest several research projects that could clarify how women experience these three important events in their lives.

10. As we discussed in this chapter, women often face a no-win situation with respect to decisions about childbearing and employment. Consider the options for three categories of women: married, lesbian, and single. What kinds of prejudices would be aimed at each category of women (e.g., a lesbian who decides to have children and to be employed full time)? Can any of these women win the complete approval of society?

Key Terms

placenta (p. 320)	benevolent sexism (p. 324)	premature birth (p. 326)	doula (p. 328)
miscarriage (p. 323)	preterm birth (p. 326)	cesarean birth (cesarean section or C-section) (p. 327)	natural childbirth (p. 329)
hostile sexism (p. 323)			infant mortality rate (p. 334)

postpartum period
(p. 339)

postpartum blues
(p. 339)

baby blues (p. 339)

postpartum
depression (p. 339)

compulsory
motherhood
(pronatalism)
(p. 342)

infertility (p. 344)

Recommended Readings

Biernat, M., Crosby, F. J., & Williams, J. C. (Eds.). (2004). The maternal wall: Research and policy perspectives on discrimination against mothers [Special issue]. *Journal of Social Issues, 60* (4). The *Journal of Social Issues* publishes special issues about a variety of social-justice concerns, and many of them focus on the psychology of women and gender. This particular special issue examines a wide variety of biases against employed women who are mothers.

Birth: Issues in Perinatal Care. This quarterly journal provides an interdisciplinary perspective on topics that psychologists have generally ignored. The articles examine women's experiences during pregnancy, childbirth, and the postpartum period; they also discuss innovative childbirth approaches.

Boston Women's Health Book Collective. (2008). *Our bodies, ourselves: Pregnancy and birth.* New York: Simon & Schuster. To prepare for writing this chapter, we read several books about pregnancy and childbirth. This one is particularly informative and not falsely cheerful. It also includes insightful descriptions of women's experiences.

Garbes, A. (2018). *Like a mother: A feminist journey through the science and culture of pregnancy.* New York, NY: HarperCollins. This delightful book covers the positives and negatives of pregnancy, childbirth, and motherhood.

Walker, R. (2007). *Baby love: Choosing motherhood after a lifetime of ambivalence.* New York: Penguin. Here is a thoughtful book that Rebecca Walker began to write after she learned that she was pregnant. It would be useful for a woman to read this book if she is considering becoming a mother, because Walker captures both the joy and the concerns about motherhood.

Answers to Demonstrations

Demonstration 10.3: Note: The name of each country is followed by its infant mortality rate (the number of infant deaths during 1 year per 1,000 live births). Australia, 3; Greece, 3; Cuba, 4; Israel, 3; Denmark, 3; Japan, 2; France, 4; Sweden, 2; Germany, 3; United States, 6; Belgium, 3; Czech Republic, 3; Ireland, 3; Italy, 3; Canada, 4.

11 Gender and Physical Health

Learning Objectives

After studying this chapter, you will be able to …

11-1 Identify how bias in the medical profession negatively affects the health of women and gender and sexual minorities.

11-2 Explain how gender is relevant for people with disabilities.

11-3 Describe how HIV and other sexually transmitted infections impact the lives of women and LGBTQ+ individuals.

11-4 Identify gender differences in substance use disorders and explain how they negatively affect physical health.

Did You Know?

- When we consider U.S. women who are 55 or older, more than half are currently experiencing one or more chronic health problems (p. 351).
- Women in the United States are more likely to die from cardiovascular disease than from breast cancer and all other forms of cancer (p. 360).
- Between 20% and 30% of U.S. and Canadian women have some form of disability (p. 365).
- A woman who has intercourse with an HIV-positive man is much more likely to become infected than a man who has intercourse with an HIV-positive woman (p. 369).
- In the United States, cigarette smoking is the most common preventable cause of death (p. 376).
- Those who have graduated from college in the United States are more likely to have tried some kind of illegal drug than those who did not finish high school (p. 380).

A woman named Samantha describes her relationship with her husband, Michael: "We love each other passionately and often. While the disability does, in reality, affect how we do things and what we are able to do together, it does not define our relationship. Assumptions are always the problem. People can assume that because I am disabled, my sexuality and my ability to enjoy and participate in sex have been taken away from me. It is fun to be part of an education process aimed at challenging this perception." Samantha has quadriplegia, which means that all four limbs are paralyzed (Boston Women's Health Book Collective, 2005, p. 216).

This chapter explores both the stereotypes and the realities about women with disabilities. We will also consider information about how gender impacts health status, sexually transmitted infections, and substance use disorders. These topics are part of **health psychology**, an interdisciplinary area in psychology that focuses on the causes of illness, the treatment of illness, illness prevention, and health improvement (Gurung, 2006; Miller et al., 2009; Sarafino, 2008). Why should health problems require special attention in a course about the psychology of women and gender? In this chapter, we will emphasize three major reasons why these health problems are important:

1. *Gender makes a difference in the kinds of health problems that people experience.* One theme of this book is that psychological gender differences are typically small. However, several biological gender differences have important consequences for people's health. For example, cisgender women may need to worry about cancer of the ovaries or the uterus, but cisgender men need to worry about prostate cancer. Transgender women and men seeking gender affirming care may require hormone therapy or surgery, whereas their cisgender peers may not.

Some consequences are more subtle. For example, the cisgender women's bodies typically have less fluid and more fat than cisgender men's bodies. This gender difference has important consequences for alcohol metabolism. Specifically, women's bodies have less fluid in which the alcohol can be distributed; it cannot be stored in fat. So, even if a man and a woman weigh the same and consume the same amount of alcohol, the woman will end up with a higher level of alcohol in her blood (L. L. Alexander et al., 2021; Sarafino, 2008).

2. *Gender makes a difference in the way a disease is diagnosed, perceived, and treated.* For example, when health-care providers diagnose a disease, they often consider the disease symptoms that occur in men to be normative, or standard (Benrud & Reddy, 1998). However, the same disease may cause a different set of symptoms in women. Ironically, women's disease symptoms are often considered deviations from the norm, consistent with our discussion of the normative male on page 67 (Porzelius, 2000).

Gender also makes a difference in the way certain diseases are perceived. For example, researchers in previous decades rarely studied osteoporosis, a bone disease found predominantly in women. As Theme 3 emphasizes, topics important to women are often understudied.

However, one cluster of women's health problems has received abundant attention: women's reproductive systems (N. G. Johnson, 2001). A physician in the late 1800s captured this perspective: "Woman is a pair of ovaries with a human being attached, where man is a human being furnished with a pair of testes" (cited by Fausto-Sterling, 1985, p. 90).

Gender also influences the actual treatment of diseases. For example, we'll learn that men are more likely than women to be treated for certain heart problems (Travis, 2005). Additionally, people who identify as LGBTQ+ are less likely than cisgender or heterosexual people to receive adequate care from the medical profession for a variety of health conditions (de Vries, Kathard, & Müller, 2020; Grant et al., 2011; Hafeez et al., 2017). This differential treatment is consistent with Theme 2 of this book.

3. *Illness is an important part of many women's experience.* A textbook on the psychology of women and gender must explore both gender comparisons and the life experiences of women. Sadly, health problems are a major concern for many women, and they become an increasingly central force as women grow older. For example, consider women in the United States who are 55 or older. More than 80% of these women experience at least one chronic health problem (Meyerowitz & Weidner, 1998; Revenson, 2001; Stanton et al., 2007). A **chronic health problem** is a long-lasting illness that cannot be completely cured. In the United States, 70% of the deaths each year can be traced to chronic illnesses (Hwang & Danoff-Burg, 2010).

In this chapter, we will explore several important components of women's physical health. In the first section, we examine how gender is related to both health care and health status. In the second section, we will emphasize the theme of variability among women, as we examine the lives of women with disabilities. In the last two sections, we will consider sexually transmitted infections and substance use disorders. The topics in this chapter may initially seem unrelated. However, they all focus on two central issues: How does gender influence people's physical health, and how does physical health influence people's lives?

11-1 Health Care and Health Status of Women and LGBTQ+ People

Learning Objectives

To identify how bias in the medical profession negatively affects the health of women and gender and sexual minorities, you can ...

11-1-1 Describe four specific sources of bias against women and gender and sexual minorities in health-care contexts.

11-1-2 Summarize how gender and economic status affect life expectancy and overall health status.

11-1-3 Explain how lack of access to health care and female genital mutilation affect women in developing countries.

11-1-4 Describe how the symptoms of cardiovascular disease vary among people of different genders.

11-1-5 Describe the primary methods by which breast cancer is identified and treated.

11-1-6 Explain why hysterectomy surgeries have a problematic history in the medical profession.

Theme 2 of this book states that women are treated differently from men. The biases against women in the health-care system provide still further evidence for that theme, both in the United States and in developing countries. In this section, we will also examine gender comparisons in life expectancy and in general health as well as several diseases that have an important impact on people's lives.

Biases Against Women and LGBTQ+ People

The medical profession has consistently been biased against women. Both women physicians and women patients have often been mistreated. A fascinating book by Mary Roth Walsh (1977) features a title based on a 1946 newspaper advertisement: *Doctors Wanted: No Women Need Apply*. The book documents the long history of attempts to keep women out of medical schools and medical practice. For example, in 1969, only 9% of medical school graduates were women. In contrast, 50 years later in 2019, 50.5% of current medical school graduates were women AAMC, 2019; Eisenberg et al., 1989; Heiser, 2019).

The medical profession has also consistently been biased against individuals who identify as LGBTQ+. For example, transgender people are more likely than cisgender people to be refused health care, be harassed in medical settings, and encounter health-care providers who lack knowledge about their specific health-care needs (de Vries, Kathard, & Müller, 2020; Grant et al., 2011). Sadly, 28% of transgender individuals report that they have postponed medical care due to discrimination in health-care settings (Grant et al., 2011).

The medical profession and the health-care system show several specific biases against women and LGBTQ+ patients. As you read about these biases, keep in mind three cautions: (1) Not every doctor is biased against women, sexual minority, and gender-nonconforming individuals; (2) some female doctors *are not* feminists; and (3) some male doctors *are* feminists. What are the biases that operate in health-care systems so that some patients often become second-class citizens?

1. *Women have often been neglected in medicine and in medical research.* Consistent with Theme 3, cisgender men's bodies have been considered normative, and they serve as the standard. With this perspective, medical experts have often assumed that women are basically identical to men, except that they are smaller … and of course they have different reproductive processes (L. L. Alexander et al., 2021; Mendelsohn et al., 1994).

Furthermore, health-care providers' decisions about women's health may be based on research that does not represent women. For instance, five large-scale studies showed that a low dose of aspirin reduces the risk of a heart attack. However, three of those studies included no women, and the other two studies did not test enough women to permit conclusions. In fact, when a large-scale study was finally conducted with women, the researchers reported that a low dose of aspirin did *not* reduce the rate of heart attacks in women (Ridker et al., 2005).

Fortunately, this neglect of women has outraged many health-care consumers and some legislators. As a result, medical schools are now more likely to emphasize women's health as part of the regular curriculum than they have in the past (Fonn, 2003; N. Rogers & Henrich, 2003). In addition, the U.S. National Institutes of Health and many other organizations require that funded research must include women, as well as members of ethnic minorities (L. L. Alexander et al., 2021; N. G. Johnson, 2001). Also, activist organizations such as The Society for Women's Health Research (2021) encourage women to become better informed about recent research and health-care strategies.

These measures won't immediately correct the centuries of neglect that health-care professionals have demonstrated toward women. However, women's health problems and concerns are now addressed more often than in previous decades. Health care is clearly an area where feminist concerns have had a clear impact on women's lives.

2. *Gender stereotypes are common in medicine.* Chapter 2 explored many of the popular beliefs about men and women. The medical profession remains attached to many of these stereotypes. For example, many physicians do not consider women's complaints to be as serious as men's complaints. Physicians may believe that women are more emotional than men or that women cannot understand information about their medical problems (Chrisler, 2001). They may believe that many common conditions affecting women, such as endometriosis, result from exaggerated or imagined symptoms (Young, Fisher, & Kirkman, 2019). Gender stereotypes keep women from receiving appropriate medical treatment. In many cases, women suffer harm from misdiagnoses, neglect, and delayed treatment for their health conditions as a result of these long-standing stereotypes within the medical profession (Dusenbery, 2018). Similarly, stereotypes about people who identify as LGBTQ+ often lead to disparate treatment by the medical community (Fingerhut & Abdou, 2017).

3. *Medical care provided to women is often inadequate or irresponsible.* Women sometimes receive too much health care, but sometimes they receive too little (Livingston, 1999; Travis et al., 2010). Specifically, some surgical procedures are performed too often. We learned in Chapter 10 that cesarean sections are performed too often during childbirth, and we'll read later in this section that hysterectomies are also more common than they need to be. As we noted earlier, the medical profession emphasizes women's reproductive systems. In addition, breast cancer patients often receive complete mastectomies, when much less invasive procedures would be just as effective (Travis et al., 2010).

In contrast, when we consider diseases that affect both women and men, the women often receive too little health care. For example, women are less likely than men to receive diagnostic testing or surgical treatment for the same severity of coronary heart disease (Dusenbery, 2018; Gan et al., 2000; Travis, 2005). The combination of "too much care" and "too little care" means that women often receive inappropriate treatment.

4. *Physician–patient communication patterns often make women feel relatively powerless.* In Chapter 6, we learned that men often interrupt women in ordinary conversations. When the man is a physician and the woman is a patient in a medical setting, women may feel especially powerless to share their concerns (Manderson, 2003b; Porzelius, 2000). For instance, women are more likely than men to report that their physicians didn't listen to them and talked down to them (Lonborg & Travis, 2007). Although there is evidence that female physicians use patient-centered language and communication styles with their patients more often than male physicians, this unfortunately does not necessarily translate to better health care (Schmid Mast & Kadji, 2018).

However, some of the research indicates no gender biases in physicians' conversational style (Roter & Hall, 1997). For example, one woman described her communication pattern with her doctor:

> Friends now marvel at my close relationship with my current doctor and my ability to talk back, question, and disagree with him and his colleagues. He respects me and trusts me to tell him what is going on, and I, in turn, trust him to listen, make suggestions, and consult with me before any action is taken. (Boston Women's Health Book Collective, 2005, p. 715)

Gender Comparisons in Life Expectancy

Let's now shift our focus to a more general question: What is the life expectancy for women and for men? Figure 11.1 shows the small but consistent gender gap in life expectancy for various groups of people in the United States. Specifically, women live about six to eight years longer than men do (WHO, 2021). The gender gap also occurs in virtually every country in the world, despite the substantial health problems that women experience in developing countries (Bird & Rieker, 2008; Klein, 2008).

But *why* do women live longer? The answer includes biological, social, and environmental factors (Etaugh, 2008; Klein, 2008; Lee, 2010). For example, cisgender women's second X chromosome may protect them from some health problems (Landrine & Klonoff, 2001; Schmerling, 2016). Gender differences in high-risk activities are also likely. For example, men are more likely to die from suicide, homicide, and motor vehicle accidents. In addition, more men than women are exposed to dangerous conditions at work, as is the case for coal miners and factory workers (Schmerling, 2016; Stanton & Courtenay, 2004; D. R. Williams, 2003).

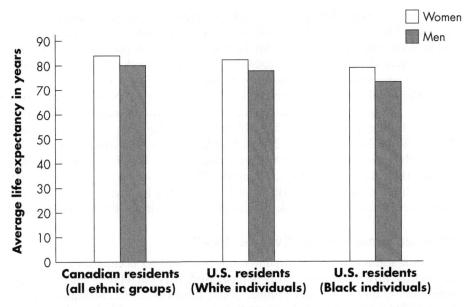

FIGURE **11.1** Average life expectancy for individuals born in 2020, in three North American populations.

Sources: Adapted from U.S Census Bureau (2020) https://www.census.gov/content/dam/Census/library/publications/2020/demo/p25-1145.pdf; Worldbank (2019) https://data.worldbank.org/indicator/SP.DYN.LE00.FE.IN?locations=CA.

In both the United States and Canada, another factor that clearly contributes to women's longevity is that women visit their health-care providers more often than men do (Lee, 2010; Lonborg & Travis, 2007; Statistics Canada, 2000; D. R. Williams, 2003). We read in earlier chapters that women are somewhat more attuned to emotions and to problems in a relationship. Compared to men, women also may be more sensitive to internal signals that might foreshadow health problems (Johnston, 2007; R. Martin & Suls, 2003; Stanton & Courtenay, 2004). In contrast, the traditional male gender role encourages men to be physically "tough," rarely complaining about minor symptoms (Marcell et al., 2007). Women may consult physicians during the early stages of a disease, before it becomes fatal.

Research on aging and life expectancy in transgender and gender-nonconforming people is limited. However, available data suggests that social stigma, lifestyle risks, and health disparities resulting from bias in health-care access and treatment may negatively impact transgender people's life expectancy and healthy aging processes (Bockting et al., 2016).

Gender Comparisons in Overall Health

We have learned that women have an advantage with respect to a longer life span. However, women in both the United States and Canada have a disadvantage with respect to **morbidity**, which is defined as generalized poor health or illness. The research demonstrates that women are more likely than men to have problems such as obesity, anemia, and respiratory illness. Women are also more likely to experience lifelong illnesses, headaches, and general fatigue (Bird & Reiker, 2008; Etaugh, 2008; Milan, 2015).

Some of this gender difference is easy to explain: Women live longer than men, so they are more likely to have nonfatal illnesses associated with old age (Crimmins et al., 2002). Some of the difference can probably be traced to the fact that morbidity is usually assessed by self-report (Brannon & Feist, 2004; Skevington, 2004). A woman may be more likely than a man to report that she is bothered by her arthritis.

Other explanations for the gender differences in morbidity are not so obvious. For example, women are the primary victims of rape, and women who have been raped are very likely to experience health problems during the years following the attack (Bird & Rieker, 2008; N. G. Johnson, 2004). In addition, an estimated 25% of U.S. women are physically abused at some point during their lifetime by a boyfriend, spouse, or domestic partner (Huecker, King, Jordan, & Smock, 2021). Economic factors also contribute to the gender differences in morbidity, as we'll learn in the following discussion. In a variety of ways, then, women are more likely than men to experience illness and poor health.

Intersectional Perspectives on Health

Economic status can be measured in terms of a person's occupation, income, or education. No matter how economic status is measured, it is correlated with life expectancy and morbidity (Adler & Conner Snibbe, 2003; Johnston, 2007; Stringhini et al., 2017). For example, U.S. residents in the top 5% income group are likely to live nine years longer than those in the bottom 10% (Gudrais, 2008).

One important factor in these correlations is the quality of health care. No country's health-care system is perfect. For example, Canadian researchers point out that their own system should emphasize disease prevention, rather than focusing primarily on treatment (Arnett et al., 2004; Romanow & Marchildon, 2003). Of the 195 countries around the world, 116 countries provide universal health care to their citizens (World Population Review, 2021). The United States is not one of them. The Affordable Care Act of 2010 expanded health-care availability to millions of U.S. citizens, reduced the number of uninsured people, and lowered health-care costs for middle-aged and older adults, as well as those of all ages with low incomes (Blumenthal, Collins, & Fowler, 2020; Kwon, Park, & McBride 2019). Although the legislation did reduce the number of uninsured adults in the United States, it still does not create a universal health-care system available to everyone, as many other industrialized and developing countries provide for their citizens. The lack of universal health care in the United States is largely responsible for two problems: The United States is currently number one in the world in the amount of money spent per person on health care, and other countries spend about half as much; but it is Number 41 as far as life expectancy is concerned (Kamal, Ramirez, & Cox, 2020; World Data, 2021).

Unfortunately, more than 32 million U.S. citizens do not have any health insurance, most commonly because they cannot afford it (CDC, 2021; Cha & Cohen, 2020). Adults who are 65 years of age and older are eligible for government-subsidized health care under the Medicare program in the United States. Adults ages 18 to 64 can obtain insurance from three possible sources: Medicaid, which is provided for people who have low incomes, insurance exchanges available through the Affordable Care Act Marketplace, or private sources, which are most commonly offered through employer sponsored insurance programs (Kaiser Family Foundation, 2021a). Men are more likely than women to have private insurance provided by their employers; private insurance furnishes the best health-care benefits (Lerner, 2009). Only 48% of women are eligible for employer-sponsored insurance, compared to 57% of men, most often because women are more likely than men to work part-time or low-wage positions that are not eligible for insurance benefits (Arons & Rosenthal, 2012). Women are also more likely than men to have either Medicaid insurance—which offers second-class benefits—or no insurance at all (Chrisler, 2001; Kaiser Family Foundation, 2021a; Lerner, 2009). Literally, health insurance sometimes makes a difference between life and death.

Women of color are especially likely to receive second-class health care (Brannon & Feist, 2004; Landrine & Klonoff, 2001; Yee & Chiriboga, 2007). For example, Native American women who live on a reservation are more likely than other women to die before the age of 45 (Smecker, 2009).

Many factors other than the quality of a person's health insurance help to explain the influence of economic status and ethnicity on both life expectancy and general health, although these factors are often intertwined. For example, affordable housing is often constructed in locations with high levels of toxic materials, and in many areas of the country, people of color and marginalized groups are more likely to live in these environments due to a history of environmental racism in the United States (Bullard, Gardezi, Chennault, & Dankbar, 2016). Also, families with low incomes often live in noisy, crowded environments; these factors are associated with poor health (Adler & Conner Snibbe, 2003; Csoboth, 2003). As you can imagine, people living in toxic environments are also more likely to experience stressful events and negative emotions. These psychological factors can lead to heart disease, as well as other health problems (Adler & Conner Snibbe, 2003; Gallo & Matthews, 2003; Miller et al., 2009). In summary, any attempt to improve the health-care system in the United States—for people of all genders—must additionally emphasize both the direct and indirect effects of intersectional forces such as economic status, ethnicity, heteronormativity, and historical patterns of racism, sexism, and ableism (López & Gadsden, 2016).

Health Issues for Women and LGBTQ+ People in Developing Countries

In developing countries, women and LBGTQ+ individuals face more severe biases than in the United States. In fact, many women and gender and sexual minorities in other countries do not need to be concerned about a health professional treating them in a biased manner because they will never even meet a physician, a nurse, or any person trained in health care. Let's consider two important topics, access to health care and female genital mutilation.

Lack of Access to Health Care

When resources are scarce, women are especially likely to suffer (Marton, 2004). Data gathered in Asia, Africa, and the Middle East demonstrate that parents are significantly more likely to seek medical care for a son than for a daughter. For example, boys in India are more than twice as likely as girls to receive medical treatment (Landrine & Klonoff, 2001). In many developing countries, only the wealthiest women have access to medical care.

Women in developing countries typically have inadequate health care. They are also more than twice as likely as men to have too little to eat ("Join the Global Effort," 2005; Marton, 2004). Women in developing countries also face a relatively high chance of dying during pregnancy or childbirth. For example, an African woman living in either Niger or Sierra Leone is about 130 times more likely to die during childbirth than a woman living in the United States—and about 360 times more likely than a woman living in Canada (World Health Organization, 2005b).

Members of gender and sexual minorities in other countries have an especially difficult time accessing adequate health care. In a systematic review of research from multiple countries, Alencar Albuquerque and colleagues (2016) found that LGBTQ+ people around the world are at higher risk for health problems due to bias and discrimination in healthcare agencies and systems, as well as a general lack of access to care.

Female Genital Mutilation

A widely discussed health issue in some developing countries is female genital mutilation. **Female genital mutilation** (also called **female genital cutting**) involves cutting or removing a section of the girl's genitals, usually part or all of the clitoris.

In some cultures, the labia minora are also removed, and the labia majora are then stitched together. (Review Chapter 9, on page 287, for a review of cisgender women's external sexual organs.) This more drastic procedure leaves only a tiny opening to allow both urine and menstrual blood to pass out of the body (S. M. James & Robertson, 2002; Johnson, 2009; Kalev, 2004). The male equivalent of this more drastic version of female genital mutilation would require removal of the entire penis and part of the skin surrounding the testicles (Whelehan, 2001).

Female genital mutilation is a controversial issue. On the one hand, some people say that people in the United States should not cast judgments about a cultural practice in another country. On the other hand, female genital mutilation clearly creates health problems for girls and women. The operation is extremely painful. It can also cause severe blood loss and infections (often leading to death), damage to other organs, long-term problems with menstruation and urination, and difficulty during childbirth (Johnson, 2009; Schiffman & Castle, 2005; Paley, 2008). Some researchers argue that female genital mutilation also increases the transmission of the HIV virus (Keown, 2007).

More than 200 million girls and women—currently living in about 30 countries throughout the world—have experienced genital mutilation (Kalev, 2004; Walley, 2002; Whelehan, 2001; World Health Organization, 2021). Most of these women live in Africa, the Middle East, and Asia. However, many have emigrated to Canada, the United States, and Europe (Johnson, 2009; Nour, 2005).

The operation is usually performed when the young girl is between the ages of 0 and 15 (World Health Organization, 2021). The girl is typically held down by women relatives. Meanwhile, an older woman performs the operation, often using an unsterilized razor blade, piece of glass, or sharp rock (Kalev, 2004). According to people in cultures that practice female genital mutilation, this procedure makes the genitals cleaner (Nour, 2005). People also believe that the operation reduces sexual activity outside marriage. In fact, women do experience less sexual pleasure if the clitoris has been removed (Walley, 2002).

The World Health Organization (2021) and other prominent health groups have condemned the practice of female genital mutilation. Some countries have reduced the percentage of girls who experience the procedure, using culturally sensitive educational techniques (El-Bushra, 2000; Gunning, 2002; Walley, 2002).

Cardiovascular Disease, Breast Cancer, and Other Specific Health Problems

So far, we have learned that gender makes a difference for both life expectancy and morbidity. Women live longer, but they experience more illness during their lifetime. Let's now examine several specific diseases and health problems that are important in women's lives. The first problem, cardiovascular disease, affects women's lives because it is such a frequent cause of death. The other three problems—breast cancer, cancer of the reproductive system, and osteoporosis—occur either exclusively or more frequently in cisgender women. Therefore, we need to examine these specific diseases in our discussion of women's health.

Cardiovascular Disease

The term **cardiovascular disease** includes heart attacks and other disorders of the heart, as well as clots and other disorders of the blood vessels. Cardiovascular disease is the major cause of death for U.S. women. In fact, it is more deadly than all forms of cancer combined (Bird & Rieker, 2008; Travis & Compton, 2001). Each year, cardiovascular disease kills about 300,000 women in the United States (CDC, 2021; L. L. Alexander et al., 2021; Hansen, 2002). In addition on average, one women dies from heart disease every 20 minutes in Canada; the rate is higher for indigenous and First Nations women than women of other ethnicities (Heart and Stroke Foundation of Canada, 2017; Norris et al., 2020).

Many people think that heart disease is a man's illness, but this myth is not correct. Men are likely to experience heart disease earlier than women do, but women run about the same risk by the time they reach 75 years of age (Bird & Rieker, 2008; Hwang & Danoff-Burg, 2010; Lee, 2010). In addition, Black women are more likely than White women to die of heart disease (Brannon & Feist, 2004).

An important problem is that men typically report chest pain when they are having a heart attack. Women may report chest pain, but they also report symptoms such as breathlessness or fatigue (CDC, 2021; Skevington, 2004). Health professionals may fail to recognize heart attacks in women if they are searching for the classic "male" symptoms.

Furthermore, as we discussed at the beginning of this chapter, men are more likely than women to receive diagnostic testing or surgical treatment for heart disease. For example, men are twice as likely as women to receive bypass surgery, even when both genders have the same medical profile (Lonborg & Travis, 2007; Travis, 2005). We know relatively little about cardiac problems in women because researchers are much more likely to study cardiac problems in men (Boston Women's Health Book Collective, 2011; Norris et al., 2020; Travis & Compton, 2001).

Women and men also behave differently after a heart attack. Men typically reduce their household chores, whereas women tend to resume their household chores more quickly (Stanton et al., 2007).

What can people do to help prevent heart disease? Some precautions include a diet that is low in salt, cholesterol, and saturated fats, maintenance of a reasonable body weight, and regular exercise (Brannon & Feist, 2004; Oldenburg & Burton, 2004). As we'll discuss later in the chapter, people who smoke cigarettes also run a high risk of heart disease.

Breast Cancer

At the beginning of this chapter, we noted that gender makes a difference in the way that certain diseases are perceived. As we've just read, many people don't associate heart disease with women. The one disease in women that receives widespread publicity is breast cancer (Hwang & Danoff-Burg, 2010).

Breast cancer is definitely an important problem that requires extensive medical research, and we all know women who have struggled with this disease. Still, health psychologists are uncertain why medical researchers—as well as the general public—focus more on breast cancer than on other illnesses that are actually more dangerous for women.

One important factor is a cultural emphasis on breasts as being "essential" to the experience of being a woman (Chrisler, 2001; Crooks & Baur, 2017).

Another factor that has led to increased amounts of research on breast cancer is the entry of more women into the medical and health professions since the 1960s. Prior to that era, male physicians and surgeons primarily relied on simple breast-removal and surgical treatments. In contrast, women scientists have focused more on researching and developing alternative treatments for breast cancer throughout the past 50 years (Osuch et al., 2012).

Each year, approximately 275,000 women in the United States are diagnosed with breast cancer and about 42,000 U.S. women die from the disease (Backus, 2002; Compas & Luecken, 2002; National Breast Cancer Foundation, 2021). Also, about 27,000 Canadian women will be diagnosed with breast cancer annually, and about 5,100 Canadian women will die from the disease (Canadian Cancer Society, 2021; Parry, 2008). Black women are less likely than White women to develop breast cancer; however, they actually have a higher death rate from it (Travis et al., 2010). Although their rate of breast cancer is lower than that of cisgender women, transgender women receiving hormone treatment are at increased risk for breast cancer over cisgender and transgender men, who can also get breast cancer (de Blok et al., 2019). An estimated 2,620 cisgender men in the United States and 240 men in Canada are diagnosed each year (Canadian Cancer Society, 2021; National Breast Cancer Foundation, 2021). Before you read further, try Demonstration 11.1.

Regular, systematic breast self-examination is an important strategy for detecting cancer. Early detection of breast cancer is important because the chances of a cure are very

---

Demonstration 11.1

Thinking About Breast Cancer

Think about and answer the following questions concerning breast cancer and its relevance in your life.

1. When was the last time you remember a discussion of breast cancer? Was the discussion a general one, or did it provide specific information about how to conduct a breast self-examination or where to go for a mammogram?
2. Have you observed any notices about breast self-examination or mammograms (e.g., in public buildings or at the student health service)?
3. If someone in your home community wanted to have a mammogram, do you know where they would go? (If you don't, you can find a nearby location by calling the American Cancer Society at 800-227-2345 or by visiting its website to find a nearby location.)
4. Think about several women over the age of 50 who are important to you. Have you ever discussed breast cancer or mammograms with them? If not, try to figure out how you might raise these issues with them soon, or identify another person who could make certain that these women have had a recent mammogram.

high if the disease is diagnosed at an early stage. If you are over the age of 20, you should examine your breasts at least once a month (L. L. Alexander et al., 2021; Keitel & Kopala, 2000). People who are menstruating should ideally examine their breasts about a week after their menstrual period is over because their breasts are likely to have normal lumps during menstruation. Figure 11.2 on page 362 provides instructions.

Breasts can also be examined using technological methods. For example, a **mammogram** is an X-ray of the breast—a picture of breast tissue—taken while the breast tissue is flattened between two plastic plates (L. L. Alexander et al., 2021). The guidelines about mammograms are continually changing. However, cisgender women over the age of 50 and transgender women over the age of 50 who have had hormonal treatment for at least 5 years are often encouraged to have a screening mammogram every year or two to detect lumps that are too small to detect by self-examination (Sonnenbrink, Shah, Goldstein, & Reisman, 2018). Men with a history of breast cancer in their family or who have specific mutations in the BRCA1 or BRCA2 genes are also encouraged to have regular mammograms after age 50, due to an increased risk of developing breast cancer (Mano et al., 2017).

Unfortunately, many women over the age of 50 do not have regular mammograms. About 72% of Canadian women and 67% of women in the United States between the ages of 50 and 69 have had a mammogram within the past two years (CDC, 2021; Shields & Wilkins, 2009). Individual differences are large, but Latina, Asian American and Pacific Islander, and Native American women of color often have lower rates for mammogram screening than Black and White women (Borrayo, 2004; CDC, 2021; Hwang & Danoff-Burg, 2010). For example, only about 50% of Asian American women in one study reported having had a mammogram, in contrast to 70% of White women (Helstrom et al., 1998). Asian American women may be less likely to have mammograms for several reasons. Many do not have health insurance that would cover the cost of the procedure. Furthermore, many Asian American women are taught from an early age not to discuss topics related to sexuality, so breast cancer is an especially forbidden topic of conversation (Ketenjian, 1999b).

Latina women may also be reluctant to perform a breast self-examination or seek breast cancer screening. For instance, many women of Mexican descent believe that it would be indecent for a health-care provider to see their unclothed breasts (Borrayo, 2004; Borrayo & Jenkins, 2003; Moadei & Harris, 2008).

When breast cancer is in an early stage, the most common treatment is a **lumpectomy**, that is, surgery that removes the cancerous lump and the immediate surrounding breast tissue. Radiation therapy or chemotherapy might also be used (Crooks & Baur, 2017). Fortunately, with earlier detection and more sophisticated procedures, women are much less likely to die from breast cancer now than in earlier decades (Backus, 2002).

Naturally, the diagnosis and treatment of breast cancer will cause some fear, anxiety, grief, depression, and anger. The treatment cycle is physically painful, and it is a socially lonely experience (Compas & Luecken, 2002; Peltason, 2008; Spira & Reed, 2003). Women often feel exhausted for several months during and after treatment (Kaelin, 2005).

As you might expect, women who have been treated for breast cancer differ widely in their reactions (Lonborg & Travis, 2007; Peltason, 2008; Stanton et al., 2007). Some women continue to worry for years afterward. For instance, one 70-year-old Black woman had chemotherapy, and she was cancer-free four years later. However, she still had persistent concerns about cancer: "It's just there, and I can't get it out of my brain, and it's just something that I've just learned to live with. It's just like sometimes you wished you could just put your brain under a faucet and just wash the kinks out because it's just sticking there" (Rosenbaum & Roos, 2000, p. 160).

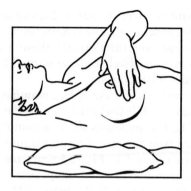 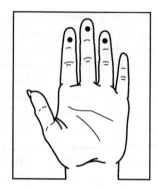

Beginning in their 20s, women should be told about the benefits and limitations of breast self-exam (BSE). Women should be aware of how their breasts normally look and feel and report any new breast changes to a health professional as soon as they are found. Finding a breast change does not necessarily mean there is a cancer.

If you choose to do BSE, the following information provides a step-by-step approach for the exam. The best time for a woman to examine her breasts is when the breasts are not tender or swollen. Women who examine their breasts should have their technique reviewed during their periodic health exams by their health-care professional.

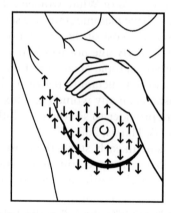

FIGURE **11.2** Performing a breast self-exam (BSE).
Source: American Cancer Society (2003). Reprinted with Permission.

Fortunately, most women who have had surgery tend to cope well, especially if they have supportive friends and family members (Bennett, 2004; Stanton et al., 2007). For instance, one study focused on Black women who had had breast-cancer surgery only two months earlier; 62% reported that they were in very good spirits (Weaver, 1998). Many women who survive cancer believe that the struggle helped them to reorder their priorities, for example, by choosing a healthier lifestyle or valuing friendships more fully

(Bird & Rieker, 2008; Lonborg & Travis, 2007). As one woman commented on her personal transformation:

> It does make you really look and see in your life what is important, what really matters. To try and do what makes you happy, gives you satisfaction in life. To tell those around you what they mean to you. Live each day to the fullest you can, don't waste a day. I don't mean live as if it's the last day you have, but cherish each one that you have. (Peltason, 2008, p. 293)

Reproductive System Cancer and Hysterectomies

Several kinds of cancer often affect women's reproductive systems. For example, **cervical cancer** affects the lower portion of the uterus. (Figure 4.1, on page 115, shows the cervix.)

In the United States, women seldom die from cervical cancer. A major reason is a highly accurate screening test called the Pap smear, administered during routine gynecology examinations. In the **Pap smear test**, the gynecologist takes a sample of cells from the cervix to determine whether they are normal, precancerous, or cancerous. When cervical cancer is detected early, it is highly curable (Crooks & Baur, 2017; Robertson et al., 2003; Schiffman & Castle, 2005). Gynecologists recommend that all cisgender women should have an annual Pap smear if they are sexually active or if they have reached the age of 18. However, many young women do not know why Pap smears are important (Blake et al., 2004). This deadly disease is not limited to older women!

In Canada, about 75% of women between the ages of 18 and 69 have had a Pap smear within the last two years (Statistics Canada, 2006w). Most White women in the United States have routine Pap smears, but millions of women without health insurance do not have this test on a regular basis (Landrine & Klonoff, 2001). For example, a 45-year-old woman remarked:

> My Mother's Day present this year was and is the best I've had in a while. My daughter got me a free Pap test…. She knew it had been years since I had one. My family's history is riddled with cancer. We don't have health insurance because it's not affordable. (Feldt, 2002, p. 92)

As we noted earlier in this chapter, U.S. women experience much more severe health problems if they do not have insurance.

Compared to White women, Latinas and other women of color are more likely to die from cancer of the cervix—especially because they are less likely to have had this screening test (Borrayo et al., 2004; Rimer et al., 2001). Throughout the world, cancer of the cervix is one of the major causes of death, especially because women in developing countries often do not have access to Pap smears (DeWeerdt, 2020).

We noted at the beginning of the chapter that gender influences the way a disease is treated and that women's reproductive systems receive more attention than other health concerns. The best example of this principle is the high rate of hysterectomies in the United States. A **hysterectomy** is the surgical removal of a woman's uterus (Elson, 2004). Some hysterectomies are advisable—for example, when advanced cancer cannot be treated by more limited surgery. However, many surgeons remove a woman's uterus when other less drastic treatments would be effective. Each year, more than 500,000 women in the United States have a hysterectomy, and it is the second most common surgery performed on women, following cesarean section (CDC, 2021). About 32% of women who are age 50 or older have had a hysterectomy (CDC, 2019). This rate is much higher than in other developed countries (Elson, 2004).

Some hysterectomies are medically necessary. Also, some women who have had hysterectomies experience only minimal psychological or physical symptoms. Consistent with our theme of individual differences, some women report that the hysterectomy removed an important part of their identity as a woman (Elson, 2004; Todkill, 2004). However, women need appropriate information about the alternatives before making decisions about whether they should have a hysterectomy.

Another disorder of the reproductive system has not received the attention it deserves. In the United States, cancer of the ovaries has the highest rate of death of all gynecological cancers (L. L. Alexander et al., 2021; Burns, 2001). Unfortunately, there is currently no reliable, valid screening test for this disorder. Furthermore, the symptoms include abdominal cramping and vomiting—so people are likely to attribute the symptoms to a less serious health problem. As a result, most ovarian cancers are not discovered until they are in an advanced stage and the cancer has spread to other parts of the body (Crooks & Baur, 2007; Robb-Nicholson, 2004).

Osteoporosis

In the disorder called **osteoporosis** (pronounced oss-tee-owe-por-*roe*-siss), the bones become less dense and more fragile. Women are roughly four times more likely than men to develop this disorder, and it is especially common among older women (L. L. Alexander et al., 2021; Fausto-Sterling, 2005). If a woman has osteoporosis, she is much more likely to experience a bone fracture, even from just tripping and falling in the bathroom. Hip fractures resulting from osteoporosis create major problems, especially because they often cause long-term disability (Raisz, 2005).

Women can reduce the risk of osteoporosis by doing regular weight-bearing exercises, such as walking or jogging. Even young women need to take adequate calcium and vitamin D to build strong bones, and they need to continue this precaution throughout their lives (Boston Women's Health Book Collective, 2011). In addition, professional organizations recommend a bone-density test when women reach the age of 65 (Raisz, 2005).

Section Summary

The Health Care and Health Status of Women

1. Women's health is a crucial issue for several reasons: (a) Women and LBGTQ+ individuals experience different illnesses than cisgender men, (b) gender influences the way a disease is treated, and (c) illness is an important factor in women's lives.
2. Health-related biases against women and members of sexual and gender minorities include the neglect of women in medicine, the prevalence of gender stereotypes in medical research, inadequate or irresponsible medical care, and problems in the physician–patient relationship.
3. U.S. women in all ethnic groups live longer than men do; this gender difference also occurs in Canada. However, women experience more health problems than men do.
4. In the United States, economic status is related to a person's health status; women of color are especially likely to receive inadequate health care.

(continues)

Section Summary *(continued)*

5. Women in developing countries often experience inadequate nutrition and health care. Female genital mutilation threatens the health of about 200 million girls and women.
6. Cardiovascular disease is the most common cause of death in women; precautions such as proper diet and exercise are important.
7. Breast cancer is relatively common in the United States and Canada, but the chances for survival are high if the cancer is detected early; most women cope reasonably well with breast cancer.
8. Pap smears are very effective in detecting early cervical cancer. Hysterectomies may be advisable in some cases of uterine cancer, but many are performed without sufficient medical justification. Ovarian cancer is an especially deadly disease.
9. Osteoporosis often leads to serious bone fractures in postmenopausal women; appropriate exercise and nutrition can reduce the risks.

11-2 Women with Disabilities

Learning Objectives

To explain how gender is relevant for people with disabilities, you can …

11-2-1 Define ableism and identify how it negatively impacts health care for people who have disabilities.

11-2-2 Analyze how common barriers to work and education affect people with disabilities.

11-2-3 Discuss how the experience of having a disability affects women's personal relationships.

In the United States, about 20,932,100 women and 19,782,700 men have a disability (Erickson, Lee, & von Schrader, 2019). In Canada, women (24%) are also more likely than men (20%) to have a disability (Morris, Fawcett, Brisebois, & Hughes, 2018). We have learned that women and men have somewhat different health-care experiences, and they also have somewhat different patterns of illness. Now let's consider how gender can be relevant when we consider individuals with disabilities.

Background Information on Disability Studies

One important theme of this book is that women vary widely from one another. We have already examined some factors that create variability: ethnicity, country of residence, economic status, and sexual orientation. Disability is an additional dimension of variability. **Disability** refers to a physical or mental impairment that limits a person's ability to perform a major life activity in the manner considered normative (Asch, 2004; Cook, 2003; Whitley & Kite, 2010). In general, the term *person with a disability* is preferable to *disabled person* (American Psychological Association, 2010). *Person with a disability* emphasizes someone's individuality first and the disability second.

The term **ableism** refers to discrimination on the basis of disability (Nabors & Pettee, 2003). For example, in the workplace, staff members often treat people with disabilities as if they were children (Whitley & Kite, 2010). Just as sexism devalues women, ableism devalues people with disabilities (Ware, 2010).

Theme 3 in this book emphasizes that women are relatively invisible. For many decades, women with disabilities were nearly invisible within the field of women's studies. **Disability studies** is an interdisciplinary field that examines disabilities from the perspective of social sciences, natural science, the arts, the humanities, education, and media studies (Siebers, 2008; B. G. Smith, 2004; Ware, 2009). Disability studies is an international discipline, in countries as diverse as Uganda, Brazil, England, and Nepal (Garland-Thomson, 2004; C. Lewis et al., 2002; Lloyd, 2006). Several books are available in the field of disability studies (M. E. Banks & Kaschak, 2003; G. A. King et al., 2003b; Olkin & Pledger, 2003; B. G. Smith & Hutchison, 2004). In addition, academic journals such as *Disability Studies Quarterly* and the *Journal of Disability Studies*, as well as multiple international journals, are devoted to publishing research in the discipline.

By some estimates, 25% of women in the United States have at least one disability (Asch et al., 2001; CDC, 2021). Women who are older adults are especially likely to have a disability. For instance, consider Canadians who are age 65 and older. An estimated 30% of women and 20% of men in this age category live with a disability (Statistics Canada, 2010c; 2010p).

The variation within the disability category is tremendous. In fact, the term *women with disabilities* is simply a social construct that links together multiple unrelated conditions (Olkin, 2008; Siebers, 2008; Whitley & Kite, 2010). In reality, life experiences may be very different for a woman who is blind, a woman who is missing an arm, and a woman who is recovering from a stroke (Asch, 2004; B. G. Smith, 2004). Still, many people judge individuals with a disability primarily in terms of that disability. As Y. King (1997) remarked, the popular culture assumes that being disabled is what these individuals *do* and *are:* "She's the one in the wheelchair."

When we consider the topic of disabilities, we also need to remind ourselves about a unity between women with disabilities and women without disabilities. Many people do not currently live with a disability. However, everyone could become disabled in a matter of seconds through an accident, a stroke, or a disease (Garland-Thomson, 2004). In other words, people who are not disabled could adopt the label "temporarily abled" (Bowleg, 1999; Siebers, 2008; Whitley & Kite, 2010).

Theorists often note that women typically live on the margins of a world in which men occupy the central territory. In many ways, women with disabilities live on the margins of those margins. As a result, they may feel that the culture considers them invisible (A. M. Bauer, 2001; Goldstein, 2001; Kisber, 2001). Women of color who have disabilities experience a triple threat, in which they constantly face sexism, racism, and ableism.

But how are disabilities related to gender? Why would the life of a woman with a disability be different from the life of a man with a disability? The following discussions of education, work, and social relationships demonstrate that disabilities can exaggerate the differential treatment of women and men (Mertens et al., 2007).

Education and Work Patterns of Women with Disabilities

Women with disabilities face barriers in pursuing an education beyond high school (Mertens et al., 2007). According to one U.S. survey, for example, only 15% of women with a disability hold at least a bachelor's degree, in contrast to 33% of women without a disability (Schur, 2004). A variety of barriers on college campuses make it difficult to pursue an education beyond high school. For example, women with disabilities often cannot find accessible buildings, wheelchair-friendly sidewalks or elevators, sign-language interpreters, and other support services (Ware, 2010).

In the United States, the civilian, noninstitutional employment rate is 15% for adult women with a disability; the comparable figure for men is 21%. In other words, the employment rates for these two groups are similar (Bureau of Labor Statistics, 2021). However, in both the United States and Canada, people with disabilities are much less likely to be employed, at 18% of the workforce, than people without disabilities, who comprise 62% of the workforce (Bureau of Labor Statistics, 2021; MacKinnon et al., 2003; Schur, 2004).

Gender and disability combine in unique ways to discriminate in the workplace against women with disabilities (Mason et al., 2004; Mertens et al., 2007; Schur, 2004). For example, Maryé (1998) described how her disability does not allow her to use her hands. Her supervisor did not invite her to attend an important meeting because he assumed that as a woman, she would need to serve as a note-taker—a function she could not perform. As she wrote, "The glass ceiling for a disabled woman turns her office into a crawl space" (p. 102).

Women with disabilities often encounter economic problems. In the United States, for example, women with disabilities have average incomes that are between 60% and 78% of the average income of men with disabilities (Mertens et al., 2007; Schur, 2004). Furthermore, women with disabilities are also unlikely to receive adequate retirement benefits.

In Chapter 7, we discussed the dilemma that lesbian women face in the workplace: Should they reveal their sexual orientation and risk discrimination? Should they try to pass as heterosexual, even though this option requires them to hide an important part of their identity? Women with invisible disabilities face a similar dilemma (Garland-Thomson, 2004; G. A. King et al., 2003a; Siebers, 2008). For instance, a woman with multiple sclerosis may not appear disabled, but she may tire easily or experience numbness or memory problems. Should she share her disability with her boss and risk patronizing comments or job discrimination? Or should she try to hide her disability, risking exhaustion or criticism for being lazy? In Chapter 7, we examined many biases that employed women face; these problems are intensified for women with disabilities.

Personal Relationships of Women with Disabilities

Throughout this book, we have emphasized how women are judged by their physical attractiveness. Cultural norms in the United States present fairly rigid and limited ideas about attractiveness. As a result, people may consider some women with disabilities to be unattractive (D. Crawford & Ostrove, 2003; Mason et al., 2004). Consequently, some women with disabilities may be excluded from the social world, as well as from some aspects of the employment world (Siebers, 2008; A. Sohn, 2005; Whitley & Kite, 2010). Heterosexual women with disabilities are less likely to date and to marry. In fact, 28% of women with disabilities live alone, in contrast to 8% of women without disabilities (Olkin, 2008; Schur, 2004).

Even less is known about the love and sexual relationships of LGBTQ+ women with disabilities. However, the research suggests that many of these individuals also have limited romantic opportunities (Asch & Fine, 1992; Chinn, 2008; Mona, Syme, & Cameron, 2014; Olkin, 2008).

Ynestra King (1997) described a vivid example of this bias against women with disabilities, with respect to romantic relationships. When she is sitting down, her disability is invisible; when she stands up, it's obvious she has difficulty walking. She commented on the reactions in social settings:

> It is especially noticeable when another individual is flirting and flattering, and has an abrupt change in affect when I stand up. I always make sure that I walk around in front of someone before I accept a date, just to save face for both of us. Once the other person perceives the disability, the switch on the sexual circuit breaker often pops off—the connection is broken. "Chemistry" is over. I have a lifetime of such experiences, and so does every other disabled woman I know. (King, 1997, p. 107)

Many people in the United States assume that people with physical disabilities are not interested in sex or not capable of engaging in sexual activity (Crooks & Baur, 2017; Olkin, 2008). Women with disabilities often complain that they do not receive adequate counseling about sexuality, and that during these discussions, their partners' needs are prioritized but their own needs are ignored (Asch et al., 2001; Mertens et al., 2007; A. Sohn, 2005). Furthermore, individuals with disabilities are at risk for sexual abuse (Mertens et al., 2007; Siebers, 2008).

Nonromantic friendships are sometimes difficult for individuals who have disabilities. For instance, adolescents report that their classmates sometimes seem to be afraid of them or they avoid certain topics of discussion (Hortman, 2007). These censored areas may include sexuality, dating, and childbearing. However, a Canadian study investigated the life satisfaction of women with disabilities who were between the ages of 25 and 54. In general, the participants reported a very high degree of satisfaction with family and friends (Crompton, 2010).

Throughout this book, we have examined how biases can have harmful effects for individuals in a less favored social group. We have learned in earlier chapters that people may be mistreated not only because of gender but also on the basis of ethnic group and sexual orientation. This is true for people with disabilities as well. According to Rosemarie Garland-Thomson (2004), "Disability, like gender and race, is everywhere, once we know how to look for it" (p. 100).

Section Summary

Women with Disabilities

1. Women with disabilities are diverse, yet they experience similar discrimination in a society that exhibits both sexism and ableism. Disabilities tend to exaggerate the differential treatment of women and men.
2. Women with disabilities may face barriers in education and in the workplace, as well as economic problems.
3. Women with invisible disabilities face a dilemma about whether to reveal their disabilities in the workplace.
4. Women with disabilities are often marginalized in the social world of love relationships, sexual desires, and friendships.

11-3 AIDS and Other Sexually Transmitted Infections

Learning Objectives

To describe how HIV and other sexually transmitted infections impact the lives of women and LGBTQ+ individuals, you can …

11-3-1 Define HIV and explain why women are biologically more susceptible to HIV infection than cisgender men.

11-3-2 Describe the biological and psychological impact that HIV infection and AIDS has on women and LGBTQ+ individuals.

11-3-3 Explain the consequences of HPV, chlamydia, genital herpes, gonorrhea, and syphilis infections on people's health.

Sexually transmitted infections have major implications for people's health. For instance, thousands of people in the United States acquire HIV each year, most often from their sexual partners. In this section, we will emphasize HIV and AIDS. However, we will also look briefly at five other sexually transmitted infections that also have important consequences for women's lives: (1) human papillomavirus, which is also called HPV or genital warts, (2) chlamydia, (3) genital herpes, (4) gonorrhea, and (5) syphilis.

Background Information on HIV and AIDS

Acquired immunodeficiency syndrome (AIDS) is a viral disease spread by infected semen, vaginal secretions, breast milk, or blood; this disease destroys the body's normal immune system (Sagrestano et al., 2008). AIDS is caused by the **human immunodeficiency virus (HIV)**, which has the potential to destroy part of the immune system. In particular, HIV invades white blood cells and reproduces itself. HIV then destroys those white blood cells—the very cells that coordinate the immune system's ability to fight infectious diseases (L. L. Alexander et al., 2021; Sagrestano et al., 2008).

For women throughout the world, the most common transmission route for HIV is vaginal or anal sex with an infected person (Sagrestano et al., 2008). HIV is also spread when drug users inject themselves with contaminated syringes. Tragically, an HIV-positive pregnant woman can also transmit the virus to her infant, for instance, during vaginal birth, or through breast feeding her infant after birth (Gross, Taylor, Tomori, & Coleman, 2019). However, the risks of HIV transmission to infants through breast feeding can be reduced when mothers use pre-exposure prophylaxis (PrEP) medications that prevent HIV transmission (World Health Organization, 2017).

Women are much more vulnerable to sexually transmitted infections than men are. By current estimates, a woman who has unprotected sexual intercourse with an HIV-infected man is between two and eight times more likely to contract HIV, compared to a man who has unprotected sexual intercourse with an HIV-infected woman (Gurung, 2006; Sagrestano et al., 2008). One reason for this gender difference is that the concentration of HIV is much greater in semen than in vaginal fluid.

Women's rates for contracting HIV/AIDS have remained stable since 2014 (CDC, 2020a). In the United States, approximately 1,173,900 people are living with HIV/AIDS, and 25% of these HIV-positive individuals are women (CDC, 2020b). In Canada, about 14,545 women are HIV-positive, which represents 23.4% of all people with HIV (CATIE, 2021).

In some parts of the world, even greater percentages of those infected with HIV are women. Worldwide, approximately 18.8 million girls and women are living with HIV, with Eastern and Southern African regions being most affected (AVERT, 2021; UNAIDS, 2018). For instance, in the African countries south of the Sahara desert, an average of 61% of HIV-positive individuals are women (AVERT, 2021). In this region, millions of heterosexual women struggle to make sense of the fact that their male partners are responsible for having infected them with a deadly virus (Long, 2009). If we consider data throughout the world, AIDS is the second leading cause of death in adolescents and young adults (World Health Organization, 2021). The only more deadly category is traffic and other accidents (R. W. Blum & Nelson-Mmari, 2004).

Figure 11.3 shows the increasing number of AIDS deaths among U.S. women since 1991. The incidence of AIDS is highest among men who have sex with men (MSM), accounting for 66% of all HIV cases (AVERT, 2021). For women, the incidence of AIDS is relatively high among both transgender and cisgender Black women; Black women account for more than half of the women who are HIV positive in the United States. The incidence is somewhat lower among Latina and White women, and equally low among Asian American and Native American women (AVERT, 2021; Grassia, 2005).

Let's now consider the medical and psychological consequences of AIDS. Then we'll explore how the risk of this disease can be reduced.

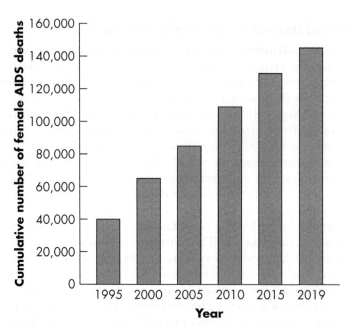

FIGURE **11.3** Cumulative AIDS deaths among girls and women ages 13+ across all ethnic groups in the United States, 1995-2019.
Source: Centers for Disease Control (2021).

Medical Aspects of HIV and AIDS

Many HIV-positive individuals have no symptoms at first, and so they do not realize that they are infected. Most people experience these symptoms of infection between 6 and 9 months later. However, some people are symptom-free for as long as 10 years. The symptoms of infection may include fatigue, rashes, unexplained fevers, unintentional weight loss, and diarrhea (L. L. Alexander et al., 2021; Kalichman, 2003; Sagrestano et al., 2008). Both men and women may have these symptoms if they are HIV positive. In addition, women who are HIV positive are likely to develop vaginal infections and cervical cancer (Crooks & Baur, 2017).

People who are HIV positive are highly contagious during the initial stages of the infection, even if they have no symptoms (Blalock & Campos, 2003). As a result, HIV-positive individuals can spread the disease to other people without realizing that they are doing so. In fact, in the United States about 15% of HIV-positive people do not know that they are infected (Kaiser Family Foundation, 2021b).

It may take 10 years or longer for an HIV infection to develop into AIDS (Crooks & Baur, 2017; Kalichman, 2003). A diagnosis of AIDS is made when a person's immune system T-cell count drops below a specified level. At this point, people are seriously ill because of the symptoms mentioned earlier and because other infections have taken advantage of a severely weakened immune system (Blalock & Campos, 2003; Crooks & Baur, 2017).

Since the beginning of the epidemic, drug therapies have been developed that prolong life for HIV-positive people. As a result, many people living with AIDS now cope with a long-term illness (Sagrestano et al., 2008). However, individuals with limited financial resources and no insurance in the United States typically have no access to those expensive medications. Women are also less likely than men to use these medications, at least partly for financial reasons (Blalock & Campos, 2003; Ciambrone, 2003).

Psychological Aspects of HIV and AIDS

HIV can damage the central nervous system, producing psychological problems such as memory loss and cognitive problems (Blalock & Campos, 2003; Sagrestano et al., 2008). As you might imagine, HIV-positive individuals are likely to experience depression, anxiety, anger, fear, and stress (Blalock & Campos, 2003; Sagrestano et al., 2008). One woman described her reactions when she received her diagnosis: "Total shock, you just go numb. ... Nothing meant anything to me. Of course, immediately you've got a death sentence; that's just what you stand there thinking" (Ciambrone, 2003, p. 24). Consistent with many diseases, high stress levels are especially likely to increase the severity of the HIV-related symptoms (Miller et al., 2009).

Some women experience a new perspective on life that is more hopeful. For instance, one woman who became an HIV/AIDS activist commented:

> My goal now is to try to help other people that have this virus and let them know that you can plan for the future—life does go on, not to give up. I've always learned that if you're a fighter you'll be okay. You have to fight and you have to want to live. ... When I finally started accepting the fact and telling people, I felt like a big burden was lifted off of my shoulder. It's like, boy, I can say it and not really be ashamed. (Ciambrone, 2003, p. 72)

People living with AIDS often report that they are stunned by insensitive reactions from other people (Ciambrone, 2003; Gahagan & Loppie, 2001). For example, family members may show no sympathy (Derlega et al., 2003; Jantarapakde et al., 2019). A 32-year-old Canadian woman was asked whether her family had been helpful. She replied, "Are you kidding, if I ask my family for help, they say stuff like you did this to yourself and now you want us to clean up after you? I don't talk to them anymore" (Gahagan & Loppie, 2001, p. 119).

However, some people are surprised by the messages of support (Sagrestano et al., 2008). For example, Runions (1996) described how she had belonged to a fundamentalist Christian church. When she went public with her personal story about AIDS, many church members wrote to her. "The letters were warm and accepting and forgiving. Bridges that I thought had been damaged beyond repair appeared to have been strengthened by the shock of my illness" (p. 67).

Be sure you have tried Demonstration 11.2 before reading further. This demonstration assesses your personal feelings about using condoms.

Preventing HIV and AIDS

At present, we have no cure for AIDS, so the only available alternative is to prevent it. However, AIDS prevention is difficult, at both the individual and the global level (Oldenburg & Burton, 2004; Sagrestano et al., 2008).

Demonstration **11.2**

Attitudes Toward Condom Use

Consider your own attitudes about condom or dental dam use in the context of sexual activity with other people. Even if you are not sexually active, think about what your own personal responses to these questions would be:

1. How do you feel about condom or dental dam use in general?
2. When was the last time that you had sexual intercourse (if any)?
3. Did you request that your sexual partner use a condom or dental dam on that occasion?
4. How do you think that your sexual partner would feel about using protection during sex?
5. Do you feel comfortable talking with your sexual partners about using protection?
6. Do you typically carry a condom or dental dam with you when you go out on a social occasion?
7. Where do you buy condoms or dental dams?
8. Is it embarrassing for you to purchase condoms or dental dams?
9. Suppose that you have been drinking and that you are about to have sexual activity with another person. Would you remember to use protection?
10. Suppose that your sexual partner says that they do not want to use a protective device. What would you do?

Source: Based on Perloff (2001).

According to surveys, some people believe that they can avoid AIDS because they can judge which sexual partners look like they might be HIV positive (L. D. Cameron & Ross-Morris, 2004; Dolan, 2005). However, it is impossible to tell whether a person is infected just by looking at them (Blalock & Campos, 2003).

One problem with AIDS prevention is that many people think, "It can't happen to me!" (Dudley et al., 2002; Perloff, 2001). When people have consumed alcohol, they especially underestimate their own personal risk (L. D. Cameron & Ross-Morris, 2004). Many people also believe that they can avoid AIDS by asking a potential sexual partner about their HIV status. However, research with HIV-positive individuals revealed that as many as 40% did not tell their sexual partners that they were HIV positive.

You can probably anticipate another problem. Many people are HIV positive and don't know it. For example, a woman may be having sex with a man who doesn't realize he is HIV positive or who may not realize that he had sex with an HIV-positive individual two months before. Basically, if a woman decides to have sex, her sexual partner is not only that individual but also all of that individual's former partners… and their partners!

As we read in Chapter 9, the abstinence-only "Just say no" approach to safer sex does not reduce teen pregnancy; it also does not reduce HIV transmission in teenagers (Coates & Szekeres, 2004). Any HIV-prevention program must include comprehensive sex education that emphasizes condom use. In general, trained professionals are more effective than peer educators in convincing people to engage in safer sex (Durantini et al., 2006).

Furthermore, education-oriented programs are significantly more persuasive than fear-oriented presentations (Albarracín et al., 2005). The programs must also emphasize strategies for reducing risky sexual interactions, as well as active participation in role-play exercises (B. T. Johnson et al., 2003; Marín, 2003). Although the overall rate of transmission has declined since 2014, adolescent girls and young women are especially at risk becoming HIV positive, due to having sexual interactions with men who are HIV-positive (UNAIDS, 2019). These men may pressure their partners or sexually assault them (DiClemente & Crosby, 2006).

Condoms can help to limit the spread of the AIDS epidemic. However, surveys show that less than 40% of women reported that they always used condoms during sexual intercourse (Kaiser Family Foundation, 2003; Noar et al., 2004). In Demonstration 11.2, we noted some of the reasons that prevent people from consistently using condoms. In many cultures, people are reluctant to discuss condom use with their potential sexual partners (Kaiser Family Foundation, 2003; Perloff, 2001).

An important problem with condom use is that men control whether they will use a condom. Throughout the world, men and women in most sexual relationships do not divide power equally. As a result, many women may not feel that they can safely insist that their partner wear a condom (R. W. Blum & Nelson-Mmari, 2004; Marín, 2003). In the United States, Latino men are especially likely to control decisions about condom use during intercourse. A program designed only for Latina women—but not Latina men—may therefore be unsuccessful (D. Castañeda, 2000a). Any HIV/AIDS-prevention program must be sensitive to the culture of the individuals that the program serves (L. A. Beatty et al., 2004; Jipguep et al., 2004).

Even regular condom use does *not* guarantee protection against AIDS because condoms can break or slip (L. L. Alexander et al., 2021). There is no perfectly safe sex, only safer sex. However, a condom is certainly better than no protection at all.

International research shows that some developing countries have successfully reduced HIV rates by emphasizing widespread education about HIV/AIDS and condom use

(D'Adesky, 2004; Smallman, 2008). These countries have used creative programs to prevent the spread of AIDS. For example, in 2005, the Argentinian government worked together with AIDS activists to publicize safe sex by creating an enormous pink condom to cover a prominent phallic-shaped tower in Buenos Aires (Smallman, 2008). Cuba also developed a variety of precautions to reduce the transmission of HIV from mothers to infants. During a 10-year period in Cuba, only 29 infants became HIV positive (Castro et al., 2008).

Other Sexually Transmitted Infections

In addition to HIV and AIDS, other STIs are important for women because women are statistically more likely than men to be infected by having sex with a partner who has one of these diseases. For example, Asian American women are four times more likely than Asian American men to have contracted an STI from a sexual partner (Spencer et al., 2007). Sexually transmitted infections also produce fewer detectable symptoms in women than in men (Crooks & Baur, 2017).

Table 11.1 lists five diseases that have particularly important consequences for women's lives. They are **HPV** (**human papillomavirus**, or **genital warts**), **chlamydia** (pronounced klah-*mih*-dee-uh), **genital herpes** (*her*-peas), **gonorrhea** (gon-uh-*ree*-uh), and **syphilis** (*siff*-ih-liss).

Women are more likely than men to have severe long-term consequences of sexually transmitted infections. For example, many women who do not seek early treatment for these infections will become infertile, or they may pass the infection on to a newborn (Crooks & Baur, 2017; R. W. Blum & Nelson-Mmari, 2004). An additional problem is that

TABLE **11.1**

Sexually Transmitted Infections (STIs) Other Than AIDS

Infection	Description (for Women)	Consequences (for Women)
HPV (Genital Warts)	Caused by various strains of the human papilloma virus; small, often painless swellings in the genital area; very common in young women; can be treated and sometimes curable.	Can lead to cervical cancer, which may lead to death. Can be passed on to newborn during delivery.
Chlamydia	Common in young women; often no symptoms, but may cause painful urination, vaginal discharge, and infertility; curable.	Can lead to infertility. Can be passed on to newborn during delivery.
Genital Herpes	Painful genital blisters, several attacks per year; can be treated, but is not currently curable.	Can lead to cervical cancer, which may lead to death. Can be passed on to newborn during delivery.
Gonorrhea	May produce vaginal discharge and pelvic pain but may not have visible symptoms; curable.	Can lead to infertility. Can be passed on to newborn during delivery.
Syphilis	Painless sores; may produce rash on the body, but may not have visible symptoms; curable.	Can be passed on to fetus prenatally and to newborn during delivery.

Sources: Based on Crooks & Baur (2017), Hyde & DeLamater (2006), Nack (2008), Rupp et al. (2005).

infections such as gonorrhea and syphilis can produce lesions in the skin, making it easier for an STI to enter the body.

The human papillomavirus, or HPV, deserves additional attention because it is the most common of the sexually transmitted diseases in the United States, especially among people between the ages of 15 and 24 (Moscicki, 2005; Nack, 2008). One study focused on women in college who reported never having sexual intercourse. Of those who then had intercourse, 30% acquired HPV within one year (Moscicki, 2005; Winer et al., 2003).

Unfortunately, however, many people are unfamiliar with HPV. But even if she does not recognize the name "human papillomavirus," a young woman who contracts HPV may eventually develop deadly cervical cancer, as discussed on pages 363 to 364 of this chapter (Crooks & Baur, 2017; Hillard & Kahn, 2005). The research shows, however, that college women are much less likely to contract HPV if their sexual partners consistently used condoms (Winer et al., 2006).

Individuals who regularly receive a Pap smear test (review pages 363–364) are more likely to receive treatment for HPV infection at an early stage. Also, a vaccine called Gardasil can prevent some forms of HPV. However, many parents seem to believe that giving their children this vaccine would encourage them to become sexually active, which reduces the likelihood of parents approving of their children becoming vaccinated (Nack, 2008; VanWormer et al., 2017).

Women who are considering a sexual relationship need to worry not only about pregnancy, but also about the very real threat of sexually transmitted infections. Some of them may simply be uncomfortable or painful. However, others may cause recurrent health problems for a woman and potential danger to her infant. Most tragically, a sexual relationship with a person who has a sexually transmitted disease might literally be deadly.

Section Summary

AIDS and Other Sexually Transmitted Diseases

1. Acquired immunodeficiency syndrome (AIDS) is caused by the human immunodeficiency virus (HIV). In unprotected sexual intercourse, cisgender and transgender women are more likely than men to contract HIV from an infected partner.
2. Most people are infected with HIV because they had vaginal or anal intercourse with an infected man or because they injected drugs. In sub-Saharan Africa, more than half of HIV-positive individuals are women.
3. People who are HIV positive may be very contagious; however, they may initially have no symptoms, so they often spread the disease. If they can afford to obtain expensive medicines, they can live much longer.
4. People living with AIDS are likely to be depressed, anxious, angry, fearful, and stressed.
5. Currently, AIDS cannot be cured. Sexually active people need to know that condoms do not offer complete protection; in addition, because of power inequities, women often cannot safely insist that their partner wear a condom. Creative AIDS-prevention programs have been successful in developing countries.

(continues)

Section Summary (continued)

6. Other sexually transmitted diseases also have long-term consequences; they include the following:

   a. HPV (human papillomavirus or genital warts) is a common infection among young people that can lead to cervical cancer. Gardasil helps to prevent some forms of HPV.
   b. Chlamydia can cause infertility.
   c. Genital herpes is not curable, and it can lead to cervical cancer.
   d. Gonorrhea can cause infertility.
   e. Syphilis may be difficult to detect in women.

11-4 Gender and Substance Use

Learning Objectives

To identify gender differences in substance use disorders and explain how they negatively affect physical health, you can …

11-4-1 Describe why smoking cigarettes increases women's likelihood of developing long-term health problems.

11-4-2 Summarize gender differences in alcohol use and health problems related to alcohol use disorders.

11-4-3 Identify gender differences in the use of substances other than alcohol and cigarettes.

Substance use is an important topic in the psychology of women for the three reasons mentioned at the beginning of the chapter:

1. The pattern of substance use is somewhat different for women and men, as we'll soon learn.
2. Substance use disorders are diagnosed differently in men and women (L. A. Beatty et al., 2006). When the patient is a woman, for example, physicians seem to be less effective in identifying problems with alcohol and illegal drugs. In addition, the screening tests that identify substance use problems are based on male norms. The tests neglect common female risk factors, such as being a victim of sexual abuse or family violence (Rheingold et al., 2004).
3. Substance use frequently causes illness and death in women. Ironically, people voluntarily smoke, drink alcohol, and use other substances, even though all of these substances may kill them.

Smoking

Cigarette smoking is the largest preventable cause of death in the United States and Canada (Belgrave & Allison, 2010; Bird & Rieker, 2008). About 201,700 U.S. women die each year from diseases related to smoking (Centers for Disease Control, 2021). Lung cancer is the best-advertised consequence of cigarette smoking, especially because only 15% of people survive more than five years after being diagnosed with lung cancer (Springen, 2004). For reasons that are not clear, smoking increases the chance of lung cancer more for women than it does for men (Cowley & Kalb, 2005; Harrell et al., 2006). Unfortunately, the rate of lung-cancer deaths is still rising among U.S. women, and worldwide, women have higher rates of lung cancer than men (Fidler-Benaoudia et al., 2020; Hwang & Danoff-Burg, 2010).

Women who smoke are more likely to die of lung cancer, several other kinds of cancer, emphysema and other lung diseases, heart disease, and stroke than women who do not smoke. Smoking also has gynecological consequences. Women who smoke increase the risk of cervical cancer, infertility, miscarriages, premature birth, and early menopause. Furthermore, babies born to women who smoke weigh less than babies born to women who do not smoke (Dodgen, 2005; Steptoe & Wardle, 2004). Older women who smoke also increase their chances of developing osteoporosis and hip fractures (Dodgen, 2005; Steptoe & Wardle, 2004).

Here is a startling statistic: Research in both Canada and the United States shows that people who smoke die an average of 10 years earlier than people who do not smoke (Bélanger et al., 2002; DiFranza & Richmond, 2008). You can understand why some people say that the tobacco industry is a business that kills its best customers!

Many women who do not smoke also suffer because of their husband's or partner's smoking habits. For example, women who do not smoke, but are married to men who do smoke, are significantly more likely to develop lung cancer and heart disease than women married to men who do not smoke (Brannon & Feist, 2004; Dodgen, 2005; Sarafino, 2008).

Every puff on a cigarette delivers a dose of nicotine, which is an addictive substance. As a result, long-term people who smoke seldom quit smoking, even with carefully designed smoking-cessation programs (DiFranza & Richmond, 2008; Dodgen, 2005; Hettema et al., 2005).

In the United States, 12.7% of women and 15.3% of men smoke cigarettes or use tobacco products (CDC, 2019). Canadian rates are comparable, with 12% for women and 16% for men (Government of Canada, 2019).

Ethnicity is related to tobacco use. In general, Native American people have the highest rates, followed by White, Black, Latina/Latino, and Asian American people. Education is also highly correlated with tobacco use: only 7% of college graduates smoke, as opposed to 22% of individuals who did not complete high school (CDC, 2019).

Why would young women want to start smoking, given the serious problems it causes? Peer influence is a major factor for adolescent girls (Kim et al., 2009). Furthermore, teenage girls often report that they smoke to control their weight and keep slim (Lee, 2010; Saules et al., 2004).

Alcohol Use

A 34-year-old woman, reflecting on her life after 7 years of sobriety, wrote the following passage in a popular online article:

> For years, after each hazy night filled with poor decisions, I'd wake and think to myself, *I have to quit drinking*, but I never actually imagined doing it.
> The errors in decision-making started out harmless enough—a public make-out session with a stranger, a sharp-tongued rebuke of a loved one—but the older I got, the more serious the

errors became. Business trips turned boozy. Car keys slipped easily into the ignition. It began to feel as if I were living two lives—only one of which I could remember (Haupt, 2018).

Alcohol use disorder refers to a pattern of alcohol use that repeatedly leads to significant impairment (American Psychiatric Association, 2013; NIAAA, 2021; Sher et al., 2005). Impairment includes missing work or school, arrests for alcohol-related crimes, or family problems (Erblich & Earleywine, 2003). Try Demonstration 11.3 before you read further.

Problems Caused by Alcohol

Alcohol has many direct effects on women's health. They include liver disease, ulcers, brain damage, high blood pressure, heart attacks, strokes, cognitive problems, and various cancers (Brannon & Feist, 2004; White, 2020; Yee & Chiriboga, 2007). Children born to mothers who use high amounts of alcohol during pregnancy are likely to have **fetal alcohol syndrome**, which is characterized by facial abnormalities, slowed physical growth, psychological abnormalities, and a higher risk of intellectual disability (Sarafino, 2008; Sher et al., 2005).

Demonstration **11.3**

Alcohol Consumption and Its Behavioral Consequences

Answer each of the following questions as accurately as possible.

1. Think about your behavior during the last two weeks. How many times have you had four or more drinks on one occasion if you are a woman or five or more drinks on one occasion if you are a man? (The operational definition of a "drink" is 12 ounces of beer or a wine cooler, 4 ounces of wine, or 1.25 ounces of liquor.)
2. Since the beginning of this school year, how many times have you personally experienced each of the following problems as a consequence of drinking alcohol?

   a. Had a hangover
   b. Missed a class
   c. Fell behind in schoolwork
   d. Did something you later regretted
   e. Forgot what you did
   f. Argued with friends
   g. Had unplanned sexual activity
   h. Failed to use protection when you had sex
   i. Damaged property
   j. Got into trouble with campus or local police
   k. Got injured or hurt
   l. Required medical treatment for an alcohol overdose

Source: Based on Wechsler et al. (1994).

Alcohol also affects women's health indirectly. For example, alcohol is a contributing factor in about 28% of all U.S. automobile fatalities each year (Centers for Disease Control and Prevention, 2020). Furthermore, when men drink heavily, they are more likely to rape or physically abuse women (Steptoe & Wardle, 2004). Alcohol abuse also increases the number of deaths from injuries, drowning, fires, violent crimes, and suicide (Jersild, 2002; Walters & Baer, 2006; M. D. Wood et al., 2001).

Gender and Alcohol

According to U.S. estimates for people older than 18, 69.5% reported that they consumed at least one drink containing alcohol during the past year (NIAAA, 2021; Substance Abuse and Mental Health Services Administration, 2019). Across all age groups, women are less likely than men to consume alcohol, although the gender gap is narrowing (Hesselbrock & Hesselbrock, 2006; Holder, 2006; King et al., 2009; NIAAA, 2021; White, 2020). The gender difference is especially large for Asian American people (Luczak et al., 2009).

However, research shows that when a man and a woman with the same body weight consume the same amount of alcohol, the woman will have a significantly higher blood alcohol level (L. L. Alexander et al., 2021; Sarafino, 2008). This means that a 150-pound woman who drinks 2 ounces of whiskey will have a higher blood alcohol level than a 150-pound male friend who drinks 2 ounces of the same whiskey. In other words, women need to be more careful than men about monitoring their alcohol consumption.

Studies on college campuses reveal that more men than women use alcohol excessively (Harrell & Karim, 2008). One of the most striking findings is the large percentage of students who had engaged in **binge drinking** (defined as five or more drinks on one occasion for men and four or more drinks on one occasion for women) during the preceding two weeks.

Surveys on college campuses show the behavioral consequences of drinking. Specifically, those who frequently binge drink are likely to report doing something they later regretted. They also report that they engaged in unplanned sexual activity and unprotected sexual intercourse (L. A. Beatty et al., 2006; Walters & Baer, 2006; Yee & Chiriboga, 2007).

Gender differences are relevant when people seek treatment for alcohol problems. Families are more likely to deny that female family members have a problem with alcohol. Physicians are also less likely to identify problem drinking in female patients than in male patients (Blume, 1998; White, 2020). In addition, society disapproves more strongly if a woman drinks excessively. Women may therefore be more reluctant to admit that they have a drinking problem (L. A. Beatty et al., 2006; Springen & Kantrowitz, 2004). Consistent with Theme 2, people react differently to male alcohol users than to female alcohol users.

Use of Other Substances

Nicotine and alcohol are the two most common substances used in the United States, but people also use other substances, such as prescription medicines. For example, consider individuals who are at least 12 years of age. A nationwide U.S. survey showed that 2% of people reported that they had misused pain relievers within the last year. In general, women and men have similar rates for the nonmedical use of psychotherapeutic drugs (Substance Abuse and Mental Health Services Administration, 2019).

When we consider illegal drugs, however, the picture changes, because men are more likely than women to use these drugs. For example, this same nationwide survey showed that 15.9%

of people aged 12 and over reported using cannabis during the previous year (Substance Abuse and Mental Health Services Administration, 2019). Of those individuals, 57.7% of men are cannabis users versus 43.3% of women (Cuttler, Mischley, & Sexton, 2016).

Educational status is related to illicit drug use. However, you might be surprised to learn that 52% of adults who graduated from college have tried some kind of illegal drug, in contrast to 38% of adults who have not completed high school (Substance Abuse and Mental Health Services Administration, 2019).

Some data suggest that women may metabolize illegal drugs differently than men do, but little research has been conducted on this topic. In addition, relatively few substance-abuse programs are designed to help women (L. L. Alexander et al., 2021; L. A. Beatty et al., 2006). Once again, women at risk for health problems are invisible, and their health needs are often ignored.

In this chapter, we have examined many health issues that are central to women's lives. We began by considering general health-care issues, showing that women are often second-class citizens in the United States. Women in developing countries face the risks of poor health care, complications during pregnancy, and female genital mutilation. In contrast, cardiovascular disease and cancer are primary concerns for women in the United States. We also learned that women with disabilities experience exaggerated discrimination. In addition, women around the world are increasingly likely to contract AIDS and other sexually transmitted infections. Finally, many women have problems with smoking, alcohol, and illegal substances. Feminist concerns have helped to make women's health problems more visible. However, information about these health problems is still incomplete.

Section Summary

Gender and Substance Use

1. Women are almost as likely as men to smoke cigarettes, a problem that has literally deadly consequences for women's health.
2. Women with alcohol use disorders face the risks of numerous health problems for themselves, as well as fetal alcohol syndrome for their children. Furthermore, people are more likely to ignore alcohol problems in women than in men.
3. Men and women are equally likely to misuse prescription drugs, whereas men are more likely than women to use illegal drugs.

Chapter Review Questions

1. This chapter starts by discussing three general trends in the medical treatment of women. Consult pages 351–352, and provide additional information about each of these trends.

2. At the beginning of this chapter, we examined gender comparisons in life expectancy, morbidity, and the number of visits to health-care providers. Summarize this information, and describe how these factors may be related.

3. One theme of this book is that men and women are often treated differently. Apply this theme to the following topics: (a) biases against women in health care, (b) women with disabilities, (c) diagnosis of specific diseases, and (d) the availability of substance-abuse programs.

4. What are some of the specific health problems that women are likely to face, and how can women reduce the chances of developing these life-threatening problems? What are other serious health problems for women who smoke or use alcohol excessively?

5. Define the terms "disability" and "ableism." How do women with disabilities differ from one another? In what ways does the life of a woman with a disability differ from the life of a woman who is does not have a disability?

6. Imagine that you are counseling high-school girls about HIV and other sexually transmitted diseases. Describe each STI and explain why a sexually active woman should be concerned about this health problem.

7. Some people argue that sexually transmitted diseases are biologically "sexist"; that is, they hurt women more than they hurt men. Provide some examples to support this statement. How does this statement also apply to smoking and alcohol use?

8. How is economic status relevant when we consider health care, morbidity, and drug therapy for people with HIV/AIDS? How is ethnicity relevant when we consider the following topics: (a) women's life expectancy, (b) women's morbidity, (c) the incidence of AIDS, and (d) substance abuse?

9. Explain why gender comparisons are complicated when we consider the topic of substance use. Before you had read the section on substance use, what did you believe about gender comparisons in this area?

10. One theme of this book is that women are relatively invisible, compared to men. Relate this theme to topics such as the general research on women's health and the specific research on women with disabilities and on women who use alcohol. In what areas are women relatively *visible?*

Key Terms

health psychology (p. 350)

chronic health problem (p. 351)

morbidity (p. 355)

female genital mutilation (p. 358)

female genital cutting (p. 358)

cardiovascular disease (p. 359)

mammogram (p. 361)

lumpectomy (p. 361)

cervical cancer (p. 363)

Pap smear test (p. 363)

hysterectomy (p. 363)

osteoporosis (p. 364)

disability (p. 365)

ableism (p. 366)

disability studies (p. 366)

acquired immunodeficiency syndrome (AIDS) (p. 369)

human immunodeficiency virus (HIV) (p. 369)

human papillomavirus (HPV) or genital warts (p. 374)

chlamydia (p. 374)

genital herpes (p. 374)

gonorrhea (p. 374)

syphilis (p. 374)

alcohol use disorder (p. 378)

fetal alcohol syndrome (p. 378)

binge drinking (p. 379)

Recommended Readings

Bird, C. E., & Rieker, P. P. (2008). *Gender and health: The effect of constrained choices and social policies.* New York: Cambridge University Press. Bird and Rieker are both sociologists, and their analysis of social-class issues is especially relevant to women's health.

Chrisler, J. C., & McCreary, D. R. (Eds.). (2010). *Handbook of gender research in psychology.* New York: Springer. This excellent handbook includes several chapters that focus on women's health. Especially relevant are the chapters on chronic illness, health behavior, and the utilization of health care.

Dusenbery, M. (2018). *Doing harm: The truth about how bad medicine and lazy science leave women dismissed, misdiagnosed, and sick.* New York: HarperCollins. This book addresses the history of women's disparate and inadequate treatment within medical profession. It highlights how medical stereotypes and lack of adequate research for women's health conditions has led to negative outcomes in terms of women's health.

Marlat, G. A., & Witkiewitz, K. (Eds.). (2009). *Addictive behaviors: New readings on etiology, prevention, and treatment.* Washington, DC: American Psychological Association. This book addresses a variety of issues such as family risk factors, the prevention of substance abuse, and treatment approaches. Gender is not central in this book, but several chapters provide useful information.

Nack, A. (2008). *Damaged goods? Women living with incurable sexually transmitted diseases.* Philadelphia: Temple University Press. Although this book discusses AIDS, its primary focus is on human papillomavirus (HPV). The author, sociologist Adina Nack, also includes many insightful interviews.

Siebers, T. (2008). *Disability theory.* Ann Arbor: University of Michigan Press. Here is a thought-provoking, interesting book that also includes examples from the media about some difficult situations encountered by people with disabilities, as well as some wonderful examples of disability rights activists.

Photographee.eu/Shutterstock.com

12 Gender and Mental Health

Learning Objectives

After studying this chapter, you will be able to ...

12-1 Describe how gender impacts individuals' experience of depression.

12-2 Summarize cultural, social, and psychological forces that contribute to the development of eating disorders.

12-3 Explain why treating psychological disorders is a gendered process.

Did You Know?

- Women in many countries around the world are two to three times more likely than men to experience major depression (pp. 385–386).
- In the United States and Canada, women are more likely to attempt suicide, but men are more likely to die from suicide (p. 386).
- After a distressing event has occurred, women are more likely than men to focus on their emotional reactions to this event (pp. 391–392).
- In many situations, a woman perceives herself as an object that can be viewed by other people (p. 394).
- As early as preschool, children typically prefer to have a friend who is below average weight, instead of above average weight (p. 395).
- White people are more likely than people of color to use mental health services (pp. 404–405).
- Feminist therapy emphasizes a fairly even distribution of power between the therapist and the client (p. 411).

Katie, a 16-year-old, described her personal history with depression:

> The experience of depression is like falling into a deep dark hole that you cannot climb out of. You scream as you fall, but it seems like no one hears you. ... Depression affects the way you interpret events. It influences the way you see yourself and the way you see other people. (Barlow & Durand, 2015, p. 217)

Meike, a 19-year-old college student, has an eating disorder. She described her experience:

> Going from a fit, healthy self, I lost nearly a third of my body weight ... I ate less and less until it was just a banana in the morning and some steamed vegetables or lettuce with vinegar on it in the evenings ... Everything hurt—physically and emotionally. Just sitting on a chair without cushioning was torture. By Thanksgiving, after a semester of teetering, I was at the bottom. I felt no love for myself, for my family and friends. (Schleiff, 2007, p. 31, p. 33)

Like many people throughout the world, these two young women are experiencing **psychological disorders**; they have emotions, thoughts, and behaviors that are typically maladaptive, distressing to themselves, and different from the social norm (Barlow & Durand, 2015). As we'll learn in this chapter, women are more likely than men to experience both depression and eating disorders. People who identify as a gender or sexual minority are also at increased risk for both depression and eating disorders when compared with their cisgender and heterosexual peers (Parker & Harriger, 2020; Yean et al., 2013). Women and LGBTQ+ individuals are also more likely to seek therapy for these disorders (Kates et al., 2018; Platt et al., 2017).

Men are more likely than women to experience a different pattern of problems. As we learned in Chapter 11, men are currently more likely than women to use alcohol and other drugs. Men are also about three times more likely than women to experience **antisocial personality disorder**, which includes behaviors that clearly violate the rights of other people; these behaviors include excessive aggressiveness, impulsiveness, and lying (Ali et al., 2010; American Psychiatric Association, 2013; Barlow & Durand, 2015). People with this disorder also believe that they are perfectly well adjusted, but everyone else in the world has a problem.

If we compile overall tallies—and include all individuals with substance use disorders —then the incidence of psychological disorders in women and men is roughly similar (Russo & Tartaro, 2008; Wilhelm, 2006). Keep in mind, however, that the specific types of disorders may differ.

In this chapter, we will focus on two categories of disorders that are more common among women, gender, and sexual minorities than cisgender and heterosexual men: depression and eating disorders. Then we will investigate both traditional and feminist approaches to treating psychological disorders.

12-1 Depression

Learning Objectives

To explain how gender impacts individuals' experience of depression, you can …

12-1-1 Describe which groups of people, on average, are more likely to experience major depressive disorder.

12-1-2 Identify the emotional, cognitive, behavioral, and physical symptoms of major depressive disorder.

12-1-3 Explain why biological factors are no longer considered relevant for understanding gender differences in depression.

12-1-4 Summarize eight factors that are associated with gender differences in depression.

12-1-5 Explain why having a ruminative style may increase someone's likelihood of developing depression.

Katie, the young woman introduced at the beginning of this chapter, is experiencing depression. A person with **major depressive disorder** has frequent episodes of hopelessness and low self-esteem; this person seldom finds pleasure in any activities (American Psychiatric Association, 2013; Whiffen & Demidenko, 2006). The World Health Organization lists depression as one of the five most prevalent mental health threats throughout the world (Sáez-Santiago & Bernal, 2003; World Health Organization, 2019).

In the United States and Canada, women are two to three times more likely than men to experience depression during their lifetime (Ali et al., 2010; Hatzenbuehler et al., 2010;

Knoll & MacLennan, 2017; Whiffen & Demidenko, 2006). Individuals who identify as sexual or gender minorities are more than twice as likely to experience depression as people who identify as cisgender or heterosexual (Hayes Skelton & Pantalone, 2018; Li, Pollitt, & Russell, 2016). Interestingly, no consistent gender differences in depression are found among young children (Hatzenbuehler et al., 2010; R. C. Kessler, 2006). However, around the time of puberty, girls and adolescents who identify as gender and sexual minorities begin reporting more depressive symptoms than cisgender boys (Irish et al., 2019). During students' first semester of college, for example, L. J. Sax and her coauthors (2002) found that 11% of women and 6% of men reported that they were frequently depressed. This gender difference continues throughout adulthood (Hatzenbuehler et al., 2010; Lapointe & Marcotte, 2000; Whiffen & Demidenko, 2006).

Gender differences in depression are substantial for all major U.S. ethnic groups: White, Latina/o, Black, Asian American, and Native American (Nolen-Hoeksema & Hilt, 2009; Sáez-Santiago & Bernal, 2003; Saluja et al., 2004). Research in Canada shows gender differences for people from British, European, and Asian ethnic backgrounds as well (Chiu, Amartey, Wang, & Kurdyak, 2018; Kornstein & Wojcik, 2002).

Furthermore, cross-cultural studies report that women are more likely than men to experience depression in countries as varied as Germany, Lebanon, Israel, Chile, South Korea, Taiwan, Uganda, and New Zealand (Kornstein & Wojcik, 2002; Nydegger, 2004; Whiffen & Demidenko, 2006; Wilhelm, 2006). Let's consider some of the characteristics of depression and then examine some explanations for the higher incidence of depression in women.

Characteristics of Depression

Depression is a disorder that includes the following emotional, cognitive, behavioral, and physical symptoms (Joorman, 2009; Mann, 2005; Merrell, 2008; Nydegger, 2008; Whiffen & Demidenko, 2006):

1. *Emotional symptoms:* feeling sad, gloomy, tearful, apathetic, irritable, and unable to experience pleasure.
2. *Cognitive symptoms:* thoughts that focus on inadequacy, worthlessness, helplessness, self-blame, and pessimism about the future. These negative thoughts interfere with normal functioning, so that people experiencing depression have trouble concentrating and making decisions. People with depression also remember negative information more accurately than positive information.
3. *Physical symptoms:* illnesses such as headaches, dizzy spells, fatigue, indigestion, and generalized pain. Some people gain weight, but other people lose weight.
4. *Behavioral symptoms:* decreased ability to do ordinary tasks, decreased productivity at work, neglected personal appearance, decreased social interactions, and sleep problems. Many individuals with depression attempt suicide. In the United States and Canada, women are typically—but not always—more likely than men to think about suicide and also more likely to attempt it. However, men are more likely to die from suicide (Berman, 2009; Canetto, 2008; Nolen-Hoeksema & Hilt, 2009). The gender difference in rates of deaths from suicide is found in most developed countries (Government of Canada, 2019; Kennedy et al., 2005; Range, 2006). However, in some countries—such as China—women are more likely than men to die from suicide (Canetto, 2008; Marecek, 2006; World Health Organization, 2009).

We should emphasize that most people have occasional episodes of extreme sadness. For example, this sadness is considered normal when a close friend or family member dies. However, these symptoms normally do not continue many years after the loss. Women who experience major depression struggle with persistent depression, often without relief (Whiffen & Demidenko, 2006). They are also likely to experience other problems such as substance use disorders, anxiety disorders, and eating disorders (Crick & Zahn-Waxler, 2003; J. R. DePaulo & Horvitz, 2002; Kornstein & Wojcik, 2002). These additional problems, in turn, may make the depression even more intense.

Depression is correlated with certain personality characteristics. For example, women who experience depression are especially likely to also have low self-esteem, traditional feminine gender typing, and little sense of control over their own lives (Malanchuk & Eccles, 2006; Travis, 2006; Whiffen & Demidenko, 2006).

Explanations for the Gender Difference in Depression

What are some of the explanations for the prevalence of depression among women? Let's begin with some biological explanations that were once thought to be important but no longer seem relevant. Then we will examine a much longer list of factors that do contribute to the gender differences in depression.

Factors No Longer Considered Relevant

Several decades ago, many theorists believed that gender differences in biological factors could explain why women are more likely than men to experience depression. For example, perhaps the gender differences could be directly traced to biochemical factors, hormonal fluctuations, or some genetic factor associated with having two X chromosomes. This perspective is consistent with the gender essentialist argument that we discussed in Chapter 1. However, careful reviews of the literature suggest that biological factors do not convincingly explain the greater prevalence of depression in women (Ali et al., 2010; Whiffen & Demidenko, 2006; Worell & Remer, 2003).[1]

Let's now consider some of the explanations that are currently thought to account for the gender differences in depression. As we frequently observe in psychology, human behavior is so complex that a single explanation is usually inadequate. All the following factors probably help to explain why the rate of depression is so much higher in women and gender and sexual minority individuals than in men.

Gender Differences in Seeking Therapy

Maybe you've thought about another potential explanation. In Chapter 11, we learned that women are more likely than men to seek medical help. Is it possible that people equally experience depression in the general population but that women and LGBTQ+ individuals are simply more likely to seek help from a therapist?

Research shows that men are less likely than women to report symptoms of depression if they think that a therapist will contact them about their potential depression (Sigmon et al., 2005). This research is consistent with other evidence that women and LGBTQ+ individuals are somewhat more likely than cisgender and heterosexual men to seek therapy

---

[1]Researchers have established that biological factors can predispose individuals to develop depression. However, men and women are similarly affected by these biological factors. For example, the clear majority of the research demonstrates no sex differences in genetic effects (e.g., Mann, 2005; Nolen-Hoeksema & Hilt, 2009).

(Addis & Mahalik, 2003; Call & Shafer, 2018; Kates et al., 2018; Mosher, 2002; Platt et al., 2017; Winerman, 2005). However, researchers have also examined the incidence of depression in the general population. Women, gender, and sexual minority individuals are still much more likely than men to experience depression (R. C. Kessler, 2006; Kornstein & Wojcik, 2002). In summary, we must search for additional factors to help explain the large gender differences in depression.

Diagnostic Biases Among Therapists and Physicians

The research suggests that therapists tend to equate "healthy adults" with "healthy adult men," whereas "healthy adult women" are rated as substantially less healthy than those two other categories (Seem & Clark, 2006). In other words—before therapists have any other information—they consider adult women to be less healthy.

Therapists and physicians also *overdiagnose* depression in women (Bacigalupe & Martin, 2021; Mojtabai, 2013). That is, therapists and physicians are more likely to supply a diagnosis of major depression for women, compared to men with similar psychological symptoms. At the same time, therapists tend to *underdiagnose* depression in men (Nydegger, 2008). That is, therapists are guided by their stereotypes about men being "tough," so they are reluctant to conclude that men have depression.

In addition, men have different behavioral manifestations of depression (Addis, 2008; Stiawa et al., 2020). Men may respond to depression by behaving aggressively, drinking alcohol excessively, or using substances. As a result, therapists may diagnose a substance use disorder, rather than depression (Bird & Rieker, 2008; McSweeney, 2004). Therapists' bias is one reason why women are more likely to be diagnosed with depression. However, many other factors also contribute to the very real gender differences in depression.

General Discrimination Against Women and LGBTQ+ Individuals

Several general forms of discrimination seem to increase the incidence of depression in women and gender and sexual minorities (Belle & Doucet, 2003; Mendelson & Muñoz, 2006; Nolen-Hoeksema, 2006). As we noted in earlier chapters, women experience general discrimination, and their accomplishments are often devalued relative to those of men. As Klonoff and her colleagues (2000) discovered, female students who frequently experience sexist treatment are especially likely to report symptoms of depression.

Furthermore, in Chapter 7 we learned that women are less likely to be hired and promoted in the workplace. In many cases, women's work is also less rewarding and prestigious. Depression is especially likely when women face barriers in their careers and when their achievements do not seem to be valued. Discrimination against women—in everyday life and in the workplace—leads women to feel that they have relatively little control over their lives (Lennon, 2006; Sue, 2010; Travis, 2006).

Women of color also experience **gendered racism**, which includes multiple intersecting forms of oppression and discrimination that is associated with an increased likelihood of depression and traumatic stress (Carr et al., 2014; Moody & Lewis, 2019; Syzmanski & Lewis, 2016).

Members of gender and sexual minority groups regularly experience discrimination across a wide variety of settings. It is estimated that LBGTQ+ individuals experience depression at twice the rate as their cisgender and heterosexual peers due to marginalization and stigma from others (King et al., 2008; Marshal et al., 2013).

Abuse and Violence

As we will emphasize in Chapter 13, many women and gender and sexual minorities are the targets of violence. Some people are sexually abused during childhood. Some people face sexual harassment at school and at work. Their partners may physically abuse them. Furthermore, a large number of women are raped, either by husbands, partners, or acquaintances they know or by people who are strangers. Interpersonal violence clearly contributes to depression (Ali et al., 2010; Mendelson & Muñoz, 2006; Hatzenbuehler et al., 2010).

A 30-year-old Latina teacher wrote the following account about how an acquaintance rape continues to affect her:

> I wake up three or four mornings a week in a state of terror. ... My last dream reminded me of a bad experience I had in college when my date drove to an isolated part of town, held me down, and threatened to beat me up unless I had sex with him. I tried to get away, but couldn't. I gave up fighting. But my reactions don't make sense. That experience was 10 years ago, and I didn't react much at the time. ... I didn't tell anyone until last week when I called the crisis line. I feel like I am going crazy. I just don't usually get this overpowered by things. (Worell & Remer, 2003, p. 204)

As you can imagine, people are likely to feel depressed and anxious if they have been raped or if they have experienced interpersonal violence, physical, or psychological abuse (J. A. Hamilton & Russo, 2006; Russo & Tartaro, 2008). In fact, it is surprising that many people who are victims of violence manage to escape the symptoms of depression.

Poverty

Throughout this book, we have emphasized how economic status influences psychological and physical well-being. In addition, people with economic problems are especially likely to experience psychological depression (Nolen-Hoeksema, 2006; Travis, 2006; Whiffen & Demidenko, 2006). Women who are economically disadvantaged have far fewer options and choices than women with sufficient financial resources (Ali et al., 2010; Belle & Dodson, 2006; Ehrenreich, 2001). Furthermore, as Chapter 7 emphasized (Belle, 2008), mothers who are unemployed in the United States struggle to raise their children under the current restrictions of the TANF policy (pp. 211–212). Try to imagine a woman who is trying to support three young children, who may be unemployed with no assistance from her partner who has deserted the family. It's easy to understand why she would experience depression. In fact, it's surprising that more women who are economically disadvantaged do *not* experience depression (V. E. O'Leary & Bhaju, 2006).

Housework

Women who experience a traditional role as a full-time homemaker often find that their chores are unstimulating and undervalued. Such unrewarding work may lead to depression (Cyranowski & Frank, 2006; Kornstein & Wojcik, 2002; Lennon, 2006). On the other hand, women who work outside the home often have the equivalent of two jobs.

We discovered in Chapter 7 that most women thrive when they are employed. However, some women who become overwhelmed with household responsibilities, in addition to a job outside the home, may develop depression (Glynn, 2018; Lennon, 2006; Nolen-Hoeksema, 2001; Travis, 2006; Weston, Zilanawala, Webb, Carvalho & McMunn, 2019). These outcomes are even more likely in times of global crisis, such as during the COVID-19 pandemic.

For example, women worldwide have experienced higher rates of depression, anxiety, and stress than men, in part due to increased work responsibilities both at home and in their jobs (Guadagni, Umilta', & Iaria, 2020; Thibaut & van Wijngaarden-Cremers, 2020).

Emphasis on Physical Appearance

Beginning in adolescence, some girls become excessively concerned about their physical appearance. As we'll read in the section on eating disorders, adolescent girls are often dissatisfied with the weight they gain during puberty. They may find their changing body shape especially unappealing in an era when female fashion models, peers, celebrities, and social media influencers regularly post and share images of bodies that are unrealistically curvy, thin, or physically fit. Adolescent girls are often aware that these body types are sometimes obtained through the process of multiple surgeries or cosmetic procedures, or that the images have been digitally photoshopped, retouched, or reshaped. Still, these unrealistic images have been shown to negatively affect girls' body image and lower their sense of body satisfaction (Kleemans, Daalmans, Carbaat, & Anschütz, 2018). This dissatisfaction may contribute to depression (Girgus & Nolen-Hoeksema, 2006; Travis, 2006; Whiffen & Demidenko, 2006). At this point, try Demonstration 12.1 before you read further.

Demonstration **12.1**

Responses to Depression

Suppose that you are in a depressed mood because of a recent personal event, such as an unexpectedly low grade on an exam, the breakup of a love relationship, or a disagreement with a close friend or relative. Check which of the following activities you are likely to engage in when you are feeling depressed:

_____ 1. Working on a hobby that takes concentration
_____ 2. Writing in a diary about how you are feeling
_____ 3. Getting away from everyone else to try to sort out your emotions
_____ 4. Doing something with your friends
_____ 5. Getting drunk or using substances
_____ 6. Telling friends about how depressed you are
_____ 7. Punching something
_____ 8. Exercising or playing sports
_____ 9. Writing a letter to someone describing your emotions
_____ 10. Engaging in reckless behavior (e g., driving more than 10 miles over the speed limit)
_____ 11. Listening to music
_____ 12. Making a list of the reasons you are sad or depressed

When you have finished, count up how many of your responses fall into the first group: Items 2, 3, 6, 9, 11, and 12. Then count up the number that fall into the second group: Items 1, 4, 5, 7, 8, and 10. The text discusses the results.

Source: Based on Nolen-Hoeksema (1990).

Women's Relationships

Women are more likely than men to feel responsible for making sure that their inter-personal relationships are going well (Crick & Zahn-Waxler, 2003; Nolen-Hoeksema & Hilt, 2009). They may believe that they ought to be more unselfish in a relation-ship rather than expressing their own personal preferences (Jack, 2003; McGann & Steil, 2006; Whiffen & Demidenko, 2006). Latina girls and women may be especially self-sacrificing (Travis, 2006).

In addition, many women become overly involved in the problems of their friends and family members. We read in Chapter 6 that women sometimes have closer relationships with their friends than men do. However, in some cases, women become so involved with others' problems that they actually neglect their own needs (McMullen, 2003; Nolen & Hilt, 2009; Whiffen, 2001).

Rumination

So far, we have discussed eight factors that help to explain why depression is more likely in women than in men. More women than men may seek therapy, and therapists and physicians may overdiagnose depression in women. In addition, women are more likely than men to be influenced by factors that increase the probability of depression. These factors—including general discrimination, abuse, poverty, housework, concern about physical appearance, and women's relationships—predispose women to depression.

Another major factor also encourages depression: Women often respond differently from men when they are experiencing a depressed mood. Demonstration 12.1 focuses on responses to depression. You may recall from Chapter 3 that parents are much more likely to encourage girls—rather than boys—to contemplate why they are sad. This factor may contribute to the development of depression in women (Hatzenbuehler et al., 2010).

Susan Nolen-Hoeksema is the major researcher on responses to depression. She proposed that depressed women are more likely than depressed men to turn inward and focus on their symptoms. They contemplate the possible causes and consequences of their emotions, an approach called a **ruminative style** of response. For example, they worry about all the things that are wrong in their life (Hatzenbuehler et al., 2010; Nolen-Hoeksema et al., 2008).

Research confirms that women are significantly more likely than men to use ruminative strategies when they are depressed (Girgus & Nolen-Hoeksema, 2006; Nolen-Hoeksema, 1990, 2003). Furthermore, a Canadian study found that Black, Chinese, and South Asian students typically ruminated more than White students (M. Conway et al., 2008). However, within each of these ethnic groups, women ruminated more than men.

The problem is that rumination can intensify a bad mood. Rumination tends to create a negative bias in people's thinking, so that pessimistic and ineffective ideas come easily to mind. People are therefore more likely to blame themselves and to feel helpless about solving their problems. This pessimistic style increases the likelihood of more long-term, serious depression (Hatzenbuehler et al., 2010; Scher et al., 2004). We also learned in the discussion about relationships that women often worry about other people's problems. Women who tend to ruminate about all these problems often make their depressed mood even worse.

Now examine your responses to Demonstration 12.1. Naturally, no 12-item ques-tionnaire can provide an accurate assessment of your style of responding to depression. However, if you checked more items in the first group, you may tend to have a ruminative style. In contrast, if you checked more items in the second group, you are probably more likely to distract yourself when you are depressed. (Incidentally, if you checked Item 1, 4, or 8, your distracting style may help lift you out of a depressed mood. However, if you checked Item 5 or 10, your response style may be less adaptive.)

What can you do if you have a ruminative style? The next time you are depressed, think briefly about the problem and then do an interesting activity that you can focus on, instead of your negative emotions. Wait until your depressed mood has lifted somewhat. Then you can think more clearly, and effectively analyze the problem that made you depressed (Nolen-Hoeksema et al., 2008). However, if your depression persists, it is recommended that you seek help from a therapist. Many campus counseling centers offer free or low-cost therapy to college students; they can also make referrals to mental health professionals in the local community.

Conclusions About Gender and Depression

Therapists may be able to help women readjust their ruminative style. But think about the other sources of gender differences, such as poverty, violence, and workload. We have learned that women, members of ethnic minority groups, and people who identify as LGBTQ+ are more likely to experience depression than cisgender and heterosexual men. In many cases, these higher rates of depression in women and gender, sexual, and ethnic minorities result from social and economic inequality present in many societies around the world. If societal inequities created the depression problem, one route to reducing the overall rates of depression in society is to work to change these inequities.

Many psychiatrists and other mental health professionals strongly emphasize biological factors, which reside inside each person. When they treat depression, they simply prescribe an antidepressant such as Prozac, rather than address the problems in society.

In contrast, feminist psychologists emphasize a different strategy: They argue that to address psychological problems, we must acknowledge that these problems occur in a social context (Ali et al., 2010; Cosgrove & Caplan, 2004; Marecek, 2006). In fact, these societal problems are intertwined with the many other gender inequities discussed throughout this textbook.

Section Summary

Depression

1. Women are more likely than men to experience depression and eating disorders; men are more likely to have problems with substance use and antisocial personality disorder.
2. Depression is two to three times more common in women and LGBTQ+ individuals than in cisgender and heterosexual men; this gender difference has been reported in a variety of ethnic groups in the United States and also in many other countries.
3. Depression includes feelings of sadness and apathy, thoughts of inadequacy and pessimism, decreased cognitive skills, physical complaints such as headaches and dizzy spells, and a potential for suicide attempts.
4. Women and men do not differ in their biological predisposition toward depression.

(continues)

Section Summary *(continued)*

5. Some likely explanations for gender differences in depression include gender differences in seeking therapy, therapists' diagnostic biases, general discrimination, violence, poverty, housework, emphasis on physical appearance, interpersonal relationships, and ruminative responses to depression. Ideally, attempts to reduce depression in women and marginalized individuals would emphasize societal problems.

12-2 Body Weight and Eating Disorders

Learning Objectives

To summarize cultural, social, and psychological forces that contribute to the development of eating disorders, you can ...

12-2-1 Identify the primary components that characterize the culture of thinness.

12-2-2 Explain how objectified body consciousness and body dissatisfaction varies across different ethnic groups.

12-2-3 Summarize common discriminatory experiences that girls and women who have above-average size bodies face.

12-2-4 Discuss why dieting is often unsuccessful.

12-2-5 Differentiate between anorexia nervosa, bulimia nervosa, and binge eating disorder.

In the first chapter of her book, Harriet Brown (2015) provides a thought-provoking anecdote about people's reactions to her daughter, who was experiencing anorexia nervosa at the time:

> More than once, when she was sick, they literally approached her in the street to praise her beauty, admire her gaunt figure, even ask her—a fourteen-year-old girl who looked like she was dying—for diet tips. Even friends who knew how ill she was commented admiringly on how gorgeous and svelte she was. It was if they couldn't help themselves. And if I hadn't seen with my own eyes how much my daughter suffered and how ill she truly was, maybe I would have found her thinness glamorous and beautiful, too. (Brown, 2015, p. 5)

The truth is that most women in the United States are preoccupied with their body weight. Most do not have one of the life-threatening eating disorders we will discuss later in this section. However, women often shift their lives away from social pleasures and professional concerns so that they can focus on their physical appearance and dieting.

Here's a second reason that the topic of body image is necessary in a textbook about the psychology of women and gender. Consistent with Theme 2, people emphasize body weight much more when they judge women than when they judge men. As Calogero and Thompson (2010) note, "The different portrayals of women's and men's bodies underscore the different lived experiences of women and men" (p. 152).

In this section, we'll first address the general topic of how many cultures place an emphasis on being thin. Then we'll consider the related issues of body weight and dieting. We need to emphasize in advance that people who are considered "overweight" do *not* have a psychological disorder. However, the emphases on women's thinness and dieting—combined with the fear of being "overweight"—are major factors in creating eating disorders. The final topics in this section focus on three categories of eating disorders: anorexia nervosa, bulimia nervosa, and binge-eating disorder.

The Culture of Thinness

Most women in the United States are concerned that they are "overweight," even if their weight is appropriate; this tendency is called the **culture of thinness** (M. Cooper, 2003). As we discovered in Chapter 4, adolescent girls often develop an intense focus on being thin. Information about the culture of thinness helps us understand why most women are extremely concerned about their physical appearance.

The extremely thin images that are portrayed in fashion magazines, on Instagram pages, and other media are an important part of the culture of thinness. For example, Kate Dillon (2000) recalled her earlier experience in fashion modeling. She was 5'11" and weighed only 125 pounds, yet she was instructed to lose 10 to 20 pounds.

Some media sources have tried to promote body positivity and counteract toxic messages, such as the "thigh gap challenge" on Instagram (Belle, 2018). However, most research demonstrates that the media emphasizes weight consciousness, thinness, and dieting in women (Choma et al., 2007; Calogero & Thompson, 2010; C. A. Smith, 2008). Other research on the media assesses how these images may influence women's views of their bodies. For instance, studies show that, when women observe images of slender women, they tend to experience higher levels of anxiety and dissatisfaction with their own bodies (Greenwood & Pietromonaco, 2004; Harper & Tiggemann, 2008; Yamamiya et al., 2005).

Let's now explore several components of the culture of thinness. Specifically, we'll consider objectified body consciousness, ethnic-group comparisons, and discrimination against women who are above average size.

Objectified Body Consciousness and Body Dissatisfaction

In Chapter 4, we noted that attractiveness is increasingly emphasized as a young woman moves through adolescence and into adulthood. Specifically, she is likely to experience **objectified body consciousness**; she tends to view herself as an object that can be looked at and judged by other people (Fredrickson & Roberts, 1997; Lindberg et al., 2006; Szymanski & Henning, 2007). Women's objectified body consciousness typically increases when they repeatedly encounter unrealistic images of women in the media (Calogero & Thompson, 2010; Clark & Tiggeman, 2008). Objectified body consciousness is especially likely when women are exposed to sexualized media, and for some girls, it can start as early as age 6 (Karsay, Knoll, & Matthes, 2018; Jongenelis & Pettigrew, 2020).

As you can imagine, women are more likely than men to perceive their bodies as objects and to be dissatisfied with their bodies (Calogero & Thompson, 2010; T. F. Davison & McCabe, 2005; Grabe et al., 2007). Unfortunately, transgender women are often vulnerable to body objectification and internalized cultural standards for female beauty that increase body dissatisfaction (Comiskey, Parent, & Tebbe, 2020). This emphasis on physical appearance can contribute to eating disorders and depression, and it also helps to explain the gender differences in the prevalence of these two categories of psychological disorders (Comiskey et al., 2020; Grabe & Hyde, 2006; Moradi & Huang, 2008).

Women of Color and Body Dissatisfaction

For many years, the research on body image focused on White populations. However, modern research also provides some information about body dissatisfaction among Black women, Latina women, and Asian American women.

Does ethnicity make a difference in women's body dissatisfaction? Shelly Grabe and Janet Hyde (2006) conducted a meta-analysis of 98 U.S. studies focusing on the relationship between ethnicity and body dissatisfaction. According to their analysis, White women were somewhat more dissatisfied with their bodies than Black women. (The d value was 0.29; as we noted in Chapter 5, this is a small effect size.) This finding is consistent with reports that Black women also believe that an average-weight woman is more attractive than a below-average-weight woman (Markey, 2004).

With respect to body dissatisfaction, the comparisons between Black women and either Latina women or Asian American women were even smaller (Grabe & Hyde, 2006). Furthermore, all the other comparisons between ethnic groups had d values close to zero. That is, White women, Asian American women, and Latina women had virtually identical levels of body dissatisfaction (Calogero & Thompson, 2010; Grabe & Hyde, 2006).

As you've read in previous chapters, any comparison of ethnic groups is complex. For instance, the difference in body dissatisfaction between Black women and White women may depend on the women's age (Roberts et al., 2006). Latina women from a wealthy South American background may be more dissatisfied with their bodies than Latina women from a lower-income Central American or Caribbean background. Asian American women may be dissatisfied with the size of their breasts, but not with their body weight (Forbes & Frederick, 2008).

Surprisingly, the results on body dissatisfaction cannot be explained by the amount of exposure to cultural norms. For instance, a study of female undergraduate students in Western Canada found that length of time living in Canada was not correlated with their body-image satisfaction. Furthermore, White Canadian women actually had more *positive* body images than Asian and South Asian women did (Kennedy et al., 2004).

Factors that appear to affect body dissatisfaction among women of color include experiences with navigating cultural norms, specific experiences of sexism and racism, parent and peer influences, and individual identity management processes (Brady et al., 2017). For example, Black women who have positive and multiculturally inclusive racial identities are less likely to experience body dissatisfaction than Black women who have internalized dominant cultural norms regarding beauty and thinness Watson, Ancis, White, & Nazari, 2013).

Discrimination Against Girls and Women Who Are Above Average Size

U.S. society is biased against women who are above average size (Rothblum & Soloway, 2009; Solovay & Rothblum, 2009). For example, most people would hesitate before making an overtly racist comment, but they might make a comment about a woman who is perceived to be above average size (Brownell, 2005; Myers & Rothblum, 2004). Furthermore, consistent with Theme 2 of this book, people discriminate more strongly against women who are above average size than against men who are similarly above average weight (Smith, 2008; Smolak, 2006).

Women who are above average size are also less likely to be hired, typically earn lower salaries, and are less likely to be promoted than women who are thin (Crandall et al., 2009; Fikkan & Rothblum, 2005). People also think that women who are larger-sized are less likely than women who are smaller-sized to have a romantic partner (Greenberg et al., 2003). This belief may partially explain why some men deliberately look for larger-sized women as "easy targets" for sexual assault (Prohaska & Gailey, 2009).

Even children in preschool and elementary school report that they would prefer to be friends with a child who is thin, rather than a child who is larger sized (Crandall et al., 2009; Latner & Schwartz, 2005; Puhl & Latner, 2007). Children bully peers who are above average size about twice as often as their slender peers (Weinstock & Krehbiel, 2009). Furthermore, children tease girls who fall into this category more than boys (Calogero & Thompson, 2010; Neumark-Sztainer & Eisenberg, 2005). Clearly, both adults' and children's perceived physical attractiveness can have widespread consequences for the way that other people treat them.

However, there's a thought-provoking interdisciplinary area called *fat studies,* which originally developed between about 2000 and 2005. **Fat studies** argues that the United States is a fat-hating culture, and that people need to rethink their approach to body weight (Mills & Fuller-Tyszkiewicz, 2017; Rothblum & Solovay, 2009; Wann, 2009). Fat studies examines popular culture, the medical profession, and the weight-loss industry, on which U.S. residents spend about $78 billion a year (La Rosa, 2020). As we'll learn in the following discussion, almost all diet programs are unsuccessful in the long run.

Body Weight and Dieting

Physicians use a variety of different measures to assess whether an individual should be categorized as "overweight." Depending on the specific measure, roughly 65 to 70% of the adult population in the United States is considered either "overweight" or "obese" (Hales, Carroll, Fryar, & Ogden, 2020; Paharia & Kase, 2008). We need to discuss the issue of body weight because it is a central topic in many women's lives. In addition, the fear of becoming "overweight" is a major factor in developing an eating disorder.

Research demonstrates that people who eat foods that are high in fat and who also do not exercise sufficiently are statistically more likely to face health risks. In addition, "overweight people" are more likely than other people to be at risk for diabetes, heart disease, and certain kinds of cancer (Paharia & Kase, 2008; Hales et al., 2020; Stice et al., 2006). However, body weight is not, in and of itself, indicative of health status. For example, some studies show that having a below-average weight leads to a higher risk of death than having an above average weight (Cao et al., 2014).

Unfortunately, it's extremely difficult to lose extra weight, and relatively few programs produce substantial weight loss (Faith et al., 2007; Gaesser, 2009). Some people engage in fad dieting. Others may seek out drastic surgical procedures that are extremely expensive. These interventions often lead to short-term success, but many people eventually regain all the weight they had lost (Paharia & Kase, 2008). People in the United States and Canada can choose from thousands of different diet plans and products, and most of them are expensive and ineffective (Lyons, 2009). Think about this: If any of these programs were truly effective, then why are there so many programs on the market?

Most people who have lost weight tend to gain it back (Gaesser, 2009; C. A. Smith, 2008). In addition, dieters may become so focused on food that they are tempted to binge. For these reasons, many clinicians encourage their clients to accept themselves, avoid further weight gain, and exercise moderately (Myers & Rothblum, 2004; C. A. Smith, 2008). Other clinicians suggest that individuals who are "overweight" should not aim for an enormous weight loss. Instead, their goal should be to remain healthy, exercise regularly, eat a balanced diet, and preserve muscle and bone mass throughout the life span (Batsis & Zagaria, 2018). Healthy bodies exist in all shapes and sizes and are not limited to a specific size or weight category.

Eating Disorders

We have examined discrimination against people based on body size, as well as the problems related to dieting. Let's now consider three kinds of eating disorders. The major symptoms of these eating disorders occur on a continuum of severity (Calogero et al., 2005; Ricciardelli & McCabe, 2004). Anorexia nervosa, bulimia nervosa, and binge-eating disorder represent the most extreme end of that continuum. However, we've noted earlier that many other women and LGBTQ+ individuals have varying degrees of body-image issues. We can place their issues on the less extreme portion of that same continuum.

There is evidence that women who experience low self-esteem and who are employed in work environments that objectify women are more likely to develop eating disorders (Syzmanski & Mikorski, 2017; Zeigler-Hill & Noser, 2015). Additionally, people who identify as LGBTQ+ are more likely to experience eating disorders than their heterosexual and cisgender peers (Parker & Harriger, 2020; Watson et al., 2015). We also know that stressful life events, such as the COVID-19 epidemic, life transitions, or other traumatic experiences, can increase the severity of eating disorder symptoms (Berge et al., 2012; Cooper et al., 2020; Degortes et al., 2014).

At the beginning of this chapter, you read about a young woman who had anorexia nervosa. A person diagnosed with **anorexia nervosa** has an extreme fear of gaining weight, and they also do not maintain an adequate body weight, defined as 85% of expected weight (American Psychiatric Association, 2013; Fairburn et al., 2008). People with this disorder typically have a distorted body image (Garfinkel, 2002; Stice, 2002). For example, one young woman with anorexia nervosa weighed only 100 pounds, yet she said:

> I look in the mirror and see myself as grotesquely fat—a real blimp. My legs and arms are really fat and I can't stand what I see. I know that others say I am too thin, but I can see myself and I have to deal with this my way. (L. L. Alexander et al., 2001, p. 64)

Approximately 75 to 95% of people with anorexia nervosa are women, and between 0.5 and 4% of adolescent girls experience anorexia nervosa. The typical age range for the onset of anorexia nervosa is 14–18 years, although concern about weight often begins many years earlier (Giovanelli & Ostertag, 2009; Jacobi, Hayward et al., 2004; Jacobi, Paul et al., 2004; Jongenelis & Pettigrew, 2020).

In the United States, this disorder is more common in White women than in Black women. However, the data about other ethnic groups is inconsistent (Jacobi, Hayward et al., 2004; Molinary, 2007; Sabik et al., 2010).

Anorexia nervosa starts in a variety of ways. For example, a comment as innocent as "Are you gaining weight?" may prompt a woman to begin a severe dieting program. Other women with anorexia trace the beginning of their disorder to a stressful life event, such as moving to a new school, or to a traumatic event, such as sexual abuse (American Psychiatric Association, 2013; Beumont, 2002). Many who develop this disorder tend to be perfectionists who are eager to please other people (Guisinger, 2003; Polivy & Herman, 2002; Stice, 2002). Their self-esteem is typically lower than in people who do not have eating disorders (Jacobi, Hayward et al., 2004; Jacobi, Paul et al., 2004).

One important medical consequence of anorexia nervosa for cisgender women is **amenorrhea** (pronounced ae-men-oh-*ree*-ah), or the cessation of menstrual periods. Other frequent medical consequences include heart, lung, kidney, and gastrointestinal disorders (American Psychiatric Association, 2013; Michel & Willard, 2003). Another common problem is osteoporosis, the bone disorder we discussed in Chapter 11. Osteoporosis is more common in women with anorexia because of their low estrogen levels and inadequate nutrition (Gordon, 2000).

Anorexia nervosa is an especially serious disorder because between 5 and 10% of people with anorexia die from it (American Psychiatric Association, 2013; Keel et al., 2003). Unfortunately, treatment for this disorder is difficult, especially because many people with anorexia also meet the criteria for major depression (Fairburn et al., 2008; Russo & Tartaro, 2008). However, when anorexia is treated during the early stages, about 75 to 90% of people can recover completely (Fairburn et al., 2008; Powers, 2002; P. F. Sullivan, 2002).

Anorexia nervosa illustrates the potentially life-threatening consequences of cultural norms regarding thinness. One father told me about his daughter, who was experiencing anorexia: "She'd rather be dead than fat."

Bulimia Nervosa

A person with **bulimia nervosa** is able to maintain a normal body weight (unlike a person with anorexia nervosa); however, they have frequent episodes of binge eating and typically use unhealthy methods to prevent weight gain. Binge eating means consuming huge amounts of food, typically 1,000 to 4,000 calories at a time (M. Cooper, 2003; Fairburn et al., 2008). The binge-eating episodes are usually secretive. People with bulimia nervosa then try to compensate for this huge food intake by vomiting or using laxatives (Stice, 2002). In between binges, they may diet or exercise excessively.

As with people with anorexia, those with bulimia tend to experience higher levels of depression and low self-esteem (Fairburn et al., 2008; Harrell & Jackson, 2008; Jacobi, Paul et al., 2004). They are also preoccupied with food, eating, and physical appearance.

At least 90% of individuals with bulimia nervosa are women, and between 1 and 5% of adolescent and young adult women develop bulimia (Hail & Le Grange, 2018; Jacobi, Hayward et al., 2004; National Institute of Mental Health, 2001). However, it's difficult to recognize that a person has bulimia, because people with bulimia typically maintain a normal body weight. They do not stand out in a crowd (Harell & Jackson, 2008; Molinary, 2007).

The medical consequences of bulimia nervosa include gastrointestinal, heart, liver, metabolism, and menstrual-cycle problems (M. Cooper, 2003; Kreipe & Birndorf, 2000).

Bulimia nervosa is typically not as life threatening as anorexia nervosa. However, bulimia is difficult to treat effectively, and it is associated with serious medical and psychological problems (R. A. Gordon, 2000; Keel et al., 2003; Tobin, 2000).

Binge-Eating Disorder

Psychologists and psychiatrists have proposed a third kind of eating disorder, called **binge-eating disorder.** People with binge-eating disorder have frequent episodes of binge eating. During these binges, they consume huge amounts of food, and they feel that they cannot control these binges. Unlike people with bulimia nervosa, they do not compensate for the binges by using unhealthy weight-loss methods, such as vomiting or the use of laxatives (Fairburn et al., 2008). As a result, those with binge-eating disorder typically gain weight over time.

Between 1 and 4% of the general population experiences binge-eating disorder. About 60 to 65% of these individuals are women. In other words, the majority are women, but the gender ratio is much less skewed toward women than the gender ratio for either anorexia nervosa or bulimia nervosa (Fairburn et al., 2008; Grilo, 2002; Kalodner, 2003). People who have binge-eating disorders are likely to experience depression and low self-esteem, similar to those with anorexia nervosa and bulimia nervosa (Grilo, 2002; Jacobi, Hayward et al., 2004; Michel & Willard, 2003). People who identify as LGBTQ+ are more likely to experience binge eating disorder than cisgender and heterosexual individuals, due to their increased exposure to heterosexist discrimination and victimization (Mason & Lewis, 2016; Parker & Harriger, 2020).

In this section on body weight and eating disorders, we have examined four groups of people who are concerned about their weight:

1. People who are above average size may try to lose weight, usually without long-term success.
2. People with anorexia nervosa try to lose weight, and they succeed, sometimes with fatal consequences.
3. People with bulimia fluctuate between eating excessive calories and restricting food intake; their weight is usually normal, but their eating habits produce numerous other health problems.
4. People with binge-eating disorder have frequent episodes of eating large amounts of food; they typically gain weight over time.

The guilt and anxiety that all four groups associate with eating might be reduced if more people were encouraged to accept and appreciate their bodies. One solution is to support cultural norms and media sources that focus less on weight issues and more on maintaining physical and psychological health. Something is clearly wrong when people with average weight begin dieting! Imagine how much more positive we might feel if people in the media had bodies that showed as much variety as the bodies we observe in real life. Imagine how wonderful it would be to glance at the covers of magazines in the grocery store and not read guilt-inducing articles titled, "Finally—An Answer to Problem Thighs" or "How to Lose 15 Pounds in Just One Month!" Now that you are familiar with the issues related to eating disorders, try Demonstration 12.2.

Demonstration **12.2**

Analyzing Your Own Attitudes Toward Body Size

Answer each of the questions in this demonstration using the following scale:

1	2	3	4	5
Never				Frequently

_____ 1. I comment about my own weight to other people.

_____ 2. I compliment other people if they seem to have lost weight.

_____ 3. If someone has gained weight, I avoid commenting about this.

_____ 4. I make jokes about people who are above average size.

_____ 5. I encourage people to feel good about their bodies, even if they do not meet the cultural norms for being thin.

_____ 6. When reading a fashion magazine, I am concerned that many of the models are too thin.

_____ 7. When someone makes a joke about people who are above average size, I express my disapproval.

_____ 8. I eat relatively little food, so that I can keep thinner than average.

_____ 9. I compliment other people when they show self-control in their eating habits.

_____ 10. When reading a magazine, I'm concerned that the photographs may be encouraging eating disorders.

Now calculate your score: Add together your ratings for Items 1, 2, 4, 8, and 9. From this sum, subtract your ratings for Items 3, 5, 6, 7, and 10. If your total score is low, congratulations! You have a positive attitude toward body-size diversity.

Source: Based on F. M. Berg (2000).

Section Summary

Body Weight and Eating Disorders

1. The "culture of thinness" is a major issue for most people in the United States. The media images of exaggerated thinness contribute to womens' "objectified body consciousness."
2. White women are somewhat more dissatisfied with their bodies than Black women, but other ethnic comparisons reveal smaller differences.

(continues)

Section Summary *(continued)*

3. People discriminate in a variety of ways against individuals who are above average size, especially against people who identify as women and LGBTQ+ individuals.
4. It's extremely difficult to lose weight without gaining it back.
5. People with anorexia nervosa have an intense fear of gaining weight, and they do not maintain an adequate body weight. They have numerous health and psychological problems, which may have fatal consequences.
6. People with bulimia nervosa binge frequently, but they maintain a normal weight because they vomit or use other methods to prevent weight gain. They typically experience health and psychological problems.
7. People with binge-eating disorder have frequent excessive binges, and they typically gain weight over time.

12-3 Treating Psychological Disorders

Learning Objectives

To explain why treating psychological disorders is a gendered process, you can …

12-3-1 Differentiate between psychotherapy and pharmacotherapy approaches to treating psychological disorders.

12-3-2 Explain how sexism, gender bias, and inappropriate relationships may negatively impact the therapy process.

12-3-3 Describe ideal components of psychotherapy with individuals who identify as LGBTQ+.

12-3-4 Summarize how microaggressions that are experienced by people of color negatively impact mental health.

12-3-5 Explain how mental health needs vary among Latino/a, Black, Asian American, and Native American people of color.

12-3-6 Summarize general strategies for creating positive therapy contexts for people of color.

12-3-7 Differentiate between psychodynamic, pharmacological, and cognitive-behavioral approaches to therapy.

12-3-8 Describe the major characteristics of feminist therapy approaches.

So far, we have discussed two categories of psychological disorders that are more common in women and gender and sexual minorities than in men: depressive disorders and eating disorders. To keep this chapter a manageable length, we omitted a third category of psychological disorders that are more common in women than in men. These are called **anxiety disorders**, conditions in which a person's anxiety is intense and persistent. For instance, one kind of anxiety disorder is called "panic disorder." In a **panic disorder**, a person experiences recurrent episodes of dread or fear, without any warning. Women are two to three times as likely as men to experience panic disorder (Craske & Barlow, 2008).

If someone seeks help for psychological problems such as depression, eating disorders, or anxiety disorders, they will probably receive psychotherapy and/or treatment with a medication. **Psychotherapy** is a process in which a therapist aims to treat psychological problems and reduce distress, most often through verbal interactions (Gilbert & Kearney, 2006). Individuals experiencing severe psychological disorders may receive therapy in a hospital. Others may receive psychotherapy for many years, while living at home. Still others choose psychotherapy during brief periods of stress in their lives.

Pharmacotherapy uses medication to treat psychological disorders. Since the mid-twentieth century, researchers have developed numerous medications to help people with psychological disorders. We will discuss both psychotherapy and pharmacotherapy later in this section.

In this section, we will first consider how sexism may influence psychotherapy, and then we will discuss psychotherapy with three important groups of women: (a) lesbian and bisexual women, (b) women with low incomes, and (c) women of color. Our final two topics focus on traditional approaches to psychotherapy and feminist therapy.

Psychotherapy and Sexism

Throughout this book, Theme 2 has emphasized that people treat women and men differently. We might hope that therapists' professional training would make them highly sensitive to potential biases. However, the research suggests that therapists often treat women in a biased manner during psychotherapy (Ali et al., 2010; American Psychological Association, 2007).

Gender and Misdiagnosis

Earlier in this chapter, we noted the potential for sexism in diagnosing psychological disorders. Specifically, therapists may over-diagnose depression in women and under-diagnose depression in men. Another problem is that therapists often rely too heavily on *The Diagnostic and Statistical Manual of Mental Disorders* (American Psychiatric Association, 2013). Unfortunately, many of the guidelines in this manual have not been scientifically tested (Ali et al., 2010; P. J. Caplan, 2008; Spiegel, 2005).

The Treatment of Women in Therapy

Gender bias may lead to misdiagnosis and to inappropriate treatment in therapy. For example, therapists may perceive men as more competent than women in work settings. Therapists may also evaluate clients in terms of how well their behavior fits traditional female and male gender stereotypes (P. J. Caplan & Cosgrove, 2004a; Ali et al., 2010). In addition, therapists often ignore poverty, discrimination, and other cultural problems that contribute to depression in women (McSweeney, 2004).

Furthermore, therapists may blame women for events beyond their control. In treating a woman who has been sexually abused, for instance, they may ask her what she did to encourage the attack. In summary, the same gender stereotypes and discriminatory behavior that operate throughout culture may also influence therapists.

Sexual Relationships Between Therapists and Clients

One of the principles of ethical conduct for psychologists and psychiatrists states that therapists must not engage in any form of sexual intimacy with their clients (Behnke, 2006;

Bersoff, 2003; Fisher, 2003). Nevertheless, surveys show that about 4% of male therapists and 1% of female therapists have had sexual relationships with their clients (Pope, 2001). As the American Psychological Association (2017) emphasizes, sexual misconduct is the most unethical form of gender bias and abuse.

We need to emphasize that most psychotherapists are ethical people who firmly believe that sexual relationships with clients are forbidden (Bersoff, 2003; Pope, 2001). As you can imagine, a woman who has been sexually exploited by a therapist is likely to feel guilty, angry, and emotionally fragile. The research shows that she also has an increased risk for suicide (Gilbert & Rader, 2001; Pope, 2001).

Sexual relationships with clients create several problems. First, these relationships emphasize the therapist's own interest, rather than the best interest of the client. Second, they demonstrate a violation of trust. Third, they are also damaging because they represent situations in which a person with power takes advantage of someone who is relatively powerless and vulnerable (Behnke, 2006; Fisher, 2003). We examine similar power inequities in Chapter 13, where we'll discuss sexual harassment, sexual assault, and abuse.

Psychotherapy with LGBTQ+ Individuals

When people who identify as a gender or sexual minority visit a therapist, they should feel just as valued and respected as any other client. In fact, ethical principles specify that psychologists must attempt to eliminate their own tendencies toward **sexual prejudice**, a negative attitude toward individuals because of their sexual orientation (Garnets, 2008; Herek, 2004; MacBride-Stewart, 2007). They must also believe that one client's lesbian relationship is just as important as another client's heterosexual relationship (C. R. Martell et al., 2004; T. L. Rogers et al., 2003). Therapists also must not try to change a person's sexual orientation or gender identity (Herek & Garnets, 2007; D. W. Sue, 2010).

Therapists must be well informed about the research on sexual orientation, gender diversity, and the importance of love relationships. In addition, they need to recognize that most LGBTQ+ people frequently experience prejudice and discrimination in their daily lives (Szymanski & Owens, 2008). Furthermore, therapists must be aware that LGBTQ+ people of color may experience different forms of sexual or gender prejudice in their own ethnic communities (Castañeda, 2008; T. L. Hughes et al., 2003). Therapists must also be knowledgeable about community resources and support groups that are available for LBGTQ+ clients.

Ideally, LGBTQ+ people should feel positive about their identities. As one lesbian woman explained,

> A healthy lesbian has to feel strong in her sexual orientation. Really strong, and feels—not necessarily clear that they're always going to be lesbian—but clear and strong and okay that at this particular point in time: "I am a lesbian and I am a happy lesbian, and I will do all the other things that every person has to about maintaining that place, that balance." (MacBride-Stewart, 2007, p. 435)

Feminists believe that people who identify as LGBTQ+ should not be treated as second-class citizens in comparison to cisgender and heterosexual people. Let's now consider how women with low incomes and women of color are also frequently treated as second-class citizens, compared to women with relatively high incomes and compared to White women.

Psychotherapy and Economic Status

As we read in Chapter 11, many women do not have health insurance. Furthermore, most insurance companies in the United States cover only a small portion of the costs for mental health care (Aponte, 2004; Brewerton, 2010; Katon & Ludman, 2003). Women also earn less than men, on average, so they often cannot afford some psychotherapy options that many men may have (American Psychological Association, 2007; V. Jackson, 2005; Nydegger, 2004).

The national health-care program in Canada is certainly more comprehensive than the U.S. system. However, their mental health coverage emphasizes drug therapy, rather than psychotherapy (Romanow & Marchildon, 2003). As a result, many women with low incomes in both the United States and Canada cannot afford psychological counseling. Even if they manage to obtain counseling, women often need to overcome barriers such as time off from work, child-care arrangements, and transportation (V. Jackson, 2005; L. Smith, 2005).

Furthermore, psychotherapists often treat economically disadvantaged women in a classist fashion. For example, therapists may assume that a woman with a low income simply needs basic resources—such as shelter and food—and that she cannot benefit by discussing psychological problems such as loneliness and depression.

Some therapists also believe in the **myth of meritocracy**, that a person's social status indicates their abilities and achievements (Lott & Bullock, 2010). In this case, a therapist might think that a client has financial problems because she has chosen not to work and not to pursue training for a better-paying job (L. Smith, 2005). Clearly, psychotherapists need to overcome classist beliefs, and they also need to receive professional training about social-class issues. Furthermore, these classist beliefs may be especially destructive for women of color.

Psychotherapy with People of Color

The United States and Canada are rapidly becoming two of the most ethnically diverse countries in the world. In the United States, for example, 24% of individuals report that they are Latina/o, Black, Asian, or Native American (U.S. Census Bureau, 2020). In Canada, 22% of individuals identify as a member of a visible minority (Statistics Canada, 2017).

If therapists in the United States want to provide high-quality care for people of color, they must be sensitive to ethnic-group differences in values and beliefs (Balls Organista et al., 2010; Brooks et al., 2004; D. W. Sue, 2004). White therapists should also acknowledge that people of color often face racial **microaggressions**, or everyday insults and other actions that convey second-class status (D. W. Sue, 2010; D. W. Sue et al., 2007).

One basic problem is that people of color are not as likely as White individuals to use mental health services, even when the ethnic groups are matched on variables such as family income (Alegría et al., 2007; Okazaki, 2009). Some of the reasons for this under-usage include: (1) reluctance to recognize that help is necessary; (2) language and economic barriers; (3) concern about discussing personal problems with therapists, especially White therapists; (4) the belief that psychological disorders could heal without therapy; and (5) the preference for other culturally specific interventions, such as prayer (Balls Organista et al., 2010; L. Smith, 2005; Snowden et al., 2007).

Most members of ethnic minority groups will not be able to choose therapists from their own background. Only about 16.4% of U.S. doctoral-level psychologists belong to ethnic minority groups (Lin, Nigrinis, Christidis, & Stamm, 2015). As a result, most people of color must consult therapists whose life experiences may be very different from their own. For instance, these therapists would not be personally familiar with the continuing racism faced by people of color (Comas-Díaz, 2000; Sue & Sue, 2003).

You can probably anticipate another problem. Some people of color do not speak fluent English, especially if they recently immigrated to the United States. Furthermore, most White therapists are not fluent in any language other than English. Language can therefore be a major barrier for many people of color (Balls Organista et al., 2010; Schwartz et al., 2010; Snowden et al., 2007). In fact, one of the most important barriers to obtaining mental-health counseling is a person's lack of fluency in English. The research shows that English fluency is even more important than health insurance in determining whether a person decides to seek counseling (Snowden et al., 2007).

To make the situation more vivid—if your own first language isn't Spanish—imagine describing your psychological problems to a therapist who speaks only Spanish. You may be able to discuss the weather, but could you describe to a Latina therapist precisely how and why you feel depressed? Could you accurately capture the subtleties of your binge-eating disorder? All these factors help to explain why people of color are less likely than White Americans to seek therapy and also why they are likely to drop out of therapy sooner (Cardemil & Sarmiento, 2009; Snowden & Yamada, 2005).

Let's consider some of the important issues that arise in therapy for four different ethnic groups: Latina, Black, Asian American, and Native American people of color. Then we'll discuss some general therapeutic issues for women of color.

Latinas

In earlier chapters, we noted that Latina/o culture sometimes emphasizes gender roles in terms of *marianismo* for women and *machismo* for men (Arredondo, 2004; Garcia-Preto, 2005; Molinary, 2007). For example, a married woman may believe that she must place her family's needs first. As a result, some Latina women may feel that they cannot accept a suggestion to spend more time addressing their own needs (G. C. N. Hall & Barongan, 2002).

Furthermore, some Latinas have come to the United States as refugees from a country besieged by war and turmoil. For example, government repression in El Salvador during the 1980s resulted in more than 75,000 deaths, as well as numerous rapes, tortures, and other human-rights abuses. A woman who escaped from El Salvador may have witnessed her sister being slaughtered, and she may have spent years in a refugee camp (Kusnir, 2005). Living through such traumatic circumstances often creates long-lasting stress-related disorders and other psychological problems (Balls Organista et al., 2010). Well-meaning therapists, even if they are fluent in Spanish, may not be prepared to provide therapy for women who have lived through political upheaval.

Black Women

Black women are likely to experience a kind of stress that is qualitatively different from the stress experienced by middle-class White women. Specifically, many Black women report stressful factors such as extreme poverty, inadequate housing, and neighborhood crime (Black & Jackson, 2005; D. W. Sue & D. Sue, 2003). Black women often experience discrimination from systemic and gendered racism, and these forms of multiple oppression have direct effects on Black women's likelihood of developing depression (Carr et al., 2014).

For example, 80% of adult Black women in one survey reported that other people had frequently made them feel inferior (D. R. Brown et al., 2003). However, heterosexual Black women may have an advantage over White women because their relationships are often more evenly balanced with respect to power (Black & Jackson, 2005; R. L. Hall & Greene, 2003).

Therapists should resist the myth that all Black women are economically disadvantaged, because an increasing percentage are upper-middle class (D. W. Sue & D. Sue, 2003). Therapists should also resist the myth that all Black women are strong and resilient (P. T. Reid, 2000). That perspective would encourage therapists to believe that their Black women clients do not really require mental health services. The Strong Black Woman schema is unfortunately associated with maladaptive perfectionism and low levels of self-compassion, which can lead to negative psychological outcomes among Black women (Yu-Hsien Liao, Wei, & Yin, 2020). In addition, research by Tawanda Greer and her coauthors (2009) shows that Black women who had frequently experienced racism were especially likely to feel anxious. In contrast, for Black men, there was no correlation between experience with racism and their level of anxiety.

Black people who emigrate from African or Caribbean countries may face additional problems. For instance, one woman emigrated with her family from Sierra Leone to a small community in Newfoundland, Canada, and she reported that many residents had never met a Black person before (Chapra & Chatterjee, 2009).

Asian American Women

We noted earlier that many Latina women are refugees from war and torture in their country of birth. Many Asian American women are also refugees. They escaped war and torture in Asian countries such as Cambodia, Laos, Sri Lanka, and East Timor (Bemak & Chung, 2004; Lee & Mock, 2005a). For instance, during the 1970s and 1980s, Southeast Asian people who speak the Hmong language immigrated to Minnesota. More than 45,000 Hmong now live in the Minneapolis–St. Paul area. As you can imagine, there are not many interpreters in mental health agencies who can speak both English and Hmong, with an appreciation of subtle nuances in both languages (Go et al., 2004).

We need to re-emphasize that individual differences among different Asian American subgroups are substantial. For example, a study conducted in California showed that Chinese, Japanese, and Korean people were more likely than other Asian subgroups to seek mental health services (Balls Organista et al., 2010; Barreto & Segal, 2005).

An important issue is that many Asian American families are strongly influenced by the traditional perspective that men should be the powerful member of the household. These families often expect women to play a passive, subordinate role (Lee & Mock, 2005a; McKenzie-Pollock, 2005; Root, 2005).

Researchers have tried to determine why Asian American people are somewhat less likely than other ethnic groups to use mental health services. They have concluded that Asian Americans are just as likely as White Americans to have mental health issues (Balls Organista, 2010; Lee & Mock, 2005a, 2005b). However, an important cultural value in many Asian groups is to maintain the honor of the family and to avoid any possibility of bringing shame to one's relatives. Psychological problems may be judged especially harshly. As a result, an Asian American woman who enters psychotherapy is basically admitting that she has failed (G. C. N. Hall & Barongan, 2002; Lee, 1999; Shibusawa, 2005).

Several Asian American mental health centers are trying outreach programs, using culturally sensitive techniques. These centers have been reasonably successful in increasing the number of community members who seek therapy (McKenzie-Pollock, 2005).

Native Americans

Among U.S. Native American and Canadian Aboriginal (First Nation) women, two major mental health issues are the relatively high rates of alcoholism and depression (Balls Organista et al., 2010; Sutton & Broken Nose, 2005; Tafoya & Del Vecchio, 2005). Two contributing factors are the high rates of unemployment and poverty in many Native communities (Winerman, 2004).

Another contributing factor is some racist governmental programs used several decades ago in both the United States and Canada (Sutton & Broken Nose, 2005; Tafoya, 2005; Tafoya & Del Vecchio, 2005). For example, many Native and Aboriginal children were taken from their families and placed in residential schools, where they were punished for speaking their own language (Tafoya, 2005). These programs encouraged children to assimilate into the White-focused mainstream and undermined their connection with the tribal elders.

A relatively small number of Native American people have become therapists. For example, Tawa Witko is a Native American woman who earned a Ph.D. degree in psychology. She then returned to live and work with the Lakota Sioux on their reservation in South Dakota. In addition to psychotherapy, she also provides counseling about substance use disorders and domestic violence (Winerman, 2004).

In addition, some White American therapists are working successfully in Native American and Canadian Aboriginal communities. They are more likely to succeed if they help to train community members to become mental health professionals (Wasserman, 1994).

General Strategies for Therapy with People of Color

Unfortunately, in the United States and Canada many disparities exist in psychological services available for people of color, as well as for people who identify as a gender or sexual minority. In an effort to reduce these disparities, the American Psychological Association has created new guidelines for psychologists to follow in treating individuals who may have different life experiences or circumstances than their own. Graduate training programs have incorporated a number of these suggestions (Aponte, 2004; Balls Organista et al., 2010; Cardemil & Sarmiento, 2009; Cervantes & Sweatt, 2004; R. L. Hall & Greene, 2003; McGoldrick et al., 2005b; Silverstein & Brooks, 2010; Singh, 2010; D. W. Sue, 2010; D. W. Sue et al., 2007; S. Sue et al., 2009). As you'll learn, many of these recommendations apply to *all* clients, not just people of color.

1. Search the client's history for strengths and skills that can facilitate the counseling process.
2. Learn about the history, experiences, religion, family dynamics, and cultural values of the client's ethnic group, and attend conference sessions on multiculturalism.
3. Understand that each ethnic category includes many subgroups that can differ substantially from one another.
4. Do not claim that you are "color blind"; doing so is hurtful and ignores the real, lived experiences of individuals who routinely experience racism, sexism, and discrimination from other people in society.

5. Show empathy, caring, respect, and appreciation for your client.
6. Be aware that some immigrants and some people of color might want to become more acculturated into society, but others want to connect more strongly with their own culture.
7. Communicate to the client that racism may have played a significant role in their life, and try to determine how the client has responded to this racism.
8. Hire bilingual staff members and paraprofessionals from the relevant ethnic communities; enlist other community professionals—such as schoolteachers—who can help to identify relevant problems in the community.

Traditional Therapies and Women

Therapists approach their work from a variety of theoretical viewpoints. A therapist's viewpoint can influence their attitudes toward women, as well as the techniques used in therapy and the goals of therapy. We'll first consider the psychodynamic approach to therapy, as well as pharmacotherapy. Then we will discuss the cognitive-behavioral approach. Our final topic will be feminist therapy.

Psychodynamic Approach

Psychodynamic therapy refers to a variety of approaches derived from Sigmund Freud's psychoanalytic theories, proposed in the early 1900s. During treatment, classic psychoanalysis requires the "patient" to free-associate, saying any thoughts that come to mind. Therapists are the "experts," and their task is to interpret these thoughts. Like Freud's psychoanalysis, current **psychodynamic therapy** focuses on unconscious and unresolved conflicts stemming from childhood; however, it emphasizes social relationships more than Freud did (Andreasen & Black, 2001).

Freud's approach presents problems for individuals who are concerned about women's mental health (P. J. Caplan & Caplan, 2009; P. J. Caplan & Cosgrove, 2004b; Chodorow, 1994; Enns, 2004a; Saguaro, 2000). For example, in Freudian theory, being a man is the norm for humans, and being a woman is less important. Furthermore, the Freudian approach blames mothers for the psychological problems that children experience, but it does not praise the positive aspects of mothers' interactions with their children.

Many modern psychodynamic theorists have redefined some of the classic Freudian concepts. You may want to read further about these more progressive approaches (Brabeck & Brabeck, 2006; Chodorow, 1999, 2000; Contratto & Rossier, 2005; Enns, 2004a; Jordan, 2000; Saguaro, 2000).

Pharmacotherapy

As we noted earlier, pharmacotherapy treats psychological disorders by using medication. However, some medications are prescribed inappropriately (Ali et al., 2010; Caplan, 2008).

Pharmacotherapy can be an important component of treating serious psychological disorders (Brewerton, 2010; Mann, 2005). For example, medication can allow clients with severe mental illness to be more receptive to therapy. Furthermore, in treating a woman with anorexia nervosa, pharmacotherapy is typically not effective while she is still severely below average weight. However, medication can be helpful—in combination with psychotherapy—when she is close to her healthy weight (Brewerton, 2010).

However, the physician must carefully select the medication, discuss it with the client, and monitor the dosage and side effects of any medications (Dunivin, 2006). Furthermore, most therapists would argue that any client with a disorder serious enough to be treated with medication should receive psychotherapy as well (P. J. Caplan & Cosgrove, 2004b; Dunivin, 2006). Incidentally, try Demonstration 12.3 before you read further.

Demonstration 12.3

Preferences About Therapists

Imagine that you have graduated from college and would like to consult a therapist for a personal problem you are experiencing. You feel that the problem is not a major one. However, you want to sort out your thoughts and emotions on this particular problem by talking with a psychotherapist. The following list describes characteristics and approaches that therapists may have. Place a check mark in front of each characteristic that you would seek out in a therapist. When you are done, consult page 414 to learn how to interpret your responses.

_____ 1. I want my therapist to believe that it's okay not to adopt a traditional gender role.

_____ 2. I would like my therapist to help me think about forces in our society that might be contributing to my problem.

_____ 3. I would like my therapist to believe that the client and the therapist should have reasonably similar power in a therapy situation.

_____ 4. My therapist should believe that women and men are similar in their capacity for assertiveness and their capacity for compassion.

_____ 5. I want my therapist to be well informed about the research on women and gender.

_____ 6. I think that my therapist should reveal relevant information about their own experiences, if the situation is appropriate.

_____ 7. I want my therapist to address relevant issues other than gender in our therapy sessions—issues such as age, economic status, ethnicity, disability, and sexual orientation.

_____ 8. My therapist should encourage me to develop relationships in which the two individuals are fairly similar in their power.

_____ 9. I want my therapist to avoid interacting with me in a gender-stereotyped fashion.

Source: Based on Enns (2004a).

Cognitive-Behavioral Approach

According to the **cognitive-behavioral approach**, psychological problems arise from maladaptive thinking (cognitive factors) and inappropriate learning (behavioral factors). This approach encourages clients to develop new behaviors and thoughts about themselves. For example, a woman who is experiencing depression and feeling lonely might be encouraged to initiate at least five social interactions within the next week (Andreasen & Black, 2001).

The cognitive-behavioral approach also encourages clients to think about any irrational thought patterns they may have. For instance, suppose that a woman is experiencing depression because she feels she is not socially skilled. A therapist may help the woman to understand alternative perspectives, such as "Just because my friend ate lunch with someone else today, it doesn't mean that I'm a loser." Well-controlled research demonstrates that cognitive-behavioral therapy (CBT) is at least as effective as medication in reducing depression and anxiety disorders (Hollon et al., 2006; Nydegger, 2008; Worell & Remer, 2003).

In addition, therapists frequently use the cognitive-behavioral approach to treat eating disorders. Well-controlled research on anorexia and bulimia nervosa shows that CBT is often more effective than pharmacotherapy (Agras & Apple, 2002; Brewerton, 2010; Wilson et al., 2007). For example, a cognitive-behavioral therapist could help a client develop behavioral strategies to reduce their compulsive eating and automatic thoughts about body image (M. Cooper, 2003; Kalodner, 2003). The therapist may also work with the client to reword negative statements (e.g., "My thighs are disgusting") into more neutral forms (e.g., "My thighs are the largest part of me").

Cognitive-behavioral therapy can also be useful for lesbian women and gay men—for instance, in helping them develop strategies for dealing with heterosexist acquaintances (C. R. Martell et al., 2004). Furthermore, many cognitive-behavioral principles can be combined with feminist therapy (Worell & Remer, 2003). Before reading further, be sure that you tried Demonstration 12.3, which begins on page 409.

Feminist Therapy

We have examined how therapists can use the psychodynamic approach, pharmacotherapy, and the cognitive-behavioral approach in treating psychological disorders. However, feminists emphasize that psychotherapists must be sensitive to gender and sexuality issues as well.

Most therapists probably believe that therapy should be nonsexist. According to the principles of **nonsexist therapy**, people of all genders and sexualities should be treated similarly, rather than in a gender-stereotyped fashion (Worell & Remer, 2003). The nonsexist therapy approach emphasizes that therapists must interact with clients in an unbiased fashion. Furthermore, therapists should be familiar with the recent research about the psychology of gender and sexualities, as well as the pervasiveness of sexism, heterosexism, gendered ageism, and racism in society (Enns, 2004a; Swim & Hyers, 2009). However, feminist therapy goes beyond nonsexist therapy in order to address these social inequalities. Demonstration 12.3 highlighted some of the differences between nonsexist therapy and feminist therapy.

Feminist therapy has three important components:

1. Clients should be treated in a nonsexist fashion, as described in the preceding paragraph.
2. Therapists must emphasize women's and gender and sexuality minority individuals' strengths, especially because they are frequently devalued in our culture.

3. The distribution of power between the client and the therapist should be as equal as possible.

Let's consider the second component of feminist therapy, that cultural norms in the United States devalue women (Brown, 2006; Cantor et al., 2004; Enns, 2004a; Nolen-Hoeksema, 2003; Rastogi & Wieling, 2005; Silverstein & Brooks, 2010; Worell & Remer, 2003). Here are five ways in which feminist therapy addresses this important principle:

1. Feminist therapists believe that women are typically less powerful than men in our culture, and women therefore have an inferior status. In reality, women have many strengths, and their major problems are *not* personal deficiencies. Instead, the problems are primarily societal ones, such as sexism, racism, ageism, heterosexism, ableism, and classism.
2. Women and men of all genders and sexualities should have equal power in their family and other social relationships; therapists must help clients gain more power.
3. Society should be changed to be less sexist; therapists should not encourage women to adjust to a sexist society by being quieter and more obedient. In other words, feminist therapy must focus on social change, as well as individual change.
4. We must work to change and improve those institutions that devalue women and people with any type of minority status, including governmental organizations, the justice system, educational systems, and the structure of the family.
5. We also need to address other important inequalities, which are based on factors such as ethnicity, age, sexual orientation, economic status, and disabilities; gender is not the only important inequality.

The third important component of feminist therapy focuses on power issues within the therapeutic relationship. In traditional psychotherapy, therapists have much more power than clients. In contrast, feminist therapy emphasizes more egalitarian interactions (Ballou, 2005; Brown, 2006; Bruns & Kaschak, 2010; Enns, 2004a; Marecek, 2001b; Rader & Gilbert, 2005; Silverstein & Brooks, 2010; Szymanski, 2003). Here are several ways in which feminist therapy tries to balance the power between the therapist and the client:

1. Whenever possible, the therapist should try to enhance the client's power in the therapeutic relationship. After all, if women clients are placed in subordinate roles in therapy, the situation simply intensifies their sense of inferior status.
2. The therapist must encourage clients to become more self-confident and independent and to develop appropriate skills to help themselves.
3. The therapist believes and demonstrates that the clients—rather than the therapist—are their own best experts on themselves.
4. When appropriate, feminist therapists may share information about their own life experiences, reducing the power discrepancy. However, a therapist's primary tasks are listening and thinking, not talking.

Feminist therapy can be a powerful tool in encouraging clients to analyze their psychological problems and to develop their personal strengths. Therapists are supposed to improve the psychological well-being of human beings. Isn't it puzzling that many therapists are not more concerned about women having an equal right to be psychologically healthy? Feminist therapists argue that more therapists—and more psychologists—need to work actively to support gender-fair legislation and greater gender equality to help reduce existing disparities in society (Nolen-Hoeksema, 2003; Silverstein & Brooks, 2010).

Section Summary

Treating Psychological Disorders

1. Gender stereotypes may encourage some therapists to misdiagnose some psychological disorders and to treat clients in a gender-biased fashion.
2. One clearly harmful violation of ethical conduct is a sexual relationship between a therapist and a client.
3. In treating LGBTQ+ clients, therapists must appreciate the importance of their clients' relationships and must also try to eliminate prejudice.
4. Many women who are economically disadvantaged cannot afford psychotherapy; furthermore, some therapists may treat clients in a classist fashion.
5. People of color are less likely than White Americans to use mental health services. Therapists must make a genuine effort to learn about other ethnic groups and other cultures, and also to convey their empathy and respect for clients who may differ from themselves.
6. Therapists can increase their skills in helping others by a variety of methods, including searching a client's history for her personal strengths, learning more about their ethnic group, and being aware of the wide range of diversity within ethnic groups.
7. The psychodynamic approach is based on Freudian theory, a framework in which men are normative and mothers are blamed for their children's psychological problems. Modern psychodynamic approaches are more progressive.
8. Pharmacotherapy may help in treating serious disorders, but it must be used with caution.
9. Cognitive-behavioral therapy emphasizes restructuring maladaptive thoughts and changing behaviors; it is effective in treating depression, eating disorders, and other psychological problems.
10. Nonsexist therapy emphasizes that therapists should treat women and men similarly, and they should avoid gender-stereotyped behavior; therapists should also be familiar with current research about the psychology of women and gender.
11. Feminist therapy proposes that (a) therapists must provide nonsexist therapy; (b) therapists must emphasize women's strengths; and (c) in therapy, power should be more equally divided between the therapist and the client.

Chapter Review Questions

1. Describe the four defining characteristics of major depression. Think of someone you know who currently seems to show no signs of depression. How would you evaluate this person, in terms of each of these four characteristics?
2. Review the factors that help to explain why women are more likely than men to develop depression. Describe which factors could be related to cultural and societal forces. How could a group of students —working on your own campus—help to reduce the impact of several of these factors?
3. Define the terms "culture of thinness" and "objectified body consciousness." Describe how these factors could contribute to eating disorders. In what ways does culture in the United States discriminate against people who are above average size?

4. Many people want to lose weight and not regain this lost weight. Describe why the issues of being above average size and dieting make these goals difficult.

5. Describe the typical characteristics of anorexia nervosa, bulimia nervosa, and binge eating disorder, as well as their medical consequences. Explain why people with these eating disorders would also be likely to experience depression.

6. Summarize the material on the unique concerns that women of color bring to a psychotherapy session. Why must therapists acknowledge individual differences within every ethnic group?

7. Based on what you have read in this chapter, why does the psychodynamic approach present major problems for those who favor a nonsexist or feminist approach to therapy?

8. Suppose that you are a feminist therapist working with a female client who is living with depression. Imagine someone who would fit this description, and describe how you would use selected principles of feminist therapy to facilitate her recovery. How might economic status be relevant in this situation?

9. Many therapists favor an eclectic approach to the treatment of psychological disorders, in which they combine elements of several approaches. If you were a therapist, how could you combine elements of cognitive-behavioral therapy and feminist therapy?

10. This chapter focused on psychological disorders. Some theorists suggest that psychologists should place more emphasis on how individuals can achieve positive mental health, rather than just avoiding disorders. Based on the information in this chapter, describe the characteristics of an individual who is mentally healthy.

Key Terms

psychological disorders (p. 384)

antisocial personality disorder (p. 385)

major depressive disorder (p. 385)

ruminative style (p. 388)

gendered racism (p. 388)

culture of thinness (p. 394)

objectified body consciousness (p. 394)

fat studies (p. 396)

anorexia nervosa (p. 397)

amenorrhea (p. 398)

bulimia nervosa (p. 398)

binge-eating disorder (p. 399)

anxiety disorders (p. 401)

panic disorder (p. 401)

psychotherapy (p. 402)

pharmacotherapy (p. 402)

sexual prejudice (p. 403)

myth of meritocracy (p. 404)

microaggressions (p. 404)

psychodynamic therapy (p. 408)

cognitive-behavioral approach (p. 410)

nonsexist therapy (p. 410)

feminist therapy (p. 410)

Recommended Readings

Balls Organista, P., Marín, G., & Chun, K. M. (2010). *The psychology of ethnic groups in the United States.* Los Angeles, CA: Sage. We strongly recommend this book for both college libraries and community libraries. It is informative and well written.

Chrisler, J. C., & McCreary, D. R. (Eds.). (2010). *Handbook of gender research in psychology.* New York: Springer. This excellent two-volume handbook includes seven chapters that are directly related to women's psychological well-being, as well as many others on related topics.

Enns, C. Z. (2004a). *Feminist theories and feminist psychotherapies* (2nd ed.). New York: Haworth. Carolyn Enns's book includes descriptions of a variety of feminist theoretical approaches, as well as feminist therapy approaches. She also includes self-testing exercises to help readers clarify their own perspectives on these approaches.

Gotlib, I. H., & Hammen, C. L. (Eds.). (2015). *Handbook of depression* (3rd ed.). New York: Guilford. We recommend this handbook if you are looking for background information on the symptoms, theory, and treatment of depression.

Rothblum, E., & Solovay, S. (Eds.). (2009). *The fat studies reader.* New York: New York University Press. No doubt the title will puzzle many people, but this book provides an interdisciplinary overview of how psychology, literature, and popular culture approach the issue of being above average weight.

Answers to Demonstrations

Interpreting Demonstration 12.3: Check your answers to Demonstration 12.3, and count how many of the following items you endorsed: Items 1, 4, 5, and 9. If you checked most of these, you tend to appreciate a nonsexist therapy approach. Now count how many of the following items you endorsed: Items 2, 3, 6, 7, and 8. Add this second number to the previous total to get a grand total. If your score is close to 9, you tend to appreciate a feminist therapy approach, in addition to nonsexist therapy.

13 Gender and Victimization

John Gomez/Shutterstock.com

Learning Objectives

After studying this chapter, you will be able to ...

13-1 Describe how sexual harassment affects individuals.

13-2 Explain how sexual assault and rape negatively affects both individuals and society.

13-3 Summarize the impact of abuse and interpersonal violence on both women and society.

Did You Know?

- Women are more likely to be sexually harassed if they work at a job where the clear majority of the employees are male (p. 421).
- Women who have been sexually harassed typically say that the harassment was moderately unpleasant, and often has long-lasting emotional effects (pp. 421–422).
- About 20% of women in the United States will be raped during their lifetime (p. 426).
- The clear majority of rape victims were previously acquainted with the person who raped them (p. 425).
- Unemployment increases the likelihood of partner abuse (p. 444).

Sexual harassment, sexual assault, interpersonal violence, and abuse are among the most terrifying events that a person could experience. These forms of violence are especially likely to occur when people are relatively powerless and vulnerable. An especially powerless group is the more than 500,000 women in the United States who are immigrant farmworkers. These women earn low wages by picking fruits and vegetables in the field. Unfortunately, female farmworkers are about 10 times more likely than other female workers to experience sexual harassment and sexual assault (Human Rights Watch, 2012).

For example, consider a Mexican American farmworker named Olivia, who lived in California. Her supervisor, Rene—also a Mexican American—repeatedly harassed and assaulted Olivia. He offered to drive her to the work site, and then he raped her. He also came to Olivia's home when her husband was at work, and he raped her again, threatening to kill her if she told anyone. When she reported these incidents to the main office, the bosses protested that she had no proof. Sexual assault is so common for female farmworkers that one woman in Iowa told a lawyer, "We thought it was normal in the United States that in order to keep your job, you had to have sex" (Clarren, 2005, p. 42).

Olivia's story describes both sexual harassment and sexual assault, two of the topics of this chapter. Sexual harassment, sexual assault, and abuse share important similarities. One similarity is that all three situations involve some form of violence—either physical or emotional.

A second similarity in these three situations is that men typically possess more power than women. Sexual harassers are usually persons with power at work or in an academic setting (DeSouza & Fansler, 2003; Foote & Goodman-Delahunty, 2005: Sigal & Annan, 2008). In rape and abusive situations, men typically have more physical power. As we read in Chapter 3, children begin to learn these messages about power and gender roles. The media also play an important role in conveying these gender stereotyped messages, because they disproportionately represent men who are influential, powerful, physically strong, and violent—especially compared to the women in the media (Galdi, Maass, & Cadinu, 2017). In a sense, sexual harassment, rape, and the abuse of women all represent a tragic exaggeration of traditional gender roles.

A third similarity focuses on entitlement, a concept we examined in Chapter 7, on women and work (p. 218). In many cultures, men have a sense of **entitlement**; based on their membership in the male social group, they believe they have a right to certain "privileges" and rewards when they interact with women (Sigal & Annan, 2008; A. J. Stewart & McDermott, 2004). For instance, a high-ranking executive may assume he has the right to fondle his administrative assistant. A male college student may assume he is entitled to force his girlfriend to have sex. A husband may believe that he is entitled to abuse his partner if they come home late from work.

Fourth, in all kinds of victimization, people are left feeling even less powerful after the violence. They have been forced to accept unwanted sexual attention, or their bodies have been violated or beaten. Powerlessness is yet another variation on one of the themes of this book: Women and gender and sexual minorities are often treated differently from cisgender, heterosexual men.

A fifth similarity is that people seldom regain power by reporting the violence committed against them. Legal proceedings are often embarrassing and humiliating; they invade someone's right to privacy even further. All these acts of violence encourage women to become more silent and more invisible (Foote & Goodman-Delahunty, 2005; T. S. Nelson, 2002). The relative invisibility of women is a theme we have emphasized repeatedly throughout this book.

The final similarity—across all three situations—is that people often blame the victim (Gravelin, Biernat, & Bucher, 2019; T. S. Nelson, 2002; J. W. White et al., 2001). A woman is sexually harassed because "those tight pants invite it." A woman is raped because she "asked for it" by her seductive behavior. A person is beaten because "they probably did something to make their partner angry." In contrast, the aggressor is often perceived as behaving "like any normal male." Although attitudes are changing, the aggressor may receive little blame for the violence.

13-1 Sexual Harassment

Learning Objectives

To describe how sexual harassment affects individuals, you can ...

13-1-1 Differentiate between quid pro quo harassment and hostile-environment harassment.

13-1-2 Describe common settings in which sexual harassment takes place.

13-1-3 Explain why sexual harassment is an important social problem.

13-1-4 Summarize statistics on how often sexual harassment occurs.

13-1-5 Describe the emotional, psychological, and occupational outcomes for women who have experienced sexual harassment.

13-1-6 Identify some ways that individuals, men, and society can help address the problem of sexual harassment.

Sexual harassment refers to unwanted gender-related behavior, such as sexual coercion, offensive sexual attention, sexual touching, and hostile verbal and physical behaviors that focus on gender (Fitzgerald et al., 2001; Gutek, 2007). Most sexual harassment situations occur in either a work setting or a school setting. According to surveys in the United States, women are between two and ten times as likely as men to report that they have been sexually harassed (Committee on Pediatric Workforce, 2006; DeSouza, 2008; Foote & Goodman-Delahunty, 2005).

The American legal system now prohibits two kinds of sexual harassment. In the first kind, called **quid pro quo harassment**, a powerful individual in a university or the workplace makes it clear that someone with less power must submit to sexual advances to obtain something, such as a good grade in a course, a job offer, or a promotion (Crosby, 2008; Rudman & Glick, 2008; Woodzicka & LaFrance, 2005).

The second kind of sexual harassment is called "hostile environment." **Hostile-environment harassment** applies to a situation in which the atmosphere at school or at work is so intimidating and unpleasant that a student or an employee cannot work effectively (Crosby, 2008; Foote & Goodman-Delahunty, 2005; M. A. Paludi, 2004). Before you read further, try Demonstration 13.1, an exercise designed to assess your thoughts about sexual harassment.

Demonstration **13.1**

Judgments About Sexual Harassment

Rate each of the six statements about sexual harassment, using the scale below. Then check the instructions at the end of the chapter, on page 452.

1	2	3	4	5

Strongly disagree   Strongly agree

_____ 1. Sexual harassment is clearly related to power.
_____ 2. Women often try to get ahead by encouraging a professor or a supervisor to be sexually interested in them.
_____ 3. Women don't have a sense of humor, and so they make a big deal out of sexual remarks and jokes in the classroom.
_____ 4. Most charges of sexual harassment are made by women who really have experienced harassment.

(continues)

> **Demonstration 13.1** *(continued)*
>
> _____ 5. Women frequently use their sexuality to tease professors and supervisors.
> _____ 6. When a female student or employee says "No" to a sexual advance from a male professor or supervisor, he should realize that she really does mean "No."
>
> Source: Based on Mazer and Percival (1989) and Kennedy and Gorzalka (2002).

Let's consider several examples of sexual harassment so that we can appreciate the variety of problems in this area.

1. *Quid pro quo sexual coercion.* A woman named Anna and her supervisor, Jason, were on a work-related trip. During this trip, Jason kept talking about sex and rubbing her shoulders and neck. She did not respond, and so he told her to loosen up. Anna later asked about opportunities in the company for promotion. Jason replied, "You'll need to loosen up and be a lot nicer to me before I can recommend you." Then he placed his arms around her waist and added, "Remember, I can make your life very easy or very difficult here" (Foote & Goodman-Delahunty, 2005, p. 54).

2. *Hostile environment in an academic setting.* At a university in Texas, a professor who taught courses in criminal justice was accused of kissing and hugging several female students. His comments were equally offensive. For example, he told one woman that "she would not know real happiness until she had sex with a married man like himself" (R. Wilson, 2004, p. A12). Notice that this example cannot be classified as quid pro quo harassment because the professor did not specify an academic reward for sexual activity.

3. *Hostile environment in the workplace.* In a study of Black female firefighters, more than 90% said that they had experienced unwanted sexual teasing, jokes, and remarks on the job (J. D. Yoder & Aniakudo, 1997). The women also reported that their male coworkers harassed them by pouring syrup into their firefighting boots and bursting in while they were using the toilet. It's likely that sexism and racism combined to create an especially hostile environment for these women. This hostile workplace variety of sexual harassment could also include suggestive remarks and nonverbal gestures (McDonald et al., 2010).

Most of this section on sexual harassment examines how men sexually harass women whom they perceive to be heterosexual. Keep in mind, however, that individuals who identify as LGBTQ+ might be sexually harassed, for example, by people in positions of power. Men can also be sexually harassed by women or by other men. For instance, a gay man may be sexually harassed by a peer. In 2010, we learned about several examples of gay men who committed suicide when they had been "outed" by a peer. However, in the most common situation, a man is harassing a woman (DeFour et al., 2003; Foote & Goodman-Delahunty, 2005; Levy, 2008; Magley et al., 2010).

You may read reports about women being harassed by their male classmates, beginning in elementary school and continuing through college; women are also harassed by their peers in the workplace (Duffy et al., 2004; Shute et al., 2008; Strauss, 2003). In addition, women are harassed in public settings by whistles and sexually explicit comments.

Those forms of harassment are certainly worrisome. In this chapter, however, we will focus on two situations in which a woman is being harassed by a man with higher status: (1) professors harassing students in college settings and (2) supervisors harassing employees in work settings. Both situations raise particular problems because they involve power inequities and reasonably long-term relationships between the woman and the harasser.

Why Is Sexual Harassment an Important Issue?

Sexual harassment is important for several reasons (Foote & Goodman-Delahunty, 2005; Magley et al., 2010; Norton, 2002; M. A. Paludi, 2004; Piran & Ross, 2006; Sigal & Annan, 2008):

1. Sexual harassment emphasizes that men typically have more power than women in our society.
2. Sexual demands are often coercive because women are offered economic or academic advantages if they comply, but harmful consequences if they say no.
3. Sexual harassment dehumanizes women and treats them in a sexist fashion; women are viewed primarily as sexual beings rather than as intelligent and competent employees or students.
4. Women are often forced to be silent, because they are afraid, and yet they need to continue either in the workplace or at school.
5. If sexual harassment occurs in a public setting, without condemnation from supervisors, many onlookers will conclude that sexist behavior is acceptable.

How Often Does Sexual Harassment Occur?

It is extremely difficult to estimate how frequently sexual harassment occurs. The boundaries of sexual harassment are often unclear. Also, people are reluctant to use the label "sexual harassment," even when they have experienced clear-cut harassment (M. A. Paludi, 2004). Furthermore, numerous cases go unreported (Gutek, 2007; Norton, 2002).

Reports of sexual harassment on college campuses suggest that between 20 and 60% of undergraduate and graduate women students have been harassed (Committee on Pediatric Workforce, 2006; Dziech, 2003; Frank et al., 1998; Rosenthal, Smidt, & Freyd, 2016). The incidence of sexual harassment in the workplace varies widely throughout the United States and Canada, depending on the employment setting. Women employed in traditionally male occupations are especially likely to experience sexual harassment (DeSouza, 2008; Foote & Goodman-Delahunty, 2005; Morgan & Gruber, 2008). For instance, women in the military frequently report sexual teasing, unwanted touching, and pressure for sexual favors. According to surveys, between 50 and 80% of women in the military said that they had experienced sexual harassment (Brownstone, Holliman, Gerber, & Monteith, 2018; Buchanan et al., 2008; Magley & Shupe, 2005; S. Nelson, 2002). The #MeToo movement in the late 2010s increased awareness of sexual harassment across a wide variety of workplaces (Daigle, 2021). Surveys suggested that 81% of women in the

United States, compared with 43% of men, had experienced some type of sexual harassment during their lifetimes (Chatterjee, 2018).

Sexual harassment is not limited to the United States. Reports come from countries such as England, Germany, the Netherlands, Australia, Pakistan, India, Taiwan, Argentina, and Turkey (Hodges, 2000; Kishwar, 1999; McDonald et al., 2010; M. A. Paludi, 2004; J. Sigal et al., 2005). In some countries around the world, up to 99% of women report that they have experienced sexual harassment, both in workplaces and public spaces (Madan & Nalla, 2016; Senthilingam, 2017). In all the cultures examined so far, one universal finding is that only a small percentage of women choose to report the sexual harassment to the authorities (Fitzgerald et al., 2001).

Women's Reactions to Being Sexually Harassed

Sexual harassment is not simply a minor inconvenience to women; it can change their lives. If a woman refuses her boss's sexual advances, she may receive a negative job evaluation, a demotion, or a transfer to another job. She may be fired or pressured into quitting (Foote & Goodman-Delahunty, 2005; Kurth et al., 2000; T. S. Nelson, 2002). A woman who has been harassed in an academic setting may drop out of school or miss classes taught or attended by the harasser (Duffy et al., 2004; Fogg, 2005; Bondestam & Lundvist, 2020).

How do women respond emotionally to sexual harassment? One woman described her sense of loneliness: "Most of the time during the harassment I felt extremely alone. I felt like no one could, or would ever understand what this man was doing to me inside my mind." Another woman reported, "I felt like running away—disappearing—becoming as unnoticeable as possible. I stopped wearing colors in my clothing—wore mostly black and gray to be less noticeable—I felt disbelief and extremely isolated from everyone" (C. V. Wright & Fitzgerald, 2007, p. 73).

Most women experience anxiety, fear, self-doubt, embarrassment, helplessness, and depression when they have been sexually harassed. Understandably, they also report reduced job satisfaction and reduced life satisfaction (Chan et al., 2008). Some develop eating disorders (Buchanan & Fitzgerald, 2008; Huerta et al., 2006). They may also feel ashamed, as if they were somehow responsible for the harassment (Collinsworth et al., 2009; Fogg, 2005; McDonald et al., 2010; Rederstorff et al., 2007). In contrast, women seldom feel responsible when they are victims of crimes such as robbery.

Understandably, a woman who has been sexually harassed may become less self-confident about her academic or occupational abilities (Duffy et al., 2004; Osman, 2004). Common physical reactions include headaches, eating disorders, substance abuse, post-traumatic stress symptoms, and sleep disturbances (Foote & Goodman-Delahunty, 2005; Lundberg-Love & Marmion, 2003; Piran & Ross, 2006; Rosenthal et al., 2016).

Another problem is that a woman's friends may not think that sexual harassment is an important problem. Researchers in a variety of countries have measured students' attitudes about sexual harassment (Levy, 2008; Russell & Trigg, 2004; Sigal et al., 2005). For example, Kennedy and Gorzalka (2002) asked students at a Canadian university to complete a 19-item questionnaire that included items similar to those in Demonstration 13.1. They found that women were more likely than men to believe that sexual harassment is a serious problem.

What to Do About Sexual Harassment

How should we address the problem of sexual harassment? Ignoring harassment won't make it disappear (Karsten & Igou, 2006). Let's consider how individual women and men can make a difference. Then we'll learn how institutions can address sexual harassment.

Individual Action

What can an individual woman do when she has experienced sexual harassment? Here are some recommendations for students who are concerned about harassment in an academic setting (Fogg, 2005; McDonald et al., 2010; M. A. Paludi, 2004):

1. Become familiar with your campus's policy on sexual harassment, and know which officials are responsible for complaints.
2. If the behavior of a professor, staff member, or another student seems questionable, discuss the situation objectively with someone you trust.
3. If the problem persists, consider informing the harasser that the sexual harassment makes you feel uncomfortable. Some experts recommend sending a formal letter to the harasser, describing your objections to the incident, and stating clearly that you want the actions to stop (Crosby, 2008). Many harassment policies cannot be legally applied unless the harasser has been informed that the behavior is unwanted and inappropriate.
4. Keep careful records of all occurrences—including specific dates and times—and keep copies of all correspondence.
5. If the problem persists, report it to the appropriate officials on campus. An institution that takes no action is responsible if another act of harassment occurs after an incident is reported.
6. Join a feminist group on campus, or help to start one. A strong support group can encourage real empowerment, reduce the chances that other students will experience sexual harassment, and help to change campus policy on this important issue.

These six suggestions can also be adapted for the workplace; employed women can take similar steps to deal with sexual harassment (Karsten & Igou, 2006). If a harasser persists, it may be necessary to say that you will report the incidents to the appropriate official. Employees may need to file a formal complaint with a supervisor, a union official, or a personnel officer. Competent legal advice may also be necessary. Fortunately, a U.S. Supreme Court decision states that employers may be held financially liable when supervisors harass employees, even when the companies are not aware of the misconduct (Fitzgerald et al., 2001). Later rulings have extended these protections to members of the LGBTQ+ community as well (Spiggle, 2020).

Some women who file a sexual harassment charge may find that their complaint is treated seriously and compassionately. Unfortunately, however, many women encounter an unsympathetic response from college administrators or company officials (Foote & Goodman-Delahunty, 2005; McDonald et al., 2010). They might be told that the event was simply a misunderstanding or that the harasser is so competent and valuable that this "minor" incident should be forgotten.

Students in women's studies courses often protest that nothing about sexual harassment seems fair. This viewpoint is absolutely correct. A woman shouldn't have to suffer the pain and embarrassment of sexual harassment, experience the quality of her work decline, and then—in many cases—find that administrators, supervisors, and the legal system do not support her.

How Men Can Help

Men who care about women and women's issues can be part of the solution. First, it is important for men to avoid behaviors that women might perceive as sexual harassment. In addition, men should speak up when they witness another man sexually harassing someone. Harassers may be more likely to stop if other men point out that they are offended by sexual harassment.

Some men believe that women often fabricate sexual-harassment cases, so they need to understand the reality about sexual harassment (Lonsway et al., 2008). Furthermore, men who work as supervisors or as counselors can support individuals who have been sexually harassed (T. S. Nelson, 2002).

If you are a male reading this book, think about what steps you might take if you learn that a woman is being sexually harassed by one of your male friends. It's difficult to tell a friend that a woman may not enjoy his comments about her body. However, if you do not comment, your silence may be interpreted as approval. You can also offer compassion and support to a friend who tells you that they have been sexually harassed.

Society's Response to the Harassment Problem

Individual people need to take action against sexual harassment. However, to stop sexual harassment more effectively, *institutions* must be firmly committed to fighting the problem (Foote & Goodman-Delahunty, 2005; Karsten & Igou, 2006). For example, women in the military typically report that their commanding officers do not treat sexual harassment as a serious problem that must be prevented (Brownstone et al., 2018; Firestone & Harris, 2003; T. S. Nelson, 2002). Clearly, most officers have not been firmly committed to stopping sexual harassment.

Universities and other organizations need to develop clear policies about sexual harassment (Committee on Pediatric Workforce, 2006; Foote & Goodman-Delahunty, 2005; Karsten & Igou, 2006; C. A. Paludi & Paludi, 2003; Rosenthal et al., 2016). They should also publicize these policies and training programs—with top administrators in attendance—on sexual harassment issues (Gutek, 2007). Students and employees should receive information about procedures to follow if they believe they have been sexually harassed. These administrators must make it clear that their organization will not tolerate sexual harassment (Kath et al., 2008).

Furthermore, public opinion needs to be changed. People should realize that they must not blame women who have been sexually harassed. The public must also realize that sexual harassment limits women's rights and opportunities in academic and work settings. Men need to know that women often do not appreciate uninvited sexual attention. In addition, behavior that a man regards as flirtation may feel more like sexual harassment to a woman (Norton, 2002). Some men who harass may not be aware that they are creating a problem. Others may believe that they have a sanction to harass because of good-natured responses from other men.

However, the real answer lies in the unequal distribution of power between men and women in societies. If we really want to eliminate sexual harassment, we must move beyond the level of trying to convince individual harassers to alter their behavior. Instead, we need to change the uneven distribution of power that encourages sexual harassment.

Section Summary

Sexual Harassment

1. Sexual harassment, rape, and abuse all focus on violence and inequalities in power—situations in which some people feel entitled to certain privileges. All of these behaviors make women and other targets of abuse feel less powerful; in addition, women are often blamed for causing the violence.
2. Two categories of sexual harassment in the workplace and in academic settings are (a) quid pro quo harassment and (b) harassment that creates a hostile environment.
3. Sexual harassment is an important issue because (a) it emphasizes gender differences in power, (b) it is coercive and dehumanizing, (c) it may force women to be silent, and (d) it may encourage onlookers to believe that sexist behavior is acceptable.
4. Sexual harassment occurs fairly often on college campuses and in the workplace; it is especially frequent for women in traditionally male occupations.
5. Women who have been sexually harassed often quit jobs or leave school; they may experience reactions such as loneliness, anxiety, fear, embarrassment, depression, shame, reduced self-confidence, and physical problems.
6. When we consider how to reduce sexual harassment, we must move beyond the individual actions of people. In addition, institutions must develop well-publicized policies. The general public must be well informed about problems related to sexual harassment, as well as the general issue of the unequal distribution of power.

13-2 Sexual Assault and Rape

Learning Objectives

To explain how sexual assault and rape negatively affect both individuals and society, you can ...

13-2-1 Explain why estimating the actual incidence of rape in society is difficult.

13-2-2 Describe when and where acquaintance rape is most likely to occur.

13-2-3 Discuss how alcohol and drug use are often associated with rape.

13-2-4 Summarize people's short-term and long-term adjustments to being raped.

13-2-5 Explain how the fear of being raped affects women's behavior.

13-2-6 Summarize common attitudes that people express about rape.

13-2-7 Explain why myths about rape, rapists, and survivors are especially problematic for women and society.

13-2-8 Discuss how child sexual abuse affects individuals.

13-2-9 Describe rape-prevention strategies that individuals and societies can implement to reduce the likelihood of rape.

Sexual assault is a comprehensive term that includes sexual touching and other forms of unwanted sexual contact. Sexual assault is typically accompanied by psychological pressure, coercion, or physical threats (O. Barnett et al., 2005; Kaufman & the Committee on Adolescence, 2008). For example, someone may say, "If you really loved me, you'd have sex with me," or they may threaten physical harm if the person they are targeting does not comply. Katz and Myhr (2008) surveyed female college students who were currently in sexual dating relationships. About 20% of these women reported that their partner had verbally coerced them to have unwanted sex on at least one occasion.

Rape is a more specific kind of sexual assault. **Rape** can be defined as sexual penetration—without the individual's consent—obtained by force or by threat of physical harm, or when the victim is incapable of giving consent (Ahrens et al., 2008; Monson et al., 2009; Worell & Remer, 2003; U.S. Department of Justice, 2012). Most of the discussion here will focus on rape. However, the inclusiveness of the term *sexual assault* helps us understand the many ways in which men have power over women's lives (J. W. White & Frabutt, 2006). Although the vast majority of rapes involve cisgender women being raped by men, it is also important to note that people of all genders can be sexually victimized by others (RAINN, 2021; Stemple & Meyer, 2014). Transgender women and men are at particularly high risk for sexual victimization; 50 to 66% of people in these gender categories report being sexually assaulted or raped at some point in their lifetimes (Grant et al., 2011; Perreault, 2020).

Although strangers commit some rapes, a rapist is more likely to be an acquaintance (Ahrens et al., 2008; J. W. White & Frabutt, 2006). In other words, people who are worried about rape need to be especially concerned about someone they already know, rather than a stranger.

A rapist may even be a woman's romantic partner. Some people believe a woman is supposed to have sex with her partner whenever they want (Platt et al., 2009). In the United States, 17 states still contain legal exemptions for marital rape when a partner is drugged or incapacitated (Carr Smyth & Karnowski, 2019). According to some estimates in the United States, between 10 and 20% of women have been raped by an intimate partner (Herrera et al., 2006; Koss, 2003; NCADV, 2020). In the United States, many of the states have a policy that a man who has forced sexual relations with a woman he knows receives a ligher sentence than a man who has forced sexual relations with a stranger (Monson et al., 2009; Polisi, 2009). The incidence of rape varies cross-culturally. Rape is typically more common in cultures where women are in subordinate roles to men throughout society (Kar & Garcia-Moreno, 2009; Rudman & Glick, 2008; Sanday, 2003).

One of the most tragic forms of rape occurs during wars and ethnic conflicts. Soldiers kill other soldiers, but they also rape women. If a woman who was raped survives, her own community may reject her (Murthi, 2009). In past decades, invading soldiers have systematically raped women in countries such as Bangladesh, Afghanistan, Bosnia, Cyprus, Guatemala, Peru, Somalia, Uganda, Rwanda, Sierra Leone, Myanmar, and the Democratic Republic of Congo (Agathangelou, 2000; Barstow, 2001; Bauchner, 2018; Borchelt, 2005; Hans, 2004; Marshall, 2010; Nikolic-Ristanovic, 2000; Winship, 2008). The stress that arises from exposure to armed conflict and interpersonal violence, including sexual violence, has been shown to increase depression, posttraumatic stress symptoms, and physical health issues in women (Mootz et al., 2019).

For example, about 2 million people in the Darfur region of Sudan were forced to leave their homes and move to refugee camps. The women in these camps have had to walk great distances away from the camps to gather wood for cooking their food. Men from the attacking militias search for these women and systematically rape them. Rape is therefore a weapon of war as well as a sexual attack on individual women (Agathangelou, 2000; Lalumiere et al., 2005).

How Often Does Rape Occur?

As you can imagine, estimating the incidence of rape is difficult. One problem is that surveys differ in their definitions of rape and sexual assault (Hamby & Koss, 2003). Another problem is that women are reluctant to indicate on a survey that they have been raped. Furthermore, only a fraction of rape survivors report the crime to the police. In the United States, for instance, only about 10 to 30% of rape survivors report the rape, depending on the group that is surveyed (Ahrens et al., 2008; Herrera et al., 2006; Ward & Lundberg-Love, 2006).

Every year in the United States, an estimated 300,000 to 730,000 women are raped or sexually assaulted (Ahrens et al., 2008; Human Rights Watch, 2008; Morgan & Oudekerk, 2019). Current estimates in both the United States and Canada suggest that between 15 and 30% of women have been raped at some point during their lives (Herrera et al., 2006; Rozee, 2005; Ullman, 2010; J. W. White & Frabutt, 2006). The data clearly demonstrate that rape is a genuine problem for women in the United States.

Demonstration 13.2

Knowledge About Rape

For each of the following statements about rape, check the space that represents your response. The correct answers appear on page 452.

	True	False
1. Women who have had a sexual relationship with a man often try to protect their reputation by claiming they have been raped.	_____	_____
2. Women cannot always prevent being raped by resisting their attackers.	_____	_____
3. Men rape because they experience uncontrollable sexual urges.	_____	_____
4. Most women secretly want to be raped.	_____	_____
5. Most rapes are not reported to the police.	_____	_____
6. A woman who is sexually experienced will not really be damaged by rape.	_____	_____
7. Women provoke rape if they dress in a sexually seductive way.	_____	_____
8. Most reported sexual assaults actually were true cases of sexual assaults.	_____	_____
9. Sexual assaults usually occur in isolated areas, away from a woman's home.	_____	_____
10. You can tell whether someone is a rapist by their appearance or general behavior.	_____	_____

Source: Based partly on Worell and Remer (2003, p. 203).

The incidence of rape is especially high for U.S. women if they are serving in the military (Brownstone et al., 2018; Campbell & Raja, 2005; Corbett, 2007; A. Wright, 2008). For instance, the data show that a U.S. female soldier who was serving in Iraq was more likely to be raped by another U.S. soldier than to be killed by enemy fire (Harman, 2008).

Before you read further, try Demonstration 13.2 to assess your knowledge about rape. Then you can check the answers at the end of the chapter.

Acquaintance Rape

Research consistently shows that a rapist is not likely to be a stranger attacking in a dark alley. Instead, a rapist may be your chemistry lab partner, your sister's boyfriend, a business acquaintance, or the neighbor next door. Surveys suggest that about 85 to 91% of female rape survivors knew the person who raped them (Koss, 2003; Black et al., 2011). Similarly, for men who experience rape, 52% know the person who raped them and 15% are raped by a stranger (Black et al., 2011). **Acquaintance rape** refers to rape by a person known to the rape survivor, who is not related by blood or marriage. For example, a woman who was a senior in high school described the following situation. A classmate had just asked her for a date, and she had turned him down.

> He got angry and told me that I was a tease and he slapped me across the face. So I pulled open the door to my car and tried to get away, but he grabbed my arm and forced me into the back seat. All I remember after that was crying and trying to push him off me. When he had finished he left me in the back seat of my car bleeding and barely conscious.
> (A. S. Kahn, 2004, p. 11)

Surveys suggest that about 15% of U.S. women will experience acquaintance rape. An additional 35 to 40% of women will experience some other form of sexual assault from an acquaintance (RAINN, 2021; Rickert et al., 2004; J. W. White & Kowalski, 1998). However, women who have been raped by a boyfriend are less likely than other rape survivors to describe the situation as a rape (Ahrens et al., 2008; Frieze, 2005; A. S. Kahn, 2004; Z. D. Peterson & Muehlenhard, 2004).

For example, researchers in Canada and the United States have studied women who had been assaulted by an acquaintance and whose experience met the legal definition for rape. Among these women, only about 40% actually classified the assault as rape (A. S. Kahn & Andreoli Mathie, 2000; Littleton et al., 2006; Shimp & Chartier, 1998). In other words, most of these women had indeed been raped, yet they did not apply that term to the assault. Furthermore, when a woman has been raped by a boyfriend or another acquaintance, she is less likely than other rape survivors to report the rape (Worell & Remer, 2003).

Some cases of acquaintance rape can probably be traced to a particular kind of miscommunication. Specifically, men are more likely than women to perceive other people as being seductive (Abbey et al., 2000, 2001; Lindgren et al., 2008). For example, Saundra may smile pleasantly when talking with Ted. Saundra may intend for her smile to convey platonic friendship. Nevertheless, Ted may interpret her behavior as a sexual invitation. Another kind of miscommunication is that some men believe that women want to have sex, even though they have clearly said "No" (Osman, 2004).

Furthermore, sexually aggressive men and men who have negative attitudes toward women are especially likely to misinterpret neutral behavior (V. Anderson et al., 2004; Jacques-Tiura et al., 2007; Lindgren et al., 2008). Unfortunately, however, people often misconstrue this information. For example, the popular media often blame women for sending the wrong messages, rather than acknowledging that men misinterpret the messages.

The findings on miscommunication have practical implications for both women and men. First, it is important for women be aware that their friendliness may be misperceived by men. Second—and even more important—men need to know that friendly verbal and nonverbal messages from a woman may simply mean "I like you," or "I enjoy talking with you," or "I'm being polite." A smile and extended eye contact do not necessarily mean "I want to have a sexual relationship with you."

The Role of Alcohol and Drugs

By some estimates, about half of rapes in the United States are associated with the use of alcohol by either the perpetrator or the rape survivor (Abbey, 2002; Davis et al., 2004; Kaufman & the Committee on Adolescence, 2008). Contexts in which alcohol and drug use are common, such as some settings on college campuses, are associated with an increased prevalence of rape (Martin, 2016).

Alcohol clearly impairs people's ability to make appropriate decisions (Abbey et al., 2002). For instance, men who have been drinking tend to overestimate a woman's interest in sexual activity. Women who have been drinking are more likely to judge a sexually aggressive situation as being relatively safe, and they are less verbally assertive (Masters et al., 2006; J. W. White & Frabutt, 2006).

You may also have read about a drug called Rohypnol (pronounced row-*hip*-noll), sometimes called "roofie" or the "date rape drug." Mixed with alcohol, Rohypnol increases sleepiness and the sensation of drunkenness (Dobbert, 2004; Ward & Lundberg-Love, 2006). In both the United States and Canada, the media have reported many cases in which Rohypnol or some similar drug has been slipped into someone's drink. The effect is like an alcohol blackout; the person typically has no recall of any events that occurred after they passed out, even a rape attack. Obviously, a drug-induced rape can have a devastating effect on a person.

Women's Reactions to Rape

A woman's reaction to rape depends on the nature of the attack, whether she knows the assailant, the threat of danger, her stage in life, whether she is well informed about rape issues, and other circumstances. However, almost all women who have been raped report that they were terrified, repulsed, confused, and overwhelmed while they were being raped (Lloyd & Emery, 2000; Ward & Lundberg-Love, 2006). Many women are afraid that they will be seriously hurt (Raitt & Zeedyk, 2000; Ullman, 2000). In fact, about 25% of women are injured (Koss, 2003).

During the rape, some women report that they feel detached from their own body (Matsakis, 2003; Ward & Lundberg-Love, 2006). One woman described her reaction to an acquaintance rape:

> The experience moved from heavy petting to forced intercourse. I realized that a fly on the wall watching would have seen two people making love. But inside I was horrified and remembered thinking to myself that this can't be happening to me. I felt like throwing-up, and I shriveled up inside of myself, so that the outside of my body and the parts he was touching were just a shell. (Funderburk, 2001, p. 263)

Short-Term Adjustment

Women report a wide range of feelings during the first few weeks after a rape. Some women have an expressive style. They show their feelings of fear, anger, and anxiety by crying and being restless (A. S. Kahn & Andreoli Mathie, 2000; Ahrens et al., 2008; Matsakis, 2003). Others hide their feelings with a calm and subdued external appearance.

The reactions of other people are crucial. Friends who think that the rape was a woman's fault are not likely to help her (Brown & Testa, 2008). For instance, one survivor's female friend asked her, "What were you wearing?" (Ullman, 2010, p. 4). This question is so commonly asked to female survivors of rape and sexual assault, that it has inspired several "What Were You Wearing?" art installations around the United States, which are designed to raise awareness of sexual victimization (Oregon State University, 2021; Vaglanos, 2017). In contrast, another survivor received emotional support from her boyfriend. He said that "He was here for me in whatever way I needed him and that we didn't have to have sex unless I wanted to" (Ullman, 2010, p. 63).

Most rape survivors feel helpless, humiliated, and devalued. Many women blame themselves for the rape (Ahrens et al., 2008; L. S. Brown, 2008; A. S. Kahn & Andreoli Mathie, 2000; Sigurvinsdottir & Ullman, 2015). For instance, one woman who had been raped by an acquaintance said, "I never thought of it as date rape until very recently. I just always thought of it as my fault that I let things get out of hand" (Lloyd & Emery, 2000, p. 119). Self-blame is a particularly troublesome reaction because, in nearly all cases, the woman did nothing to encourage the assault.

Immediately following a rape, a cisgender woman may experience physical pain, and she may also experience gynecological symptoms, such as vaginal discharge and generalized pain. Realistically, women who have been raped may worry about possible pregnancy, as well as HIV and other sexually transmitted diseases (Kaufman & the Committee on Adolescence, 2008). However, many women are too upset or too ashamed to seek medical attention. Women who do go to a hospital may be treated in a caring manner, but some report that the members of the hospital staff were unsympathetic (Boston Women's Health Book Collective, 2011).

A woman who has been raped must also decide whether to report the crime to the police. Women often decide not to make an official report because "it wouldn't do any good." They believe that the criminal justice system won't handle the case effectively, that officials won't believe them, and that they might be embarrassed by the verifying procedure (Konradi, 2007). These fears may be realistic. The legal system often harasses and frightens women who have been raped, often minimizes their distress, and often blames victims rather than supporting them. However, a growing number of women have reported that they were treated with compassion and respect (Konradi, 2007; Ullman, 2010).

Long-Term Adjustment

The effects of a rape do not disappear suddenly. The physical and mental aftereffects may last for years (Ward & Lundberg-Love, 2006). Common physical health problems include pelvic pain, excessive menstrual bleeding, vaginal infections, complications during pregnancy, gastrointestinal problems, and headaches (Reed, 2009; Ullman & Brecklin, 2003; E. A. Walker et al., 2004).

Women who have been raped are also likely to experience depression, excessive weight loss, eating disorders, substance abuse, and sexual dysfunction (Ahrens et al., 2008;

Herrera et al., 2006; Ullman & Brecklin, 2003). Some people who have been raped may engage in high-risk sexual behavior (Rheingold et al., 2004; Ullman & Brecklin, 2003). They are also more likely to attempt suicide (Ahrens et al., 2008; Grant et al., 2011; Ullman, 2004).

Many rape survivors also meet the criteria for a psychological disorder called **post-traumatic stress disorder (PTSD)**, a pattern of symptoms such as intense fear, heightened anxiety, and emotional numbing after a traumatic event (Ahrens et al., 2008; Olff et al., 2007; Littleton & Breitkopf, 2006). People experiencing PTSD following a rape may report that they keep re-experiencing the rape, either in nightmares or in thoughts intruding during daily activities. Their memories of the rape may seem vivid and emotionally intense (Ahrens et al., 2008; Schnurr & Green, 2004). However—consistent with Theme 4—individual differences are striking. For instance, many women report that they feel "more normal" within 3 months of the assault, but some people will continue to have symptoms for several years (Frieze, 2005; Ozer & Weiss, 2004).

Many women seek professional psychotherapy to reduce persistent symptoms. Controlled studies indicate that several kinds of psychotherapy are effective (Ullman, 2010). Many approaches use components of the cognitive-behavioral approach, as discussed in Chapter 12. For example, the therapist may ask the client to gradually confront the painful memories. Then the therapist helps them manage the anxieties that arise as they create a mental image of the traumatic event (Enns, 2004a). Group counseling can also be beneficial, because people can share their concerns with others who have survived similar experiences (Funderburk, 2001).

Some women who are raped manage to transform their terrifying experience in a way that makes them stronger, more determined, and more resilient (Ahrens et al., 2008; Slater et al., 2003; Ullman, 2010). Many survivors choose to speak out against violence—for example, at a forum on a college campus. As Funderburk (2001) wrote:

> Besides being a therapeutic experience in its own right, speaking out helps transform self-blame to anger and can galvanize the campus to making a commitment to social change through education and awareness. (Funderburk, 2001, p. 278)

Fear of Rape

So far, our discussion of rape has focused on women who have been raped. However, we also need to consider that all women suffer because of the threat of rape (Beneke, 1997; Rozee, 2008). Young girls and elderly women can be raped. Furthermore, many women are raped in the "safety" of their own homes—the one location where they are supposed to feel most secure.

Surveys in both the United States and Canada confirm women's fear of rape and perceived danger (Benoit et al., 2015; Frieze, 2005; M. B. Harris & Miller, 2000). Men are often astonished to learn about the large number of safety measures that women employ to avoid being raped (Rozee, 2008). One problem is that women take numerous precautions against rape by a stranger but they take significantly fewer precautions to avoid rape by an acquaintance, even though they correctly acknowledge that acquaintance rape is more common (Rozee, 2008).

Fear of rape controls women's behavior and restricts what they can do, no matter where they live. Sadly, the fear of rape drastically reduces women's sense of freedom and power (Rozee, 2008).

Demonstration **13.3**

Assigning Responsibility for Rape

Read the first scenario in this demonstration. Then decide who is responsible for the occurrence of the rape, Jordan or Cheyenne. If you believe that Jordan is entirely responsible, assign a value of 100% to the Jordan column and 0% to the Cheyenne column. If they are both equally responsible, assign a value of 50% to each one. If Cheyenne is entirely responsible, assign a value of 0% to the Jordan column and 100% to the Cheyenne column. Use any values between 0% and 100%, as long as the two values sum to 100. To make the situations comparable, assume that both Jordan and Cheyenne are college students in all five scenarios. After completing the first scenario, read and evaluate each subsequent one.

Jordan   Cheyenne

_____ _____   1. Cheyenne is walking back to her dorm from the library at 9:00 P.M., taking a route that everyone considers safe. As she passes the science building, Jordan leaps out, knocks her down, drags her to an unlit area, and rapes her.

_____ _____   2. Cheyenne is at a party, where she meets a pleasant-looking student named Jordan. After dancing for a while, he suggests they go outside to cool off. No one else is outside. Jordan knocks her down, drags her to an unlit area, and rapes her.

_____ _____   3. Cheyenne is at a party, and she is wearing a very short skirt. She meets a pleasant-looking student named Jordan. After dancing for a while, he suggests they go outside to cool off. No one else is outside. Jordan knocks her down, drags her to an unlit area, and rapes her.

_____ _____   4. Cheyenne is on a first date with Jordan, whom she knows slightly from her history class. After a movie, they go out for an elegant late-night meal. They decide to split the cost of both the movie and the meal. In the car on the way home, Jordan stops in a secluded area. Cheyenne tries to escape once she realizes what is happening. However, Jordan is much larger than she is, and he pins her down and rapes her.

(continues)

> **Demonstration 13.3** *(continued)*
>
> _____ _____ 5. Cheyenne is on a first date with Jordan, whom she knows slightly from her history class. After the movie, they go out for an elegant late-night meal. Jordan pays for the cost of both the movie and the meal. In the car on the way home, Jordan stops in a secluded area. Cheyenne tries to escape once she realizes what is happening. However, Jordan is much larger than she is, and he holds her down and rapes her.

The Public's Attitudes About Rape

Before you read further, try Demonstration 13.3 above, which examines your own perspectives on rape.

Women who are raped are often doubly victimized, first by the assailant and later by the attitudes of other people (R. Campbell & Raja, 2005; J. W. White & Frabutt, 2006; Ullman, 2010). The survivor may find that her own family, her friends, the court system, and society all tend to blame her and treat her negatively because of something that was not her fault (Gravelin et al., 2019). These responses are particularly damaging at a time when she needs help and compassion. In fact, this "second victimization" increases the likelihood that a woman will develop post-traumatic stress disorder (R. Campbell & Raja, 2005). People who identify as LGBTQ+ face similar outcomes and victimization from others who tend to blame them for being raped instead of providing assistance and support (Balsam, Lehavot, & Beadnell, 2011; Messinger & Koon-Magnin, 2019).

The legal system's treatment of rape is mostly beyond the scope of this book. However, there are numerous reports of injustice and mistreatment. For example, a New York City judge once recommended leniency for a man who had forcibly sodomized a woman who had cognitive disabilities. Astonishingly, the judge said, "there was no violence here" (Rhode, 1997, p. 122).

People differ in their attitudes about rape. For instance, people with traditional gender roles place a greater proportion of the blame on the woman who has been raped (Gravelin et al., 2019; A. J. Lambert & Raichle, 2000; Simonson & Subich, 1999). People who agree with rape myths and perceive low levels of similarity with victims are also more likely to blame individuals for being raped (Gravelin et al., 2019).

The research also shows that men are somewhat more likely than women to blame the woman who has been raped (Emmers-Sommer et al., 2005; W. H. George & Martínez, 2002; Gravelin et al., 2019). For example, Alan J. Lambert and Katherine Raichle (2000) asked students at a Midwestern university to read an acquaintance rape scenario in which students named Bill and Donna begin talking at a party and then go to her apartment. They undress. Then Donna says she does not want to have sex. However, Bill continues, despite

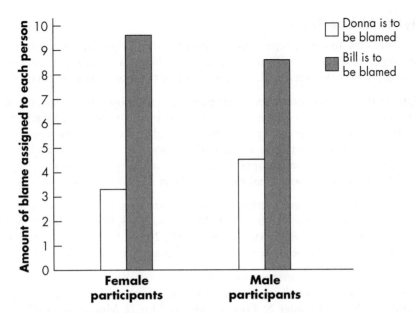

FIGURE **13.1** Responses to an acquaintance rape scenario, as a function of the participant's gender. (Note: 0 = Not at all to be blamed; 10 = very much to be blamed.)

Source: Based on A. J. Lambert and Raichle (2000).

her frequent pleading for him to stop. Participants were asked how much they thought each person could be blamed for what happened. As Figure 13.1 demonstrates, men are somewhat more likely than women to blame Donna.

People's attitudes about rape also depend on the circumstances surrounding the assault. For instance, college students are more likely to blame a woman for a sexual assault if she was verbally coerced, rather than physically forced (Katz et al., 2007).

Furthermore, people are much more likely to blame the woman who has been raped in an acquaintance rape, rather than in a stranger rape (L. A. Morris, 1997; Wallace, 1999). Compare your answers to the first and second scenario in Demonstration 13.3 on page 431. In the first scenario, did you assign all (or almost all) of the blame to Jordan? Did you shift the blame somewhat when Cheyenne had known Jordan for perhaps 30 minutes?

Next think about your response for Scenario 3, in which Cheyenne was wearing a short skirt. People are likely to hold a woman more responsible for a rape if she is wearing revealing clothing, rather than more conservative clothing (Workman & Freeburg, 1999).

Now think about whether your assignment of blame differed for Scenarios 4 and 5. In general, people are more likely to hold a woman responsible for a rape if the man paid for the date (Ahrens et al., 2008; L. A. Morris, 1997; Parrot, 1999). Let's say that the evening cost $100. In Scenario 4, they therefore each paid $50. In Scenario 5, Jordan paid $100. If Jordan pays $50 extra, does he have the right to rape Cheyenne?

Myths About Rape

Numerous myths about rape, rapists, and survivors help to shape the kind of attitudes that we have just examined. As you might imagine, these rape myths can intensify the anguish of a woman who has been raped. Here are four of the more common myths:

Myth 1: Rapists are strangers—that is, people unknown to the victim. We noted earlier that about 85 to 91% of rapes are committed by acquaintances (Black et al., 2011; Koss, 2003). However, the percentage may be even higher because women are less likely to report a rape that was committed by a person they know (Z. D. Peterson & Muehlenhard, 2004). Furthermore, if someone is raped by a former sexual partner, many people believe that it doesn't actually count as a "real rape" (Krahé et al., 2007; Temkin & Krahé, 2008).

Myth 2: Women ask to be raped; they could avoid rape if they wanted to. Some people believe that women invite rape (Frieze, 2005; Matsakis, 2003; Ullman, 2010). Many video games feature women who invite sexual assault (Dill, 2009). Furthermore, students believe that a woman is asking for rape if she is wearing "suggestive" clothing (Maurer & Robinson, 2008).

Myth 3: Women who consent to sexual intercourse often claim—later on—that they were raped. Basically, this myth suggests that women don't mind telling a lie and getting men in trouble (DeMarni Cromer & Freyd, 2007; Kahlor & Morrison, 2007; Temkin & Krahé, 2008). As one male college student commented, "Women have the ability to call rape just because they weren't sure if they should have sex" (Clark & Carroll, 2008, p. 624). According to this myth, unless a woman genuinely struggles, she is basically saying "yes" to intercourse (Clark & Carroll, 2008).

Myth 4: Pornography has no effect on men's likelihood to rape. According to research, this myth is false. In fact, pornography that emphasizes violence can definitely be harmful. It can increase men's likelihood of sexual assault, as well as other forms of violence (B. A. Scott, 2008; J. W. White & Frabutt, 2006). Pornography seems to be especially dangerous for men who are high in hostility and high in promiscuity (Malamuth, 1998). Pornography can also provide men with "rape scripts," to show them specific techniques for sexual assault (Bourke, 2007).

Pornography is clearly a complex social, moral, and legal issue (B. A. Scott, 2008; J. W. White & Frabutt, 2006). However, pornography is not simply an innocent form of entertainment.

Child Sexual Abuse

So far, we have focused on the sexual abuse of college-age adolescents, as well as adult women. We also need to discuss **child sexual abuse**, which occurs when an adult engages in any kind of sexual contact with a child; this contact includes sexual touching, stimulation of the genitals, and intercourse.

Child sexual abuse is one of the most devastating forms of sexual violence. For example, when a girl named Sashima was 9 years old, her mother's boyfriend moved into their house. At first, the boyfriend began by checking on Sashima during the night but later attempted to have sexual intercourse with her. With the help of a concerned teacher, Sashima reported the events to child protective services. The mother's boyfriend was later arrested (O. Barnett et al., 2005).

Child sexual abuse is particularly cruel because, in most cases, children are abused by relatives, neighbors, and caretakers (Freyd et al., 2005). These abusers are the very individuals who should be protecting them, nurturing them, and acting in their best interests.

The incidence of child sexual abuse depends on the precise definition of the term. Estimations are also difficult because only a fraction of the cases are reported (O. Barnett et al., 2005; Frieze, 2005; Ullman, 2010).

In the past few decades, we've learned that numerous young boys have been sexually assaulted by trusted adult men. However, the overall assault rates are typically higher for young girls (Ward & Lundberg-Love, 2006). In fact, estimates suggest that about 15 to 30% of all women in the United States and Canada have experienced some form of child sexual abuse by the time they were 18 years old (O. Barnett et al., 2005; Benoit et al., 2015; Herrera et al., 2006; Lemieux & Byers, 2008; Olio, 2004). According to the research, ethnicity does not have a consistent effect on the rate of child sexual abuse (Doll et al., 2004).

Incest is a specific kind of child sexual abuse; again, the definitions vary. One accepted definition is that **incest** refers to sexual contact between biologically related individuals; this contact includes sexual touching, stimulation of the genitals, or intercourse (Frieze, 2005). Unfortunately, relatives commit a large proportion of child sexual abuse incidents—including rape (Olafson, 2004).

Sexual abuse can profoundly affect a child, both immediately and over the long term. The immediate psychological consequences of child sexual abuse include fear, anger, depression, betrayal, and guilt. Nightmares and other sleep disturbances are also common. As you might expect, many victims also stop trusting other people (Slater et al., 2003; Ullman, 2010; Ward & Lundgren-Love, 2006).

The long-term consequences of child sexual abuse may include post-traumatic stress disorder, which we discussed on page 432 (Stern, 2010). Other common symptoms include depression, anxiety disorders, eating disorders, substance abuse, sexual dysfunction, and risky sexual behavior (Black et al., 2009; Lemieux & Byers, 2008; Ward & Lundgren-Love, 2006). Child sexual abuse also affects the long-term physical health of adult women (O. Barnett et al., 2005; Herrera et al., 2006; Zurbriggen & Freyd, 2004).

Some children who have been sexually abused may forget their memory of that experience, especially if the abuser was a close relative or other trusted adult. However, they may recover that memory when a later event triggers recall or during the context of therapy during adulthood (L. S. Brown, 2008; DeMarni Cromer & Freyd, 2007; Freyd et al., 2005; Goodman, Gonzalves, & Wolpe, 2019; Stern, 2010). In other cases, people may "remember" events that never really happened during their childhood. This is known as "false memory" and is especially likely if the event is plausible (Brainerd & Reyna, 2005; Loftus et al., 2008; McNally, 2003).

One major problem is that we cannot easily determine whether a memory of childhood abuse is accurate. Children are abused in private settings without witnesses. Also, we cannot conduct research about child sexual abuse in a fashion that is both realistic and ethical. Most psychologists in the United States and Canada acknowledge the complexity of these issues. They argue that both recovered memory and false memory can occur (e.g., Enns, 2004b; Frieze, 2005).

The Prevention of Sexual Assault and Rape

We've examined several important characteristics of rape; what can people do to prevent it? Rape prevention is an issue both for individual women and for people throughout society. Table 13.1 lists some precautions that individual women can take; it is based on much longer lists available in several resources. More than 1,100 different rape-prevention strategies have been listed, and the advice is often confusing and conflicting (Basile et al., 2016; Corcoran & Mahlstedt, 1999; Fischhoff, 1992). Furthermore, no specific set of guidelines can prevent rape, although some strategies may reduce the dangers or likelihood of being raped (Gidycz et al., 2006). Let's first consider how people can attempt to avoid rape by strangers and next examine strategies for making acquaintance rape less likely. Then we'll discuss how society can work to prevent rape.

Individuals' Prevention of Rape by Strangers

An important issue can be called the "blame-the-victim problem." Notice that many of the items in Table 13.1 will force women to limit their own freedom. For instance, women should not hitchhike or walk in unlighted areas. Why should women—the potential victims—be the ones who have to restrict their behavior? This complaint cannot be answered satisfactorily (Koss, 2003; Rozee, 2008). The situation definitely *is* unjust. However, the reality is that rape is less likely if women take these precautions. This injustice also emphasizes that the real solutions would require changes in society, rather than modifying only a woman's personal behavior.

The research also shows that women significantly reduce their chances of being raped if they try to block, push, or incapacitate their assailants. Women who fight back are also likely to recover their psychological well-being more rapidly (Crooks & Baur, 2017; Gavey, 2005; Rozee, 2005).

Resources on rape avoidance also recommend training in self-defense, especially because self-defense affords women greater empowerment and personal competence (Crooks & Baur, 2017; Gidycz et al., 2006; Ullman, 2010). In a rape situation, a woman must quickly assess the specific situation, as well as her own physical strength, before deciding whether to resist. However, even if a woman is raped, *it is never her fault.*

Research on **empowerment self-defense (ESD) training** suggests that active resistance rape and assault prevention programs are particularly effective for helping women develop resistance to rape and assault (Berke & DeFour, 2021). Comprehensive ESD programs teach women strategies for avoiding the full continuum of sexual violence, from harassment and assault to rape. They also situate the problem of sexual violence in the broader societal and cultural context, and focus on holding perpetrators responsible for their violent assaults on others. They also empower women and gender and sexual minorities to focus on their bodies as a source of strength, rather than as liabilities (Berke & DeFour, 2021).

Individuals' Prevention of Acquaintance Rape

Women may feel comforted to think that they can protect themselves from rape by locking their doors, practicing self-defense, and avoiding late-night walks in dangerous areas. However, they also need to protect themselves from the more frequent problem: being raped by someone they know (Messman-Moore & Brown, 2006).

Unfortunately, people must use a different set of strategies to protect themselves from an acquaintance rape (Rozee, 2005). One precaution is to avoid a relationship with a person who talks negatively about women in general or with a domineering person who insults you and ignores what you say. These people are likely to ignore your refusals if you say you do not want to have sex (Adams-Curtis & Forbes, 2004; Crooks & Baur, 2017).

Some precautions on dating safety may sound obvious, but they can decrease the chances of acquaintance rape. When you are just getting to know someone, go to public

TABLE **13.1**

Safety Precautions to Avoid a Rape Confrontation with a Stranger

Note: Read the section on individuals' prevention of rape by strangers (page 436) before you read the following information. Keep in mind that these suggestions are presented from the view of potential victims. However, the ultimate responsibility for avoiding rape in society falls on rapists themselves. For balance, the comedian Sarah Silverman's viral tweet from 2015 presents an alternative perspective on how to prevent rape from the perpetrator's perspective (Bennett-Smith, 2016). For other modern initiatives, visit the Men Can Stop Rape Foundation website online, which provides additional insight on how men can reduce rape within modern societies.

General Precautions

1. Before an emergency arises, locate the nearest Rape Crisis Center or similar organization to obtain material on rape prevention.
2. If you have a cell phone, keep it with you when you are alone.
3. Make certain that your consumption of alcohol or other drugs does not endanger your alertness. When people use drugs or alcohol before a rape attack, they typically experience more severe bodily injury.
4. Take a self-defense course, and learn the vulnerable body parts of a potential attacker.
5. If you are attacked, do not be afraid to be rude. Instead, yell loudly and throw any available object at the attacker.
6. People should avoid hitchhiking, and they should try to avoid walking in unlighted areas.

Precautions at Home

1. Make certain to use secure locks on doors and windows.
2. Ask repair or delivery personnel for identification before you open the door; do not let strangers inside your residence without proper identification.
3. If you live in an apartment, be aware of your surroundings at all times and don't enter a deserted basement or laundry room. Insist that the apartment management keep hallways, entrances, and grounds well lit.

Precautions on the Street

1. When you are walking, walk purposefully; make it clear that you know your destination. Be alert to your surroundings.
2. Avoid being alone on the streets or on campus late at night. If you cannot avoid being alone, carry a whistle that will make a loud noise or a "practical" weapon such as an umbrella, a pen, or keys.
3. If a car is following you, quickly turn around and then walk in the opposite direction to the nearest open store or neighbor.

Precautions in Cars and on Buses or Subways

1. Keep car doors locked, even when you are riding as a passenger.
2. Keep your gas tank filled and the car in good working order. If you have car trouble, call 911 or another emergency number.
3. If you are being followed while driving, don't pull into your own driveway. Instead, drive to the nearest police or fire station and honk your horn.
4. At bus or transit stations, stay in well-lit sections, near change booths or near a group of people.

Sources: Based on L. L. Alexander et al. (2021), Boston Women's Health Book Collective (2011), Crooks and Baur (2017), Parrot (1999), Rozee (2005), and Ullman (2010).

places with a group of people. If possible, agree in advance that everyone will leave together at the end of the event. Monitor your alcohol intake, and make sure that no one can slip a drug into your drink (Boston Women's Health Book Collective, 2011; Crooks & Baur, 2017). Also, take some time to think about a backup plan *before* a situation becomes threatening. What would your options be? Throughout a relationship, communicate with your dating partner about any sexual activities that seem appropriate or inappropriate (Abbey, 2002; Kennett et al., 2009).

In the previous section, we discussed effective ways of preventing rape by strangers. When the attacker is an acquaintance, they may respond to verbal assertiveness. For example, a woman can shout something such as, "Stop it right now! This is rape, and I'm calling the police!" Screaming or running away may also be effective.

In an ideal world, women could trust their dates, their classmates, and their friends. In the real world, the clear majority of men would never rape an acquaintance. However, some do, and women must be prepared for this possibility.

Society's Prevention of Rape

An individual may avoid rape by following certain precautions. However, solutions at the individual level mean that women will continue to live in fear of being raped (Rozee, 2008). To prevent rape, we need to take a broader approach, encouraging people to value women and men equally. We must acknowledge that a violent society—which often devalues women and gender and sexual minorities—will tend to encourage rape (O. Barnett et al., 2005; Frieze, 2005; Gravelin et al., 2019; Ullman, 2010). Our list starts with concrete suggestions and then considers some problems that require more fundamental changes (Boston Women's Health Book Collective, 2011; Kaufman & the Committee on Adolescence; Rozee, 2005; Temkin & Krahé, 2008; Ullman, 2010):

1. Professionals who work with children and adolescents should be alert for evidence of sexual abuse.
2. Hospitals and medical providers should be sensitive to the emotional and physical needs of people who have been raped.
3. Laws must be reformed so that the legal process is less stressful, less likely to blame the victim, and more supportive of the victim.
4. Education about rape needs to be improved, beginning in middle school (Anderson & Whiston, 2005; Konradi, 2007; Temkin & Krahé, 2008). Students need this information when they are young because they typically form their attitudes toward rape before they reach high school. To be effective, these rape-prevention programs must continue throughout high school and college. They must emphasize that men *can* control their sexual impulses and that women and gender and sexual minorities must not be blamed for rape (L. A. Anderson & Whiston, 2005). These programs must also emphasize the relatively high frequency of acquaintance rape (Messman-Moore & Brown, 2006).
5. Men's groups must become more involved in rape prevention (Louwagie, 2008). On some college campuses, fraternities will join together with campus women's groups to organize a sexual-assault awareness day or a "Take Back the Night" event (Abbey & McAuslan, 2004; Marine, 2004; Ullman, 2010). Men and men's organizations need to emphasize this important quotation: "If you're not part of the solution, you're part of the problem." Programs focusing on men have also been created in India, Brazil, and Cambodia (The Population Council, 2008; Tarrant, 2009).

6. Violence must be less glorified in the media. We now recognize that there is violence on the Internet, as well as violence in films, video games, TV shows, and popular music. This violence is widely recognized, yet the situation has not improved in recent years (Dill et al., 2005; Escobar-Chaves et al., 2005; Rozee, 2008; Ullman, 2010). We must emphasize that violent "entertainment" encourages aggression against women.

7. Rape crisis centers need to receive more funding, so that they can provide much more extensive education in our communities (Ullman, 2010).

8. Ultimately, leaders in society must direct more attention toward the needs of women. As we've emphasized throughout this book, women are relatively underpaid, powerless, and invisible. Their needs are often trivialized and ignored. Every woman should be able to feel that her body is safe from attack and that she has the same freedom of movement that men have. Our culture must not tolerate violence toward women.

Section Summary

Sexual Assault and Rape

1. Rape is more common in cultures where women have relatively little power; invading soldiers have systematically raped women during wartime.

2. According to U.S. and Canadian estimates, between 15 and 30% of women have been raped at some point during their lives.

3. Frequently, women who have been raped by an acquaintance do not consider the assault to be a "real" rape. Some instances of acquaintance rape can be traced to misinterpretations of sexual interest.

4. Alcohol and other drugs increase the likelihood of sexual assault.

5. Women who have been raped report that, during the assault, they felt terrified, confused, and overwhelmed. Afterward, they often feel helpless and devalued. Long-term consequences for a rape survivor may include post-traumatic stress disorder and physical health problems, although individual differences are substantial.

6. Because of the threat of rape, many women feel unsafe, and they restrict their activities.

7. A person who has been raped may be blamed by their family, the legal system, and the general public; people's attitudes about rape depend on factors such as gender, and whether a stranger or an acquaintance raped the person.

8. Some widely held ideas about rape are not consistent with the research findings. In reality, rapists are often acquaintances; people do not "ask" to be raped; people are not likely to lie about being raped; and pornography can increase the incidence of rape.

9. Child sexual abuse has both immediate and long-term effects on mental and physical health; some memories of child sexual abuse can be forgotten and then recovered later, but some adults may construct false memories of abuse that did not occur.

(continues)

Section Summary *(continued)*

10. Safety precautions that may prevent rape by a stranger typically limit women's freedom at home and in public places; however, it is important not to blame the person who has been raped. Empowerment self-defense training can be an effective strategy for women in avoiding assault and rape by others.
11. Precautions for reducing the likelihood of acquaintance rape include avoiding men who downgrade women; dating in groups at the beginning of a relationship; and being verbally assertive.
12. Ultimately, the number of rapes can be reduced only by greater societal attention to women's needs. The issues include increasing the sensitivity of relevant professionals, educating students, and encouraging men to become more active.
13. The media needs to reduce their emphasis on gender-based violence, and women's issues must receive more attention.

13-3 The Abuse of Women

Learning Objectives

To summarize the impact of abuse and interpersonal violence on both women and society, you can ...

13-3-1 Explain how societies estimate the prevalence of abuse and intimate partner violence.

13-3-2 Describe people's reactions to abusive experiences.

13-3-3 Discuss family variables and personality characteristics that are associated with higher rates of reported abuse.

13-3-4 Compare and contrast public attitudes about the abuse of women among various countries around the world.

13-3-5 Summarize why commonly accepted myths about abuse are inaccurate.

13-3-6 Describe some evidence-based strategies for reducing intimate partner violence.

13-3-7 Discuss some reasons why U.S. society has been unable to reduce the rate of interpersonal violence and abuse.

Consider the following passage, in which a woman described how her husband had abused her:

> Little by little, he isolated me from my friends, he convinced me to quit working, he complained about how I kept the house, he kept track of the mileage on the car to make sure that I wasn't going anywhere. Eventually, when the beatings were regular and severe, I had no one to turn to, and I felt completely alone. (Boston Women's Health Book Collective, 2005)

The terms **abuse of women** and **intimate partner violence** refer to intentional acts that injure someone; these acts include physical, psychological, and sexual abuse. (We discussed sexual abuse in the previous section.) These two terms are broader than many similar terms. For example, the term *domestic violence* implies that two people are living together. Therefore, this term seems to exclude the kind of violence that often occurs in dating relationships, including high school and college students (Roberts, 2007; J. W. White & Frabutt, 2006). A second term, *battered women,* also implies *physical* abuse (J. W. White et al., 2001). However, many women who have been abused report that the emotional abuse is the most destructive component of the abusive relationship (Offman & Matheson, 2004; K. D. O'Leary & Maiuro, 2001).

Physical abuse can include hitting, kicking, burning, pushing, choking, throwing objects, and using a weapon. Emotional abuse can include humiliation, name calling, intimidation, extreme jealousy, refusal to speak, and isolating someone from friends and family members (D. A. Hines & Malley-Morrison, 2005; Stahly, 2008; Straus, 2005). Another form of emotional abuse focuses on finances, for example, when a man withholds money or destroys his wife's credit cards (Castañeda & Burns-Glover, 2004; Mandel, 2009). It is important to know that—in a substantial percentage of intimate relationships—men sexually assault their female partner, in addition to using other forms of violence (J. Katz et al., 2008).

Because of space limitations, in this section we will focus primarily on male violence against women within the context of heterosexual relationships. The research demonstrates that some women abuse their male partners. However, most research shows that men abuse their female partners more frequently and more severely (McHugh et al., 2008; Statistics Canada, 2021). For example, men are about nine times as likely as women to assault a former spouse (Loseke & Kurz, 2005). Research has also found that intimate partner violence is not limited to cisgender individuals in heterosexual relationships. People in lesbian and gay relationships can also experience abuse from their partners (D. A. Hines & Malley-Morrison, 2005; Oswald, Fonseca, & Hardesty, 2010; Peplau & Fingerhut, 2007; Whitton et al., 2019). Before you read further, try Demonstration 13.4.

Demonstration 13.4

Thinking About Your Own Romantic Relationship

As you can imagine, no simple questionnaire can assess whether a relationship shows signs of abuse. However, read the following questions and determine whether they may apply to a current relationship, a previous relationship, or to a couple whom you know well. Does your partner:

1. Make fun of you or make demeaning comments when other people are present?
2. Tell you that everything is your fault?
3. Check up on you at work or other locations, to make certain that you are at the place where you said you'd be?
4. Make you feel unsafe in the current relationship?
5. Make you feel that they would explode if you did the wrong thing?

(continues)

Demonstration 13.4 *(continued)*

6. Act very suspicious about any potential romantic relationship with another person?
7. Try to keep you from developing nonromantic friendships with other people?
8. Try to make you do things you don't want to do?
9. Criticize you frequently?
10. Decide what you will wear, eat, or buy—when you have expressed a preference for something else?
11. Threaten to hurt you?
12. Intentionally hurt you physically?

Sources: Frieze (2005), Shaw and Lee (2001), and Warshaw (2001).

How Often Does the Abuse of Women Occur?

Earlier in this chapter, we discussed the difficulty of estimating how many women experience sexual harassment and rape. Most women believe that they must not let others know that they have been abused; this silence prevents researchers from obtaining accurate data about violence in intimate relationships (Jiwani, 2000). According to estimates, however, about 20 to 35% of women in the United States and Canada will experience abuse during their lifetime (Christopher & Lloyd, 2000; NCADV, 2020; Statistics Canada, 2021). To consider the statistics another way, male partners physically abuse between 1 million and 3 million U.S. women each year (NCADV, 2020; Roberts, 2007; Stahly, 2008; J. W. White & Frabutt, 2006).

Between 30 and 55% of women who are treated in U.S. hospital emergency departments have injuries related to domestic violence. Furthermore, pregnancy actually increases the risk of abuse. As many as 20% of all pregnant women experience physical or sexual abuse. These kinds of abuse sometimes cause substantial birth abnormalities (Logan et al., 2006; J. W. White & Frabutt, 2006).

According to Canadian and U.S. surveys, boys abuse their girlfriends as early as elementary school, and the abuse continues through high school and college (DeKeseredy & Schwartz, 1998, 2002; Frieze, 2005; J. Katz, Carino, & Hilton, 2002). For instance, a large-scale survey of Canadian university students revealed that 31% of the women had been pushed, grabbed, or shoved by someone they were dating. Emotional abuse was even more common: 65% of the women said they had been degraded in front of friends or family, and 65% had experienced insults or swearing (DeKeseredy & Schwartz, 1998). Many women report that the emotional abuse is worse than physical abuse (Burks, 2006). The abuse of women is not limited to the United States and Canada. The rates of abuse in European countries are similar to the North American rate (O. Barnett et al., 2005). Data gathered in Asia, Latin America, and Africa reveal even higher rates of abuse (e.g., O. Barnett et al., 2005; Ferrer, 2007; Krahé et al., 2005; Levy, 2008; Parrot & Cummings, 2006). Women in Mexico and Central American countries also experience high levels of intimate partner and gendered violence, as well as femicide, which sometimes forces them to emigrate from their own countries and seek refuge elsewhere to preserve their physical and mental health (Green & Viani, 2007; Lee & Au, 2007; Westbrook, 2020). Global statistics indicate that the three most dangerous subregions of the world for women are located in Central American, Caribbean, and South American countries (Westbrook, 2020; Widmer & Pavesi, 2016).

Throughout the world, women are especially likely to experience abuse in the turmoil of a war or a natural disaster, such as the tsunami that hit southern Asia in 2004, the massive earthquake that devastated Haiti in 2010, or throughout the COVID-19 epidemic (Campbell et al., 2016; Bourgault, Peterman, & O'Donnell, 2021). As one woman said, "The silence regarding violence against women is louder than the tsunami waves" (Chew, 2005, p. 1).

In many countries, more than half of adult women reported that a partner had physically assaulted them. For example, an interviewer asked a man in South Korea if he had beaten his wife. He replied:

> I was married at 28, and I'm 52 now. How could I have been married all these years and not beaten my wife? … For me, it's better to release that anger and get it over with. Otherwise, I just get sick inside. (Kristof, 1996, p. 17A)

Note how this man felt entitled to batter his wife (Stahly, 2008). He never considered whether the abuse was also better for his wife.

Women's Reactions to Abuse

As you might expect, women typically react to abuse with fear, depression, and mistrust. Women who have been abused may be hyper-alert, searching for signs that their partner may be ready to strike again (Martz & Saraurer, 2002; Statistics Canada, 2021). Understandably, women in long-term violent relationships report that they are dissatisfied with these relationships (S. L. Williams & Frieze, 2005). Women who have been abused typically feel anxious, isolated, and low in self-esteem. Many of these women also develop depression or other post-traumatic stress symptoms (Stahly, 2008; Stark, 2009).

Women who have been abused also experience many problems with their physical health. Women may suffer from bruises, cuts, burns, broken bones, bullet wounds, and brain damage as a direct result of an assault (Chrisler & Ferguson, 2006; Stark, 2009). Abusers may even prevent women from seeking medical care. Many months afterward, women may still experience headaches, sleep disturbances, extreme fatigue, abdominal pain, pelvic pain, gynecological problems, and other chronic disorders (O. Barnett et al., 2005; Logan et al., 2006). Naturally, these physical problems may intensify their psychological problems. These physical problems may also prevent women from going to work, resulting in numerous additional problems (Mighty, 2004; Riger et al., 2004; Wathen, MacGregor, & MacMurrie, 2015).

Characteristics Related to Abusive Relationships

Researchers have examined several factors related to the abuse of women. For example, some family characteristics may be associated with abuse. In addition, certain personal attributes are especially common among men who abuse their partners.

Family Variables Associated with Abuse

Reported abuse is somewhat more common among families with low incomes, although the relationship between abuse and economic status is complex (Logan et al., 2006; Marmion & Faulkner, 2006; Stahly, 2008). Furthermore, families with high incomes might be less likely to report abuse. It's clear, however, that no woman is immune. For example, a female professor at a prestigious college described her own experiences, when she was married to a well-educated man who was verbally and physically abusive for 12 years. When she finally left her husband, he committed suicide (Bates, 2005).

The relationship between ethnicity and family violence is both complex and inconsistent (Flores-Ortiz, 2004; Logan et al., 2006). For instance, Statistics Canada (2021) noted that Aboriginal/First Nations women are three times as likely as other Canadian women to report domestic violence. In the United States, Native American women provided higher estimates of domestic violence for their ethnic group, compared to estimates from White Americans (Tehee & Willis Esqueda, 2008). However, many analyses do not take economic status into account, and we have just learned that economic status is somewhat related to patterns of abuse.

In contrast, the number of reported cases of domestic abuse is relatively low in Asian American communities (O. Barnett et al., 2005; Marmion & Faulkner, 2006). One reason may be that Asian American families are extremely reluctant to let anyone outside the immediate family know about domestic problems (McHugh & Bartoszek, 2000). According to Asian American researchers, many Asian cultures believe that women should accept their suffering and endure their hardships. This value system would discourage women from reporting domestic violence (G. C. N. Hall, 2002; Tran & Des Jardins, 2000).

Black women experience higher lifetime rates of physical violence from their intimate partners than women in other ethnic groups (Green, 2017). This outcome is especially likely when their partners sexually objectify Black women and use that objectification to justify abuse within their relationships (Cheeseborough, Overstreet, & Ward, 2020).

Personal Characteristics of Male Abusers

One of the most commonly reported characteristics of male abusers is that they feel they are entitled to hurt their partners. From their egocentric perspective, their own needs come first (Kilmartin & Allison, 2007; Stahly, 2008). A good example of this male entitlement perspective is the Korean man who felt he was better off releasing his anger by beating his wife (p. 443).

Abusers are also likely to believe that the man should be the head of the family, along with other traditional concepts about gender roles (D. A. Hines & Malley-Morrison, 2005; Stark, 2009). Not surprisingly, abusers have more positive attitudes toward physical and verbal aggression, compared to men who are not abusers (D. A. Hines & Malley-Morrison, 2005; J. W. White & Frabutt, 2006). Furthermore, abusers are more likely than nonabusers to have witnessed family violence during childhood (Cares, 2009; Kilmartin & Allison, 2007; Stark, 2009).

Situational factors also increase the likelihood of partner abuse. For example, men who are unemployed have a relatively high rate of domestic violence (Frieze, 2005; Marin & Russo, 1999). Men who have served in the Armed Forces in a war zone are especially likely to abuse their partner (Alvarez, 2008).

Research also suggests that men who drink alcohol excessively are more likely to abuse women (D. A. Hines & Malley-Morrison, 2005; J. W. White & Frabutt, 2006). It's possible that alcohol plays an important role because it affects judgment and other cognitive processes. However, alcohol may not directly *cause* violence. For instance, some men simply use alcohol as an excuse for their violence (Gelles & Cavanaugh, 2005; Roberts, 2007). A man might try to justify his violence by saying, "I don't know what got into me. It must have been the liquor."

The Public's Attitudes About the Abuse of Women

In earlier chapters, we discussed the negative impact of the media on such issues as children's beliefs about gender, as well as adults' gender stereotypes and body images. In contrast, research in the United States suggests that the media have had a generally positive impact on knowledge about domestic violence (Goldfarb, 2005; Rapoza, 2004). For example, 93% of U.S. residents in a nationwide survey said that they had learned from media coverage that domestic violence is a serious problem (E. Klein et al., 1997). We should be pleased when feminist educational efforts combine with the media and legal reform to change societal attitudes (Frieze, 2005; C. M. Sullivan, 2006; Yllö, 2005). In a Canadian public opinion survey, for instance, 77% of the respondents said that the prevention of family violence should be an important priority for the federal government (Dookie, 2004).

In general, women are more likely than men to have negative attitudes toward the abuse of women. In contrast, men are more likely than women to say that a woman must have done something to deserve the punishment (Frieze, 2005; D. A. Hines & Malley-Morrison, 2005).

A study by Nayak and her colleagues (2003) assessed attitudes toward men who physically abuse their wives. These researchers gathered data from college classrooms in four countries: the United States, India, Japan, and Kuwait. Figure 13.2 shows the students' tendency to believe that wives deserve to be physically abused. Consistent with the other research, the women in each country were less likely than the men to believe that wives deserved abuse. Furthermore, students in the United States were less likely than students in the other three countries to endorse abuse. However, are the cross-national differences as large as you would have expected?

Myths About the Abuse of Women

We have already discussed the evidence against several commonly accepted myths about the abuse of women. For example, each of the following four myths is *not correct* because the research *contradicts* these myths:

Myth 1: Abuse is rare.

Myth 2: Men experience as much abuse as women.

Myth 3: Abuse is limited to the economically disadvantaged social classes.

Myth 4: Abuse is much more common among ethnic minority groups than among White Americans.

Let's examine two other myths. In each case, think how the myth encourages people to blame women for being abused.

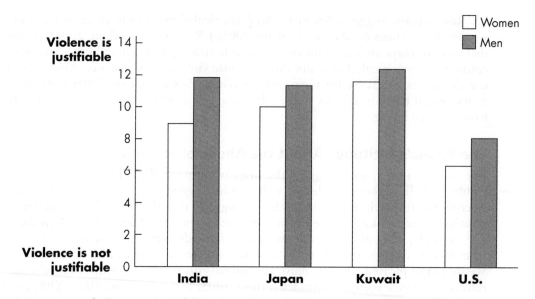

FIGURE **13.2** College students' attitudes about whether a man's physical violence toward his wife is justifiable, as a function of gender and country of residence. (Note: High scores violence is justifiable; low scores = violence is not justifiable.)

Source: From M. B. Nayak et al. (2003).

Myth 5: Women who are abused deserve to be beaten and humiliated. According to this myth, when a woman behaves in a manner that does not fit within the traditional gendered boundaries in heterosexual relationships, she "deserves" to be beaten. In other words, people may blame the woman's behavior, not the man's response (O. Barnett et al., 2005; Grothues & Marmion, 2006; Stahly, 2008). A student in a psychology of women course once related an incident in which she had described a wife-abuse case to a group of friends. Specifically, a husband had seriously injured his wife because dinner was not ready as soon as he came home from work. A male friend in this student's group—whom the student had previously considered enlightened about feminism—responded, "Yes, but she really should have prepared dinner on time."

Myth 6: Women who are abused could easily leave, if they really wanted to. This myth ignores both the interpersonal factors and the practical factors that prevent a woman from leaving a relationship. An woman who is abused may sincerely believe that her partner is basically a good person who can be reformed (Frieze, 2005; Stahly, 2008).

Many women who are abused also face practical barriers. A woman may have no place to go, no money, and no way of escaping (O. Barnett et al., 2005; Frieze, 2005). Another important concern is that the abuser may threaten to retaliate if she leaves. In fact, the research shows that the majority of abusers become even more violent after a woman has moved out of the home (Grothues & Marmion, 2006; D. A. Hines & Malley-Morrison, 2005; Stahly, 2008).

Reducing Intimate Partner Violence

Some women remain in abusive relationships, and some may seek support from family members or friends. A woman's strategies for handling abuse depend on her family background. For example, some families emphasize persevering in unpleasant situations and hiding domestic problems (O. Barnett et al., 2005). Community members and religious leaders may oppose the breakup of a marriage (McCallum & Lauzon, 2005). In these circumstances, women are less likely to leave an abusive relationship.

Beginning in the 1970s, the U.S. criminal justice system began prosecuting abuse cases and requiring the abusers to attend "batterer intervention programs." There are approximately 2,000 programs nationwide that focus on the abuser. Some useful resources are available (e.g., Wexler, 2006); however, there has been little systematic research on their effectiveness (Maxwell et al., 2009; Rosenbaum & Kunkel, 2009). Meta-analytic review of studies that have examined the effectiveness of batterer intervention programs suggest these programs have mixed results in actually reducing intimate partner violence (Babcock, Green, & Robie, 2004).

An abusive relationship seldom improves spontaneously. What options does a woman have for herself? We'll discuss three of them: (1) therapy; (2) using services in the community, such as a shelter for women who were abused; and (3) leaving the relationship.

Therapy

Women often seek the services of therapists, who are usually aware that society's attitudes can encourage the abuse of women. Ideally, therapists who work with women who have been abused will adopt a feminist-therapy approach (refer to pp. 410–411). Therapists ideally should respect a woman's strengths and difficulties. They should also help women think about themselves with compassion, rather than with criticism. Like other forms of women-centered therapy, this approach empowers women to pursue their own goals, rather than simply focusing on other people's needs (Frieze, 2005; Logan et al., 2006).

Consider the feminist-therapy approach that Rinfret-Raynor and Cantin (1997) used in working with French Canadian women who were abused and who had decided to remain in the relationship. A major message throughout therapy was that the abuser, not the victim, is responsible for the violence. The therapists also worked to increase the women's self-esteem and sense of independence. Compared to women who had received standard nonsexist therapy, the women who had received feminist therapy experienced a greater decrease in physical violence.

Psychotherapists acknowledge that there is no "one-size-fits-all" approach to therapy for partner abuse. However, cognitive-behavioral therapy is often an effective approach (refer to p. 410). In some cases, group therapy can also be helpful (Murphy et al., 2009). However, in many cases, even the most competent therapist cannot reduce the overall level of physical or psychological violence in an abusive relationship.

Services for Women Who Have Been Abused

Most communities in the United States provide services for women who have been abused. Some communities also have shelters where a woman who was abused and her children can go for safety, support, and information about social services available locally. Many shelters also offer counseling services and support groups for the residents

(O. Barnett et al., 2005; C. M. Sullivan, 2006). On a typical day in 2016, for example, more than 41,000 women and children were living in a U.S. shelter for women who have been abused (Rogers, 2019).

In 2014, Canada had about 627 shelters that focus on domestic violence (Beattie & Hutchins, 2015). The United States—with about nine times the population of Canada—has only about 3,000 shelters (U.S. Department of Health and Human Services, 2021).

Unfortunately, these shelters operate on extremely limited budgets, and we need hundreds of additional shelters throughout Canada and the United States. Historically, there has been limited funding allocated by many national governments for women's shelters and other relevant services. These facilities must therefore struggle to locate funding from individuals and organizations in the community (Logan et al., 2006). Due to capacity limits, thousands of women are turned away each year from shelters that are filled (Beattie & Hutchins, 2015; Marmion, 2006). Many of these women become homeless (Toro, 2007). Others return to their homes, where they risk being abused once again.

Deciding to Leave a Relationship

Many women decide that abuse is too high a price to pay for the advantages of remaining in a relationship. Many women reach a crisis point after a particularly violent episode (Lloyd & Emery, 2000). For instance, one woman decided to leave after her husband broke her ribs (Martz & Saraurer, 2002).

Some women decide to leave after they have been attacked in front of their children. For example, one woman left after her husband threatened to kill her in front of her children. Others leave after their partner breaks a promise about stopping the abuse or after they realize that the relationship will not improve (O. Barnett et al., 2005).

Unfortunately, people are so intrigued by the question, "Why do women who are battered stay?" that they forget to ask other important questions (Stahly, 2008). Some of these questions include "Why are men who are violent allowed to stay?" and "How can societies make it clear that emotional and physical abuse is not acceptable?"

Society's Response to the Problem of Abuse

In recent years, the criminal justice system and the general public have become much more aware that abuse is a serious problem. Still, government policies have no consistent plan for providing shelters, services, and assistance for women who have been abused. These policies also do not require counseling for the abusers. Government officials and agencies must publicize the fact that abuse of any kind is unacceptable.

It would be helpful if high schools and colleges required antiviolence programs that address sexual assault and family violence. Programs also need to be developed for children who have witnessed family violence (Foshee et al., 2009).

Unfortunately, community organizations are often silent about the issue of women who have been abused. Imagine what could happen if religious groups, parent-teacher associations, and service organizations (such as the Rotary Club and the Kiwanis) were to sponsor programs on domestic violence. These organizations often set the moral tone for a community, and they could send a strong message that abuse of women cannot be tolerated (Marmion, 2006).

One positive development is that in modern times, physicians pay more attention to the issue of women who were abused (Kaufman & the Committee on Adolescence, 2008;

Logan et al., 2006). For example, physicians are now encouraged to screen all women by telling them that partner abuse is a very important health problem, so it is now common for physicians to ask all of their patients a few questions about their personal lives. This issue is especially important for physicians, because partner abuse is a major reason that women seek medical attention (Williamson, 2009). Physicians should be less likely to ignore the evidence of abuse now that a new norm of concern has been established.

Individual men can also make a difference (Kilmartin & Allison, 2007; Poling et al., 2002). For example, James Poling describes how he and two male colleagues "moved from a lack of awareness of abusive behaviors, to a period of growing awareness because of the honest sharing of women about their experiences of violence, to belief in a set of principles that opened our eyes." As a result, they incorporated antiviolence messages into the religious services that they conduct.

Concern about the abuse of women is emerging more slowly in developing countries. For instance, most countries do not offer legal protection for women who have been abused (R. J. R. Levesque, 2001). Additionally, countries that tend toward nondemocratic political structures and that economically have relatively low and middle incomes, relative to other countries, tend to have the most societal acceptance toward interpersonal violence and abuse of women (Sardinha & Nájera Catalán, 2018).

Ultimately, however, any attempt to solve the problem of abuse must acknowledge that the power imbalance in intimate relationships reflects the power imbalance in our society (Goldfarb, 2005; Pickup, 2001). In addition, our culture trains some men to control their intimate partners through physical and emotional abuse. Some television and Internet programs, music videos, advertisements, news reports, and other media reinforce the images of men's violence toward women. We can help to counteract these attitudes by encouraging the media to provide less violent entertainment and to focus on responsible news reporting when covering events that involve gender-based violence (Menon, Pattnaik, Bascarane, & Padhy, 2020; Swift & Gold, 2021; Sutherland et al., 2019). We must work toward a world in which violence is not directed at women as a group in order to keep them powerless.

Section Summary

The Abuse of Women

1. About one-quarter of women in the United States and Canada will experience abuse during their lifetime; abuse is also common in dating relationships; abuse is more likely in some regions of the world, including Asia, Latin America, and Africa.
2. Women who have been abused may feel afraid, depressed, and anxious; they also experience many physical health problems.
3. Abuse is somewhat correlated with economic status, but its relationship with ethnicity is complex; male abusers typically have a sense of entitlement; unemployed men and men who have served in military war zones are at risk for abusing their partners.
4. Most people in the United States and Canada consider abuse to be a serious issue; women are more likely than men to have negative attitudes about abuse, and country of residence is also related to attitudes.

(continues)

Section Summary *(continued)*

5. Two additional myths about women who were abused—which the research does not support—are that women who were abused deserve to be beaten and that they could easily leave the relationship.
6. The U.S. criminal justice system is now more likely to require batterers to attend battering-intervention programs than in previous decades.
7. Therapy for women who have been abused focuses on reducing self-criticism and emphasizing their own needs.
8. Shelters for women who have been abused are helpful, but they are poorly funded; many women decide to leave an abusive relationship after they reach a specific crisis point.
9. Government policies have no uniform provisions about shelters or services for women who were abused; health-care providers now have better training about abuse issues.
10. As in other issues of violence, the problem of women who were abused requires gender equality at the societal level and reduced violence in our culture.

Chapter Review Questions

1. Throughout this chapter, we emphasized that people often blame female survivors for problems that are beyond the control of these women. Describe how this process operates in sexual harassment, rape, and the abuse of women.
2. According to the introduction of this chapter, a culture that values men more than women encourages some men to feel that they are entitled to certain privileges.
3. Explain how this sense of entitlement is relevant in sexual harassment, rape, and the abuse of women.
4. What are the two general categories of sexual harassment? Provide at least one example for each category, based on the recent media or on reports from friends. How do these examples illustrate why sexual harassment is an important issue?
5. Summarize the information about acquaintance rape and child sexual abuse. What does this information tell us about the balance of power and sexual violence in close personal relationships?

6. What are some of the common myths about sexual harassment, rape, and abuse? What do all these myths reveal about society's attitudes toward men and women?
7. In this chapter, we examined attitudes about rape and abuse. Identify any similarities that apply to both of these topics. Also, comment on gender comparisons in these attitudes and the relationship between gender roles and these attitudes.
8. What information do we have about sexual harassment, rape, and abuse, with respect to countries outside Canada and the United States? Is this information substantially different from information about violence against women in these two North American countries?
9. Imagine that you have been appointed to a national committee to address the problems of sexual harassment, rape, and abuse. What recommendations would you make for government policy, the legal

system, universities, business institutions, the media, and educational programs? Provide several of your own suggestions in addition to those mentioned in this chapter.

10. According to Theme 3 of your textbook, women are less visible than men in many important areas; topics important in women's lives are also considered relatively unimportant. How much did you already know about the topics of sexual harassment, rape, and abuse before the course for which you are reading this book? What are some factors that encourage these three topics to be relatively invisible?

11. Think about a high-school girl whom you know well. Imagine that she is about to go off to college. What kind of information could you supply from this chapter that would be helpful for her to know, with respect to violence against women? Now think about a high-school boy whom you know. If he were preparing to go to college, what information would you supply? Provide information about how he could avoid violence against women and how he could support women who have experienced violence. (Better still, figure out how you can have an actual conversation about these topics with those individuals!)

Key Terms

entitlement (p. 417)

sexual harassment (p. 418)

quid pro quo harassment (p. 418)

hostile-environment harassment (p. 418)

sexual assault (p. 424)

rape (p. 425)

acquaintance rape (p. 427)

post-traumatic stress disorder (PTSD) (p. 430)

child sexual abuse (p. 434)

incest (p. 435)

empowerment self-defense training (p. 436)

abuse of women (p. 440)

intimate partner violence (p. 440)

Recommended Readings

Chrisler, J. C., & Golden, C., (Eds.). (2018). *Lectures on the psychology of women* (5th ed.). Long Grove, IL: Waveland Press. This wonderful resource book includes 22 chapters on topics relevant to women's lives. The chapters on fear of rape, pornography, and the abuse of women are particularly relevant to the current chapter.

Denmark, F. L., & Paludi, M. A. (Eds.). (2017). *Psychology of women: A handbook of issues and theories* (3rd ed.). Westport, CT: Praeger. You'll find many interesting chapters in this book. The ones on rape, intimate partner violence, and sexual harassment are especially related to violence against women.

Stark, E., & Buzawa, E. S. (Eds.). (2009). *Violence against women in families and relationships* (Volumes 1–4). Santa Barbara, CA: ABC-CLIO. This four-volume set explores such topics as victimization, the community response, the context of the family, criminal justice issues, and media representations of family violence.

Ullman, S. E. (2010). *Talking about sexual assault: Society's response to survivors*. Washington, DC: American Psychological Association. We strongly recommend this book, which provides a review of the research on sexual assault, as well as Ullman's own research and quotations from women who have experienced sexual assault.

Answers to Demonstrations

Demonstration 13.1: Calculate a subtotal by adding together your ratings for items 1, 4, and 6. Then calculate an overall score by subtracting the ratings that you gave for items 2, 3, and 5. If your overall score is negative, you tend to be tolerant of sexual harassment. If your overall score is positive, you are aware that sexual harassment can be a serious problem.

Demonstration 13.2: 1. False; 2. True; 3. False; 4. False; 5. True; 6. False; 7. False; 8. True; 9. False; 10. False.

iStockPhoto/FatCamera

14 Women and Older Adulthood

Learning Objectives

After studying this chapter, you will be able to ...

14-1 Summarize commonly held attitudes about older women.

14-2 Describe gender differences in financial security during retirement.

14-3 Explain how menopause and hormonal changes at midlife affect the aging process for older adults.

14-4 Describe how gender affects people's social relationships during older adulthood.

Did You Know?

- According to the current research, young people in Japan and South Korea believe that older people may be pleasant, but not very smart (p. 460).
- The research shows that men usually have fewer retirement problems than women do (p. 462).
- Few women experience moderate depression, called "the empty-nest syndrome," when their children move away from home (p. 470).
- Older White American women are less likely than Asian Americans and Latina Americans to live with younger family members (p. 473).
- Older women often experience health, financial, and social problems, but most of them are reasonably satisfied with their lives (p. 475).

A middle-aged woman described her thoughts about growing older: I want to use my time well and live in a way that is true to my values. Some women face this question in college. For me, I just wanted to get married and have children. What do I want to do now? I want to feel I am leaving a legacy. It hit me full force at mid-life. (Boston Women's Health Book Collective, 2005, pp. 527–528)

Another woman, aged 67, said that she has "been gifted with a wonderful long-term marriage." She currently wants to develop "a passion, something that I do and like to do, that does not directly involve my family, something that is all about me. I need this to keep going now and feel like there is a future." (Browne-Miller, 2010, pp. 142–143)

In this chapter, we will explore the experiences of women in midlife and older adulthood, and we will discover many examples of the energy and sense of purpose revealed in these two quotations. Throughout this textbook, we have emphasized the contrast between people's stereotypes about women and the reality of women's lives. This contrast is also obvious when we examine the lives of older women.

No clear-cut age spans define middle age and old age. However, one fairly standard guideline is that middle age begins at about 40 and that older adulthood begins at about 60 or 65 (Etaugh & Bridges, 2006; Lachman, 2004; Takamura, 2007).

Consistent with our invisibility theme, psychological research has typically ignored older people, especially older women (Bugental & Hehman, 2007; Lachman, 2004;

Takamura, 2007). Feminist research has also paid little attention to older women (Calasanti & Slevin, 2006; Stewart & Newton, 2010; Street, 2007). For instance, articles about women over 40 seldom appear in prominent journals such as *Psychology of Women Quarterly* and *Sex Roles*. This neglect is unfortunate, because the average life expectancy for a woman in North America and Europe is around 80 to 84 years (Arias, Tejada-Vera, & Ahmad, 2021; United Nations Population Fund, 2021). In other words, about half of a woman's life has been largely ignored.

The absence of information is also unfortunate because the United States has so many older women. According to 2019 Census data, the United States had approximately 30 million women and 24 million men over the age of 65—roughly 25% more women than men (U.S. Census Bureau, 2021). The comparable figures for Canada—in the 2020 Census—were 6.8 million women and 6.6 million men over age 65 (Statistics Canada, 2020). An increasing number of women live beyond middle age and typically into their 70s, 80s, and older. Therefore, we need to examine the lives of older women in any discussion about the psychology of women.

In general, this chapter focuses on older women in the United States and Canada. As you might guess, we have relatively abundant information about the millions of people older than 65 who live in the economically and technologically developed countries within North America, Europe, and Asia. Unfortunately, we have little information about the millions of older people who live in countries outside of those regions (Takamura, 2007).

Several earlier chapters in this textbook have examined other aspects of older women's lives. Specifically, in Chapter 8, we discussed long-lasting romantic relationships, and in Chapter 9, we learned about sexuality and aging. In Chapter 11, we explored many issues relevant to older women's health, including heart disease, osteoporosis, cancer of the reproductive system, and breast cancer.

In this chapter, we'll focus on four additional topics: (1) attitudes toward older women, (2) retirement and financial issues, (3) menopause, and (4) social aspects of older women's lives.

14-1 Attitudes Toward Older Women

Learning Objectives

To summarize commonly held attitudes about older women, you can ...

14-1-1 Describe how ageism affects the representation of older women in media sources.

14-1-2 Analyze situations in which the double standard of aging shapes people's judgments about aging adults.

14-1-3 Explain how culture affects people's perceptions of aging people.

Ageism is a bias based on age, most often a bias against people who are older (Cruikshank, 2013; T. D. Nelson, 2009; Palmore, 2001, 2004). Common examples of ageism include negative stereotypes, myths, emotions, attitudes, and discrimination. For example, young people often think that older adults are typically grouchy and tired, and that they tend to feel sorry for themselves (Andreoletti, 2010).

Younger people may also avoid interacting with older individuals, and they often tell jokes about older people (Bugental & Hehman, 2007; Bytheway, 2005; Sneed & Whitbourne, 2005). We already mentioned one example of ageism: that researchers generally avoid studying older people. Another example of ageism is that many people infantilize older adults and speak to them in slow, very simple sentences, as if they are talking to a young child (Cruikshank, 2013; Hummert et al., 2004; Whitley & Kite, 2010).

Furthermore, many physicians believe that older individuals complain too much about relatively minor medical problems (Calasanti & Sleven, 2006; Jorgensen, 2001; Zebrowitz & Montepare, 2000). Physicians also treat older patients with less respect and concern, compared to younger patients (Bugental & Hehman, 2007; Pasupathi & Löckenhoff, 2002; T. L. Thompson et al., 2004). Unfortunately, many psychotherapists also treat older clients with less respect (Brown, 2008).

Ageism is an ironic bias, because older people constitute the only stigmatized social group that all people will join eventually—unless we happen to die early. If we have negative attitudes toward older people, we will probably have negative attitudes toward ourselves as we grow older (Andreoletti, 2010; Calasanti & Sleven, 2006; Cruikshank, 2013). Furthermore, if our ageism prevents us from interacting with older people, we won't realize that many ageist assumptions are not correct (H. Giles & Reid, 2005; Hagestad & Uhlenberg, 2005). Unfortunately, however, ageism is studied much less than either racism or sexism (Hedge et al., 2006; T. D. Nelson, 2009).

We'll begin this section on attitudes by considering how the media treats older women. Then we'll examine whether people respond more negatively to older women than to older men. Finally, we'll learn that older women may be treated more positively in some other cultures.

Older Women and the Media

Try Demonstration 14.1 to discover how the media represents older women. For example, older women are usually missing from the programs and advertisements on television

---

Demonstration 14.1

Older Women in the Media

Between now and the end of this academic term, keep a written record of how the media portrays both middle-aged women and older women. Be sure to include several kinds of programs (soap operas, game shows, situation comedies, dramas, shows during prime time, and Internet shows), as well as advertisements.

Pay attention to the number of older women portrayed and what they do. Are they working outside the home? Do they have interests, hobbies, and important concerns, or are they mainly busy being nurturant? Are they portrayed as intelligent or absent-minded? Do they enjoy the friendship of other women—the way that real older women do? Do they seem "real," or are they represented in a stereotypical fashion?

(Cruikshank, 2013; Kaid & Garner, 2004; R. Levine, 2004). When you finally find a TV show that features older women, most of those women will be concerned about cookie recipes or trivial complaints, rather than issues of greater significance (Whitley & Kite, 2010).

We all know spirited, accomplished older women in real life—women who lead active, purposeful lives consistent with the two quotations at the beginning of this chapter. However, your inspection of media's older women may not reveal many women of that caliber (Bedford, 2003; Cruikshank, 2013; J. D. Robinson et al., 2004). Many of you who are reading this book are older women, and you may have figured out that women like yourself are relatively invisible in the media (Kjaersgaard, 2005; J. D. Robinson et al., 2004). It's possible that older women may be more prominent as the majority of the "baby boomer" women reach their late 60s, but the trends so far are not hopeful (Andreoletti, 2010; Cruikshank, 2013; Nelson, 2009).

Older women sometimes appear in the fashion magazines, primarily in advertisements for age-concealing products (Chrisler, 2007a). These ads are designed to make older women feel especially inadequate (Cruikshank, 2013; Etaugh & Bridges, 2001). To hide signs of age, the ads say, women should dye their hair and have facelifts. In fact, one surgical procedure removes fat from a woman's thighs or buttocks and injects it into her lips, to restore a youthful fullness. Just imagine: You could be the first in your neighborhood to wear your hips on your lips!

We shouldn't be surprised, then, when many older women themselves show ageism. Sadly, they are often biased against people their own age (H. Giles & Reid, 2005; Whitbourne & Sneed, 2002). Most older women do not list "physical appearance" as their most important concern (Chrisler, 2007a). However, some older women do internalize the ageist messages about womens' inferior status within society (Cruikshank, 2013; Levy, 2009; Levy et al., 2009; Nelson, 2009). For example, studies have shown that media exposure and aging anxiety are two factors that directly influence women's attitudes about cosmetic surgery during middle age (Slevic & Tiggemann, 2010).

The Double Standard of Aging

As we've learned, people in the United States typically have negative views about the aging process. Some theorists have proposed that people judge older women even more harshly than older men, a discrepancy called the **double standard of aging** (Andreoletti, 2010; Whitbourne & Skultety, 2006; Whitley & Kite, 2010). For example, people tend to think that wrinkles in a man's face reveal character and maturity. However, people often believe that wrinkles in a woman's face send a negative message (Erber, 2005; Etaugh & Bridges, 2006). After all, the ideal woman's face should be unblemished and show no signs of previous experiences or emotions!

Does the research provide evidence for the double standard of aging? This is a difficult question to answer because our stereotypes about older men and women are complicated. As you'll learn, these stereotypes depend on the particular attribute we are judging, and how we measure the judgments (Kite et al., 2005; D. J. Schneider, 2004; Whitley & Kite, 2010). Let's consider two areas in which the double standard of aging may operate: (1) personality characteristics and (2) potential as a romantic partner.

Personality Characteristics

In a classic study, Hummert and her colleagues (1997) showed that people have a double standard of aging about personality characteristics. These researchers assembled photographs of men and women who represented different age groups. Let's consider specifically the part of this study in which the photographs being judged (the targets) were individuals in either their 60s or 70s, and they had neutral facial expressions. The participants in this study included men and women whose ages ranged from 18 through 96. They were asked to place each photograph next to one of six cards that described either a positive stereotype (e.g., a person who was lively, sociable, and interesting) or a negative stereotype (e.g., a person who was depressed, afraid, and lonely).

Figure 14.1 displays the average number of positive stereotypes that the participants selected. (The participants' age did not have a major impact on judgments, so Figure 14.1 combines the judgments of all participants.) As you can tell, people selected far fewer positive stereotypes for the older group of women than for all of the other three groups.

A large-scale meta-analysis by Mary Kite and her colleagues (2005) reveals a double standard of aging in some characteristics, but not in others. If a double standard of aging exists, then people should evaluate an old woman much more negatively than a young woman. At the same time, they should evaluate an old man only slightly more negatively than a young man. In other words, the "drop" should be larger for female targets than for male targets. Kite and her coauthors found that people did demonstrate a larger drop for female targets in two conditions: (1) when the people rated the male and female targets on characteristics such as generosity or friendliness and (2) when the people rated how willing they would be to interact with the male and female targets.

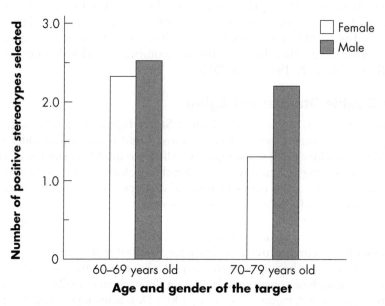

FIGURE **14.1** Average number of positive stereotypes, as a function of target age and target gender. (Note: Maximum positive score = 3.0.)

Source: Based on Hummert et al. (1997).

However, Kite and her colleagues found some surprising results when people rated the target men and women on intelligence, memory skills, and other characteristics related to competence. Specifically, the drop was larger for male targets than for female targets. In other words, people rated older men as being much less competent than younger men; in contrast, they rated older women and younger women about the same. We have learned throughout this book that people often undervalue women's competence. Should we be pleased that people think that women do not become even *less* competent as they grow older?

Potential as a Romantic Partner

Mary Kite and her colleagues (2005) suggested that the double standard of aging would be especially likely to operate when people judge whether men and women are physically attractive. However, there were not enough formal studies to allow a meta-analysis about attractiveness. One study reported that older women were much more critical than older men about how their aging bodies appeared (Halliwell & Dittmar, 2003).

The film industry clearly shows the double standard of aging, because they feature older men far more than older women, typically as the romantic leads (Cruikshank, 2013). Consider an analysis of the 100 most popular films of 2002 (Lauzen & Dozier, 2005). Older men are represented fairly; 45% of the major male actors in these films were older than 40, and 51% of the U.S. male population is in this category. In contrast, 34% of the major female actors were older than 40, although more than half of the U.S. female population is in this category. Think about the recent films you have experienced that include a heterosexual couple who are romantically and/or sexually involved. Can you think of many films in which the woman is older than the man?

Lesbian women also report that people react negatively when one partner is much older than the other. A 41-year-old woman wrote:

> I set about telling my friends that I am a lesbian and, at the same time, that I love a 63-year-old woman. The questions, stated or implied: Am I looking for a mother? Is she looking for some security in her old age? Is lesbian love, then, really asexual? (Macdonald & Rich, 2001, p. 11)

The double standard of aging also applies to sexuality because men often believe that an aging woman would not be a desirable sex partner (Bugental & Hehman, 2007; Teuscher & Teuscher, 2007). As we noted in Chapter 9, people admire an older man's interest in sexuality, but they condemn the same interest shown by an older woman. Older women therefore face a particular disadvantage with respect to sexuality. Not only are they considered to be sexually unattractive, but they are also expected to express minimal interest in sexuality.

In this discussion, we've read that older women are downgraded when people judge how pleasant someone is and whether they would enjoy interacting with that person. However, older men are downgraded in judgments about competence. When we consider physical attractiveness and romantic potential, the older women are again downgraded. Note that the double standard of aging is, in fact, a variant of Theme 2 of this book: In general, people react differently to women than they do to men. Furthermore, the differential treatment may increase as men and women grow older.

Cross-Cultural Views of Older Women

In this book, we have often focused on women in the United States and Canada. However, when we explore other cultures, we sometimes find useful alternative models for viewing older women. As Cruikshank (2013) writes, "The way you age depends on where you live" (p. 9). In many of these cultures, a woman's power within the family may increase as she grows older (Uba, 1994). For example, in some subcultures in African countries such as Nigeria and Kenya, older women are quite powerful (Calasanti & Slevin, 2001; Cruikshank, 2013).

These positive attitudes in other cultures could have important implications for cognitive functioning. In one study, for example, older women showed little memory decline in China, a culture that had positive attitudes toward older people in the early 1990s, when this study was conducted (B. R. Levy & Langer, 1994). In contrast, suppose that a culture does not expect older women to be very intelligent. These expectations may indirectly encourage older women to perform less well on a variety of cognitive tasks (Gilleard & Higgs, 2000).

Unfortunately, modernization can bring about a change for the worse (Bugenthal & Hehman, 2007). A more recent study focuses on attitudes toward older people—both women and men—in Hong Kong, Japan, and South Korea. These three East Asian countries have traditionally emphasized respect for older people. However, Cuddy and her coauthors (2005) found that young people in these countries judged their elders to be warm and good natured, but not very competent or intelligent. Young people in East Asia may treat older people with respect, but their attitudes may sometimes be negative (Nelson, 2009).

Unfortunately, research has apparently not examined whether young people in other cultures have more negative attitudes toward older women than toward older men. As a result, we do not know whether they show a double standard of aging.

Section Summary

Attitudes Toward Older Women

1. Researchers typically ignore older adults. Ageism is a bias against people, based on their age, and it is primarily directed toward older people.
2. The media under-represents and misrepresents older women—for example, in the movies and in magazines.
3. The double standard of aging proposes that people judge older women more harshly than they do older men. The evidence supports this double standard in some areas, such as judgments about the person's generosity and friendliness, but not in judgments about competence.
4. The double standard of aging also applies when people assess physical attractiveness; an older man is considered more appropriate as a romantic or sexual partner, compared to an older woman.
5. Cross-cultural ideas about aging seem to be in transition. In some cultures outside the United States and Canada, an older woman's power increases within the family as she grows older. However, in some Asian countries, older adults (both men and women) are considered to be warm, but not very competent.

14-2 Older Women, Retirement, and Financial Issues

Learning Objectives

To describe gender differences in financial security during retirement, you can ...

14-2-1 Discuss factors that impact women's planning for retirement.

14-2-2 Summarize major gender differences in people's adjustment to retirement.

14-2-3 Explain why women are more likely to experience financial insecurity during retirement than men.

Think about the topic of women and retirement for a moment. Have you ever read a short story or a book about a woman retiring from her job? How many television and Internet shows, plays, or movies focus on this issue? Women are somewhat missing from the popular lore about retirement—and from the research (Etaugh, 2008; Moen & Roehling, 2005; Whitbourne & Skultety, 2006). Once again, we have evidence for the relative invisibility of women (Sugar, 2007).

We need to emphasize that the concept of retirement has changed during various economic crises since 2000. Both men and women are finding that their retirement funds have shrunk substantially. It's not yet clear whether there are gender differences in the impact of the economic problems.

In any event, the invisibility of retired women may change now that so many women work outside the home. For example, about 71% of U.S. women between the ages of 50 and 54 are employed in jobs outside the home (Bureau of Labor Statistics, 2019). The media typically lags behind reality, but maybe we'll soon have a movie that includes a retirement party for a woman! Let's first consider several components of retirement, and then we'll focus on the economic issues that older women face.

Planning for Retirement

Women retire for a number of reasons, such as personal health problems and the appeal of free time (Etaugh, 2008; Price & Joo, 2005). Many women retire early to take care of relatives with health problems (Kim & Moen, 2001b; Sugar, 2007; Whitbourne & Skultety, 2006). Many women in middle age "retire" early because they are fired when a company is downsizing (R. Levine, 2004).

One worrisome gender difference is that women are less likely than men to seek information about retirement benefits before they retire (Etaugh, 2008; Kim & Moen, 2001a, 2001b). An important reason is that many women in heterosexual marriages assume that their husbands will be responsible for financial planning (Onyx & Benton, 1999). This avoidance may be a major problem because, as we'll soon learn, most women receive much lower retirement benefits than men do.

Adjusting to Retirement

Consistent with Theme 4 of this book, women differ widely in their reactions to retirement (Bauer-Maglin & Radosh, 2003b). Many women welcome retirement as an opportunity to relax, pursue new interests, do volunteer work, focus on social-justice issues, and enjoy interactions with friends.

Some studies report no gender differences in adjustment to retirement (e.g., Reitzes & Mutran, 2004). However, most of the research suggests that women tend to experience more retirement problems than men. Women may also need more time to adapt to retirement (Etaugh, 2008; Price & Joo, 2005). They may need time to feel comfortable simply enjoying projects, without feeling guilty about being "selfish" (S. B. Levine, 2005). As Sweet and Moen (2007) suggest, older women experience this kind of ambivalence during many of their life-transition phases.

One reason for gender differences in adjusting to retirement is that many women have lower incomes, so they often experience financial problems (Calasanti & Slevin, 2001). Another reason is that retired women in heterosexual marriages perform more housework than their retired husbands (Bernard & Phillipson, 2004; Cleveland, 2008; Cruikshank, 2013), and few women are inspired by housework. As one woman commented, "When a married couple retire, the women seem to spend most of the time doing housework etc., whereas men *do* retire" (Skucha & Bernard, 2000, p. 32).

When professional women retire, they frequently report that they miss their professional identity (Bauer-Maglin & Radosh, 2003b; Whitbourne & Skultety, 2006). Barbara Rubin had been a successful college professor in New York City. She reports on her emotions during her first year of retirement:

> Cut loose from an identity that had been carefully crafted and hard won, I became shaky as I suddenly questioned who I was now. Would I ever do anything of real importance again, anything as compelling as what I had already done? I went to a Manhattan party just around that time, and the host introduced me to another guest … "She used to be a chair of women's studies." (B. Rubin, 2003, p. 190)

As you can imagine, a woman's adjustment during retirement depends on her reasons for retirement. If a woman retires because she wants more time for herself and her leisure interests, she will probably adjust well to retirement. In contrast, if a woman retires because she needs to care for a sick relative, she is less likely to enjoy her retirement (Bauer-Maglin & Radosh, 2003a).

Significant life events, such as divorce or the death of family members, also influence a woman's adjustment to retirement. However, after heterosexual married couples have been retired for at least 2 years, both women and men are usually happier with their lives and their marriages, compared with couples who have not yet retired (Kim & Moen, 2001a; Moen et al., 2001).

Research on LGBTQ+ couples suggest similar outcomes in retirement satisfaction. However, same-sex couples tend to retire at asynchronous times more often than opposite sex couples, who tend to retire at similar times (Kridahl & Kolk, 2018).

We still have many unanswered questions about women and retirement. For example, how can we encourage women to learn more about their retirement benefits? What successful strategies do married women use when they negotiate a more equal sharing of housework during retirement? How can women best maintain their social connections from work? And what kinds of activities are most likely to help women feel more satisfied with retirement?

Financial Issues

Older Canadian women have a better economic situation than older women in the United States. For example, the poverty rate for Canadian women over the age of 65 has decreased since 2000; 16.3% are in the low-income category (Canadian Women's Foundation, 2018). Furthermore, 39.5% of employed women in Canada have a pension plan, compared to 38% of employed men (Fox & Moyser, 2018).

In contrast, many older women in the United States face economic difficulties. For U.S. women, the average annual income is about 82% of the incomes earned by men (Bureau of Labor Statistics, 2017). When U.S. women retire, they also receive lower Social Security benefits than men do, based on these accumulated differences in their overall lifetime incomes due to the gender wage gap (Enda & Gale, 2020; Hartmann & Lee, 2003).

The other major source of income for older women is private pension plans; employers contribute to these pension plans, based on earned income. Unfortunately, most employed women do not have jobs with pension plans. In the United States, the prevalence of private pension plans has declined since 2000; only 21% of people over 65 can expect this form of income during retirement (Napoletano & Curry, 2020; Pension Rights Center, 2019).

The gender differences in factors such as Social Security and pension plans have an enormous financial and psychological impact. In fact, after working for 40 years, the average man could potentially have a retirement fund that is roughly $1,000,000 more than the average woman's retirement fund (Sugar, 2007). Longitudinal studies of psychological well-being in retirement suggest that people who perceive that they have enough financial resources in retirement experience higher levels of life satisfaction and well-being than those who are economically disadvantaged (Kubicek, Korunka, Raymo, & Hoonakker, 2011). As a group, women are more likely to experience economic disadvantages than men during their retirement years.

Economic problems are even more serious for women of color (Applewhite et al., 2009; Cruikshank, 2013; Markham, 2006; Polivka, 2010). For example, very few Black and Latina women have a pension plan (Canetto, 2001a; Older Women's League, 2006a).

Let's consider several other important reasons that U.S. women have fewer financial resources than men during older adulthood (Applewhite et al., 2009; Cruikshank, 2013; Markham, 2006; Moen & Roehling, 2005; Sugar, 2007):

1. Many middle-aged women have unexpected layoffs—without a source of income (Moen & Roehling, 2005).
2. Women are not compensated for their unpaid work in the home.
3. Many women are either divorced or widowed; as a result, they have limited financial resources. For widows, the husband's health-care expenses may have depleted the family finances.
4. Women live longer. Compared to men, their total savings must be spread across a greater number of years.
5. As we learned in Chapter 11, women are more likely to have chronic illnesses, and the expense of treatment and medications further decreases their usable income.
6. Due to the gender wage gap throughout women's working careers, the accumulated effects of being undercompensated for labor outside the home leads to fewer financial resources in retirement.

Naturally, we need to remind ourselves about individual differences. Some older women in the United States and Canada are well-off. However, several miles away, other older women rarely have a nutritious meal. Furthermore, throughout the developing world, many older women have lived their entire lives without enough to eat (Hedge et al., 2006; United Nations, 2007; Vos et al., 2008).

Section Summary

Older Women, Retirement, and Financial Issues

1. The issue of women's retirement is relatively invisible in both the media and the psychological research.
2. Women are less likely than men to seek information about retirement benefits.
3. Although individual differences are large, women frequently experience more adjustment problems in retirement than men do, especially if they encounter financial difficulties.
4. In general, older women in Canada have a better economic situation than older women in the United States. Many older women in the United States live in poverty.
5. In the United States, older women are likely to have lower incomes than older men because of such factors as lower salaries when they were employed, lower income from Social Security, lack of pension plans, unpaid work in the home, and chronic illness.

14-3 Menopause

Learning Objectives

To explain how menopause and hormonal changes at midlife affect the aging process for older adults, you can ...

14-3-1   Describe common physical symptoms that accompany menopause.

14-3-2   Identify the major reasons why hormone replacement therapy is controversial.

14-3-3   Explain why bias in the medical literature has led to negative perceptions of menopause.

14-3-4   Summarize variations in people's psychological reactions to menopause.

So far, our study of older adulthood has examined two topics that are central to older women: (1) how other people react to older women and represent them in the media and (2) how older women experience retirement and economic issues. Let's now turn our attention to menopause. Compared to the first two topics, menopause is usually less important in women's lives.

As cisgender women grow older, their ovaries gradually produce less estrogen and progesterone, so that women no longer menstruate on a regular basis (Baram, 2005; Kurpius & Nicpon, 2003). Anyone with female reproductive anatomy, including cisgender women, nonbinary individuals, and transgender men who are not using gender affirming hormone therapy, enters **menopause** when they have stopped having menstrual periods for 12 months. Most people experience menopause between the ages of 45 and 55, with the average being 51 (Dell, 2005; Derry, 2004; Quintanilla et al., 2004). People who have had hysterectomies prior to this age sometimes enter menopause earlier than normal, depending on whether they retain their ovaries (Mishra et al., 2017).

Transgender women who experience gender affirming hormone therapy typically do not experience menopause in the traditional sense, as estrogen and other hormones associated with hormone therapy are typically administered for life (Iwamoto et al., 2019; Mohamed & Hunter, 2018). There is some evidence that transgender women may be at slightly increased risk of heart attacks and strokes during middle and late adulthood, due to long-term use of estrogens (Connelly et al., 2019; Mass et al., 2021).

Let's consider four components of menopause. We'll begin with the physical symptoms and next discuss why hormone replacement therapy is no longer widely recommended for cisgender women. We'll then consider people's attitudes toward menopause, ending with a discussion of cisgender women's psychological reactions to menopause.

Physical Changes During Menopause

Several common physical symptoms accompany menopause. The most common symptom is the **hot flash,** a sensation of heat coming from within the body. Heavy perspiration may accompany hot flashes, which can sometimes disrupt sleep (Chrisler, 2008a; Crooks & Baur, 2017; Lachman, 2004). However, the frequency and the intensity of hot flashes usually decrease after 1 or 2 years (Boston Women's Health Book Collective, 2011; Derry, 2004). The menopausal transition can last several years and occurs in a series of stages that begins with perimenopause and ends with a complete cessation of monthly menstrual cycles (Gunter, 2021; Santoro, 2016).

Other physical changes during menopause may include osteoporosis (which we discussed in Chapter 11), vaginal dryness, thinning of the vaginal tissues, dyspareunia, headaches, urinary symptoms, and fatigue (Chrisler, 2008; Dell, 2005; Santoro, 2016; Stanton et al., 2002). This list of physical symptoms sounds frightening, but some people report none of these symptoms, and many people report only one or two symptoms. Throughout this book, we have emphasized individual differences in gynecological issues such as menarche, menstrual pain, premenstrual syndrome, pregnancy, and childbirth. People's reactions to the physical changes of menopause show similar variation (Crooks & Baur, 2017; Caplan & Caplan, 2009; Derry, 2004). These individual differences provide additional evidence for Theme 4 of this book.

Why Hormone Replacement Therapy Is Controversial

Between about 1990 and 2001, health-care providers often recommended that cisgender women should take hormones during and after menopause (Houck, 2006; Lachman, 2004). **Hormone replacement therapy (HRT)** is a term that usually refers to a combination of estrogen and progestin, although some forms of HRT involve the use of only estrogen. Hormone replacement therapy relieves some of the physical symptoms of menopause, such as hot flashes. Prior to 2002, the research also seemed to show that hormones offered additional health benefits, such as reducing the risk of heart disease.

However, people concerned about women's health were waiting to learn the results of several long-term research projects. One of the largest of these projects was the Women's Health Initiative (WHI) study, which included more than 16,000 women. In this carefully designed study, half of the women were given pills for hormone replacement therapy. The other half were in the control group; they were given placebo pills, which had no active ingredients.

In May 2002, the WHI researchers suddenly halted the study—more than 3 years before the scheduled completion date of the original phase of the study. After examining their results, the researchers discovered that the estrogen-progestin combination did not prevent heart disease. In fact, it was associated with an increased risk of heart attacks, strokes, and blood clots, as well as a slightly increased risk of breast cancer. This combination of medication did reduce the risk of hip fractures, but not enough to offset the increase in the other risks (Cheung, 2005; Heiss et al., 2008; Writing Group for the Women's Health Initiative Investigators, 2002).

The WHI authors recommended that women should stop taking hormone-replacement medication. Other research confirmed that hormone replacement therapy had no beneficial effect on other measures, such as physical pain, sleep disturbances, and reported mental health (Hays et al., 2003).

Heiss and his colleagues (2008) conducted a follow-up study with the same women, three years after the first phase of the WHI study had been halted. This study reported approximately the same results, with more risks than benefits. Other research suggests that hormone replacement therapy can also increase the risk of Alzheimer's disease (Hogervorst, 2006; Travis et al., 2010).

Naturally, the negative results for hormone replacement therapy left millions of women in industrialized countries angry and puzzled (Chrisler, 2008a; S. B. Levine, 2005; Seaman, 2003; Solomon & Dluhy, 2003). Why hadn't earlier researchers conducted the appropriate studies? Why hadn't the drug companies discovered the potentially harmful effects of this hormone combination?

At present, health-care professionals usually do not recommend hormone replacement therapy for cisgender women. Instead, they encourage women to eat nutritious food and exercise appropriately (Chrisler, 2008a). Longer-term studies have provided additional evidence that hormone replacement therapy is associated with an increased risk of breast cancer; some studies suggest that the timing of HRT is important, a phenomenon known as the *timing hypothesis* (Cagnacci & Venier, 2019; Collaborative Group on Hormonal Factors in Breast Cancer, 2019; Mehta, Chester, & Kling, 2019; Vinogradova, Coupland, & Hippisley-Cox, 2020).

In summary, we have learned an important lesson: Be cautious about the claims that drug companies make, especially in the absence of empirical data from clinical trials (Naughton et al., 2005; Seaman, 2003).

Contemporary Attitudes About Menopause

You can assess your friends' attitudes toward menopause by trying Demonstration 14.2 on page 467. Menopause is no longer a taboo subject, but our students in their 20s report that they rarely discuss menopause with their friends. Furthermore, many women who are experiencing menopause say that they do not have detailed information about menopause.

Some women don't even discuss menopause with their friends (Chrisler, 2008a; Koch & Mansfield, 2004). In contrast, Dillaway (2007) found that the majority of the women in her midwestern U.S. sample knew about their mother's experiences with menopause.

Unfortunately, the medical literature has a long history of representing menopause negatively—as if menopause were a chronic illness (Derry, 2004; Dillaway, 2005; M. M. Gergen & Gergen, 2006; S. Greene, 2003). Self-help books and other popular media frequently echo this negative portrayal of menopause. These sources suggest that a woman who is experiencing menopause is plagued by wildly fluctuating hormones, which force her to be grouchy, highly anxious, and depressed (Caplan & Caplan, 2009; Houck, 2006).

Another problem is that the media often portrays worst-case scenarios, which contribute to the public's negative attitudes toward menopause. The media also perpetuates another related myth: that menopausal women are no longer interested in sexual activity. In Chapter 9, though, we noted that women who have sexual partners typically remain sexually active during older adulthood.

Given the negative representation of menopause in both medicine and the media, you won't be surprised to learn that the general public has similar negative attitudes. For example, Amy Marcus-Newhall and her colleagues (2001) asked people to list words that they would associate with each of three middle-aged groups of people. (Demonstration 14.2 is based on this study.) Then people evaluated each term on a rating scale.

Attitudes toward 45- to 55-year-old women (described as menopausal) were significantly more negative than attitudes toward both 45- to 55-year-old women (with no mention of menopause) and 45- to 55-year-old men. For example, they believed that menopausal women would be significantly less likely than members of the other two groups to have hobbies or to be attractive, and significantly more likely to express negative emotions. In Demonstration 14.2, do your friends show this same trend?

Women's Psychological Reactions to Menopause

At the beginning of this chapter, we emphasized that attitudes toward older women are often negative; they do not accurately describe the characteristics of real-world older women. Similarly, we find that the media's attitude toward menopause does not accurately

---

Demonstration 14.2

Attitudes Toward Menopause

For this demonstration, you will need at least six friends to participate in a brief study on people's attitudes toward typical middle-aged individuals. Test at least two people in each of the three conditions.

Tell the people in the first condition, "Please list items that you associate with men in the age range of 45 to 55 years. You can list words that describe their personality, appearance, attitudes, interests, emotions, and behaviors." After a couple of minutes, tell them to go back over those items and give a rating to indicate how positive or negative each characteristic is. Instruct them to use a rating scale where 1 is very negative, 3 is neutral, and 5 is very positive.

Repeat these instructions with people in two additional conditions. For the second condition, substitute the phrase "women in the age range of 45 to 55 years." For the third condition, substitute the phrase "menopausal women in the age range of 45 to 55 years."

After you have tested everyone, calculate an "average rating" for each of the three middle-aged conditions. Do your three conditions differ?

Source: Based on Marcus-Newhall et al. (2001, p. 704).

describe women's actual experiences during menopause (Caplan & Caplan, 2009; Hvas, 2001; Stanton et al., 2002). Some people report psychological symptoms such as depression, irritability, and mood swings. However, we have no evidence that normal menopause—by itself—causes these symptoms.

In this chapter, we have already noted a number of depressing factors in the lives of older women, including attitudes toward older women and women's economic status. Women also experience health problems, divorce, and the death of relatives and friends. All these stressful factors are more important than menopause itself in determining the psychological status of women during middle age (Avis, 2003; Glazer et al., 2002).

Hot flashes may keep a small percentage of women awake at night, and therefore make them more sleepy the next day (Caplan & Caplan, 2009). However, most women do not report depression or other negative psychological reactions to menopause (Avis et al., 2004; G. Robinson, 2002). For example, a 50-year-old woman provided her perspective on menopause: "I was well into my menopause before I realized what was happening. My symptoms were so minor and rather vague. I didn't understand all the hype about symptoms" (L. L. Alexander et al., 2001, p. 398).

Some women are relieved that they no longer need to be worried about becoming pregnant. Other women regard menopause as a life event that encourages them to evaluate their lives and decide whether they want to change directions (Rich & Mervyn, 1999; Zerbe, 1999). Lotte Hvas (2001) asked Danish women to describe their experiences with menopause. About half described at least one positive component. For instance, a 51-year-old woman said:

> Physically I have obtained a great strength passing the menopause—my sexual life has become more fun—I know for sure what I want—I look forward to becoming a grandmother soon, I am about to change my job, and I look forward to it. (Hvas, 2001, p. 14)

Similarly, Quintanilla and her colleagues (2004) interviewed 35 U.S. women about their own experiences with menopause. Two women provided negative descriptions about feeling "out of control." The remaining 33 women provided either positive or neutral descriptions: for example, that menopause is "something women should almost look forward to because it is going to be a change for the better" (p. 113). In contrast, both the medical world and the media ignore the potentially positive aspects of menopause (Sherwin, 2001).

Some research explores how women of color experience menopause. In a large-scale study, Barbara Sommer and her colleagues (1999) analyzed telephone interviews that had been conducted with more than 16,000 middle-aged women throughout the United States. Ethnic-group differences were small but statistically significant. Black women had the most positive attitudes; White and Latina women were intermediate; and Asian American women were least positive.

Women from Greece, southern Mexico, and several other cultures outside the United States and Canada seem to have relatively positive views, especially if older women are valued in the culture (S. Greene, 2003; G. Robinson, 2002). For example, Lamb (2000) studied women in a town in the West Bengal region of India. Young women and older women uniformly described menopause in positive terms because menopause meant that they were free of the hassles of menstruation and that they could participate in religious ceremonies that are forbidden to menstruating women. Alternative viewpoints such as this one help us to understand how each culture constructs menopause according to its own values. Multicultural and cross-cultural perspectives also provide us with some positive cultural attitudes.

Section Summary

Menopause

1. Menopause is the cessation of menstrual periods; common physical symptoms of menopause include hot flashes, osteoporosis, genital changes, headaches, and fatigue.
2. For most post-menopausal people, hormone replacement therapy produces more health risks than health benefits.
3. Both medicine and the media have represented menopause negatively, and the general public usually has negative reactions to the phrase "menopausal women."
4. Contrary to folklore, menopause does not cause psychological symptoms such as depression and irritability. Many people have some positive reactions to menopause. Small ethnic-group differences have been reported in the United States, and women in some parts of the world may have relatively positive reactions to menopause.

14-4 Social Relationships in Older Women's Lives

Learning Objectives

To describe how gender affects people's social relationships during older adulthood, you can ...

14-4-1 Describe how the family relationships of daughters, mothers, and grandmothers change during older adulthood.

14-4-2 Explain how the death of a spouse or intimate partner affects people's lives.

14-4-3 Summarize differences in older adulthood experiences among women of color.

14-4-4 Explain how the paradox of well-being in older adulthood can lead to successful aging.

14-4-5 Identify factors that may help older adults rewrite their life stories.

In this chapter, we have considered how society conceptualizes older women, as well as women's experiences as they pass through menopause and retire from the workforce. Now let's examine the changing social world of older women. As a woman grows older, how do her family relationships evolve, as a daughter, a mother, and a grandmother? How do women respond to the death of a spouse or other intimate partner? Do women of color and White women have similar experiences? How happy are women with their lives? Throughout this section, you will discover substantial evidence for our theme of individual differences (Kjaersgaard, 2005).

Family Relationships

In Chapter 8, on love relationships, we explored one family role that is important for many women: being a wife. In that chapter, we examined some characteristics of happy long-term relationships. We also examined the relationships of LGBTQ+ women. Let's now explore other important family roles for many older women—their roles as daughters, mothers, and grandmothers.

Older Women as Daughters

We usually think of adult women's roles as mothers and grandmothers. However, the majority of adult women are also daughters. Most of the research on the daughter role focuses on adult women who take care of their older parents. Many women caregivers now spend more years caring for their parents than caring for their children (Crose, 2003).

The term **sandwich generation** refers to middle-aged people, especially women, who find themselves responsible for both their dependent children and their aging parents (Whitbourne, 2008). Daughters are much more likely than sons to become caretakers for an older parent who is in poor health (Cruikshank, 2013; Etaugh, 2008; Fortinsky et al., 2007). In many cases, women take time off from paid employment, often creating problems at work and reducing their own retirement funds (Cleveland, 2008; Cruikshank, 2013). Because women usually spend much more time on these tasks than men do, taking care of older parents is really a women's issue.

Many of the resources on women's caregiving roles emphasize that the tasks are unpleasant and burdensome for middle-aged daughters. In fact, providing care for others is often stressful and time-consuming. It can therefore have negative effects on the caregiver's physical and mental health (Bouldin & Andresen, 2010; E. M. Brody, 2004; Fortinsky et al., 2007; Miller-Day, 2004).

However, studies have also found that many daughters willingly accept this responsibility, especially when they feel that their parents have raised them with so much love and generosity (Musil et al., 2005; Whitbourne, 2008). Many women take on these roles due to a sense of **filial responsibility**, which involves feeling obligated to take care of family members based on social norms or personal belief systems (Funk, Chappell, & Liu, 2013). They also feel satisfied that they can provide their parents with good care (Fingerman, 2003; Menzies, 2005). According to research in British Columbia, the clear majority of caregivers reported that they found aspects of their work to be rewarding. Many reported, for example, that they felt closer to the person whom they were assisting (Chappell et al., 2008). Similarly, a colleague commented on the challenges of missing work so that she could take care of her severely ill older mother. As she wrote:

> I considered myself blessed to have been able to give so much to my mother and to provide her hospice care in her home. She died in my arms. Yes it was stressful. Yes it was difficult. And, yes, I had these positive feelings—as well as negative feelings—at the time I was doing this. But I have no regrets and would do it again without thinking about it. (L. Skinner, personal communication, 1999)

A small number of researchers have begun to explore other aspects of the relationship between grown children and their parents—beyond the caretaking role (Fingerman, 2003; Fingerman et al., 2007; Hunter et al., 2002). Unfortunately, however, the media generally ignores the social interactions between middle-aged people and their parents. Aside from an occasional brief reference, how often have you observed or read about a relationship between an adult woman and her mother in which they were interacting as adults?

Older Women as Mothers

Much of the earlier research and theory on middle-aged women focused on the **empty nest**, or the period after children are no longer living at home. Note that the name *empty nest* implies that a woman's identity focuses completely on being a mother. Years ago, researchers were eager to demonstrate that mothers felt depressed when children left home.

In reality, however, the research reveals the same individual differences that our other discussions of women's lives have uncovered (Theme 4). In general, though, research confirms that the empty nest does not cause depression. In fact, middle-aged mothers whose children have left home tend to be as happy as or even slightly happier than middle-aged mothers who have at least one child at home (Canetto, 2003; Gergen, 2008; Stewart & Newton, 2010). Naturally, mothers worry when an adult child has marital problems or loses a job (Pillemer et al., 2007). However, most mothers still feel deeply connected with their children, even when those children no longer live at home (Pruchno & Rosenbaum, 2003). Our students who are in their early 20s are often dismayed to learn that their mothers may be somewhat happier after the children leave home. Please do not conclude that women are overjoyed with their children's departure. Mothers may indeed be saddened. However, serious depression is rare. Instead, mothers learn to reshape their lives around new interests and activities as their children move into adulthood (Johnston-Robledo, 2000; Stewart & Newton, 2010).

These positive psychological outcomes are similar to outcomes found among women who remained child-free throughout their lives. Whether women have chosen to raise children or not during their young adult years, middle age provides a new opportunity for women to reinvent their lives, accomplish long-term goals, and maintain generativity (Moore & Radtke, 2015).

Older Women as Grandmothers

According to one of the traditional stereotypes, grandmothers are cheerful white-haired old ladies who bestow cookies and affection on their grandchildren. According to another stereotype, grandmothers are fussy, frail, and helpless (Cruikshank, 2013; Denmark, 2002; P. K. Smith & Drew, 2002). Neither of these stereotypes captures the wide variety of skills, interests, and personality characteristics that are typical of real grandmothers.

Many women who have children eventually become grandmothers for about one-third of their lives (P. K. Smith & Drew, 2002). Compared to grandfathers, grandmothers are typically more involved with their grandchildren (P. K. Smith & Drew, 2002). Furthermore, about 8% of children younger than 18 live in a home where a grandparent is the head of the household (Wu, 2018). However, once again, we have relatively little research on this role.

Grandmothers are likely to impart advice that emphasizes moral values and social responsibility (Belgrave & Allison, 2010; Erber, 2005; Fingerman, 2003). However, our theme of individual differences is evident in patterns of grandmothering. Some women argue that good grandparents should not interfere with their grandchildren's upbringing, but others feel it is their duty to advise (Erber, 2005; Whitbourne, 2008). In Black and Native American families, grandmothers may be expected to play an especially important role in supporting and advising their grandchildren (P. K. Smith & Drew, 2002; Trotman & Brody, 2002).

According to the research, grandmothers almost always report that being a grandparent is much more fun and much more relaxing than being a parent (Brott, 2006; Whitbourne, 2008). After all, grandmothers do not need to be responsible for rearing a child on a daily basis. As one grandmother said, "I don't have to be on the front lines anymore, I can just watch the show" (Miller-Day, 2004, p. 81).

The Death of an Intimate Partner and Coping with Bereavement

According to the research on married heterosexual women, the death of a spouse is usually one of the most traumatic and stressful events of their lives (Carr & Ha, 2006; Hansson & Stroebe, 2007; Whitbourne, 2008). Women are more likely to become widows than men are to become widowers. Several factors explain this discrepancy. For example, women live longer, they typically marry men older than themselves, and they are less likely to remarry following the death of a spouse (Carr & Ha, 2006; Freund & Riediger, 2003). As a result, U.S. Census data show that among people 75 years and older, 58% of women but only 28% of men report having been widowed at some point in their lives (Gurrentz & Mayol Garcia, 2021). The ratio in other regions of the world is even more extreme. For instance, 10% of all girls and women older than age 14 in Africa are widows (The World Bank, 2018).

When a woman's partner dies, she faces the pain, grief, and mourning that accompany bereavement. She may feel emotionally exhausted and physically weakened, especially if she was an active caregiver during her partner's final weeks (Christakis & Allison, 2006; Pruchno & Rosenbaum, 2003). Loneliness is one of the major problems for widows (Bedford & Blieszner, 2000; R. Levine, 2004). Widows also report that they often feel awkward in social situations where most people are with a spouse.

When a spouse dies, people are likely to experience loneliness, grief, stress, and health problems. Adjustment to widowhood is especially difficult when people have been happily married, with little interpersonal conflict (Pruchno & Rosenbaum, 2003).

Researchers know relatively little about the grieving process for LGBTQ+ partners (Bristowe, Marshall, & Harding, 2016). One reason is that many older individuals who identify as LGBTQ+ found their life partners during prior eras when most people condemned same-gender relationships (Claasen, 2005; Whipple, 2006). Older lesbian women of color are especially missing from the research (R. L. Hall & Fine, 2005).

Consider the situation of Marilyn, whose partner, Cheryl, had died prior to the legalization of same-sex marriage in the United States that occurred in 2015. Marilyn described her dilemma:

> I am a widow. The law does not say so. My tax form does not say so. Neither do any of the countless forms that I fill out that include marital status say so. But every time I check off the box that says single, I want to scream and white it out and write "widow." But I am a lesbian who has lost her female partner, so in most places I am not accorded the status of widow. ... It does not seem to matter that we lived in a monogamous, loving relationship for thirty-one years, or that we coparented three wonderful children. (Whipple, 2006, p. 129)

Unfortunately, even though same-sex marriage is now legal at the federal level in the United States, barriers to grieving still remain in some areas of the country. Our culture's heterosexism is likely to deny LGBTQ+ individuals the widespread social support that is typically offered to heterosexual women whose husbands have died. For instance, one woman teaching in a small rural school was afraid she would lose her job if she revealed her grief after the death of her partner (Deevey, 2000). They had spent years concealing their romantic relationship, and now she could not publicly express her sorrow. Grieving without being able to publicly show those emotions or receive social support from others is called **disenfranchised grief**, and it is unfortunately a common experience among LGBTQ+ individuals who have lost a life partner or spouse (Bristowe et al., 2016).

We find enormous individual differences in bereavement, as in all important transitions in women's lives (Siegel, 2004; Stroebe et al., 2005). Many women are deeply depressed, long after the death of an intimate partner. However, some women discover a hidden strength that aids their recovery. For example, a 48-year-old woman wrote:

> I think that when you lose a loved one, it's a rebirth for yourself. You can't always dwell on the loss of the loved one. You have to look forward to what you are going to do with your life now. ... Every day's a little learning experience for myself, of doing new things and learning new things as a single person. (Nolen- Hoeksema & Larson, 1999, p. 149)

Older Women of Color

In discussing older women of color, we need to emphasize the substantial individual differences within each ethnic group (Iwamasa & Sorocco, 2002). We also need to realize the potential challenges of conducting research about this topic. For example, Delores Mullings (2004) is a young Caribbean Canadian, and she wanted to learn more about older women who shared her ethnic background. She describes numerous ways in which she was able to convey her genuine respect for the participants in her study, including her choice of clothing, specific choice of words, and conversational patterns.

We noted earlier in this chapter that Latina and Black older women are much more likely than White older women to live in poverty (Applewhite et al., 2009; Cruikshank, 2013; Markham, 2006; Polivka, 2010). Consequently, many older women of color face a daily struggle in paying for housing, health care, transportation, and even enough food to eat.

However, older women of color also benefit from an advantage: They are more likely than White women to have family members living nearby, who can provide assistance and support. They are also more likely to live in the same home as younger family members (Armstrong, 2001; Saperstein, 2002; Trotman, 2002).

Latina Women

Latina grandmothers are generally treated with respect, and they typically enjoy their social role. However, they often describe the role as "confining" or "limiting," especially if they must take on child-care responsibilities.

Older Latina women living in the United States are expected to provide help to children and grandchildren (Angel & Torres-Gil, 2010; Harm, 2001; Zajicek et al., 2006). Similarly, older women are expected to seek help from younger relatives (Sánchez, 2001).

Black Women

Older Black women are represented by two opposing stereotypes (Ralston, 1997; Trotman, 2002). One stereotype portrays them as victims of poverty and urban decay. The other stereotype portrays them as superhuman individuals who surmount obstacles through hard work and a good heart. Neither portrayal captures the complexity of their actual lives.

In general, older Black women are likely to be active in religious groups and other community organizations (Ai et al., 2010; Armstrong, 2001). In addition, Black women are often closely involved in the lives of their grandchildren (McWright, 2002; P. K. Smith & Drew, 2002). These women frequently give their grandchildren social support, monitor their activities, discipline them, and encourage them to achieve. However, many Black grandmothers report that they resent being the primary caretaker for grandchildren, especially if they only recently finished rearing their own children (Barer, 2001; Calasanti & Slevin, 2001; Harm, 2001).

Asian American Women

When we consider older Asian American women, we discover additional evidence of diversity within each ethnic group. For example, an older South Asian woman from India may be a retired physician. In contrast, relatively few older women from Laos have completed high school (Kagawa-Singer et al., 1997). Similarly, older Japanese Americans have a higher average income than older Vietnamese Americans (Cruikshank, 2013).

If older Asian Americans are not fluent in English, a younger English-speaking relative is expected to accompany them to a store or a doctor's appointment (Armstrong, 2001; Saperstein, 2002; Yee & Chiriboga, 2007). Furthermore, young Asian Americans are usually more likely than White Americans to express respect older people. However, it's not clear whether this respect translates into greater life satisfaction for Asian American elders (Iwamasa & Sorocco, 2002).

Native American and First Nation Women

Researchers probably know the least about Native American, First Nation, and Aboriginal women (Polacca, 2001). In the United States, many older Native American women live in rural areas or on reservations, where they typically assume the roles of grandmother, caregiver, educator, and wisdom keeper (Conway-Turner, 1999; Polacca, 2001). Native American grandmothers are more likely to actively rear their grandchildren than grandmothers from any other ethnic group in the United States (Byers, 2010; Dennis & Brewer, 2017).

A study of Apache grandmothers living on a reservation in Arizona emphasizes the strong bond between grandmothers and their grandchildren (Bahr, 1994). Many Apache children live with their grandparents, because parents often leave the reservation to seek employment in an urban setting. Most grandmothers in Bahr's (1994) study reported that they felt great satisfaction in caring for their grandchildren. These grandmothers are expected to be wise, energetic, and resourceful, especially in transmitting their cultural heritage to their grandchildren. In turn, young Native Americans are more likely than young White Americans to believe that they have a responsibility to take care of older relatives (Gardiner et al., 1998; Polacca, 2001).

Throughout this chapter, we have discussed the invisibility of older women as a group. Older women of color are even less visible, due to historical bias and lack of intersectional perspectives in research. To fully understand the complexity of older women's experiences within various communities and cultures, it would be helpful for future researchers studying the lives of women to focus on all aspects their lived experiences in middle and late adulthood.

Satisfaction with Life

If you browse through some of the topics discussed in this book, you'll read that many older women have every right to be unhappy. Chapter 11 described physical problems such as breast cancer and osteoporosis, which are relatively common among older women. In the current chapter, we have discovered that women may be unhappy about retiring.

Many worry about the health of their parents. Many will mourn the loss of a spouse or a life partner.

Many older women, especially women of color, are likely to face economic crises. Even women who do not have any of these problems are likely to experience negative reactions from others because they live in a culture that rejects older women's wrinkles and other signs of aging (Gergen, 2008).

In reality, however, most middle-aged and older women are reasonably satisfied with their lives (Bourque et al., 2005; Ko et al., 2007; Miner-Rubino et al., 2004; Whitbourne & Sneed, 2002). Furthermore, older women are actually *less* likely than younger women to experience depression (D. G. Myers, 2000).

The research on life satisfaction demonstrates the **paradox of well-being**: Many older women report high life satisfaction, despite the objective difficulties they encounter (Carstensen & Mikels, 2005; Kahana et al., 2005; Whitbourne, 2008, 2010). Unfortunately, as Stewart and Newton (2010) note, researchers know little about the well-being of women who have experienced lifelong poverty.

Several factors help to explain why most older women are at least reasonably happy. Specifically, they have learned how to cope effectively with negative emotions and how to spend time on activities they enjoy. They have also adjusted their goals so that they are more realistic. In addition, they can maintain a positive view of themselves, even when they encounter disappointments (Dark-Freudeman, 2010; Magai, 2001; Whitbourne, 2010).

A relatively new focus in research about older people is called "successful aging." Although definitions vary, **successful aging** means that a person maximizes gains and minimizes losses as they grow older (Dark-Freudeman, 2010; Freund & Riediger, 2003; Whitbourne, 2008, 2010). For example, an older woman could demonstrate successful aging if:

1. She is satisfied with various aspects of her life, such as her family and friends.
2. She is optimistic, and she believes she is achieving her personal goals.
3. She is healthy, and she is cognitively competent.
4. She is satisfied with her income and living conditions.
5. She is involved in social causes that make life better for other people, so that she can have a sense of purpose in her life.

Throughout this book, we have emphasized the theme of individual variation. Women also vary in the ways they achieve happiness. They do not share a universal ready-made blueprint for happiness (Charles & Pasupathi, 2003; S. B. Levine, 2005). One woman might find happiness through her spouse and children, whereas another might be equally happy with a less traditional lifestyle.

Rewriting Our Life Stories

Many young women think they know exactly where their lives are heading, and many women's lives do reveal a pattern of continuity and predictability. However, many women find that their lives take an unexpected route (Whitbourne, 2010). Most middle-aged women welcome new challenges, and they are more confident than in earlier years (S. B. Levine, 2005; A. J. Stewart et al., 2001). Furthermore, middle-aged women often report that the feminist movement has helped them feel more powerful and self-confident (S. B. Levine, 2005; A. M. Young et al., 2001).

Yes, some middle-aged women say that—several years earlier—they had regrets about their life path. However, if they make life changes, and they rewrite their life stories, they are typically more satisfied than those who continued to live with their regrets (S. B. Levine, 2005; A. J. Stewart & Vandewater, 1999; Whitbourne, 2010).

For example, at the age of 46, Linda N. Edelstein (1999) faced the possibility of cancer. Fortunately, the tumor turned out to be benign. She reported that the incident forced her to question what she really wanted and how she should pursue these dreams. As she wrote, "The sadness and hopelessness some women experience in the middle years does not come from trying and failing, but from not trying" (p. 195). Older women have rewritten their life stories by developing greater appreciation for their loved ones and by developing new interests (K. J. Gergen & Gergen, 2004; Whitbourne, 2010).

It is important to emphasize, however, that older women in the United States would be more likely to create positive, productive life stories if our society truly valued older women. In a country of such enormous wealth and resources, it is unfortunate that many women of all ages, but especially during late adulthood, still struggle to obtain adequate food, housing, and health care. For the last demonstration of this chapter, try Demonstration 14.3, when you have a convenient opportunity.

Demonstration **14.3**

The Life Stories of Older Women

The instructions for this demonstration are more open-ended than for the previous demonstrations. Think of a woman you know fairly well who is at least 40 years old. Ask if you might interview her at a convenient time.

Before the interview, select some of this demonstration's sample questions, keeping in mind that a few questions may be too personal. Also, construct several other questions based on the information in this chapter. Before you begin the interview, be sure to emphasize that she can choose not to answer any question you ask.

Sample Questions

1. What was the happiest time in your life?
2. When you were 20, did you think that your life would take you along the pathway you have been going?
3. Is there anything you would have done differently if you had the chance to relive part of your life?
4. Has your self-confidence changed since you were 20 or 30 years old?
5. If you were 20 years old, living in today's world, what kind of choices would you make?
6. (If relevant) When your children left home, what kinds of emotional reactions did you have?

(continues)

Demonstration 14.3 *(continued)*

7. (If relevant) When you retired from your job, what kinds of emotional reactions did you have?
8. Do you feel that you are still searching for a sense of who you are?
9. Do you feel that people treat you differently because of your age and your gender?
10. Is there a question about your life that I somehow didn't ask—one that is personally interesting to you?

Sources: Questions based on A. J. Stewart and Vandewater (1999) and A. J. Stewart et al. (2001).

Final Words

To conclude this chapter, a 69-year-old friend reflected on her life and on old age. At the age of 58, Anne and her husband, Duane, decided to leave their comfortable community in Rochester, New York, to work in the South for several organizations that are concerned with civil rights and social justice. She wrote about this period in her life:

> When our children were through college and on their own, our feeling was that it was time to close out the marketplace phase of our lives. We never had the empty-nest feeling. It was, instead, a kind of liberation, a time to move into a new phase. Just as marriage had been a new phase, followed by parenthood, this was another.
>
> The caring, the sharing of concerns, the readiness to be of help to each other when necessary, would continue with our children, unchanged by the fact that we were no longer living under one roof, but we were ready to move on, just as they were. We had both done a great deal of volunteer work in our free time for many years, and now we had the opportunity to do it full-time.

After 10 years of social-justice work in the South, Anne and Duane retired and moved back north. She commented on this transition:

> "Retirement" has many advantages. It's possible to be involved in many activities, yet not be pressured by them. We set our own schedules. We're free of regimentation. If something interesting to do comes up, we can do that and shift other commitments around. It's a more flexible, less rigid, less scheduled life.
>
> At the age of 69, I still don't feel "old," although chronologically, I'm not "young." I think one ages—given reasonable health—as one has been gradually aging in all the years before, very much depending on the quality of life one has built. My interests haven't changed, except that we have the added joy of six grandchildren in our lives. Older people are as diverse as young people. Differences between them remain; previous likes and dislikes remain, for the most part. I am still me, "old" or not, though I feel that I have become more understanding, less judgmental, more open to new experiences, still trying to grow as a person.
>
> We have begun to experience the loss of relatives and friends, and chronic and serious illnesses are beginning to appear among our associates. It's sad, of course, but it has the positive side of drawing us closer to those of our families and friends who are still in our lives, makes us more loving, more willing to overlook small irritants, more giving. ...

Section Summary

Social Relationships in Older Women's Lives

1. During middle age, daughters are more likely than sons to become caregivers for older parents. Research emphasizes the negative aspects of this caregiver role, but many women identify positive aspects.
2. Some women experience the empty-nest effect, but most women are relatively happy after their children leave home.
3. Women differ widely in their grandmothering styles, but many grandmothers believe that they should convey moral values and social responsibility to their grandchildren.
4. Most married women find that the death of a spouse is traumatic, and loneliness is a frequent problem. When people who identify as LGBTQ+ lose a life partner, they may have the added burden of needing to hide their grief.
5. Older women of color are disproportionately likely to experience poverty. However, they are more likely than older White women to have the support of an extended family. Many older women of color live with younger family members.
6. Older Latinas are expected to help with children and grandchildren and to seek help when they need it. Older Black women are likely to be active in community organizations, and many help rear their grandchildren. Older Asian American women also seek help from younger relatives. Many older Native American women actively rear and share their cultural heritage with their grandchildren.
7. Despite many problems, middle-aged and older women are typically just as satisfied with their lives as younger women are; this phenomenon is called "the paradox of well-being."
8. The term "successful aging" refers to qualities such as optimism, good health, and projects that help others. Many women rethink their lives during middle age or later, and they make choices that take them in new directions.

Chapter Review Questions

1. One theme of this book is that women tend to be relatively invisible in society compared with men. Discuss how this tendency is especially true for older women, pointing out topics that have not received enough attention in each of these areas: (a) representation in the media, (b) research on retirement, and (c) the lives of older women of color. Then add to the list any other areas of older women's lives that seem important to you and were not covered in this chapter.

2. What is the double standard of aging? When does it seem most likely to operate, and when does it not apply? What other aspects of women's lives—not mentioned in this chapter—might be affected by the double standard of aging?

3. From your knowledge about retirement, describe a woman who is likely to adjust well to retirement. Then describe a woman who is likely to adjust poorly to retirement.

4. Describe the economic situation of older women, and list factors that help to explain the gender differences in income for older men and women.

5. Think about any women you know who have retired from their paid employment. How do their lives match the information on retirement that this chapter discussed, with respect to the timing of their retirement, their financial resources during later adulthood, and their adjustment to retirement?

6. What are some of the physical symptoms of menopause? Imagine that a middle-aged friend is now experiencing menopause. What information would you tell her about hormone replacement therapy?

7. What psychological reactions do women have to menopause? How does this information compare with (a) your previous knowledge about menopause before reading this chapter and (b) the general public's attitudes toward menopause?

8. Research in the psychology of women has historically been too heavily focused on the experiences of White American, middle-class women. What did you learn in this chapter about the lives of older women of color, economically disadvantaged women, and women in other cultures?

9. The theme of individual differences has been prominent throughout this book. However, some researchers argue that individual differences increase during our lives. Examine the topics outlined on page 453, and describe the nature of those individual differences, where relevant.

10. In this chapter, we have discussed many legitimate reasons why older women might be dissatisfied with their lives. List as many of these as you can. Then suggest why the paradox of well-being applies to many older women.

Key Terms

ageism (p. 455)

double standard of aging (p. 457)

menopause (p. 464)

hot flash (p. 465)

hormone replacement therapy (p. 465)

sandwich generation (p. 470)

filial responsibility (p. 470)

empty nest (p. 470)

disenfranchised grief (p. 472)

paradox of well-being (p. 475)

successful aging (p. 475)

Recommended Readings

Cavanaugh, J. C., & Cavanaugh, C. K. (Eds.). (2010). *Aging in America* (Vols. 1–3). Santa Barbara, CA: ABC-Clio. We strongly recommend this superb three-volume series, especially because of its comprehensive scope and its emphasis on social justice. Sample chapters include age stereotypes, successful aging, retirement issues, caregiving, and mental health.

Cruikshank, M. (2013). *Learning to be old* (3rd ed.). Lanham, MD: Rowman & Littlefield. If you are interested in stereotypes about older people, this book is excellent for you! Other topics include the politics of healthy aging and a feminist's approach to gerontology.

Gunter, J. (2021). *The menopause manifesto: Own your health with facts and feminism*. New York, NY: Kensington Press. We highly recommend this witty and informative book, which provides a complete overview of the health changes that occur throughout the process of menopause. Dr. Jen Gunter is an OB/GYN who specializes in women's health across the lifespan.

Stewart, A. J., & Newton, N. J. (2010). Gender, adult development, and aging. In J. C. Chrisler & D. R. McCreary (Eds.), *Handbook of gender research in psychology* (Vol. 1, pp. 559–580). New York: Springer. This superb chapter focuses on how gender is relevant in the aging process, including topics such as aging bodies, family roles, and well-being.

Whitbourne, S. K. (2010). *The search for fulfillment.* New York: Ballantine. Susan K. Whitbourne has published widely in the area of adult development and aging. She wrote this book for a general audience, and it provides some interesting perspectives about creatively assessing your life experiences and future directions.

15 Moving Onward...

Mr Doomits/Shutterstock.com

Learning Objectives

After studying this chapter, you will be able to …

15-1 Identify factors that will shape the future of the discipline of the psychology of women and gender.

15-2 Explain how women of color have shaped the feminist movement.

15-3 Describe the current and future status of the men's movement in the United States.

15-4 Summarize current trends in feminism.

Did You Know?

- In psychology research about women of color, White American women have often served as the standard of comparison (p. 485).
- Chicana feminism has been active in the United States since the early 1970s (p. 486).
- In Asian American families, fathers are often expected to make the decisions in a family, which makes it difficult for daughters to express their feminist beliefs (p. 487).
- When women from some ethnic groups become feminist activists, the men in their community often tell them that this activism is a threat to ethnic unity (pp. 487–488).
- One branch of the men's movement, called the "profeminists," argues that rigid gender roles can harm men as well as women (p. 491).
- The religious approach to the men's movement emphasizes that men must take back their roles as family leaders and women should be followers (p. 492).
- According to both qualitative and quantitative research, students say that their women's studies courses have increased their feminist identity (pp. 494–495).

You have now read 14 chapters about the lives of girls and women, from their prenatal development through old age. To gain a perspective on all the diverse statistics, research studies, theories, and personal testimonies, you may find it useful to focus on one central question: Have women's lives improved in recent years? To answer this question, let's consider some representative information—both uplifting and depressing—on the lives of women in the modern era:

- Women now receive 52.9% of all Ph.D. degrees in the United States and outnumber men in graduate programs by a ratio of 141 to 100. However, men still earn more Ph.D. degrees in the fields of business, engineering, mathematics and computer science, and physical and earth sciences (Perry, 2020).
- In Multan, Pakistan, a tribal council was distressed that a young boy had been walking with a woman from a higher-caste family. To punish the boy's "crime," the tribal council ordered that his older *sister*, Mukhtaran Bibi, now known as Mukhtār Mā'ī, be sentenced to gang rape. Four men raped her repeatedly. Tradition demanded that

she commit suicide. However, she chose to sue her rapists in court, and they were convicted, although the Pakistani Supreme Court overturned the ruling in 2011 and provoked international outrage. Mukhtār used the $8,300 awarded to her by the government to found a school for girls. Her ongoing efforts to educate women turned into the Mukhtār Mā'ī Women's Welfare Organisation. This humanitarian foundation provides shelter and education for rape, violence, and abuse survivors (Kristof, 2008; Mukhtaran Bibi, 2021).

- The Global Fund for Women (2021) is an organization, located in San Francisco, that supports human rights by investing in organizations throughout the world. They have raised money to fund thousands of grass roots organizations that focus on social justice, equality and peace.

As these examples suggest, women's lives have improved considerably in some areas, yet the progress is often slow. Let's begin this chapter by discussing the status of the discipline we call the psychology of women and gender. Then we'll examine how women of color perceive and practice feminism. Our third section explores several different components of the men's movement. The final section looks at current trends in the women's movement, in both the United States and other regions of the world.

15-1 The Future of the Discipline of the Psychology of Women and Gender

Learning Objectives

To identify factors that will shape the future of the discipline of the psychology of women and gender, you can …

15-1-1 Discuss how increasing numbers of women in psychology may impact feminist theory and research.

15-1-2 Explain how multicultural, intersectional, and nonbinary perspectives will shape future research in the discipline.

As we noted in Chapter 1, the discipline of the psychology of women and gender is relatively young when compared to other specialty disciplines in psychology. Most college courses with that title were offered for the first time in the 1970s or 1980s. Two major journals—*Psychology of Women Quarterly* and *Sex Roles*—published their first issues during this period. The most popular topic during this era was gender comparisons (McCreary & Chrisler, 2010; Rutherford, 2007; Rutherford & Granek, 2010).

People who teach courses in the psychology of women or the psychology of gender often emphasize the strong connection they immediately felt with this emerging discipline (e.g., Baker, 2006; Deaux, 2001; Hyde, 2001). For example, Letitia Anne Peplau said, "Feminist perspectives helped me understand my own life experiences and relationships in new and more insightful ways. … Feminist activism sought to improve the lives of women and to work toward a more just society that places a high value on women as well as men" (Peplau, 1994, p. 44).

This passion about the psychology of women and gender has continued to grow during subsequent decades (Stewart & Dottolo, 2006). Thousands of professors and scholars throughout the United States and Canada now share this passion for teaching and studying the psychology of women and gender. At present, for example, the American Psychological Association Division on the Psychology of Women has over 2,000 dynamic and diverse members.

Two topics related to the future of our discipline are (1) the increasing number of women entering psychology and (2) the need to emphasize a more multicultural, intersectional, and nonbinary approach to studying the psychology of women and gender.

The Increased Number of Women in Psychology

Between 1920 and 1974, women earned only 23% of all psychology Ph.D. degrees in the United States (Baker, 2006). Fortunately, the picture has changed. Now they earn 74% of these degrees in the United States and Canada (Fowler et al., 2018). The gender ratio for psychology faculty members still favors men, but it may approach equality as many of the current women in graduate school become faculty members.

The increasing number of women in psychology does not necessarily *guarantee* a strong feminist discipline. There is evidence that gender stereotypes are changing over time, especially stereotypes about women (Bhatia & Bhatia, 2021; Eagly et al., 2020). But as we have learned throughout this book, people often hold similar stereotypes about gender. In addition, a survey of Canadian graduate students showed that the women and the men reported similar attitudes about their career plans (Singer et al., 2005). However, the increasing number of women entering psychology has certainly contributed to the growing support for feminist theory and research.

Increasing Multicultural, Intersectional, and Nonbinary Research Perspectives

In constructing the discipline of psychology of women and gender, feminists originally hoped to create a new perspective that values women's and men's lives equally. A continuing problem, however, has been that the psychology of women and gender has typically centered research and theory around the experiences of educated, heterosexual, nondisabled, middle-class White American women (Olkin, 2006; Rutherford & Granek, 2010; Signorella, 2020; Stewart & Dottolo, 2006). After all, these earlier psychologists—as well as the college women whom they typically studied in previous decades—were historically most likely to be educated, heterosexual, nondisabled, middle-class White American women (Enns, 2004a).

In recent years, however, many scholars have moved away from the traditional research population of White American heterosexual women to examine additional populations, many of whom have been historically marginalized by both society and science (e.g., Hurtado & Cervantez, 2009; E. Martínez, 2008; Rojas, 2009). An increasing number of publications emphasize intersectionality, as women of color experience gender differently than White American women (Crenshaw, 1989; Collins, 2015; Stewart & Dottolo, 2006).

However, much research on the experiences of women of color, LGBTQ+ individuals, women with disabilities, and women who are economically disadvantaged is still framed within an "othering" context. As a discipline, we need to decolonize the creation of knowledge; decenter the experiences of White, middle-class, and heterosexual women; move beyond the gender binary; and include disabled perspectives in our research (Else-Quest & Hyde, 2016; Fernández, Sonn, Carolissen, & Stevens, 2021; Hyde et al., 2019; Olkin, 2014). We also need to make a conscious effort to cite scholars of color who use intersectional perspectives in their work (Moradi et al., 2020; Signorella, 2020).

Additionally, scholars within the broader discipline of psychology have argued that much of the knowledge generated about the human condition thus far is disproportionately based on data collected from WEIRD samples. WEIRD samples include data from people who live in Western, Educated, Industrialized, Rich, and Democratic societies (Rad, Martingano, & Ginges, 2018). The experiences of women living within these societies are unlikely to generalize to women around the world.

Another problem with a group-comparisons approach is that psychologists often select topics for research in which the group that is not WEIRD, heterosexual, White, binary, economically privileged, or nondisabled is presented in a way that emphasizes negative aspects of experiences among people among those groups. For example, studies on Native Americans and Canadian First Nations people occasionally focus on women's strengths, for instance, about skillful mothering among Oneida women in Canada (Sunseri, 2008). Still, most of the research focuses on topics such as alcoholism and suicide.

In summary, the psychology of women and gender must not repeat the errors made by earlier generations of psychologists when they ignored women. Consistent with Theme 4, we need to value the diversity of girls and women who are included within the category called "female," those who identify as LGBTQ+ or disabled, and those who live within a wide range of economic, geographic, and cultural contexts. In the next section, we'll focus on a related topic: how women of color respond to the feminist movement.

Section Summary

The Future of the Discipline of the Psychology of Women and Gender

1. The first courses in the psychology of women were taught in the 1970s; people in this area are committed to its continued growth.
2. Psychology has shown a strong increase in the percentage of Ph.D. degrees that women earn. This trend encourages teaching and research about feminism.
3. The discipline of psychology of women needs to emphasize the diversity of backgrounds that women represent, rather than centering on educated, heterosexual, nondisabled women from middle-class White American backgrounds.

15-2 Women of Color and the Feminist Movement

Learning Objectives

To explain how women of color have shaped the feminist movement, you can …

15-2-1 Discuss how the Chicana/o and Mujerista feminist movements characterize Latina feminisms.

15-2-2 Describe the major characteristics of Black feminisms in the United States.

15-2-3   Explain why Asian American feminisms do not necessarily match with traditional Asian American value systems.

15-2-4   Describe how characteristics of Native American feminisms differ from other types of feminism.

Throughout this book, we have learned that women from different ethnic groups have diverse life experiences. Similarly, Latina women, Black women, Asian American, and Native American women offer differing perspectives on feminism. They also may report that they feel marginalized by issues that have been traditionally emphasized by "mainstream" White feminism (Collins, 2006; Enns, 2004a).

What many women of color have accurately recognized and documented is that we are still living in an era where people from various ethnic backgrounds are not treated equitably, due to the intertwined effects of systemic racism, sexism, Eurocentrism, ableism, and ageism still present in society (Ferber, 2007; Spates, 2012). In this section, we will explore some feminist perspectives that are associated with women who identify with various ethnic groups. As we explore this section, keep in mind that perspectives vary widely within each ethnic group, and no one feminist perspective can effectively capture the broad range of experiences that are reflected in people's lives. However, we will discuss a few of the major perspectives within each group.

Latina/o Feminisms

Most U.S. students learn something about Black history and the civil rights movement in high school, although what is taught to students across the 50 U.S. states is highly inconsistent and contains significant omissions of historical events and information (Duncan, Zawistowski, & Luibrand, 2020; King, 2017). Students are even less likely to learn about the history of Latinas/os. The situation is also complex, because people who identify with this ethnicity have often come from many different countries. For example, in New York State, most people from a Latin American background emigrated from Puerto Rico or the Dominican Republic. The people living in these two islands have elected women to be vice presidents and governors, and feminism may be a familiar concept (Lopez, 2006).

The Mujerista feminism movement developed among Latina women who felt marginalized by traditional White feminism. *Mujerismo* translates as "Latina womanism," and the central perspective of this feminist approach is inclusion of diverse perspectives, a focus on interdisciplinary scholarship, and an emphasis on self-definition and self-determination (Bryant-Davis & Comas-Díaz, 2016).

If you live in the western part of the United States, you may know about the Chicana/o movement, which specifically addresses the concerns of Mexican Americans. Chicana feminism has a longer history than most people may realize. In 1971, for example, Chicana feminists organized a successful national conference in Houston, Texas (E. Martínez, 2008; Roth, 2004).

When women began to participate in the Chicana/o movement, they started questioning their traditional roles. They also protested that this movement ignores women's issues (Blea, 2003; Enns, 2004a; Hurtado & Cervantez, 2009). In addition, these women acknowledged that Chicana feminism would need to address both race and class, in addition to gender (Moraga, 1993; Roth, 2004).

Chicano men have often misinterpreted the Chicana feminist movement as a threat to the political unity of the Chicana/o movement. In fact, Chicano male activists may label these women *vendidas,* or "sellouts." They might also accuse Chicana feminists of "acting like White women" (E. Martínez, 1995; McKee & Stone, 2007). However, many college courses in Chicana/o studies now acknowledge the important contributions of Chicana women (E. Martínez, 2008; Saldívar-Hull, 2000).

Black Feminisms

A Black feminist scholar, bell hooks, recalls giving a lecture in which she described how feminism had changed her life. A Black female student then rose to give an impassioned speech against feminism. The student said that feminism addressed the needs of White women only, with whom she had nothing in common (hooks, 1994).

Many Black women do not feel connected with historical feminist perspectives in their daily lives (Belgrave & Allison, 2010; hooks, 2015). Black women sometimes report that their experiences are too different from the experiences of White women, who often benefit from economic and social privileges that are built into U.S. society from centuries of structural racism (Cole & Guy-Sheftall, 2003; Collins, 2006; Roth, 2004). Black women also report that they feel no connection with racist White women (hooks, 2015; Roth, 2004). These feelings are grounded in the historical truth that many early White feminists either ignored issues that uniquely affected Black women and other people of color, or were themselves supportive of racist policies and belief systems (Cooper, 2018; Kendall, 2020).

In addition, Black women may be reluctant to criticize Black men, who already experience negative reactions from White individuals (Collins, 2006; Rosen, 2000). Furthermore, Black men may argue that feminism draws Black women away from the issue of combatting racism, a goal that the Black men perceive to be more important (Cole & Guy-Sheftall, 2006). *Womanism* is a form of Black feminism that acknowledges the historical invisibility of Black women and other women of color within the broader waves of feminism (Walker, 1983). This feminist perspective seeks to acknowledge the role of relationships with others, including men, in fighting sexism, racism, and systems of oppression within society.

Black feminists and other feminists of color have been at the forefront of the fourth wave of feminism, which is defined by both intersectional and transnational approaches to understanding how gender, ethnicity, social class, ability status, geography, and sexuality are intertwined in shaping the lives of individuals living within societal systems (Collins, 2015; Collins & Bilge, 2020; Crenshaw, 1989; Nash, 2019). You may remember our discussion of intersectionality in Chapter 1. *Transnational feminism* seeks to decenter Western epistemology by focusing on how historical and colonial systems of oppression shape the lives of women and other people who identify with groups that have historically held little power within societies around the world (Enns, Comas Díaz, & Bryant-Davis, 2020; Kaur Hundle, Szeman, & Pares Hoare, 2019).

Asian American Feminisms

Asian American women face different challenges in identifying with the feminist movement. In many Asian cultures, fathers make the decisions for their family. In contrast, women are expected to be relatively passive, invisible, and supportive of men (Balls Organista et al., 2010; Chu, 2004; McKee & Stone, 2007). Amita Handa (2003) describes the difficulties of growing up as a teenager in Toronto, with parents who had emigrated from the Punjabi region of India. She commented that she did not fit people's expectations about either Western teenagers or good South Asian girls.

When Asian American women do express feminist perspectives, community members are likely to criticize them. These critics accuse them of diluting the resources in the Asian American community and harming the working relationships between Asian women and men (Chow, 1991).

Furthermore, many women with an Asian background are not familiar with the feminist movement. This issue is especially likely if they recently immigrated to the United States or Canada (G. C. N. Hall & Barongan, 2002; J. Lee, 2001). For example, Pramila Aggarwal (1990) described how she discovered a way to discuss feminist issues with women who had recently immigrated to Canada from India. Aggarwal, a bilingual student, had been hired to teach English to Punjabi women who were working in a garment factory in Toronto. During these English classes, Aggarwal discovered that these women were interested in women's issues, such as the division of labor in the home and sexual harassment in the workplace. From this experience, Aggarwal concluded that feminist organizers must be sensitive to the specific needs of women, rather than imposing their own personal viewpoint.

Some regions in the United States and Canada have had a substantial Asian population for many decades. As a result, feminism may be more visible in these communities. During the 1970s, for example, universities such as UC Berkeley, UCLA, and San Francisco State began to offer courses about Asian American women (Chu, 2004). College students who complete these courses are likely to acquire a sophisticated perspective on both feminism and racism, as Asian American feminists express cross-racial solidarity with other women of color and promote intersectional perspectives (Fujiwara & Roshanravan, 2018).

Native American Feminisms

In this section, we will use the term *Native American* to refer to individuals who identify as American Indian, Native American, Indigenous, or First Nations peoples who inhabited North America prior to European colonization. Although this term refers to all peoples who lived in North America prior to colonization and is considered the most inclusive, it is not without controversy. The term *Native American* was assigned by others and often reflects **ethnic gloss**, which occurs when people incorrectly infer that all members of an ethnic group share a common set of characteristics (Jackson, 2006). The more than 570 tribes distributed across the continent vary individually in whether they prefer the terms *American Indian, Native American, Indigenous,* or *First Nations* peoples. Keep in mind that it is most preferable to use individual tribal names and identities whenever possible (Native Knot, 2021).

Native American feminisms are rooted in philosophies of resistance, decolonization, community, Indigenous sovereignty, and intersectional environmentalism (Gearon, 2021). These perspectives celebrate the strength and solidarity of Indigenous women, who for centuries have preserved Native cultures and natural resources amid a backdrop of historical oppression, colonization, and collective trauma experienced by their communities.

Factors that are specific to Native American feminisms involve focusing on issues unique to Native communities, including the epidemic of missing and murdered girls, women, and two-spirit individuals. It is estimated that up to 80% of Native American women in the United States and Canada have experienced interpersonal violence (Coalition to Stop Violence Against Native Women, 2021; d'Entremont, 2020).

Another central perspective in Native American feminisms is appreciation for environmentalism and connection with the Earth (Thomas, 2021). This perspective argues that traditional male-dominated, hierarchical, capitalistic, and colonial forces have taken advantage of the Earth's resources much as they have treated women—as resources to be exploited for financial, social, and political gain. Native American women from the Standing Rock Sioux reservation are representative of this perspective. These women were largely responsible for coordinating protests against the Dakota Access Pipeline, with a goal of preserving water resources for future generations (Dennis & Bell, 2020; Privott, 2019).

Many Native American cultures are matriarchal and egalitarian, so traditional feminisms that are grounded in resisting or transforming patriarchal systems may not apply. Other Native American women are reluctant to label themselves as feminists in the traditional sense, because they perceive that traditional White feminism reinforces colonial oppression, white supremacy, and capitalism (Gearon, 2021). For example, in describing why she is not a feminist, a Diné woman writes:

> To assist in aspiring to the twenty-first century Navajo female being is the role I have found myself in as an adult Navajo and Hopi woman. Recently I have witnessed modern Diné women labeling themselves "feminists." I am not a feminist, that term is a germ in my opinion and has no place in our Diné culture. The origins of white American feminism are rooted in racism against the black man. (Yazzie, 2018)

In summary, women of color may identify feminist issues in their lives although they may be reluctant to label themselves as feminists. They may find it difficult to become feminist activists because activism is not consistent with their culture or because the men in their culture might believe that feminism threatens the efforts to unify their ethnic group. In addition, they may feel that feminist groups that are organized by White women may not be sensitive to the concerns of women of color.

Fortunately, however, the situation is gradually changing, and women from all ethnic groups are now writing about how feminism can transform the lives of women of color (Enns, 2004a; Kirk & Okazawa-Rey, 2001; Rojas, 2009). In the words of Black feminists Johnetta Betsch Cole and Beverly Guy-Sheftall (2003), "We believe it is possible to free ourselves as a community from the traps of sexism and heterosexism even as we continue our struggle against the ever present threats of racial inequality and poverty" (p. 70).

At the same time, feminists from all ethnic backgrounds acknowledge that contemporary feminism must extend beyond gender issues. Claire Kirch, who works with a feminist publisher, addresses this perspective:

> Feminism today is about social justice. Not justice just for women, but for all people. It is many voices saying one thing: Peace on earth, economic justice now, and social justice for all. It is about a living wage, national health-care, the love of oneself as a political act, and the promotion of ecological justice. (cited in Braun, 2003, p. 24)

Section Summary

Women of Color and the Feminist Movement

1. Chicano men may accuse feminists of undermining the Chicana/o movement. College courses on Chicana issues now emphasize the contributions of Chicanas.

(continues)

Section Summary *(continued)*

2. Many Black women do not report a connection with feminism because they believe that their lives are too different from the lives of White American women. They are also reluctant to criticize Black men.
3. Asian American women may believe that feminist activism is not consistent with the traditional role of women in Asian cultures; critics may accuse Asian feminists of undermining the unity in their community.
4. Native American women may not identify with traditional feminist perspectives that represent Westernized value systems. They are instead focused on Native American and Indigenous feminisms, which focus on preserving community, family, and intergenerational traditions.
5. An increasing number of women of color are writing about feminism; they emphasize that feminism is an important component of social justice.

15-3 The Men's Movement

Learning Objectives

To describe the current and future status of the men's movement in the United States, you can …

15-3-1 Describe factors that represent the profeminist approach to understanding men's gendered experiences.

15-3-2 Explain how the mythopoetic approach describes men's gender roles.

15-3-3 Discuss how religious approaches within the men's movement differ from profeminist and mythopoetic approaches.

Beginning in the 1970s, some men began examining masculine gender roles and their implications for men's lives (Cochran, 2010; Smiler & Kilmartin, 2019; O'Neil, 2008). These investigations inspired a new academic field, called men's studies. **Men's studies** is a collection of scholarly activities—such as teaching courses and conducting research—that focus on men's lives. Men's studies often emphasizes gender-role socialization, gender-role conflict, the sexism problem, and ethnic diversity (Smiler & Kilmartin, 2019; A. J. Lott, 2003; White, 2008).

Men's studies also explores areas in which men's behaviors are maladaptive. For example, as we discovered in Chapters 11 and 12, men are less likely than women to seek help for health and psychological problems (Brooks, 2010; Levant et al., 2006; A. J. Lott, 2003; Smiler & Kilmartin, 2019; Yousaf, Popat, & Hunter, 2015). Several resources present more details on men's studies (e.g., J. S. Kahn, 2009; Smiler & Kilmartin, 2019; O'Neil, 2008; Tarrant, 2009). Some resources focus specifically on men of color (Lemons, 2008; Poulson-Bryant, 2005; White, 2008) and men who have immigrated to the United States (Chuang & Moreno, 2008).

Just as there is no unitary women's movement, we also find no unitary, single-focus men's movement (Kahn, 2009; Smiler & Kilmartin, 2019). Three strands within the men's movement are commonly mentioned: (1) the profeminists, (2) the mythopoetic movement, and (3) the religiously oriented approach. Students who are learning about the psychology of women need to know that some men's groups serve as allies, whereas others may be antagonists.

Profeminist Approaches

The **profeminists** support feminism, and they want to eliminate destructive aspects of gender, such as gender stereotypes, gender inequalities, and gender-related violence (Smiler & Kilmartin, 2019). Profeminists emphasize that strict gender roles can hurt both men and women (Brooks, 2010). They also believe that men must actively work toward gender equality throughout their lifetime (Lemons, 2008).

At the national level, the largest profeminist organization is the National Organization of Men Against Sexism (NOMAS). This group focuses on issues such as equal pay. They also hold workshops on gender equality, and they raise funds for women's shelters (Cochran, 2010; J. S. Kahn, 2009).

Within psychology, the most visible profeminist group is called the Society for the Psychological Study of Men and Masculinity (SPSMM, Division 51 of the American Psychological Association, 2021). According to its mission statement, this organization examines how gender can constrict men's lives, limiting their full potential. In addition, this organization is committed to supporting women, gender and sexual minorities, and people of color. They also emphasize that people of all genders function best and have the richest relationships if they can move beyond the traditional definitions of gender roles. They are particularly interested in exploring how hegemonic masculinity norms, which involve displaying aggression, independence, invulnerability, and emotional repression, are harmful to men's physical and psychological health (Springer & Mouzon, 2011; Yousaf et al., 2015). As individuals, profeminist men can serve as allies. **Allies** are people who provide support to groups other than their own (Smiler & Kilmartin, 2019). Try Demonstration 15.1 to explore this concept in more detail.

Demonstration **15.1**

Identifying Allies

As we note in the previous paragraph, allies are people who provide support to groups other than their own group. Begin this demonstration by thinking of several men you know personally who are likely to provide support to women. (If you are a man or nonbinary, you may be able to include yourself in this list.)

Write down each man's name and then list some specific things that this individual has done to support girls and women. Then repeat this exercise by thinking about White people who are likely to provide support to people of color; identify their specific contributions. Continue this process with several other social groups that frequently experience biased treatment. Some representative groups would be LGBTQ+ individuals, immigrants, and people with disabilities.

Profeminist men can also work together to organize public actions. For example, the White Ribbon Campaign (2021) began when a small group of men in Canada began wearing white ribbons after the murder of 14 women at École Polytechnique in Montreal in 1989.[1] Within just six weeks, about 100,000 men throughout Canada were wearing white ribbons. White Ribbon Campaign groups can now be found in more than 55 countries throughout the world. These groups continue to examine issues related to male violence. For example, here is a description about the values that are especially important to the men of the White Ribbon Campaign (2021):

> Within all of our work with men and boys, we enhance awareness of the increased risk female-identified, trans, non-conforming folks have of multiple forms of violence, due to their perceived gender identity. To fully understand the root causes, forms and impacts of gender-based violence, we must consider all social categories which intersect with gender, including race, class, sexualities, status, abilities, age. We acknowledge that men do not experience power in the same ways.

Mythopoetic Approaches

The profeminist men focus on how traditional binary gender roles hurt people of all genders and sexualities. In contrast, the mythopoetic men focus on how these gender roles hurt men personally. Men who favor the **mythopoetic approaches** believe that modern men should use myths, storytelling, and poetry to develop their own well-being and spiritual growth (Smiler & Kilmartin, 2019 Brooks, 2010; Kilmartin, 2010; Tarrant, 2009). To achieve this growth, men join all-male gatherings. Their goal is for the men to work through their psychological difficulties and focus on male role models (J. S. Kahn, 2009). In general, the men who adopt the mythopoetic approach believe that profeminist men focus too much on women's issues, instead of their own gender issues (J. S. Kahn, 2009; Smiler & Kilmartin, 2019).

Many men in the mythopoetic movement express somewhat feminist views. However, the majority of these men are relatively wealthy, middle-aged White American heterosexual cisgender men. Compared to most other people, they have greater economic resources, and they have benefited more than other groups in U.S. society (Smiler & Kilmartin, 2019).

Religious Approaches

The religiously oriented approaches to the men's movement have become more visible in recent years. A few of these religious groups emphasize gender equality. In general, however, the **religious approaches** argue that men should take back their roles as head of the household so that they can become leaders in their family, church, and community (Brooks, 2010; Kahn, 2009). As a result, they argue that women should accept the role of being followers.

Among the religious approaches, the most visible is the Promise Keepers (Brooks, 2010; J. S. Kahn, 2009; Metzger, 2002; White, 2008). Their huge rallies usually take place in football stadiums, and the messages are strongly traditional. Men are told to be assertive about taking back their "natural" role, and they are encouraged to invite male friends to attend future rallies. The Promise Keeper website (2021) lists branches in U.S. cities such as Kansas City, Dallas, Colorado Springs, and Atlanta, as well as in Canada and New Zealand.

---

[1] In 1989, a man named Marc Lepin entered a classroom in the engineering school at École Polytechnique, in Montreal, Canada. He forced the female students to line up along a wall. Shouting "You are all feminists," he shot them all. He then tracked down other women in the building, killing a total of 14 women.

The Promise Keeper rallies emphasize essentialism—that men and women are different because women were created for men (Smiler & Kilmartin, 2019).

The Promise Keepers and other religiously based forms of the men's movement may voice some admirable statements, such as racial reconciliation and encouraging men to become more actively involved in nurturing their children. However, these groups typically want to reduce the rights of women (Brooks, 2010; White, 2008).

How do college students react to these different men's groups? In a classic study, Rickabaugh (1994) asked undergraduates at a California university to read descriptions of several men. Each description represented a different strand of the men's movement. Both men and women gave the highest rating to the profeminist man. They saw the profeminist man as both nurturant and competent—a finding that should be encouraging to profeminist male students who are reading this book.

Section Summary

The Men's Movement

1. Men's studies includes scholarly activities—such as teaching courses and conducting research—that focus on men's lives and the issues they encounter.
2. Three major strands within the men's movement are (a) the profeminists, who believe that gender roles hurt both men and women, (b) the mythopoetic approach, which focuses on men's spiritual growth, and (c) religious approaches, such as the Promise Keepers.

15-4 Current Trends in Feminism

Learning Objectives

To summarize current trends in feminism, you can ...

15-4-1 Explain why women's studies courses positively impact the students who take them.

15-4-2 Discuss characteristics of the first four waves of feminist thought and theory.

15-4-3 Identify examples of how the global feminist movement has helped improve women's lives.

15-4-4 Describe some ways in which people can promote feminist values in everyday life.

Is feminism thriving, more than two decades into the twenty-first century? What about issues important to women? Let's consider four perspectives on these questions: (1) women's studies courses, (2) the women's movement in the United States and Canada, (3) the women's movement at the international level, and (4) how you can contribute to the well-being of girls and women.

Women's Studies Courses in the United States

Thousands of women's studies courses are offered at colleges and universities throughout the United States. The American Academy of Arts and Sciences (2017) lists about 283 U.S. colleges and universities that have official women's studies programs and grant degrees in women and gender studies. Women's studies is now a well-established field, and it enrolls about 109,000 undergraduate students each year (American Academy of Arts and Sciences, 2017). Furthermore, numerous women's studies courses are available at the graduate level. Each year, around 21,000 students enroll in graduate level courses, and about 50 programs offer either a Master's or a Ph.D. degree in women's studies (American Academy of Arts and Sciences, 2017; National Women's Studies Association, 2021).

Students often comment that they gain a new perspective from women's studies courses (Chrisler, 2007; Dodwell, 2003; Stake, 2007; N. A. Stewart, 2007). In these courses, students discover feminism, and they learn to appreciate the connections between the scholarly resources and their personal experiences (Collins, 2006; Enns & Forrest, 2005; Zucker & Stewart, 2007).

Women of color sometimes comment that their women's studies courses help them understand both gender and ethnicity issues (Elfman, 2009). For example, a Chicana student from Wisconsin commented on her women's studies course:

> I am a Chicana; not only must I deal with racism but I must also live in a sexist world. I come from a family with strong conservative views compared to other families in the U.S. … Machismo is very prominent and sometimes cannot be seen but it is there. I never really thought about important feminist issues in high school. But I always knew that women were oppressed in our society. I saw it in my own home. It was not until I broke away from home that I began to think about my identity. I must say that my first real exposure to feminist ideas was when I left home for college. It is here where I am learning and trying to understand feminist ideas. (Rhoades, 1999, p. 68)

Research using quantitative methods confirms that these courses have a significant impact on students' lives. For instance, people enrolled in women's studies courses are significantly more likely than similar students (enrolled in other courses) to develop a nontraditional attitude toward gender roles. They are also more likely to develop a strong feminist identity after taking the course (Malkin & Stake, 2004; Stake, 2007; Stake & Hoffmann, 2001). Other research shows that people of all genders are equally likely to benefit from these women's studies courses (Stake, 2007; Stake & Malkin, 2003).

In addition, women's studies courses enhance self-confidence and a sense of control over one's life (Malkin & Stake, 2004; Zucker & Stewart, 2007). Finally, students emphasize that their women's studies courses encourage critical thinking (Eudey, 2007; Sinacore & Boatwright, 2005; Stake & Hoffmann, 2000; Yoder et al., 2007).

Michelle Fine is an especially creative feminist psychologist. She and her colleagues have documented the impact of women's studies in an unusual setting: Bedford Women's Correctional Facility, a maximum-security prison located in New York State (M. Fine, 2007a; M. Fine & Torre, 2006; M. Fine et al., 2001). As part of an educational program, these women had read novels by Alice Walker and discussed postmodern philosophy. In 2013, she was awarded the American Psychological Association Award for Distinguished Contributions to Research in Public Policy for her efforts to change women's lives through education (M. Fine, 2013a).

Unfortunately, the U.S. government stopped the financial support for programs like this, although private foundations and public institutions stepped in to keep funding

Fine's program and similar programs as part of the Public Science Project (Fine, 2013a). After release from prison, those women who had participated in the educational program were only 24% as likely to be imprisoned for new crimes, compared to nonparticipants (M. Fine, 2013b). You can read more about the various social justice projects funded by the Public Science Project initiative by searching for this organization on the Internet.

In summary, college students report that their women's studies courses are both thought-provoking and informative. These courses also change students' attitudes, self-confidence, and critical-thinking ability. In a prison setting, women's studies courses have the potential to completely change women's lives.

The Women's Movement in the United States

The antislavery movement of the 1830s inspired the first wave of the feminist movement in North America. Women such as Susan B. Anthony and Elizabeth Cady Stanton created strategies for political organizing, and they saw clear links between freedom for slaves and freedom for women (Enns, 2004a; Kravetz & Marecek, 2001). However, their concerns were not answered for almost a century. For instance, U.S. women did not win the right to vote until August 1920, with the ratification of the Nineteenth Amendment to the U.S. Constitution.

The second wave of the women's movement in the United States emerged from the attempts to resolve important social problems during the 1960s. Women were active in the civil rights movement and in protesting the war in Vietnam. As in the previous century, this focus on issues of social justice made women in the United States and Canada more aware that they were second-class citizens (Collins, 2009; Rebick, 2005). In Canada, the National Action Committee on the Status of Women (NAC) was founded in 1972. It has addressed issues such as women's shelters, immigrant women, lesbian groups, international solidarity, and student issues (S. John, personal communication, 2010; National Action Committee, 2006; Rebick, 2005).

The National Organization for Women (NOW) was founded in 1966, and it remains one of the most important women's rights organizations in the United States. The scope of modern feminist organizations is impressive. Some groups, such as NOW, have a general focus that addresses issues such as violence against women, reproductive rights, and workplace problems. Other groups emphasize more specific issues. For example, Emily's List is an organization that raises money to help elect progressive feminist women to the U.S. Congress and other important leadership positions.

The feminist historian Linda Nicholson (2010) has argued that the wave metaphor may have outlived its usefulness to describe how feminist philosophies have evolved over time. However, many scholars suggest that the third wave of feminism arose in the 1990s and was led by the feminist punk subculture and Generation Xers (Heywood & Drake, 1997; Walker, 1995). Third wave feminism highlighted the concept of male privilege in society, embraced intersectionality, questioned the gender binary, argued for anti-essentialism, and included postmodernist perspectives (Gillis, Howie, & Munford, 2007). The rise of the modern Internet during this time period also provided a social communication mechanism for expanding traditional feminist philosophies and promoting more inclusive spaces for the LBGTQ+ community, people of color, and international feminists.

We are now in the fourth wave of feminism, in which feminist groups in the United States are focused on a broader array of issues and are therefore less coherent than previous waves (Abrahams, 2017; Grady, 2018). Various areas of focus include the abuse of women, antimilitarism, rape culture, greater representation of marginalized people, women's health, reproductive rights, women's spirituality, socioeconomic inequality, educational disparities, women of color, older women, LGBTQ+ concerns, immigration issues, antipoverty problems, and community problems (Collins, 2009; S. M. Evans, 2003). Some groups emphasize **ecofeminism**, an approach that opposes the way that humans destroy other animals and natural resources. Also, feminist communities have created a variety of feminist-run organizations. These include feminist therapy groups, theater groups, and music festivals. Feminism is clearly visible, especially on college campuses and in large cities (Collins, 2009; Roof, 2007). In fact, seek out organizations and women's studies courses on your own campus!

Critics of the women's movement argue that feminism specifies a rigid set of regulations. However, there is no single, unified version of feminism (Collins, 2009, 2015; Jervis, 2004/2005). For example, feminists disagree among themselves about many important issues. Some of these issues include whether women should be encouraged to join the military and whether pornography should be regulated (R. C. Barnett & Rivers, 2004; Reinharz & Kulick, 2007). Feminist principles argue that we should respect women and their life choices.

Critics of the women's movement also argue that women and men are now being treated equally; therefore, feminists should just stop complaining. A stream of antifeminist messages from the media has created a backlash within the general population in both the United States and Canada. Unfortunately, this backlash undercuts the genuine progress that the women's movement has made in the past few decades (Reese, 2021; Seely, 2007). This misinformation about feminism also affects many people who respect women and believe that women and men should be socially, economically, and legally equal (A. N. Zucker, 2004). Try Demonstration 15.2 to identify how several of your friends feel about feminism.

In summary, the U.S. feminist movement has grown and diversified considerably in recent decades, despite the attacks from critics. Fortunately, too, feminists in the United States and Canada now emphasize a global and transnational approach: Women face discrimination in every country, and we must work to change this problem.

Demonstration **15.2**

Diversity of Views About Feminism

At the top of several pieces of paper, write these instructions: "Please define feminism in your own words, and describe how feminism is relevant or irrelevant in your life." Distribute one page to each of several friends, and ask them to provide a written reply. (You may wish to tell them to omit their names from the sheets or use other precautions, so that their descriptions are anonymous.) Among those who have positive views of feminism, can you identify a variety of perspectives? (Check pp. 6–7 to remind yourself about various kinds of feminism.) Among those with negative views, can you think how the media would have influenced their perspectives?

The Women's Movement Worldwide

In New Zealand, women won the right to vote in 1893. Australia, Canada, and many European countries followed within the next three decades. However, women living in Kuwait were not granted the right to vote until 2005. Women have been elected or appointed as heads of state in more than 80 countries—among them, India, Haiti, Nicaragua, Bolivia, Turkey, Iceland, Great Britain, and Canada—but not the United States. Throughout the world, however, women seldom hold a substantial number of seats in national legislatures. In summary, women are a long way from equality when we consider official positions within national governments.

Women's grassroots activism has had impressive consequences in countries outside North America. Consider the Mothers and Grandmothers of the Plaza de Mayo, a group of women whose children "disappeared" during the military dictatorship in Argentina between 1976 and 1983. More than 30,000 people were killed during that era. Many of them were young people who were secretly murdered because they had opposed the government. The government had forbidden all public demonstrations, yet these women risked their lives by gathering at the Plaza de Mayo in Buenos Aires every Thursday, holding large photos of their missing children. The bravery of these Argentinian women ultimately helped end that terrifying regime, and it helped women in countries such as El Salvador and Guatemala to become activists (Brabeck & Rogers, 2000; Moghadam, 2009).

This mothers' group in Argentina also inspired a group of Mexican American women who called themselves "Mothers of East Los Angeles." These U.S. women successfully blocked the construction of a hazardous-waste incinerator that was planned within their community (Pardo, 2005). Notice, then, that political strategies can spread from developing countries to the United States, rather than only in the reverse direction (Brownhill & Turner, 2003; Mendez, 2005).

Throughout the world, groups of women are working to improve women's lives. We now have rich resources describing women's global activism (e.g., Durán et al., 2007; Essed et al., 2005; Kristof & WuDunn, 2009; Mendez, 2005; Moghadam, 2009).

A superb group called the Global Fund for Women (2021) has provided small grants for thousands of projects developed by women in countries throughout the world. Here are some representative examples from a recent list of the fund's projects:

- Worldwide, the fund has partnered with local feminist groups to help women during the COVID-19 pandemic, as women have been disproportionately affected by increased workloads throughout the global crisis.
- In Peru, the project has funded initiatives to end sexual and gender-based violence.
- In Cameroon, the fund provides financial support for the Moving in Feminism with Adolescent Leaders in Action (MIFALI) program, which empowers adolescent girls facing prejudice and discrimination.
- In India, the fund works with local organizations to institute legal protections for domestic workers, who have been severely impacted by COVID-19 and are subject to exploitation.

Women in developing countries share many of the same perspectives and concerns that women in North America and Europe express. However, women in these countries must also overcome basic survival problems. Some of the subtle points of U.S. feminism may seem irrelevant to a woman in India who believes that she must give her son more food than her daughter so that he can grow strong in order to support the family (Kristof & WuDunn, 2009). These points may also seem irrelevant for a woman in Myanmar who must work under harsh conditions for much less than $1 a day, making sneakers for a prestigious American company.

In recent decades, people in wealthy countries have increasingly begun to realize an important issue: People in the rest of the world are suffering intensely in order to make U.S. lives more comfortable or more entertaining (Mendez, 2005). In Chapter 7, we considered the exploitation of women who work in sweatshops. A more terrifying form of exploitation is called **trafficking**, or the sale and displacement of human beings for illegal purposes.

Trafficking is clearly an international women's issue, but the world has not made systematic efforts toward addressing this problem. An estimated 24.9 million people worldwide are trafficked each year and experience this modern form of slavery. People are trafficked primarily for the purpose of labor, sexual exploitation, and state-sponsored labor (Human Rights First, 2017).

However, a small percentage of these women—the victims of trafficking—manage to escape. A small percentage of these escaped women manage to change their lives. Consider the case of Srey Rath, a Cambodian woman who had been sold to a brothel in Thailand. She escaped and returned home to Cambodia. With a loan from a U.S. organization, she bought a cart so that she could sell shirts, toys, and snacks. Nicholas Kristof and Sheryl WuDunn (2009) emphasize that Srey Rath's transformed life illustrates an important truth: "Women aren't the problem but the solution. The plight of girls is no more a tragedy than an opportunity" (p. xviii).

Helping to Change the Future: Becoming an Activist

So far in this section on some trends in women's issues, we have examined women's studies courses, the women's movement in the United States, and the women's movement worldwide. In most psychology courses, students remain passive as they read about the future of a discipline. This time it's different: *You* can be part of the solution—if you're not already involved—rather than assuming that someone else will do the work. For example, at Bennett College in North Carolina, a group of Black women decided to develop an educational program to celebrate National American Indian Heritage Month (Malveaux, 2006). Here are just a few of many other options:

- Subscribe to a feminist magazine, such as *Ms. Magazine* or *Canadian Woman Studies/Les cahiers de la femme*. It will inform you about political activities that you may want to support, and the articles will keep you thinking about feminist issues.
- Visit a website or follow social media accounts on feminist activism and find a topic that matches your interests. Then speak out and become involved!
- Talk with friends and relatives about feminist issues. In our everyday conversations, we need to make many decisions. If someone makes a sexist, ageist, ableist, classist, or racist remark, we can take a small activist step by deciding not to join in the laughter. Even better, we can respond with a comment such as, "That's not funny—it hurts people."
- Serve as a mentor to a girl or a younger woman. Some people choose to work on more formal projects, for example, as long-term volunteers at a soup kitchen for families who are economically disadvantaged (Lott & Webster, 2006). Others mentor through organizations such as Big Brothers Big Sisters, Girls on the Run, or Girls, Inc., or work as coaches for girls' sports.

- Give gifts that provide information about girls and women. For instance, send a gift subscription to *New Moon Girls* to any girl between the ages of about 9 and 12 (refer to p. 103). Buy any book from the A Mighty Girl booklist of about 4,000 titles for any girl you know. These titles are written to support and empower young girls.
- Help fight negative representations of women. When you observe an offensive advertisement, for example, e-mail the company to complain or post a negative review of the ad. Also, when you observe positive ad, send a compliment to the company.
- Be a "critical consumer" when you read or observe reports about women in the media. Review the research biases in Figure 1.3, and ask yourself whether the conclusions in the report seem justified. If you'd like to express your discontent—or possibly your approval!—post an Internet comment or write a letter to the editor of a newspaper or magazine. You may also wish to comment on the ratio of men to women in that particular news source (Berg, 2009). You now have more information about women's lives than most other individuals in your community, so you can share your knowledge.
- Join a women's group on campus or in your community—or help to start one. Work with the group to make certain that diversity issues are an integral part of your mission.
- Organize an event that focuses on a feminist issue, such as sexual violence on your own college campus (Chrisler & Segrest, 2008). Be aware that people on your campus may have more—or less—feminist perspectives than you suspect (Kilmartin & Allison, 2007; Kilmartin et al., 2008.)

Remember: No one individual can tackle all the problems that women and other people who are members of marginalized groups face. Also, change does not happen overnight. Celebrate the social-justice victories, and share these victories with other like-minded people (Lott & Webster, 2006; Marsella, 2006; Schwebel, 2008). Also, keep in mind a quotation attributed to anthropologist Margaret Mead: "Never doubt that a small group of thoughtful, committed citizens can change the world; indeed, it's the only thing that ever has."

Section Summary

Current Trends in Feminism

1. According to the research, women's studies courses can change people's attitudes and self-confidence; they can also change women's lives.
2. The first wave of the feminist movement in North America arose out of the anti-slavery movement, and it eventually led to the passage of the Nineteenth Amendment to the U.S. Constitution.
3. The second wave of the feminist movement arose out of the civil rights movement and the antiwar movement; feminist groups in the third and fourth waves have addressed a wide variety of issues concerned with women and other marginalized people.
4. Women hold relatively few national leadership positions throughout the world; grassroots women's organizations have achieved many victories, but important problems—such as trafficking—are still widespread.
5. Students can improve women's lives by methods such as talking about gender discrimination, mentoring girls and younger women, and organizing feminist events.

Chapter Review Questions

1. What are the trends with respect to the gender ratio for psychology Ph.D. degrees? What is the current gender ratio for the psychology faculty and for psychology majors at your own college or university? Why might the changing gender ratio help the women's movement?

2. People concerned about the psychology of women have emphasized that the discipline should include more multicultural research. What are some problems that can arise when researchers use traditional approaches to study people of color?

3. In the second section of this chapter, we focused on women of color and feminism, and we mentioned that most students have little exposure to research on ethnic groups other than Black people. Before you enrolled in a course on the psychology of women (or the psychology of gender), what kind of information did you learn in high school or college about ethnicity? What have you learned outside class in the popular media? Did this information about people of color focus more on men or women?

4. Why do women of color face special challenges in identifying with the feminist movement? Why would men of color oppose women from their ethnic group who want to be active feminists?

5. Describe the three basic strands within the men's movement. Which would be likely to support the growth of the women's movement? Which would oppose it? Which might consider it irrelevant? Do you have any evidence of the men's movement in your community or in your academic institution?

6. Briefly trace the history of the women's movement in the United States. What issues were important to the early activists? Then comment on the women's movement worldwide. What kinds of concerns have these groups addressed?

7. In several parts of this chapter, we examined attitudes toward feminist issues. Why do you think that people in the United States and throughout the world are reluctant to call themselves feminists?

8. Identify an issue related to women and girls that is especially important to you. If you wanted to increase people's awareness about this issue, what strategies could you adopt from the section on becoming an activist?
(These final two questions require you to review the entire textbook.)

9. In this chapter, we focused on the current trends with respect to women and gender. To help yourself review this book, go back through the 15 chapters. Note which specific developments are moving in a positive direction and which are moving in a negative direction.

10. You will need to set aside several hours for this final task: On separate pieces of paper, list each of the four themes of this book. Then skim through each of the 15 chapters and note any mention of the themes on the appropriate piece of paper. (You can determine whether your lists are complete by checking the entries for Themes 1, 2, 3, and 4 in the subject index.) After you have completed that task, try to synthesize the material within each of the four themes.

Key Terms

ethnic gloss (p. 488)	allies (p. 491)	religious approaches (p. 492)	trafficking (p. 498)
men's studies (p. 490)	mythopoetic approaches (p. 492)		
profeminists (p. 491)		ecofeminism (p. 496)	

Recommended Readings

Enns, C. Z., & Sinacore, A. L. (Eds.). (2005). *Teaching and social justice: Integrating multi-cultural and feminist theories in the classroom.* Washington, DC: American Psychological Association. Here is an excellent resource that illustrates how feminist theory can be applied to the college classroom, while emphasizing multicultural approaches.

Kristof, N. D., & WuDunn, S. (2009). *Half the sky: Turning oppression into opportunity for women worldwide.* New York: Knopf. Nicholas Kristof and Sheryl WuDunn won a Pulitzer Prize in journalism for their coverage of events in China in the *New York Times.* Their book, *Half the Sky,* also examines gender issues in countries such as Pakistan, Congo, and Afghanistan.

Martínez, E. (2008). *500 years of Chicana women's history/500 años de la mujer Chicana* (bilingual edition). New Brunswick, NJ: Rutgers University Press. "Betita" Martínez is an important leader in the area of Chicana feminism, and this book is richly illustrated with photos of Chicana women and the history of Chicana feminism. An added benefit of this edition is that the text is in both English and Spanish.

Smiler, A., & Kilmartin, C. (2019). *The masculine self* (6th ed.). Cornwall-on-Hudson, NY: Sloan. This excellent textbook provides a concise, profeminist summary of the research on the psychology of men and masculinities. Smiler and Kilmartin's description of the various groups within the men's movement is especially useful.

References

Abbey, A. (2002). Alcohol-related sexual assault: A common problem among college students. *Journal of Studies on Alcohol, 14* (Suppl.), 118–128.

Abbey, A., & McAuslan, P. (2004). A longitudinal examination of male college students' perpetration of sexual assault. *Journal of Consulting and Clinical Psychology, 72,* 747–756.

Abbey, A., Zawacki, T., & McAuslan, P. (2000). Alcohol's effects on sexual perception. *Journal of Studies on Alcohol, 61,* 688–697.

Abbey, A., et al. (2001). Attitudinal, experiential, and situational predictors of sexual assault perpetration. *Journal of Interpersonal Violence, 16,* 784–807.

Abbey, A., et al. (2002). Alcohol-involved rapes: Are they more violent? *Psychology of Women Quarterly, 26,* 99–109.

Abel, M. H., & Meltzer, A. L. (2007). Student ratings of a male and female professors' lecture on sex discrimination in the workforce. *Sex Roles, 57,* 173–180.

Abrahams, J. (2017, August). Everything you wanted to know about fourth wave feminism—but were afraid to ask. *Prospect Magazine.* Retrieved October 5, 2021 from https://www.prospectmagazine.co.uk/magazine/everything-wanted-know-fourth-wave-feminism

Adair, L. S., & Gordon-Larsen, P. (2001). Maturational timing and overweight prevalence in U.S. adolescent girls. *American*

Journal of Public Health, 91, 642–644.

Adams, A. (1995). Maternal bonds: Recent literature on mothering. *Signs, 20,* 414–427.

Adams, K. L., & Ware, N. C. (2000). Sexism and the English language: The linguistic implications of being a woman. In A. Minas (Ed.), *Gender basics* (pp. 70–78). Belmont, CA: Wadsworth/Thomson Learning.

Adams, S., Juebli, J., Boyle, P. A., & Fivush, R. (1995). Gender differences in parent-child conversations about past emotions: A longitudinal investigation. *Sex Roles, 33,* 309–323.

Adams-Curtis, L. E., & Forbes, G. B. (2004). College women's experiences of sexual coercion. *Trauma, Violence, & Abuse, 5,* 91–122.

Addis, M. E. (2008). Gender and depression in men. *Clinical Psychology: Science and Practice, 15,* 153–168.

Addis, M. E., & Mahalik, J. R. (2003). Men, masculinity, and the contexts of help seeking. *American Psychologist, 58,* 5–14.

Adler, J. A. (2006). Daughter/wife/mother or sage/immortal/Bodhisattva? Women in the teaching of Chinese religions. *ASIANetwork Exchange,* Vol. XIV, no. 2, 11-16.

Adler, N. E., & Conner Snibbe, A. (2003). The role of psychosocial processes in explaining the gradient between socioeconomic status and health. *Current*

Directions in Psychological Science, 12, 119–123.

Adler, N. E., Ozer, E. J., & Tschann, J. (2003). Abortion among adolescents. *American Psychologist, 58,* 211–217.

Adler, N. E., & Smith, L. B. (1998). Abortion. In E. A. Blechman & K. D. Brownell (Eds.), *Behavioral medicine and women: A comprehensive handbook* (pp. 510–514). New York: Guilford.

Agars, M. D. (2004). Reconsidering the impact of gender stereotypes on the advancement of women in organizations. *Psychology of Women Quarterly, 28,* 103–111.

Agathangelou, A. M. (2000). Nationalist narratives and (dis)-appearing women. *Canadian Woman Studies/ Les cahiers de la femme, 19*(Winter), 12–27.

Aggarwal, P. (1990). English classes for immigrant women: A feminist organizing tool. *Fireweed, 30,* 95–100.

Agras, W. S., & Apple, R. F. (2002). Understanding and treating eating disorders. In F. K. Kaslow (Ed.), *Comprehensive handbook of psychotherapy: Cognitive-behavioral approaches* (Vol. 2, pp. 189–212). New York: Wiley.

Ahmed, L. (1992). *Women and gender in Islam: The historical roots of a modern debate.* Yale University Press.

Ahrens, C. E., Dean, K., Rozee, P. D., & McKenzie, M. (2008). Understanding and preventing rape. In F. L. Denmark & M. A. Paludi (Eds.), *Psychology of women: A handbook of issues and theories* (2nd ed., pp. 509–554). Westport, CT: Praeger.

Ahrens, C. J. C., & Ryff, C. D. (2006). Multiple roles and well-being: Sociodemographic and psychological moderators. *Sex Roles, 55,* 801–815.

Ai, A. L., Wink, P., & Ardelt, M. (2010). Spirituality and aging: A journey for meaning through deep interconnection in humanity. In J. C. Cavanaugh & C. K. Cava-naugh (Eds.), *Aging in America* (Vol. 3). Santa Barbara, CA: ABC-CLIO.

Albarracín, D., et al. (2005). A test of major assumptions about behavior change: A comprehensive look at the effects of passive and active HIV-prevention interventions since the beginning of the epidemic. *Psychological Bulletin, 131,* 856–897.

Alden, P. B. (2000). Crossing the moon. In R. Ratner (Ed.), *Bearing life: Women's writings on childlessness* (pp. 106–111). New York: Feminist Press.

Alegría, et al. (2007). Correlates of past-year mental service use among Latinos: Results from the National Latino and Asian American Study. *American Journal of Public Health, 97,* 75–83.

Alencar Albuquerque, G., de Lima Garcia, C., da Silva Quirino, G., Alves, M. J., Belém, J. M., dos Santos Figueiredo, F. W., da Silva Paiva, L., do Nascimento, V. B., da Silva Maciel, É., Valenti, V. E., de Abreu, L. C., & Adami, F. (2016). Access to health services by lesbian, gay, bisexual, and transgender persons: systematic literature review. *BMC International Health and Human Rights, 16,* 2.

Alexander, L. L., LaRosa, J. H., & Bader, H. (2001). *New dimensions in women's health* (2nd ed.). Boston: Jones and Bartlett.

Alexander, L. L., LaRosa, J. H., Bader, H., Garfield, S., & Alexander, W. J. (2021). *New dimensions in women's health* (8th ed.).

Burlington, MA: Jones and Bartlett.

Alexander, S. H. (1999). Messages to women on love and marriage from women's magazines. In M. Meyers (Ed.), *Mediated women: Representations in popular culture* (pp. 25–37). Cresskill, NJ: Hampton Press.

Algoe, S. B., Buswell, B. N., & DeLamater, J. D. (2000). Gender and job status as contextual cues for the interpretation of facial expression of emotion. *Sex Roles, 42,* 183–208.

Ali, A. (2007, November). Feminists reread the Quran. *The Progressive,* 29–31.

Alhusen, J. L. Bower, K., Epstein, E., & Sharps, P. (2016). Racial discrimination and adverse birth outcomes: An integrative review. *Journal of Midwifery and Women's Health, 61,* 707-720.

Ali, A., Caplan, P. J., & Fagnant, R. (2010). Gender stereotypes in diagnostic criteria. In J. C. Chrisler & D. R. McCreary (Eds.), *Handbook of gender research in psychology* (Vol. 2, pp. 91–109). New York: Springer.

Allen, K. R. (1994). Feminist reflections on lifelong single women. In D. L. Sollie & L. A. Leslie (Eds.), *Gender, families, and close relationships: Feminist research journeys* (pp. 97–119). Thousand Oaks, CA: Sage.

Allen, M., & Burrell, N. A. (2002). Sexual orientation of the parent: The impact on the child. In M. Allen, R. W. Preiss, B. M. Gayle, & N. A. Burrell (Eds.), *Interpersonal communication research: Advances through meta-analysis* (pp. 125–143). Mahwah, NJ: Erlbaum.

Allen, M., Emmers-Summer, T. M., & Crowell, T. L. (2002). Couples negotiating safer sex behaviors: A meta-analysis of the impact of conversation and gender. In M. Allen, R. W. Preiss, B. M. Gayle, & N. A. Burrell (Eds.), *Interpersonal communication research: Advances through meta-analysis*

(pp. 263–279). Mahwah, NJ: Erlbaum.

Allgeier, E. R., & Allgeier, A. R. (2000). *Sexual interactions* (5th ed.). Boston: Houghton Mifflin.

Alvarez, L. (2008). *Despite Army's assurances, violence at home.* Retrieved November 23, 2008, from http://www.truthout .org/112408L

Amato, P. R., Booth, A., Johnson, D. R., & Rogers, S. J. (2007). *Alone together: How marriage in America is changing.* Cambridge, MA: Harvard University Press.

Amato, P. R., Johnson, D. R., Booth, A., & Rogers, S. J. (2003). Continuity and change in marital quality between 1980 and 2000. *Journal of Marriage and Family, 65,* 1–22.

American Academy of Arts and Sciences. (2017). The state of the humanities in four-year colleges and universities – 2017. *American Academy of Arts and Sciences.* Retrieved October 5, 2021 from https://www.amacad .org/sites/default/files/media /document/2020-05/hds3_the _state_of_the_humanities_in _colleges_and_universities.pdf

American Academy of Pediatrics. (2001). WIC Program. *Pediatrics, 108,* 1216–1217.

American Academy of Pediatrics. (2002a). Coparent or second-parent adoption by same-sex parents. *Pediatrics, 109,* 339–340.

American Academy of Pediatrics. (2002b). Technical report: Coparent or second-parent adoption by same-sex parents. *Pediatrics, 109,* 341–344.

American Academy of Pediatrics. (2005). Breastfeeding and the use of human milk. *Pediatrics, 115,* 496–506.

American Association of University Professors. (2020). *Data snapshot: Full-time women faculty and faculty of color.* Retrieved October 3, 2021 from https://www.aaup.org/news/data -snapshot-full-time-women

-faculty-and-faculty-color#
.YHZ92ehKhPY

American Cancer Society. (2011).
Breast cancer: Early detection.
Retrieved February 10, 2011,
from http:// www.cancer
.org/Cancer/Breast Cancer
/MoreInformation/Breast
CancerEarlyDetection/breast
-cancer-early-detection-acs-recs-bse

American College of Obstetricians
and Gynecologists. (2015).
Access to contraception:
Committee opinion no. 615.
Obstetrics and Gynecology, 125,
250-255.

American Immigration Council.
(2017). *The impact of immigrant
women on America's labor force*.
Retrieved October 3, 2021 from
https://www.americanimmigration
council.org/research/impact
-immigrant-women-americas
-labor-force

American Psychiatric Association.
(2013). *Diagnostic and statistical manual of mental disorders*
(DSM-V, 5th ed.). Washington,
DC: Author.

American Psychological Association.
(2001). *Publication manual of
the American Psychological
Association* (5th ed.). Washington, DC: Author.

American Psychological Association.
(2004). *Resolution on sexual orientation and marriage*. Retrieved
June 8, 2005, from www.apa
.org/ releases/gaymarriage_reso
.pdf

American Psychological Association.
(2007). Guidelines for psychological practice with girls and
women. *American Psychologist,
62*, 949–979.

American Psychological Association.
(2015). Guidelines for
psychological practice with
transgender and gender nonconforming people. *American
Psychologist, 70*, 832–864.

American Psychological Association.
(2020). *Publication manual of
the American Psychological
Association* (7th ed.).
Washington, DC: Author.

American Psychological Association.
(2017). *Ethical principles of
psychologists and code of conduct*. Washington, DC: Author.
Retrieved October 5, 2021 from
https://www.apa.org/ethics/code/

American Psychological Association
(2020). Degrees in Psychology
[interactive data tool]. http://
www.apa.org/workforce/data
-tools/degrees-psychology.aspx

Anderson, B. (2003). Just another job?
The commodification of domes-
tic labor. In B. Ehrenreich & A.
R. Hochschild (Eds.), *Global
woman* (pp. 104–114).
New York: Metropolitan Books.

Anderson, C. A., & Bushman, B.
J. (2002). Human aggression.
*Annual Review of Psychology,
53*, 27–51.

Anderson, D. A., & Hamilton, M.
(2005). Gender role stereotyping
of parents in children's picture
books: The invisible father. *Sex
Roles, 52*, 145–151.

Anderson, K. J. (2010). *Benign
bigotry: The psychology of
subtle prejudice*. New York:
Cambridge.

Anderson, K. J., & Leaper, C. (1998).
Meta-analyses of gender effects
on conversational interruption:
Who, what, when, where, and
how. *Sex Roles, 39*, 225–252.

Anderson, L. A., & Whiston, S. C.
(2005). Sexual assault education
programs: A meta-analytic examination of their effectiveness.
*Psychology of Women Quarterly,
29*, 374–388.

Andreasen, N. C., & Black, D. W.
(2001). *Introductory textbook
of psychiatry* (3rd ed.). Washington, DC: American Psychiatric
Publishing.

Anderson, S. E., Dallal, G. E., &
Must, A. (2003). Relative weight
and race influence average age
at menarche: Results from two
nationally representative surveys
of US girls studied 25 years
apart. *Pediatrics, 111*, 844–850.

Anderson, V., Simpson-Taylor, D., &
Herrmann, D. J. (2004). Gender,
age, and rape-supportive rules.
Sex Roles, 50, 77–90.

Andreoletti, C. (2010). The content
and consequences of age stereo-
types. In J. C. Cavanaugh & C.
K. Cava-naugh (Eds.), *Aging in
America* (Vol. 1, pp. 135–155).
Santa Barbara, CA: ABC-CLIO.

Ang, C-S., Lee, K-F., & Lie, X. (2020).
Understanding singleness: A
phenomenological study of single
women in Beijing and Singapore.
The Qualitative Report, 25,
3080-3100.

Angel, J. L., & Torres-Gil, F. (2010).
Hispanic aging and social policy.
In J. C. Cavanaugh & C. K.
Cava-naugh (Eds.), *Aging in
America* (Vol. 3, pp. 1–19). Santa
Barbara, CA: ABC-CLIO.

Angus Reid Institute. (2018). *I
don't: Four-in-ten Canadian
adults have never married,
and aren't sure they want to*.
Retrieved October 4, 2021
from https://angusreid.org/
marriage-trends-canada/

Anthis, K. S. (2002). The role of sexist
discrimination in adult women's
identity development. *Sex Roles,
47*, 477–484.

Antonsen, A. N., Zdaniuk, B., Yule,
M., & Brotto, L. A. (2020). Ace
and aro: Understanding differences in romantic attractions
among persons identifying as
asexual. *Archives of Sexual
Behavior, 49*, 1615–1630.

Anyaso, H. H. (2008, November 13).
Self-navigating the terrain. *Diverse
Issues in Higher Education*,
23–29.

Aponte, J. F. (2004). The role of
culture in the treatment of culturally diverse populations. In
U. P. Gielen, J. M. Fish, & J. G.
Draguns (Eds.), *Handbook of
culture, therapy, and healing*
(pp. 103–120). Mahwah, NJ:
Erlbaum.

Apostolou, M., O, J., & Esposito,
G. (2020). Singles' reasons for
being single: Empirical evidence
from an evolutionary perspective. *Frontiers in Psychology, 11*,
1-13.

Apparala, M. L., Reifman, A., &
Munsch, J. (2003). Cross-
national comparison of attitudes

toward fathers' and mothers' participation in household tasks and childcare. *Sex Roles, 48,* 189–203.

Appelman, H. (2008, July/August). Teen angst? *Rochester Review,* 32–35.

Applewhite, S. R., Biggs, M. J. G., & Herrera, A. P. (2009). Health and mental health perspectives on elderly Latinos in the United States. In F. A. Villarruel et al. (Eds.), *Handbook of U.S. Latino psychology* (pp. 235–249). Thousand Oaks, CA: Sage.

Arbuckle, J., & Williams, B. D. (2003). Students' perceptions of expressiveness: Age and gender effects on teacher evaluations. *Sex Roles, 49,* 507–516.

Archer, J. (2004). Sex differences in aggression in real-world settings: A meta-analytic review. *Review of General Psychology, 8,* 291–322.

Archer, J., & Coyne, S. M. (2005). An integrated review of indirect, relational, and social aggression. *Personality and Social Psychology Review, 9,* 212–230.

Archer, J., & Lloyd, B. (2002). *Sex and gender* (2nd ed.). New York: Cambridge University Press.

Arias, E., MacDorman, M. F., Strobino, D. M., & Guyer, B. (2003). Annual summary of vital statistics—2002. *Pediatrics, 112,* 1215–1230.

Arias, E., Tejada-Vera, B., & Ahmad, F. (2021). *Provisional life expectancy estimates for January through June 2020.* National Vital Statistics Rapid Release, Report No. 010. Centers for Disease Control. Retrieved October 5, 2021 from https://www.cdc.gov/nchs/data/vsrr/VSRR10-508.pdf

Aries, E. (1996). *Men and women in interaction: Reconsidering the differences.* New York: Oxford University Press.

Aries, E. (1998). Gender differences in interaction. In D. J. Canary & K. Dindia (Eds.), *Sex differences and similarities in communication* (pp. 65–81). Mahwah, NJ: Erlbaum.

Arima, A. N. (2003). Gender stereotypes in Japanese television advertisements. *Sex Roles, 49,* 81–90.

Armstrong, M. J. (2001). Ethnic minority women as they age. In J. D. Garner & S. O. Mercer (Eds.), *Women as they age* (2nd ed., pp. 97–111). New York: Haworth.

Arnett, J. L., Nicholson, I. R., & Breault, L. (2004). Psychology's role in health in Canada: Reactions to Romanow and Marchildon. *Canadian Psychology/Psychologie Canadienne, 45,* 228–232.

Arons, J., & Rosenthal, L. (2012). *The health insurance compensation gap: How unequal health care coverage for women increases the gender wage gap.* Center for American Progress. Retrieved October 5, 2021 from https://cdn.americanprogress.org/wp-content/uploads/issues/2012/04/pdf/health_insurance_gap.pdf?_ga=2.73106011.934572687.1622227255-138176192.1615663203

Arredondo, P. (2004). Psychotherapy with Chicanas. In R. J. Velásquez, L. M. Arellano, & B. W. McNeill (Eds.), *The handbook of Chicana/o psychology and mental health* (pp. 231–250). Mahwah, NJ: Erlbaum.

Asian Center for Human Rights (ACHR). (2016). *Female infanticide worldwide: The case for action by the UN Human Rights Council.* Retrieved October 3, 2021 from https://www.transcend.org/tms/2016/07/female-infanticide-worldwide-the-case-for-action-by-the-un-human-rights-council/

Asch, A. (2004). Critical race theory, feminism, and disability. In B. G. Smith & B. Hutchison (Eds.), *Gendering disability* (pp. 9–44). New Brunswick, NJ: Rutgers University Press.

Asch, A., & Fine, M. (1992). Beyond pedestals: Revisiting the lives of women with disabilities. In M. Fine (Ed.), *Disruptive voices: The possibilities of feminist research* (pp. 139–171). Ann Arbor: University of Michigan Press.

Asch, A., & McCarthy, H. (2003). Infusing disability issues into the psychology curriculum. In P. Bronste & K. Quina (Eds.), *Teaching gender and multicultural awareness* (2nd ed., pp. 253–269). Washington, DC: American Psychological Association.

Asch, A., Perkins, T. S., Fine, M., & Rousso, H. (2001). Disabilities and women: Deconstructing myths and reconstructing realities. In J. Worell (Ed.), *Encyclopedia of women and gender* (pp. 345–354). San Diego: Academic Press.

Association for American Medical Colleges. (2019). *2019 Fall Applicant, Matriculant, and Enrollment Data Tables.* Retrieved October 5, 2021 from https://www.aamc.org/system/files/2019-12/2019%20AAMC%20Fall%20Applicant%2C%20Matriculant%2C%20and%20Enrollment%20Data%20Tables_0.pdf

Astin, H. S., & Lindholm, J. A. (2001). Academic aspirations and degree attainment of women. In J. Worell (Ed.), *Encyclopedia of women and gender* (pp. 15–27). San Diego: Academic Press.

Athenstaedt, U., Haas, E., & Schwab, S. (2004). Gender role self-concept and gender-typed communication behavior in mixed-sex and same-sex dyads. *Sex Roles, 50,* 37–52.

Atwater, L. E., et al. (2004). Men's and women's perceptions of the gender typing of management subroles. *Sex Roles, 50,* 191–199.

Aubeeluck, A., & Maguire, M. (2002). The Menstrual Joy Questionnaire items alone can positively prime reporting of menstrual attitudes and symptoms. *Psychology of Women Quarterly, 26,* 160–162.

Aubrey, J. S. (2004). Sex and punishment: An examination of sexual consequences and the sexual double standard in teen programming. *Sex Roles, 50,* 505–514.

Auster, C. J., & Ohm, S. C. (2000). Masculinity and femininity in contemporary American society: A reevaluation using the Bem Sex-Role Inventory. *Sex Roles, 43,* 499–528.

AVERT. (2021). *Women and girls, HIV and AIDS.* Retrieved October 5, 2021, from https://www.avert.org/professionals/hiv-social-issues/key-affected-populations/women

Avery, A., Zimmermann, K., Underwood, P. W., & Magnus, J. H. (2009). Confident commitment is a key factor for sustained breast-feeding. *Birth, 36,* 141–148.

Avis, N. E. (2003). Depression during the menopausal transition. *Psychology of Women Quarterly, 27,* 91–100.

Avis, N. E., et al. (2004). Quality of life in diverse groups of midlife women: Assessing the influence of menopause, health status and psychosocial and demographic factors. *Quality of Life Research, 13,* 933–946.

Ayala, J. (2006). Confianza, consejos, and contradictions: Gender and sexuality lessons between Latina adolescent daughters and mothers. In J. Denner & B. L. Guzmán (Eds.), *Latina girls: Voices of adolescent strength in the United States* (pp. 29–43). New York: New York University Press.

Babcock, J. C., Green, C. E., & Robie, C. (2004). Does batterers' treatment work? A meta-analytic review of domestic violence treatment. *Clinical Psychology Review, 23,* 1023-1053.

Baber, K. M. (2000). Women's sexualities. In M. Biaggio & M. Hersen (Eds.), *Issues in the psychology of women* (pp. 145–171). New York: Kluwer Academic/Plenum.

Baber, K. M., & Tucker, C. J. (2006). The social roles questionnaire: A new approach to measuring attitudes toward gender. *Sex Roles, 54,* 459–467.

Baca Zinn, M., & Eitzen, D. S. (2002). *Diversity in families* (6th ed.). Boston: Allyn & Bacon.

Baca Zinn, M., Hondagneu-Sotelo, P., & Messner, M. A. (2001). Gender through the prism of difference. In M. L. Anderson & P. H. Collins (Eds.), *Race, class, and gender* (4th ed., pp. 168–176). Belmont, CA: Wadsworth.

Bachand, L. L., & Caron, S. L. (2001). Ties that bind: A qualitative study of happy long-term marriages. *Contemporary Family Therapy, 23,* 105–121.

Backus, V. P. (2002). Psychiatric aspects of breast cancer. *Harvard Review of Psychiatry, 10,* 307–314.

Bacigalupe, A., & Martín, U. (2021). Gender inequalities in depression/anxiety and the consumption of psychotropic drugs: Are we medicalising women's mental health? *Scandinavian Journal of Public Health, 49,* 317-324.

Badgett, M. V. L. (2008). Bringing all families to work today: Equality for gay and lesbian workers and families. In A. Marcus-Newhall, D. F. Halpern, & S. J. Tan (Eds.), *The changing realities of work and family: A multidisciplinary approach* (pp. 140–154). Malden, MA: Blackwell.

Baer, J., & Kaufman, J. C. (2008). Gender differences in creativity. *The Journal of Creative Behavior, 42,* 75–105.

Bahr, K. S. (1994). The strengths of Apache grandmothers: Observations on commitment, culture, and caretaking. *Journal of Comparative Family Studies, 25,* 233–248.

Baijko, M. S. (2020, September 17). More same-sex parents are raising kids and out-earning straight couples. Bay Area Reporter. Retrieved October 5, 2021 from https://www.ebar.com/news/latest_news/297294

Bailey, J. A., et al. (2008). Men's and women's patterns of substance use around pregnancy. *Birth, 35,* 50–59.

Bailey, J. M., Dunne, M. P., & Martin, N. G. (2000). Genetic and environmental influences on sexual orientation and its correlates in an Australian twin sample. *Journal of Personality and Social Psychology, 78,* 524–536.

Bailey, J. M., Pillard, R. C., Neale, M. C., & Agyei, Y. (1993). Heritable factors influence sexual orientation in women. *Archives of General Psychiatry, 50,* 217–223.

Baird-Windle, P., & Bader, E. J. (2001). *Targets of hatred: Antiabortion terrorism.* New York: Palgrave.

Bajko, M. S. (2020, September 17). More same-sex parents are raising kids and out-earning straight couples. *Bay Area Reporter.* Retrieved October 4, 2021 from https://www.ebar.com/news/latest_news//297294

Baker, C. N. (2005). Images of women's sexuality in advertisements: A content analysis of Black-and White-oriented women's and men's magazines. *Sex Roles, 52,* 13–27.

Baker, N. L. (2006). Feminist psychology in the service of women: Staying engaged without getting married. *Psychology of Women Quarterly, 30,* 1–14.

Baker, K., McGovern, A., Gruberg, S., & Cray, A. (2016, August 9). *The Medicaid program and LGBT communities: Overview and policy recommendations.* Center for American Progress. Retrieved October 3, 2021 from https://www.americanprogress.org/issues/lgbtq-rights/reports/2016/08/09/142424/the-medicaid-program-and-lgbt-communities-overview-and-policy-recommendations/

Baker-Sperry, L. (2007). Production of meaning through peer interaction: Children and Walt Disney's *Cinderella. Sex Roles, 56,* 717–727.

Baldwin, J., & DeSouza, E. (2001). Modelo de María and machismo: The social construction of gender in Brazil. *Revista*

Interamericana de Psicología/Interamerican Journal of Psychology, 35, 9–29.

Ballou, M. (2005). Threats and challenges to feminist therapy. In M. Hill & M. Ballou (Eds.), *The foundation and future of feminist therapy* (pp. 201–210). Binghamton, NY: Haworth.

Balls Organista, P., Marín, G., & Chun, K. M. (2010). *The psychology of ethnic groups in the United States.* Los Angeles, CA: Sage.

Balsam, K. F., Beauchaine, T. P., Mickey, R. M., & Rothblum, E. D. (2005). Mental health of lesbian, gay, bisexual, and heterosexual siblings: Effects of gender, sexual orientation, and family. *Journal of Abnormal Psychology, 114,* 471–476.

Balsam, K. F., Beauchaine, T. P., Rothblum, E. D., & Solomon, S. E. (2008). Three-year follow-up of same-sex couples who had civil unions in Vermont, same-sex couples not in civil unions, and heterosexual married couples. *Developmental Psychology, 44,* 102–116.

Balsam, K. F., Lehavot, K., & Beadnell, B. (2011). Sexual revictimization and mental health: A comparison of lesbians, gay men, and heterosexual women. *Journal of Interpersonal Violence, 26,* 1798-1814.

Balsam, K. F., Rothblum, E., & Wickham, R. E. (2017). Longitudinal predictors of relationship dissolution among same-sex and heterosexual couples. *Couple and Family Psychology: Research and Practice, 6,* 247-257.

Bancroft, J., Loftus, J., & Long, J. S. (2003). Distress about sex: A national survey of women in heterosexual relationships. *Archives of Sexual Behavior, 32,* 193–208.

Bandura, A., & Bussey, K. (2004). On broadening the cognitive, motivational, and sociostructural scope of theorizing about gender development and functioning. *Psychological Bulletin, 130,* 691–701.

Banks, C., & Arnold, P. (2001). Opinions towards sexual partners with a large age difference. *Marriage and Family Review, 33,* 5–17.

Banks, M. E., & Kaschak, E. (Eds.). (2003). *Women with visible and invisible disabilities.* New York: Haworth.

Bao, X. (2003). Sweatshops in Sunset Park. In D. E. Bender & R. A. Greenwald (Eds.), *Sweatshop USA: The American sweatshop in historical and global perspective* (pp. 117–139). New York: Routledge.

Baram, D. A. (2005). Physiology and symptoms of menopause. In D. E. Stewart (Ed.), *Menopause: A mental health practitioner's guide* (pp. 15–32). Washington, DC: American Psychiatric Press.

Barber, B. L., & Eccles, J. S. (2003). The joy of romance: Healthy adolescent relationships as an educational agenda. In P. Florsheim (Ed.), *Adolescent romantic relations and sexual behavior* (pp. 355–370). Mahwah, NJ: Erlbaum.

Barber, J. S., Axinn, W. G., & Thornton, A. (1999). Unwanted childbearing, health, and mother-child relationships. *Journal of Health and Social Behavior, 40,* 231–257.

Barber, N. (2017). Cross-national variation in attitudes to premarital sex: Economic development, disease risk, and marriage strength. *Cross-Cultural Research, 52,* 259-273.

Barbuto, J. E., Jr., Fritz, S. M., Matkin, G. S., & Marx, D. B. (2007). Effects of gender, education, and age upon leaders' use of influence tactics and full range leadership behaviors. *Sex Roles, 56,* 71–83.

Barel, E., & Tzischinsky, O. (2018). Age and sex differences in verbal and visuospatial abilities. *Advances in Cognitive Psychology, 14,* 51-61.

Barer, B. M. (2001). The "grands and greats" of very old black grandmothers. *Journal of Aging Studies, 15,* 1–11.

Bargad, A., & Hyde, J. S. (1991). A study of feminist identity development in women. *Psychology of Women Quarterly, 15,* 181–201.

Barlow, D. H., & Durand, V. M. (2015). *Abnormal psychology* (8th ed.). Cengage Learning.

Barnett, O., Miller-Perrin, C. L., & Perrin, R. D. (2005). *Family violence across the lifespan* (2nd ed.). Thousand Oaks, CA: Sage.

Barnett, R. C. (2004). Preface: Women and work: Where are we, where did we come from, and where are we going. *Journal of Social Issues, 60,* 667–674.

Barnett, R. C., & Hyde, J. S. (2001). Women, men, work, and family: An expansionist theory. *American Psychologist, 56,* 781–796.

Barnett, R. C., & Rivers, C. (2004). *Same difference: How gender myths are hurting our relationships, our children, and our jobs.* New York: Basic Books.

Barretto, R. M., & Segal, S. P. (2005). Use of mental health services by Asian Americans. *Psychiatric Services, 56,* 746–748.

Barstow, A. L. (2001, Winter). *War's dirty secret: Rape, prostitution, and other crimes against women.* New York: Women's Ink.

Bartell, R. (2005). Abstinence-only-until-marriage programs. *Informed Choice, 1.*

Bartlett, S. J., et al. (2004). Maternal depressive symptoms and adherence to therapy in inner-city children with asthma. *Pediatrics, 113,* 229–237.

Bartoli, A. M. (2006). The dating game: Similarities and differences in dating scripts among college students. *Sexuality & Culture, 10,* 54–80.

Bartsch, R. A., Burnett, T., Diller, T. R., & Rankin Williams, E. (2000). Gender representation in television commercials: Updating an update. *Sex Roles, 43,* 735–743.

Basile, K. C., DeGue, S., Jones, K., Freire, K., Dills, J., Smith, S. G., & Raiford, J. L. (2016). *STOP SV: A technical package to prevent sexual violence.* National Center for Injury Prevention and

Control: Centers for Disease Control. Retrieved October 5, 2021 from https://www.cdc.gov /violenceprevention/pdf/SV -Prevention-Technical-Package.pdf

Basow, S. A. (2001). Androcentrism. In J. Worell (Ed.), *Encyclopedia of women and gender* (pp. 125–135). San Diego: Academic Press.

Basow, S. A. (2004a). Gender dynamics in the classroom. In J. C. Chrisler, C. Golden, & P. D. Rozee (Eds.), *Lectures on the psychology of women* (3rd ed., pp. 45–55). Boston: McGraw-Hill.

Basow, S. A. (2004b). The hidden curriculum: Gender in the classroom. In M. Paludi (Ed.), *Praeger guide to the psychology of gender* (pp. 117–131). Westport, CT: Praeger.

Basow, S. A. (2006). Gender role and gender identity development. In J. Worell & C. D. Goodheart (Eds.), *Handbook of girls' and women's psychological health: Gender and well-being across the life span* (pp. 242–251). New York: Oxford University Press.

Basow, S. A., & Johnson, K. (2000). Predictors of homophobia in female college students. *Sex Roles, 42,* 391–404.

Basow, S. A., Phelan, J. E., & Capotosto, L. (2006). Gender patterns in college students' choices of their best and worst professors. *Psychology of Women Quarterly, 30,* 25–35.

Basow, S. A., et al. (2007). Perceptions of relational and physical aggression among college students: Effects of gender of perpetrator, target, and perceiver. *Psychology of Women Quarterly, 31,* 85–95.

Basson, R. (2006). Sexual desire and arousal disorders in women. *New England Journal of Medicine, 354,* 1497–1506.

Basson, R. (2007). Sexual desire/ arousal disorders in women. In S. R. Lei-blum (Ed.), *Principles and practice of sex therapy* (4th ed., pp. 25–53). New York: Guilford.

Bates, M. (2005, September 9). Tenured and battered. *Chronicle of Higher Education,* pp. C1, C4.

Batsis, J. A., & Zagaria, A. B. (2018). Addressing obesity in aging patients. *Medical Clinics of North America, 102,* 65-85.

Bauchner, S. (2018, April 16). *Rape puts Myanmar army on UN 'list of shame.'* Human Rights Watch. https://www.hrw.org/news /2018/04/16/rape-puts-myanmar -army-un-list-shame#

Bauer, A. M. (2001). "Tell them we're girls": The invisibility of girls with disabilities. In P. O'Reilly, E. M. Penn, & K. deMarrais (Eds.), *Educating young adolescent girls* (pp. 29–45). Mahwah, NJ: Erlbaum.

Bauer, C. C., & Baltes, B. B. (2002). Reducing the effects of gender stereotypes on performance evaluations. *Sex Roles, 47,* 465–476.

Bauer-Maglin, N., & Radosh, A. (2003a). Introduction. In N. Bauer- Maglin & A. Radosh (Eds.), *Women confronting retirement: A nontraditional guide* (pp. 1–30). New Brunswick, NJ: Rutgers University Press.

Bauer-Maglin, N., & Radosh, A. (Eds.). (2003b). *Women confronting retirement: A nontraditional guide.* New Brunswick, NJ: Rutgers University Press.

Baumeister, R. F. (2000). Gender differences in erotic plasticity: The female sex drive as socially flexible and responsive. *Psychological Bulletin, 126,* 347–374.

Bay-Cheng, L. Y., & Zucker, A. N. (2007). Feminism between the sheets: Sexual attitudes among feminists, nonfeminists, and egalitarians. *Psychology of Women Quarterly, 31,* 157–163.

Bays, A. (2017). Perceptions, emotions, and behaviors toward women based on parental status. *Sex Roles, 76,* 138-155.

Beall, A. E. (1993). A social constructionist view of gender. In A. E. Beall & R. J. Sternberg (Eds.), *The psychology of gender* (2nd ed., pp. 127–147). New York: Guilford.

Beall, A. E., Eagly, A. H., & Sternberg, R. J. (2004). Introduction. In A. H. Eagly, A. E. Beall, & R. J. Sternberg (Eds.), *The psychology of gender* (2nd ed., pp. 1–8). New York: Guilford.

Beals, K. P., Impett, E. A., & Peplau, L. A. (2002). Lesbians in love: Why some relationships endure and others end. *Journal of Lesbian Studies, 6,* 53–64.

Beals, K. P., & Peplau, L. A. (2005). Identity support, identity devaluation, and well-being among lesbians. *Psychology of Women Quarterly, 29,* 140–148.

Beattie, S., & Hutchins, H. (2015). *Shelters for abused women in Canada, 2014.* Statistics Canada Catalogue no. 85-002-X ISSN 1209-6393. Retrieved October 5, 2021 from https://www150 .statcan.gc.ca/n1/en/pub/85 -002-x/2015001/article /14207-eng.pdf?st=_uHdi-oe

Beatty, L. A., Wetherington, C. L., Jones, D. J., & Roman, A. B. (2006). Substance use and abuse by girls and women. In J. Worell & C. D. Goodheart (Eds.), *Handbook of girls' and women's psychological health: Gender and well-being across the life span* (pp. 113–121). New York: Oxford University Press.

Beatty, L. A., Wheeler, D., & Gaiter, J. (2004). HIV prevention research for African Americans: Current and future directions. *Journal of Black Psychology, 30,* 40–58.

Becker, D. V., et al. (2007). The confounded nature of angry men and happy women. *Journal of Personality and Social Psychology, 92,* 179–190.

Becker, E., Rankin, E., & Rickel, A. U. (1998). *High-risk sexual behavior: Interventions with vulnerable populations.* New York: Plenum.

Becker, S. W., & Eagly, A. H. (2004). The heroism of women and men. *American Psychologist, 59,* 163–178.

Beckman, L. J. (2006). Women's reproductive health: Issues, findings, and controversies. In J. Worell & C. D. Goodheart (Eds.), *Handbook of girls' and women's psychological health: Gender and well-being across the life span* (pp. 330–338). New York: Oxford University Press.

Beckman, L. J., & Harvey, S. M. (Eds.). (2005). Current reproductive technologies: Psychological, ethical, cultural and political considerations [special issue]. *Journal of Social Issues, 61*(1).

Beckman, L. J., Harvey, S. M., Satre, S. J., & Walker, M. A. (1999). Cultural beliefs about social influence strategies of Mexican immigrant women and their heterosexual partners. *Sex Roles, 40*, 871–892.

Bedford, V. H. (2003). Men and women in old age: Incorporating aging into psychology of gender courses. In S. K. Whitbourne & J. Cavanaugh (Eds.), *Integrating aging topics into psychology: A practical guide for teaching undergraduates* (pp. 159–172). Washington, DC: American Psychological Association.

Bedford, V. H., & Blieszner, R. (2000). Older adults and their families. In D. H. Demo, K. R. Allen, & M. A. Fine (Eds.), *Handbook of family diversity* (pp. 216–232). New York: Oxford University Press.

Behnke, S. (2006, June). The discipline of ethics and the prohibition against becoming sexually involved with patients. *Monitor on Psychology,* 86–87.

Bélanger, A., et al. (2002). Gender differences in disability-free life expectancy for selected risk factors and chronic conditions in Canada. In S. B. Laditka (Ed.), *Health expectations for older women: International perspectives* (pp. 61–83). Binghamton, NY: Haworth.

Belansky, E. S., & Boggiano, A. K. (1994). Predicting helping behaviors: The role of gender and instrumental/ expressive self-schemata. *Sex Roles, 30*, 647–661.

Belgrave, F. Z., & Allison, K. W. (2010). *African American psychology: From Africa to America* (2nd ed.). Thousand Oaks, CA: Sage.

Bell, J., et al. (2014). *Religion in Latin America: Widespread change in in a historically Catholic region.* Pew Research Center. Retrieved October 4, 2021 from https://www.pewresearch.org/wp-content/uploads/sites/7/2014/11/Religion-in-Latin-America-11-12-PM-full-PDF.pdf

Bell, N. J., O'Neal, K. K., Feng, D., & Schoenrock, C. J. (1999). Gender and sexual risk. *Sex Roles, 41*, 313–332.

Bellamy, C. (2000). *The state of the world's children 2000.* New York: United Nations Children's Fund.

Belle, D. (2008). Poor women in a wealthy nation. In J. C. Chrisler, C. Golden, & P. D. Rozee (Eds.), *Lectures on the psychology of women* (4th ed., pp. 26–41). Boston, MA: McGraw-Hill.

Belle, D., & Dodson, L. (2006). Poor women and girls in a wealthy nation. In J. Worell & C. D. Goodheart (Eds.), *Handbook of girls' and women's psychological health: Gender and well-being across the life span* (pp. 122–126). New York: Oxford University Press.

Belle, D., & Doucet, J. (2003). Poverty, inequality, and discrimination as sources of depression among U.S. women. *Psychology of Women Quarterly, 27*, 101–113.

Belle, E. (2018). Instagram side-by-side shows how to get a thigh gap. *Teen Vogue.* Retrieved October 5, 2021 from https://www.teenvogue.com/story/instagram-side-by-side-shows-how-to-get-a-thigh-gap

Bem, S. L. (1974). The measurement of psychological androgyny. *Journal of Consulting and Clinical Psychology, 42*, 155–162.

Bem, S. L. (1977). On the utility of alternative procedures for assessing psychological androgyny. *Journal of Consulting and Clinical Psychology, 45*, 196–205.

Bem, S. L. (1981). Gender schema theory: A cognitive account of sex typing. *Psychological Review, 88*, 354–364.

Bem, S. L. (1983). Gender schema theory and its implications for child development: Raising gender aschematic children in a gender-schematic society. *Signs, 8*, 598–616.

Bem, S. L. (1993). *The lenses of gender: Transforming the debate on sexual inequality.* New Haven, CT: Yale University Press.

Bem, S. L. (1998). *An unconventional family.* New Haven, CT: Yale University Press.

Bem, S. L. (2008). Transforming the debate on sexual inequality: From biological difference to institutionalized androcentrism. In J. C. Chrisler, C. Golden, & P. D. Rozee (Eds.), *Lectures on the psychology of women* (4th ed., pp. 2–15). Boston, MA: McGraw-Hill.

Bender, D. E., & Greenwald, R. A. (2003). Introduction: Sweatshop USA: The American sweatshop in global and historical perspective. In D. E. Bender & R. A. Greenwald (Eds.), *Sweatshop USA: The American sweatshop in historical and global perspective* (pp. 1–16). New York: Routledge.

Beneke, T. (1997). Men on rape. In M. Baca Zinn, P. Hondagneu-Sotelo, & M. A. Messner (Eds.), *Through the prism of difference: Readings on sex and gender* (pp. 130–135). Boston: Allyn & Bacon.

Benjamin, L. T., Jr. (2007). *A brief history of modern psychology.* Malden, MA: Blackwell.

Bennett, L. (2007, Fall). Love Your Body turns 10: Sex, stereotypes and beauty. *National NOW Foundation Times,* 5.

Bennett, L. (2007). *The feminine mistake: Are we giving up too much?* New York: Hyperion.

Bennett, P. (2004). Psychological interventions in patients with chronic illness. In A. Kaptein & J. Weinman (Eds.), *Health psychology* (pp. 337–357). Malden, MA: Blackwell.

Bennett-Smith, M. (2016, March 23). *Sarah Silverman's rape tips for men really annoyed a lot of men.* Quartz Media. Retrieved October 5, 2021 from https://qz.com/368240/sarah-silvermans-rape-tips-for-men-really-annoyed-a-lot-of-men/

Benoit, C. Shumka, L., Phillips, R., Kennedy, M. C., & Belle-Isle, L. (2015). *Issue brief: Sexual violence against women in Canada.* Government of Canada. Retrieved October 5, 2021 from https://cfc-swc.gc.ca/svawc-vcsfc/issue-brief-en.pdf

Benrud, L. M., & Reddy, D. M. (1998). Differential explanations of illness in women and men. *Sex Roles, 38,* 375–386.

Berenson, C. (2002). What's in a name? Bisexual women define their terms. *Journal of Bisexuality, 2,* 9–21.

Berg, B. J. (2009). *Sexism in America: Alive, well, and ruining our future.* Chicago: Lawrence Hill Books.

Berg, F. M. (2000). *Women afraid to eat: Breaking free in today's weight-obsessed world.* Hettinger, ND: Healthy Weight Network.

Berg, J. H., Stephen, W. G., & Dodson, M. (1981). Attributional modesty in women. *Psychology of Women Quarterly, 5,* 711–727.

Berge, J. M., Loth, K., Hanson, C., Croll-Lampert, J., & Neumark-Sztainer, D. (2012). Family life cycle transitions and the onset of eating disorders: a retrospective grounded theory approach. *Journal of Clinical Nursing, 21,* 1355–1363.

Bemak, F., & Chung, E. C. (2004). Culturally oriented psychotherapy with refugees. In U. P. Gielen, J. M. Fish, & J. G. Draguns (Eds.), *Handbook of culture, therapy, and healing* (pp. 121–132). Mahwah, NJ: Erlbaum.

Berger, R. (2004). *Immigrant women tell their stories.* New York: Haworth.

Bergevin, T. A., Bukowski, W. M., & Karavasilis, L. (2003). Childhood sexual abuse and pubertal timing: Implications for long-term psychosocial adjustment. In C. Hayward (Ed.), *Gender differences at puberty* (pp. 187–216). New York: Cambridge University Press.

Bergman, B. (2003). The validation of the women workplace culture questionnaire: Gender-related stress and health for Swedish working women. *Sex Roles, 49,* 287–297.

Bergman, B., Ahmad, F., & Stewart, D. E. (2003). Physician health, stress and gender at a university hospital. *Journal of Psychosomatic Research, 54,* 171–178.

Bergmann, B. R. (2006). Discrimination through the economist's eye? In F. J. Crosby, M. S. Stockdale, & S. A. Ropp (Eds.), *Sex discrimination in the workplace: Multidisciplinary perspectives* (pp. 213–234). Malden, MA: Blackwell.

Bergum, V. (1997). *A child on her mind: The experience of becoming a mother.* Westport, CT: Bergin & Garvey.

Berke, D. S., & DeFour, D. (2021). Teaching about empowerment self-defense training for sexual assault prevention: Recommendations for feminist instruction in psychology. *Psychology of Women Quarterly, 45,* 387–394.

Berkman, B. (2004). Celebrating the many roles of women. In L. Flanders (Ed.), *The W effect* (pp. 185–187). New York: Feminist Press.

Berman, A. L. (2009). Depression and suicide. In I. H. Gotlib & C. L. Hammen (Eds.), *Handbook of depression* (2nd ed., pp. 510–530). New York: Guilford.

Berman, P. W. (1980). Are women more responsive than men to the young? A review of developmental and situational variables. *Psychological Bulletin, 88,* 668–695.

Bernard, M., & Phillipson, C. (2004). Retirement and leisure. In J. F. Nussbaum & J. Coupland (Eds.), *Handbook of communication and aging research* (2nd ed., pp. 353–381). Mahwah, NJ: Erlbaum.

Bersoff, D. N. (2003). *Ethical conflicts in psychology.* Washington, DC: American Psychological Association.

Best, D. L., & Thomas, J. J. (2004). Cultural diversity and cross-cultural perspectives. In A. H. Eagly, A. E. Beall, & R. J. Sternberg (Eds.), *The psychology of gender* (2nd ed., pp. 296–327). New York: Guilford.

Betz, N. E. (1994). Basic issues and concepts in career counseling for women. In W. B. Walsh & S. H. Osipow (Eds.), *Career counseling for women* (pp. 1–41). Hillsdale, NJ: Erlbaum.

Betz, N. E. (2006). Women's career development. In J. Worell & C. D. Goodheart (Eds.), *Handbook of girls' and women's psychological health: Gender and well-being across the life span* (pp. 312–320). New York: Oxford University Press.

Betz, N. E. (2008). Women's career development. In F. L. Denmark & M. P. Paludi (Eds.), *Psychology of women: A handbook of issues and theories* (pp. 717–752). Westport, CT: Praeger.

Beumont, P. J. V. (2002). Clinical presentation of anorexia nervosa and bulimia nervosa. In C. G. Fairburn & K. D. Brownell (Eds.), *Eating disorders and obesity: A comprehensive handbook* (2nd ed., pp. 162–170). New York: Guilford.

Beyer, C. E., et al. (1996). Gender representation in illustrations, text, and topic areas in sexuality education curricula. *Journal of School Health, 66,* 361–364.

Beyer, S. (1998). Gender differences in self-perception and negative recall biases. *Sex Roles, 38,* 103–133.

Beyer, S. (1998/1999). Gender differences in causal attribution by college students of performance on course examinations. *Current Psychology: Developmental, Learning, Personality, Social, 17,* 346–358.

Beyer, S. (1999b). Gender differences in the accuracy of grade expectancies and evaluation. *Sex Roles, 41,* 279–296.

Bhanot, R., & Jovanovic, J. (2005). Do parents' academic gender stereotypes influence whether they intrude on their children's homework? *Sex Roles, 52,* 597–607.

Bhatia, N., & Bhatia, S. (2021). Changes in gender stereotypes over time: A computational analysis. *Psychology of Women Quarterly, 45,* 106-125.

Bhattacharjee, Y. (2007a). U.S. agencies quiz universities on the status of women in science. *Science, 315,* 1776.

Bhattacharjee, Y. (2007b). Women are scarce in new NAS class. *Science, 316,* 817.

Białecka-Pikul, M., Stępień-Nycz1, M., Sikorska, I., Topolewska-Siedzik, E., Cieciuch, J. (2019). Change and consistency of self-esteem in early and middle adolescence in the context of school transition. *Journal of Youth and Adolescence, 48,* 1605-1618.

Biehl, M., et al. (1997). Matsumoto and Ekman's Japanese and Caucasian facial expressions of emotion (JAC-FEE): Reliability data and cross-national differences. *Journal of Nonverbal Behavior, 21,* 3–21.

Bigler, R. S. (1995). The role of classification skill in moderating environmental influences on children's gender stereotyping: A study of the functional use of gender in the classroom. *Child Development, 66,* 1072–1087.

Bigler, R. S. (1999a). Psychological interventions designed to counter sexism in children: Empirical limitations and theoretical foundations. In W. B. Swann, Jr., J. H. Langlois, & L. A. Gilbert (Eds.), *Sexism and stereotypes in modern society* (pp. 129–151). Washington, DC: American Psychological Association.

Bilbao, J. A. (2003, June). Maquilas are like Aspirin: Temporary pain relief but no cure. *Envío.* 11–16.

Birchard, K. (2004, January 9). Canada's billion-dollar controversy. *Chronicle of Higher Education,* pp. A38–A39.

Birchard, K. (2006, January 13). Native suspicion. *Chronicle of Higher Education,* pp. A46–A49.

Bird, C. E. (1999). Gender, household labor, and psychological distress: The impact of the amount and division of housework. *Journal of Health and Social Behavior, 40,* 32–45.

Bird, C. E., & Rieker, P. P. (2008). *Gender and health: The effect of constrained choices and social policies.* New York: Cambridge University Press.

Bisom-Rapp, S., Stockdale, M. S., & Crosby, F. J. (2007). A critical look at organizational responses to and remedies for sex discrimination. In F. J. Crosby, M. S. Stockdale, & S. A. Ropp (Eds.), *Sex discrimination in the workplace* (pp. 273–293). Malden, MA: Blackwell.

Black, L., & Jackson, V. (2005). Families of African origin. In M. McGoldrick, J. Giordano, & N. Garcia-Preto (Eds.), *Ethnicity and family therapy* (3rd ed., pp. 77–86). New York: Guilford.

Black, M., et al. (2009). Sexual intercourse among adolescents maltreated before age 12: A prospective investigation. *Pediatrics, 124,* 941–949.

Black, M. C., Basile, K. C., Breiding, M. J., Smith, S. G., Walters, M. L., Merrick, M. T., Chen, J., & Stevens, M. R. (2011). *The national intimate partner and sexual violence survey (NISVS): 2010 summary report.* National Center for Injury Prevention and Control, Centers for Disease Control and Prevention. Retrieved October 5, 2021 from https://www.nsvrc.org/sites/default/files/2021-04/NISVS_Report2010-a.pdf

Blades, J., & Rowe-Finkbeiner, K. (2006). *The motherhood manifesto.* New York: Nation Books.

Blair, I. V. (2001). Implicit stereotypes and prejudice. In G. B. Moskowitz (Ed.), *Cognitive social psychology* (pp. 359–374). Mahwah, NJ: Erlbaum.

Blais, D. (2006, Fall). Ivory tower. *Teaching Tolerance,* 19–22.

Blake, D. R., Weber, B. M., & Fletcher, K. E. (2004). Adolescent and young adult women' s misunderstanding of the term Pap smear. *Archives of Pediatrics and Adolescent Medicine, 158,* 966–970.

Blakemore, J. E. O. (1998). The influence of gender and parental attitudes on preschool children's interest in babies: Observations in natural settings. *Sex Roles, 38,* 73–94.

Blakemore, J. E. O. (2003). Children's beliefs about violating gender norms: Boys shouldn't look like girls, and girls shouldn't act like boys. *Sex Roles, 48,* 411–419.

Blakemore, J. E. O., Berenbaum, S. A., & Liben, L. S. (2009). *Gender development.* New York: Psychology Press.

Blakemore, J. E. O., & Centers, R. E. (2005). Characteristics of boys' and girls' toys. *Sex Roles, 53,* 619–633.

Blakemore, J. E. O., & Hill, C. A. (2008). The child gender socialization scale: A measure to compare traditional and feminist parents. *Sex Roles, 58,* 192–207.

Blakemore, J. E. O., Lawton, C. A., & Vartanian, L. R. O. (2005). I can't wait to get married: Gender differences in drive to marry. *Sex Roles, 53,* 327–335.

Blalock, A. C., & Campos, P. E. (2003). Human Immunodeficiency Virus and Acquired

Immune Deficiency Syndrome. In L. M. Cohen, D. E. McChargue, & F. L. Collins, Jr. (Eds.), *The health psychology handbook* (pp. 383–396). Thousand Oaks, CA: Sage.

Blank, R., & Slipp, S. (1994). *Voices of diversity: Real people talk about problems and solutions in a workplace where everyone is not alike.* New York: American.

Blau, F. D., Brinton, M. C., & Grusky, D. B. (2006). The declining significance of gender? In F. D. Blau, M. C. Brinton, & D. B. Grusky (Eds.), *The declining significance of gender?* (pp. 3–34). New York: Russell Sage.

Blau, F. D., & Kahn, L. M. (2006). The gender pay gap: Going, going . . . but not gone. In F. D. Blau, M. C. Brinton, & D. B. Grusky (Eds.), *The declining significance of gender?* (pp. 37–66). New York: Russell Sage.

Blayo, C., & Blayo, Y. (2003). The social pressure to abort. In A. M. Basu (Ed.), *The sociocultural and political aspects of abortion: Global perspectives* (pp. 237–247). Westport, CT: Praeger.

Blea, I. (2003). *The feminization of racism: Promoting world peace in America.* Westport, CT: Praeger.

Bleakley, A., Hennessy, M., & Fishbein, M. (2006). Public opinion on sex education in US schools. *Archives of Pediatric and Adolescent Medicine, 160,* 1151–1156.

Bleidorn, W., Arslan, R. C., Denissen, J. J. A., Rentfrow, P. J., Gebauer, J. E., Potter, J., & Gosling, S. D. (2016). Age and gender differences in self-esteem—A cross-cultural window. *Journal of Personality and Social Psychology, 111,* 396–410.

Blizzard, R. M. (2002). Intersex issues: A series of continuing conundrums. *Pediatrics, 110,* 616–621.

Blosnich, J. R., Nasuti, L. J., Mays, V. M., & Cochran, S. D. (2016) Suicidality and sexual orientation: Characteristics of symptom severity, disclosure, and timing

across the life course. *American Journal of Orthopsychiatry, 86,* 69-78.

Blum, R. W., & Nelson-Mmari, K. (2004). Adolescent health from an international perspective. In R. M. Lerner & L. Steinberg (Eds.), *Handbook of adolescent psychology* (2nd ed., pp. 553–586). Hoboken, NJ: Wiley.

Blume, S. B. (1998, March). Alcoholism in women. *Harvard Mental Health Letter, 5–7.*

Blumenthal, D. Collins, S. R., & Fowler, E. J. (2020). The affordable care act at 10 years – its coverage and access provisions. *New England Journal of Medicine, 382,* 963-969.

Bobo, M., Hildreth, B. L., & Durodoye, B. (1998). Changing patterns in career choices among African-American, Hispanic, and Anglo children. *Professional School Counseling, 1,* 37–42.

Bociurkiw, M. (2005, Winter/Spring). It' s not about the sex. *Canadian Woman Studies/Les cahiers de la femme, 24,* 15–21.

Bockting, W., Coleman, E., Deutsch, M. B., Guillamon, A., Meyer, I., Meyer, W., Reisner, S., Sevelius, J., & Ettner, R. (2016). Adult development and quality of life of transgender and gender nonconforming people. *Current Opinion in Endocrinology, Diabetes and Obesity, 23,* 188-197.

Boesch, D., & Phadke, S. (2021). *When women lose all the jobs.* Center for American Progress.

Bogle, K. A. (2008, March 21). "Hooking up": What educators need to know. *Chronicle of Higher Education,* pp. 32.

Bohan, J. S. (1996). *Psychology and sexual orientation: Coming to terms.* New York: Routledge.

Bohan, J. S. (2002). Sex differences and/ in the self: Classic themes, feminist variations, postmodern challenges. *Psychology of Women Quarterly, 26,* 74–88.

Boisnier, A. D. (2003). Race and women's identity development: Distinguishing between feminism

and womanism among Black and White women. *Sex Roles, 49,* 211-218.

Bolden, T. (2002). *33 things every girl should know about women's history.* New York: Crown.

Bondestam, F., & Lundqvist, M. (2020). Sexual harassment in higher education – a systematic review. *European Journal of Higher Education, 10,* 397-419.

Bonebright, T. L., Thompson, J. L., & Leger, D. W. (1996). Gender stereotypes in the expression and perception of vocal affect. *Sex Roles, 34,* 429–445.

Bontempo, D. E., & D'Augelli, A. R. (2002). Effects of at-school victimization and sexual orientation on lesbian, gay, or bisexual youths' health risk behavior. *Journal of Adolescent Health, 30,* 364–374.

Boot, T. (1999). Black or African American: What's in a name? In Y. Alaniz & N. Wong (Eds.), *Voices of color* (pp. 69–72). Seattle: Red Letter Press.

Borchelt, G. (2005). Sexual violence against women in war and armed conflict. In A. Barnes (Ed.), *The handbook of women, psychology, and the law* (pp. 293–327). San Francisco: Jossey-Bass.

Boris, E. (2003, July). Caring for the caretakers. *Women's Review of Books, 20,* 21.

Borrayo, E. A. (2004). Where's Maria? A video to increase awareness about breast cancer and mammography screening among low-literacy Latinas. *Preventive Medicine, 39,* 99–110.

Borrayo, E. A., & Jenkins, S. R. (2003). Feeling frugal: Socio-economic status, acculturation, and cultural health beliefs among women of Mexican descent. *Cultural Diversity and Ethnic Minority Psychology, 9,* 197–206.

Borrayo, E. A., Thomas, J. J., & Lawsin, C. (2004). Cervical cancer screening among Latinas: The importance of referral and participation in parallel cancer screening behaviors. *Women & Health, 39,* 13–29.

Bosacki, S. L., & Moore, C. (2004). Preschoolers' understanding of simple and complex emotions: Links with gender and language. *Sex Roles, 50,* 659–675.

Bosak, J., & Sczesny, S. (2008). Am I the right candidate? Self-ascribed fit of women and men to a leadership position. *Sex Roles, 58,* 682–688.

Bosco, A., Longoni, A. M., & Vecchi, T. (2004). Gender effects in spatial orientation: Cognitive profiles and mental strategies. *Applied Cognitive Psychology, 18,* 519–532.

Bosley-Smith, E. R., & Reczek, C. (2018). Before and after "I Do": Marriage processes for mid-life gay and lesbian married couples. *Journal of Homosexuality, 65,* 1985–2004.

Boston, L. B., Chambers, S., Canetto, S. S., & Slinkard, B. (2001, August). *That kind of woman: Stereotypical representations in computer magazine advertising.* Paper presented at the annual meeting of the American Psychological Association, San Francisco.

Boston Women's Health Book Collective. (2005). *Our bodies, ourselves* (4th ed.). New York: Touchstone.

Boston Women's Health Book Collective. (2011). *Our bodies, ourselves* (5th ed.). New York: Simon & Schuster.

Boston Women's Health Book Collective. (2008). *Our bodies, ourselves: Pregnancy and birth.* New York: Simon & Schuster.

Botta, R. A. (2003). For your health? The relationship between magazine reading and adolescents' body image and eating disturbances. *Sex Roles, 48,* 389–399.

Bouldin, E. D., & Andresen, E. (2010). Caregiving and health. In J. C. Cavanaugh & C. K. Cavanaugh (Eds.), *Aging in America* (Vol. 2, pp. 81–99). Santa Barbara, CA: ABC–CLIO.

Bourgault, S., Peterman, A., & O'Donnell, M. (2021). *Violence against women and children during COVID-19: One year on and 100 papers in: A fourth research round up.* Center for Global Development. Retrieved October 5, 2021 from https://www.cgdev.org/sites/default/files/vawc-fourth-roundup.pdf

Bourke, J. (2007). *Rape: Sex, violence, history.* Berkeley, CA: Shoemaker Hoard.

Bourque, P., Pushkar, D., Bonneville, L., & Béland, F. (2005). Contextual effects on life satisfaction of older men and women. *Canadian Journal on Aging/La revue canadienne du viellissement, 24,* 31–44.

Bowleg, L. (1999). "When I look at you, I don't see race" and other diverse tales from the introduction to women's studies classroom. In B. S. Winkler & C. DiPalma (Eds.), *Teaching introduction to women's studies: Expectations and strategies* (pp. 111–122). Westport, CT: Bergin & Garvey.

Bowleg, L. (2008). When Black + lesbian + woman? Black lesbian woman: The methodological challenges of qualitative and quantitative inter-sectionality research. *Sex Roles, 59,* 312–325.

Bowleg, L., Lucas, K. J., & Tschann, J. M. (2004). "The ball was always in his court" : An exploratory analysis of relational scripts, sexual scripts, and condom use among African American women. *Psychology of Women Quarterly, 28,* 70–82.

Bowles, H. R., Babcock, L., & Lai, L. (2007). Social incentives for gender differences in the propensity to initiate negotiations: Sometimes it does hurt to ask. *Organizational Behavior and Human Decision Processes, 103,* 84–101.

Boyatzis, C. J., & Eades, J. (1999). Gender differences in preschoolers' and kindergartners' artistic production and preference. *Sex Roles, 41,* 627–638.

Brabeck, M. M., & Brabeck, K. M. (2006). Women and relationships. In J. Worell & C. D. Goodheart (Eds.), *Handbook of girls' and women's psychological health: Gender and well-being across the life span* (pp. 208–217). New York: Oxford University Press.

Brabeck, M. M., & Rogers, L. (2000). Human rights as a moral issue: Lessons for moral educators from human rights work. *Journal of Moral Education, 29,* 167–182.

Brabeck, M. M., & Shore, E. L. (2002). Gender differences in intellectual and moral development? The evidence that refutes the claim. In J. Demick & C. Andreoletti (Eds.), *Handbook of adult development* (pp. 351–368). New York: Plenum.

Brabeck, M. M., & Ting, K. (2000). Feminist ethics: Lenses for examining ethical psychological practice. In M. M. Brabeck (Ed.), *Practicing feminist ethics in psychology* (pp. 17–35). Washington, DC: American Psychological Association.

Bradbury, T., Rogge, R., & Lawrence, E. (2001). Reconsidering the role of conflict in marriage. In A. Booth, A. C. Crouter, & M. Clements (Eds.), *Couples in conflict* (pp. 59–81). Mahwah, NJ: Erlbaum.

Brady, J. L., Kaya, A., Iwamoto, D., Park, A., Fox, L., & Moorhead, M. (2017). Asian American women's body image experiences: A qualitative intersectionality study. *Psychology of Women Quarterly, 41,* 479-496.

Brady, K. L., & Eisler, R. M. (1995). Gender bias in the college classroom: A critical review of the literature and implications for future research. *Journal of Research and Development in Education, 29,* 9–19.

Brady, K. L., & Eisler, R. M. (1999). Sex and gender in the college classroom: A quantitative analysis of faculty–student interactions and perceptions. *Journal of Educational Psychology, 91,* 127–145.

Brady, S. S., & Halpern-Felsher, B. L. (2007). Adolescents' reported consequences of having oral sex versus vaginal sex. *Pediatrics, 119,* 229–236.

Bragger, J. D., Kutcher, E., Morgan, J., & Firth, P. (2002). The effects of the structured interview on reducing biases against pregnant job applicants. *Sex Roles, 46,* 215–226. Brain responses vary by sexual orientation, new research shows. (2005, May 10). *Wall Street Journal,* D4.

Brainerd, C. J., & Reyna, V. F. (2005). *The science of false memory.* New York: Oxford University Press.

Brannon, L., & Feist, J. (2004). *Health psychology: An introduction to behavior and health* (5th ed.). Belmont, CA: Thomson Wadsworth.

Braun, N. (2003, Mid-Winter). The new culture: Today's feminist presses embody activism and critical thinking. *Fore Word Magazine,* 24–27.

Brehm, S. S., Kassin, S., & Fein, S. (2005). *Social psychology* (6th ed.). Boston: Houghton Mifflin.

Brehm, S. S., Miller, R. S., Perlman, D., & Campbell, S. M. (2002). *Intimate relationships* (3rd ed.). Boston: McGraw-Hill.

Brescoll, V. L., & Uhlmann, E. L. (2005). Attitudes toward traditional and nontraditional parents. *Psychology of Women Quarterly, 29,* 436–445.

Brescoll, V., & LaFrance, M. (2004). The correlates and consequences of newspaper reports of research on sex differences. *Psychological Science, 15,* 515–520.

Bretl, D. J., & Cantor, J. (1988). The portrayal of men and women in U.S. television commercials: A recent content analysis and trends over 15 years. *Sex Roles, 18,* 595–609.

Brewerton, T. D. (2010, June 21). Eating disorders. *Audio-Digest Psychiatry, 39*(12).

Bridges, J. S. (1993). Pink or blue: Gender-stereotypic perceptions of infants as conveyed by birth congratulations cards. *Psychology of Women Quarterly, 17,* 193–205.

Briere, J., & Lanktree, C. (1983). Sex-role related effects of sex bias in language. *Sex Roles, 9,* 625–632.

Bristowe, K., Marshall, S., & Harding, R. (2016). The bereavement experiences of lesbian, gay, bisexual and/or trans* people who have lost a partner: A systematic review, thematic synthesis and modelling of the literature. *Palliative Medicine, 30,* 730–744.

Briton, N. J., & Hall, J. A. (1995). Beliefs about female and male nonverbal communication. *Sex Roles, 32,* 79–90.

Brody, E. M. (2004). *Women in the middle: Their parent care years* (2nd ed.). New York: Springer.

Brody, L. R. (1999). *Gender, emotion, and the family.* Cambridge, MA: Harvard University Press.

Brody, L. R., & Hall, J. A. (2000). Gender, emotion, and expression. In M. Lewis & J. M. Haviland-Jones (Eds.), *Handbook of emotions* (2nd ed., pp. 338–349). New York: Guilford Press.

Brody, L. R., Hall, J. A., & Stokes, L. R. (2016). Gender and emotion: Theory, findings, and context. In L. F. Barrett, M. Lewis, & J. M. Haviland-Jones (Eds.), *Handbook of emotions* (4th ed., pp. 362-392). New York, NY: Guilford.

Bronstein, P. A. (2006). The family environment: Where gender role socialization begins. In J. Worell & C. D. Goodheart (Eds.), *Handbook of girls' and women's psychological health: Gender and well-being across the life span* (pp. 262–271). New York: Oxford University Press.

Bronstein, P. A., Briones, M., Brooks, T., & Cowan, B. (1996). Gender and family factors as predictors of late adolescent emotional expressiveness and adjustment: A longitudinal study. *Sex Roles, 34,* 739–765.

Bronstein, P. A., Fox, B. J., Kamon, J. L., & Knolls, M. L. (2007). Parenting and gender as predictors of moral courage in late adolescence: A longitudinal study. *Sex Roles, 56,* 661–674.

Brooks, B. L., Mintz, A. R., & Dobson, K. S. (2004). Diversity training in Canadian predoctoral clinical psychology internships: A survey of directors of internship training. *Canadian Psychology/Psychologie canadienne, 45,* 308–312.

Brooks, G. R. (2010). *Beyond the crisis of masculinity.* Washington, DC: American Psychological Association.

Brooks-Gunn, J., Han, W., & Waldfogel, J. (2002). Maternal employment and child cognitive outcomes in the first three years of the NICHD Study of Early Child Care. *Child Development, 73,* 1050–1072.

Brott, J. S. (2006). New grandmother. In J. A. Weinberg (Ed.), *Still going strong* (pp. 221–223). New York: Hayworth.

Brotto, L. A., Knudson, G., Inskip, J., Rhodes, K., & Erksine. Y. (2010). Asexuality: A mixed methods approach. *Archives of Sexual Behavior, 39,* 599-618.

Brotto, L., & Yule, M. A. (2017). Asexuality: Sexual orientation, paraphilia, sexual dysfunction, or none of the above? *Archives of Sexual Behavior, 46,* 619-628.

Brown, A. L., & Testa, M. (2008). Social influences on judgments of rape victims: The role of the negative and positive social reactions of others. *Sex Roles, 58,* 490–500.

Brown, B. B. (2004). Adolescents' relationships with peers. In R. M. Lerner & L. Steinberg (Eds.), *Handbook of adolescent psychology* (2nd ed., pp. 363–394). Hoboken, NJ: Wiley.

Brown, B. B., Dolcini, M. M., & Leventhal, A. (1997). Transformations in peer relationships at adolescence: Implications for health-related behavior. In J. Schulenberg, J. L. Maggs, & K. Hurrelmann (Eds.), *Health risks and developmental transitions during adolescence* (pp. 161–189). New York: Cambridge University Press.

Brown, D. R., Keith, V. M., Jackson, J. S., & Gary, L. E. (2003). (Dis)respected and (dis)regarded: Experiences of racism and psychological distress. In D. R. Brown & V. M. Keith (Eds.), *In and out of our right minds: The mental health of African American women* (pp. 85–98). New York: Columbia University Press.

Brown, H. (2015). *Body of truth: How science, history, and culture drive our obsession with weight – and what we can do about it.* Boston, MA: Da Capo Press.

Brown, J. D., et al. (2006). Sexy media matter: Exposure to sexual content in music, movies, television, and magazines predicts Black and White adolescents' sexual behavior. *Pediatrics, 117,* 1018–1027.

Brown, K. A., Dewookler, A. V., Baker, N., & Dodich, C. (2017). The female athlete triad: Special considerations for adolescent female athletes. *Translational Pediatrics, 6*(3), 144-149.

Brown, L. M. (1998). *Raising their voices: The politics of girls' anger.* Cambridge, MA: Harvard University Press.

Brown, L. M., Way, N., & Duff, J. L. (1999). The others in my I: Adolescent girls' friendships and peer relations. In N. G. Johnson, M. C. Roberts, & J. Worell (Eds.), *Beyond appearance: A new look at adolescent girls* (pp. 205–225). Washington, DC: American Psychological Association.

Brown, L. S. (2000). Dangerousness, impotence, silence, and invisibility: Heterosexism in the construction of women's sexuality.

In C. B. Travis & J. W. White (Eds.), *Sexuality, society, and feminism* (pp. 273–297). Washington, DC: American Psychological Association.

Brown, L. S. (2006). Still subversive after all these years: The relevance of feminist therapy in the age of evidence-based practice. *Psychology of Women Quarterly, 30,* 15–24.

Brown, L. S. (2008). *Cultural competence in trauma therapy: Beyond the flashback.* Washington, DC: American Psychological Association.

Browne-Miller, A. (2010). *Will you still need me? Feeling wanted, loved, and meaningful as we age.* West-port, CT: Praeger.

Brownell, K. D. (2005). Introduction. In K. D. Brownell, R. M. Puhl, M. B. Schwartz, & L. Rudd (Eds.), *Weight bias: Nature, consequences, and remedies* (pp. 1–11). New York: Guilford.

Brownhill, L. S., & Turner, T. E. (2003, Fall/Winter). Mau Mau women rise again: The reassertion of commoning in twenty-first century Kenya. *Canadian Woman Studies/ Les cahiers de la femme, 23,* 168–176.

Brownlow, S., Jacobi, T., & Rogers, M. (2000). Science anxiety as a function of gender and experience. *Sex Roles, 42,* 119–131.

Brownlow, S., & Miderski, C. A. (2002). How gender and college chemistry experience influence mental rotation ability. *Themes in Education, 3,* 133–140.

Brownlow, S., Rosamond, J. A., & Parker, J. A. (2003). Gender-linked linguistic behavior in television interviews. *Sex Roles, 49,* 121–132.

Brownlow, S., Smith, T. J., & Ellis, B. R. (2002). How interest in science negatively influences perceptions of women. *Journal of Science Education and Technology, 11,* 135–144.

Brownlow, S., Whitener, R., & Rupert, J. M. (1998). "I'll take gender differences for $1000! " :

Domain-specific intellectual success on " Jeopardy. " *Sex Roles, 38,* 269–285.

Brownstone, L. M., Holliman, B. D., Gerber, H. R., Monteith, L. L. (2018). The phenomenology of military sexual trauma among women veterans. *Psychology of Women Quarterly, 42,* 399-413.

Bruhaker, L., & Smith, J. M. H. (2004). *Gender in the early medieval world: East and west* (pp. 300–900). New York: Cambridge University Press.

Bruns, C. M., & Kaschak, E. (2010). Feminist psychotherapies: Theory, research, and practice. In J. C. Chrisler & D. R. McCreary (Eds.), *Handbook of gender research in psychology* (Vol. 2, pp. 187–219). New York: Springer.

Bryant, A. N. (2003). Changes in attitudes toward women's roles: Predicting gender-role traditionalism among college students. *Sex Roles, 48,* 131–142.

Bryant, C. M., & Wickrama, K. A. S. (2005). Marital relationships of African Americans: A contextual approach. In V. C. McLoyd, N. E. Hill, & K. A. Dodge (Eds.), *African American family life* (pp. 111–134). New York: Guilford.

Bryant-Davis, T., and Comas-Díaz, L. (Eds.). (2016). *Womanist and Mujerista psychologies: Voices of fire, acts of courage.* Washington, DC: American Psychological Association.

Bub, K. L., & McCartney, K. (2004). On childcare as a support for maternal employment wages and hours. *Journal of Social Issues, 60,* 819–824.

Buchanan, N. T., & Fitzgerald, L. F. (2008). Effects of racial and sexual harassment on work and the psychological well-being of African American women. *Journal of Occupational Health Psychology, 13,* 137–151.

Buchanan, N. T., Settles, I. H., & Woods, K. C. (2008). Comparing sexual harassment subtypes among Black and White women by military rank: Double jeopardy, the Jezebel, and the cult of true womanhood. *Psychology of Women Quarterly, 32,* 347–361.

Buchanan, T. (2005). The paradox of the contented female worker in a traditionally female industry. *Sociological Spectrum, 25,* 677–713.

Buchanan, T., & Selmon, N. (2008). Race and gender differences in self-efficacy: Assessing the role of gender role attitudes and family background. *Sex Roles, 58,* 822–836.

Buckley, T. R., & Carter, R. T. (2005). Black adolescent girls: Do gender role and racial identity impact their self-esteem? *Sex Roles, 53,* 647–661.

Bueno, J. (2019). *The brink of being: Talking about miscarriage.* New York: Penguin Books.

Bugental, D. B., & Hehman, J. A. (2007). Ageism: A review of research and policy implications. *Social Issues and Policy Review, 1,* 172–216.

Bullard, R., Gardezi, M., Chennault, C., & Dankbar, H. (2016). Climate change and environmental justice: A conversation with Dr. Robert Bullard. *Journal of Critical Thought and Praxis, 5*(2).

Bullock, H. E., Wyche, K. F., & Williams, W. R. (2001). Media images of the poor. *Journal of Social Issues, 57,* 229–246.

Bureau of Labor Statistics. (2004b). *Women in the labor force: A data-book.* Washington, DC: U.S. Department of Labor.

Bureau of Labor Statistics (2008b). *Married-couple families by presence and relationship of employed members, 2007.* Retrieved December 2, 2010, from http://www.bls.gov/ opub /ted/2008/jun/wk1/art01.txt

Bureau of Labor Statistics (2009a, October 14). *TED: The Editor's Desk.* Retrieved November 19, 2010, from http://www.bls.gov / opub/ted/2009/ted_20091014 _ data.htm

Bureau of Labor Statistics. (2009b, August 7). *Women and men in management, professional, and related occupations, 2008.* Retrieved November 19, 2010, from http://www.bls.gov/opub /ted/2009/ted_20090807.htm

Bureau of Labor Statistics. (2010a). *Employed persons by detailed occupation, sex, race, and Hispanic or Latino ethnicity, Tables 7.1, 7.2, 7.3.* Retrieved November 30, 2010, from http:// www.bls.gov/cps/ cpsaat11.pdf

Bureau of Labor Statistics (2010b). *Employment status of the civilian noninstitutionalized population by age, sex, and race.* Retrieved December 24, 2010, from http:// www.bls.gov/cps/ cpsaat3.pdf

Bureau of Labor Statistics. (2015). *Hispanics and Latinos in industries and occupations.* Retrieved October 4, 2021 from https:// www.bls.gov/opub/ted/2015 /hispanics-and-latinos-in -industries-and-occupations.htm

Bureau of Labor Statistics. (2017). *Women's and men's earnings by age in 2016.* U.S. Department of Labor, The Economics Daily. Retrieved October 5, 2021 form https://www.bls.gov/opub/ ted/2017/womens-and-mens -earnings-by-age-in-2016.htm

Bureau of Labor Statistics. (2019). *Women in the labor force: A databook.* Bureau of Labor Statistics Report 1084. Retrieved October 5, 2021 from https://www.bls.gov/opub /reports/womens-databook /2019/home.htm

Bureau of Labor Statistics. (2020). *Labor force statistics from the current population survey: Table 39, median weekly earnings of full-time wage and salary workers by detailed occupation and sex.* Bureau of Labor Statistics. Retrieved October 3, 2021 from https://www.bls.gov/cps /cpsaat39.htm

Bureau of Labor Statistics. (2021). *Employment characteristics of families – 2020.* Bureau of Labor Statistics. Retrieved October 3, 2021 from https://www.bls.gov /news.release/pdf/famee.pdf

Bureau of Labor Statistics. (2021). *Table 1. Employment status of the civilian noninstitutional population by disability status and selected characteristics, 2020 annual averages.* Retrieved October 5, 2021 from https:// www.bls.gov/news.release/pdf /disabl.pdf

Burgess, E. O. (2004). Sexuality in mid-life and later life couples. In J. H. Harvey, A. Wenzel, & S. Sprecher (Eds.), *The handbook of sexuality in close relationships* (pp. 437–454). Mahwah, NJ: Erlbaum.

Burgess, M. C. R., Sterner, S. P., & Burgess, S. R. (2007). Sex, lies, and video games: The portrayal of male and female characters on video game covers. *Sex Roles, 57,* 419–433.

Burks, B. K. (2006). Emotional abuse of women. In P. K. Lundberg-Love & S. L. Marmion (Eds.), *"Intimate" violence against women: When spouses, partners, or lovers attack* (pp. 15–29). Westport, CT: Praeger.

Burlingame-Lee, L. J., & Canetto, S. S. (2005). Narratives of gender in computer advertisements. In E. Cole & J. Henderson Daniel (Eds.), *Media, women, and girls: Implications for feminist psychology* (pp. 85–99). Washington, DC: American Psychological Association.

Burn, S. M. (1996). *The social psychology of gender.* New York: McGraw-Hill.

Burn, S. M., Aboud, R., & Moyles, C. (2000). The relationship between gender, social identity, and support for feminism. *Sex Roles, 42,* 1081–1089.

Burn, S. M., & Busso, J. (2005). Ambivalent sexism, scriptural literalism, and religiosity. *Psychology of Women Quarterly, 29,* 412–418.

Burn, S. M., & Ward, Z. A. (2005). Men's conformity to traditional masculinity and relationship satisfaction. *Psychology of Men and Masculinity, 6,* 254–263.

Burns, L. H. (2001). Gynecologic oncology. In N. L. Stotland & D. E. Stewart (Eds.), *Psychological aspects of women's health care* (pp. 307–329). Washington, DC: American Psychiatric Press.

Burpee, L. C., & Langer, E. J. (2005). Mindfulness and marital satisfaction. *Journal of Adult Development, 12,* 43–51.

Bursik, K. (2000, August). *Gender, gender role, and ego level: Individual differences in feminism.* Paper presented at the annual convention of the American Psychological Association, Washington, DC.

Buss, D. M. (1998). The psychology of human mate selection: Exploring the complexity of the strategic repertoire. In C. Crawford & D. L. Krebs (Eds.), *Handbook of evolutionary psychology: Ideas, issues, and applications* (pp. 405–429). Mahwah, NJ: Erlbaum.

Buss, D. M. (2000). *The dangerous passion: Why jealousy is as necessary as love and sex.* New York: Free Press.

Buss, D. M., & Schmitt, D. P. (2019). Mate preferences and their behavioral manifestations. *Annual Review of Psychology, 70:1,* 77-110.

Bussey, K., & Bandura, A. (1999). Social cognitive theory of gender development and differentiation. *Psychological Review, 106,* 676–713.

Bussey, K., & Bandura, A. (2004). Social cognitive theory of gender development and functioning. In A. H. Eagly, A. E. Beall, & R. J. Sternberg (Eds.). *The psychology of gender* (2nd ed., pp. 92–120). New York: Guilford.

Buttner, E. H., & McEnally, M. (1996). The interactive effect of influence tactic, applicant gender, and type of job on hiring recommendations. *Sex Roles, 34,* 581–591.

By the numbers. (2006, January 12). *Diverse Issues in Higher Education, 36.*

Byers, E. S., & Demmons, S. (1999). Sexual satisfaction and sexual self-disclosure within dating relationships. *Journal of Sex Research, 36,* 180–189.

Byers, L. (2010). Native American grandmothers: Tradition and contemporary necessity. *Journal of Ethnic & Cultural Diversity in Social Work, 19,* 305-316.

Bylsma, W. H., & Major, B. (1992). Two routes to eliminating gender differences in personal entitlement: Social comparisons and performance evaluations. *Psychology of Women Quarterly, 16,* 193–200.

Byrne, A. (2009). Perfidious and pernicious singlism [Review of the book *Singled out: How singles are stereotyped, stigmatized, and ignored, and still live happily ever* after]. *Sex Roles, 60,* 760–763.

Byrne, A., & Carr, D. (2005). Caught in the cultural lag: The stigma of singlehood. *Psychological Inquiry, 16,* 84–141.

Byrnes, J. P. (2004). Gender differences in math: Cognitive processes in an expanded framework. In A. M. Gallagher & J. C. Kaufman (Eds.), *Gender differences in mathematics: An integrative psychological approach* (pp. 73–98). New York: Cambridge University Press.

Bytheway, B. (2005). Ageism and age categorization. *Journal of Social Issues, 61,* 361–374.

Cacciari, C., & Padovani, R. (2007). Further evidence of gender stereotype priming in language: Semantic facilitation and inhibition in Italian role nouns. *Applied Psycholinguistics, 20,* 277-293.

Cadinu, M., Maass, A., Rosabianca, A., & Kiesner, J. (2005). Why do women underperform under stereotype threat? Evidence for the role of negative thinking. *Psychological Science, 16,* 572–578.

Cagnacci, A., & Venier, M. (2019). The controversial history of hormone replacement therapy. *Medicina (Kaunas, Lithuania), 55,* 602.

Cahan, S., & Ganor, Y. (1995). Cognitive gender differences among Israeli children. *Sex Roles, 32,* 469–484.

Calasanti, T. M., & Slevin, K. F. (2001). *Gender, social inequalities, and aging.* Walnut Creek, CA: AltaMira Press.

Calabrese, S. K., Meyer, I. H., Overstreet, N. M., Haile, R., & Hansen, N. B. (2015). Exploring discrimination and mental health disparities faced by Black sexual minority women using a minority stress framework. *Psychology of Women Quarterly, 39,* 287-304.

Calasanti, T. M., & Slevin, K. F. (2006). Introduction: Age matters. In T. M. Calasanti & K. F. Slevin (Eds.), *Age matters: Realigning feminist thinking* (pp. 1–17). New York: Routledge.

Caldwell, J. C., & Caldwell, P. (2003). Introduction: Induced abortion in a changing world. In A. M. Basu (Ed.), *The sociocultural and political aspects of abortion: Global perspectives* (pp. 1–13). Westport, CT: Praeger.

Call, J. B., & Shafer, K. (2018). Gendered manifestations of depression and help seeking among men. *American Journal of Men's Health, 12,* 41-51.

Calogero, R. M., Davis, W. N., & Thompson, J. K. (2005). The role of self-objectification in the experience of women with eating disorders. *Sex Roles, 52,* 43–50.

Calogero, R. M., & Thompson, J. K. (2010). Gender and body image. In J. C. Chrisler & D. R. McCreary (Eds.), *Handbook of gender research in psychology* (Vol. 2, pp. 153–184). New York: Springer.

Cao, S., Moineddin, R., Urquia, M. L., Razak, F., & Ray, J. G. (2014). J-shapedness: An often missed, often miscalculated relation: The example of weight and mortality. Journal of Epidemiology and Community Health, 68, 683-690.

Cameron, L. D., & Ross-Morris, R. (2004). Illness-related cognition and behaviour. In A. Kaptein & J. Weinman (Eds.), *Health psychology* (pp. 84–110). Malden, MA: Blackwell.

Campbell, A. (2002). *A mind of her own: The evolutionary psychology of women.* New York: Oxford University Press.

Campbell, C. R., & Henry, J. W. (1999). Gender differences in self-attributions: Relationship of gender to attributional consistency, style, and expectations for performance in a college course. *Sex Roles, 41,* 95–104.

Campbell, D. W., Campbell, J. C., Yarandi, H. N., O'Connor, A. L., Dollar, E., Killion, C., Sloand, E., Callwood, G. B., Cesar, N. M., Hassan, M., & Gary, F. (2016). Violence and abuse of internally displaced women survivors of the 2010 Haiti earthquake. *International Journal of Public Health, 61,* 981–992.

Campbell, R., & Raja, S. (2005). The sexual assault and secondary victimization of female veterans: Help-seeking experiences with military and civilian social systems. *Psychology of Women Quarterly, 29,* 97–106.

Canadian Cancer Society. (2021). *Breast cancer statistics.* Retrieved October 5, 2021 from https://cancer.ca/en/cancer-information/cancer-types/breast/statistics

Canadian Press. (2016, August 4). Fewer Canadian mothers work outside home than those in many rich countries. CBC News. Retrieved October 3, 2021 from https://www.cbc.ca/news/business/mothers-work-outside-home-1.3707227

Canadian Women's Foundation. (2018). *Fact sheet: Women and poverty in Canada.* Retrieved October 5, 2021 from https://canadianwomen.org/wp-content/uploads/2018/09/Fact-Sheet-WOMEN-POVERTY-September-2018.pdf

Canetto, S. S. (2001). Older adult women: Issues, resources, and challenges. In R. K. Unger (Ed.), *Handbook of the psychology of women and gender* (pp. 183–197). New York: Wiley.

Canetto, S. S. (2003). Older adulthood. In L. Slater, J. H. Daniel, & A. E. Banks (Eds.), *The complete guide to mental health for women* (pp. 56–64). Boston: Beacon Press.

Canetto, S. S. (2008). Women and suicidal behavior: A cultural analysis. *American Journal of Orthopsychiatry, 78,* 259–266.

Canetto, S. S., Timpson, W. M., Borrayo, E. A., & Yang, R. K. (2003). Teaching about human diversity: Lessons learned and recommendations. In W. M. Timpson, S. S. Canetto, E. A. Borrayo, & R. Yang (Eds.), *Teaching diversity: Challenges and complexities, identities and integrity* (pp. 189–205). Madison, WI: Atwood.

Cann, A. (1993). Evaluative expectations and the gender schema: Is failed inconsistency better? *Sex Roles, 28,* 667–678.

Cantor, D., et al. (2004). *Finding your voice: A woman's guide to using self-talk for fulfilling relationships, work, and life.* Hoboken, NJ: Wiley.

Caplan, P. J. (2000). *The new don't blame mother: Mending the mother-daughter relationship.* New York: Routledge.

Caplan, P. J. (2001). Motherhood: Its changing face. In J. Worell (Ed.), *Encyclopedia of women and gender* (pp. 783–794). San Diego: Academic Press.

Caplan, P. J. (2008, Summer). Pathologizing your period. *Ms. Magazine,* 63–64.

Caplan, P. J. (2010). Teaching critical thinking about psychology of sex and gender. *Psychology of Women Quarterly, 34,* 553–557.

Caplan, P. J., & Caplan, J. B. (2009). *Thinking critically about research on sex and gender* (3rd ed.). Boston, MA: Pearson.

Caplan, P. J., & Cosgrove, L. (2004b). Is this really necessary? In P. J. Caplan & L. Cosgrove (Eds.), *Bias in psychiatric diagnosis* (pp. xix–xxxiii). Lanham, MD: Jason Aronson.

Carbajal, P. C. (2020, September 29). *From Hispanic to Latine: Hispanic heritage month and the terms that bind us.* New York Public Library. Retrieved September 28, 2021 from https://www.nypl.org/blog/2020/09/29/hispanic-heritage-month-terms-bind-us

Cardemil, E. V., & Sarmiento, I. A. (2009). Clinical approaches to working with Latino adults. In F. A. Villarruel et al. (Ed.), *Handbook of U.S. Latino psychology* (pp. 329–361). Los Angeles: Sage.

Cardus. (2020). *The Canadian marriage map.* Retrieved October 4, 2021 from https://www.cardus.ca/research/family/reports/the-canadian-marriage-map/

Cares, A. C. (2009). The "transmission" of intimate partner violence across generations. In E. Stark & E. S. Buzawa (Eds.), *Violence against women in families and relationships* (Vol. 2, pp. 23–39). Santa Barbara, CA: ABC-CLIO.

Carli, L. L. (1990). Gender, language, and influence. *Journal of Personality and Social Psychology, 59,* 941–951.

Carli, L. L. (1999). Gender, interpersonal power, and social influence. *Journal of Social Issues, 55,* 81–99.

Carli, L. L. (2001). Gender and social influence. *Journal of Social Issues, 57,* 725–741.

Carli, L. L., & Bukatko, D. (2000). Gender, communication and social influence: A developmental perspective. In T. Eckes & H. M. Trautner (Eds.), *The developmental social psychology of gender* (pp. 295–331). Mahwah, NJ: Erlbaum.

Carli, L. L., & Eagly, A. H. (2002). Gender effects on social influence and emergent leadership. In

G. N. Powell (Ed.), *Handbook of gender and work* (3rd ed., pp. 203–222). Thousand Oaks, CA: Sage.

Carli, L. L., LaFleur, S. J., & Loeber, C. C. (1995). Nonverbal behavior, gender, and influence. *Journal of Personality and Social Psychology, 68,* 1030–1041.

Carlo, G., Raffaeli, M., Laible, D. J., & Meyer, K. A. (1999). Why are girls less physically aggressive than boys? Personality and parenting mediators of physical aggression. *Sex Roles, 40,* 711–729.

Carmichael, M. (2004, January 26). No girls please. *Newsweek,* p. 50.

Carney, D. R., Cuddy, A. J. C., & Yap, A. J. (2015). Review and summary of research on the embodied effects of expansive (vs. contractive) nonverbal displays. *Psychological Science, 26,* 657-663.

Carpenter, L. M. (1998). From girls into women: Scripts for sexuality and romance in *Seventeen* magazine. *Journal of Sex Research, 35,* 158–168.

Carpenter, L. M. (2005). *Virginity lost: An intimate portrait of first sexual experience.* New York: New York University Press.

Carr, D., & Ha, J. (2006). Bereavement. In J. Worell & C. D. Goodheart (Eds.), *Handbook of girls' and women's psychological health: Gender and well-being across the life span* (pp. 397–405). New York: Oxford University Press.

Carr, E. R., Szymanski, D. M., Taha, F., West, L. M., & Kaslow, N. J. (2014). Understanding the link between multiple oppressions and depression among African American women: The role of internalization. *Psychology of Women Quarterly, 38,* 233-245.

Carr Smyth, J., & Karnowski, S. (2019, May 4). Some states seek to close loopholes in marital rape laws. Associated Press. Retrieved October 5, 2021 from https://apnews.com/article/north-america-us-news-ap-top-news-laws-marriage-3a11fee6d-0e449ce81f6c8a50601c687

Carroll, J. L. (2005). *Sexuality now: Embracing diversity.* Belmont, CA: Wadsworth.

Carstensen, L. L., & Mikels, J. A. (2005). At the intersection of emotion and cognition: Aging and the positivity effect. *Current Directions in Psychological Science, 14,* 117–121.

Carver, P. R., Yunger, J. L., & Perry, D. G. (2003). Gender identity and adjustment in middle childhood. *Sex Roles, 49,* 95–109.

Casad, B. J. (2008). Issues and trends in work-family integration. In A. Marcus-Newhall, D. F. Halpern, & Sherylle J. Tan (Eds.), *The changing realities of work and family: A multidisciplinary approach* (pp. 277–292). Malden, MA: Blackwell.

Casey, T. (1998). *Pride and joy: The lives and passions of women without children.* Hillsboro, OR: Beyond Words Publishing.

Castañeda, D. (2000). The close relationship context and HIV/AIDS risk reduction among Mexican Americans. *Sex Roles, 42,* 551–580.

Castañeda, D. (2008). Gender issues among Latinas. In J. C. Chrisler, C. Golden, & P. D. Rozee (Eds.), *Lectures on the psychology of women* (4th ed., pp. 250–267). Boston, MA: McGraw Hill.

Castañeda, D., & Burns-Glover, A. (2004). Gender, sexuality, and intimate relationships. In M. A. Paludi (Ed.), *Praeger guide to the psychology of gender* (pp. 69–90). Westport, CT: Praeger.

Castañeda, D., & Collins, B. E. (1998). The effects of gender, ethnicity, and a close relationship theme on perceptions of persons introducing a condom. *Sex Roles, 39,* 369–390.

Castro, A., Khawja, J., & González-Núñez, I. (2008, July/August). Giving birth, contesting stigma: Cuban women living with HIV. *NACLA Report on the Americas,* pp. 25–29.

CATIE. (2021). *The epidemiology of HIV in Canada: Fact sheet.* Canadian AIDS Treatment Information Exchange. Retrieved October 5, 2021 from https://www.catie.ca/sites/default/files/epi-hiv-02242021-en.pdf

Caughlin, J. P., & Huston, T. L. (2006). The affective structure of marriage. In A. L. Vangelisti & D. Perlman (Eds.), *The Cambridge handbook of personal relationships* (pp. 131–155). New York: Cambridge University Press.

Cavanaugh, J. C., & Cavanaugh, C. K. (Eds.). (2010). *Aging in America* (Vols. 1–4). Santa Barbara, CA: ABC-CLIO.

Ceballo, R. (1999). "The only Black woman walking the face of the earth who cannot have a baby?" In M. Romero & A. Stewart (Eds.), *Women's untold stories: Outside the master narrative.* New York: Routledge.

Ceballo, R., Graham, E. T., & Hart, J. (2015). Silent and infertile: An intersectional analysis of the experiences of socioeconomically diverse African American women with infertility. *Psychology of Women Quarterly, 39,* 497-511.

Ceballo, R., Lansford, J. E., Abbey, A., & Stewart, A. J. (2004). Gaining a child: Comparing the experiences of biological parents, adoptive parents, and stepparents. *Family Relations, 53,* 38–48.

Ceci, S. J., Ginther, D. K., Kahn, S., & Williams, W. M. (2014). Women in academic science: A changing landscape. *Psychological Science in the Public Interest, 15,* 75–141.

Ceci, S. J., & Williams, W. M. (2007a). Are we moving closer and closer apart? Shared evidence leads to conflicting views. In C. J. Ceci & W. M. Williams (Eds.), *Why aren't more women in science? Top researchers debate the evidence* (pp. 213–236). Washington, DC: American Psychological Association.

Ceci, S. J., & Williams, W. M. (Eds.). (2007b). *Why aren't more women in science? Top researchers debate the evidence.* Washington, DC: American Psychological Association.

Center on Budget and Policy Priorities. (2021). Policy basics: Temporary assistance for needy families. CBPP. Retrieved October 3, 2021 from https://www.cbpp.org /research/family-income-support /temporary-assistance-for-needy -families

Centers for Disease Control. (2008). *Youth Risk Behavior Surveillance—United States, 2007.* Retrieved August 19, 2009, from http://www. cdc.gov/mmwr /preview/mmwrhtml / ss5704a1.htm

Centers for Disease Control and Prevention. (2010a). *Healthy youth: Alcohol and drug use.* Retrieved December 19, 2010, from http:// www.cdc.gov/HealthyYouth /alco-holdrug/index.htm

Centers for Disease Control and Prevention. (2010b). *Women and tobacco.* Retrieved December 19, 2010, from http://www.cdc .gov/ tobacco/data_statistics /fact_sheets/ populations/women /index.htm

Centers for Disease Control and Prevention. (2017). *Breastfeeding among U.S. children born 2010–2017, CDC national immunization survey.* CDC. Retrieved October 4, 2021 from https:// www.cdc.gov/breastfeeding/data /nis_data/results.html

Centers for Disease Control and Prevention. (2019). *Current cigarette smoking among adults in the United States.* CDC. Retrieved October 5, 2021 from https://www.cdc.gov/tobacco /data_statistics/fact_sheets/adult _data/cig_smoking/index.htm

Centers for Disease Control and Prevention. (2019). QuickStats: Percentage of women aged ≥50 years who have had a hysterectomy, by race/ethnicity and year – National Health Interview Survey, United States, 2008 and 2019. *Morbidity and Mortality Weekly Report, 68,* 935.

Centers for Disease Control and Prevention. (2020a). HIV in the United States and dependent areas. *CDC.* Retrieved October 5, 2021 from https://www.cdc .gov/hiv/statistics/overview /ataglance.html

Centers for Disease Control and Prevention. (2020b). Estimated HIV incidence and prevalence in the United States, 2014–2018. *HIV Surveillance Supplemental Report, 25*(No. 1). Retrieved October 5, 2021 from http:// www.cdc.gov/hiv/library/reports /hiv-surveillance.html

Centers for Disease Control and Prevention. (2020). *Impaired driving: Get the facts.* CDC Transportation Safety. Retrieved October 5, 2021 from https:// www.cdc.gov/transportationsafety /impaired_driving/impaired-drv _factsheet.html

Centers for Disease Control and Prevention. (2021). *Health insurance coverage: Data for the U.S.* CDC. Retrieved October 5, 2021 from https://www.cdc.gov/nchs /fastats/health-insurance.htm

Centers for Disease Control and Prevention. (2021). *Mammography: Table 33. Use of mammography among women aged 40 and over, by selected characteristics: United States, selected years 1987–2018.* National Center for Health Statistics. Retrieved October 5, 2021 from https://www.cdc.gov/nchs /data/hus/2019/033-508.pdf

Centers for Disease Control and Prevention. (2021). *Women and heart disease.* Centers for Disease Control. Retrieved October 5, 2021 https://www.cdc.gov /heartdisease/women.htm

Cervantes, J. M., & Sweatt, L. I. (2004). Family therapy with Chicana/os. In R. J. Velásquez, L. M. Arellano, & B. W. McNeill (Eds.), *The handbook of Chicana/o psychology and mental health* (pp. 285–322). Mahwah, NJ: Erlbaum.

Cha, A. E., & Cohen, R. A. (2020). Reasons for being uninsured among adults aged 18-64 in the United States, 2019. *National Center for Health Statistics Data Brief No. 382.* Centers for Disease Control.

Chaillet, N., & Dumont, A. (2007). Evidence-based strategies for reducing cesarean section rates: A meta-analysis. *Birth, 34,* 53–64.

Challenging cases: Family benefits of a doula present at the birth of a child. (2004). *Pediatrics, 114,* 1488–1491.

Chalmers, B. (2002). How often must we ask for sensitive care before we get it? *Birth, 29,* 79–82.

Chalmers, B., et al. (2009). Breastfeeding rates and hospital breastfeeding practices in Canada: A national survey of women. *Birth, 36,* 122–140.

Chambers, W. (2005). *Educating MENA: The benefits of female education and how it can be improved in the Middle East.* Unpublished paper, University of Georgia, Athens, GA.

Chan, C. S. (2003). Psychological issues of Asian Americans. In P. Bronstein & K. Quina (Eds.), *Teaching gender and multicultural awareness* (pp. 179–193). Washington, DC: American Psychological Association.

Chan, C. S. (2008). In J. C. Chrisler, C. Golden, & P. D. Rozee (Eds.), *Lectures on the psychology of women* (4th ed., pp. 220–231). Boston, MA: McGraw Hill.

Chan, D. K.-S., Lam, C. B., Chow, S. Y., & Cheung, S. F. (2008). Examining the job-related, psychological, and physical outcomes of workplace sexual harassment: A meta-analytic review. *Psychology of Women Quarterly, 32,* 362–376.

Chance, C., & Fiese, B. H. (1999). Gender-stereotyped lessons about emotion in family narratives. *Narrative Inquiry, 9,* 243–255.

Chang, G. (2016). *Disposable domestics: Immigrant women*

workers in the global economy, 2nd ed. Chicago, IL: Haymarket Books.

Chang, C., & Hitchon, J. C. B. (2004). When does gender count? Further insights into gender schematic processing of female candidates' political advertisements. *Sex Roles, 51,* 197–208.

Chappell, N., McDonald, L., & Stones, M. (2008). *Aging in contemporary Canada* (2nd ed.). Toronto: Pearson Education Canada.

Chapra, A., & Chatterjee, S. (2009, Spring/Summer). Talking race, talking colour. *Canadian Woman Studies/Les cahiers de la femme,* 27, 14–20.

Charles, S. T., & Pasupathi, M. (2003). Age-related patterns of variability in self-descriptions: Implications for everyday affect experience. *Psychology and Aging, 18,* 524–536.

Charles, V. E., Polis, C. B., Sridhara, S. K., & Blum, R. W. (2008). Abortion and long-term mental health outcomes: A systematic review of the evidence. *Contraception, 78,* 436–450.

Chatard, A., Guimond, S., & Selim-begovic, L. (2007). "How good are you in math? " The effect of gender stereotypes on students' recollection of their school marks. *Journal of Experimental Social Psychology, 43,* 1017–1024.

Chatterjee, R. (2018, February 18). *A new survey finds 81% of women have experienced sexual harassment.* The Two Way: NPR. Retrieved October 5, 2021 from https://www.npr.org/sections /thetwo-way/2018/02/21/587671849 /a-new-survey-finds-eighty -percent-of-women-have -experienced-sexual-harassment

Cheeseborough, T., Overstreet, N. & Ward, L. M. (2020). Interpersonal sexual objectification, jezebel stereotype endorsement, and justification of intimate partner violence toward women.

Psychology of Women Quarterly, 44, 203-216.

Chen, W., & Adler, J. L. (2019). Assessment of screen exposure in young children, 1997 to 2014. *JAMA Pediatrics, 173,* 391-393.

Chen, H., Kasen, S., & Cohen, P. (2007). Life values and mental health: A longitudinal study comparing chronically ill women to women without chronic disease. *Psychology & Health, 24,* 1–11.

Cheng, A. W.., Chang, J., O'Brien, J., Budgazad, M. S., & Tsai, J. (2017). Model minority stereotype: Influence on perceived mental health needs of Asian Americans. *Journal of Immigrant Mental Health, 19,* 572–581.

Cherney, I. D. (2005). Children's and adults' recall of sex-stereotyped toy pictures: Effects of presentation and memory task. *Infant and Child Development, 14,* 11–27.

Cherney, I. D., & London, K. (2006). Gender-linked differences in the toys, television shows, computer games, and outdoor activities of 5- to 13-year-old children. *Sex Roles, 54,* 717–726.

Cherng, H-Y., S. & Halpin, P. F. (2016). The importance of minority teachers: Student perceptions of minority versus white teachers. *Educational Researcher, 45,* 407-420.

Chethik, N. (2006). *VoiceMale.* New York: Simon & Schuster.

Cheung, A. M. (2005). Medical aspects of perimenopause and menopause. In D. E. Stewart (Ed.), *Menopause: A mental health practitioner's guide* (pp. 105–142). Washington, DC: American Psychiatric Press.

Chew, L. (2005, April). Breaking the wave of silence: How women are regrouping in the aftermath of the tsunami. *Raising Our Voices Newsletter,* pp. 1–11.

Chin, J. L. (2004). 2003 Division 35 presidential address: Feminist leadership: Feminist visions and diverse voices. *Psychology of Women Quarterly, 28,* 1–8.

Chin, J. L. (2007). Conclusion: Transforming leadership with diverse feminist voices. In J. L. Chin, B. Lott, J. K. Rice, & J. Sanchez-Hucles (Eds.), *Women and leadership: Transforming visions and diverse voices* (pp. 355–362). Malden, MA: Blackwell.

Chinn, S. E. (2004). Feeling her way: Audre Lorde and the power of touch. In B. G. Smith & B. Hutchison (Eds.), *Gendering disability* (pp. 192–215). New Brunswick, NJ: Rutgers University Press.

Chipman, S. F. (2004). Research on the women and mathematics issue: A personal case history. In A. M. Gallagher & J. C. Kaufman (Eds.), *Gender differences in mathematics: An integrative psychological approach* (pp. 1–24). New York: Cambridge University Press.

Chisholm, J., & Greene, B. (2008). Women of color: Perspectives on " multiple identities" in psychological theory, research, and practice. In F. L. Denmark & M. A. Paludi (Eds.), *Psychology of women: A handbook of issues and theories* (2nd ed., pp. 40–69). Westport, CT: Praeger.

Chiu, M., Amartey, A., Wang, X., & Kurdyak, P. (2018). Ethnic differences in mental health status and service utilization: A population-based study in Ontario, Canada. *The Canadian Journal of Psychiatry/ La Revue Canadienne de Psychiatrie, 63,* 481-491.

Chivers, M. L. (2017). The specificity of women's sexual response and its relationship with sexual orientations: A review and ten hypotheses. *Archives of Sexual Behavior, 46,* 1161-1179.

Chodorow, N. J. (1994). *Femininities, masculinities, sexualities: Freud and beyond.* Lexington: University Press of Kentucky.

Chodorow, N. J. (1999). *The power of feelings: Personal meaning in psychoanalysis, gender, and culture.* New Haven, CT: Yale University Press.

Chodorow, N. J. (2000). The psychodynamics of the family. In S. Saguaro (Ed.), *Psychoanalysis and woman: A reader* (pp. 108–127). New York: New York University Press.

Choma, B. L., Foster, M. D., & Radford, E. (2007). Use of objectification theory to examine the effects of a media literacy intervention on women. *Sex Roles, 56*, 581–591.

Chonody, J. M., Killian, M., Gabb, J., & Dunk-West, P. (2020) Relationship quality and sexuality: A latent profile analysis of long-term heterosexual and LGB long-term partnerships. *Journal of Evidence-Based Social Work, 17*, 203-225.

Choo, P., Levine, T., & Hatfield, E. (1996). Gender, love schemas, and reactions to romantic breakups. *Journal of Social Behavior and Personality, 11*, 143–160.

Chow, E. N. (1991). The development of feminist consciousness among Asian American women. In J. Lorber & S. A. Farrell (Eds.), *The social construction of gender* (pp. 255–268). Newbury Park, CA: Sage.

Chrisler, J. C. (2001). Gendered bodies and physical health. In R. K. Unger (Ed.), *Handbook of the psychology of women and gender* (pp. 289–301). New York: Wiley.

Chrisler, J. C. (2007a). Body image issues of women over 50. In V. Muhlbauer & C. J. Chrisler (Eds.), *Women over 50: Psychological perspectives* (pp. 6–25). New York: Springer.

Chrisler, J. C. (2007b, Spring). The new "F word." *The Feminist Psychologist*, pp. 1–2, 30.

Chrisler, J. C. (2017). The menstrual cycle. In F. L. Denmark & M. A. Paludi (Eds.), *Psychology of women: A handbook of issues and theories* (3rd ed., pp. 193-232). Santa Barbara, CA: ABC-CLIO.

Chrisler, J. C. (2008b). PMS as a culture-bound syndrome. In J. C. Chrisler, C. Golden, & P. D. Rozee (Eds.), *Lectures on the psychology of women* (4th ed., pp. 154–171). Boston: McGraw-Hill.

Chrisler, J. C., & Caplan, P. (2002). The strange case of Dr. Jekyll and Ms. Hyde: How PMS became a cultural phenomenon and a psychiatric disorder. *Annual Review of Sex Research, 13*, 274–306.

Chrisler, J. C., & Clapp, S. K. (2008). When the boss is a woman. In M. A. Paludi (Ed.), *The psychology of women at work* (Vol. 1, pp. 39–65). Westport, CT: Praeger.

Chrisler, J. C., & Ferguson, S. (2006). Violence against women as a public health issue. *Annals of the New York Academy of Sciences, 1087*, 235–249.

Chrisler, J. C., & Golden, C. (Eds.). (2018). *Lectures on the psychology of women* (5th ed.). Long Grove, IL: Waveland Press.

Chrisler, J. C., Johnston, I. K., Champagne, N. M., & Preston, K. E. (1994). Menstrual joy: The construct and its consequences. *Psychology of Women Quarterly, 18*, 375–387.

Chrisler, J. C., & Levy, K. B. (1990). The media construct a menstrual monster: A content analysis of PMS articles in the popular press. *Women and Health, 16*, 89–104.

Chrisler, J. C., & McCreary, D. R. (Eds.). (2010). *Handbook of gender research in psychology.* New York: Springer.

Chrisler, J. C., & Segrest, M. (2008). "A" is for activism: Classroom-based approaches to preventing campus violence. In M. A. Paludi (Ed.), *Understanding and preventing campus violence* (pp. 95–98). Westport, CT: Praeger.

Chrisler, J. C., & Smith, C. A. (2004). Feminism and psychology. In M. A. Paludi (Ed.), *Praeger guide to the psychology of gender* (pp. 271–291). Westport, CT: Praeger.

Chrisler, J. C., et al. (2006). The PMS illusion: Social cognition maintains social construction. *Sex Roles, 54*, 371–376.

Christakis, N. A., & Allison, P. D. (2006). Mortality after the hospitalization of a spouse. *New England Journal of Medicine, 354*, 719–730.

Christopher, F. S., & Lloyd, S. A. (2000). Physical and sexual aggression in relationships. In C. Hendrick & S. S. Hendrick (Eds.), *Close relationships* (pp. 331–356). Thousand Oaks, CA: Sage.

Chu, J. (2004). Asian American women's studies courses. In L. T. Võ et al. (Eds.), *Asian American women: The frontiers reader* (pp. 201–213). Lincoln: University of Nebraska Press.

Chuang, S. S., & Moreno, R. P. (Eds.). (2008). *On new shores: Understanding immigrant fathers in North America.* Lanham, MD: Lexington.

Chumlea, W. C., et al. (2003). Age at menarche and racial comparisons in US girls. *Pediatrics, 111*, 110–113.

Ciambrone, D. (2003). *Women's experiences with HIV/AIDS: Mending fractured selves.* Binghamton, NY: Haworth.

Cisneros, S. (2001). Only daughter. In S. M. Shaw & J. Lee (Eds.), *Women's voices, feminist visions* (pp. 301–303). Mountain View, CA: Mayfield.

Claasen, C. (2005). *Whistling women: A study of the lives of older lesbians.* New York: Haworth.

Clark, J., & Zehr, D. (1993). Other women can: Discrepant performance predictions for self and same-sex other. *Journal of College Student Development, 34*, 31–35.

Clark, L., & Tiggemann, M. (2008). Sociocultural and individual psychological predictors of body image in young girls: A prospective study. *Developmental Psychology, 44*, 1124–1134.

Clark, M. D., & Carroll, M. H. (2008). Acquaintance rape

scripts of women and men: Similarities and differences. *Sex Roles, 58,* 616–625.

Clark, M. S., & Graham, S. M. (2005). Do researchers neglect singles? Can we do better? *Psychological Inquiry, 16,* 131–136.

Clark, R. A. (1993). Men's and women's self-confidence in persuasive, comforting, and justificatory communicative tasks. *Sex Roles, 28,* 553–567.

Clark, R. A. (1998). A comparison of topics and objectives in a cross section of young men's and women's everyday conversations. In D. J. Canary & K. Dindia (Eds.), *Sex differences and similarities in communication* (pp. 303–319). Mahwah, NJ: Erlbaum.

Clark, R., Guilmain, J., Saucier, P. K., & Tavarez, J. (2003). Two steps forward, one step back: The presence of female characters and gender stereotyping in award-winning picture books between the 1930s and the 1960s. *Sex Roles, 49,* 439–449.

Clarren, R. (2005, Summer). The green motel. *Ms. Magazine,* pp. 41–45.

Clearfield, M. W., & Nelson, N. M. (2006). Sex differences in mothers' speech and play behavior with 6-, 9-, and 14-month-old infants. *Sex Roles, 54,* 127–137.

Clements, A. M., et al. (2006). Sex differences in cerebral laterality of language and visuospatial processing. *Brain and Language, 98,* 150–158.

Cleveland, J. N. (2008). Age, work, and family: Balancing unique challenges for the twenty-first century. In A. Marcus-Newhall, D. F. Halpern, & S. J. Tan (Eds.), *The changing realities of work and family* (pp. 108–139). Malden, MA: Blackwell.

Cleveland, J. N., Stockdale, M., & Murphy, K. R. (2000). *Women and men in organizations.* Mahwah, NJ: Erlbaum.

Clinchy, B. M., & Norem, J. K. (Eds.). (1998). *The gender and psychology reader.* New York: New York University Press.

Coalition to Stop Violence Against Native Women. (2021). Missing and murdered Indigenous women, girls, and two-spirit. *CSVANW.* Retrieved October 5, 2021 from https://www.csvanw.org/mmiw

Coates, T. J., & Szekeres, G. (2004). A plan for the next generation of HIV prevention research: Seven key policy investigative challenges. *American Psychologist, 59,* 747–757.

Cocco, M. (2004, May 4). Scandal shows women acting like men. *Liberal Opinion Week,* p. 20.

Cochran, S. D., & Mays, V. M. (2006). Estimating prevalence of mental and substance-using disorders among lesbians and gay men from existing national health data. In A. M. Omoto & H. S. Kurtzman (Eds.), *Sexual orientation and mental health* (pp. 143–165). Washington DC: American Psychological Association.

Cochran, S. V. (2010). Emergence and development of the psychology of men. In J. C. Chrisler & D. R. McCreary (Eds.), *Handbook of gender research in psychology* (Vol. 1, pp. 43–58). New York: Springer.

Coffin, F. (1997). Drywall rocker and taper. In M. Martin (Ed.), *Hard-hatted women: Life on the job* (pp. 63–70). Seattle: Seal Press.

Cohen, M. (2008). *College students' attitudes toward feminism and self-identification as feminists.* Unpublished manuscript, SUNY Geneseo, Geneseo, NY.

Colapinto, J. (2000). *As nature made him: The boy who was raised as a girl.* New York: HarperCollins.

Cole, E. R. (2009). Intersectionality and research in psychology. *American Psychologist, 64,* 170–180.

Cole, E. R., et al. (2007). Vive la différence? Genetic explanations for perceived gender differences in nurturance. *Sex Roles, 57,* 211–222.

Cole, J. B., & Guy-Sheftall, B. (2003). *Gender talk: The struggle for women's equality in African American communities.* New York: Ballantine Books.

Coleman, M., Ganong, L., & Leon, K. (2006). Divorce and postdivorce relationships. In A. L. Vangelisti & D. Perlman (Eds.), *The Cambridge handbook of personal relationships* (pp. 157–173). New York: Cambridge University Press.

Colen, S. (1997). "With respect and feelings": Voices of West Indian child care and domestic workers in New York City. In M. Crawford & R. Unger (Eds.), *In our own words: Readings on the psychology of women and gender* (pp. 199–218). New York: McGraw-Hill.

Collaborative Group on Hormonal Factors in Breast Cancer. (2019). Type and timing of menopausal hormone therapy and breast cancer risk: Individual participant meta-analysis of the worldwide epidemiological evidence. *The Lancet, 394,* 1159-1168.

Colley, A., et al. (2002). Gender-linked differences in everyday memory performance: Effort makes the difference. *Sex Roles, 47,* 577–582.

Collins, G. (2009). *When everything changed.* New York: Little, Brown and Company.

Collins, P. H. (1991). The meaning of motherhood in Black culture and Black mother-daughter relationships. In P. Bell-Scott et al. (Eds.), *Double stitch: Black women write about mothers and daughters* (pp. 42–60). Boston: Beacon Press.

Collins, P. H. (2000). *Black feminist thought: Knowledge, consciousness, and the politics of empowerment* (2nd ed.). New York, NY: Routledge.

Collins, P. H. (2006). *From Black power to hip hop.* Philadelphia: Temple.

Collins, P. H. (2015). Intersectionality's definitional dilemmas. *Annual Review of Sociology, 41,* 1-20.

Collins, P. H., & Bilge, S. (2020). *Intersectionality* (2nd ed). Medford, MA: Polity.

Collins, R. L., Strasburger, V. C., Brown, J. D., Donnerstein, E., Lenhart, A., & Ward, L. M. (2017). Sexual media and childhood well-being and health. *Pediatrics, 140*(2), 162-166.

Collins, W. A., & Laursen, B. (2004). Parent-adolescent relationships and influences. In R. M. Lerner & L. Steinberg (Eds.), *Handbook of adolescent psychology* (2nd ed., pp. 331–361). Hoboken, NJ: Wiley.

Collins, W. A., & Laursen, B. (2006). Parent-adolescent relationships. In P. Noller & J. A. Feeney (Eds.), *Close relationships: Functions, forms, and processes* (pp. 111–125). New York: Psychology Press.

Collins, W. A., & Sroufe, L. A. (1999). Capacity for intimate relationships: A developmental construction. In W. Furman, B. B. Brown, & C. Feiring (Eds.), *The development of romantic relationships in adolescence* (pp. 125–147). New York: Cambridge University Press.

Collins, W. A., & Steinberg, L. (2006). Adolescent development in interpersonal context. In W. Damon & R. M. Lerner (Series Eds.), & N. Eisenberg (Vol. Ed.), *Handbook of child psychology: Vol. 3. Social, emotional, and personality development* (6th ed., pp. 1003–1067). Hoboken, NJ: Wiley.

Collinsworth, L. L., Fitzgerald, L. F., & Drasgow, F. (2009). In harm's way: Factors related to psychological distress following sexual harassment. *Psychology of Women Quarterly, 33*, 475–490.

Collison, M. N.-K. (2000, February 3). The " other Asians." *Black Issues in Higher Education*, pp. 20–24.

Coltrane, S. (1998). *Gender and families*. Thousand Oaks, CA: Pine Forge Press.

Coltrane, S., & Adams, M. (2001a). Men, women, and housework. In D. Vannoy (Ed.), *Gender mosaics: Social perspectives* (pp. 145–154). New York: Roxbury.

Coltrane, S., & Adams, M. (2001b). Men's family work: Child-centered fathering and the sharing of domestic labor. In R. Hertz & N. L. Marshall (Eds.), *Working families: The transformation of the American home* (pp. 72–99). Berkeley: University of California Press.

Coltrane, S., & Adams, M. (2008). *Gender and families* (2nd ed.). Lanham, MD: Rowman & Littlefield.

Coltrane, S., & Messineo, M. (2000). The perpetuation of subtle prejudice: Race and gender imagery in 1990s television advertising. *Sex Roles, 42*, 363–389.

Colwell, M. J., & Lindsey, E. W. (2005). Preschool children's pretend and physical play and sex of play partner: Connections to peer competence. *Sex Roles, 52*, 497–509.

Comas-Díaz, L. (2000). An ethnopolitical approach to working with people of color. *American Psychologist, 55*, 1319–1325.

Comiskey, A., Parent, M. C., & Tebbe, E. A. (2020). An inhospitable world: Exploring a model of objectification theory with trans women. *Psychology of Women Quarterly, 44*, 105-116.

Committee on Pediatric Workforce. (2006). Prevention of sexual harassment in the workplace and educational setting. *Pediatrics, 118*, 1752–1756.

Compas, B. E., & Luecken, L. (2002). Psychological adjustment to breast cancer. *Current Directions in Psychological Science, 11*, 111–114.

Compian, L., & Hayward, C. (2003). Gender differences in opposite sex relationships: Interactions with puberty. In C. Hayward (Ed.), *Gender differences at puberty* (pp. 77–92). New York: Cambridge University Press.

Condon, J. T., & Corkindale, C. (1997). The correlates of antenatal attachment in pregnant women. *British Journal of Medical Psychology, 70*, 359–372.

Condry, J. C., & Condry, S. (1976). Sex differences: A study of the eye of the beholder. *Child Development, 47*, 812–819.

Conley, F. K. (1998). *Walking out on the boys*. New York: Farrar, Straus & Giroux.

Connelly, P. J., Freel, E. M., Perry, C., Ewan, J., Touyz, R. M., Currie, G., & Delles, C. (2019). Gender-affirming hormone therapy, vascular health, and cardiovascular disease in transgender adults. *Hypertension, 74*, 1266-1274.

Conrad, S., & Milburn, M. (2001). *Sexual intelligence*. New York: Crown.

Contratto, S., & Rossier, J. (2005). Early trends in feminist therapy theory and practice. In M. Hill & M. Ballou (Eds.), *The foundation and future of feminist therapy* (pp. 7–26). Binghamton, NY: Haworth.

Conway-Turner, K. (1999). Older women of color: A feminist exploration of the intersections of personal, familial, and community life. In J. D. Garner (Ed.), *Fundamentals of feminist gerontology* (pp. 115–130). New York: Haworth.

Conway, M., Alfonsi, G., Pushkar, D., & Giannopoulos, C. (2008). Rumination on sadness and dimensions of communality and agency: Comparing White and visible minority individuals in a Canadian context. *Sex Roles, 58*, 738–749.

Cook, J. A. (2003). Depression, disability, and rehabilitation services for women. *Psychology of Women Quarterly, 27*, 121–129.

Cooper, B. (2018). *Eloquent rage: A Black feminist discovers her superpower*. New York: Picador.

Cooper, J., & Weaver, K. D. (2003). *Gender and computers: Understanding the digital divide*. Mahwah, NJ: Erlbaum.

Cooper, M. (2003). *The psychology of bulimia nervosa*. Oxford, England: Oxford University Press.

Cope-Farrar, K. M., & Kunkel, D. (2002). Sexual messages in teens' favorite prime-time television programs. In J. D. Brown, J. R. Steele, & K. Walsh-Childers (Eds.), *Sexual teens, sexual media: Investigating media's influence on adolescent sexuality* (pp. 59–78). Mahwah, NJ: Erlbaum.

Cooper, M., Reilly, E. E., Siegel, J. A., Coniglio, K., Sadeh-Sharvit, S., Pisetsky, E. M., & Anderson, L. M. (2020). Eating disorders during the COVID-19 pandemic and quarantine: an overview of risks and recommendations for treatment and early intervention, *Eating Disorders*. DOI: 10.1080/10640266.2020.1790271

Copen, C. E., Chandra, A, & Febo-Vazquez, I. (2016). Sexual behavior, sexual attraction, and sexual orientation among adults aged 18-44 in the United States: Data from the 2011-2013 National Survey of Family Growth. *National Health Statistics Reports, 88*, 1-14.

Corbett, C., Hill, C., & St. Rose, A. (2008). *Where the girls are: The facts about gender equity in education.* Washington, DC: American Association for University Women.

Corbett, S. (2007). *The women's war.* Retrieved March 18, 2007, from http://www.truthout.org/docs_2006/031807C.shtml

Corcoran, C. B., & Mahlstedt, D. (1999). Preventing sexual assault on campus: A feminist perspective. In C. Forden, A. E. Hunter, & B. Birns (Eds.), *Readings in the psychology of women* (pp. 289–299). Boston: Allyn & Bacon.

Corcoran, C. B., & Thompson, A. R. (2004). "What's race got to do, got to do with it?" Denial of racism on predominantly White college campuses. In J. L. Chin (Ed.), *The psychology of prejudice and discrimination* (Vol. 1, pp. 137–176). Westport, CT: Praeger.

Correll, S. J., Benard, S., & Paik, I. (2007). Getting a job: Is there a motherhood penalty? *American Journal of Sociology, 112*, 1297–1338.

Cosgrove, L., & Caplan, P. J. (2004). Medicalizing menstrual distress. In P. J. Caplan & L. Cosgrove (Eds.), *Bias in psychiatric diagnosis* (pp. 221–230). Lanham, MD: Jason Aronson.

Cosgrove, L., & Riddle, B. (2001a). *Constructions of femininity and experiences of menstrual distress.* Paper presented at the Society for Menstrual Cycle Research, Avon, CT.

Cosgrove, L., & Riddle, B. (2001b). *Libidinal and bleeding bodies: Deconstructing menstrual cycle research.* Paper presented at the annual meeting of the American Psychological Association, San Francisco.

Costa, D., Cooper, D., & Shierholz, H. (2014). *Facts about immigration and the U.S. economy: Answers to frequently asked questions.* Economic Policy Institute. Retrieved October 3, 2021 from https://files.epi.org/pdf/68129.pdf

Costos, D., Ackerman, R., & Paradis, L. (2002). Recollections of menarche: Communication between mothers and daughters regarding menstruation. *Sex Roles, 46*, 49–45.

Cota, A. A., Reid, A., & Dion, K. L. (1991). Construct validity of a diagnostic ratio measure of gender stereotypes. *Sex Roles, 25*, 225–235.

Cowan, C. P., & Cowan, P. A. (1992). *When partners become parents: The big life change for couples.* New York: Basic Books.

Cowan, G., & Khatchadourian, D. (2003). Empathy, ways of knowing, and interdependence as mediators of gender differences in attitudes toward hate speech and freedom of speech. *Psychology of Women Quarterly, 27*, 300–308.

Cox, A. (2018). *Cracking the boy code: How to understand and talk to boys.* Gabriola Island,

BC, Canada: New Society Publishers.

Cramer, K. M., Million, E., & Perreault, L. A. (2002). Perceptions of musicians: Gender stereotypes and social role theory. *Psychology of Music, 30*, 164–174.

Crandall, C. S., & Eshleman, A. (2003). A justification-suppression model of the expression and experience of prejudice. *Psychological Bulletin, 129*, 414–446.

Crandall, C. S., Nierman, A., & Hebl, M. (2009). Anti-fat prejudice. In T. D. Nelson (Ed.), *Handbook of prejudice, stereotyping, and discrimination* (pp. 469–487). New York: Psychology Press.

Craske, M. C., & Barlow, D. H. (2008). Panic disorder and agoraphobia. In D. H. Barlow (Ed.), *Clinical handbook of psychological disorders* (pp. 1–64). New York: Guilford.

Crawford, D., & Ostrove, J. M. (2003). Representation of disability and the interpersonal relationships of women with disabilities. In M. E. Banks & E. Kaschak (Eds.), *Women with visible and invisible disabilities* (pp. 179–194). New York: Haworth.

Crawford, M. (1995). *Talking difference: On gender and language.* Thousand Oaks, CA: Sage.

Crawford, M. (2001). Gender and language. In R. K. Unger (Ed.), *Handbook of the psychology of women and gender* (pp. 228–244). New York: Wiley.

Crawford, M. (2010). *Sex trafficking in South Asia: Telling Maya's story.* New York: Routledge.

Crawford, M., & MacLeod, M. (1990). Gender in the college classroom: An assessment of the "chilly climate" for women. *Sex Roles, 23*, 101–122.

Crenshaw, K. (1989). Demarginalizing the intersection of race and sex: A black feminist critique of antidiscrimination doctrine, feminist theory and antiracist politics. *University of Chicago Legal Forum: Vol. 1989: Iss. 1*, Article 8.

Crenshaw, K. W. (2007). Framing affirmative action. *Michigan Law Review First Impressions, 105*, 123-133.

Crenshaw, K. (2017). *On intersectionality: Essential writings*. The New Press: New York.

Crick, N. R., Casas, J. F., & Nelson, D. A. (2002). Toward a more comprehensive understanding of peer maltreatment: Studies of relational victimization. *Current Directions in Psychological Science, 11*, 98–101.

Crick, N. R., & Nelson, D. A. (2002). Relational and physical victimization within friendships: Nobody told me there'd be friends like these. *Journal of Abnormal Child Psychology, 30*, 599–607.

Crick, N. R., & Rose, A. J. (2000). Toward a gender-balanced approach to the study of social-emotional development: A look at relational aggression. In P. M. Miller & E. K. Scholnick (Eds.), *Toward a feminist developmental psychology* (pp. 153–168). New York: Routledge.

Crick, N. R., & Zahn-Waxler, C. (2003). The development of psychopathology in females and males: Current progress and future challenges. *Development and Psychopathology, 15*, 719–742.

Crick, N. R., et al. (2004). Relational aggression in early childhood. In M. Putallaz & K. L. Bierman (Eds.), *Aggression, antisocial behavior, and violence among girls* (pp. 71–89). New York: Guilford.

Crimmins, E. M., Kim, J. K., & Hagedorn, A. (2002). Life with and without disease: Women experience more of both. In S. B. Laditka (Ed.), *Health expectations for older women: International perspectives* (pp. 47–59). Binghamton, NY: Haworth.

Critchley, H. O. D., Babayev, E., Bulun, S. E., Clark, S., Garcia-Grau, I., Gregersen, P., Kilcoyne, A., Kim, J-Y., J., Lavender, M., Marsh, E., Matteson, K. A., Maybin, J. A., Metz, C. N., Moreno, I., Silk, K., Sommer, M., Simon, C., Tariyal, R., Taylor, H. S., Wagner, G. P., & Griffith, L. G. (2020). Menstruation: Science and society. *American Journal of Obstetrics and Gynecology, 223*, 624-664.

Crocker, J., & Park, L. E. (2004a). The costly pursuit of self-esteem. *Psychological Bulletin, 130*, 292–414.

Crocker, J., & Park, L. E. (2004b). Reaping the benefits of pursuing self-esteem without the costs? *Psychological Bulletin, 130*, 430–434.

Crockett, L. J., Raffaeli, M., & Moilanen, K. (2002). Adolescent sexuality: Behavior and meaning. In G. R. Adams & M. Berzonsky (Eds.), *Blackwell handbook of adolescence*. Oxford, England: Blackwell.

Croll, E. (2000). *Endangered daughters: Discrimination and development in Asia*. New York: Routledge.

Crombie, G., et al. (2005). Predictors of young adolescents' math grades and course enrollment intentions: Gender similarities and differences. *Sex Roles, 52*, 351–367.

Crompton, S. (2010). Living with disability series: Life satisfaction of working-age women with disabilities. *Canadian Social Trends*. Catalogue no. 11-008-X, Statistics Canada. Retrieved January 6, from http://www.statcan.gc.ca/pub/ 11-008-x/2010001/article/11124-eng.htm

Crooks, R., & Baur, K. (2005). *Our sexuality* (9th ed.). Belmont, CA: Wadsworth.

Crooks, R., & Baur, K. (2017). *Our sexuality* (13th ed.). Cengage Learning.

Crosby, F. J. (2004). *Affirmative action is dead; long live affirmative action*. New Haven, CT: Yale University Press.

Crosby, F. J. (2008). Sex discrimination at work. In J. C. Chrisler, C. Golden, & P. D. Rozee (Eds.), *Lectures on the psychology of women* (4th ed., pp. 42–57). Boston: McGraw-Hill.

Crosby, F. J., & Sabattini, L. (2006). Family and work balance. In J. Worell & C. D. Goodheart (Eds.), *Handbook of girls' and women's psychological health: Gender and well-being across the life span* (pp. 350–358). New York: Oxford University Press.

Crosby, F. J., Iyer, A., Clayton, S., & Downing, R. A. (2003). Affirmative action: Psychological data and the policy debates. *American Psychologist, 58*, 93–115.

Crosby, F. J., Iyer, A., & Sincharoen, S. (2006). Understanding affirmative action. *Annual Review of Psychology, 57*, 585–611.

Crose, R. (2003). Teaching the psychology of later life. In P. Bronstein & K. Quina (Eds.), *Teaching gender and multicultural awareness* (pp. 271–283). Washington, DC: American Psychological Association.

Cross, S. E. (2001). Training the scientists and engineers of tomorrow: A person-situation approach. *Journal of Applied Social Psychology, 31*, 296–323.

Cross, S. E., & Vick, N. V. (2001). The interdependent self-construal and social support: The case of persistence in engineering. *Personality and Social Psychology Bulletin, 27*, 820–832.

Crouch, S. R., Waters, E., McNair, R., Power, J., & Davis, E. (2014). Parent-reported measures of child health and wellbeing in same-sex parent families: A cross-sectional survey. *BMC Public Health, 14*, Article 635.

Crowley, K., Callanan, M. A., Tenenbaum, H. R., & Allen, E. (2001). Parents explain more often to boys than to girls during shared scientific thinking. *Psychological Science, 12*, 258–261.

Cruikshank, M. (2013). *Learning to be old* (3rd ed.). Lanham, MD: Rowman & Littlefield.

Csoboth, C. T. (2003). Women's health issues. In L. M. Cohen,

D. E. McChargue, & F. L. Collins, Jr. (Eds.), *The health psychology handbook* (pp. 469–484). Thousand Oaks, CA: Sage.

Cuddy, A. J. C., & Fiske, S. T. (2004). When professionals become mothers, warmth doesn't cut the ice. *Journal of Social Issues, 60,* 701–718.

Cuddy, A. J. C., Norton, M. I., & Fiske, S. T. (2005). This old stereotype: The pervasiveness and persistence of the elderly stereotype. *Journal of Social Issues, 61,* 267–285.

Cull, P. (1997). Carpenter. In M. Martin (Ed.), *Hard-hatted women: Life on the job* (pp. 45–54). Seattle: Seal Press.

Cummings, N. A., & O'Donohue, W. T. (2008). *Eleven blunders that cripple psychotherapy in America.* New York: Routledge.

Cunningham, J., & Macan, T. (2007). Effects of applicant pregnancy on hiring decisions and interview ratings. *Sex Roles, 57,* 497–508.

Cunningham, B. C., Ralph, J., Mulvaney Hoyer, K, & Sparks, D. (2015). *Gender differences in science, technology, engineering, and mathematics (STEM) interest, credits earned, and NAEP performance in the 12th grade.* National Center for Education Statistics. Retrieved October 3, 2021 from https://nces.ed.gov/pubs2015/2015075.pdf

Cushner, K. (2003). *Human diversity in action.* Boston: McGraw-Hill.

Cutrona, C. E., Russell, D. W., & Gardner, K. A. (2005). The relationship enhancement mode of social support. In T. A. Revenson, K. Kayser, & G. Bodenmann (Eds.), *Couples coping with stress* (pp. 73–95). Washington, DC: American Psychological Association.

Cuttler, C., Mischley, L. K., & Sexton, M. (2016). Sex differences in cannabis use and effects: A cross-sectional survey of cannabis users. *Cannabis and Cannabinoid Research, 1,* 166–175.

Cyranowski, J. M., & Frank, E. (2006). Targeting populations of women for prevention and treatment of depression. In C. M. Mazure & G. P. Keita (Eds.), *Understanding depression* (pp. 71–112). Washington, DC: American Psychological Association.

D'Adesky, A. (Eds.). (2004). *Moving mountains: The race to treat global AIDS.* New York: Verso.

D'Augelli, A. R. (2002). Mental health problems among lesbian, gay, and bisexual youths ages 14 to 21. *Clinical Child Psychology and Psychiatry, 7,* 1359–1045.

D'Augelli, A. R. (2003). Lesbian and bisexual female youths aged 14 to 21: Developmental challenges and victimization experiences. *Journal of Lesbian Studies, 7,* 9–29.

D'Augelli, A. R., Pilkington, N. W., & Hershberger, S. L. (2002). Incidence and mental health impact of sexual orientation victimization of lesbian, gay, and bisexual youths in high school. *School Psychology Quarterly, 17,* 148–167.

Dahlberg, K., Berg, M., & Lundgren, I. (1999). Commentary: Studying maternal experiences of childbirth. *Birth, 26,* 215–225.

Daigle, L. E. (2021). *Special issue:* Research on sexual violence in the #MeToo era: Prevention and innovative methodologies. *American Journal of Criminal Justice, 46,* 2-5.

Daly, F. Y. (2001). Perspectives of Native American women on race and gender. In G. Kirk & M. Okazawa-Rey (Eds.), *Women's lives: Multicultural perspectives* (2nd ed., pp. 60–68). Mountain View, CA: Mayfield.

Daminger, A. (2019). The cognitive dimension of household labor. *American Sociological Review, 84,* 609-633.

Dark-Freudeman, A. (2010). Successful aging. In J. C. Cavanaugh & C. K. Cavanaugh (Eds.), *Aging in America* (Vol. 1, pp. 232–254). Santa Barbara, CA: ABC-CLIO.

Dasgupta, N., & Rivera, L. M. (2006a). From automatic antigay prejudice to behavior: The moderating role of conscious beliefs about gender and behavioral control. *Journal of Personality and Social Psychology, 91,* 268–280.

Dasgupta, N., & Rivera, L. M. (2006b). When social context matters: The influence of long-term contact and short-term exposure to admired outgroup members on implicit attitudes and behavioral intentions. *Social Cognition, 26,* 112–123.

Daubman, K. A., Heatherington, L., & Ahn, A. (1992). Gender and the self-presentation of academic achievement. *Sex Roles, 27,* 187–204.

Davey, F. H. (1998). Young women's expected and preferred patterns of employment and child care. *Sex Roles, 38,* 95–102.

David, H. P., Dytrych, Z., & Matejcek, Z. (2003). Born unwanted: Observations from the Prague study. *American Psychologist, 58,* 224–229.

David, H. P., Dytrych, Z., Matejcek, Z., & Schüller, V. (Eds.). (1988). *Born unwanted: Developmental effects of denied abortion.* New York: Springer.

David, H. P., & Lee, E. (2001). Abortion and its health effects. In J. Worell (Ed.), *Encyclopedia of women and gender* (pp. 1–14). San Diego, CA: Academic Press.

David, H. P., & Russo, N. F. (2003). Psychology, population, and reproductive behavior. *American Psychologist, 58,* 193–196.

Davies, C. (2002). When is a map not a map? Task and language in spatial interpretation with digital map displays. *Applied Cognitive Psychology, 16,* 273–285.

Davies, P. G., & Spencer, S. J. (2004). The gender-gap artifact: Women's underperformance in quantitative domains through the lens of stereotype threat. In A. M. Gallagher & J. C. Kaufman (Eds.), *Gender differences in mathematics: An integrative psychological approach* (pp. 172–188). New York: Cambridge University Press.

Davies, P. G., Spencer, S. J., & Steele, C. M. (2005). Clearing the air: Identity safety moderates the effects of stereotype threat on women's leadership aspirations. *Journal of Personality and Social Psychology, 88*, 276–287.

Davis, J. T. M., Hines, M. (2020). How large are gender differences in toy preferences? A systematic review and meta-analysis of toy preference research. *Archives of Sexual Behavior, 49*, 373–394.

Davis, K. C., George, W. H., & Norris, J. (2004). Women's responses to unwanted sexual advances: The role of alcohol and inhibition conflict. *Psychology of Women Quarterly, 22*, 333–334.

Davison, T. F., & McCabe, M. P. (2005). Relationship between men's and women's body image and their psychological, social, and sexual functioning. *Sex Roles, 52*, 463–475.

Davison, K. K., Susman, E. J., & Birch, L. L. (2003). Percent body fat at age 5 predicts earlier pubertal development among girls at age 9. *Pediatrics, 111*, 815–821.

Dayhoff, S. A. (1983). Sexist language and person perceptions: Evaluation of candidates from newspaper articles. *Sex Roles, 9*, 543–555.

d'Entremont, D. (2020). Yukon releases MMIWG2S+ strategy in response to national inquiry. *CBC News*. Retrieved October 5, 2021 from https://www.cbc.ca /news/canada/north/yukon -mmiwg2s-strategy-national -inquiry-1.5835588

De Backer, C. J. S., Nelissen, M., & Fisher, M. L. (2007). Let's talk about sex: A study on the recall of gossip about potential mates and sexual rivals. *Sex Roles, 56*, 781–791.

de Beauvoir, S. (1961). *The second sex*. New York: Bantam Books.

de Blok, C. J. M., Wiepjes, C. M., Nota, N. M., van Engelen, K., Adank, M. A., Dreijerink, K. M. A., et al. (2019). Breast cancer risk in transgender people receiving hormone treatment: Nationwide cohort study in the Netherlands. *BMJ, 365*:11652.

de Guzman, M. R. T., et al. (2004). Gender and age differences in Brazilian children's friendship nominations and peer sociometric ratings. *Sex Roles, 51*, 217–225.

De las Fuentes, C., Barón, A., Jr., & Vásquez, M. J. T. (2003). Teaching Latino psychology. In P. Bronstein & K. Quina (Eds.), *Teaching gender and multicultural awareness* (pp. 207–220). Washington, DC: American Psychological Association.

De Lisi, R., & McGillicuddy-De Lisi, A. (2002). Sex differences in mathematical abilities and achievement. In A. McGillicuddy-De Lisi & R. De Lisi (Eds.), *Biology, society, and behavior: The development of sex differences in cognition* (pp. 155–181). Westport, CT: Ablex Publishing.

de Marneffe, D. (2004). *Maternal desire: On children, love, and the inner life*. New York: Little, Brown.

de Vries, D. A., Peter, J., de Graaf, H., & Nikken, P. (2016). Adolescents' social network site use, peer appearance-related feedback, and body dissatisfaction: Testing a mediation model. *Journal of Youth and Adolescence, 45*, 211-224.

de Vries, E., Kathard, H., & Muller, A. (2020). Debate: Why should gender-affirming health care be included in health science curricula? *BMC Medical Education, 20*:51.

DealsInsight Team. (2020, April 15). *Tips for women to effectively manage work-from-home and family*. DealsInsight. Retrieved

October 3, 2021 from https:// www.dealsinsight.com/manage -work-from-home-and-family/

Deaux, K. (1979). Self-evaluation of male and female managers. *Sex Roles, 5*, 571–580.

Deaux, K. (1995). How basic can you be? The evolution of research on gender stereotypes. *Journal of Social Issues, 51*, 11–20.

Deaux, K. (2001). Autobiographical perspectives. In A. N. O'Connell (Ed.), *Models of achievement: Reflections of eminent women in psychology* (Vol. 3, pp. 202–218). Mahwah, NJ: Erlbaum.

Deaux, K. (2006). *To be an immigrant*. New York: Russell Sage.

DeBare, D. (2009). The evolution of the shelter movement. In E. Stark & E. S. Buzawa (Eds.), *Violence against women in families and relationships* (Vol. 1, pp. 15–32). Santa Barbara, CA: ABC-CLIO.

DeBlaere, C., & Moradi, B. (2008). Structures of the schedules of racist and sexist events: Confirmatory factor analyses of African American women's responses. *Psychology of Women Quarterly, 32*, 83–94.

Deckman, S. L., Fulmer, E. F., Kirby, K., Hoover, K., & Mackall, A. S. (2018). Numbers are just not enough: A critical analysis of race, gender, and sexuality in elementary and middle school health textbooks, *Educational Studies, 54*, 285-302.

Deevey, S. (2000). Cultural variation in lesbian bereavement experiences in Ohio. *Journal of the Gay and Lesbian Medical Association, 4*, 9–17.

DeFour, D. C. (2008). Challenges for women of color. In M. A. Paludi (Ed.), *The psychology of women at work: Challenges and solutions for our female workforce* (pp. 109–119). Westport, CT: Praeger.

DeFour, D. C., David, G., Diaz, F. J., & Thompkins, S. (2003). The interface of race, sex, sexual orientation, and ethnicity in understanding sexual harassment. In M. A. Paludi & C. A. Paludi (Eds.), *Academic and workplace sexual harassment* (pp. 31–45). Westport, CT: Praeger.

DeFrain, J., & Olson, D. H. (1999). Contemporary family patterns and relationships. In M. Sussman, S. K. Steinmetz, & G. W. Peterson (Eds.), *Handbook of marriage and the family* (2nd ed., pp. 309–326). New York: Plenum.

Defreyne, J., Elaut, E., Heijer, M. D., Kreukels, B., Fisher, A. D., & T'Sjoen, G. (2021). Sexual orientation in transgender individuals: Results from the longitudinal ENIGI study. *International Journal of Impotence Research.* https://doi.org/10.1038/s41443-020-00402-7

Degortes, D., Santonastaso, P., Zanetti, T., Tenconi, E., Veronese, A., Favaro, A. (2014). Stressful life events and binge eating disorder. *European Eating Disorders Review, 22,* 378-382.

DeKeseredy, W. S., & Schwartz, M. D. (1998). *Woman abuse on campus: Results from the Canadian national survey.* Thousand Oaks, CA: Sage.

DeKeseredy, W. S., & Schwartz, M. D. (2002). The incidence and prevalence of woman abuse in Canadian courtship. In K. M. J. McKenna & J. Larkin (Eds.), *Violence against women: New Canadian perspectives* (pp. 93–122). Toronto, ON: Inanna Publications and Education.

DeLamater, J., & Hyde, J. S. (2004). Conceptual and theoretical issues in studying sexuality in close relationships. In J. H. Harvey, A. Wenzel, & S. Sprecher (Eds.), *The handbook of sexuality in close relationships* (pp. 7–30). Mahwah, NJ: Erlbaum.

Delaney, C. (2000). Making babies in a Turkish village. In J. DeLoache & A. Gottlieb (Eds.), *A world of babies: Imagined childcare guides for seven societies* (pp. 117–144). New York: Cambridge University Press.

Delaney, J., Lupton, M. J., & Toth, E. (1988). *The curse: A cultural history of menstruation* (2nd ed.). Urbana: University of Illinois Press.

Delk, J. L., Madden, R. B., Livingston, M., & Ryan, T. T. (1986). Adult perceptions of the infant as a function of gender labeling and observer gender. *Sex Roles, 15,* 527–534.

Dell, D. L. (2005). Gynecologic aspects of perimenopause and menopause. In D. E. Stewart (Ed.), *Menopause: A mental health practitioner's guide* (pp. 143–164). Washington, DC: American Psychiatric Press.

DeLoache, J., & Gottlieb, A. (Eds.). (2000). *A world of babies.* New York: Cambridge University Press.

Demarest, J., & Glinos, F. (1992). Gender and sex role differences in young adult reactions towards " newborns" in a pretend situation. *Psychological Reports, 71,* 727–737.

DeMarni Cromer, L., & Freyd, J. J. (2007). What influences believing child sexual abuse disclosures? The roles of depicted memory, persistence, participant gender, trauma history, and sexism. *Psychology of Women Quarterly, 31,* 13–22.

Denham, S. A. (1998). *Emotional development in young children.* New York: Guilford.

Denmark, F. L. (2002, March). *Myths of aging.* Paper presented at the annual convention of the Southeastern Psychological Association.

Denmark, F. L., & Paludi, M. A. (Eds.). (2017). *Psychology of women: A handbook of issues and theories* (3rd ed.). Santa Barbara, CA: ABC-CLIO.

Denmark, F. L., Klara, M., Baron, E., & Cambareri-Fernandez, L. (2008). Historical development of the psychology of women. In F. L. Denmark & M. A. Paludi (Eds.), *Psychology of women:*

A handbook of issues and theories (2nd ed., pp. 3–39). Westport, CT: Praeger.

Denner, J., & Griffin, A. (2003). The role of gender in enhancing program strategies for healthy youth development. In F. Villarruel, D. F. Perkins, L. M. Borden, & J. G. Keith (Eds.), *Community youth development* (pp. 118–144). Thousand Oaks, CA: Sage.

Denner, J., & Guzmán, B. L. (Eds.). (2006). *Latina girls: Voices of adolescent strength in the United States.* New York: New York University Press.

Dennerstein, L., Alexander, J. L., & Kotz, K. (2003). The menopause and sexual functioning: A review of the population-based studies. *Annual Review of Sex Research, 14,* 64–82.

Dennis, M. K., & Bell, F. M. (2020). Indigenous women, water protectors, and reciprocal responsibilities. *Social Work, 65,* 378-386.

Dennis, M. K., & Brewer, J. P. (2017). Rearing generations: Lakota grandparents' commitment to family and community. *Journal of Cross Cultural Gerontology, 32,* 95-113.

Denton, T. C. (1990). Bonding and supportive relationships among black professional women: Rituals of restoration. *Journal of Organizational Behavior, 11,* 447–457.

Department of Health and Family Planning. (2010). *Health status of Kerala.* Retrieved December 12, 2010, from http://www.kerala.gov.in/dept_health/healthstatus.htm

DePaulo, B. M. (2006). *Singled out: How singles are stereotyped, stigmatized, and ignored, and still live happily ever after.* New York: St. Martin's Press.

DePaulo, B. M., & Morris, W. L. (2005). Singles in society and in science. *Psychological Inquiry, 16,* 57–83.

DePaulo, B. M., & Morris, W. L. (2006). The unrecognized

stereotyping and discrimination against singles. *Current Directions in Psychological Science, 15,* 251–254.

DePaulo, J. R., Jr., & Horvitz, L. A. (2002). *Understanding depression.* New York: Wiley.

Deprez, L. S., Butler, S. S., & Smith, R. J. (2004). Securing higher education for women on welfare in Maine. In V. Polakow, S. S. Butler, L. S. Deprez, & P. Kahn (Eds.), *Shut out: Low income mothers and higher education in post-welfare America* (pp. 217–236). Albany, NY: State University of New York Press.

Derlega, V., Winstead, B. A., Oldfield, E. C., & Barbee, A. P. (2003). Close relationships and social support in coping with HIV: A test of sensitive interaction systems theory. *AIDS and Behavior, 7,* 119–129.

Derry, P. S. (2004). Coping with distress during perimenopause. In J. C. Chrisler (Ed.), *From menarche to menopause: The female body in feminist therapy* (pp. 165–177). New York: Haworth.

des Rivieres-Pigeon, C., Saurel-Cubizolles, M., & Lelong, N. (2004). Considering a simple strategy for detection of women at risk of psychological distress after childbirth. *Birth, 31,* 34–42.

Désert, M., & Leyens, J. P. (2006). Social comparisons across cultures I: Gender stereotypes in high and low power cultures. In S. Guimond (Ed.), *Social comparison and social psychology* (pp. 303–317). New York: Cambridge University Press.

Desmarais, S., & Curtis, J. (2001). Gender and perceived income entitlement among full-time workers: Analysis for Canadian national samples, 1984 and 1994. *Basic and Applied Social Psychology, 23,* 157–168.

DeSouza, E. (2008). Workplace incivility, sexual harassment, and racial microaggression: The interface of three literatures. In M. A. Paludi (Ed.), *The psychology of women at work: Challenges and solutions for our female workforce* (Vol. 2, pp. 65–83). Westport, CT: Praeger.

DeSouza, E., & Fansler, A. G. (2003). Contrapower sexual harassment: A survey of students and faculty members. *Sex Roles, 48,* 529–542.

Deutsch, F. M. (1999). *Halving it all: How equally shared parenting works.* Cambridge, MA: Harvard University Press.

Deutsch, F. M. (2001). Equally shared parenting. *Current Directions in Psychological Science, 10,* 25–28.

Deutsch, F. M., & Saxon, S. E. (1998a). The double standard of praise and criticism for mothers and fathers. *Psychology of Women Quarterly, 22,* 665–683.

Deutsch, F. M., & Saxon, S. E. (1998b). Traditional ideologies, nontraditional lives. *Sex Roles, 38,* 331–362.

Deutsch, F. M., Servis, L. J., & Payne, J. D. (2001). Paternal participation in child care and its effects on children's self-esteem and attitudes toward gendered roles. *Journal of Family Issues, 22,* 1000–1024.

Deveny, K. (2008, October 6). So where's the epidemic? *Newsweek,* p. 61.

Devos, T., & Banaji, M. R. (2005). American = White? *Journal of Personality and Social Psychology, 88,* 447–466.

DeWeerdt, S. (2020). A global drive toward elimination. *Nature, 580,* S2-S4.

Dey, J. G., & Hill, C. (2007). Behind the pay gap. Washington, DC: American Association of University Women Educational Foundation.

Dhruvarajan, V. (1992). Conjugal power among first generation Hindu Asian Indians in a Canadian city. *International Journal of Sociology of the Family, 22,* 1–33.

Diamond, L. M. (2002). What we got wrong about sexual identity development: Unexpected findings from a longitudinal study of young women. In A. Omoto & H. Kurtz-man (Eds.), *Recent research on sexual orientation.* Washington, DC: American Psychological Association.

Diamond, L. M. (2004). Emerging perspectives on distinctions between romantic love and sexual desire. *Current Directions in Psychological Science, 13,* 116–119.

Diamond, L. M. (2005). A new view of lesbian subtypes: Stable versus fluid identity trajectories over an 8-year period. *Psychology of Women Quarterly, 29,* 119–128.

Diamond, L. M. (2006). The intimate same-sex relationships of sexual minorities. In A. L. Vangelisti & D. Perlman (Eds.), *The Cambridge handbook of personal relationships* (pp. 293–312). New York: Cambridge University Press.

Diamond, L. M. (2007). A dynamical systems approach to the development and expression of female same-sex sexuality. *Perspectives on Psychological Science, 2,* 142–157.

Diamond, L. M. (2008). *Sexual fluidity: Understanding women's love and desire.* Cambridge, MA: Harvard University Press.

Diamond, L. M. (2008). Female bisexuality from adolescence to adulthood: Results from a 10-year longitudinal study. *Developmental Psychology, 44*(1), 5-14.

Diamond, L. M., & Blair, K. L. (2018). The intimate relationships of sexual and gender minorities. In A. V. Vangelisti, & D. Perlman (Eds.), *The Cambridge Handbook of Personal Relationships* (pp. 199-210). Cambridge University Press.

Diamond, L. M., & Rosky, C. J. (2016). Scrutinizing immutability: Research on sexual orientation and U.S. legal advocacy for sexual minorities. *Journal of Sex Research, 53,* 363-391.

Diamond, M. (1996). Prenatal predisposition and the clinical management of some pediatric conditions. *Journal of Sex and Marital Therapy, 22*, 139–147.

DiClemente, R. J., & Crosby, R. A. (2006). Preventing HIV infection in adolescents: What works for uninfected teens. In M. E. Lyon & L. J. D'Angelo (Eds.), *Teenagers, HIV, and AIDS: Insights from youths living with the virus* (pp. 143–161). Westport, CT: Praeger.

Diekman, A. B., Eagly, A. H., Mladinic, A., & Ferreira, M. C. (2005). Dynamic stereotypes about women and men in Latin America and the United States. *Journal of Cross-Cultural Psychology, 36*, 209–226.

Diekman, A. B., & Goodfriend, W. (2006). Rolling with the changes: A role congruity perspective on gender norms. *Psychology of Women Quarterly, 30*, 369–383.

Diekman, A. B., McDonald, M., & Gardner, W. L. (2000). Love means never having to be careful: The relationship between reading romance novels and safe sex behavior. *Psychology of Women Quarterly, 24*, 179–188.

Diekman, A. B., & Murnen, S. K. (2004). Learning to be little women and little men: The inequitable gender equality of nonsexist children's literature. *Sex Roles, 50*, 373–385.

DiFranza, J. R., & Richmond, J. B. (2008). Let the children be heard: Lessons from studies of the early onset of tobacco addiction. *Pediatrics, 121*, 623–624.

Dill, K. E. (2009). Violent video games, rape myth acceptance, and negative attitudes toward women. In E. Stark & E. S. Buzawa (Eds.), *Violence against women in families and relationships: The media and cultural attitudes* (Vol. 4, pp. 135–140). Santa Barbara, CA: Praeger.

Dill, K. E., Gentile, D. A., Richter, W. A., & Dill, J. C. (2005). Violence, sex, race, and age in popular video games: A content analysis. In E. Cole & J. H. Daniel (Eds.),

Featuring females: Feminist analyses of media (pp. 115–130). Washington, DC: American Psychological Association.

Dill, K. E., & Thill, K. P. (2007). Video game characteristics and the socialization of gender roles: Young people's perceptions mirror sexist media depictions. *Sex Roles, 57*, 851–864.

Dillaway, H. E. (2005). (Un)changing menopausal bodies: How women think and act in the face of a reproductive transition and gendered beauty ideals. *Sex Roles, 53*, 1–17.

Dillaway, H. E. (2007). "Am I similar to my mother? " How women make sense of menopause using family background. *Women & Health, 46*, 79–97.

Dillon, K. (2000). Sizing myself up: Tales of a plus-size model. In O. Edut (Ed.), *Body outlaws: Young women write about body image and identity* (pp. 232–239). Seattle: Seal Press.

Dindia, K., & Allen, M. (1992). Sex differences in self-disclosure: A meta-analysis. *Psychological Bulletin, 112*, 106–124.

Dindia, K., & Emmers-Sommer, T. M. (2006). What partners do to maintain their close relationships. In P. Noller & J. A. Feeney (Eds.), *Close relationships: Functions, forms, and processes* (pp. 305–324). New York: Psychology Press.

Dingel, M. J. (2006). Gendered experiences in the science classroom. In J. M. Bystydzienski & S. R. Bird (Eds.), *Removing barriers: Women in academic science, technology, engineering, and mathematics* (pp. 161–176). Bloomington: Indiana University Press.

Dingfelder, S. F. (2004, February). Programmed for psychopathology? *Monitor on Psychology*, p. 56.

Dion, K. K., & Dion, K. L. (2001a). Gender and cultural adaptation in immigrant families. *Journal of Social Issues, 57*, 511–521.

Dion, K. K., & Dion, K. L. (2001b). Gender and relationships. In R.

K. Unger (Ed.), *Handbook of the psychology of women and gender* (pp. 256–271). New York: Wiley.

Dion, K. K., & Dion, K. L. (2004). Gender, immigrant generation, and ethnocultural identity. *Sex Roles, 50*, 347–355.

Dion, K. L. (2003). Prejudice, racism, and discrimination. In I. B. Weiner (Ed.), *Handbook of psychology* (Vol. 6, pp. 507–536). Hoboken, NJ: Wiley.

Dion, K. L., & Dion, K. K. (1993). Gender and ethnocultural comparisons in styles of love. *Psychology of Women Quarterly, 17*, 463–473.

DiPietro, J. A. (2004). The role of prenatal maternal stress in child development. *Current Directions in Psychological Science, 13*, 71–74.

D'Lima, T., Solotaroff, J. L., Pande, R. P. (2020). For the sake of family and tradition: Honour killings in India and Pakistan. *ANTYAJAA: Indian Journal of Women and Social Change, 5*, 22-39.

Djen, V. (2007, Anniversary Issue). Finding Clara: A new database of women artists. *Women in the Arts*, p. 42.

Dobbert, D. L. (2004). *Halting the sexual predators among us*. Westport, CT: Praeger.

Dodd, E. H., Giuliano, T. A., Boutell, J. M., & Moran, B. A. (2001). Respected or rejected: Perceptions of women who confront sexist remarks. *Sex Roles, 45*, 567–577.

Dodgen, C. E. (2005). *Nicotine dependence*. Washington, DC: American Psychological Association.

Dodson, J. E. (1997). Conceptualizations of African American families. In H. P. McAdoo (Ed.), *Black families* (3rd ed., pp. 67–82). Thousand Oaks, CA: Sage.

Dodwell, K. (2003). Marketing and teaching a women's literature course to culturally conservative students. *Feminist Teacher, 14*, 234–247.

Dolan, K. A. (2005). *Lesbian women and sexual health: The social* construction of risk and susceptibility. New York: Haworth.

Doll, L. S., Koenig, L. J., & Purcell, D. W. (2004). Child sexual abuse and adult sexual risk: Where are we now? In L. J. Koenig, L. S. Doll, A. O'Leary, & W. Pequegnat (Eds.), *From child sexual abuse to adult sexual risk: Trauma, revictimization, and intervention* (pp. 3–10). Washington, DC: American Psychological Association.

Dookie, I. J. (2004). Canada. In K. Malley-Morrison (Ed.), *International perspectives on family violence and abuse* (pp. 431–449). Mahwah, NJ: Erlbaum.

Douglas, E. (2001, July/August). HIV/AIDS: A new report from CDC, the response from Congress, and psychology's role in the solution. *Psychological Science Agenda*, p. 12.

Douglas, S. J., & Michaels, M. W. (2004). *The mommy myth: The idealization of motherhood and how it has undermined women.* New York: Free Press.

Dowdall, J. (2003, June 20). Gender and the administrative search. *Chronicle of Higher Education*, p. C3.

Dowling, C. (2000). *The frailty myth: Women approaching physical equality.* New York: Random House.

Doyle, J. A. (1995). *The male experience* (3rd ed.). Madison, WI: Brown & Benchmark.

Drake, P., Driscoll, A. K., & Mathews, T. J. (2018). Cigarette smoking during pregnancy: United States, 2016. *National Center for Health Statistics Data Brief No. 305.* Retrieved October 4, 2021 from https://www.cdc.gov/nchs/data/databriefs/db305.pdf

Dryden, C. (1999). *Being married, doing gender.* London: Routledge.

Dubé, E. M., Savin-Williams, R. C., & Diamond, L. M. (2001). Intimacy development, gender, and ethnicity among sexual-minority youths. In A. R. D'Augelli & C. J. Patterson (Eds.), *Lesbian,*

gay, and bisexual identities and youth (pp. 129–152). New York: Oxford University Press.

Dube, K. (2004, June 18). What feminism means to today's undergraduates. *Chronicle of Higher Education*, p. B5.

Ducharme, J. K., & Kollar, M. M. (2012). Does the "marriage benefit" extend to same-sex union? Evidence from a sample of married lesbian couples in Massachusetts. *Journal of Homosexuality, 59*, 580-591.

Duck, S., & Wright, P. H. (1993). Reexamining gender differences in same-gender friendships: A close look at two kinds of data. *Sex Roles, 28*, 709–727.

Dudley, C., O'Sullivan, L. F., & Moreau, D. (2002). Does familiarity breed complacency? HIV knowledge, personal contact, and sexual risk behavior of psychiatrically referred Latino adolescent girls. *Hispanic Journal of Behavioral Sciences, 24*, 353–368.

Duehr, E. E., & Bono, J. E. (2006). Men, women, and managers: Are stereotypes finally changing? *Personnel Psychology, 59*, 815–846.

Duffy, J., Wareham, S., & Walsh, M. (2004). Psychological consequences for high school students of having been sexually harassed. *Sex Roles, 50*, 811–821.

Duffy, J., Warren, K., & Walsh, M. (2001). Classroom interactions: Gender of teacher, gender of student, and classroom subject. *Sex Roles, 45*, 579–593.

Duffy, S. A., & Keir, J. A. (2004). Violating stereotypes: Eye movements and comprehension processes when text conflicts with world knowledge. *Memory & Cognition, 32*, 551–559.

Duncan, J., Zawistowski, C., & Luibrand, S (2020, February 19). *50 states, 50 ways of teaching America's past.* CBS News. Retrieved October 5, 2021 from https://www.cbsnews.com/news/us-history-how-teaching-americas-past-varies-across-the-country/

Dunivin, D. L. (2006). Psychopharma-cotherapy and women: Issues for consideration. In J. Worell & C. D. Goodheart (Eds.), *Handbook of girls' and women's psychological health: Gender and well-being across the life span* (pp. 447–454). New York: Oxford University Press.

Dunning, D., & Sherman, D. A. (1997). Stereotypes and tacit inference. *Journal of Personality and Social Psychology, 73*, 459–471.

Duong, T. C. (2004). My multiple identity disorder. In K. K. Kumashiro (Ed.), *Restoried selves: Autobiographies of queer Asian/Pacific American activists* (pp. 47–52). New York: Harrington Park Press.

Durán, L. A., Payne, N. D., & Russo, A. (Eds.). (2007). *Building feminist movements and organizations: Global perspectives.* London: Zed Books.

Durantini, M. R., et al. (2006). Conceptualizing the influence of social agents of behavior change: A meta-analysis of the effectiveness of HIV-prevention interventionists for different groups. *Psychological Bulletin, 132*, 212–248.

Dusenbery, M. (2018). *Doing harm: The truth about how bad medicine and lazy science leave women dismissed, misdiagnosed, and sick.* New York: HarperCollins.

Dyke, L. S., & Murphy, S. A. (2006). How we define success: A qualitative study of what matters most to women and men. *Sex Roles, 55*, 357–371.

Dziech, B. W. (2003). Sexual harassment on college campuses. In M. A. Paludi & C. A. Paludi (Eds.), *Academic and workplace sexual harassment* (pp. 147–171). Westport, CT: Praeger.

Eagly, A. H. (2001). Social role theory of sex differences and similarities. In J. Worell (Ed.), *Encyclopedia of women and gender* (pp. 1069–1078). San Diego: Academic Press.

Eagly, A. H. (2004). Prejudice: Toward a more inclusive understanding. In A. H. Eagly, R. M. Baron, & V. L. Hamilton (Eds.), *The social psychology of group identity and social conflict* (pp. 45–64). Washington, DC: American Psychological Association.

Eagly, A. H. (2007). Female leadership advantage and disadvantage: Resolving the contradictions. *Psychology of Women Quarterly, 31,* 1–12.

Eagly, A. H., & Carli, L. L. (2007). *Through the labyrinth: The truth about how women become leaders.* Boston: Harvard Business School Press.

Eagly, A. H., & Crowley, M. (1986). Gender and helping behavior: A meta-analytic review of the social psychological literature. *Psychological Bulletin, 100,* 283–308.

Eagly, A. H., & Diekman, A. B. (2006). Examining gender gaps in sociopolitical attitudes: It's not Mars and Venus. *Feminism & Psychology, 16,* 26–34.

Eagly, A. H., Johannesen-Schmidt, M. C., & van Engen, M. L. (2003). Transformational, transactional, and laissez-faire leadership styles: A meta-analysis comparing women and men. *Psychological Bulletin, 129,* 569–591.

Eagly, A. H., & Karau, S. J. (2002). Role congruity theory of prejudice toward female leaders. *Psychological Review, 109,* 573–598.

Eagly, A. H., & Koenig, A. M. (2008). Gender prejudice: On the risks of occupying incongruent roles. In E. Borgida & S. T. Fiske (Eds.), *Beyond common sense: Psychological science in the courtroom* (pp. 63–81). Malden, MA: Blackwell.

Eagly, A. H., Makhijani, M. G., & Klonsky, B. G. (1992). Gender and the evaluation of leaders: A meta-analysis. *Psychological Bulletin, 111,* 3–22.

Eagly, A. H., & Mladinic, A. (1994). Are people prejudiced against women? Some answers from research on attitudes, gender stereotypes, and judgments of competence. In W. Stroebe & M. Hewstone (Eds.*), European review of social psychology.* New York: Wiley.

Eagly, A. H., Nater, C., Miller, D. I., Kaufmann, M., & Sczesny, S. (2020). Gender stereotypes have changed: A cross-temporal meta-analysis of U.S. public opinion polls from 1946 to 2018. *American Psychologist, 75,* 301–315.

Eagly, A. H., & Wood, W. (1999). The origins of sex differences in human behavior: Evolved dispositions versus social roles. *American Psychologist, 54,* 408–423.

Easton, D., O'Sullivan, L. F., & Parker, R. G. (2002). Sexualities and sexual health/lessons from history: Emergence of sexuality as a sexual health and political issue. In D. Miller & J. Green (Eds.), *The psychology of sexual health* (pp. 53–67). Malden, MA: Blackwell.

Eastwick, P. W., & Finkel, E. J. (2008). Sex differences in mate preferences revisited: Do people know what they initially desire in a romantic partner? *Journal of Personality and Social Psychology, 94,* 245–264.

Eastwick, P. W., et al. (2006). Is traditional gender ideology associated with sex-typed mate preferences? A test in nine nations. *Sex Roles, 54,* 603–614.

Eccles, J. S. (1987). Gender roles and women's achievement-related decisions. *Psychology of Women Quarterly, 11,* 135–172.

Eccles, J. S. (1994). Understanding women's educational and occupational choices. *Psychology of Women Quarterly, 18,* 585–609.

Eccles, J. S. (2001). Achievement. In J. Worell (Ed.), *Encyclopedia of women and gender* (pp. 43–53). San Diego: Academic Press.

Eccles, J. S. (2004). Schools, academic motivation, and stage-environment fit. In R. M. Lerner & L. Steinberg (Eds.), *Handbook of adolescent psychology* (2nd ed., pp. 125–153). Hoboken, NJ: Wiley.

Eccles, J. (2007). Where are all the women? Gender differences in participation in physical science and engineering. In C. J. Ceci & W. M. Williams (Eds.), *Why aren't more women in science? Top researchers debate the evidence* (pp. 199–210). Washington, DC: American Psychological Association.

Eccles, J. S., Jacobs, J. E., & Harold, R. D. (1990). Gender-role stereotypes, expectancy effects, and parents' socialization of gender differences. *Journal of Social Issues, 46,* 183–201.

Eccles, J. S., Wigfield, A., & Byrnes, J. (2003). Cognitive development in adolescence. In I. B. Weiner (Ed.), *Handbook of psychology* (Vol. 6, pp. 325–350). Hoboken, NJ: Wiley.

Eccles, J. S., et al. (2000). Gender-roles socialization in the family: A longitudinal approach. In T. Eckes & H. M. Trautner (Eds.), *The developmental social psychology of gender* (pp. 333–360). Mahwah, NJ: Erlbaum.

Eckert, P., & McConnell-Ginet, S. (2003). *Language and gender.* New York: Cambridge University Press.

Edelstein, L. N. (1999). *The art of midlife.* Westport, CT: Bergin & Garvey.

EducationData.org. (2019). *Education attainment statistics.* [Data Set]. https://educationdata.org /education-attainment-statistics #bachelors-degree

Edwards, C. P., Knoche, L., & Kumuru, A. (2001). Play patterns and gender. In J. Worell (Ed.), *Encyclopedia of women and gender.* San Diego: Academic Press.

Edwards, N., & Sim-Jones, N. (1998). Smoking and smoking relapse during pregnancy and postpartum: Results of a qualitative study. *Birth, 25,* 94–100.

Edwards, R., & Hamilton, M. A. (2004). You need to understand my gender role: An empirical test of Tannen' s model of gender and communication. *Sex Roles, 50,* 491–504.

Edwards, T. M. (2000, August 28). Flying solo. *Time,* pp. 47–53.

Ehrenreich, B. (2001). *Nickel and dimed: On (not) getting by in America.* New York: Metropolitan Books.

Einav, S., & Hood, B. M. (2008). Tell-tale eyes: Children's attribution of gaze aversion as a lying cue. *Developmental Psychology, 44,* 1655–1667.

Eisenberg, N., Fabes, R., & Shea, C. (1989). Gender differences in empathy and prosocial moral reasoning: Empirical investigations. In M. M. Brabeck (Ed.), *Who cares? Theory, research, and educational implications of the ethic of care* (pp. 127–143). New York: Praeger.

Eisenberg, N., Fabes, R. A., & Spinrad, T. L. (2006). Prosocial development. In W. Damon, R. M. Lerner (Series Ed.), & N. Eisenberg (Vol. Ed.), *Handbook of child psychology: Vol. 3. Social, emotional, and personality development* (6th ed., pp. 933–1002). Hoboken, NJ: Wiley.

Eisenberg, N., Martin, C. L., & Fabes, R. A. (1996). Gender development and gender effects. In D. C. Berliner & R. C. Calfee (Eds.), *Handbook of educational psychology* (pp. 358–396). New York: Macmillan.

Eisenberg, S. (1998). *We'll call you if we need you: Experiences of women working construction.* Ithaca, NY: Cornell University Press.

El-Bushra, J. (2000). Rethinking gender and development practice for the twenty-first century. In C. Sweetman (Ed.), *Gender in the 21st century* (pp. 55–62). Oxford, England: Oxfam.

El-Safty, M. (2004). Women in Egypt: Islamic rights versus cultural practice. *Sex Roles, 51,* 273–281.

Elfman, L. (2009, March 5). A "second wave" of feminism. *Diverse,* 10–11.

Ellis, B. J. (2004). Timing of pubertal maturation in girls: An integrated life history approach. *Psychological Bulletin, 130,* 920–958.

Ellis, L., et al. (2008). *Sex differences: Summarizing more than a century of scientific research.* New York: Psychology Press.

Ellison, C. R. (2001). A research inquiry into some American women's sexual concerns and problems. In E. Kaschak & L. Tiefer (Eds.), *A new view of women's sexual problems* (pp. 147–159). New York: Haworth.

Ellsberg, M., et al. (1998). *¿Cómo atender a las mujeres que viven situaciones de violencia doméstica? [How to attend to women who live in violent domestic situations.].* Managua, Nicaragua: Arco Producciones.

Else-Quest, N. M., & Hyde, J. S. (2016). Intersectionality in quantitative psychological research: I. Theoretical and epistemological issues. *Psychology of Women Quarterly, 40,* 155-170.

Else-Quest, N. M., Hyde, J. S., & Clark, R. (2003). Breastfeeding, bonding, and the mother-infant relationship. *Merrill-Palmer Quarterly, 49,* 495–517.

Else-Quest, N. M., Hyde, J. S., Goldsmith, H. H., & Van Hulle, C. (2006). Gender differences in temperament: A meta-analysis. *Psychological Bulletin, 132,* 33–72.

Elson, J. (2004). *Am I still a woman? Hysterectomy and gender identity.* Philadelphia: Temple University Press.

Emmers-Sommer, T. M., et al. (2005). The impact of film manipulation on men's and women's attitudes toward women and film editing. *Sex Roles, 52,* 683–695.

Enda, G., & Gale, W. G. (2020). *How does gender equality affect women in retirement?* The Brookings Institution. Retrieved October 5, 2021 from https:// www.brookings.edu/essay/ how-does-gender-equality-affect -women-in-retirement/

England, P. (2006). Toward gender equality: Progress and bottlenecks. In F. D. Blau, M. C. Brinton, & D. B. Grusky (Eds.), *The declining significance of gender?* (pp. 245–264). New York: Russell Sage.

English, J., & Swangin, B. (2019). One woman and six newborns die every two hours from complications during pregnancy or childbirth in Yemen. *UNICEF.* Retrieved October 4, 2021 from https://www.unicef.org/press -releases/one-woman-and-six -newborns-die-every-two-hours -complications-during -pregnancy-or

Enjuris. (2020). *Law school rankings by female enrollment.* Retrieved October 3, 2021 from https:// www.enjuris.com/students/ law-school-women-enrollment -2020.html

Enns, C. Z. (2004a). *Feminist theories and feminist psychotherapies* (2nd ed.). New York: Haworth.

Enns, C. Z. (2004b). The politics and psychology of false memory syndrome. In J. C. Chrisler, C. Golden, & P. D. Rozee (Eds.), *Lectures on the psychology of women* (3rd ed., pp. 357–373). New York: McGraw-Hill.

Enns, C. Z., Comas Díaz, L., & Bryant-Davis, T. (2020). Transnational feminist theory and practice: An introduction. *Women & Therapy, 44,* 11-26.

Enns, C. Z., & Forrest, L. M. (2005). Toward defining and integrating multicultural and feminist pedagogy. In C. Z. Enns & A. L. Sinacore (Eds.), *Teaching and social justice: Integrating multicultural and feminist theories in the classroom* (pp. 3–23). Washington, DC: American Psychological Association.

Enns, C. Z., & Sinacore, A. L. (2001). Feminist theories. In J. Worell (Ed.), *Encyclopedia of women and gender* (pp. 469–480). San Diego: Academic Press.

Enns, C. Z., & Sinacore, A. L. (Eds.). (2005). *Teaching and social justice: Integrating multi-cultural and feminist theories in the classroom.* Washington, DC: American Psychological Association.

Enright, E. (2004, July/August). A house divided. *AARP Magazine,* 62–65.

Entwisle, D. R., Alexander, K. L., & Olson, L. S. (2007). Early schooling: The handicap of being poor and male. *Sociology of Education, 80,* 114–138.

Erber, J. T. (2005). *Aging & older adulthood.* Belmont, CA: Thomson/ Wadsworth.

Erblich, J., & Earleywine, M. (2003). Alcohol problems. In L. M. Cohen, D. E. McChargue, & F. L. Collins, Jr. (Eds.), *The health psychology handbook* (pp. 79–100). Thousand Oaks, CA: Sage.

Erchull, M. J., Chrisler, J. C., Gorman, J. A., & Johnston-Robledo, I. (2002). Education and advertising: A content analysis of commercially produced booklets about menstruation. *Journal of Early Adolescence, 22,* 455–474.

Erdley, C. A., & Day, H. J. (2017). Friendship in childhood and adolescence. In M. Hojjat & A. Moyer (Eds.), *The psychology of friendship* (pp. 3-19). New York, NY: Oxford University Press.

Erickson, W., Lee, C., & von Schrader, S. (2019). *2017 disability status report: United States.* Ithaca, NY: Cornell University Yang-Tan Institute on Employment and Disability (YTI).

Erkut, S., Marx, F., & Fields, J. P. (2001). A delicate balance: How teachers can support Middle school girls' confidence and competence. In P. O'Reilly, E. M. Penn, & K. deMarrais (Eds.), *Educating young adolescent girls* (pp. 83–101). Mahwah, NJ: Erlbaum.

Erler, M. C., & Kowaleski, M. (Eds.). (2003). *Gendering the master narrative: Women and power in the Middle Ages.* Ithaca, NY: Cornell University Press.

Escobar-Chaves, S. L., et al. (2005). Impact of the media on

adolescent sexual attitudes and behaviors. *Pediatrics, 116* (Suppl.), 297–326.

Espinosa, L. L., Turk, J. M., Taylor, M., & Chessman, H. M. (2020). *Race and ethnicity in higher education: A status report.* American Council on Education. Retrieved October 3, 2021 from https://www.acenet .edu/Research-Insights /Pages/Race-and-Ethnicity-in -Higher-Education.aspx

Essed, P., Goldberg, D. T., & Kobayashi, A. (2005). *A companion to gender studies.* Malden, MA: Blackwell.

Estrada, F., Bäckman, O., & Nilsson, A. (2016). The darker side of equality? The declining gender gap in crime: Historical trends and an enhanced analysis of staggered birth cohorts. *British Journal of Criminology, 56,* 1272-1290.

Etaugh, C. A. (2008). Women in the middle and later years. In F. L. Denmark & M. A. Paludi (Eds.), *Psychology of women: A handbook of issues and theories* (2nd ed., pp. 271–302). Westport, CT: Praeger.

Etaugh, C. A., & Bridges, J. S. (2001). Midlife transitions. In J. Worell (Ed.), *Encyclopedia of women and aging* (pp. 759–769). San Diego: Academic Press.

Etaugh, C. A., & Bridges, J. S. (2006). Midlife transitions. In J. Worell & C. D. Goodheart (Eds.), *Handbook of girls' and women's psychological health: Gender and well-being across the life span* (pp. 359–367). New York: Oxford University Press.

Etaugh, C. A., & Liss, M. B. (1992). Home, school, and playroom: Training grounds for adult gender roles. *Sex Roles, 26,* 129–147.

Etson, T. D. (2003, December 18). Sharing the responsibility: Increasing Black male student enrollment. *Black Issues in Higher Education,* p. 124.

Etzkowitz, H., Kemelgor, C., & Uzzi, B. (2000). *Athena unbound: The advancement of women in science*

and technology. New York: Cambridge University Press.

Evans, D. K., Akmal, M., and Jakiela, P. (2019). *Gender gaps in education: The long view. CGD Working Paper 523.* Washington, DC: Center for Global Development. Retrieved October 3, 2021 from https://www.cgdev.org /publication/gender-gaps -education-long-view

Eudey, B. (2007). Gender equity strategies for diverse populations: Overview. In S. S. Klein (Ed.), *Handbook for achieving gender equity through education* (2nd ed., pp. 445–463). Mahwah, NJ: Erlbaum.

Evans, C. D., & Diekman, A. B. (2009). On motivated role selection: Gender beliefs, distant goals, and career preferences. *Psychology of Women Quarterly, 33,* 235–249.

Evans, E. M., Schweingruber, H., & Stevenson, H. W. (2002). Gender differences in interest and knowledge acquisition: The United States, Taiwan, and Japan. *Sex Roles, 47,* 153–167.

Evans, S. M. (2003). *Tidal wave: How women changed America at century's end.* New York: Free Press.

Evelyn, J. (2000, August 3). Double standard reform. *Black Issues in Higher Education,* p. 6.

Ex, C. T. G. M., & Janssens, J. M. A. M. (2000). Young females' images of motherhood. *Sex Roles, 43,* 865–890.

Fabes, R. A., & Martin, C. L. (2000). *Exploring child development: Transactions and transformations.* Boston: Allyn & Bacon.

Fabes, R. A., Martin, C. L., & Hanish, L. D. (2003). Young children's play qualities in same-, other-, and mixed-sex peer groups. *Child Development, 74,* 921–932.

Fagot, B. I., Rodgers, C. S., & Leinbach, M. D. (2000). Theories of gender socialization. In T. Eckes & H. M. Trautner (Eds.), *The developmental social psychology of gender* (pp. 65–89). Mahwah, NJ: Erlbaum.

Fairburn, C. G., Cooper, Z., Shafran, R., & Wilson, G. T. (2008). Eating disorders: A transdiagnostic protocol. In D. H. Barlow (Ed.), *Clinical handbook of psychological disorders* (pp. 578–614). New York: Guilford.

Faith, M. Y., Fontaine, K. R., Baskin, M. L., & Allison, D. B. (2007). Toward the reduction of population obesity: Macrolevel environmental approaches of the problems of food, eating, and obesity. *Psychological Bulletin, 133*, 205–226.

Family Planning Advocates of New York State. (2005). *Funding for reproductive health care.* Retrieved July 14, 2005, from http://www.fpaofnys.org /publications/fact_sheets.html

Fales, M. R., Frederick, D. A., Garcia, J. R., Gildersleeve, K. A., Haselton, M. G., & Fisher, H. (2016). Mating markets and bargaining hands: Mate preference for attractiveness and resources in two national U. S. studies. *Personality and Individual Differences, 88*, 78-87.

Farber, N. (2003). *Adolescent pregnancy: Policy and prevention services.* New York: Springer.

Fassinger, R. E. (2002). Hitting the ceiling: Gendered barriers to occupational entry, advancement, and achievement. In L. Diamant & J. A. Lee (Eds.), *The psychology of sex, gender, and jobs* (pp. 21–45). Westport, CT: Praeger.

Fassinger, R. E., & Arseneau, J. P. (2008). Diverse women's sexualities. In F. L. Denmark & M. A. Paludi (Eds.), *Psychology of women: A handbook of issues and theories* (pp. 484–505). Westport, CT: Praeger.

Fausto-Sterling, A. (1985). *Myths of gender: Biological theories about women and men.* New York: Basic Books.

Fausto-Sterling, A. (2005). The bare bones of sex: Part 1—sex and gender. *Signs, 30*, 1492–1517.

Favreau, O. E. (1993). Do the N's justify the means? Null hypothesis testing applied to sex and other differences. *Canadian Psychology/Psychologie canadienne, 34*, 64–78.

Favreau, O. E. (1997). Sex and gender comparisons: Does null hypothesis testing create a false dichotomy? *Feminism and Psychology, 7*, 63–81.

Favreau, O. E., & Everett, J. C. (1996). A tale of two tails. *American Psychologist, 51*, 268–269.

Fazio, R. H., & Olson, M. A. (2003). Implicit measures in social cognition research: Their meaning and use. *Annual Review of Psychology, 54*, 297–327.

Fears, D. (2003, September 17). The power of a label. *The Washington Post National Weekly Edition, 29.*

Fechner, P. Y. (2003). The biology of puberty: New developments in sex differences. In C. Hayward (Ed.), *Gender differences at puberty* (pp. 17–28). New York: Cambridge University Press.

Federman, D. D. (2004). Three facets of sexual differentiation. *New England Journal of Medicine, 350*, 323–324.

Federman, D. D. (2006). The biology of human sex differences. *New England Journal of Medicine, 354*, 1507–1514.

Feeney, J. A., Hohaus, L., Noller, P., & Alexander, R. P. (2001). *Becoming parents: Exploring the bonds between mothers, fathers, and their infants.* New York: Cambridge University Press.

Fehr, B. (2004). Intimacy expectation in same-sex friendships: A prototype interaction-pattern model. *Journal of Personality and Social Psychology, 86*, 265–285.

Feingold, A. (1988). Cognitive gender differences are disappearing. *American Psychologist, 43*, 95–103.

Feingold, A. (1994). Gender differences in personality: A meta-analysis. *Psychological Bulletin, 116*, 429–456.

Feiring, C. (1996). Concepts of romance in 15-year-old adolescents. *Journal of Research on Adolescents, 6*, 181–200.

Feiring, C. (1998). Gender identity and the development of romantic relationships in adolescence. In W. Furman, B. B. Brown, & C. Feiring (Eds.), *Contemporary perspectives in adolescent romantic relationships.* Cambridge, England: Cambridge University Press.

Feiring, C. (1999). Other-sex friendship networks and the development of romantic relationships in adolescence. *Journal of Youth and Adolescence, 28*, 495–512.

Feldt, G. (2002). *Behind every choice is a story.* Denton, TX: University of North Texas Press.

Fencl, H., & Scheel, K. R. (2006). Making sense of retention: An examination of undergraduate women's participation in physics courses. In J. M. Bystydzienski & S. R. Bird (Eds.), *Removing barriers: Women in academic science, technology, engineering, and mathematics* (pp. 287–302). Bloomington, IN: Indiana University Press.

Feng, J., Spence, I., & Pratt, J. (2007). Playing an action video game reduces gender differences in spatial cognition. *Psychological Science, 18*, 850–855.

Fenigstein, A., & Preston, M. (2007). The desired number of sexual partners as a function of gender, sexual risks, and the meaning of " ideal." *Journal of Sex Research, 44*, 89–95.

Ferber, A. L. (2007). Color-blind racism and post-feminism: The contemporary politics of inequality. In M. T. Segal & T. A. Martinez (Eds.), *Intersections of gender, race, and class* (pp. 551–556). Los Angeles, CA: Roxbury.

Ferguson, C. J., Cruz, A. M., & Rueda, S. M. (2008). Gender, video game playing habits and visual memory tasks. *Sex Roles, 58*, 279–286.

Ferguson, S. J. (2000). Challenging traditional marriage: Never married Chinese American and

Japanese American women. *Gender and Society, 14,* 136–159.

Fernández, J. S., Sonn, C. C., Carolissen, R., & Stevens, G. (2021). Roots and routes toward decoloniality within and outside psychology praxis. *Review of General Psychology,* 1-15.

Ferrer, D. V. (2007). Validating coping strategies and empowering Latino battered women in Puerto Rico. In A. R. Roberts (Ed.), *Battered women and their families* (3rd ed., pp. 563–590). New York: Springer.

Fessler, A. (2006). *The girls who went away: The hidden history of women who surrendered children for adoption in the decades before Roe v. Wade.* New York: Penguin.

Fidler-Benaoudia, M. M., Torre, L. A., Bray, F., Ferlay, J., Jemal, A. (2020). Lung cancer incidence in young women vs. young men: A systematic analysis in 40 countries. *International Journal of Cancer. 147,* 811-819.

Fields, C. D. (2002, January 31). Sexual responsibility on campus. *Black Issues in Higher Education,* 18–24.

Fiese, B. H., & Skillman, G. (2000). Gender differences in family stories: Moderating influence of parent gender role and child gender. *Sex Roles, 43,* 267–283.

Figert, A. E. (1996). *Women and the ownership of PMS: The structuring of a psychiatric disorder.* New York: Aldine de Gruyter.

Fikkan, J., & Rothblum, E. (2005). Weight bias in employment. In K. D. Brownell, R. M. Puhl, M. B. Schwartz, & L. Rudd (Eds.), *Weight bias: Nature, consequences, and remedies* (pp. 15–28). New York: Guilford.

Fikslin, R. (2021). Toward an intersectional science of reproductive norms: Generating research across the natalism spectrum. *Psychology of Women Quarterly, 45,* 308-324.

Fincham, F. D. (2004). Communication in marriage. In A. L. Vangelisti (Ed.), *Handbook of family communication* (pp. 83–103). Mahwah, NJ: Erlbaum.

Fincham, F. D., & Beach, S. R. H. (1999). Conflict in marriage: Implications for working with couples. *Annual Review of Psychology, 50,* 47–77.

Fine, M. A. (2000). Divorce and single parenting. In C. Hendrick & S. S. Hendrick (Eds.), *Close relationships* (pp. 138–152). Thousand Oaks, CA: Sage.

Fine, M. (2007a). Feminist designs for difference. In S. N. Hesse-Biber (Ed.), *Handbook of feminist research: Theory and praxis* (pp. 613–619). Thousand Oaks, CA: Sage.

Fine, J. (2007b). Worker centers and immigrant women. In D. S. Cobble (Ed.), *The sex of class: Women transforming American labor* (pp. 211–230). Ithaca, NY: Cornell University Press.

Fine, M. (2013a). Award for Distinguished Contributions to Research in Public Policy. *American Psychologist, 68,* 686-687.

Fine, M. (2013b). Echoes of Bedford: A 20-year social psychology memoir on participatory action research hatched behind bars. *American Psychologist, 68,* 687-698.

Fine, M., & Burns, A. (2003). Class notes: Toward a critical psychology of class and schooling. *Journal of Social Issues, 59,* 841–860.

Fine, M. A., & Carney, S. (2001). Women, gender, and the law: Toward a feminist rethinking of responsibility. In R. K. Unger (Ed.), *Handbook of the psychology of women and gender* (pp. 388–409). New York: Wiley.

Fine, M., & McClelland, S. I. (2007). The politics of teen women's sexuality: Public policy and the adolescent female body. *Emory Law Journal, 56,* 99–1038.

Fine, M., Roberts, R., & Weis, L. (2000). Refusing the betrayal: Latinas redefining gender, sexuality, culture and resistance. *Review of Education/Psychology/ Cultural Studies, 22,* 87–119.

Fine, M., & Torre, M. E. (2001). Remembering exclusions: Participatory action research in public institutions. *Qualitative Research in Psychology, 1,* 15–37.

Fine, M., & Torre, M. E. (2006). Intimate details: Participatory action research in prison. *Action Research, 4,* 253–269.

Fine, M., et al. (2001). *Changing minds: The impact of college in a maximum security prison.* New York: The Graduate School and University Center, City University of New York.

Fingerhut, A. W., & Abdou, C. M. (2017). The role of healthcare stereotype threat and social identity threat in LGB disparities. *Journal of Social Issues, 73,* 493-507.

Fingerhut, A. W., Peplau, L. A., & Ghavami, N. (2005). A dual-identity framework for understanding lesbian experience. *Psychology of Women Quarterly, 29,* 129–139.

Fingerman, K. L. (2003). *Mothers and their adult daughters: Mixed emotions, enduring bonds.* New York: Springer.

Fingerman, K. L., et al. (2007). Parents' and offspring's perceptions of change and continuity when parents experience the transition to old age. *Interpersonal Relations across the Life Course, 12,* 275–306.

Fingerson, L. (2006). *Girls in power: Gender, body, and menstruation in adolescence.* Albany: State University of New York Press.

Finnie, R., Lascelles, E., & Sweetman, A. (2005). *Who goes? The direct and indirect impact of family background on access to postsecondary education.* (Catalogue #11F0019MIE no. 237). Ottawa: Statistics Canada.

Firestone, J. M., & Harris, R. J. (2003). Personal responses to structural problems: Organizational climate and sexual harassment in the U.S. Military, 1988 and 1995. *Gender, Work, and Organization, 10,* 42–64.

Fischhoff, B. (1992). Giving advice: Decision theory perspectives on sexual assault. *American Psychologist, 47,* 577–588.

Fisher-Thompson, D., & Burke, T. A. (1998). Experimenter influences and children's cross-gender behavior. *Sex Roles, 39,* 669–684.

Fisher, C. B. (2003). *Decoding the ethics code: A practical guide for psychologists.* Thousand Oaks, CA: Sage.

Fiske, S. T. (1993). Social cognition and social perception. *Annual Review of Psychology, 44,* 155–194.

Fiske, S. T. (2004). *Social beings: A core motives approach to social psychology.* Hoboken, NJ: Wiley.

Fiske, S. T., Cuddy, A. J. C., Glick, P., & Xu, J. (2002). A model of (often mixed) stereotype content: Competence and warmth respectively follow from perceived status and competition. *Journal of Personality and Social Psychology, 82,* 878–902.

Fiske, S. T., & Stevens, L. E. (1993). What's so special about sex? Gender stereotyping and discrimination. In S. Oskamp & M. Costanzo (Eds.), *Gender issues in contemporary society* (pp. 173–196). New-bury Park, CA: Sage.

Fiske, S. T., et al. (1993). Accuracy and objectivity on behalf of the APA. *American Psychologist, 48,* 55–56.

Fitch, R. H., Cowell, P. E., & Denenberg, V. H. (1998). The female phenotype: Nature's default? *Developmental Neuropsychology, 14,* 213–231.

Fitness, J. (2006). Emotion and cognition in close relationships. In P. Noller & J. A. Feeney (Eds.), *Close relationships: Functions, forms, and processes* (pp. 285–303). New York: Psychology Press.

Fitzgerald, L. F., Collinsworth, L. L., & Harned, M. S. (2001). Sexual harassment. In J. Worell (Ed.), *Encyclopedia of women and gender* (pp. 991–1004). San Diego: Academic Press.

Fivush, R. (1989). Exploring sex differences in the emotional content of mother-child conversations about the past. *Sex Roles, 20,* 675–691.

Fivush, R., & Buckner, J. P. (2000). Gender, sadness, and depression: The development of emotional focus through gendered discourse. In A. H. Fischer (Ed.), *Gender and emotion: Social psychological perspectives* (pp. 232–253). Cambridge, England: Cambridge University Press.

Fivush, R., Brotman, M. A., Buckner, J. P., & Goodman, S. H. (2000). Gender differences in parent-child emotion narratives. *Sex Roles, 42,* 233–253.

Fivush, R., & Nelson, K. (2004). Culture and language in the emergence of autobiographical memory. *Psychological Science, 15,* 573–577.

Flannagan, D., & Perese, S. (1998). Emotional references in mother-daughter and mother-son dyads' conversations about school. *Sex Roles, 39,* 353–367.

Fletcher, G. (2002). *The new science of intimate relationships.* Malden, MA: Blackwell.

Fletcher, G., & Boyes, A. D. (2008). Is love blind? Reality and illusion in intimate relationships. In J. P. Forgas & J. Fitness (Eds.), *Social relationships: Cognitive, affective, and motivational processes* (pp. 101–114). New York: Psychology Press.

Fletcher, T. D., & Major, D. A. (2004). Medical students' motivations to volunteer: An examination of the nature of gender differences. *Sex Roles, 51,* 109–114.

Flores, L. Y., & O'Brien, K. M. (2002). The career development of Mexican American adolescent women: A test of social cognitive career theory. *Journal of Counseling Psychology, 49,* 14–27.

Flores-Ortiz, Y. (1998). Voices from the couch: The co-creation of a Chicana psychology. In C. Trujillo (Ed.), *Living Chicana theory* (pp. 102–122). Berkeley, CA: Third Woman Press.

Flores-Ortiz, Y. (2004). Domestic violence in Chicana/o families. In R. J. Velásquez, L. M. Arellano, & B. W. McNeill (Eds.), *The handbook of Chicana/o psychology and mental health* (pp. 267–284). Mahwah, NJ: Erlbaum.

Florsheim, P. (2003). Adolescent romantic and sexual behavior: What we know and where we go from here. In P. Florsheim (Ed.), *Adolescent romantic relations and sexual behavior: Theory, research, and practical implications* (pp. 371–385). Mahwah, NJ: Erlbaum.

Foels, R., & Tomcho, T. J. (2005). Gender, interdependent self-construals, and collective self-esteem: Women and men are mostly the same. *Self and Identity, 4,* 213–225.

Fogg, P. (2005, April 29). Don't stand so close to me. *Chronicle of Higher Education,* pp. A10–A12.

Foley, S., Kope, S. A., & Sugrue, D. P. (2002). *Sex matters for women: A complete guide to taking care of your sexual self.* New York: Guilford.

Fonn, S. (2003). Not only what you do, but how you do it: Working with health care practitioners on gender equality. In L. Manderson (Ed.), *Teaching gender, teaching women's health* (pp. 105–120). Binghamton, NY: Haworth.

Fontes, L. A. (2001). The new view and Latina sexualities: ¡Pero no soy una máquina! In E. Kaschak & L. Tiefer (Eds.), *A new view of women's sexual problems* (pp. 33–37). New York: Haworth.

Foote, W. E., & Goodman-Delahunty, J. (2005). *Evaluating sexual harassment: Psychological, social, and legal considerations in forensic examinations.* Washington, DC: American Psychological Association.

association between socioeconomic status and physical health: Do negative emotions play a role? *Psychological Bulletin, 129,* 10–51.

Gan, S. C., et al. (2000). Treatment of acute myocardial infarction and 30-day mortality among women and men. *New England Journal of Medicine, 343,* 8–15.

Ganahl, D. J., Prinsen, T. J., & Netzley, S. B. (2003). A content analysis of prime time commercials: A contextual framework of gender representation. *Sex Roles, 49,* 545–551.

Gannon, L., & Ekstrom, B. (1993). Attitudes toward menopause. The influence of sociocultural paradigms. *Psychology of Women Quarterly, 17,* 275–288.

Ganong, L. H., & Coleman, M. (1995). The content of mother stereotypes. *Sex Roles, 32,* 495–512.

Ganong, L. H., & Coleman, M. (1999). *Changing families, changing responsibilities: Family obligations following divorce and remarriage.* Mahwah, NJ: Erlbaum.

Garbes, A. (2018). *Like a mother: A feminist journey through the science and culture of pregnancy.* New York, NY: HarperCollins.

Garcia, J. R., Reiber, C., Massey, S. G., & Merriwether, A. M. (2012). Sexual hookup culture: A review. *Review of General Psychology, 16,* 161-176.

Garcia-Navarro, L. (Host), & Jay-Green (Guest). (2014). Same-sex couples may have more egalitarian relationships. [*All Things Considered*]. American University, Washington, DC.

Garcia-Preto, N. (2005). Puerto Rican families. In M. McGoldrick, J. Giordano, & N. Garcia-Preto (Eds.), *Ethnicity and family therapy* (3rd ed., pp. 242–255). New York: Guilford.

Gardiner, H. W., Mutter, J. D., & Kosmitzki, C. (1998). *Lives across cultures: Cross-cultural human development.* Boston: Allyn & Bacon.

Gardner, A. (2009). *FDA approves Plan B pill for 17-year-olds.* Retrieved April 20, 2009, from http://www. truthout.org/docs

Gardner, W. L., & Gabriel, S. (2004). Gender differences in relational and collective interdependence. In A. H. Eagly, A. E. Beall, & R. J. Sternberg (Eds.), *The psychology of gender* (2nd ed., pp. 169–191). New York: Guilford.

Garfinkel, P. E. (2002). Classification and diagnosis of eating disorders. In C. G. Fairburn & K. D. Brownell (Eds.), *Eating disorders and obesity: A comprehensive handbook* (2nd ed., pp. 155–161). New York: Guilford.

Garg, S., & Anand, T. (2015). Menstruation related myths in India: Strategies for combating it. *Journal of Family Medicine and Primary Care, 4,* 184-186.

Garland-Thomson, R. (2004). Integrating disability, transforming feminist theory. In B. G. Smith & B. Hutchison (Eds.), *Gendering disability* (pp. 73–103). New Brunswick, NJ: Rutgers University Press.

Garner, P. W., & Estep, K. M. (2001). Empathy and emotional expressivity. In J. Worell (Ed.), *Encyclopedia of women and gender* (pp. 391–402). San Diego: Academic Press.

Garnets, L. D. (2008). Life as a lesbian: What does gender have to do with it? In J. C. Chrisler, C. Golden, & P. D. Rozee (Eds.), *Lectures on the psychology of women* (4th ed., pp. 232–249). Boston, MA: McGraw-Hill.

Garrod, A., Smulyan, L., Powers, S., & Kilkenny, R. (1992). *Adolescent portraits.* Boston: Allyn & Bacon.

Garst, J., & Bodenhausen, G. V. (1997). Advertising's effects on men's gender role attitudes. *Sex Roles, 36,* 551–572.

Gastil, J. (1990). Generic pronouns and sexist language: The oxymoronic character of masculine generics. *Sex Roles, 23,* 629–643.

Gates, G. J., & Kastanis, A. (2013). *LGBT Latino/a individuals and Latino/a same-sex couples.* The Williams Institute. Retrieved October 4, 2021 from https://escholarship.org/uc/item/93m0w231

Gavey, N. (2005). *Just sex? The cultural scaffolding of rape.* New York: Routledge.

Gearon, J. (2021, February 11). Indigenous feminism is our culture. *Stanford Social Innovation Review.* Retrieved October 5, 2021 from https://ssir.org/articles/entry/indigenous_feminism_is_our_culture

Geary, D. C. (2005). Evolution of life-history trade-offs in mate attractiveness and health: Comment on Weeden & Sabini (2005). *Psychological Bulletin, 131,* 654–657.

Geiger, T. C., Zimmer-Gembeck, M., & Crick, N. R. (2004). The science of relational aggression: Can we guide intervention? In M. M. Moretti, C. L. Odgers, & M. A. Jackson (Eds.), *Girls and aggression: Contributing factors and intervention principles* (pp. 27–40). New York: Kluwer Academic/Plenum.

Gelles, R. J., & Cavanaugh, M. M. (2005). Association is not causation. In D. R. Loseke, R. J. Gelles, & M. M. Cavanaugh (Eds.), *Current controversies on family violence* (2nd ed., pp. 175–189). Thousand Oaks, CA: Sage.

Gelman, S. A., Taylor, M. G., & Nguyen, S. P. (2004). Mother-child conversations about gender. *Monographs of the Society for Research in Child Development, 69*(1, Serial No. 275). New Jersey: Wiley-Blackwell.

Gender affects educational learning styles, researchers confirm. (1995, October). *Women in Higher Education, 7.*

General Accounting Office. (2004, January 23). *Defense of marriage act: Update to prior report* (Document GAO/OGC-97-16). Washington, DC: Author.

Genesoni, L., & Tallandini, M. A. (2009). Men's psychological transition to fatherhood: An analysis of the literature, 1989-2008. *Birth, 36,* 305–317.

George, D., Carroll, P., Kersnick, R., & Calderon, K. (1998). Gender-related patterns of helping among friends. *Psychology of Women Quarterly, 22,* 685–704.

George, W. H., & Martínez, L. J. (2002). Victim blaming in rape: Effects of victim and perpetrator race, type of rape, and participant racism. *Psychology of Women Quarterly, 26,* 110–119.

Gerber, G. L. (2001). *Women and men police officers: Status, gender, and personality.* Westport, CT: Praeger.

Gergen, K. J., & Gergen, M. M. (2004). *Social construction: Entering the dialogue.* Chagrin Falls, OH: Taos Institute Publications.

Gergen, M. (2008). Positive aging for women. In J. C. Chrisler, C. Golden, & P. D. Rozee (Eds.), *Lectures on the psychology of women* (3rd ed., pp. 377–301). Boston: McGraw-Hill.

Gergen, M. (2010). Teaching psychology of gender from a social constructionist standpoint. *Psychology of Women Quarterly, 34,* 261–264.

Gergen, M., & Gergen, K. J. (2006). Positive aging: Reconstructing the life course. In J. Worell & C. D. Goodheart (Eds.), *Handbook of girls' and women's psychological health: Gender and well-being across the life span* (pp. 416–424). New York: Oxford University Press.

Gernsbacher, M. A., & Kaschak, M. P. (2003). Neuroimaging studies of language production and comprehension. *Annual Review of Psychology, 54,* 91–114.

Gianakos, I. (2001). Predictors of career decision-making self-efficacy. *Journal of Career Assessment, 9,* 101–114.

Ghavami, N., & Peplau, L. A. (2013). An intersectional analysis of gender and ethnic stereotypes: Testing three hypotheses. *Psychology of Women Quarterly, 37,* 113-127.

Gibbon, M. (1999). *Feminist perspectives on language.* London: Longman.

Gibbons, J. L., Stiles, D. A., & Shkodriani, G. M. (1991). Adolescents' attitudes toward family and gender roles: An international comparison. *Sex Roles, 25,* 625–643.

Gibbons, J. L., Wilson, S. L., & Rufener, C. A. (2006). Gender attitudes mediate gender differences in attitudes toward adoption in Guatemala. *Sex Roles, 54,* 139–145.

Gibson, C. E., Losee, J., & Vitiello, C. (2014). A replication attempt of stereotype susceptibility (Shih, Pittinsky, & Ambady, 1999): Identity salience and shifts in quantitative performance. *Social Psychology, 45,* 194-198.

Gibson, P. R. (2011). The diversity watch: Finding your inner isms. *Psychology of Women Quarterly, 35,* 158–161.

Gibson, P., & Lindberg, A. (2006, Fall). Confronting the-isms. *Teaching Tolerance, 15.*

Gidycz, C. A., et al. (2006). The evaluation of a sexual assault self-defense and risk-reduction program for college women: A prospective study. *Psychology of Women Quarterly, 30,* 172–186.

Gilbert, L. A., & Kearney, L. K. (2006). The psychotherapeutic relationship as a positive and powerful resource for girls and women. In J. Worell & C. D. Goodheart (Eds.), *Handbook of girls' and women's psychological health: Gender and well-being across the life span* (pp. 229–238). New York: Oxford University Press.

Gilbert, L. A., & Rader, J. (2001). Counseling and psychotherapy: Gender, race/ethnicity, and sexuality. In J. Worell (Ed.), *Encyclopedia of women and gender* (pp. 265–277). San Diego: Academic Press.

Giles, H., & Reid, S. A. (2005). Ageism across the lifespan: Towards a self-categorization model of ageing. *Journal of Social Issues, 61,* 389–404.

Gilleard, C., & Higgs, P. (2000). *Cultures of ageing: Self, citizen, and the body.* Harlow, England: Prentice Hall.

Gillem, A. R. (2008). Triple jeopardy in the lives of biracial Black/White women. In J. C. Chrisler, C. Golden, & P. D. Rozee (Eds.), *Lectures on the psychology of women* (4th ed., pp. 268–285). Boston, MA: McGraw-Hill.

Gilligan, C. (1982). *In a different voice.* Cambridge, MA: Harvard University Press.

Gilligan, C., & Attanucci, J. (1988). Two moral orientations: Gender differences and similarities. *Merrill-Palmer Quarterly, 34,* 223–237.

Gillis, S., Howie, G., & Munford, R. (Eds.). (2007). *Third wave feminism: A critical exploration, 2nd ed.* Basingstoke, UK: Palgrave Macmillan.

Giovanelli, D., & Ostertag, S. (2009). Controlling the body: Media representations, body size, and self-discipline. In E. Rothblum & S. Solovay (Eds.), *The fat studies reader* (pp. 289–296). New York: New York University Press.

Girgus, J. S., & Nolen-Hoeksema, S. (2006). Cognition and depression. In C. L. M. Keyes & S. H. Goodman (Eds.), *Women and depression: A handbook for the social, behavioral, and biomedical sciences* (pp. 147–175). New York: Cambridge University Press.

Giscombé, C. L., & Lobel, M. (2005). Explaining disproportionately high rates of adverse birth outcomes among African Americans: The impact of stress, racism, and related factors in pregnancy. *Psychological Bulletin, 131,* 662–683.

Gjerdingen, D. W., & Center, B. A. (2005). First-time parents' post-partum changes in employment, child-care, and housework responsibilities. *Social Science Research, 34,* 103–116.

Glascock, J., & Preston-Schreck, C. (2004). Gender and racial stereotypes in daily newspaper comics: A time-honored tradition? *Sex Roles, 51,* 423–431.

Glaser, J. (2005). Understanding prejudice and discrimination [Review of the book *Understanding Prejudice and Discrimination*]. *Analysis of Social Issues and Public Policy, 5,* 277–279.

Glass, V., & Few-Demo, A. L. (2013). Complexities of informal social support arrangements for Black lesbian couples. *Family Relations, 62,* 714-726.

Glazer, G., et al. (2002). The Ohio mid-life women's study. *Health Care for Women International, 23,* 612–630.

Gleeson, K., & Frith, H. (2004). Pretty in pink: Young women presenting mature sexual identities. In A. Harris (Ed.), *All about the girl: Culture, power, and identity* (pp. 103–113). New York: Routledge.

Glenn, D. (2004, April 30). A dangerous surplus of sons? *Chronicle of Higher Education,* pp. A14-A16, A-18.

Glick, P. (2006). Ambivalent sexism, power distance, and gender inequality across cultures. In S. Guimond (Ed.), *Social comparison and social psychology* (pp. 283–302). New York: Cambridge University Press.

Glick, P., & Fiske, S. T. (1996). The ambivalent sexism inventory: Differentiating hostile and benevolent sexism. *Journal of Personality and Social Psychology, 70,* 491–512.

Glick, P., & Fiske, S. T. (2001a). An ambivalent alliance: Hostile and benevolent sexism as complementary justifications for gender inequality. *American Psychologist, 56,* 109–118.

Glick, P., & Fiske, S. T. (2001b). Ambivalent sexism. *Advances in Experimental Social Psychology, 33,* 115–188.

Glick, P., & Fiske, S. T. (2007). Sex discrimination: The psychological approach. In F. J. Crosby, M. S. Stockdale, & S. Ann Ropp (Eds.), *Sex discrimination in the workplace.* Malden, MA: Blackwell.

Glick, P., et al. (2000). Beyond prejudice as simple antipathy: Hostile and benevolent sexism across cultures. *Journal of Personality and Social Psychology, 79,* 763–775.

Glick, P., et al. (2004). Bad but bold: Ambivalent attitudes toward men predict gender inequality in 16 nations. *Journal of Personality and Social Psychology, 86,* 713–728.

Global Fund for Women. (2021). *Success stories.* Retrieved October 5, 2021 from https://www.globalfundforwomen.org/

Go, M., Dunnigan, T., & Schuchman, K. M. (2004). Bias in counseling Hmong clients with limited English proficiency. In J. L. Chin (Ed.), *The psychology of prejudice and discrimination* (Vol. 2, pp. 109–136). Westport, CT: Praeger.

Glynn, S. J. (2018). *An unequal division of labor: How equitable workplace policies would benefit working mothers.* Center for American Progress. Retrieved October 5, 2021 from https://www.american-progress.org/issues/women/reports/2018/05/18/450972/unequal-division-labor/

Goldberg, P. A. (1968). Are women prejudiced against women? *Transaction, 5,* 28–30.

Golden, C. (1996). What's in a name? Sexual self-identification among women. In R. C. Savin-Williams & K. M. Cohen (Eds.), *The lives of lesbians, gays, and bisexuals* (pp. 229–249). Fort Worth, TX: Harcourt Brace.

Golden, C. (2008). The intersexed and the transgendered: Rethinking sex/ gender. In J. C. Chrisler, C. Golden, & P. D. Rozee (Eds.), *Lectures on the psychology of women* (4th ed., pp. 2–15). Boston, MA: McGraw-Hill.

Goldenberg, J. L., & Roberts, T. (2004). The beast within the beauty. In J. Greenberg, S. L. Koole, & T. Pyszczynski (Eds.), *Handbook of experimental existential psychology* (pp. 71–85). New York: Guilford.

Goldenberg, R. L., & Culhane, J. R. (2005). Editorial: Prepregnancy health status and the risk of preterm delivery. *Archives of Pediatric and Adolescent Medicine, 159,* 89–90.

Goldfarb, P. (2005). Intimacy and injury: Legal interventions for battered women. In A. Barnes (Ed.), *The handbook of women, psychology, and the law* (pp. 212–264). San Francisco: Jossey-Bass.

Goldman, B. M., Gutek, B. A., Stein, J. H., & Lewis, K. (2006). Employment discrimination in organizations: Antecedents and consequences. *Journal of Management, 32,* 786–830.

Goldrick-Jones, A. (2002). *Men who believe in feminism.* Westport, CT: Praeger.

Goldstein, L. A. (2001, Fall). "And you can quote me on that. " *Michigan Today,* pp. 10–11.

Goldwasser, A. (Eds.). (2007). *Red: The next generation of American writers—teenage girls—on what fires up their lives today.* New York: Hudson Street Press.

Golombok, S., & Fivush, R. (1994). *Gender development.* New York: Cambridge University Press.

Golombok, S., & Hines, M. (2002). Sex differences in social behavior. In P. K. Smith & C. H. Hart (Eds.), *Blackwell handbook of childhood social development* (pp. 117–136). Malden, MA: Blackwell.

Golombok, S., et al. (2003). Children with lesbian parents: A community study. *Developmental Psychology, 39,* 20–33.

Golub, S. (1992). *Periods: From menarche to menopause.* Newbury Park, CA: Sage.

Gonzales, P. M., Blanton, H., & Williams, K. J. (2002). The effects of stereotype threat and double-minority status on the test performance of Latino women. *Personality and Social Psychology Bulletin, 28,* 659–670.

Gonzalez, A. Q., & Koestner, R. (2005). Parental preference for sex of newborn as reflected in positive affect in birth announcements. *Sex Roles, 52,* 407–411.

Good, C., Aronson, J., & Inzlicht, M. (2003). Improving adolescents' standardized test performance: An intervention to reduce the effects of stereotype threat. *Applied Developmental Psychology, 24,* 645–662.

Gooden, A. M., & Gooden, M. A. (2001). Gender representation in notable children's picture books: 1995-1999. *Sex Roles, 45,* 89–101.

Goodman, G. S., et al. (2003). A prospective study of memory for child sexual abuse. *Psychological Science, 14,* 113–118.

Goodman, G. S., Gonzalves, L., & Wolpe, S. (2019). False memories and true memories of childhood trauma: Balancing the risks. *Clinical Psychological Science, 7,* 29-31.

Gordon, R. A. (2000). *Eating disorders* (2nd ed.). Oxford, England: Blackwell.

Gorlick, C. A. (1995). Divorce: Options available, constraints forced, pathways taken. In N. Mandell & A. Duffy (Ed.), *Canadian families: Diversity, conflict, and change* (pp. 211–234). Toronto: Harcourt Brace Canada.

Gorney, C. (1998). *Articles of faith: A frontline history of the abortion wars.* New York: Simon & Schuster.

Gorman, A. (2021a). *The hill we climb: An inaugural poem for the country.* New York: Viking.

Gorman, A. [@TheAmandaGorman]. (2021b, March 5). *A security guard tailed me on my walk home tonight. He demanded if I lived there because "you look suspicious." I showed my keys & buzzed myself into my building. He left, no apology. This is the reality of black girls: One day you're called an icon, the next day, a threat.* [Tweet]. Twitter.

Gotlib, I. H., & Hammen, C. L. (Eds.) (2009). *Handbook of depression* (2nd ed.). New York: Guilford.

Gottfried, A. E., & Gottfried, A. W. (2008). The upside of maternal and dual-earner employment: A focus on positive family adaptations, home environments, and child development in the Fullerton Longitudinal Study. In A. Marcus- Newhall, D. F. Halpern, & J. Sherylle (Eds.), *The changing realities of work and family: A multidisciplinary approach* (pp. 25–42). Malden, MA: Blackwell.

Gottheil, M., Steinberg, R., & Granger, L. (1999). An exploration of clinicians' diagnostic approaches to premenstrual symptomatology. *Canadian Journal of Behavioural Sciences, 31,* 254–262.

Gottlieb, A. (2020). Menstrual taboos: Moving beyond the curse. In C. Bobel, I. T. Winkler, B. Fahs, K. A. Hasson, E. A. Kissling, & T. A. Roberts (Eds.). *The Palgrave Handbook of Critical Menstruation Studies* (pp. 143-162). Singapore: Palgrave Macmillan.

Government of Canada. (2019). *Canadian tobacco and nicotine survey: A summary of results for 2019.* Retrieved October 5, 2021 from https://www.canada.ca/en/health-canada/services/canadian-tobacco-nicotine-survey/2019-summary.html

Government of Canada. (2019). *Suicide in Canada. Government of Canada.* Retrieved October 5, 2021 from https://www.canada.ca/en/public-health/services/suicide-prevention/suicide-canada.html

Grabe, S., & Else-Quest, N. M. (2012). The role of transnational feminism in psychology: Complementary visions. *Psychology of Women Quarterly, 36,* 158-161.

Grabe, S., & Hyde, J. S. (2006). Ethnicity and body dissatisfaction among women in the United States: A meta-analysis. *Psychological Bulletin, 132,* 622–640.

Grabe, S., Hyde, J. S., & Lindberg, S. M. (2006). Body objectification and depression in adolescents: The role of gender, shame, and rumination. *Psychology of Women Quarterly, 31,* 164–175.

Grabe, S., Hyde, J. S., & Lindberg, S. M. (2007). Body objectification and depression in adolescents: The role of gender, shame, and rumination. *Psychology of Women Quarterly, 31,* 164–175.

Grady, C. (2018, July 20). The waves of feminism, and why people keep fighting over them, explained. *Vox.* Retrieved October 5, 2021 from https://www.vox.com/2018/3/20/16955588/feminism-waves-explained-first-second-third-fourth

Graham-Kevan, N., & Archer, J. (2005). Investigating three explanations of women's relationship aggression. *Psychology of Women Quarterly, 29,* 270–277.

Grant, L. (1994). Helpers, enforcers, and go-betweens: Black females in elementary school classrooms. In M. Baca Zinn & B. T. Dill (Eds.), *Women of color in U.S. Society* (pp. 43–63). Philadelphia: Temple University Press.

Grant, J. M., Mottet, L. A., Tanis, J., Harrison, J., Herman, J. L., & Keisling, M. (2011). *Injustice at every turn: A report on the national transgender discrimination survey.* Washington: National Center for Transgender Equality and National Gay and Lesbian Task Force, 2011. Retrieved October 5, 2021 from https://transequality.org/sites/default/files/docs/resources/NTDS_Report.pdf

Grassia, T. (2005, September). Heterosexual Black women and

teens: The face of the U.S. AIDS epidemic. *Infectious Diseases in Children, 67*–68.

Gravelin, C. R., Biernat, M., & Bucher, C. E. (2019). Blaming the victim of acquaintance rape: Individual, situational, and sociocultural factors. *Frontiers in Psychology, 9*:2422.

Gray, J. (1992). *Men are from Mars, women are from Venus.* New York: HarperCollins.

Grayson, D. A. (2001). Squeaky wheel versus invisibility: Gender bias in teacher-student interactions. In H. Rousso & M. L. Wehmeyer (Eds.), *Double jeopardy: Addressing gender equity in special education* (pp. 155–183). Albany, NY: SUNY Press.

Green, D. L., & Viani, M. W. (2007). Venezuelan American abusive relationships: Assessment and treatment. In A. R. Roberts (Ed.), *Battered women and their families* (3rd ed., pp. 509–528). New York: Springer.

Green, S. (2017). *Violence against Black women – many types, far-reaching effects.* Institute for Women's Policy Research. Retrieved October 5, 2021 from https://iwpr.org/iwpr-issues /race-ethnicity-gender-and -economy/violence-against-black -women-many-types-far-reaching -effects/

Greenberg, B. S., & Worrell, T. R. (2005). The portrayal of weight in the media and its social impact. In K. D. Brownell, R. M. Puhl, M. B. Schwartz, & L. Rudd (Eds.), *Weight bias: Nature, consequences, and remedies* (pp. 42–53). New York: Guilford.

Greenberg, B. S., et al. (2003). Portrayals of overweight and obese individuals on commercial television. *American Journal of Public Health, 93,* 1342–1348.

Greene, B. (2000). African American lesbian and bisexual women. *Journal of Social Issues, 56,* 239–249.

Greene, K. (2004). The politics of birth. *AWP Newsletter,* pp. 6, 18.

Greene, K., & Faulkner, S. L. (2005). Gender, belief in the sexual double standard, and sexual talk in heterosexual dating relationships. *Sex Roles, 53,* 239–251.

Greene, S. (2003). *The psychological development of girls and women: Rethinking change in time.* New York: Routledge.

Greenwald, A. G., McGee, D. E., & Schwartz, J. L. K. (1998). Measuring individual differences in implicit cognition. The Implicit Association Test. *Journal of Personality and Social Psychology, 74,* 1464–1480.

Greenwald, A. G., & Nosek, B. A. (2001). Health of the Implicit Association Test at age 3. *Zeitschrift für Experimentelle Psychologie, 48,* 85-93.

Greenwood, R. M., Adshead, M., & Jay, S. (2017). Immigrant women's experiences of acculturative stress: Ordinary privileges, overt discrimination, and psychological well-being. *Psychology of Women Quarterly, 41,* 497-512.

Greenwood, D. N., & Pietromonaco, P. R. (2004). The interplay among attachment orientation, idealized media images of women, and body dissatisfaction: A social psychological analysis. In L. J. Shurm (Ed.), *The psychology of entertainment media* (pp. 291–308). Mahwah, NJ: Erlbaum.

Greer, T. M., Laseter, A., & Asiamah, D. (2009). Gender as a moderator of the relationship between race-related stress and mental health symptoms for African Americans. *Psychology of Women Quarterly, 33,* 295–307.

Gregory, E. (2007). *Ready: Why women are embracing the new later motherhood.* New York: Basic Books.

Greitemeyer, T. (2007). What do men and women want in a partner? Are educated partners always more desirable? *Journal of Experimental Social Psychology, 43,* 180–194.

Gresky, D. M., Ten Eyck, L. L., Lord, C. G., & McIntyre, R. B. (2005).

Effects of salient multiple identities on women's performance under mathematics stereotype threat. *Sex Roles, 53,* 703–716.

Grilo, C. M. (2002). Binge eating disorder. In C. G. Fairburn & K. D. Brownell (Eds.), *Eating disorders and obesity: A comprehensive handbook* (2nd ed., pp. 178–182). New York: Guilford.

Grolnick, W. S., Gurland, S. T., Jacob, K. F., & Decourcey, W. (2002), The development of self-determination in Middle childhood and adolescence. In A. Wigfield & J. S. Eccles (Eds.), *Development of achievement motivation* (pp. 147–171). San Diego, CA: Academic Press.

Gross, M. S., Taylor, H. A., Tomori, C., & Coleman, J. S. (2019). Breastfeeding with HIV: An evidence-based case for new policy. *Journal of Law, Medicine, and Ethics, 47,* 152-160.

Grote, N. K., & Frieze, I. H. (1994). The measurement of friendship-based love in intimate relationships. *Personal Relationships, 1,* 275–300.

Grothues, C. A., & Marmion, S. L. (2006). Dismantling the myths about intimate violence against women. In P. K. Lundberg-Love & S. L. Marmion (Eds.), *Intimate violence against women: When spouses, partners, or lovers attack* (pp. 9–14). Westport, CT: Praeger.

Grusec, J. E., & Lytton, H. (1988). *Social development.* New York: Springer.

Guadagni, V., Umiltà, A., & Iaria, G. (2020) Sleep quality, empathy, and mood during the isolation period of the COVID-19 Pandemic in the Canadian population: Females and women suffered the most. *Frontiers in Global Women's Health, 1*:585938.

Gudrais, E. (2008). *Unequal America.* Retrieved February 3, 2010, from www.truthout.org/article /unequal-America

Guimond, S., et al. (2006). Social comparison, self-stereotyping, and gender differences in self-construals. *Journal of Personality and Social Psychology, 90,* 221–242.

Guimond, S., et al. (2007). Culture, gender, and the self: Variations and impact of social comparison processes. *Journal of Personality and Social Psychology, 92,* 1118–1134.

Guisinger, S. (2003). Adapted to flee famine: Adding an evolutionary perspective on anorexia nervosa. *Psychological Review, 110,* 745–761.

Gunning, I. R. (2002). Female genital surgeries: Eradication measures at the Western local level—a cautionary tale. In S. M. James & C. C. Robertson (Eds.), *Genital cutting and transnational sisterhood* (pp. 114–125). Urbana: University of Illinois Press.

Gunter, B., Harrison, J., & Wykes, M. (2003). *Violence on television: Distribution, form, context, and themes.* Mahwah, NJ: Erlbaum.

Gunter, J. (2021). *The menopause manifesto: Own your health with facts and feminism.* New York, NY: Kensington Press.

Gupta, S. R. (1999). Forged by fire: Indian-American women reflect on their marriages, divorces, and on rebuilding lives. In S. R. Gupta (Ed.), *Emerging voices: South Asian American women redefine self, family, and community* (pp. 193–221). Walnut Creek, CA: AltaMira Press.

Gurrentz, B., & Mayol-Garcia, Y. (2021). *Marriage, divorce, and widowhood remain prevalent among older populations.* U. S. Census Bureau. Retrieved October 5, 2021 from https://www.census.gov/library/stories/2021/04/love-and-loss-among-older-adults.html

Gurung, R. A. R. (2006). *Health psychology: A cultural approach.* Belmont, CA: Wadsworth.

Gutek, B. A. (2001). Working environments. In J. Worell (Ed.), *Encyclopedia of women and gender* (pp. 1191–1204). San Diego: Academic Press.

Gutek, B. A. (2007). How can we make our research on sexual harassment more useful in legal decision making? In R. L. Wiener, B. H. Bornstein, R. Schopp, & S. L. Willborn (Eds.), *Social consciousness in legal decision making: Psychological perspectives* (pp. 153–170). New York: Springer.

Gutek, B. A., & Gilliland, C. (2007). Work versus the family: Keeping the balance. In S. Gilliland, D. Steiner, & D. Skarlicki (Eds.), *Managing social and ethical issues in organizations* (pp. 53–82). Greenwich, CT: Information Age Publishers.

Guthrie, R. V. (1998). *Even the rat was white: A historical view of psychology* (2nd ed.). Boston: Allyn & Bacon.

Guttmacher Institute. (2001). *Can more progress be made? Teenage sexual and reproductive behavior in developed countries: Executive summary.* New York: Author.

Guttmacher Institute. (2004). *U.S. teenage pregnancy statistics: Overall trends, trends by race and ethnicity and state-by-state information.* New York: Author.

Guttmacher Institute. (2005). *Get "in the know": 20 questions about pregnancy, contraception and abortion.* Retrieved July 11, 2005, from http://www. guttmacher.org/in-the-know/index

Guttmacher Institute. (2008). *Facts on contraceptive use.* Retrieved September 9, 2009, from http://www.gutt-macher.org/pubs/fb_contr_use.html

Guttmacher Institute. (2015). *Adolescent pregnancy and its outcomes across countries, 2015.* Retrieved October 4, 2021 from https://www.guttmacher.org/fact-sheet/adolescent-pregnancy-and-its-outcomes-across-countries.

Guttmacher Institute. (2017). *American adolescents' sources of sexual health information.* Retrieved October 4, 2021 from https://www.guttmacher.org/fact-sheet/facts-american-teens-sources-information-about-sex#

Haas, J. S., et al. (2005). Prepregnancy health status and the risk of preterm delivery. *Archives of Pediatric and Adolescent Medicine, 159,* 58–63.

Hackney, K. J., Daniels, S. R., Paustian-Underdahl, S. C., Perrewé, P. L., Mandeville, A., & Eaton, A. A. (2021). Examining the effects of perceived pregnancy discrimination on mother and baby health. *Journal of Applied Psychology, 106,* 774–783.

Hafeez, H., Zeshan, M., Tahir, M. A., et al. (2017) Health care disparities among lesbian, gay, bisexual, and transgender youth: A literature review. *Cureus 9:* e1184.

Hafiz, S., & Paarlberg, M. (2017). *The human trafficking of domestic workers in the United States: Findings from the beyond survival campaign.* Institute for Policy Studies and the National Domestic Workers Alliance. Retrieved October 3, 2021 from https://ips-dc.org/wp-content/uploads/2017/03/Beyond-Survival-2017-Report_FINAL_PROOF-1-1.pdf

Hafter, D. M. (1979). An overview of women's history. In M. Richmond-Abbott (Ed.), *The American woman* (pp. 1–27). New York: Holt, Rinehart & Winston.

Haley, H. (2001, June). *Crisscrossing gender lines and color lines: A test of the subordinate male target hypothesis.* Paper presented at the meeting of the American Psychological Society, Toronto, Ontario.

Hail, L., & Le Grange, D. (2018). Bulimia nervosa in adolescents: Prevalence and treatment challenges. *Adolescent Health, Medicine, and Therapeutics, 9,* 11-16.

Haley-Banez, L., & Garrett, J. (2002). *Lesbians in committed relationships: Extraordinary couples, ordinary lives.* Binghamton, NY: Haworth.

Hales, C. M., Carroll, M. D., Fryar, C. D., & Ogden, C. L. (2020).

Prevalence of obesity and severe obesity among adults: United States, 2017-2018. NCHS Data Brief, no 360. National Center for Health Statistics. Retrieved October 5, 2021 from https://www.cdc.gov/nchs/products/databriefs/db360.htm

Hall, G. C. N., & Barongan, C. (2002). *Multicultural psychology.* Upper Saddle River, NJ: Prentice Hall.

Hall, G. S. (1906). The question of coeducation. *Munsey's Magazine, 588–592.*

Hall, J. A. (1984). *Nonverbal sex differences: Communication accuracy and expressive style.* Baltimore: Johns Hopkins University Press.

Hall, J. A. (1987). On explaining gender differences: The case of nonverbal communication. In P. Shaver & C. Hendrick (Eds.), *Sex and gender* (pp. 177–200). Newbury Park, CA: Sage.

Hall, J. A. (1998). How big are nonverbal sex differences? The case of smiling and sensitivity to nonverbal cues. In D. J. Canary & K. Dindia (Eds.), *Sex differences and similarities in communication* (pp. 155–177). Mahwah, NJ: Erlbaum.

Hall, J. A. (2006). Nonverbal behavior, status, and gender: How do we understand their relations? *Psychology of Women Quarterly, 30,* 384–391.

Hall, J. A., & Carter, J. D. (1999). Gender-stereotype accuracy as an individual difference. *Journal of Personality and Social Psychology, 77,* 350–359.

Hall, J. A., Carter, J. D., & Horgan, T. G. (2000). Gender differences in nonverbal communication of emotion. In A. H. Fischer (Ed.), *Gender and emotion: Social psychological perspectives* (pp. 97–117). New York: Cambridge University Press.

Hall, J. A., Coats, E. J., & LeBeau, L. S. (2005). Nonverbal behavior and the vertical dimension of social relations: A meta-analysis. *Psychological Bulletin, 131,* 898–924.

Hall, J. A., & Halberstadt, A. G. (1986). Smiling and gazing. In J. S. Hyde & M. C. Linn (Eds.), *The psychology of gender: Advances through meta-analysis* (pp. 136–158). Baltimore: Johns Hopkins University Press.

Hall, J. A., & Halberstadt, A. G. (1997). Subordination and nonverbal sensitivity: A hypothesis in search of support. In M. R. Walsh (Ed.), *Women, men, and gender: Ongoing debates* (pp. 120–133). New Haven, CT: Yale University Press.

Hall, J. A., Smith LeBeau, L., Gordon Reinoso, J. G., & Thayer, F. (2001). Status, gender, and nonverbal behavior in candid and posed photographs: A study of conversations between university employees. *Sex Roles, 44,* 677–692.

Hall, R. L. (2008). Sweating it out. In J. C. Chrisler, C. Golden, & P. D. Rozee (Eds.), *Lectures on the psychology of women* (4th ed., pp. 42–57). Boston, MA: McGraw-Hill.

Hall, R. L., & Fine, M. (2005). The stories we tell: The lives and friendship of two older black lesbians. *Psychology of Women Quarterly, 29,* 177–187.

Hall, R. L., & Greene, B. (2002). Not any one thing: The complex legacy of social class on African American lesbian relationships. *Journal of Lesbian Studies, 6,* 65–74.

Hall, R. L., & Greene, B. (2003). Contemporary African American families. In L. B. Silverstein & T. J. Goodrich (Eds.), *Feminist family therapy: Empowerment in social context* (pp. 107–120). Washington, DC: American Psychological Association.

Halpern, C. T. (2003). Biological influences on adolescent romantic and sexual behavior. In P. Florsheim (Ed.), *Adolescent romantic relations and sexual behavior* (pp. 57–84). Mahwah, NJ: Erlbaum.

Halpern, D. F. (1985). The influence of sex-role stereotypes on prose recall. *Sex Roles, 12,* 363–375.

Halpern, D. F. (1997). Sex differences in intelligence: Implications for education. *American Psychologist, 52,* 1091–1102.

Halpern, D. F. (2000). *Sex differences in cognitive abilities* (3rd ed.). Mahwah, NJ: Erlbaum.

Halpern, D. F. (2001). Sex difference research: Cognitive abilities. In J. Worell (Ed.), *The encyclopedia of women and gender* (pp. 963–971). San Diego: Academic Press.

Halpern, D. F. (2004a). A cognitive-process taxonomy for sex differences in cognitive abilities. *Current Directions inPsychologicalScience,13,* 135–139.

Halpern, D. F. (2004b, February). I dare you to try this at home (or at work). *Monitor on Psychology, 5.*

Halpern, D. F. (2005). Psychology at the intersection of work and family: Recommendations for employers, working families, and policymakers. *American Psychologist, 60,* 397–409.

Halpern, D. F. (2006a). Assessing gender gaps in learning and academic achievement. In P. A. Alexander & P. H. Winne (Eds.), *Handbook of educational psychology* (pp. 635–652). Mahwah, NJ: Erlbaum.

Halpern, D. F. (2006b). Girls and academic success: Changing patterns of academic achievement. In J. Worell & C. D. Goodheart (Eds.), *Handbook of girls' and women's psychological health: Gender and well-being across the life span* (pp. 272–282). New York: Oxford University Press.

Halpern, D. F. (2007). Science, sex, and good sense: Why women are under-represented in some areas of science and math. In C. J. Ceci & W. M. Williams (Eds.), *Why aren't more women in science? Top researchers debate the evidence* (pp. 121–130). Washington, DC: American Psychological Association.

Halpern, D. F. (2008). Nurturing careers in psychology: Combining work and family. *Educational Psychology Review, 20,* 57–64.

Halpern, D. F., Aronson, J., et al. (2007). *Encouraging girls in math and science.* Washington, DC: National Center for Education Research.

Halpern, D. F., Benbow, C. P., et al. (2007). The science of sex differences in science and mathematics. *Psychological Science in the Public Interest, 8,* 1–51.

Halpern, D. F., & Collaer, M. L. (2005). Sex differences in visuospatial abilities. In P. Shah & A. Miyake (Eds.), *The Cambridge handbook of visuo-spatial thinking* (pp. 170–212). New York: Cambridge University Press.

Halpern, D. F., & Ikier, S. (2002). Causes, correlates, and caveats: Understanding the development of sex differences in cognition. In A. McGillicuddy-De Lisi & R. De Lisi (Eds.), *Biology, society, and behavior: The development of sex differences in cognition* (pp. 3–19). Westport, CT: Ablex Publishing.

Halpern, D. F., & Tan, U. (2001). Stereotypes and steroids: Using a psychobiosocial model to understand cognitive sex differences. *Brain and Cognition, 45,* 392–414.

Halpern, D. F., Tan, S. J., & Carsten, M. (2008). California paid family leave: Is it working for caregivers? In A. Marcus-Newhall, D. F. Halpern, & S. J. Tan (Eds.), *The changing realities of work and family* (pp. 159–174). Malden, MA: Blackwell.

Hambright, M. K., & Decker, J. D. (2002). The unprotected: The sexual harassment of lesbians and gays. In L. Diamant & J. A. Lee (Eds.), *The psychology of sex, gender, and jobs* (pp. 121–140). Westport, CT: Praeger.

Hamilton, B. E. (2021). Total fertility rates, by maternal educational attainment and race and hispanic origin: United States, 2019. *National Vital Statistics Reports,* 70(5). Retrieved October 4, 2021 from https://www.cdc.gov/nchs/data/nvsr/nvsr70/nvsr70-05-508.pdf

Hamilton, B. E., et al. (2007). Annual summary of vital statistics: 2005. *Pediatrics, 119,* 345–360.

Hamilton, J. A., & Russo, N. F. (2006). Women and depression: Research, theory, and social policy. In C. L. M. Keyes & S. H. Goodman (Eds.), *Women and depression: A handbook for the social, behavioral, and bio-medical sciences* (pp. 479–522). New York: Cambridge University Press.

Hamilton, J. G., & Lobel, M. (2008). Types, patterns, and predictors of coping with stress during pregnancy: Examination of the revised prenatal coping inventory in a diverse sample. *Journal of Psychosomatic Obstetrics & Gynecology, 29,* 97–104.

Hamilton, M. C. (1991). Masculine bias in the attribution of personhood: People = male, male = people. *Psychology of Women Quarterly, 15,* 393–402.

Hamilton, M. C. (2001). Sex-related difference research: Personality. In J. Worell (Ed.), *Encyclopedia of women and gender* (pp. 973-981). San Diego: Academic Press.

Hamilton, M. C., Anderson, D., Broaddus, M., & Young, K. (2006). Gender stereotyping and under-representation of female characters in 200 popular children's picture books: A 21st century update. *Sex Roles, 55,* 757–765.

Hamon, R. R., & Ingoldsby, B. B. (Eds.). (2003). *Mate selection across cultures.* Thousand Oaks, CA: Sage.

Hampson, E., & Moffat, S. D. (2004). The psychobiology of gender: Cognitive effects of reproductive hormones in the adult nervous system. In A. H. Eagly, A. E. Beall, & R. J. Sternberg (Eds.), *The psychology of gender* (2nd ed., pp. 38–64). New York: Guilford.

Hansen, S. (2002). Cardiovascular disease. In S. G. Kornstein & A. H. Clayton (Eds.), *Women's mental health* (pp. 422–436). New York: Guilford.

Hancock, A. B., & Rubin, B. A. (2015). Influence of communication partner's gender on language. *Journal of Language and Social Psychology, 34,* 46-64.

Haney-Caron, E., & Heilbrun, K. (2014). Lesbian and gay parents and determination of child custody: The changing legal landscape and implications for policy and practice. *Psychology of Sexual Orientation and Gender Diversity, 1,* 19-29.

Hanks, A., Solomon, D, & Weller, C. E. (2018). *Systematic inequality: How America's structural racism helped create the Black-White wealth gap.* Center for American Progress. Retrieved October 4, 2021 from https://www.americanprogress.org/issues/race/reports/2018/02/21/447051/systematic-inequality/

Hanley, N. A., Hagan, D., Clement-Jones, M. M., Ball, S. G., Strachan, T., Salas-Cortés, L., McElreavey, K., ... Wilson, D. I. (2000). SRY, SOX9, and DAX1 expression patterns during human sex determination and gonadal development. *Mechanisms of Development, 91*(1–2), 403-407.

Hantsoo, L., & Epperson, C. N. (2015). Premenstrual dysphoric disorder: Etiology and treatment. *Current Psychiatry Reports, 17,* 87.

Hardie, E. A. (1997). Prevalence and predictors of cyclic and noncyclic affective change. *Psychology of Women Quarterly, 21,* 299–314.

Hare-Mustin, R. T., & Marecek, J. (1994). Asking the right questions: Feminist psychology and sex differences. *Feminism and Psychology, 4,* 531–537.

Harman, J. (2008, April 23). Rapists and bullies wreck the ranks. *Liberal Opinion Weekly,* pp. 10–11.

Harper, B., & Tiggemann, M. (2008). The effect of thin ideal media images on women's self-objecti-fication, mood, and body image. *Sex Roles, 58,* 649–657.

Harper, C. C., Weiss, D. C., Speidel, J. J., & Raine-Bennett, T. (2008). Over-the-counter access to emergency contraception for teens. *Contraception, 77,* 230–233.

Harper, M., & Schoeman, W. J. (2003). Influences of gender as a basic-level category in person perception on the gender belief system. *Sex Roles, 49,* 517–526.

Harrell, Z. A. T., & Jackson, B. (2008). Thinking fat and feeling blue: Eating behaviors, ruminative coping, and depressive symptoms in college women. *Sex Roles, 58,* 658–665.

Harrell, Z. A. T., & Karim, N. M. (2008). Is gender relevant only for problem alcohol behaviors? An examination of correlates of alcohol use among college students. *Addictive Behaviors, 33,* 359–365.

Harris, M. G. (1994). Cholas, Mexican-American girls, and gangs. *Sex Roles, 30,* 289–301.

Harris, R. J., & Firestone, J. M. (1998). Changes in predictors of gender role ideologies among women: A multi-variate analysis. *Sex Roles, 38,* 239–252.

Hart, L. (2008). Workforce issues: In my own voice. In M. A. Paludi (Ed.), *The psychology of women at work* (Vol. 3, pp. 143–148). Westport, CT: Praeger.

Hartman, H., & Hartman, M. (2007). Is teamwork a female-friendly pedagogy? In I. Welpe, B. Reschka, & J. Larkin (Eds.), *Gender and engineering: Strategies and possibilities* (pp. 73–91). Frankfurt: Peter Lang.

Hartman, H., & Hartman, M. (2008). How undergraduate engineering students perceive women's (and men's) problems in science, math and engineering. *Sex Roles, 58,* 251–265.

Hartmann, H., & Lee, S. (2003, April). *Social security: The largest source of income for both women and men in retirement*

(Briefing Paper #D455). Washington, DC: Institute for Women's Policy Research.

Hartup, W. W. (1999). Foreword. In W. Furman, B. B. Brown, & C. Feiring (Eds.), *The development of romantic relationships in adolescence* (pp. xi–xv). New York: Cambridge University Press.

Harvey, J. H., & Weber, A. L. (2002). *Odyssey of the heart: Close relationships in the 21st century* (2nd ed.). Mahwah, NJ: Erlbaum.

Harvey, P. D. (2000). *Let every child be wanted.* Westport, CT: Auburn House.

Harville, E. W., Xiong, X., & Buekens, P. (2009). Hurricane Katrina and perinatal health. *Birth, 36,* 325–331.

Harville, M. L., & Rienzi, B. M. (2000). Equal worth and gracious submission: Judeo-Christian attitudes toward employed women. *Psychology of Women Quarterly, 24,* 145–147.

Harwood, R., et al. (2002). Parenting among Latino families in the U.S. In M. H. Bornstein (Ed.), *Handbook of parenting* (2nd ed., Vol. 4, pp. 21–46). Mahwah, NJ: Erlbaum.

Hase, M. (2001). Student resistance and nationalism in the classroom: Some reflections on globalizing the curriculum. *Feminist Teacher, 13,* 90–107.

Hatcher, R. A., et al. (2004). *Contraceptive technology* (18th rev ed.). New York: Ardent Media.

Hatfield, E., & Rapson, R. L. (1993). *Love, sex, and intimacy: Their psychology, biology, and history.* New York: HarperCollins.

Hatfield, E., & Rapson, R. L. (1996). *Love and sex: Cross-cultural perspectives.* Boston: Allyn & Bacon.

Hatfield, E., & Rapson, R. L. (2005). *Love and sex: Cross-cultural perspectives.* Lanham, MD: University Press of America.

Hatfield, E., & Rapson, R. L. (2006). Passionate love, sexual desire, and mate selection: Cross-cultural and historical perspectives.

In P. Noller & J. A. Feeney (Eds.), *Close relationships: Functions, forms, and processes* (pp. 227–243). New York: Psychology Press.

Hatfield, E., Rapson, R. L., & Le, Y. C. L. (2008). Emotional contagion and empathy. In J. Decety & W. Ickes (Eds.), *The social neuroscience of empathy* (pp. 28–51). Boston, MA: MIT Press.

Hatfield, E., Rapson, R. L., & Martel, L. D. (2007). Passionate love and sexual desire. In S. Kitayama & D. Cohen (Eds.), *Handbook of cultural psychology* (pp. 760–779). New York: Guilford Press.

Hatfield, E., & Sprecher, S. (1995). Men's and women's preferences in marital partners in the United States, Russia, and Japan. *Journal of Cross-Cultural Psychology, 26,* 728–750.

Hatzenbuehler, M. L., Hilt, L. M., & Nolen-Hoeksema, S. (2010). Gender, sexual orientation, and vulnerability to depression. In J. C. Chrisler & D. R. McCreary (Eds.), *Handbook of gender research in psychology* (Vol. 2, pp. 133–151). New York: Springer.

Haugen, E. N., Schmutzer, P. A., & Wenzel, A. (2004). Sexuality and the partner relationship during pregnancy and the postpartum period. In J. H. Harvey, A. Wenzel, & S. Sprecher (Eds.), *The handbook of sexuality in close relationships* (pp. 411–435). Mahwah, NJ: Erlbaum.

Haupt, A. (2018, February 6). 8 women share what made them finally decide to get sober. *Women's Health Magazine.* Retrieved October 5, 2021 from https://www.womenshealthmag.com/health/a19996261/sobriety-quotes/

Hauser, D. (2009). Five years of abstinence-only-until-marriage education: Assessing the impact. In J. W. White (Ed.), *Taking sides: Clashing views in gender* (4th ed., pp. 342–348). Boston: McGraw-Hill.

Hawkins, B. D. (1994, November 3). An evening with Gwendolyn Brooks. *Black Issues in Higher Education*, 16–21.

Hayden, J. M., Singer, J. A., & Chrisler, J. C. (2006). The transmission of birth stories from mother to daughter: Self-esteem and mother-daughter attachment. *Sex Roles, 55,* 373–383.

Hayes Skelton, S., & Pantalone, D. (2018). Anxiety and depression in sexual and gender minority individuals. *Anxiety and Depression Association of America.* Retrieved October 5, 2021 from https://adaa.org/sexual-gender-minority-individuals

Hazen, C., Campa, M., & Hit-Yaish, N. (2006). Attachment across the lifespan. In P. Noller & J. A. Feeney (Eds.), *Close relationships: Functions, forms, and processes* (pp. 189–209). New York: Psychology Press.

Hearn, K. D., O'Sullivan, L. F., & Dudley, C. D. (2003). Assessing reliability of early adolescent girls' reports of romantic and sexual behavior. *Archives of Sexual Behavior, 32,* 513–521.

Heart and Stroke Foundation of Canada. (2017). Ms. Understood: Women's hearts are victims of a system that is ill-equipped to diagnose, treat and support them. *Heart & Stroke 2018 Heart Report.* Retrieved October 5, 2021 from https://www.heartandstroke.ca/-/media/pdf-files/canada/2018-heart-month/hs_2018-heart-report_en.ashx?rev=71bed5e2bcf148b4a0bf5082e50de6c6

Heatherington, L., Burns, A. B., & Gustafson, T. B. (1998). When another stumbles: Gender and self-presentation to vulnerable others. *Sex Roles, 38,* 889–913.

Heatherington, L., et al. (1993). Two investigations of "female modesty" in achievement situations. *Sex Roles, 29,* 739–754.

Hebl, M. R., Kazama, S. M., Singletary, S. L., & Glick, P. (2007). Hostile and benevolent reactions toward pregnant women: Complementary interpersonal punishments and rewards that maintain traditional roles. *Journal of Applied Psychology, 92,* 1499–1511.

Heck, K. E., Schoendorf, K. C., Chávez, G. F., & Braverman, P. (2003). Does postpartum length of stay affect breastfeeding duration? A population-based study. *Birth, 30,* 153–159.

Heckert, T. M., et al. (2002). Gender differences in anticipated salary: Role of salary estimates for others, job characteristics, career paths, and job inputs. *Sex Roles, 47,* 139–151.

Hedges, L., & Nowell, A. (1995). Sex differences in mental test scores, variability, and numbers of high-scoring individuals. *Science, 269,* 41–45.

Hedley, M. (2002a). The geometry of gendered conflict in popular film: 1986–2000. *Sex Roles, 47,* 201–217.

Hedley, M. (2002b). Gendered conflict resolution in popular film: Epiphanies of female deference. *The Journal of American and Contemporary Cultures, 25,* 363–374.

Heilman, M. E., Wallen, A. S., Fuchs, D., & Tamkins, M. M. (2004). Penalties for success: Reactions to women who succeed at male gender-typed tasks. *Journal of Applied Psychology, 89,* 416–427.

Heilman, M. F., & Okimoto, T. G. (2008). Motherhood: A potential source of bias in employment decisions. *Journal of Applied Psychology, 93,* 189–198.

Heiman, J. B. (2007). Orgasmic disorders in women. In S. R. Leiblum (Ed.), *Principles and practice of sex therapy* (4th ed., pp. 25–53). New York: Guilford.

Heiser, S. (2019). *The majority of U.S. medical school students are women, new data show.* American Association of Medical Colleges. Retrieved October 3, 2021 from https://www.aamc.org/news-insights/press-releases/majority-us-medical-students-are-women-new-data-show

Heiss, G., et al. (2008). Health risks and benefits 3 years after stopping randomized treatment with estrogen and progestin. *JAMA, 299,* 1036–1045.

Hellenga, K., Aber, M. S., & Rhodes, J. E. (2002). African American adolescent mothers' vocational aspiration-expectation gap: Individual, social and environmental influences. *Psychology of Women Quarterly, 26,* 200–212.

Helstrom, A. W., Coffey, C., & Jorgannathan, P. (1998). Asian-American women's health. In A. Blechman & K. D. Brownell (Eds.), *Behavioral medicine and women: A comprehensive handbook* (pp. 826–832). New York: Guilford.

Helwig, A. A. (1998). Gender-role stereotyping: Testing theory with a longitudinal sample. *Sex Roles, 38,* 403–423.

Helwig-Larsen, M., Gunningham, S. J., Carrico, A., & Pergram, A. M. (2004). To nod or not to nod: An observational study of nonverbal communication and status in female and male college students. *Psychology of Women Quarterly, 28,* 358–361.

Henderson-King, D., & Zhermer, N. (2003). Feminist consciousness among Russians and Americans. *Sex Roles, 48,* 143–155.

Hendrick, C., & Hendrick, S. (1996). Gender and the experience of heterosexual love. In J. T. Wood (Ed.), *Gendered relationships* (pp. 131–148). Mountain View, CA: Mayfield.

Hendrick, S. (2006). Love, intimacy, and partners. In J. Worell & C. D. Goodheart (Eds.), *Handbook of girls' and women's psychological health: Gender and well-being across the life span* (pp. 321–329). New York: Oxford University Press.

Henrie, R. L., Aron, R. H., Nelson, B. D., & Poole, D. A. (1997). Gender-related knowledge variations within geography. *Sex Roles, 36,* 605–623.

Herbert, S. E. (1996). Lesbian sexuality. In R. P. Cabaj & T. S. Stein (Eds.), *Textbook of homosexuality and mental health* (pp. 723–742). Washington, DC: American Psychiatric Press.

Herek, G. M. (1996). Why tell if you're not asked? Self-disclosure, inter-group contact, and heterosexuals' attitudes toward lesbians and gay men. In G. M. Herek, J. B. Jobe, & R. M. Carney (Eds.), *Out in force: Sexual orientation and the military* (pp. 197–225). Chicago: University of Chicago Press.

Herek, G. M. (2002a). Gender gaps in public opinion about lesbians and gay men. *Public Opinion Quarterly, 66,* 40–66.

Herek, G. M. (2002b). Heterosexuals' attitudes toward bisexual men and women in the United States. *The Journal of Sex Research, 38,* 264–272.

Herek, G. M. (2004). Beyond "homophobia" : Thinking about sexual prejudice and stigma in the twenty-first century. *Sexuality Research & Social Policy, 1,* 6–24.

Herek, G. M. (2006). Legal recognition of same-sex relationships in the United States. *American Psychologist, 61,* 607–621.

Herek, G. M. (2007). Confronting sexual stigma and prejudice: Theory and practice. *Journal of Social Issues, 63,* 905–925.

Herek, G. M. (2009a). Hate crimes and stigma-related experiences among sexual minority adults in the United States: Prevalence from a national probability sample. *Journal of Interpersonal Violence, 24,* 54–74.

Herek, G. M. (2009b). Sexual prejudice. In T. D. Nelson (Ed.), *Handbook of prejudice, stereotyping, and discrimination* (pp. 441–467). New York: Psychology Press.

Herek, G. M., Cogan, J. C., & Gillis, J. R. (2002). Victim experiences in hate crimes based on sexual orientation. *Journal of Social Issues, 38,* 319–339.

Herek, G. M., & Garnets, L. D. (2007). Sexual orientation and mental health. *Annual Review of Clinical Psychology, 3,* 353–375.

Herlitz, A., & Rehnman, J. (2008). Sex differences in episodic memory. *Current Directions in Psychological Science, 17,* 52–54.

Herlitz, A., & Yonker, J. E. (2002). Sex differences in episodic memory: The influence of intelligence. *Journal of Clinical and Experimental Neuro-psychology, 24,* 107–114.

Herlitz, A., Airaksinen, E., & Nordstrom, E. (1999). Sex differences in episodic memory: The impact of verbal and visuospatial ability. *Neuropsychology, 13,* 590–597.

Herrmann, D. J., Crawford, M., & Holdsworth, M. (1992). Gender-linked differences in everyday memory performance. *British Journal of Psychology, 83,* 221–231.

Hershberger, S. L. (2001). Biological factors in the development of sexual orientation. In A. R. D'Augelli & C. J. Patterson (Eds.), *Lesbian, gay, and bisexual identities and youth* (pp. 27–51). New York: Oxford University Press.

Hesse-Biber, S., & Carter, G. L. (2000). *Working women in America: Split dreams.* New York: Oxford University Press.

Hesselbrock, V. M., & Hesselbrock, M. N. (2006). Developmental perspectives on the risk for developing substance abuse problems. In W. R. Miller & K. M. Carroll (Eds.), *Rethinking substance abuse* (pp. 97–114). New York: Guilford.

Hetsroni, A. (2007a). Sexual content on mainstream TV advertising: A cross-cultural comparison. *Sex Roles, 57,* 201–210.

Hetsroni, A. (2007b). Three decades of sexual content on prime-time network programming: A longitudinal meta-analytic review. *Journal of Communication, 57,* 318–348.

Hettema, J., Steele, J., & Miller, W. R. (2005). Motivational interviewing. *Annual Review of Clinical Psychology, 1,* 91–111.

Hewitt, E. C., & Moore, L. D. (2002). The role of lay theories of the etiologies of homosexuality in attitudes towards lesbians and gay men. *Journal of Lesbian Studies, 6,* 59–72.

Hewstone, M., Rubin, M., & Willis, H. (2002). Intergroup bias. *Annual Review of Psychology, 53,* 575–604.

Heyman, G. D. (2001). Children's interpretation of ambiguous behavior: Evidence for a " boys are bad" bias. *Social Development, 10,* 230–247.

Heywood, L, & Drake, J. (Eds.). (1997). *Third wave agenda: Being feminist, doing feminism.* Minneapolis: University of Minnesota Press.

Hickman, S. E., & Muehlenhard, C. L. (1999). " By the semi-mystical appearance of a condom" : How young women and men communicate sexual consent in heterosexual situations. *Journal of Sex Research, 36,* 258–272.

Higgins, L. T., Zheng, M., Liu, Y., & Sun, C. H. (2002). Attitudes to marriage and sexual behaviors: A survey of gender and culture differences in China and United Kingdom. *Sex Roles, 46,* 75–89.

Hill, A. C., Laird, A. R., & Robinson, J. L. (2014). Gender differences in working memory networks: A BrainMap meta-analysis. *Biological Psychology, 102,* 18-29.

Hill, C. A. (2008). *Human sexuality: Personality and social psychological perspectives.* Thousand Oaks, CA: Sage.

Hill, N. A., Woodson, K. M., Ferguson, A. D., & Parks Jr., C. W. (2012). Intimate partner abuse among African American lesbians: Prevalence, risk factors, theory, and resilience *Journal of Family Violence, 27,* 401-413.

Hill, S. A. (2002). Teaching and doing gender in African American families. *Sex Roles, 47,* 493–506.

Hillard, P. J. A., & Kahn, J. A. (2005). Understanding and preventing human papillomavirus infection during adolescence and young adulthood. *Journal of Adolescent Health, 37,* S1-S2.

Hilton, J. L., & von Hippel, W. (1996). Stereotypes. *Annual Review of Psychology, 47,* 237–271.

Hines, M. (2004). *Brain gender.* New York: Oxford University Press.

Hines, M. (2007). Do sex difference in cognition cause the shortage of women in science? In C. J. Ceci & W. M. Williams (Eds.), *Why aren't more women in science? Top researchers debate the evidence* (pp. 101–112). Washington, DC: American Psychological Association.

Hirsch, P., Koch, I., & Karbach, J. (2019). Putting a stereotype to the test: The case of gender differences in multitasking costs in task-switching and dual-task situations. *PLoS ONE 14*(8): e0220150.

Hochschild, J. L. (2003). Social class in public schools. *Journal of Social Issues, 59,* 821–840.

Hoff, T., & Greene, L. (2000). *Sex education in America.* Menlo Park, CA: Henry J. Kaiser Family Foundation.

Hoffkling, A., Obedin-Maliver, J., & Sevelius, J. M. (2017). From erasure to opportunity: A qualitative study of the experiences of transgender men around pregnancy and recommendations for providers. *BMC Pregnancy and Childbirth, 17*(Suppl 2):332.

Hoffnung, M. (1992). *What's a mother to do? Conversations on work and family.* Pasadena, CA: Trilogy.

Hoffnung, M. (1995). Motherhood: Contemporary conflict for women. In J. Freeman (Ed.), *Women: A feminist perspective* (pp. 162–181). Mountain View, CA: Mayfield.

Hoffnung, M. (2000, March). *Motherhood and career: Changes in college women's thoughts over time.* Paper presented at the annual meeting of the Eastern Psychological Association, Baltimore, MD.

Hoffnung, M. (2003). Studying women's lives: College to seven years after. In E. S. Adler & R. Clark (Eds.), *How it's done: An invitation to social research* (pp. 74–78). Pacific Grove, CA: Wadsworth.

Hoffnung, M. (2004). Wanting it all: Career, marriage, and motherhood during college-educated women's 20s. *Sex Roles, 50,* 711–723.

Hoffnung, M. (2006). What's in a name? Marital name choice revisited. *Sex Roles, 55,* 817–825.

Hoffnung, M. (2010). *Great expectations: Career, marriage, and motherhood during college-educated women's 30s.* Unpublished manuscript.

Hoffnung, M. (in press). Teaching about motherhood: Revisioning family. *Psychology of Women Quarterly, 35.*

Hogervorst, E. (2006). The short-lived effects of hormone therapy on cognitive function. In N. L. Rasgon (Ed.), *The effects of estrogen on brain function* (pp. 46–78). Baltimore, MD: Johns Hopkins University Press.

Hogue, M., & Lord, R. G. (2007). A multilevel, complexity theory approach to understanding gender bias in leadership. *The Leadership Quarterly, 18,* 370–390.

Hogue, M., & Yoder, J. D. (2003). The role of status in producing depressed entitlement in women's and men's pay allocations. *Psychology of Women Quarterly, 27,* 330–337.

Holder, H. D. (2006). Racial and gender differences in substance abuse: What should communities do about them? In W. R. Miller & K. M. Carroll (Eds.), *Rethinking substance abuse* (pp. 153–165). New York: Guilford.

Holliday, B. G., & Holmes, A. L. (2003). A tale of challenge and change: A history and chronology of ethnic minorities in psychology in the United States. In G. Bernal, J. E. Trimble, A. K. Burley, & F. T. L. Leong (Eds.), *Handbook of racial and ethnic minority psychology* (pp. 15–64). Thousand Oaks, CA: Sage.

Hollingworth, L. S. (1914). *Functional periodicity: An experimental study of mental and motor abilities of women during menstruation* (Contributions to Education No. 69, pp. v-14, 86–101). New York: Teachers College, Columbia University.

Hollon, S. D., Stewart, M. O., & Strunk, D. (2006). Enduring effects for cognitive behavior therapy in the treatment of depression and anxiety. *Annual Review of Psychology, 57,* 285–315.

Hom, A. Y. (2003). Stories from the homefront: Perspectives of Asian-American parents with lesbian daughters and gay sons. In L. D. Garnets & D. C. Kimmel (Eds.), *Psychological perspectives on lesbian, gay, and bisexual experiences* (2nd ed., pp. 549–570). New York: Columbia University Press.

Hood, A. (1995). It's a wonderful divorce. In P. Kaganoff & S. Spano (Eds.), *Women and divorce* (pp. 119–133). New York: Harcourt Brace.

Hooks, B. (2015). *Feminism is for everybody: Passionate politics.* New York: Routledge.

Hoover, E. (2004, October 15). Bates calls its SAT-optional policy a boon. *Chronicle of Higher Education,* pp. A32–A33.

Hopkins, A. B. (2007). Opposing views, strongly held. In F. J. Crosby, M. S. Stockdale, & S. A. Ropp (Eds.), *Sex discrimination in the workplace* (pp. 59–67). Malden, MA: Blackwell.

Horgan, J. (2004, November 26). Do our genes influence behavior? Why we want to think they do. *Chronicle of Higher Education,* pp. B12–B13.

Horowitz, J. M., Graf, N., & Livingston, G. (2019). *Marriage and cohabitation in the United States*. Pew Research Center. Retrieved October 4, 2021 from https://www.pewresearch.org/social-trends/2019/11/06/marriage-and-cohabitation-in-the-u-s/

Hortman, T. (2007). Muscle. In A. Goldwasser (Ed.), *Red: The next generation of American writers — teenage girls—on what fires up their lives today* (pp. 12–15). New York: Hudson Street Press.

Horvath, M., & Ryan, A. M. (2003). Antecedents and potential moderators of the relationship between attitudes and hiring discrimination on the basis of sexual orientation. *Sex Roles, 48,* 115–130.

Houck, J. A. (2006). *Hot and bothered: Women, medicine and menopause in modern America.* Cambridge, MA: Harvard University Press.

Houseman, B. L. (2003). *Mother's milk: Breastfeeding controversies in American culture.* New York: Routledge.

Hovland, R., et al. (2005). Gender role portrayals in American and Korean advertisements. *Sex Roles, 53,* 887–899.

Howe, F. (2001). *The politics of women's studies: Testimony from thirty founding mothers.* New York: Feminist Press.

Hoyert, D. L., Daniel, I., & Tully, P. (2000). Maternal mortality, United States and Canada, 1982-1997. *Birth, 27,* 4–11.

Hoynes, W. (1999, September/October). The cost of survival. *Extra!,* pp. 11–23.

Hoyt, C. L., & Blascovich, J. (2007). Leadership efficacy and women leaders' responses to stereotype activation. *Group Processes and Intergroup Relations, 10,* 595–616.

Hoyt, C. L., & Murphy, S. E. (2016). Managing to clear the air: Stereotype threat, women, and leadership. *The Leadership Quarterly, 72,* 387-399.

Hudson, V. M., & den Boer, A. M. (2004). *Bare branches: Security implications of Asia's surplus male population.* Cambridge, MA: MIT Press.

Huecker, M. R., King, K. C., Jordan, G. A., & Smock, W. (2021). Domestic violence. *StatPearls* [Internet]. Treasure Island (FL): StatPearls Publishing.

Huerta, M., et al. (2006). Sex and power in the academy: Modeling sexual harassment in the lives of college women. *Personality and Social Psychology Bulletin, 32,* 616–628.

Hughes, F. M., & Seta, C. E. (2003). Gender stereotypes: Children's perceptions of future compensatory behavior following violations of gender roles. *Sex Roles, 49,* 685–691.

Hughes, T. L., Matthews, A. K., Razzano, L., & Aranda, F. (2003). Psychological distress in African American lesbian and heterosexual women. In T. L. Hughes, C. Smith, & A. Dan (Eds.), *Mental health issues for sexual minority women: Redefining women's mental health* (pp. 51–68). New York: Haworth.

Humphreys, T. (2007). Perception of sexual consent: The impact of relationship history and gender. *Journal of Health Research, 44,* 307–315.

Human Rights Campaign. (2021). *Marriage equality around the world.* Retrieved October 4, 2021 from https://www.hrc.org/resources/marriage-equality-around-the-world

Human Rights Watch. (2012). *Cultivating fear: The vulnerability of immigrant farmworkers in the US to sexual violence and sexual harassment.* Retrieved October 5, 2021 from https://www.hrw.org/sites/default/files/reports/us0512ForUpload_1.pdf

Human Rights First. (2017). *Human trafficking by the numbers: Fact sheet.* Retrieved October 5, 2021 from https://www.humanrightsfirst.org/sites/default/files/TraffickingbytheNumbers.pdf

Humphreys, T., & Herold, E. (2007). Sexual consent in heterosexual relationships: Development of a new measure. *Sex Roles, 57,* 30–315.

Hung, S., Morrison, D. R., Whittington, L. A., & Fein, S. B. (2002). Prepartum work, job characteristics, and risk of cesarean delivery. *Birth, 29,* 10–17.

Hunt, A. (2007). Sleeves. In A. Goldwasser (Ed.), *Red: The next generation of American writers —teenage girls—on what fires up their lives today* (pp. 3–7). New York: Hudson Street Press.

Hunt, G., & Boris, M. B. (2007). The lesbian, gay, bisexual, and trans-gender challenge to American labor. In D. S. Cobble (Ed.), *The sex of class: Women transforming American labor* (pp. 81–98). Ithaca, NY: Cornell University Press.

Huntemann, N., & Morgan, M. (2001). Mass media and identity development. In D. G. Singer & J. L. Singer (Eds.), *Handbook on children and the media* (pp. 309–322). Thousand Oaks, CA: Sage.

Hunter College Women's Studies Collective. (1995). *Women's realities, women's choices* (2nd ed.). New York: Oxford University Press.

Hurtado, A. (2003). *Voicing Chicana feminisms: Young women speak out on sexuality and identity.* New York: New York University Press.

Hurtado, S. (2005). The next generation of diversity and intergroup relations research. *Journal of Social Issues, 61,* 595–610.

Hurtz, W., & Durkin, K. (1997). Gender role stereotyping in Australian radio commercials. *Sex Roles, 36,* 103–114.

Hurtz, W., & Durkin, K. (2004). The effects of gender-stereotyped radio commercials. *Journal of Applied Social Psychology, 34,* 1974–1992.

Huston, T. L., & Holmes, E. K. (2004). Becoming parents.

In A. L. Vangelisti (Ed.), *Handbook of family communication* (pp. 105–133). Mahwah, NJ: Erlbaum.

Huston, T. L., & Melz, H. (2004). The case for (promoting) marriage: The devil is in the details. *Journal of Marriage and Family, 66,* 943–958.

Huttenlocher, J., et al. (1991). Early vocabulary growth: Relation to language input and gender. *Developmental Psychology, 27,* 236–248.

Hwang, V. S., & Danoff-Burg, S. (2010). Gender issues in the diagnosis and treatment of chronic illnesses. In J. C. Chrisler & D. R. McCreary (Eds.), *Handbook of gender research in psychology* (pp. 541–560). New York: Springer.

Hyams, M. (2006). La escuela: Young Latina women negotiating identities in school. In J. Denner & B. L. Guzmán (Eds.), *Latina girls: Voices of adolescent strength in the United States* (pp. 93–108). New York: New York University Press.

Hyde, J. S. (1981). How large are cognitive gender differences? A meta-analysis using w^2 and d. *American Psychologist, 36,* 892–901.

Hyde, J. S. (2002). Another good evolution story [Review of the book *The dangerous passion: Why jealousy is as necessary as love and sex*]. *Psychology of Women Quarterly, 26,* 170.

Hyde, J. S. (2005a). The gender similarities hypothesis. *American Psychologist, 60,* 581–592.

Hyde, J. S. (2005b). The genetics of sexual orientation. In J. S. Hyde (Ed.), *Biological substrates of human sexuality* (pp. 9–20). Washington, DC: American Psychological Association.

Hyde, J. S. (2007). Women in science: Gender similarities in abilities and sociocultural forces. In C. J. Ceci & W. M. Williams (Eds.), *Why aren't more women in science? Top researchers debate*

the evidence (pp. 131–145). Washington, DC: American Psychological Association.

Hyde, J. S., Bigler, R., Joel, D., Tate, C. C., & van Anders, S. M. (2019). The future of sex and gender in psychology: Five challenges to the gender binary. *American Psychologist, 74,* 171-193.

Hyde, J. S., & DeLamater, J. D. (2006). *Understanding human sexuality* (9th ed.). New York: McGraw-Hill.

Hyde, J. S., & Grabe, S. (2008). Meta-analysis in the psychology of women. In F. L. Denmark & M. A. Paludi (Eds.), *Psychology of women: A handbook of issues and theories* (2nd ed., pp. 142–173). Westport, CT: Praeger.

Hyde, J. S., & Jaffee, S. R. (2000). Becoming a heterosexual adult: The experiences of young women. *Journal of Social Issues, 56,* 283–296.

Hyde, J. S., & Kling, K. C. (2001). Women, motivation, and achievement. *Psychology of Women Quarterly, 25,* 364–378.

Hyde, J. S., & Lindberg, S. M. (2007). Facts and assumptions about the nature of gender differences and the implications for gender equity. In S. S. Klein (Ed.), *Handbook for achieving gender equity through education* (2nd ed., pp. 19–32). Mahwah, NJ: Erlbaum.

Hyde, J. S., & Linn, M. C. (1988). Gender differences in verbal ability: A meta-analysis. *Psychological Bulletin, 104,* 53–69.

Hyde, J. S., & Mezulis, A. H. (2001). Gender difference research. In J. Worell (Ed.), *Encyclopedia of women and gender* (pp. 551–559). San Diego: Academic Press.

Hyde, J. S., & Oliver, M. B. (2000). Gender differences in sexuality: Results from meta-analysis. In C. B. Travis & J. W. White (Eds.), *Sexuality, society, and feminism* (pp. 57–77). Washington, DC: American Psychological Association.

Hyde, J. S., et al. (1990). Gender differences in mathematics

performance: A meta-analysis. *Psychological Bulletin, 107,* 139–155.

Hyde, J. S., et al. (2008). Gender similarities characterize math performance. *Science, 321 ,* 494–495.

Hynie, M., Lydon, J. E., & Taradash, A. (1997). Commitment, intimacy, and women's perceptions of premarital sex and contraceptive readiness. *Psychology of Women Quarterly, 21,* 447–464.

Ibish, H. (Ed.). (2008). *Report on hate crimes and discrimination against Arab Americans* (pp. 2003–2007). Washington, DC: American-Arab Anti-Discrimination Committee Research Institute.

Ibroscheva, E. (2007). Caught between East and West? Portrayals of gender in Bulgarian television advertisements. *Sex Roles, 57,* 409–418.

Idle, T., Wood, E., & Desmarais, S. (1993). Gender role socialization in toy play situations: Mothers and fathers with their sons and daughters. *Sex Roles, 28,* 679–691.

Immigrants Are Us. (n.d.). *Sarahi Salamanca.* Retrieved October 3, 2021 from https://www .immigrantsareus.org/immigrant -bios/sarahi-salamanca/

Impett, E. A., & Peplau, L. A. (2002). Why some women consent to unwanted sex with a dating partner: Insights from attachment theory. *Psychology of Women Quarterly, 26,* 360–370.

Impett, E. A., & Peplau, L. A. (2003). Sexual compliance: Gender, motivational, and relationship perspectives. *Journal of Sex Research, 40,* 87–100.

Impett, E. A., & Peplau, L. A. (2006). " His" and " her" relationships? A review of the empirical evidence. In A. L. Vangelisti & D. Perlman (Eds.), *The Cambridge handbook of personal relationships* (pp. 273–291). New York: Cambridge University Press.

Impett, E. A., Peplau, L. A., & Gable, S. L. (2005). Approach and avoidance sexual motives: Implications for personal and interpersonal well-being. *Personal Relationships, 12,* 465–482.

Impett, E. A., Schooler, D., & Tolman, D. L. (2006). To be seen and not heard: Femininity ideology and adolescent girls' sexual health. *Archives of Sexual Behavior, 35,* 131–144.

Impett, E. A., Strachman, A., Finkel, E. J., & Gable, S. L. (2008). Maintaining sexual desire in intimate relationships: The importance of approach goals. *Journal of Personality and Social Psychology, 94,* 808–823.

Impett, E. A., & Tolman, D. L. (2006). Late adolescent girls' sexual experiences and sexual satisfaction. *Journal of Adolescent Research, 21,* 628–646.

India Abroad. (2009, July 17). *Matrimonial bride.* Retrieved July 17, 2009, from http://www.indiaab-road.com/CLASSIFIED/current-listing/2910.shtml

Ineichen, B., Pierce, M., & Lawrenson, R. (1997). Teenage mothers as breastfeeders: Attitudes and behavior. *Journal of Adolescence, 20,* 505–509.

Institute for Women's Policy Research. (2009, April). *Fact sheet.* Washington, DC: Author.

Institute for Women's Policy Research. (2010, September). *Fact sheet: The gender wage gap.* Retrieved January, 2011, from http://www.iwpr.org/pdf/C350.pdf

Irish, M., Solmi, F., Mars, B., King, M., Lewis, G., Pearson, R. M., Pitman, A., Rowe, S., Srinivasan, R., & Lewis, G. (2019). Depression and self-harm from adolescence to young adulthood in sexual minorities compared with heterosexuals in the UK: A population-based cohort study. *Lancet Child and Adolescent Health, 3,* 91-98.

Iwamoto, S. J., Defreyne, J., Rothman, M. S., Van Schuylenbergh, J., Van de Bruaene, L., Motmans, J., & T'Sjoen, G. (2019). Health considerations for transgender women and remaining unknowns: A narrative review. *Therapeutic Advances in Endocrinology and Metabolism, 10,* 2042018819871166.

Jack, D. C. (2003). The anger of hope and the anger of despair. In M. Stoppard & L. M. McMullen (Eds.), *Situating sadness: Women and depression in social context* (pp. 62–87). New York: New York University Press.

Jacklin, C. N., & Maccoby, E. E. (1983). Issues of gender differentiation. In M. D. Levine, W. B. Carey, A. C. Crocker, & R. T. Gross (Eds.), *Developmental behavioral pediatrics* (pp. 175–184). Philadelphia: Saunders.

Jackson, V. (2005). Robbing Peter to pay Paul. In M. P. Mirkin, K. L. Suyemoto, & B. F. Okun (Eds.), *Psychotherapy with women: Exploring diverse contexts and identities* (pp. 237–253). New York: Guilford.

Jackson, Y. (2006). Ethnic gloss. In *Encyclopedia of multicultural psychology* (Vol. 1, pp. 178-179). SAGE Publications, Inc.

Jacobi, C., Hayward, C., de Zwaan, M., Kraemer, H. C., & Agras, W. S. (2004). Coming to terms with risk factors for eating disorders: Application of risk terminology and suggestions for a general taxonomy. *Psychological Bulletin, 130,* 19–65.

Jacobi, C., Paul, T., de Zwaan, M., Nutzinger, D. O., & Dahme, B. (2004). Specificity of self-concept disturbances in eating disorders. *International Journal of Eating Disorders, 35,* 204–210.

Jacobs, J. E., et al. (2004). "I can, but I don't want to. " In A. M. Gallagher & J. C. Kaufman (Eds.), *Gender differences in mathematics: An integrative psychological approach* (pp. 246–263). New York: Cambridge University Press.

Jacques-Tiura, A. J., Abbey, A., Parkhill, M. R., & Zawacki, T. (2007). Why do some men misperceive women's sexual intentions more frequently than others do? An application of the confluence model. *Personality and Social Psychology Bulletin, 33,* 1467–1480.

Jaffee, K. D., Shires, D. A., & Stroumsa, D. (2016). Discrimination and delayed health care among transgender women and men: Implications for improving medical education and health care delivery. *Medical Care, 54,* 1010-1016.

Jaffee, S., & Hyde, J. S. (2000). Gender differences in moral orientation: A meta-analysis. *Psychological Bulletin, 126,* 703–726.

Jaffee, S., et al. (1999). The view from down here: Feminist graduate students consider innovative methodologies. *Psychology of Women Quarterly, 23,* 423–430.

James, S. E., Herman, J. L., Rankin, S., Keisling, M., Mottet, L., & Anafi, M. (2016). *The Report of the 2015 U.S. Transgender Survey.* Washington, DC: National Center for Transgender Equality.

James, K. (2006, February). Canadian cultures. *Observer,* pp. 17–18, 20.

James, S. M., & Robertson, C. C. (2002). Introduction: Reimagining transnational sisterhood. In S. M. James & C. C. Robertson (Eds.), *Genital cutting and transnational sisterhood* (pp. 5–15). Urbana: University of Illinois Press.

Jankowiak, W. R., & Paladino, T. (2008). Desiring sex, longing for love: A tripartite conundrum. In W. R. Jankowiak (Ed.), *Intimacies: Love and sex across cultures* (pp. 1–36). New York: Columbia University Press.

Jantarapakde, J.. Pancharoen, C., Teeratakulpisarn, S., et al. (2019). An integrated approach to HIV disclosure for HIV-affected families in Thailand. *Journal of the International Association of Providers of AIDS Care (JIAPAC), 18,* 1-7.

Janz, T. A., & Pyke, S. W. (2000). A scale to assess student perceptions of academic climates. *Canadian Journal of Higher Education, 30,* 89–122.

Jay, T. (2000). *Why we curse.* Philadelphia: John Benjamins.

Jayakody, R., & Cabrera, N. (2002). What are the choices for low-income families? Cohabitation, marriage, and remaining single. In A. Booth & A. C. Crouter (Eds.), *Just living together* (pp. 85–95). Mahwah, NJ: Erlbaum.

Jensen, R. (2017). *The end of patriarchy: Radical feminism for men.* North Melbourne, Victoria, Australia: Spinefex Press.

Jersild, D. (2002, May 31). Alcohol in the vulnerable lives of college women. *Chronicle of Higher Education,* pp. B10–B11.

Jipguep, M.-C., Sanders-Phillips, K., & Cotton, L. (2004). Another look at HIV in African American women: The impact of psychosocial and contextual factors. *Journal of Black Psychology, 30,* 366–385.

Johannesen-Schmidt, M. C., & Eagly, A. H. (2002). Another look at sex differences in preferred mate characteristics: The effects of endorsing the traditional female gender role. *Psychology of Women Quarterly, 26,* 322–328.

Johnson, A. G. (2001). *Privilege, power, and differences.* Mountain View, CA: Mayfield.

Johnson, B. T., et al. (2003). Interventions to reduce sexual risk for the human immunodeficiency virus in adolescents, 1985–2000. *Archives of Pediatric and Adolescent Medicine, 157,* 381–388.

Johnson, C. (2009). Female genital cutting. In A. Goldstein, C. Pukall, & I. Goldstein (Eds.), *Female sexual pain disorders* (pp. 235–243). Malden, MA: Blackwell.

Johnson, D., & Piore, A. (2004, October 18). Home in two worlds. *Newsweek,* pp. 52–54.

Johnson, K. L., & Tassinary, L. G. (2005). Perceiving sex directly and indirectly: Meaning in motion and morphology. *Psychological Science, 16,* 890–897.

Johnson, M. E., & Dowling-Guyer, S. (1996). Effects of inclusive vs. exclusive language on evaluations of the counselor. *Sex Roles, 34,* 407–418.

Johnson, M., & Helgeson, V. S. (2002). Sex differences in response to evaluative feedback: A field study. *Psychology of Women Quarterly, 26,* 242–251.

Johnson, N. G. (2001, October). Changing outcomes in women's health. *APA Monitor,* p. 5.

Johnson, N. G. (2004). Introduction: Psychology and health—taking the initiative to bring it together. In R. H. Rozensky, N. G. Johnson, C. D. Goodheart, & W. R. Hammond (Eds.), *Psychology builds a healthy world* (pp. 3–31). Washington, DC: American Psychological Association.

Johnson, S. M., & O'Connor, E. (2001). *For lesbian parents: Your guide to helping your family grow up happy, healthy, and proud.* New York: Guilford.

Johnson, S. M., & O'Connor, E. (2002). *The gay baby boom: The psychology of gay parenthood.* New York: New York University Press.

Johnson, S. P., & Moore, D. A. (2020). Spatial thinking in infancy: Origins and development of mental rotation between 3 and 10 months of age. *Cognitive Research: Principles and Implications, 5,* 10. https://doi.org/10.1186/s41235-020-00212-x

Johnson, W., Carothers, A., & Deary, I. J. (2008). Sex differences in variability in general intelligence: A new look at the old question. *Perspectives on Psychological Science, 3,* 518–531.

Johnston-Robledo, I. (2000). From postpartum depression to the empty nest syndrome: The motherhood mystique revisited. In J. C. Chrisler, C. Golden, & P. D. Rozee (Eds.), *Lectures on the psychology of women* (2nd ed., pp. 128–147). Boston: McGraw-Hill.

Johnston, D. D., & Swanson, D. H. (2002, November). *Defining mother: The experience of mothering ideologies by work status.* Paper presented at the annual meeting of the National Communication Association, New Orleans, LA.

Johnston, D. D., & Swanson, D. H. (2003a). Invisible mothers: A content analysis of motherhood ideologies and myths in magazines. *Sex Roles, 49,* 21–33.

Johnston, D. D., & Swanson, D. H. (2003b). Undermining mothers: A content analysis of the representation of mothers in magazines. *Mass Communication & Society, 6,* 243–265.

Johnston, D. D., & Swanson, D. H. (2004). Moms hating moms: The internalization of mother war rhetoric. *Sex Roles, 51,* 497–509.

Johnston, D. D., & Swanson, D. H. (2006). Constructing the "good mother" : The experience of mothering ideologies by work status. *Sex Roles, 54,* 509–519.

Johnston, D. D., & Swanson, D. H. (2007). Cognitive acrobatics in the construction of worker-mother identity. *Sex Roles, 57,* 447–450.

Johnston, D. D., & Swanson, D. H. (2008). Where are the mommies? A content analysis of women's magazines. In L. B. Arnold (Ed.), *Family communication: Theory and research* (pp. 395–403). Boston: Pearson.

Johnston, M. L. (2007). SES, race/ethnicity, and health. In M. Texler Segal & T. A. Martinez (Eds.), *Intersections of gender, race, and class* (pp. 323–334). Los Angeles, CA: Roxbury.

Johnston-Robledo, I., & Barnack, J. (2004). Psychological issues in childbirth: Potential roles for psychotherapists. *Women & Therapy, 27,* 133–150.

Johnston-Robledo, I., & Chrisler, J. (2017). The menstrual mark: Menstruation as social stigma. *Sex Roles, 68,* 1-10.

Johnston-Robledo, I., & Fred, V. (2008). Self-objectification and lower income pregnant women's breastfeeding attitudes. *Journal of Applied Social Psychology, 38*, 1–21.

Join the global effort to end poverty and promote development. (2005, Summer). *MADRE*, 7–10.

Jokela, M., Kivimäki, M., Elovainio, M., & Keltikangas-Jarvinen, L. (2009). Personality and having children; A two-way relation ship. *Journal of Personality and Social Psychology, 96*, 218–230.

Jonegenelis, M. I., & Pettigrew, S. (2020). Body image and eating disturbances in children: The role of self-objectification. *Psychology of Women Quarterly, 44*, 339-402.

Jones, J., Doss, B. D., & Christensen, A. (2001). Integrative behavioral couple therapy. In J. Harvey & A. Wenzel (Eds.), *Close romantic relationships: Maintenance and enhancement* (pp. 321–344). Mahwah, NJ: Erlbaum.

Jones, S. (2003). Identities of race, class, and gender inside and outside the math classroom: A girls' math club as a hybrid possibility. *Feminist Teacher, 14*, 220–233.

Joorman, J. (2009). Cognitive aspects of depression. In I. H. Gotlib & C. L. Hammen (Eds.), *Handbook of depression* (2nd ed., pp. 298–321). New York: Guilford.

Joos, C. M., Wodzinski, A. M., Wadsworth, M. E., & Dorn, L. D. (2018). Neither antecedent nor consequence: Developmental integration of chronic stress, pubertal timing, and conditionally adapted stress response. *Developmental Review, 48*, 1-3.

Jordan, J. V. (1997). The relational model is a source of empowerment for women. In M. R. Walsh (Ed.), *Women, men, and gender: Ongoing debates* (pp. 373–379). New Haven, CT: Yale University Press.

Jordan, J. V. (2000). The role of mutual empathy in relational/ cultural therapy. *Journal of Clinical Psychology, 56*, 1005–1016.

Joyner, K., & Laumann, E. O. (2002). Teenage sex and the sexual revolution. In E. O. Laumann & R. T. Michael (Eds.), *Sex, love, and health in America* (pp. 41–71). Chicago: University of Chicago Press.

Jussim, L., et al. (2000). Stigma and self-fulfilling prophecies. In T. F. Heatherton, R. E. Kleck, M. R. Hebl, & J. G. Hull (Eds.), *The social psychology of stigma* (pp. 374–418). New York: Guilford.

Kaelin, C. (2005, April). When a breast cancer expert gets breast cancer. *Harvard Women's Health Watch*, pp. 4–6.

Kagawa-Singer, M., Hikoyeda, N., & Tanjasiri, S. P. (1997). Aging, chronic conditions, and physical disabilities in Asian and Pacific Islander Americans. In K. S. Markides & M. R. Miranda (Eds.), *Minorities, aging, and health* (pp. 149–180). Thousand Oaks, CA: Sage.

Kahana, E., et al. (2005). Successful aging in the face of chronic disease. In M. L. Wykle, P. J. Whitehouse, & D. L. Morris (Eds.), *Successful aging through the life span* (pp. 101–123). New York: Springer.

Kahn, A. S. (2004). 2003 Carolyn Sherif Award Address: What college women do and do not experience as rape. *Psychology of Women Quarterly, 28*, 9–15.

Kahn, A. S., & Andreoli Mathie, V. (2000). Understanding the unacknowledged rape victim. In C. B. Travis & J. W. White (Eds.), *Sexuality, society, and feminism* (pp. 377–403). Washington, DC: American Psychological Association.

Kahn, A. S., & Yoder, J. D. (1989). The psychology of women and conservatism. *Psychology of Women Quarterly, 13*, 417–432.

Kahn, J. S. (2009). *An introduction to masculinities*. Malden, MA: Wiley-Blackwell.

Kahne, H. (2004). Low-wage single-mother families in this jobless recovery: Can improved social policies help? *Analysis of Social Issues and Public Policy, 4*, 47–68.

Kaid, L. L., & Garner, J. (2004). The portrayal of older adults in political advertising. Media usage patterns and portrayals of seniors. In J. F. Nussbaum & J. Coupland (Eds.), *Handbook of communication and aging research* (2nd ed., pp. 407–421). Mahwah, NJ: Erlbaum.

Kail, R. V. (2010). *Children and their development* (5th ed.). Upper Saddle River, NJ: Prentice Hall.

Kail, R. V., Jr., Carter, P., & Pellegrino, J. (1979). The locus of sex differences in spatial ability. *Perception and Psychophysics, 26*, 182–186.

Kaiser Family Foundation. (2003). *National survey of adolescents and young adults: Sexual knowledge, attitudes, and experiences.* Menlo Park, CA: Author.

Kaiser Family Foundation. (2021a). Women's health insurance coverage. *KFF Women's Health Policy Fact Sheet.* Retrieved October 5, 2021 from https://www.kff.org /womens-health-policy/fact-sheet /womens-health-insurance -coverage/

Kaiser Family Foundation. (2021b). The HIV/AIDS epidemic in the United States: The basics. Retrieved October 5, 2021 from https://www.kff.org/hivaids/fact -sheet/the-hivaids-epidemic-in -the-united-states-the-basics/

Kaiser, G., Janda, C., Kleinstäuber, M., & Weise, C. (2018). Clusters of premenstrual symptoms in women with PMDD: Appearance, stability and association with impairment. *Journal of Psychosomatic Research, 115*, 38-43.

Kalat, J. W., & Shiota, M. N. (2007). *Emotion.* Belmont, CA: Thomson Wadsworth.

Kalev, H. D. (2004). Cultural rights or human rights: The case of female genital mutilation. *Sex Roles, 31*, 339–348.

Kalichman, S. C. (2003). *The inside story on AIDS.* Washington, DC: American Psychological Association.

Kalick, S. M., Zebrowitz, L. A., Langlois, J. H., & Johnson, R. M. (1998). Does human face attractiveness honestly advertise health? *Psychological Science, 9,* 8–13.

Kalodner, C. R. (2003). *Too fat or too thin? A reference guide to eating disorders.* Westport, CT: Greenwood.

Kamal, R., Ramirez, G., & Cox, C. (2020). *How does health care spending in the U.S. compare to other countries?* Peterson KKF Health System Tracker. https://www.healthsystemtracker.org/chart-collection/health-spending-u-s-compare-countries/#item-start

Kamen, P. (2000). *Her way: Young women remake the sexual revolution.* New York: New York University Press.

Kantrowitz, B. (2004, January 26). One, two, three or more? *Newsweek,* pp. 52–53.

Kaplan, J., & Aronson, D. (1994, Spring). The numbers gap. *Teaching Tolerance,* 21–27.

Kaplan, P. S., Bachorowski, J., Smoski, M. J., & Hudenko, W. J. (2002). Infants of depressed mothers, although competent learners, fail to learn in response to their own mothers' infant-directed speech. *Psychological Science, 13,* 268–271.

Kar, H. L., & Garcia-Moreno, C. (2009). Partner aggression across cultures. In K. D. O'Leary & E. M. Woodin (Eds.), *Psychological and physical aggression in couples: Causes and interventions* (pp. 59–75). Washington, DC: American Psychological Association.

Karney, B. R., & Bradbury, T. M. (2004). Trajectories of change during the early years of marriage. In R. D. Conger, F. O. Lorenz, & K. A. S. Wickrama (Eds.), *Continuity and change in family relationships* (pp. 65–96). Mahwah, NJ: Erlbaum.

Karniol, R., Gabay, R., Ochion, Y., & Harari, Y. (1998). Is gender or gender-role orientation a better predictor of empathy in adolescence? *Sex Roles, 39,* 45–59.

Karraker, K. H., Vogel, D. A., & Lake, M. A. (1995). Parents' gender-stereotyped perceptions of newborns: The eye of the beholder revisited. *Sex Roles, 33,* 687–701.

Karsay, K., Knoll, J., & Matthes, J. (2018). Sexualizing media use and self-objectification: A meta-analysis. *Psychology of Women Quarterly, 42,* 9-28.

Karsten, M. F. (2006). *Management, gender, and race in the 21st century.* Lanham, MD: University Press of America.

Karsten, M. F., & Igou, F. P. (2006). Equal employment opportunity and harassment. In M. F. Karsten (Ed.), *Management, gender, and race in the 21st century* (pp. 54–89). Lanthan, MD: University Press of America.

Kaschak, E., & Tiefer, L. (2001). *A new view of women's sexual problems.* New York: Haworth.

Kashimada, K., & Koopman, P. (2010). Sry: The master switch in mammalian sex determination. *Development, 137,* 3921-3930.

Kasser, T., & Sharma, Y. S. (1999). Reproductive freedom, educational equality, and females' preferences for resource-acquisition characteristics in mates. *Psychological Science, 10,* 374–377.

Kastanis, A. & Gates, G. J. (2013). *LGBT Asian and Pacific Islander individuals and same-sex couples.* The Williams Institute. Retrieved October 4, 2021 from https://williamsinstitute.law.ucla.edu/publications/lgbt-api-people-couples/

Kates, J., Ranji, U., Beamesderfer, A., Salganicoff, A., & Dawson, L. (2018). *Health and access to care and coverage for lesbian, gay, bisexual, and transgender individuals in the U.S.* Kaiser Family Foundation. Retrieved October 5, 2021 from https://www.kff.org/racial-equity-and-health-policy/issue-brief/health-and-access-to-care-and-coverage-for-lesbian-gay-bisexual-and-transgender-individuals-in-the-u-s/

Kath, L. M., et al. (2008). Cross-level, three-way interactions among workgroup climate, gender, and frequency of harassment on job-related outcomes of sexual harassment. *Journal of Occupational and Organizational Psychology, 82,* 159–192.

Katon, W. J., & Ludman, E. J. (2003). Improving services for women with depression in primary care settings. *Psychology of Women Quarterly, 27,* 114–120.

Katz, J., Carino, A., & Hilton, A. (2002). Perceived verbal conflict behaviors associated with physical aggression and sexual coercion in dating relationships: A gender-sensitive analysis. *Violence and Victims, 17,* 93–109.

Katz, J., Moore, J. A., & May, P. (2008). Physical and sexual covictimization from dating partners: A distinct type of intimate abuse? *Violence Against Women, 14,* 963–980.

Katz, J., Moore, J. A., & Tkachuk, S. (2007). Verbal sexual coercion and perceived victim responsibility: Mediating effects of perceived control. *Sex Roles, 57,* 235–247.

Katz, J., & Myhr, L. (2008). Perceived conflict patterns and relationship quality associated with verbal sexual coercion by male dating partners. *Journal of Interpersonal Violence, 23,* 780–797.

Katz-Wise, K. L., & Hyde, J. S. (2015). Sexual fluidity and related attitudes and beliefs among young adults with a same-gender orientation. *Archives of Sexual Behavior, 44,* 1459-1470.

Katz, P. A. (2003). Racists or tolerant multiculturalists? How do they begin? *American Psychologist, 58,* 897–909.

Katz, P. A., Boggiano, A., & Silvern, L. (1993). Theories of female personality. In F. L. Denmark & M. A. Paludi (Eds.), *Psychology of women: A handbook of issues and theories* (pp. 247–280). Westport, CT: Greenwood Press.

Katz, P. A., & Kofkin, J. A. (1997). Race, gender, and young children. In S. Luthar, J. A. Baruck, D. Cicchetti, & J. Weisz (Eds.), *Developmental psychopathology: Perspectives on adjustment, risk, and disorder* (pp. 51–74). New York: Cambridge University Press.

Kaufman, G. (1999). The portrayal of men's family roles in television commercials. *Sex Roles, 41,* 439–458.

Kaufman, M., & the Committee on Adolescence. (2008). Care of the adolescent sexual assault victim. *Pediatrics, 122,* 462–470.

Kaur Hundle, A. K., Szeman, I., & Pares Hoare, J. (2019). What is the transnational in transnational feminist research? *Feminist Review, 121,* 3-8.

Kcomt, L., Gorey, K. M., Barrett, B. J., & McCabe, S. E. (2020). Health-care avoidance due to anticipated discrimination among transgender people: A call to create trans-affirmative environments. *SSM - Population Health, 11,* 100608.

Kendall, F. E. (2012). *Understanding white privilege: Creating pathways to authentic relationships across race.* Hoboken, NJ: Taylor & Francis.

Keel, P. K., et al. (2003). Predictors of mortality in eating disorders. *Archives of General Psychiatry, 60,* 179–183.

Keitel, M. A., & Kopala, M. (2000). *Counseling women with breast cancer.* Thousand Oaks, CA: Sage.

Kelly, J. R., & Hutson-Comeaux, S. L. (2000). The appropriateness of emotional expression in women and men: The double-bind of emotion. *Journal of Social Behavior and Personality, 15,* 515–528.

Kelly, Y., Zilanawala, A, Sacker, A, Hiatt, R. & Viner, R. (2017). Early puberty in 11-year-old girls: Millennium Cohort Study findings. *Archives of Disease in Childhood, 102,* 232-237.

Kendall-Tackett, K. A. (2005). *Depression in new mothers: Causes, consequences, and treatment alternatives.* New York: Haworth.

Kendall, M. (2020). Hood feminism: Notes from the women that a movement forgot. New York: Viking.

Kennedy, M. A., & Gorzalka, B. B. (2002). Asian and non-Asian attitudes toward rape, sexual harassment, and sexuality. *Sex Roles, 46,* 227–238.

Kennedy, M. A., Parhar, K. K., Samra, J., & Gorzalka, B. (2005). Suicide ideation in different generations of immigrants. *Canadian Journal of Psychiatry, 50,* 353–356.

Kennedy, M. A., Templeton, L., Gandhi, A., & Gorzalka, B. B. (2004). Asian body image satisfaction: Ethnic and gender differences across Chinese, Indo-Asian and European descent students. *Eating Disorders: The Journal of Treatment and Prevention, 12,* 321–336.

Kennett, D. J., Humphreys, T., & Patchell, M. (2009). The role of learned resourcefulness in helping female undergraduates deal with unwanted sexual activity. *Sex Education, 9,* 341–353.

Keown, M. K. (2007). *Health activists link spread of HIV-AIDS to FGM.* Retrieved August 11, 2007, from www.truthout.org /issues_06/ 081007HA.shtml

Kessler, R. C. (2006). The epidemiology of depression among women. In C. L. M. Keyes & S. H. Goodman (Eds.), *Women and depression: A handbook for the social, behavioral, and bio-medical sciences* (pp. 22–37). New York: Cambridge University Press.

Kessler, S. J. (1998). *Lessons from the intersexed.* Piscataway, NJ: Rutgers University Press.

Kessler-Harris, A. (2007, December 7). Do we still need women's history? *Chronicle of Higher Education,* pp. B6–B7.

Ketenjian, T. (1999). Interview of Patsy Mink. In G. Null & B. Seaman(Eds.), *For women only: Your guide to health empowerment* (pp. 1042–1045). New York: Seven Stories Press.

Ketz, K., & Israel, T. (2002). The relationship between women's sexual identity and perceived wellness. *Journal of Bisexuality, 2,* 227–242.

Kidd, E., & Lum, J. A. G. (2008). Sex differences in past tense overregularization. *Developmental Science, 11,* 882–889.

Kiefer, A., & Shih, M. (2006). Gender differences in persistence and attributions in stereotype relevant contexts. *Sex Roles, 54,* 859–868.

Kiener R. (2011). Honor killings: Can murders of women and girls be stopped? *CQ Global Researcher [Internet], 5,* 183-208.

Kikuzawa, S. (2006). Multiple roles and mental health in cross-cultural perspective. The elderly in the United States and Japan. *Journal of Health and Social Behavior, 47,* 62–76.

Kilbourne, J. (2003). Advertising and disconnection. In T. Reichert & J. Lambiase (Eds.), *Sex in advertising* (pp. 173–180). Mahwah, NJ: Erlbaum.

Killeen, L. A., López-Zafra, E., & Eagly, A. H. (2006). Envisioning oneself as a leader: Comparisons of women and men in Spain and the United States. *Psychology of Women Quarterly, 30,* 312–322.

Kilmartin, C. (2007). *The masculine self* (3rd ed.). Cornwall-on-Hudson, NY: Sloan Publishing.

Kilmartin, C. (2008). A real time social norms intervention to reduce male sexism. *Sex Roles, 59,* 264–273.

Kilmartin, C., & Allison, J. (2007). *Men's violence against women:*

Theory, research, and activism. Mahwah, NJ: Erlbaum.

Kim, J. E., & Moen, P. (2001a). Is retirement good or bad for subjective well-being? *Current Directions in Psychological Science, 10,* 83–86.

Kim, J. E., & Moen, P. (2001b). Moving into retirement: Preparation and transitions in late mid-life. In M. E. Lachman (Ed.), *Handbook of midlife development* (pp. 487–527). New York: Wiley.

Kim, J. L., & Ward, L. M. (2004). Pleasure reading: Associations between young women's sexual attitudes and their reading of contemporary women's magazines. *Psychology of Women Quarterly, 28,* 48–58.

Kim, J. L., et al. (2007). From sex to sexuality: Exposing the heterosexual script on primetime network television. *Journal of Sex Research, 44,* 145–157.

Kim, K., & Lowry, D. T. (2005). Television commercials as a lagging social indicator: Gender role stereotypes in Korean television advertising. *Sex Roles, 53,* 901–910.

Kim, M. J., Fleming, C. B., & Catalano, R. F. (2009). Individual and social influences on progression to daily smoking during adolescence. *Pediatrics, 124,* 895–902.

Kimball, M. M. (1989). A new perspective on women's math achievement. *Psychological Bulletin, 105,* 198–214.

Kimball, M. M. (1995). *Feminist visions of gender similarities and differences.* Binghamton, NY: Haworth.

Kimball, M. M. (2003). Feminists rethink gender. In D. B. Hill & M. J. Kral (Eds.), *About psychology: Essays at the crossroads of history, theory, and philosophy* (pp. 127–146). Albany, NY: State University of New York Press

Kimmel, E. B. (2007). How did a nice girl like you . . .? In F. J. Crosby, M. S. Stockdale, & S. A. Ropp (Eds.), *Sex discrimination in the workplace: Multidisciplinary*

perspectives (pp. 83–95). Malden, MA: Blackwell.

Kimura, D. (1992, September). Sex differences in the brain. *Scientific American, 267,* 118–125.

King, G. A., Brown, E. G., & Smith, L. K. (2003a). Introduction: An invitation to learn from the turning points of people with disabilities. In G. A. King, E. G. Brown, & L. K. Smith (Eds.), *Resilience: Learning from people with disabilities and the turning points in their lives* (pp. 1–6). Westport, CT: Praeger.

King, G. A., Brown, E. G., & Smith, L. K. (Eds.). (2003b). *Resilience: Learning from people with disabilities and the turning points in their lives.* Westport, CT: Praeger.

King, L. J. (2017). The status of Black history in U.S. schools and society. *Social Education, 81,* 14-18.

King, M., Semlyen, J., Tai, S. S., Killaspy, H., Osborn, D., Popelyuk, D., & Nazareth, I. (2008). A systematic review of mental disorder, suicide, and deliberate self harm in lesbian, gay and bisexual people. *BMC Psychiatry, 8,* 70.

King, S. M., et al. (2009). Etiological contributions to heavy drinking from late adolescence to young adulthood. In G. A. Marlat & K. Witkiewitz (Eds.), *Addictive behaviors: New readings on etiology, prevention, and treatment* (pp. 89–116). Washington, DC: American Psychological Association.

King, Y. (1997). The other body: Reflections on difference, disability, and identity politics. In M. Crawford & R. Unger (Eds.), *In our own words: Readings on the psychology of women and gender* (pp. 107–111). New York: McGraw-Hill.

Kingsberg, S. (2002). The impact of aging of sexual function in women and their partners. *Archives of Sexual Behavior, 33,* 431–437.

Kirk, G., & Okazawa-Rey, M. (2001). *Women's lives: Multicultural*

perspectives (2nd ed.). Mountain View, CA: Mayfield.

Kisber, S. (2001, Spring). Reflections on my experience as a disabled feminist psychologist. *Association for Women in Psychology Newsletter,* pp. 4–5.

Kishwar, M. (1999). *Off the beaten track: Rethinking gender justice for Indian women.* New Delhi: Oxford University Press.

Kissling, E. A. (2002). On the rag on screen: Menarche in film and television. *Sex Roles, 46,* 5–12.

Kissling, E. A. (2003). Menstrual taboo. In J. J. Ponzetti, Jr. (Ed.), *International encyclopedia of marriage and family* (2nd ed., Vol. 3, pp. 1123–1126). New York: Macmillan Reference USA.

Kissling, E. A. (2006). *Capitalizing on the curse: The business of menstruation.* Boulder, CO: Lynne Rienner Publishers.

Kite, M. E. (1994). When perceptions meet reality: Individual differences in reactions to lesbians and gay men. In B. Greene & G. M. Herek (Eds.), *Contemporary perspectives on gay and lesbian psychology* (pp. 25–53). Newbury Park, CA: Sage.

Kite, M. E., & Deaux, K. (1986). Attitudes toward homosexuality: Assessment and behavioral consequences. *Basic and Applied Social Psychology, 7,* 137–162.

Kite, M., Deaux, K., & Haines, E. L. (2008). Gender stereotypes. In F. L. Denmark & M. A. Paludi (Eds.), *Psychology of women: A handbook of issues and theories* (2nd ed., pp. 205–236). Westport, CT: Praeger.

Kite, M. E., Stockdale, G. D., Whitley, B. E., Jr., & Johnson, B. T. (2005). Attitudes toward younger and older adults: An updated meta-analytic review. *Journal of Social Issues, 61,* 241–266.

Kite, M. E., & Whitley, B. E., Jr. (2002). Do heterosexual women and men differ in their attitudes toward homosexuality? A conceptual and methodological analysis. In L. D. Garnets & D. C. Kimmel (Eds.), *Psychological perspectives on lesbian, gay, and bisexual experiences* (2nd ed., pp. 165–187). New York: Columbia University Press.

Kitzinger, C., & Wilkinson, S. (1997). Transitions from heterosexuality to lesbianism: The discursive production of lesbian identities. In M. R. Walsh (Ed.), *Women, men, and gender: Ongoing debates* (pp. 188–203). New Haven, CT: Yale University Press.

Kitzinger, S. (1995). *Ourselves as mothers: The universal experience of motherhood*. Reading, MA: Addison Wesley.

Kitzinger, S. (2003). *The complete book of pregnancy and childbirth* (4th ed.). New York: Knopf.

Kitzmann, K. M., & Gaylord, N. K. (2001). Divorce and child custody. In J. Worell (Ed.), *Encyclopedia of women and gender* (pp. 355–367). San Diego: Academic Press.

Kjaersgaard, K. (2005). Aging to perfection or perfectly aged? The image of women growing older on television. In E. Cole & J. H. Daniel (Eds.), *Featuring females: Feminist analyses of media* (pp. 199–210). Washington, DC: American Psychological Association.

Klaus, M. H., Kennell, J. H., & Klaus, P. H. (2002). *The doula book: How a trained labor companion can help you have a shorter, easier, and healthier birth* (2nd ed.). Cambridge, MA: Perseus Publishing.

Klebanoff, M. A., Shiono, P. H., & Rhoads, G. G. (1990). Outcomes of pregnancy in a national sample of resident physicians. *New England Journal of Medicine, 323*, 1040–1045.

Kleemans, M., Daalmans, S., Carbaat, I., & Anschütz, D. (2018). Picture perfect: The direct effect of manipulated Instagram photos on body image in adolescent girls, *Media Psychology, 21*, 93-110.

Klein, A. G. (2002). *A forgotten voice: A biography of Leta Stetter Hollingworth*. Scottsdale, AZ: Great Potential Press.

Klein, E., Campbell, J., Soler, E., & Ghez, M. (1997). *Ending domestic violence: Changing public perceptions/halting the epidemic*. Thousand Oaks, CA: Sage.

Klein, G. (2020, July 13). Remembering Sandra Bland and Breonna Taylor and demanding justice. *MS Magazine*. Retrieved September 28, 2021 from https://msmagazine.com/2020/07/13/remembering-sandra-bland-and-breonna-taylor-and-demanding-justice/

Klein, J. D., et al. (2005). Adolescent pregnancy: Current trends and issues. *Pediatrics, 116*, 281–286.

Klein, K. J. K., & Hodges, S. D. (2001). Gender differences, motivation, and empathic accuracy: When it pays to understand. *Personality and Social Psychology Bulletin, 27*, 720–730.

Klein, M. C. (2004). Quick fix culture: The cesarean-section-on-demand debate. *Birth, 31*, 161–164.

Klein, M. H., Hyde, J. S., Essex, M. J., & Clark, R. (1998). Maternity leave, role quality, work involvement, and mental health one year after delivery. *Psychology of Women Quarterly, 22*, 239–266.

Klein, S. L. (Ed.). (2008). Sex differences infectious and autoimmune diseases. In J. R. Becker et al. (Eds.), *Sex differences in the brain from genes to behavior* (pp. 329–353). New York: Oxford.

Klein, S. S. (2007). *Handbook for achieving gender equity through education* (2nd ed.). Mahwah, NJ: Erlbaum.

Kling, K. C., & Hyde, J. S. (2001). Self-esteem. In J. Worell (Ed.), *Encyclopedia of women and gender*. San Diego: Academic Press.

Kling, K. C., Hyde, J. S., Showers, C., & Buswell, B. (1999). Gender differences in self-esteem: A meta-analysis. *Psychological Bulletin, 125*, 470–500.

Klinger, R. L. (1996). Lesbian couples. In R. P. Cabaj & T. S. Stein (Eds.), *Textbook of homosexuality and mental health* (pp. 339–352). Washington, DC: American Psychiatric Press.

Klonis, S., Endo, J., Cosby, F., & Worell, J. (1997). Feminism as life raft. *Psychology of Women Quarterly, 21*, 333–345.

Klonis, S. C., Plant, E. A., & Devine, P. G. (2005). Internal and external motivation to respond without sexism. *Personality and Social Psychology Bulletin, 31*, 1237–1249.

Klonoff, E. A., Landrine, H., & Campbell, R. (2000). Sexist discrimination may account for well-known gender differences in psychiatric symptoms. *Psychology of Women Quarterly, 24*, 93–99.

Knight, J. L., & Giuliano, T. A. (2001). He's a Laker; she's a "looker": The consequences of gender-stereotypical portrayals of male and female athletes by the print media. *Sex Roles, 45*, 217–229.

Knight, M. (2004, Winter). Black self-employed women in the twenty-first century: A critical approach. *Canadian Woman Studies/Les cahiers de la femme, 23*, 104–110.

Ko, K. J., et al. (2007). Profiles of successful aging in middle-aged and older adult married couples. *Psychology and Aging, 22*, 705–718.

Knoll, A. D., & MacLennan, R. N. (2017). Prevalence and correlates of depression in Canada: Findings from the Canadian Community Health Survey. *Canadian Psychology/Psychologie canadienne, 58*, 116–123.

Koch, P. B., & Mansfield, P. K. (2004). Facing the unknown: Social support during the menopausal transition. In J. C. Chrisler (Ed.), *From menarche to menopause: The female body in feminist therapy* (pp. 179–194). New York: Haworth.

Kohlberg, L. (1966). A cognitive-developmental analysis of

children's sex-role concepts and attitudes. In E. E. Maccoby (Ed.), *The development of sex differences* (pp. 82–173). Stanford, CA: Stanford University Press.

Kohlberg, L. (1981). *The philosophy of moral development: Essays on moral development* (Vols. 1 & 2). San Francisco: Harper & Row.

Kohlberg, L. (1984). *Essays on moral development: The psychology of moral development* (Vol. 2). San Francisco: Freeman.

Kohler, P. K, Manhart, L. E, & Lafferty, W. E. (2008). Abstinence-only and comprehensive sex education and the initiation of sexual activity and teen pregnancy. *Journal of Adolescent Health, 42,* 344-351.

Konrad, A. M., & Linnehan, F. (1999). Affirmative action: History, effects, and attitudes. In G. N. Powell (Ed.), *Handbook of gender and work* (pp. 429–452). Thousand Oaks, CA: Sage.

Konradi, A. (2007). *Taking the stand: Rape survivors and the prosecution of rapists.* Westport, CT: Praeger.

Kornblau, I. S., Pearson, H, C., & Redecki Breithopf, C. (2007). Demographic, behavioral, and physical correlates of body esteem among low-income female adolescents. *Journal of Adolescent Health, 41,* 566–570.

Kornstein, S. G., & Wojcik, B. A. (2002). Depression. In S. G. Kornstein & A. H. Clayton (Eds.), *Women's mental health: A comprehensive textbook* (pp. 147–165). New York: Guilford.

Koss, M. P. (2003). Evolutionary models of why men rape: Acknowledging the complexities. In C. B. Travis (Ed.), *Evolution, gender, and rape* (pp. 191–205). Cambridge, MA: MIT Press.

Kossek, E. E., Meece, D., Barratt, M. E., & Prince, B. E. (2005). U.S. Latino migrant farm workers: Managing acculturative stress and conserving work-family resources. In S. A. Y. Poelmans (Ed.), *Work and family: An international research perspective* (pp. 47–70). Mahwah, NJ: Erlbaum.

Krahé, B., Bieneck, S., & Möller, I. (2005). Understanding gender and intimate partner violence from an international perspective. *Sex Roles, 52,* 807–827.

Krahé, B., Temkin, J., & Bieneck, S. (2007). Schema-driven information processing in judgements about rape. *Applied Cognitive Psychology, 31,* 601–619.

Kravetz, D., & Marecek, J. (2001). The feminist movement. In J. Worell (Ed.), *Encyclopedia of women and gender* (pp. 457–468). San Diego: Academic Press.

Kreipe, R. E., & Birndorf, S. A. (2000). Eating disorders in adolescents and young adults. *Medical Clinics of North America, 84,* 1027–1049.

Kridahl, L., & Kolk, M. (2018). Retirement coordination in opposite-sex and same-sex married couples: Evidence from Swedish registers. *Advances in Life Course Research, 38,* 22-36.

Krieger, L. H. (2007). The watched variable improves: On eliminating sex discrimination in employment. In F. J. Crosby, M. S. Stockdale, & S. A. Ropp (Eds.), *Sex discrimination in the workplace* (pp. 295–329). Malden, MA: Blackwell.

Krishman, A., & Sweeney, C. J. (1998). Gender differences in fear of success imagery and other achievement-related background variables among medical students. *Sex Roles, 39,* 299–310.

Kristof, N. (1996, December 9). Wife-beating still common practice in much of Korea. *San Jose Mercury News,* pp. 17A.

Kristof, N. (2008). *Giving thanks to heroes.* Retrieved December 25, 2010, from http://www .mercycorps. org/inthenews/15149 ?ource= 13296&gclid=CP -Ktd-yh6YCFU1-5QodBBm2nw

Kristof, N., & WuDunn, S. (2009). *Half the sky: Turning oppression into opportunity for women worldwide.* New York: Knopf.

Kruse, L., Denk, C. E., Feldman-Winter, L., & Rotondo, F. M. (2005). Comparing sociodemographic and hospital influences on breastfeeding initiation. *Birth, 32,* 81–85.

Kubicek, B., Korunka, C., Raymo, J. M., & Hoonakker, P. (2011). Psychological well-being in retirement: The effects of personal and gendered contextual resources. *Journal of Occupational Health Psychology, 16,* 230-246.

Kuchynka, S. L., Salomon, K., Bosson, J. K., El-Hout, M., Kiebel, E., Cooperman, C., & Toomey, R. (2018). Hostile and benevolent sexism and college women's STEM outcomes. *Psychology of Women Quarterly, 42,* 72-87.

Kuck, V., Marzabadi, C. H., Buckner, J. P., & Nolan, S. A. (2007). A review and study on graduate training and academic hiring of chemists. *Journal of Chemical Education, 84,* 277–284.

Kuhn, J. (2008, Fall). Fighting sexism in elementary schools. *The Feminist Psychologist, 7,* 28.

Kunda, Z. (1999). *Social cognition: Making sense of people.* Cambridge, MA: MIT Press.

Kunda, Z., & Sherman-Williams, B. (1993). Stereotypes and the construal of individuating information. *Personality and Social Psychology Bulletin, 19,* 90–99.

Kundanis, R. M. (2003). *Children, teens, families, and mass media.* Mahwah, NJ: Erlbaum.

Kunkel, A. W., & Burleson, B. R. (1998). Social support and the emotional lives of men and women: An assessment of the different cultures perspective. In D. J. Canary & K. Dindia (Eds.), *Sex differences and similarities in communication* (pp. 101–125). Mahwah, NJ: Erlbaum.

Kurdek, L. A. (1995). Assessing multiple determinants of relationship commitment in cohabiting gay, cohabiting lesbian, dating heterosexual, and married heterosexual couples. *Family Relations, 44,* 261–266.

Kurdek, L. A. (2005). Gender and marital satisfaction early in marriage: A growth curve approach. *Journal of Marriage and Family, 67,* 68–84.

Kurpius, S. E. R., & Nicpon, M. F. (2003). Menopause and the lives of midlife women. In M. Kopala & M. A. Keitel (Eds.), *Handbook of counseling women* (pp. 269–276). Thousand Oaks, CA: Sage.

Kurth, S. B., Spiller, B. B., & Travis, C. B. (2000). Consent, power, and sexual scripts: Deconstructing sexual harassment. In C. B. Travis & J. W. White (Eds.), *Sexuality, society, and feminism* (pp. 323–354). Washington, DC: American Psychological Association.

Kusnir, D. (2005). Salvadoran families. In M. McGoldrick, J. Giordano, & N. Garcia-Preto (Eds.), *Ethnicity and family therapy* (3rd ed., pp. 256–265). New York: Guilford.

Kwa, L. (1994). Adolescent females' perceptions of competence: What is defined as healthy and achieving. In J. Gallivan, S. D. Crozier, & V. M. Lalande (Eds.), *Women, girls, and achievement* (pp. 121–132). North York, Canada: Captus University Publications.

Kwon, E. Park, S. & McBride, T. D. (2019). Effects of the affordable care act on health insurance coverage among middle-aged adults. *International Journal of Health Services, 49,* 712-732.

La Greca, A. M., Mackay, E. R., & Miller, K. B. (2006). The interplay of physical and psychosocial development. In J. Worell & C. D. Goodheart (Eds.), *Handbook of girls' and women's psychological health: Gender and well-being across the life span* (pp. 252–261). New York: Oxford University Press.

Lacampagne, C. B., et al. (2007). Gender equity in mathematics. In S. S. Klein (Ed.), *Handbook for achieving gender equity through education* (2nd ed., pp. 235–253). Mahwah, NJ: Erlbaum.

Lacasse, A., et al. (2009). Determinants of early medical management of nausea and vomiting of pregnancy. *Birth, 36,* 70–77.

Lachman, M. E. (2004). Development in midlife. *Annual Review of Psychology, 55,* 305–351.

Laflamme, D., Pomerleau, A., & Malcuit, G. (2002). A comparison of fathers' and mothers' involvement in childcare and stimulation behaviors during free-play with their infants at 9 and 15 months. *Sex Roles, 47,* 507–518.

LaFrance, M., Hecht, M. A., & Paluck, E. L. (2003). The contingent smile: A meta-analysis of sex differences in smiling. *Psychological Bulletin, 129,* 305–334.

LaFrance, M., & Henley, N. M. (1997). On oppressing hypotheses: Or, differences in nonverbal sensitivity revisited. In M. R. Walsh (Ed.), *Women, men, and gender: Ongoing debates* (pp. 104–119). New Haven, CT: Yale University Press.

LaFrance, M., Paluck, E. L., & Brescoll, V. (2004). Sex changes: A current perspective on the psychology of gender. In A. H. Eagly, A. E. Beall, & R. J. Sternberg (Eds.), *The psychology of gender* (2nd ed., pp. 328–344). New York: Guilford.

LaFrance, M., & Vial, A. C. (2016). Gender and nonverbal behavior. In D. Matsumoto, H. C. Hwang, & M. G. Frank (Eds.), *APA handbook of nonverbal communication* (pp. 139-161). Washington DC: American Psychological Association.

Lakoff, R. T. (1990). *Talking power: The politics of language in our lives.* New York: Basic Books.

Lalumiere, M., Harris., G. T., Quinsey, V. L., & Rice, M. E. (2005). *The causes of rape: Understanding individual differences in male propensity for sexual aggression.* Washington, DC: American Psychological Association.

Lamb, S. (2000). *White saris and sweet mangoes: Aging, gender, and body in North India.* Berkeley: University of California Press.

Lamb, S. (2008, June 27). The "right" sexuality for girls. *Chronicle of Higher Education,* pp. B14–B15.

Lamb, S., & Brown, L. M. (2006). *Packaging girlhood: Rescuing our daughters from marketers' schemes.* New York: St. Martin's Press.

Lambdin, J. R., et al. (2003). The Animal = Male hypothesis: Children's and adults' beliefs about the sex of non-sex-specific stuffed animals. *Sex Roles, 48,* 471–482.

Lambert, A. J., & Raichle, K. (2000). The role of political ideology in mediating judgments of blame in rape victims and their assailants: A test of the just world, personal responsibility, and legitimization hypothesis. *Personality and Social Psychology Bulletin, 26,* 853–863.

Lambert, J. C. (2000, May 2). Self-made? Male myth. *City Newspaper,* p. 6.

Lamke, L. K., Sollie, D. L., Durbin, R. G., & Fitzpatrick, J. A. (1994). Masculinity, femininity, and relationship satisfaction: The mediating role of interpersonal competence. *Journal of Social and Personal Relationships, 11,* 535–554.

Lance, L. M. (1998). Gender differences in heterosexual dating: A content analysis of personal ads. *Journal of Men's Studies, 6,* 297–305.

Landau, S. C., Tapias, M. P., & McGhee, B. T. (2006). Birth control within reach: A national survey on women's attitudes toward and interest in pharmacy access to hormonal contraception. *Contraception, 74,* 463–470.

Landrine, H., & Klonoff, E. A. (1997). *Discrimination against women: Prevalence, consequences, remedies.* Thousand Oaks, CA: Sage.

Landrine, H., & Klonoff, E. A. (2001). Health and health care: How gender makes women sick. In J. Worell (Ed.), *Encyclopedia of women and gender* (pp. 577–592). San Diego: Academic Press.

Lane, K. A., Kang, J., & Banaji, M. R. (2007). Implicit social cognition and the law. *Annual Review of Law Social Science, 3*, 427–451.

Lapointe, V., & Marcotte, D. (2000). Gender-typed characteristics and coping strategies of depressed adolescents. *European Review of Applied Psychology, 50*, 451–460.

Larson, M. S. (2003). Gender, race, and aggression in television commercials that feature children. *Sex Roles, 48*, 67–75.

LaRosa, J. (2020, June 3). $72 billion U.S. weight loss industry pivots to survive pandemic. *Market Research Blog.* Retrieved October 5, 2021 from https://blog.marketresearch.com/71-billion-u.s.-weight-loss-market-pivots-to-survive-pandemic

Larson, R. W., Clore, G. L., & Wood, G. A. (1999). The emotions of romantic relationships: Do they wreak havoc on adolescents? In W. Furman, B. D. Brown, & C. Feiring (Eds.), *The development of romantic relationships in adolescence.* New York: Cambridge University Press.

Larsson, M., Lövdén, M., & Lars-Göran, N. (2003). Sex differences in recollective experience for olfactory and verbal information. *Acta Psychologica, 112*, 89–103.

Latner, J. D., & Schwartz, M. B. (2005). Weight bias in a child's world. In K. D. Brownell, R. M. Puhl, M. B. Schwartz, & L. Rudd (Eds.), *Weight bias: Nature, consequences, and remedies* (pp. 54–67). New York: Guilford.

Laube, H., Massoni, K., Sprague, J., & Ferber, A. L. (2007). The impact of gender on the evaluation of teaching: What we know and what we do. *National Women's Studies Association Journal, 19*, 87–104.

Laumann, E. O., Gagnon, J. H., Michael, R. T., & Michaels, S. (1994). *The social organization of sexuality: Sexual practices in the United States.* Chicago: University of Chicago Press.

Laumann, E. O., Paik, A., & Rosen, R. C. (2002). Sexual dysfunction in the United States: Prevalence and predictors. In E. O. Laumann & R. T. Michael (Eds.), *Sex, love, and health in America* (pp. 352–376). Chicago: University of Chicago Press.

Lauzen, M. M., & Dozier, D. M. (2002). You look mahvelous: An examination of gender and appearance comments in the 1999–2000 prime-time season. *Sex Roles, 46*, 429–437.

Lauzen, M. M., & Dozier, D. M. (2005). Maintaining the double standard: Portrayals of age and gender in popular films. *Sex Roles, 52*, 437–446.

Lawless, J. L., & Fox, R. L. (2005). *It takes a candidate: Why women don't run for office.* New York: Cambridge University Press.

Lawrence, A. A. (2008). Gender identity disorders in adults: Diagnosis and treatment. In D. L. Rowland & L. Incrocci (Eds.), *Handbook of sexual and gender identity disorders* (pp. 423–456). Hoboken, NJ: Wiley.

Lawrence, R. A. (1998). Breastfeeding. In E. A. Blechman & K. D. Brownell (Eds.), *Behavioral medicine and women: A comprehensive handbook* (pp. 495–500). New York: Guilford.

Lawton, C. A., & Hatcher., D. W. (2005). Gender differences in integration of images in visuospatial memory. *Sex Roles, 13*, 717–725.

Lawton, C. A., & Kallai, J. (2002). Gender differences in way finding strategies and anxiety about way finding: A cross-cultural comparison. *Sex Roles, 47*, 389–401.

Lawton, C. A., & Morrin, K. A. (1999). Gender differences in pointing accuracy in computer-simulated 3D mazes. *Sex Roles, 40*, 73–92.

Leaper, C. (2002). Parenting girls and boys. In M. H. Bornstein (Ed.), *Handbook of parenting* (Vol. 1). Mahwah, NJ: Erlbaum.

Leaper, C., Anderson, K. J., & Sanders, P. (1998). Moderators of gender effects on parents' talk to their children: A meta-analysis. *Developmental Psychology, 34*, 3–27.

Leaper, C., & Brown, C. S. (2008). Perceived experiences with sexism among adolescent girls. *Child Development, 79*, 685–704.

Leaper, C., & Robnett, R. (2011). Women are more likely than men to use tentative language, aren't they? A meta-analysis testing for gender differences and moderators. *Psychology of Women Quarterly, 35*, 129-142.

Lederman, R. P. (1996). *Psychosocial adaptation in pregnancy* (2nd ed.). New York: Springer.

Lee, C. (2010). Gender, health, and health behaviors. In J. C. Chrisler & D. R. McCreary (Eds.), *Handbook of gender research in psychology* (pp. 471–493). New York: Springer.

Lee, E. (2003). *Abortion, motherhood, and mental health.* New York: Aldine de Gruyter.

Lee, E., & Mock, M. R. (2005a). Asian families: An overview. In M. McGoldrick, J. Giordano, & N. Garcia-Preto (Eds.), *Ethnicity and family therapy* (3rd ed., pp. 269–289). New York: Guilford.

Lee, E., & Mock, M. R. (2005b). Chinese families. In M. McGoldrick, J. Giordano, & N. Garcia-Preto (Eds.), *Ethnicity and family therapy* (3rd ed., pp. 302–318). New York: Guilford.

Lee, J. (2001). Beyond bean counting. In S. M. Shaw & J. Lee (Eds.), *Women's voices, feminist visions* (pp. 36–39). Mountain View, CA: Mayfield.

Lee, M.-Y., & Au, P. (2007). Chinese battered women in North America. In A. R. Roberts (Ed.), *Battered women and their families* (3rd ed., pp. 529–562). New York: Springer.

Lee, W. M. L. (1999). *An introduction to multicultural counseling.* Philadelphia: Taylor & Francis.

Lee, Y. G., & Bhargava, V. (2004). Leisure time: Do married and single individuals spend it differently? *Family and Consumer Sciences Research Journal, 32,* 254–274.

LeEspiritu, Y. (2001). Ideological racism and cultural resistance. In M. L. Anderson & P. H. Collins (Eds.), *Race, class, and gender* (4th ed., pp. 191–201). Belmont, CA: Wadsworth.

Leifer, M. (1980). *Psychological effects of motherhood.* New York: Praeger.

Lein, L., & Schexnayder, D. (2007). *Life after welfare: Reform and the persistence of poverty.* Austin: University of Texas Press.

Lemieux, S. R., & Byers, E. S. (2008). The sexual well-being of women who have experienced child sexual abuse. *Psychology of Women Quarterly, 32,* 126–144.

Lemons, G. L. (2008). *Black male outsider teaching as a profeminist man: A memoir.* Albany: State University of New York Press.

Lennon, M. C. (2006). Women, work, and depression. In C. L. M. Keyes & S. H. Goodman (Eds.), *Women and depression: A handbook for the social, behavioral, and biomedical sciences* (pp. 309–327). New York: Cambridge University Press.

Lerner, H. (1989). *Women in therapy.* New York: Harper & Row.

Lerner, S. (2009). *Why women need health care reform.* Retrieved August 24, 2009, from http://www.truthout.org/082409E?n

Lesbian, gay, bisexual, and transgendered youth issues. (2001, April/May). *Siecus Report Supplement, 29,* 1–5.

Lesch, E., & van der Watt, A. S. (2018). Living single: A phenomenological study of a group of South African single women. *Feminism & Psychology, 28,* 390-408.

Leung, A., Sakkas, D., Pang, S., Thornton, K., & Resetkova, N. (2019). Assisted reproductive technology outcomes in female-to-male transgender patients compared with cisgender patients: A new frontier in reproductive medicine. *Fertility and Sterility, 112*(5), 858-865.

Leung, P., & Adashi, E. (Eds.). (2019). *The ovary,* 3rd ed. Elsevier.

Levant, R. F., et al. (2006). The normative male alexithymia scale. *Psychology of Men & Masculinity, 7,* 212–234.

Levant, R. F., Majors, R. G., & Kelley, M. L. (1998). Masculinity ideology among young African American and European American women and men in different regions of the United States. *Cultural Diversity and Mental Health, 4,* 227–236.

LeVay, S. (1996). *The use and abuse of research into homosexuality.* Cambridge, MA: MIT Press.

Levering, M. (1994). Women, the state, and religion today in the People's Republic of China. In A. Sharma (Ed.), *Today's woman in world religions* (pp. 171–224). Albany, NY: State University of New York Press.

Levesque, M. J., & Lowe, C. A. (1999). Face-ism as a determinant of interpersonal perceptions: The influence of context on facial prominence effects. *Sex Roles, 41,* 241–259.

Levesque, R. J. R. (2001). *Culture and family violence.* Washington, DC: American Psychological Association.

Levin, R. J. (2008). Critically revisiting aspects of the human sexual response cycle of Masters and Johnson: Correcting errors and suggesting modifications. *Sexual and Relationship Therapy, 23,* 393-399.

Levine, F., & Le De Simone, L. (1991). The effects of experimenter gender on pain report in male and female subjects. *Pain, 44,* 69–72.

Levine, R. (2004). *Growing older with dignity and vitality.* Westport, CT: Praeger.

Levine, S. B. (2005). *Inventing the rest of our lives: Women in second adulthood.* New York: Viking.

Levitt, H. M., & Ware, K. N. (2006). Religious leaders' perspectives on marriage, divorce, and intimate partner violence. *Psychology of Women Quarterly, 30,* 212–222.

Levstik, L. S. (2001). Daily acts of ordinary courage: Gender-equitable practice in the social studies classroom. In P. O'Reilly, E. M. Penn, & K. deMarrais (Eds.), *Educating young adolescent girls* (pp. 189–211). Mahwah, NJ: Erlbaum.

Levy, B. (2008). *Women and violence.* Berkeley, CA: Seal Press.

Levy, B. R. (2009). Stereotype embodiment: A psychosocial approach to aging. *Current Directions in Psychological Science, 18,* 332–336.

Levy, B. R., & Banaji, M. R. (2002). Implicit ageism. In T. Nelson (Ed.), *Ageism: Stereotyping and prejudice against older persons* (pp. 49–75). Cambridge, MA: MIT Press.

Levy, B. R., & Langer, E. (1994). Aging free from negative stereotypes: Successful memory in China and among the American deaf. *Journal of Personality and Social Psychology, 66,* 989–997.

Levy, B. R., Zonderman, A. B., Slade, M. D., & Ferrucci, L. (2009). Age stereotypes held earlier in life predict cardiovascular events in later life. *Psychological Science, 20,* 296–298.

Levy, G. D., Sadovsky, A. L., & Troseth, G. L. (2000). Aspects of young children's perceptions of gender-type occupations. *Sex Roles, 42,* 993–1006.

Lewin, C., & Herlitz, A. (2002). Sex differences in face recognition —women's faces make the difference. *Brain and Cognition, 50,* 121–128.

Lewis, C., Crawford, J., & Sygall, S. (2002). *Loud, proud and passionate.* New York: Women, Ink.

Lewis, C., Scully, D., & Condor, S. (1992). Sex stereotyping of infants: A re-examination. *Journal of Reproductive and Infant Psychology, 10,* 53–63.

Lewis, J. M., Wallerstein, J. S., & Johnson-Reitz, L. (2004). Communication in divorced and single-parent families. In A. L. Vangelisti (Ed.), *Handbook of family communication* (pp. 197–214). Mahwah, NJ: Erlbaum.

Lewis, K. G., & Moon, S. (1997). Always single and single again women: A qualitative study. *Journal of Marital and Family Therapy, 23,* 115–134.

Li, A. K. F., & Adamson, G. (1995). Motivational patterns related to gifted students' learning of mathematics, science, and English: An examination of gender differences. *Journal for the Education of the Gifted, 18,* 284–297.

Li, C., & Kerpelman, J. (2007). Parental influences on young women's certainty about their career aspirations. *Sex Roles, 56,* 105–115.

Li, G., Pollitt, A. M., & Russell, S. T. (2016). Depression and sexual orientation during young adulthood: Diversity among sexual minority subgroups and the role of gender. *Archives of Sexual Behavior, 45,* 697-711.

Li, N. P., & Kenrick, D. T. (2006). Sex similarities and differences in preferences for short-term mates: What, whether, and why. *Journal of Personality and Social Psychology, 90,* 468–489.

Li, R., & Grummer-Strawn, L. (2002). Racial and ethnic disparities in breastfeeding among United States infants: Third national health and nutrition examination survey, 1988–1994. *Birth, 29,* 251–257.

Liben, L. S., & Bigler, R. S. (2002). The developmental course of gender differentiation. *Monographs of the Society for Research in Child Development, 67*(2, Serial No. 269).

Liben, L. S., Bigler, R. S., & Krogh, H. R. (2002). Language at work: Children's gendered interpretations of occupational titles. *Child Development, 73,* 810–828.

Lieu, N. T. (2004). Remembering "the nation" through pageantry. In L.

T. Võ et al. (Eds.), *Asian American women: The frontiers reader.* Lincoln: University of Nebraska Press.

Light, A. D., Obedin-Maliver, J., Sevelius, J. M., & Kerns, J. K. (2014). Transgender men who experienced pregnancy after female-to-male gender transitioning. *Obstetrics & Gynecology, 124,* 1120-1127.

Lightdale, J. R., & Prentice, D. A. (1994). Rethinking sex differences in aggression: Aggressive behavior in the absence of social roles. *Personality and Social Psychology Bulletin, 20,* 34–44.

Lilliecreutz, C., Larén, J., Sydsjö, G., & Josefsson, A. (2016). Effect of maternal stress during pregnancy on the risk for preterm birth. *BMC Pregnancy and Childbirth, 16*:5. DOI 10.1186/s12884 -015-0775-x

Lim, I.-S. (1997). Korean immigrant women's challenge to gender inequality at home: The interplay of economic resources, gender, and family. *Gender and Society, 11 ,* 31–51.

Lim, S., Cortina, L. M., & Magley, V. L. (2008). Personal and workgroup incivility: Impact on work and health outcomes. *Journal of Applied Psychology, 93,* 95–107.

Lindberg, S. M., Hyde, J. S., & McKinley, N. M. (2006). A measure of objectified body consciousness for preadolescent and adolescent youth. *Psychology of Women Quarterly, 30,* 65–76.

Lin, L., Nigrinis, A., Christidis, P., & Stamm, K. (2015). Demographics of the U.S. psychology workforce: Findings from the American community survey. *American Psychological Association Center for Workforce Studies.* Retrieved October 5, 2021 from https://www.apa .org/workforce/publications /13-demographics/report.pdf

Lindberg, S. M., Hyde, J. S., Peterson, J. L., & Linn, M. C. (2010). New trends in gender and mathematics performance: A meta-analysis. *Psychological Bulletin, 136*(6), 1123-1135.

Lindgren, K. P., Parkhill, M. R., George, W. H., & Hendershot, C. S. (2008). Gender differences in perceptions of sexual intent: A qualitative review and integration. *Psychology of Women Quarterly, 32,* 423–439.

Lips, H. M. (2001). Power: Social and interpersonal aspects. In J. Worell (Ed.), *Encyclopedia of women and gender* (pp. 847–858). San Diego: Academic Press.

Lips, H. M. (2003). The gender pay gap: Concrete indicator of women's progress toward equality. *Analyses of Social Issues and Public Policy, 3,* 87–109.

Lips, H. M. (2004). The gender gap in possible selves: Divergence of academic self-views among high school and university students. *Sex Roles, 50,* 357–371.

Lips, H. M., & Keener, E. (2007). Effects of gender and dominance on leadership emergence: Incentives make a difference. *Sex Roles, 56,* 563–571.

List of countries and territories by fertility rate. (2009). Retrieved September 9, 2009, from http:// en. wikipedia.org/wiki/List_of _ countries_and_territories _ by_fertility_rate

Littleton, H., Axsom, D., Breitkopf, C. R., & Berenson, A. (2006). Rape acknowledgment and postassault experiences: How acknowledgment status relates to disclosure, coping, worldview, and reactions received from others. *Violence and Victims, 21,* 761–778.

Littleton, H., & Breitkopf, C. R. (2006). Coping with the experience of rape. *Psychology of Women Quarterly, 30,* 106–116.

Livingston, M. (1999). How to think about women's health. In C. Forden, A. E. Hunter, & B. Birns (Eds.), *Readings in the psychology of women: Dimensions of the female experience* (pp. 244–253). Boston: Allyn & Bacon.

Livingston, G. (2018). *They're waiting longer, but U.S. women today more likely to have children than a decade ago.* Pew Research

Center. Retrieved October 4, 2021 from https://www .pewresearch.org/social-trends /2018/01/18/theyre-waiting -longer-but-u-s-women-today -more-likely-to-have-children -than-a-decade-ago/

Livingston, G., & Thomas, D. (2019). *Among 41 countries, only U.S. lacks paid parental leave.* Pew Research Center. Retrieved October 4, 2021 from https:// www.pewresearch.org/fact -tank/2019/12/16/u-s-lacks -mandated-paid-parental-leave/

Lloyd, M. (2006, August 11). Slowly enabling the disabled. *Chronicle of Higher Education,* pp. A35–A37.

Lloyd, S. A., & Emery, B. C. (2000). *The dark side of courtship: Physical and sexual aggression.* Thousand Oaks, CA: Sage.

Lobel, M., & DeLuca, R. S. (2007). Psychosocial sequelae of cesarean delivery: Review and analysis of their causes and implications. *Social Science & Medicine, 64,* 2272–2284.

Lobel, M., Hamilton, J. G., & Cannella, D. T. (2008). Psychosocial perspectives on pregnancy: Prenatal maternal stress and coping. *Social and Personality Psychology Compass, 2,* 1–24.

Lobel, T. E., et al. (2000). Gender schema and social judgments: A developmental study of children from Hong Kong. *Sex Roles, 43,* 19–42.

Lobo, R. A. (2005). Potential options for preservation of fertility in women. *New England Journal of Medicine, 353,* 64–73.

Loeb, S., Fuller, B., Kagan, S. L., & Carrol, B. (2004). Child care in poor communities: Early learning effects of type, quality, and stability. *Child Development, 75,* 47–65.

Loftus, E. F. (2004, February). Evidently enough. *American Psychological Society Newsletter,* pp. 8.

Loftus, E. F., Garry, M., & Hayne, H. (2008). Repressed and recovered memory. In E. Borgida & S. T. Fiske (Eds.), *Beyond common sense: Psychological science in the courtroom* (pp. 177–194). Malden, MA: Blackwell.

Logan, T. K., Walker, R., Jordan, C. E., & Leukefeld, C. G. (2006). *Women and victimization: Contributing factors, interventions, and implications.* Washington, DC: American Psychological Association.

Lonborg, S. D., & Travis, C. B. (2007). Living longer, healthier lives. In V. Muhlbauer & J. C. Chrisler (Eds.), *Women over 50: Psychological perspectives* (pp. 53–78). New York: Springer.

Long, C. (2009). "I don't know who to blame" : HIV-positive South African women navigating heterosexual infection. *Psychology of Women Quarterly, 33,* 321–333.

Lonner, W. J. (2003). Teaching cross-cultural psychology. In P. Bronstein & K. Quina (Eds.), *Teaching gender and multicultural awareness* (pp. 169–179). Washington, DC: American Psychological Association.

Lonsway, K. A., Cortina, L. M., & Magley, V. J. (2008). Sexual harassment mythology: Definition, conceptualization, and measurement. *Sex Roles, 58,* 599–615.

Lopez, N. (2006). Resistance to race and gender oppression: Dominican high school girls in New York City. In J. Denner & B. L. Guzmán (Eds.), *Latina girls: Voices of adolescent strength in the United States* (pp. 79–92). New York: New York University Press.

López, N., & Gadsden, V. L. (2016). Health inequities, social determinants, and intersectionality. *NAM Perspectives.* Discussion Paper, National Academy of Medicine, Washington, DC.

LoPiccolo, J. (2002). Integrative sex therapy: A postmodern model. In J. Lebow (Ed.), *Comprehensive handbook of psychotherapy* (Vol. 4). New York: Wiley.

Lorber, J. (2005a). *Breaking the bowls.* New York: Norton.

Lorber, J. (2005b). *Gender inequality: Feminist theories and politics* (3rd ed.). Los Angeles: Roxbury.

Lorde, A. (2001). Age, race, class, and sex: Women redefining difference. In M. L. Anderson & P. H. Collins (Eds.), *Race, class, and gender* (4th ed., pp. 177–184). Belmont, CA: Wadsworth.

Loseke, D. R., & Kurz, D. (2005). Men's violence toward women is the serious social problem. In D. R. Loseke, R. J. Gelles, & M. M. Cavanaugh (Eds.), *Current controversies on family violence* (2nd ed., pp. 79–95). Thousand Oaks, CA: Sage.

Lott, A. J. (2003). A course on men and masculinity. In P. Bronstein & K. Quina (Eds.), *Teaching gender and multicultural awareness* (pp. 299–312). Washington, DC: American Psychological Association.

Lott, B. (1987). Sexist discrimination as distancing behavior: I. A laboratory demonstration. *Psychology of Women Quarterly, 11,* 47–58.

Lott, B. (1996). Politics or science? The question of gender sameness/ difference. *American Psychologist, 51,* 155–156.

Lott, B. (2000). Global connections: The significance of women's poverty. In J. C. Chrisler, C. Golden, & P. D. Rozee (Eds.), *Lectures on the psychology of women* (2nd ed., pp. 27–36). Boston: McGraw-Hill.

Lott, B. (2002). Cognitive and behavioral distancing from the poor. *American Psychologist, 57,* 100–110.

Lott, B. (2003). Recognizing and welcoming the standpoint of low-income parents in the public schools. *Journal of Educational and Psychological Consultation, 14,* 91–104.

Lott, B., & Bullock, H. (2010). Social class and women's lives. *Psychology of Women Quarterly, 34,* 421–424.

Lott, B., & Maluso, D. (1993). The social learning of gender. In A. E. Beall & R. J. Sternberg (Eds.), *The psychology of gender* (pp. 99–123). New York: Guilford.

Lott, B., & Maluso, D. (1995). Introduction: Framing the questions. In B. Lott & D. Maluso (Eds.), *The social psychology of interpersonal discrimination* (pp. 1–11). New York: Guilford.

Lott, B., & Maluso, D. (2001). Gender development: Social learning. In J. Worell (Ed.), *Encyclopedia of women and gender* (pp. 537–549). San Diego: Academic Press.

Lott, B., & Saxon, S. (2002). The influence of ethnicity, social class, and context on judgments about U.S. women. *Journal of Social Psychology, 142,* 481–499.

Lott, B., & Webster, K. (2006). Carry the banner where it can be seen: Small wins for social justice. *Social Justice Research, 19,* 123–134.

Louwagie, P. (2008). *Sexual assault on campus: Culture change 101.* Retrieved November 11, 2008, from http://www.truthout.org/111008WA

Lovell, V., Hartmann, H., & Werschkul, M. (2007). More than raising the floor: The persistence of gender inequalities in the low-wage labor market. In D. S. Cobble (Ed.), *The sex of class: Women transforming American labor* (pp. 35–57). Ithaca, NY: Cornell University Press.

Lubinski, D., et al. (2001). Men and women at promise for scientific excellence: Similarity not dissimilarity. *Psychological Science, 12,* 309–317.

Luce, A., Cash, M., Hundley, V., Cheyne, H., van Teijlingen, E., & Angell, C. (2016). "Is it realistic?" The portrayal of pregnancy and childbirth in the media. *BMC Pregnancy Childbirth, 16:*40.

Luczak, S. E., Glatt, S. J., & Wall, T. L. (2009). Meta-analyses of ALDH2 and ADHIB with alcohol dependence in Asians. In

G. A. Marlatt & K. Witkiewitz (Eds.), *Addictive behaviors: New readings on etiology, prevention, and treatment* (pp. 677–712). Washington, DC: American Psychological Association.

Luker, K. (1996). *Dubious conceptions: The politics of teenage pregnancy.* Cambridge, MA: Harvard University Press.

Lundberg-Love, P., & Faulkner, D. L. (2008). Stress and health. In M. A. Paludi (Ed.), *The psychology of women at work* (Vol. 3, pp. 59–83). Westport, CT: Praeger.

Lundberg-Love, P., & Marmion, S. (2003). Sexual harassment in the private sector. In M. A. Paludi & C. A. Paludi (Eds.), *Academic and workplace sexual harassment* (pp. 77–101). Westport, CT: Praeger.

Lundeberg, M. A., Fox, P. W., Brown, A. C., & Elbedour, S. (2000). Cultural influences on confidence: Country and gender. *Journal of Educational Psychology, 92,* 152–159.

Lyons, B. H., Walters, M. L., Jack, S. P. D., Petrosky, E., Blair, J. M., & Ivey-Stephenson, A. Z. (2019). Suicides among lesbian and gay male individuals: Findings from the national violent death reporting system. *American Journal of Preventive Medicine, 56,* 512-521.

Lyons, P. (2009). Prescription for harm: Industry influence, public health policy, and the "obesity epidemic. " In E. Rothblum & S. Solovay (Eds.), *The fat studies reader* (pp. 75–87). New York: New York University Press.

Macalister, H. E. (2003). In defense of ambiguity: Understanding bi-sexuality's invisibility through cognitive psychology. *Journal of Bisexuality, 3,* 23–32.

MacBride-Stewart, S. (2007). Que(e)rying the meaning of lesbian health: Individual(izing) and community discourses. In V. Clarke & E. Peel (Eds.), *Out in psychology: Lesbians, gay, bisexual, trans and queer perspectives*

(pp. 427–443). Chichester, West Sussex, England: Wiley.

Maccoby, E. E. (1998). *The two sexes: Growing up apart, coming together.* Cambridge, MA: Harvard University Press.

Maccoby, E. E. (2002). Gender and group process: A developmental perspective. *Current Directions in Psychological Science, 11,* 54–58.

Maccoby, E. E., & Jacklin, C. N. (1974). *The psychology of sex differences.* Stanford, CA: Stanford University Press.

MacDermid, S. M., Leslie, L. A., & Bissonette, L. (2001). Walking the walk: Insights from research on helping clients navigate work and family. *Journal of Feminist Therapy, 13,* 21–40.

Macdonald, B., & Rich, C. (2001). *Look me in the eye: Old women, aging, and ageism (expanded ed.).* Denver, CO: Spinsters Ink.

MacGeorge, E. L. (2003). Gender differences in attributions and emotions in helping contexts. *Sex Roles, 48,* 175–182.

MacGeorge, E. L. (2004). The myth of gender cultures: Similarities outweigh differences in men's and women's provision of and responses to supportive communication. *Sex Roles, 50,* 143–175.

MacGeorge, E. L., Gillihan, S. J., Samter, W., & Clark, R. A. (2003). Skill deficit or differential motivation? *Communication Research, 30,* 273–303.

MacIntosh, H., Reissing, E. D., & Andruff, H. (2010). Same-sex marriage in Canada: The impact of legal marriage on the first cohort of gay and lesbian Canadians to wed. *Canadian Journal of Human Sexuality, 19,* 79–90.

MacKay, N. J., & Covell, K. (1997). The impact of women in advertisements on attitudes toward women. *Sex Roles, 36,* 573–583.

Mackey, R. A., Diemer, M. A., & O'Brien, B. A. (2000). Psychological intimacy in the lasting relationships of heterosexual and same-gender couples. *Sex Roles, 43*, 201–227.

MacKinnon, E., Brown, E. G., Polgar, J. M., & Havens, L. (2003). "Choral music" for community change. In G. A. King, E. G. Brown, & L. K. Smith (Eds.), *Resilience: Learning from people with disabilities and the turning points in their lives* (pp. 129–151). Westport, CT: Praeger.

MacLachlan, A. J. (2006). The graduate experience of women in STEM and how it could be improved. In J. M. Bystydzienski & S. R. Bird (Eds.), *Removing barriers: Women in academic science, technology, engineering, and mathematics* (pp. 237–253). Bloomington: Indiana University Press.

MacLaughlin, D. T., & Donahoe, P. K. (2004). Sex determination and differentiation. *New England Journal of Medicine, 350*, 367–378.

Macrae, C. N., & Bodenhausen, G. V. (2000). Social cognition: Thinking categorically about others. *Annual Review of Psychology, 51*, 93–120.

Madan, M., & Nalla, M. K. (2016). Sexual harassment in public spaces: Examining gender differences in perceived seriousness and victimization. *International Criminal Justice Review, 26*, 80-97.

Madden, M. E., & Hyde, J. S. (1998). Integrating gender and ethnicity into psychology courses. *Psychology of Women Quarterly, 22*, 1–12.

Madi, B. C., Sandall, J., Bennett, R., & MacLeod, C. (1999). Effects of female relative support in labor: A randomized controlled trial. *Birth, 26*, 4–8.

Madu, B. N., & Kasanga, L. A. (2005). Sex differences in the acquisition of English as a second language. *Gender & Behaviour, 3*, 442–452.

Magai, C. (2001). Emotions over the life span. In J. E. Birren & K. W. Schaie (Eds.), *Handbook of the psychology of aging* (5th ed., pp. 399–426). San Diego: Academic Press.

Magley, V. J., Gallus, J. A., & Bunk, J. A. (2010). The gendered nature of workplace mistreatment. In J. C. Chrisler & D. R. McCreary (Eds.), *Handbook of gender research in psychology* (Vol. 2, pp. 423–441). New York: Springer.

Magley, V. J., & Shupe, E. I. (2005). Self-labeling sexual harassment. *Sex Roles, 53*, 173–189.

Mah, K., & Binik, Y. (2002). Do all orgasms feel alike? Evaluating a two-dimensional model of orgasm experience across gender and sexual context. *Journal of Sex Research, 39*, 104–113.

Mahaffy, K. A., & Ward, S. K. (2002). The gendering of adolescents' childbearing and educational plans: Reciprocal effects and the influence of social context. *Sex Roles, 46*, 403–417.

Maitland, S., et al. (2004). Selective sex differences in declarative memory. *Memory & Cognition, 32*, 1160–1169.

Major, B. (1998). Personal resilience, cognitive appraisals, and coping: An integrative model of adjustment to abortion. *Journal of Personality and Social Psychology, 74*, 735–752.

Major, B., Barr, L., Zubek, J., & Babey, S. H. (1999). Gender and self-esteem: A meta-analysis. In W. B. Swann, Jr., J. H. Langlois, & L. A. Gilbert (Eds.), *Sexism and stereotypes in modern society* (pp. 223–253). Washington, DC: American Psychological Association.

Makarova, E., Aeschlimann, B., & Herzog, W. (2019). The gender gap in STEM fields: The impact of the gender stereotype of math and science on secondary students' career aspirations. *Frontiers in Education, 10*: 60. https://doi.org/10.3389/feduc .2019.00060

Makwana, B., Lee, Y., Parkin, S., & Farmer, L. (2018). Selfie-esteem: The relationship between body dissatisfaction and social media in adolescent and young women. *The Inquisitive Mind, 35*(1). Retrieved October 3, 2021 from https://www.in-mind.org/article/ selfie-esteem-the-relationship -between-body-dissatisfaction -and-social-media-in -adolescent

Malamuth, N. M. (1998). The confluence model as an organizing framework for research on sexually aggressive men: Risk moderators, imagined aggression, and pornography consumption. In R. G. Geen & E. Donnerstein (Eds.), *Human aggression: Theories, research, and implications for social policy* (pp. 229–245). San Diego: Academic Press.

Malanchuk, O., & Eccles, J. S. (2006). Self-esteem. In J. Worell & C. D. Goodheart (Eds.), *Handbook of girls' and women's psychological health: Gender and well-being across the life span* (pp. 149–156). New York: Oxford University Press.

Malkin, C., & Stake, J. E. (2004). Changes in attitudes and self-confidence in the women's and gender studies classroom: The role of teacher alliance and student cohesion. *Sex Roles, 50*, 455–468.

Malveaux, J. (2006, January 12). Dimensions of diversity: When you teach, you learn. *Diverse Education, 39*.

Mandel, D. (2009). Batterers and the lives of their children. In E. Stark & E. S. Buzawa (Eds.), *Violence against women in families and relationships* (Vol. 2, pp. 67–93). Santa Barbara, CA: ABC-CLIO.

Manderson, L. (2003). Teaching gender, teaching women's health: Introduction. In L. Manderson (Ed.), *Teaching gender, teaching women's health* (pp. 1–9). Binghamton, NY: Haworth.

Mann, J. J. (2005). The medical management of depression. New England Journal of Medicine, 353, 1819–1834.

Mano, R., Benjaminov, O., Kedar, I., Bar, Y., Sela, S., Ozalvo, R., Baniel, J., & Margel, D. (2017). PD07-10 malignancies in male BRCA mutation carriers – results from a prospectively screened cohort of patients enrolled to a dedicated male BRCA clinic. *The Journal of Urology, 197*, No. 4S Supplement, e131-e132.

Mansfield, P. K., Koch, P. B., & Voda, A. M. (1998). Qualities midlife women desire in their sexual relationships and their changing sexual response. Psychology of Women Quarterly, 22, 285–303.

Mantsios, G. (2001). Media magic: Making class invisible. In M. L. Andersen & P. H. Collins (Eds.), *Race, class, and gender* (pp. 333–341). Belmont, CA: Wadsworth.

Marcell, A. V., Ford, C. A., Pleck, J. H., & Sonenstein, F. L. (2007). Masculine beliefs, parental communication, and male adolescents' health care. *Pediatrics, 119*, 966–975.

Marcus-Newhall, A., Halpern, D. F., & Tan, S. J. (Eds.). (2008). *The changing realities of work and family*. Malden, MA: Wiley-Blackwell.

Marcus-Newhall, A., Thompson, S., & Thomas, C. (2001). Examining a gender stereotype: Menopausal women. *Journal of Applied Social Psychology, 31*, 698–719.

Marecek, J., Crawford, M., & Popp, D. (2004). On the construction of gender, sex, and sexualities. In A. H. Eagly, A. E. Beall, & R. J. Sternberg (Eds.), *The psychology of gender* (2nd ed., pp. 192–216). New York: Guilford.

Marecek, J. (2001a). After the facts: Psychology and the study of gender. *Canadian Psychology/Psychologie canadienne, 42*, 254–267.

Marecek, J. (2001b). Disorderly constructs: Feminist frameworks for clinical psychology. In R. K. Unger (Ed.), *Handbook of women and gender* (pp. 303–329). New York: Wiley.

Marecek, J., et al. (2003). Psychology of women and gender. In I. B. Weiner (Ed.), *Handbook of psychology* (Vol. 1, pp. 249–268). Hoboken, NJ: Wiley.

Marecek, J. (2006). Young women's suicide in Sri Lanka: Cultural, ecological, and psychological factors. *Asian Journal of Counselling, 13*, 63–92.

Marecek, J., Crawford, M., & Popp, D. (2004). On the construction of gender, sex, and sexualities. In A. H. Eagly, A. E. Beall, & R. J. Sternberg (Eds.), *The psychology of gender* (2nd ed., pp. 192–216). New York: Guilford.

Marin, A. J., & Russo, N. F. (1999). Feminist perspectives on male violence against women. In M. Harway & J. M. O'Neil (Eds.), *What causes men's violence against women?* (pp. 18–35). Thousand Oaks, CA: Sage.

Marín, B. V. (2003). Challenges of HIV prevention in diverse communities. In G. Bernal, J. E. Trimble, A. K. Burlew, & F. T. L. Leong (Eds.), *Handbook of racial and ethnic minority psychology* (pp. 608–620). Thousand Oaks, CA: Sage.

Marine, S. (2004, November 26). Waking up from the nightmare of rape. *Chronicle of Higher Education*, p. B5.

Markey, C. N. (2004). Culture and the development of eating disorders: A tripartite model. *Eating Disorders, 12*, 139–156.

Markham, B. (2006). Older women and security. In J. Worell & C. D. Goodheart (Eds.), *Handbook of girls' and women's psychological health: Gender and well-being across the life span* (pp. 388–396). New York: Oxford University Press.

Marks, M. J., & Fraley, R. C. (2005). The sexual double standard: Fact or fiction? *Sex Roles, 52*, 175–186.

Marks, M. J., & Fraley, R. C. (2006). Confirmation bias and the sexual double standard. *Sex Roles, 54*, 19–26.

Marks, N. F. (1996). Flying solo at midlife: Gender, marital status, and psychological well-being. *Journal of Marriage and the Family, 58*, 917–932.

Markus, H. R. (2008). Pride, prejudice, and ambivalence: Toward a unified theory of race and ethnicity. *American Psychologist, 63*, 651–670.

Marlat, G. A., & Witkiewitz, K. (Eds.). (2009). *Addictive behaviors: New readings on etiology, prevention, and treatment*. Washington, DC: American Psychological Association.

Marleau, J. D., & Saucier, J.-F. (2002). Preference for a firstborn boy in Western societies. *Journal of Bio-social Science, 34*, 13–27.

Marlino, D., & Wilson, F. (2006). Career expectations of Latina adolescents: Results from a nationwide study. In J. Denner & B. L. Guzmán (Eds.), *Latina girls: Voices of adolescent strength in the United States* (pp. 109–137). New York: New York University Press.

Marmion, S. L. (2006). To the future. In P. K. Lundberg-Love & S. L. Marmion (Eds.), *"Intimate" violence against women: When spouses, partners, or lovers attack*. Westport, CT: Praeger.

Marmion, S. L., & Faulkner, D. L. (2006). Effects of class and culture on intimate partner violence. In P. K. Lundberg-Love & S. L. Marmion (Eds.), *"Intimate" violence against women: When spouses, partners, or lovers attack*. Westport, CT: Praeger.

Marple, L., & Latchmore, V. (2005, Summer/Fall). LGBTQ activism: Small town social change. *Canadian Woman Studies/Les cahiers de la femme, 24*, 55–58.

Marsa, L. (2007, Spring). He thinks, she thinks. *Discover Magazine*, pp. 30–34.

Marsella, A. J. (2006). Justice in a global age: Becoming counselors to the world. *Counselling Psychology Quarterly, 19*, 121–132.

Marshal, M. P., Dermody, S. S., Cheong, J., Burton, C. M.,

Friedman, M. S., Aranda, F., & Hughes, T. L. (2013). Trajectories of depressive symptoms and suicidality among heterosexual and sexual minority youth. *Journal of Youth and Adolescence, 42,* 1243-1256.

Marshall L. (2010, April 15). *The "other" terrorism: Militarism and violence against women.* Retrieved April 15, 2010, from http://www.truthout.org/the-other-terrorism-militarism-and-violence-against-women58608

Marshall, N. L. (2004). The quality of early child care and children's development. *Current Directions in Psychological Science, 13,* 165–168.

Marshall, T. C. (2010). Gender, peer relations, and intimate romantic relationships. In J. C. Chrisler & D. R. McCreary (Eds.), *Handbook of gender research in psychology* (pp. 281–310). New York: Springer.

Martell, C. R., Safren, S. A., & Prince, S. E. (2004). *Cognitive-behavioral therapies with lesbian, gay, and bisexual clients.* New York: Guilford.

Martin, C. L., & Fabes, R. A. (2001). The stability and consequences of young children's same-sex peer interactions. *Developmental Psychology, 37,* 431–446.

Martin, C. L., & Ruble, D. (2004). Children's search for gender cues. *Current Directions in Psychological Science, 13,* 67–70.

Martin, C. L., Ruble, D. N., & Szkrybalo, J. (2002). Cognitive theories of early gender development. *Psychological Bulletin, 128,* 903–933.

Martin, C. L., Ruble, D. N., & Szkrybalo, J. (2004). Recognizing the centrality of gender identity and stereotype knowledge in gender development and moving toward theoretical integration. *Psychological Bulletin, 130,* 702–710.

Martin, J. A., Hamilton, B. E., Osterman, M. J. K., & Driscoll, A. K. (2019). *National Vital Statistics Reports: Births: Final data for 2018.* Centers for Disease Control. https://www.cdc.gov/nchs/data/nvsr/nvsr68/nvsr68_13-508.pdf

Martin, J. A., Hamilton, B. E., Osterman, M. J. K., & Driscoll, A. K. (2021). *Births: Final data for 2019.* National Vital Statistics Report, 70(2), Centers for Disease Control. Retrieved October 4, 2021 from https://www.cdc.gov/nchs/data/nvsr/nvsr70/nvsr70-02-508.pdf

Martin, P. Y. (2016). The rape prone culture of academic contexts: Fraternities and athletics. *Gender and Society, 30,* 30-43.

Martin, R., & Suls, J. (2003). How gender stereotypes influence self-regulation of cardiac health care-seeking and adaptation. In L. D. Cameron & H. Leventhal (Eds.), *The self-regulation of health and illness behaviour* (pp. 220–241). New York: Routledge.

Martin, S. F. (2004). *Refugee women* (2nd ed.). Lanham, MD: Lexington.

Martínez, E. (1995). In pursuit of Latina liberation. *Signs: Journal of Women in Culture and Society, 20,* 1019–1028.

Martinez, E. (2008). *500 Years of Chicana women's history/500 años de la mujer Chicana* (bilingual edition). New Brunswick, NJ: Rutgers University Press.

Martinez, R., Johnston-Robledo, I., Ulsh, H. M., & Chrisler, J. C. (2000). Singing "the baby blues": A content analysis of popular press articles about postpartum affective disturbances. *Women and Health, 31,* 37–56.

Martino, S. C., et al. (2005). Social cognitive processes mediating the relationship between exposure to television content and adolescents' sexual behavior. *Journal of Personality and Social Psychology, 89,* 914–924.

Marton, K. (2004, May 10). A worldwide gender gap. *Newsweek,* pp. 94.

Martz, D. J. F., & Sarauer, D. B. (2002). Domestic violence and the experiences of rural women in East Central Saskatchewan. In K. M. J. McKenna & J. Larkin (Eds.), *Violence against women: New Canadian perspectives* (pp. 163–196). Toronto, ON: Inanna Publications and Education.

Marx, D. M., & Stapel, D. A. (2006a). Distinguishing stereotype threat from priming effects: On the role of the social self and threat-based concerns. *Journal of Personality and Social Psychology, 91,* 243–254.

Marx, D. M., & Stapel, D. A. (2006b). It depends on your perspective: The role of self-relevance in stereotype-based underperformance. *Journal of Experimental Social Psychology, 42,* 768–775.

Mason, A., et al. (2004). Prejudice toward people with disabilities. In J. L. Chin (Ed.), *The psychology of prejudice and discrimination* (Vol. 4, pp. 51–93). Westport, CT: Praeger.

Mason, T. B., & Lewis, R. J. (2016). Minority stress, body shame, and binge eating among lesbian women: Social anxiety as a linking mechanism. *Psychology of Women Quarterly, 40,* 428-440.

Mass, A. H. E. M., Rosano, G., Cifkova, R., Chieffo, A., van Dijken, D., … Collins, P. (2021). Cardiovascular health after menopause transition, pregnancy disorders, and other gynaecologic conditions: A consensus document from European cardiologists, gynaecologists, and endocrinologists. *European Heart Journal, 42,* 967-984.

Masser, B., & Abrams, D. (2004). Reinforcing the glass ceiling: The consequences of hostile sexism for female managerial candidates. *Sex Roles, 51,* 609–615.

Masser, B., Grass, K., & Nesic, M. (2007). "We like you, but we don't want you"—The impact of pregnancy in the workplace. *Sex Roles, 57,* 703–712.

Masters, N. T., Norris, J., Stoner, S. A., & George, W. H. (2006). How does it end? Women project the outcome of a sexual assault scenario. *Psychology of Women Quarterly, 30,* 291–302.

Masters, W. H., & Johnson, V. E. (1966). *Human sexual response.* Boston: Little, Brown.

Mathur, A. K., Reichle, J., Strawn, J., & Wiseley, C. (2004). Credentials count: How California's community colleges help parents move from welfare to self-sufficiency. In V. Polakow, S. S. Butler, L. S. Deprez, & P. Kahn (Eds.), *Shut out: Low income mothers and higher education in post-welfare America* (pp. 149–170). Albany, NY: State University of New York Press.

Maticka-Tyndale, E., Herold, E. S., & Mewhinney, D. (1998). Casual sex on spring break: Intentions and behaviors of Canadian students. *Journal of Sex Research, 35,* 254–264.

Maticka-Tyndale, E., McKay, A., & Barrett, M. (2001). *Teenage sexual and reproductive behavior in developed countries: Country report for Canada.* New York: Alan Guttmacher Institute.

Matlin, M. W. (2003). From menarche to menopause: Misconceptions about women's reproductive lives. *Psychology Science, 45,* 106–122.

Matlin, M. W. (2009). *Cognition* (7th ed.). Hoboken: Wiley.

Matsakis, A. (2003). *The rape recovery handbook: Step-by-step help for survivors of sexual assault.* Oakland, CA: New Harbinger.

Matsumoto, D., & Juang, L. (2004). *Culture and psychology* (3rd ed.). Belmont, CA: Wadsworth.

Matsumoto, D., & Juang, L. (2008). *Culture and psychology* (4th ed.). Belmont, CA: Thomson Wadsworth.

Matteson, A. V., & Moradi, B. (2005). Examining the structure of the schedule of sexist events: Replication and extension. *Psychology of Women Quarterly, 29,* 47–57.

Matthews, A. K., Hughes, T. L., & Tartaro, J. (2006). Sexual behavior and sexual dysfunction on a community sample of lesbian and heterosexual women. In A. M. Omoto & H. S. Kurtzman (Eds.), *Sexual orientation and mental health* (pp. 185–205). Washington, DC: American Psychological Association.

Maurer, T. W., & Robinson, D. W. (2008). Effects of attire, alcohol, and gender on perceptions of date rape. *Sex Roles, 58,* 423–434.

Mauthner, N. S. (2002). *The darkest days of my life: Stories of postpartum depression.* Cambridge, MA: Harvard University Press.

Maxwell, C. D., Robinson, A. L., & Klein, A. R. (2009). The prosecution of domestic violence across time. In E. Stark & E. S. Buzawa (Eds.), *Violence against women in families and relationships* (Vol. 3, pp. 91–113). Santa Barbara, CA: ABC-CLIO.

Mazrekaj, D., De Witte, K., & Cabus, S. (2020). School outcomes of children raised by same-sex parents: Evidence from administrative panel data. *American Sociological Review, 85,* 830-856.

McAdoo, H. P. (2002). African American parenting. In M. H. Bornstein (Ed.), *Handbook of parenting* (2nd ed., Vol. 4, pp. 47–58). Mahwah, NJ: Erlbaum.

McAdoo, J. L. (1993). Decision making and marital satisfaction in African American families. In H. P. McAdoo (Ed.), *Family ethnicity: Strength in diversity* (pp. 109–119). New-bury Park, CA: Sage.

McCallum, M., & Lauzon, A. (2005, Summer/Fall). If there's no mark, there's no crime. *Canadian Woman Studies/Les cahiers de la femme, 25,* 130–135.

McCarthy, B., & McCarthy, E. J. (2006). *Getting it right this time.* New York: Routledge.

McClure, E. B. (2000). A meta-analytic review of sex differences in facial expression processing and their development in infants, children, and adolescence. *Psychological Bulletin, 126,* 424–453.

McCormick, N. B. (1994). *Sexual salvation: Affirming women's sexual rights and pleasures.* Westport, CT: Praeger.

McCoyd, J. L. M., Curran, L., & Munch, S. (2020). They say, "If you don't relax ... you're going to make something bad happen": Women's emotion management during medically high-risk pregnancy, *Psychology of Women Quarterly, 44,* 117-129.

McCreary, D. R., & Chrisler, J. C. (2010). Introduction. In J. C. Chrisler & D. R. McCreary (Eds.), *Handbook of gender research in psychology* (Vol. 1, pp. 19–41). New York: Springer.

McCreight, B. S. (2005). Perinatal grief and emotional labour: A study of nurses' experiences in gynae wards. *International Journal of Nursing Studies, 42,* 439–448.

McDonald, P., Graham, T., & Martin, B. (2010). Outrage management in cases of sexual harassment as revealed in judicial decisions. *Psychology of Women Quarterly, 34,* 165–180.

McDougall, J., DeWit, D. J., & Ebanks, C. E. (1999). Parental preferences for sex of children in Canada. *Sex Roles, 41,* 615–626.

McFarland, J., Hussar, B., de Brey, C., Snyder, T., Wang, X., Wilkinson-Flicker, S., Gebrekristos, S., Zhang, J., Rathbun, A., Barmer, A., Bullock Mann, F., & Hinz, S. (2017). The Condition of Education 2017 (NCES 2017- 144). U.S. Department of Education. Washington, DC: National Center for Education Statistics. Retrieved October 3, 2021 from https://nces.ed.gov/pubsearch /pubsinfo.asp?pubid=2017144.

McGann, V. L., & Steil, J. M. (2006). The sense of entitlement: Implications for gender equity and psychological well-being. In J. Worell & C. D. Goodheart (Eds.), *Handbook of girls' and women's psychological health: Gender and well-being across the life span* (pp. 175–182). New York: Oxford University Press.

McGlone, M. S., Aronson, J., & Kobrynowicz, E. (2006). Stereotype threat and the gender gap in political knowledge. *Psychology of Women Quarterly, 30,* 392–398.

McGoldrick, M., Giordano, J., & Garcia-Preto, N. (2005b). Overview: Ethnicity and family therapy. In M. McGoldrick, J. Giordano, & N. Garcia-Preto (Eds.), *Ethnicity and family therapy* (3rd ed., pp. 1–40). New York: Guilford.

McGuinness, C. (1998). Cognition. In K. Trew & J. Kremer (Eds.), *Gender and psychology* (pp. 66–81). London: Arnold Publishers.

McHale, S. M., Dariotis, J., & Kauh, T. J. (2002). Social development and social relationships in middle childhood. In I. B. Weiner (Ed.), *Handbook of psychology* (Vol. 6, pp. 241–265). Hoboken, NJ: Wiley.

McHugh, M. C. (2006). What do women want? A new view of women's sexual problems. *Sex Roles, 54,* 361–369.

McHugh, M. C., & Bartoszek, T. A. R. (2000). Intimate violence. In M. Biaggio & M. Hersen (Eds.), *Issues in the psychology of women* (pp. 115–142). New York: Kluwer Academic/Plenum.

McHugh, M. C., & Cosgrove, L. (1998). Research for women: Feminist methods. In D. M. Ashcraft (Ed.), *Women's work: A survey of scholarship by and about women* (pp. 19–43). New York: Haworth.

McHugh, M. C., Livingston, N., & Frieze, I. H. (2008). Intimate partner violence: Perspectives on research and intervention. In F. L. Denmark & M. A. Paludi (Eds.), *Psychology of women: A handbook of issues and theories* (2nd ed.). Westport CT: Praeger.

McIntosh, P. (2001). White privilege and male privilege. In S. M. Shaw & J. Lee (Eds.), *Women's voices, feminist visions* (pp.

78–86). Mountain View, CA: Mayfield.

McKee, N. P., & Stone, L. (2007). *Gender and culture in America* (3rd ed.). Cornwall-on-Hudson, NY: Sloan.

McKenry, P. C., & McKelvey, M. W. (2003). The psychosocial well-being of Black and White mothers following marital dissolution: A brief report of a follow-up study. *Psychology of Women Quarterly, 27,* 31–36.

McKenzie-Pollock, L. (2005). Cambodian families. In M. McGoldrick, J. Giordano, & N. Garcia-Preto (Eds.), *Ethnicity and family therapy* (3rd ed., pp. 290–301). New York: Guilford.

McLeod, B. A. (2003, Fall/Winter). First Nations women and sustainability on the Canadian prairies. *Canadian Woman Studies/ Les cahiers de la femme, 23,* 47–54.

McLoyd, V. C., Hill, N. E., & Dodge, K. A. (2005). Introduction: Conceptualizations of African American families. In H. P. McAdoo (Ed.), *Black families* (3rd ed., pp. 67–82). Thousand Oaks, CA: Sage.

McMahon, M. (1995). *Engendering motherhood: Identity and self-transformation in women's lives.* New York: Guilford.

McMullen, L. N. (2003). "Depressed" women's constructions of the deficient self. In J. M. Stoppard & L. M. McMullen (Eds.), *Situating sadness: Women and depression in social context* (pp. 17–38). New York: New York University Press.

McNally, R. J. (2003). *Remembering trauma.* Cambridge, MA: Harvard University Press.

McSweeney, S. (2004). Depression in women. In P. J. Caplan & L. Cos-grove (Eds.), *Bias in psychiatric diagnosis* (pp. 183–188). Lanham, MD: Jason Aronson.

McWright, L. (2002). African American grandmothers' and grandfathers' influence in the value socialization of grandchildren.

In H. P. McAdoo (Ed.), *Black children* (2nd ed., pp. 27–44). Thousand Oaks, CA: Sage.

Medland, S. E., Geffen, G., & McFarland, K. (2002). Lateralization of speech production using verbal/manual dual tasks: Meta-analysis of sex differences and practice effects. *Neuropsychologia, 40,* 1233–1239.

Mednick, M. T., & Thomas, V. (1993). Women and the psychology of achievement: A view from the eighties. In F. L. Denmark & M. A. Paludi (Eds.), *Psychology of women: A handbook of issues and theories* (pp. 585–626). Westport, CT: Greenwood Press.

Meece, J. L., & Scantlebury, K. (2006). Gender and schooling: Progress and persistent barriers. In J. Worell & C. D. Goodheart (Eds.), *Handbook of girls' and women's psychological health: Gender and well-being across the life span* (pp. 283–291). New York: Oxford University Press.

Megan, C. E. (2000, November). Childless by choice. *Ms. Magazine,* pp. 43–46.

Mehl, M. R., et al. (2007). Are women really more talkative than men? *Science, 317,* 82.

Mehta, J. M., Chester, R. C., Kling, J. M. (2019). The timing hypothesis: Hormone therapy for treating symptomatic women during menopause and its relationship to cardiovascular disease. *Journal of Women's Health, 28,* 705-711.

Meinz, E. J., & Salthouse, T. A. (1998). Is age kinder to females than to males? *Psychonomic Bulletin and Review, 5,* 56–70.

Meireish, Katz-Wise, & Woulfe, (2017). Bisexual-specific minority stressors, psychological distress, and suicidality in bisexual individuals: The mediating role of loneliness. *Prevention Research, 18,* 716-725.

Melender, H. (2002). Experiences of fears associated with pregnancy and childbirth: A study of 329 pregnant women. *Birth, 29,* 101–111.

Mendelsohn, K. D., et al. (1994). Sex and gender bias in anatomy and physical diagnosis text illustrations. *Journal of the American Medical Association, 272,* 1267–1270.

Mendelson, T., & Muñoz, R. F. (2006). Prevention of depression in women. In C. L. M. Keyes & S. H. Goodman (Eds.), *Women and depression: A handbook for the social, behavioral, and biomedical sciences* (pp. 450–478). New York: Cambridge University Press.

Mendez, J. B. (2005). *From the revolution to the maquiladoras: Gender, labor, and globalization in Nicaragua.* Durham, NC: Duke University Press.

Mendola, P., et al. (1998). Risk of recurrent spontaneous abortion, cigarette smoking, and genetic polymorphisms in NAT2 and GSTMI. *Epidemiology, 9,* 666–668.

Mengel, F., Sauermann, J., & Zölitz, U. (2019). Gender bias in teaching evaluations. *Journal of the European Economic Association, 17,* 535-566.

Menon, V., Pattnaik, J. I., Bascarane, S., & Padhy, S. K. (2021). Role of media in preventing gender-based violence and crimes during the COVID-19 pandemic. *Asian Journal of Psychiatry, 54,* 102449.

Menzies, C. H. (2005, Winter). Caregiving and being in touch: Lessons from my 85–year-old mum and me. *Canadian Woman Studies/Les cahiers de la femme, 24,* 122–126.

Merrell, K. W. (2008). *Helping students overcome depression and anxiety* (2nd ed.). New York: Guilford.

Merritt, R. D., & Harrison, T. W. (2006). Gender and ethnicity attributions to a gender- and ethnicity-unspecified individual: Is there a people = white male bias? *Sex Roles, 54,* 787–797.

Merritt, R. D., & Kok, C. J. (1995). Attribution of gender to a gender-unspecified individual: An evaluation of the people = male hypothesis. *Sex Roles, 33,* 145–157.

Merskin, D. (1999). Adolescence, advertising, and the ideology of menstruation. *Sex Roles, 40,* 941–957.

Mertens, D. M., Wilson, A., & Mounty, J. (2007). Gender equity for people with disabilities. In S. S. Klein (Ed.), *Handbook for achieving gender equity through education* (2nd ed., pp. 583–604). Mahwah, NJ: Erlbaum.

Mervis, J. (2007). U.S. national medals-for men only? *Science, 316,* 1683.

Messinger, A. M., & Koon-Magnin, S. (2019). Sexual violence in LGBTQ communities. In W. T. O'Donohue & P. A. Schewe, (Eds.), *Handbook of sexual assault and sexual assault prevention* (pp. 661-674). Springer.Messman-Moore, T. L., & Brown, A. L. (2006). Risk perception, rape, and sexual revictimization: A prospective study of college women. *Psychology of Women Quarterly, 30,* 159–172.

Metzger, T. (2002, June 19–25). The cross and the Y chromosome: Promise keepers storm Rochester. *City Newspaper,* pp. 10–12.

Meyer, I. L. (2003). Prejudice, social stress, and mental health in lesbian, gay, and bisexual populations: Conceptual issues and research evidence. *Psychological Bulletin, 129,* 674–697.

Meyerowitz, B. E., & Weidner, G. (1998). Section editors' overview. In E. A. Blechman & K. D. Brownell (Eds.), *Behavioral medicine and women: A comprehensive handbook* (pp. 537–545). New York: Guilford.

Meyersson Milgrom, E. M., & Petersen, T. (2006). The glass ceiling in the United States and Sweden: Lessons from the family-friendly corner of the world, 1970 to 1990. In F. D. Blau, M. C. Brinton, & D. B. Grusky (Eds.), *The declining significance of gender?* (pp. 156–211). New York: Russell Sage.

Mezulis, A. H., Abramson, L. Y., Hyde, J. S., & Hankin, B. L. (2004). Is there a universal positivity bias in attributions? A meta-analytic review of individual, developmental, and cultural differences in the self-serving attributional bias. *Psychological Bulletin, 139,* 711–747.

Michel, D. M., & Willard, S. G. (2003). *When dieting becomes dangerous.* New Haven, CT: Yale University Press.

Mighty, E. J. (2004). Working with abuse: Workplace responses to family violence. In M. L. Stirling, C. A. Cameron, N. Nason-Clark, & B. Miedema (Eds.), *Partnering for change* (pp. 111–132). Toronto: University of Toronto Press.

Milan, A. (2015). Women in Canada: A gender-based statistical report. *Statistics Canada.* Retrieved October 5, 2021 from https://www150.statcan.gc.ca/n1/en/pub/89-503-x/2015001/article/14152-eng.pdf?st=ORM19jik

Milar, K. S. (2000). The first generation of women psychologists and the psychology of women. *American Psychologist, 55,* 616–619.

Milburn, S. S., Carney, D. R., & Ramirez, A. M. (2001). Even in modern media, the picture is still the same: A content analysis of clipart images. *Sex Roles, 44,* 277–294.

Miles, L. K. (2009). Who is approachable? *Journal of Experimental Social Psychology, 45,* 262–266.

Milkman, R. (2007). Two worlds of unionism: Women and the new labor movement. In D. S. Cobble (Ed.), *The sex of class: Women transforming American labor* (pp. 63–80). Ithaca, NY: Cornell University Press.

Millard, J. E., & Grant, P. R. (2006). The stereotypes of Black and White women in fashion magazine photographs: The pose of the model and the impression she creates. *Sex Roles, 54,* 659–673.

Miller, C. C. (2018). *The U.S. fertility rate is down, yet more women are mothers.* New York Times. Retrieved October 4, 2021 from https://www.nytimes.com/2018/01/18/upshot/the-us-fertility-rate-is-down-yet-more-women-are-mothers.html

Miller, C. F., Trautner, H. M., & Ruble, D. N. (2006). The role of gender stereotypes in children's preferences and behavior. In L. Balter & C. S, Tamis-LeMonda (Eds.), *Child psychology: A handbook of contemporary issues* (2nd ed.). New York: Psychology Press.

Miller, D. T., Taylor, B., & Buck, M. L. (1991). Gender gaps: Who needs to be explained? *Journal of Personality and Social Psychology, 61,* 5–12.

Miller, E. J., Smith, J. E., & Trembath, D. L. (2000). The "skinny" on body size requests in personal ads. *Sex Roles, 43,* 129–141.

Miller, G., Chen, E., & Cole, S. W. (2009). Health psychology: Developing biologically plausible models linking the social world and physical health. *Annual Review of Psychology, 60,* 501–524.

Miller, J., & Chamberlin, M. (2000). Women are teachers, men are professors: A study of student perceptions. *Teaching Sociology, 28,* 283–298.

Miller, L. C., Putcha-Bhagavatula, A., & Pedersen, W. C. (2002). Men's and women's mating preferences: Distinct evolutionary mechanisms. *Current Directions in Psychological Science, 11,* 88–93.

Miller, L. J. (2002). Postpartum depression. *JAMA, 287,* 762–765.

Miller, R. S., Perlman, D., & Brehm, S. S. (2004). *Intimate relationships* (4th ed.). Boston: McGraw-Hill.

Miller-Day, M. A. (2004). *Communication among grandmothers, mothers, and adult daughters.* Mahwah, NJ: Erlbaum.

Miller-Johnson, S., Moore, B. L., Underwood, M. K., & Coie, J. D.

(2005). African-American girls and physical aggression: Does stability of childhood aggression predict later negative outcomes? In D. J. Pepler, K. C. Madsen, C. Webster, & K. S. Levene (Eds.), *The development and treatment of girlhood aggression* (pp. 75–101). Mahwah, NJ: Erlbaum.

Mills, J. L. (1999). Cocaine, smoking, and spontaneous abortion. *New England Journal of Medicine, 340,* 380–381.

Mills, J., & Fuller-Tyszkiewicz, M. (2017). Fat talk and body image disturbance: A systematic review and meta-analysis. *Psychology of Women Quarterly, 41,* 114-129.

Mills, R. S. L., Pedersen, J., & Grusec, J. E. (1989). Sex differences in reasoning and emotion about altruism. *Sex Roles, 20,* 603–621.

Mills, S. (2003). *Gender and politeness.* New York: Cambridge University Press.

Miner-Rubino, K., Winter, D. G., & Stewart, A. J. (2004). Gender, social class, and the subjective experience of aging: Self-perceived personality change from early adulthood to late mid-life. *Personality and Social Psychology Bulletin, 30,* 1599–1610.

Minton, H. L. (2000). Psychology and gender at the turn of the century. *American Psychologist, 55,* 613–615.

Mishel, L, & Wolfe, J. (2019). *CEO Compensation has grown 940% since 1978: Typical worker has compensation has grown only 12% during that time.* Economic Policy Institute. Retrieved September 28, 2021 from https://files.epi.org/pdf/171191.pdf

Mishra, G. D., Pandeya, N., Dobson, A. J., Chung, H-F., Anderson, D., Kih, D., Sandin, S., Giles, G. G., Bruinsma, F., Hayashi, K., Lee, J. S., Mizunuma, H., Cade, J. E., Burley, V., Greenwood, D. C., Goodman, A., … Weiderpass, E. (2017). Early menarche, nulliparity and the risk for premature

and early natural menopause. *Human Reproduction, 32,* 679-686.

Mitchell, K., & Martin, J. (2018). Gender bias in student evaluations. *Political Science & Politics, 51,* 648-652.

Mitte, K. (2005). Meta-analysis of cognitive-behavioral treatments for generalized anxiety disorder: A comparison with pharmacotherapy. *Psychological Bulletin, 131,* 785–795.

Moadei, A. B., & Harris, M. S. (2008). Cancer. In B. A. Boyer & M. Indira Paharia (Eds.), *Comprehensive handbook of clinical health psychology* (pp. 153–178). Hoboken, NJ: Wiley.

Moen, P. (2008). It's constraints, not choices. *Science, 319,* 903–904.

Moen, P., Kim, J. E., & Hofmeister, H. (2001). Couples' work/retirement transitions, gender, and marital quality. *Social Psychology Quarterly, 64,* 55–71.

Moen, P., & Roehling, P. (2005). *The career mystique: Cracks in the American dream.* Lanham, MD: Rowman & Littlefield.

Moghadam, V. M. (2009). *Globalism and social movements.* Lanham, MD: Rowman & Littlefield.

Mohamed, S., & Hunter, M. S. (2018). Transgender women's experiences and beliefs about hormone therapy through and beyond mid-age: An exploratory UK study. *The International Journal of Transgenderism, 20,* 98–107.

Mojtabai, R. (2013). Clinician-identified depression in community settings: Concordance with structured-interview diagnoses. *Psychotherapy and Psychosomatics, 82,* 161-169.

Molinary, R. (2007). *Hijas americanas: Beauty, body image, and growing up Latina.* Emeryville, CA: Seal Press.

Mollen, D. (2014). Reproductive rights and informed consent: Toward a more inclusive discourse. *Analyses of Social Issues and Public Policy, 14,* 162-182.

Mona, L. R., Syme, M. L., & Cameron, R. P. (2014). Sexuality and disability: A disability-affirmative approach to sex therapy. In Y. M. Binik, & K. S. K. Hall (Eds.), *Principles and practice of sex therapy* (pp. 457-481). The Guilford Press.

Monson, C. M., Langhinrichsen-Rohling, J., & Taft, C. T. (2009). Sexual aggression in intimate relationships. In K. D. O'Leary & E. M. Woodin (Eds.), *Psychological and physical aggression in couples: Causes and interventions* (pp. 37–57). Washington, DC: American Psychological Association.

Monsour, M. (1992). Meanings of intimacy in cross- and same-sex friendships. *Journal of Social and Personal Relationships, 9,* 277–295.

Monsour, M. (2002). *Women and men as friends.* Mahwah, NJ: Erlbaum.

Monteith, M. J., & Voils, C. I. (2001). Exerting control over prejudiced responses. In G. B. Moskowitz (Ed.), *Cognitive social psychology* (pp. 375–388). Mahwah, NJ: Erlbaum.

Moody, A. T., & Lewis, J. A. (2019). Gendered racial microaggressions and traumatic stress symptoms among Black women. *Psychology of Women Quarterly, 43,* 201-214.

Mooney, M., & Rivas-Drake, D. (2008, March 28). Colleges need to recognize, and serve, the 3 kinds of Latino students. *Chronicle of Higher Education,* pp. A37–A39.

Moore, J. A., & Radtke, H. L. (2015). Starting "real" life: Women negotiating a successful midlife single identity. *Psychology of Women Quarterly, 39,* 305-319.

Mootz, J. J., Muhanguzi, F., Greenfield, B., Gill, M., Gonzalez, M. B., Panko, P., Onyango Mangen, P., Wainberg, M. L., & Khoshnood, K. (2019). Armed conflict, intimate partner violence, and mental distress of women in Northeastern Uganda: A mixed methods study. *Psychology of Women Quarterly, 43,* 457-471.

Moradi, B., & Huang, Y.-P. (2008). Objectification theory and psychology of women: A decade of advances and future directions. *Psychology of Women Quarterly, 32,* 377–398.

Moradi, B., Parent, M. C., Weis, A. S., Ouch, S., & Broad, K. L. (2020). Mapping the travels of intersectionality scholarship: A citation network analysis. *Psychology of Women Quarterly, 44,* 151-169.

Moraga, C. (1993). Women's subordination through the lens of sex/gender, sexuality, class, and race: Multicultural feminism. In A. M. Jaggar & P. S. Rothenberg (Eds.), *Feminist frameworks: Alternative theoretical accounts of the relations between women and men* (3rd ed., pp. 203–212). New York: McGraw-Hill.

Morales, K. J., Gordon, M. C., & Bates, G. W. (2007). Postcesarean delivery adhesions associated with delayed delivery of infant. *American Journal of Obstetrics & Gynecology, 196,* 461e1–461e6.

Morandini, J. S., Blaszczynski, A., & Dar-Nimrod, I. (2016): Who adopts queer and pansexual sexual identities? *The Journal of Sex Research, 54,* 911-922.

Morgan, B. L. (1998). A three-generational study of tomboy behavior. *Sex Roles, 39,* 787–800.

Morgan, P., & Gruber, J. (2008). Sexual harassment and male dominance: Toward an ecological approach. In M. A. Paludi (Ed.), *The psychology of women at work: Challenges and solutions for our female workforce* (Vol. 2, pp. 85–107). Westport, CT: Praeger.

Morgan, R. E., & Oudekerk, B. A. (2019). *Criminal victimization, 2018.* U. S. Department of Justice. Retrieved October 5, 2021 from https://www.nsvrc.org/sites/default/files/2021-04/cv18.pdf

Morison, T., Macleod, C., Lynch, I., Mijas, M., & Shiyakumar, S. T. (2016). Stigma resistance in online childfree communities: The limitations of choice rhetoric. *Psychology of Women Quarterly, 40,* 184-198.

Morling, B., Kitayama, S., & Miyamoto, Y. (2003). American and Japanese women use different coping strategies during normal pregnancy. *Personality and Social Psychology Bulletin, 29,* 1533–1546.

Morokoff, P. J. (2000). A cultural context for sexual assertiveness in women. In C. B. Travis & J. W. White (Eds.), *Sexuality, society, and feminism* (pp. 299–319). Washington, DC: American Psychological Association.

Morokoff, P. J., et al. (1997). Sexual Assertiveness Scale for women: Development and validation. *Journal of Personality and Social Psychology, 73,* 790–804.

Morr Serewicz, M. C., & Gale, E. (2008). First-date scripts: Gender roles, context, and relationship. *Sex Roles, 58,* 149–164.

Morris, J. F. (2000, August). *Lesbian women of color in communities: Social activities and mental health services.* Paper presented at the annual convention of the American Psychological Association, Washington, DC.

Morris, J. F., & Hart, S. (2003). Defending claims about mental health. In M. R. Stevenson & J. C. Cogan (Eds.), *Everyday activism: A handbook for lesbian, gay, and bisexual people and their allies* (pp. 57–78). New York: Routledge.

Morris, J. F., Waldo, C. R., & Rothblum, E. D. (2001). A model of predictors and outcomes of outness among lesbian and bisexual women. *American Journal of Orthopsychiatry, 71,* 61–71.

Morris, L. A. (1997). *The male heterosexual.* Thousand Oaks, CA: Sage.

Morris, S., Fawcett, G., Brisebois, L., & Hughes, J. (2018). A demographic, employment and income profile of Canadians with disabilities aged 15 years and over, 2017. Statistics Canada. Retrieved October 5, 2021 from https://www150.statcan .gc.ca/n1/pub/89-654-x/89-654 -x2018002-eng.htm

Morris, T., & McInerney, K. (2010). Media representations of pregnancy and childbirth: An analysis of reality television programs. *Birth, 37,* 134–140.

Morris, W. L., DePaulo, B. M., Hertel, J., & Taylor, L. C. (2008). Singlism—another problem that has no name: Prejudice, stereotypes, and discrimination against singles. In T. G. Morrison & M. A. Morrison (Eds.), *The psychology of modern prejudice* (pp. 165-194). Hauppauge, NY: Nova Science.

Morris, W. L., Sinclair, S., & DePaulo, B. M. (2007). No shelter for singles: The perceived legitimacy of marital status discrimination. *Group Processes and Intergroup Relations, 10,* 457–470.

Morrissey, T. W. (2017). Child care and parent labor force participation: A review of the research literature. *Review of Economics of the Household, 15,* 1-24.

Morrison, M. M., & Shaffer, D. R. (2003). Gender-role congruence and self-referencing as determinants of advertising effectiveness. *Sex Roles, 49,* 265–275.

Morrongiello, B. A., & Hogg, K. (2004). Mothers' reactions to children misbehaving in ways that can lead to injury. *Sex Roles, 50,* 103–118.

Mortenson, G., & Relin, D. O. (2006). *Three cups of tea: One man's mission to fight terrorism and build nations—one school at a time.* New York: Viking.

Moscicki, A. B. (2005). Impact of HPV infection in adolescent populations. *Journal of Adolescent Health, 37,* S3–S9.

Mosher, C. E. (2002). Impact of gender and problem severity upon intervention selection. *Sex Roles, 46,* 113–119.

Mosher, C. E., & Danoff-Burg, S. (2005). Agentic and communal

personality traits: Relations to attitudes toward sex and sexual experiences. *Sex Roles, 52,* 121–129.

Moss-Racusin, C. A., Schofield, C. A., Brown, S. S., & O'Brien, K. A., (2020). Breast is (viewed as) best: Demonstrating formula feeding stigma. *Psychology of Women Quarterly, 44,* 503-520.

Moyser, M. (2017). Women and paid work. Statistics Canada. Retrieved October 3, 2021 from https://www150.statcan.gc.ca/n1/ pub/89-503-x/2015001/article /14694-eng.htm

Mozurkewich, E. L., et al. (2000). Working conditions and adverse pregnancy outcome: A meta-analysis. *Obstetrics and Gynecology, 95,* 623–635.

Msengi, C. M., Arthur-Okur, H., Killion, L., & Schoer, J. (2015). Educating immigrant women through social support. *SAGE Open, Oct-Dec,* 1-8.

Mueller, K. A., & Yoder, J. D. (1997). Gendered norms for family size, employment, and occupation: Are there personal costs for violating them? *Sex Roles, 36,* 207–220.

Mueller, K. A., & Yoder, J. D. (1999). Stigmatization of non-normative family size status. *Sex Roles, 41 ,* 901–919.

Mukhtaran Bibi. (2021). *Profiles of Famous Pakistanis.* Retrieved October 5, 2021 from https:// profilepk.com/mukhtaran-bibi

Mulac, A., Bradac, J. J., & Gibbons, P. (2001). Empirical support for the gender-as-culture hypothesis. *Human Communication Research, 27,* 121–152.

Mulama J. (2008, November 17). *Africa: Gender budgeting still finding its feet.* Retrieved November 17, 2008, from http:// www.truthout.org/111908WA

Mullings, D. V. (2004, Winter). Situating older Caribbean Canadian women in feminist research: A reflection. *Canadian Woman Studies/Les cahiers de la femme, 23,* 134–139.

Mundy, L. (2007). *Everything conceivable: How assisted reproduction is changing men, women, and the world.* New York: Knopf.

Munk-Olsen, T., et al. (2011). Induced first-trimester abortion and risk of mental disorder. *New England Journal of Medicine, 364,* 332–339.

Murkoff, H., Eisenberg, A., & Hathaway, S. (2002). *What to expect when you're expecting.* New York: Workman.

Murphy, C. M., Meis, L. A., & Eckhardt, C. I. (2009). Individualized services and individual therapy for partner abuse perpetrators. In K. D. O'Leary & E. M. Woodin (Eds.), *Psychological and physical aggressions in couples: Causes and interventions* (pp. 211–231). Washington, DC: American Psychological Association.

Murphy, C. P. (2003). *Lavinia Fontana: A painter and her patrons in sixteenth-century Bologna.* New Haven, CT: Yale University Press.

Murphy, E. F. (2005). *Getting even: Why women don't get paid like men—and what to do about it.* New York: Simon & Schuster.

Murphy, E. M. (2003). Being born female is dangerous for your health. *American Psychologist, 58,* 205–210.

Murphy, M. C., Steele, C. M., & Gross, J. J. (2007). Signaling threat: How situational cues affect women in math, science, and engineering settings. *Psychological Science, 18,* 879–885.

Murray, L. (2008, October 8). *From homeless to Harvard.* Talk given at YWCA Empowering Women, Rochester, NY.

Murthi, M. (2009). Who is to blame ? Rape of Hindu-Muslim women in interethnic violence in India. *Psychology of Women Quarterly, 33,* 453–462.

Musil, C. M., Warner, C. B., Stoller, E. P., & Andersson, T. E. (2005). Women and intergenerational care giving in families:

Structures, ethnicity, and building family ties. In M. L. Wykle, P. J. Whitehouse, & D. L. Morris (Eds.), *Successful aging through the life span* (pp. 143–158). New York: Springer.

Morris, S., Fawcett, G., Brisebois, L., & Hughes, J. (2018). *A demographic, employment and income profile of Canadians with disabilities aged 15 years and over, 2017.* Statistics Canada. Retrieved October 5, 2021 from https://www150.statcan .gc.ca/n1/pub/89-654-x/89-654 -x2018002-eng.htm

Mwangi, M. W. (1996). Gender roles portrayed in Kenyan television commercials. *Sex Roles, 34,* 205–214.

Myers, A. M., & Rothblum, E. D. (2004). Coping with prejudice and discrimination based on weight. In J. L. Chin (Ed.), *The psychology of prejudice and discrimination* (Vol. 4, pp. 111–134). Westport, CT: Praeger.

Myers, D. G. (2000). *The American paradox.* New Haven, CT: Yale University Press.

Myersson Milgrom. E-M., & Peterson, T. (2006). Is there a glass ceiling for women in Sweden? Life cycle and/or cohort effects. In F. Blau, M. Brinton, & D. Grusky (Eds.), *The declining significance of gender?* New York: Russell Sage.

Nabors, N., & Pettee, M. F. (2003). Womanist therapy with African American women with disabilities. In M. E. Banks & E. Kaschak (Eds.), *Women with visible and invisible disabilities* (pp. 331–341). New York: Haworth.

Nack, A. (2008). *Damaged goods? Women living with incurable sexually transmitted diseases.* Philadelphia: Temple University Press.

Nahata, L., Chen, D., Moravek, M. B., Quinn, G. P., Sutter, M. E., Taylor, J., Tishelman, A. C., & Gomez-Lobo., V. (2019). Understudied and under-reported:

Fertility issues in transgender youth – a narrative review. *Journal of Pediatrics, 205,* 265-271.

Naidoo, J. C. (2000). The problem of Canada in the new millennium: Socio-psychological challenges for visible minority women. *Psychologia, 8,* 1–19.

Nance, M. (2007, December 13). Unmasking the model minority myth. *Diverse,* 10–12.

Nancekivell, S. E., Shah, P., & Gelman, S. A. (2019). Maybe they're born with it, or maybe it's experience: Toward a deeper understanding of the learning styles myth. *Journal of Educational Psychology, 112,* 221-235.

Napoletano, E., & Curry, B. (2020, December 16). *How the gender income gap affects women's retirement.* Forbes Magazine. Retrieved October 5, 2021 from https://www .forbes.com/advisor/retirement/ retirement-gender-income-gap/

Nash, J. C. (2019). *Black feminism reimagined: After intersectionality.* Durham, NC: Duke University Press.

Nassif, A., & Gunter, B. (2008). Gender representation in television advertisements in Britain and Saudi Arabia. *Sex Roles, 58,* 752–760.

National Breast Cancer Foundation. (2021). Facts about breast cancer in the United States. *NBCF Fact Sheet.* Retrieved October 5, 2021 from https://www.nationalbreast cancer.org/breast-cancer-facts

National Center on Parent, Family, and Community Engagement. (2020). *Healthy gender development and young children: A guide for early childhood programs and professionals.* Retrieved October 3, 2021 from https://eclkc.ohs.acf.hhs.gov/ publication/healthy-gender -development-young-children

National Coalition Against Domestic Violence (NCADV). (2020). *Domestic violence.* Retrieved October 5, 2021 from https:// assets.speakcdn.com/assets

/2497/domestic_violence -2020080709350855.pdf ?1596811079991

National Committee on Pay Equity. (2021). *The wage gap over time.* Retrieved October 3, 2021 from https://www.pay-equity.org/

National Institute on Alcohol Abuse and Alcoholism. (2021). *Understanding alcohol use disorder.* NIAAA. Retrieved October 5, 2021 from https://www.niaaa .nih.gov/alcohols-effects-health /alcohol-use-disorder

National Institute of Mental Health. (2001). *Eating disorders: Facts about eating disorders and the search for solutions.* Bethesda, MD: Author.

National Women's Health Information Center. (2010). *Women and HIV/ AIDS.* Retrieved December 18, 2010, from http:// www.women-shealth.gov/hiv/ worldwide/#regions

National Women's Studies Association. (2021). *About NWSA.* Retrieved October 5, 2021 from https://www.nwsa.org /page/about-NWSA

Native Knot. (2021). *'Native American' or 'American Indian'? Native Knot.* Retrieved October 5, 2021 from https://www.nativeknot.com/ news/Native-American-News/ Native-American-or-American -Indian-How-to-Talk-About -Indigenous-.html

Naughton, M. J., Jones, A. S., & Shumaker, S. A. (2005). When practices, promises, profits, and policies outpace hard evidence: The post-menopausal hormone debate. *Journal of Social Issues, 61,* 159–179.

Navarro, M. (2004, September 19). When gender isn't a given. *New York Times,* pp. 9–1, 9–6.

Nayak, M. B., Byrne, C. A., Martin, M. K., & Abraham, A. G. (2003). Attitudes toward violence against women: A cross-nation study. *Sex Roles, 49,* 333–342.

Needle, R. B., & Walker, L. E. A. (2008). *Abortion counseling: A clinician's guide to psychology, legislation, politics, and competency.* New York: Springer.

Neff, L. A., & Karney, B. R. (2005). To know you is to love you: The implications of global adoration and specific accuracy for marital relationships. *Journal of Personality and Social Psychology, 88,* 480–497.

Nelson, A. L., & Marshall, J. R. (2004). Impaired fertility. In R. A. Hatcher et al. (Eds.), *Contraceptive technology* (18th ed., pp. 651–671). New York: Ardent Media.

Nelson, D. L., & Burke, R. J. (2002). A framework for examining gender, work stress, and health. In D. L. Nelson & R. J. Burke (Eds.), *Gender, work stress, and health* (pp. 3–14). Washington, DC: American Psychological Association.

Nelson, J. A., et al. (2008). Identity in action: Predictors of feminist self-identification and collective action. *Sex Roles, 58,* 721–728.

Nelson, M. R., & Paek, H.-J. (2005). Cross-cultural differences in sexual advertising content in a transnational women's magazine. *Sex Roles, 53,* 371–383.

Nelson, T. D. (2009). Ageism. In T. D. Nelson (Ed.), *Handbook of prejudice, stereotyping, and discrimination* (pp. 431–440). New York: Psychology Press.

Nelson, T., Cardemil, E. V., & Adeoye, C. T. (2016). Rethinking strength: Black women's perceptions of the "Strong Black Woman" role. *Psychology of Women Quarterly, 40,* 551-563.

Nelson, T. S. (2002). *For love of country: Confronting rape and sexual harassment in the U.S. Military.* New York: Haworth.

Nencel, L. (2005). Heterosexuality. In P. Essed, D. T. Goldberg, & A. Kobayashi (Eds.), *A companion to gender studies* (pp. 132–142). Malden, MA: Blackwell.

Ness, I. (2003). Globalization and worker organization in New York City's garment industry. In

D. E. Bender & R. A. Greenwald (Eds.), *Sweatshop USA: The American sweatshop in historical and global perspective* (pp. 169–182). New York: Routledge.

Ness, R. B., et al. (1999). Cocaine and tobacco use and the risk of spontaneous abortion. *New England Journal of Medicine, 340,* 333–339.

Neumark-Sztainer, D., & Eisenberg, M. (2005). Weight bias in a teen's world. In K. D. Brownell, R. M. Puhl, M. B. Schwartz, & L. Rudd (Eds.), *Weight bias: Nature, consequences, and remedies* (pp. 68–79). New York: Guilford.

New England tribal college would be the first to serve Eastern tribes. (2004, December 16). *Black Issues in Higher Education, 20.*

Newcombe, N. S. (2007a). Developmental psychology meets the mommy wars. *Journal of Applied Developmental Psychology, 28,* 553–555.

Newcombe, N. S. (2007b). Taking science seriously: Straight thinking about spatial sex differences. In C. J. Ceci & W. M. Williams (Eds.), *Why aren't more women in science? Top researchers debate the evidence* (pp. 69–77). Washington, DC: American Psychological Association.

Newcombe, N. S., Mathason, L., & Terlecki, M. (2002). Maximization of spatial competence: More important than finding the cause of sex differences. In A. McGillicuddy-De Lisi & R. De Lisi (Eds.), *Biology, society, and behavior: The development of sex differences in cognition* (pp. 183–206). Westport, CT: Ablex Publishing.

Newland, M. C., & Rasmussen, E. B. (2003). Behavior in adulthood and during aging is affected by contaminant exposure in utero. *Current Directions in Psychological Science, 12,* 212–217.

Newman, M. L., Groom, C. J., Handelman, L. D., & Pennebaker, J. W. (2008). Gender differences

in language use: An analysis of 14,000 text samples. *Discourse Processes, 45,* 211–236.

Newport, F. (2018). *Slight preference for having boy children persists in U.S.* [Data Set]. Gallup. Retrieved October 3, 2021 from https://news.gallup .com/poll/236513/slight -preference-having-boy-children -persists.aspx

Newtson, R. L., & Keith, P. M. (1997). Single women in later life. In J. M. Coyle (Ed.), *Handbook on women and aging* (pp. 385–399). Westport, CT: Greenwood Press.

Nguyen, T. (2005). *We are all suspects now: Untold stories from immigrant communities after 9/11.* Boston: Beacon Press.

NICHD Early Child Care Research Network. (2001). Nonmaternal care and family factors in early development. *Applied Developmental Psychology, 22,* 457–492.

NICHD Early Child Care Research Network. (2002). Child-care structure process outcome: Direct and indirect effects of child-care quality on young children's development. *Psychological Science, 13,* 199–206.

NICHD Early Child Care Research Network. (2004). Type of child care and children's development at 54 months. *Early Childhood Research Quarterly, 19,* 203–230.

NICHD Early Child Care Research Network. (2005). *Child care and child development: Results from the NICHD study of early child care and youth development.* New York: Guilford.

NICHD Early Child Care Research Network. (2006). Child-care effect sizes for the NICHD study of early child care and youth development. *American Psychologist, 61,* 99–116.

Nichols, M., & Shernoff, M. (2007). Therapy with sexual minorities: Queering practice. In S. Leiblum (Ed.), *Principles and practice of sex therapy* (4th ed.,). New York: Guilford.

Nichols, S. L., & Good, T. L. (2004). *America's teenagers—myths and realities.* Mahwah, NJ: Erlbaum.

Niedzwienska, A. (2003). Gender differences in vivid memories. *Sex Roles, 49,* 321–331.

Nicholson, L. (2010). Feminism in "waves": Useful metaphor or not? *New Politics, 12*(4), No. 48.

Nielsen, L. B. (2002). Subtle, pervasive, harmful: Racist and sexist remarks as hate speech. *Journal of Social Issues, 58,* 265–280.

Niemann, Y. F., et al. (1994). Use of free responses and cluster analysis to determine stereotypes of eight groups. *Personality and Social Psychology Bulletin, 20,* 379–390.

Nikolic-Ristanovic, V. (2000, Winter). Victimization by war rape. *Canadian Woman Studies/Les cahiers de la femme, 19,* 28–35.

Nishihara, R., & Okubo, M. (2015). A study on personal space in virtual space based on personality. *Procedia Manufacturing, 3,* 2183-2190.

Nisbett, R. E., Aronson, J., Blair, C., Dickens, W., Flynn, J., Halpern, D. F., & Turkheimer, E. (2012). Intelligence: New findings and theoretical developments. *American Psychologist, 67*(2), 130-159.

Noar, S. M., Zimmerman, R. S., & Atwood, K. A. (2004). Safer sex and sexually transmitted infections from a relationship perspective. In J. H. Harvey, A. Wenzel, & S. Sprecher (Eds.), *The handbook of sexuality in close relationships* (pp. 519–544). Mahwah, NJ: Erlbaum.

Noe-Bustamante, Flores, A., & Shah, S. (2017). *Facts on Hispanics of Mexican origin in the United States.* Pew Research Center. Retrieved September 28, 2021 from https://www.pewresearch.org/hispanic/fact-sheet/u-s-hispanics-facts-on-mexican-origin-latinos/

Nolan, S. A., Buckner, J. P., Marzabadi, C. H., & Kuck, V. J. (2008). Training and mentoring of chemists: A study of gender disparity. *Sex Roles, 58,* 235–259.

Nolen-Hoeksema, S. (1990). *Sex differences in depression.* Stanford, CA: Stanford University Press.

Nolen-Hoeksema, S. (2001). Gender differences in depression. *Current Directions in Psychological Science, 10,* 173–176.

Nolen-Hoeksema, S. (2003). *Women who think too much: How to break free of overthinking and reclaim your life.* New York: Holt.

Nolen-Hoeksema, S. (2006). The etiology of gender differences in depression. In C. M. Mazure & G. P. Keita (Eds.), *Understanding depression* (pp. 9–43). Washington, DC: American Psychological Association.

Nolen-Hoeksema, S., & Hilt, L. M. (2009). Gender differences in depression. In I. H. Gotlib & C. L. Hammen (Eds.), *Handbook of depression* (2nd ed., pp. 386–404). New York: Guilford.

Nolen-Hoeksema, S., & Larson, J. (1999). *Coping with loss.* Mahwah, NJ: Erlbaum.

Nolen-Hoeksema, S., Wisco, B. E., & Lyubomirsky, S. (2008). Rethinking rumination. *Perspectives on Psychological Science, 3,* 400–424.

Noller, P. (2006). Marital relationships. In P. Noller & J. A. Feeney (Eds.), *Close relationships: Functions, forms and processes* (pp. 67–88). New York: Psychology Press.

Noller, P., & Feeney, J. A. (2002). Communication, relationship concerns, and satisfaction in early marriage. In A. L. Vangelisti, H. T. Reis, & M. A. Fitzpatrick (Eds.), *Stability and change in relationships* (pp. 129–155). New York: Cambridge.

Nordvik, H., & Amponsah, B. (1998). Gender differences in spatial activity among university students in an egalitarian educational system. *Sex Roles, 38,* 1009–1023.

Norris, C. M., et al. (2020). State of the science in women's cardiovascular disease: A Canadian perspective on the influence of sex and gender. *Journal of the American Heart Association, 9,* e015634.

Norton, S. (2002). Women exposed: Sexual harassment and female vulnerability. In L. Diamant & J. A. Lee (Eds.), *The psychology of sex, gender, and jobs* (pp. 83–101). Westport, CT: Praeger.

Nosek, B. A., Banaji, M. R., & Greenwald, A. G. (2002). Math = male, me = female, therefore math ≠ me. *Journal of Personality and Social Psychology, 83,* 44–59.

Nosek, B. A., Greenwald, A. G., & Banaji, M. R. (2007). The Implicit Association Test at age 7: A methodological and conceptual review. In J. A. Bargh (Ed.), *Social psychology and the unconscious: The automaticity of higher mental processes* (pp. 265–292). New York: Psychology Press.

Notzon, F. C. (2008). Quickstats: Rates of cesarean deliveries—selected countries, 2005. *Birth, 35,* 336–337.

Nour, N. M. (2005). Female genital cutting is both a health and human rights issue. In Boston Women's Health Book Collective (Eds.), *Our bodies, ourselves* (4th ed., pp. 644–655). New York: Touchstone.

Nussbaum, M. (2000, September 8). Globalization debate ignores the education of women. *Chronicle of Higher Education,* pp. B16–B17.

Nydegger, R. (2004). Gender and mental health: Incidence and treatment issues. In M. A. Paludi (Ed.), *Praeger guide to the psychology of gender* (pp. 93–116). Westport, CT: Praeger.

Nydegger, R. (2008). *Understanding and treating depression: Ways to find hope and help.* Westport, CT: Praeger.

O'Brien, M., et al. (2000). Gender-role cognition in three-year-old boys and girls. *Sex Roles, 42,* 1007–1025.

Ocampo, C., et al. (2003). Diversity research in Teaching of Psychology: Summary and agenda. *Teaching of Psychology, 30,* 5–18.

Ochman, J. M. (1996). The effects of nongender-role stereotyped, same-sex role models in storybooks on the self-esteem of children in grade three. *Sex Roles, 35,* 711–735.

O'Connell,, A. N. (2001). *Models of achievement: Reflections of eminent women in psychology* (Vol. 3). Mahwah, NJ: Erlbaum.

Odgers, C. L., et al. (2008). Is it important to prevent early exposure to drugs and alcohol among adolescents? *Psychological Science, 19,* 1037–1044.

Offman, A., & Kleinplatz, P. J. (2004, Spring). Does PMDD belong in the DSM? Challenging the medicalization of women's bodies. *Canadian Journal of Human Sexuality, 13,* 17–27.

Offman, A., & Matheson, K. (2004). The sexual self-perceptions of young women experiencing abuse in dating relationships. *Sex Roles, 51 ,* 551–560.

Oggins, J., Veroff, J., & Leber, D. (1993). Perceptions of marital interaction among Black and White newlyweds. *Journal of Personality and Social Psychology, 65,* 494–511.

Ogletree, S. (2015). Gender role attitudes and expectations for marriage. *Journal of Research on Women and Gender, 5,* 71-82.

O'Hara, M. W., & Stuart, S. (1999). Pregnancy and postpartum. In R. G. Robinson & W. R. Yates (Eds.), *Psychiatric treatment of the medically ill* (pp. 253–277). New York: Marcel Dekker.

Okahana, H., & Zhou, E. (2018). *Graduate enrollment and degrees: 2007-2017.* Washington, DC: Council of Graduate Schools. Retrieved October 3, 2021 from https://cgsnet.org/ckfinder/userfiles/files/CGS_GED17_Report.pdf

Okazaki, S. (2009). Impact of racism on ethnic minority mental health.

Perspectives on Psychological Science, 4, 103–107.

Oksman, J. C. (2002). *An analysis of the portrayal of menstruation in menstrual product advertisements.* Unpublished manuscript, SUNY, Geneseo, NY.

Olafson, E. (2004). Child sexual abuse. In B. J. Cling (Ed.), *Sexualized violence against women and children* (pp. 151–187). New York: Guilford.

O'Leary, K. D., & Maiuro, R. D. (Eds.). (2001). *Psychological abuse in violent domestic relations.* New York: Springer.

O'Leary, V. E., & Bhaju, J. (2006). Resilience and empowerment. In J. Worell & C. D. Goodheart (Eds.), *Handbook of girls' and women's psychological health: Gender and well-being across the life span* (pp. 157–165). New York: Oxford University Press.

Oldenburg, B., & Burton, N. W. (2004). Primary prevention. In A. Kaptein & J. Weinman (Eds.), *Health psychology* (pp. 305–336). Malden, MA: Blackwell.

Older Women's League. (2006). *Older women and poverty.* Retrieved March 7, 2006, from http://www.owl-national.org/poverty.html

Olff, M., Langeland, W., Draijer, N., & Gersons, B. P. R. (2007). Gender differences in posttraumatic stress disorder. *Psychological Bulletin, 133 ,* 183–204.

Olio, K. A. (2004). The truth about "false memory syndrome." In P. J. Caplan & L. Cosgrove (Eds.), *Bias in psychiatric diagnosis* (pp. 163–169). Lanham, MD: Jason Aronson.

Oliver, M. B., & Hyde, J. S. (1993). Gender differences in sexuality: A meta-analysis. *Psychological Bulletin, 114,* 29–51.

Olkin, R. (2006). Physical or systemic disabilities. In J. Worell & C. D. Goodheart (Eds.), *Handbook of girls' and women's psychological health: Gender and well-being across the life span* (pp. 94–102). New York: Oxford University Press.

Olkin, R. (2008). Women with disabilities. In J. C. Chrisler, C. Golden, & P. D. Rozee (Eds.), *Lectures on the psychology of women* (4th ed., pp. 190–203). Boston, MA: McGraw Hill.

Olkin, R. (2014). What should we teach when we teach about women with disabilities? *Women & Therapy, 37,* 94-108.

Olkin, R., & Pledger, C. (2003). Can disability studies and psychology join hands? *American Psychologist, 58,* 296–304.

Olson, J. E., et al. (2007). Belief in equality for women as related to economic factors in Central and Eastern Europe and the United States. *Sex Roles, 56,* 297–308.

Olson, K. R., & Dweck, C. S. (2008). A blueprint for social cognitive development. *Perspectives on Psychological Science, 3,* 193–202.

O'Neil, J. M. (2008). Summarizing 25 years of research on men's gender role conflict using the Gender Role Conflict Scale. *The Counseling Psychologist, 36,* 358–445.

Online. (2004, September 17). *Chronicle of Higher Education,* p. A29.

Ontiveros, M. L. (2007). Female immigrant workers and the law: Limits and opportunities. In D. S. Cobble (Ed.), *The sex of class: Women transforming American labor* (pp. 235–252). Ithaca, NY: Cornell University Press.

Onyx, J., & Benton, P. (1999). What does retirement mean for women? In J. Onyx, R. Leonard, & R. Reed (Eds.), *Revisioning aging: Empowering of older women* (pp. 93–108). New York: Peter Lang.

Oregon State University. (2021, June). *What were you wearing? Installation history.* Oregon State University Department of Forestry.

Organisation for Economic Cooperation and Development. (2019). *Education at a glance 2019: OECD indicators.* OECD Publishing, Paris. Retrieved October 3, 2021 from https://doi.org/10.1787/f8d7880d-en

Organisation for Economic Cooperation and Development. (2021). *Health at a glance, 2019: Cesarian sections.* OECD. Retrieved October 4, 2021 from https://www.oecd-ilibrary.org/sites/fa1f7281-en/index.html?itemId=/content/component/fa1f7281-en

Ormerod, A. J., Collinsworth, L. J., & Perry, L. A. (2008). Critical climate: Relations among sexual harassment, climate, and outcomes for high school girls and boys. *Psychology of Women Quarterly, 32,* 113–125.

Orozco, A. E. (1999). Mexican blood runs through my veins. In D. L. Galindo & M. D. Gonzales (Eds.), *Speaking chicana: Voice, power, and identity* (pp. 106–120). Tucson: University of Arizona Press.

Osman, S. L. (2004). Victim resistance: Theory and data on understanding perceptions of sexual harassment. *Sex Roles, 50,* 267–275.

Ostenson, R. S. (2008). Who's in and who's out: The results of oppression. In J. C. Chrisler, C. Golden, & P. D. Rozee (Eds.), *Lectures on the psychology of women* (4th ed., pp. 16–25). Boston, MA: McGraw-Hill.

Osterhout, L., Bersick, M., & McLaughlin, J. (1997). Brain potentials reflect violations of gender stereotypes. *Memory & Cognition, 25,* 273–285.

Osterman, M. J. K., & Martin, J. A. (2018). Timing and adequacy of prenatal care in the United States, 2016. *National Vital Statistics Reports, 67*(3). Retrieved October 4, 2021 from https://www.cdc.gov/nchs/data/nvsr/nvsr67/nvsr67_03.pdf

Ostrove, J. M., & Cole, E. R. (2003). Privileging class: Toward a critical psychology of social class in the context of education. *Journal of Social Issues, 59,* 677–692.

Ostrov, J. M., Crick, N. R., & Keating, C. F. (2005). Gender-biased perceptions of preschoolers' behavior: How much is aggression and pro-social behavior in the eye of the beholder? *Sex Roles, 52,* 393–398.

Ostrov, J. M., et al. (2004). An observational study of delivered and received aggression, gender, and social-psychological adjustment in preschool: " This white crayon doesn't work . . . ." *Early Childhood Research Quarterly, 19,* 355–371.

Osuch, J. R., Silk, K., Price, C., Barlow, J., Miller, K., Hernick, A., & Fonfa, A. (2012). A historical perspective on breast cancer activism in the United States: From education and support to partnership in scientific research. *Journal of Women's Health, 21,* 355–362.

Oswald, D. L., Baalbaki, M., & Kirkman, M. (2019). Experiences with benevolent sexism: Scale development and associations with women's well-being. *Sex Roles, 80,* 362–380.

Oswald, R. F., Fonseca, C. A., & Hardesty, J. L. (2010). Lesbian mothers' counseling experiences in the context of intimate partner violence. *Psychology of Women Quarterly, 34,* 286–296

O'Sullivan, L. F., & Gaines, M. E. (1998). Decision-making in college students' heterosexual dating relationship: Ambivalence about engaging in sexual activity. *Journal of Social and Personal Relationships, 15,* 347–363.

O'Sullivan, L. F., Graber, J. A., & Brooks-Gunn, J. (2001). Adolescent gender development. In J. Worell (Ed.), *Encyclopedia of women and gender* (pp. 55–67). San Diego: Academic Press.

O'Sullivan, L. F., McCrudden, M. C., & Tolman., D. L. (2006). To your sexual health! Incorporating sexuality into the health perspective. In J. Worell & C. D. Goodheart (Eds.), *Handbook of girls' and women's psychological health: Gender and well-being across the life span* (pp. 192–207). New York: Oxford University Press.

O'Sullivan, L. F., & Meyer-Bahlburg, H. F. L. (2003). African-American and Latina inner-city girls' reports of romantic and sexual development. *Journal of Social and Personal Relationships, 20,* 221–238.

Oswald, D. L. (2008). Gender stereotypes and women's reports of liking and ability in traditionally masculine and feminine occupations. *Psychology of Women Quarterly, 32,* 196–203.

Oswald, D. L., & Linstedt, K. (2006). The content and function of gender self-stereotypes: An exploratory investigation. *Sex Roles, 54,* 447–458.

Ottati, V., Claypool, H. M., & Gingrich, B. (2005). Effects of a group stereotype on memory for behaviors performed by a group member. *European Journal of Social Psychology, 35,* 797–808.

Ozer, E. J., & Weiss, D. S. (2004). Who develops posttraumatic stress disorder. *Current Directions in Psychological Science, 13,* 169–172.

Pachankis, J. E. (2007). The psychological implications of concealing a stigma: A cognitive-affective-behavioral model. *Psychological Bulletin, 133,* 328–345.

Padavic, I., & Reskin, B. (2002). *Women and men at work* (2nd ed.). Thousand Oaks, CA: Pine Forge Press.

Paharia, M. I., & Kase, L. (2008). Obesity. In B. A. Boyer & M. I. Paharia (Eds.), *Comprehensive handbook of clinical health psychology* (pp. 81–103). Hoboken, NJ: Wiley.

Paik, H. (2001). The history of children's use of electronic media. In D. G. Singer & J. L. Singer (Eds.), *Handbook on children and the media* (pp. 7–27). Thousand Oaks, CA: Sage.

Pak, J. (2019). *The Chinese workers who make your shoes.* Marketplace. Retrieved October 3, 2021 from https://www.marketplace.org/2019/10/02/the-chinese-workers-who-make-your-shoes/

Paley, A. R. (2008). For Kurdish girls, a painful ancient ritual. *The Washington Post*, pp. A9.

Palmore, E. (2001). The ageism survey: First findings. *The Gerontologist, 41*, 572–575.

Palmore, E. (2004). Research note: Ageism in Canada and the United States. *Journal of Cross-Cultural Gerontology, 19*, 41–46.

Paludi, C. A., Jr., & Paludi, M. A. (2003). Developing and enforcing effective policies, procedures, and training programs for educational institutions and businesses. In M. A. Paludi & C. A. Paludi (Eds.), *Academic and workplace sexual harassment* (pp. 175–198). Westport, CT: Praeger.

Paludi, M. A. (Ed.). (2008). *The psychology of women at work* (Vols. 1–3). Westport, CT: Praeger.

Paludi, M. A. (2004). Sexual harassment of college students: Cultural similarities and differences. In J. C. Chrisler, C. Golden, & P. D. Rozee (Eds.), *Lectures on the psychology of women* (3rd ed., pp. 332–355). New York: McGraw-Hill.

Pardo, M. (2005). Mexican American women, grassroots community activists: Mothers of East Los Angeles. In M. Baca Zinn, P. Hondagneu-Sotelo, & M. A. Messner (Eds.), *Gender through the prism of difference* (3rd ed., pp. 541–546). New York: Oxford University Press.

Park, J., & Liao, T. F. (2000). The effect of multiple roles of South Korean married women professors: Role changes and the factors which influence potential role gratification and strain. *Sex Roles, 43*, 571–591.

Parke, R. D. (2004). Development in the family. *Annual Review of Psychology, 55*, 365–399.

Parker, K. (2018). *Women in majority-male workplaces report higher rates of gender discrimination*. *Pew Research Center*. Retrieved October 3, 2021 from https://www.pewresearch.org/ fact-tank/2018/03/07/women-in-majority-male-workplaces-report-higher-rates-of-gender-discrimination/

Parker, L. L., & Harriger, J. A. (2020). Eating disorders and disordered eating behaviors in the LGBT population: A review of the literature. *Journal of Eating Disorders, 8*, 51.

Parks, J. B., & Roberton, M. A. (1998a). Contemporary arguments against nonsexist language: Blaubergs (1980) revisited. *Sex Roles, 39*, 445–461.

Parks, J. B., & Roberton, M. A. (1998b). Influence of age, gender, and context on attitudes toward sexist/nonsexist language: Is sport a special case? *Sex Roles, 38*, 477–494.

Parks, J. B., & Roberton, M. A. (2000). Development and validation of an instrument to measure attitudes toward sexist/ nonsexist language. *Sex Roles, 42*, 415–438.

Parrot, A. (1999). *Coping with date and acquaintance rape*. New York: Rosen Publishing Group.

Parrot, A., & Cummings, N. (2006). *Forsaken females: The global brutalization of women*. Lanham, MD: Rowman & Littlefield.

Parry, D. C. (2005). Work, leisure, and support groups: An examination of the ways women with infertility respond to pronatalist ideology. *Sex Roles, 53*, 337–346.

Parry, D. C. (2008). The contribution of dragon boat racing to women's health and breast cancer survivorship. *Qualitative Health Research, 18*, 222–223.

Pasch, L. (2001). Confronting fertility problems: Current research and future challenges. In A. Baum, T. A. Revenson, & J. E. Singer (Eds.), *Handbook of health psychology* (pp. 559–570). Mahwah, NJ: Erlbaum.

Pasterski, V. (2008). Disorders of sex development and atypical sex differentiation. In D. L. Rowland & L. Incrocci (Ed.), *Handbook of sexual and gender identity disorders* (pp. 354–376). Hoboken, NJ: Wiley.

Pasupathi, M., & Lockenhoff, C. E. (2002). Ageist behavior. In T. D. Nelson (Ed.), *Ageism: Stereotyping and prejudice against older persons* (pp. 201–246). Cambridge, MA: MIT Press.

Pattatucci, A. M., & Hamer, D. H. (1995). Development and familiality of sexual orientation in females. *Behavior Genetics, 25*, 407–420.

Patterson, C. J. (2003). Children of lesbian and gay parents. In L. D. Garnets & D. C. Kimmel (Eds.), *Psychological perspectives on lesbian, gay, and bisexual experiences* (2nd ed., pp. 497–548). New York: Columbia University Press.

Patterson, G. A. (2008, November 13). Managing motherhood and tenure. *Diverse Issues in Higher Education* 16–18.

Pauwels, A. (1998). *Women changing language*. London: Longman.

Pauwels, H. R. M. (2008). *The goddess as role model: Sita and Radha in scripture and on screen*. New York: Oxford University Press.

Pawelski, J. G., et al. (2006). The effects of marriage, civil union, and domestic partnership laws on the health and well-being of children. *Pediatrics, 118*, 349–364.

Pearson, J. (2006). Personal control, self-efficacy in sexual negotiation, and contraceptive risk among adolescents: The role of gender. *Sex Roles, 54*, 615–625.

Pechilis, K. (Ed.). (2004). *The graceful guru: Hindu female gurus in India and the United States*. New York: Oxford University Press.

Pedersen, W. C, Miller, L. C, & Putcha-Bhagavatula, & Yang, Y. (2002). Evolved sex differences in the number of partners desired? *Psychological Science, 13*, 157–161.

Peirce, K. (1990). A feminist theoretical perspective on the socialization of teenage girls through *Seventeen* magazine. *Sex Roles, 23,* 491–500.

Pelletier, R., Patterson, M., & Môyser, M. (2019). *The gender wage gap in Canada: 1998-2018.* Statistics Canada. Retrieved October 3, 2021 from https://www150 .statcan.gc.ca/n1/pub/75-004-m/75 -004-m2019004-eng.htm

Peltason, R. (2008). *I am not my breast cancer.* New York: Harper Collins.

Peña, M. (1998). Class, gender, and machismo: The "treacherous woman" folklore of Mexican male workers. In M. S. Kimmel & M. A. Messner (Eds.), *Men's lives* (4th ed., pp. 273–284). Boston: Allyn & Bacon.

Peñacoba Puente, C., Carmona Monge, F. J., Carretero Abellán, I., & Marín Morales, D. (2011). Effects of personality on psychiatric and somatic symptoms in pregnant women: The role of pregnancy worries. *Psychology of Women Quarterly, 35,* 293-302.

Pension Rights Center. (2019). *How many American workers participate in workplace retirement plans?* Retrieved October 5, 2021 http://www.pensionrights .org/publications/statistic /how-many-american-workers -participate-workplace -retirement-plans

Peplau, L. A. (1994). Men and women in love. In D. L. Sollie & L. A. Leslie (Eds.), *Gender, families, and close relationships: Feminist research journeys* (pp. 19–49). Thousand Oaks, CA: Sage.

Peplau, L. A. (2001). Rethinking women's sexual orientation: An interdisciplinary, relationship-focused approach. *Personal Relationships, 8,* 1–19.

Peplau, L. A. (2003). Human sexuality: How do men and women differ? *Current Directions in Psychological Science, 12,* 37–40.

Peplau, L. A., & Beals, K. P. (2001). Lesbians, gay men, and bisexuals in relationships. In J. Worell

(Ed.), *Encyclopedia of women and gender* (pp. 657–666). San Diego: Academic Press.

Peplau, L. A., & Beals, K. P. (2004). The family lives of lesbians and gay men. In A. L. Vangelisti (Ed.), *Handbook of family communication* (pp. 233–248). Mahwah, NJ: Erlbaum.

Peplau, L. A., Cochran, S. D., & Mays, V. M. (1997). A national survey of the intimate relationships of African-American lesbians and gay men. In B. Greene (Ed.), *Ethnic and cultural diversity among lesbians and gay men* (pp. 11–38). Thousand Oaks, CA: Sage.

Peplau, L. A., & Fingerhut, A. W. (2004). The paradox of the lesbian worker. *Journal of Social Issues, 60,* 719–735.

Peplau, L. A., & Fingerhut, A. W. (2007). The close relationships of lesbians and gay men. *Annual Review of Psychology, 58,* 405–424.

Peplau, L. A., & Garnets, L. D. (2000). A new paradigm for understanding women's sexuality and sexual orientation. *Journal of Social Issues, 56,* 329–350.

Peplau, L. A., & Spalding, L. R. (2000). The close relationships of lesbians, gay men, and bisexuals. In C. Hendrick & S. S. Hendrick (Eds.), *Close relationships* (pp. 111–123). Thousand Oaks, CA: Sage.

Peplau, L. A., Veniegas, R. C, Taylor, P. L., & DeBro, S. C. (1999). Sociocultural perspectives on the lives of women and men. In L. A. Peplau et al. (Eds.), *Gender, culture, and ethnicity: Current research about women and men* (pp. 23–37). Mountain View, CA: Mayfield.

Perloff, R. M. (2001). *Persuading people to have safer sex: Applications of social science to the AIDS crisis.* Mahwah, NJ: Erlbaum.

Perreault, S. (2020). *Gender-based violence: Sexual and physical assault in Canada's territories,*

2018. Canadian Centre for Justice and Community Safety Statistics. Statistics Canada Catalogue no. 85-002-X. Retrieved October 5, 2021, https:// www150.statcan.gc.ca/n1/en /pub/85-002-x/2020001/article /00012-eng.pdf?st=e0Dvawi0

Perry, M. J. (2020). *Women earned majority of doctoral degrees in 2019 for 11th straight year and outnumber men in grad school 141 to 100.* American Enterprise Institute. Retrieved October 5, 2021 from https:// www.aei.org/carpe-diem/women -earned-majority-of-doctoral -degrees-in-2019-for-11th -straight-year-and-outnumber -men-in-grad-school-141-to-100/

Perry-Jenkins, M., Pierce, C. P., & Goldberg, A. E. (2004). Discourse on diapers and dirty laundry: Family communication about child care and housework. In A. L. Vangelisti (Ed.), *Handbook of family communication* (pp. 541–561). Mahwah, NJ: Erlbaum.

Perse, E. M. (2001). *Media effects and society.* Mahwah, NJ: Erlbaum.

Pessin, L. (2018). Changing gender norms and marriage dynamics in the United States. *Journal of Marriage and Family, 80,* 25-41.

Petersen, E. E., Davis, N. L., Goodman, D., et al. (2019). Racial/ ethnic disparities in pregnancy-related deaths – United States, 2007-2016. *Morbidity Mortal Weekly Report, 68,* 762-765.

Peterson, J. (2018). Gender difference in verbal performance: A meta-analysis of United States state performance assessments. *Educational Psychology Review, 30,* 1269-1281.

Peterson, J., & Hyde, J. S. (2010a). Gender differences in sexuality. In J. C. Chrisler & D. R. McCreary (Eds.), *Handbook of gender research in psychology* (Vol. 2, pp. 471–491). New York: Springer.

Peterson, J., & Hyde, J. S. (2010b). A meta-analytic review of research on gender differences in sexuality, 1993–2007. *Psychological Bulletin, 136,* 21–38.

Peterson, Z. D., & Muehlenhard, C. L. (2004). Was it rape? The function of women's rape myth acceptance and definitions of sex in labeling their own experiences. *Sex Roles, 51,* 129–144.

Phelan, J. E., Moss-Racusin, C. A., & Rudman, L. A. (2008). Competent yet out in the cold: Shifting criteria for hiring reflect backlash toward agentic women. *Psychology of Women Quarterly, 32,* 406–413.

Philbin, M., Meier, E., Hoffman, S., & Boverie, P. (1995). A survey of gender and learning styles. *Sex Roles, 32,* 485–494.

Philipp, D. A., & Carr, M. L. (2001). Normal and medically complicated pregnancies. In N. L. Stotland & D. E. Stewart (Eds.), *Psychological aspects of women's health care: The interface between psychiatry and obstetrics and gynecology* (2nd ed., pp. 13–32). Washington, DC: American Psychiatric Publishing.

Pickup, F. (2001). *Ending violence against women: A challenge for development and humanitarian work.* Oxford, England: Oxfam.

Pierce, W. D., Sydie, R. A., Stratkotter, R., & Krull, C. (2003). Social concepts and judgments: A semantic differential analysis of the concepts feminist, man, and woman. *Psychology of Women Quarterly, 27,* 338–346.

Pillemer, K., et al. (2007). Capturing the complexity of intergenerational relations: Exploring ambivalence within later-life families. *Journal of Social Issues, 63,* 775–791.

Pincus, J. (2000). Childbirth advice literature as it relates to two child-bearing ideologies. *Birth, 27,* 209–213.

Piran, N., & Ross, E. (2006). From girlhood to womanhood: Multiple transitions in context. In J. Worell & C. D. Goodheart (Eds.), *Handbook of girls' and women's psychological health: Gender and well-being across the life span* (pp. 301–310). New York: Oxford University Press.

Place, S. S., Todd, P. M., Penke, L., & Asendorpf, J. B. (2009). The ability to judge the romantic interest of others. *Psychological Science, 20,* 22–26.

Planned Parenthood. (2009). *Planned Parenthood Federation of America statement on the murder of Dr. George Tiller.* Retrieved December 12, 2010, from http://www.plannedparenthood.org/about-US/newsroom/press-releases/planned-parenthood-federation-America-statement-murder-dr-george-tiller-27643.htm

Planned Parenthood. (2010). *Morning-after pill (emergency contraception).* Retrieved December 12, 2010, from http://www.plannedparenthood.org/health-topics/emergency-contra-ception-morning-after-pill-4363.asp

Plant, E. A., Hyde, J. S., Keltner, D., & Devine, P. G. (2000). The gender stereotyping of emotions. *Psychology of Women Quarterly, 24,* 81–92.

Platt, L. F., Wolf, J. K., & Scheitle, C. P.. (2017). Patterns of mental health care utilization among sexual orientation minority groups. *Journal of Homosexuality, 65,* 135-153.

Platt, M., Barton, J., & Freyd, J. (2009). A betrayal trauma perspective on domestic violence. In E. Stark & E. S. Buzawa (Eds.), *Violence against women in families and relationships* (Vol. 1, pp. 185–207). Santa Barbara, CA: ABC-CLIO.

Pleck, J. H., & Masciadrelli, B. P. (2004). Paternal involvement: Levels, origins, and consequences. In M. E. Lamb (Ed.), *The role of the father in child development* (4th ed., pp. 222–271). New York: Wiley.

Pobojewski, S. (2008, Spring). The first 21 days. *Medicine at Michigan,* 22–27.

Poelmans, S. A. Y. (Ed.). (2005). *Work and family: An international research perspective.* Mahwah, NJ: Erlbaum.

Pogrebin, L. C. (1997, September/October). Endless love. *Ms. Magazine,* pp. 36–37.

Poggi, L., Goutaudier, N., Séjourné, N., & Chabrol, H. (2018). When fear of childbirth is pathological: The fear continuum. *Maternal and Child Health Journal, 22,* 772-778.

Pohl, W. (2004). Gender and ethnicity in the early Middle ages. In L. Brubaker & J. M. H. Smith (Eds.), *Gender in the early medieval world: East and west, 300–900* (pp. 23–43). New York: Cambridge University Press.

Polacca, M. (2001). American Indian and Alaska native elderly. In L. K. Olson (Ed.), *Age through ethnic lenses: Caring for the elderly in a multicultural society* (pp. 112–122). Lanham, MD: Rowman & Littlefield.

Poling, J. N., Grundy, C., & Min, H. (2002). Men helping men to become pro-feminist. In J. N. Poling & C. C. Neuger (Eds.), *Men's work in preventing violence against women* (pp. 107–122). New York: Haworth.

Polisi, C. J. (2009, July 1). *Spousal rape laws continue to evolve.* Retrieved April 29, 2010, from http://www.truthout.org/070309E?n

Polivka, L. (2010). Neoliberalism and the new politics of aging and retirement security. In J. C. Cavanaugh & C. K. Cavanaugh (Eds.), *Aging in America* (Vol. 3, pp. 160–202). Santa Barbara, CA: ABC-CLIO.

Polivy, J., & Herman, C. P. (2002). Experimental studies of dieting. In C. G. Fairburn & K. D. Brownell (Eds.), *Eating disorders and obesity: A comprehensive handbook* (2nd ed., pp. 84–87). New York: Guilford.

Pollack, W. (1998). *Real boys.* New York: Random House.

Pollard, M. S., & Morgan, S. P. (2002). Emerging parental

gender indifference? Sex composition of children and the third birth. *American Sociological Review, 67,* 600–613.

Pollitt, K. (2004). U.S. feminism lite: Claiming independence, asserting personal choice. In L. Flanders (Ed.), *The W effect: Bush's war on women* (pp. 280–284). New York: Feminist Press.

Pomerleau, A., Bolduc, D., Malcuit, G., & Cossette, L. (1990). Pink or blue: Environmental gender stereotypes in the first two years of life. *Sex Roles, 22,* 359–367.

Pomeroy, J. (2007). *Italian women artists from Renaissance to Baroque* (pp. 16–23). Washington DC: National Museum of Women in the Arts.

Pomfret, J. (2001, June 3). China's boy boom tied to ultrasound machines. *Dallas Morning News,* p. 31A.

Pope, K. (2001). Sex between therapists and clients. In J. Worell (Ed.), *Encyclopedia of women and gender* (pp. 955–962). San Diego: Academic Press.

Popenoe, D., & Whitehead, B. D. (2002). *The state of our unions.* Piscataway, NJ: National Marriage Project.

Population Council. (2008, September). Involving men as partners against violence. *Momentum,* pp. 4–5.

Poran, M. A. (2002). Denying diversity: Perceptions of beauty and social comparison processes among Latina, Black, and White women. *Sex Roles, 47,* 65–81.

Poran, M. A. (2006). The politics of protection: Body image, social pressures, and the misrepresentation of young Black women. *Sex Roles, 55,* 739–755.

Porter, N., & Daniel, J. H. (2007). Developing transformational leaders: Theory to practice. In J. L. Chin, B. Lott, J. K. Rice, & J. Sanchez-Hucles (Eds.), *Women and leadership: Transforming visions and diverse voices* (pp. 245–263).

Malden, MA: Blackwell. Porzelius, L. K. (2000). Physical health issues for women. In M. Biaggio & M. Hersen (Eds.), *Issues in the psychology of women* (pp. 229–249). New York: Plenum.

Poulson-Bryant, S. (2005). *Hung: A meditation on the measure of Black men in America.* New York: Doubleday.

Powell, G. N., & Graves, L. M. (2003). *Women and men in management* (3rd ed.). Thousand Oaks, CA: Sage.

Powers, P. S. (2002). Eating disorders. In S. G. Kornstein & A. H. Clayton (Eds.), *Women's mental health: A comprehensive textbook* (pp. 244–262). New York: Guilford.

Powlishta, K. K. (1995). Inter-group processes in childhood: Social categorization and sex role development. *Developmental Psychology, 31,* 781–788.

Powlishta, K. K. (2000). The effect of target age on the activation of gender stereotypes. *Sex Roles, 42,* 271–282.

Powlishta, K. K., et al. (2001). From infancy through middle childhood: The role of cognitive and social factors in becoming gendered. In R. K. Unger (Ed.), *Handbook of the psychology of women and gender* (pp. 116–132). New York: Wiley.

Pozner, J. L. (2001, March/April). Cosmetic coverage. *Extra!,* pp. 8–10.

Prager, K. J., & Roberts, L. J. (2004). Deep intimate connection: Self and intimacy in couple relationships. In D. J. Mashek & A. Aron (Eds.), *Handbook of closeness and intimacy* (pp. 43–60). Mahwah, NJ: Erlbaum.

Preston, A. E. (2004). *Leaving science.* New York: Russell Sage Foundation.

Prezbindowski, K. S., & Prezbindowski, A. K. (2001). Educating young adolescent girls about lesbian, bisexual, and gay issues. In P. O'Reilly, E. M. Penn, & K. deMarrais (Eds.), *Educating

young adolescent girls* (pp. 47–80). Mahwah, NJ: Erlbaum.

Price, C. A., & Joo, E. (2005). Exploring the relationship between marital status and women's retirement satisfaction. *International Journal of Aging and Human Development, 61,* 37–55.

Prince, C. J. (2004). Media myths: The truth about the opt-out hype. *NAFE Magazine,* 14–17.

Privott, M. (2019). An ethos of responsibility and Indigenous women water protectors in the #NoDAPL movement. *American Indian Quarterly, 43*(1), 74-100.

Prohaska, A., & Gailey, J. (2009). Fat women as "easy targets": Achieving masculinity through hogging. In E. Rothblum & S. Solovay (Eds.), *The fat studies reader* (pp. 158–166). New York: New York University Press.

Pruchno, R., & Rosenbaum, J. (2003). Social relationships in adulthood and old age. In R. M. Lerner, M. Ann Easterbrooks, & J. Mistry (Eds.), *Handbook of psychology* (Vol. 6, pp. 487–508). New York: Wiley.

Puchner, L., & Klein, N. A. (2012). Skirting the issue: Teachers' experiences "addressing sexuality in middle school language arts." *Research in Middle School Education Online, 36,* 1-16.

Puhl, R. M., & Lamer, J. D. (2007). Stigma, obesity, and the health of the nation's children. *Psychological Bulletin, 133,* 557–580.

Pulera, D. (2002). *Visible differences: Why race will matter to Americans in the twenty-first century.* New York: Continuum.

Pyke, S. W. (1998, June). *The inferior sex: Psychology's construction of gender.* Paper presented at the annual convention of the Canadian Psychological Association, Edmonton, Canada.

Pyke, S. W. (2001). Feminist psychology in Canada: Early days. *Canadian Psychology/Psychologie canadienne, 42,* 268–275.

Quatman, T., & Watson, C. M. (2001). Gender differences

in adolescent self-esteem: An exploration of domains. *Journal of Genetic Psychology, 162,* 93–117.

Quindlen, A. (2001, December 17). The terrorists here at home. *Newsweek,* p. 78.

Quindlen, A. (2005, February 21). The good enough mother. *Newsweek,* pp. 50–51.

Quindlen, A. (2008). Pregnant in New York. In S. Macdonald Strong (Ed.), *The maternal is political* (pp. 285–288). Berkeley, CA: Seal Press.

Quindlen, A. (2009, March 7). Let's talk about sex. *Newsweek,* p. 76.

Quinn, J. M., & Wagner, R. K. (2015). Gender differences in reading impairment and in the identification of impaired readers: Results from a large-scale study of at-risk readers. *Journal of Learning Disabilities, 48*(4), 433-445.

Quintanilla, K., Cano, N. F., & Ivy, D. K. (2004). The defining of menopause. In P. Buzzanelli, H. Sterk, & L. H. Turner (Eds.), *Gender in applied communication contexts* (pp. 99–125). Thousand Oaks, CA: Sage.

Rad, M. S., Martingano, A. J., & Ginges, J. (2018). Toward a psychology of *Homo sapiens*: Making psychological science more representative of the human population. *Proceedings of the National Academy of Sciences, 115,* 11401-11405.

Rader, J., & Gilbert, L. A. (2005). The egalitarian relationship in feminist therapy. *Psychology of Women Quarterly, 29,* 427–435.

Radini et al., (2019). Medieval women's early involvement in manuscript production suggested by lapis lazuli identification in dental calculus. *Science Advances, 5*(1). eaau7126. DOI: 10.1126/sciadv.aau7126

Raffaelli, M. (2005). Adolescent dating experiences described by Latino college students. *Journal of Adolescence, 28,* 559–572.

Raffaelli, M., & Green, S. (2003). Parent-adolescent communication about sex: Retrospective reports by Latino college students. *Journal of Marriage and Family, 65,* 474–481.

Raffaelli, M., & Ontai, L. L. (2004). Gender socialization in Latino/a families: Results from two retrospective studies. *Sex Roles, 50,* 287–299.

RAINN. (2021, June). *Victims of sexual violence: Statistics.* Retrieved October 5, 2021 from https://www.rainn.org/statistics/victims-sexual-violence

Raisz, L. G. (2005). Screening for osteoporosis. *New England Journal of Medicine, 353,* 164–171.

Raitt, F. E., & Zeedyk, S. (2000). *The implicit relation of psychology and law: Women and syndrome evidence.* London: Routledge.

Raj, A., Gomez, C, & Silverman, J. G. (2008). Driven to a fiery death: The tragedy of self-immolation in Afghanistan. *New England Journal of Medicine, 358,* 2201–2203.

Rajvanshi, D. (2005, May/June). Sorry state of women's health. *Manushi, 148,* pp. 30–31.

Ralston, P. A. (1997). Midlife and older Black women. In J. M. Coyle (Ed.), *Handbook on women and aging* (pp. 273–289). Westport, CT: Greenwood Press.

Range, L. M. (2006). Women and suicide. In J. Worell & C. D. Good-heart (Eds.), *Handbook of girls' and women's psychological health: Gender and well-being across the life span* (pp. 129–136). New York: Oxford University Press.

Rankin, L. E., & Eagly, A. H. (2008). Is his heroism hailed and hers hidden? Women, men, and the social construction of heroism. *Psychology of Women Quarterly, 32,* 414–422.

Rapoza, K. A. (2004). The United States. In K. Malley-Morrison (Ed.), *International perspectives on family violence and abuse* (pp. 451–470). Mahwah, NJ: Erlbaum.

Raque-Bogdan, T. A., & Hoffman, M. L. (2015). The relationship among infertility, self-compassion, and well-being for women with primary or secondary infertility. *Psychology of Women Quarterly, 39,* 484-496.

Rastogi, M., & Wieling, E. (Eds.). (2005). *Voices of color: First-person accounts of ethnic minority therapists.* Thousand Oaks, CA: Sage.

Ratner, L. (2004). Failing low income students: Education and training in the age of reform. In V. Polakow, S. S. Butler, L. S. Deprez, & P. Kahn (Eds.), *Shut out: Low income mothers and higher education in post-welfare America* (pp. 45–74). Albany: State University of New York Press.

Rauer, A. J., & Volling, B. L. (2005). The role of husbands' and wives' emotional expressivity in the marital relationship. *Sex Roles, 52,* 577–587.

Rebick, J. (2005). *Ten thousand roses: The making of a feminist revolution.* Toronto: Penguin Canada.

Rederstorff, J. C, Buchanan, N. T., & Settles, I. H. (2007). The moderating roles of race and gender-role attitudes in the relationship between sexual harassment and psychological well-being. *Psychology of Women Quarterly, 31,* 50–61.

Reed, B. D. (2009). Dyspareunia and sexual/physical abuse. In A. Goldstein, C. Pukall, & I. Goldstein (Eds.), *Female sexual pain disorders* (pp. 213–217). Hoboken, NJ: Blackwell.

Reed, S. J., Miller, R. L., & Timm, T. (2011). Identity and agency: The meaning and value of pregnancy for young Black lesbians. *Psychology of Women Quarterly, 35,* 571-581.

Reese, H. (2021, March 17). *Backlash then, Backlash now.* JSTOR Daily. Retrieved October 5, 2021 from https://daily.jstor.org/backlash-then-backlash-now/

Regalado, Z. (2007). Pots and pans. A. Goldwasser (Ed.), *Red: The* next generation of American writers— teenage girls—on what fires up their lives today (pp. 62–65). New York: Hudson Street Press.

Regan, P. C, & Berscheid, E. (1997). Gender differences in characteristics desired in a potential sexual and marriage partner. *Journal of Psychology and Human Sexuality, 9, 25–37.*

Reid, P. T. (2000). Foreword. In L. C. Jackson & B. Greene (Eds.), *Psychotherapy with African American women* (pp. xiii–xv). New York: Guilford.

Reid, A., & Purcell, N. (2004). Pathways to feminist identification. *Sex Roles, 50, 759–769.*

Reid, P. T., Cooper, S. M., & Banks, K. H. (2008). Girls to women: Developmental theory, research, and issues. In F. L. Denmark & M. A. Paludi (Eds.), *Psychology of women: A handbook of issues and theories* (2nd ed., pp. 237–270). Westport, CT: Praeger.

Reilly, D., Neumann, D. L., & Andrews, G. (2019). Gender differences in reading and writing achievement: Evidence from the National Assessment of Educational Progress (NAEP). *American Psychologist, 74, 445-458.*

Reinharz, S., & Kulick, R. (2007). Feminist designs for difference. In S. N. Hesse-Biber (Ed.), *Handbook of feminist research: Theory and praxis* (pp. 257–275). Thousand Oaks, CA: Sage.

Reis, S. M. (1998). *Work left undone: Choices and compromises of talented females.* Mansfield Center, CT: Creative Learning Press.

Reis, H. T., & Aron, A. (2008). Love: What is it, why does it matter, and how does it operate? *Perspectives on Psychological Science, 3, 80–86.*

Reiser, C. (2001). *Reflections on anger: Women and men in a changing society.* Westport, CT: Praeger.

Reitzes, D. C., & Mutran, E. J. (2004). The transition to retirement: Stages and factors that influence retirement adjustment.

International Journal of Aging and Human Development, 59, 63–84.

Remillard, A. M., & Lamb, S. (2005). Adolescent girls' coping with relational aggression. *Sex Roles, 53, 221–229.*

Rensenbrink, C. W. (2001). *All in our places: Feminist challenges in elementary school classrooms.* Lanham, MD: Rowman & Littlefield.

Revenson, T. A. (2001). Chronic illness adjustment. In J. Worell (Ed.), *Encyclopedia of women and gender* (pp. 245–255). San Diego: Academic Press.

Rheingold, A. A., Acierno, R., & Resnick, H. S. (2004). Trauma, posttraumatic stress disorder, and health risk behaviors. In P. P. Schnurr & B. L. Green (Eds.), *Trauma and health: Physical health consequences of exposure to extreme stress* (pp. 217–243). Washington, DC: American Psychological Association.

Rhoades, K. A. (1999). Border zones: Identification, resistance, and transgressive teaching in introductory women's studies courses. In B. S. Winkler & C. DiPalma (Eds.), *Teaching introduction to women's studies* (pp. 61–71). Westport, CT: Bergin & Garvey.

Rhode, D. L. (1997). *Speaking of sex: The denial of gender inequality.* Cambridge, MA: Harvard University Press.

Rhode, D. L., & Williams, J. C. (2007). Legal perspectives on employment discrimination. In F. J. Crosby, M. S. Stockdale, & S. A. Ropp (Eds.), *Sex discrimination in the workplace* (pp. 235–270). Malden, MA: Blackwell.

Rhodes, G. (2006). The evolutionary psychology of facial beauty. *Annual Review of Psychology, 57, 199–226.*

Rhodes, J. E., Davis, A. A., Prescott, L. R., & Spencer, R. (2007). Caring connections: Mentoring relationships in the lives of urban girls. In B. J. R. Leadbeater & N. Way (Eds.), *Urban girls*

revisited: Building strengths (pp. 142–156). New York: New York University Press.

Ricciardelli, L. A., & McCabe, M. P. (2004). A biopsychosocial model of disordered eating and the pursuit of muscularity in adolescent boys. *Psychological Bulletin, 130, 179–205.*

Rice, J. K. (2001, Summer). Cross-cultural perspectives: Global divorce and the feminization of poverty. *International Psychology Reporter, 14–16.*

Rice, J. K., & Else-Quest, N. (2006). The mixed messages of motherhood. In J. Worell & C. Goodheart (Eds.), *Handbook of girls' and women's psychological health: Gender and well-being across the life span* (pp. 339–349). New York: Oxford University Press.

Rich, P., & Mervyn, F. (1999). *The healing journey through menopause.* New York: Wiley.

Richardson, D. S. (2005). The myth of female passivity: Thirty years of revelations about female aggression. *Psychology of Women Quarterly, 29, 238–247.*

Richardson, H. R. L., Beazley, R. P., Delaney, M. E., & Langille, D. B. (1997). Factors influencing condom use among students attending high school in Nova Scotia. *Canadian Journal of Human Sexuality, 6, 185–197.*

Rickabaugh, C. A. (1994). Just who is this guy, anyway? Stereotypes of the men's movement. *Sex Roles, 30, 459–470.*

Rickert, V. I., Wiemann, C. M., Vaughan, R. D., & White, J. W. (2004). Rates and risk factors for sexual violence among an ethnically diverse sample of adolescents. *Archives of Pediatric and Adolescent Medicine, 158, 1132–1139.*

Ridker, P. M., et al. (2005). A randomized trial of low-dose aspirin in the primary prevention of cardiovascular disease in women. *New England Journal of Medicine, 352, 1293–1304.*

Riger, S., Staggs, S. L., & Schewe, P. (2004). Intimate partner violence as an obstacle to employment among mothers affected by welfare reform. *Journal of Social Issues, 60,* 801–818.

Riggs, J. M. (2001). *Who's going to care for the children? College students' expectations for future employment and family roles.* Paper presented at the annual meeting of the Eastern Psychological Association.

Riggs, J. M. (2005). Impressions of mothers and fathers on the periphery of child care. *Psychology of Women Quarterly, 29,* 58–62.

Rimer, B. K., McBride, C., & Crump, C. (2001). Women's health promotion. In A. Baum, T. A. Revenson, & J. E. Singer (Eds.), *Handbook of health psychology* (pp. 519–539). Mahwah, NJ: Erlbaum.

Rinfret-Raynor, M., & Cantin, S. (1997). Feminist therapy for battered women. In G. K. Kantor & J. L. Jasinski (Eds.), *Out of the darkness: Contemporary perspectives on family violence* (pp. 219–234). Thousand Oaks, CA: Sage.

Rist, R. C. (2000). Author's introduction: The enduring dilemmas of class and color in American education. *Harvard Educational Review, 70,* 257–265.

Ritchie, A. (2017). *Invisible no more: Police violence against Black women and women of color.* Boston, MA: Beacon Press.

Rivero, A. J., Kaminski, P. L., & York, C. D. (2004, August). *Sex and gender differences in actual and perceived leader effectiveness: Self-and subordinate views.* Paper presented at the annual convention of the American Psychological Association, Honolulu, HI.

Robb-Nicholson, C. (2004, September). Screening for ovarian cancer. *Harvard Women's Health Watch, 5.*

Roberts, A., Cash, T. F., Feingold, A., & Johnson, B. T. (2006). Are Black-White differences in females' body dissatisfaction decreasing? A meta-analytic review. *Journal of Counseling and Clinical Psychology, 74,* 1121–1131.

Roberts, A. R. (2007). Overview and new directions for intervening on behalf of battered women. In A. R. Roberts (Ed.), *Battered women and their families* (3rd ed., pp. 3–31). New York: Springer.

Roberts, C. (2008). *Ladies of liberty: The women who shaped our nation.* New York: HarperCollins.

Roberts, J. E., & Bell, M. A. (2000). Sex differences on a computerized mental rotation task disappear with computer familiarization. *Perceptual and Motor Skills, 91*(3, Pt 2), 1027-1034.

Roberts, J. E., & Bell, M. A. (2003). Two- and three-dimensional mental rotation tasks lead to different parietal laterality for men and women. *International Journal of Psychophysiology, 50,* 235-246.

Roberts, M. C., et al. (2004). Family health through injury and violence prevention at home. In R. H. Rozensky, N. G. Johnson, C. D. Goodheart, & W. R. Hammond (Eds.), *Psychology builds a healthy world* (pp. 77–104). Washington, DC: American Psychological Association.

Roberts, T. (1991). Gender and the influence of evaluations on self-assessments in achievement settings. *Psychological Bulletin, 109,* 297–308.

Roberts, T., & Gettman, J. Y. (2004). Mere exposure: Gender differences in the negative effects of priming a state of self-objectification. *Sex Roles, 51,* 17–27.

Roberts, T., & Waters, P. L. (2004). Self-objectification and that "not so fresh feeling": Feminist therapeutic interventions for health female embodiment. *Women and Therapy, 27,* 5–21.

Roberts, T., Goldenberg, J. L., Power, C, & Pyszczynski, T. (2002). "Feminine protection": The effects of menstruation on attitudes toward women. *Psychology of Women Quarterly, 26,* 131–139.

Roberts, T., & Nolen-Hoeksema, S. (1989). Sex differences in reactions to evaluative feedback. *Sex Roles, 21,* 725–747.

Robertson, K., O'Connor, V., Hegarty, K., & Gunn, J. (2003). Women teaching women's health. In L. Manderson (Ed.), *Teaching gender, teaching women's health* (pp. 49–65). Binghamton, NY: Haworth.

Robin, L., & Hamner, K. (2000). Bisexuality: Identities and community. In V. A. Wall & N. J. Evans (Eds.), *Toward acceptance: Sexual orientation issues on campus* (pp. 245–259). Lanham, MD: American College Personnel Association.

Robinson, G. (2002). Cross-cultural perspectives on menopause. In A. E. Hunter & C. Forden (Eds.), *Readings in the psychology of gender* (pp. 140–149). Boston: Allyn & Bacon.

Robinson, G. E., & Stewart, D. S. (2001). Postpartum disorders. In N. L. Stotland & D. E. Stewart (Ed.), *Psychological aspects of women's health care* (pp. 117–139). Washington, DC: American Psychiatric Press.

Robinson, J. D., Skill, T., & Turner, J. W. (2004). Media usage patterns and portrayals of seniors. In J. F. Nussbaum & J. Coupland (Eds.), *Handbook of communication and aging research* (2nd ed., pp. 423–446). Mahwah, NJ: Erlbaum.

Robinson, M. D., & Johnson, J. T. (1997). Is it emotion or is it stress? Gender stereotypes and the perception of subjective experience. *Sex Roles, 36,* 235–258.

Rogers, L. (2001). *Sexing the brain.* New York: Columbia University Press.

Rogers, L. L. (2019). *Transitional housing programs and*

empowering survivors of domestic violence. United States Department of Justice Archives. Retrieved October 5, 2021 from https://www.justice.gov/archives /ovw/blog/transitional-housing -programs-and-empowering -survivors-domestic-violence

Rogers, N., & Henrich, J. (2003). Teaching women's health into the 21st century. In L. Manderson (Ed.), *Teaching gender, teaching women's health* (pp. 11–21). Binghamton, NY: Haworth.

Rogers, S. J. (1996). Mothers' work hours and marital quality: Variations by family structure and family size. *Journal of Marriage and the Family, 58,* 606–617.

Rogers, S. J., & DeBoer, D. D. (2001). Changes in wives' income: Effects on marital happiness, psychological well-being, and the risk of divorce. *Journal of Marriage and Family, 63,* 458–472.

Rogers, T. B., Kuiper, N. A., & Kirker, W. S. (1977). Self-reference and the encoding of personal information. *Journal of Personality and Social Psychology, 35,* 677–688.

Rogers, T. L., Emanuel, K., & Bradford, J. (2003). Sexual minorities seeking services: A retrospective study of the mental health concerns of lesbian and bisexual women. *Journal of Lesbian Studies, 7,* 127–146.

Rojas, M. (2009). *Women of color and feminism.* Berkeley, CA: Seal Press.

Romaine, S. (1999). *Communicating gender.* Mahwah, NJ: Erlbaum.

Romanow, R. J., & Marchildon, G. P. (2003). Psychological services and the future of health care in Canada. *Canadian Psychology /Psychologie canadienne, 44,* 283–295.

Roof, J. (2007). Authority and representation in feminist research. In S. N. Hesse-Biber (Ed.), *Handbook of feminist research: Theory and praxis* (pp. 425–442). Thousand Oaks, CA: Sage.

Root, M. P. P. (2005). Filipino families. In M. McGoldrick, J. Giordano, & N. Garcia-Preto (Eds.), *Ethnicity and family therapy* (3rd ed., pp. 269–289). New York: Guilford.

Rose, A. J & Rudolph, K. D. (2006). A review of sex differences in peer relationship processes: Potential trade-offs for the emotional and behavioral development of girls and boys. *Psychological Bulletin, 132,* 98–131.

Rose, S. (2000). Heterosexism and the study of women's romantic and friend relationships. *Journal of Social Issues, 56,* 315–328.

Rose, S. M. (2008). Crossing the color line in women's friendships. In J. C. Chrisler, C. Golden, & P. D. Rozee (Eds.), *Lectures on the psychology of women* (4th ed., pp. 300–321). Boston, MA: McGraw-Hill.

Rose, T. (2003). *Longing to tell: Black women talk about sexuality and intimacy.* New York: Farrar, Straus & Giroux.

Rosen, R. (2000). *The world split open: How the modern women's movement changed America.* New York: Viking.

Rosenbaum, A., & Kunkel, T. S. (2009). Group interventions for intimate partner violence. In K. D. O'Leary & E. M. Woodin (Eds.), *Psychological and physical aggressions in couples: Causes and interventions* (pp. 191–210). Washington, DC: American Psychological Association.

Rosenbaum, M. E., & Roos, G. M. (2000). Women's experiences of breast cancer. In A. S. Kasper & S. J. Ferguson (Eds.), *Breast cancer: Society shapes an epidemic* (pp. 153–181). New York: St. Martin's.

Rosenfeld, M. J. (2014). Couple longevity in the era of same-sex marriage in the U.S. *Journal of Marriage and Family, 76,* 905-918.

Rosenfield, A., Min, C. J., & Freedman, L. P. (2007). Making

motherhood safe in developing countries. *New England Journal of Medicine, 356,* 1395–1397.

Rosenthal, M. N., Smidt, A. M., & Freyd, J. J. (2016). Still second class: Sexual harassment of graduate students. *Psychology of Women Quarterly, 40,* 364-377.

Rosenthal, R. (1993). Interpersonal expectations: Some antecedents and some consequences. In P. D. Blank (Ed.), *Interpersonal expectations: Theory, research, and applications* (pp. 3–24). New York: Cambridge University Press.

Rosette, A. S., Mueller, J. S., & Lebel, R. D. (2015). Are male leaders penalized for seeking help? The influence of gender and asking behaviors on competence perceptions. *The Leadership Quarterly, 26,* 749-762.

Rostosky, S. S., & Travis, C. B. (2000). Menopause and sexuality: Ageism and sexism unite. In C. B. Travis & J. W. White (Eds.), *Sexuality, society, and feminism* (pp. 181–209). Washington, DC: American Psychological Association.

Roter, D. L., & Hall, J. A. (1997). Gender differences in patient-physician communication. In S. J. Gallant, G. P. Keita, & R. Royak-Schaler (Eds.), *Health care for women* (pp. 57–71). Washington, DC: American Psychological Association.

Roth, B. (2004). *Separate roads to feminism: Black, Chicana, and White feminist movements in America's second wave.* New York: Cambridge University Press.

Rothblum, E. D. (2000). Sexual orientation and sex in women's lives: Conceptual and methodological issues. *Journal of Social Issues, 56,* 193–204.

Rothblum, E. D., & Factor, R. (2001). Lesbians and their sisters as a control group. *Psychological Science, 12,* 63–69.

Rothblum, E., & Solovay, S. (Eds.). (2009). *The fat studies reader.*

New York: New York University Press.

Rousar, E. E., III, & Aron, A. (1990, July). *Valuing, altruism, and the concept of love*. Paper presented at the Fifth International Conference on Personal Relationships, Oxford, England.

Rouse, L. P. (2002). *Marital and sexual lifestyles in the United States*. Binghamton, NY: Haworth.

Rowe-Murray, H. J., & Fisher, J. R. W. (2002). Baby-friendly hospital practices: Cesarean section is a persistent barrier to early initiation of breastfeeding. *Birth, 29*, 124–131.

Royo-Vela, M., Aldás-Manzano, J., Küster-Boluda, I., & Vila-Lopez, N. (2007). Gender role portrayals and sexism in Spanish magazines. *Equal Opportunities International, 26*, 633–652.

Royo-Vela, M., Romero, M. J. M., & Giner, E. C. (2006, September). Advertising content as a socialization agent: Potential reinforcement of gender stereotypes. *ESIC Market*, 81–106.

Rozee, P. D. (2005). Rape resistance: Successes and challenges. In A. Barnes (Ed.), *The handbook of women, psychology, and the law* (pp. 265–279). San Francisco: Jossey-Bass.

Rozee, P. D. (2008). Women's fear of rape: Cause, consequences, and coping. In J. C. Chrisler, C. Golden, & P. D. Rozee (Eds.), *Lectures on the psychology of women* (4th ed., pp. 322–337). Boston: McGraw-Hill.

Rozee, P. D., Golden, C., & Chrisler, J. C. (2008). Introduction. In J. C. Chrisler, C. Golden, & P. D. Rozee (Eds.), *Lectures on the psychology of women* (4th ed., pp. viii-xiv). Boston, MA: McGraw-Hill.

Rubin, B. (2003). Every day a Sunday? Reflections on a first year of retirement. In N. Bauer-Maglin & A. Radosh (Eds.), *Women confronting retirement: A nontraditional guide* (pp. 187–200). New Brunswick, NJ: Rutgers University Press.

Ruble, D. N., & Martin, C. L. (1998). Gender development. In W. Damon (Series Ed.) & N. Eisenberg (Vol. Ed.), *Handbook of child psychology: Vol. 4. Social, emotional, and personality development* (pp. 933–1016). New York: Wiley.

Ruble, D. N., Martin, C. L., & Berenbaum, S. A. (2006). Gender development. In W. Damon & R. M. Lerner (Series Eds.), & N. Eisenberg (Vol. Ed.), *Handbook of child psychology: Vol. 3. Social, emotional, and personality development* (6th ed., pp. 858–952). Hoboken, NJ: Wiley.

Ruble, D. N., et al. (2004). The development of a sense of "we": The emergence and implications of children's collective identity. In M. Bennett & F. Sani (Eds.), *The development of the social self* (pp. 29–76). New York: Psychology Press.

Rudman, L. A., & Glick, P. (2008). *The social psychology of gender: How power and intimacy shape gender relations*. New York: Guilford.

Rudman, L. A., & Phelan, J. E. (2007). The interpersonal power of feminism: Is feminism good for romantic relationships? *Sex Roles, 57*, 787–799.

Ruffins, P. (2007, March 8). A real fear. *Diverse Issues in Higher Education*, pp. 17–19.

Runions, D. (1996). HIV/AIDS: A personal perspective. In L. D. Long & E. M. Ankrah (Eds.), *Women's experiences with HIV/AIDS* (pp. 56–72). New York: Columbia University Press.

Runkle, S. (2004). Manufactured beauties: India's integration into the global beauty industry. *Manushi*, Issue 143, pp. 14–24.

Runte, M. (1998). Women with disabilities: Alone on the playground. *Canadian Women Studies/Les cahiers de la femme, 18*, 101–105.

Rupp, R. E., Stanberry, L. R., & Rosenthal, S. L. (2005). Vaccines for sexually transmitted infections. *Pediatric Annals, 34*, 818–824.

Russell, B. L., & Trigg, K. Y. (2004). Tolerance of sexual harassment: An examination of gender differences, ambivalent sexism, social dominance, and gender roles. *Sex Roles, 50*, 565–573.

Russell-Brown, K. (2004). *Underground codes: Race, crime and related fires*. New York: New York University Press.

Russo, N. F. (2008a). Foreword. In R. B. Needle & L. E. A. Walker (Eds.), *Abortion counseling: A clinician's guide to psychology, legislation, politics, and competency* (pp. xiii–xxi). New York: Springer.

Russo, N. F. (2008b). Understanding emotional responses after abortion. In J. C. Chrisler, C. Golden, & P. D. Rozee (Eds.), *Lectures on the psychology of women* (4th ed., pp. 172–189). New York: Boston.

Russo, N. F., & Tartaro, J. (2008). Women and mental health. In F. L. Denmark & M. A. Paludi (Eds.), *Psychology of women: A handbook of issues and theories* (2nd ed., pp. 440–483). Westport, CT: Praeger.

Rust, P. C. (1996). Monogamy and polyamory: Relationship issues for bisexuals. In B. A. Firestein (Ed.), *Bisexuality: The psychology and politics of an invisible minority* (pp. 127–148). Thousand Oaks, CA: Sage.

Rust, P. C. (2000). Bisexuality: A contemporary paradox for women. *Journal of Social Issues, 56*, 205–221.

Ruth, S. (2001). *Issues in feminism: An introduction to women's studies* (5th ed.). Mountain View, CA: Mayfield.

Rutherford, A. (2007). Feminist questions, feminist answers: Toward a redefinition. *Feminism & Psychology, 17*, 459–464.

Rutherford, A., & Granek, L. (2010). Emergence and development of the psychology of women. In J. C. Chrisler & D. R. McCreary

(Eds.), *Handbook of gender research in psychology* (Vol. 1, pp. 19–41). New York: Springer.

Saad, L. (2015). *Children a key factor in women's desire to work outside the home.* Gallup. Retrieved October 3, 2021 from https://news.gallup.com/poll/186050/children-key-factor-women-desire-work-outside-home.aspx

Sabattini, L., & Leaper, C. (2004). The relation between mothers' and fathers' parenting styles and their division of labor in the home: Young adults' retrospective reports. *Sex Roles, 50,* 217–225.

Sabik, N. J., Cole, E. R., & Ward, L. M. (2010). Are all minority women equally buffered from negative body image? Intra-ethnic moderators of the buffering hypothesis. *Psychology of Women Quarterly, 34,* 139–151.

Sadker, D., Sadker, M., & Zittleman, K. R. (2009). *Still failing at fairness: How gender bias cheats girls and boys in school and what we can do about it.* New York, NY: Scribner.

Sadker, D. M., & Zittleman, K. (2007a). Practical strategies for detecting and correcting gender bias in your classroom. In D. M. Sadker & E. S. Silber (Eds.), *Gender in the classroom: Foundations, skills, methods, and strategies across the curriculum* (pp. 259–275). Mahwah, NJ: Erlbaum.

Sadker, D. M., & Zittleman, K. (2007b). The treatment of gender education in teacher education. In S. S. Klein (Ed.), *Handbook for achieving gender equity through education* (2nd ed., pp. 131–149). Mahwah, NJ: Erlbaum.

Sadker, M., & Sadker, D. (1994). *Failing at fairness: How America's schools cheat girls.* New York: Scribner's.

Sáez-Santiago, E., & Bernal, G. (2003). Depression in ethnic minorities. In G. Bernal, J. E. Trimble, A. K. Burlew, & F. T. L. Leong (Eds.), *Handbook of racial and ethnic minority psychology* (pp. 406–428). Thousand Oaks, CA: Sage.

Sagrestano, L. M., Rogers, A., & Service, A. (2008). HIV/AIDS. In B. A. Boyer & M. Indira Paharia (Eds.), *Comprehensive handbook of clinical health psychology* (pp. 201–228). Hoboken, NJ : Wiley.

Saguaro, S. (Ed.). (2000). *Psychoanalysis and woman: A reader.* New York: New York University Press.

Saldívar-Hull, S. (2000). *Feminism on the border.* Berkeley: University of California Press.

Saleh, S. (1972). Women in Islam: Their role in religious and traditional culture. *International Journal of Sociology and the Family, 2,* 193-201.

Salomon, K., Burgess, K. D., & Bosson, J. K. (2015). Flash fire and slow burn: Women's cardiovascular reactivity and recovery following hostile and benevolent sexism. *Journal of Experimental Psychology: General, 144,* 469–479.

Saluja, G., et al. (2004). Prevalence of and risk factors for depressive symptoms among young adolescents. *Archives of Pediatric and Adolescent Medicine, 158,* 760–765.

Sánchez, C. D. (2001). Puerto Rican elderly. In L. K. Olson (Ed.), *Age through ethnic lenses: Caring for the elderly in a multicultural society* (pp. 86–94). Lanham, MD: Rowman & Littlefield.

Sanchez, D. T., Crocker, J., & Boike, K. R. (2005). Doing gender in the bedroom: Investing in gender norms and the sexual experience. *Personality and Social Psychology Bulletin, 31,* 1445–1455.

Sanchez, D. T., Kiefer, A. K., & Ybarra, O. (2006). Sexual submissiveness in women: Costs for sexual autonomy and arousal. *Personality and Social Psychology Bulletin, 32,* 512–524.

Sanday, P. R. (2003). Rape-free versus rape-prone: How culture makes a difference. In C. B. Travis (Ed.), *Evolution, gender, and rape*

(pp. 337–361). Cambridge, MA: MIT Press.

Sandberg, D. (2019). *When women lead, firms win.* S&P Global. Retrieved October 3, 2021 from https://www.spglobal.com/_division_assets/images/special-editorial/iif-2019/whenwomenlead_.pdf

Sandnabba, N. K., & Ahlberg, C. (1999). Parents' attitudes and expectations about children's cross-gender behavior. *Sex Roles, 40,* 249–263.

Santelli, J. S., Kantor, L. M., Grilo, S. A., Speizer, I. S., Lindberg, L. D., Heitel, J., Schalet, A. T., Maureen E. Lyon, M. E., Mason-Jones, A. J., McGovern, T., Heck, C. J., Rogers, J. & Ott, M. A. (2017). Abstinence-only-until-marriage: An updated review of U.S. policies and programs and their impact. *Journal of Adolescent Health, 61,* 273-280.

Santoro, K. B. (1992). *Thoughts on being a mommy.* Interlaken, NY: Windswept Press.

Santoro, N. (2016). Perimenopause: From research to practice. *Journal of Women's Health, 25,* 332-339.

Saperstein, A. R. (2002). Racial & ethnic diversity. In E. M. Brody (Ed.), *Women in the middle* (2nd ed., pp. 274–286). New York: Springer.

Sarafino, E. P. (2008). *Health psychology: Biopsychosocial interactions* (6th ed.). Hoboken, NJ: Wiley.

Sardinha, L., & Nájera Catalán, H. (2018). Attitudes towards domestic violence in 49 low- and middle-income countries: A gendered analysis of prevalence and country-level correlates. *PLoS ONE 13*(10): e0206101.

Saris, R. N., & Johnston-Robledo, I. (2000). Poor women are still shut out of mainstream psychology. *Psychology of Women Quarterly, 24,* 233–235.

Sarkeesian, A., & Petit, C. (2019, June 14.) Female representation in videogames isn't getting any better. *Wired.* Retrieved September

28, 2001 from https://www
.wired.com/story/e3-2019-female
-representation-videogames/

Saules, K. K., et al. (2004). Relationship
of onset of cigarette smoking
during college to alcohol use, dieting concerns, and depressed mood.
Addictive Behaviors, 29, 893–899.

Saunders, S., & Mulligan, B. (2008,
September 25). The quest for
fair pay. *New York Teacher,* pp.
3, 16.

Savage, L. (2019). *Female offenders in
Canada, 2017.* Statistics Canada.
Retrieved October 3, 2021 from
https://www150.statcan.gc.ca
/n1/pub/85-002-x/2019001/article
/00001-eng.htm

Savic, I., Berglund, H., & Lindström,
P. (2005). Brain response to
putative pheromones in homo-
sexual men. *Proceedings of the
National Academy of Sciences
of the United States of America,
102,* 7356–7361.

Savin-Williams, R. C. (1998). The disclosure to families of same-sex attractions by lesbian, gay, and bisexual
youths. *Journal of Research on
Adolescence, 8,* 49–68.

Savin-Williams, R. C. (2001). *Mom,
Dad. I'm gay. How families
negotiate coming out.* Washington, DC: American Psychological
Association.

Savin-Williams, R. C. (2007). Girl-on-
girl sexuality. In B. J. R. Leadbeater & N. Way (Eds.), *Urban
girls revisited: Building strengths*
(pp. 301–318). New York: New
York University Press.

Savin-Williams, R. C, & Dubé, E. M.
(1998). Parental reactions to
their child's disclosure of a gay/
lesbian identity. *Family Relations, 47,* 7–13.

Savin-Williams, R. C, & Esterberg,
K. G. (2000). Lesbian, gay, and
bisexual families. In D. H. Demo,
K. R. Allen, & M. A. Fine (Eds.),
Handbook of family diversity
(pp. 197–215). New York:
Oxford University Press.

Sawyer, D. F. (1996). *Women and
religion in the first Christian centuries.* London: Routledge.

Sax, L. L., & Bryant, A. N. (2003,
November). *The impact of
college on sex-atypical career
choices of men and women.*
Paper presented at the annual
meeting of the Association for
the Study of Higher Education,
Portland, OR.

Sax, L. J., Bryant, A. N., & Gilmartin,
S. K. (2002, November). *A longitudinal investigation of emotional
health among male and female
first-year college students.* Paper
presented at the Annual Meeting
of the Association for the Study of
Higher Education, Sacramento, CA.

Scarborough, E., & Furumoto, L.
(1987). *Untold lives: The first
generation of American women
psychologists.* New York:
Columbia University Press.

Scarr, S. (1997). Rules of evidence: A
larger context for the statistical
debate. *Psychological Science, 8,*
16–17.

Schafer, E., Vogel, M. K., Veigas, S., &
Hausafus, C. (1998). Volunteer
peer counselors increase breastfeeding duration among rural
low-income women. *Birth, 25,*
101–106.

Schaller, M., & Conway, L. G., III
(2001). From cognition to culture: The origins of stereotypes
that really matter. In G. B. Moskowitz (Ed.), *Cognitive social
psychology* (pp. 163–176). Mahwah, NJ: Erlbaum.

Schank, J. C. (2006). Do human menstrual-cycle pheromones exist?
Human Nature, 17, 448–470.

Scharrer, E., Kim, D. D., Lin, K.-M., &
Liu, Z. (2006). Working hard or
hardly working? Gender, humor,
and the performance of domestic
chores in television commercials.
*Mass Communication & Society,
9,* 215–238.

Scher, C. D., Segal, Z. V., & Ingram,
R. E. (2004). Beck's theory
of depression. In R. L. Leahy
(Ed.), *Contemporary cognitive
therapy* (pp. 27–44). New York:
Guilford.

Schiffman, M., & Castle, P. E.
(2005). The promise of global

cervical-cancer prevention. *New
England Journal of Medicine,
353,* 2101–2104.

Schilt, K., & Westbrook, L. (2009).
Doing gender, doing heteronormativity: "Gender normals,"
transgender people, and the
social maintenance of heterosexuality. *Gender and Society, 23,*
440–464.

Schleiff, M. (2007). The "beautiful"
cause of death that had me dying
for a while. In A. Goldwasser
(Ed.), *Red: The next generation
of American writers—teenage
girls—on what fires up their lives
today* (pp. 31–36). New York:
Hudson Street Press.

Schlenker, J. A., Caron, S. L., &
Halteman, W. A. (1998). A feminist analysis of *Seventeen* magazine: Content analysis from 1945
to 1995. *Sex Roles, 38,* 135–149.

Schmader, T., Whitehead, J., & Wysocki,
V. H. (2007). A linguistic comparison of letters of recommendation
for male and female chemistry and
biochemistry job applicants. *Sex
Roles, 57,* 509–514.

Schmerling, R. H. (2016, February
19). Why men often die earlier
than women. *Harvard Health
Publishing.* Retrieved October 5,
2021 from https://www.health
.harvard.edu/blog/why-men
-often-die-earlier-than-women
-201602199137

Schmid Mast, M. (2005). The world
according to men: It is hierarchical and stereotypical. *Sex Roles,
53,* 919–924.

Schmid Mast, M., & Hall, J. A.
(2006). Women's advantage at
remembering others' appearance:
A systematic look at the why and
when of a gender difference. *Personality and Social Psychology
Bulletin, 32,* 353–364.

Schmid Mast, M., & Kadji, K.
(2018). How female and male
physicians' communication is
perceived differently. *Patient
Education and Counseling, 101,*
1697-1701.

Schmidt, U. (2002). Risk factors
for eating disorders. In

C. G. Fairburn & K. D. Brownell (Eds.), *Eating disorders and obesity: A comprehensive handbook* (2nd ed., pp. 247–250). New York: Guilford.

Schmitt, D. P. (2008). Attachment matters: Patterns of romantic attachment across gender, geography, and cultural forms. In J. P. Forgas & J. Fitness (Eds.), *Social relationships: Cognitive, affective, and motivational processes* (pp. 75–97). New York: Psychology Press.

Schmitt, M. T., Branscombe, N. R., Kobrynowicz, D., & Owen, S. (2002). Perceiving discrimination against one's gender group has different implications for well-being in women and men. *Personality and Social Psychology Bulletin, 28,* 197–210.

Schmookler, T., & Bursik, K. (2007). The value of monogamy in emerging adulthood: A gendered perspective. *Journal of Social and Personal Relationships, 24,* 819–835.

Schneider, D. J. (2004). *The psychology of stereotyping.* New York: Guilford.

Schneider, M. S. (2001). Toward a reconceptualization of the coming-out process for adolescent females. In A. R. D'Augelli & C. J. Patterson (Eds.), *Lesbian, gay, and bisexual identities and youth* (pp. 71–96). New York: Oxford University Press.

Schnurr, P. P., & Green, B. L. (2004). Understanding relationships among trauma, posttraumatic stress disorder, and health outcomes. In P. P. Schnurr & B. L. Green (Eds.), *Trauma and health: Physical health consequences of exposure to extreme stress* (pp. 247–275). Washington, DC: American Psychological Association.

Schur, L. (2004). Is there still a "double handicap"? Economic, social, and political disparities experienced by women with disabilities. In B. G. Smith & B. Hutchison (Eds.), *Gendering*

disability (pp. 253–271). New Brunswick, NJ: Rutgers University Press.

Schwartz, P. (1994). *Peer marriage: How love between equals really works.* New York: Free Press.

Schwartz, P. (2007). *Prime: Adventures and advice on sex, love, and the sensual years.* New York: HarperCollins.

Schwartz, P., & Rutter, V. (1998). *The gender of sexuality.* Thousand Oaks, CA: Pine Forge Press.

Schwartz, S. J., et al. (2010). Rethinking the concept of acculturation: Implications for theory and research. *American Psychologist, 65,* 237–251.

Schwebel, M. (2008). Peace activists: Maintaining morale. *Peace & Conflict, 14,* 215–223.

Scott, B. A. (2008). Women and pornography : What we don't know can hurt us. In J. C. Chrisler, C. Golden, & P. D. Rozee (Eds.), *Lectures on the psychology of women* (4th ed., pp. 338–355). Boston: McGraw-Hill.

Scott, J. A., Shaker, I., & Reid, M. (2004). Parental attitudes toward breastfeeding: Their association with feeding outcome at hospital discharge. *Birth, 31* , 125–131.

Sczesny, S. (2003). A closer look beneath the surface: Various facets of the think-manager-think-male stereotype. *Sex Roles, 49,* 353–363.

Seaman, B. (2003). *The greatest experiment ever performed on women: Exploding the estrogen myth.* New York: Hyperion.

Sechzer, J., & Rabinowitz, V. C. (2008). Feminist perspectives on research methods. In F. L. Denmark & M. A. Paludi (Eds.), *Psychology of women: A handbook of issues and theories* (2nd ed., pp. 93–141). Westport, CT: Praeger.

Sechzer, J. A. (2004). "Islam and woman: Where tradition meets modernity" : History and interpretations of Islamic women's status. *Sex Roles, 51,* 263–272.

Sedgh, G., Finer, L. B., Bankole, A., Eilers, M. A., & Singh, S. (2015).

Adolescent pregnancy, birth, and abortion rates across countries: Levels and recent trends. *Journal of Adolescent Health, 56,* 223-230.

Seely, M. (2007). *Fight like a girl: How to be a fearless feminist.* New York: NYU Press.

Seem, S. R., & Clark, M. D. (2006). Healthy women, healthy men, and healthy adults: An evaluation of gender role stereotypes in the twenty-first century. *Sex Roles, 55,* 247–258.

Seidman, G. W. (2007). *Beyond the boycott: Labor rights, human rights, and transnational activism.* New York: Russell Sage Foundation.

Senthilingam, M. (2017, November 29). *Sexual harassment: How it stands across the globe.* CNN. Retrieved October 5, 2021 from https://www.cnn .com/2017/11/25/health /sexual-harassment-violence -abuse-global-levels/index.html

Serbin, L. A., Poulin-Dubois, D., & Eichstedt, J. A. (2002). Infants' response to gender-inconsistent events. *Infancy, 3,* 531–542.

Settles, I. (2006). Use of an intersectional framework to understand Black women's racial and gender identities. *Sex Roles, 54,* 589–601.

Settles, I., Cortina, L. M., Malley, J., & Stewart, A. J. (2006). The climate for women in academic science: The good, the bad, and the changeable. *Psychology of Women Quarterly, 30,* 47–58.

Sewell, K. K., McGarrity, L. A., & Strassberg, D. S. (2017). Sexual behavior, definitions of sex, and the role of self-partner context among lesbian, gay, and bisexual adults. *The Journal of Sex Research, 54,* 825-831.

Sewell, K. K., & Strassberg, D. (2015). How do heterosexual undergraduate students define having sex? A new approach to an old question. *The Journal of Sex Research, 52,* 507-516.

Shapiro, A. F., Gottman, J. M., & Carrére, S. (2000). The baby and the marriage: Identifying factors that buffer against decline in marital satisfaction after the first baby arrives. *Journal of Family Psychology, 14,* 59–70.

Shapka, J. D., Domene, J. F., & Keating, D. P. (2008). Gender, mathematics achievement, and the educational and occupational aspirations of Canadian youth. In H. M. G. Watt & J. S. Eccles (Eds.), *Gender and occupational outcomes: Longitudinal assessments of individual, social, and cultural influences* (pp. 27–54). Washington, DC: American Psychological Association.

Shaywitz, B. A., et al. (1995). Sex differences in the functional organization of the brain for language. *Nature, 373,* 607–609.

Shaywitz, S. E., Shaywitz, B. A., Fletcher, J. M., & Escobar, M. D. (1990). Prevalence of reading disability in boys and girls. *Journal of the American Medical Association, 264,* 998–1002.

Sheldon, J. P. (2004). Gender stereotypes in educational software for young children. *Sex Roles, 51,* 433–444.

Sher, K. L., Grekin, E. R., & Williams, N. A. (2005). The development of alcohol use disorders. *Annual Review of Clinical Psychology, 1,* 493–523.

Sherman, J. W. (2001). The dynamic relationship between stereotype efficiency and mental representation. In G. B. Moskowitz (Ed.), *Cognitive social psychology* (pp. 177–190). Mahwah, NJ: Erlbaum.

Sherwin, B. B. (2001). Menopause: Myths and realities. In N. Stotland & D. E. Stewart (Eds.), *Psychological aspects of women's health care* (2nd ed., pp. 241–259). Washington, DC: American Psychiatric Press.

Shibusawa, R. (2005). Japanese families. In M. McGoldrick, J. Giordano, & N. Garcia-Preto (Eds.), *Ethnicity and family therapy* (3rd ed., pp. 339–348). New York: Guilford.

Shields, M. & Wilkins, K. (2009, September). An update on mammography use in Canada. *Statistics Canada, Catalogue no. 82-003-XPE Health Reports, 20*(3).

Shields, S. A. (2002). *Speaking from the heart: Gender and the social meaning of emotion.* New York: Cambridge University Press.

Shields, S. A. (2008). Gender: An intersectionality perspective. *Sex Roles, 59,* 301–311.

Shields, S. A., Schuberth, R. L., & Conrad, D. R. (2006). The women's studies Ph.D. in North America: Archive II. *NWSA Journal, 18,* 190–206.

Shifren, J., & Ferrari, N. A. (2004, May 10). A better sex life. *Newsweek,* pp. 86–89.

Shih, M., Pittinksy, T. L., & Ambady, N. (1999). Stereotype susceptibility: Identity salience and shifts in quantitative performance. *Psychological Science, 10,* 80–83.

Shih, M., & Sanchez, D. T. (2005). Perspectives and research on the positive and negative implications of having multiple racial identities. *Psychological Bulletin, 131*, 569–591.

Shimp, L., & Chartier, B. (1998, June). *Unacknowledged rape and sexual assault in a sample of university women.* Paper presented at the annual convention of the Canadian Psychological Association, Edmonton, Alberta.

Shulman, J. L., & Horne, S. G. (2003). The use of self-pleasure: Masturbation and body image among African American and European American women. *Psychology of Women Quarterly, 27,* 262–269.

Shute, R., Owens, L., & Slee, P. (2008). Everyday victimization of adolescent girls by boys: Sexual harassment, bullying or aggression? *Sex Roles, 58,* 477–489.

Siebers, T. (2008). *Disability theory.* Ann Arbor: University of Michigan Press.

Siegel, R. J. (2004). Ageism in psychiatric diagnosis. In P. J. Caplan & L. Cosgrove (Eds.), *Bias in psychiatric diagnosis* (pp. 89–97). Lanham, MD: Jason Aronson.

Siegel, R. J., Choldin, S., & Orost, J. H. (1995). The impact of three patriarchal religions on women. In J. C. Chrisler & A. H. Hemstreet (Eds.), *Variation on a theme: Diversity and the psychology of women* (pp. 107–144). Albany, NY: State University of New York Press.

Sieverding, J. A., Adler, N., With, S., & Ellen, J. (2005). The influence of parental monitoring on adolescent sexual initiation. *Archives of Pediatrics and Adolescent Medicine, 159,* 724–729.

Sigal, J., & Annan, V., Jr. (2008). Violence against women: International workplace sexual harassment and domestic violence. In F. L. Denmark & M. A. Paludi (Eds.), *Psychology of women: A handbook of issues and theories* (2nd ed., pp. 590–622). Westport, CT: Praeger.

Sigal, J. J., Perry, J. C., Rossignol, M., & Ouimet, M. C. (2003). Unwanted infants: Psychological and physical consequences of inadequate orphanage care 50 years later. *American Journal of Orthopsychiatry, 73,* 3–12.

Sigal, J., et al. (2005). Cross-cultural reactions to academic sexual harassment: Effects of individualist vs. collectivist culture and gender of participants. *Sex Roles, 52,* 201–215.

Sigmon, S. T., et al. (2005). Gender differences in self-reports of depression: The response bias hypothesis revisited. *Sex Roles, 53,* 401–411.

Sigmon, S. T., Dorhofer, D. M., et al. (2000). Psychophysiological, somatic, and affective changes across the menstrual cycle in women with panic disorder. *Journal of Consulting and Clinical Psychology, 68,* 425–431.

Sigmon, S. T., Rohan, K. J., et al. (2000). Menstrual reactivity: The role of gender specificity, anxiety sensitivity, and somatic concerns in self-reported menstrual distress. *Sex Roles, 43,* 143–161.

Signorella, M. L. (2020). Toward a more just feminism. *Psychology of Women Quarterly, 44,* 256-265.

Signorielli, N., & Lears, M. (1992). Children, television, and conceptions about chores: Attitudes and behaviors. *Sex Roles, 27,* 157–170.

Sigurvinsdottir, R., & Ullman, S. E. (2015). Social reactions, self-blame, and problem drinking in adult sexual assault survivors. *Psychology of Violence, 5,* 192-198.

Silbert, A., & Dubé, C. M. (2021). *The power gap among top earners at America's elite universities: 2021 study.* Eos Foundation. Retrieved September 28, 2021 from https://www .womenspowergap.org/wp -content/uploads/2021/02/WPG-Power-Gap-at-Elite -Universities-2021-Study-4.pdf

Silverstein, L. B., & Brooks, G. R. (2010). Gender issues in family therapy and couples counseling. In J. C. Chrisler & D. R. McCreary (Eds.), *Handbook of gender research in psychology* (Vol. 2, pp. 253–277). New York: Springer.

Simkin, P., et al. (2008). *Pregnancy, child birth and the newborn: The complete guide.* New York: Simon & Schuster.

Simon, R. W. (2008, Spring). The joys of parenthood, reconsidered. *Contexts,* pp. 40–45.

Simonson, K., & Subich, L. M. (1999). Rape perceptions as a function of gender-role traditionality and victim-perpetrator association. *Sex Roles, 40,* 617–634.

Sinacore, A. L., & Boatwright, K. J. (2005). The feminist classroom: Feminist strategies and student responses. In C. Z. Enns & A. L. Sinacore (Eds.), *Teaching and social justice: Integrating multicultural and feminist theories in the classroom* (pp. 109–124). Washington, DC: American Psychological Association.

Sincharoen, S., & Crosby, F. J. (2001). Affirmative action. In J. Worell (Ed.), *Encyclopedia of women and gender* (pp. 69–79). San Diego: Academic Press.

Singer, A. R., Cassin, S. E., & Dobson, K. S. (2005). The role of gender in the career aspirations of professional psychology graduates: Are there more similarities than differences? *Canadian Psychology/Psychologie canadienne, 46,* 215–222.

Singer, D. G., & Singer, J. L. (2001). Introduction: Why a handbook on children and the media? In D. G. Singer & J. L. Singer (Eds.), *Handbook on children and the media* (pp. xi–xvii). Thousand Oaks, CA: Sage.

Singh, A. A. (2010). Teaching social justice advocacy: Using the metaphor of a quilt. *Psychology of Women Quarterly, 34,* 550–553.

Singh, S., & Darroch, J. E. (2000). Adolescent pregnancy and child-bearing: Levels and trends in developed countries. *Family Planning Perspectives, 32,* 14–23.

Singh, S., Henshaw, S. K., & Brentsen, K. (2003). Abortion: A worldwide overview. In A. M. Basu (Ed.), *The sociocultural and political aspects of abortion: Global perspectives* (pp. 15–47). Westport, CT: Praeger.

Singh, B., Keaney, T., & Rossi, A. M. (2018). Male body contouring. *Journal of Drugs in Dermatology, 14,* 1052-1059.

Sirin, S. R., & Fine, M. (2007). Hyphenated selves: Muslim-American youth negotiating identities on the fault lines of global conflict. *Applied Developmental Science, 11,* 151–163.

Sirin, S. R., & Fine, M. (2008). *Muslim American youth: Understanding hyphenated identities through multiple methods.* New York: New York University Press.

Skevington, S. M. (2004). Pain and symptom perception. In A. Kaptein & J. Weinman (Eds.), *Health psychology* (pp. 182–206). Malden, MA: Blackwell.

Skinner, L. (1999). Personal communication.

Skrypnek, B. J., & Snyder, M. (1982). On the self-perpetuating nature of stereotypes about women and men. *Journal of Experimental Social Psychology, 18,* 277–291.

Skucha, J., & Bernard, M. (2000). "Women's work" and the transition to retirement. In M. Bernard, J. Phillips, L. Machin, & V. H. Davies (Eds.), *Women ageing: Changing identities, challenging myths* (pp. 23–39). London: Routledge.

Slater, L., Henderson-Daniel, J., & Banks, A. E. (2003). *The complete guide to mental health for women.* Boston: Beacon Press.

Slevic, J., & Tiggemann, M. (2010). Attitudes toward cosmetic surgery in middle-aged women: Body image, aging anxiety, and the media. *Psychology of Women Quarterly, 34,* 65-74.

Slusser, W. M., & Lange, L. (2002). Breastfeeding in the United States today: Are families prepared? In N. Halfon, K. T. McLearn, & M. A. Schuster (Eds.), *Child rearing in America: Challenges facing parents with young children* (pp. 178–216). New York: Cambridge University Press.

Smallman, S. (2008, July/August). A case for guarded optimism: HIV/AIDS in Latin America. *NACLA Report on the Americas,* 14–19.

Smecker, F. J. (2009). *Health care, not assimilation: American Indians and Alaskan Natives in the wake of health care reform.* Retrieved November 14, 2009, from http:// www.truthout.org/1114096

Smetana, J. G., Campione-Barr, N., & Metzger, A. (2006). Adolescent development in interpersonal and societal contexts. *Annual Review of Psychology, 57,* 255–284.

Smetana, J. G., Daddis, C, & Chuang, S. S. (2003). "Clean your room!" A longitudinal investigation of adolescent-parent conflict and conflict resolution in middle-class African American families. *Journal of Adolescent Research, 18*, 631–650.

Smiler, A., & Kilmartin, C. (2019). *The masculine self* (6th ed.). Cornwall-on-Hudson, NY: Sloan.

Smith, A. (2021). *U.S. House of Representatives passes paycheck fairness act*. Society for Human Resource Management. Retrieved October 3, 2021 from https://www.shrm.org/resource-sandtools/legal-and-compliance/employment-law/pages/house-passes-paycheck-fairness-act-2021.aspx

Smith, A. (2011). Against the law: Indigenous feminism and the nation-state. In G. Coulthard, J. Lasky, A. Lewis, and V. Watts (Eds.). *Affinities: A Journal of Radical Theory, Culture, and Action 5*(1). Special Issue on Anarch@Indigenism, 56-69.

Smith, B. G. (2004). Introduction. In B. G. Smith & B. Hutchison (Eds.), *Gendering disability* (pp. 1–7). New Brunswick, NJ: Rutgers University Press.

Smith, B. G., & Hutchison, B. (Eds.). (2004). *Gendering disability*. New Brunswick, NJ: Rutgers University Press.

Smith, C. A. (2008). Women, weight, and body image. In J. C. Chrisler, C. Golden, & P. D. Rozee (Eds.), *Lectures on the psychology of women* (4th ed., pp. 116–135). Boston: McGraw-Hill.

Smith, C. A., & Stillman, S. (2002). What do women want? The effects of gender and sexual orientation on the desirability of physical attributes in the personal ads of women. *Sex Roles, 46*, 337–342.

Smith, C. J., Noll, J. A., & Bryant, J. B. (1999). The effect of social context on gender self-concept. *Sex Roles, 40*, 499–512.

Smith, G. J. (1985). Facial and full-length ratings of attractiveness related to the social interactions

of young children. *Sex Roles, 12*, 287–293.

Smith, J. L. (2004). Understanding the process of stereotype threat: A review of mediational variables and new performance goal directions. *Educational Psychology Review, 16*, 177–206.

Smith, J. L., & Johnson, C. S. (2006). A stereotype boost or choking under pressure? Positive gender stereotypes and men who are low in domain identification. *Basic and Applied Social Psychology, 28*, 51–63.

Smith, J. L., Morgan, C. L., & White, P. H. (2005). Investigating a measure of computer technology domain identification: A tool for understanding gender differences and stereotypes. *Educational and Psychological Measurement, 65*, 336–355.

Smith, J. L., Samsone, C, & White, P. H. (2007). The stereotyped task engagement process: The role of interest and achievement motivation. *Journal of Educational Psychology, 99*, 99–114.

Smith, L. (2005). Psychotherapy, classism, and the poor: Conspicuous by their absence. *American Psychologist, 60*, 687–696.

Smith, P. K., & Drew, L. M. (2002). Grandparenthood. In M. H. Bornstein (Ed.), *Handbook of parenting* (2nd ed., Vol. 3, pp. 141–172). Mahwah, NJ: Erlbaum.

Smith, P., Wilhelm, D., & Rodgers, R. J. (2014). Development of mammalian ovary. *Journal of Endocrinology, 221*, R145-R161.

Smith, S. D. (2004). Sexually underrepresented youth: Understanding gay, lesbian, bisexual, transgendered, and questioning (GLBT-Q) youth. In J. L. Chin (Ed.), *The psychology of prejudice and discrimination* (Vol. 3, pp. 151–199). Westport, CT: Praeger.

Smith, S. E., & Huston, T. L. (2004). How and why marriages change over time: Shifting patterns of companionship. In R. D. Conger,

F. O. Lorenz, & K. A. S. Wickrama (Eds.), *Continuity and change in family relationships* (pp. 145–180). Mahwah, NJ: Erlbaum.

Smithsonian Institute. (2007). *Do all Indians live in tipis? Questions & answers from the National Museum of the American Indian*. New York: HarperCollins.

Smock, P. J & Gupta, S. (2002). Cohabitation in contemporary North America. In A. Booth & A. C. Crouter (Eds.), *Just living together* (pp. 53–84). Mahwah, NJ: Erlbaum.

Smolak, L. (2006). Body image. In J. Worell & C. D. Goodheart (Eds.), *Handbook of girls' and women's psychological health: Gender and well-being across the life span* (pp. 69–76). New York: Oxford University Press.

Sneed, J. R., & Whitbourne, S. K. (2005). Models of the aging self. *Journal of Social Issues, 61*, 375–388.

Snowden, L. R., Masland, M., & Guerrero, R. (2007). Federal civil rights policy and mental health treatment access for persons with limited English proficiency. *American Psychologist, 67*, 109–117.

Snowden, L. R., & Yamada, A. (2005). Cultural differences in access to care. *Annual Review of Clinical Psychology, 1*, 143–166.

Society for the Psychological Study of Men and Masculinity. (2010). *Mission statement*. Retrieved September 6, 2010, from http://www.apa.org/divisions/div51/aboutus/mission. htm

Society for Women's Health Research. (2020). *Homepage*. Retrieved October 5, 2021 from https://swhr.org/

Soet, J. E., Brack, G. A., & Dilorio, C. (2003). Prevalence and predictors of women's experience of psychological trauma during child birth. *Birth, 30*, 36–46.

Sohn, A. (2005, January 3). Obstacle course. *New York Magazine*, p. 58.

Solheim, B. O. (2000). *On top of the world: Women's political leadership in Scandinavia and beyond.* West-port, CT: Greenwood Press.

Solomon, C. G., & Dluhy, R. G. (2003). Rethinking postmenopausal hormone therapy. *New England Journal of Medicine, 348,* 579–580.

Sommer, B., et al. (1999). Attitudes toward menopause and aging across ethnic/racial groups. *Psychosomatic Medicine, 61,* 868–875.

Sommer, I. E. C., Aleman, A., Bouma, A., & Kahn, R. S. (2004). Do women really have more bilateral language representation than men? A meta-analysis of functional imaging studies. *Brain, 127,* 1845–1852.

Sommer, M., Hirsch, J. S., Nathanson, C., & Parker, R. G. (2015). Comfortably, safely, and without shame: Defining menstrual hygiene management as a public health issue. *American Journal of Public Health, 105,* 1302-1311.

Song, H. (2001). The mother-daughter relationship as a resource for Korean women's career aspirations. *Sex Roles, 44,* 79–97.

Sonnenblick, E. B., Shah, A. D., Goldstein, Z., & Reisman, T. (2018). Breast imaging of transgender individuals: A review. *Current Radiology Reports, 6*(1), 1.

Spates, K. (2012). "The missing link": The exclusion of Black women in psychological research and the implications for Black women's mental health. *SAGE Open,* July-September 2012: 1-8.

Spencer, J. M., Zimet, G. G., Aalsma, M. C., & Orr, D. P. (2002). Self-esteem as a predictor of initiation of coitus in early adolescents. *Pediatrics, 109,* 581–584.

Spencer, M. L., Inoue, Y., & McField, G. P. (2007). Achieving gender equity for Asian and Pacific Islander Americans. In S. S. Klein (Ed.), *Handbook for achieving gender equity through education* (2nd ed., pp. 501–524). Mahwah, NJ: Erlbaum.

Spiegel, A. (2005, January 3). The dictionary of disorder. *New Yorker,* 56–63.

Spiggle, T. (2020, June 17). The supreme court rules that federal law protects LGBTQ+ workers from discrimination. *Forbes Magazine.* Retrieved October 5, 2021 from https://www.forbes .com/sites/tomspiggle/2020/06/17 /the-supreme-court-rules-that -federal-law-protects-lgbtq -workers-from-discrimination /?sh=119c4fb59850

Spira, J. L., & Reed, G. M. (2003). *Group psychotherapy for women with breast cancer.* Washington, DC: American Psychological Association.

Sprague, J., & Massoni, K. (2005). Student evaluations and gendered expectations: What we can't count can hurt us. *Sex Roles, 53,* 779–793.

Sprecher, S. (2006). Sexuality in close relationships. In P. Noller & J. A. Feeney (Eds.), *Close relationships: Functions, forms, and processes* (pp. 267–284). New York: Psychology Press.

Sprecher, S., & Sedikides, C. (1993). Gender differences in perceptions of emotionality: The case of close heterosexual relationships. *Sex Roles, 28,* 511–530.

Sprimont, D. (2020, April 8). Prenatal care in developing countries. *Borgen Magazine.* Retrieved October 4, 2021 from https:// www.borgenmagazine.com /prenatal-care-in-developing -countries/

Springen, K. (2004, May 10). Women, cigarettes and death. *Newsweek,* p. 69.

Springen, K., & Kantrowitz, B. (2004, May 10). Alcohol's deadly triple threat. *Newsweek,* pp. 90–92.

Springer, K. W., & Mouzon, D. M. (2011). "Macho men" and preventive health care: Implications for older men in different social classes. *Journal of Health and Social Behavior, 52,* 212-227.

Stacey, J. (2000). The handbook's tail: Toward revels or a requiem for family diversity? In D. H. Demo, K. R. Allen, & M. A. Fine (Eds.), *Handbook of family diversity* (pp. 424–439). New York: Oxford University Press.

Stacey, J., & Biblarz, T. J. (2001). (How) does the sexual orientation of parents matter? *American Sociological Review, 66,* 159–183.

Stahly, G. B. (2008). Battered women: Why don't they just leave? In J. C. Chrisler, C. Golden, & P. D. Rozee (Eds.), *Lectures on the psychology of women* (4th ed., pp. 356–375). Boston: McGraw-Hill.

Stake, J. E. (2003). Understanding male bias against girls and women in science. *Journal of Applied Social Psychology, 33,* 667–682.

Stake, J. E. (2007). Predictors of change in feminist activism through women's and gender studies. *Sex Roles, 57,* 43–54.

Stake, J. E., & Hoffmann, F. L. (2000). Putting feminist pedagogy to the test. *Psychology of Women Quarterly, 24,* 30–38.

Stake, J. E., & Hoffmann, F. L. (2001). Changes in student social attitudes, activism, and personal confidence in higher education: The role of women's studies. *American Educational Research Journal, 38,* 411–436.

Stake, J. E., & Malkin, C. (2003). Students' quality of experience and perceptions of intolerance and bias in the women's and gender studies classroom. *Psychology of Women Quarterly, 27,* 174–185.

Stake, J. E., & Nickens, S. D. (2005). Adolescent girls' and boys' science peer relationships and perceptions of the possible self as scientist. *Sex Roles, 52,* 1–11.

Stankiewicz, J. M., & Rosselli, F. (2008). Women as sex objects and victims in print advertisements. *Sex Roles, 58,* 579–589.

Stanton, A. L., & Courtenay, W. (2004). Gender, stress, and health. In R. H. Rozensky, N. G. Johnson, C. D. Goodheart, & W.

R. Hammond (Eds.), *Psychology builds a healthy world* (pp. 105–135). Washington, DC: American Psychological Association.

Stanton, A. L., Lobel, M., Sears, S., & DeLuca, R. S. (2002). Psychosocial aspects of selected issues in women's reproductive health: Current status and future directions. *Journal of Consulting and Clinical Psychology, 70,* 751–770.

Stanton, A. L., Revenson, T. A., & Tennen, H. (2007). Health psychology: Psychological adjustment to chronic disease. *Annual Review of Psychology, 58,* 565–592.

Stark, E. (2009). *Coercive control: How men entrap women in personal life.* New York: Oxford University Press.

Stark, E., & Buzawa, E. S. (Eds.). (2009). *Violence against women in families and relationships* (Volumes 1–4). Santa Barbara, CA: ABC-CLIO.

Starr, T. (1991). *The "natural inferiority" of women: Outrageous pronouncements by misguided males.* New York: Poseidon Press.

Statista. (2019). *Women in selected national parliaments (lower or upper houses) as of December 2019.* [Data Set]. https://www .statista.com/statistics/267028 /women-in-selected-national -parliaments/

Statistics Canada. (2000). *Women in Canada 2000: A gender-based statistical report.* Ottawa, Ontario, Canada: Author.

Statistics Canada. (2004). *Women in Canada: Work chapter updates 2003* (Catalogue no. 89F0133XIE). Ottawa, Ontario, Canada: Author.

Statistics Canada (2005). *2001 Census: Standard data products.* Retrieved May 3, 2005, from http://www12.statcan.ca/english /census01/ products/

Statistics Canada. (2006). *Women in Canada: A gender-based statistical report.* (5th ed.). Ottawa:

Author. Retrieved October 5, 2021 from http://www.statcan .gc.ca/pub/89-503-x/89-503 -x2005001-eng.pdf

Statistics Canada. (2010b). *Canada's population estimates: Age and sex.* Retrieved February 17, 2010, from http://www.statcan .gc.ca/daily-quo-tidien/091127 /t091127b2-eng.htm

Statistics Canada (2010d). *Population by marital status and sex.* Retrieved December 10, 2010, from http:// www40.statcan.ca /l01/cst01/ famil01-eng.htm

Statistics Canada. (2016). Education in Canada: Key results from the 2016 Census. Retrieved October 3, 2021 from https:// www150.statcan.gc.ca /n1/daily-quotidien/171129 /dq171129a-eng.htm

Statistics Canada. (2016). *Same-sex couples in Canada in 2016.* Statistics Canada. Retrieved October 4, 2021 from https:// www12.statcan.gc.ca/census -recensement/2016/as-sa/98-200 -x/2016007/98-200-x2016007 -eng.cfm

Statistics Canada. (2017). *Immigration and ethnocultural diversity: Key results from the 2016 census.* Statistics Canada. Retrieved October 5, 2021 from https://www150.statcan.gc.ca/ n1/daily-quotidien/171025 /dq171025b-eng.htm?indid =14428-3&indgeo=0

Statistics Canada. (2020). *Population estimates on July 1st, by age and sex.* Table 17-10-0005-01. Retrieved October 5, 2021 from https://www150 .statcan.gc.ca/t1/tbl1/en/ tv.action?pid=1710000501

Statistics Canada. (2021). *Family violence in Canada: A statistical profile, 2019.* Retrieved October 5, 2021 from https://www150 .statcan.gc.ca/n1/en/daily -quotidien/210302/dq210302d -eng.pdf?st=a_KGpUZL

Stayton, W. R., Haffner, D. W., & McNiff, S. S. (2008). Sexuality and reproductive health of men

and women. In B. A. Boyer & M. I. Paharia (Eds.), *Comprehensive handbook of clinical health psychology* (pp. 425–451). Hoboken, NJ: Wiley.

Steele, C. M. (1997). A threat in the air: How stereotypes shape intellectual identity and performance. *American Psychologist, 52,* 613–629.

Steele, C. M., Spencer, S. J., & Aronson, J. (2002). Contending with group image: The psychology of stereotype and social identity threat. *Advances in Experimental Social Psychology, 34,* 379–440.

Steele, J., James, J. B., & Barnett, R. C. (2002). Learning in a man's world: Examining the perceptions of undergraduate women in male-dominated academic areas. *Psychology of Women Quarterly, 26,* 46–50.

Steil, J. M. (2000). Contemporary marriage: Still an unequal partnership. In C. Hendrick & S. S. Hendrick (Eds.), *Close relationships: A sourcebook* (pp. 125–136). Thousand Oaks, CA: Sage.

Steil, J. M. (2001a). Family forms and member well-being: A research agenda for the decade of behavior. *Psychology of Women Quarterly, 25,* 344–363.

Steil, J. M. (2001b). Marriage: Still "his" and "hers"? In J. Worell (Ed.), *Encyclopedia of women and gender* (pp. 677–686). San Diego: Academic Press.

Steinberg, J. R., True, M., & Russo, N. F. (2008). Work and family roles: Selected issues. In F. L. Denmark & M. A. Paludi (Eds.), *Psychology of women: A handbook of issues and theories* (2nd ed., pp. 652–700). Westport, CT: Praeger.

Steinpreis, R. H., Anders, K. A., & Ritzke, D. (1999). The impact of gender on the review of the curricula vitae of job applicants and tenure candidates: A national empirical study. *Sex Roles, 41,* 509–528.

Stemple, L., & Meyer, I. H. (2014). The sexual victimization of men in America: New data challenge old assumptions. *American Journal of Public Health, 104,* e19–e26.

Stephenson, J. (2000). *Women's roots: The history of women in Western civilization* (5th ed.). Fullerton, CA: Diemer, Smith Publishing.

Steptoe, A., & Wardle, J. (2004). Health-related behaviour: Prevalence and links with disease. In A. Kaptein & J. Weinman (Eds.), *Health psychology* (pp. 22–51). Malden, MA: Blackwell.

Stern, J. (2010). *Denial.* New York: HarperCollins.

Stern, M., & Karraker, M. K. (1989). Sex stereotyping of infants: A review of gender labeling studies. *Sex Roles, 20,* 501–522.

Sternberg, R. J. (1998). *Cupid's arrow: The course of love through time.* New York: Cambridge University Press.

Stevens, A. (2008, July 3). Single moms' poverty spikes after welfare overhaul. Retrieved June 26, 2009, from http://www.truthout.org/docs

Stevens, T., Wang, K., Olivárez. A., Jr., & Hamman, D. (2007). Use of self-perspectives and their sources to predict the mathematics enrollment intentions of girls and boys. *Sex Roles, 56,* 351–363.

Stevenson, J. (2021, January 17). *Canada has 29th highest divorce rate out of 87 countries: Survey.* Toronto Sun. Retrieved October 4, 2021 from https://torontosun.com/news/national/canadas-divorce-rate-29th-out-of-87-countries-survey

Stewart, A. J., & Dottolo, A. L. (2006). Feminist psychology. *Signs, 31,* 493–509.

Stewart, A. J., & LaVaque-Manty, D. (2008). Advancing women faculty in science and engineering: An effort in institutional transformation. In H. M. G. Watt & J. S. Eccles (Eds.), *Gender and occupational outcomes: Longitudinal assessments of individual, social, and cultural influences* (pp. 299–322). Washington, DC: American Psychological Association.

Stewart, A. J., & McDermott, C. (2004). Gender in psychology. *Annual Review of Psychology, 55,* 519–544.

Stewart, A. J., & Newton, N. J. (2010). Gender, adult development, and aging. In J. C. Chrisler & D. R. McCreary (Eds.), *Handbook of gender research in psychology* (Vol. 1, pp. 559–580). New York: Springer.

Stewart, A. J., Ostrove, J. M., & Helson, R. (2001). Middle aging in women: Patterns of personality change from the 30s to the 50s. *Journal of Adult Development, 8,* 23–37.

Stewart, A. J., & Vandewater, E. A. (1999). "If I had it to do over again": Midlife review, midcourse corrections, and women's well-being in midlife. *Journal of Personality and Social Psychology, 76,* 270–283.

Stewart, N. A. (2007, Spring). Transform the world. *Ms. Magazine,* pp. 65–66.

Stewart, S., & Jambunathan, J. (1996). Hmong women and postpartum depression. *Health Care for Women International, 17,* 319–330.

Stewart, T. L., & Vassar, P. M. (2000). The effect of occupational status cues on memory for male and female targets. *Psychology of Women Quarterly, 24,* 161–169.

Stewart, T. L., Vassar, P. M., Sanchez, D. T., & David, S. E. (2000). Attitude toward women's societal roles moderates the effect of gender cues on target individuation. *Journal of Personality and Social Psychology, 79,* 143–157.

Stiawa, M., Müller-Stierlin, A., Staiger, T. *et al.* (2020). Mental health professionals view about the impact of male gender for the treatment of men with depression - a qualitative study. *BMC Psychiatry, 20,* 276.

Stice, E. (2002). Risk and maintenance factors for eating pathology: A meta-analytic review. *Psychological Bulletin, 128,* 825–848.

Stice, E., Shaw, H., & Marti, C. N. (2006). A meta-analytic review of obesity prevention programs for children and adolescents: The skinny on interventions that work. *Psychological Bulletin, 132,* 667–681.

Stolzenberg, E. B., Aragon, M. C., Romo, E., Couch, V., McLennan, D., Eagan, M. K., & Kang, N. (2020). *The American Freshman: National Norms Fall 2019.* Higher Education Research Institute, Los Angeles, UCLA.

Stone, P. (2007). *Opting out? Why women really quit careers and head home.* Berkeley, CA: University of California Press.

Straus, M. A. (2005). Women's violence toward men is a serious social problem. In D. R. Loseke, R. J. Gelles, & M. M. Cavanaugh (Eds.), *Current controversies on family violence* (2nd ed., pp. 55–77). Thousand Oaks, CA: Sage.

Straus, M. B. (2007). *Girls in crisis: Intervention and hope.* New York: Norton.

Strauss, S. (2003). Sexual harassment in K-12. In M. A. Paludi & C. A. Paludi (Eds.), *Academic and workplace sexual harassment* (pp. 175–198). Westport, CT: Praeger.

Strebeigh, F. (2009). *Taking inequality to court.* New York: W. W. Norton.

Street, D. A. (2007). Sociological approaches to understanding age and aging. In J. A. Blackburn & C. N. Dulmus (Eds.), *Handbook of gerontology: Evidence-based approaches to theory, practice, and policy* (pp. 143–168). Hoboken, NJ: Wiley.

Street, S., Kimmel, E. B., & Kromrey, J. D. (1995). Revisiting university student gender role perceptions. *Sex Roles, 33,* 183–201.

Streissguth, A. P., et al. (1999). The long-term neurocognitive consequences of prenatal alcohol exposure: A 14-year study. *Psychological Science, 10,* 186–190.

Stringhini, S., et al. (2017). Socioeconomic status and the 25 × 25 risk factors as determinants of premature mortality: A multicohort study and meta-analysis of 1.7 million men and women. *The Lancet, 389,* 1229-1237.

Strober, M. H. (2003). Rethinking economics through a feminist lens. In E. Mutari & D. M. Figart (Eds.), *Women and the economy* (pp. 5–12). Armonk, NY: M. E. Sharpe.

Stroebe, M., Schut, H., & Stroebe, W. (2005). Attachment in coping with bereavement: A theoretical integration. *Review of General Psychology, 9,* 48–66.

Stromquist, N. P. (2007). Gender equity education globally. In S. S. Klein (Ed.), *Handbook for achieving gender equity through education* (2nd ed., pp. 33–42). Mahwah, NJ: Erlbaum.

Strouse, J. (1999, August 16). She got game. *New Yorker,* pp. 36–40.

Subrahmanyam, K., Greenfield, P. M., Kraut, R., & Gross, E. (2002). The impact of computer use on children's and adolescents' development. In S. L. Calvert, A. B. Jordan, & R. R. Cocking (Eds.), *Children in the digital age: Influence of electronic media on development* (pp. 3–33). Westport, CT: Praeger.

Substance Abuse and Mental Health Services Administration. (2019). *Key substance use and mental health indicators in the United States: Results from the 2018 National Survey on Drug Use and Health.* HHS Publication No. PEP19-5068, NSDUH Series H-54. Rockville, MD: Center for Behavioral Health Statistics and Quality, Substance Abuse and Mental Health Services Administration.

Such, E. (2006). Leisure and fatherhood in dual-earner families. *Leisure Studies, 25,* 185–199.

Sue, D. W. (2004). Whiteness and ethnocentric monoculturalism:

Making the " invisible" visible. *American Psychologist, 59,* 761–769.

Sue, D. W. (2010). Microaggressions in everyday life: *Race, gender, and sexual orientation.* Hoboken, NJ: Wiley.

Sue, D. W., & Sue, D. (2003). *Counseling the culturally diverse: Theory and practice* (4th ed.). New York: Wiley.

Sue, D. W., et al. (2007). Racial microaggressions in everyday life: Implications for clinical practice. *American Psychologist, 62,* 271–286.

Sue, S., Zane, N. H., Hall, G. C. N., & Berger, L. K. (2009). The case for cultural competency in psychotherapeutic interventions. *Annual Review of Psychology, 60,* 525–548.

Sugar, J. A. (2007). Work and retirement: Challenges and opportunities for women over 50. Body image issues of women over 50. In V. Muhlbauer & C. J. Chrisler (Eds.), *Women over 50: Psychological perspectives* (pp. 164–181). New York: Springer.

Sullivan, C. M. (2006). Interventions to address intimate partner violence: The current state of the field. In J. R. Lutzker (Ed.), *Preventing violence: Research and evidence-based intervention strategies* (pp. 195–212). Washington, DC: American Psychological Association.

Sullivan, E. (2018, February 5). *Doritos, for her.* NPR. Retrieved September 28, 2021 from https://www.npr.org/sections/thetwo-way/2018/02/05/583399141/doritos-for-her

Sullivan, M. (2004). *The family of woman: Lesbian mothers, their children, and the undoing of gender.* Berkeley: University of California Press.

Sullivan, P. F. (2002). Course and outcome of anorexia nervosa and bulimia nervosa. In C. G. Fairburn & K. D. Brownell (Eds.), *Eating disorders and obesity: A comprehensive handbook*

(2nd ed., pp. 226–230). New York: Guilford.

Summers-Effler, E. (2004). Little girls in women's bodies: Social interaction and the strategizing of early breast development. *Sex Roles, 51,* 29–44.

Sunseri, L. (2008, Winter/Spring). Sky woman lives on: Contemporary examples of mothering the nation. *Canadian Woman Studies/Les cahiers de la femme, 26,* 21–30.

Surra, C. A., Gray, C. R,, Cottle, N., & Boettcher, T. M. J. (2004). Research on mate selection and premarital relationships: What do we really know? In A. L. Vangelisti (Ed.), *Handbook of family communication* (pp. 53–82). Mahwah, NJ: Erlbaum.

Susskind, J. E. (2003). Children's perception of gender-based illusory correlations: Enhancing preexisting relationships between gender and behavior. *Sex Roles, 48,* 483–494.

Sutherland, G., Easteal, P., Holland, K., & Vaughan, C. (2019). Mediated representations of violence against women in the mainstream news in Australia. *BMC Public Health, 19:* 502.

Sutton, C. T., & Broken Nose, M. A. (2005). American Indian families: An overview. In M. McGoldrick, J. Giordano, & N. Garcia-Preto (Eds.), *Ethnicity and family therapy* (3rd ed., pp. 43–54). New York: Guilford.

Swanson, D. H., & Johnston, D. D. (2003). Mothering in the ivy tower: Interviews with academic mothers. *Journal of the Association for Research on Mothering, 5,* 63–75.

Swearingen-Hilker, N., & Yoder, J. D. (2002). Understanding the context of unbalanced domestic contributions: The influence of perceiver's attitudes, target's gender, and presentational format. *Sex Roles, 46,* 91–98.

Sweet, S., & Moen, P. (2007). Integrating educational careers in work and family: Women's return to school and family life quality. *Community, Work, and Family, 10,* 231–250.

Sweetman, C. (1998). Editorial. In C. Sweetman (Ed.), *Gender, education, and training* (pp. 2–8). Oxford, England: Oxfam.

Swim, J. K., Borgida, E., Maruyama, G., & Myers, D. G. (1989). Joan McKay versus John McKay: Do gender stereotypes bias evaluations? *Psychological Bulletin, 105,* 409–429.

Sweney, M. (2016, June 22). Unilever vows to drop sexist stereotypes from its ads. *The Guardian.* Retrieved September 28, 2021 from https://www.theguardian .com/media/2016/jun/22/ unilever-sexist-stereotypes -ads-sunsilk-dove-lynx

Swift, & Gold. (2021, January 11). *Not an object: On sexualization and exploitation of women and girls.* UNICEF USA. Retrieved October 5, 2021 from https:// www.unicefusa.org/stories /not-object-sexualization -and-exploitation-women-and -girls/30366

Swim, J. K., & Hyers, L. L. (2009). Sexism. In T. D. Nelson (Ed.), *Handbook of prejudice, stereotyping, and discrimination* (pp. 407–430). New York: Psychology Press.

Swim, J. K., Hyers, L. L., Cohen, L. L., & Ferguson, M. J. (2001). Everyday sexism: Evidence for its incidence, nature, and psychological impact from three daily diary studies. *Journal of Social Issues, 57,* 31–53.

Swim, J. K., Mallet, R., Russo-Devosa, Y., & Stangor, C. (2005). Judgments of sexism: A comparison of the subtlety of sexism measures and sources of variability in judgments of sexism. *Psychology of Women Quarterly, 29,* 406–411.

Swim, J. K., Mallet, R., & Stangor, C. (2004). Understanding subtle sexism: Detection and use of sexist language. *Sex Roles, 51,* 117–128.

Swim, J. K., & Sanna, L. J. (1996). He's skilled, she's lucky: A meta-analysis of observers' attributions for women's and men's successes and failures. *Personality and Social Psychology Bulletin, 22,* 507–551.

Sy, S. R. (2006). Family and work influences on the transition to college among Latina adolescents. *Hispanic Journal of Behavioral Sciences, 28,* 368–386.

Sy, S. R., & Brittian, A. (2008). The impact of family obligations on young women's decisions during the transition to college: A comparison of Latina, European American, and Asian American students. *Sex Roles, 58,* 729–737.

Sy, S. R., & Romero, J. (2008). Family responsibilities among Latina college students from immigrant families. *Journal of Hispanic Higher Education, 7,* 212–227.

Symonds, P. V. (1996). Journey to the land of light: Birth among Hmong women. In P. L. Rice & L. Manderson (Eds.), *Maternity and reproductive health in Asian societies* (pp. 103–123). Amsterdam: Harwood Academic.

Szameitat, A. J., Hamaida, Y., Tulley, R. S., Saylik, R., & Otermans, P. C. J. (2015). "Women are better than men" - public beliefs on gender differences and other aspects in multitasking. *PLoS ONE 10*(10): e0140371.

Szymanski, D. M. (2003). The feminist supervision scale: Rational/theoretical approach. *Psychology of Women Quarterly, 27,* 221–232.

Szymanski, D. M., & Henning, S. L. (2007). The role of self-objectification in women's depression: A test of objectification theory. *Sex Roles, 56,* 45–53.

Szymanski, D. M., & Lewis, J. A. (2016). Gendered racism, coping, identity centrality, and African American college women's psychological distress. *Psychology of Women Quarterly, 40,* 229-243.

Syzmanski, D. M., & Mikorski, R. (2017). Sexually objectifying

environments: Power, rumination, and waitresses' anxiety and disordered eating. *Psychology of Women Quarterly, 41,* 314-324.

Szymanski, D. M., & Owens, G. P. (2008). Do coping styles moderate or mediate the relationship between internalized heterosexism and sexual minority women's psychological distress? *Psychology of Women Quarterly, 32,* 95–104.

Tafoya, N. (2005). Native American women. In M. P. Mirkin, K. L. Suyemoto, & B. F. Okun (Eds.), *Psychotherapy with women: Exploring diverse contexts and identities* (pp. 297–312). New York: Guilford.

Tafoya, N., & Del Vecchio, A. (2005). Back to the future: An examination of the Native American holocaust experience. In M. McGoldrick, J. Giordano, & N. Garcia-Preto (Eds.), *Ethnicity and family therapy* (3rd ed., pp. 55–63). New York: Guilford.

Takagi, D. Y. (2001). Maiden voyage: Excursion into sexuality and identity politics in Asian America. In M. L. Andersen & P. H. Collins (Eds.), *Race, class, and gender* (4th ed.). Belmont, CA: Wadsworth/ Thomson.

Takamura, J. C. (2007). Global challenges for an aging population. In J. A. Blackburn & C. N. Dulmus (Eds.), *Handbook of gerontology: Evidence-based approaches to theory, practice, and policy* (pp. 545–564). Hoboken, NJ: Wiley.

Tan, S. J. (2008). The myths and realities of material employment. In A. Marcus-Newhall, D. F. Halpern, & Sherylle J. Tan (Eds.), *The changing realities of work and family: A multidisciplinary approach* (pp. 9–24). Malden, MA: Blackwell.

Tang, M. (2021). Addressing skewed sex ratio at birth in China: Practices and challenges. *China Population and Development Studies, 4,* 319–326.

Tannen, D. (1994). *Gender and discourse.* New York: Oxford University Press.

Tarrant, S. (2009). *Men and feminism.* Berkeley, CA: Seal Press.

Tatum, B. D. (1992, Spring). Talking about race, learning about racism: The application of racial identity development theory in the classroom. *Harvard Educational Review, 62,* 1–24.

Tavris, C. (1992). *The mismeasure of woman.* New York: Simon & Schuster.

Taylor, D. (2005). Premenstrual symptoms and syndromes: Guidelines for symptom management and self care. *Advances in the Study of Medicine, 5,* 228–241.

Taylor, J. M., Gilligan, C, & Sullivan, A. M. (1995). *Between voice and silence: Women and girls, race and relationships.* Cambridge, MA: Harvard University Press.

Taylor, L. D. (2005). All for him: Articles about sex in American lad magazines. *Sex Roles, 52,* 153–163.

Taylor, P., Lopez, M. H., Martínez, J., & Velasco, G. (2012). *When labels don't fit: Hispanics and their views of identity.* Pew Research Center. Retrieved September 28, 2021 from https://www.pewresearch.org/hispanic/2012/04/04/when-labels-dont-fit-hispanics-and-their-views-of-identity/

Taylor, S. E. (2002). *The tending instinct.* New York: Henry Holt.

TEDxMenloPark (2019, November 22). *Sarahi Espinoza Salamanca: Nation of immigrants.* [Video]. YouTube. https://www.youtube.com/watch?v=PpUfAB6MeEA

Tehee, M., & Willis Esqueda, C. (2008). American Indian and European American women's perceptions of domestic violence. *Journal of Family Violence, 23,* 25–35.

Temkin, J., & Krahé, B. (2008). *Sexual assault and the justice gap: A question of attitude.* Portland, OR: Hart.

Tenenbaum, H. R., & Leaper, C. (1997). Mothers' and fathers' questions to their child in Mexican-descent families: Moderators of cognitive demand during play. *Hispanic Journal of Behavioral Sciences, 19,* 318–332.

Tenenbaum, H. R., & Leaper, C. (2003). Parent-child conversations about science. The socialization of gender inequities. *Developmental Psychology, 39,* 34–47.

Tenenbaum, H. R., Snow, C. E., Roach, K. A., & Kurland, B. (2005). Talking and reading science: Longitudinal data on sex differences in mother-child conversations in low-income families. *Applied Developmental Psychology, 26,* 1–19.

Terlecki, M. S., & Newcombe, N. S. (2005) How important is the digital divide? The relation of computer and videogame usage to gender differences in mental rotation ability. *Sex Roles, 53,* 433–441.

Terlecki, M. S., Newcombe, N, S., & Little, M. (2008). Durable and generalized effects of spatial experience on mental rotation: Gender differences in growth patterns. *Applied Cognitive Psychology, 22,* 996, 1031.

Teuscher, U., & Teuscher, C. (2007). Reconsidering the double standard of aging: Effects of gender and sexual orientation on facial attractiveness ratings. *Personality and Individual Differences, 42,* 631–639.

The College Board. (2020). *SAT suite of assessments annual report.* Retrieved October 3, 2021 from https://reports.collegeboard.org/pdf/2020-total-group-sat-suite-assessments-annual-report.pdf

The Tucker Center for Research on Girls and Women in Sport & tptMN. (2014). *Media coverage & female athletes.* [Film]. University of Minnesota & tptMN.

The White Ribbon Campaign (2021). *The White Ribbon Campaign: Working to end violence against women.* Retrieved October 5, 2021 from https://www.whiteribbon.ca/

The Williams Institute, UCLA School of Law. (2019). *LGBT demographic data interactive.* The Williams Institute. Retrieved October 4, 2021 from https://williamsinstitute.law.ucla.edu/visualization/lgbt-stats/?topic=SS#about-the-data

The World Bank. (2019). *Adolescent fertility rates (births per 1,000 women ages 10-19).* Retrieved October 4, 2021 from https://data.worldbank.org/indicator/SP.ADO.TFRT

The World Bank. (2019). *Pregnant women receiving prenatal care.* World Bank Group. Retrieved October 4, 2021 from https://data.worldbank.org/indicator/SH.STA.ANVC.ZS

The World Bank. (2021). *Mortality rate, infant (per 1,000 live births).* World Bank. Retrieved October 4, 2021 from https://data.worldbank.org/indicator/SP.DYN.IMRT.IN

The World Bank. (2021). *Labor force participation rate, female (% of female population ages 15+).* International Labour Organization, ILOSTAT database. Retrieved October 3, 2021 from https://data.worldbank.org/indicator/SL.TLF.CACT.FE.Zs

The World Bank. (2018). *Invisible and excluded: The fate of widows and divorcees in Africa.* The World Bank. Retrieved October 5, 2021 from https://www.worldbank.org/en/news/feature/2018/01/20/invisible-and-excluded-the-fate-of-widows-and-divorcees-in-africa

Thibaut, F., & van Wijngaarden-Cremers, P. J. M. (2020). Women's mental health in the time of Covid-19 pandemic. *Frontiers in Global Women's Health, 1:*588372.

Thilers, P. P., MacDonald, S. W. S., & Herlitz, A. (2007). Sex differences in cognition: The role of handedness. *Physiology & Behavior, 93,* 105–109.

This year's freshmen at 4-year colleges: A statistical profile. (2007, January 26). *Chronicle of Higher Education,* pp. 40–41.

Thoman, D. B., White, P. H., Yamawaki, N., & Koishi, H. (2008). Variations of gender-math stereotype content affect women's vulnerability to stereotype threat. *Sex Roles, 58,* 702–712.

Thomas, L. (2021, April 22). Intersectional environmentalism is the urgent way forward. *Marie Claire.* Retrieved October 5, 2021 from https://www.marieclaire .com/politics/a36176067 /what-is-intersectional -environmentalism/

Thompson, H. B. (1903). *The mental traits of sex.* Chicago: University of Chicago Press.

Thompson, J. F., Roberts, C. L., Currie, M., & Ellwood, D. A. (2002). Prevalence and persistence of health problems after childbirth: Associations with parity and method of birth. *Birth, 29,* 83–94.

Thompson, T. L., Robinson, J. D., & Beisecker, A. F. (2004). The older patient-physician interaction. In J. F. Nussbaum & J. Coupland (Eds.), *Handbook of communication and aging research* (2nd ed., pp. 451–477). Mahwah, NJ: Erlbaum.

Thomson, R., Murachver, T., & Green, J. (2001). Where is the gender in gendered language? *Psychological Science, 12,* 171–175.

Thorp, S. R., Krause, E. D., Cukrowicz, K. C., & Lynch, T. R. (2004). Postpartum partner support, demand-withdraw communication, and maternal stress. *Psychology of Women Quarterly, 28,* 362–369.

Thorpe, K., Barsky, J., & Boudreau, R. (1998, April). *Women's health: Occupational and life experiences— Women in transition.* Paper presented at the International Research Utilization Conference, Toronto, Canada.

Tiefer, L. (1996). Towards a feminist sex therapy. *Women and Therapy, 19,* 53–64.

Tiefer, L. (2001). A new view of women's sexual problems: Why new? Why now? *Journal of Sex Research, 38,* 89–96.

Tiefer, L. (2004). *Sex is not a natural act and other essays.* Boulder, CO: Westview Press.

Tiefer, L. (2006). Female Sexual Dysfunction: A case study of disease mongering and activist resistance. PLoS [Public Library of Science] *Medicine, 3,* 436–440.

Tiffany, K. (2019, June 18). Gender stereotypes have been banned from British ads. What does that mean? *Vox.* Retrieved September 28, 2021 from https://www.vox.com/the -goods/2019/6/18/18684088/ uk-gender-stereotype-ad-ban -sexism-advertising-history

Tiggemann, M., & Boundy, M. (2008). Effect of environment and appearance compliment on college women's self-objectification, mood, body shame, and cognitive performance. *Psychology of Women Quarterly, 32,* 399–405

Timmerman, L. M. (2002). Comparing the production of power in language on the basis of sex. In M. Allen, R. W. Preiss, B. M. Gayle, & N. A. Burrell (Eds.), *Interpersonal communication research: Advances through meta-analysis* (pp. 73–88). Mahwah, NJ: Erlbaum.

Tjaden, P., & Thoennes, N. (2000). *Extent, nature, and consequences of intimate partner violence: Findings from the National Violence against Women Survey.* Washington, DC: National Institute of Justice.

Tobin, D. L. (2000). *Coping strategies for bulimia nervosa.* Washington, DC: American Psychological Association.

Todkill, A. M. (2004, April). Me and my uterus [Review of *Am I still a woman? Hysterectomy and gender identity*]. *Women's Review of Books,* pp. 16–17.

Toller, P. W., Suter, E. A., & Trautman, T. C. (2004). Gender role identity and attitudes toward feminism. *Sex Roles, 51,* 85–90.

Tolman, D. L. (2002). *Dilemmas of desire: Teenage girls talk about sexuality.* Cambridge, MA: Harvard University Press.

Tolman, D. L., & Diamond, L. (2001a). Desegregating sexuality research: Cultural and biological perspectives on gender and desire. *Annual Review of Sex Research, 12,* 33–74.

Tolman, D. L., & Diamond, L. (2001b). Sexuality and sexual desire. In J. Worell (Ed.), *Encyclopedia of women and gender* (pp. 1005–1021). San Diego: Academic Press.

Tolman, D. L., Impett, E. A., Tracy, A., & Michael, A. (2006). Looking good, sounding good: Femininity ideology and adolescent girls' mental health. *Psychology of Women Quarterly, 30,* 85–95.

Toro, P. A. (2007). Toward an international understanding of homelessness. *Journal of Social Issues, 63,* 461–481.

Torres, E. E. (2003). *Chicana without apology: The new Chicana cultural studies.* New York: Routledge.

Townsend, J. W. (2003). Reproductive behavior in the context of global population. *American Psychologist, 58,* 197–204.

Tracy, A. J., & Erkut, S. (2002). Gender and race patterns in the pathways from sports participation to self-esteem. *Sociological Perspectives, 45,* 445–466.

Tran, C. G., & Des Jardins, K. (2000). Domestic violence in Vietnamese refugee and Korean immigrant communities. In J. L. Chin (Ed.), *Relationships among Asian American women* (pp. 71–96). Washington, DC: American Psychological Association.

Trautner, H. M., & Eckes, T. (2000). Putting gender development into context: Problems and prospects. In T. Eckes & H. M. Trautner (Eds.), *The developmental social psychology of gender* (pp. 419–435). Mahwah, NJ: Erlbaum.

Trautner, H. M., et al. (2005). Rigidity and flexibility of gender stereotypes in childhood: Developmental or differential? *Infant and Child Development, 14,* 365–381.

Travis, C. B. (2005). 2004 Carolyn Sherif award address: Heart disease and gender inequity. *Psychology of Women Quarterly, 29,* 15–23.

Travis, C. B. (2006). Risks to healthy development: The somber planes of life. In J. Worell & C. D. Goodheart (Eds.), *Handbook of girls' and women's psychological health: Gender and well-being across the life span* (pp. 15–24). New York: Oxford University Press.

Travis, C. B., & Compton, J. D. (2001). Feminism and health in the decade of behavior. *Psychology of Women Quarterly, 25,* 312–323.

Travis, C. B., Gressley, D. L., & Crumpler, C. A. (1991). Feminist contributions to health psychology. *Psychology of Women Quarterly, 15,* 557–566.

Travis, C. B., & Meginnis-Payne, K. L. (2001). Beauty politics and patriarchy: The impact on women's lives. In J. Worell (Ed.), *Encyclopedia of women and gender* (pp. 189–200). San Diego: Academic Press.

Travis, C. B., Meltzer, A. L., & Howerton, D. M. (2010). Gender issues in health care utilization. In J. C. Chrisler & D. R. McCreary (Eds.), *Handbook of gender research in psychology* (pp. 517–540). New York: Springer.

Trimble, J. E. (2003). Infusing American Indian and Alaska Native topics into the psychology curriculum. In P. Bronstein & K. Quina (Eds.), *Teaching gender and multicultural awareness* (pp. 221–236).Washington, DC: American Psychological Association.

Trotman, F. K. (2002). Old, African American, and female: Political,

economic, and historical contexts. In F. K. Trotman & C. M. Brody (Eds.), *Psychotherapy and counseling with older women* (pp. 70–86). New York: Springer.

Trotman, F. K., & Brody, C. M. (2002). Cross-cultural perspectives: Grandmothers. In F. K. Trotman & C. M. Brody (Eds.), *Psychotherapy and counseling with older women* (pp. 41–57). New York: Springer.

Tucker, M. B., & James, A. D. (2005). New families, new functions: Postmodern African American families in context. In V. C. McLoyd, N. E. Hill, & K. A. Dodge (Eds.), *African American family life: Ecological and cultural diversity* (pp. 86–108). New York: Guilford.

Tugend, A. (2019, October 9). *Questioning their fairness, a record number of colleges stop requiring the SAT and ACT.* The Hechinger Report. Retrieved October 3, 2021 from https://hechingerreport.org/questioning-their-fairness-a-record-number-of-colleges-stop-requiring-the-sat-and-act/

Tulloch, H. E., McCaul, K. D., Miltenberger, R. G., & Smyth, J. M. (2004). Partner communication skills and condom use among college couples. *Journal of American College Health, 23*–268.

Turk, C. (2004, April 5). A woman can learn anything a man can. *Newsweek,* p. 12.

Twenge, J. M., Sherman, R. A., & Wells, B. E. (2015). Changes in American adults' sexual behavior and attitudes, 1972–2012. *Archives of Sexual Behavior, 44,* 2273–2285.

Twenge, J., M., Sherman, R. A.., & Wells, B. E. (2017). Declines in sexual frequency among American adults, 1989-2014. *Archives of Sexual Behavior, 46,* 2389–2401.

Tyre, P. (2004, April 19). No longer most likely to succeed. *Newsweek,* p. 59.

U.S. Census Bureau. (2005). *Statistical abstract of the United States: 2004–2005.* Washington, DC: Author.

U. S. Census Bureau. (2020). *Historical marital status tables.* U.S. Census Bureau. Retrieved October 4, 2021 from https://www.census.gov/data/tables/time-series/demo/families/marital.html

U. S. Census Bureau. (2020). *Quick Facts.* U. S. Census. Retrieved October 5, 2021 from https://www.census.gov/quickfacts/fact/table/US/IPE120219

U.S. Census Bureau. (2021). *National population by characteristics: 2010-2019.* U.S. Census. Retrieved October 5, 2021 https://www.census.gov/data/tables/time-series/demo/popest/2010s-national-detail.html

Uba, L. (1994). *Asian Americans: Personality patterns, identity, and mental health.* New York: Guilford.

Ueda P., Mercer C. H., Ghaznavi C., Herbenick D. (2020). Trends in frequency of sexual activity and number of sexual partners among adults aged 18 to 44 years in the US, 2000-2018. *JAMA Network Open,* 3(6): e203833.

Ullman, M. T., Miranda, R. A., & Travers, M. L. (2008). Sex differences in the neurocognition of language. In J. Becker et al. (Eds.), *Sex differences in the brain from genes to behavior* (pp. 291–309). New York: Oxford.

Ullman, S. E. (2000). Psychometric characteristics of the social reactions questionnaire: A measure of reactions to sexual assault victims. *Psychology of Women Quarterly, 24,* 257–271.

Ullman, S. E. (2004). Sexual assault victimization and suicidal behavior in women: A review of the literature. *Aggression and Violent Behavior, 9,* 331–351.

Ullman, S. E. (2010). *Talking about sexual assault: Society's response to survivors.* Washington DC: American Psychological Association.

Ullman, S. E., & Brecklin, L. R. (2003). Sexual assault history and health-related outcomes in a national sample of women. *Psychology of Women Quarterly, 27,* 46–57.

Umberson, D., Thomeer, M. B., & Lodge, A. C. (2015). Intimacy and emotion work in lesbian, gay, and heterosexual relationships. *Journal of Marriage and Family, 77,* 542-556.

UNAIDS. (2018). *Women and girls and HIV.* United Nations. Retrieved October 5, 2021 from https://www.unaids.org /sites/default/files/media_asset /women_girls_hiv_en.pdf

UNAIDS. (2019). *Women and HIV: A spotlight on adolescent girls and young women.* UNAIDS. Retrieved October 5, 2021 from https://www.unaids.org/sites/ default/files/media_asset/2019 _women-and-hiv_en.pdf

Underwood, M. K. (2003). *Social aggression among girls.* New York: Guilford.

Underwood, M. K. (2004). Gender and peer relationships: Are the two gender cultures really all that different? In J. B. Kupersmidt & K. A. Dodge (Eds.), *Children's peer relations: From development to intervention* (pp. 21–36). Washington, DC: American Psychological Association.

UNESCO Institute for Statistics. (2010, September 7). *International Literacy Day celebrated on September 8.* Retrieved November 17, 2010, from http:// www.uis.unesco.org/ev.php? ID=8107_201&ID2=DO_TOPIC

Unger, R. K. (1997). The three-sided mirror: Feminists looking at psychologists looking at women. In R. Fuller, P. N. Walsh, & P. McGinley (Eds.), *A century of psychology: Progress, paradigms, and prospects for the new millennium* (pp. 16–35). New York: Routledge.

Unger, R. K. (1998). *Resisting gender: Twenty-five years of feminist psychology.* London: Sage.

United Nations. (2000). *The world's women 2000: Trends and statistics.* New York: Author.

United Nations. (2005). *World fertility patterns 2004.* New York: Author.

United Nations. (2007). *World economic and social survey 2007: Development in an ageing world.* New York: Author.

United Nations. (2015). *Free & equal campaign fact sheet: Intersex* (PDF). Office of the High Commissioner for Human Rights. Retrieved October 3, 2021 from https://www.unfe.org/wp-content /uploads/2017/05/UNFE -Intersex.pdf

United Nations Children's Fund. (2013). *Making education a priority in the post-2015 development agenda: Report of the global thematic consultation on education in the post-2015 development agenda.* Retrieved October 3, 2021 from https:// unesdoc.unesco.org/ark:/48223/ pf0000223024

United Nations Population Fund. (2021). *World population dashboard: Life expectancy at birth (years), 2021, female.* Retrieved October 5, 2021 from https://www.unfpa.org/data/ world-population-dashboard

United States Department of Health and Human Services. (2021). *National domestic violence hotline.* Retrieved October 5, 2021 from https://www.acf .hhs.gov/fysb/programs/family -violence-prevention-services/ programs/ndvh

United States Department of Justice. (2012). *An updated definition of rape.* US DOJ Archives. Retrieved October 5, 2021 from https://www .justice.gov/archives/opa/blog/ updated-definition-rape

United States Department of Justice, Federal Bureau of Investigation. (2020). *Crime in the United States, 2019.* Retrieved October 3, 2021 from https://ucr.fbi.gov /crime-in-the-u.s/2019 /crime-in-the-u.s.-2019/ topic-pages/about-cius

Uray, N., & Burnaz, S. (2003). An analysis of the portrayal of gender roles in Turkish television advertisements. *Sex Roles, 48,* 77–87.

Urban Indian Health Institute. (2016). *Community health profile: National aggregate of urban Indian health program service areas.* Seattle, WA: Urban Indian Health Institute. Retrieved October 4, 2021 from http:// www.uihi.org/wp-content /uploads/2017/08/UIHI _CHP_2016_Electronic _20170825.pdf

Urbaniak, G. C, & Kilmann, P. R. (2003). Physical attractiveness and the "nice guy paradox": Do nice guys really finish last? *Sex Roles, 49,* 413–426.

Useem, A. (2005, Summer). Holy radical. *Ms. Magazine,* pp. 18–27.

Ussher, J. M. (2006). *Managing the monstrous feminine: Regulating the reproductive body.* London: Routledge.

Vaglanos, A. (2017, September). *Art exhibit powerfully answers the question 'What were you wearing?'* Huffington Post. Retrieved October 5, 2021 from https://www.huffpost .com/entry/powerful-art-exhibit -powerfully-answers-the -question-what-were-you -wearing_n_59baddd2e4b02 da0e1405d2a

Valian, V. (1998). *Why so slow?: The advancement of women.* Cambridge, MA: MIT Press.

Valian, V. (2006). Beyond gender schemas: Improving the advancement of women in academia. In J. M. Bystydzienski & S. R. Bird (Eds.), *Removing barriers: Women in academic science, technology, engineering, and mathematics* (pp. 320–332). Bloomington: Indiana University Press.

Valls-Fernández, F., & Martínez-Vicente, J. M. (2007). Gender stereotypes in Spanish television commercials. *Sex Roles, 56,* 691–699.

Van Blyderveen, S., & Wood, J. (2001). *Gender differences in the tendency to generate self evaluations based on the views of others in the autobiographical memories of events.* Paper presented at the annual convention of the Canadian Psychological Association. Ste-Fey, Quebec.

Van de gaer, E., Pustjens, H., & Van Damme, J. (2007). Impact of attitudes of peers on language achievement: Gender differences. *Journal of Educational Research, 101,* 78–90.

Van der Pas, D., & Aaldering, L. (2020). Gender differences in political media coverage: A meta-analysis. *Journal of Communication, 70,* 114-143.

Van Evra, J. P. (2004). *Television and child development* (3rd ed.). Mahwah, NJ: Erlbaum.

Van Rooy, D., et al. (2003). A recurrent connectionist model of group biases. *Psychological Review, 110,* 536–563.

Van Vugt, M., & Spisak, B. R. (2008). Sex differences in the emergence of leadership during competitions within and between groups. *Psychological Science, 19,* 854–858.

Vance, E. B., & Wagner, N. N. (1977). Written descriptions of orgasm: A study of sex differences. In D. Byrne & L. A. Byrne (Eds.), *Exploring human sexuality* (pp. 201–212). New York: Thomas Y. Crowell.

Vang, C. Y. (2008). *Hmong in Minnesota.* Minneapolis: Minnesota Historical Society.

Vangelisti, A. L. (2006). Relationship dissolution: Antecedents, processes, and consequences. In A. L. Vangelisti & D. Perlman (Eds.), *The Cambridge handbook of personal relationships* (pp. 353-374). Mahwah, NJ: Erlbaum.

Vangelisti, A. L., & Perlman, D. (Eds.). (2006). *The Cambridge handbook of personal relationships.* Mahwah, NJ: Erlbaum.

Van Wormer, J. J., Bendixsen, C. G., Vickers, E. R., Stokley, S., McNeil, M. M., Gee, J., Belongia, E. A., & McLean, H. Q. (2017). Association between parent attitudes and receipt of human papillomavirus vaccine in adolescents. *BMC Public Health, 17,* 766.

Vargas, J. A. G. (1999). Who is the Puerto Rican woman and how is she?: Shall Hollywood respond? In M. Meyers (Ed.), *Mediated woman: Representations in popular culture* (pp. 111–132). Cresskill, NJ: Hampton Press.

Vasquez, M. J. T. (2002). Latinas: Exercise and empowerment from a feminist psychodynamic perspective. In R. L. Hall & C. A. Oglesby (Eds.), *Exercise and sport in feminist therapy* (pp. 23–38). Binghamton, NY: Haworth Press.

Vasquez, M. J. T., & De las Fuentes, C. (1999). American-born Asian, African, Latina, and American Indian adolescent girls: Challenges and strengths. In N. G. Johnson, M. C. Roberts, & J. Worell (Eds.), *Beyond appearance: A new look at adolescent girls* (pp. 151–173). Washington, DC: American Psychological Association.

Vasta, R., Knott, J. A., & Gaze, C. E. (1996). Can spatial training erase the gender differences on the water-level task? *Psychology of Women Quarterly, 20,* 549–567.

Verhofstadt, L. L., Buysse, A., & Ickes, W. (2007). Social support in couples: An examination of gender differences using self-report and observational methods. *Sex Roles, 57,* 267–282.

Viers, D., & Prouty, A. M. (2001). We've come a long way? An overview of research on dual-career couples' stressors and strengths. *Journal of Feminist Family Therapy, 13,* 169–190.

Vigorito, A. J., & Curry, T. J. (1998). Marketing masculinity: Gender identity and popular magazines. *Sex Roles, 39,* 135–152.

Villani, S. L. (1997). *Motherhood at the crossroads: Meeting the challenge of a changing role.* New York: Plenum.

Vinogradova, Y., Coupland, C., & Hippisley-Cox, J. (2020). Use of hormone replacement therapy and risk of breast cancer: Nested case-control studies using the QResearch and CPRD databases. *British Medical Journal, 371*:m3873.

Võ, L. T., & Scichitano, M. (2004). Introduction: Reimagining Asian American women's experiences. In L. T. Võ & M. Scichitano (Eds.), *Asian American women: The Frontiers reader.* Lincoln: University of Nebraska Press.

Voelker, D., K., Reel, J. J., & Greenleaf, C. (2015). Weight status and body image perceptions in adolescents: Current perspectives. *Adolescent Health, Medicine and Therapeutics, 6,* 149–158.

Vohs, K. D., & Baumeister, R. F. (2004). Sexual passion, intimacy, and gender. In D. J. Mashek & A. Aron (Eds.), *Handbook of closeness and intimacy* (pp. 189–199). Mahwah, NJ: Erlbaum.

Vos, R., Ocampo, J. A., & Cortez, A. L. (2008). *Ageing and development.* London: Zed Books.

Voyer, D., Nolan, C., & Voyer, S. (2000). The relation between experience and spatial performance in men and women. *Sex Roles, 43,* 891–915.

Voyer, D., Posma, A., Brake, B., & Imperato-McGinley, J. (2007). Gender differences in object location memory: A meta-analysis. *Psychonomic Bulletin & Review, 14,* 23–38.

Voyer, D., Voyer, S., & Bryden, M. P. (1995). Magnitude of sex differences in spatial abilities: A meta-analysis and consideration of critical variables. *Psychological Bulletin, 117,* 250–270.

Voyer, D., Voyer, S. D., & Saint-Aubin, J. (2017). Sex differences in visual-spatial working memory: A meta-analysis. *Psychonomic Bulletin Review, 24,* 307-334.

Wade, C., & Cirese, S. (1991). *Human sexuality* (2nd ed.). San Diego: Harcourt Brace Jovanovich.

Wade, C., & Tavris, C. (1999). Gender and culture. In L. A. Peplau et al. (Eds.), *Gender, culture, and ethnicity: Current research about women and men* (pp. 15–22). Mountain View, CA: Mayfield.

Wainer, H., & Steinberg, L. S. (1992). Sex differences in performance on the mathematics section of the Scholastic Aptitude Test: A bidirectional validity study. *Harvard Educational Review, 62,* 323–336.

Walker, A. (1983). *In search of our mothers' gardens: Womanist prose.* New York: Harcourt Inc.

Walker, A. (2008, March 7*). Lest we forget: An open letter to my sisters who are brave.* Retrieved April 6, 2008, from http://www .truthout. org/docs

Walker, A. E. (1998). *The menstrual cycle.* New York: Routledge.

Walker, E. A., Newman, E., & Koss, M. P. (2004). Costs and health care utilization associated with traumatic experiences. In P. P. Schnurr & B. L. Green (Eds.), *Trauma and health: Physical health consequences of exposure to extreme stress* (pp. 43–69). Washington, DC: American Psychological Association.

Walker, R. (Ed.). (1995). *To be real: Telling the truth and changing the face of feminism.* New York: Anchor.

Walker, R. (2007). *Baby love: Choosing motherhood after a lifetime of ambivalence.* New York: Riverhead.

Walker, R., Turnbull, D., & Wilkinson, C. (2002). Strategies to address global cesarean section rates: A review of the evidence. *Birth, 29,* 28–39.

Wallace, H. (1999). *Family violence: Legal, medical, and social perspectives* (2nd ed.). Boston: Allyn & Bacon.

Walley, C. J. (2002). Searching for " voices" : Feminism, anthropology, and the global debate over female genital operations. In S. M. James & C. C. Robertson (Eds.), *Genital cutting and transnational sisterhood* (pp. 17–53). Urbana: University of Illinois Press.

Walsh, M. R. (1977). *Doctors wanted: No women need apply.* New Haven, CT: Yale University Press.

Walsh, M. R. (1987). Introduction. In M. R. Walsh (Ed.), *The psychology of women: Ongoing debates* (pp. 1–15). New Haven, CT: Yale University Press.

Walsh, M. R. (1990). Women in medicine since Flexner. *New York State Journal of Medicine, 90,* 302–308.

Walter, K. V., Conroy-Beam, D., Buss, D. M., Asao, K., Sorokowska, A., Sorokowski, P., Aavik, T., Akello, G., Alhabahba, M. M., Alm, C., Amjad, N., Anjum, A., Atama, C. S., Duyar. D. A., Ayebare, R., Batres, C., Bendixen, M., Bensafia, A., Bizumic, B. … Zupanc̆ic, M. (2020). Sex differences in mate preferences across 45 countries: A large-scale replication. *Psychological Science, 31,* 408–423.

Walters, K. L., & Simoni, J. M. (1993). Lesbian and gay male group identity attitudes and self-esteem: Implications for counseling. *Journal of Counseling Psychology, 40,* 94–99.

Walters, S. T., & Baer, J. S. (2006). *Talking with college students about alcohol.* New York: Guilford.

Walton, M. D., et al. (1988). Physical stigma and the pregnancy role: Receiving help from strangers. *Sex Roles, 18,* 323–331.

Wang, W. (2020). *More than one-third of prime-age Americans have never married.* Institute for Family Studies. Retrieved October 4, 2021 from https:// ifstudies.org/ifs-admin/ resources/final2-ifs-single -americansbrief2020.pdf

Wang, L., & Widener, A. (2019, May 12). The struggle to keep women in academia. *Chemical & Engineering News, 97*(19). Retrieved October 3, 2021 from https://cen.acs.org/ careers/diversity/struggle -keep-women-academia/97/i19

Wang, S., Chen, C., Chin, C., & Lee, S. (2005). Impact of postpartum depression on the mother-infant couple. *Birth, 32,* 39–44.

Wangu, M. B. (2003). From curiosity to devotion: The many meanings of Kali. *Manushi, 134,* 14–18.

Wann, M. (2009). Foreword: Fat studies: An invitation to revolution. In E. Rothblum & S. Solovay (Eds.), *The fat studies reader* (pp. xi–xxv). New York: New York University Press.

Ward, C. N., & Lundberg-Love, P. K. (2006). Sexual abuse of women. In P. K. Lundberg-Love & S. L. Marmion (Eds.), *"Intimate" violence against women: When spouses, partners, or lovers attack* (pp. 47–68). Westport, CT: Praeger.

Ward, L. M. (1999). [Review of the book *The two sexes: Growing up apart, coming together.]* *Sex Roles, 40,* 657–659.

Ward, L. M. & Freedman, K. (2006). Using TV as a guide: Associations between television viewing and adolescents' sexual attitudes and behavior. *Journal of Research on Adolescence, 16,* 133–156.

Ward, L. M., & Harrison, K. (2005). The impact of media use on girls' beliefs about gender roles, their bodies, and sexual relationships: A research synthesis. In E. Cole & J. H. Daniel (Eds.), *Featuring females: Feminist analyses of media* (pp. 3–23). Washington DC: American Psychological Association.

Ware, L. (2009). The hegemonic impulse for health and well-being: A saga of the less well and the less worthy. In S. R. Steinberg (Ed.), *Diversity and multiculturalism: A reader* (pp. 363–376). New York: Peter Lang.

Warin, J. (2000). The attainment of self-consistency through gender in young children. *Sex Roles, 42,* 209–230.

Warner, J. (2005, February 21). The myth of the perfect mother. *Newsweek,* pp. 42–47.

Warner, L., & Shields, S. A. (2007). The perception of crying in women and men: Angry tears, sad tears, and the " right way" to weep. In U. Hess & P. Philippot (Eds.), *Group dynamics and emotional expression.* New York: Cambridge University Press.

Warren, E., & Tyagi, A. W. (2003). *The two-income trap.* New York: Basic Books.

Warshaw, C. (2001). Women and violence. In N. L. Stotland & D. E. Stewart (Eds.), *Psychological aspects of women's health care* (2nd ed., pp. 477–548). Washington, DC: American Psychiatric Press.

Wasserman, E. B. (1994). Personal reflections of an Anglo therapist in Indian country. In J. Adleman & G. Enguídanos (Eds.), *Racism in the lives of women* (pp. 23–32). New York: Haworth.

Wathen, C. N., MacGregor, J. C., & MacQuarrie, B. J. (2015). The impact of domestic violence in the workplace: Results from a Pan-Canadian survey. *Journal of Occupational and Environmental Medicine, 57,* e65–e71.

Watson, C. M., Quatman, T., & Edler, E. (2002). Career aspirations of adolescent girls: Effects of achievement level, grade, and single-sex school environment. *Sex Roles, 46,* 323–335.

Watson, L. B., Ancis, J. R., White, D. N., & Nazari, N. (2013). Racial identity buffers African American women from body image problems and disordered eating. *Psychology of Women Quarterly, 37,* 337-350.

Watson, L. B., Grotewiel, M., Farrell, M. Marshik, J., & Schneider, M. (2015). Experiences of sexual objectification, minority stress, and disordered eating among sexual minority women. *Psychology of Women Quarterly, 39,* 458-470.

Watson, P. J., Biderman, M. D., & Sawrie, S. M. (1994). Empathy, sex role orientation, and narcissism. *Sex Roles, 30,* 701–723.

Way, N. (1998). *Everyday courage: The lives and stories of urban teenagers.* New York: New York University Press.

Wayne, L. D. (2005, Winter/Spring). Neutral pronouns: A modest proposal whose time has come. *Canadian Woman Studies/Les cahiers de la femme, 24,* 85–99.

Weatherall, A. (2002). *Gender, language, and discourse.* New York: Routledge.

Weaver, G. D. (1998, August). *Emotional health of older African American women with breast cancer.* Paper presented at the annual convention of the American Psychological Association, San Francisco, CA.

Webb, D. A., et al. (2008). Postpartum physical symptoms in new mothers: Their relationship to functional limitations and emotional well-being. *Birth, 35,* 179–187.

Webster, J., Pritchard, M., Creedy, D., & East, C. (2003). A simplified predictive index for the detection of women at risk for postnatal depression. *Birth, 30,* 101–108.

Weedon, C. (1999). *Feminism, theory, and the politics of difference.* Malden, MA: Blackwell.

Weichold, K., Silbereisen, R. K., & Schmitt-Rodermund, E. (2003). Short-term and long-term consequences of early versus late physical maturation in adolescents. In C. Hayward (Ed.), *Gender differences at puberty* (pp. 241–276). New York: Cambridge University Press.

Weinshenker, M. N. (2005). Imagining family roles: Parental influences on the expectations of adolescents in dual-earner families. In B. Schneider & Linda J. Waite (Eds.), *Being together, working apart: Dual-career families and the work-life balance* (pp. 365–388). Cambridge, UK: Cambridge University Press.

Weinshenker, M. N. (2006). Adolescents' expectations about mothers' employment: Life course patterns and parental influence. *Sex Roles, 54,* 845–857.

Weinstock, J. S. (2003). Lesbian, gay, bisexual, transgender, and intersex issues in the psychology curriculum. In P. Bronstein & K. Quina (Eds.), *Teaching gender and multicultural awareness* (pp. 285–297). Washington, DC: American Psychological Association.

Weinstock, J., & Krehbiel, M. (2009). Fat youth as common targets for bullying. In E. Rothblum & S. Solovay (Eds.), *The fat studies reader* (pp. 120–126). New York: New York University Press.

Weisgram, E. S., & Bigler, R. S. (2007). Effects of learning about gender discrimination on adolescent girls' attitudes toward and interest in science. *Psychology of Women Quarterly, 31,* 262–269.

Wekerle, C, & Avgoustis, E. (2003). Child maltreatment, adolescent dating, and adolescent dating violence. In P. Florsheim (Ed.), *Adolescent romantic relations and sexual behavior* (pp. 213–241). Mahwah, NJ: Erlbaum.

Welcoming women: Former students laud engineering mentor. (2004, September/October). *Stanford Alumni Magazine,* pp. 22–24.

Welsh, D. P., Rostosky, S. S., & Kawaguchi, M. C. (2000). A normative perspective of adolescent girls' developing sexuality. In C. B. Tavris & J. W. White (Eds.), *Sexuality, society, and feminism* (pp. 111–166). Washington, DC: American Psychological Association.

Wenniger, M. D., & Conroy, M. H. (2001). *Gender equity or bust! On the road to campus leadership with women in higher education.* San Francisco: Jossey-Bass.

Wessler, S. L., & De Andrade, L. L. (2006). Slurs, stereotypes, and student interventions: Examining the dynamics, impact, and prevention of harassment in middle and high school. *Journal of Social Issues, 62*, 511–532.

West, C. M. (2008). Mammy, Jezebel, Sapphire, and their homegirls. In J. C. Chrisler, C. Golden, & P. D. Rozee (Eds.), *Lectures on the psychology of women* (3rd ed., pp. 287–321). Boston: McGraw-Hill.

West, C, & Zimmerman, D. H. (1998a). Doing gender. In B. M. Clinchy & J. K. Norem (Eds.), *The gender and psychology reader* (pp. 104–124). New York: New York University Press.

West, C, & Zimmerman, D. H. (1998b). Women's place in everyday talk: Reflections on parent-child interaction. In J. Coates (Ed.), *Language and gender: A reader* (pp. 165–175). Malden, MA: Blackwell.

West, M., & Fernández, M. (1997). *Reflexión Cristiana: ¿ Cómo ayudar a una mujer maltratada?* [Christian reflection: How to help an abused woman.] Managua, Nicaragua: Red de Mujeres contra la Violencia.

Westbrook, J. (2020, February 27). *How Mexico and Central America's femicide epidemic drives and complicates the migrant crisis.* The New Humanitarian. Retrieved October 5, 2021 from https://www.thenewhumanitarian .org/news-feature/2020/02/27/ Femicide-migration-Central -America-Mexico-US-Mexico -women-violence

Wester, S. R., Vogel, D. L., Pressly, P. K., & Heesacker, M. (2002). Sex differences in emotion: A critical review of the literature and implications for counseling psychology. *The Counseling Psychologist, 30*, 630–652.

Weston, G., Zilanawala, A., Webb, E., Carvalho, L. A., & McMunn, A. (2019). Long work hours, weekend working and depressive symptoms in men and women: Findings from a UK population-based study. *Journal of Epidemiology and Community Health, 73*, 465-474.

Wetchler, J. D. (2007). Avoiding sex discrimination litigation and defending sex discrimination suits. In F. J. Crosby, M. S. Stockdale, & S. A. Ropp (Eds.), *Sex discrimination in the workplace: Multidisciplinary perspectives* (pp. 7–17). Malden, MA: Blackwell.

Wexler, D. B. (2006). *Stop domestic violence: Group leader's manual.* New York: Norton.

Whatley, M. H., & Henken, E. R. (2000). *Did you hear about the girl who . . . ? Contemporary legends, folklore, and human sexuality.* New York: New York University Press.

Wheelan, S. A., & Verdi, A. F. (1992). Differences in male and female patterns of communication in groups: A methodological artifact? *Sex Roles, 27*, 1–15.

Wheeler, C. (1994, September/October). How much ink do women get? *Executive Female, 51.*

Whelehan, P. (2001). Cross-cultural sexual practices. In J. Worell (Ed.), *Encyclopedia of women and gender* (pp. 291–302). San Diego: Academic Press.

Whiffen, V. E. (2001). Depression. In J. Worell (Ed.), *Encyclopedia of women and gender* (pp. 303–314). San Diego: Academic Press.

Whiffen, V. E., & Demidenko, N. (2006). Mood disturbance across the life span. In J. Worell & C. D. Goodheart (Eds.), *Handbook of girls' and women's psychological health: Gender and well-being across the life span* (pp. 51–59). New York: Oxford University Press.

Whipple, V. (2006). *Lesbian widows: Invisible grief.* Binghamton, NY: Haworth.

Whitaker, S., Shapiro, V. B., & Shields, J. P. (2016). School-based protective factors related to suicide for lesbian, gay, and bisexual adolescents. *Journal of Adolescent Health, 58*, 63-68.

Whitbourne, S. K. (2005). *Adult development and aging: Biopsychosocial perspectives* (2nd ed.). Hoboken, NJ: Wiley.

Whitbourne, S. K. (2008). *Adult development and aging: Biopsychosocial perspectives* (3rd ed.). Hoboken, NJ: Wiley.

Whitbourne, S. K. (2010). *The search for fulfillment.* New York: Ballantine.

Whitbourne, S. K., & Skultety, K. M. (2006). Aging and identity: How women face later life transitions. In J. Worell & C. D. Goodheart (Eds.), *Handbook of girls' and women's psychological health: Gender and well-being across the life span* (pp. 370–378). New York: Oxford University Press.

Whitbourne, S. K., & Sneed, J. R. (2002). The paradox of well-being, identity processes, and stereotype threat: Ageism and its potential relationship to the self and later life. In T. D. Nelson (Ed.), *Ageism: Stereotyping and prejudice against older persons* (pp. 247–273). Cambridge, MA: MIT Press.

White, A. M. (2008). *Ain't I a feminist? African American men speak out on fatherhood, friendship, forgiveness, and freedom.* Albany: State University of New York Press.

White A. M. (2020). Gender differences in the epidemiology of alcohol use and related harms in the United States. *Alcohol Research: Current Reviews, 40*, 01.

White, J. W. (2001). Aggression and gender. In J. Worell (Ed.), *Encyclopedia of women and gender* (pp. 81–93). San Diego: Academic Press.

White, J. W. (2009). *Taking sides: Clashing views in gender* (4th ed.). New York: McGraw-Hill.

White, J. W., Bondurant, B., & Travis, C. B. (2000). *Social constructions of sexuality: Unpacking hidden meanings.* In C. B. Travis & J. W. White (Eds.), *Sexuality, society, and feminism* (pp. 11–33). Washington, DC: American Psychological Association.

White, J. W., Donat, P. L. N., & Bondurant, B. (2001). A

developmental examination of violence against girls and women. In R. K. Unger (Ed.), *Handbook of the psychology of women and gender* (pp. 343–357). New York: Wiley.

White, J. W., & Frabutt, J. M. (2006). Violence against girls and women: An integrative developmental perspective. In J. Worell & C. D. Goodheart (Eds.), *Handbook of girls' and women's psychological health: Gender and well-being across the life span* (pp. 85–93). New York: Oxford University Press.

White, J. W., & Kowalski, R. M. (1998). Male violence toward women: An integrated perspective. In R. G. Geen & E. Donnerstein (Eds.), *Human aggression: Theories, research, and implications for social policy* (pp. 203–228). San Diego: Academic Press.

White, L., & Rogers, S. J. (2000). Economic circumstances and family outcomes: A review of the 1990s. *Journal of Marriage and the Family, 62,* 1035–1051.

Whitehead, B. D. (2003). *Why there are no good men left: The romantic plight of the new single woman.* New York: Broadway.

Whitley, B. E., Jr., & Ægisdóttir, S. (2000). The gender belief system, authoritarianism, social dominance orientation, and heterosexuals' attitudes toward lesbians and gay men. *Sex Roles, 42,* 947–967.

Whitley, B. E., Jr., & Kite, M. E. (2010). *The psychology of prejudice and discrimination* (2nd ed.). Belmont, CA: Wadsworth Cengage.

Whitley, B. E., Jr., McHugh, M. C., & Frieze, I. H. (1986). Assessing the theoretical models for sex differences in causal attributions of success and failure. In J. S. Hyde & M. C. Linn (Eds.), *The psychology of gender: Advances through meta-analysis* (pp. 102–135). Baltimore: Johns Hopkins University Press.

Whitton, S. W., Dyar, C., Mustanski, B., & Newcomb, M. E. (2019). Intimate partner violence experiences of sexual and gender minority adolescents and young adults assigned female at birth. *Psychology of Women Quarterly, 43,* 232-249.

Why don't I have a boyfriend? (And how do I get one?). (2001, August). *Twist,* pp. 26–27.

Wickett, M. (2001). Uncovering bias in the classroom: A personal journey. In H. Rousso & M. L. Wehmeyer (Eds.), *Double jeopardy: Addressing gender equity in special education* (pp. 261–268). Albany, NJ: SUNY Press.

Wickrama., K. A., Bryant, C. M., Conger, R. D., & Brennim, J. M. (2004). Change and continuity in marital relationships during the middle years. In R. D. Conger, F. O. Lorenz, & K. A. S. Wickrama (Eds.), *Continuity and change in family relationships* (pp. 123–143). Mahwah, NJ: Erlbaum.

Widen, S. C., & Russell, J. A. (2002). Gender and preschoolers' perception of emotion. *Merrill-Palmer Quarterly, 48,* 248–262.

Widmer, E. D., Treas, J., & Newcomb, R. (1998). Attitudes toward non-marital sex in 24 countries. *Journal of Sex Research, 35,* 349–358.

Widmer, M., & Pavesi, I. (2016). A gendered analysis of violent deaths. *Small Arms Survey Research Notes, 63,* 1-8.

Wiesner-Hanks, M. E. (2019). *Women and gender in early modern Europe* (4th ed.). New York: Cambridge University Press.

Wigfield, A., Battle, A., Keller, L. B., & Eccles, J. S. (2002). Sex differences in motivation, self-concept, career aspiration, and career choice: Implications for cognitive development. In A. McGillicuddy-De Lisi & R. De Lisi (Eds.), *Biology, society, and behavior: The development of sex differences in cognition* (pp. 93–124). Westport, CT: Ablex Publishing.

Wigfield, A., et al. (2015). Development of achievement motivation and engagement. In R. M. Lerner (Series Eds.) & M. Lamb (Vol. Ed.), *Handbook of child psychology and developmental science: Vol. 3. Socioemotional processes* (7th ed., pp. 657–700). Hoboken, NJ: Wiley.

Wilbers, J., Bugg, G., Nance, T., & Hamilton, M. C. (2003, November). *Sexism in titles of address: Dr. or professor?* Paper presented at the meeting of the Kentucky Academy of Science, Louisville.

Wilchins, R. A. (2004). *Queer theory, gender theory.* Los Angeles: Alyson Books.

Wilde, A., & Deikman, A. B. (2005). Cross-cultural similarities and differences in dynamic stereotypes: A comparison between Germany and the United States. *Psychology of Women Quarterly, 29,* 188–196.

Wildgrube, M. (2008). On work-life balance: In my own voice. In M. A. Paludi (Ed.), *The psychology of women at work* (Vol. 1, pp. 31–38). Westport, CT: Praeger.

Wilhelm, K. (2006). Depression: From nosology to global burden. In C. L. M. Keyes & S. H. Goodman (Eds.), *Women and depression: A handbook for the social, behavioral, and biomedical sciences* (pp. 3–21). New York: Cambridge University Press.

Willemsen, T. M. (1998). Widening the gender gap: Teenage magazines for girls and boys. *Sex Roles, 38,* 851–861.

Willetts, M. C., Sprecher, S., & Beck, E. D. (2004). Overview of sexual practices and attitudes within relational contexts. In J. H. Harvey, A. Wenzel, & S. Sprecher (Eds.), *The handbook of sexuality in close relationships* (pp. 57–85). Mahwah, NJ: Erlbaum.

Williams, C. L. (1998). The glass escalator: Hidden advantages for men in the "female" positions. In M. S. Kimmel & M. A. Messner (Eds.), *Men's lives* (4th ed., pp. 285–299). Boston: Allyn & Bacon.

Williams, D. R. (2003). The health of men: Structured inequalities and opportunities. *American Journal of Public Health, 9,* 724–731.

Williams, J. E., & Best, D. L. (1990). *Measuring sex stereotypes: A multinational study* (Rev. ed.). Newbury Park, CA: Sage.

Williams, J. E., Satterwhite, R. C., & Best, D. L. (1999). Pancultural gender stereotypes revisited: The five factor model. *Sex Roles, 40,* 513–525.

Williams, R. B. (2007, November 29). Tribal colleges: The model for cultural- and community-based education reform. *Diverse Issues in Higher Education,* p. 41.

Williams, S. L., & Frieze, I. H. (2005). Patterns of violent relationships, psychological distress, and marital satisfaction in a national sample of men and women. *Sex Roles, 52,* 771–784.

Williamson, E. (2009). The health system response to domestic violence. In E. Stark & E. S. Buzawa (Eds.), *Violence against women in families and relationships* (Vol. 1, pp. 163–184). Santa Barbara, CA: ABC-CLIO.

Willingham, W. W., & Cole, N. S. (1997). *Gender and fair assessment.* Mahwah, NJ: Erlbaum.

Wilson, G. T., Grilo, C. M., & Vitousek, K. M. (2007). Psychological treatment of eating disorders. *American Psychologist, 62,* 199–216.

Wilson, R. (2004, July 2). Students sue professor and U. of Texas in harassment case. *Chronicle of Higher Education,* A12.

Wilson, R. (2009, July 10). Is having more than 2 children an unspoken taboo? *Chronicle of Higher Education,* B16–B19.

Wincze, J. P., & Carey, M. P. (2001). *Sexual dysfunction: A guide for assessment and treatment* (2nd ed.). New York: Guilford.

Winer, R. L., et al. (2003). Genital human papillomavirus infection: Incidence and risk factors in a cohort of female university students. *American Journal of Epidemiology, 157,* 218–226.

Winer, R. L., et al. (2006). Condom use and the risk of genital human papillomavirus infection in young women. *New England Journal of Medicine, 354,* 2645–2666.

Winerman, L. (2004, September). Back to her roots. *American Psychologist, 59,* 46–47.

Winerman, L. (2005, June). Helping men to help themselves. *Monitor on Psychology,* pp. 57–68.

Winship, M. (2008). "The greatest silence: Rape in the Congo" illuminates and devastates. Retrieved April 29, 2010, from http://www. truthout.org/docs_2006/040108H. html

Winstead, B. A., Derlega, V. J., & Rose, S. (1997). *Gender and close relationships.* Thousand Oaks, CA: Sage.

Winstead, B. A., & Griffin, J. L. (2001). Friendship styles. In J. Worell (Ed.), *Encyclopedia of women and gender* (pp. 481–492). San Diego: Academic Press.

Winston, A. S. (Ed.). (2003). *Defining difference: Race and racism in the history of psychology.* Washington, DC: American Psychological Association.

Winter, D. D. (1996). *Ecological psychology: Healing the split between planet and self.* New York: HarperCollins.

Winters, A. M., & Duck, S. (2001). You ****! Swearing as an aversive and a relational activity. In R. M. Kowalski (Ed.), *Behaving badly* (pp. 59–77). Washington, DC: American Psychological Association.

Wise, D., & Stake, J. E. (2002). The moderating roles of personal and social resources on the relationship between dual expectations (for instrumentality and expressiveness) and well-being. *Journal of Social Psychology, 142,* 109–119.

Wise, P. H. (2002). Prenatal care, delivery, and birth outcomes. In N. Halfon, K. T. McLearn, & M. A. Schuster (Eds.), *Child rearing in America* (pp. 263–292). New York: Cambridge University Press.

Wise, T. (2008). *This is your nation on White privilege.* Retrieved September 15, 2008, from http://www. redroom.com/blog/tim-wise/this-your-nation-white-privilege

Wodak, R. (2005). Discourse. In P. Essed, D. T. Goldberg, & A. Kobayashi (Eds.), *A companion to gender studies* (pp. 519–529). Malden, MA: Blackwell.

Wolf, N. (2001). *Misconceptions.* New York: Doubleday.

Women's Media Center. (2019). *The status of women in the U.S. media 2019.* Retrieved September 28, 2021 from https://www.womensmediacenter.com/assets/site/from-bsd/WMCStatusofWomeninUSMedia2019.pdf

Wonder Girls. (2007, Fall). *American Educator,* p. 4.

Wood, E., Desmarais, S., & Gugula, S. (2002). The impact of parenting experience on gender stereotyped toy play of children. *Sex Roles, 47,* 39–49.

Wood, W., & Eagly, A. H. (2010). Gender. In S. T. Fiske, D. T. Gilbert, & G. Lindzey (Eds.), *Handbook of social psychology* (Vol. 1, pp. 629–667). Hoboken, NJ: Wiley.

Wood, M. D., Vinson, D. C, & Sher, K. J. (2001). Alcohol use and misuse. In A. Baum, T. A. Revenson, & J. E. Singer (Eds.), *Handbook of health psychology* (pp. 281–318). Mahwah, NJ: Erlbaum.

Woodzicka, J. A. (2008). Sex differences in self-awareness of smiling during a mock job interview. *Journal of Nonverbal Behavior, 32,* 109–121.

Woodzicka, J. A., & LaFrance, M. (2005). The effects of subtle sexual harassment on women's performance in a job interview. *Sex Roles, 53,* 67–77.

Woolf, S. E., & Maisto, S. A. (2008). Gender differences in condom use behavior? The role of power and partner-type. *Sex Roles, 58,* 689–701.

Woollett, A., & Marshall, H. (1997). Discourses of pregnancy and childbirth. In L. Yardley (Ed.), *Material discourses of health and illness* (pp. 176–198). London: Routledge.

Woolley, H. T. (1910). Psychological literature: A review of the recent literature on the psychology of sex. *Psychological Bulletin, 7,* 335–342.

Word, C. H., Zanna, M. P., & Cooper, J. (1974). The nonverbal mediation of self-fulfilling prophecies in interracial interaction. *Journal of Experimental Social Psychology, 10,* 109–120.

Worell, J. & Remer, P. P. (2003). *Feminist perspectives in therapy: Empowering diverse women* (2nd ed.). New York: Wiley.

Workman, J. E., & Freeburg, E. W. (1999). An examination of date rape, victim dress, and perceiver variables within the context of attribution theory. *Sex Roles, 41,* 261–277.

World Data. (2021). *Life expectancy for men and women.* [Database]. Retrieved October 5, 2021 from https://www.worlddata.info/life-expectancy.php

World Health Organization. (2005b). *World health report 2005 statistical annex.* Retrieved September 7, 2005, from http://www.who.int/ whr/2005/annex/en/index.html

World Health Organization. (2009). *Women and health: Today's evidence, tomorrow's agenda.* Retrieved October 5, 2021 from https://apps.who.int/iris/bitstream/handle/10665/70119/WHO_IER_MHI_STM.09.1_eng.pdf;sequence=1

World Health Organization. (2016). *Pregnant women must be able to access the right care at the right time, says WHO.* Retrieved October 4, 2021 from https://www.who.int/news/item/07-11-2016-pregnant-women-must-be

-able-to-access-the-right-care-at-the-right-time-says-who

World Health Organization. (2017). *Preventing HIV during pregnancy and pregnancy in the context of prep.* Retrieved October 5, 2021 from https://apps.who.int/iris/bitstream/handle/10665/255866/WHO-HIV-2017.09-eng.pdf

World Health Organization. (2018). *Infant mortality.* Retrieved October 4, 2021 from https://www.who.int/data/gho/data/themes/topics/indicator-groups/indicator-group-details/GHO/infant-mortality#:~:text=Globally%2C%20the%20infant%20mortality%20rate,to%204.0%20million%20in%202018.

World Health Organization. (2019). *Mental disorders.* Retrieved October 5, 2021 from https://www.who.int/news-room/fact-sheets/detail/mental-disorders

World Health Organization (2019). *Trends in maternal mortality: 2000–2017.* Retrieved October 4, 2021 from https://www.unfpa.org/featured-publication/trends-maternal-mortality-2000-2017

World Health Organization. (2021). *Adolescent health.* Retrieved October 5, 2021 from https://www.who.int/health-topics/adolescent-health#tab=tab_1

World Health Organization. (2021). *Female life expectancy: Situation and trends.* World Health Organization Global Health Observatory Data. Retrieved October 5, 2021 from https://www.who.int/data/gho/data/themes/topics/indicator-groups/indicator-group-details/GHO/life-expectancy-and-healthy-life-expectancy

World Health Organization. (2021). *Female genital mutilation.* Retrieved October 5, 2021 from https://www.who.int/news-room/fact-sheets/detail/female-genital-mutilation.

Worldometer. (2020). *Canada demographics.* Retrieved October 4,

2021 from https://www.worldometers.info/demographics/canada-demographics/

World Population Review. (2021). *Countries with universal health care 2021.* [World Population Review database]. Retrieved October 5, 2021 from https://worldpopulationreview.com/country-rankings/countries-with-universal-healthcare

Wosinska, W., Dabul, A. J., Whetstone-Dion, M. R., & Cialdini, R. B. (1996). Self-presentational responses to success in the organization: The costs and benefits of modesty. *Basic and Applied Social Psychology, 18,* 229–242.

Wright, A. (2008, April 28). *Is there an Army cover-up of rape and murder of women soldiers?* Retrieved April 28, 2008, from http://www.truth-out.org/docs_2006/042808A.shtml

Wright, C. V., & Fitzgerald, L. F. (2007). Angry and afraid: Women's appraisal of sexual harassment during litigation. *Psychology of Women Quarterly, 31,* 73–84.

Wright, K. (1997, February). Anticipatory guidance: Developing a healthy sexuality. *Pediatric Annals,* pp. S142–S145.

Wright, P. H. (1998). Toward an expanded orientation to the study of sex differences in friendship. In D. J. Canary & K. Dindia (Eds.), *Sex differences and similarities in communication* (pp. 41–63). Mahwah, NJ: Erlbaum.

Wright, R., et al. (2008). Training generalized spatial skills. *Psychonomic Bulletin & Review, 15,* 768–771.

Writing Group for the Women's Health Initiative Investigators. (2002). Risks and benefits of estrogen plus progestin in healthy postmenopausal women. *Journal of the American Medical Association, 288,* 321–333.

Wu, H. (2018). Grandchildren living in a grandparent-headed household. *Family Profiles,* FP-18-01. Bowling Green,

OH: National Center for Family & Marriage Research.

Yamamiya, Y., et al. (2005). Women's exposure to thin-and-beautiful media images: Body image effects of media-ideal internalization and impact-reduction interventions, *Body Image, 2,* 74–80.

Yang, Z., & Schank, J. C. (2006). Women do not synchronize their menstrual cycles. *Human Nature, 17,* 433–447.

Yarkin, K. L., Town, J. P., & Wallston, B. S. (1982). Blacks and women must try harder: Stimulus persons' race and sex attributions of causality. *Personality and Social Psychology Bulletin, 8,* 21–30.

Yazzie, V. (2018, October 25). Letters: Feminism is against our culture. *Navajo Times.* Retrieved October 5, 2021 from https://navajotimes.com/opinion/letters/letters-feminism-is-against-our-culture/

Yean, C., Benau, E. M., Dakanalis, A., Hormes, J. M., Perone, J., & Timko, C. A. (2013). The relationship of sex and sexual orientation to self-esteem, body shape satisfaction, and eating disorder symptomatology. *Frontiers in Psychology, 4,* 1–11.

Yee, B., & Chiriboga, D. A. (2007). Issues of diversity in health psychology and aging. In C. M. Aid-win, C. L. Park, & A. Spiro III (Eds.), *Handbook of health psychology and aging* (pp. 286–312). New York: Guilford.

Yllö, K. A. (2005). Through a feminist lens: Gender, diversity and violence: Extending the feminist framework. In D. R. Loseke, R. J. Gelles, & M. M. Cavanaugh (Eds.), *Current controversies on family violence* (2nd ed., pp. 19–34). Thousand Oaks, CA: Sage.

Yoder, J. D. (2000). Women and work. In M. Biaggio & M. Hersen (Eds.), *Issues in the psychology of women* (pp. 71–91). New York: Kluwer Academic/Plenum.

Yoder, J. D. (2002). 2001 Division 35 presidential address: Context

matters: Understanding tokenism processes and their impact on women's work. *Psychology of Women Quarterly, 26,* 1–8.

Yoder, J. D., & Aniakudo, P. (1997). " Outsider within" the firehouse: Subordination and difference in the social interactions of African American women firefighters. *Gender and Society, 11,* 324–341.

Yoder, J. D., & Berendsen, L. L. (2001). " Outsider within" the firehouse: African American and White women firefighters. *Psychology of Women Quarterly, 25,* 27–36.

Yoder, J. D., Christopher, J., & Holmes, J. D. (2008). Are television commercials still achievement scripts for women? *Psychology of Women Quarterly, 32,* 303–311.

Yoder, J. D., Fischer, A. R., Kahn, A. S., & Groden, J. (2007). Changes in students' explanations for gender differences after taking a psychology of women class: More constructionist and less essentialist. *Psychology of Women Quarterly, 31,* 415–425.

Yoder, J. D., & Kahn, A. S. (2003). Making gender comparisons more meaningful: A call for more attention to social context. *Psychology of Women Quarterly, 27,* 281–290.

Yoder, J. D., & McDonald, T. W. (1998). Measuring sexist discrimination in the workplace: Support for the validity of the schedule of sexist events. *Psychology of Women Quarterly, 22,* 487–491.

Yoder, J. D., Perry, R. L., & Saal, E. I. (2007). What good is a feminist identity?: Women's feminist identification and role expectations for intimate and sexual relationships. *Sex Roles, 57,* 365–372.

Yoder, J. D., Schleicher, T. L., & McDonald, T. W. (1998). Empowering token women leaders: The importance of organizationally legitimated credibility. *Psychology of Women Quarterly, 22,* 209–222.

Young, A. M., Stewart, A. J., & Miner-Rubino, K. (2001). Women's understandings of their own divorces: A developmental perspective. In D. P. McAdams, R. Josselson, & A. Lieblich (Eds.), *Turns in the road: Narrative studies of lives in transition* (pp. 203–226).Washington, DC: American Psychological Association.

Young, D. (1982). *Changing childbirth: Family birth in the hospital.* Rochester, NY: Childbirth Graphics.

Young, D. (2003). The push against vaginal birth. *Birth, 30,* 149–152.

Young, D. (2009). What is normal childbirth and do we need more statements about it? *Birth, 36,* 1–3.

Young, J., & Bursik, K. (2000). Identity development and life plan maturity: A comparison of women athletes and nonathletes. *Sex Roles, 43,* 241–254.

Young, J. E., Rygh, J. L., Weinberger, A. D., & Beck, A. T. (2008). Cognitive therapy for depression. In D. H. Barlow (Ed.), *Clinical handbook of psychological disorders* (pp. 250–305). New York: Guilford.

Young, K., Fisher, J., & Kirkman, M. (2019). "Do mad people get endo or does endo make you mad?": Clinicians' discursive constructions of medicine and women with endometriosis. *Feminism & Psychology, 29,* 337-356.

Young, P. D. (2005). Religion. In P. Essed, D. T. Goldberg, & Audrey Kobayashi (Eds.), *A companion to gender studies* (pp. 509–518). Malden, MA: Blackwell.

Yousaf, O., Popat, A., & Hunter, M. S. (2015). An investigation of masculinity attitudes, gender, and attitudes toward psychological help-seeking. *Psychology of Men & Masculinity, 16,* 234–237.

Yu-Hsin Liao, K. Wei, M., & Yin, M. (2020). The misunderstood schema of the Strong Black Woman: Exploring its mental health consequences and coping responses among African American women. *Psychology of Women Quarterly, 44*, 84-104.

Zaal, M., Salah, T., & Fine, M. (2007). The weight of the hyphen: Freedom, fusion, and responsibility embodied by young Muslim-American women during a time of surveillance. *Applied Development Science, 11*, 164–177.

Zack, N. (2005). *Inclusive feminism: A third wave theory of women's commonality.* Lanham, MD: Rowman & Littlefield.

Zajicek, A., Calasaanti, T., Ginther, C., & Summers, J. (2006). Intersectionality and age relations: Unpaid care work and Chicanas. In T. M. Calasanti & K. F. Slevin (Eds.), *Age matters: Realigning feminist thinking* (pp. 175–197). New York: Routledge.

Zakriski, A. L., Wright, J. C., & Underwood, M. K. (2005). Gender similarities and differences in children's social behavior: Finding personality in contextualized patterns of adaptation. *Journal of Personality and Social Psychology, 88*, 844–855.

Zandy, J. (2001). "Women have always sewed" : The production of clothing and the work of women. In J. Zandy (Ed.), *What we hold in common: An introduction to working-class studies* (pp. 148–153). New York: Feminist Press.

Zarembka, J. M. (2003). America's dirty work: Migrant maids and modern-day slavery. In B. Ehrenreich & A. R. Hochschild (Eds.), *Global woman* (pp. 142–153). New York: Metropolitan Books.

Zebrowitz, L. A., & Montepare, J. M. (2000). "Too young, too old": Stigmatizing adolescents and elders. In T. F. Heatherton, et al.

(Eds.), *The social psychology of stigma* (pp. 334–373). New York: Guilford.

Zeigler, M. (2008, July 17). Knifing called " honor attack" : Afghan immigrant accused of trying to kill sister for being "bad Muslim." *Rochester Democrat and Chronicle*, pp. A1–A2.

Zeigler-Hill, V., & Noser, A. (2015). Will I ever think I'm thin enough? A moderated mediation study of women's contingent self-esteem, body image discrepancies, and disordered eating. *Psychology of Women Quarterly, 39*, 109-118.

Zeldes, K., & Norsigian, J. (2008). Encouraging women to consider a less medicalized approach to childbirth without turning them off: Challenges to producing *Our bodies, ourselves: Pregnancy and Birth. Birth, 35*, 245–249.

Zell, E., Krizan, Z., & Teeter, K. (2015). Evaluating gender similarities and differences using metasynthesis. *American Psychologist, 70*, 10-20.

Zeng, Y., & Hesketh, T. (2016). The effects of China's universal two-child policy. *Lancet, 388*(10054), 1930-1938.

Zerbe, K. J. (1999). *Women's mental health in primary care.* Philadelphia: W. B. Saunders.

Zhao, F., Franco, H., Rodriguez, K. F., Brown, P. R., Tsai, M-J., Tsai, S. Y., & Yao, H. H.-C. (2017). Elimination of the male reproductive tract in the female embryo is promoted by COUP-TFII in mice. *Science, 357*(6352), 717-720.

Zheng, L., & Su, Y. (2018). Patterns of asexuality in China: Sexual activity, sexual and romantic attraction, and sexual desire. *Archives of Sexual Behavior, 47*, 1265–1276.

Zhou, L.-Y. (2006). American and Chinese college students' anticipations of their postgraduate education, career, and future family roles. *Sex Roles, 55*, 95–110.

Ziegler, L. (2008, April 2). *On-screen sex ratios add up to one big minus.* Retrieved April 2, 2008, from http://www.truthout.org/docs

Zigerell, L. J. (2018). Black and White discrimination in the United States: Evidence from an archive of survey experiment studies. *Research and Politics, January-March*, 1-7.

Zittleman, K. (2007). Teachers, students, and Title IX: A promise for fairness. In D. M. Sadker & E. S. Silber (Eds.), *Gender in the classroom* (pp. 73–107). Mahwah, NJ: Erlbaum.

Zucker, A. N. (2004). Disavowing social identities: What it means when women say, "I'm not a feminist, but." *Psychology of Women Quarterly, 28*, 423–436.

Zucker, A. N., & Stewart, A. J. (2007). Growing up and growing older: Feminism as a context for women's lives. *Psychology of Women Quarterly*, 137–145.

Zurbriggen, E. L., & Freyd, J. J. (2004). The link between child sexual abuse and risky sexual behavior: The role of dissociative tendencies, information-processing effects, and consensual sex decision mechanisms. In L. J. Koenig, L. S. Doll, A. O' Leary, & W. Pequegn (Eds.), *From child sexual abuse to adult sexual risk: Trauma, revictimization, and intervention* (pp. 135–157). Washington, DC: American Psychological Association.

Glossary

A

ableism: bias or discrimination against people with disabilities

abuse of women: intentional acts that injure someone, including physical, psychological, and sexual abuse; includes *intimate partner violence*

access discrimination: refers to discrimination used in hiring—for example, rejecting well-qualified applicants or offering them less attractive positions

achievement motivation: desire to accomplish something on your own and to do it well

acquaintance rape: rape by a person known to the rape survivor, who is not related by blood or marriage

acquired immunodeficiency syndrome (AIDS): a viral disease spread by infected semen, vaginal secretions, breast milk, or blood; AIDS destroys the body's normal immune system and is caused by the HIV virus

adolescence: transition phase between childhood and adulthood that is accompanied by psychological, social and emotional changes

affirmative action: process by which an employer makes special efforts to consider qualified members of underrepresented groups during hiring, as well as during decisions about salary and promotion; occurs when employers actively work to remove any barriers that prevent genuine equality of opportunity

ageism: bias based on a person's chronological age

agency: term that describes a concern with your own self-interests; includes characteristics such as *self-confidence* and *competitiveness*

aggression: behavior that is directed toward another person, with the intention of doing harm to that person

alcohol use disorder: refers to a pattern of alcohol use that repeatedly leads to significant impairment, including missing work or school, arrests for alcohol-related crimes, or family problems

allies: people who provide support to groups other than their own

altruism: unselfish behavior that benefits others at some cost to the individual

ambivalent sexism: sexism that reflects a mixture of negative and positive attitudes toward women, and combines aspects of both *hostile sexism* and *benevolent sexism*

amenorrhea: the cessation of menstrual periods, often associated with *anorexia nervosa*

androcentric generic: in languages, the use of masculine nouns and pronouns to refer to all human beings—of all genders—instead of referring only to men; also known as the *masculine generic*

androcentrism: belief system in which the male experience is treated as the norm in society; also known as the *normative-male problem*

androgen: one of the male sex hormones

androgen insensitivity syndrome: a condition in which genetic males (XY) produce normal amounts of androgen, but their bodies do not respond to androgen, the genital tubercle does not grow into a penis, and the external genitals appear female

androgynous: describes a person who scores high on both femininity and masculinity scales; most often associated with Bem's Sex-Role Inventory

anorexia nervosa: eating disorder characterized by an extreme fear of gaining weight, inadequate body weight (defined as 85% of expected weight), and a distorted body image

antisocial personality disorder: personality disorder in which someone engages in behaviors that clearly violate the rights of other people, including excessive aggressiveness, impulsiveness, and lying

anxiety disorders: psychological disorders in which a person's anxiety is intense and persistent

asexuality: a sexual orientation in which people have low sexual attraction to others

attributions: explanations and beliefs about the causes of your own or others' behavior

B

baby blues: a short-lasting change in mood that usually occurs during the first 10 days after childbirth; symptoms include crying, sadness, insomnia, irritability, anxiety, and a lack of confidence, as well as feeling overwhelmed; also called *postpartum blues*

benevolent sexism: more subtle kind of sexism that argues for women's special niceness and purity; primarily directed toward traditional women, such as stay-at-home-mothers

binge drinking: alcohol drinking patterns defined as five or more drinks on one occasion for men and four or more drinks on one occasion for women

binge-eating disorder: eating disorder characterized by frequent episodes of binge eating, but unlike *bulimia nervosa,* without compensation for those binges by using unhealthy weight-loss methods such as vomiting or the use of laxatives

bisexuality: a sexual orientation characterized by psychological, emotional, and sexual attraction to both women and men

bisexual woman: a cisgender or transgender woman who is psychologically, emotionally, and sexually attracted to both women and men

box-score approach: a summary method in which researchers read through all the appropriate studies on a given topic, consider both statistically meaningful and nonmeaningful results, and draw conclusions based on a tally of their outcomes; also called the *counting approach*

boys' code: a set of rigid rules about how boys should speak and behave

bulimia nervosa: eating disorder characterized by an ability to maintain a normal body weight, but involving frequent episodes of secretive binge eating (i.e., consuming 1,000 to 4,000 calories at a time) and unhealthy methods to prevent weight gain such as using laxatives, dieting, or excessive exercise

C

cardiovascular disease: leading cause of death for U.S. women that includes heart attacks and other disorders of the heart, as well as clots and other disorders of the blood vessels

care approach: approach to moral decision-making in which individuals are interrelated with other people in a web of connections; often associated with Carol Gilligan's theory

cervical cancer: cancer that affects the lower portion of the uterus

cesarean birth (cesarean section or C-section): surgical birth technique in which a physician makes an incision through the woman's abdomen and into the uterus to deliver the baby

child sexual abuse: occurs when an adult engages in any kind of sexual contact with a child; this contact includes sexual touching, stimulation of the genitals, and intercourse

chilly classroom climate: occurs when female students receive a message from teachers or faculty that they have entered a male-dominated environment where they are not welcome, may be treated differently than men, or may feel ignored and devalued in the classroom

chlamydia: curable sexually transmitted infection that often causes no symptoms, but may cause painful urination, vaginal discharge, and infertility; can cause infertility if left untreated and can be passed to a newborn during vaginal delivery

chronic health problem: a long-lasting illness that cannot be completely cured

cisgender: refers to individuals who have a match between the sex they were assigned at birth, their reproductive anatomy or biological sex, and their gender identity

classism: bias that is based on a person's socioeconomic status or social class

clitoris: a small sensitive organ that plays a central role in women's orgasms

cognitive-behavioral approach: therapeutic approach emphasizing that psychological problems arise from irrational thoughts and maladaptive thinking (cognitive factors) and inappropriate learning (behavioral factors), and encourages clients to develop new behaviors and thoughts about themselves

cognitive developmental approach: theoretical perspective proposing that children are active thinkers who seek information from their environment, try to make sense of this information, and organize it in a coherent fashion

cognitive restructuring: sex therapy technique in which a therapist tries to change people's inappropriately negative thoughts about some aspect of sexuality and also reduce thoughts that interfere with sexual activity and pleasure

communion: term that emphasizes a concern for your relationship with other people; includes characteristics such as *gentle* and *warm*

comparable worth: argument that women and men should receive equal pay for different jobs when those different jobs are comparable (i.e., when the jobs require equal training and equal ability)

compulsory motherhood: belief that all women should have children; also called *pronatalism*

confounding variable: any characteristic, other than the central variable being studied, that is not equivalent under all conditions and has the potential to influence the study's result

congenital adrenal hyperplasia: condition in which genetic females (XX) receive as much androgen as males do during prenatal development, and this excess androgen causes their genitals to appear somewhat masculine at birth

contractive posture: nonverbal posture that conveys submissiveness, such as keeping one's legs together with arms and hands close to one's body

counting approach: a summary method in which researchers read through all the appropriate studies on a given topic, consider both statistically meaningful and nonmeaningful results, and draw conclusions based on a tally of their outcomes; also called the *box-score approach*

critical thinking: a form of thinking in which individuals test ideas or possible solutions for errors, or consider a problem from multiple points of view; involves conceptualizing, analyzing, synthesizing, and evaluating information

cultural feminism: form of feminism that emphasizes the positive qualities that are presumed to be stronger in women than in men—qualities such as nurturing, social cooperation, and care-taking rather than aggression

cultural identity: facet of identity that incorporates ideas and customs associated with a social grouping such as country of origin, ethnic group, geographic region, or religion

culture of thinness: societal norms that emphasize an intense focus on being thin and concern about physical appearance and weight, even when one's weight is appropriate

D

decoding ability: ability or skill in interpreting another person's nonverbal behavior and figuring out what emotion that person is feeling

demisexuality: a sexual orientation in which someone is only sexually attracted to a person with whom they have formed a strong emotional connection

denial of personal disadvantage: occurs when someone is reluctant to acknowledge that they personally are the victim of discriminatory treatment from an employer

differences perspective: theoretical perspective proposing that men and women are generally different in their intellectual and social abilities

disability: refers to a physical or mental impairment that limits a person's ability to perform a major life activity in the manner considered normative

disability studies: an interdisciplinary field that examines disabilities from the perspective of the social sciences, natural science, the arts, the humanities, education, and media studies

discrimination: differential treatment of the members of different groups that often involves negative, hostile, and injurious treatment of people in the rejected groups

disenfranchised grief: grieving without being able to publicly show those emotions or receive social support from others

doing gender: active, dynamic process that occurs when expressing one's gender during interactions with other people

double standard of aging: cultural norm by which people judge older women even more harshly than older men

doula: a woman experienced in childbirth who provides continuous support to a family throughout labor and delivery

dynamical systems approach: proposes that a woman may experience new sexual feelings that occur in specific situations, and then she thinks about these experiences, eventually creating a new perspective about her sexuality

dysmenorrhea: menstrual pain that typically refers to painful cramps in the abdomen that may also include headache, nausea, dizziness, fatigue, and pain in the lower back

E

ecofeminism: a feminist approach that opposes the way that humans destroy other animals and natural resources

egalitarian marriage: marital structure that emphasizes companionship, sharing, and friendship, where which both partners share power equally, de-emphasize traditional gender roles, and have equal responsibility for housework, child care, finances, and decision making

emergency contraception: hormone pills that prevent pregnancy by inhibiting ovulation and by producing other changes in the cervix and the uterus

empathy: a person's ability to understand the emotion that another person is feeling, experience that same emotion, and feel concerned about that person's well-being

employed women: women who work for pay; employed women may receive a salary or be self-employed

empowerment self-defense (ESD) training: training programs that help women develop resistance to rape and assault, teach women strategies for avoiding sexual violence, situate the problem of sexual violence in the broader societal and cultural context, and empower women and gender and sexual minorities to focus on their bodies as a source of strength, rather than as liabilities

empty nest: the period after which children are no longer living at home with their childhood caregivers

entitlement: perception that someone deserves greater power simply because they are members of a particular group

essentialism: theoretical perspective that gender is a basic, unchangeable, and stable characteristic that resides within an individual, rather than in social or cultural structures, and that all members of a gender category share the same psychological characteristics

estrogen: one of the female sex hormones

ethnic gloss: occurs when people incorrectly infer that all members of an ethnic group share a common set of characteristics

evolutionary-psychology approach: theoretical perspective that argues various species gradually change over the course of many generations so that they can adapt better to their environment and succeed in passing on their genes to the next generation

excitement phase: first phase of the sexual response cycle, in which people become sexually aroused by touching and erotic thoughts and blood rushes to the genital region, causing *vasocongestion*

expansive posture: posture which is linked to feelings of power and dominance, such as sitting or standing with legs apart, and moving hands and arms away from the body

explicit gender stereotypes: stereotypes that are expressed when you are overtly aware that you are being tested

F

fat studies: area of scholarly inquiry and critical analysis that argues that the United States is a fat-hating culture, and that people need to rethink their approach to body weight; examines popular culture, the medical profession, and the weight-loss industry

feedback loop: self-regulatory cycle that regulates hormone release in which low levels of a particular hormone signals a brain structure to produce more of that hormone; when the level of a hormone is too high, a brain structure begins a chain of events that decreases that hormone

female genital cutting or mutilation: surgical procedure that involves cutting or removing a section of a girl's genitals, usually including part or all of the clitoris, but also sometimes including removal of the labia minora and stitching the labia majora together

female orgasmic disorder: condition in which a woman experiences sexual excitement, but she does not reach orgasm and is currently unhappy about her sexual experiences; also called *anorgasmia* or *orgasmic dysfunction*

feminism: the principle that values women's experiences and ideas; feminism emphasizes that women, men, and people of all genders should be socially, economically, and legally equal

feminist social identity: identity that incorporates a feminist world view

feminist therapy: therapeutic approach in which clients are treated in a nonsexist fashion, women's and gender and sexuality minority individuals' strengths are emphasized, and the distribution of power between the client and the therapist is as equal as possible

fetal alcohol syndrome: condition in which children born to mothers who use high amounts of alcohol during pregnancy experience facial abnormalities, slowed physical growth, psychological abnormalities, and a higher risk of intellectual disability

filial responsibility: situation in which people feel obligated to take care of family members based on social norms or personal belief systems

fluid lesbians: according to Lisa Diamond's research, lesbian women who questioned or changed their lesbian sexual identity at some point during development

frequency distribution: statistical representation that shows how many people in a sample receive each score

G

gender: psychological characteristics and social categories that human culture creates; implies the psychological, behavioral, social, and cultural traits associated with being male, female, or nonbinary

gender as a stimulus variable: treatment of gender as a characteristic of a person to which other people react

gender as a subject variable: treatment of gender as a characteristic within a person that influences the way they act

gender bias: general term that reflects stereotypes, prejudice, and discriminatory practices directed against people of a particular sex or gender, usually women

genderqueer: refers to individuals who express a gender identity that is beyond the traditional binary and is not exclusively male or female

gender identity: one's self-identification and labeling as male, female, or nonbinary; influenced by both sociocultural and biological forces

gender nonconforming: refers to individuals who do not identify as transgender, but also do not conform to traditional gender norms

gender polarization: cognitive tendency to divide the world into two groups—male and female—and to perceive all males as being similar, all females as being similar, and the two gender categories as being different from each other

gender-role spillover: occurs when beliefs about gender roles and characteristics spread to the work setting

gender schemas: cognitive organizational frameworks in which gender is organized into conceptual categories,

most often *female* and *male*, and that encourage people to think and act in gender-stereotyped ways that are consistent with their gender schemas

gender segregation: tendency to associate with other people of the same gender, observed most often among children

gender stereotypes: the relatively fixed and overly simplified beliefs, generalizations, and assumptions that we associate with women, men, and nonbinary, transgender, or genderqueer people

gender typing: process by which children acquire their knowledge about gender and how they develop their gender-related personality characteristics, preferences, skills, behaviors, and self-concepts

gendered racism: a specific form of racism that includes multiple intersecting forms of oppression and discrimination, and is associated with an increased likelihood of depression and traumatic stress

genital herpes: sexually transmitted infection that causes painful genital blisters, and often several attacks per year; can lead to cervical cancer and can be passed to a newborn during vaginal delivery

glass ceiling: an invisible but rigid barrier that seems to prevent women and people of color from reaching the top levels in many professional organizations

glass escalator: applies to men who enter occupational fields that are often associated with women, such as nursing, teaching, library science, and social work; in these occupations, men are often quickly promoted to management or more prestigious positions

gonads: male and female sex glands

gonorrhea: curable sexually transmitted infection that may lead to vaginal discharge and pelvic pain but may not have visible symptoms; can cause infertility if left untreated and can be passed to a newborn during vaginal delivery

H

health psychology: an interdisciplinary area in psychology that focuses on the causes of illness, the treatment of illness, illness prevention, and health improvement

heroism: risking one's life for the welfare of other people

heterosexism: a belief system that devalues lesbian women, gay men, and bisexual women—any group that is not heterosexual; also called *sexual prejudice*

heterosexuality: a sexual orientation in which a cisgender man or woman experiences sexual attraction for someone of the opposite sex or gender

hooking up: usually refers to a sexual encounter in which two people—who are not in an established relationship or are uncommitted—have sexual interactions that may range from behaviors such as nongenital touching to oral sex or intercourse

hormone replacement therapy (HRT): a term that usually refers to the administration of a combination of estrogen and progestin, although some forms of HRT involve the use of only estrogen; hormone replacement therapy relieves some of the physical symptoms of menopause, such as hot flashes

hostile-environment harassment: a form of sexual harassment that applies to a situation in which the atmosphere at school or at work is so intimidating and unpleasant that a student or an employee cannot work effectively

hostile sexism: blatant kind of sexism based on the idea that women should be subservient to men and should "know their place"; primarily directed toward nontraditional women, such as female professionals and feminists

hot flash: common symptom of menopause in which people experience a sensation of heat coming from within the body

human immunodeficiency virus (HIV): virus that causes acquired immunodeficiency syndrome; HIV destroys white blood cells that coordinate the immune system's ability to fight infectious diseases

human papillomavirus (HPV) or genital warts: sexually transmitted infection caused by various strains of the human papilloma virus that causes small, often painless swellings in the genital area; can lead to cervical cancer and can be passed to a newborn during vaginal delivery

hysterectomy: the surgical removal of a woman's uterus; may be *total* (includes removal of the cervix), *subtotal* (includes only removal of the uterus above the cervix), or *radical* (includes removal of part of the vagina, along with the uterus and cervix)

I

identity: self-rating of personal characteristics in the physical, psychological, and social dimensions

implicit gender stereotypes: automatic stereotypes you reveal when you are not aware that your gender stereotypes are being assessed

incest: refers to sexual contact between biologically related individuals; this contact includes sexual touching, stimulation of the genitals, or intercourse

individual approach: explanations for occupational segregation that argue that female socialization encourages women to develop personality traits and skills that are inappropriate for "male occupations"; also called *person-centered explanations*

infancy: the period between birth and 18 months of life

infant mortality rate: the annual number of deaths prior to the first birthday, per 1,000 live births

infertility: failure to conceive or become pregnant after 1 year of heterosexual intercourse without using contraception

intersectionality: theoretical perspective emphasizing that each person belongs to multiple social groups based on categories such as ethnicity, gender, sexual orientation, ability, age, and social class

intersex: refers to individuals who are born with reproductive anatomy or genitals that do not necessarily match their genes, sex chromosomes, or hormones, or they have bodies that are not consistently male or female, or are atypical of cisgender women and men

intersex individual: someone who is born with sex characteristics that are not clearly female or male

intimate partner violence: physical, psychological, and sexual abuse of a partner with whom someone has an intimate relationship

intrinsic motivation: tendency to work on a task for your own satisfaction, rather than for rewards such as money or praise

J

justice approach: approach to moral decision-making where each individual is part of a hierarchy in which some people have more power and influence than others; often associated with Carol Gilligan's theory

L

labyrinth metaphor: metaphor that women in search of an occupational promotion will encounter many difficulties along the route, including dead ends, detours, and puzzling pathways

lateralization: one-sided preferences influenced by the two halves (or hemispheres) of the brain that function somewhat differently

lesbian woman: a cisgender or transgender woman who is psychologically, emotionally, and sexually attracted to other women

liberal feminism: form of feminism that emphasizes the goal of gender equality, giving women and men the same legal rights and opportunities

low sexual desire: condition in which a person has little interest in sexual activity and is distressed by this lack of desire

lumpectomy: surgery that removes a cancerous lump and the immediate surrounding breast tissue

M

machismo: in Latina/o heterosexual relationships, the belief that men must show their manhood by being strong, sexual, and dominant over women

major depressive disorder: psychological disorder in which a person experiences frequent episodes of hopelessness and low self-esteem, and may not find pleasure in previously pleasurable activities

mammogram: procedure administered to screen for breast cancer that involves taking an X-ray of the breast—a picture of breast tissue—while the breast tissue is flattened between two plastic plates

marianismo: in Latina/o heterosexual relationships, the belief that women must remain chaste until marriage, be passive and long suffering, and give up their own needs to help their husbands and children

maquiladoras (maquilas): sweatshops located in Latin America, that are typically run by U.S. corporations

masculine generic: in languages, the use of masculine nouns and pronouns to refer to all human beings—of all genders—instead of referring only to men; also known as the *androcentric generic*

menarche: major biological milestone of puberty in which girls begin to menstruate

menopause: developmental change at midlife that occurs when cisgender women have stopped having menstrual periods for a period of 12 months; most people experience menopause between the ages of 45 and 55, with the average being 51

men's studies: a collection of scholarly activities—such as teaching courses and conducting research—that focus on men's lives; often emphasize gender-role socialization, gender-role conflict, the sexism problem, and ethnic diversity

mental rotation: ability to cognitively rotate a two- or three-dimensional figure rapidly and accurately

meta-analysis: a statistical method for integrating numerous studies on a single topic; yields a single number that tells us whether a particular variable has an overall effect

microaggressions: everyday insults and other actions that convey second-class status

miscarriage: an unintended termination of pregnancy—prior to the 24th week of pregnancy— before the fetus is viable and developed enough to survive after birth

modeling: type of learning in which children learn by observing others and imitating them; also called *observational learning*

morbidity: generalized poor health or illness that negatively affects one's life span

myth of meritocracy: myth that a person's social status indicates their abilities and achievements

mythopoetic approaches: men's studies approach proposing that modern men should use myths, storytelling, and poetry to develop their own well-being and spiritual growth

N

natural childbirth: birthing method that emphasizes empathic health-care providers who encourage empowerment and education about pregnancy and childbirth, relaxation techniques and exercises designed to strengthen muscles, controlled breathing and other focusing techniques to reduce pain, and social support from a partner or person trained as a caregiver

nonemployed women: women who are not paid for their work; they may do work for their families in their own homes, or for volunteer organizations, but they receive no money for these services

nonverbal communication: all forms of human communication that do not focus on actual words; includes tone of voice, facial expression, body language, and interpersonal distance from others

nonsexist therapy: therapeutic approach emphasizing that people of all genders and sexualities should be treated similarly, rather than in a gender-stereotyped fashion

normative-male problem: portrayal of men as the standard of comparison in society, whereas women are "the second sex"; also called *androcentrism*

nurturance: a kind of helping in which someone gives care to another person, usually someone who is younger or less competent at performing a particular task

O

objectified body consciousness: a tendency to view oneself as an object that can be looked at and judged by other people; typically increases when someone repeatedly encounters unrealistic images of women in the media

observational learning: type of learning in which children learn by observing others and imitating them; also called *modeling*

occupational segregation: occurs when men and women tend to choose different occupations

operational definition: description of exactly how researchers will measure or observe a variable (or characteristic) in a scientific study

orgasmic phase: third phase of the sexual response cycle in which the uterus and the outer part of the vagina contract strongly at intervals roughly a second apart, leading to the experience of orgasm

osteoporosis: degenerative bone disorder in which a person's bones become less dense and more fragile

ova: eggs in the reproductive system

ovaries: organs in the female reproductive system containing follicles that hold the *ova*, or eggs, and produce estrogen and progesterone

ovulation: on about the 14th day of the menstrual cycle, process by which an *ova*, or egg, breaks out of its follicle, moves into a fallopian tube, and then into the uterus

P

panic disorder: anxiety disorder in which a person experiences recurrent episodes of dread or fear, often without any warning

pansexuality: a sexual orientation in which someone experiences sexual, romantic, or emotional attraction toward someone's personality, regardless of their sexual orientation or gender identity

Pap smear test: removal of a small sample of cells from the cervix to determine whether they are normal, precancerous, or cancerous

paradox of well-being: paradox that many older women report high life satisfaction, despite the objective difficulties they encounter

peer group: other people of approximately one's own age

personal space: refers to the invisible boundary around each person—a boundary that other people should not invade during ordinary social interactions

person-centered explanations: explanations for occupational segregation that argue that female socialization encourages women to develop personality traits and skills that are inappropriate for "male occupations"; also called the *individual approach*

pharmacotherapy: therapeutic approach in which medication is used to treat psychological disorders

physical aggression: intentional aggression that could physically harm another person

placenta: organ in prenatal development that is connected to the growing embryo/fetus, and allows oxygen and nutrients to pass from the mother to the developing embryo/fetus

plateau phase: second phase of the sexual response cycle, in which the clitoris becomes extremely sensitive, shortens and draws back under the clitoral hood

postpartum blues: a short-lasting change in mood that usually occurs during the first 10 days after childbirth; symptoms include crying, sadness, insomnia, irritability, anxiety, and a lack of confidence, as well as feeling overwhelmed; also called *baby blues*

postpartum depression: a more intense and serious experience of depression that usually begins to develop within 6 months after childbirth and may last for many months; symptoms include feelings of extreme sadness, exhaustion, sleep disturbances, despair, lack of interest in enjoyable activities, loss of interest in the baby, and feelings of guilt

postpartum period: period following birth which extends from 0 to 6 weeks after birth

post-traumatic stress disorder (PTSD): a pattern of symptoms such as intense fear, heightened anxiety, and emotional numbing after a traumatic event

practical significance: occurs when the results of a research study have some meaningful and useful implications for the real world

prejudice: an emotional reaction or attitude, often negative, that people have toward a particular group of people

premature birth: birth that occurs at less than 37 weeks' gestation, which places a child at risk for medical complications; also called *preterm birth*

premenstrual syndrome (PMS): the cyclical set of symptoms that may occur a few days before menstruating that often includes headaches, breast soreness, swelling, nausea, increased sensitivity to pain, allergies, and acne, as well as psychological reactions such as depression, irritability, anxiety, dizziness, and low energy

prenatal period: developmental period spanning from conception to birth

preterm birth: birth that occurs at less than 37 weeks' gestation, which places a child at risk for medical complications; also called *premature birth*

pronatalism: belief that all women should have children; also called *compulsory motherhood*

profeminists: individuals who support feminism, want to eliminate destructive aspects of gender (i.e., gender stereotypes, gender inequalities, and gender-related violence), and who emphasize that strict gender roles can hurt both men and women

prostaglandins: substances that the body produces in high concentrations just before menstruation that can cause severe cramps

psychodynamic therapy: therapeutic approach that focuses on unconscious and unresolved conflicts stemming from childhood and emphasizes social relationships

psychological disorders: conditions in which individuals experience emotions, thoughts, and behaviors that are typically maladaptive, distressing to themselves, and different from the social norm

psychotherapy: a therapeutic process in which a therapist aims to treat a client's psychological problems and reduce distress, most often through verbal interactions

puberty: stage of physical development when changes that lead to sexual maturity occur and secondary sex characteristics begin to appear

Q

quid pro quo harassment: from the Latin, literally "one thing for another"; a form of sexual harassment in which a person with less power in a social or professional situation must submit to implicit or explicit sexual demands in exchange for positive professional outcomes

R

racism: bias against people on the basis of their racial or ethnic group

radical feminism: form of feminism that argues that the basic cause of women's oppression lies deep in the entire sex and gender structural system in society, rather than in superficial laws and policies

rape: defined as sexual penetration without the individual's consent, obtained by force or by threat of physical harm, or when the victim is incapable of giving consent

reading disability: refers to poor reading skills that are not accounted for by the level of general intelligence

relational aggression: aggression that could harm another person through intentionally manipulating interpersonal relationships, such as friendships

religious approaches: men's studies approach arguing that men should take back their roles as head of the household so that they can become leaders in their family, church, and community

researcher expectancy: pre-existing biases researchers bring to a research study that can influence the outcome

resolution phase: fourth phase of the sexual response cycle in which the sexual organs return to their earlier unstimulated size; the resolution phase may last 30 minutes or more

reverse discrimination: rare situation that occurs when women or other qualified minorities are hired instead of a more highly qualified man or member of a majority group

role congruity theory: Alice Eagly's theory that people tend to perceive women in leadership positions as not behaving in a manner consistent with the "female" role in society, which leads to prejudice against women leaders

role strain: stress which occurs when people have difficulty fulfilling all their different role obligations

ruminative style: a cognitive style associated with depression, in which people turn inward and focus on their symptoms, contemplate the possible causes and consequences of their emotions, and worry about all the things that are wrong in their life

S

sandwich generation: refers to middle-aged people, especially women, who find themselves responsible for both their dependent children and their aging parents

sapiosexuality: a sexual orientation in which someone finds intelligence sexually attractive or arousing, independent of other factors such as appearance

schema: a general concept that we use to organize our thoughts and attitudes about a topic

secondary sex characteristics: features of the body related to reproduction but not directly involved in it; includes characteristics such as breast development, facial hair, and pubic hair

self-disclosure: revealing information about oneself to another person

self-efficacy: a person's belief that they have the ability to achieve a goal, and that they are competent and effective

self-esteem: a measure of how much you like and value yourself

self-fulfilling prophecy: occurs when expectations about someone may lead them to act in ways that confirm your original expectation

self-objectification: occurs when women are judged on the basis of their attractiveness, and they subsequently adopt an observer's view of their body—as if their body were an object

sex: relatively narrow term that typically refers to physical and biological characteristics relating to reproductive anatomy, such as sex chromosomes or sex organs

sexism: bias against people on the basis of their gender or sex

sex chromosomes: 23rd pair of chromosomes that determine whether the embryo will be genetically female or male

sexual assault: unwanted sexual contact, which includes sexual touching as well as *rape*

sexual desire: a need to engage in sexual activities, for either emotional or physical pleasure

sexual disorder: a disturbance in sexual arousal or in sexual responding that causes mental distress; also called *sexual dysfunction*

sexual double standard: belief that men and women should be judged differently for their sexual behavior

sexual harassment: refers to unwanted gender-related behavior, such as sexual coercion, offensive sexual attention, sexual touching, and hostile verbal and physical behaviors that focus on gender

sexual minority: anyone who has a same-gender attraction (i.e., lesbian women, gay men, bisexual women, bisexual men), or who expresses any other nonheterosexual orientation (i.e., pansexual, sapiosexual, demisexual, asexual)

sexual prejudice: a negative attitude or belief system that devalues someone because of their sexual orientation and occurs most often toward lesbian women, gay men, and bisexual people—any group that is not heterosexual; also called *heterosexism*

sexual script: describes the social and cultural norms for sexual behavior, which we learn by growing up in a culture

similarities perspective: belief that men and women are generally more similar than dissimilar in their intellectual and social skills

singlism: bias against people who are not married

situation-centered explanations: explanations for occupational segregation that argue that the characteristics of an organizational situation (i.e., *labyrinths, sticky floors, glass ceilings, and treatment discrimination*) explain why women are rarely employed in traditionally masculine occupations; also called the *structural approach*

social cognitive approach: perspective that focuses on cognitive errors and provides a useful theoretical explanation for gender stereotypes and stereotypes based on categories such as ethnicity, sexual orientation, economic status, disability status, and age

social constructionism: theoretical perspective that individuals and cultures construct or invent their own versions of reality based on prior experiences, social interactions, and beliefs

social constructionist approach: process by which we construct or invent our own versions of reality, based on prior experiences, social interactions, and beliefs; often focuses on language as a mechanism for categorizing our experiences

social learning approach: theoretical perspective that children are rewarded for "gender-appropriate" behavior and punished for "gender-inappropriate" behavior, and that children observe and imitate the behavior of people from their own gender category

social justice: perspective that expresses concern about the well-being of a large group of people who experience discrimination and danger, such as people of color, people who identify as LGBTQ+, people who have been displaced from their home countries, and people who are living in a war zone

social role: a culture's shared expectations about the behavior of a group that occupies a particular social category, for example, the social categories of "men" and "women"

social-roles approach: theoretical perspective that men and women often occupy different social roles in societies; they are also socialized differently and experience different social opportunities and social disadvantages

spatial abilities: cognitive abilities that include understanding, perceiving, and manipulating shapes and figures

spatial perception: cognitive abilities that involve identifying spatial locations without being distracted by irrelevant information

spatial visualization: cognitive abilities that require complex processing of spatially presented information such as embedded-figures or complex visual arrays

stable lesbians: according to Lisa Diamond's research, lesbian women who focused their interest on girls and women during childhood, and whose interest continued during adolescence

statistical significance: occurs when the results of a research study are not likely to occur by chance alone

stereotypes: the relatively fixed and overly simplified beliefs, generalizations, and assumptions that we associate with particular groups of people

stereotype threat: occurs when someone's task performance is negatively affected they are reminded of a negative stereotype about a group to which that person belongs; expectation that one's performance on a task will reflect badly on the larger member group to which a person belongs

sticky floor: describes the situation of women who are employed in low-level jobs with no chance of promotion

structural approach: explanations for occupational segregation that argue that the characteristics of an organizational situation (i.e., *labyrinths, sticky floors, glass ceilings, and treatment discrimination*) explain why women are rarely employed in traditionally masculine occupations; also called *situation-centered explanations*

successful aging: process by which a person maximizes gains and minimizes losses as they grow older

sweatshop: a factory that violates labor laws regarding wages and working conditions

syphilis: curable sexually transmitted infection that causes painless sores and may produce rash on the body, but may not have visible symptoms; can be passed to fetus prenatally and to newborn during delivery

T

traditional marriage: heterosexual marital structure in which a husband is more dominant than the wife, and both partners maintain traditional gender roles, such as the wife making most of the decisions about housework and child care, but the husband having ultimate authority in family decisions

trafficking: a form of interpersonal exploitation that involves the sale and displacement of human beings for illegal purposes

trans: an umbrella term for anyone on the transgender spectrum, which may include people who identify as transgender, gender nonconforming, genderqueer, cross-dressing, gender fluid, pangender, polygender, two-spirit, androgynous, or any other nonbinary identity

transactional style of leadership: leadership style in which leaders clarify the tasks that employees must accomplish, rewarding them when they meet the appropriate objectives and correcting them when they do not meet these objectives

transformational style of leadership: leadership style in which leaders inspire employees, gain their trust, and encourage them to develop their potential skills

transgender: refers to individuals whose gender identity, expression, or behavior does not conform to the sex they were assigned at birth

transgender person: someone who moves across or beyond the gender boundaries as they are traditionally defined in U.S. culture, or anyone who does not identify with the gender they were assigned at birth

treatment discrimination: discrimination that people may encounter after they have already obtained a job

tribal colleges: 2- and 4-year college institutions that provide a transition between native culture and the predominately White "mainstream" culture

U

U.S.-centered nationalism: belief system that the United States is dominant over all other countries in the world, which are believed to have lower status

uterus: the organ in which a fetus develops

V

vagina: a flexible canal through which menstrual fluid passes in cisgender women; during heterosexual intercourse, the penis enters the vagina, and during vaginal birth, the infant passes out through the canal

validity: degree to which a test measures what it is supposed to measure

variable: any characteristic of a person or object that can take on different categories, levels, or values and that can be quantified or measured

vasocongestion: during the sexual response cycle, swelling caused by the accumulation of blood in the genital regions

verbal fluency: naming objects that meet certain criteria, such as beginning with the letter *S*

W

White-as-normative concept: recognition that Whiteness is presented throughout society as the normal standard in U.S. culture

White-privilege concept: recognition that society is structured to give White people certain status and privileges in society based on their skin color

women-of-color feminisms: intersectional feminisms that emphasize how historical forms of oppression, ethnicity, and social class intersect in shaping people's lives

working women: women who are employed (who work for pay) or nonemployed (who do not receive pay for their services)

Name Index

This index includes names of people, government agencies, and organizations.

Morris, W. L., 276, 278
Morrison, D. R., 324
Morrison, M. M., 47
Morrissey, T. W., 211
Morrongiello, B.A., 92
Mortenson, G., 100
Moscicki, A. B., 375
Mosher, C. E., 290, 388
Moss-Racusin, C. A., 213, 338
Motmans, J., 465
Mottet, L., 37
Mottet, L. A., 351, 353, 425, 430
Mounty, J., 366–368
Mouzon, D. M., 491
Moyles, C., 126
Moyser, M., 217, 224, 233, 463
Mozurkewich, E. L., 324
Msengi, C. M., 211
Muehlenhard, C. L., 299, 427, 434
Mueller, J. S., 37
Mueller, K. A., 343
Muhanguzi, F., 425
Mukhtaran Bibi, 483
Mulac, A., 177, 178
Mulama J., 99
Müller-Stierlin, A., 388
Mulligan, B., 225
Mullings, D. V., 473
Mulvaney Hoyer, K, 154, 162
Munch, S., 322
Mundy, L., 344, 345
Munford, R., 495
Munk-Olsen, T., 312
Muñoz, R. F., 388, 389
Munsch, J., 235
Murachver, T., 177
Murkoff, H., 320
Murnen, S. K., 101
Murphy, A. M., 447
Murphy, C. P., 39, 312
Murphy, E. F., 216–218
Murphy, E. M., 311
Murphy, K. R., 214, 222, 239
Murphy, S. A., 165, 168
Murphy, S. E., 200
Murray, L., 134
Murthi, M., 425
Musil, C. M., 470
Must, A., 114
Mustanski, B., 441
Mutran, E. J., 462
Mutter, J. D., 474
Mwangi, M. W., 47
Myers, A. M., 396, 397
Myers, D. G., 475
Myersson Milgrom. E-M., 231
Myersson Milgrom, E. M., 231
Myhr, L., 425

Nabors, N., 366
Nack, A., 375
Nahata, L., 114
Naidoo, J. C., 211
Nájera Catalán, H., 449
Nalla, M. K., 421
Nance, M., 17
Nance, T., 220
Nancekivell, S. E., 150

Nash, J. C., 487
Nassif, A., 47
Nasuti, L. J., 266
Nater, C., 484
Nathanson, C., 114
National Breast Cancer Foundation, 360
National Coalition Against Domestic
    Violence (NCADV), 425, 442
National Committee on Pay Equity, 208, 216
National Institute of Mental Health, 398
National Women's Studies Association, 494
Naughton, M. J., 466
Navarro, M., 82
Nazareth, I., 388
Nazari, N., 395
Neale, M. C., 273
Needle, R. B., 312
Neff, L. A., 256
Nelissen, M., 248
Nelson, A. L., 344, 345
Nelson, B. D., 551
Nelson, D. A., 197
Nelson, D. L., 240
Nelson, J. A., 126
Nelson, K., 91, 151
Nelson, M. R., 47, 205, 295
Nelson-Mmari, K., 370, 373, 374
Nelson, N. M., 91
Nelson, T., 336
Nelson, T. D., 455, 456, 457, 460
Nelson, T. S., 417, 420, 421, 423
Nencel, L., 272
Ness, I., 226
Ness, R. B., 311
Netzley, S. B., 46, 47
Neumann, D. L., 153
Neumark-Sztainer, D., 396, 397
New England Tribal College, 133
Newcomb, M. E., 441
Newcomb, R., 291
Newcombe, N. S., 160, 161, 237
Newland, M. C., 322
Newman, E., 429
Newman, M. L., 178, 179
Newport, F., 83
Newton, N. J., 455, 471, 475
Newtson, R. L., 279
Nguyen, S. P., 87, 88, 105, 106
Nguyen, T., 127
NICHD Early Child Care Research
    Network, 237, 238
Nichols, M., 302
Nichols, S. L., 295, 298, 309, 313
Nicholson, I. R., 356
Nicholson, L., 495
Nickens, S. D., 131
Nicpon, M. F., 464
Nielsen, L. B., 61
Nierman, A., 396
Nigrinis, A., 405
Nikolic-Ristanovic, V., 425
Nisbett, R. E., 150
Nishihara, R., 180
Noar, S. M., 373
Noe-Bustamante, 16
Nolan, C., 158
Nolan, S. A., 229

Nolen-Hoeksema, S., 91, 166, 167, 385, 386,
    387, 388, 389, 390, 391, 392, 411, 473
Noll, J. A., 71
Noller, P., 256, 257, 320–322, 326, 335, 340
Nordstrom, E., 158
Nordvik, H., 158
Norris, C. M., 359
Norris, J., 428
Norsigian, J., 328
Norton, M. I., 460
Nosek, B. A., 55–56, 146
Noser, A., 397
Nour, N. M., 358
Nowell, A., 153
Nussbaum, M., 99
Nutzinger, D. O., 397, 398
Nydegger, R., 386, 388, 404, 410

Obedin-Maliver, J., 319
O'Brien, B. A., 268
O'Brien, J., 17
O'Brien, K. A., 338
O'Brien, M., 108
Ocampo, C., 5
Ocampo, J. A., 463
Ochion, Y., 189
Ochman, J. M., 102
O'Connell, A. N., 222
O'Connor, A. L., 443
O'Connor, E., 336, 337
O'Connor, V., 363
Odgers, C. L., 308
O'Donnell, M., 443
O'Donohue, W. T., 100
Offman, A., 118, 303, 441
Ogletree, S., 258
O'Hara, M. W., 339
Ohm, S. C., 71
Okahana, H., 131
Okazaki, S., 404
Okimoto, T. G., 340
Oksman, J. C., 121
Okubo, M., 180
Olafson, E., 435
Oldenburg, B., 359, 372
Older Women's League, 463
Oldfield, E. C., 371
O'Leary, K. D., 441
O'Leary, V. E., 389
Olio, K. A., 435
Olivárez. A., Jr., 166
Oliver, M. B., 298, 299
Olkin, R., 5, 366, 367, 368, 484, 485
Olson, D. H., 276
Olson, K. R., 87
Olson, L. S., 98
Olson, M. A., 55
O'Neal, K. K., 308
O'Neil, J. M., 490
Online, 46
Ontai, L. L., 93
Onyango Mangen, P., 425
Onyx, J., 461
Oregon State University, 429
Ormerod, A. J., 130
Orost, J. H., 42
Orozco, A. E., 14
Orr, D. P., 297

Subject Index

For names of both people and organizations, *see* the Name Index.

Bisexuality, definition of, 62
Blacks
  achievement motivation of, 164
  affirmative action for, 214
  birth control and, 307
  body dissatisfaction and, 395
  breast cancer and, 359, 362
  breastfeeding and, 338
  cardiovascular disease and, 359
  childbirth and, 326–327
  churches of, 268
  depression and, 386, 391
  divorce and, 256, 261, 262
  eating disorders and, 397
  education of, 98, 112, 132, 161
  employment of, 211, 230, 324, 336
  ethnicity and, 16–17
  families of, 259, 335, 406, 473–474
  feminism and, 487
  gender stereotypes of, 53
  gender typing and, 93
  heterosexual relationships of, during
    adolescence, 138
  higher education for, 132
  housework by, 234
  infertility and, 345
  interpersonal relationships of, 135, 406
  intersectionality and identity of Black
    women, 71
  leadership by, 201
  as lesbians, 268
  marriage and, 256, 259–260
  media portrayal of, 48
  menarche and, 114
  menopause and, 468
  motherhood and, 335–336
  in music videos, 125
  as older women and grandmothers, 463,
    471, 473–474
  participation in community
    organizations by, 473–474, 487
  population of, in U.S. and Canada,
    14–15, 17, 405
  poverty of, 259, 262, 406, 473–474
  pregnancy of, 322, 324
  psychotherapy for, 406
  racism against, 5, 16–17, 406, 487
  as research participants, 23
  salary discrimination and, 216
  self-esteem of, 123
  sex education and, 294
  sexism against, 61
  sexual harassment of, 220, 419
  sexuality and sexual behavior of, 138,
    297
  as single women, 279
  smoking by, 322
  social class of, 406
  stereotypes of, 406, 473–474
Blaming the victim, 445
Body. See also Eating disorders
  adolescents' body image, 124
  attitudes on body size, 400
  culture of thinness, 124, 390,
    393–400
  depression and emphasis on, 390

  gender bias in media portrayal of,
    47–48
  male body as normative, 359
  objectified body consciousness and body
    dissatisfaction, 395
  secondary sex characteristics of, 114
Body image, 124, 410
Body posture, 179, 180
Bolivia, 497
Bone-density test, 364
Books
  for children, 101–103
  romance novels, 298, 309
Bosnia, 425
Botswana, 328
Box-score approach, 148
Brain lateralization, 160
Brazil, 52, 95, 438
Breaking up, 252–254, 268
Breast cancer, 338, 354, 359–363, 466, 474
Breast self-examination, 360–362
Breastfeeding, 337–338
Britain. See Great Britain/United Kingdom
BSRI (Bem Sex-Role Inventory), 70, 71
Bulgaria, 47
Bulimia nervosa, 398–399
Bullying, 130

C-section (cesarean section), 329, 338, 354
Cambodia, 406, 438, 498
Canada. See also Canadian research; First
    Nation (Canadian)
  abortion in, 311, 311n
  abuse of women in, 441, 444, 447
  adolescent birthrates and abortion in,
    305, 306, 311n
  bisexuals in, 140
  breast cancer in, 359
  cardiovascular disease in, 359
  Carnegie Hero Medal in, 188
  child care in, 236
  child sexual abuse in, 435
  childbirth in, 324, 327, 357
  crimes in, 196
  depression in, 386
  divorce in, 261, 262
  employed women in, 462–463
  Employment Equity programs in, 214
  employment of women in, 209, 210,
    211, 224, 236
  ethnic origins of residents of, 14, 15, 18,
    211, 386, 406
  feminism in, 126, 495, 497
  fertility rate of, 311
  health care in, 355, 406
  higher education in, 131, 133, 213
  immigrants in, 211, 357, 488
  infant mortality rate in, 333
  lesbians in, 140, 270, 336
  life expectancy in, 355
  mammograms in, 361
  marriage in, 255, 270
  maternal deaths in, 334, 357
  math education in, 154
  morbidity in, 355
  mothers' employment in, 236

  older women in, 455, 462–463
  Pap smear test in, 364
  pension plans in, 463
  political power of women in, 497
  population of, 15
  poverty in, 462–463
  pregnant women in, 324
  programs on gender and sexual diversity
    in, 64
  psychology of women as discipline in, 11
  psychology Ph.D. programs in, 484
  rape in, 427, 428
  salary discrimination in, 217, 217n
  same-gender marriages in, 270
  sexual behavior of adolescents and
    young adults in, 297, 310
  single women in, 276
  smoking in, 322
  suicide in, 386
  sweatshops in, 227
  White Ribbon Campaign in, 492, 492n
  women's studies in, 494–495
  working past retirement in, 459
Canadian research. See also Canada
  abuse of women, 445
  altruism, 187–188
  childbirth, 328
  communication about sexuality, 299
  decoding ability, 183
  depression, 391
  employed women, 218
  gender comparisons, 158
  gender segregation, 94
  household tasks performed by men, 234
  ideal romantic partners, 248
  menstrual joy, 120
  older women, 473
  parental preference about sex of
    children, 83
  personal definitions of success, 168
  premarital sex, 291
  rape, 428
  role strain, 238–239
  self-disclosure, 193
  sexism, 57–58
  sexual harassment, 421
  spatial abilities, 158
Canadian Woman Studies/Les cahiers de la
    femme, 12, 498
Canary Islands, 100
Cancer, 338, 354, 358–364, 396, 466, 474
Cardiovascular disease, 359
Care approach to moral decisions, 190
Career aspirations, 133–134. See also
    Work
Caribbean, 225, 406
Caring. See Helping and caring
Carnegie Hero Medal, 188
CBT. See Cognitive-behavioral therapy
    (CBT)
Central America. See Latin America; and
    specific countries
Cervical cancer, 363
Cervix, 115, 326
Cesarean birth, 329, 338
Cesarean section (C-section), 329, 338, 354

enrollment statistics for, 132
ethnicity of students in, 112, 132–133
faculty in, 132, 213
fat studies in, 396
Institutional Review Board policies in, 31n
law schools, 209–210
leadership training in, 200
medical schools, 209, 352
men's studies in, 490
Ph.D. degrees for women, 12, 482, 484
psychology of women courses in, 11, 498–499
sexual harassment in, 417–424
tribal colleges, 133
women's studies in, 11, 494–495
The Hill We Climb, 17
Hinduism, 41, 42. *See also* Religion
Hiring patterns, 212–215. *See also* Work
Hispanics, 16. *See also* Chicanas/os; Latinas/os; Mexican Americans
History
feminist historians, 39
gender biases throughout, 38–40
invisibility of women in, 38–39
philosophers' representation of women throughout, 39–40
of psychology of women, 10–12
Hmong tribe, 17, 336, 406
Homemakers, 341, 389
Homophobia. *See* Heterosexism
Homosexuality. *See* Gay males; Lesbians
Hong Kong, 460
Hooking up, 298
Hormone replacement therapy (HRT), 466
Hormones
gender comparisons and, 160
menopause and, 466
menstrual cycle and, 115
pregnancy and, 320
premenstrual syndrome (PMS) and, 118
prenatal sex development and, 80
sexual desire and, 289–290, 301
sexual orientation and, 273
Hostile sexism, 59, 324
Hot flash, 465, 468
Household tasks. *See also* Homemakers
employed women and, 233–235
equal sharing of, 257
ethnicity and, 233
list of, 233
men's responsibilities for, 233–235, 258
HPV (human papillomavirus, or genital warts), 374
Human immunodeficiency virus (HIV), 369–374
Human Sexual Response (Masters and Johnson), 287
Hypothalamus, 114
Hypothesis, 21–22. *See also* Research
Hysterectomy, 354, 363–364

IAT. *See* Implicit Association Test (IAT)
Iceland, 270, 497
Identity
during adolescence, 122–129
cultural identity, 127–128

definition of, 122–123
feminist identity, 125–126
gender identity, 88
transgender identity, 128–129
Illiteracy. *See* Education
Illnesses. *See* Physical health; and specific illnesses
Illusion of gender differences, 29. *See also* Theme 2 (differential treatment)
Immigrants. *See also specific ethnic* groups
discrimination against, 211
education of, 133, 211
employment of, 211, 226
families of, 336
female genital mutilation and, 358
feminism and, 488
higher education for, 133
marriage of, 260
Native American, 488–489
psychotherapy with, 406
Implicit Association Test (IAT), 55–56, 63
Implicit gender stereotypes, 55–56
Incest, 435
Income. *See* Poverty; Salary; Social class
Independence in children, 92, 239
India
abuse of women in, 445, 446
arranged marriages in, 248
beauty pageant in, 127
emigration from, 17, 474, 487–488
family structure in, 260
favoritism toward boys in, 84, 357, 497
fertility rate in, 310
health care for boys versus girls in, 357
literacy rate in, 310
menopause in, 468
older women in, 468, 474
PMS in, 118
political power for women in, 497
prostitutes in, 497–498
rape prevention in, 438
sex-negative culture in, 302
sexual harassment in, 421
India Abroad, 248
Indians (originating in Indian Subcontinent). *See* South Asians
Indians (originating in North America). *See* First Nation (Canadian); Native Americans
Individual approach, 231
Individual differences. *See* Theme 4 (variability/individual differences)
Infancy. *See also* Childbirth; Childhood
care of infants by mothers, 333–335
clothing for girls, 100
definition of, 79
female infanticide, 84
knowledge about gender during, 105
mortality rate for infants, 332–333
parental preferences about sex of children, 83–84
people's responses to infant girls and boys, 83–86
people's stereotypes about infant girls and boys, 84–86

Infant mortality rate, 332–333, 334
Infanticide, 84
Infertility, 344–345
Institutional Review Board, 31n
Insurance. *See* Health insurance
Intelligence, 150, 247. *See also* Cognitive abilities
Interaction patterns. *See* Communication patterns; Friendships; Interpersonal relationships; Love relationships
Intercourse. *See* Sexuality
International issues. *See* Cross-cultural patterns; and specific countries
Internet, 284, 296
Interpersonal relationships. *See also* Friendships; Love relationships; Marriage
of Blacks, 406
depression and, 391
during adolescence, 135–140
gender discrimination in, 61
moral judgments about, 190
relational aggression, 196–197
Interruptions, 177
Intersectional research, 484–485
Intersectionality, 18, 54, 71, 268
Intersex, 62
Intersex individuals, 82
Intimacy. *See* Friendships; Love relationships; Marriage; Sexuality
Intimate partner violence, 440. *See also* Abuse of women
Intrinsic motivation, 164
Invisibility. *See* Theme 3 (invisibility)
IQs, 150
Iraq, 19, 196
Ireland, 291, 333
Islam, 41, 42. *See also* Muslims; Religion
Israel, 333, 386
Italy, 333

Japan
abuse of women in, 445, 446
characteristics of ideal marriage partner in, 248–249
emigration from, 17
employment of women in, 209, 239
gender difference in decoding ability in, 183
infant mortality rate in, 333
media in, 47
older women in, 460
salary discrimination in, 217
Japanese Americans, 17, 406, 474. *See also* Asian Americans
Jews. *See* Judaism
Jobs. *See* Work
Joy
and breakup of love relationship, 253
childbirth and, 335
marriage and, 255
menstrual joy, 119, 120
pregnancy and, 320–322
Judaism, 40. *See also* Religion
Justice. *See* Social justice
Justice approach to moral decisions, 190